Springer Texts in Business and Economics

More information about this series at http://www.springer.com/series/10099

Efraim Turban · Jon Outland · David King
Jae Kyu Lee · Ting-Peng Liang
Deborrah C. Turban

Electronic Commerce 2018

A Managerial and Social Networks
Perspective

Ninth Edition

 Springer

Efraim Turban
University of Hawaii
Kihei, HI, USA

David King
JDA Software
Scottsdale, AZ, USA

Ting-Peng Liang
National Sun Yat-sen University
Kaohsiung, Taiwan

Jon Outland
Herzing University
Rapid City, SD, USA

Jae Kyu Lee
School of Business
Yonsei University
Seodaemun-gu, Seoul, Korea

Deborrah C. Turban
Turban Company Inc.
Kihei, HI, USA

ISSN 2192-4333   ISSN 2192-4341   (electronic)
Springer Texts in Business and Economics
ISBN 978-3-319-58714-1   ISBN 978-3-319-58715-8   (eBook)
DOI 10.1007/978-3-319-58715-8

Library of Congress Control Number: 2017943371

This Springer imprint is published by Springer Nature
The registered company is Springer International Publishing AG
The registered company address is: Gewerbestrasse 11, 6330 Cham, Switzerland

Preface

Electronic commerce, the topic of this book, has grown rapidly, with companies like Facebook, Google, Pinterest, LinkedIn, Uber, Alibaba Group, and Amazon.com setting new levels of performance every year.

Electronic commerce (EC) is a business model in which transactions take place over electronic networks, mostly the Internet. It includes the process of electronically buying and selling goods, services, and information. Certain EC applications, such as online buying and selling stocks and airline tickets, are reaching maturity, some even exceeding non-Internet trade volume. However, EC is not just about buying and selling; it also is about electronically innovating, communicating, collaborating, and discovering information. It is about e-learning, e-customer service, e-government, social networking, problem-solving, and much more. EC is having an impact on a significant portion of the world, affecting businesses, professions, trade, and, of course, people. It is undoubtedly improving our quality of life.

A most important development in EC since 2014 is the phenomenal growth of social network services, especially Facebook, Google+, and Twitter. Also impressive is the trend toward conducting EC via mobile devices. Another major development is the global expansion of EC, especially in China, where you can find the world's largest EC company. In addition, attention is given to artificial intelligence and its applications and to smart commerce as well as to the use of analytics and big data to enhance EC. Finally, some emerging EC business models are transforming industries (e.g., travel, banking, fashion, and transportation).

In the ninth edition (2017–2018), we bring forth the latest trends in e-commerce, including smart commerce, social commerce, social collaboration, shared economy, innovations, and mobility.

What's New in This Edition?

The following are the major changes in this edition:

New Chapters

1. Smart (intelligent) commerce (Chap. 7) is emerging as an important development.
2. EC Strategy, Globalization, SMEs, and Implementation (Chap. 14) replaces Chaps. 13 and 14 in the eighth edition.

- **Chapters with major changes:**
  Chapter 5 includes two new sections about sharing economy and e-health. Also, completely upgraded was the P2P section. The topic of collaborative commerce was transferred to Chap. 4.
  Chapter 6 was streamlined for m-commerce activities and applications. Several sections were transferred to new Chap. 7. Much attention is given to mobile apps.

Chapter 10 (old Chap. 9) is concentrating on marketing and advertising in EC instead of online behavior. Chap. 12 (EC payment) was completely restructured with major attention given to digital currencies.

Chapter 13 (EC order fulfillment) was reorganized and updated to include robotics, 3D printing, and drones.

New Topics

Many new topics were added in all chapters, while obsolete topics were deleted.

Here is a small sample of new topics: the changing retailing landscape, virtual reality applications, robot advisors, chatbots, virtual personal assistants, fitness trackers, Nest (of Google), augmented reality application, fake content, Internet of things (IoT) applications, Pokemon GO craze, drop-shipping, ransomware, 3D printing for mass customization, robots in EC warehouses, drones and robots for deliveries, and new advertisement methods.

New Cases

We replaced more than 20 cases (e.g., new cases: Airbnb, Uber, Costco global payments, Bitcoin, money transfer via smartphones in Africa, Instagram, and Pokemon GO).

To emphasize the importance of security in EC, ransomware and DDoS attack cases are added.

New Coauthor

Dr. Jon Outland is bringing considerable expertise in the area of e-marketing.

The Book's Learning Objectives (Learning Outcomes)

Upon completion of this book, the reader will be able to:

1. Define all types of e-commerce systems and describe their major business and revenue models, drivers, and benefits.
2. Describe all the major mechanisms that are used in executing e-commerce.
3. Describe all methods and models of selling products and services online from business to individual customers.
4. Understand all online business-to-business activities, including selling, procurement, auctions, and collaboration.
5. Describe EC activities other than selling online, such as e-government, e-learning/e-training, e-health, and sharing economy.
6. Describe the importance of mobile commerce and its content and implementation.
7. Describe the major applications of artificial intelligence in EC.
8. Describe social networks, social customers, and social software as facilitators of social commerce.
9. Describe the landscape of social commerce applications, including social shopping and advertising, social CRM, social entertainment, and crowdsourcing.
10. Describe social enterprise systems.
11. Describe the connected e-commerce and Internet of things and its smart applications.
12. Understand online consumer behavior.

13. Describe marketing and advertising in the Web environment.
14. Describe security issues and their solutions in e-commerce, including EC fraud protection.
15. Describe the use of e-payments, including mobile payments, and digital currency in e-commerce.
16. Understand order fulfillment in e-commerce and its relationship to supply chain management.
17. Understand e-commerce strategy and describe its process and steps, including justification, planning, implementation, and assessment.
18. Describe the global aspects of e-commerce.
19. Explain the issues of using e-commerce by small- and medium-sized companies.
20. Understand the ethical, legal, social, and business environments within which e-commerce operates.

Features of This Book

Several features are unique to this book.

Most Comprehensive EC Textbook

This is the most comprehensive EC textbook available. It covers more topics than any other text, and it provides numerous examples and case studies as well as hundreds of links to resources and references.

Managerial Orientation

e-Commerce can be approached from two major perspectives: technological and managerial. This text uses the second approach. Most of the presentations are about EC applications and their implementation. However, we do recognize the importance of the technology; therefore, we present the essentials of security in Chap. 12 and the essentials of infrastructure and systems development in Chaps. 2 and 14. We also provide some detailed technology material in the five online tutorials on the book's website (**affordable-ecommerce-textbook.com**). Managerial issues are also provided at the end of each chapter.

Experienced Coauthors and Contributors

In contrast to other EC books written by one or two authors who claim to be polymaths, we have a diversified global team of authors who are experts in a variety of fields, including an expert on e-marketing and a senior consultant of an e-commerce-related company. All contributions were copyedited to assure quality and uniformity.

Real-World Orientation

Extensive, vivid examples from large corporations, small businesses from different industries and services, governments, and nonprofit agencies from all over the world make concepts come alive. These examples, which were collected by both academicians and practitioners, show the students the capabilities of EC, its cost and justification, and the innovative ways corporations are using EC in their operations.

Solid Theoretical Background and Research Suggestions

Throughout the book, we present the theoretical foundations necessary for understanding EC, ranging from consumer behavior to the economic theory of competition. Furthermore, we provide many website resources, numerous exercises, and extensive references and links to supplement the theoretical resources.

Most Up-to-Date and Current Topics

This book presents the most current topics relating to EC, as evidenced by the many citations from 2015, 2016, and 2017. Finally, we introduce some of the most promising newcomer companies to e-commerce such as Instagram, Line, Waze, Volusion, Uber, Airbnb, and Shopify.

Social Media and Commerce

In addition to the two full chapters on this topic, we present EC social media and commerce topics in all chapters.

Integrated Systems

In contrast to other EC books that highlight isolated Internet-based systems, we emphasize integrated systems that support the entire life cycle of e-commerce. Social network-based systems are also highlighted, as are the latest developments in global EC, mobile commerce, and mobile apps.

Global Perspective

The importance of global competition, partnerships, and trade is increasing rapidly. EC facilitates exporting and importing, the management of multinational companies, and electronic trading and payments around the globe. International examples are provided throughout the book. The world's largest e-commerce company, the Alibaba Group, is featured in Chap. 4. Our authors and contributors are from the United States, Macau (China), Korea, Taiwan, Brazil, and the Philippines. Examples and cases presented are from over 20 countries. Cross-border EC is discussed in several chapters, including money transfers.

Small- and Middle-Sized Companies

Throughout the book, we provide discussions and examples of small- and middle-sized companies in addition to the large ones.

The Public Sector

In numerous places, we cover the topic of e-commerce in governments and other public and not-for-profit organizations. We added the use of AI-based systems in these organizations.

Interdisciplinary Approach

e-Commerce is interdisciplinary in nature, and we illustrate this throughout the book. Major EC-related disciplines include accounting, finance, information systems, marketing, management, operations management, and human resources management. In addition, some nonbusiness disciplines are touched upon, especially public administration, computer science, sociology, engineering, psychology, political science, and law. Economics also plays a major role in the understanding of EC.

EC Failures and Lessons Learned

In addition to EC success stories, we also present EC failures and, wherever possible, analyze the causes of those failures with lessons learned (e.g., in the opening case to Chap. 16).

Online Tutorials

We provide five technology-related online tutorials (instead of 12 in EC2012).

The following tutorials are not related to any specific chapter. They cover the essentials of EC technologies and provide a guide to relevant resources:

T1—eCRM
T2—EC technology: EDI, Extranet, RFID, and cloud computing
T3—business intelligence and analytics, data, text, and Web mining
T4—competition in cyberspace.
T5—e-collaboration

The tutorials are available at **affordable-ecommerce-textbook.com**.

User-Friendliness

While covering all major EC topics, this book is clear, simple, and well organized. It provides all the basic definitions of terms as well as logical and conceptual support. Furthermore, the book is easy to understand and is full of real-world examples that keep the reader's interest. Relevant review questions are provided at the end of each section so the reader can pause to digest the new material.

Links, Links, Links, and References

In this book, the reader will find several hundred links to useful resources supplementing all topics and providing up-to-date information. Note: With so many links, some may change over time. Also, you will find numerous references (e.g., about 200 in the new Chap. 7).

Other Outstanding Features

1. Five to ten topics for individual discussions and seven to twelve class discussion and debate issues are available in each chapter.
2. A class assignment that involves the opening case is available at the end of each chapter.

3. A class assignment that requires watching one or more short videos (3 to 10 min) about a certain technology or a mini case, followed by questions or some other student engagement, is included.
4. Videos related to specific topics are suggested in the text, some related to cases.
5. Over 100 real-world examples on specific topics and subtopics are used.
6. Learning objectives for the entire book are provided in this preface.

Organization of the Book

The book is divided into 15 chapters grouped into five parts.

Part 1: Introduction to e-Commerce and e-Marketplaces

In Part 1, we provide an overview of today's business environment as well as the fundamentals of EC and some of its terminology (Chap. 1). A discussion of electronic markets and their impacts is provided in Chap. 2, where special attention is given to EC mechanisms ranging from traditional shopping carts to social networks. We also introduce augmented reality and crowdsourcing platforms for EC in this chapter.

Part 2: E-Commerce Applications

In Part 2, we describe EC applications in three chapters. Chapter 3 addresses e-tailing and electronic service industries (e.g., e-travel, e-banking) as they relate to individual consumers. In Chap. 4, we examine the major B2B models, including online auctions, online trading, e-procurement, online marketplaces, and collaborative commerce. In Chap. 5, we present several innovative and emerging applications, such as e-government, e-learning, sharing economy, and P2P. A new section is dedicated to shared economy applications.

Part 3: Emerging EC Platforms

Chapter 6 explores the developing applications in the world of wireless EC (m-commerce, l-commerce, and pervasive computing). Chapter 7 is new. It introduces the topic of artificial intelligence chatbots, virtual personal assistants, and Internet of things in e-commerce. In Chap. 8, we explore the world of social media marketing and social CRM. Chapter 9 covers enterprise social networks, crowdsourcing, and some social media applications.

Part 4: EC Support Services

There are four chapters in this part. Chapter 10 is dedicated to online consumer behavior, market research, e-marketing methods, and e-advertising. Chapter 11 begins with a discussion of the need to protect EC systems. It also describes various types of attacks on e-commerce systems and their users, including fraud, and how to minimize these risks through appropriate security protection programs. The chapter also deals with the various aspects of cyberwars. Chapter 12 describes major EC payment issues and methods including mobile payments and digital currencies. Chapter 13 concentrates on order fulfillment, supply chain improvement, the role of 3D printing in mass customization, robots in EC warehousing and fulfillment, and the role of drones in delivery.

Part 5: E-Commerce Strategy and Implementation

Chapter 14 discusses the process of EC strategy and strategic issues in implementing EC including justification and cost–benefit analysis and systems acquisitions and developments. The chapter also presents global EC and EC for small businesses. Chapter 15 deals with legal, ethical, and societal issues concentrating on regulatory issues, privacy, and green IT.

Learning Aids

The text offers the student a number of learning aids:

- **Chapter Outlines.** A listing of the main headings ("Content") at the beginning of each chapter provides a quick overview of the major topics covered.
- **Chapter Learning Objectives.** Learning objectives at the beginning of each chapter help students focus their efforts and alert them to the important concepts to be discussed. Additionally, note the newly added learning objectives for the entire book.
- **Opening Cases.** Each chapter opens with a real-world example that illustrates the importance of EC to modern corporations. These cases were carefully chosen to call attention to some of the major topics to be covered in the chapters. Following each opening case is a short section titled "Lessons Learned from the Case" that relates the important issues in the case to the forthcoming content of the chapter. Finally, questions for the case are provided at the end of each chapter.
- **EC Application Cases.** In-chapter cases highlight real-world problems encountered by organizations as companies develop and implement EC. Questions follow each case to help direct the student's attention to the implications of the case material. Also, the cases deal with organizational problems and their solutions.
- **Real-World Examples.** Dozens of examples illustrate how EC concepts and tools are applied. These are usually linked to detailed descriptions and sources.
- **Figures and Tables.** Numerous eye-catching figures and tables extend and supplement the text presentation.
- **Review Questions.** Each section in each chapter ends with a series of review questions about that particular section. These questions are intended to help students summarize the concepts introduced and digest the essentials of each section before moving on to another topic.
- **Glossary and Key Terms.** Each key term is defined in the text when it first appears. In addition, an alphabetical glossary of key terms appears at the end of the book, with a page reference to the location where the term is discussed.
- **Managerial Issues.** At the end of every chapter, we explore some of the special concerns managers face as they prepare to do business in cyberspace. These issues are framed as questions to maximize the readers' active participation.
- **Chapter Summary.** The chapter summary is linked one-to-one with the learning objectives introduced at the beginning of each chapter.
- **End-of-Chapter Exercises.** Different types of questions measure the students' comprehension and their ability to apply the learned knowledge. Discussion Questions by individual students are intended to challenge them to express their thinking about relevant topics. Topics for Class Discussion and Debates promote dialogs and develop critical thinking skills. Internet Exercises are challenging assignments that require students to surf the Internet and apply what they have learned. Over 250 hands-on exercises send students to interesting websites to conduct research, learn about applications, download demos, or research state-of-the-art technology. The Team Assignments and Projects are thought-provoking group projects designed to foster teamwork.
- **Closing Cases.** Each chapter ends with a comprehensive case, which is presented somewhat more in depth than the in-chapter EC application cases. Questions follow each case relating the case to the topics covered in the chapter.

Supplementary Materials

The following support materials are also available:

- The **Instructor's Manual**, written by Jon Outland, includes answers to all review and discussion questions, exercises, and case questions.
- **Test bank** which was prepared by Jon Outland is available to support this text.
- The **PowerPoint Lecture Notes** highlight the important areas and are related to the text learning objectives. These are initially prepared by Judy Whiteside and updated to this edition by Jon Outland.

Companion Website: affordable-ecommerce-textbook.com

The book is supported by a companion website that includes:

- Five online tutorials

Content Contributors

The following individuals contributed material for this edition:

- Linda Lai provides material to Chaps. 8 and 14.
- Fabio Cipriani contributed his eCRM and social CRM slides to Chaps. 1 and 8.
- Judy Whiteside updated material in several chapters and conducted supporting research.
- Ivan C. Seballos II contributed the new illustrations and helped in updating several chapters.

Acknowledgments

Many individuals helped us create this text. Faculty feedback was solicited via written reviews and through individual interviews. We are grateful to them for their contributions.

Several individuals helped us with the research and the administrative work. We thank all these individuals for their dedication and excellent performance shown throughout the project. We also recognize the various organizations and corporations that provided us with their permission to reproduce material. We appreciate the assistance provided by the Springer team under the leadership of Neil Levine and Matthew Amboy. We also recognize the assistance of Ramesh Sharda who advises us about the previous edition.

Reviews

The previous editions of the book were reviewed by many professors. We thank all of them.

Kihei, HI, USA	Efraim Turban
Rapid City, SD, USA	Jon Outland
Scottsdale, AZ, USA	David King
Seodaemun-gu, Seoul, Korea	Jae Kyu Lee
Kaohsiung, Taiwan	Ting-Peng Liang
Kihei, HI, USA	Deborrah C. Turban

Contents

Part IV   EC Support Services

Introduction to E-Commerce and E-Marketplaces

Overview of Electronic Commerce

1

Contents

Learning Objectives

Upon completion of this chapter, you will be able to:

1. Define electronic commerce (EC) and describe its various categories.
2. Describe and discuss the content and framework of EC.
3. Describe the major types of EC transactions.
4. Describe the drivers of EC.
5. Discuss the benefits of EC to individuals, organizations, and society.
6. Discuss social computing.
7. Describe social commerce and social software.
8. Understand the elements of the digital world.
9. Describe some EC business models.
10. List and describe the major limitations of EC.

© Springer International Publishing AG 2018

E. Turban et al., *Electronic Commerce 2018*, Springer Texts in Business and Economics, DOI 10.1007/978-3-319-58715-8_1

OPENING CASE
HOW STARBUCKS IS CHANGING TO A DIGITAL AND SOCIAL ENTERPRISE

Starbucks is the world's largest coffee house chain, with 23,768 retail stores (July 17, 2016; see **news.starbucks.com/uploads/documents/AboutUs-Company_Timeline-Q42015.pdf**). Many people view Starbucks as a traditional store where customers drop in, place an order, pay for coffee or other products, consume their choices in the store, and go on about their business. The opposite is actually true. Starbucks is turning itself into a digital and social company.

For a long time, Starbucks was known to be appealing to young people because of the free Wi-Fi Internet access provided in its US and Canadian stores. However, lately, the company has embarked on several digital initiatives to become a truly tech-savvy company.

The Problem

Starting in 2007, the company's operating income declined sharply (from over $1 billion in 2007 to $504 million in 2008 and $560 million in 2009). This decline was caused not only by the economic slowdown but also by the increased competition (e.g., from Green Mountain Coffee Roasters), which intensified even during the recession. Excellent coffee and customer service helped, but only in the short run. A better solution was needed.

Starbucks realized that better interaction with its customers was necessary and decided to solve the problem via digitization.

The Solution: Going Digital and Social

Today, Starbucks considers itself as a technology company. Its CEO and major executives come from pure technology companies! (See La Monica 2015). In addition to traditional measures to improve its operation and margin, the company resorted to *electronic commerce*, meaning the use of computerized systems to conduct and support its business. The company appointed a senior executive with the title of Chief Digital Officer to oversee its digital activities. It also created the Digital Venture Group to conduct the technical implementation and maintenance. For details, see Sung (2014).

The Electronic Commerce Initiatives

Starbucks deployed several e-commerce projects; the major ones follow.

Online Store

Starbucks sells many of their products online at **store.starbucks.com**. These offerings include coffee, tea, and Starbucks equipment and merchandise. The store has been in operation for years, using a typical shopping cart (called My Bag), but in August 2011, the company completely redesigned the webstore to make shopping more convenient and easy. In addition, customers (individual or companies) can schedule deliveries of standard and special items. Customers can order rare and exquisite coffee that is available only in some US stores. Finally, online customers get exclusive promotions.

The eGift Card Program

Customers can buy Starbucks customized gift cards digitally (e.g., a gift card for a friend's birthday is auto delivered on the desired date). Payments can be made with a credit card, through PayPal, or the Starbucks app for mobile devices. The gift card is sent to the recipient via e-mail or postal mail.

The recipients can print the card and go shopping at a Starbucks physical store and transfer the gift amount to their Starbucks' card or to a Starbucks electronic gift card (see **starbucks.com/card**).

Loyalty Program

Like airlines and other vendors, the company offers a loyalty program (My Starbucks Rewards). Those who reach the gold level receive extra benefits. The program is managed electronically.

Mobile Payments

Customers can pay at Starbucks stores with prepaid (stored value) cards, similar to those used in transportation, or pay from their smartphones using the Starbucks mobile app. Payment is made by selecting "touch to pay" and holding up the barcode on the device screen to a scanner at the register. The system is connected automatically to a debit or credit card. The system works only in company-owned stores (2016). The mobile payment is connected with the loyalty program. Over 25% of all purchases in 2016 were made with mobile payments.

Social Media Projects

Starbucks realized the importance of social media that uses Internet-based systems to support social interactions and user involvement and engagement (Chap. 7). Thus, it started several initiatives to foster customer relationships based on the needs, wants, and preferences of its existing and future customers. The following are some representative activities. The company develops their social relationship marketing via social media (Samuely 2015b).

Exploiting Collective Intelligence

My Starbucks Idea (**mystarbucksidea.force.com**) is a platform in which a community of over 300,000 consumers and employees can make suggestions for improvements, vote for the suggestions, ask questions, collaborate on projects, and express their complaints and frustrations. The community generated 70,000 ideas in its first year, ranging from thoughts on the company's reward cards and elimination of paper cups to ways to improve customer service. The site also provides statistics on the ideas generated, by category, as well as their status (under review, reviewed, in the works, and launched). The company may provide incentives for certain generated ideas. For example, Starbucks offered $20,000 in prizes for the best idea concerning the reuse of its used coffee cups. This initiative is based on the technology of *collective intelligence*, also known as *crowdsourcing* (see Chaps. 2 and 8), and is supported by the "Ideas in Action" blog. This blog is written by employees who discuss ideas submitted to **blogs.starbucks.com/blogs/Customer**.

Starbucks' Activities on Facebook

Starbucks maintains a strong social media presence on Facebook (**facebook.com/Starbucks/**), with over 36 million "likes" (as of February 2017). The company uploads videos, blog posts, photos, promotions, product highlights, and special deals. The millions of people who "like" Starbucks on Facebook verify that the company has one of the most popular fan pages (see current statistics at (**fanpagelist.com** and at **facebook.com/Starbucks/**). Starbucks offers one of the best online marketing communication experiences on Facebook to date as well as mobile commerce engagements. Starbucks posts diversified information on its Facebook page, whether it is content, questions, or updates. The company also advertises on its Facebook page (e.g., contests, events, new products).

Starbucks' Presence on LinkedIn and Google+

Starbucks has a profile on LinkedIn site with over 767,000 followers (February 2017). It provides business data about the company, lists new hires in managerial positions, and advertises other available jobs. Starbucks is also active on Google+. It provides business data about the company, shows employee profiles, and advertises available jobs. Note that Starbucks is regularly assessing the cost-benefit of advertising on social networks.

Starbucks' Activities on Twitter

In February 2017, Starbucks had over 11.9 million followers (follow @starbucks) on Twitter (**twitter.com/starbucks**). Whenever the company has some new update or marketing campaign, the company posts a tweet (e.g., discounted drinks). By October 2013, Starbucks was the number one retailer to follow on Twitter. In November 2013, Starbucks gave away a $5 gift certificate to 100,000 customers who tweeted a coffee to one of their friends or followers (see **blissxo.com/free-stuff/deals/cash-back-and-rebates/free-5oo-starbucks-gift-card**).

Starbucks' Activities on YouTube, Flickr, Pinterest, and Instagram

Starbucks has a presence on both YouTube (**youtube.com/Starbucks**) and Flickr (**flickr.com/groups/starbuckscoffeecompany**), with a selection of videos and photos for viewing. It also runs advertising campaigns there. Finally, Starbucks has about 13.1 million followers (February 2017) on the photo-sharing company Instagram (**instagram.com/Starbucks**).

Starbucks Digital Network

When customers are at Starbucks, they have more than Wi-Fi—they get access to the Starbucks Digital Network from all major mobile devices, including tablets and smartphones (see **starbucks.com/coffeehouse/wireless-internet/starbucks-digital-network**). The Network, in partnership with Yahoo!, features free premium online content, such as news, entertainment, business, health, and even local neighborhood information channels. In 2014, Starbucks switched to Google Wi-Fi, to give their customers faster Wi-Fi and network speeds.

Global Activities

Being a global company, Starbucks is known for its several country-oriented projects. For example, in December 2015, the company launched e-commerce for China on Tmall (an Alibaba company). For more on how Starbucks is using mobile commerce, see Strout (2015).

Early Adoption of Foursquare: A Failure

Not all Starbucks social media projects were successes. For example, the company decided to be an early adopter of geolocation by working with Foursquare (Chap. 7). The initiative simply did not work, and the project ended in mid-2010. The company experimented in the UK with a similar location company called Placecast. As of fall 2011, Starbucks had a better understanding of the opportunities and the limitations, so it may decide to try geolocation again with Facebook Places, or it may revive the Foursquare project.

The Results

Starbucks turned sales around by effectively integrating the digital and the physical worlds. In 2010, its operating income almost tripled ($1.437 billion versus $560 million in 2009) and so did its stock price. In 2011, the operating income reached $1.7 billion. Since then, the operating income is increasing rapidly. Sales are lifting due to digital and social media promotions. By 2017, sales increase sharply.

The company's social media initiatives are widely recognized. In 2012, it was listed by *Fortune Magazine* as one of the top social media stars (per **archive.fortune.com/galleries/2012/fortune/1205/gallery.500-social-media.fortune/5.html**), and in 2008, it was awarded the 2008 Groundswell Award by Forrester Research. In 2014, the company's strategy received the top spot on many reviewers' lists, driving sales to new highlights (see Samuely 2015b). The site is very popular on Facebook, where it has millions of fans (sometimes more popular than pop icon Lady Gaga). Starbucks attributes its success to ten philosophical guidelines that drive its social media efforts.

Sources: Based on Brohan (2015), Panagiotaropoulou (2015), Samuely (2015a, b), Sung (2014), Strout (2015), Moth (2013).Welch and Buvat (2015), Allison (2013), **mystarbucksidea.force.com**, **blogs.starbucks.com/blogs/Customer**, and **starbucks.com** (accessed February 2017).

LESSONS LEARNED FROM THE CASE

The Starbucks.com case illustrates the story of a large retailer that is transforming into a digital and social enterprise. Doing business electronically is one of the major activities of e-commerce, the subject of this book. The case demonstrates several topics you will learn about in this chapter and throughout the book. These are:

1. There are multiple activities in EC, including selling online, customer service, and collaborative intelligence.
2. The case shows major benefits to both buyers and sellers. This is typical in EC.
3. The EC capabilities include the ability to offer products and services in many locations, including overseas, to many customers, individuals, and businesses. You can do so because you can have a larger customer base online and people can buy from anywhere at any time.
4. In a regular store, you pay and pick up the merchandise or service. On Starbucks.com and other webstores, you order and pay, and the product is shipped to you. Therefore, order fulfillment needs to be very efficient and timely.
5. Being digital can be very useful, but a greater benefit can be achieved by extending the conversion to lead to a socially oriented enterprise. Both approaches constitute the backbone of electronic commerce.

In this opening chapter, we describe the essentials of EC, some of which were illustrated in this case. We present some of the drivers and benefits of EC and explain their impact on the technology. Special attention is provided to the emergence of the social economy, sharing economy, social networks, and social enterprises. Finally, we describe the outline of this book.

1.1 ELECTRONIC COMMERCE: DEFINITIONS AND CONCEPTS

As early as 2002, management guru Peter Drucker (2002) forecasted that e-commerce (EC) would significantly impact the way that business would be done. And indeed, the world is embracing EC, which makes Drucker's prediction a reality.

Defining Electronic Commerce

Electronic commerce (EC) refers to using the Internet and other networks (e.g., intranets) to purchase, sell, transport, or trade data, goods, or services. For an overview, see Plunkett (2017). In addition, watch the video titled "What is E-Commerce?" at **youtube.com/watch?v=3wZw2IRb0Vg**. EC is often confused with e-business, which is defined next.

Defining e-Business

Some people view the term *commerce* as describing only buying and selling transactions conducted between business partners. If this definition of commerce were used, the term *electronic commerce* would be fairly narrow. Thus, many use the term *e-business* instead. **e-Business** refers to a broader definition of EC, not just the buying and selling of goods and services but conducting all kinds of business online such as servicing customers, collaborating with business partners, delivering e-learning, and conducting electronic transactions within organizations. However, others view e-business only as comprising those activities that do not involve buying or selling over the Internet, such as collaboration and intrabusiness activities; that is, it is a *complement* of the narrowly defined e-commerce. In its narrow definitions, e-commerce can be viewed as a subset of e-business. In this book, we use the broadest meaning of electronic commerce, which is basically equivalent to the broadest definition of e-business. The two terms will be used interchangeably throughout the text.

Major EC Concepts

Several other concepts are frequently used in conjunction with EC. The major ones are as follows.

Pure Versus Partial EC

EC can be either pure or partial depending on the nature of its three major activities: ordering and payments, order fulfillment, and delivery to customers. Each activity can be done physically or digitally. Thus, there are eight possible combinations as shown in Table 1.1. If all activities are digital, we have pure EC; if none are digital, we have no EC; otherwise, we have partial EC.

If there is at least one digital dimension, we consider the situation EC, but only partial EC. For example, purchasing a computer from Dell's website or a book from Amazon.com is partial EC, because the merchandise is physically delivered. However, buying an e-book from Amazon.com or a software product from microsoft.com is pure EC, because ordering, processing, and delivery to the buyer are all digital. Note that many companies operate in two or more of the classifications. For example, Jaguar has a 3D application for self-configuration of cars online, prior to production shopping (see Vizard 2013).

Table 1.1 Classifications of e-commerce

Activity	1	2	3	4	5	6	7	8
Ordering, payment	P	D	D	D	D	P	P	P
Order fulfillment	P	D	D	P	P	D	P	D
Delivery (shipment)	P	D	P	P	D	D	D	D
Type of EC	Non-EC	Pure EC	Partial EC					

Legend: *P* physical, *D* digital

EC Organizations

Purely physical organizations (companies) are referred to as **brick-and-mortar (or old economy) organizations**, whereas companies that are engaged only in EC are considered **virtual (pure-play) organizations**. **Click-and-mortar (click-and-brick) organizations** are those that conduct some EC activities, usually as an additional marketing channel. Gradually, many brick-and-mortar companies are changing to click-and-mortar ones (e.g., GAP, Walmart, Target).

Cyberspace

Cyberspace is the nonphysical environment where EC is conducted by using computers and networks. The mechanisms used in cyberspace to conduct e-commerce are described in Chap. 2. The most important mechanisms are the Web, electronic market places, social networks, and communication tools.

Electronic Markets and Networks

EC can be conducted in an **electronic market (e-marketplace)**, an online location where buyers and sellers conduct commercial transactions such as selling goods, services, or information. Any individual can also open a private market selling products or services online. Electronic markets can also match individuals to others or to jobs. They usually are owned by independent owners. Electronic markets are connected to sellers and buyers via the Internet or to its counterpart within organizations, an *intranet*. An **intranet** is a corporate or government internal network that uses Internet tools, such as Web browsers and Internet protocols. Another computer environment is an **extranet**, a network that uses Internet technology to link intranets of several organizations in a secure manner (see Online Tutorial T2).

SECTION 1.1 REVIEW QUESTIONS

1. Define EC and e-business.
2. Distinguish between pure and partial EC.
3. Define click-and-mortar and brick-and-mortar organizations.
4. Define electronic markets.
5. Define intranets and extranets.

1.2   THE ELECTRONIC COMMERCE FIELD: GROWTH, CONTENT, CLASSIFICATION, AND A BRIEF HISTORY

According to the US Census Bureau (2016), e-commerce sales in 2014 accounted for over 60% of total sales of all manufacturing activities in the United States, over 22% of merchant wholesalers, 6.4% of all retailing (vs. 5.9% in 2013), and 2% of all sales in selected service industries. The grand total of EC in 2014 has been $7692 billion as seen in Fig. 1.1. Notice the sharp increase in manufacturing compared to other sectors. In addition, note that EC is growing much faster than the total of all commerce by about 16–17% annually. For a more detailed breakdown, see the US Census Bureau annual report as well as Plunkett (2017).

There is a clear trend that online retail sales are taking business from traditional retailers. Today, more and more people are buying online. For statistics about e-commerce on the Internet, see **internetworldstats.com/stats.htm**.

According to *Ecommerce Europe*, September 5, 2012, European online retail sales will double to €323 billion by 2018.

The Content and Framework of e-Commerce

Classifying e-commerce aids the understanding of this diversified field. In general, selling and buying electronically can be either business-to-consumer (B2C) or business-to-business (B2B). Online transactions are made between businesses and individual consumers in B2C, such as when a person purchases a coffee at **store.starbucks.com** or a computer at **dell.com**. In B2B, business transactions are made online between businesses, such as when Dell electronically buys parts from its suppliers. Dell also collaborates electronically with its partners and provides customer service online e-CRM (see Online Tutorial T1). Several other types of EC will be described later in this chapter.

Fig. 1.1   e-Commerce as
percent of total value:
(2005–2014) (Source: **census.
gov/content/dam/Census/
library/publications/2016/
econ/e14-estats.pdf**, accessed
March 2017)

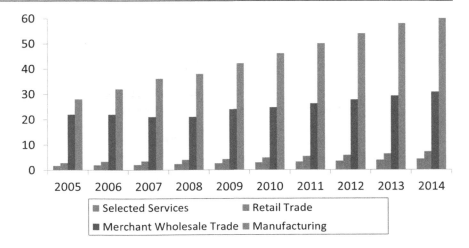

The total EC shipments grew 16.5% in 2013. comScore reported that US retail commerce online increased 17% in QI 2012 as compared to a year earlier. EC is growing in all areas. Similar results can be found in many industries, companies, and countries (e.g., see periodic reports at comScore and BizReport) and Ahmad (2014, an infographic). e-Commerce is exploding globally. According to a press release of **ecommerce-europe.eu/press** of May 23, 2013, European e-commerce grew by 19% in 2012 reaching €312 billion (see **ecommerce-europe.eu/press-item/european-e-commerce-to-reach-e-312-billion-in-2012-19-growth**). According to Stanley and Ritacca (2014), e-commerce in China is exploding, reaching $600 billion by the end of 2013. Finally, in several developing countries, EC is becoming a major economic asset.

1. **People**. Sellers, buyers, intermediaries, information systems and technology specialists, other employees, and any other participants.
2. **Public policy**. Legal and other policy and regulatory issues, such as privacy protection and taxation, which are determined by governments. Included are technical standards and compliance.
3. **Marketing and advertising**. Like any other business, EC usually requires the support of marketing and advertising. This is especially important in B2C online transactions, in which the buyers and sellers usually do not know each other.
4. **Support services**. Many services are needed to support EC. These range from content creation to payments to order delivery.
5. **Business partnerships**. Joint ventures, exchanges, and business partnerships of various types are common in EC. These occur frequently throughout the *supply chain* (i.e., the interactions between a company and its suppliers, customers, and other partners).

An EC Framework

The EC field is diverse, involving many activities, organizational units, and technologies. Therefore, a framework that describes its contents can be useful. Figure 1.2 introduces one such framework.

As shown in the figure, there are many EC applications (top of figure), which will be illustrated throughout the book. To perform these applications, companies need the right information, infrastructure, and support services. Figure 1.2 shows that EC applications are supported by infrastructure and by the following five support areas (shown as pillars in the figure):

The infrastructure for EC is shown at the bottom of the figure. *Infrastructure* describes the hardware, software, and networks used in EC. All of these components require good *management practices*. This means that companies need to plan, organize, motivate, devise strategy, and restructure processes, as needed, to optimize the business use of EC models and strategies.

Classification of EC by the Nature of the Transactions and the Relationships Among Participants

A common classification of EC is by the type of the transactions and the transacting members. The major types of EC transactions are listed below.

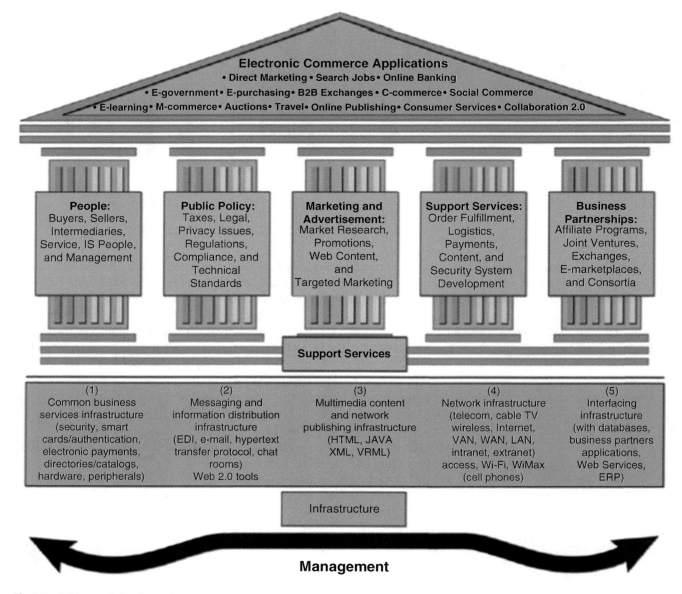

Fig. 1.2 A framework for electronic commerce

Business-to-Business (B2B)

Business-to-business (B2B) EC refers to transactions between and among organizations. Today, about 85% of EC volume is B2B. For Dell, the entire wholesale transaction is B2B. Dell buys most of its parts through e-commerce and sells its products to businesses (B2B) and individuals (B2C) using e-commerce.

Business-to-Consumer (B2C)

Business-to-consumer (B2C) EC includes retail transactions of products or services from businesses to individual shoppers. The typical shopper at Amazon.com is this type. Since the sellers are usually retailers, we also call this **e-tailing**.

Consumer-to-Business (C2B)

In **consumer-to-business (C2B)**, people use the Internet to sell products or services to organizations. Alternatively, individuals use C2B to request bids on products or services. Priceline.com is a well-known organizer of C2B travel service transactions, where people place a request for offers at a price they are willing to pay for a specific trip.

Intrabusiness EC

The **intrabusiness EC** category refers to EC transactions among various organizational departments and individuals in one company.

Business-to-Employees (B2E)

The **business-to-employees (B2E)** category refers to the delivery of services, information, or products from organizations to their employees. A major category of employees is *mobile employees*, such as field representatives or repair employees that go on to customers. EC support to such employees is also called *business-to-mobile employees (B2ME)*.

Drop-shipping

In this model, a seller advertises and sells a product to a buyer and collects the payment. Then, the seller transfers the orders to a supplier and pays the wholesale price. The supplier packs and delivers the product to the buyer. For details, see Chap. 3.

Consumer-to-Consumer (C2C)

In the **consumer-to-consumer (C2C)** EC category, individual consumers sell to or buy from other consumers. Examples of C2C include individuals selling computers, musical instruments, or personal services online. eBay sales and auctions are mostly C2C as are the ads on Craigslist.

Collaborative Commerce

Collaborative commerce (c-commerce) refers to online activities and communications done by parties working to attain the same goal. For example, business partners may design a new product together.

e-Government

In **e-government** EC, a government agency buys or provides goods, services, or information from or to businesses (G2B) or from or to individual citizens (G2C). Governments can deal also with other governments (G2G).

The previous categories are illustrated in Fig. 1.3. Many examples of the various types of EC transactions will be presented throughout this book.

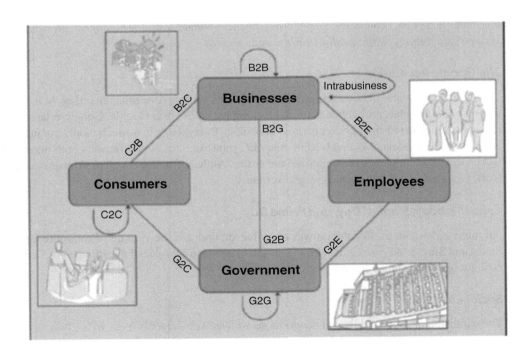

Fig. 1.3 Categories of transactions in e-commerce

A Brief History of EC

The pioneering of e-commerce applications can be tracked to the early 1970s when money was transferred electronically, mostly among financial institutions (known as *electronic funds transfer [EFT]*), whereby funds could be routed electronically from one organization to another. However, the use of these applications was limited to large corporations, financial institutions, and a few other daring businesses. Then came *electronic data interchange (EDI)*, a technology used to enable the electronic transfer of routine documents. EDI later expanded from financial transactions to other types of transactions (see Online Tutorial T2 for more on EDI). More new EC applications followed, ranging from travel reservation systems to online stock trading.

The Internet appeared on the scene in 1969, as an experiment by the US government, and its initial users were mostly academic researchers and other scientists. Some users started to place personal classifieds on the Internet. A major milestone in the development of EC was the appearance of the World Wide Web (the "Web") in the early 1990s. This allowed companies to have a presence on the Internet with both text and photos. When the Internet became commercialized and users began flocking to participate in the World Wide Web in the early 1990s, the term *electronic commerce* was introduced. EC applications rapidly expanded. A large number of so-called dot-coms, or *Internet start-ups*, also appeared. Today, all companies in the developing countries have presence on the Web. Many of these sites contain tens of thousands of pages and links. In 1999, the emphasis of EC shifted from B2C to B2B, and in 2001 from B2B to B2E, c-commerce, e-government, e-learning, and m-commerce. In 2005, social networks started to receive quite a bit of attention, as did m-commerce and wireless applications. As of 2009, EC added social commerce channels. An example is the increasing commercial activities on Facebook and Twitter. Given the nature of technology and Internet usage, EC will undoubtedly continue to grow, adding new business models and introducing change. More and more EC successes are emerging. For a comprehensive ready reference guide to EC including statistics, trends, and in-depth profiles of hundreds of companies, see plunkettresearch.com/ecommerce-internet-technology-market-research/industry-and-business-data and **en.wikipedia.org/wiki/E-commerce**.

While looking at the history of EC, one must keep in mind the following:

The Global Nature of EC

EC activities can be seen between and within countries. In fact, the largest EC company in the world is Alibaba Group of China (see Chap. 4). See also Tse (2015).

The Interdisciplinary Nature of EC

From just the brief overview of the EC framework and classification, you can probably see that EC is related to several different disciplines. The major academic EC disciplines include the following: *accounting, business law, computer science, consumer behavior, economics, engineering, finance, human resource management, management, management information systems, marketing, public administration*, and *robotics*.

The Google Revolution

During its early years, EC was impacted by companies such as Amazon.com, eBay, AOL, and Yahoo!. However, since 2001, no other company has probably had more of an impact on EC than Google. Google-related Web searches are targeting advertisements much better than its competitors are doing. Today, Google is much more than just a search engine; it employs many innovative EC models, it is involved in many EC joint ventures, and it impacts both organizational activities and individual lives. Google's companies are organized under the "Alphabet" name. In 2016, Alphabet included Google, Calico, Google X, Nest, Google Capital, Fiber, and Google Ventures.

Cyber Monday, Singles' Day, and Prime Day

An interesting evidence for the growth of online shopping is the volume of shopping during Cyber Monday in the United States and Singles' Day in China (11/11). In 2016, Amazon introduced the *Prime Day*. On July 12, 2016, the daily sales were 60% more than on any other previous day.

Social Commerce

The explosion of social media and networks, as well as Web 2.0 tools (e.g., wikis, blogs), resulted in new ways of conducting e-commerce by making it social. Several new and modified EC models were created, rejuvenating the field as described in several chapters in the book, especially in Chaps. 8 and 9 and in Turban et al. (2016).

EC Failures

Starting in 1999, a large number of EC companies, especially e-tailing and B2B exchanges, began to fail. Well-known B2C failures include Drkoop, MarchFirst, eToys, and Boo. Well-known B2B failures include Webvan, Chemdex, Ventro, and VerticalNet. (Incidentally, the history of these pioneering companies is documented by David Kirsch in his Business Plan Archive (**businessplanarchive.org**). A survey regarding failures of dot-coms in 1998–2005 found that 62% of dot-coms lacked financial skills and 50% had little experience with marketing. Similarly, many companies failed to have satisfactory order fulfillment and enough inventory to meet the fluctuating and increasing demand for their products. The situation today (2017) is about the same in many small and medium companies. The reasons for these and other EC failures are discussed in Chaps. 3, 4, and 14. As of 2008, many start-ups related to Web 2.0 and social commerce started to collapse (see **blogs. cioinsight.com/it-management/startup-deathwatch-20.html**).

Does the large number of failures mean that EC's days are numbered? Absolutely not! First, the dot-com failure rate is declining sharply. Second, the EC field is basically experiencing consolidation as companies test different business models and organizational structures. Third, some pure EC companies, including giants such as Amazon.com and Netflix, are expanding operations and generating increased sales. Finally, the click-and-mortar model seems to work very well, especially in e-tailing (e.g., Gap, Walmart, Target, Apple, HP, and Best Buy).

EC Successes

The last few years have seen the rise of extremely successful EC companies such as eBay, Pandora, Zillow, Google+, Facebook, Amazon.com, Pay Pal, Pinterest, VeriSign, LinkedIn, and E*TRADE. Click-and-mortar companies such as Cisco, Walmart, General Electric, IBM, Intel, and Schwab also have seen great success. Additional success stories include start-ups such as Alloy.com (a young adult-oriented portal), Blue Nile (jewelry), Ticketmaster, Amazon.com, Net-a-Porter (Case 1.1), Expedia, Yelp, Uber, Airbnb, TripAdvisor, and Grubhub.

CASE 1.1: EC APPLICATION
NET-A-PORTER: DRESS FOR SUCCESS

Will a woman buy a $2000 dress online without trying it on? Net-a-Porter (a UK online retailer, known as "the Net") bet on it and proved that today's women will purchase their dresses (for success) online, especially if the luxury clothing and accessories are international brands such as Jimmy Choo or Calvin Klein (see Pressler 2015).

The Opportunity

When talking about e-commerce (EC), most people think about buying online books, vitamins, CDs, or other commodity items. And this indeed was what people bought in the mid-1990s, when EC began. But in 2000, Natalie Massenet, a fashion journalist, saw an opportunity because of the success of luxury online stores such as Blue Nile (see Chap. 2) and the fact that professional women are very busy and willing to do more purchasing online.

The Solution

Natalie decided to open an online business for luxury fashion. She created a comprehensive, socially oriented, e-tailing site, naming it Net-a-Porter.

According to **net-a-porter.com**, some experts, and the company:

- Opened an e-tailing store.
- Offered merchandise from over 350 top designers, where most offline stores offer a few dozen.
- Offered its own designs in addition to others.
- Arranged global distribution systems to over 170 countries.
- Opened physical stores in London and New York to support the online business.
- Arranged same-day delivery in London and New York and overnight delivery elsewhere.
- Organized very fast cycle time for producing and introducing new clothes and other products that match customers' preference.

- Devised prediction methods of fashion trends based on customer feedback through social media.
- Ran online fashion shows.
- Developed superb inventory and sales tracking systems based on dashboards.
- Offered an online fashion magazine.
- Discovered what customers really want via social networks (Chap. 7) and fulfilled their needs.
- Offered large discounts.
- Developed a presence on Facebook and app for iPhone.
- Has 771,000 followers on Google + (February 2017).
- Has 6 million visitors each month (February 2017).
- Experiences 750,000 downloads per month on iPhone.
- Started augmented reality shopping windows in several global cities as of 2012 (see **digitalbuzzblog.com/net-a-porter-augmented-reality-shopping-windows**). On this same site, you can watch the video "Window Shop" and download the Net-a-Porter iPhone/iPad app.
- Note: Melania Trump is a regular customer of the store. She purchased her RNC dress there in July 2016. (See Ilyashov 2016, and watch the video there).
- As of 2010, the company is taking advantage of the social media environment that is changing the fashion industry.

The Results

Customers now come from over 170 countries, and revenue and profits are increasing rapidly. Several million visitors come to the site every week. The "Net" became profitable after 1 year—a very rare case in e-tailing. During the economic crisis of 2009, the Net's total sales were up 45% versus a 14% decrease for one of its major competitors (Neiman Marcus; Web and paper catalog sales). The company was so successful that luxury goods company Richemont Corp. purchased a 93% stake in the business. In October 2015, the company merged with the YOOX Group (**yooxgroup.com**).

In June 2010, when the company celebrated its tenth anniversary, it opened a new website dedicated to menswear. With success comes competition, and the Net's competitors include Bluefly (low prices), Shopbop (an Amazon.com company, but it lacks the Net's prestige), and high-end department stores with their own online stores (Nordstrom, Neiman Marcus). However, the Net has the highest prestige and growth rate. A major threat may come from eBay, which has been reaching out to high-end designers about creating their own virtual stores (hosted by eBay) where they can sell at fixed prices and also use auctions. Finally, note that in the late 2010, Amazon.com created Amazon Fashion, a store that offers designer brands at a discount. To stay on top of the competition, the Net is planning new ventures and expanding its business model to include children's clothes. Net-a-Porter is an example of the revolution that is occurring in the fashion industry. Another example is Polyvore, whose case is presented in Chap. 8. For details on these new business models, see **businessoffashion.com/2012/01/e-commerce-week-the-rise-of-new-business-models.html**.

Sources: Based on Davis (2016), Pressler (2015), **en.wikipedia.org/wiki/YOOX_Net-a-Porter_Group** (accessed February 2017).

Questions

1. Why would you buy (or not buy) from Net-a-Porter?
2. Watch the video "The Future of Shopping" (**youtube.com/watch?v=_Te-NCAC3a4**). How would you integrate this development with Net-a-Porter?
3. List both the advantages and disadvantages of the Net's physical stores.
4. It is said that the Net is playing a significant role in transforming how designers reach customers. Explain why.
5. Read the benefits of EC to customers (Sect. 2). Which ones are the most relevant here?
6. What EC capabilities are helping the Net and its designers?
7. Analyze the competition in the high-end fashion market.
8. What is the importance of globalization in this case?
9. Imitators are springing up on all sides. Even eBay and Amazon.com are expanding their fashion e-tailing efforts. What strategy do you suggest for the Net?

SECTION 1.2 REVIEW QUESTIONS

1. List the major components of the EC framework.
2. List the major transactional types of EC.
3. Describe the major landmarks in EC history.
4. List some EC successes and failures.

1.3 DRIVERS AND BENEFITS OF E-COMMERCE

The tremendous explosion of EC can be explained by its drivers and characteristics, benefits, and changes in the business environment.

The Drivers of e-Commerce

Although EC is only about 24 years old, it is expected to have nonstoppable growth, and it expands consistently into new areas of our life. The question is why. What drives EC?

EC is driven by many factors depending on the industry, company, and application involved. The major drivers are shown in the self-explanatory Fig. 1.4, together with the section and/or chapter where details are presented.

The Benefits of e-Commerce

There are many benefits of EC, and they continue to increase with time. We elected to organize them in three categories:

EC provides benefits to *organizations*, *individual customers*, and *society*. These benefits are summarized in Table 1.2.

Opportunities for Entrepreneurs

A major benefit of EC is the creation of opportunities to start a business in an unconventional ways. The new business models permit entrepreneurs to open businesses with little money and experience and grow them rapidly. Many entrepreneurs are making some big money online.

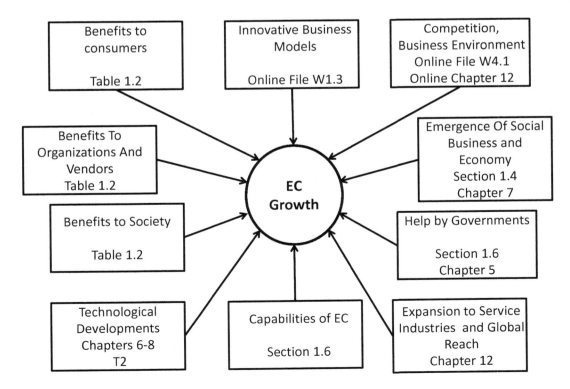

Fig. 1.4 The major drivers of e-commerce growth

Table 1.2 Benefits of e-commerce

Benefit	Description
Benefits to organizations	
Global reach	Quickly locating customers and business partners at reasonable cost worldwide
Cost reduction	Lower cost of information processing, storage, and distribution
Facilitate problem-solving	Solve complex problems that have remained unsolved
Supply chain improvements	Reduce delays, inventories, and cost
Business always open	Open 24/7/365; no overtime or other costs
Customization/personalization	Make order for customer preference
Ability to innovate, use new business models	Facilitate innovation and enable unique business models
Lower communication costs	The Internet is cheaper then VAN private lines
Efficient procurement	Saves time and reduces costs by enabling e-procurement
Improved customer service and relationship	Direct interaction with customers, better CRM
Help SME to compete	EC may help small companies to compete against large ones by using special business models
Lower inventories	Using customization inventories can be minimized
Lower cost of distributing digitizable product	Delivery online can be 90% cheaper; save paperworks
Provide competitive advantage	Lower prices, better service, improve brand image
Benefits to consumers	
Availability	Huge selection to choose from (vendor, products, information styles)
Ubiquity	Can shop any time from any place
Self-configuration	Can self-customize products
Find bargains	Use comparison engine; pay less
Real-time delivery	Download digital products quickly
No sales tax	Sometimes; changing
Enable telecommuting	Can work or study at home or any place
Social interaction and engagement	In social networks, get reviews, recommendations
Find unique items	Using online auctions, collectible items can be found
Comfortable shopping	Shop at your leisure without pushy sales clerks bothering you; open 24/7
Benefits to society	
Enable telecommuting	Facilitate work at home; less traffic, pollution
More and better public services	Provided by e-government (e.g., e-health)
Improved homeland security	Facilitate domestic security
Increased standard of living	Can buy more and cheaper goods/services, get better education
Close the digital divide	Allow people in rural areas and developing countries to use more services and purchase what they really like
Home shipping	Less travel, air pollution

Example: Fish Flops

Madison Robinson was a 15-year-old ninth grader when she opened the business, both online and offline. She designs the footwear herself. Madison uses her Twitter account and tweets about Fish Flops. After only 2 years of operation, the business became profitable enough to pay for Madison's college expenses. For details, see Burke (2013).

EC as a Provider of Efficiency, Effectiveness, and Competitive Advantage

The benefits of EC may result in significant changes in the way business is conducted. These changes may positively impact corporate operations resulting in a competitive advantage for the firms using EC (see Chap. 14) as well as more efficient governments and nonprofit organizations.

SECTION 1.3 REVIEW QUESTIONS

1. List the major drivers of EC.
2. List five benefits each to customers, organizations, and society.
3. From your knowledge, describe some technological developments that facilitate EC.
4. Identify additional benefits to society.

1.4 SOCIAL COMPUTING AND COMMERCE

The first generation of EC involved mainly trading, e-services, and corporate-sponsored collaboration. Currently, we are moving into the second generation of EC, which we call e-Commerce 2.0. It is based on Web 2.0 tools, social media, social networks, and virtual worlds—all the offspring of social computing.

Social Computing

Social computing refers to a computing system that involves social interactions and behaviors. It is performed with a set of tools that includes blogs, wikis, social network services, other *social software tools*, and social marketplaces (see Chap. 8). Whereas traditional computing systems concentrate on business processes, particularly transaction processing and increases in productivity, social computing concentrates on improving collaboration and interaction among people and on user-generated content. In social computing and commerce, people work together over the Internet, consult with specialists, and locate goods and services recommended by their friends.

Example: Social Computing Helps Travel

Advances in social computing impact travel operations and decisions. Travelers can share good travel experiences or warn others of bad experiences using sites such as **tripadvisor.com**. Special travel-oriented social networks such as WAYN are very popular among travelers.

In social computing, information is mostly generated by individuals and is available to all, usually for free. The major implementation tools of social computing are Web 2.0 and social media.

Web 2.0

The term *Web 2.0* was coined by O'Reilly Media in 2004. **Web 2.0** is the second generation of Internet-based tools and services that enable users to easily generate content, share media, and communicate and collaborate, in innovative ways.

O'Reilly divided Web 2.0 into four levels and provided examples of each. Some view Web 2.0 as a new digital ecosystem, which can be described through five Cs: creativity, connectivity, collaboration, convergence, and community.

The major tools of Web 2.0 are described in Chap. 2, and the applications are described in most other chapters. In addition, browse **enterpriseirregulars.com/author/dion** for an open forum about the Internet, society, collective intelligence, and the future.

Social Media

The term **social media** has several definitions. A popular definition is that social media involves user-generated online text, image, audio, and video content that are delivered via Web 2.0 platforms and tools. This media is used primarily for social interactions and conversations such as sharing opinions, experiences, insights, and perceptions and for online collaboration. Therefore, it is a powerful force for socialization. A key element is that users produce, control, and manage content. Additional definitions, descriptions, and references and a framework are provided in Chaps. 2 and 8 and in Turban et al. (2016).

The Difference Between Social Media and Web 2.0

Note that the concept of Web 2.0 is related to the concept of social media; many people equate the two terms and use them interchangeably. However, some people point to the differences. While social media uses Web 2.0 and its tools and technologies, the social media concept includes the philosophy of connected people, the interactions among them, the social support provided, the digital content that is created by users, and so forth.

Example: How Oprah Is Using Social Media to Build Her Business

According to Bertelsen (2014), Oprah Winfrey is integrating social media activities with everything she does, to encourage interactions of people with different platforms (e.g., Facebook, Twitter). Oprah is rewarding people based on their online engagement (e.g., posting comments). She is using Facebook polls and getting bloggers involved. Oprah is also actively using Twitter to interact with her followers.

Social Networks and Social Networking Services

The most interesting e-commerce application in recent years has been the emergence of social and enterprise social networks. Originating from online communities, these networks are growing rapidly and providing many new EC initiatives, revenue models, and business models (see **sustainablebrands.com/news_and_views/blog/13-hot-business-model-innovations-follow-2013**).

A **social network** is a social entity composed of nodes (which are generally individuals, groups, or organizations) that are connected by links such as hobbies, friendship, or profession. The structures are often very complex.

In its simplest form, a social network can be described by an image of the nodes and links. The network can also be used to describe Facebook's *social graph* (see description on Facebook.com).

Social Networking Services

Social networking services (SNSs), such as LinkedIn and Facebook, provide and host a Web space for communities of people to build their homepages for free. SNSs also provide basic support tools for conducting different activities and allow many vendors to provide apps. Social networks are people oriented but increasingly are used for commercial purposes also. For example, many performers, notably Justin Bieber, were discovered on YouTube. Initially, social networks were used solely for social activities. Today, corporations have a great interest in the business aspects of social networks (e.g., see **linkedin.com**, a network used for recruiting, and collaboration and Facebook for advertising).

The following are examples of representative social networking services:

- **Facebook.com**: The most visited social networking website.
- **YouTube.com** and **metacafe.com**: Users can upload and view video clips.
- **Flickr.com**: Users share and comment on photos.
- **LinkedIn.com**: The major enterprise-oriented social network.
- **Habbo.com**: Entertaining country-specific sites for kids and adults.
- **Pinterest.com**: Provides a platform for organizing and sharing images.
- *Google* + (**plus.google.com**): A business-oriented social network.
- **MySpace.com**: Facilitates socialization and entertainment for people of all ages.
- **Instagram.com**: Provides a platform for sharing photos and videos.

Social Networking

We define **social networking** as the execution of any Web 2.0 activity, such as blogging or having a presence in a social network. It also includes all activities conducted in social networks.

Enterprise Social Networks

Business-oriented social networks can be public, such as LinkedIn.com. As such, they are owned and managed by an independent company. Another type of business-oriented social network is private, owned by corporations, and operated inside them. These are known as *enterprise social networks* (e.g., My Starbucks Idea). These can be directed toward customers and/or company employees.

Example: A Customer-Oriented Enterprise Social Network

Carnival Cruise Line sponsors a social networking site (**carnival.com/funville**) to attract cruise fans. Visitors use the site to exchange opinions, organize groups for trips, and much more. It cost the company $300,000 to set up the site, but the initial cost was covered by increased business within a year.

Social Commerce

Social commerce (SC), also known as *social business*, refers to e-commerce transactions delivered via social media. Social commerce is considered a subset of e-commerce by some. More specifically, it is a combination of e-commerce, e-marketing, the supporting technologies, and social media content. This definition is illustrated in Fig. 1.5. The figure shows that social

Fig. 1.5 The foundation of social commerce

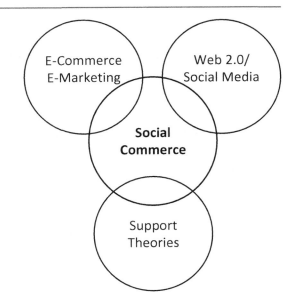

commerce is created from the integration of e-commerce and e-marketing using Web 2.0/social media applications. The integration is supported by theories such as social capital, social psychology, consumer behavior, and online collaboration, resulting in a set of useful applications that drive social commerce.

We will return to social commerce in Chaps. 8 and 9.

The following are some examples of social commerce:

- Hilton Garden Inn introduced in 2016 Instagram-based photo map (GFI Travel Guide) to assist in advertising their hotels.
- Dell Computer claims to have made $6.5 million by selling computers on Twitter in 2 years. Also, Dell generates ideas from community members at its *Idea Storm* site.
- Procter & Gamble sells its Max Factor brand cosmetics on Facebook.
- Disney allows people to book certain tickets on Facebook without leaving the social network.
- PepsiCo gives live notifications when its customers are close to physical stores (grocery, restaurants, gas stations) that sell Pepsi products. Then, PepsiCo sends coupons and discount information to the customers.
- Starbucks is using extensive promotions on Facebook including generating ideas from the members via its My Starbucks Idea website (see the opening case for details).
- Mountain Dew attracts video game lovers and sport enthusiasts via Dewmocracy contests. The company also uses the most dedicated community members to contribute ideas. The company used Facebook, Twitter, and YouTube to interact with consumers and engage them.
- Target used Twitter to promote their fall fashion show in New York with videos and ads. The show was streamed live on Facebook.
- Levi's advertises on Facebook based on "what people think their friends would like."
- Wendy's uses Facebook and Twitter to award $50 gift cards to people who have the funniest and quirkiest responses to Wendy's published challenges online.

Overall, the vast majority of US companies have a presence on Facebook (see **emarketer.com** for periodic reports). For more applications, see Chaps. 8 and 9and Turban et al. (2016). For a free guide, go to **pixtree.com/shoppable-galleries**.

The Major Tools of Web 2.0

Web 2.0 uses dozens of tools such as wikis, RSS feeds, blogs, and microblogs (e.g., Twitter). With microblogging, you can transmit short messages (up to 140 characters) to a list of recipients via the Internet and wireless or wireline devices. As of 2009, Twitter became a major Web 2.0 tool with diversified business applications.

SECTION 1.4 REVIEW QUESTIONS

1. Define social computing and list its characteristics.
2. Define Web 2.0 and list its attributes.
3. Define social networks.
4. Describe the capabilities of social networking services (SNSs).
5. Describe Facebook. Why is it so popular?
6. What is an enterprise social network?
7. Define social commerce.

1.5   THE DIGITAL AND SOCIAL WORLDS: ECONOMY, ENTERPRISES, AND SOCIETY

e-Commerce, including e-Commerce 2.0, is facilitated by developments in the digital and social economy. For an overview, see videos titled "Did You Know" of the latest updated information.

The digital revolution is upon us. We see it every day at home and work, in businesses, in schools, in hospitals, on the roads, and in entertainment. For an overview, see Sidhu (2015). Next, we describe three elements of the digital world: economy, enterprises, and society.

The Digital Economy

The **digital economy**, also known as the *Internet economy*, is an economy based on online transactions, mostly e-commerce. It includes digital wireline or wireless communication networks (e.g., the Internet, intranets, extranets, and VANs), computers, software, and other related information technologies. This digital economy displays the following characteristics:

- Many digitizable products—books, databases, magazines, information, electronic games, and software—are delivered over a digital infrastructure anytime, anywhere in the world, interconnected by a global grid. We are moving from analog to digital; even the media is going digital (TV as of February 2009).
- Information is transformed into a commodity.
- Financial transactions are now digitized, and chips are embedded in many products (e.g., cameras, cars). Knowledge is codified.
- Work and business processes are organized in new and innovative ways.
- Disruptive innovation is occurring in many industries (see Manyika et al. 2013).

Table 1.3 summarizes the major characteristics of the digital economy.

The digital revolution also enables many innovations, and new ones appear almost daily, improving business processes and productivity. The digital revolution provides the necessary technologies for EC and creates major changes in the business environment, as described in section "Electronic Commerce Business Models"

Sharing Economy

Sharing economy refers to an economic system constructed around the concept of sharing goods and services among the participating people. Also known as "collaborative consumption" and "collaborative economy," such systems appear in different forms and frequently use information technologies in their operations. Well-known examples are ride sharing

Table 1.3 Major characteristics of the digital economy

Area	Description
Globalization	Global communication and collaboration; global electronic marketplaces and competition
Digitization	Music, books, pictures, software, videos, and more are digitized for fast and inexpensive storage and distribution
Speed	A move to real-time transactions, thanks to digitized documents, products, and services. Many business processes are expedited by 90% or more
Information overload and intelligent search	Although the amount of information generated is accelerating, intelligent search tools can help users find what people need
Markets	Markets are moving online. Physical marketplaces are being replaced or supplemented by electronic markets; new markets are being created, increasing competition
Business models and processes	New and improved business models and processes provide opportunities to new companies and industries
Innovation	Digital and Internet-based innovations continue at a rapid pace. More patents are being granted than ever before
Obsolescence	The fast pace of innovation creates a high rate of obsolescence
Opportunities	Opportunities abound in almost all aspects of life and operations
Fraud	Criminals employ a slew of innovative schemes on the Internet. Cybercons are everywhere
Wars	Conventional wars are changing to cyberwars or are complemented by them
Organizations	Organizations are moving to digital enterprises and social businesses

(e.g., Uber), money lending (Lending Club), and accommodation sharing (Airbnb). The essentials of this concept are described in Chap. 5. For an overview, see Howard (2015) and PWC's free e-book (2015).

The major benefits for participants are cost reduction for buyers and the ability to sell more for sellers. Societal benefits include reduction of carbon footprint (e.g., in ride sharing), increase recycling, and increase social interactions. For comprehensive coverage, see **en.wikipedia.org/wiki/Sharing_economy**.

Sharing Economy and e-Commerce
Several EC models and companies are based on the concept of the sharing economy. Examples include Uber (for ride sharing), Yerdle (a sharing economy free marketplace), Kickstarter (for crowdfunding), Krrb (a P2P marketplace), and Knok and Love Home Swap for home swapping. Money lending is growing rapidly (Lending Club). Vacation rental is a large area where home and condo owners provide short-term rentals possibly for an exchange or renting (e.g., see Airbnb, HomeAway, and VRBO).

For descriptions, examples, and cases, see Chap. 5.

Example: Swedish Farmers Go Online
According to Willgren (2013), traditional farmers in Sweden created a social network called "MinFarm" (My Farm). The network allows communication between the farmers and their customers. It also allows people that grow their own food to tell their stories and ask for advice. Customers can visit farms and shop there; they can also order online. The network promotes self-sustainability.

The Social Impact

The digital revolution is accompanied by social impacts that resulted in part by improved communication and collaboration tools offered by social media. For example, smartphones reduce the digital divide. In addition to productivity improvement in the economy, one can see some major social changes, such as the mass participation in social networks. One impact is the creation of the *social enterprise* (see **centreforsocialenterprise.com/what-is-social-enterprise**).

The Apps Society
New apps change the way that people communicate, work, and play. People are looking for apps for thousands of new uses.

The Digital Enterprise

One of the major impacts of EC is the creation of the digital enterprise that accompanies the social enterprise.

The term *digital enterprise* has several definitions. It usually refers to an enterprise, such as Amazon.com, Google, Facebook, or Ticketmaster, which uses computers and information systems to automate most of its business processes.

Table 1.4 The digital versus brick-and-mortar enterprises

Brick-and-mortar organizations	Digital organizations
Selling in physical stores	Selling online
Selling tangible goods	Selling digital goods online as well
Internal inventory/production planning	Online collaborative inventory and production planning
Paper catalogs	Smart electronic catalogs
Physical marketplace	Electronic marketplace
Use of telephone, fax, VANs, and traditional EDI	Use of computers, smartphones, the Internet, and extranets and EDI
Physical auctions, infrequently	Online auctions, everywhere, any time
Broker-based services, transactions	Electronic infomediaries, value-added services
Paper-based billing and payments	Electronic billing and payments
Paper-based tendering	Electronic tendering (reverse auctions)
Push production, starting with demand forecasting	Pull production, starting with an order (build to order)
Mass production (standard products)	Mass customization, build to order
Physical-based commission marketing	Affiliated, virtual marketing
Word-of-mouth, slow, and limited advertisement	Explosive viral marketing, in particular in social networks
Linear supply chains	Hub-based supply chains
Large amount of capital needed for mass production	Less capital needed for build to order; payments can be collected before production starts
Large fixed cost required for plant operation	Small fixed cost required for smaller and less complex plant operation
Customers' value proposition is frequently a mismatch (cost > value)	Perfect match of customers' value proposition (cost < = value)

The **digital enterprise** is a relatively new business model that uses IT to gain competitive advantage by increasing employee productivity, improving efficiency and effectiveness of business processes, and providing better interactivity between vendors and customers. The major characteristics of a digital enterprise are listed in Table 1.4, where they are compared with those of a traditional enterprise. See also Olanrewaju et al. (2014).

Note that the term *enterprise* refers to any kind of organization, public or private, small or large. An enterprise can be a manufacturing plant, a hospital, a university, a TV network, an entire city, or an entire country. For example, Singapore is one of the seven countries considered digital; see Estopace (2016). They are all moving toward being digitized.

A digital enterprise uses networks of computers in EC to facilitate the following:

- All business partners are reached via the Internet or a group of secured intranets, called an extranet, or value-added private communication lines.
- All internal communication is done via an intranet, which is the counterpart of the Internet inside the company.

Most companies' data and EC transactions are done via the Internet and extranets. Many companies employ a **corporate portal**, which is a gateway for customers, employees, and partners to reach corporate information and to communicate with the company.

A key concern of many companies today is how to transform themselves into digital (or at least partially digital) enterprises. The concept of the digital enterprise is related to the concept of social business.

The Social Business (Enterprise)

The concept of social business has several definitions and characteristics. We present only a few of them.

The Social Business Forum's Definition

The concept of social business was developed decades ago and was not related to computers. Today, the Social Business Forum defines **social business** as "an organization that has put in place the strategies, technologies, and processes to systematically engage all the individuals of its ecosystem (employees, customers, partners, suppliers) to maximize the cocreated value." See **2013.socialbusinessforum.com/social-business-manifesto**. The Forum also discusses the implication of this definition and its relevance inside, across, and outside organizations. Note that the efficient creation of value using technology is emphasized. The Forum conducts annual conferences.

IBM's Approach

IBM has been recognized by the research company IDC as the market share leader in social software platform providers. IBM and IDC include in their joint definition the following characteristics: use of emerging technologies such as social software, social-oriented organizational culture, and improvements of business processes. The IBM effort also concentrates on improved collaboration. The basic idea is that social media networks and social customers require organizations to drastically change the way they work to become a social business that can exploit the opportunities created by the digital and social revolutions. IBM is helping organizations become social businesses (e.g., see **ibm.com/social-business/us/en**). IBM has an extensive "social business video library"; two interesting videos are recommended for a better understanding of the concept:

1. "How Do You Become a Social Business?"—by Sandy Carter from IBM (1:04 min) at **youtube.com/watch?v= OZy0dNQbotg**
2. "Social Business @ IBM"—an interview with Luis Suarez (8:50 min) at **youtube.com/watch?v=enudW2gHek0**

These are used in Team Assignment #4 at the end of this chapter. Both are useful for understanding of the concept.

The Social Enterprise

The concept of social business is frequently equated to and sometimes confused with the term *social enterprise*. Many use the two terms interchangeably. The main goal of a **social enterprise** is to focus on social issues. These enterprises generate revenue. The profits do not go to owners and shareholders but are put back into the company and used toward building positive social change. The *Social Enterprise Alliance* provides details at **se-alliance.org/why**. It seems that the above definition emphasizes the social goals.

The Digital Revolution and Society

The final, and perhaps most important, element of the *digital world* is people and the way they work and live. Clearly, the digital revolution has changed almost any activity one can think of—work, play, shopping, entertainment, travel, medical care, education, and much more. Just think about your digital phone, camera, TV, car, home, and almost anything else. It is only natural that people are utilizing technology and EC at an increasing rate. Let us take a look at some examples:

- Google has developed cars that drive themselves automatically in traffic (autonomous vehicles). The cars are being tested in several states, including California, and were approved in the state of Nevada in the summer of 2012. See Bridges and Sherman (2016) on how these will change the world. For an overview and potential benefits, including safety, see Neckermann (2015). For details, see Chap. 7.
- AeroMobile is planning a flying car for 2017 that will use several e-business features (see Smith 2015).Flying cars are planned now by several other companies.
- As of 2008, high school girls are able to solicit feedback from their friends regarding dozens of different prom dresses that have been displayed by Sears on Facebook.
- Washers and dryers in some college dorms are controlled via the Internet. Students can sign in at **esuds.net** or use their smartphone to check the availability of laundry machines (or get alerts). Furthermore, they can receive e-mail or SMS alerts when their wash and dry cycles are complete. Some systems can even inject premeasured amounts of detergent and fabric softener at the right cycle time.
- Hailing a taxi in South Florida and other major cities is much easier today. As of August 2012, you can e-hail a taxi if you have a smartphone with an application by ZabCab (**zabcab.com**). All you have to do is to push one button. Your exact location (on a map) will appear automatically on the portable device screen of all subscribing taxi drivers. There is no cost for the user. ZabCab collaborates with taxi drivers and individual drivers (see Vermontbiz News 2016). It competes with Uber. (See Chap. 5).
- Several hundreds of millions of active users are downloading songs, games, and videos on Apple's iTunes store (a selection of over 52 million songs, TV episodes, etc.). The store also serves 575 million mobile devices users. Total revenue is estimated to reach $13 billion in 2017. The store is considered the most popular music store in the world. Since its inception in 2003, it has sold over 33 billion songs as of spring 2017. At the same time, the iPhone store has offered over 1.2 million apps.

- Ford Company is using the "MyFord Touch" system to calculate the fastest, shortest, and most fuel-efficient way to get from a given place to a destination. The system charts a route that avoids congestion (based on historical and real-time traffic data). Results are shown on a dashboard. Initial deployment can be seen in recent models of Ford Focus.
- A new Japanese hotel is staffed entirely by robots (see Moscaritolo 2015).
- As of 2014, guests in several Starwood Hotels & Resorts and other big hotel chains can enter their rooms by using a smartphone as a room key.
- Pokémon GO is a smartphone game based on augmented reality (Chap. 2). Hundreds of millions of people play this game, which was invented in Japan.
- An international research project is developing a computerized system that enables the monitoring of patients at home in real time, conducting of diagnosis, and providing of medical advice. The objective is to reduce traffic to medical facilities while increasing the quality of care. The project is managed in Israel with collaboration of experts from several European countries. For details, see **haifa.ac.il/index.php/en**.
- Union Pacific, the largest US railroad company, is using a large number of sensors on their trains and other equipment to collect data that is transmitted via wireless and wireline networks to a data center. There, an analysis is performed to determine optimal preventive maintenance by using *predictive analytics*. The analysis increased the annual revenue by $35 million.
- Water loss involving many influencing variables in the Valley of the Moon Water District in California has been considerably reduced by using smart analytical computing from IBM.
- Supermarket shoppers in Finland are using camera-equipped smartphones that can scan the bar code of an item to find its ingredients, nutrient value, and the exercise time needed to burn the consumed calories.
- Bicycle computers (by Bridgestone Cycle Co.) can automatically keep track of your travel distance, speed, time, and calorie consumption. For cycling communities, see **bikewire.net** and **cyclingforum.com**.
- Champions of the World Series of Poker used to be people in their 50s and 60s who spent years playing the game to gain the experience needed to win. However, in 2009, Joe Cada from the United States won the main event at the World Series of Poker, at the age of 21. To gain experience quickly, Cada plays extensively online. Joe McKeehen won in 2015, at the age of 24.

The above list can be extended to hundreds or even thousands of items.

Some Impacts of the Digital and Social Worlds

Of the many impacts of the digital and social worlds, here we will describe only two: the disruptive impacts of e-commerce and the social customers.

Disruptive Impacts of e-Commerce

Digital technologies in general, and EC and related technologies such as m-commerce and social commerce, may have a disruptive impact on economies, industries, business models, and people (see the 2013 'Disruptive Technologies' video at **mckinsey.com/insights/high_tech_telecoms_internet/disruptive_technologies**). See also McCafferty (2015). For a 2014 video interview of MIT's Andrew McAfee and McKinsey's James Manyika titled "Why Every Leader Should Care about Digitization and Disruptive Innovation," see **mckinsey.com/business-functions/business-technology/our-insights/why-every-leader-should-care-about-digitization-and-disruptive-innovation**. For a discussion and examples, see Chap. 5.

The Social Customer

An important component in the digital society is the *social customer*. **Social customers** (sometimes called *digital customers*) are usually members of social networks who share opinions about products, services, and vendors, do online social shopping, and understand their rights and how to use the wisdom and power of social communities to their benefit. The number of social customers is increasing exponentially due to wireless shopping, new online shopping models (Chap. 8), and communication tools (see Chap. 2). The highlights of the social customers are shown in Fig. 1.6.

Fig. 1.6 The social customer (Source: Courtesy of F. Cipriani, "Social CRM: Concept, Benefits, and Approach to Adopt," November 2008. slideshare. net/fhcipriani/social-crm-presentation-761,225; accessed March 2017; used with permission)

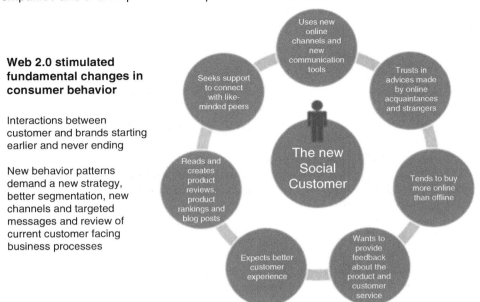

Being connected, customers realized that they could ask more from companies and share opinions about products and services

Web 2.0 stimulated fundamental changes in consumer behavior

Interactions between customer and brands starting earlier and never ending

New behavior patterns demand a new strategy, better segmentation, new channels and targeted messages and review of current customer facing business processes

As the figure illustrates, social customers expect better service and are willing to provide feedback and product reviews, and they connect with like-minded peers. This new behavior pattern requires a new strategy for marketing, communications, and customer service. For example, Phillips Corp. is digitally transforming itself to put the customers first (see Baldwin 2016).

The social customer is participatory and has active involvement in the shopping process both as a buyer and as an influencer. Individuals can be influenced by friends, friends of friends, and even friends of friends of friends. Merchants must understand how these consumers differ from conventional customers and therefore use appropriate e-commerce marketing strategy as well as superb customer service. Procedures, guidelines, and software are publically available for social CRM (e.g., see **en.wikipedia.org/wiki/Social_CRM**).

SECTION 1.5 REVIEW QUESTIONS

1. Define the digital revolution and list its components.
2. List the characteristics of the digital economy.
3. What is the social economy?
4. Define a digital enterprise and relate it to social business.
5. Describe the social enterprise.
6. Compare traditional and digital enterprises.
7. Describe the digital society.
8. Describe how EC technologies can disrupt industries.
9. Describe social customers.

1.6   ELECTRONIC COMMERCE BUSINESS MODELS

One of the major characteristics of EC is that it facilitates the creation of new business models. A **business model** describes the manner in which business is done to generate revenue and create value. This is accomplished by attaining organizational objectives. A key area is attracting enough customers to buy the organization's products or services. Several different EC business models are possible, depending on the company, the industry, and so on. Business models can be found in existing businesses as well as in proposed ones. See Lazazzera (2015).

Note: The January–February 2011 issue of *Harvard Business Review* is dedicated to business model innovations (five articles), including several topics related to e-commerce.

The Structure and Properties of Business Models

A comprehensive business model (for a proposal company) may include some or all of the following components as illustrated in Fig. 1.7:

- A description of the *customers* to be served and their *value proposition*. Also, how these customers can be reached and supported
- A description of all *products* and *services* the business plans to deliver. Also, what the differentiating aspects of the products are
- The company's growth strategies
- A description of the required *business process* and the distribution infrastructure (including human resources)
- A list of the *resources* required, their cost, and availability (including human resources)
- A description of the organization's *supply chains*, including *suppliers* and other *business partners*
- The value chain structure
- The relevant markets with a list of the major competitors and their market share. Also, market strategies and strengths/weaknesses of the company
- The competitive advantage offered by the business model including pricing and selling strategies
- The anticipated organizational changes and any resistance to change
- A description of the revenues expected (*revenue model*), sources of funding, and the *financial viability*

Models also include a *value proposition*, which is a description of the benefits of using the specific model (tangible and intangible), both to the customers and to the organization. A detailed discussion and examples of business models and their relationship to business plans are presented at **en.wikipedia.org/wiki/Business_model**.

This chapter presents two of the models' elements: *revenue models* and *value propositions*.

Fig. 1.7 The major components of a business model

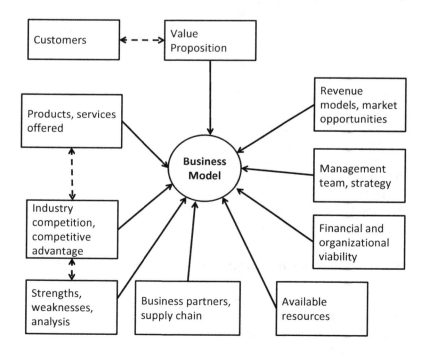

Revenue Models

A revenue model specifies how the organization, or an EC project, will generate revenue. For example, the revenue model for Net-a-Porter shows revenue from online sales of luxury dresses. The major revenue models are shown in the shaded area that follows:

Sales. Companies generate revenue from selling products or services on their websites. An example is when Net-a-Porter, Starbucks, Amazon.com, or Godiva sells a product online.

Transaction fees. Commissions are based on the volume of transactions made. For example, when a homeowner sells a house, he or she typically pays a transaction fee to the broker. The higher the value of the sale, the higher the total transaction fee. Alternatively, transaction fees can be levied *per transaction*. With online stock trades, for example, there is usually a fixed fee per trade, regardless of the volume.

Subscription fees. Customers pay a fixed amount, usually monthly, to get some type of service. An example would be the fee you pay to an Internet access provider (fixed monthly payments).

Advertising fees. Companies charge others for allowing them to place a banner on their sites.

Affiliate fees. Companies receive commissions for referring customers to certain websites. A good program is available at Amazon.com.

Licensing fees. Another revenue source is licensing fees (e.g., see **progress.com/datadirect-connectors**). Licensing fees can be assessed as an annual fee or a per usage fee. Microsoft receives fees from each workstation that uses Windows NT, for example.

Other revenue sources. Some companies allow people to play games for a fee or to watch a sports competition in real time for a fee (e.g., see **espn.go.com**).

A company uses its *revenue model* to describe how it will generate revenue and its *business model* to describe the *process* it will use to do so.

Innovative Revenue Models for Individuals

The Internet allows for innovative revenue models, some of which can be utilized even by individuals, as demonstrated by the following example:

Example: buy low, sell high

This strategy has been known for generations, but now you have a better chance. How about buying stuff cheap on Craigslist (or other online classified ad sites) and reselling it for a 50–200% profit at an auction on eBay? Try it; you might make money. Some people make it even bigger. The person who bought the domain name *pizza.com* for $20 in 1994 sold it for $2.6 million in April 2008 (one of the many he purchased). The revenue model can be part of the value proposition or it may supplement it.

Value Proposition

Business models also include a value-proposition statement. A **value proposition** refers to the benefits, including the intangible ones that a company hopes to derive from using its business model. In B2C EC, for example, the *customer value proposition* defines how a company's product or service fulfills the needs of customers. In other words, it describes the total benefits to the customer. The *value proposition* is an important part of the marketing plan of any product or service. For 50 value propositions in B2C e-commerce, see Davis (2012).

Functions of a Business Model

Business models have the following major functions or objectives:

- Describe the supply and value chains.
- Formulate the venture's competitive strategy and its long-range plans.
- Present the customer value proposition.
- Identify who will use the technology for what purpose; specify the revenue-generation process, where the company will operate.
- Estimate the cost structure and amount and profit potential.

Typical EC Business Models

There are many types of EC business models. Examples and details of EC business models can be found throughout this text and provided by Rappa (2010). The following are common models.

1. **Online direct marketing**. The most obvious EC model is that of selling products or services online. Sales may be from a *manufacturer* to a customer, eliminating intermediaries or physical stores (e.g., Dell), or from *retailers* to consumers, making distribution more efficient (e.g., Net-a-Porter, Walmart online). This model is especially efficient for digitizable products and services (those that can be delivered electronically). This model has several variations (see Chaps. 3 and 4) and uses different mechanisms (e.g., auctions). It is practiced in B2C (where it is called *e-tailing*).

Example

As of 2016, farmers in India can reach customers directly as part of agriculture reform. For details, see Biswas (2016).

2. **Electronic tendering systems**. Large organizational buyers usually make large-volume or large-value purchases through a **tendering (bidding) system**, also known as a *reverse auction*. Such tendering can be done online, saving time and money. Pioneered by General Electric Corp., e-tendering systems are gaining popularity. Indeed, many government agencies mandate that most of their procurement must be done through e-tendering. (Details are provided in Chap. 4).

3. **Electronic marketplaces and exchanges**. Electronic marketplaces existed in isolated applications for decades (e.g., stock and commodities exchanges). However, as of 1996, hundreds of e-marketplaces (old and new) have introduced new methods and efficiencies to the trading process. If they are well organized and managed, e-marketplaces can provide significant benefits to both buyers and sellers. Of special interest are vertical marketplaces that concentrate on one industry. For example, Net-a-Porter is a marketplace for dresses and related items. Its customers are mostly individuals. For details, see Chaps. 3 and 4.

4. **Viral advertising and marketing**. According to the viral marketing model, people use e-mail and social networks to spread word-of-mouth advertising. It is basically Web-based *word-of-mouth* advertising and is popular in social networks.

5. **Group purchasing**. Group purchasing is a well-known offline method, both in B2C and B2B. It is based on the concept of quantity discounts ("cheaper by the dozen"). The Internet model allows individuals to get together so they can gain the large-quantity advantage. This model was not popular in B2C until 2010 when Groupon introduced a modified model in which people are grouped around special deals, as illustrated in Chap. 8. Note that the model is very popular in China.

A company may use several EC models as demonstrated in the Starbucks opening case, the NFL closing case, and the Dell case.

Classification of Business Models in e-Commerce

Rappa (2010) classified the EC business models into eight categories:
1. Brokerage: Market makers that charge fee for their services.
2. Advertising: Websites that provide content and charge advertisers for related ads.

3. Infomediary: Provides information and/or infrastructure that help buyers and/or sellers and charge for their services.
4. Merchant—retailers (such as Walmart or Amazon): These buy the products and sell them at profit.
5. Direct model: Sells without intermediaries.
6. Affiliate: Paying website owners to place banners. Share fees received from advertisers.
7. Community: A social media-based model that utilizes Web 2.0 tools, social networks, and the characteristics presented in Chap. 8.

Rappa (2010) further provides examples of each plus their revenue models. In addition, he presents the major varieties in each category.

SECTION 1.6 REVIEW QUESTIONS

1. What is a business model? Describe its functions and properties.
2. Describe a revenue model and a value proposition. How are they related?
3. Describe the following business models: direct marketing, tendering system, electronic exchanges, viral marketing, and social networking/commerce.
4. Identify some business models related to buying and those related to selling.
5. Describe how viral marketing works.

1.7   THE LIMITATIONS, IMPACTS, AND THE FUTURE OF E-COMMERCE

As indicated in section "The Electronic Commerce Field: Growth, Content, Classification, and a Brief History" there are some limitations and failures in EC.

The Limitations and Barriers of EC

Barriers to EC are either non-technological or technological. Representative major barriers are listed in Table 1.5.
    One important area that may limit some EC project is ethics.

Ethical Issues

Ethical issues can create pressures or constraints on EC business operations. Yet some ethical sites increase trust and help EC vendors. **Ethics** relates to standards of right and wrong. Ethics is a difficult concept, because what is considered ethical by one person may seem unethical to another. Likewise, what is considered ethical in one country may be unethical in another. See Chap. 15. Also, security issues are important (see Chap. 11).

Table 1.5 Limitations of electronic commerce

Technological limitations	Non-technological limitations
Need for universal standards for quality, security, and reliability	Security and privacy concerns deter customers from buying
The telecommunications bandwidth may be insufficient, especially for m-commerce, videos, and graphics	Lack of trust in sellers, in computers, and paperless faceless transactions hinders buying
Software development tools are still evolving	Resistance to change
It is difficult to integrate Internet and EC software with some existing (especially legacy) applications and databases	Many legal and public policy issues are not resolved or are not clear
Special Web servers are needed in addition to the network servers, which add to the cost of EC	National and international government regulations sometimes get in the way Global competition intensifies
Internet accessibility is still expensive and/or inconvenient for many	It is difficult to measure some of the costs and benefits of EC
Large-scale B2C requires special automated warehouses for order fulfillment	Not enough customers. Lack of collaboration along the supply chain

Implementing EC may raise ethical issues ranging from monitoring employee's e-mail to invasion of privacy of millions of customers whose data are stored in private and public databases. In implementing EC, it is necessary to pay attention to these issues and recognize that some of them may limit, or even prohibit, the use of EC. An example of this can be seen in the attempted implementation of RFID tags (Online Tutorial T2) in retail stores due to the potential invasion of buyers' privacy.

Overcoming the Barriers

Despite these barriers, EC is expanding rapidly. As experience accumulates and technology improves, the cost-benefit ratio of EC will increase, resulting in even greater rates of EC adoption.

Why Study e-Commerce?

The major reason to study e-commerce is that it is rapidly growing and impacting many businesses and marketing operations. The percentage of EC of total commerce transactions is increasing rapidly, and some predict that most future commerce will be online. Thus, any businessperson or a business student should learn about this field.

This is why the academic area of e-commerce that started around 1995 with only a few courses and textbooks is growing rapidly. Today, many universities offer EC courses and complete programs in e-commerce or e-business (e.g., majors in e-commerce, minors in e-commerce and certificate programs; see University of Virginia, University of Maine, University of Arkansas). Recently, e-commerce topics have been integrated into all functional fields (e.g., Internet marketing, electronic financial markets). The reason for this proliferation is that e-commerce is penetrating more and more into business areas, services, and governments. Finally, it is a fascinating field with its innovative business models.

However, there are also some very tangible benefits to increased knowledge of EC. First, your chances of getting a good (or better) job are higher. The demand for both technical and managerial EC skills is growing rapidly and so are the salaries (e.g., see salary comparison sites such as **salary.com** and **careerbuilder.com/insights**. Hundreds of well-paying open positions are available in areas related to social media, social networking, and social commerce. Second, your chances for a promotion could be higher if you understand EC and know how to seize its opportunities. Finally, it gives you a chance to become a billionaire, like the founders of Google, Facebook, YouTube, Amazon.com, and Alibaba, or to make a great deal of money on eBay. You can make money simply by selling online. And, you can do online business even while you are a student (See **jetpens.com**). Even some teenagers practice successful EC. An example is Diane Keng, an entrepreneur from Cupertino Monte Vista High School in California, who initiated three successful Web 2.0 start-up companies, making substantial money.

In 2016, a 9-year-old sold thousands of boxes of Girl Scout Cookies on the Internet instead of going door to door.

There are many other opportunities for young people to make money from EC in addition to the examples in this book and selling on eBay. Experts suggest the following ways to earn extra cash online: (1) sell your craft; (2) make money from your talent; (3) be a nurse on call; (4) write, edit, or proofread; (5) design graphics and websites; (6) tutor kids or adults; (7) give advice; (8) provide customer service; (9) launch a blog; (10) give your opinion (for a fee); (11) search the Internet; and (12) do online tasks. For 21 ways to make money online, see Adams (2016). See also **shop.com** and Staff (2017). A growing EC model that can be used by individuals is drop-shipping (see Bennet 2016 and Chap. 3 for details).

Many opportunities are available in the areas of social media and commerce.

The Future of EC

According to the World Trade Organization (INAS 2016), e-commerce can play a pivotal role in fostering economic growth and raising living standards, particularly for developing countries. This is one factor that contributes to EC's bright future.

Several economic, technological, and societal trends impact EC and shape its direction. For example, most experts agree that the shift from EC to mobile commerce is inevitable. In addition, many believe in the future of social commerce, as a major component of e-commerce. There will be a surge in the use of e-commerce in developing countries (mostly thanks to smartphones and tablets as well as e-payment systems). e-Commerce will win its battle against conventional retailing. Finally, e-commerce will increase its global reach.

EC will impact some industries more than others will. This impact is changing with time. For example, major impacts in the past 8 years were felt in travel, retail, stock brokering, and banking. Next are movies, healthcare, book publishing, and electronic payments. Today's predictions about the future size of EC, provided by respected analysts such as comScore, eMarketer.com, and Forrester, vary. For a list of sites that provide such predictions and other EC statistics, see Table 3.1.

The number of Internet users worldwide was estimated to be around 3 billion in the late 2016 and 3.5 billion in 2017 (see Plunkett 2017 and **internetworldstats.com**). With more people on the Internet, EC will increase.

eMarketer forecasted that almost 85% of all Internet users in the United States would shop online in 2016. The repercussions of the 2008–2013 financial meltdown have motivated people to shop online and look for bargains where price comparison is easy and fast (e.g., try to find the price of an item on Amazon.com). Another important factor is the increase of mobile devices and especially smartphones. EC growth would come not only from B2C but also from B2B and from newer applications such as e-government, e-learning, B2E, social commerce, and c-commerce. The total volume of EC has been growing every year by 13–16% in spite of the failures of individual companies and initiatives and the economic slowdown.

Finally, different business environment factors facilitate EC.

The future of EC depends on technological, organizational, and societal trends (e.g., see Fei and Chung 2015). Gartner Inc. publishes a list of the "Top 10 Strategic Technology Trends" every year. Both the 2015 and 2016 lists include several EC topics (e.g., mobile apps, Internet of Things). See also McCafferty (2016) for the top trends of 2016.

A final note: The future of EC depends on the accessibility to the Internet. Facebook's laser drones could bring the Internet to 5 billion people (see CBS 2015). Kelly (2016) lists 12 technological forces that shape our future. For more on the future of EC, see Chap. 15.

SECTION 1.7 REVIEW QUESTIONS

1. List the major technological and non-technological barriers and limitations to EC.
2. Describe some of the benefits of studying EC.
3. How can EC help entrepreneurship?
4. Summarize the major points involved with the future of e-commerce.

1.8 OVERVIEW OF THIS BOOK

This book is composed of 16 chapters grouped into six parts, as shown in Fig. 1.8. Additional content, including online supplemental material for each chapter, is available online on the book's website (**affordable-ecommerce-textbook.com/turban**).

The specific parts and chapters of this textbook are as follows:

Part I: Introduction to e-Commerce and e-Marketplaces

This part of the book includes an overview of EC and its content, benefits, limitations, and drivers, which are presented in Chap. 1. Chapter 2 presents electronic markets and their mechanisms, such as electronic catalogs and auctions. This chapter also includes a presentation of Web 2.0 tools of social networks and some emerging technologies.

Part II: EC Applications

This section includes three chapters. Chapter 3 describes e-tailing (B2C), including some of its most innovative applications for selling products online. It also describes the delivery of services, such as online banking, travel, and insurance. In Chap. 4, we introduce B2B EC and describe company-centric models (one buyer, many sellers; one seller, many buyers) as well as electronic exchanges (many buyers and many sellers). e-Government, e-learning, management health, sharing economy models, and P2P are the major subjects of Chap. 5.

Part III: Emerging EC Delivery Platforms

In addition to traditional EC delivery platforms, described in Part II, we present in the four chapters of Part III the following topics: Chap. 6 covers the area of mobile commerce. In Chap. 7, we cover the emerging areas of AI-based smart commerce and the related topic of the Internet of Things and its EC applications. The areas of social commerce and social media marketing are covered in Chap. 8. Enterprise social commerce and other applications are presented in Chap. 9.

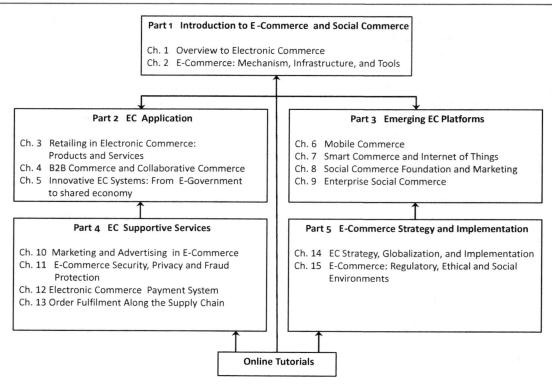

Fig. 1.8 Plan of the book

Part IV: EC Support Services

Part IV examines the issues involving the support services needed for EC applications in three chapters. Chapter 10 explains consumer behavior in cyberspace, online market research, and Internet advertising. Chapter 11 delves into EC security and fraud protection. Chapter 12 discusses electronic payments. Order fulfillment is covered in Chap. 13.

Part V: EC Strategy and Implementation

Part V includes two chapters. Chapter 14 examines e-strategy and planning, including going global and the impact of EC on small businesses. It also deals with implementation issues. The last chapter, Chap. 15, deals with ethical and regulatory issues that include privacy protection, intellectual property, and fake content. Also covered are some societal-related issues. The chapter also provides an overview of the future of EC.

Online Mini Tutorials

Five tutorials are available on the book's website (**affordable-ecommerce-textbook.com/turban**).
T1 e-CRM
T2 EC Technology: EDI, Extranet, RFID, and Cloud Computing
T3 Business Intelligence and Analytics
T4 Competition in cyberspace
T5 e-Collaboration

MANAGERIAL ISSUES

Some managerial issues related to this introductory chapter are as follows:

1. **Why is B2B e-commerce so essential and successful?** B2B EC is essential for several reasons. First, some B2B models are easier to implement than B2C models. The volume and value of transactions are much larger in B2B than in B2C, and the potential savings are larger and easier to justify. In contrast with B2C, which has several major problems, ranging from channel conflict with existing distributors to fraud to a lack of a critical mass of buyers, there are much fewer problems in these areas. Many companies can start B2B by simply buying from existing online stores and B2B exchanges or by selling electronically joining existing marketplaces or an auction house. The problem is determining *what* and *where* to buy or sell online.

2. **Which EC business projects work best?** Beginning in the early 2000s, the news was awash with stories about the failure of many dot-coms and EC projects. Industry consolidation often occurs after a "gold rush." About 100 years ago, hundreds of companies tried to manufacture cars, following Ford's success in the United States; however, only three survived. The important thing is to learn from the successes and failures of others and discover the right business model for each endeavor.

3. **How can we exploit social commerce?** There are major possibilities here. Some companies even open their own social networks. Advertising is probably the first thing to consider. Recruiting can be a promising avenue as well. Offering discounted products and services should also be considered. Providing customer service and conducting market research can be a useful activity as well. Making customers and selling to them can be beneficial. Finally, the ultimate goal is associating the social network with commerce so that revenue can be created.

4. **What are the top challenges of EC today?** The top ten technical issues for EC (in order of their importance) are security, adequate infrastructure, virtualization, back-end systems integration, more intelligent software, cloud computing, data warehousing and mining, scalability, and content distribution. The top ten managerial issues for EC are justification, budgets, project deadlines, keeping up with technology, privacy issues, unrealistic management expectations, training, reaching new customers, improving customer services, and finding qualified EC employees. Most of these issues are discussed throughout this book.

SUMMARY

In this chapter, you learned about the following EC issues as they relate to the chapter's learning objectives.

1. **Definition of EC and description of its various categories**. EC involves conducting transactions electronically. Its major categories are pure versus partial EC, Internet versus non-Internet, and electronic markets versus company-based systems.

2. **The content and framework of EC**. The applications of EC, and there are many, are based on infrastructures and are supported by people; public policy and technical standards; marketing and advertising; support services, such as logistics, security, and payment services; and business partners—all tied together by management.

3. **The major types of EC transactions**. The major types of EC transactions are B2B, B2C, C2C, m-commerce, intrabusiness commerce, B2E, c-commerce, e-government, social commerce, and e-learning.

4. **The drivers of EC**. EC is a major product of the digital and technological revolutions, which enables companies to simultaneously increase both growth and profits. These revolutions enable digitization of products, services, and information. A major driver of EC is the changing business environment. The rapid change is due to technological breakthroughs, globalization, societal changes, deregulation, and more. The changing business environment forces organizations to respond. Many traditional responses may not be sufficient because of the magnitude of the pressures and the pace of the changes involved. Therefore, organizations must frequently innovate and reengineer their operations. EC, due to its characteristics, is a necessary partner for this process.

   Finally, EC is driven due to its ability to provide a much needed strategic advantage so organizations can compete better.

5. **Benefits of EC to organizations, consumers, and society**. EC offers numerous benefits to all participants. Because these benefits are substantial, it looks as though EC is here to stay and cannot be ignored. In addition, organizations can go into remote and global markets for both selling and buying at better prices. Organizations can speed time to market to gain a competitive advantage. They can improve the internal and external supply chain as well as increase collaboration. Finally, they can better comply with government regulations.

6. **e-Commerce 2.0 and social media**. This refers to the use of social computing in business, often using Web 2.0 tools (such as blogs, wikis) with its social media framework, as well as the emergence of enterprise social networking and commercial activities in virtual worlds. Social and business networks attract huge numbers of visitors.

7. **Describe social commerce and social software**. Companies are beginning to exploit the opportunity of conducting business transactions in social networks and by using social software such as blogs. Major areas are advertising, shopping, customer service, recruiting, and collaboration.

8. **The elements of the digital world**. The major elements of the digital world are the digital economy, digital enterprises, and digital society. They are diversified and expanding rapidly.

    The digital world is accompanied by social businesses and social customers.

9. **The major EC business models**. The major EC business models include online direct marketing, electronic tendering systems, name-your-own-price, affiliate marketing, viral marketing, group purchasing, online auctions, mass customization (make-to-order), electronic exchanges, supply chain improvers, finding the best price, value-chain integration, value-chain providers, information brokers, bartering, deep discounting, and membership.

10. **Limitations of e-commerce**. The major limitations of EC are the resistance to new technology, fear of fraud, integration with other IT systems may be difficult, costly order fulfillment, privacy issues, unclear regulatory issues, lack of trust in computers and unknown business partners, difficulties to justify EC initiatives, and lack of employees who are skilled in EC.

KEY TERMS

Brick-and-mortar (old economy) organizations
Business model
Business-to-business (B2B)
Business-to-consumer (B2C)
Business-to-employee (B2E)
Click-and-mortar (click-and-brick) organizations
Collaborative commerce (c-commerce)
Consumer-to-business (C2B)
Consumer-to-consumer (C2C)
Corporate portal
Digital economy
Digital enterprise
e-Business
e-Government
e-Tailing
Electronic commerce (EC)
Electronic market (e-marketplace)
Ethics
Extranet
Intrabusiness EC
Intranet
Sharing economy
Social business
Social commerce (SC)
Social computing
Social (digital) customer
Social enterprise
Social media
Social network
Social networking
Social networking services (SNSs)
Tendering (bidding) system
Value proposition
Virtual (pure-play) organizations
Web 2.0

DISCUSSION QUESTIONS

1. Compare brick-and-mortar and click-and-mortar organizations.
2. Why is buying with a smart card from a vending machine considered EC?
3. Explain how EC can reduce cycle time, improve employees' empowerment, and facilitate customer service.
4. Compare and contrast viral marketing with affiliate marketing.
5. Identify the contribution of Web 2.0. What does it add to EC?
6. Discuss the reasons companies embark on social commerce.
7. Distinguish an enterprise social network from a public one such as Facebook.
8. Carefully examine the non-technological limitations of EC. Which are company dependent and which are generic?
9. Relate the social customer to social business.

TOPICS FOR CLASS DISCUSSION AND DEBATES

1. How can EC be both a business pressure and an organizational response to other business pressures?
2. Debate: Does digital business eliminate the "human touch" in trading? In addition, if "yes," is this really bad?
3. Why do companies frequently change their business models? What are the advantages? The disadvantages?
4. Debate: EC eliminates more jobs than it creates. Should we restrict its use and growth?
5. Debate: Will online fashion hurt traditional fashion retailers?
6. Search for information on the enterprise of the future. Start with **ibm.com**. In one or two pages, summarize how the enterprise of the future differs from today's enterprise.
7. Investigate why the 1 day sales during Singles' Day in China generated more than twice the money generated on Cyber Monday in the United States.
8. Discuss the impacts of EC on the fashion industry.
9. Visit **packdog.com** and **entirelypets.com/dogtoys.html**. Compare the two sites and relate their contents to the digital society.

INTERNET EXERCISES

1. Enter **http://www.excitingcommerce.comwww.excitingcommerce.com** and find recent information about emerging EC models and the future of the field.
2. Visit **amazon.com** and locate recent information in the following areas:
   (a) Find the five top-selling books on EC.
   (b) Find a review of one of these books.
   (c) Review the personalized services you can get from Amazon.com, and describe the benefits you receive from shopping there.
   (d) Review the products directory.
3. Visit **priceline.com** and **zappos.com**, and identify the various business revenue models used by both. Discuss their advantages.
4. Go to **nike.com** and design your own shoes. Next, visit **products.office.com** and create your own business card. Finally, enter **jaguar.com** and configure the car of your dreams. What are the advantages of each activity? The disadvantages?
5. Try to save on your next purchase. Visit **pricegrabber.com**, **yub.com**, and **buyerzone.com**. Which site do you prefer? Why?
6. Enter **espn.go.com**, **123greetings.com**, and **facebook.com**, and identify and list all the revenue sources on each of the companies' sites.
7. Enter **philatino.com**, **stampauctioncentral.com**, and **statusint.com**. Identify the business model(s) and revenue models they use. What are the benefits to sellers? To buyers?
8. Go to **zipcar.com**. What can this site help you do?
9. Enter **digitalenterprise.org**. Prepare a report regarding the latest EC models and developments.
10. Visit some websites that offer employment opportunities in EC (such as **execunet.com** and **monster.com**). Compare the EC salaries to salaries offered to accountants. For other information on EC salaries, check *Computerworld*'s annual salary survey and **salary.com**.

11. Visit **bluenile.com**, **diamond.com**, and **jewelryexchange.com**. Compare the sites. Comment on the similarities and the differences.

12. Visit **tickets-online.com**, **ticketmaster.com**, **tickets-online.com**, and other sites that sell event tickets online. Assess the competition in online ticket sales. What services do the different sites provide?

13. Enter the Timberland Company (**timberland.com**), and design a pair of boots. Compare it to building your own sneakers at **nike.com**. Compare these sites to **zappos.com/shoes**.

14. Examine two or three of the following sites: **prosper.com**, **paperbackswap.com**, **bigvine.net**, etc. Compare their business and revenue models.

TEAM ASSIGNMENT AND PROJECTS

1. Read the opening case and answer the following questions:

   (a) In what ways do you think Starbucks increases its brand recognition with its EC initiatives?
   (b) Some criticize My Starbucks Idea as an ineffective "show off." Find information about the pros and cons of the program. (See the Starbucks Ideas in Action Blog).
   (c) Starbucks initiates discussions on Facebook about nonbusiness topics such as the marriage equality bill. Why?
   (d) Discuss how customers are being kept involved and engaged in the various EC initiatives.
   (e) Starbucks believes that its digital and social initiatives are "highly innovative and cause dramatic changes in consumer behavior." Discuss.

2. Each team will research two EC success stories. Members of the group should examine companies that operate solely online and some that extensively utilize a click-and-mortar strategy. Each team should identify the critical success factors for their companies and present a report to the other teams.

3. Watch the video *E-Commerce Part 1* (10:03 min) at **youtube.com/watch?v=gOVh-r03zxQ**.

   (a) Update all the data shown in the video.
   (b) What fundamental change is introduced by EC?
   (c) What is the first mover advantage discussed in the video?
   (d) Amazon.com and other companies that lost money during the time the video was made are making a lot of money today; find out why.
   (e) Identify all the EC business models discussed in the video.
   (f) How can one conduct an EC business from home?
   (g) EC is considered a disruptor. In what ways?

4. Conduct a search on "social business." Start at **eweek.com**. Divide the work between several teams; each team covers one topic, and each team writes a report.

5. Research the status of self-driven cars. Outline the pro and con points. Why this is considered EC? Give a presentation.

6. Research the impact of e-commerce on the auto industry, including self-driven cars (read Gao et al. 2016).

7. Write a report. Compare Net-a-Porter with buying fashion products on Amazon and other websites that discount designer items. In addition, see what Groupon offers in this area. Analyze the competitive advantage of each. Write a report.

8. Compare ride sharing companies (e.g., Uber) to ZabCab.

CLOSING CASE: E-COMMERCE AT THE NATIONAL FOOTBALL LEAGUE (NFL)

Professional sports are multibillion-dollar businesses in the United States, and they are growing rapidly in many other countries. The National Football League (NFL), which consists of 32 teams, is a premier brand of the most popular sport in the United States—football. The NFL uses e-commerce and other information technologies extensively to run its business efficiently. The following are some examples of e-commerce activities the NFL conducts both at the corporate level and at the individual team level.

Selling Online

In addition to the official store (**nflshop.com**) and the individual team stores (e.g., the Atlanta Falcons), there are dozens of independent stores that sell authentic, as well as replicas, of jerseys, hats, shirts, and other team merchandise. Most of these sales are done online, which enables you to buy your favorite team's items from anywhere; you can also save with coupons. It is basically a multibillion-dollar B2C business, supported by search and shopping tools (see Chap. 2), including price comparisons (e.g., compare prices at **bizrate.com/electronics-cases-bags**). In 2015, the NFL players association picked EC giant fanatics to be the lead manufacturer and seller of licensed merchandise (Bloomberg News 2016).

Several online stores sell tickets for NFL events, including resale tickets. For example, see **ticketsnow.com/nfl-tickets**.

Selling in China

In October 2013, the NFL opened its official online store in China (**nfl.world.tmall.com**). To embark on this venture, the NFL used two partners: Export Now to handle all the administration of the transactions and Tmall.com (China's leading EC seller with over 500 million registered members).

Information, News, and Social Commerce

The NFL is on Facebook where there is a company description and many posts by its fans. It is also on Twitter where you can find information on upcoming NFL events and be one of its over 23,000,000+ followers. You can also get local news, including real-time sports scores texted to your smartphone. The popularity of social media used by players created a need for a policy regarding the use of social networks before and after (but not during) games. For the policy, see the article titled "Social Media Before, After Games" at **sports.espn.go.com/nfl/news/story?id=4435401**. For the use of social commerce in the NFL business, see Brennan (2014).

Videos and Fantasy Games

Madden NFL 11 is a video game available across all major consoles with an adaptation for iPhone and iPad versions of the game. See also the Game Pass. For details, see **en.wikipedia.org/wiki/Madden_NFL_11**. Related to these games are the NFL fantasy games that are available for free at **fantasy.nfl.com**. For livestreaming, see Baysinger (2015).

Smartphone Experience

Smartphones, and especially iPhones, now allow users to go online to view games in real time (some are costly). You can also use the iPhone to view photos in the stadium that are projected on a TV and much more. NFL mobile is a well-known option.

Wireless Applications in Stadiums

Several stadiums are equipped with state-of-the-art wireless systems. One example is the University of Phoenix Stadium, which is the home of the Arizona Cardinals. Fans can access many high-definition TVs in real time. Fans with smartphones can get real-time scores or purchase food and other merchandise. The system also enables employees to process ticket sales quickly. In addition, fans can watch the game while buying food in the stadium. The Cardinal's marketing department can advertise the forthcoming games and other events on the system. It also delivers data to coaches as needed during games. A similar system (used in the Sun Life Stadium, home of the Miami Dolphins) enables personalized replay during games (see the video about a special portable device titled "Miami Dolphins Transform Sun Life Stadium into Entertainment Destination for Fans" at **youtube.com/watch?v=t2qErS7f17Y**). Also, you can order food online, have it delivered to your seat, and pay for it electronically. Finally, you can play fantasy games while in the stadium. These EC applications are designed to make fans happy and to generate revenue.

Other Applications

The NFL uses many other EC applications for the management of transportation to the Super Bowl, security implementation, procurement (B2B), providing e-CRM, and much more.

For an interesting infographic on the Super Bowl NFL business, see Bathe (2015).

Sources: Based on Bathe (2015), Baysinger (2015), and material collected on Facebook and Twitter (accessed February 2017).

Questions

1. Identify all applications related to B2C in online stores (see Roggio 2013 to get started).
2. Identify all B2C applications inside the stadium.
3. Identify all B2E applications inside the stadium.
4. Relate online game playing to EC at the NFL.
5. Compare the NFL information available on Facebook to that available on Instagram.
6. Find additional NFL-related applications not cited in this case.
7. Enter **www.ignify.com/Atlanta_Falcons_eCommerce_Case_Study.html**. Read the case "Atlanta Falcons E-Commerce Case Study," then go to the Falcons' online store, and describe all major EC models that are used there.
8. Find information on social commerce at the NFL.
9. Compare *Madden NFL 11* with NFL fantasy games.

REFERENCES

Adams, R. L. "21 Legit Ways to Make Money Online." *Forbes.com*, October 11, 2016.

Ahmad, I. "100 Most Startling Tech Facts, Figures, and Statistics from 2013 [Infographic]." January 2, 2014. **socialmediatoday.com/irfan-ahmad/2033741/100-most-startling-tech-facts-figures-and-statistics-2013-infographic** (accessed February 2017).

Allison, M., "Starbucks Presses Social Media Onward." *The Seattle Times*, April 27, 2013. **seattletimes.com/html/businesstechnology/2020862483_starbuckssocialxml.html** (accessed February 2017).

Baldwin, C. "Philips Is Digitally Transforming to Put the Customer First." *Essential Retail*, June 8, 2016.

Bathe, M. "eCommerce Community: NFL Super Bowl & eCommerce." *The Jibe*, January 28, 2015. **thejibe.com/blog/15/01/ecommerce-community-nfl-super-bowl-ecommerce-infographic** (accessed February 2017).

Baysinger, T. "Here's How the NFL is Beefing Up Its Digital Presence: More Live Streaming and a New Premium Mobile Subscription." *AdWeek*, September 6, 2015. **adweek.com/tv-video/here-s-how-nfl-beefing-its-digital-presence-166733** (accessed February 2017).

Bennet, A. *Online DropShipping Income 2016: How To Make Money via E-Commerce Without Having Your Own Product.* Seattle, WA: Amazon Digital Services, 2016.

Bertelsen, M. "8 Surprising Social Media Lessons You'll Learn from Oprah." *Social Media Revolver*, December 23, 2014. **socialmediarevolver.com/surprising-social-media-lessons-oprah** (accessed February 2017).

Biswas, S. P. "Maharashtra: Farmers to Go the E-Commerce Way, Reach Customers Directly." *The Indian Express*, July 10, 2016.

Bloomberg News. "E-Commerce Giant Fanatics Scores a New Deal with the NFL." *E-Commerce World*, April 15, 2016.

Brennan, B. "The Effect of the 2014/15 NFL American Football Season on E-Commerce and Retail Companies." *Conversocial*, October 15, 2014. **conversocial.com/blog/the-effect-of-the-2014/15-nfl-american-football-season-for-ecommerce-and-retail-companies#.VtoWdPkrI2w** (accessed February 2017).

Bridges, R., and A. Sherman. *Driverless Car Revolution: Buy Mobility, Not Metal*, Kindle Edition. Seattle, WA: Amazon Digital Services, 2016.

Brohan, M. "Starbucks Wants Its Fill of Mobile-First Customers." *Internet Retailer*, November 4, 2015.

Burke, A. "How a 15-Year-Old Entrepreneur Got Her Product into Nordstrom." *Yahoo! News*, December 23, 2013. **news.yahoo.com/blogs/profit-minded/15-old-entrepreneur-got-her-product-nordstrom-233738356.html** (accessed February 2017).

CBS. "Facebook's Laser Drones Could Bring Internet to 5 Billion People." *CBS SF Bay Area*, March 26, 2015. **sanfrancisco.cbslocal.com/2015/03/26/facebook-drones-lasers-internet** (accessed February 2017).

Davis, A. "50 Value Propositions for Ecommerce Retailers." *CPC Strategy*, July 12, 2012. **cpcstrategy.com/blog/2012/07/50-value-propositions-for-ecommerce-retailers** (accessed February 2017).

Davis, B. "The Most Powerful Woman You've Never Heard of: Scarily Well-Connected Net-A-Porter Founder Natalie Massenet Changed the Way You Shop and Now She's Set Her Sights on Politics." *Daily Mail*, February 19, 2016.

Drucker, P. *Managing in the Next Society.* New York: Truman Talley Books, 2002.

Estopace, E. "Singapore Among World's 7 Most Digital Savvy Countries." *eGov Innovation*, July 19, 2016.

Fei, X., and J.-Y. Chung. *IT for Future e-Business Management.* Heidelberg, Berlin: Springer Link, 2015.

Gao, P., H.-W. Kaas, D. Mohr, and D. Wee. "Disruptive Trends That Will Transform the Auto Industry." *McKinsey Company*, January 2016.

Howard, B. *We-Commerce: How to Create, Collaborate, and Succeed in the Sharing Economy.* Westminster, London: Tarcher Perigee, 2015.

Ilyashov , A. "Melania Trump's RNC Dress is Very Different from Past Potential FLOTUS' Looks." *Refinery 29*, July 19, 2016.

INAS. "E-Commerce Development Can Stimulate Growth: WTO." *Business Standard*, July 6, 2016.

Kelly, K. "The Internet Is Still at the Beginning of Its Beginning." *LinkedIn*, June 4, 2016. **linkedin.com/pulse/internet-still-beginning-its-kevin-kelly** (accessed February 2017).

La Monica, P.R. "Starbucks Is Morphing into a Tech Company." *CNN Money*, January 23, 2015. **money.cnn.com/2015/01/23/investing/starbucks-kevin-johnson** (accessed February 2017).

Lazazzera, R. "How to Choose an Ecommerce Business Model." *Shopify*, February 19, 2015. **shopify.com/blog/17240328-how-to-choose-an-ecommerce-business-model** (accessed February 2017).

Manyika, J., M. Chui, J. Bughin, R. Dobbes, P. Bisson, and A. Marrs. "Disruptive Technologies: Advances That Will Transform Life, Business, and the Global Economy." *Report - McKinsey Global Institute*. May (2013). **mckinsey.com/insights/business_technology/disruptive-technologies** (accessed February 2017).

McCafferty, D. "How Technology Disrupts Work-Life-Balance." *Baseline*, May 25, 2015.

McCafferty, D. "The Top 9 Tech Trends for 2016." *Baseline*, January 26, 2016.

Moscaritolo, A. "Futuristic Japanese Hotel Staffed Entirely by Robots." *PCMag*, February 5, 2015. **pcmag.com/article2/0,2817,2476347,00.asp** (accessed February 2017).

Moth, D. "How Starbucks Uses Pinterest, Facebook, Twitter and Google+." *Econsultancy.com*, March 6, 2013. **econsultancy.com/blog/62281-how-starbucks-uses-pinterest-facebook-twitter-and-google#i.1k5vbfsm0ndjpt** (accessed February 2017).

Neckermann, L. *The Mobility Revolution: Zero Emissions, Zero Accidents, Zero Ownership*. Leicester, UK: Matador, 2015.

Olanrewaju, T., K. Smaje, and P. Willmott. "The Seven Traits of Effective Digital Enterprises." *McKinsey Company Article*, May 2014.

Panagiotaropoulou, S. "Starbucks Case Study: Innovation in CRM Strategies, Means of Enabling E-Commerce. *LinkedIn*, September 22, 2015. **linkedin.com/pulse/starbucks-case-study-innovation-crm-strategies-means-stavroula** (accessed February 2017).

Plunkett, J. W. *Plunkett's E-Commerce & Internet Business Almanac 2017 (Plunkett's E-Commerce and Internet Business Almanac)*, Houston, TX: Plunkett Research Ltd., February 17, 2017.

Pressler, J. "The World is not Enough for Net-a-Porter." *Nymag.com/Thecut/*, August 11, 2015.

PWC. "The Sharing Economy," *eBook*, 2015. **pwc-consumer-intelligence-series-the-sharing-economy.pdf** (accessed February 2017).

Rappa, M. "Business Models on the Web." January 17, 2010. **digitalenterprise.org/models/models.html** (accessed February 2017).

Roggio, A. "9 Ecommerce Lessons from NFL Online Shops." *Practical Ecommerce*, November 6, 2013. **practicalecommerce.com/article/60509-9-Ecommerce-Lessons-from-NFL-Online-Shops** (accessed February 2017).

Samuely, A. "How Starbucks' Social Strategy Won the Holidays and Drove Sales." *Mobile Commerce Daily*, January 20, 2015a.

Samuely, A. "Starbucks Heats Up Social Relationship Marketing." *Mobile Commerce Daily*, April 15, 2015b.

Sidhu, I. *The Digital Revolution: How Connected Digital Innovations are Transforming Your Industry, Company & Career*. London: Pearson FT Press, 2015.

Smith, A. "This Flying Car Will Be Ready for Take Off in 2017." *CNN Money*, March 17, 2015. **money.cnn.com/2015/03/17/autos/aeromobil-flying-car/index.html?iid=surge-story-summary** (accessed February 2017).

Staff. "75 Legitimate Ways to Earn Money at Home (Updated for 2017)." *MoneyPantry.com*, March 2, 2017.

Stanley, T. and R. Ritacca. "E-Commerce in China: Driving a New Consumer Culture." *KPMG Report*, January 2014.

Strout, A. "Follow the Leader: How Starbucks is Dominating Mobile Commerce." *Mobile Marketing*, August 13, 2015. **marketingland.com/follow-leader-starbucks-dominating-mobile-commerce-136784** (accessed February 2017).

Sung, B. "What E-Commerce Businesses Can Learn from Starbucks." *Unity E-Commerce*, September 9, 2014.

Tse, E. *China's Disruptors: How Alibaba, Xiaomi, Tencent, and Other Companies Are Changing the Rules of Business*. Westminster, London: Portfolio, 2015.

Turban, E., et al. *Social Commerce*. New York: Springer, 2016.

U.S. Census Bureau. "E-Stats 2014 Report: Measuring the Electronic Economy." June 7, 2016. **census.gov/content/dam/Census/library/publications/2016/econ/e14-estats.pdf** (accessed March 2017).

Vizard, M. "Jaguar Launches Virtual Shopping Experiences." *CIO Insight*, June 5, 2013.

Vermontbiz News. "ZabCab Taxi App Reaches 10,000 Rides in Burlington, Partners with Dunwright Taxi and Independent Drivers." *Vermontbiz*, January 12, 2016.

Welch, M., and J. Buvat. "Starbucks: Taking the 'Starbucks Experience' Digital." eBook: *Capgemini Consulting*, November 23, 2015. **ebooks.capgemini-consulting.com/dm/Starbucks.pdf** (accessed February 2017).

Willgren, S. "Farmers Online: Old Traditions, Modern Technology." *The Epoch Times* (Toronto, Canada), June 18–19, 2013.

E-Commerce: Mechanisms, Platforms, and Tools

2

Contents

Learning Objectives

Upon completion of this chapter, you will be able to:

1. Describe the major electronic commerce (EC) activities and processes and the mechanisms that support them.
2. Define e-marketplaces and list their components.
3. List the major types of e-marketplaces and describe their features.
4. Describe electronic catalogs, search engines, and shopping carts.
5. Describe the major types of auctions and list their characteristics.
6. Discuss the benefits and limitations of e-auctions.
7. Describe bartering and negotiating online.
8. Describe virtual communities.
9. Describe social networks as EC mechanisms.
10. Describe the emerging technologies of augmented reality and crowdsourcing.
11. Describe Web 3.0 and define Web 4.0 and Web 5.0.

© Springer International Publishing AG 2018
E. Turban et al., *Electronic Commerce 2018*, Springer Texts in Business and Economics, DOI 10.1007/978-3-319-58715-8_2

OPENING CASE PINTEREST
A NEW KID ON THE E-COMMERCE BLOCK

An e-commerce site that talked about a great deal since 2011 is Pinterest.

The Opportunity

Pinterest is a social bookmarking website where users "pin" images on a virtual "pinboard." The social bookmarking of images has been practiced on the Internet all over the world, for several years. The company's founders saw the business potential and the success of similar companies in Brazil and China. Furthermore, they succeeded in attracting initial venture capital to expand the business. For a guide, see Ahmad (2016) or Kissmetrics (2015), and for statistics, see Smith (2016).

The Solution

Pinterest is a company that provides virtual pinboards that allow users to organize and share images found on the Web (referred to as "pins"). The pinned images ("boards") are organized by any category the user wants and placed on a virtual pinboard, just like on a real bulletin board. For example, one can collect pictures of sailboats and pin them on one pinboard, with appropriate text explanation. You can collect decorations for your home on another pinboard, while you collect Chinese recipes on a third pinboard. Millions of people create pinboards, and anyone can search and view them. You can also add friends to your account and "follow" them. According to their website, "Pinterest is a tool for collecting and organizing the things that inspire you" (see **about.pinterest.com**). For more about what Pinterest is and how it works, see **makeuseof.com/tag/your-guide-to-pinterest**.

Having many visitors and a rapid growth rate are necessary but not sufficient for EC success. Viable business and revenue models are also needed.

The Business and Revenue Models

Pinterest is privately held, and it does not have to report its business or revenue models to the public. But analysts are able to evaluate the companies actions, and it appears that the company's current priority is user growth and experimentation with advertising methods (Tarver 2015). Many people speculate about (or suggest) revenue opportunities for the company, some of which are provided next.

Marketing Models

With several marketing models available, it appears that Pinterest's current focus is on both "cost-per-engagement" (CPE) and "cost-per-action" (CPA) models (D'Onfro 2015). Under these systems, advertisers only pay the site when users are actively engaging in promoted content. This is designed to shift the risk to Pinterest, ensuring that they efficiently target promoted content to users.

Selling Data for Market Research and Analysis

Several experts suggested selling customer data available on Pinterest to retailers who can use analytics, including data mining, to conduct market research using this data. Customer data may reveal important statistical associations and relationships between consumer behavior, content (e.g., product recommendations, personalization, ads), and services and products provided.

Other Suggestions for Doing Business on Pinterest

- Hootsuite provides a comprehensive listing of methods to use Pinterest for business marketing at **blog.hootsuite.com/how-to-use-pinterest-for-business**.
- Hub Spot (**hubspot.com**) offers a free e-book titled "How to Use Pinterest for Business" (**offers.hubspot.com/how-to-use-pinterest-for-business**). It includes information such as how to create a Pinterest business account and how Pinterest works.
- Wikipedia lists several potential revenue sources at **en.wikipedia.org/wiki/Pinterest**.
- For more suggestions, see **business.pinterest.com/en/pinterest-guides**.

Using Pinterest for Advertising and Marketing

Most of the suggestions cited above, as well as suggestions by others, concentrate on advertising and marketing opportunities. For comprehensive coverage, see McDonald (2015) and Cario (2013).

Results and Managerial Issues

Pinterest is one of the fastest growing social network ever. As of March 2016, the total number of monthly Pinterest users worldwide was 110 million **linkedin.com/pulse/pinterest-2016-statistics-110million-monthly-users-ivonne-teoh**).

Similar reports on this amazing growth rate and popularity are provided by comScore and other reporting companies. Some leaked financial reports in 2015 indicated that the company would have $169 million in total revenue in 2015 and a projected $2.8 billion in annual revenue by 2018 (Roof 2015).

In October 2014, the valuation of Pinterest was $11 billion. If the company can continue to add users and generate significant revenue, it probably will go to the IPO route, in which case the valuation may be much higher (Mangalindan 2016). Let us look now at some managerial issues facing the company. Representative managerial issues are:

Legal Concerns

Many people collect images from the Internet to build their pinboards (and possibly a brand) without asking permission from the content creators, giving them an attribute, or compensating them. Some of the collected material is formally copyrighted; other material may be considered copyrighted. A similar problem exists with material used on Facebook or by bloggers. According to Pinterest's "Terms of Use," members are "solely responsible for what they pin and repin." Furthermore, users must have explicit permission from the owners of contents to post them. Note that Pinterest places all blame and potential legal fees on its users (who may have to pay the legal fees incurred by Pinterest also). Pinterest has taken several steps to alleviate the legal concerns of users. The company is continuously adding measures to minimize the legal problems. For example, in May 2012, the company added a feature that facilitates the attribution of credit to content creators. Finally, legal concerns may include dealing with the spammers who are busy on the site. But even with these features, users are still counseled to ensure that their pins meet copyright guidelines (see **turbofuture.com/internet/how-to-use-pinterest-copyright-legally**).

The Competition

The popularity of Pinterest has resulted in many attempts to clone the company. Since the core concept is basically image sharing, it may not be patentable; therefore, competitors try to jump into niche markets. For example, Juxtapost (**juxtapost. com**) is similar in function to Pinterest, but focuses more on photography. Foodgawker (**foodgawker.com**) focuses on cooking and dining, while Liqurious (**liqurious.com**) focuses on drinks. We Heart It (**weheartit.com**) is a Brazilian company (operating in the United States) that is very similar to Pinterest. An emerging competitor is Fancy (**fancy.com**), which partnered with Google + in 2013. Companies such as Facebook and Google may initiate a competitive service. Some believe that Pinterest may take business away from both Facebook and Twitter due to its better match with the business world.

Conclusion

Pinterest is more business oriented than Facebook or Twitter and visitors tend to buy more from there, although the latter companies drive more visitors to their sites. It seems that Pinterest has some potential benefits for small businesses (e.g., designers). Many companies already use Pinterest to derive benefits. However, these applications do not currently provide any revenue to Pinterest. The success of Pinterest will be determined by its revenue model and the company's profitability.

Sources: Based on Mangalindan (2016), McDonald (2015), Roof (2015), and Tarver (2015).

LESSONS LEARNED FROM THE CASE

Pinterest is a social network that connects people who find interesting images on the Web and organized them on virtual boards. At the same time, Pinterest is a platform on which several activities of EC can be supported. For example, companies can build pinboards that promote their brands. Pinterest can be used as a platform for facilitating innovations via idea generation and sharing.

2.1   ELECTRONIC COMMERCE MECHANISMS: AN OVERVIEW

The many EC models and types of transactions presented in Chap. 1 are enabled by several mechanisms. To begin with, most applications are conducted on the Internet. In addition, the generic enablers of any information system including databases, networks, security, software and server software, operating systems, hardware (Web servers), and hosting services need to be established. Added to the above are the specific EC mechanisms presented in this chapter, such as electronic markets, shopping carts, e-catalogs, and support services such as payment and order fulfillment. In addition to all of the above, there are different methods for executing EC, such as buying at a fixed price or at an auction, and each method has a different support mechanism. Finally, there are the Web 2.0-based collaboration and communication mechanisms (e.g., Twitter) and special platforms such as the one used by Pinterest. In this chapter, we describe the major EC and social commerce mechanisms so that you will be able to understand their uses in the forthcoming chapters.

EC Activities and Support Mechanisms

EC activities are divided here into six categories, which are listed on the left side of Fig. 2.1. Each activity is supported by one or more EC mechanisms, which are shown on the right side of Fig. 2.1, along with the section number in this chapter where they are presented. Additional mechanisms exist for special activities, such as payment and order fulfillment and security.

In the next section, we describe online markets. Before we do this, however, we will describe what happens during a typical purchasing process.

The Online Purchasing Process

Customers buy goods online in different ways. The most common is purchasing from e-catalogs at fixed prices. Sometimes prices may be negotiated or discounted. Another way to determine price is *dynamic pricing*, which refers to non-fixed prices such as those in auctions or stock (commodity) exchanges.

The process starts with a buyer logging on to a seller's website, registering (if needed), and entering an online catalog or the buyer's "My Account." E-catalogs can be very large, so using a search engine may be useful. Buyers usually like to compare prices; therefore, an online price comparison service can be useful (now available on smartphones). Some sellers (e.g., American Airlines, Amazon.com) provide price comparisons showing competitors. If not satisfied, the buyer may abandon the seller's site. If satisfied, the buyer will place the chosen item in a virtual *shopping cart* (or bag). The buyer may return to the seller's catalog to choose more items. Each selected item is placed in the shopping cart. When the item selection is completed, the buyer goes to a checkout page, where a shipment option is selected from a menu (e.g., standard, next day). Finally, a payment option is selected. For example, **newegg.com** allows you to pay by credit card, PayPal, check after billing, in installments, and so on. After checking all the details for accuracy, the buyer *submits* the order.

The major mechanisms that support this process are described in Sections "Customer Shopping Mechanisms: Webstores, Malls, and Portals" and "Merchant Solutions: Electronic Catalogs, Search Engines, and Shopping Carts" of this chapter. The place where buying and selling occurs is called an *e-marketplace*, which we introduce next.

SECTION 2.1 REVIEW QUESTIONS

1. List the major EC activities.
2. List the major EC mechanisms.
3. Describe the online purchasing process.

2.2   E-MARKETPLACES

Markets (electronic or otherwise) have four major functions: (1) enabling transactions to occur by providing a meeting place for buyers and sellers; (2) enabling the flow of relevant information; (3) providing services associated with market transactions, such as payments and escrow; and (4) providing auxiliary services such as legal, auditing, and security.

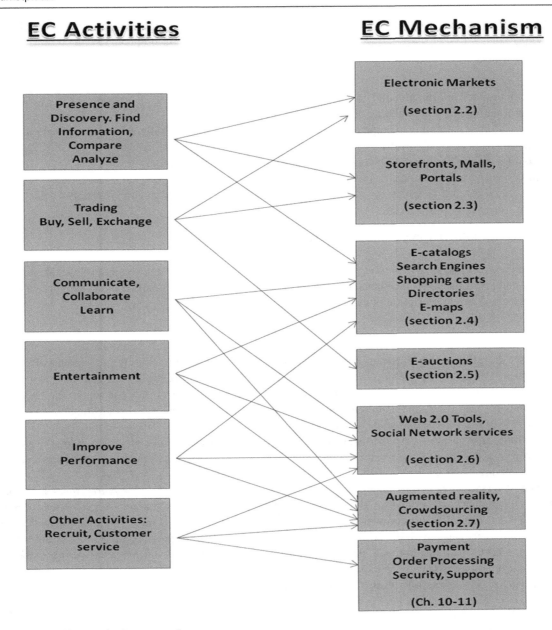

Fig. 2.1 The EC activities–mechanism connection

Electronic Markets

The *electronic market* is the major venue for conducting EC transactions. An **e-marketplace** (also called *e-market*, *virtual market*, or *marketspace*) is an electronic space where sellers and buyers meet and conduct different types of transactions. Customers receive goods and services for money (or for other goods and services, if bartering is used). The functions of an e-market are the same as those of a physical marketplace; however, computerized systems tend to make electronic markets much more efficient by providing more updated information and various support services, such as rapid and smooth executions of transactions.

The emergence of *electronic marketplaces*, especially Web-based ones, has changed several of the processes used in trading and supply chains. In many cases, these changes, driven by technology, have frequently resulted in:

- Lower search time for information and cost to buyers
- Reduced information misunderstanding between sellers and buyers
- Possible reduction in the time gap between purchase and possession of physical products purchased online (especially if the product can be digitized)
- The ability of market participants to be in different locations while trading online
- The ability to conduct transactions at any time (24/7) from any place

The Components and Participants in E-Marketplaces

The major components and players in a *marketspace* are customers, sellers, products and services (physical or digital), infrastructure, a front-end and a back-end mechanism, intermediaries and other business partners, and support services such as security and payments. A brief description of each follows:

- **Customers.** Several billions of Internet users worldwide are potential buyers of goods and services offered on the Internet. These consumers are looking for bargains, customized items, collectors' items, entertainment, socialization, and more. The social customers have more power than regular customers. They can search for detailed information, compare prices, bid, and sometimes negotiate. Buying organizations are also customers, accounting for more than 85% of EC volume and value activities.
- **Sellers.** Millions of webstores are advertising and offering a huge variety of items. These stores are owned by companies, government agencies, or individuals. Every day it is possible to find new offerings of products and services. Sellers can sell directly from their websites or from public e-marketplaces.
- **Products and services.** One of the major differences between the *marketplace* and the *marketspace* is the possible digitization of products and services in a marketspace. Although both types of markets can sell physical products, they can also sell **digital products**, which are goods that can be transformed into a digital format. However, in marketspaces, buyers can buy digitized products online, anytime and from any place in seconds, and receive the purchased goods instantly. In addition to the digitization of software, music, and airline tickets, it is possible to digitize dozens of other products and services.
- **Infrastructure.** The marketspace infrastructure includes electronic networks, databases, hardware, software, and more.
- **Front end.** Customers interact with a marketspace via a **front end.** The major components of the front end can include the seller's portal, electronic catalogs, a shopping cart, a search engine, an auction engine, a payment gateway, and all other activities related to placing orders.
- **Back end.** All the activities that are related to order aggregation and fulfillment, inventory management, purchasing from suppliers, accounting and finance, insurance, payment processing, packaging, and delivery are done in what is termed the **back end** of the business.
- **Intermediaries.** In marketing, an **intermediary** is typically a third party that operates between sellers and buyers. The role of electronic intermediaries is frequently different from that of regular intermediaries (such as wholesalers or retailers), as will be seen throughout the text. For example, online intermediaries create and manage the online markets. They help match buyers and sellers, provide escrow services, and help customers and/or sellers complete transactions. Physical intermediaries may be eliminated and their jobs be computerized (fully or partially) as described next.

Disintermediation and Reintermediation

Intermediaries usually provide three types of services: (1) they provide relevant information about demand: supply, prices, and trading requirements; (2) they help match sellers and buyers; and/or (3) they offer value-added services such as transfer of products, escrow, payment arrangements, consulting, or assistance in finding a business partner. In general, the first and second types of services can be fully automated, and thus it is likely to be assumed by e-marketplaces, infomediaries, and portals that provide free or low-fee services. The third type requires expertise, such as knowledge of the industry, the market, the products, and the technological trends and therefore can only be partially automated.

Intermediaries that provide only (or mainly) the first two types of services may be eliminated; this phenomenon is called **disintermediation**. An example is the airline industry and its push for selling electronic tickets directly by the airlines. Most airlines require customers to pay $25 or more per ticket processed by an employee via telephone. This results in the *disintermediation* of many travel agents from the purchasing process. In another example, discount stockbrokers that only execute trades manually are disappearing. However, brokers who manage electronic intermediation are not only surviving but may also be prospering (e.g., **travelocity.com** and **expedia.com** in the travel industry and **tdameritrade.com** in stock trading). This phenomenon, in which disintermediated entities or newcomers take on new intermediary roles, is called *reintermediation.*

Disintermediation is more likely to occur in supply chains involving several intermediaries, as illustrated by Case 2.1.

CASE 2.1: EC APPLICATION
BLUE NILE INC.: CHANGE AND ADAPTATION IN THE ONLINE JEWELRY INDUSTRY

Blue Nile Inc. (**bluenile.com**), a pure-play online e-tailer that specializes in diamonds and jewelry, capitalized on online diamond sales as a dot-com start-up in 1999. The company is a textbook case of how EC fundamentally changes the way that an industry conducts its business. For information about the company, see **quotes.wsj.com/NILE/company-people**.

Changing the Industry

Using the B2C EC model—eliminating the need for physical stores—Blue Nile was able to offer discounts of 35%, yet it became profitable in a short time. The critical success factors for the company included its ability to offer large discounts, a huge selection of diamonds online and provides more information about diamonds than its brick-and-mortar competitors. The combination of a 30-day 100% money-back guarantee and a comprehensive set of online tools like live chat, payment options, build-your-own engagement ring, gift ideas, and mobile applications (**m.bluenile.com**) helped the company win over customers.

In order to sell $473 million in jewelry in 1 year, a traditional retail chain needs over 300 stores and over 3000 employees. Blue Nile does it with one 10,000-square-foot warehouse and 301 employees. The company also bypasses the industry's complex supply chain, in which a diamond may pass through five or more middlemen before reaching a retailer. Because they are a large buyer, they can deal directly with original suppliers.

The company became the eighth-largest specialty jewelry company in the United States and went public in 2004 (one of the most successful IPOs of that year). Blue Nile's sales reached $129 million in 2003and expanded to $473 million in 2015 (a 367% increase over). Historically the company responded well to market changes; while sales fell during the economic downturn in 2008, in 2009 and 2010 the company rallied again with a 2.3% growth.

Adapting to the Market

Changes in the market and competition have kept Blue Nile on its toes. Noticing the company's success, other retailers have entered the space, using many of the same tools Blue Nile pioneered. This includes both general online retailers such as **overstock.com** and **amazon.com**, as well as direct online jewelry retailers such as **jamesallen.com** and **abazias.com**. Additionally, traditional brick-and-mortar retailers such as **jared.com** and **tiffany.com** are significantly expanding their online presence.

Additionally, changes in the market overall may have an effect on Blue Nile's prospects. One of the Company's primary markets is engagement rings. Demographic trends show that the rates of marriage in the United States are decreasing (Yarrow 2015), and this may be one of the reasons behind lower sales from the company. In the first quarter of 2016, engagement ring sales were down 7%, representing the loss of $58 million (Tu 2016).

To combat these trends, Blue Nile is rethinking its pure-play model and is introducing the idea of "Retail-Reimagined" webrooms, hybrid physical/online presences in large retail markets (Blue Nile 2016). These webrooms seek to provide the same variety and customization options available online, while using a physical location to drive visits and customer confidence.

Sources: Based on Bloomberg (2004), Tu (2016), **en.wikipedia.org/wiki/Blue_Nile_Company**, and **bluenile.com/about-blue-nile** (both accessed December 2016).

Questions

1. Using the classification of EC (Section "The Electronic Commerce Field: Growth, Content, Classification, and a Brief History", Chap. 1), how would you classify the Blue Nile's business historically? Today?
2. In what ways is the company changing its industry?
3. What are the critical success factors of the company?
4. Competition between Blue Nile and Amazon.com will continue to increase. In your opinion, which one will win? (Visit their websites and see how they sell jewelry.)
5. Compare the following three sites: **diamond.com**, **abazias.com**, and **bluenile.com**.
6. Follow the performance of Blue Nile's stock since 2003 (symbol: NILE, go to **money.cnn.com**). Compare it to the performance of the total market and the averages of the industry. What is your conclusion?
7. Do you feel that the "Retail Reimagined" locations will be successful? Why?

Types of E-Marketplaces

The term *marketplace* differs once it referred to on the Web. It is sometimes referred to as e-marketplace or marketspace. We distinguish two types of e-marketplaces: private and public.

Private E-Marketplaces

Private e-marketplaces are those owned and operated by a single company. **Starbucks.com**, **dell.com**, **target.com**, and **united.com** sell from their websites. Private markets are either sell-side or buy-side. In a **sell-side e-marketplace** , a company (e.g., **net-a-porter.com** or **cisco.com**) will sell either standard or customized products to individuals (B2C) or to businesses (B2B); this type of selling is considered to be *one-to-many*. In a **buy-side e-marketplace** , a company purchases from many potential suppliers; this type of purchasing is considered to be *many-to-one*, and it is a B2B activity. For example, some hotels buy their supplies from approved vendors that come to its e-market. Walmart (**walmart.com**) buys goods from thousands of suppliers. Private marketplaces can be open only to selected members and are not publicly regulated.

Public E-Marketplaces

Public e-marketplaces are often owned by a third party (not a seller or a buyer) or by a small group of buying or selling companies, and they serve many sellers and many buyers. They are open to the public and sometimes are regulated by the government.

SECTION 2.2 REVIEW QUESTIONS

1. Define e-marketplace and describe its attributes.
2. What is the difference between a physical marketplace and an e-marketplace (marketspace)?
3. List the components of a marketspace.
4. Define a digital product and provide five examples.
5. Describe private versus public e-markets.

2.3 CUSTOMER SHOPPING MECHANISMS: WEBSTORES, MALLS, AND PORTALS

Several kinds of interactions exist among sellers, buyers, and e-marketplaces. The major B2C mechanisms are *webstores* (*storefronts*) and *Internet malls*. Let us elaborate on these, as well as on the gateways to e-marketplaces—portals.

Webstores

A **webstore** (or **storefront**) refers to a single company's (or individual seller's) website where products and services are sold.

Webstores may target an industry, a location, or a niche market (e.g., **cattoys.com**). The webstore may belong to a manufacturer (e.g., **geappliances.com** and **dell.com**), to a retailer (e.g., **amazon.com**), to individuals selling from home, or to other types of business. Note that some companies refer to their webstores as *portals*.

A webstore includes tools known as *merchant software that* are necessary for conducting online sales. The most common tools are an *electronic catalog*; a *search engine* that helps the consumer find products in the catalog; an *electronic shopping cart* for holding items until checkout; *e-auction facilities* where auctions take place; a *payment gateway* where payment arrangements can be made; a *shipment center* where shipping arrangements are made; and *customer services*, which include product and warranty information and CRM.

Microsites

A *microsite* is a Web page(s) that acts as a supplement to a primary website, but is external to it. It expands on the content by adding editorial, commercial videos, or educational and training material.

Electronic Malls

In addition to shopping at individual webstores, consumers can shop in electronic malls (e-malls). Similar to malls in the physical world, an **e-mall (online mall)** is an online shopping location where many stores present their catalogs. The mall charges commission from the sellers based on their sale volume. For example, the Emall of Maine (**emallsofamerica.com/ emallofmaine.htm**) is an e-mall that aggregates products, services, and providers in the state of Maine. It contains a directory of vacation services and product categories and the vendors in each category. When a consumer indicates the category he or she is interested in, the consumer is transferred to the appropriate independent *webstore*. This kind of mall does not provide any shared services; it is merely a directory. Other malls, such as **choicemall.com** or **etsy.com**, do provide some shared services. Both **yahoo.com** and **ebay.com** operate electronic malls.

Web (Information) Portals

A *portal* is an information gateway that is used in e-marketplaces, webstores, and other types of EC (e.g., in e-collaboration, intrabusiness, and e-learning). A **Web (information) portal** is a single point of access, through a Web browser, to critical business information located inside and outside of organizations. This information is aggregated and is accessed and presented in a consistent way. Many Web portals personalize for users. Note that wireless devices are becoming portals for both enterprise and Internet access. A schematic view of a portal is shown in Fig. 2.2. Information sources (external and internal) are shown on the left side, and integrated and process data are shown as output on the monitor's screen. Web portals offer some useful services such as e-mail, news, stock prices, entertainment, shopping capabilities, and so forth.

Types of Portals

Portals can assume many shapes. One way to distinguish among them is to look at their content, which can vary from narrow to broad, and their community or audience, which also can differ. The major types of portals are as follows:

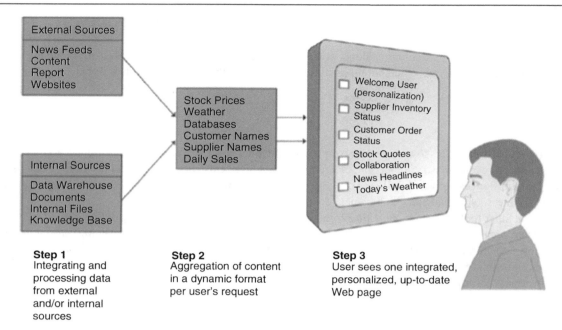

Fig. 2.2 How a portal works

- **Commercial (public) portals.** These popular portals offer content for anyone. Although they can be customized by the user, they are still intended for broad audiences and offer fairly routine content, some in real time (e.g., a stock ticker and news). Examples of such sites are **yahoo.com**, **google.com**, and **msn.com**.
- **Corporate (private) portals.** Corporate portals provide organized access to internal corporate information. These also are known as *enterprise portals* or *enterprise information portals*. Corporate portals appear in different forms. Examples of e-commerce portals can be found at **ibm.com/software/products/en/websphere-portal-family**.
- **Patient portals.** Several companies offer patient portals, for example, WebMD and **myUCLAhealth.org**. Patients have access to their personal information. The UCLA portal also allows communication between patients and their caregivers.
- **Publishing portals.** These portals are intended for communities with specific interests and involve relatively little customization of content; however, they provide extensive online search features and some interactive capabilities. Examples of such sites are **techweb.com** and **zdnet.com**.
- **Mobile portals. Mobile portals** are portals that are accessible from mobile devices. An increasing number of portals are accessible via mobile devices.
- **Voice portals. Voice portals** are websites, usually portals, with audio interfaces. This means that they can be accessed by a standard telephone or a cell phone. AOLbyPhone (**aolbyphone.com**) is an example of a service that allows users to retrieve e-mail, news, and other content from AOL via telephone. It uses both speech recognition and text-to-speech technologies. Products by companies such as Microsoft's Tellme (**tmaa.com/microsoftand-247inc.html**) offer access to the Internet from telephones, as well as tools to build voice portals. Voice portals are especially popular for 1–800 numbers (enterprise 800 numbers) that provide self-service to customers with information available in Internet databases (e.g., finding your balance or last deposit made at your bank).
- **Knowledge portals.** Knowledge portals enable easy access to knowledge by company employees and facilitate collaboration.
- **Board portals.** These portals support decision making (see Questex 2015).
- **Communities' portals.** These are usually parts of online communities. They are dedicated to some theme and may be sponsored by a vendor such as Sony. An example is **gamespot.com/portal.**

The Roles and Value of Intermediaries in E-Marketplaces

The two major types of *online intermediaries* are brokers and infomediaries.

Brokers

A *broker* in EC is a person or a company that facilitates transactions between buyers and sellers. The following are different types of brokers:

- **Trading**. A company that aids online trading (e.g., E*TRADE or eBay).
- **Organization of online malls**. A company that organizes many online stores in one place (e.g., Yahoo! Shopping and Alibaba.com).
- **Comparison agent**. A company that helps consumers compare prices, encourages user comments, and provides customer service at different stores (e.g., Bizrate for a great diversity of products and Hotwire, Inc. for travel-related products and services.
- **Shopping aids provider**. A company that helps online shopping by providing escrow, payments, shipping, and security (e.g., PuntoMio, Inc.) for global shoppers.
- **Matching services**. These services match entities such as jobs to applicants, and buyers to sellers.

Distributors in B2B

A special type of intermediary in e-commerce is the B2B *e-distributor*. These intermediaries connect manufacturers with business buyers (customers), such as retailers (or resellers in the computer industry). **E-distributors** aggregate product information from many manufacturers, sometimes thousands of them, in the e-distributor's catalog. An example is W.W. Grainger (**grainger.com**). The distributor buys the products and then sells them, as supermarkets do.

SECTION 2.3 REVIEW QUESTIONS

1. Describe webstores and e-malls.
2. List the various types of webstores and e-malls.
3. What are Web (information) portals? List the major types.
4. Describe e-distributors.

2.4 MERCHANT SOLUTIONS: ELECTRONIC CATALOGS, SEARCH ENGINES, AND SHOPPING CARTS

To enable selling online, a website usually needs *EC merchant server software*. Merchant software includes several tools and platforms. Such software offers basic tools that include electronic catalogs, search engines, and shopping carts; all are intended to facilitate the electronic trading process.

One example of such software is osCommerce, which is open-source software (see **oscommerce.com**). For a list of merchant software vendors, see **cmscritic.com/dir/ecommerce-software.**

Electronic Catalogs

Catalogs have been printed on paper for generations. Recently, electronic catalogs on a DVD (or CD-ROM) and on the Internet have gained popularity. **Electronic catalogs (e-catalogs)** consist of a product database, directory, and a presentation function. They are the backbone of most e-commerce sales sites. For merchants, the objective of e-catalogs is to advertise and promote products and services. For the customer, the purpose of such catalogs is to locate information on products and services. E-catalogs can be searched quickly with the help of search engines. Some offer tools for interactions. For an example, see InfiniSys "Change My Image" for Microsoft Windows at **en.infinisys.co.jp/product/cmimage** and for Macintosh at **en.infinisys.co.jp/product/cmimage_mac**.

Most early online catalogs were static presentations of text and messages from paper catalogs. However, online catalogs have evolved to become more dynamic, customizable, and integrated with selling and buying procedures, shopping carts, order taking, and payment. E-catalogs may include video clips. The tools for building them are being integrated with merchant software suites and Web hosting tools (e.g., see **smallbusiness.yahoo.com/ecommerce**). Examples of a simple product catalog can be seen at JetPens (**jetpens.com** and Starbucks Store (**store.starbucks.com**).

Although used only occasionally in B2C commerce, customized catalogs are used frequently in B2B e-commerce.

EC Search Activities, Types, and Engines

Search activities are popular in EC, and many tools for conducting searches are available. Several studies revealed that 95% of shoppers conduct research online before making any purchase. Consumers may search inside one company's catalog to find a product or service, or use Google or Bing to find companies that sell the product they need. Here we describe only the essentials for EC search. For a video illustration, see "Google Commerce Search" (2:15 min) at **youtube.com/watch?v=gj7qrotOmVY**. To read publications on electronic research and e-commerce at the Research at Google website, see **research.google.com/pubs/EconomicsandElectronicCommerce.html**. Let us now look at three major types of searches.

Types of EC Searches

The three major types of EC searches are *Internet/Web search*, *enterprise search*, and *desktop search*.

Internet/Web search. This is the most popular search that involves looking for any documents on the Web. According to Pew Research Internet Project (**pewinternet.org**) and other statistical sites (e.g., see **infoplease.com/ipa/A0921862.html**), finding information is one of the most frequent activities done on the Web.

Enterprise search. An **enterprise search** describes the search for information *within* the files and databases of an organization. For example, Google has a powerful Search Appliance (known as GSA).

Desktop search. A **desktop search** involves a search of a user's own computer files (e.g., using **copernic.com** or **windows.microsoft.com/en-us/windows7/products/features/windows-search**). Searching for documents is done by looking through all the information that is available on the user's PC. A simple example is the ability to search all files related to your e-mail archive. A search also can be extended to photos, USB ports, and Word documents.

Search Engines

Customers look for information (e.g., requests for product information or pricing) in similar ways. This type of request is repetitive, and answering such requests manually is costly. Search engines deliver answers economically and efficiently by matching questions with frequently asked question (FAQ) templates, which respond with "canned" answers. In general, a **search engine** is a computer program that can access databases of Internet or intranet resources, search for specific information or keywords, and report the results.

Google and Bing are the most popular search engines in the United States. Baidu is the primary search engine in China. Portals such as Yahoo! and MSN have their own search engines. Special search engines organized to answer certain questions or search in specified areas include **ask.com**, **aol.com**, and **looksmart.com**. Thousands of different public search engines are available (see **searchengineguide.com**). Each of these tools excels in one, or a few, area. These can be very specialized with different capabilities. In addition, many companies have their own enterprise search engines.

Voice-Powered Search

To ease searching, especially when using a smartphone, Google introduced a voice-powered tool (Google Voice Search; **google.com/insidesearch/features/voicesearch/index-chrome.html**) that allows you to skip the keyboard altogether. The first product was included as part of iPhone's mobile search application. It allows you to talk into your phone and ask any question, and the results of your query are provided on your iPhone. In addition to asking questions by talking into your iPhone, you can also listen to search engine results. For an example of Apple's intelligent personal assistant, "Siri," see **apple.com/ios/siri** and **imore.com/siri**. Several language translators use a similar technology.

Video and Mobile Search

There are dozens of dedicated search tools and sites that will search for videos and other images. Some of them, such as bing.com/videos, will search across multiple sites; others, such as YouTube, will search only for their own content. For a list of over 40 sites, see **thesearchenginelist.com/video-search**. For another example, the search engine Bing has a search feature that allows you to listen to more than 5 million full-length songs.

Mobile Search

Several search engines are adapted to mobile search. Notable are Google, Yippy, and Yahoo!

Visual Shopping Search Engine

Visual search means looking for information that is presented visually (photos, images, etc.) For an overview, see **scholarpedia.org/article/Visual_search**. This technology can be used to support e-commerce. For example, **google.com/shopping** provides a visual search engine based on machine learning and computer vision that focuses on consumer products.

Visual search is popular when conducted on mobile devices.

Social Network Search Engines

Social network search, also known as *social search*, is a class of online search engines that help people find material about social networking activities, such as in user-generated content, discussion groups, or recommendations. Like all search engines, these organize, prioritize, and filter search results. Examples of such search engines are **socialmention.com**, "real-time social media search and analysis"; **yoname.com**, "people search across social networks, blogs, and more"; and **bing.com/explore/social**. For an overview, see the blog "Social Media: The Next Best Search Engine" business2community.com/social-media/social-media-next-best-search-engine-01427662 . For a discussion of the benefits and concerns, see **en.wikipedia.org/wiki/Social_search**.

Shopping Carts

An **electronic shopping cart** (also known as *shopping bag* or *shopping basket*) is a software that allows customers to accumulate items they wish to buy before they arrange payment and checkout, much like a shopping cart in a supermarket. The electronic shopping cart software program automatically calculates the total cost and adds tax and shipping charges when applicable. Customers can review and revise their shopping list before finalizing their purchase by clicking on the "submit" button.

Shopping carts for B2C are fairly simple (visit **amazon.com** to see an example), but for B2B, a shopping cart may be more complex. Shopping cart software is sold or provided free to store builders as an independent component outside a merchant suite (e.g., see **networksolutions.com/e-commerce/index-v3.jsp** – "create an online store now," **shopify.com**, and **squarespace.com**). It also is embedded in merchants' servers, such as **smallbusiness.yahoo.com/ecommerce**. Free online shopping carts (trials and demos) are available at **volusion.com** and **1freecart.com**. For shopping cart applications for Facebook, see **ecwid.com/facebook-app.html**.

Product Configuration (Self-Customization)

A key characteristic of EC is the ability to self-customize products and services, as **dell.com**, **nike.com**, or **jaguarusa.com**. Manufacturers like to produce customized products in economical and rapid ways so that the price of their products will be competitive.

Questions and Answers Online

Intelligent search engines can answer users' questions. A leading engine is **ask.com**, a subsidiary of IAC. The Q&A service matches answers from the database to questions users ask. For details, see **ask.com** and **answers.ask.com**. A competing engine is **answers.com**, a question and answer (Q&A) site, which comprises **wikianswers.com**. Wiki Answers is a community-generated social knowledge Q&A platform available in several languages. People ask questions on the platform and the community answers them. Another similar platform is **answers.wikia.com/wiki/Wikianswers**.

SECTION 2.4 REVIEW QUESTIONS

1. List and briefly describe the dimensions by which electronic catalogs can be classified.
2. List the benefits of e-catalogs.
3. Describe an electronic shopping cart.
4. Describe voice- and vision-related search engines.
5. What is self-customization?

2.5   AUCTIONS, BARTERING, AND NEGOTIATING ONLINE

One of the most interesting market mechanisms in e-commerce is the electronic auction. Auctions are used in B2C, B2B, C2C, G2B, and G2C.

Definition and Characteristics

An *online auction* is an electronic space where sellers and buyers meet and conduct different types of transactions. This market mechanism uses a competitive process where a seller solicits consecutive bids from buyers (forward e-auctions) or a buyer solicits bids from sellers (reverse e-auctions). A wide variety of online markets qualify as auctions using this definition. Prices are determined dynamically by the bids. Auctions, an established method of commerce for generations, deal with products and services when conventional marketing channels are ineffective or inefficient. For example, e-auctions can expedite the clearance of items that need to be liquidated or sold quickly. Rare coins, stamps, and other collectibles are frequently sold at e-auctions.

There are several types of auctions, each with its own specialties and procedures. (For coverage, see **en.wikipedia.org/ wiki/Online_auction_business_model**.) Auctions can be conducted on *public* auction sites, such as **ebay.com**, or on *private* auction sites, which may be "by invitation only."

Dynamic Pricing

One major characteristic of auctions is that they are based on dynamic pricing. **Dynamic pricing** refers to prices that are not fixed, but are allowed to fluctuate, and are determined by supply and demand. In contrast, catalog prices are fixed, as are prices in department stores, supermarkets, and most webstores.

Dynamic pricing appears in several forms. Perhaps the oldest forms are negotiation and bargaining, which have been practiced for many generations in open-air markets. The most popular today are the online auctions.

Traditional Auctions Versus E-Auctions

Traditional, physical auctions are still very popular. However, the volume traded on e-auctions is significantly larger and continues to increase. In addition, person-to-person auctions are done mostly online.

Limitations of Traditional Offline Auctions

Traditional offline auctions, regardless of their type, have several limitations. They usually last only a few minutes, or even seconds, for each item sold. This rapid process may give potential buyers little time to make a decision, so they may decide not to bid. Therefore, sellers may not get the highest possible price; bidders may not get what they really want, or they may pay too much for the items. Additionally, in many cases, the bidders do not have much time to examine the goods before placing a bid. Bidders have difficulty learning about specific auctions and cannot compare what is being offered at each location. Bidders must usually be physically present at auctions; thus, many potential bidders are excluded.

Similarly, it may be difficult for sellers to move goods to an auction site. Commissions are fairly high because a physical location must be rented, the auction needs to be advertised, and an auctioneer and other employees need to be paid. Electronic auctioning removes or lessens these drawbacks.

Electronic Auctions

The Internet provides an infrastructure for executing auctions electronically at lower cost, with a wide array of support services, and with many more participating sellers and buyers than physical auctions. Individual consumers and corporations can both participate in this rapidly growing and very convenient form of e-commerce.

Electronic auctions (e-auctions) are similar to offline auctions except that they are conducted online. E-auctions (or online auctions) have been in existence since the 1980s over LANs (e.g., for the historical perspective in flowers; see Saarinen et al. 2006). Host sites on the Web, which were started in 1995, serve as brokers, offering services for sellers to post their goods for sale and enabling buyers to bid on those items.

Major online auction sites, such as eBay, offer consumer products, electronic parts, artwork, vacation packages, airline tickets, and collectibles, as well as excess supplies and inventories that are being auctioned off by businesses. Another type of B2B online auction is used to trade special types of commodities, such as electricity transmission capacities and gas and energy options (e.g., see **energyauctionexchange.com**). Furthermore, conventional business practices that traditionally have relied on contracts and fixed prices increasingly are converted into auctions with bidding for online procurements.

For a comparison of 10 online auction sites, see **online-auction-sites.toptenreviews.com**.

Types of Auctions

It is customary to classify auctions into the following major types based on how many buyers and sellers are involved.

One Buyer, One Seller

In this configuration, one can use negotiation, bargaining, or bartering. The resulting price will be determined by each party's bargaining power, supply and demand in the item's market, and (possibly) business environment factors.

One Seller, Many Potential Buyers

In this configuration, the seller uses a **forward auction** , which is an auction where a seller entertains bids from multiple buyers. (Because forward auctions are the most common and traditional form, they often are simply called *auctions*.) The four major types of forward auctions are *English* and *Yankee* auctions, in which bidding prices increase as the auction progresses, and *Dutch* and *free-fall* auctions, in which bidding prices decline as the auction progresses. Each of these can be used for either liquidation or for market efficiency.

Example: Warren Buffet's Annual Power Lunch Auctions

Every year, Warren Buffet, the famous US investment guru, has an auction with the prize being a lunch with him; the winner may also bring along up to seven friends. The winner pays big money for the honor. The money is donated to a charity called the Glide Foundation, which helps the poor and homeless in San Francisco. In the past, Buffett charged $30,000 per group. Since July 2003, Buffett has placed the invitation on an online auction (eBay). In 2003, bidders pushed the bid from $30,000 to $250,100. The highest winning bid in both 2012 and 2016 was the record-setting amount of $3,456,789, both won by an anonymous bidders. In addition to benefiting the needy, the auction provides an opportunity for people (with money) to meet Mr. Buffett.

One Buyer, Many Potential Sellers

Two popular types of auctions in which there is one buyer and many potential sellers are reverse auctions (tendering) and name-your-own-price auctions.

Reverse Auctions

When there is one buyer and many potential sellers, a **reverse auction (bidding** or **tendering system**) is in place. In a reverse auction, the buyer places an item he or she wants to buy for a bid (or *tender*) on a *request for quote* (RFQ) system. Potential suppliers bid on the item, reducing the price sequentially (see Fig. 2.3). In electronic bidding in a reverse auction, several rounds of bidding may take place until the bidders do not reduce the price any further. The winning supplier is the one with the lowest bid (assuming that only price is considered). Reverse auctions are primarily a B2B or G2B mechanism.

Fig. 2.3 The reverse auction process

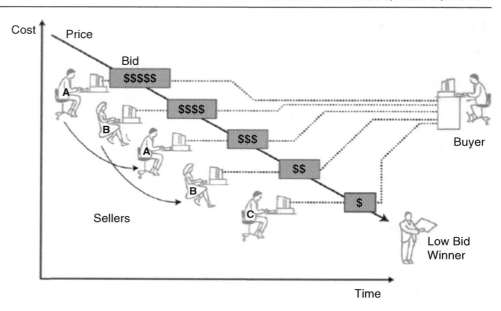

The Name-Your-Own-Price Model

Priceline.com pioneered the **name-your-own-price model** . In this model, a would-be buyer specifies the price (and other terms) that he or she is willing to pay to any willing and able seller. For example, Priceline.com (**priceline.com**) presents consumers' requests to sellers, who fill as much of the guaranteed demand as they wish at prices and terms agreed upon by buyers. The sellers may come up with counter offers managed by Priceline. Alternatively, Priceline.com searches its own database that contains the participating vendors' lowest prices and tries to match supplies with requests. This is basically a C2B model, although some businesses also use it.

Many Sellers, Many Buyers

When there are many sellers and many buyers, buyers and their bidding prices are matched with sellers and their asking prices based on the quantities on both sides. Stock and commodity markets are typical examples of this configuration. Buyers and sellers may be individuals or businesses. Such an auction is also called a **double auction**.

Penny Auctions

A *bidding fee auction*, also called a **penny auction**, is a new type of online forward auction in which participants must pay a small nonrefundable fee each time they place a bid (usually in small increments above the previous bid). When the auction-planned time expires, the last participant to have placed a bid wins the item paying the final bid price, which is usually significantly lower than the retail price of the item. For a tutorial, see the video titled "BidBidSold Penny Auction Site Tutorial" (7:35 min) at **youtu.be/UeC1w0h2UbY**.

Because most bidders will receive nothing in return for their paid bids, some observers have stated that the fee spent on the bid is actually equivalent to a lottery or wager. The auctioneer receives income both in the form of the fees collected for each participant bidder as well as in the form of a seller's commission for the winning bid. Examples of penny auction companies are **happybidday.com** and **quibids.com/en**. At **bestpennyauctionsites.org**, you can find a list of several penny auction companies. Some companies allow the auction's unsuccessful bidders to use all their bidding fees toward a purchase of items at regular or slightly discounted prices. Users need to be careful of scams. For additional information, see **en.wikipedia.org/wiki/Bidding_fee_auction**.

Several other innovative auctions are available.

Benefits of E-Auctions

E-auctions are becoming important selling and buying channels for many companies and individuals. E-auctions enable buyers to access goods and services anywhere auctions are conducted. Moreover, almost perfect market information is available about prices, products, current supply and demand, and so on. These characteristics provide benefits to all.

The auction culture seems to revolutionize the way customers buy, sell, and obtain what they want. A listing of the benefits of e-auctions to sellers, buyers, and e-auctioneers is provided in Table 2.1.

Table 2.1 Benefits of e-auctions

Benefits to sellers	Benefits to buyers	Benefits to E-auctioneers
Increased revenues from broadening bidder base and shortening cycle time. Can sell anywhere globally	Opportunities to find unique items and collectibles	Higher repeat purchases. **marketresearch.com** found that auction sites, such as eBay, tend to garner higher repeat-purchase rates than the top B2C sites, such as Amazon.com
Opportunity to bargain instead of selling at a fixed price. Can sell at any time and conduct frequent auctions	Entertainment. Participation in e-auctions can be entertaining and exciting (e.g., virtual live auction site **tophatter.com**)	High "stickiness" to the website (the tendency of customers to stay at sites longer and come back more often). Auction sites are frequently "stickier" than fixed-priced sites. Stickier sites generate more ad revenue for the e-auctioneer
Optimal price setting determined by the market (more buyers, more information)	Convenience. Buyers can bid from anywhere, even using a mobile device; they do not have to travel to a physical auction place	Easy expansion of the auction business
Sellers can gain more customer dollars by offering items directly (saves on the commission to intermediaries; also, physical auctions are very expensive compared to e-auctions)	Anonymity. With the help of a third party, buyers can remain anonymous	
Can liquidate large quantities quickly	Possibility of finding bargains, for both individuals and organizations	
Improved customer relationship and loyalty (in the case of specialized B2B auction sites and electronic exchanges)		

Limitations of E-Auctions

E-auctions have several limitations. The most significant limitations are minimal security, the possibility of fraud, and limited participation.

Minimal Security

Some of the auctions conducted on the Internet are not secure because most are done in an unencrypted (or poorly protected) environment. This means that credit card numbers can be stolen during the payment process. Payment methods such as PayPal (**paypal.com**) can be used to solve the problem. In addition, some B2B auctions are conducted over highly secure private lines.

Possibility of Fraud

In many cases, auction items are unique, used, or antique. Because the buyer cannot see and touch the items, the buyer may receive something different than he/she had in mind. In addition, products may be defective. Buyers may also commit fraud (e.g., by receiving goods or services without paying for them). Thus, the fraud rate in e-auctions is relatively high. For a discussion of e-auction fraud and fraud prevention, see **fraud.org/scams/internet-fraud/online-auctions**. For general information on Internet fraud in general, see **fraud.org/learn/internet-fraud**, and for information for sellers, see **fraud.org/component/content/article/2-uncategorised/62-seller-beware**. Lately, several people have warned about fraud on penny auctions sites. For examples of scams, see **tomuse.com/penny-auction-fraud-scam-cheat-bidders**.

Limited Participation

Some auctions are by invitation only; others are open only to dealers. Limited participation may be a disadvantage to sellers, who usually benefit from as large a pool of buyers as possible. Buyers also may be unhappy if they are excluded from participation.

Online Bartering

Bartering, the exchange of goods and services, is the oldest method of trade. Today, it is done primarily between organizations. The problem with bartering is that it is difficult to match trading partners. Businesses and individuals may use classified ads to advertise what they need and what they offer in exchange, but they still may not be able to find what they want. Intermediaries may be helpful, but they are expensive (20–30% commissions) and very slow.

E-bartering (electronic bartering)—bartering conducted online—can improve the matching process by attracting more partners to the barter. In addition, matching can be done faster, and as a result, better matches can be found. Items that are frequently bartered online include office space, storage, and factory space; unused facilities; and labor, products, and banner ads. (Note that e-bartering may have tax implications that need to be considered.)

E-bartering is usually done in a **bartering exchange**, a marketplace where an intermediary arranges the transactions. These exchanges can be very effective. Representative bartering websites include **u-exchange.com** "Trade Anything, Pay Nothing," **swapace.com** "Swap anything for anything," and **barterdepot.com**. The typical bartering process works like this: First, the company tells the bartering exchange what it wants to offer. The exchange then assesses the value of the company's products or services and offers it certain "points" or "bartering dollars." The company can use the "points" to buy the things it needs from a participating member in the exchange.

Bartering sites must be financially secure; otherwise, users may not have a chance to use the points they accumulate. (For further details, see **virtualbarter.net** and **barternews.com**.)

Online Negotiating

Dynamic prices also can be determined by *negotiation*. Negotiated pricing is commonly used for expensive or specialized products. Negotiated prices also are popular when large quantities are purchased. Much like auctions, negotiated prices result from interactions and bargaining among sellers and buyers. Negotiation also deals with terms, such as the payment method, timing, and credit. Negotiation is a well-known process in the offline world (e.g., in real estate, automobile purchases, and contract work). A simple peer-to-peer (P2P) negotiation can be seen at **ioffer.com**.

SECTION 2.5 REVIEW QUESTIONS

1. Define auctions and describe how they work.
2. Describe the benefits of e-auctions over traditional (offline) auctions.
3. List the four major types of auctions.
4. Distinguish between forward and reverse auctions.
5. Describe the "name-your-own-price" auction model.
6. Describe penny auctions.
7. List the major benefits of auctions to buyers, sellers, and auctioneers.
8. What are the major limitations of auctions?
9. Define bartering and describe the advantages of e-bartering.
10. Explain the role of online negotiation in EC.

2.6   VIRTUAL COMMUNITIES AND SOCIAL NETWORKS

A *community* is a group of people with common interests who interact with one another. A **virtual community** is one where the interaction takes place over a computer network, mainly the Internet. Virtual communities parallel typical physical communities, such as neighborhoods, clubs, or associations, but people do not meet face-to-face. Instead, they meet online. Virtual communities offer several ways for members to interact, collaborate, and trade (see Table 2.2 for types of virtual communities).

Characteristics of Traditional Online Communities and Their Classification

Most virtual communities are Internet-based, known also as *Internet communities*.

Hundreds of thousands of communities exist on the Internet, and the number is growing rapidly. Pure-play Internet communities may have thousands, or even hundreds of millions, of members. By early 2016 (its 12th anniversary), Facebook had grown to about 1 billion active members around the world. This is one major difference from traditional purely physical communities, which usually are much smaller. Another difference is that offline communities frequently are confined to one geographic location, whereas only a few online communities are geographically confined.

Table 2.2 Types of virtual communities

Community type	Description
Transaction and other business activities	Facilitate buying and selling. Combines an information portal with an infrastructure for trading. Members are buyers, sellers, intermediaries, etc., who are focused on a specific commercial area (e.g., fishing)
Purpose or interest	No trading, just exchange of information on a topic of mutual interest. Examples: Investors consult The Motley Fool (**fool.com**) for financial advice; music lovers go to **mp3.com**
Relations or practices	Members are organized around certain life experiences. Examples: **ivillage.com** caters to women and **seniornet.com** is for senior citizens. Professional communities also belong to this category. Examples: **aboutus.org/Isworld.org** is a space for information systems faculty, students, and professionals
Fantasy/role-playing	Members share imaginary environments. For examples on sports fantasy teams **espn.com**, see **games.yahoo.com** and **horseracegame.com**
Social networks	Members communicate, collaborate, create, share, form groups, entertain, and more. Facebook is the leader
Virtual worlds	Members use avatars to represent themselves in a simulated 3D environment where they can play games, conduct business, socialize, and fantasize about whatever they like

Classifications of Virtual Communities

Virtual communities can be classified in several ways.

Public Versus Private Communities

Communities can be designated as *public*, meaning that their membership is open to anyone. The owner of the community may be a privately held corporation (e.g., Twitter), public for profit organizations, or nonprofit organizations. Many of the large social networks, including Facebook, belong to the public for profit category.

In contrast, *private* communities belong to a company, an association, or a group of companies, and their membership is limited to people who meet certain requirements (e.g., work for a particular employer or work in a particular profession). Private communities may be internal (e.g., only employees can be members) or external (for customers and suppliers).

Classification Categories

Another option is to classify the members as *traders*, *players*, *just friends*, *enthusiasts*, or *friends in need*. A more common classification recognizes six types of Internet communities: (1) transaction, (2) purpose or interest, (3) relations or practices, (4) fantasy, (5) social networks, and (6) virtual worlds.

The most popular type of virtual community today is the social networking service, the subject of our next section.

Social Networking Service (Sites)

A social network is a virtual community whose members interact, share, and exhibit social behaviors. They are hosted by social networking sites (or services).

A Definition and Basic Information

A *social network* (or *service*) site as a Web-based company, such as Facebook, that provides free Web space and tools for its community members to build profiles, interact, share, connect, and create and publish content.

A preliminary list of the characteristics and capabilities of social networking sites (SNAs) was provided in section "Drivers and Benefits of e-Commerce" of Chap. 1. More capabilities are provided in this section.

SNAs are also known as *social networks*, and they appear in a variety of forms; the most well-known, most social-oriented, network is Facebook. LinkedIn is a business-oriented network.

A Global Phenomenon

Although Facebook, Pinterest, Twitter, Google+, and other social networks attract the majority of media attention in the United States, they also have many members in other countries. Other country-based social networking sites are proliferating and growing in popularity worldwide. For example, **renren.com** and **us.weibo.com** are large communities in China; **mixi.jp** has been widely adopted in Japan and **vk.com** in Europe (primarily in Russia). Dutch users have embraced **hyves.nl**; and Nasza Klasa (**nk.pl**) has captured Poland. **Hi5.com**, a social network (now part of Tagged), has been popular in Latin America, the United States, South America, and Europe. **Migente.com** is an English language site geared toward the Hispanic community. Additionally, previously popular communication and community services have begun implementing social networking features. For example, the Chinese instant messaging service **qq.com** became one of the largest social networking services in the world once it added profiles and made friends visible to one another. Finally, Cyworld conquered the Korean market by adding "buddies."

Representative Capabilities and Services Provided by Social Networking Sites

Social networking sites provide many capabilities and services such as:

- Users can construct a Web page where they present their profile to the public.
- Users can create a circle of friends who are linked together.
- The site provides discussion forums (by subgroup, by topic).
- Photo, video, and document viewing and sharing (streaming videos, user-supplied videos) are supported.
- Wikis can be used to jointly create documents.
- Blogs can be used for discussion, dissemination of information, and much more.
- These sites offer community e-mail and instant messaging (IM) capabilities.
- Experts can be made available to answer member queries.
- Consumers can rate and comment on products and services.
- Online voting may be available to poll member opinions.
- The site may provide an e-newsletter.
- The site supports conference (group) chatting, combined with document and image sharing.
- Message and bulletin board services are available for posting information to groups and individuals on the website.
- The site provides storage for content, including photos, videos, and music.
- Users can bookmark self-created content.
- Users can find other networks, friends, or topics of interest.

These capabilities can make social networks user-friendly.

Business-Oriented Public Social Networks

Business-oriented social networks, also known as *professional social networks*, are social networks whose primary objective is to facilitate business. The prime example here is **linkedin.com**, which provides business connections and enables recruiting and finding jobs. Another example is **craigslist.org**, the largest classified ad site, which offers many social-oriented features (see Case 2.2 later in this section). Another example is The Brainyard, a place for executives to find news, knowledge, and contacts. Finally, **doximity.com** is a medical network for US physicians and healthcare professionals. Businesses are using business social networks to advertise their brands as well as making and enhancing contacts globally.

Some Capabilities of Business-Oriented Networks

With Web 2.0 tools, companies can engage users in new innovative ways. More direct communication is achieved by offering additional ways for consumers to engage and interact among themselves and with organizations. For example, a company can:

- Encourage consumers to rate and comment on products and services.
- Allow consumers to create their own topic areas and build communities (forums) around shared interests possibly related to a company's products.
- Hire bloggers or staff editors who can lead discussions about customer feedback.
- Provide incentives such as sweepstakes and contests for customers to get involved in new product (service) design and marketing campaigns.
- Encourage user-made videos about products/services and offer prizes for winning video ads.
- Provide interesting stories in e-newsletters.

An interesting business-oriented company that uses classified ads is **craigslist.org**, which is described in Case 2.2.

CASE 2.2: EC APPLICATION
CRAIGSLIST: THE ULTIMATE ONLINE-CLASSIFIED COMMUNITY

If you want to find (or offer) a job, housing, goods and services, social activities, romance, advice, and much more in over 700 local sites in 13 languages, and in more than 70 countries worldwide (2016 data), go to Craigslist (**craigslist.org**). The site has much more information than you will find in newspapers. According to their website, Craigslist receives 80 million new classified ads every month. Each month there are more than 60 million visitors to the site in the United States alone (see **craigslist.org/about/factsheet**). Finally, there are over 50 billion page views per month. For more statistics, see **alexa.com/siteinfo/craigslist.org**. According to Alexa.com, Craigslist is the eleventh most visited site in the United States.

In addition, Craigslist features over 100 topical discussion forums with more than 200 million user postings. Every day, people from 700 local sites in 70 countries worldwide check classified ads and interact on forums. Craigslist is considered by many as one of the few websites that could change the world because it is simply a free social-oriented, popular, and useful notice site. Although many other sites offer free classifieds, no other site comes close to Craigslist.

Users cite the following reasons for the popularity of Craigslist:

- It gives people a voice.
- It is consistent and champions down-to-earth values.
- It illustrates simplicity.
- It has social networking capabilities.
- It can be used for free in most cases (you can post free ads, except for business; for rent, or for sale ads in a few large cities; some employment ads; and for adult and therapeutic services).

For more information, see **craigslist.org/about/factsheet**.

As an example of the site's benefits, we provide the personal experience of one of the authors, who needed to rent his condo in Long Beach, California. The usual process to get the condo rented would take 2–4 weeks and $400 to $700 in newspaper ads, plus ads in local online sites for rental services. With Craigslist, it took less than a week at no cost. As more people discover Craigslist, the traditional newspaper-based classified ad industry will probably be the loser; ad rates may become lower, and fewer ads will be printed.

In some cities, Craigslist charges for "help wanted" ads and apartments listed by brokers. In addition, Craigslist may charge for ads with rich media features.

Concerns About Craigslist

Critics charge that some users post illegitimate or false ads on the site and the Craigslist staff are unable to effectively monitor this practice. Some users have complained about questionable ads and scams being posted. Craigslist also attracts criminals seeking to commit fraud by paying with bad checks. The anonymity of Craigslist's users as well as the lack of ratings encourages unlawful acts.

Another concern is that adult services make up a significant portion of the total traffic on the site and may involve illegal activities, especially concerning minors. With the sheer volume of users and ads posted per day, such monitoring is not possible given the modest workforce of only 40 plus that the site employs (data of 2016). (As of September 8, 2010, Craigslist has been trying to control such activities.)

On the other side, many supporters contend that attempts to control Craigslist may simply cause users to use other, less-regulated sites.

In China, a company called 58.com Inc. (**58.com**) is modeled after Craigslist and provides similar information and generates sizeable revenue and profits. The company is listed in the NYSE under the symbol WUBA.

Sources: Based on Liedtke (2009), Seamans and Zhu (2014), and **craigslist.org** (accessed January 2017).

Questions

1. Identify the business model used by Craigslist.
2. Visit **craigslist.org** and identify the social network and business network elements.
3. What do you like about the site? What do you dislike about it?
4. Why is Craigslist considered by some as a site that "could change the world?"
5. What are some of the risks and limitations of using this site?

Private (or Enterprise) Social Networks

In addition to public-oriented business social networks such as LinkedIn and Craigslist, there are many private social networks (also called enterprise networks) within organizations. Other companies with notable internal networks for employees only include Northwestern Mutual. According to the company, they have an internal blog ("Mutualblog") and a Yammer account internally, which is used by over 1000 employees to dialog and make connections on nonproprietary topics. Private networks are for employees, business partners, and customers.

Business Models and Services Related to Social Networking

Social networking sites provide innovative business models, ranging from customer reviews of food and night life in India (**burrp.mumbai.com**) to users who dress up paper dolls that look like celebrities (**stardoll.com**). New revenue models are being created almost daily. Although some generate limited revenue, others succeed. Lately, the Pinterest model has become popular.

Many communities attract advertisers. For example, **vivapets.com** attracts pet lovers with wiki contributions in its attempt to catalog all pet breeds. The site attracts hundreds of thousands of unique visitors per month. Obviously, pet food-related vendors are interested in placing ads there.

Some of the popular social-oriented services are:

1. **Reddit.com** is a community-based website that takes short reports from members on podcasts, news articles, and videos, which are then voted on by other participants. Reddit is available on a website, iPhone apps, and Android apps.
2. **Xanga.com** hosts blogs, photo blogs, and social networking profiles. Users of Xanga are referred to as "Xangans." Xanga was originally launched as a site for sharing book and music reviews. Today it is one of the most popular blogging and networking services, with an estimated 10,000,000–100,000,000 users worldwide. Xanga has a very popular blogring in Hong Kong, Macao, and Singapore. (A *blogring* links together a number of blogs that share mutual interests and can be searched by subject matter).

Mobile Social Commerce

Mobile computing is growing faster than any other type of EC computing. According to Cisco (2016), mobile data traffic will grow 827% (to 30.6 exabytes per month in 2020 from 3.7 exabytes per month in 2015). This clearly boosts mobile commerce. According to Taylor (2015), 90% of smartphone consumers used them to shop online. In subsequent chapters, we will discuss many mobile applications. Instagram is considered an important factor in the future of mobile social commerce. Here we present the basic definitions, technologies, and a few examples.

Mobile Social Networking

Mobile social networking refers to social networking where members chat and connect with one another using any mobile device. Most major social networking websites now offer mobile services. By Q1 2016, Facebook had 1.44 billion mobile users out of a total 1.59 billion monthly active users (see **venturebeat.com/2016/01/27/over-half-of-facebook-users-access-the-service-only-on-mobile** and **newsroom.fb.com/Company-info**). Some social networking sites offer mobile-only services (e.g., **path.com** and **javagala.ru**).

Mobile social networking is especially popular in Japan, South Korea, and China, generally due to better data pricing (flat rates are widespread in Japan). In Japan and South Korea, where 4G networks offer more bandwidth, the leaders in social networking are **mixi.jp** and Mobage by Dena (**mbga.jp**). Numerous other mobile social networking sites have been launched in Japan. For statistics on the exponential growth of mobile social networks, see **comscore.com**.

Experts predict that mobile social networks will experience explosive growth in the future.

Mobile Enterprise Networks

Several companies have developed (or fully sponsor) mobile-based social networks. For example, Coca-Cola has a social network that can only be accessed by mobile devices. There Coca-Cola employees attempt to influence young people to buy Coke's products.

Examples of Social Mobile Commerce Applications

There are several types of social mobile applications. Illustrative examples are provided next.

Example 1: IBM

IBM is a leader in social commerce adoption on mobile devices. Following are some examples of IBM's initiatives.

- IBM Mobile Connect (formerly IBM Lotus Mobile Connect) (social media and social networks building software, abbreviated as Connect) is popular in industry. Customers can get immediate access to blogs, wikis, and other tools. They can also share photos, videos, and files on major mobile devices (e.g., Android, iOS).
- IBM Connections allows people to generate and vote on ideas at work (see **ibm.com/connections/blogs/SametimeBlog/?lang=en**).
- The capabilities in IBM Connections 5.0, such as Moderations, or Ideation Blogs, enable workers to embrace networks of engaged people.

Example 2: Social Networks

With the current technology, we also see a trend toward sophisticated interactions of Internet social networks with images, voice, and videos. This is expected to be a powerful managerial and marketing feature in the near future.

Recent Innovative Tools and Platforms for Social Networking

A large number of software tools and platforms are available for social networking. Well-known tools are blogs, microblogs, and wikis. Note that the capabilities of these tools are improving continuously. Here we provide a representative list of recent innovative tools:

- **Snapchat.com**—A mobile photo messaging service for "chatting" with friends through photos, videos, and captions "like 'texting' with pictures or videos" (see **webtrends.about.com/od/Iphone-Apps/a/What-Is-Snapchat.htm**).
- **WhatsApp.com**—According to its website, WhatsApp is a cross platform free mobile messaging app for smartphones. Users can form groups and send each other unlimited images and video and audio media messages. The company was acquired by Facebook in 2014 for around $19 billion. WhatsApp was used by over 1 billion people each month in January 2016 (Ahmed 2016).
- **Ortsbo.com**—Enabler of real-time conversational translation mainly in social media.
- **Droid Translator (droid-translator.tiwinnovations.com)**—Translates phone calls, video chats (e.g., Skype), and text conversations into 29 different languages (for more information, see Petroff 2014).
- **Tagged.com**—A maker of *social discovery* products that enable people to meet and socialize with other people through playing games, browsing features, shared interests, and more. You can share tags, browse profiles, and exchange virtual gifts.
- **Viber.com**, **line.me/en**, etc.—Companies that provide free voice only of video calling for mobile devices and desktops (e.g., Viber for Desktop).

- **Instagram.com**—A free platform for sharing photos and videos. As a social network, it allows for the creation of a review section, etc., (Acquired by Facebook in 2012.)
- **Rocketium.com** focuses on the simple creation of videos with overlaid text.
- **Screenr.com** allows for the simple creation of screen-capture videos with audio for how-to creation.
- **Hshtags.com** ("A social media search engine dedicated to hashtags")—Enables users to see in real time all public content related to any keyword and join any related public conversation in real time (see **digitaltrends.com/social-media/new-search-engine-like-google-social-web**).

Mobile Community Activities

In many mobile social networks, devices can be utilized to conduct the same activities that are performed in a nonmobile settings. Customers can even create their own mobile community.

Mobile video sharing, which sometimes is combined with photo sharing, is a new technological and social trend. Mobile video-sharing portals are becoming popular (e.g., see **myubo.com**). Many social networking sites offer mobile features.

For 2016 statistics about social commerce, see **bazaarvoice.com/research-and-insight/social-commerce-statistics**.

SECTION 2.6 REVIEW QUESTIONS

1. Define virtual communities and describe their characteristics.
2. List the major types of virtual communities.
3. Define social network.
4. Describe mobile social commerce.
5. List some major social networking sites.
6. Describe the global nature of social networks.
7. Describe social networking.
8. Describe mobile social networking and commerce.

2.7 EMERGING EC PLATFORMS: AUGMENTED REALITY AND CROWDSOURCING

Several technologies are used as platforms that enable innovative EC applications. Here we present two.

Augmented Reality

An increasing number of business applications use the technology of *augmented reality* (AR). See Malik (2016) for more details. The term AR has several definitions depending on its field of applications. According to Wikipedia, **augmented reality** is "a live or indirect view of a physical, real-world environment whose elements are *augmented* (or supplemented) by computer-generated sensory input such as sound, video, graphics or GPS data" (see **en.wikipedia.org/wiki/Augmented_reality**). Such an arrangement helps people enhance the sensory perception of reality. The computerized layer can be seen through an application on mobile devices such as smartphones, webcams, or 3D glasses (including 3D TV). Google developed augmented reality (AR) glasses called "Google Glass."

Applications in E-Commerce

The major applications in e-commerce are in the areas of advertising and marketing (for details, see Bauer in 2016 and Corpuz in 2015). There are potentially many other areas of applications. For example, Bauer (2016) describes several marketing applications that use the technology to better engage potential customers. Google's AR is being used by several companies. For example, Walgreens is using AR for improving customer loyalty (see Kaye 2014). Finally, Wikipedia lists many e-commerce-related applications of AR.

Example 1: Net-a-Porter

This innovative company is using an iPhone/iPad app to view an AR "shopping window." As can be seen in the video "Net-A-Porter Augmented Reality Shopping Windows" (1:37 min) available at **digitalbuzzblog.com/net-a-porter-augmented-reality-shopping-windows**, customers at the company's physical store can point the mobile device camera at a clothing display (e.g., in the stores or store windows), and see a 360 degree view of the clothes. They also can see presentations at fashion shows, price, availability, and other relevant information. Furthermore, the window shoppers can immediately buy the clothing online using their mobile device (for the download, see **itunes.apple.com/ne/app/net-a-porter/id318597939?mt=8**).

Example 2: IKEA

IKEA uses AR to show how its furniture can fit in your house. For details on this mobile devices app, see Truong (2013) and watch the video "Place IKEA Furniture in Your Home with Augmented Reality" at **youtube.com/watch?v=vDNzTasuYEw**. The technology used is made by Snapshot, a free app for iOS systems.

Example 3: CastAR

Using AR technology, CastAR is able to produce more interactive tabletop gaming environments for users in a small area. See a demonstrations at **youtu.be/hL1qT0TK6aw** and **youtu.be/A4TAppwUMWU**.

Applications in Social Gaming

AR is already used in several applications. According to **t-immersion.com/augmented-reality/use-cases/social-augmented-reality-games**, social AR gaming is a superb tool for generating marketing leads and brand recognition because of the huge number of players engaged in games connected with a product.

Virtual Reality (VR)

Often confused with augmented reality is *virtual reality*. **Virtual reality** is a computer-generated simulation of a real-life environment in which users can be immersed. People feel like they are inside the environment and they can manipulate it (e.g., see Parisi 2016). To experience VR, user must wear special glasses and handsets. The technology has been around for decades but was used mainly for computer games. Lately, however, VR is moving to be an EC element (e.g., see Williams 2016). An example is Facebook's Oculus, which is experimenting with commercial applications. This is an example of combining social commerce and virtual reality. For details, see Meola (2016).

Comparing AR and VR

According to McKalin (2015), both technologies are similar in their goal of immersing the users. But they do it in different ways and for different purpose. For details see McKalin (2015), Boyajian (2015), and Aukstakalnis (2016).

Crowdsourcing

Another platform for e-commerce is crowdsourcing. Crowdsourcing is a platform for collective intelligence in e-commerce and social commerce (see the industry website **crowdsourcing.org**). Here we present the essentials of the technology.

Definitions and Major Concepts

The term *crowd* refers to a large group of people such as a group of consumers, employees of a corporation, or members of a social network who offer expertise.

AR is developed into apps for mobile devices to blend digital components into real worlds.

Crowdsourcing utilizes crowds to collectively execute tasks such as solving problems, innovating, or getting large projects completed by dividing the work among many people. The term was coined by Jeff Howe in June 2006 (Howe 2008). In the crowdsourcing process, the initiator recruits a crowd (e.g., customers) to create content, a cumbersome task (e.g., translating Wikipedia articles), or in research and development. This is based on the idea that two heads are better than one. The collective intelligence of large groups is assumed to be able to solve complex problems at low cost (Aitamurto et al. 2016; Blokdijk 2015; Zeref 2015).

Fig. 2.4 The elements
of crowdsourcing

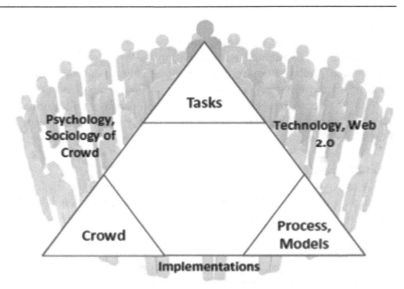

Fig. 2.5 A typical
crowdsourcing process

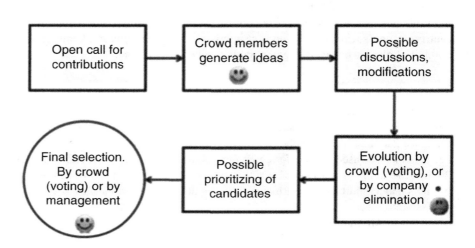

The basic elements of crowdsourcing are illustrated in Fig. 2.4. Three elements are involved: the task(s) to be carried out; the crowd, which is used to work on the task; and the models and processes used by the crowd to execute the task. These elements are connected by features related to the tasks and the crowd (such as the psychology of the crowd), the technologies used (such as idea generation and voting), and implementation issues such as incentives paid to the participants.

The Process of Crowdsourcing

Crowdsourcing can be viewed as a collective problem-solving or work sharing process and usually is conducted as a Web-based activity. In a typical use of crowdsourcing, problems are broadcasted either to a known crowd (e.g., employees or business partners) or to an *unknown* group of participants (e.g., expert problem solvers or consumers). The communication usually starts as an open call for solutions or ideas (see first step in Fig. 2.5). The members of the crowd are organized as an online community, and the members submit individual work (e.g., solutions). The crowd may also discuss the solutions and may vote for a final short list. Alternatively, the short list is then prioritized (e.g., ranked). The final selection can be made by the crowd or by management (Fig. 2.5). The winning individuals in the crowd are well compensated, either monetarily or with special recognition. In other cases, the only rewards may be the satisfaction with a job well done. The use of crowd-sourcing can yield results from amateurs or unrecognized professionals.

Example: Starbucks

Starbucks introduced My Starbucks Idea (**mystarbucksidea.force.com**), a social media site designed to solicit ideas and feedback from customers. The site was built around four key themes: (1) ideas are user generated; (2) users can vote to short list ideas, discussing them before and/or after the vote; and (3) company employees act as "idea partners," providing answers to questions and leading discussions.

The crowd's idea generation process is visible to the entire Starbucks community. The members can see the status of each proposal.

An overview of crowdsourcing is provided in a video titled "Crowdsourcing and Crowdfunding Explained" (3:48 min) at **youtu.be/−38uPkyH9vI**, also see **crowdsourcing.org** and Crowdsortium (**crowdsortium.org**). These specialists have developed best practices for the industry.

Benefits of Crowdsourcing

The major perceived benefits of crowdsourcing include the following:

- Problems can be analyzed or solved at comparative little cost. (Payment can be determined by the results; however, sometimes there is no monetary payment, just praise or accolades).
- Solutions can be reached quickly since many people work on the needed research project simultaneously. Also, designs of products may be expedited.
- The contributing crowd may reside within the organization; therefore, talents may be discovered.
- By listening to the crowd, organizations gain firsthand insight into the desires of their customers (or employees). There is built-in market research when the crowd is composed of customers.
- Crowdsourcing can tap into the global world of ideas. The crowd may include business partners, customers, academicians, etc., and the members of the crowd can reside in different countries.
- Customers tend to be more loyal if they participate in a company's problem-solving project.

Uses of Crowdsourcing in E-Commerce

There are several EC applications of crowdsourcing—notable is the creation of Wikipedia. Corners (2015) and Fitchard (2015) present many successful applications.

SECTION 2.7 REVIEW QUESTIONS

1. Define augmented reality.
2. Describe how AR can facilitate EC.
3. Define crowdsourcing.
4. List the elements of crowdsourcing.
5. Describe the process of crowdsourcing.
6. What are the major benefits of crowdsourcing?
7. How is crowdsourcing used in EC?

2.8   THE FUTURE: WEB 3.0, WEB 4.0, AND WEB 5.0

Web 2.0 is here. What's next? The answer is a still-unknown entity referred to as *Web 3.0*, the future wave of Internet applications. Some of the desired capabilities of Web 3.0 will be discussed later in this section. In general, there is optimism about the future of the use of the Web 3.0 to facilitate EC (see **siliconangle.com/blog/2013/08/02/the-future-of-ecommerce-with-web-3-0** and **wired.com/insights/2014/09/e-commerce-to-web-3-0**).

Web 3.0: What Does the Future Hold?

Web 3.0 is projected to deliver a new generation of business applications that will see business and social computing converge. Web 3.0 could change the manner in which people live and work as well as the organizations where they work, and it may even revolutionize social networking (see 1stwebdesigner 2015).

According to several experts, Web 3.0 could have the following capabilities:

- Make current applications smarter by introducing new intelligent features.
- Provide easier and faster interaction, collaboration, and user engagement.
- Facilitate intelligent-based powerful search engines.
- Provide more user-friendly application–creation and human–computer interaction capabilities.
- Increase the wisdom and creativity of people.
- Enable smarter machines (Gartner 2016).
- Enable much wider bandwidth.
- Enable better visualization including 3D tools.
- Simplify the use of mobile computing and mobile commerce.

For additional capabilities, see O'Connell's (2015) slideshow.

Web 3.0 and the Semantic Web

One of the major possible platforms of Web 3.0 technologies is the *Semantic Web*. The term was presented by the inventor of the Web, Tim Berners-Lee, who visualized the Semantic Web as the platform for making the Web smarter. There is no standard definition of **Semantic Web**. It is basically a group of methods that focus on machines (in contrast with Web 2.0 that focuses on people). The technology attempts to enable computers to understand the semantics (i.e., the meaning) of information, by using natural language understanding tools. For a video titled "Evolution Web 1.0, Web 2.0 to Web 3.0" (3.58 min), see **youtube.com/watch?v=bsNcjya56v8**.

Concerns

The following are a few concerns regarding the implementation of Web 3.0 and the future of EC.

- **Future threats.** According to the authors' experiences, the following trends may slow the growth of EC and Web 3.0 and may even cripple the Internet.
- **Security and privacy concerns.** Shoppers, as users of e-banking and other services, and members of social networks, worry about online security and privacy. The Web needs to be made safer.
- **Lack of net neutrality.** If the big telecommunications companies are allowed to charge companies for a guarantee of faster access, critics fear that small innovative Web companies could be demolished by the big companies that can afford to pay more for efficient Internet usage. **Copyright complaints. T**he legal problems of YouTube, Craigslist, Wikipedia, and others may result in a loss of originality, dedication, and creativity of user-generated content.
- **Insufficient connectivity.** Upstream bandwidths are still constraining applications, making uploading of video files a time-consuming task.
- **Language fitness.** There will be a need to reconsider the existing spoken languages with Web 3.0 taxonomies and schemes.
- **Standards.** There will be a need for architectural standards for Web 3.0.

Therefore, some believe that the Semantic Web will never work (see the 91 min video at **youtube.com/watch?v=oKiXpO2rbJM**).

Despite these concerns, Web 3.0 and e-commerce could thrive due to several innovations in the technological environment.

The Technological Environment

The future of EC and the Semantic Web is dependent on how far the relevant information technology advances (e.g., see Gartner 2016). Of the many predictions, we cite two here. Also, see Gartner's annual reports about Strategic Technology Trends at **gartner.com/technology/research**.

Web 4.0

Web 4.0 is the Web generation after Web 3.0. It is still an unknown entity. It is known as Symbiotic Web. Several futurists, including Daniel Burrus (see a video at **bigthink.com/big-think-tv/web-40-the-ultra-intelligent-electronic-agent-is-coming**), view the primary business driver of Web 4.0 as vastly more powerful electronic agents. These agents will work to integrate and personalize all of an individual's interactions with technology (Fowler and Rodd 2015).

For a discussion, see Koren (2013) or Edwards (2013).

Web 5.0

According to Patel (2013), "Web 5.0 is still an underground idea in progress and there is no exact definition of how it would be. Web 5.0 can be considered as a Symbionet Web, decentralized." Patel provides some technical information. Additional details and a comparison are provided at **flatworldbusiness.wordpress.com/flat-education/previously/web-1-0-vs-web-2-0-vs-web-3-0-a-bird-eye-on-the-definition**.

SECTION 2.8 REVIEW QUESTIONS

1. What is Web 3.0, and how will it differ from Web 2.0?
2. Define Semantic Web.
3. List the major potential inhibitors and concerns of e-commerce and Web 3.0.
4. What are the major influencing computing and IT trends?
5. What are Web 4.0 and Web 5.0?

MANAGERIAL ISSUES

Some managerial issues related to this chapter are as follows.

1. **Should we use auctions for selling?** A major strategic issue is whether to use auctions as sales channels. Auctions do have some limitations, and forward auctions may create conflicts with other distribution channels. If a company decides to use auctions, it needs to select auction mechanisms and determine a pricing strategy. These decisions determine the success of the auctions and the ability to attract and retain visitors on the selling site. Auctions also require support services. Decisions about how to provide these services and to what extent to use business partners are critical to the success of high-volume auctions.
2. **Should we barter?** Bartering can be an interesting strategy, especially for companies that lack cash, need special material or machinery, and have surplus resources. However, the valuation of what is bought or sold may be hard to determine, and the tax implications in some countries are not clear.
3. **How do we select merchant software?** There are many products and vendors on the market. Small businesses should consider offers from Yahoo! or eBay since the software is combined with hosting and offers exposure to the vendor-managed e-market. The functionalities of the software as well as the ease of building webstores need to be examined.
4. **How can we use Facebook and other social networks in our business?** The many possibilities are mostly in marketing and advertising. Any progressive organization should examine and experiment with social networking.

SUMMARY

In this chapter, you learned about the following EC issues as they relate to the chapter's learning objectives.

1. **Activities and mechanisms.** The major activities are information dissemination and presence, online trading, collaboration, entertainment, and search. The major mechanisms are marketplaces, webstores, shopping carts, catalogs, search engines, Web 2.0 tools, and virtual worlds.

   Most of the activities are between sellers and buyers. However, there also are collaboration activities among supply chain members as well as among people within organizations. EC attempts to automate the interaction process for the above activities.

2. **E-marketplaces and their components.** An e-marketplace or marketspace is a virtual market that does not suffer from limitations of space, time, or borders. As such, it can be very efficient and effective. Its major components include customers, sellers, products (some digital), infrastructure, front-end processes, back-end activities, electronic intermediaries, other business partners, and support services.

   The role of intermediaries will change as e-markets develop: Some will be eliminated (disintermediation); others will change their roles and prosper (reintermediation). In the B2B area, for example, e-distributors connect manufacturers with buyers by aggregating e-catalogs of many suppliers. New value-added services that range from content creation to syndication are mushrooming.

3. **The major types of e-marketplaces.** In the B2C area, there are webstores and e-malls. In the B2B area, there are private and public e-marketplaces, which may be vertical (within one industry) or horizontal (across different industries). Exchanges are the platform for many buyers and sellers to meet and trade. Different types of portals provide access to e-marketplaces.

4. **Electronic catalogs, search engines, and shopping carts.** The major mechanisms in e-markets are e-catalogs, search engines, software (intelligent) agents, and electronic shopping carts. These mechanisms, which are known as merchant suites, facilitate EC by providing a user-friendly and efficient shopping environment.

5. **Types of auctions and their characteristics.** In forward auctions, bids from buyers are placed sequentially, either in increasing mode or in decreasing mode. In reverse auctions, buyers place an RFQ, and suppliers submit offers in one or several rounds. In name-your-own-price auctions, buyers specify how much they are willing to pay for a product or service, and an intermediary tries to find a supplier to fulfill the request. Penny auctions are forward auctions where a small fee is paid each time a bid is made. The final member to bid wins the auction when the designated time is up.

6. **The benefits and limitations of auctions.** The major benefits for sellers are the ability to reach many buyers, sell quickly, and save on intermediary commissions. Buyers have excellent access to auctions and a chance to obtain bargains and collectibles while shopping from their homes. The major limitation is the possibility of fraud.

7. **Bartering and negotiating.** Electronic bartering can greatly facilitate the swapping of goods and services among organizations, thanks to improved search and matching capabilities, which is managed by bartering exchanges. Software agents can facilitate online negotiation.

8. **The structure and role of virtual communities.** Virtual communities create new types of business opportunities. They bring people with similar interests together at one website. (Such groups are a natural target for advertisers and marketers.) Using chat rooms, discussion spaces, and so forth, members can exchange opinions about certain products and services. Of special interest are communities of transactions, whose interest is the promotion of commercial buying and selling. Virtual communities can foster customer loyalty. This may increase sales of products made by vendors that sponsor communities and facilitate customer feedback for improving service and business operations.

9. **Social networks as EC mechanisms.** These are very large Internet communities that enable the sharing of content, including text, videos, and photos, and promote online socialization and interaction. Hundreds of social networks are emerging around the world, competing for advertising money. Millions of corporations advertise, entertain, and even sell on social networks.

   Business-oriented communities concentrate on business issues, both in one country and around the world (e.g., recruiting, finding business partners). Social marketplaces meld social networks and some aspects of business. Notable business-oriented social networks are LinkedIn and XING. Some companies are active in public social networks such as Facebook. Other companies own and operate their own social networks within the company, which are known as enterprise social networks. Their members are usually employees and retirees. They are used mainly for collaboration, knowledge creation and preservation, training, and socialization. Many large companies have such networks (e.g., IBM, Wells Fargo, Northwestern Mutual).

10. **Augmented reality (AR) and crowdsourcing**. These emerging technologies facilitate two types of EC activities. AR blends visual aspects of computer and physical worlds. Thus, it can facilitate advertisement and presentation of information. It works by pointing a mobile device (e.g., smartphone) to a product or building and adds information to what you see (e.g., 360 degree view, price tag). Crowdsourcing solicits the wisdom of the crowd for idea generation or problem-solving. It also is used to divide a large task among many people, each of whom is executing a different, small subtask.

11. **Web 3.0 and Web 4.0**. Web 3.0, the next generation of the Web, will combine social and business computing. It will be more portable and personal, with powerful search engines, increased clout, and greater connectivity with the wireless environment and on-demand applications. Knowledge management will be one of its main pillars. The Semantic Web will play a major role in Web 3.0 applications. Web 3.0 and its applications will depend on IT trends such as the developments in cloud computing, utility computing, parallel processing, and machine intelligence. Web 4.0 is a futuristic Web that will be built on ubiquitous and intelligent systems. It will connect "islands" of intelligence from different sources.

KEY TERMS

Augmented reality
Back end
Bartering
Bartering exchange
Business-oriented social network
Buy-side e-marketplace
Crowdsourcing
Desktop search
Digital products
Disintermediation
Double auction
Dynamic pricing
E-bartering (electronic bartering)
E-distributor
E-mall (online mall)
E-marketplace
Electronic auction (e-auction)
Electronic catalog (e-catalog)
Electronic shopping cart
Enterprise search
Forward auction
Front end
Intermediary
Mobile portal
Mobile social networking
Name-your-own-price model
Penny auction
Reverse auction (bidding or tendering system)
Search engine
Sell-side e-marketplace
Semantic Web
Virtual community
Virtual reality
Voice portal
Web 3.0
Web 4.0
Web (information) portal
Webstore (storefront)

DISCUSSION QUESTIONS

1. Compare physical marketplaces with marketspaces. What are the advantages and limitations of each?
2. Discuss the competitive advantage of Craigslist using classified ads.
3. Describe the advantages of Web 3.0 over Web 1.0 and Web 2.0.
4. Discuss the need for portals in EC.
5. How do business-oriented networks differ from regular social networks such as Facebook?
6. Why are social marketplaces considered to be a Web 2.0 application?
7. Discuss the following statement: "Technically, you can put together a portal in a weekend, but culturally there are a slew of things to consider; therefore it takes much longer."
8. Discuss the pros and cons of selling cars via auctions.

   Discuss the differences between virtual reality and augmented reality.

TOPICS FOR CLASS DISCUSSION AND DEBATES

1. Compare and contrast the efficiency of traditional markets with that of digital markets.
2. Some claim that social networking, especially microblogging and social networking sites, displace the traditional electronic bulletin board systems. Discuss.
3. Discuss the advantages of dynamic pricing strategy over fixed pricing. What are the potential disadvantages of dynamic pricing?
4. Enter Facebook and search for companies that do auctions on the site. Identify the different types of auctions on the site.
5. What is the advantage of a business using eBay instead of conducting auctions from its own site? Distinguish between C2C and B2B cases.
6. Debate: Should companies build in-house social networks for external activities or use existing public social networks?
7. Debate: Should Craigslist and YouTube monitor and control what users publish there? Who will pay the cost?
8. Debate: Social networking services can provide good security to enterprise social networks. However, security may limit users' creativity and disrupt the business. Should a company use such a service?
9. Debate: Some research suggests that the use of public social networks by employees during work hours can be good for a business because employees develop relationships and share information, which increases productivity and innovation. Others say it is a waste of time and ban the use of Facebook, YouTube, and other such sites at work.
10. Debate the business value of social networking.
11. Debate: Facebook and Twitter compete for advertisers' money. Which one has a better chance to get more ad money and why?
12. Some of the largest social media networks exist in China (**qq.com**, **qzone.qq.com**, **us.weibo.com**, **weixin.qq.com**, and **renren.com**). Find information about these networks and list their properties. How do they differ from US social networks?

INTERNET EXERCISES

1. Enter **droid-translator.tiwinnovations.com** and **tranzactive.com** and compare their translation capabilities.
2. Examine how bartering is conducted online at **tradeaway.com**, **barterquest.com**, and **u-exchange.com**. Compare and contrast the functionalities and ease of use of these sites.
3. Enter **volusion.com** and identify all specific e-commerce mechanisms (or solutions) provided by the company.
4. Enter **respond.com** and request a product or a service. Once you receive replies, select the best deal. You have no obligation to buy. Write a short report based on your experience.
5. Enter **dtsearch.com** and find its capabilities. What type(s) of search does it conduct (e.g., desktop, enterprise, general)?
6. Enter **cars.com**. List all services available to both sellers and buyers of cars. Compare it to **carsdirect.com**. Finally, identify the revenue sources of both sites.

7. Enter **ups.com**.

    (a) Find out what information is available to customers before they send a package.
    (b) Find out about the "package tracking" system; be specific.
    (c) Compute the cost of delivering a 10″ × 20″ × 15″ box, weighing 40 pounds, from your hometown to Long Beach, California. Compare the cost for the fastest delivery option with to the lowest possible delivery cost.
    (d) Prepare a spreadsheet using Excel for two different types of calculations available on the UPS site. Enter data to solve for two different calculations.

8. Enter **magicleap.com** and find the company's activities in augmented reality. Write a report.
9. Enter **truecar.com** and review the services they provide to car buyers. Write a report.
10. Enter **ibm.com** and **oracle.com**. Prepare a list of the major products available for building corporate portals.
11. Enter **go.sap.com/index.html** and find the key capabilities of its enterprise portals. List the benefits of using five of the capabilities of SAP's portals.
12. Enter **networksolutions.com**. View the shopping cart demo. What features impress you the most and why? What related services does it provide? Compare it to **storefront.net**, **nexternal.com**, and **ecwid.com**.
13. Enter the website of a social networking service of your choice. Build a homepage. Add a chat room and a message board to your site using the free tools provided. Describe the other capabilities available. Make at least five new friends.
14. Enter **vivapets.com** and **dogster.com** and compare their offerings.
15. Enter **w3.org**. Find material about Semantic Web (SW); check their RDF/FAQ and search for some applications. Write a report.
16. Enter **zippycart.com** and read the article "13 Ecommerce Link Building Tactics for Your Online Store" at **zippycart.com/ecommerce-news/1430-13-ways-to-gain-inbound-links-to-your-online-store.html**. Write a brief summary.

TEAM ASSIGNMENTS AND PROJECTS

1. **Assignment for the Opening Case**
   Read the opening case and answer the following questions:

   (a) Why is Pinterest considered a social network?
   (b) What are the company's business and revenue models?
   (c) How can manufacturers advertise on Pinterest?
   (d) Compare Pinterest and We Heart It. Pay attention to the business models.
   (e) Pinterest has a large amount of money. How does it use this money on its website to increase its competitive advantage?

2. Assign each group a large e-tailer (e.g., Amazon.com, Walmart.com, Target.com, Dell.com, Apple.com, and HP.com). Trace the purchasing process. Look at the catalogs, search engines, shopping carts, Web 2.0 features, and any other mechanisms that improve e-shopping. Prepare a presentation that includes recommendations for improving the existing process.

3. Compare the shopping carts from Shopopify, Big Commerce, and Open Cart. Distinguish between hosted and self-hosted carts. Watch the O'Reilly Media video titled "Online Communities: The Tribalization of Business" (Part 1 is 6:15 min; Parts 2 and 3 are optional) at **youtube.com/watch?v=qQJvKyytMXU** and answer the following questions:

   (a) Why is the term tribalization used in the video?
   (b) What are virtual communities?
   (c) How can traditional businesses benefit from online communities?
   (d) What is the value of communities for the customers?
   (e) Compare social vs. marketing frameworks.
   (f) How are virtual communities aligned with the businesses?
   (g) Discuss the issues of measurements, metrics, and CSFs.
   (h) Optional: View Part 2 (**youtube.com/watch?v=U0JsT8mfZHc#t=15**) and Part 3 (**youtube.com/watch?v=AeE9VWQY9Tc**) (6:50 and 10:24 min respectively), and summarize the major topics discussed.

4. The team's mission is to analyze Pinterest's U.S. and global competition, including similar companies in China and Brazil. Begin by looking at **weheartit.com**. Look at another country of your choice. Comment on the cultural differences. Write a report.

5. There are many applications of augmented reality. Find current ones and classify them by areas (e.g., marketing). Make a class presentation.

CLOSING CASE: DRIVING CUSTOMER ENGAGEMENT WITH AUGMENTED REALITY AT TESCO

The Problem

Businesses are constantly searching for new products and services that can be used to recruit and retain customers. These products and services can be used to grow profits or act as "loss leaders" to bring customers into the store. Grocery stores are very price competitive, especially in more mature economies such as Britain.

Tesco is a world leading retailer of groceries and other goods with locations in 11 countries (www.tescoplc.com/about-us/our-businesses). Britain is one of the company's primary markets, and completion in the market is growing. These changes are being driven primarily by the growth of discounters such as Aldi and Lidi. With these competitors focusing of price completion, it is becoming more important for more traditional retailers such as Tesco to build store traffic by offering unique goods and services (Telegraph 2017).

Disney is global entertainment and media brand well known for their movies, television programs, resorts, and products (**thewaltdisneycompany.com/about/#our-businesses**). One of Disney's most recent animated features was the movie Frozen, which earned over $1.2 billion worldwide since its release in 2013. The movie and its characters still enjoy a strong popularity with fans, especially children.

The Solution

Tesco has identified the need to create unique promotions to drive traffic to its locations and brokered a partnership with Disney to help create a unique offering that was meant to showcase new augmented reality technology deployed by Engine Creative (2016). The store provided the opportunity for customers to receive a free sticker folder and stickers related to the themes and characters in the Frozen movie. Using the free Tesco Discover Augmented Reality app, customers were able to interactive with the stickers through different 3D scenes. Additionally, the app is designed to take interactive selfies with their favorite Frozen characters (youtube.com/watch?v=P0Zq8YFmiWk).

The Results

The promotion was a success on multiple levels. First, it drove significant traffic into stores, and supplies of stickers were exhausted in many locations. Second, the promotion drove significant downloads of the Tesco Discover Augmented Reality app. While the app was initially used for the Frozen promotion, it also contained a number of additional augmented realty functions designed to be used on an ongoing basis. These features included enabling shoppers to discover great videos of their favorite recipes, Scan-to-Shop gift guides, magazines and catalogs, enter exclusive competitions, and play a range of interactive games that can only be accessed by scanning Tesco products and publications.

Sources: Based on Creative Engine (2016) and Telegraph (2017).

Questions

1. How does price completion drive the need to compete in other areas?
2. Why would Tesco partner with Disney to drive traffic to its locations?
3. Why did Tesco use an expended set of features (beyond the promotion) in its app?
4. Do you think augmented reality applications can help Tesco differentiate itself?

REFERENCES

1stwebdesigner. "A Brief Introduction to Web 3.0." August 14, 2015. **1stwebdesigner.com/web-3-introduction** (accessed December 2016).

Ahmad, I. "Optimizing Pins on Pinterest: Make Each Pin Count for Higher Reach [Infographic]." *Social Media Today*, February 25, 2016.

Ahmed, M. "One in Seven People on Earth Use WhatsApp Each Month." *Business ETC*, February 2, 2016. **bidnessetc.com/authors/mohid-ahmed** (accessed December 2016).

Aitamurto, T., H. Landemore, J. S. Galli (2016). "Unmasking the Crowd: Participants' Motivation Factors, Expectations, and Profile in a Crowdsourced Law Reform." *Information, Communication & Society*. **thefinnishexperiment.com/2016/09/21/motivation-factors-for-participation-in-crowdsourced-policymaking** (accessed December 2016)

Aukstakalnis, S. *Practical Augmented Reality: A Guide to the Technologies, Applications and Human Factors for AR and VR (Usability)*. Boston, MA: Addison Wesley Professional, 2016.

Bauer, T. "Is Augmented Reality Part of Your 2017 Marketing Plan? Maybe It Should Be." *Localytics*. December 16, 2016. **info.localytics.com/blog/is-augmented-reality-part-of-your-2017-marketing-plan-maybe-it-should-be-0** (accessed January 2017)

Bloomberg. "Jewelry Heist." Special Report E-Biz, May 9, 2004. **businessweek.com/stories/2004-05-09/jewelry-heist** (accessed December 2016).

Blue Nile. "Blue Nile Expands "Retail Reimagined" Concept to D.C.-Metro Area." June 13, 2016. **investor.bluenile.com/releasedetail.cfm?ReleaseID=975478** (accessed December 2016)

Boyajian, L. "Virtual Reality vs. Augmented Reality." *Augment.com*, October 6, 2015. **augment.com/blog/virtual-reality-vs-augmented-reality** (accessed December 2016).

Blokdijk, B. *Crowdsourcing - Simple Steps to Win, Insights and Opportunities for Maxing Out Success*. New York, New York: Complete Publishing, 2015.

Cario, J. E. *Pinterest Marketing: An Hour a Day*. Hoboken, NJ: Sybex, 2013.

Cisco. "Cisco Visual Networking Index: Global Mobile Data Traffic Forecast Update, 2015–2020 White Paper." February 1, 2016. **cisco.com/c/en/us/solutions/collateral/service-provider/visual-networking-index-vni/mobile-white-paper-c11-520862.html** (accessed December 2016).

Corners, B. "4 Killer Ways Retailers Benefit From Crowdsourcing." *Crowdsource*. February 5, 2015. **crowdsource.com/blog/2015/02/4-killer-ways-retailers-benefit-crowdsourcing** (accessed December 2016).

Corpuz, J. "Best Augmented Reality Apps." *Tom's Guide*, April 28, 2015. **tomsguide.com/us/pictures-story/657-best-augmented-reality-apps.html** (accessed December 2016).

D'Onfro, J. "Why $11 billion Pinterest thinks it has the 'best kind of business model'." Business Insider, May 19, 2015. **finance.yahoo.com/news/why-11-billion-pinterest-thinks-165432347.html** (accessed December 2016).

Edwards, J. What Might Web 4.0 Look Like and Should You be Preparing?" *IMedia*. May 18, 2013. **imediaconnection.com/articles/ported-articles/red-dot-articles/2013/may/what-might-web-40-look-like-and-should-you-be-preparing/#sthash.oS4FadBL.dpuf** (accessed December 2016).

Engine Creative. "Tesco Brings Disney Frozen to Life with Augmented Reality Magic." November 22, 2016. http://www.enginecreative.co.uk/blog/tesco-brings-disney-frozen-life-augmented-reality-magic (accessed December 2016).

Fitchard, K. "8 Crowdsourcing Apps (Besides OpenSignal) We Love." *OpenSignal Blog*, July 9, 2015. **opensignal.com/blog/2015/07/09/8-crowdsourcing-apps-besides-opensignals-love** (accessed December 2016).

Fowler, N. & Rodd, E. "Web 4.0: The Ultra-Intelligent Electronic Agent is Coming" *ThinkBig*. March 1, 2015. **bigthink.com/big-think-tv/web-40-the-ultra-intelligent-electronic-agent-is-coming** (accessed December 2016).

Gartner. "Gartner Identifies the Top 10 Strategic Technology Trends for 2016." **gartner.com/newsroom/id/3482617** (accessed December 2016).

Howe, J. *Crowdsourcing: Why the Power of the Crowd is Driving the Future of Business*. New York: Crown Business, 2008.

Kaye, K. "Walgreens Tests Google's Augmented Reality for Loyal." *Adage.com*, July 1, 2014. **adage.com/article/datadriven-marketing/walgreens-tests-google-s-augmented-reality-loyalty-app/293961** (accessed December 2016).

Koren, J. "From Web 4.0 and Beyond." *Integrating Educational Technology and Digital Learning* January 20, 2013. **slideshare.net/joh5700/educational-technology-and-digital-learning-16077621** (accessed December 2016).

Kissmetrics, "The Ultimate Pinterest Marketing Guide: How to Improve Your Reach and Promote Your Brand" January 17, 2015. **blog.kissmetrics.com/ultimate-pinterest-marketing-guide** (accessed December 2016).

Liedtke, M. "Study: Craigslist Revenue to Climb 23 Pct to $100M." June 10, 2009. **thestreet.com/story/10511645/1/study-craigslist-revenue-to-climb-23-pct-to-100m.html** (accessed December 2016).

Malik, A. *Augmented Reality for Dummies*. Hoboken, NJ: For Dummies, June 2016.

Mangalindan, J.P. "How Pinterest can justify its $11 billion valuation and set itself up for an IPO" Yahoo Finance. October 17, 2016. **finance.yahoo.com/news/pinterest-may-be-gearing-up-for-ipo-175408938.html** (accessed December 2016).

McDonald, J, *Pinterest Marketing Workbook: How to Use Pinterest for Business*, New York: CreateSpace, 2015.

McKalin, V. "Augmented Reality vs. Virtual Reality: What Are the Differences and Similarities?" *Tech Times*, 2015.

Meola, A. "Inside Facebook's Marriage of Social Media and Virtual Reality." *Business Insider*, February 23, 2016.

O'Connell, J. "The Next Big Thing is Web 3.0: Catch It If You Can." *IWBNet*, 62 slides, 2015.

Parisi, T. *Learning Virtual Reality: Development Immersive Experiences and Applications for Desktop, Web and Mobile*. Sebastopol, CA: O'Reilly Media, November 2016.

Patel, K. "Incremental Journey for World Wide Web: Introduced with Wen 1.0 to Recent Web 5.0- A Survey Paper." *International Journal of Advanced Research in Computer Science and Software Engineering*, 3(10), October 2013.

Petroff, A. "Want to Chat in 29 Languages?" *CNN Money*, January 2, 2014. **money.cnn.com/2014/01/02/technology/translation-service-app** (accessed December 2016).

Questex. "Board Portals: Decision-Making Has a New Ally." *Diligent*, 2015. **diligent.com/new/board-portals:Decision-making-has-a-new-ally** (accessed December 2016).

Roof, K. "Leaked Pinterest Documents Show Revenue, Growth Forecasts." *TechCrunch*. October 16, 2015. **techcrunch.com/2015/10/16/leaked-pinterest-documents-show-revenue-growth-forecasts** (accessed December 2016).

Saarinen, T., M. Tinnilä, and A. Tseng, (Eds.). *Managing Business in a Multi-Channel World: Success Factors for E-Business*. Hershey, PA: Idea Group, Inc., 2006.

Seamans, R., and F. Zhu. (2014). Responses to Entry in Multi-Sided Markets: The Impact of Craigslist on Local Newspapers. *Management Science*, 60(2).

Smith, C. "270 Amazing Pinterest Statistics and Facts." *Expanded Ramblings*, November 17, 2016. **expandedramblings.com/index.php/pinterest-stats** (accessed December 2016).

Tarver, E. "An Inside Look at Pinterest's Business Model." *Investopedia*. August 18, 2015. **investopedia.com/articles/investing/081815/inside-look-pinterests-business-model.asp** (accessed December 2016).

Taylor, G. "More Than 90% Of Consumers Use Smartphones While Shopping in Stores." *Retail Touchpoints,* August 20, 2015. **retailtouchpoints. com/topics/mobile/more-than-90-of-consumers-use-smartphones-while-shopping-in-stores** (accessed December 2016).

Telegraph, "The Battle Is Only Just Beginning for Britain's 'Big Four' Supermarkets." *The Telegraph*. January 2, 2017. **telegraph.co.uk/finance/ newsbysector/retailandconsumer/11590348/The-battle-is-only-just-beginning-for-Britains-big-four-supermarkets.html**   (accessed January 2017).

Truong, A. "Today's Most Innovative Company: IKEA Uses Augmented Reality to Show How Furniture Fits in a Room." July 26, 2013. **fastcompany.com/3014930/most-innovative-companies/todays-most-innovative-company-ikea-uses-augmented-reality-to-show** (accessed December 2016).

Tu, J. "Blue Nile Reports Lower Sales and Profit." *The Seattle Times*, May 5, 2016. **seattletimes.com/business/retail/blue-nile-reports-lower-sales-and-profit** (accessed December 2016).

Williams, M. "VR Just Got Serious and You Should Be Paying Attention." *IT World*, February 24, 2016.

Yarrow, A. "Falling Marriage Rates Reveal Economic Fault Lines." *The New York Times*. Feburary 6, 2015. **nytimes.com/2015/02/08/fashion/ weddings/falling-marriage-rates-reveal-economic-fault-lines.html?_r=0** (accessed December 2016).

Zeref, L. *Mindsharing: The Art of Crowdsourcing Everything*. Westminster, London: Portfolio, 2015.

Part II

E-Commerce Applications

Retailing in Electronic Commerce: Products and Services

Contents

Learning Objectives

Upon completion of this chapter, you will be able to:

1. Describe electronic retailing (e-tailing) and its characteristics.
2. Classify the primary e-tailing business models.
3. Describe how online travel and tourism services operate and how they influence the industry.
4. Discuss the online employment market, including its participants and benefits.
5. Describe online real estate services.
6. Discuss online stock trading services.
7. Discuss cyberbanking and online personal finance.
8. Describe on-demand delivery of groceries and similar perishable products and services related to them.
9. Describe the delivery of digital products such as online entertainment.
10. Discuss various online consumer aids, including price comparison sites.
11. Describe the impact of e-tailing on retail competition.
12. Describe disintermediation and other B2C strategic issues.

© Springer International Publishing AG 2018

E. Turban et al., *Electronic Commerce 2018*, Springer Texts in Business and Economics, DOI 10.1007/978-3-319-58715-8_3

OPENING CASE
AMAZON.COM—E-COMMERCE INNOVATOR

The Problem

In the early 1990s, entrepreneur Jeff Bezos saw an opportunity rather than a business problem. He decided that books were the most logical product for selling online, because they were the same product, regardless of how or where they were purchased. In July 1995, Bezos started Amazon.com (**amazon.com**) and began selling books online. Over the years, the company has continually improved, expanded, changed its business model, and expanded its product selection, improving customer experience and adding new products and services and business alliances. The company also recognized the importance of order fulfillment and warehousing early on. It has invested billions of dollars building physical warehouses and distribution centers designed for shipping packages to millions of customers. In 2012, the company started same-day delivery from its new distribution center and in 2016 piloted the use of drones for this purpose. After 2000, the company added information technology products and services, notably Kindle e-reader family, Fire TV, Echo, and Web Services (cloud technologies). The company maintains a listing of its new and innovative products and services at **amazon.com/p/feature/tv76jef8gz289rm**. In 2015, Amazon continued to heavily invest in Prime Video to actively compete with Netflix and Hulu (Trefis 2015). Amazon.com's challenge was, and still is, to profitably sell many consumer products and services online.

The Solution: Innovations and Reaching Out to Customers

To meet the goals of increasing sales and market penetration, Amazon must focus on making products easier to buy for its existing customers, creating new customers and innovating new products and services for all customers to purchase. All of these activities require different types of innovation, a concept that is held in high regard at the company. For example, see this interesting talk from Jeff Bezos on the importance of innovation and entrepreneurship in technology companies (**youtu.be/_KEKkVrzeU8**).

Making Buying Easier

The company's initial innovations were all based on the idea of making products easy to search, select, purchase, and ship. Amazon was a leader in the development of easy-to-use website searching, as well as accurate keyword searches for products. Key features of Amazon.com are easy browsing, searching, and ordering; useful product information, reviews, recommendations, and other personalization techniques; a very large selection of products and the ability to compare prices; low prices; secure payment system; efficient order fulfillment; and an easy product return arrangement. From this foundation, the company added one-click ordering (**amazon.com/p/feature/7smbfan9c84m7rd**), which made it easy for existing customers to quickly order products without the hassle of going through multiple checkout screens. The company also created Amazon Prime (**amazon.com/p/feature/zh395rdnqt6b8ea**), a service that allows free 2-day shipping on many products for a small annual fee. A unique example of a product and service offered is Amazon Dash Buttons (**amazon.com/ddb/learn-more**), a Wi-Fi-connected device that reorders products with the press of a button. Each Dash Button is paired with a unique product and allows for easy repeat ordering of often-used home products.

Amazon.com is also recognized as an online leader in providing personalized services and CRM. When a customer revisits Amazon.com, a cookie file identifies the user and says, for example, "Welcome back, Sarah Shopper," and then proceeds to recommend new books on topics similar to past purchases. You may receive recommendations for cheaper products. For example, a customer who buys printer toner for $30 a unit regularly might be directed to a vendor that sells four units for a total of $65. Amazon also provides detailed product descriptions and ratings to help consumers make informed purchase decisions. The site has an efficient search engine and other shopping aids. Amazon.com has a state-of-the-art warehousing system that gives the company an advantage over the competition.

These and other innovations are designed to streamline the shopping experience for customers and reduce any barriers that would stop them from purchasing products. This strategy is designed to help increase total sales for existing customers.

Creating New Customers

Other innovations are meant to help drive additional market share in the form of new customers. In addition to all the features that make shopping easy for existing customers, Amazon has attempted to entice customers that would have otherwise shopped at other retailers to shop with them. These features are primarily focused on increasing the diversity and types of products available at the site. In addition to selling products sourced by Amazon, the company works with affiliates that can provide a more diverse array of products in more niche areas; this can include items such as unique home decor, clothing, and jewelry. Amazon has also embraced the idea of supporting new and unique products through Amazon Launchpad (**amazon.com/p/feature/kzwyhyjs7ore8d6**), a service that allows customers to purchase goods and services from start-up companies, many of which can be found nowhere else.

New Products and Services

The company's final set of innovations is the creation of new goods and services that are either wholly unique or Amazon-branded products that compete with others. Some unique goods include the Amazon Echo (**amazon.com/p/feature/ofoyqn-7wjy2p39a**), a voice recognition device that is also linked to multiple applications on the Web. Other offerings are meant to both compete with other brands in the space and drive the utilization of Amazon products. One example is the Kindle Fire tablet line that both competes with other tablets, for example, Apple and Samsung, and also drives the use of Amazon products such as e-books and digital video. Another example is the Fire TV (**amazon.com/p/feature/7n5tkm4ugzff7bo**), a Wi-Fi-based streaming device that easily allows users to access both subscription and paid content through Amazon Prime.

The Results

Since he started Amazon, Jeff Bezos has received numerous recognitions including the 1999 *Time* magazine "Person of the Year" and the "Businessperson of The Year" by *Forbes* in 2012 (see **content.time.com/time/specials/packages/0,28757,2023311,00.html** and **fortune.com/2012/11/16/business-person-of-the-year.fortune/2.html**). In January 2002, Amazon.com declared its first profit—for the 2001 fourth quarter. Since then, the company has remained profitable despite its huge investments in distribution centers and other initiatives. Amazon.com reported that despite adverse US and global economic conditions, its annual revenue for 2015 had increased 721% from 2007, and in the third quarter of 2016, the company posted a $252 million profit. The company can boast of having over 230,000 employees, 304 million accounts, and 186 million unique monthly visitors; 81% of US Internet users have an account, and the Kindle has 74% market share for e-book readers (see **statista.com/topics/846/amazon**).

But Amazon and Jeff Bezos cannot afford to rest on their laurels. There is major competition in the marketplace, and everyone has their eyes set on Amazon. Many new and existing companies want to expand their market share in online retailing, and one of the ways that they can do this is by competing with Amazon. One example is Walmart (**walmart.com**). While Walmart does not have the same online presence that Amazon does, they may be able to leverage their brick-and-mortar locations to their advantage. One way they might do this is through ship-to-store services or local customer support (Petro 2016). Amazon is also at a disadvantage because of its wide product breadth. This means that niche retailers may be able to target particular markets and possibly serve them better than Amazon could. Another example is Newegg (see **newegg.com**). This site specializes in computers, computer hardware, and technology. Because they serve a specific niche market, they may be able to provide more specific services and support than a large, multifaceted company like Amazon. Amazon's financial performance has also started to dip. While still very profitable, the company missed its earnings estimate in the third quarter of 2016. Instead of returning a profit of $0.78 a share, the company only returns to profit of $0.52 a share. While the company is still very financially sound, this was enough to decrease the stock price (Fiegerman 2016).

Even with these challenges, Amazon is poised to continue its growth into the future. By continuing to leverage its strong customer base, unique technologies, and spirit of invention, Jeff Bezos' company has proved to be a true innovator in e-commerce.

Sources: Based on Fiegerman (2016), Trefis (2015), and **amazon.com** (accessed January 2017).

LESSONS LEARNED FROM THE CASE

The case of Amazon.com, the most recognized name of all e-tailers in the world, demonstrates the evolution of e-tailing, some of the problems encountered by e-tailers, and the solutions that a company can employ to expand its business. It also is indicative of some key trends in Internet retailing. For example, there is fierce competition online. Amazon.com is successful because of its size, innovations, personalization, order fulfillment, and customer service. The biggest online retailer is still growing and becoming more dominant. E-tailing, as demonstrated by the Amazon.com case, continues its double-digit, year-over-year growth rate despite the global economic downturn. This is, in part, because sales are shifting away from physical stores. In this chapter, we look at the delivery of both products and services online to individual customers. We also discuss e-tailing successes and failures.

3.1   INTERNET MARKETING AND B2C ELECTRONIC RETAILING

The Amazon.com case illustrates how commerce can be conducted on the Internet. Indeed, the amount and percentage of goods and services sold on the Internet are increasing rapidly, despite the failure of many dot-com companies. **internetworldstats.com** estimates that there are over 7.26 billion Internet users worldwide and over 357 million in North America as of April 2016 (see **internetworldstats.com/stats.htm**). Forrester Research estimates that US shoppers will spend $327 million online in 2016, a 62% increase over 2012. Experts also forecast that global B2C sales will be over $2.35 trillion globally in 2018, especially due to the growth in China. Some think that as the number of Internet users reaches saturation, the rate of increase of online shopping may slow down. However, this may not be the case. In fact, the rise of social and mobile shopping seems to have accelerated the pace of B2C (see **forbes.com/sites/theyec/2016/05/27/mobile-commerce-trends-for-the-second-half-of-2016/#569dcc315bde**). In addition, the economic downturn may increase online shopping as a means of saving money (e.g., save on gas if you do not need to drive to a physical store or an online merchant may have a better price than a brick-and-mortar retailer). Finally, global B2C is still increasing rapidly, and many companies view these international markets as major sources of growth in the years ahead. Therefore, one of the challenges facing e-tailers is increasing the amount of money each person spends online. Companies have many benefits from selling their goods and services online. Innovative marketing models and strategies and a better understanding of online consumer behavior are critical success factors in B2C.

Overview of Electronic Retailing

A retailer is a sales *intermediary* between manufacturers and customers. Even though many manufacturers sell directly to consumers, they usually do so to supplement their major sales through wholesalers and retailers. In the physical world, retailing is done in stores (or factory outlets) that customers must visit physically in order to make a purchase, although sometimes customers may order by phone. Companies that produce a large number of products for millions of customers, such as Procter & Gamble, must use retailers for efficient product distribution. However, even if a company sells relatively few different types of products (e.g., Apple computers), it still might need retailers to reach a large number of customers who are scattered in many locations.

Catalog (mail-order) sales offer companies the opportunity to reach more customers and give customers a chance to buy from home. Catalog retailers do not need a physical store with staff; online shopping has created the need for electronic catalogs. Retailing conducted over the Internet is called **electronic retailing (e-tailing)**, and sellers who conduct retail business online are called **e-tailers**, as illustrated in the opening case. E-tailing can be conducted through catalogs that have fixed prices as well as online via auctions. E-tailing helps manufacturers (e.g., Dell) sell directly to customers. This chapter examines the various types of e-tailing and related issues.

Note that the distinction between B2C and B2B EC may be unclear. For example, Amazon.com sells to both individuals and to organizations. Walmart (**walmart.com**) sells to both individuals and businesses (via Sam's Club). Dell sells its computers to both consumers and businesses from **dell.com**, Staples sells to both markets at **staples.com**, and insurance sites sell to both individuals and corporations.

Size and Growth of the B2C Market

B2C e-commerce is growing rapidly, especially in developing countries (e.g., China, Russia, and India).

The statistics for the volume of B2C EC sales, including forecasts for future sales, come from many sources. Reported amounts of online sales *deviate substantially* based on how the numbers are derived, and thus it is often difficult to obtain a consistent and accurate picture of the growth of EC. Some of the variation stems from the use of different definitions and classifications of EC. Another issue is how the items for sale are categorized. Some sources combine certain products and services; others do not or use different methods. Some sources include online travel sales in the statistics for EC retail; others do not. Sometimes different time periods are used in the measurement. Therefore, when reading data about B2C EC sales, it is important that care is taken in interpreting the figures.

Developments in B2C E-Commerce

The first generation of B2C e-commerce sold books, software, and music—simple to understand, small items (known as commodity items) that were easily shipped to consumers. The second wave of online growth started in 2000, as consumers started researching and buying complex products such as furniture, large appliances, and expensive clothing. Today consumers research product information and purchase online from categories such as bedding, spas, expensive jewelry, designer clothes, appliances, cars, flooring, big-screen TVs, and building supplies. Consumers are also buying many services such as college educations, insurance policies, and streaming entertainment.

Characteristics and Advantages of Successful E-Tailing

Many of the same success factors that apply to physical retailing also apply to e-tailing. In addition, a scalable and secure infrastructure is needed. However, e-tailers can offer special consumer services not offered by traditional retailers. For a comparison of e-tailing and retailing, including advantages, see Table 3.1.

Goods with the following characteristics are expected to sell the most:

- Brand name recognition (e.g., Apple, Dell, Sony). A service guarantee provided by well-known vendors (e.g., Amazon.com, BlueNile.com). For example, return policies and expedited delivery and free shipping
- Digitized format (e.g., software, music, e-books, or videos)
- Relatively inexpensive items (e.g., office supplies, vitamins)
- Frequently purchased items (e.g., books, cosmetics, office supplies, prescription drugs)
- Commodities for which physical inspection is not necessary (e.g., books, CDs, airline tickets)
- Well-known packaged items that you normally do not open in a physical store (e.g., canned or sealed foods, chocolates, vitamins)

Table 3.1 Retailing versus e-tailing

Factor	Retailers	E-tailers
Increase of sales volume	Expansion of locations, stores, and space	Going out of their regular area and even globally to find customers
More visitors but less revenue	Expand marketing efforts to turn "window shoppers" into active shoppers	Expand marketing communications to turn viewers into shoppers
Use of technology	Automation store technologies such as POS, self-check, and information kiosks	Ordering, payments, and fulfillment systems
		Comparisons and customer testimonials
		Instant delivery of digital products
Customer relations and handling of complaints	Face-to-face, stable contacts	Anonymous contacts, less stability
	More tolerance of disputes due to face-to-face contacts	More responsiveness to complaints due to potential negative publicity via social media platforms (e.g., Facebook, Twitter)
Competition	Local competition	More competitors
	Fewer competitors	Intense due to comparisons and price reductions
		Global competition
Customer base	Local area customers	Wide-area (possibly global) customers
	Lack of anonymity	Anonymity most of the time
	High increase of customer loyalty	Easy to switch brands (less loyalty)
Supply chain cost	High cost, interruptions	Lower cost, more efficient
Customization and personalization	Expensive and slow	Fast, more efficient
	Not very popular	Popular
Price changing	Expensive and slow, not done often	Inexpensive, can be done anytime
Adaptability to market trends	Slow	Rapid

Sources: Based on Ingham et al. (2015) and authors' experiences

Advantages of E-Tailing

E-tailing provides advantages to both sellers and buyers.

The major advantages to sellers are:

- Lower product cost, thus increasing competitive advantage.
- Reach more customers, many outside the vendor's region, including going global. For example, some Chinese and Taiwanese e-tailers operate sites that sell electronic products all over the world (e.g., E-Way Technology Systems Corp.; **ewayco.com**).
- Change prices and catalogs quickly, including the visual presentation. Such flexibility increases competitive advantage.
- Lower supply chain costs.
- Provide customers with a wealth of information online as a self-service option, thus saving customer service costs.
- React quickly to customer needs, complaints, tastes, and so forth.
- Provide customization of products and services, self-configuration, and personalization of customer care.
- Recommendation of alternate or complementary products based on a customer's history and preferences
- Enable small companies to compete with larger companies.
- Better understand customers and interact with them.
- Sell specialized items countrywide or even worldwide (e.g., surfing-related merchandise by the Australian company **surfstitch.com**).
- Engage customers in interesting search, comparison, and discussion activities.
- Contact customers who are not reachable by traditional methods of communication.

The major benefits to the buyers are to:

- Pay less than in traditional or even discount stores.
- Find products/services not available in local stores.
- Shop globally: compare prices and services.
- Shop anytime and from anywhere.
- Find it unnecessary to go to the store wasting time and gasoline and being pressured by salespeople.
- Create their own designs and products (e.g., see **vistaprint.com**).
- Find collectors' items.
- Buy in groups: buy with friends and engage in social shopping.

The next section examines the major business models that have proven successful in e-tailing.

SECTION 3.1 REVIEW QUESTIONS

1. Describe the nature of B2C EC.
2. What are the characteristics of high-volume products and services?
3. Describe the major trends in B2C.
4. Why is B2C also called e-tailing?
5. List the major characteristics of B2C.
6. What are the benefits of B2C for both buyers and sellers?

3.2   E-TAILING BUSINESS MODELS

In order to understand e-tailing better, let us look at it from the point of view of a retailer or a manufacturer that sells to individual consumers (see Fig. 3.1). The seller has its own organization and must also buy materials, goods, and services from others, usually businesses (B2B in Fig. 3.1). As also shown in the figure, e-tailing, which is basically B2C (right side of the figure), is done between the seller (a retailer or a manufacturer) and an individual buyer. The figure shows other EC transactions and related activities that may affect e-tailing. Retailing businesses, like other businesses, are driven by a business model. A **business model** is a description of how an organization intends to generate revenue through its business operations.

In this section, we will look at the various B2C models and their classifications.

Classification of Models by Distribution Channel

E-tailing business models can be classified in several ways. For example, some classify e-tailers by the nature of the business (e.g., general-purpose versus specialty e-tailing) or by the scope of the sales region covered (global versus regional), whereas others use classification by revenue sources. Here we classify the models by the distribution channel used, distinguishing five categories:

1. **Traditional mail-order retailers that also sell online.** For example, J.C. Penny and Lands' End also sell on the Internet.
2. **Direct marketing by manufacturers.** Manufacturers such as Dell, LEGO, and Godiva market directly online from their webstore to customers, in addition to selling via retailers.
3. **Pure-play e-tailers.** These e-tailers sell only online. Amazon.com is an example of a pure-play e-tailer (see opening case).
4. **Click-and-mortar ("brick-and-click") retailers.** These are retailers that open webstores to supplement their regular business activities (e.g., **walmart.com** and **homedepot.com**). However, we are now seeing a reverse trend: Some pure-play e-tailers are creating physical storefronts. For example, Apple opened physical stores, and Dell sells its products at

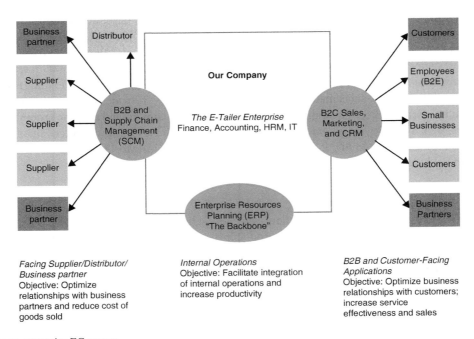

Facing Supplier/Distributor/
Business partner
Objective: Optimize
relationships with business
partners and reduce cost of
goods sold

Internal Operations
Objective: Facilitate integration
of internal operations and
increase productivity

B2B and Customer-Facing
Applications
Objective: Optimize business
relationships with customers;
increase service
effectiveness and sales

Fig. 3.1   E-tailing as an enterprise EC system

partner store locations, such as Best Buy and Staples. The idea of selling both online and offline is part of a model or strategy known as a **multichannel business model**. Using this strategy, the company offers several options for the customer to shop, including over the Internet. This strategy gives customers the opportunity to select the marketing channel with which they are most comfortable. For more on multichannel, see the white paper at **enterpriseinnovation.net/whitepaper/multichannel-customer**).

5. **Convergence and Omnichannel.** This is a hybrid form of pure-play e-tailers as they begin to utilize physical locations for specific markets or products.
6. **Internet (online) malls.** These malls include many stores on one website.

   Note that in direct marketing of any type, sellers and buyers have a chance to interact directly and better understand each other.
7. **Flash sales.** In any of the above categories, sellers can offer steep discounts via an intermediary or directly to the consumers. These discounts exist in several varieties.

Our examination of each of these distribution channel categories follows.

Direct Marketing by Mail-Order Companies

In a broad sense, **direct marketing** describes marketing that takes place without physical stores. Direct marketers take orders directly from consumers, frequently bypassing traditional intermediaries. Sellers can be retailers or manufacturers.

Direct Sales by Manufacturers and Make to Order

Many manufacturers are selling directly to customers. Dell, HP, and other computer manufacturers use this method. It is usually combined with self-configuration of products (customized, build to order). The major success factor of this model is the ability to offer customized products at a reasonable cost.

Virtual (Pure-Play) E-Tailers

Virtual (pure-play) e-tailers are companies with direct online sales that do not need physical stores. Amazon.com is a prime example of this type of e-tailer. Virtual e-tailers have the advantage of low fixed costs. However, one drawback can be a lack of an efficient order fulfillment system. Virtual e-tailers can be *general-purpose* (such as Amazon.com or Rakuten.com) or *specialized* e-tailers (such as DogToys.com).

General-purpose pure-play companies can be very large. Amazon.com is one example. Another example is Rakuten Ichiba, Japan's largest online mall that offers more than 50 million products made by over 33,000 merchants. In May 2010, the Japanese company acquired US-based Buy.com (which is now known as Rakuten.com Shopping). The combined company offers more than 90 million products made by over 35,000 merchants worldwide. Thousands of other companies operate as pure-play e-tailers. Examples are Australian companies **dealsdirect.com.au** and **asiabookroom.com**.

Specialty e-tailers, such as CatToys.com (**cattoys.com**), can operate in a very narrow market. Blue Nile is another example. Such specialized businesses would find it difficult to survive in the physical world because they would not have enough customers and could not hold a large variety of stock.

Drop-Shipping

Drop-shipping is a form of pure-play e-commerce where a business sells products that they do not stock or ship. Instead, after the order is placed, the company directs a third-party drop-shipper to pull the item from their warehouse and ship it to the customer. This type of arrangement provides a very low barrier of entry to the e-tailer because they do not manage any logistics or carry any stock risk. They are free to focus on front-end marketing only. Shopify is a major supporter of this model; for more information about drop-shipping, see **shopify.com/guides/dropshipping**.

Click-and-Mortar Retailers and Multichanneling

This is probably the most commonly used model of e-tailing competing with pure-play e-tailers. Examples are Walmart.com, Target.com, and thousands of other retailers that offer products and services online as an additional sales channel. This strategy is gaining momentum, but it is not always successful for large companies. A prime example is Best Buy (see section "The New Face of Retail Competition: Retailers versus E-Tailers").

A **click-and-mortar retailer** is a combination of both the traditional retailer and a webstore.

A **brick-and-mortar retailer** conducts business exclusively in the physical world. In some cases, sellers also might operate a traditional mail-order business.

In today's digital economy, *click-and-mortar* retailers sell via stores, through phone calls, over the Internet, and via mobile devices. A firm that operates both physical stores and an online e-tail site is a click-and-mortar business selling in a *multichannel business model*. Examples of retailers going from brick and mortar only to brick and click are department stores, such as Macy's (**macys.com**) and Sears (**sears.com**), as well as discount stores, such as Walmart (**walmart.com**) and Target (**target.com**). It also includes supermarkets and all other types of retailing.

Convergence and Omnichannel

Historically, it was easy to separate different types of retailers based on their primary locations and channels through which they sold to the public. This is changing with the idea of convergence (also referred to as "omnichannel"). As technologies have advanced and retailers have become savvier to the needs and preferences of customers, the lines between pure-play e-commerce, brick-and-mortar commerce, and click-and-mortar commerce are beginning to blur (see **meldstudios.com. au/2012/08/27/future-retail-blurring-boundary-online-offline**).

Retailers that were traditionally pure play (like Amazon) have begun to build storefronts in specific areas for specific types of products. Additionally, technologies, especially those associated with mobile apps, allow customers to interact with physical products and Web-based services and systems at the same time. Forrester research found that 61% of all shoppers still enjoy interacting with both physical products and sales associates at retail locations and that merchants can continue to be successful if they are able to cater to this audience without the threat of "showrooming" products (Forrester Research 2015). Showrooming is when customers come into a store to review a product and then leave to purchase it online, often from another vendor. As the different methods to market and sell to customers continue to converge, retailers will be better able to meet customer needs as well as leveraging the advantages of both technology and their physical locations (Brown 2016).

For more details on this trend, see the video titled "The Rebirth of Retail, and the Convergence of Online and Offline Technology" from the National Retail Federation (45:03 min) at **youtu.be/KuZy_bGpnRU**.

Retailing in Online Malls

There are two types of online malls: referring directories and malls with shared shopping services.

Referring Directories

This type of virtual mall contains a directory organized by product type. Banner ads at the mall site advertise the products or vendors. When users click on the product and/or a specific store, they are transferred to the webstore of the seller, where they can complete the transaction. Examples of referring directories can be found at **bedandbreakfast.com**. Either the stores listed in a directory own the directory collectively or they pay a subscription fee or a commission to the organizing third party for maintaining the site and advertising their products. This type of e-tailing is a kind of affiliate marketing (see **shopping24.de**).

Malls with Shared Services

In online malls with shared services, a consumer can find a product, order and pay for it, and arrange for shipment. The hosting mall provides these services.

Ideally, the customer would like to go to different stores in the same mall, use one shopping cart, and pay only once. This arrangement is possible, for example, in Yahoo! Small Business (see **smallbusiness.yahoo.com/ecommerce**) and **bingshop.com**. With the availability of e-commerce software and outsourced logistics services, the popularity of online malls is shrinking.

Other B2C Models and Special Retailing

Several other business models are used in B2C. They are discussed in various places throughout the book. Some of these models also are used in B2B, B2B2C, G2B, and other types of EC.

B2C Social Shopping

Social shopping activities are facilitated by new or improved business models, (e.g., see Turban et al. 2016; and Zimmerman and Singh 2015). For example, B2C sites such as **amazon.com** and **netflix.com** provide consumers with extensive social context and engagement opportunities, such as product ratings. Using blogs, wikis, discussion groups, and Twitter, retailers can help customers find and recommend shopping opportunities. Typical new or improved models created by social media tools are summarized below.

Flash Deals (Deals of the Day)

These are sales in which companies offer heavily discounted products to consumers for a limited time (usually 24–72 h), directly or via intermediaries such as Groupon. The discounts are so large that the sellers hope that people will spread the news to their friends (see **woot.com**).

Online Group Buying

In these depressed economic times, more people are using the Internet as a smart way to save money. Using online *group buying*, it is easy to join a group of buyers to get volume discounts. There are several start-ups in this market: **yipit.com** and **livingsocial.com**. Other sites that used pure group buy are now concentrating on flash deal sales. For example, see Groupon, **dealradar.com**, and **myhabit.com**.

Personalized Event Shopping

Event shopping is the B2C model in which sales are designed to meet the needs of special events (e.g., a wedding, Black Friday). This model may be combined with group purchasing (to lower the customers' cost). Two variations of this online model are *private shopping clubs* and *group gifting online*.

Private Shopping Clubs

An online **private shopping club**, like an offline shopping club (e.g., Costco), enables members to shop at a discount, frequently for short periods of time (just few hours or days). Members may need to register before they are invited to see the special offers. To assure quality, many clubs buy directly from the manufacturers.

Examples of such clubs are Gilt (**gilt.com**) in the United States (see Wieczner and Bellstrom 2010) and KupiVIP (**kupi-vip.ru**) in Russia.

Private shopping clubs can be organized in different ways (e.g., see **beststreet.com**). For details, see **en.wikipedia.org/wiki/Private_shopping_club**.

Group Gifting Online

In many cases, a group of friends can collaborate on gifts for events such as a wedding. To help coordinate the group activities and select the gifts, one can use sites like **frumus.com** and **socialgift.com**.

Location-Based E-Commerce

Location-based e-commerce (l-commerce) is a wireless-based technology used by vendors to send advertisements relevant to the location where customers are at a given time by using GPS. The technology is a part of mobile commerce. The model was unsuccessful until social networking emerged. Today, companies such as Foursquare provide l-commerce services.

Drop-Shipping

Drop-shipping is an EC model where an e-tailer (the seller) sells a product and then buys it from a supplier who packs and sends the product to the buyer.

The Process of Drop-Shipping

The process is composed of the following steps:

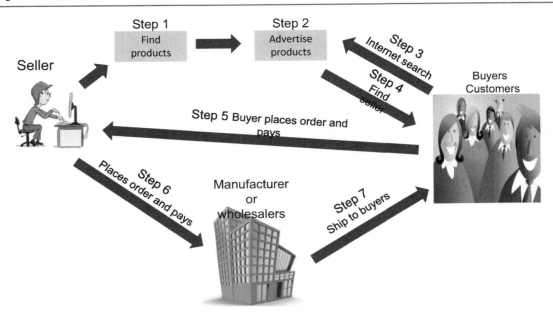

Fig. 3.2 How drop-shipping works

Step 1. The e-tailer (seller) finds a product and a supplier to buy it from.
Step 2. The e-tailer advertises the product on its own website and/or on popular sites (such as eBay).
Step 3. A buyer searches for a product online.
Step 4. The buyer (buyers) finds the product in a search.
Step 5. The buyer orders the product and pays for it to the e-tailer.
Step 6. The e-tailer transfers the order to a wholesaler, manufacturer, or a drop-shipping vendor (the supplier) and pays for it (the wholesale price).
Step 7. The supplier acquires, packs, and ships the product to the buyer.

The seven-step process is illustrated in Fig. 3.2.

The Participants in the Process

The following are the major participants:

1. **The seller**. The seller can be an individual who sells to individual customer (kind of P2P). The seller advertises on its own website or on popular websites.
   The seller can also be a retailer who uses the model as one of a multichannel, or it can be a small retailer who practices drop-shipping only.
2. **The buyer**. The customers are usually individual people who buy small quantities for themselves.
3. **The supplier**. It can be a manufacturer, wholesaler, or another vendor that acts as a third party and plays the activities of order fulfillment.
4. **The directory provider**. Several companies help people to find suppliers and products. They usually charge a fee for their service (monthly or per search). The directory providers can perform the order fulfillment as well (see Zorzini 2017).
5. **A website builder**. If the sellers do many transactions, it makes sense for them to build a website. They can use it for advertisements, payment collection from the buyers, communication with the buyers and suppliers, transferring orders and payments to the supplier, and conducting other store management activities.

A major store builder that specializes in supporting drop-shipping is *Shopify*. The company has detailed guides for the various activities in the process. For a website selection and management, see **ecommerce-platforms.com/ecommerce-selling-advice/setup-drop-shipping-ecommerce-website/**.

The Benefits of Drop-Shipping

The major benefits are:

- Less capital is required (increase in cash flow).
- Easy to get started.
- Easy to scale the business (expand or contract).
- Good yearning potential.
- You need very little resources and space.
- You pay suppliers only after you get paid.
- Low overhead.
- Flexible location.
- No need to fulfill the order.
- No need to keep inventory.
- Increase lifetime value of customers.
- Enable expansion to new (including global) markets.
- Having another sales channel.

For discussion, see **multichannelmerchant.com/opsandfulfillment/7-business-advantages-drop-shipping-14042015/**.

The Disadvantages of Drop-Shipping

The major disadvantages are:

- If anything goes wrong, it is your fault.
- You do not see what the supplier ships.
- People may do exactly what you do (competition!).
- Returns from customers can be complex.
- You lose control over quality and speed of shipments.
- You must provide good customer service that may be costly if you have many customers.
- The difference between the prices you charge and what you pay to the supplier can be too small.

Some Suggestions for Implementation

Shopify provides several guides for how to do drop-shipping:

(a) You start with an understanding of the process **shopify.com/guides/dropshipping/understanding-dropshipping/**.
(b) You need to find products and suppliers **shopify.com/guides/dropshipping/finding-suppliers/**.
(c) You need to advertise and possibly sell on eBay, Amazon, etc. **shopify.com/guides/dropshipping/evaluating-sales-channels/**.
(d) Find the right e-commerce platform **ecommerce-platforms.com/ecommerce-selling-advice/setup-drop-shipping-ecommerce-website/**.

The model is very popular with many individuals and small businesses. (For over 25% of small businesses, drop-shipping is the major sales channel.)

For a guide to drop-shipping, see **shopify.com/guides/dropshipping/** and novatechwholesale.com. For an overview, see Williams (2016). For how you can make money from drop-shipping, see Bennet (2016). This model provides a very low barrier of entry to sellers, since it is very easy for competitors to start a business. To succeed, however, the seller needs to find the right products and makes sure that the price differential between the retail and wholesale is large enough.

SECTION 3.2 REVIEW QUESTIONS

1. List the B2C distribution channel models.
2. Describe how traditional mail-order firms are transforming or adding online options.
3. Describe the direct marketing model used by manufacturers.
4. Describe virtual e-tailing.
5. Describe the click-and-mortar approach. Compare it to a pure e-tailing model.
6. Describe the different types of e-malls.
7. Describe flash sales (daily deals).
8. Describe B2C social shopping models.
9. Describe the drop-shipping process.
10. List the major advantages and disadvantages.

3.3   ONLINE TRAVEL AND TOURISM (HOSPITALITY) SERVICES

Online services are provided by many travel vendors. Some major travel-related websites are **expedia.com**, **travelocity.com**, **tripadvisor.com**, and **priceline.com**. All major airlines sell their tickets online. Other services are vacation packages (e.g., **blue-hawaii.com**), train schedules and reservations (e.g., **amtrak.com**), car rental agencies (e.g., **autoeurope.com**), hotels (e.g., **marriott.com**), commercial portals (e.g., **cnn.com/TRAVEL**), and tour companies (e.g., **atlastravelweb.com**). Publishers of travel guides such as **lonelyplanet.com**, **fodors.com**, and **tripadvisor.com** provide considerable amounts of travel-related information on their websites, as well as selling travel services. The competition is fierce, but there is also collaboration. For example, in 2012, TripAdvisor helped New Orleans hotels to attract more guests. For an overview of the travel industry in 2016, see the presentation at **slideshare.net/yoramw/online-travel-report-by-dealroom-june-2016**.

Example: TripAdvisor
According to comScore Media Metrix (in November of 2016), TripAdvisor (**tripadvisor.com**) is the world's largest travel site. The company provides trip advice generated from actual travelers. This is a global site with more than 350 million visitors a month. For history, features, and more facts, see **tripadvisor.com/PressCenter-c4-Fact_Sheet.html**.

Example: Qunar.com
Qunar (**qunar.com**) is the world's largest Chinese-language travel platform. The site provides services similar to those provided by TripAdvisor, such as travel information, travel arrangements, and in-depth search (see **www.qunar.com/site/en/Qunar.in.China_1.1.shtml**).

Characteristics of Online Travel

Online travel services generate income from commissions, advertising fees, lead generation payments, subscription fees, site membership fees, etc.

With rapid growth and increasing success, the online travel industry is very popular, although online travel companies cite revenue loss due to fraud as their biggest concern. Consumers themselves can fall prey to online travel fraud. However, competition among online travel e-tailers is intense and has low margins. In addition, customer loyalty and difference in prices make it more difficult to survive. Thus, guaranteed best rates and the provision of loyalty programs are becoming a necessity.

Three important trends will drive further changes in the online travel industry. First, online travel agents may try to differentiate themselves by providing superior customer service. Second, they provide easy search capabilities (e.g., for best prices). Third, online travel companies are likely to use social media tools to provide content to travelers and would-be travelers.

Services Provided

Online travel agencies offer almost all the same services delivered by conventional travel agencies, from providing general information to reserving and purchasing travel accommodations and event tickets. In addition, they often provide services that most conventional travel agencies do not offer, such as travel tips and reviews provided by other travelers, fare tracking (free e-mail alerts on low fares), expert opinions, detailed driving maps, and directions (see **airbnb.com**; a website that connects travelers and lists accommodations around the world, chat rooms, and bulletin boards).

Example: HomeAway.com, Inc.

HomeAway, Inc. (**homeaway.com**) is a marketplace for the vacation rental industry. This online marketplace hosts 1.26 million paid listings offering vacation rental homes in 196 countries (April 2016 data). The basic idea is to offer travelers vacation homes at affordable prices. For example, you can rent a whole vacation house at less than half the price of a hotel. The site connects property managers and owners with travelers. Besides the United States, the company has subsidiaries in several countries, such as the United Kingdom, France, and Spain. It has both short and longer stay rentals. For details, see **homeaway.com**.

Other special services include:

- **Combined booking.** Most travel services allow you to book flights, rental cars, and hotels at the same time. Often by combining these different aspects of a trip, customers are able to secure a lower price than if they booked these services independently.
- **Wireless services.** Many airlines (e.g., Cathay Pacific, Delta, and Qantas) allow passengers to access the Internet during flights with mobile devices (usually for a fee).
- **Advance check-in.** Most airlines provide advance online check-in. You can print your boarding pass within 24 h prior to departure. Alternatively, you can use a smartphone (or a tablet) to download the boarding pass to your cell phone and then submit your phone to the security with your ID. The security department has electronic scanners that read the boarding pass from your smartphone and let you board the plane.
- **Direct marketing.** Airlines sell electronic tickets (or "e-tickets") over the Internet. When customers purchase electronic tickets online (or by phone), all they have to do is print the boarding pass or enter their credit card at an *electronic kiosk* to get a boarding pass there.
- **Alliances and consortia.** Airlines and other travel companies are creating alliances with one another (e.g., **staralliance.com**) to increase sales or reduce purchasing costs for purchases made over the Internet.

Using Mobile Devices

The use of these is increasing rapidly, with hundreds of apps related to comparing prices, making reservations, looking at travel reviews, and finding the best travel deals available (see **tomsguide.com/us/pictures-story/491-best-travel-apps.html** for a list of 50 ultimate travel apps). The growth in the use of mobile apps in the travel industry has paralleled their growth overall. Today, 25% of travel bookings are completed with a mobile app, and that percentage is expected to rise in the future (Diaz 2016). All major travel companies offer apps with feature similar to their browser-based websites (see a comparison of available apps at **digitaltrends.com/mobile/best-travel-apps**).

Social Travel Networks

Travelers are using sites like Facebook, YouTube, Twitter, Gogobot, Flickr, Foursquare, and TripAdvisor to plan their trips and share experiences (both good and bad) afterward. For example, all major airlines have pages on Facebook that provide information and news about their airline and offer their customers a community to meet other travelers and share experiences (e.g., see **facebook.com/AmericanAirlines**).

Several social networks have travel channels that cater to travelers. Travelers can use these channels to share details of their trips and review their accommodations, travel providers, and recreational activities. An example of such networks is **wikitravel.org**, which features a travel channel that uses a wiki allowing any Internet reader to create, update, edit, and illustrate *any* article on the website ("the travel guide you write"). For a comprehensive resource on travel, see **tripadvisor.com**. Other social networks available exclusively for travelers are Trip Wolf, Trip Hub (a blog dedicated to group travel), TripAdvisor, VirtualTourist, BootsnAll, and Lonely Planet.

These social media connections to travel are becoming a critical factor in customer's decisions on travel locations and suppliers (Sablich 2016). These networks are providing customers with a volume of trusted advice that was not possible before, and these shared opinions are having a major impact on how the industry handles customer service (see **independenttraveler.com/travel-tips/travelers-ed/how-social-media-is-changing-travel**). Vendors that are able to exploit this trend have found that word-of-mouth advertising can significantly increase booking. One method that many encourage is the use of their mobile apps, especially sharing pictures and videos (Morrison 2015). In that survey, it was found that:

- 52% of users said friends' Facebook photos inspired travel plans.
- 76% photo vacation photos to social networks.
- 51% said Twitter influenced consideration of a travel brand.
- 92% of customers trust earned media above all other forms of travel advertising.

CASE 3.1: EC APPLICATION
ZILLOW—UNIQUE TOOLS FOR THE REAL ESTATE MARKETPLACE

Zillow (**Zillow.com**) is an online real estate database company that was founded in 2006. The website acts as a marketplace for many different types of real estate including homes and apartments: for sale and for rent. The site is unique when compared to more traditional real estate websites because it aggregates available properties across multiple databases and also allows users to enter their own properties for sale or rent. Additionally, the site provides a wide variety of features relating to design/decor.

Unlike a traditional real estate broker, the website does not generate profit through the sale of properties. Instead the website generates the majority of its profits through advertising sales and subscriptions. This can be for individual sellers, agents, or mortgage lenders. In the first quarter of 2016, the company recorded total revenue of 168 million, a 25% increase from the same time period in 2015 (see **investors.zillowgroup.com/releasedetail.cfm?releaseid=968880**). During this time, the website had more than 166 million unique users across its multiple brands (Zillow, Trulia, StreetEasy, and HotPads).

Because the company depends on advertising revenue to drive profitability, it is important for the website to provide an enticing set of features for potential users. While many of these features are similar to other real estate brokers, the ability to search for available properties, Zillow has added additional features to help set it apart. Some of these tools are targeted at agents. The premier agent platform provides a suite of online tools that allow agents and brokers to manage their teams and available properties (Zillow Group 2016). Other features are targeted at individual users. These features can include referral agent's comma advice on purchasing and maintaining properties and inspirations on home design.

One very unique feature of Zillow is the ability to estimate the value of an existing property. The system aggregates information from past property sales, the current state of the market, and real estate tax appraisals to estimate the value of a property. While this is a good estimate of property value, it is not exact. Other professionals in the field feel that this feature may give homeowners an unrealistic expectation of what a property's sale price might be. Zillow and others are working on ways to further refine the model to generate more accurate results using a larger amount of available data (Corcoran and Liu 2014).

Zillow continues to develop and enhance a diverse set of online features that it hopes will continue to drive users to its website, thus allowing it to grow.

Questions

1. What is Zillow's business model?
2. Why is it important for Zillow to provide a variety of features?
3. Should Zillow continue to offer the value estimation tool?

Benefits, Limitations, and Competition in Online Travel Services

The benefits of online travel services to travelers and travel providers are extensive. The amount of free information is voluminous and is accessible at any time from any place. Shoppers can find the lowest prices. Travel providers also benefit by eliminating commissions and selling otherwise empty spaces. Finally, processing fees are reduced.

Online travel services do have some limitations. First, complex trips are difficult to arrange and may not be available on some sites because they require complicated arrangements. Therefore, the need for travel agents as intermediaries remains, at least for the time being.

Competition in Online Travel

The competition in online travel is intense. In addition to well-known pure players such as Expedia (**expedia.com**), Priceline (**priceline.com**), and Hotels.com (**hotels.com**), there are thousands of travel-related sites online. Many service providers have their own sites, related websites advertise travel sites, and tourist guides sell services or direct users to them. In such a competitive environment, online businesses may fail (e.g., Travel-Ticker folded in September 2012). This competitive environment is compounded by the rise of travel aggregator websites; these services search a large number of sites to find the best price (see **independenttraveler.com/travel-tips/travelers-ed/the-aggregators-are-coming**). This type of service forces many travel sites to price match and compete of other metrics such as site features or customer service. For information on how to use a travel aggregator website, see **tripbadger.com/smart-travel-tips/10-best-travel-sites** or a video tutorial on using a popular site, KAYAK **kayak.com** at **youtu.be/xFSjY5MxwAk**.

Corporate Travel

The corporate travel market is huge, and its online portion has been growing rapidly in recent years. Corporations can use all the online travel services mentioned earlier where they may receive special services. Companies can enable employees to plan and book their own trips to save time and money. Using online optimization tools provided by travel companies, such as those offered by American Express (**amexglobalbusinesstravel.com**), companies can try to reduce travel costs even further. Expedia via Egencia TripNavigator (**egencia.com**), Travelocity (**travelocity.com**), and Orbitz (**orbitzforbusiness.com**) also offer software tools for corporate planning and booking. TripAdvisor for Business (**tripadvisor.com/Owners**) provides information to the tourism and hospitality industries. TripAdvisor TripConnect offers a way for businesses to compete for bookings and generate new business by bringing visitors directly to their online booking pages. Many companies use these services to help simplify reservations but also to control costs. Expenses are a significant concern for many companies, and online corporate reservation systems can reduce time spent on bookings, as well as enforcing travel rules and cost ceilings (for more details on controlling costs, see **gbta.org/usa/About/Pages/TheValueofTravelManagement.aspx**).

Example: American Express's Business Travel Helps URS Corp. to Survive Hurricanes

In order to repair the damage caused by Hurricane Katrina, URS Corporation (a large engineering and architectural design firm) realized that they needed an automated system to identify travelers in need of immediate assistance. A solution was found by implementing American Express Business Traveler's TrackPoint system (**trackpoint.amexgbt.com**), which "enables companies to quickly interface impacted travelers, pinpoint their locations, and review their itineraries" (see **businesstravel.americanexpress.com/se/files/2011/11/CS_URSCorp-US.pdf**).

SECTION 3.3 REVIEW QUESTIONS

1. What travel services are available online that are not available offline?
2. List the benefits of online travel services to travelers and to service providers.
3. How do social networks facilitate travel?
4. Describe corporate online travel services.
5. Describe the competition in online travel services.

3.4   EMPLOYMENT AND THE ONLINE JOB MARKET

The online job market connects job seekers with potential employers. An online job market is now very popular with both job seekers and employers. In addition to job ads posted online and placement services available through specialized websites (such as **careerbuilder.com** and **hotjobs.com**), larger companies are building career portals on their corporate websites as a way of reducing recruitment costs and expediting the time to fill vacancies. Additionally, many applicants and employers are taking to social media networks to search for positions and find applicants. Advantages of the online job market over the traditional one are listed in Table 3.2.

The Internet Job Market

The Internet offers a comprehensive and large environment for job seekers and for recruiters. Nearly all *Fortune 500* companies now use the Internet for some of their recruitment activities. Online resources are the most popular recruitment option for many companies. Since 2000, online job recruitment revenues and volume significantly overtook print ad classifieds.

Table 3.2 Traditional versus online job markets

Characteristic	Traditional job market	Online job market
Cost	Expensive, especially in prime space	Can be very inexpensive
Life cycle	Short	Long
Place	Usually local and limited if global	Global
Context updating	Can be complex, expensive	Fast, simple, inexpensive
Space for details	Limited	Large
Ease of search by applicant	Difficult, especially for out-of-town applicants	Quick and easy
Ability of employers to find applicants	May be very difficult, especially for out-of-town applicants	Easy
Matching of supply and demand	Difficult	Easy
Reliability	Low, material can get lost in mail	High
Communication speed between employees and employers	Can be slow	Fast
Ability of employees to compare jobs	Limited	Easy, fast

In 2017, it is estimated that over 88% of available positions in the United States will be posted online. Tens of thousands of job-related sites are active in the United States alone. Note that many sites provide free lists of available positions. The US market is dominated by several major players, especially as Monster acquired Yahoo! HotJobs and CareerBuilder. However, socially oriented sites such as Craigslist, LinkedIn, Twitter, and Facebook are becoming very important online recruitment sites (see **askingsmarterquestions.com/how-to-recruit-online-finding-talent-with-facebook-twitter-study**).

Online Job Markets on Social Networks

According to Del Castillo (2016), 25% of job seekers use social media as their primary job search tool, and 70% of 18–34-year-olds found their last job through social media. Recruiters are also rapidly adopting, with 92% using LinkedIn, 54% using Facebook, and 24% using Google+. LinkedIn reports in 2016 that hiring managers are moving to social networks not only to find the best candidate but also because finding quality candidates is becoming more competitive (see the presentation at **business.linkedin.com/content/dam/business/talent-solutions/global/en_us/c/pdfs/GRT16_GlobalRecruiting_100815.pdf**). Facebook has many features that help people find jobs and help employers find candidates. One such feature is Jobcast (**jobcast.net**), which is an app for companies to place on their Facebook page to recruit candidates. The app, which has different types of plans (free and paid), offers social sharing to LinkedIn and Twitter, as well as to Facebook. Their app on Facebook is for jobseekers and employers to connect, and they also have interesting articles regarding the job market. (See **facebook.com/jobcastnet**.) Another way for employers and jobseekers to connect via Facebook is through a company called FindEmployment (**facebook.com/findemployment**), which also offers tips and suggestions for job seekers. A similar service is provided by **linkedin.com/job**. Craigslist, for example, claims more than one million new job listings every month. The LinkedIn search engine can help employers find appropriate candidates quickly.

While LinkedIn was previously seen as the preferred outlet to search for positions and applicants, the tools provided by Facebook are helping to challenge that superiority (Costine 2016). While LinkedIn is considered to be more professional and easier to search by recruiters, Facebook has a larger and more active user base. But, some Facebook users are concerned about the co-mingling of their personal and professional lives. While this may have some effect, many believe that Facebook may grow to parity with LinkedIn, especially with younger users (see **linkhumans.com/blog/rise-facebook-recruitment**). LinkedIn is looking to counter this trend with several new features, including a new effort aimed at younger users looking for their first position out of college (see **students.linkedin.com**).

For more on social networking activities in recruiting, see Budzienski (2015).

In addition, *job referral social networking* sites solve the need for finding the right people for the job (e.g., **jobster.com**). These sites provide job seekers opportunities to promote themselves and their areas of expertise, as well as help them be discovered by employers. The site's algorithms enable headhunters to analyze qualified applicants by different criteria. When a job offer is made, the job referral site receives referral fees. Lately, the use of Twitter as an aid for job searches has increased. Bortz (2014) provides a strategy for job seekers and for how to use Twitter to access recruiters and increase job seekers' visibility (also see **jobmob.co.il/blog/beginners-guide-find-a-job-with-twitter**).

Table 3.3 Advantages of the electronic job market for job seekers and employers

Advantages for job seekers	Advantages for employers
Can discover a large number of job openings	Can reach a large number of job seekers
Can communicate directly and quickly with potential employers	Can reduce recruitment costs
Can market themselves quickly to appropriate employers (e.g., **quintcareers.com**)	Can reduce application processing costs by using electronic application forms
Can post résumés for large-volume distribution (e.g., at **careerbuilder.com**	Can provide greater equal opportunity for job seekers
	Opportunity of finding highly skilled employees who match the job requirements
Can search for available positions any time	Can describe positions in great detail
Can obtain several support services at no cost (e.g., **careerbuilder.com** and **monster.com** provide free career planning services)	Can interview candidates online (e.g., using video teleconferencing)
Can determine appropriate salaries in the marketplace (e.g., use **salary.com** and **rileyguide.com**; look for salary surveys)	Can arrange for testing online
	Can view salary surveys for recruiting strategies
Can learn how to behave in an interview (**greatvoice.com**)	
Can access social network groups dedicated to electronic job markets	Can use existing staff to refer applicants

Sources: Based on Taylor (2016), Princeton University (2016), and the authors' experiences

Global Online Portals for Job Placement

The Internet is very helpful for anyone looking for a job in another country. An interesting global site for placing/finding jobs in different countries is **xing.com**. The electronic job market may increase employee turnover and its costs. Finally, recruiting online is more complicated than most people think, mainly because there are so many résumés online. To facilitate recruitment, top recruiters are seeking the benefits of using new tools like video conferencing to interview and connect with candidates from remote locations.

Benefits and Limitations of the Electronic Job Market

The online job market has many benefits for both job seekers and recruiters. The major advantages are shown in Table 3.3. For more on the advantages of attending job fairs, see **careercast.com/career-news/how-rock-virtual-job-fair**. For benefits of virtual recruiting, see **smallbusiness.chron.com/advantages-virtual-recruitment-16632.html**.

The electronic job market also has a few limitations, such as security and privacy. Posted résumés and employer-employee communications are usually not encrypted. Thus, confidentiality and data protection cannot be guaranteed. It is also possible that someone at a job seeker's current place of employment (e.g., his or her boss) could find out that that person is job hunting. LinkedIn, for example, provides privacy protection, enabling job seekers to determine who can see their résumé online. Additionally, while many positions are posted online, LinkedIn reports that 85% of jobs are still filled through networking activities, either before or after a posted position is applied for (see the report at **linkedin.com/pulse/new-survey-reveals-85-all-jobs-filled-via-networking-lou-adler**). Users of other social sites, such as Facebook, may be concerned that personal information, photos, and events may be scrutinized by potential employers (see **repnup.com/blog/2015/09/09/employers-can-find-your-facebook-profile-set-to-private**).

For tips on how to protect your privacy while job hunting, see **guides.wsj.com/careers/how-to-start-a-job-search/how-to-protect-your-privacy-when-job-hunting** or **youtu.be/xJH-YXsjH3k**.

SECTION 3.4 REVIEW QUESTIONS

1. What are the driving forces of the electronic job market?
2. What are the major advantages of the electronic job market to the candidate? To employers?
3. Why is LinkedIn so useful for job seekers and for employees? List the specific tools provided by EC to job seekers.
4. List the specific tools provided by recruiters.
5. What are the limitations of electronic job markets?

3.5 ONLINE REAL ESTATE, INSURANCE, AND STOCK TRADING

Online infrastructures enable additional marketing channels and new business models and provide new capabilities. The infrastructures provide a different way of delivering products and services. Some major services are presented in this and the following section.

Real Estate Online

Changes in online real estate information search and transactions significantly impact the way that business is conducted.

To get some idea of the changes, see **realtor.org/research-and-statistics**, and for statistics on the growth of the online and offline real estate markets, see **realtor.org/research-and-statistics/research-reports**. For example, in 2015, 74% of all realtors used social media tools regularly. Additional studies by the National Association of Realtors® (NAR) have shown that over 42% of real estate buyers begin their searches for properties on the Internet and 87% of all recent buyers used the Internet at some point in their home search (National Association of Realtors® 2015).

E-commerce and the Internet are slowly but surely having an ever-increasing impact on the real estate industry. For example, despite the changes that are beginning to emerge, real estate agents have not been disintermediated. Home buyers today tend to use both real estate agents and the Internet. One possible impact is declining commissions that sellers pay agents (Harney 2017).

Zillow, Craigslist, and Other Web 2.0 Real Estate Services

Craigslist (**craigslist.org**), Zillow (**zillow.com**), and Trulia (**trulia.com**) are examples of Web 2.0 free real estate services. Both reduce the use of newspaper classified advertising and allow buyers to find housing information and do price and location comparisons on their own.

Zillow operates the "Make Me Move" (**zillow.com/make-me-move**) service (free) that allows you to see for what price you would be willing to sell your home without actually putting it on the market (**zillow.com/wikipages/What-is-Make-Me-Move**). Homeowners may be motivated to sell when they see the price they can get when they list their homes (anonymously). Sellers can see prices of similar homes. Buyers can contact the sellers via anonymous e-mail. The company also provides free listings (including photos). Users can also participate in a blog or wiki, start a discussion, and engage in other social-oriented activities. Zillow also offers mortgage calculators and current loan rates. Zillow makes money from advertisers and was listed on the stock market in 2012. Zillow has several competitors (e.g., **ziprealty.com** and **listingbook.com**). Zillow offers its brand via more than a dozen websites (e.g., **zillow.com/homes/for_rent** and **agentfolio.com**). Zillow generates revenue by selling ads on its companion websites.

Craigslist has a major classified section for real estate ("for sale" and "for rent" listings). Listings are free except in some large cities, where brokers must pay a fee for placing ads.

Other entrants to the online real estate market include auction sites. While these types of services had existed in the past (**ebay.com**), they were less successful due to the complicated nature of real estate and buyers desire to thoroughly inspect the product. New sites like **realtybid.com** use the technology available today, including extensive photos and videos, to help facilitate this process.

Many real estate service sites are embracing the use of augmented reality and virtual reality in advertising their listings. These systems allow customers to interact in an interactive virtual environment when being shown a property or as they consider it. These systems are being cautiously adopted, especially in more competitive environments (Mazzara 2015). These systems are provided by companies like AR Pandora (**arpandora.com**) and VR Global (**vrglobal.com/real-estate**). For a guide on how augmented reality can be used when selling a home, see the guide at **crcbr.org/augmented-reality-enhancing-the-real-estate-experience**. An example video of an augmented reality tour is available at **youtu.be/TRoK-L0m-zg**.

Insurance Online

An increasing number of companies use the Internet to offer standard insurance policies, such as auto, home, life, or health, at a substantial discount, mostly to individuals. Furthermore, third-party aggregators offer free comparisons of available policies. Several large insurance and risk-management companies offer comprehensive insurance contracts online (e.g., **allstate.com**, **ensurance.com**, **statefarm.com/insurance**, **progressive.com/insurance-choices**, **geico.com**). Although many people do not trust the faceless insurance agent, others are eager to take advantage of the reduced premiums. Many insurance companies use a dual strategy, using sales agents in the field but also selling online. (e.g., advertising on e-mails and Google searches.) Like real estate brokers, insurance brokers send unsolicited e-mails to millions of people. The stiff competition will probably reduce the commission for the surviving agents. Different types of insurance are harder to quote, home insurance, for example. Other types such as car insurance are more straightforward, and quote aggregators are able to search multiple providers at a single time (see **thezebra.com** for an example).

Example
The insurance industry has seen that over 86% of potential insurance customers are researching and gathering information on the Internet. Thus, insurance companies are trying to capitalize on this trend. Many insurance companies are quickly rolling out a variety of online tools to meet this need (**bain.com/publications/articles/for-insurance-companies-the-day-of-digital-reckoning.aspx**).

Online Stock Trading and Investments

The commission for an online trade is between $1 and $15 ("dirt-cheap brokers") to $15–$30 ("mid-priced discount brokers"), compared with an average fee of $100–$200 per trade from a full-service broker (see **investopedia.com/university/broker/broker1.asp**). With online trading, there are no busy telephone lines, and the chance to err is small, because there is no oral communication in a frequently noisy environment. Orders can be placed from anywhere, at any time, and there is no biased broker to push a sale. Furthermore, investors can find a considerable amount of free research information about specific companies or mutual funds. Many services provided to online traders include online statements, tax-related calculations, extensive research on industries, real-time news, and even tutoring on how to trade (e.g., check **etrade.com** or **google.com/finance**).

How does online trading work? Let us say an investor has an account with Charles Schwab. The investor accesses Schwab's website (**schwab.com**), enters an account number and password, and clicks on "stock trading." Using a menu, the investor enters the details of the order (buy, sell, margin or cash, price limit, or market order). The computer tells the investor the current (real-time) "ask" and "bid" prices, just as a broker would do over the telephone, and the investor can approve or reject the transaction. See a video on Schwab's online tools at **youtu.be/sqqmY8I8gxU**. You can also download a full report of state of online brokerage platforms at **scivantage.com/celent-defines-the-state-of-online-brokerage-platforms-in-new-report**.The flow chart of this process is shown in Fig. 3.3.

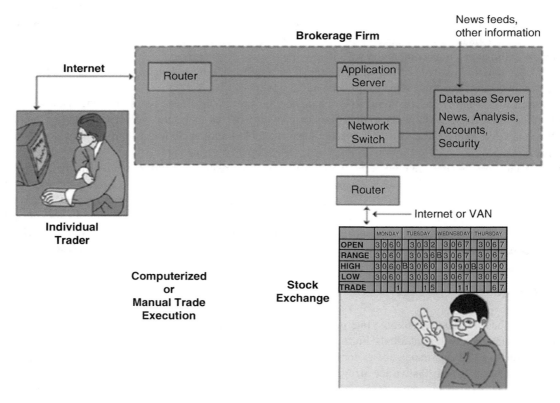

Fig. 3.3 Online electronic stock trading

A new breed of online investing sites is based on the concept of actively managed investments (generally only available to high net worth individuals) that rely on computer trading algorithms to manage trading activity and minimize taxable income. These firms hope to strike a middle ground between index fund investing and active individual trading. Current market leaders include **wealthfront.com** and **betterment.com**.

Some companies, including Schwab, are now also licensed as exchanges. This allows them to match the selling and buying orders of their own customers for many securities in 1–2 s. Some well-known companies that offer online trading are E*TRADE, TD Ameritrade, Scottrade, and ShareBuilder.

With the rapid pace of adoption of mobile computing, mobile stock trading is becoming more and more popular (e.g., see the mobile offering from E*TRADE). For example, users can pay bills and purchase stocks.

SECTION 3.5 REVIEW QUESTIONS

1. List the major online real estate applications.
2. What are the advantages of selling insurance online?
3. What are the advantages of online stock trading?

3.6 ONLINE BANKING AND PERSONAL FINANCE

Electronic (online) banking (e-banking) refers to conducting banking activities online. Consumers can use e-banking to check their accounts, pay bills online, secure a loan, transfer money, and much more. Sixty-one percent of US adult Internet users bank and pay bills online (**pewinternet.org/files/old-media/Files/Reports/2013/PIP_OnlineBanking.pdf**), and 46% of US customers have made a mobile payment (see **pewtrusts.org/en/research-and-analysis/issue-briefs/2016/05/who-uses-mobile-payments**). Several sites have tools that can help you with personal finance and budgeting. Examples are **mint.com**, **geezeo.com**, and **kiplinger.com**.

E-Banking

E-banking saves users' time and money. For banks, it offers a rapid and inexpensive strategy to acquire out-of-the-area customers. In addition, the banks may need fewer branches or employees. Many physical banks now offer online banking services, and some use EC as a major competitive strategy.

Online banking in general has been embraced worldwide, including developing countries. For example, online banking in China is increasing rapidly in popularity, especially among China's new educated middle class who live in the more developed cities. It is facilitated by the use of smartphones and other mobile devices. (See **hsbc.com.cn/1/2/personal-banking/e-banking/personal-internet-banking** and Bank of China **boc.cn/en**.)

Online Banking Capabilities

Banking applications can be divided into the following categories: informational, administrative, transactional, portal, and others. In general, the larger the bank, the more services are offered online.

Many banks have diligently added services to help grow acceptance and use of this format, which is less expensive for them than having employees and branches. While the initial efforts in online banking were little more than online statements, the features available today have expanded greatly. These features include the ability to pay bills, transfer money, open new accounts, take out loans, research banking investments, and check credit scores (see **gobankingrates.com/banking/history-online-banking**). Many of these services are designed to allow customers to support themselves without the need for interaction with bank employees. Some banks are extending this thinking further and using AI-driven systems to support customers. For example, Singapore's POSB Bank launched an AI chatbot that answers customer questions through Facebook Messenger. The company hopes that this system will provide customers with the information they need while eliminating the need for employees (see **enterpriseinnovation.net/article/posb-launches-its-first-ai-driven-chatbot-facebook-messenger-860619969**).

Pure Virtual Banks

Virtual banks have no physical location and conduct only online transactions. Security First Network Bank (SFNB) was the first such bank to offer secure banking transactions on the Web. Amid the consolidation that has taken place in the banking industry, SFNB has since been purchased and now is a part of RBC Bank (**rbcbank.com**). Other representative virtual banks in the United States are the First Internet Bank (**firstib.com**) and Bank of Internet USA (**bankofinternet.com**).

However, more than 97% of the hundreds of pure-play virtual banks failed by 2003 due to a lack of financial viability. Many more failed during 2007–2012. The most successful banks seem to be of the click-and-mortar type (e.g., Wells Fargo, City Corp, HSBC).

Virtual banking can be done with new business models, one of which is P2P lending.

P2P Lending

The introduction of online banking enables the move of personal loans to the Web in what is called *online person-to-person money lending* or in short *P2P lending*. This model allows people to lend money and to borrow from each other via the Internet. For how P2P loans work, see **thebalance.com/how-peer-to-peer-loans-work-315730** and **youtu.be/G1eXrutcJTI**.

Examples

Two examples of peer-to-peer (P2P) online lending are Zopa Limited in the United Kingdom (**zopa.com**) and Prosper Marketplace in the United States (**prosper.com**). Note that despite the global credit crunch of 2008–2012 and the fact that neither has a government-backed guarantee, both Zopa and Prosper are enjoying solid growth. For example, as of May 2016, Zopa's 53,000 active members had lent more than £1.45 billion at negotiated rates to UK customers, mainly for car payments, credit card debts, and home improvements. The default rate of these P2P lenders is very low (e.g., Zopa's historical bad debt is 0.19% since 2010) since money is lent only to the most credit-worthy borrowers. For Prosper's company overview, see **prosper.com/about**.

A word of caution about virtual banking, including P2P lending: Before sending money to any cyberbank, especially one that promises high interest rates for your deposits, make sure that the bank is a legitimate one. Another important factor is to understand the policies and risks associated with both P2P lending and the individual lending company. For more information on trends and risks, see (**moneyandbanking.com/commentary/2015/3/16/the-cloudy-future-of-peer-to-peer-lending**).

CASE 3.2: EC APPLICATION
SECURITY FOR ONLINE BANK TRANSACTIONS

Banks provide extensive security measures to their customers. The following describes some of the safeguards provided.

Customers accessing a bank system online must go through encryption provided by SSL (Secure Socket Layer) and digital certificate verification. The verification process assures users each time they sign on that they are indeed connected to their specific bank. The customer inquiry message then goes through an external firewall. Once the log-on screen is reached, a user ID and a password are required. This information flows through a direct Web server and then goes through an internal firewall to the bank's application server. This process is illustrated in Fig. 3.4.

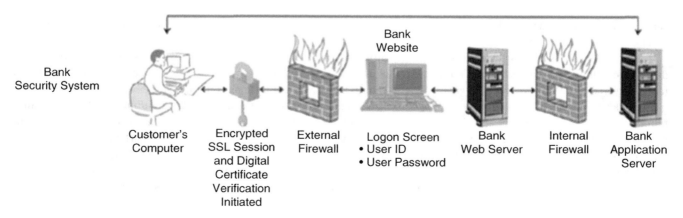

Fig. 3.4 Security for online banking transactions

Information is shared among banks' business partners only for legitimate business purposes.

Banks do not capture information provided by customers when conducting hypothetical scenarios using planning tools (to ensure privacy). Many banks use cookies to learn about their customers; however, customers can control both the collection and in some cases the use of such information. In addition, most banks provide suggestions on how users can increase security (e.g., by using a browser that supports 128-bit encryption).

With the increased use of mobile devices, the threat of security risks has increased. Banks are creating innovative solutions. For example, in January 2009, Bank of America introduced "SafePass," a feature that can generate a six-digit, one-time passcode that is necessary to complete an online transaction. The passcode is delivered via text message to your mobile device. (See **bankofamerica.com/privacy/online-mobile-banking-privacy/safepass.go**.) A similar device is offered by other financial institutions.

Another concern of banks is larger-scale attacks in the form of DDOS, phishing, and malware attacks. The Bank of England recently simulated a significant cyberattack and found that they may be lacking several areas. Experts recommend that financial institutions adopt five best practices to better combat these threats (Reeves 2014). These include:

1. Drive better risk assessment.
2. Adopt strong authentication standards.
3. Take a layered approach.
4. Explore advanced authentication techniques.
5. Enhance customer awareness and education.

Even with these institutional safeguards, it is also important for individuals to maintain good security habits as well. For more information on online banking security, download the "Online Banking Guide" from First Commonwealth Bank (**fcbanking.com/media/Online-Banking-Guide.pdf**</URL>) or see Zaharia (2016).

Questions

1. Why is security so important for a bank?
2. Why is there a need for two firewalls?
3. Who is protected by the bank's security system—the customer, the bank, or both? Elaborate.
4. What might be the limitations of such a security system?

Example

Some banks have multistage security systems. For example, the Central Pacific Bank (**centralpacificbank.com**) asks you to log in (with your ID) and then answer security questions to which you previously provided the answers. You then see an image on the screen that you preselected. If you do not recognize the image and a preestablished phrase, you know you have not accessed the real bank. If all answers are provided satisfactorily, you provide a password to enter your account.

Risks

Online banks, as well as click-and-mortar banks, might carry some risks and problems, especially in international banking. The first is the risk of hackers accessing their accounts. In addition, some believe that virtual banks carry a *liquidity* risk (the risk of not having sufficient funds to pay obligations as they become due) and could be more susceptible to panic withdrawals. Regulators are grappling with the safeguards that need to be imposed on e-banking.

Online Billing and Bill Paying

The popularity of e-payments is growing rapidly. The number of checks the US Federal Reserve System processes has been decreasing, while the volume of commercial Automated Clearing House (ACH) transactions has been increasing. Many people prefer online payments of monthly bills such as mortgage payments, car loans, telephone, utilities, rent, credit cards, cable, TV, and so on. The recipients of such payments are equally eager to receive money online because online payments are received much more regularly and timely and have lower processing costs.

Another method for paying bills via the Internet is electronic billing or electronic bill payment and presentment (EBPP). With this method, the consumer makes payments at each biller's website, either with a credit card or by giving the biller enough information to complete an electronic withdrawal directly from the consumer's bank account. The biller sends the invoice to the customer via e-mail or a hosting service site. The customer then authorizes and initiates a payment via an automatic authorization, e-check, and so forth.

Taxes

One important area in personal finance is advice about and computation of taxes. Dozens of sites are available to help people with their federal tax preparations. Many sites will help people legally reduce their taxes. The following list offers some sites worth checking:

- **irs.gov**: The official website of the Internal Revenue Service.
- **taxsites.com**: A massive directory of tax-related information, research, and services.
- **fairmark.com**: A tax guide for investors.
- **taxaudit.com**: IRS tax audit help and audit assistance.

Mobile Banking

Mobile banking is a system that enables people to conduct financial transactions from a smartphone or other wireless mobile device. Many of the recent developments are in the area of mobile banking. Topics such as payments from smartphones and handling micropayments have revolutionized the financial systems. In 2016, 43% of mobile phone owners with a bank account used a mobile application; this was up to 39% from the previous year. You can download the report from the Federal Reserve at **federalreserve.gov/econresdata/consumers-and-mobile-financial-services-report-201603.pdf**. For a comparison of different mobile banking apps, see **magnifymoney.com/blog/consumer-watchdog/best-worst-mobile-banking-apps-100-banks-credit-unions**.

SECTION 3.6 REVIEW QUESTIONS

1. List the capabilities of online banking. Which of these capabilities would be most beneficial to you?
2. How are banks protecting customer data and transactions?
3. Define a P2P loan system.
4. How are banking transactions protected?
5. What is mobile banking?

3.7   ON-DEMAND DELIVERY OF PRODUCTS, DIGITAL ITEMS, ENTERTAINMENT, AND GAMING

This section examines B2C delivery issues related to on-demand items, such as perishable products, as well as the delivery of digitizable items, entertainment, and games.

On-Demand Delivery of Products

Most e-tailers use third-party logistics carriers to deliver products to customers. They might use the postal system within their country, or they might use private shippers such as UPS, FedEx, or DHL. Deliveries can be made within days or overnight. Customers are frequently asked to pay for expedited shipments (unless they have a "premium" subscription, such as Amazon.com Prime; **amazon.com/Prime**).

Some e-tailers and direct marketing manufacturers own a fleet of delivery vehicles in order to provide faster service or cut delivery costs to the consumer. According to Mark Sebba, CEO of Net-a-Porter (**net-a-porter.com**), the company prefers "to do as much as possible in-house, which includes operating their own delivery vans for customers in London and Manhattan" (see **net-a-porter-brand.blogspot.com/2013/05/some-more-current-content.html**). Such firms provide either regular deliveries or will deliver items on demand (e.g., auto parts). They might also provide additional services to increase the value proposition for the buyers. An example in this category is an online grocer, or *e-grocer*. An **e-grocer** is a grocer that takes orders online and provides deliveries on a daily or other regular schedules or within a very short period of time, sometimes within an hour. Home delivery of food from restaurants or pizza parlors is another example. In addition, office supply stores, repair parts distributors (e.g., for cars), and pharmaceutical suppliers promise speedy, same-day delivery.

An express delivery option is referred to as an **on-demand delivery service**. In such a case, the delivery must be done quickly after an order is received. A variation of this model is same-day delivery. According to this model, delivery is done faster than "overnight" but slower than the 30–60 min expected with on-demand delivery of pizzas, fresh flowers, or auto repair parts. E-grocers often deliver using the same-day delivery model.

Speed of Delivery

Speed of delivery is critical not only for groceries and perishable items but also for other on-demand and large items. For example, **uber.com** is an on-demand traveler's delivery service. Since 2013, they have also partnered with retailers like Home Depot and Oleander (see **newsroom.uber.com/uae/ubertree** and **businessinsider.com/uber-christmas-tree-delivery-britain-pines-and-needles-app-2015-12**)to deliver Christmas trees.

The fastest delivery in the future may be by drones. Amazon.com, UPS, and Google are exploring this phenomenon. In 2014, Facebook decided to "jump on the bandwagon" with the purchase of drone maker Titan Aerospace for $60 million (see **forbes.com/sites/briansolomon/2014/03/04/facebook-follows-amazon-google-into-drones-with-60-million-purchase**). Amazon leads the market in this area and has successfully completed a commercial drone delivery in late 2016 (see **mashable.com/2016/12/14/amazon-first-drone-delivery**). Additionally, nonretail companies are beginning to explore this market. An example is Flirtey (**flirtey.com**) that recently raised $16 million in VC capital to provide both services and hardware (see **techcrunch.com/2017/01/18/drone-delivery-startup-flirtey-raises-16-million-to-become-a-next-gen-ups/**).

Online Delivery of Digital Products, Entertainment, and Media

Certain goods, such as software, music, or news stories, can be distributed in physical format (such as hard copy, CD-ROM, DVD, and newsprint), or they can be digitized and delivered over the Internet. Online delivery is much cheaper and saves sellers storage room, handling, and distribution costs.

Online Entertainment

Online entertainment is growing rapidly and is now the most popular medium in the United States among young people between the ages of 8 and 17. There are many kinds of Internet entertainment. It is difficult to categorize them precisely because there is a mixture of entertainment types, delivery modes, and personal taste. All these must be considered when deciding whether something is entertainment or not and what kind of entertainment it is. Some online entertainment is interactive, in that the user is engaged in it. PricewaterhouseCoopers (2016) predicts that the global entertainment and media industry spending will reach over $172 billion in 2020 in the United States alone. This includes cinema, video games, music, and TV/video. Video games have the largest predicted growth at 3.6% between 2015 and 2020.

All forms of traditional entertainment are now available over the Internet. However, some have become much more popular in the new environment due to the capabilities of technology. For example, Facebook's online games attract millions of players.

iTunes

iTunes (**apple.com/itunes**) is a media management software by Apple that includes an online store for buying music and other media. The program also enables you to organize and play the digital items you downloaded. Note that iTunes and similar services have basically crushed the music industry (see **money.cnn.com/2013/04/25/technology/itunes-music-decline**), similar to the way **netflix.com** has impacted the sale of DVDs and CDs. A 2014 study by Asymco found at **asymco.com/2014/02/10/fortune-130** discovered that iTunes is more profitable than Xerox and Time Warner Cable (see **wallstcheatsheet.com/stocks/study-itunes-is-more-profitable-than-xerox-and-time-warner-cable.html/?a=viewall**).

Online Ticketing

This popular service enables customers to buy tickets for events (e.g., sports, music, theater) by using a computer or mobile device. Companies such as Ticketmaster, Inc. are active in this area. Fandango is a company that sells movie theater tickets.

Internet TV and Internet Radio

Two similar streaming technologies are popular on the Web: Internet TV and Internet radio.

Internet TV

Internet TV is the delivery of TV content via the Internet by video streaming technologies. The content includes TV shows, sporting events, movies, and other videos. Several video-on-demand and subscription services, such as **netflix.com**, **hulu.com**, and **hulu.com/plus**, as well as **amazon.com/Prime-Instant-Video**, offer this service. For a comprehensive description of Internet TV, see **wisegeek.org/what-is-internet-tv.htm**. The major advantage is the ability to select what and when to view content and the ability to do so from computers, tablets, smartphones, Blu-ray consoles, Apple TV (**apple.com/appletv**), Roku (**roku.com**), Google Chromecast (**google.com/intl/en/chrome/devices/chromecast**), Aereo (**aereo.com**), and so forth.

Internet Radio

Known by several other names, **Internet radio** refers to audio content transmitted live via the Internet. It is a broadcasting service that enables users to listen online to thousands of radio stations (e.g., over 4000 in Europe; see **listenlive.eu**). The service can broadcast anything that is on the radio stations plus broadcasts from organizations, governments, and even individuals (**radio.about.com/od/listentoradioonline/qt/bl-InternetRadio.htm**). Internet radio has the same copyright issues as those of Internet TV. Note that in many cases, there is an agreement between the content creators and the distributors (e.g., Warner Music and Apple reached an iTunes Radio deal in 2013; see **cnet.com/news/apple-reaches-iradio-deal-with-warner-music-suggesting-wwdc-launch** and **apple.com/itunes/itunes-radio**).

Pandora Radio

Pandora is a leading free Internet radio that delivers music not only from radio stations but also from many other sources. The core of the service is the *Music Genome Project*. According to **pandora.com/about**, the project is an inclusive analysis of thousands of musical pieces. All the music in the project is available on Pandora for your listening pleasure.

Pandora is actually a music streaming and automated music recommendation service that in 2016 is available only in the United States, Australia, and New Zealand. Users can create up to 100 personalized stations that play prearranged selections. In February 2014, the company opened up its content submission process to independent artists (see **submit.pandora.com**, **help.pandora.com/customer/portal/articles/24802-information-for-artists-submitting-to-pandora**, and Hockenson (2014)). For Pandora's Help Center, see **help.pandora.com**.

Various e-tailers offer songs for sale to Pandora's listeners. You can access Pandora through many streaming media devices. You can enjoy Pandora for free on the Web, on home-listening devices, and on most mobile devices. Pandora One (**pandora.com/one**) has a monthly fee, but the benefits include ad-free service and higher-quality audio. Pandora is a profitable business. Its subscriber base continues to grow; in March of 2014, it had 75.3 million active listeners (**investor.pandora.com/file/Index?KeyFile=22417465**).

Social Television (TV)

Social TV is an emerging social media technology that enables several TV viewers who are in different locations to interactively share experiences such as discussions, reviews, and recommendations while watching the same show simultaneously. According to Mashable.com (**mashable.com/category/social-tv**), social TV is "the union of television and social media" and refers to "the phenomenon of people communicating with each other while watching a TV show or discussing with each other about television content using the Internet as a medium of communication." The communication can be done via texting in social networks, smartphones, tablets, etc. Social TV combines broadcast television programs and user-generated content with rich social media.

Characteristics of Social TV

Social TV has several unique characteristics:

- The possibility of discovering new video content and sharing this discovery with friends.
- Most social TV activities are done in real time by watching content and commenting on it to others, even if the viewers are in different locations.
- Social TV allows people to connect in a unique way, with other people who share the same interests.

Social TV is attracting an ample number of viewers. (The number of traditional television viewers is declining due to Internet viewing.)

Adult Entertainment

Online adult entertainment is probably the most profitable B2C model (usually with no or little advertisement; viewers pay subscription fees), and it accounts for a large percentage of Internet use. Adult content sites are popular because they provide a large and vivid selection, low fees (even free), and anonymity for those who watch. This popularity may cause a problem for some companies. According to reports by market research firms that monitor the industry, such as Forrester Research, IDC, Datamonitor, Mediabistro Inc., and Nielsen, viewers are willing to pay substantial fees to view adult sites.

Internet Gaming

Internet gaming is comprised of all forms of gaming such as arcade gaming, lotteries, casino gaming, and promotional incentives. Between 2008 and 2016, online gambling revenue continued to increase despite the bad economy. The global online gambling industry grew 8% during 2013 to reach $35.5 billion. According to Statistica.com (2016), the online gaming market will reach almost $56.1 billion in 2018. The ease of access and use of broadband services throughout the world in recent years has been vital to the expansion of online gaming.

Legal Aspects

Online gambling is booming despite the fact that it is illegal in almost all US states. In 2013, Delaware and Nevada were the first US states to allow some online gambling, followed by New Jersey (in October 2013, Delaware became the first state to allow a "full suite" of Internet gambling). In February 2014, both Delaware and Nevada signed a deal to allow interstate online gambling. Delaware reported $1.8 million in state revenue in 2015. Note that federal law limits online gambling to players while they are physically within a given state. (This can be verified by using geolocation software.) Therefore, if one state allows online gambling, you can play only when you are in that state. Online gambling is legal in other countries (e.g., Australia). By 2015, at least seven US states had pending legislation that would legalize online gambling.

Source: Based on Ruddock (2016), Fox News (2014), and Pempus (2016).

SECTION 3.7 REVIEW QUESTIONS

1. Describe on-demand delivery services.
2. Describe digital goods and their delivery process(es).
3. What are the benefits and limitations of digital delivery of software, music, and so forth?
4. What are the major forms of online entertainment?
5. Describe Internet TV, social TV, and Internet radio.
6. Describe Internet gambling and its challenges.

3.8   ONLINE PURCHASING DECISION AIDS

Many sites and tools are available to help consumers with online purchasing decisions. Some sites offer price comparisons as their primary tool (e.g., **pricerunner.co.uk** and **shopzilla.com**); others evaluate services, trust, quality, and other factors. Shopping portals, shopping robots ("shopbots"), business rating sites, trust verification sites, friends' advice in social networks, and other shopping aids are available also. The major types are discussed next.

Shopping Portals

Shopping portals are gateways to webstores and e-malls. Specifically, they host many online stores simultaneously. Like any other portal, they can be comprehensive or niche oriented. Comprehensive, or general-purpose, portals have links to many different sellers and present and evaluate a broad range of products. An example of a comprehensive portal is eCOST. com (**ecost.com**). Several public portals also offer shopping opportunities and comparison aids. Examples are **shopping.com** (part of the eBay Commerce Network), **shopping.yahoo.com**, and **pricegrabber.com**. eBay (**ebay.com**) is a shopping portal also because it offers shopping at fixed prices as well as auctions. Several of these evaluation companies have purchasing shopbots or other, smaller shopping aids and have incorporated them into their portals.

Some shopping portals offer specialized items with links to certain products (e.g., books, phones) or services (universities, hospitals). Such portals also help customers conduct research. Examples include **zdnet.com/topic-reviews** and **shopper. cnet.com** for computers, appliances, and electronics. The advantage of niche shopping portals is their ability to specialize in a certain line of products.

For a comprehensive site with information on e-retailers, B2B, marketing, etc., see Internet Retailer (**internetretailer.com**).

Price and Quality Comparison by Shopbot Software Agents

Savvy Internet shoppers may want to find bargain shopping. **Shopping robots** (**shopping agents, shopbots**) are search engines that look for the lowest prices or other search criteria. Different shopbots use different search methods. For example, mySimon (**mysimon.com**) searches the Web to find the best prices and availability for thousands of popular items.

Google Enterprise Search and Enterprise Search Appliance

Google Enterprise Search helps companies search all internal and public-facing information.

Search is facilitated by a powerful server called Enterprise Search Appliance which enables many flexible search options including the search of some foreign languages.

A similar service is offered by SearchSpring (**searchspring.net**).

"Spy" Services

In this context, "spy" services are not the CIA or MI5. Rather, they are services that visit websites for customers, at their direction, and notify them of their findings. Web surfers and shoppers constantly monitor sites for new information, special sales, ending times of auctions, stock market updates, and so on, but visiting the sites to monitor them is time-consuming. Several sites will track stock prices or airline special sales and send e-mails accordingly. For example, **money.cnn.com**, **pcworld.com**, **expedia.com**, and alerts at **google.com/alerts** will send people personalized e-mail alerts.

Of course, one of the most effective ways to "spy" on Internet users is to introduce cookies and spyware to their computers.

Ratings, Reviews, and Recommendation Sites

Ratings and reviews by friends, even by people that you do not know (e.g., experts or independent third-party evaluators), are usually available for social shoppers. In addition, any user has an opportunity to contribute reviews and participate in relevant discussions. The tools for conducting ratings and reviews, which are presented next, are based on Charlton (2015), **bazaarvoice.com/solutions/conversations**, and the authors' experiences. The major types of tools and methods are:

- **Customer ratings and reviews.** Customer ratings are popular; they can be found on product (or service) pages or on independent review sites (e.g., TripAdvisor) and/or in customer news feeds (e.g., Amazon.com, Buzzillions, and Epinions). Customer ratings can be summarized by votes or polls.
- **Customer testimonials.** Customer experiences are typically published on vendors' sites and third-party sites such as TripAdvisor. Some sites encourage discussion (e.g., Bazaarvoice Connections; **bazaarvoice.com/solutions/connections**).
- **Expert ratings and reviews.** Ratings or reviews can also be generated by domain experts and appear in different online publications.
- **Sponsored reviews.** These reviews are written by paid bloggers or domain experts. Advertisers and bloggers can find each other by searching through websites such as **sponsoredreviews.com**, which connects bloggers with marketers and advertisers.
- **Conversational marketing.** People communicate via e-mail, blog, live chat, discussion groups, and tweets. Monitoring conversations may yield rich data for market research and customer service. An example of a conversational marketing platform is Adobe Campaign (**adobe.com/solutions/campaign-management.html**, formerly Neolane).
- **Video product review.** Reviews can be generated by using videos. YouTube offers reviews that are uploaded, viewed, commented on, and shared.
- **Bloggers' post-reviews.** This is a questionable method, however, since some bloggers are paid and may use a biased approach. However, many bloggers have reputations as unbiased sources. For example, you can see a list of 100 product review blogs for books at **blog.feedspot.com/bookreview_blogs/**.

Many websites rate various e-tailers and online products based on multiple criteria. Bizrate (**bizrate.com**) and Consumer Reports Online (**consumerreports.org**) are well-known rating sites. Bizrate.com organized a network of shoppers that reports on various sellers and uses the compiled results in its evaluations. Note that different rating sites provide different rankings. Alexa Internet, Inc. (**alexa.com**; an Amazon.com company) computes Web traffic rank; see **alexa.com/pro/insight**.

Comparison Shopping Websites

A large number of websites provide price comparisons for products and services (e.g., online tickets, cruises). Online retailers such as Amazon.com also provide price comparisons and so do many other sites (e.g., **nextag.com, pricegrabber.com, mysimon.com**). FreePriceAlerts.com (**freepricealerts.com**) is a price comparison app.

Social Network Influence

Social networks can play an important role in influencing customer purchases both through referrals and requests for information. While these systems are not as defined and regimented as other purchasing aids, they can be significantly more influential. Based on a new report by Deloitte Digital (2015), the dollar impact of comparison shopping due to digital and mobile use was over $2.67 trillion. This amount included the use of digital and mobile devices to comparison shop, as well as social media influences. Another recent survey by PricewaterhouseCoopers indicated that 45% of respondents were influenced by reading reviews, comments, and feedback on products and services (eMarketer 2016). Both studies indicate that it is important for retailers to cultivate positive reviews and feedback of their products and services, as well as encourage happy customers to be vocal about their opinions.

Trust Verification Sites

With so many sellers online, many consumers are not sure whom they should trust. A number of companies evaluate and verify the trustworthiness of various e-tailers. One such company is TRUSTe (**truste.com**). The TRUSTe seal appears at the bottom of each TRUSTe-approved e-tailer's website. E-tailers pay TRUSTe for the use of the seal (which they call a "Trustmark"). TRUSTe's 1300 plus members hope that consumers will use the seal as an assurance and as a proxy for actual research into their conduct of business, privacy policy, and personal information protection. Trust sites grant a *trust seal* for a business to display, demonstrating to customers the level of quality. For an overview of the services TRUSTe provides, see the video at **youtu.be/tT89ZvX1C7E?list=PLr7xw10POYs7r265jYCgrKX7m7GBOacJz**. TRUSTe now offers a service for mobile devices, called TRUSTed apps (**truste.com/products-and-services/enterprise-privacy/TRUSTed-apps**), which provide ongoing monitoring and safeguarding of brands to ensure that merchants' mobile apps are trusted by consumers.

Some comprehensive trust verification sites are Symantec Corporation's VeriSign (**verisign.com**) and BBBOnline (**bbb.org**). VeriSign tends to be the most widely used. Other sources of trust verification include Secure Assure (**secureassure.co.uk**), which charges yearly fees. In addition, Ernst & Young, the global public accounting firm, has services for auditing e-tailers in order to offer some guarantee of the integrity of their business practices. Other sites that perform similar services are **trust-guard.com** and **trust-verified.org**. For the results of a 2013 survey on which site seal people trust the most, conducted using Google Consumer Surveys, is reported at **baymard.com/blog/site-seal-trust**.

Concerns About Reviews, Ratings, and Recommendations

Some people raise the issue of how accurate reported reviews and recommendations are. On some sites, fake reviews and claims are suspected to encompass 30–40% of the total reviews. In 2012, however, Yelp unveiled its Consumer Alerts, which shows warnings to users when they find businesses who have paid for reviews (see **webpronews.com/just-how-bad-is-yelps-fake-review-problem-2014-01**). As of mid-January 2014, Yelp has issued almost 300 Consumer Alerts. (For an example of a Consumer Alert, see **searchengineland.com/yelp-turns-up-the-heat-285-consumer-alerts-issued-over-fake-reviews-181706**.) There is also a concern about businesses paying money to bloggers for producing reviews. Some claim that such reviews may be biased. Another concern is that in cases of a small number of reviewers, a bias (positive or negative) may exist. Finally, it is wise to look at bloggers' review sites. As a side note, Amazon.com has compiled a list of the "Funniest Reviews" posted on their site, on products ranging from banana slicers to horsehead masks (see **amazon.com/gp/feature.html?ie=UTF8&docId=1001250201**).

Other Shopping Assisting Tools

Other digital intermediaries assist buyers or sellers, or both, with research and purchase processes. For example, escrow services (e.g., **escrow.com** and **safefunds.com**) assist buyers and sellers with the exchange of items and money. A trusted third party frequently is needed to facilitate the proper exchange of money and goods or to verify information. (Remember that trading partners usually do not even see each other.) Escrow sites may also provide payment processing support, as well as letters of credit.

- Similar to Craigslist, Angie's List (**angieslist.com**) helps its members find high-quality service companies and healthcare professional services in over 700 categories. Although there is a fee, its advantage over free review sites is there are no anonymous reviews and their data is certified, "so you get the whole story" (see **angieslist.com/how-it-works.htm**). **Angieslist.com** also provides a complaint resolution service and discounts from highly rated service companies. They also offer live support through a call center.
- To organize store information in a standard, easy-to-see, and understandable format, vendors can use tools such as **facebook.com/thefind/**. Shoppers can use the same tools to search once and compare products at every store, finding the best deals.

Another shopping tool is a *wallet*—in this case, an *electronic wallet*—which is a program that contains the shopper's information. To expedite online shopping, consumers can use electronic wallets so that they do not need to reenter the information each time they shop. Although sites such as Amazon.com offer their own specialized wallets, Microsoft Passport has two services, "a Single Sign-On service that allows members to use a single name and password to sign on to a growing number of participating websites, and a Wallet service that members can use to make fast, convenient online purchases."

Example: Yelp

Yelp (**yelp.com**) is a search engine whose mission is to help people find local (in a specific city) qualified services ranging from mechanics to restaurants to hairstylists based on recommendations of fellow locals. It connects people with businesses. Community members, known as "Yelpers," write reviews of the businesses and then rate them. Yelpers also find events and special offers and can connect with each other by posting "conversations" on different topics (e.g., to "talk" with someone from Los Angeles, see **yelp.com/talk/la**). For details, see **yelp.com/faq**.

Aggregators

These are sites that aggregate information from many other sites and bring them to one place. Yipit (**yipit.com**) is a free "e-mail based daily aggregator" that gathers deals ("every deal in your city") on products from daily deal sites such as Groupon, Living Social, etc. Tell Yipit what you want, and they will alert you when there are deals that match, usually at a fraction of the retail price (**yipit.com/about**).

Digital Coupons

Shoppers are introduced to a new generation of coupons, which can be described as "no clip and no print." This is how it works. You register, for example, with the "Just-For-U" program at Safeway. You click on the special sale items or on the coupon of a product you want. When you go into Safeway and buy any of the products you clicked on (if they are available), you automatically receive a 10–20% discount. SavingStar Inc. (**savingstar.com**) and CoolSavings (**coolsavings.com**) offer similar nationwide services in the United States.

Self-Service

One of the major benefits of EC is that it facilitates self-service. By providing tools that enhance self-service, customers can improve their online shopping experience. Examples of self-service tools are configuration tools, calculators (e.g., for cost), FAQs, virtual online real-time assistants, application tools, and site searches.

SECTION 3.8 REVIEW QUESTIONS

1. Define shopping portals and provide two examples.
2. What are shopbots?
3. Explain the role of business and website ratings, reviews, recommendations, and site verification tools in the purchase decision process.
4. Why are escrow services useful for online purchases? Describe "spy" services in B2C EC.
5. How can a site motivate people to contribute their opinions on products and vendors?
6. Describe digital coupons.

3.9   THE NEW FACE OF RETAIL COMPETITION: RETAILERS VERSUS E-TAILERS

The introduction of B2C intensified the competition in the retail market. Prices are declining, while companies are disappearing or changing. For example, many retailers are adding an online channel to their offline offerings or adding Internet-only options. Adding an online retail channel helps, but many well-known retailers such as Best Buy, J.C. Penney, RadioShack, Sears, Staples, and Office Depot still are forced to close numerous physical stores and are struggling to survive (e.g., see **clark. com/major-retailers-closing-2017**, **usatoday.com/story/money/business/2014/03/12/retailers-store-closings/6333865** and Schoon 2014). Let us first look at an overview of the competition.

The Online Versus Offline Competition: An Overview

The Oxford Handbook of the Digital Economy from **oxfordhandbooks.com** provides a comprehensive study by Lieber and Syverson (2012), which describes the nature of the competition as well as the interplay of online and offline retail markets. They also look at the characteristics of online shoppers and the changes in both the demand and supply. The major variables studied in the Oxford Handbook are:

- **Customers' search cost.** With today's shopping search and comparison engines and the use of mobile devices, the search cost to customers is very low, and its importance in the competition is probably declining.
- **Delivery time.** Order fulfillment in physical stores is usually immediate for physical goods. However, online companies are constantly reducing the time between purchase and consumption. Sometime in the future, delivery will be by drones. Amazon has been experimenting with this technology and completed its first commercial drone delivery in December

2016 (**wsj.com/articles/amazon-conducts-first-commercial-drone-delivery-1481725956**). In the meantime, e-tailers are developing efficient same-day delivery services, at least in the large metropolitan areas. Additionally, in 2013, Amazon. com partnered with the US Postal Service for Sunday delivery to Los Angeles and New York metropolitan areas, with service to extend to other cities in 2014 (see **usatoday.com/story/tech/2013/11/11/amazon-Sunday-delivery-usps/3479055**). Google Shopping Express (**google.com/shopping/express**) is a same-day delivery service in the San Francisco and San Jose areas, challenging similar services offered by Amazon.com and eBay (see Hsu 2014).

Obviously the delivery time of digitizable products is very fast in e-tailing. This is an important factor since prices and the quality of products sold online are getting to be similar in different stores, so delivery time becomes an important factor.

- **Distribution costs.** Traditional retailers need to spend money to build (or rent) stores, have inventory, advertise, etc. On the other hand, e-tailers need to pay for packing and shipments, but their advertising costs and inventory costs are lower. These costs vary, depending on the products, the geographical location, and more. The distribution costs can be an important factor in the competition.
  - **Tax differences.** The advantage of online shopping is diminishing as the trend is to levy a tax on out of state online products. For example, Amazon is now charging sales tax in many US states (see **startribune.com/smaller-states-rejoice-as-amazon-finally-collects-sales-tax/412087413**).
- **Price.** Not only do online vendors offer lower prices on the same goods, but they also may create a price conflict within click-and-mortar companies (see Section "Issues in E-Tailing and Lessons Learned").
- **Information available to buyers.** While buyers cannot physically examine goods they buy online, they can use the Internet to obtain considerable information on what they plan to purchase. In general, this is not a major factor in most transactions.
- **Other influencing factors.** Several other factors are important in the competition. For example, who the sellers are, who the buyers are, the distribution channels used, consumer satisfaction, level of consumer loyalty, and the relationship between the sellers' online and offline marketing channels are all important. Finally, the shopping trends clearly indicate that more people are shopping online and spending more money doing so (e.g., see Moseti 2014). Younger people especially are turning to the so-called showrooming, meaning that shoppers go to a physical store to examine goods and check prices. Then they buy online at a lower price (see Isidore 2014). Shoppers are using apps on their mobile devices to compare prices (see Schwartz in 2015; and for some of the apps used, see **verizonwireless.com/news/article/2014/01/showrooming-trend.html**). Customers in general prefer to "touch and feel" items before they purchase them online (see **cnbc.com/id/100597529**).

Global Competition

As of 2016, we are seeing an increase in online global competition. For example, several Chinese companies are offering consumer electronic products at a discount when compared to what you can get at Amazon.com. After acquiring Buy.com, Japanese company Rakuten (**rakuten.com**) is competing in the US market by offering their website in English.

Retailers Versus E-Tailers

Since the beginning of EC in the mid-1990s, it has become clear that in certain industries, e-tailing will hurt brick-and-mortar retailers. Blue Nile is an example of disrupting the jewelry industry. Stock brokerages and travel agents also have become victims to pure-play competitors. Amazon.com initially concentrated on books, eliminating bookstores such as Borders. Today, Amazon.com is competing with thousands of retailers, including giants such as Walmart (see Petro 2016). *Encyclopedia Britannica* and many others no longer have printed editions. The initial line of defense for traditional retailers was to become a "click and brick," namely, adding an online distribution channel to their physical presence. This helped some department stores and specialty stores, but not all.

Convergence and Omnichannel

Historically, pure-play e-tailors began to build brick-and-mortar locations for specific products and markets where they felt the physical presence of goods would aid competition against other retailers.

Examples of Click-and-Brick Retailers

Most large retailers have already migrated to be click-and-brick companies. Let us look at several examples.

Best Buy

Best Buy, like Walmart, Target, and others, added an online marketing channel. However, in contrast with GAP, Best Buy was not successful. One reason is that the company operates large-scale stores. Consumers come to the stores, examine the products, and go home and order them online ("showrooming") on Amazon.com because it is much cheaper. In summer 2012, Best Buy reduced its prices to match those of Amazon.com. The result was that in August 2012, Best Buy, which is one of the world's largest electronic retailers, saw its profit going down 91% in 1 year. Thus, the company decided to close 50 of its stores and also is moving to smaller stores to cut expenses. After this downturn, the company changed its strategy and has been significantly more successful. The "Renew Blue" campaign focused on two major areas to compete: pricing and specialty shops. Best Buy continues to price-match other retailers in the hopes of driving in-store sales. Additionally the company has lobbied states to institute sales taxes on online merchants to level the playing field. The company has also created "stores-within-stores," with electronic giants Samsung and Microsoft opening their own stores within Best Buy stores. These changes have had a positive effect, and as late 2016, the company's stock has started to rebound (see **forbes.com/sites/ panosmourdoukoutas/2016/11/19/sorry-amazon-fans-best-buy-is-still-alive-and-rising/#31c493df3419**).

SM Chain of Malls in the Philippines

According to Magdirila (2014), this huge chain **smsupermalls.com** (over 230 malls and supermarkets across the Philippines) is launching full-scale online operations in 2016. The company seeks to expand its large footprint in the Philippines with continued growth in China and other Asian counties. SM hopes to expand with the growing acceptance of e-commerce in these markets (see **techinasia.com/philippines-sm-malls-preparing-huge-ecommerce-entry** and **bloomberg.com/news/ articles/2014-02-25/billionaire-sy-goes-online-as-web-draws-shoppers**).

Other Strategies

According to PYMNTS.com (see **pymnts.com/news/retail/2016/mobile-apps-employees-brick-and-mortar-retail**), many retailers are providing apps that help shoppers locate and pay for items, while they are inside physical stores. The retailers can also provide digital discount coupons and make it easier for shoppers to place online orders for out-of-stock merchandise. For more on these strategies, see Hudson (2016).

What Can Traditional Retailers Do?

In addition to opening online channels and closing the least profitable stores, traditional companies have a few strategies to defend themselves. Here are representative examples:

Can Small Businesses Survive?

While large retailers such as Best Buy and hhgregg may go out of business, some small businesses may survive. Small businesses such as **dogtoys.com** and **dell.com** were pioneers of e-commerce and are still doing well. It seems that the success of small e-tailers is related to a strategy that includes:

- Niche markets. Products that cannot be produced in mass production (e.g., non-commodities) should be considered by a small business (e.g., provide custom-made and specialized products).
- Faster delivery than Amazon. Uniquely distributed products in local markets are ideal for small companies. (However, now, Amazon offers same-day delivery in select cities via its "Local Express Delivery" service.)
- Protect privacy. Amazon tracks customers' movements on the Web.
- Concentrate on local markets.
- Provide outstanding customer service.
- Prices should be competitive.
- Maintain their reputation using such strategies as many small companies have done; either pure play, brick and mortar, or click and brick can survive and succeed.

Going Global

Some small companies (e.g., DogToys.com) have many global customers. Big companies, like Amazon.com, are also very active globally. For example, according to Brohan (2015), Amazon.com is Europe's largest online retailer with sales of over $3.08 billion. Large companies acquire local EC companies or need to enter into joint ventures with them.

Examples

Ralph Lauren Corporation (**ralphlauren.com**), apparel designer, manufacturer, and retailer, is selling aggressively online in Europe. In 2013, it started to sell online in Japan. Online sales increased about 6% to $889 million in Q4 2015, leading other distribution channels (**internetretailer.com/2016/05/13/e-commerce-leads-ralph-laurens-q4-retail-sales-gain**).

Conclusion

According to Isidore (2014) and many others, the future of brick-and-mortar retail does not look good. Many stores already have gone out of business. In addition, many retailers will go out of business sooner or later. Note that the online business is becoming more diversified. For example, Amazon.com is experimenting with the same-day delivery of vegetables and fruits, and China's e-commerce companies are moving on to banking (see Riley et al. 2014).

SECTION 3.9 REVIEW QUESTIONS

1. What are the major advantages of e-tailers over retailers?
2. Why is offline retailing in bad shape?
3. Discuss some strategies for small businesses to survive and succeed.
4. Why do e-tailers go global?

3.10   ISSUES IN E-TAILING AND LESSONS LEARNED

The following are representative issues and problems (and some lessons learned from them) that need to be addressed when conducting B2C EC.

Disintermediation and Reintermediation

Disintermediation refers to the removal of an intermediary that is responsible for certain activities between trading partners (usually in a supply chain). As shown in part B of Fig. 3.5, a manufacturer can bypass wholesalers and retailers, selling directly to consumers. Thus, B2C may drive regular retailers out of business. According to Lieber and Syverson (2012), half of the US travel agencies went out of business between 1997 and 2007 due to online competition.

However, consumers might have problems selecting an online vendor, vendors might have problems delivering goods to customers, and both might need an escrow service to ensure the transactions. Thus, new types of intermediaries might be needed, and services might be provided by new or by traditional intermediaries. This new activity is called **reintermediation**. It is pictured in part C of Fig. 3.5. An example of a company that provides these new roles of intermediation is Edmunds (**edmunds.com**), which provides consumers with information about cars (e.g., price comparisons, ratings, and the dealer costs). Another example would be travel agents who can arrange complicated trips, provide longer periods for holding reservations, arrange special tours, and spot deals. Such new role-playing companies can grow rapidly, while traditional intermediaries decline.

Resistance to Change

Intermediaries that may be eliminated, or their status and pay may decrease, might resist the change. One example is the computerization of the Chicago Mercantile Exchange (CME) and the Chicago Board of Trade (CBOT). The resistance by brokers there has been going on for a long time.

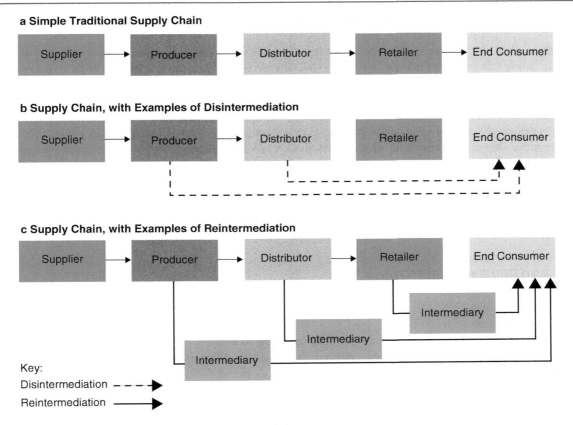

Fig. 3.5 Disintermediation and reintermediation in the B2C supply chain

Channel Conflict

Many traditional retailers establish a supplemental marketing channel when they start selling online. Similarly, some manufacturers have instituted direct marketing initiatives parallel with their established channels of distribution, such as retailers or dealers. In such cases, *channel conflict* can occur. **Channel conflict** refers to the case in which online sales damage the well-being of an existing channel partner. The extent of this conflict varies according to the nature of the industry and the characteristics of particular firms, but sometimes a move to sell online can damage old, valued relationships between trading partners. Channel conflict may occur when a move to online trading simply shifts a company's customers from their traditional stores to an online environment, thus cannibalizing the sales from the former and potentially negatively affecting the traditional outlets by rendering them less profitable. One model that can solve the conflict is to allow ordering and payment online, but the item is delivered to a physical store for pickup.

Product and Service Customization and Personalization

The Internet also allows for easy self-configuration ("design it your way"). This creates a large demand for customized products and services. Manufacturers can meet that demand by using a *mass customization* strategy (see **en.wikipedia.org/wiki/ Build_to_order** and the white paper at **enterpriseinnovation.net/whitepaper/online-commerce-plotting-course-person- alization**). As indicated earlier, many companies offer customized products on their websites.

In conclusion, e-tailing is growing rapidly as an additional marketing channel. In other words, the *click-and-brick model is* a successful one regardless of the conflicts cited. For more about e-tailing and multichanneling retailing, see **dmsretail. com/etailing.htm**.

Lessons Learned from Failures and Lack of Success of E-Tailers

As in the physical world, companies can also fail when doing business online. Although thousands of companies have evolved their online strategies into mature websites with extensive interactive features that add value to the consumer purchasing process, many other sites remain simple "brochureware" sites with limited interactivity. Many traditional companies are in a transitional stage. Mature transactional systems include features for payment processing, order fulfillment, logistics, inventory management, and a host of other services. In most cases, a company must replicate each of its physical business processes and design several more that can be performed online only. Today's environment includes sophisticated access to order information, shipping information, product information, and more through Web pages, touch-tone phones, Web-enabled smartphones, and tablets over wireless networks. Faced with all of these variables, the challenges to profitably implementing EC can be daunting.

A traditional brick-and-mortar store with a mature website that uses a successful click-and-mortar strategy such as those used by Target, Walmart, and Staples can create a successful multichannel business whose benefits can be enjoyed by customers who like to have options on how to buy.

SECTION 3.10 REVIEW QUESTIONS

1. Define disintermediation.
2. Describe reintermediation.
3. Describe channel conflict and other conflicts that may appear in e-tailing.
4. Explain personalization and customization opportunities in e-tailing. What are their benefits to customers?
5. What makes click-and-mortar companies successful?

MANAGERIAL ISSUES

Some managerial issues related to this chapter are as follows:

1. **What are the limitations of e-tailing? Where is e-tailing going?** In Korea, Internet retailing has become the second most important distribution channel, exceeding the national sales volume of all department stores. In many countries, B2C is the fastest growing form of retailing. The question is what will be the limits of e-tailing? The market concentration has already begun, setting a high bar for new e-tailers. However, small businesses can easily start their online channel as part of a stable e-mall service platform when they find a niche opportunity.

   Because many easy sources of funding have dried up and revenue models are being scrutinized, vendor consolidation will continue until greater stability within the e-tailing sector occurs. Ultimately, there will likely be a smaller number of larger sellers with comprehensive general sites (e.g., Amazon.com) and many smaller, specialized niche sites (e.g., Net-a-Porter, Blue Nile).

2. **How should we introduce wireless shopping?** In some countries (e.g., Japan, Korea, Finland, United States), shopping from smartphones is already very popular. In other countries, mobile shopping is not popular yet, although the platform itself may be available. Alternative channels (multichannel marketing) and a culture of a variety of communication channels are developing in many countries, facilitating mobile strategies. In addition, because the younger generation prefers the mobile platform, strategies for the younger generation need to be considered. Offering mobile shopping might not be simple or appropriate to all businesses, but it certainly will be dominant in the future.

3. **Do we have ethics and privacy guidelines?** Ethical issues are extremely important online, just as they are offline. In traditional systems, people play a significant role in ensuring the ethical behavior of buyers and sellers. Will online ethics and the rules of etiquette be sufficient to guide behavior on the Internet? Only time will tell. For example, as job applicant information travels over the Internet, security and privacy become even more important. It is the management's job to make sure that information from applicants is secure. Moreover, e-tailers need to establish guidelines for protecting the privacy of customers who visit their websites. Security and privacy must be priorities.

4. **How will intermediaries act in cyberspace?** The role of online intermediaries has become more and more important. In the banking, stock trading, job market, travel industry, and book sales sectors, the Internet has become an essential service channel. These intermediary services create new business opportunities for sellers and intermediaries.

5. **Should we try to capitalize on social networks?** Many organizations and individuals began advertising or selling products and services on Facebook and other social networks. Although large companies currently are concentrating on advertising, some are experimenting with B2C sales. Social commerce may become an extremely important marketing channel and should be at least experimented with by retailers.

6. **How should we manage multichannel marketing to avoid channel and/or price conflicts?** Managing multichannels requires a strategy on handling different types of transactions in the most appropriate and cost-effective way. Changing channels needs to be done together with appropriate conflict management.

7. **What are the major potential limitations of the growth of B2C EC?** First, the limitations depend on market demands for online products. The saturation effect may be strong. Second, the cost and availability of Internet access may influence growth. Third, cultural differences and habits may deter or slow down e-shopping. Fourth, the ease of B2C shopping is important, and fifth, the availability of payments and order fulfillment infrastructure are critical success factors.

8. **How to deal with "big data"?** A large amount of data is collected in B2C and is growing rapidly. It is necessary to extract valuable information and knowledge from this data. The technologies that are used belong mostly to the category of business intelligence (BI); they range from data and Web mining to several other analytical tools.

SUMMARY

In this chapter, you learned about the following EC issues as they relate to the chapter's learning objectives.

1. **The scope and characteristics of e-tailing.** E-tailing, the online selling of products and services, is growing rapidly. Computers, software, and electronics are the major items sold online. Books, CDs, toys, office supplies, and other standard commodities also sell well. Even more successful are services that are sold online, such as airline tickets and travel services, stock trading, and some financial services.

2. **Classify e-tailing business models.** The major e-tailing business models can be classified by distribution channel—a manufacturer or mail-order company selling directly to consumers, pure-play (virtual) e-tailing, a click-and-mortar strategy with both online and traditional channels, and online malls that provide either referring directories or shared services. Social commerce facilitates group buying and location shopping.

3. **How online travel/tourism services operate.** Most services available through a physical travel agency also are available online. However, customers can get additional information more quickly using online resources. Customers can even submit bids to travel providers (e.g., using the C2B business model). Finally, travelers can compare prices, participate in online activities, read other travelers' recommendations, and view user-generated videos. Lately, social travel is becoming popular, with travelers learning from each other and organizing trips accordingly.

4. **The online employment market and its benefits.** The online job market is growing rapidly. The major benefits for employers are the ability to quickly reach a large number of job seekers at a low cost, conduct remote video interviews, and even conduct preemployment qualification tests. Finally, résumés can be checked and matched against job requirements. Millions of job offers posted on the Internet help job seekers, who also can post their résumés for recruiters. Recruiting in social networks, especially LinkedIn and Facebook, is growing rapidly.

5. **The electronic real estate marketplace.** In most cases, the online real estate marketplace supports traditional operations. However, both buyers and sellers can save time and effort by using the electronic markets. Buyers can purchase properties in several locations much more easily than without the Internet, and in some situations, they have access to less expensive services (insurance, mortgages, etc.). Eventually, agents' commissions on regular transactions are expected to decline as a result of the electronic market for real estate, as more online sales directly by owner become popular.

6. **Online trading of stocks and bonds.** One of the fastest growing online businesses is the online trading of securities. It is inexpensive, convenient, and supported by a tremendous amount of financial and advisory information. Trading is very fast and efficient, almost fully automated, and is moving toward 24/7 global trading. However, security breaches are more possible, so good security protection is essential.

7. **Cyberbanking and online personal finance.** Branch banking is on the decline due to less expensive, more convenient online banking as the world becomes more accustomed to and trusting in cyberbanking. Today, most routine banking services can be done from anywhere. Banks can reach customers in remote places, and customers can conduct transactions with banks outside their community. This makes the financial markets more efficient. Online personal finance applications, such as bill paying, monitoring of accounts, and tax preparation, also are very popular.

8. **On-demand delivery service.** On-demand delivery service is needed when items are perishable or when delivering medicine, express documents, or urgently needed supplies. One example of on-demand delivery is e-groceries; these may be ordered online and are shipped or ready for store pickup within 24 h or less.

9. **Delivery of digital products.** Anything that can be digitized can be successfully delivered online. Delivery of digital products such as music, software, e-books, movies, and other entertainments online has been a success. Some print media, such as electronic versions of magazines or electronic books, also are successful when digitized and delivered electronically.

10. **Aiding consumer purchase decisions.** Purchase decision aids include shopping portals, shopbots and comparison agents, business rating sites, recommendations (including electronic ones), trust verification sites, and other tools. Tools include real-time mobile devices and extensive support from social networks.

11. **The new face of retail competition.** The surge in B2C has resulted in pressure on traditional retailers to add online channels and reduce prices. Even large companies such as Best Buy are struggling. The online retail giants, Amazon.com and eBay, are becoming more aggressive and competitive (e.g., adding same-day delivery), so their consumers are enjoying lower prices and better service. Traditional retailers also need a strategy to deal with the intense competition. New competition is also coming from Chinese and other foreign online vendors.

12. **Disintermediation and other B2C strategic issues.** Direct electronic marketing by manufacturers results in disintermediation by removing wholesalers and retailers. However, online reintermediaries provide additional services and value, such as helping consumers select among multiple vendors. Traditional retailers may feel threatened or pressured when manufacturers decide to sell directly to customers online; such direct selling can cause channel conflict. Pricing of online and offline products and services is also an issue that frequently needs to be addressed.

KEY TERMS

Brick-and-mortar retailer
Business model
Channel conflict
Click-and-mortar retailer
Direct marketing
Disintermediation
Drop-shipping
E-grocer
Electronic (online) banking (e-banking)
Electronic retailing (e-tailing)
E-tailers
Event shopping
Internet radio
Internet TV
Location-based e-commerce (l-commerce)
Multichannel business model
On-demand delivery service
Private shopping club
Reintermediation
Shopping portals
Shopping robots (shopping agents, shopbots)
Social TV
Virtual (pure-play) e-tailers

DISCUSSION QUESTIONS

1. Discuss the importance of comparison tools, product reviews, and customer ratings in online shopping.
2. Discuss the advantages of a specialized e-tailer, such as DogToys.com (**dogtoys.com**). Could such a store survive in the physical world? Why or why not?
3. Use Google to find the benefits of travel-related social networking sites. Discuss five of them.
4. Discuss the benefits of **salary.com**. Are there any disadvantages?
5. Why are online travel services a popular Internet application? Why do so many websites provide free travel information?
6. Compare the advantages and disadvantages of online stock trading with offline trading.
7. Compare the advantages and disadvantages of distributing digitizable products electronically versus physical delivery.
8. Do you trust your personal data on social networks such as **linkedin.com** or **facebook.com**? How do you protect your privacy?
9. Many companies encourage their customers to buy products and services online, sometimes "pushing" them to do so. Why?
10. Would you use **monster.com** or **linkedin.com** for recruiting, or would you rather use a traditional agency? Why?
11. Travel social network WAYN (**wayn.com**) says that it is a bridge between two social sites: Facebook and TripAdvisor. Discuss.
12. Do you use your social network when you decide which products to purchase? How? Is this more valid to you than professional reviews? Why?

TOPICS FOR CLASS DISCUSSION AND DEBATES

1. Discuss the advantages of established click-and-mortar companies such as Walmart over pure-play e-tailers such as Amazon.com. What are the disadvantages of click-and-brick retailers as compared with pure-play e-tailers? Also debate: Competition between pure-play e-tailers (e.g., Amazon.com, Blue Nile) and traditional retailers such as HP, Walmart, and other department stores that have added the Web as a part of a multichannel business model. Who may win? Under what assumptions?
2. Online employment services make it easy to change jobs; therefore, turnover rates may increase. This could result in total higher costs for employers because of increased costs for recruiting and training new employees and the need to pay higher salaries and wages to attract or keep existing employees. What can companies do to minimize this problem?
3. Discuss each of the following as limiting factors on the growth of B2C EC: (a) Too much competition, (b) expensive technology, (c) people need desktop computers to shop online (but smartphones are changing this situation), (d) people need the social interaction of face-to-face shopping, (e) many people cannot afford Internet access, and (f) the fear of fraud and security breaching.
4. Debate: Some employers ask job applicants permission to log into their Facebook account during an in-person interview; others ask for complete, unfiltered access to the entire Facebook account. Some US states propose legislation (several already have passed laws) banning employers (and universities) from using a prospective employee's Facebook content as selection criteria.
5. In April 2012, TripAdvisor announced on its website that it is the world's largest social travel site. Some people say that WAYN is the only truly social travel network. Compare the social networking activities of both sites. Debate the issue.
6. Debate: Should online sales be an independent division in a click-and-mortar firm?
7. Debate: What is the future of Amazon.com?
8. Debate: Will omnichannel retailing destroy brick-and-mortar retailers?
9. Some love digital coupons; others say the idea is waste of time since coupons are not available for the products they want to buy. Research the topic and debate the value of digital versus paper coupons.
10. Investigate the impact of online casinos on physical ones. Discuss.

INTERNET EXERCISES

1. Many consumer portals offer advice and ratings on products or e-tailers. Identify and examine two separate general-consumer portals that look at sites, and compare prices or other purchase criteria. Try to find and compare prices for some digital cameras, microwave ovens, and MP3 players. Visit **yippy.com**. How can this site help with your shopping? Summarize your experience. Comment on the strong and weak points of such shopping tools.

2. Visit **landsend.com**, and prepare a customized order for an item of clothing. Describe the process. Do you think this will result in better-fitting clothes? Do you think this personalization feature will lead to greater sales volume for Lands' End?

3. Make your résumé accessible to millions of people. Consult **asktheheadhunter.com** or **careerbuilder.com** for help rewriting your résumé. See **monster.com** for ideas about planning your career. Get prepared for an online job interview, and look at **monster-tronics.com** for interesting capabilities. Use the Web to determine what salary you can get in the city of your choice for the kind of job you want.

4. Visit **move.com**, **decisionaide.com**, or a similar site, and compute the monthly mortgage payment on a 30-year loan at 5.5% fixed interest. Also check current interest rates. Estimate your closing costs on a $200,000 loan. Compare the monthly payments of the fixed rate with that of an adjustable rate for the first year. Finally, compute your total payments if you take the loan for 15 years at the going rate. Compare it with a 30-year mortgage. Comment on the difference.

5. Access the Virtual Trader game at **virtualtrader.co.uk**, and register for the Internet stock game. You will be bankrolled with a virtual £100,000 in a trading account every month. You can play other investment games at **investopedia.com/simulator** or find and create a free stock market game at **marketwatch.com/game**. Comment on your experiences.

6. Evaluate **prosper.com** and **leandingclub.com**. Read the comparison at **lendingmemo.com/lending-club-vs-prosper**. Would you consider P2P lending? Why? Which service would you use?

7. Compare the price of a specific Sony digital camera at **shopping.com**, **mysimon.com**, **bizrate.com**, and **pricegrabber.com**. Which site locates the best deal? Where do you get the best information?

8. Enter **vineyardvines.com**. Identify all multichannels used in their retail operations. List the benefits to the company.

9. Enter **bazaarvoice.com**, and find how consumers can engage in a dialog. Look at its Q&A functionality in both "Conversations" and "Connections." Write a report based on your findings.

10. Enter **couchsurfing.org**, and examine how they connect potential travelers with hosts. Discuss the things that you like and the limitations of this service. Compare with home swapping sites such as **homeexchange.com**.

11. Enter **zillow.com/corp/ZillowPortfolio.htm**, and see Zillow's portfolio. Examine their capabilities and the benefits to consumers. Write a report.

12. How can LinkedIn and Facebook help job seekers? How can they help employers? Relate your answers to what you can find on **indeed.com**.

13. Compare the sites **yelp.com** and **epinions.com**.

14. Visit **hayneedle.com**. What kind of a mall is this?

15. Enter **layar.com**. Find information about Layar Creator and other products that can support B2C shopping. Write a report.

16. Enter **play.google.com/store**. Relate the offerings of this site to topics in this chapter.

TEAM ASSIGNMENTS AND PROJECTS

1. Assignment for the Opening Case

   Read the opening case and answer the following questions:

   (a) What are Amazon.com's critical success factors? Is its decision to offer a much broader selection of items a good marketing strategy? With the increased services and diversification, do you think the company will be able to concentrate on its core competency of enhancing the Amazon.com brand? What about their long-term vs. short-term strategy?

   (b) Amazon.com operates Zappos (**zappos.com**) as a separate entity. Does this make sense? Why or why not?

   (c) Visit **amazon.com**, and identify at least three specific elements of its personalization and customization features. Browse specific books on one particular subject, leave the site, and then go back and revisit the site. What do you see? Are these features likely to encourage you to purchase more books in the future from Amazon.com? Check the 1-Click feature and other shopping aids provided. List the features and discuss how they may lead to increased sales.

   (d) Which innovative product do you feel will have the biggest impact for Amazon? Why?

(e) Check all the personalization features on Amazon.com. List their advantages.

(f) Find the technology-oriented activities at Amazon.com (e.g., Echo, making e-readers). List the major ones and discuss the logic of such offerings.

(g) Find some recent material on Amazon.com's marketing strategy, and discuss your findings.

(h) Examine social networking activities on Amazon.com. What are their purposes?

(i) Examine Amazon Web Services. Why do you think the company offers this service?

2. Each team will investigate the services of two online car-selling sites (from the following list or other sites). When the teams have finished, they should bring their research together and discuss their findings.

(a) Buying new cars through an intermediary (**autobytel.com**/URL> or **carsdirect.com**)

(b) Buying used cars **autotrader.com**

(c) Buying used cars from auto dealers (**manheim.com**)

(d) Automobile rating sites (**carsdirect.com** and **fueleconomy.gov**)

(e) Car-buying portals **thecarportal.com** and **cars.com**

(f) Buying collector cars **classiccars.com** and **antiquecar.com**

3. Each team (or team member) will review two or three travel-oriented social networks (e.g., **world66.com, virtualtourist.com, bootsnall.com, tripadvisor.com, travel.tripcase.com**, Lonely Planet's Thorn Tree travel forum **lonelyplanet.com/thorntree, wayn.com**, and **budgetglobetrotting.com**). Compare their functionalities. Then read Jong (2016), and examine the various issues raised in this paper including emerging trends. Write a report.

4. Each team will represent a broker-based area (e.g., real estate, insurance, stocks, employment). Each team will find a new development that has occurred within the assigned area over the most recent 3 months. Look for vendor announcements on these sites, and search for new happenings in each area. In addition, examine the relevant business news at **bloomberg.com**. After completing your research, as a team, prepare a report on disintermediation in your assigned area.

5. Watch the video "Internet Marketing and E-Commerce with Tom Antion Part One" (9:06 min) at **youtube.com/watch?v=tc1u9eqpf68** (part two at **youtube.com/watch?v=7jmK0_QTguk** is optional), and answer the following questions:

(a) What revenue sources are cited?

(b) What B2C revenue sources that you are aware of are not cited?

(c) What are the two "affiliate" models? Compare these two models.

(d) Why is eBay so great for selling?

(e) Comment on the suggestions for products/services you can sell from your home.

(f) What problems and limitations do you see for conducting business from your home?

6. View some videos about future retail shopping (both offline and online). Discuss what B2C e-commerce may look like in the future, considering future shopping innovations (e.g., see Google's view on changes in retail at **youtu.be/O7fSDKBddpU**).

7. Your mission is to help people find jobs online. Each team evaluates several job sites and lists their capabilities and shortcomings. (Starting list: **craigslist.org, careerbuilder.com, dice.com, glassdoor.com, linkedin.com, mediabistro.com, monster.com, simplyhired.com**, and **tweetmyjobs.com**.) In addition, check virtual job fairs such as "Monster Virtual Job Fair" (**virtualjobfair.be**).

8. Watch the video "How to get a job using Linkedin" (see **youtu.be/uQ8ULVpAsvE**) on how to find a job using social networking.

(a) Do you feel this is a valid approach? Why?

(b) What would you change in this approach?

(c) Would this work in your field or demographic area?

9. The team(s) investigates Pandora Radio (**pandora.com**). Concentrate on:

(a) All sources of music they can stream.

(b) All devices that can be used to access Pandora.

(c) Their business model and competitiveness.

(d) Present your findings. Watch the video "on how to find a job using social networking."

CLOSING CASE: ETSY—A SOCIAL-ORIENTED B2C MARKETPLACE

Etsy is an online marketplace where designers across the world sell unique handcrafted jewelry, clothing, vintage items (20 years or older), art, prints and posters, handmade goods, craft supplies, and more. According to its website, Etsy has created a community of sellers, each with a virtual storefront. The sellers are usually independent designers who sell small quantities of unique handcrafted goods. Etsy can be viewed as a designer's virtual fair where creators have their own virtual store with an "about" link, so buyers can learn about the shop, read reviews, and contact the seller with any questions. Each seller may offer a link to their Facebook or Instagram page, so potential buyers can see products available to purchase. (To better understand selling on Etsy, see the following video: **youtu.be/6_95qiLdVec.**) This is how Etsy emphasizes its social presence. For tips on social networking success on Etsy, see **blog.etsy.com/en/tags/etsy-success-social-networking**.

The Company's Mission

According to **etsy.com/about**, the company's mission is "to re-imagine commerce in ways that build a more fulfilling and lasting world." In 2012, Etsy became a "Certified B Corporation," which is "a new kind of company that uses the power of business to solve social and environmental problems" (see **blog.etsy.com/news/2012/etsy-joins-the-b-corporation-movement**).

The Community

According to **etsy.com/community**, Etsy is more than a marketplace. It is a community of artists, creators, collectors, thinkers, and doers. Members are encouraged to share ideas, attend events (in your area), and join streaming workshops. Community members can post comments and stories. Etsy describes itself as "the marketplace we make together."

Etsy uses several social media tools and networks. For example, in April 2009, it organized an "Etsy Day" promotion on Twitter. In March 2011, the company introduced a Facebook-type social networking system called "People Search," a tool for people to search through all Etsy buyers and sellers and add people to their "Circle." This addition resulted in criticism regarding privacy and subsequently to the protection of such personal information on Etsy's site. For more details, see **huffingtonpost.com/2011/03/15/etsy-privacy-debacle-site_n_836277.html**. In 2016, the company launched its first international social campaign focused on the variety of expressions of individual globally. This campaign was meant to help expand the service to both international buyers and sellers (see **adweek.com/news/advertising-branding/etsys-first-global-campaign-expression-individuality-just-stuff-it-sells-173404**).

The Business and Revenue Models

Etsy is a for-profit private company. Although there is no membership fee, Etsy charges 20¢ for each item listed for 4 months or until that item sells. There is an additional fee of 3.5% of the sale price of that item once that item is sold, and if the seller uses the site's payment system (called Direct Checkout), there is an additional 3% fee (or more, depending on location of bank account) per transaction (see **etsy.com/sell**). Etsy went public in 2015 to mixed reviews (Barinka & Cao 2016). Experts speculate that the slip in stock price is a combination of initial overvaluation and lingering concerns about the company's ability to grow long term.

Competition

Many of Etsy's direct competitors are located outside the United States (e.g., German-based DaWanda, **en.dawanda.com**; Swiss-based Ezebee.com, **ezebee.com**; and Australian-based Zibbet **zibbet.com**). See details at **en.wikipedia.org/wiki/Etsy**. In the United States, many handcraft creators sell on eBay and Amazon.com. Some competing websites sell only selected items like clothing, jewelry, and art (see **bonanza.com** for clothing). Etsy has an official blog (see **blog.etsy.com/en**). It has a presence on Facebook (**facebook.com/Etsy**) and Twitter (**twitter.com/etsy**). As of mid-2016, the company has over 955,200 followers on Pinterest (see **pinterest.com/etsy**) where there are thousands of pins about Etsy merchandise organized on almost 70 boards.

Conclusion

In addition to the "People Search" privacy issue, the company was criticized for insufficient fraud detection efforts. For example, only original creations are allowed to be sold on Etsy, while reselling items is forbidden. Etsy is now insisting on transparency from all of its vendors and will continue to investigate all shops "flagged" for possible violations (see **blog.etsy. com/news/2013/a-frank-conversation-about-resellers/?ref=about_blog_title**). Despite the criticism, the company is growing rapidly. Etsy now operates in Germany, France, and Australia and plans expansion to other countries.

    Sources: Based on Barinka & Cao (2016), Chow (2014), Feldmann (2014), **en.wikipedia.org/wiki/Etsy**, and **etsy.com/ blog/news** (both accessed January 2017).

Questions

1. Explain why the company has been compared to a cross between Amazon.com, eBay, and a grandma's basement.
2. Examine the mission of the company, and explain what the company is doing to attain its mission.
3. The sellers in this case are mostly small businesses. As such, Etsy is considered a B2C company. However, it can also be viewed as an enabler of P2P. Explain.
4. Compare and contrast similar transactions conducted on Etsy and on eBay.
5. Enter **storenvy.com** and look at their markets. Compare this site with Etsy. Write a report.
6. Investigate the connection between Pinterest and Etsy. Start with Feldmann (2014). Write a report.

REFERENCES

Barinka, A. and Cao, J., "Etsy Sinks to Low Since IPO as Lockup Ends, Investors Bail" Bloomberg. January 11, 2016. **bloomberg.com/news/ articles/2016-01-11/etsy-plunges-to-lowest-since-ipo-as-lockup-ends-investors-bail/** (accessed January 2017).

Bennet, A. Online DropShipping Income 2016: How To Make via E-Commerce Without Having Your Own Product. Seattle, WA: Amazon Digital Services, 2016.

Bortz, D. "Tweet Yourself to a New Job." February 6, 2014. **money.cnn.com/2014/01/01/pf/twitter-job.moneymag** (accessed January 2017).

Brohan, M. "Amazon Builds Up Its European Marketplace." April 30, 2015. **internetretailer.com/2015/04/30/amazon-builds-its-european-marketplace** (accessed January 2017).

Brown, S. "Why 2016 Will Be the Year Online and Offline Retail Converge." Norwest Venture Partners, April 12, 2016. **nvp.com/blog/2016-will-year-online-offline-retail-converge** (accessed January 2017).

Budzienski, J. "3 Ways to Be Constantly Recruiting Star Talent Through Social Media." April 23, 2015. **entrepreneur.com/article/245295** (accessed January 2017).

Charlton, G. "Ecommerce Consumer Reviews: Why You Need Them and How to Use Them." July, 8, 2015. **econsultancy.com/blog/9366-ecommerce-consumer-reviews-why-you-need-them-and-how-to-use-them** (accessed January 2017).

Chow, C. "The Website Etsy.com a Virtual Craft Shop for Designers and Shoppers Alike." *San Jose Mercury News*, February 5, 2014. **mercurynews.com/campbell/ci_25072351/website-etsy-com-virtual-craft-shop-designers-and** (accessed January 2017).

Corcoran, C., & F. Liu. (2014). "Accuracy of Zillow's Home Value Estimates." Real Estate Issues, 39(1), 45–49, 2–3, 6.

Costine, J. "Facebook Threatens LinkedIn with Job Opening Features." TechCrunch, November 7, 2016. **techcrunch.com/2016/11/07/jobbook/** (accessed January 2017)

Del Castillo, C. "2016 Social Recruitment Trends Forecast." February 10, 2016. **resources.workable.com/blog/2016-social-recruitment-trends-forecast** (accessed January 2017).

Deloitte Digital. "Navigating the New Digital Divide." Deloitte Development, 2015. **deloitte.com/content/dam/Deloitte/us/Documents/consumer-business/us-cb-navigating-the-new-digital-divide-051315.pdf** (accessed January 2017).

Diaz, L. "3 Trends Shaping the Online Travel Industry." Optimizely, July 18, 2016. **blog.optimizely.com/2016/07/18/online-travel-industry-trends** (accessed January 2017).

eMarketer. "How Social Media Influences Shopping Behavior." eMarketer, March 17, 2016. **emarketer.com/Article/How-Social-Media-Influences-Shopping-Behavior/1013718** (accessed January 2017).

Feldmann, A. "Etsy Expands Reach and Sales for Its Seller Community." *Pinterest for Business*, 2014. **business.pinterest.com/case-study-etsy** (accessed January 2017).

Fiegerman, S. "Amazon stock tanks after disappointing profit." CNNTech, October 28, 2016. **money.cnn.com/2016/10/27/technology/amazon-earnings** (accessed January 2017).

Forrester Research. "The State of Retailing Online 2015: Marketing and Merchandising." Forrester Research, December 2015.

Fox News. "Nevada, Delaware Sign Deal to Allow Interstate Online Gambling." February 25, 2014. **foxnews.com/politics/2014/02/25/raising-stakes-nevada-and-delaware-sign-agreement-to-allow-interstate-online** (accessed January 2017).

Harney, K. "Average Real Estate Commissions Dropping to Low 5 Percent Range." *Chicago Tribune*, January 10, 2017. **chicagotribune.com/ classified/realestate/ct-re-0115-kenneth-harney-column-20170112-column.html** (accessed January 2017).

Hockenson, L. "Updated: Pandora Opens Submission Process to Independent Artists." February 7, 2014. **gigaom.com/2014/02/07/Pandora-opens-submission-process-to-independent-artists** (accessed January 2017).

Hsu, T. "Google Expands Same-Day Delivery Test to Southern California." January 23, 2014. **latimes.com/business/money/la-fi-mo-google-delivery-los-angeles-20140123,0,190849.story#axzz2yN0AT1zE** (accessed January 2017).

Hudson, M., "Can Brick and Mortar Compete with Online?" October 19, 2016. **thebalance.com/can-brick-and-mortar-compete-with-online-2890023** (accessed January 2017).

Ingham, J., J. Cadieux, A. M. Berrada. (2015). "e-Shopping Acceptance." *Journal of Information and Management*, 52(1), 44–60.

Isidore, C. "Everything Must Go: There's a Flood of Store Closings." March 7, 2014. **money.cnn.com/2014/03/07/news/companies/retail-store-closings** (accessed January 2017).

Jong, A. "Global Bus Distribution Shifts Gears to Online." November 2016. **phocuswright.com/Free-Travel-Research/Global-Bus-Distribution-Shifts-Gears-to-Online/** (accessed January 2017).

Lieber, E., and C. Syverson. *Online versus Offline Competition: The Oxford Handbook of the Digital Economy*. New York: Oxford University Press, 2012.

Magdirila, P. "After Creating Biggest Chain of Malls in Philippines, SM Plans to Conquer E-Commerce." February 27, 2014. **techinasia.com/Philippines-sm-malls-preparing-huge-ecommerce-entry/** (accessed January 2017).

Mazzara, B. "What Is Augmented Reality and Virtual Reality Real Estate?" Bisnow, October 15, 2015. **bisnow.com/new-york/news/technology/what-is-augmented-reality-and-virtual-reality-real-estate-50994/** (accessed January 2017).

Morrison, K. "Social Media and Travel Go Hand in Hand." *AdWeek*, August 17, 2015. **adweek.com/digital/social-media-and-travel-go-hand-in-hand-infographic/** (accessed January 2017).

Moseti, W. M. "Struggling Retailers Report Change in Shopping Trends." February 2, 2014. **sproutwired.com/struggling-retailers-report-change-in-shopping-trends/185173/** (accessed January 2017).

National Association of Realtors. "Highlights from the 2015 Profile of Home Buyers and Sellers." November 5, 2015. **realtor.org/reports/highlights-from-the-2015-profile-of-home-buyers-and-sellers/** (accessed January 2017).

Pempus, B. "Delaware Online Gaming Yields $1.8M In 2015." Jan 19, 2016. **cardplayer.com/poker-news/19884-delaware-online-gaming-yields-1-8m-in-2015/** (accessed January 2017).

Petro, G., "Amazon Vs. Walmart: Clash Of The Titans." August 25, 2016. **forbes.com/sites/gregpetro/2016/08/25/amazon-vs-walmart-clash-of-the-titans/#724c903518d9** (accessed January 2017).

Princeton University (Career Services). "Using Social Media to Network & Search." 2016. http://**careerservices.princeton.edu/undergraduate-students/internship-job-search/social-media** (accessed May 2016).

PricewaterhouseCoopers. "Global Entertainment and Media Outlook 2016–2020: US Edition." 2016. **pwc.com/us/en/industry/entertainment-media/publications/global-entertainment-media-outlook.html** (accessed January 2017).

Reeves, M., "Top 5 Security Practices for Financial Institutions to Defeat Online Identity Attacks." February 10, 2014. **entrust.com/top-5-security-practices-financial-institutions-defeat-online-identity-attacks** (accessed January 2017).

Riley, C., Y. Yang, and P. Chiou. "China's Big Tech Moves onto Banks' Turf." February 27, 2014. **money.cnn.com/2014/02/27/news/economy/china-alibaba-bank** (accessed January 2017).

Ruddock, S. "Three Years in the Making: A Retrospective Look at New Jersey's Legal Online Gambling Market." November 30, 2016. **online-pokerreport.com/22910/nj-online-gambling-websites-timeline/** (accessed January 2017).

Sablich, J. "5 Ways Social Media Can Help You Travel." *The New York Times*, October, 18, 2016. **nytimes.com/2016/10/19/travel/travel-tips-social-media.html?_r=0/** (accessed January 2017).

Schwartz, S. "Price-Match Apps Help Holiday Shoppers Find Bargains." December 1, 2015. **cnbc.com/2015/12/01/retail-price-comparison-apps-empower-shoppers.html/** (accessed January 2017).

Schoon, R. "RadioShack Announces It's Closing 1000's of Stores: Mistakes and E-Commerce Competition to Blame." March 5, 2014. **latinpost.com/articles/8316/20140305/radioshack-announces-its-closing-1000s-of-stores-mistakes-and-e-commerce-competition-to-blame.htm/** (accessed January 2017).

Statistica.com. "Size of Online Gaming Market from 2003 to 2018." 2016. **statista.com/statistics/270728/market-volume-of-online-gaming-worldwide/** (accessed January 2017).

Taylor, N. "Hiring in the Digital Age: What's Next for Recruiting?" January 11, 2016. **businessnewsdaily.com/6975-future-of-recruiting.html/** (accessed January 2017).

Trefis, T. "Streaming Partners Program: Amazon's New Initiative To Drive Prime Memberships?" December 23, 2015. **forbes.com/sites/greatspeculations/2015/12/23/streaming-partners-program-amazons-new-initiative-to-drive-prime-memberships/#5b652661303a/** (accessed January 2017).

Turban, E., J. Strauss, and L. Lai. *Social Commerce*. New York: Springer, 2016.

Wieczner, J., and K. Bellstrom. "The Mall Goes High-Tech." SmartMoney, November 2010.

Williams, M. DropShipping: The Ultimate DropShipping Blueprint Made Simple (Dropshipping for Beginners. Dropshipping with Amazon, Dropshiiping Suppliers). [Kindle Edition]. Seattle, WA: Amazon Digital Services, 2016

Zaharia, Z. "15 Steps to Maximize your Financial Data Protection" Heimdal Security, 2016. **heimdalsecurity.com/blog/online-financial-security-guide** (accessed January 2017).

Zillow Group. "Zillow Group's Premier Agent App Celebrates First Anniversary with Major Feature Update; Brings Third Party Leads to the App." Dec 12, 2016. **prnewswire.com/news-releases/zillow-groups-premier-agent-app-celebrates-first-anniversary-with-major-feature-update-brings-third-party-leads-to-the-app-300376411.html** (accessed January 2017).

Zimmerman, J. and S. Singh. *Social Media Marketing for Dummies,* 3rd edition. Hoboken, NJ: Wiley, 2015.

Zorzini, C. "Best Drop Shipping Companies (February 2017)." Ecommerce Platforms, February 1, 2017.

Business-to-Business E-Commerce

4

Contents

Learning Objectives

Upon completion of this chapter, you will be able to:

1. Describe the B2B field.
2. Describe the major types of B2B models.
3. Discuss the models and characteristics of the sell-side marketplace, including auctions.
4. Describe sell-side intermediaries.
5. Describe the characteristics of the buy-side marketplace and e-procurement.
6. Explain how reverse auctions work in B2B.
7. Describe B2B aggregation and group purchasing models.
8. Define exchanges and describe their major types.
9. Describe third-party exchanges.
10. Describe how B2B can benefit from social networking and Web 2.0.
11. Describe collaborative commerce.

© Springer International Publishing AG 2018
E. Turban et al., *Electronic Commerce 2018*, Springer Texts in Business and Economics, DOI 10.1007/978-3-319-58715-8_4

OPENING CASE
ALIBABA.COM—THE WORLD'S LARGEST B2B MARKETPLACE

Alibaba Group is a collection of Internet-based e-commerce companies, some of which are B2B (notably Alibaba.com); the others are B2C and EC services (e.g., payments). For a company overview, see **alibabagroup.com/en/about/overview**. The company started as a portal for connecting Chinese manufacturers with buyers from other countries. By 2014, Alibaba Group became the world's largest e-commerce enterprise and in 2016 has surpassed Walmart as the world's largest retailer. Its business-to-business (B2B) operation (Alibaba.com) is the world's largest marketplace. The fascinating story of the company is described by Clark (2016) and by Erisman (2015). The company describes itself as:

> We provide the fundamental technology infrastructure and marketing reach to help merchants, brands and other businesses that provide products, services and digital content to leverage the power of the Internet to engage with their users and customers. Our businesses are comprised of core commerce, cloud computing, digital media and entertainment, innovation initiatives and others. Through investee affiliates, we also participate in the logistics and local services sectors.
> (from **alibabagroup.com/en/about/overview**)

The Opportunity

The Alibaba Group was started in 1999 by Jack Ma and his partners. Ma envisioned an opportunity to connect foreign buyers with Chinese manufacturers, especially the small ones. These companies wanted to go global but did not know how to do it. The initial business was Alibaba.com, a B2B portal, which later on developed into a comprehensive B2B marketplace. The Alibaba Group also added a consumer-to-consumer (C2C) marketplace called Taobao (**taobao.com**). In 2004, Alibaba added the "Alipay Cross-Border E-Payment Service" (**alipay.com**). In 2007, the Alibaba Group founded the Internet-based business management software company Alisoft (**alisoft.com**), followed by Tmall.com (**tmall.com**), a giant B2C platform. The company established a cloud computing platform and restructured over time. In 2014 Alibaba Group had an IPO in the USA raising over $20 billion. In 2015 the company's valuation was over $158 million compared to Amazon's valuation of $249 million. This case concentrates on Alibaba.com, the B2B company (herein "Alibaba.com").

The Solution

Alibaba.com is an online marketplace composed of a platform for buyers and sellers, a community, and B2B services. The company's mission is to provide all the necessary support for buyers, suppliers, and traders. The components and role of the company are illustrated in Fig. 4.1.

- **Suppliers:** Post their catalogs, company information, special promotions, etc. on the suppliers' space. Alibaba.com helps to reach international buyers. Suppliers can get free online training.

Fig. 4.1 The role of Alibaba.com in B2B

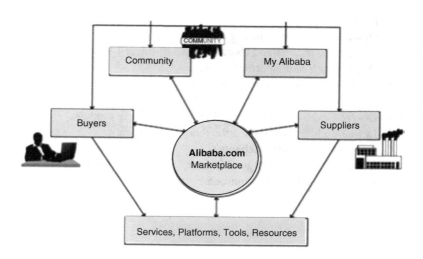

- **Buyers:** Search for potential products and suppliers and also have the option to post what they need (requests) on the buyers' space and get quotes from suppliers. Buyers can verify the suppliers' worthiness (see a video about suppliers' assessment at **sa.alibaba.com**). Alibaba.com provides inspection services with reliable experts. Buyers can compare prices and terms of service as well.
- **Services for buyers and suppliers:** Alibaba.com helps to communicate, negotiate, and assist in reaching a deal. They also arrange the payment process, insurance, and delivery details. Alibaba.com provides all the technology necessary to support the activities on its site. It also provides services such as escrow and handling customer complaints.
- **My Alibaba:** A personal communication and trade management tool on Alibaba.com. It is now separated for buyers and suppliers.
- **Tools and resources:** Alibaba.com provides information and tools for export and import. It also provides a tradeshow channel.
- **Alibaba cloud computing and other infrastructure:** The company is a developer of cloud computing services. The company is committed to supporting the growth of Alibaba Group companies and providing a comprehensive suite of Internet-based EC-oriented computing services, which include e-commerce data mining, high-speed massive e-commerce data processing capabilities, and data customization.
- **Alipay (alipay.com)** is a cross-border online payment platform, mainly used by buyers and sellers engaging in e-commerce transactions. It offers an easy, safe, and secure way for millions of individuals and businesses to make and receive payments on the Internet. By 2016, Alipay had 400 million registered users who made over 519 billion monthly payments and mobile users, through Mobile Alipay. Mobile Alipay is now the largest mobile platform in the world (see **chinainternetwatch.com/6183/alipay-the-largest-mobile-payments-platform-in-the-world**).
- Alibaba.com Secure Payment (an escrow service; **alibaba.com/escrow/buyer.html**) is a service that holds the payment to the seller until both parties have confirmed that the transaction is complete. Alibaba Escrow Service also has a Dispute and Refund process if the buyer does not receive the goods or is unhappy with the delivery. For more information about the Escrow Service and the Dispute and Refund process, see **alibaba.com/help/safety_security/products/escrow/faq.html**.

Alipay also offers an online global payment solution to help buyers or sellers outside China to do business in China. Alipay supports transactions in 28 major foreign currencies (December 2016).

The Database

The center of Alibaba.com is its huge database, which is basically horizontal information organized into dozens of industry categories, including agriculture, apparel and fashion, automobiles, and toys. Each industry category is further divided into subcategories (over 800 in total). For example, the toy category includes items such as dolls, electronic pets, and wooden toys. Each subcategory includes classified postings organized into four groups: sellers, buyers, agents, and cooperation. Each group may include many companies and products. (Some categories have thousands of product postings.) A powerful search engine helps navigate the database.

Community Services

Alibaba.com provides the following major features all related to import and export: free e-mail, help center, 24-h online intelligent robot to assist with answering questions, tutorials for traders, Trade Alert free updates to your inbox, news, tradeshow information, legal information, arbitration, forums and discussion groups, trade trends, and so on. In addition, a supplier can create a personalized company Web page as well as a "product showroom"; members also can post their own marketing leads (where to buy and sell). Alibaba.com also offers the TradeManager mobile app (**trademanager.alibaba.com**), which is their Instant Messaging tool. TradeManager can be used to chat with buyers in real time, get real-time translation, easily search for buyers and suppliers, and get the latest trade results. The TradeManager app is provided in multiple languages and at relatively low fees (the IM is free). For details, see Clark (2016) and **alibaba.com/help/features-trademanager.html**.

According to DYC Software Studio (**chat-translator.com**), DYC sells translation software called ChatTranslator for TradeManager, which is available in 40 languages. It can translate and send messages in any foreign language and translate replies from one language into the user's language. (For information about features and to purchase and download the software, see **chat-translator.com/products/chat-translator-trademanager.html** and **download.cnet.com/Chat-Translator-for-TradeManager/3000-20424_4-75212643.html**). To see the new features of TradeManager, see **trademanager.alibaba.com/features/introduction.htm**. To see more about the tools and features Alibaba offers to help buyers and sellers, see **alibaba.com/help/alibaba-features.html**. Note: A free translator is available at **facebook.com/FreeTranslator**.

The Competition

Many companies are attempting to rival Alibaba. For example, JD.com (**jd.com**; which merged with Tencent) is China's second largest e-commerce company. (It is used for both B2B and B2C.) **Trade.gov.cn/product.html** is a comprehensive e-commerce platform, used mainly to promote domestic and overseas trade, and Made-in-China.com (**made-in-china.com**), another world leading B2B portal, is another competitor. In the international market, companies such as TradeBanq (**tradebanq.com**), EC21 (**ec21.com**), Hubwoo (**hubwoo.com**), and Allactiontrade.com (**allactiontrade.com**) are all competing.

A recent development is conjecture that Alibaba may begin competing with Amazon and other B2C retailers on the United States. These rumors have spawned many interesting comparisons on the two companies (see **cnbc.com/2016/05/05/a-tale-of-two-companies-matching-up-alibaba-vs-amazon.html** and **qz.com/545687/alibaba-vs-amazon-how-the-worlds-two-online-shopping-giants-stack-up/**).

The Results

By 2016, Alibaba.com covered over 5200 product categories and had about 280 million registered, active buyers. The company conducts business in over 240 countries and regions, and it employs more than 35,000 people.

Sources: Based on Chen (2016), Erisman (2015), **crunchbase.com/organization/alibaba**, **buyer.alibaba.com**, and **seller.alibaba.com** (all accessed January 2017).

Note: For ten things to know about Jack Ma, see **mashable.com/2014/09/17/jack-ma/#JlbtV2i29PqC**.

LESSONS LEARNED FROM THE CASE

B2B e-commerce, which constitutes over 85% of all EC volume, is composed of different types of marketplaces and trading methods. The opening case illustrates a marketplace for many buyers and sellers to make transactions. The case presents the technology support provided for the B2B marketplace. In addition, the case describes information about support services (e.g., escrow services). The case illustrates the services provided for sellers (which are discussed in more detail in sections "B2B Marketing: Sell-Side E-Marketplaces" and "Selling via E-Auctions") and the services for buyers (described in sections "One-from-Many: E-Procurement at Buy-Side E-Marketplaces", "Reverse Auctions at Buy-Side E-Marketplaces (E-Tendering)", and "Other E-Procurement Methods"). The case also demonstrates the role of marketplaces (sections "B2B Exchanges (E-Marketplaces): Definitions and Concept" and "B2B in Web 2.0 and Social Networking"). All the major EC buying and selling B2B methods as well as types of B2B marketplaces and portals are described in this chapter. Finally, we relate B2B to social networking and other support services.

4.1   CONCEPTS, CHARACTERISTICS, AND MODELS OF B2B E-COMMERCE

B2B EC has some special characteristics as well as specific models, components, and concepts. The major ones are described next.

Basic B2B Concepts and Process

Business-to-business e-commerce (B2B EC), also known as *eB2B* (*electronic B2B*), or just B2B, refers to transactions between businesses conducted electronically over the Internet, extranets, intranets, or private networks. Such transactions may take place between a business and its supply chain partners, as well as between a business and a government and with any other business. In this context, a *business* refers to any organization, private, public, profit, or nonprofit. In B2B, companies aim to computerize trading transactions and communication and collaboration processes in order to increase efficiency and effectiveness. B2B EC is very different and more complex than B2C. It is much more difficult to sell to a company than to individuals. For a comprehensive discussion, see Wirthwein and Bannon (2014).

Key business drivers for electronic B2B (some of which were shown in the opening case) are the need to reduce cost, the need to gain competitive advantage, the availability of a secure Internet platform (i.e., the extranet), and the private and public B2B e-marketplaces. In addition, there is the need for collaboration between business partners, the need to reduce transaction time and delays along the supply chain, and the emergence of effective technologies for interactions and systems integration. Several large companies have developed efficient B2B buying and selling systems. An example is "Dell PremierConnect" that is illustrated in the video "Dell Enterprise Resource Planning (ERP) Procurement Systems" at youtube.com/watch?v=vGMHs6gj_1o.

For B2B statistics see Pick (2015) and **ecommerceandb2b.com/b2b-e-commerce-trends-statistics**.

The Basic Types of B2B Transactions and Activities

The number of sellers and buyers and the form of participation used in B2B determine the five basic B2B transaction activity types:

1. **Sell-side.** One seller to many buyers
2. **Buy-side.** One buyer from many sellers
3. **Marketplaces or exchanges.** Many sellers to many buyers
4. **Supply chain improvements**
5. **Collaborative commerce**

The last two categories include activities other than buying or selling inside organizations and among business partners. They include, for example, removing obstacles from the supply chain, communicating, collaborating, sharing information for joint design and planning, and so forth.

Figure 4.2 illustrates these five B2B types. A brief explanation follows.

Fig. 4.2 Five types of B2B e-commerce

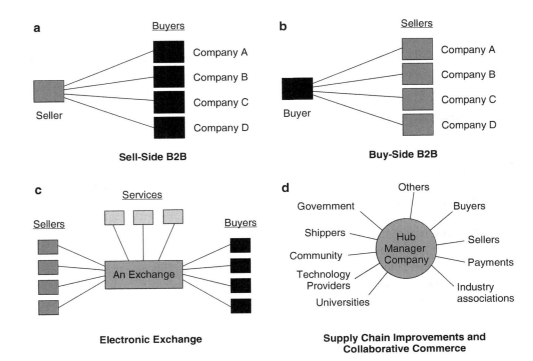

The Basic Types of B2B E-Marketplaces and Services

The following are the descriptions of the basic types of B2B e-marketplaces:

One-to-Many and Many-to-One: Private E-Marketplaces

In one-to-many and many-to-one markets, one company does either all the selling (*sell-side market*) or all the buying (*buy-side market*). Because EC is focused on a single company's buying or selling needs, this type of EC is also referred to as **company-centric EC**. Company-centric marketplaces—both sell-side and buy-side—are discussed in sections "B2B Marketing: Sell-Side E-Marketplaces", "Selling via E-Auctions", "One-from-Many: E-Procurement at Buy-Side E-Marketplaces", "Reverse Auctions at Buy-Side E-Marketplaces (E-Tendering)", and "Other E-Procurement Methods".

Many-to-Many: Public Exchanges (or E-Marketplaces)

In many-to-many e-marketplaces, many buyers and many sellers meet electronically to trade with one another. There are different types of such *e-marketplaces*, which are also known as **exchanges** (**trading communities** or **trading exchanges**). We will use the term *exchanges* in this book. Exchanges are usually marketplaces owned and run by a third party or by a consortium. They are described in more detail in section "B2B Exchanges (E-Marketplaces): Definitions and Concept". **Public e-marketplaces** are open to all interested parties (sellers and buyers). Alibaba.com is an example of an exchange.

Supply Chain Improvers and Collaborative Commerce

B2B transactions are conducted frequently along segments of the supply chain. Therefore, B2B initiatives need to be examined in light of other supply chain activities such as procurement of raw materials, fulfilling orders, shipments, and logistics. For example, Liz Claiborne, Inc. (retail fashion company) digitized its entire supply chain, reaping substantial results (see case study at **gxs.com/assets/uploads/pdfs/caseStudies/CS_L_Claiborne_GXS.pdf**). Many firms see supply-side improvements as a method to decrease costs and hopefully increase revenues. These actions can be helpful, but firms need to ensure that supply-side improvements will truly have the greatest impacts (see **sites.tcs.com/insights/perspectives/entrepreneurial-cio-supply-chain-management-setting-up-b2b**).

Collaboration

Businesses deal with other businesses for purposes beyond just selling or buying. One example is that of *collaborative commerce*, which includes communication, joint design, planning, and information sharing among business partners (see section "Collaborative Commerce").

Market Size and Content of B2B

The US Census Bureau estimates B2B online sales to be about 40% of the total B2B volume depending on the type (e.g., 49% in manufacturing). Chemicals, computer electronics, utilities, agriculture, shipping and warehousing, motor vehicles, petrochemicals, paper and office products, and food are the leading items in B2B. According to the authors' experience and several sources, the dollar value of B2B comprises at least 85% of the total transaction value of all e-commerce, and in some countries, it is over 90% for a total of about $20 trillion worldwide. Even with this volume of transactions, many believe that the B2B space is still maturing and that continued IT improvements will drive future growth (eMarketer 2016a), with total US sales in 2020 projected to be $1.1 trillion. For statistics, see Pick (2015) and Econsultancy (2017).

B2B EC is now in its sixth generation, as shown in Fig. 4.3. This generation includes collaboration with suppliers, buyers, government, and other business partners via extensive use of mobile computing; use of blogs, wikis, and other Web 2.0 tools; deployment of in-house social networks; use of public social networks such as LinkedIn and Facebook; and increased use of intelligent systems. In addition, the sixth generation is capitalizing on mobile computing, especially tablets and smartphones.

Many believe that the seventh generation of B2B will rely on technologies that are common to B2C. These include greater links with professional social networks and a larger reliance on mobile applications (Paradis 2016 and **contalog.com/blog/b2b-ecommerce-trends-2016**). These IT advancements will both help grow the demand side as well as streamlining the supply side of a company's operations. Greater availability and lower cost of other technologies that are dissimilar from B2C will also play a role. The use of RFID throughout the supply chain is an example (Parekh 2016).

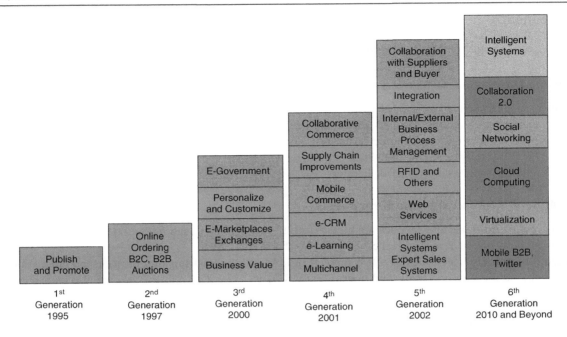

Fig. 4.3 Generations of B2B e-commerce

Fig. 4.4 The components
of B2B

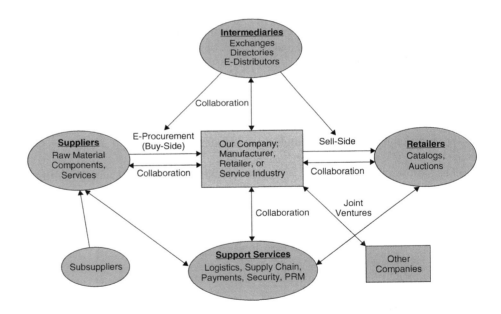

The B2B field is very diverse, depending on the industry, products and services transacted, volume, method used, and more. The diversity can be seen in Fig. 4.4 where we distinguish five major components: Our company, which may be the manufacturer, retailer, service provider, and so forth, is shown in the center. It has suppliers (on the left) and retailers (on the right). Our company operations are supported by different services (bottom), and we may work with several intermediaries (top of Fig. 4.4). The solid lines show the flow of information.

B2B Components

Next, we present various components of B2B commerce.

Parties to the Transaction: Sellers, Buyers, and Intermediaries

B2B commerce can be conducted *directly* between a *customer* and a *manufacturer* or it can be conducted via an *online intermediary*. An **online intermediary** is a third-party entity that serves as transaction broker between the buyer and seller; it can apply to either a virtual or click-and-mortar business. Some of the electronic intermediaries for individual consumers can also be used for B2B by replacing the individual consumers with business customers. Aggregations of buyers or sellers are typical B2B activities conducted by intermediaries.

Types of Materials Traded: What Do Firms Buy?

Two major types of materials and supplies are traded in B2B markets: *direct* and *indirect*. **Direct materials** are materials used in making products, such as steel in a car or paper in a book.

  Indirect materials are items, such as office supplies or light bulbs, which support operation and production. They normally are used in **maintenance, repair, and operation (MRO)** activities. Collectively, they are also known as *nonproduction materials*.

B2B Marketplaces and Platforms

B2B transactions are frequently conducted in marketplaces such as Alibaba.com. B2B marketplaces can be classified as *vertical* or *horizontal*. **Vertical marketplaces** are those for one particular industry or industry segment. Examples include marketplaces specializing in electronics, cars, hospital supplies, steel, or chemicals. **Horizontal marketplaces** are those in which trading is in a service or a product that is used in many types of industries. Examples are office supplies, cleaning materials, or paint. Alibaba.com is an example of a horizontal marketplace.

  The types of materials traded and the types of B2B transactions are used to define the B2B marketplaces. One way of classifying these markets is:

- *Strategic (systematic) sourcing* and indirect materials = MRO hubs (horizontal markets for MRO)
- Systematic sourcing and direct materials = vertical markets for direct materials
- *Spot buying* and indirect materials = horizontal markets for spot sourcing
- Spot sourcing and direct materials = vertical markets

The various characteristics of B2B transactions are presented in summary form in Table 4.1.

Table 4.1 Summary of B2B characteristics

Parties to transactions	Types of transactions
Direct, seller to buyer, or buyer to seller	Spot buying
Via intermediaries	Strategic sourcing
B2B 2C: A business sells to a business but delivers to individual consumers	
Types of materials sold	**Direction of trade**
Direct materials and supplies	Vertical
Indirect (MROs)	Horizontal
Number and form of participation	**Degree of openness**
One-to-many: sell-side (e-storefront)	Private exchanges, restricted
Many-to-one: buy-side	Private exchanges, restricted
Many-to-many: exchanges	Public exchanges, open to all
Many, connected: collaborative, supply chain	Private (usually), can be public

Online Service Industries in B2B

In addition to trading products between businesses, services also can be provided electronically in B2B. Just as service industries such as travel, banking, insurance, real estate, and stock trading can be conducted electronically for individuals, they also can be conducted electronically for businesses. The major B2B services are:

- **Travel and hospitality services.** Many large corporations arrange their travel electronically through corporate travel agents. For instance, American Express Global Business Travel offers several tools to help corporate travel managers plan and control their employees' travel. In addition to traditional scheduling and control tools, American Express offers the following EC-based tools: (**amexglobalbusinesstravel.com/total-program-management**):
- *TrackPoint* enables locating a traveler in real time.
- *Travel Alert* provides travel advisories and updates, such as weather conditions and delays.
- *Info Point* (**businesstravel.americanexpress.com/info-point**) is a website that includes detailed information about countries and cities around the world.
- *Meetings and Events* (**amexglobalbusinesstravel.com/meetings-and-events**) assists in managing meetings, including searching for venues.
- *American Express* has a presence on social networks (e.g., Facebook, Twitter, YouTube).
- *Egencia LLC* (**egencia.com/en**) (an Expedia company) partners with organizations to optimize the organizations' total travel activities by providing advice and travel management software. For details, see (**egencia.com/en/about-egencia**).
- Expedia (**expedia.com**), Travelocity (**travelocity.com**), Orbitz (**orbitz.com**), and other online travel services provide similar services for both B2C and B2B.
- **Real estate.** Commercial real estate transactions can be large and complex. Therefore, the Web might not be able to replace existing human agents completely. Instead, the Web can help businesses find the right properties, compare properties, and assist in negotiations. Some government-run foreclosed real estate auctions are open to dealers only and are conducted online.
- **Financial services.** Internet banking can be an efficient way of making business payments, transferring funds, or performing other financial transactions. For example, electronic funds transfer (EFT), which provides for electronic payments, is popular with businesses, as are electronic letters of credit. Transaction fees over the Internet are less costly than any other alternative method. Businesses can also purchase insurance online, from both pure online insurance companies and from click-and-mortar ones.
- **Banking and online financing.** Business loans can be solicited online from lenders. Because of the economic downturn, it is difficult for some business owners (even those with excellent credit scores) to obtain loans; therefore, they may turn to companies like Biz2Credit (**biz2credit.com**), a company that helps small businesses grow. Biz2Credit is an online credit marketplace that matches loan applicants with over 1200 lenders (see **biz2credit.com/about** and **cnbc.com/id/101009116**). Several sites, such as Garage Technology Ventures, LLC (**garage.com**), provide information about venture capital. Institutional investors use the Internet for certain trading activities.
- Recruiting and staffing services. Many companies provide services to businesses to assist them in finding full- and part-time employees. These services can be full service (see **kellyservices.us**) or can provide infrastructure and support to HR staff (see **icims.com**).
- **Other online services.** Consulting services, law firms, accounting firms, medical services, and others sell enterprise knowledge and special services online. Many other online services, such as the purchase of electronic stamps (similar to metered postage but generated on a computer), are available online (see **stamps.com**).

The Benefits and Limitations of B2B

The benefits of B2B are for buyers, sellers, or for both, and they depend on which model is used. In general, though, the major benefits of B2B (the beneficiaries are marked after each benefit: S = seller, B = buyer, J = joint) are that it:

- Creates new sales opportunities (S).
- Decreases the time and cost of managing customer accounts (S).
- Eliminates paper and reduces administrative costs (J).
- Expedites processing and reduces trading cycle time (J).
- Lowers search costs and time for buyers to find products and vendors (B).
- Increases productivity of employees dealing with buying and/or selling (J).
- Reduces errors and improves quality of service (J).
- Allows for enhanced customer service (J).
- Makes product configuration easier (B).
- Reduces marketing and sales costs (S).
- Reduces inventory levels and costs (J).
- Reduces purchasing costs by cutting down on use of intermediaries (B).
- Enables customized e-catalogs with different prices for different customers (J).
- Increases production flexibility, permitting on demand delivery (S).
- Reduces procurement costs (B).
- Facilitates customization via self-configuration (J).
- Provides for efficient customer service (B).
- Increases opportunities for collaboration (J).
- Data collected can help make operations more efficient (B).
- Web-based EC is more affordable than traditional EDI (J).
- Allows more business partners to be reached than with EDI (J).
- Reaches a more geographically dispersed customer base (S).
- Provides a better means of communication with other media (J).
- Provides 24/7 coverage of the shop front (J).
- Helps equalize small enterprises (B).

(For more details, see **ecommerceandb2b.com/3-benefits-of-b2b-e-commerce-may-not-considered**, **insitesoft.com/blog/10-benefits-of-b2b-e-commerce** and **thebalance.com/business-to-business-ecommerce-1141703**.)

B2B EC development has limitations as well, especially regarding channel conflict and the operation of public exchanges. Furthermore, personal face-to-face interactions may be needed but are unavailable. Some companies are attempting to offset the potential disadvantages of the lack of sales contact by using VOIP and video systems integrated into B2B CRMs (like **gotomeeting.com**). These interpersonal interactions have the ability to solidify long-term partnerships (see **cluteinstitute.com/ojs/index.php/IBER/article/view/3236**) as well as initial client meetings (Fullerton 2016).

Implementing e-B2B might eliminate the distributor or the retailer, which could be a benefit to the seller and the buyer (though not a benefit to the distributor or retailer). This phenomenon is referred to as *disintermediation*. The benefits and limitations of B2B depend on such variables as who buys what items and in what quantities, who are the suppliers, how often a company buys, and so forth.

SECTION 4.1 REVIEW QUESTIONS

1. Define B2B.
2. Discuss the following: spot buying versus strategic sourcing, direct materials versus indirect materials, and vertical markets versus horizontal markets.

3. What are company-centric marketplaces? Are they public or private?
4. Define B2B exchanges.
5. Relate the supply chain to B2B transactions.
6. List the benefits and limitations of B2B.
7. State two benefits to Whirlpool and their customers from the portal.

4.2 B2B MARKETING: SELL-SIDE E-MARKETPLACES

A major portion of B2B is selling in what is known as *B2B marketing*. *B2B marketing* refers to marketing by manufacturers and wholesalers along the sell-side of the supply chain. A variety of methods exist. For information, see the periodic reports from eMarketer, such as eMarketer (2016b).

Sell-Side Models

In the B2C model, a manufacturer or a retailer electronically sells directly to consumers from a *storefront* (or *webstore*). In a B2B **sell-side e-marketplace,** a business sells products and services to business customers electronically, frequently over an extranet. The seller can be a raw material producer selling to manufacturers or a manufacturer selling to an intermediary such as a wholesaler, a retailer, or an individual business. Intel (**intel.com**), Exxon (**exxon.com**), Cisco Systems, Inc. (**cisco.com**), and Dell (**dell.com**) are examples of such sellers. Alternatively, the seller can be a distributor selling to retailers or businesses (e.g., W.W. Grainger, Inc. (**grainger.com**). In either case, sell-side e-marketplaces involve one seller and many potential buyers. In this model, both individual consumers and business buyers might use either the same private sell-side marketplace (e.g., **dell.com**) or a public marketplace.

The one-to-many model has three major marketing methods: (1) selling from *electronic catalogs* with fixed prices, (2) selling via *forward auctions*, and (3) one-to-one selling, usually under a *negotiated* long-term contract. Such one-to-one negotiation is familiar: The buying company negotiates the price, quantity, payments, delivery, and quality terms with the selling company. We describe the first method in this section and the second method in section "Selling via E-Auctions".

For 33 case studies, see Petersen (2015).

B2B Sellers

Sellers in the sell-side marketplace may be click-and-mortar manufacturers or intermediaries (e.g., distributors or wholesalers). The intermediaries may even be pure online companies (e.g., Alibaba.com).

We now turn our attention to the most common sell-side method—selling online from a company's e-catalog.

Sales from Catalogs: Webstores

Companies can use the Internet to sell directly from their online catalog. A company might offer one catalog for all customers or a *customized catalog* for each large customer (possibly both). For example, Staples (**staples.com**), an office supply vendor, offers its business customers a personalized software catalog of about 100,000 products at different pricing schemes (see their ordering site at **order.staplesadvantage.com**).

Many companies use a multichannel marketing strategy where one channel is e-commerce.

In selling online to business buyers, manufacturers might encounter a similar problem to that of B2C sellers, namely, conflict with the regular distribution channels, including corporate dealers (channel conflict). To avoid conflicts, some companies advertise online but sell only in physical stores.

Examples

Amazon (**amazon.com**) is best known for its B2C sales, but the company is launching a large portal to target B2B customers. Amazon hopes to be able to tap into this large potential market while leveraging its existing technology and distribution infrastructure (Demery 2016a). Another example is NewEgg (**newegg.com** and **neweggbusiness.com**), which is historically known for provided technology products to individuals. This company is also targeting business users with a dedicated webstore and B2B services. They also hope to leverage existing system to enter the B2B marketplace (Demery 2016).

Distributors' Catalogs

Webstores are used by manufacturers (e.g., Gregg's Cycles) or by *distributors*. Distributors in B2B are similar to retailers in B2C. They can be general (like W.W. Grainger; see section "B2B Marketing: Sell-Side E-Marketplaces"), or they can concentrate on one area, much like Toys "R" Us (**toysrus.com**) in B2C.

Example

Stone Wheel (**stonewheel.com**) distributes over 100,000 different auto parts from 15 warehouses serving over 3500 independent repair shops in the Midwest region of the United States. They deliver within 30 min, using their own vehicles. Using the e-catalog, customers can order the exact part, saving time and minimizing misunderstandings and errors.

Self-Service Portals

Portals are used for several purposes, one of which is to enable business partners to conduct self-service, as is shown in the following example:

Example

Atomic Software (**atomicsoftware.com**) needed to create a responsive and engaging portal for its customers who were being provided with business automation services. It was important for customers to have quick access to self-help services and incident reporting and tracking.

To build this system, the company partnered with ServiceNow (**servicenow.com**) and used their platform to create a portal for customers. The resulting system included all the required customer facing system to manage the knowledge base and ticketing system. On the back end, the system integrated with Atomic's CRM to provide visibility of use and issues to both the sales team and customer support.

The resulting system allowed for easier communication with customers and a significant reduction to the time required to manage customer issues. Over 80% of help requests were addressed within the system, and the average time to resolution was decreased.

Based on **servicenow.com/content/dam/servicenow/documents/case-studies/cs_SN_Automic.pdf**.

Benefits and Limitations of Online Sales from Catalogs

Successful examples of the B2B online direct sales model include manufacturers, such as Dell, Intel, IBM, and Cisco, and distributors, such as Ingram Micro (**ingrammicro.com/IMD_WASWeb/jsp/login/corporate.jsp**) that sells to value-added retailers; the retailer adds some service along with the product. Sellers that use this model can be successful as long as they have a solid reputation in the market and a large enough group of loyal customers. Catalogs in B2B environments can often be customized to meet the needs of individual customers. This drives efficiency at the buy-side and may increase customer loyalty (see **rightoninteractive.com/customer-lifecycle-marketing/customize-and-personalize-b2b-buyer**).

While the benefits of direct online sales are similar to that of B2C, there are limitations also. One of the major issues facing direct sellers is finding buyers. Many companies know how to advertise using traditional channels but are still learning how to contact would-be business buyers online. (Note: This is where Alibaba.com and similar companies provide help.) In addition, B2B sellers may experience channel conflicts with their existing distribution systems. Another limitation is that if traditional electronic data interchange (EDI)—the computer-to-computer direct transfer of business documents—is used, the cost might be passed on to the customers, and they could become reluctant to go online. The solution to this problem is transferring documents over extranets and using an Internet-based EDI. Finally, the number of business partners online must be large enough to justify the system infrastructure and operation and maintenance expenses.

Comprehensive Sell-Side Systems

Sell-side systems must provide several essential functionalities that enable B2B vendors to execute sales efficiently, provide outstanding customer service, allow integration with existing IT systems, and provide integration with non-Internet sales systems. For an example of such a system provided by Sterling Commerce (an IBM Company), see **ibm.com/software/info/sterling-commerce**.

Selling Via Distributors and Other Intermediaries

Manufacturers can sell directly to other businesses, and they do so if the customers are large buyers. However, manufacturers frequently use intermediaries to distribute their products to a large number of smaller buyers. The intermediaries buy products from many other manufacturers and aggregate those products into one catalog from which they sell to customers or to retailers. Many of these distributors also are selling online via webstores.

Some well-known online distributors for businesses are Sam's Club (**samsclub.com**), Avnet (**avnet.com**), and W.W. Grainger (**grainger.com**). Many e-distributors sell in horizontal markets, meaning that they sell to businesses in a variety of industries. However, some distributors sell to businesses that specialize in one industry (vertical market), such as Boeing PART Page (see **boeing.com/assets/pdf/commercial/aviationservices/brochures/MaterialsOptimization.pdf**) or ChemNet (see **http://www.chemnet.com**). Most intermediaries sell at fixed prices; however, some offer quantity discounts and negotiated prices or conduct auctions.

SECTION 4.2 REVIEW QUESTIONS

1. What are buy-side and sell-side transactions? How do they differ?
2. List the types of sell-side B2B transaction models.
3. Describe customer service in B2B systems.
4. Describe the direct online B2B sales process from catalogs.
5. Discuss the benefits and limitations of direct online B2B sales from catalogs.
6. What are the advantages of using intermediaries in B2B sales?

4.3   SELLING VIA E-AUCTIONS

Auctions are gaining popularity both as B2B buying and as sales channels. Some major B2B auction issues are discussed in this section.

The Benefits of Auctions on the Sell Side

Many companies use *forward auctions* to liquidate their surplus products or capital assets. In such a situation, items are usually displayed on an auction site (private or public) for quick clearance. Forward auctions offer the following benefits to B2B sellers:

- **Revenue generation.** Forward auctions support and expand online and overall sales. Forward auctions also offer businesses a new venue to quickly and easily dispose of excess, obsolete, and returned products (e.g., see **liquidation.com**).
- **Cost savings.** In addition to generating new revenue, conducting e-auctions reduces the costs of selling the auctioned items, which helps increase the seller's profits.
- **Increased "stickiness."** Forward auctions give websites increased "stickiness," namely, potential buyers stay there longer. *Stickiness* is a characteristic that measures customer loyalty to a site that eventually results in higher revenue.
- **Member acquisition and retention.** Registered members of auctions can invite their business contacts. In addition, auction software aids enable sellers to search and report on virtually every relevant auction activity. Such information can be analyzed and used for business strategy.

Forward auctions can be conducted in two ways. A company can conduct its forward auctions from its own website or it can sell from an intermediary auction site, such as **liquidation.com**, **bstock.com**, and **ebay.com**. Let us examine these options.

Auctioning from the Company's Own Site

For large and well-known companies that frequently conduct auctions, it makes sense to build an auction mechanism on the company's own website. Why should a company pay a commission to an intermediary if the intermediary cannot provide the company with added value? Of course, if a company decides to auction from its own site, it will have to pay for infrastructure and operate and maintain the auction site. Note that, if the company already has an electronic marketplace for selling from e-catalogs, the additional cost for conducting auctions might not be too high.

Using Intermediaries in Auctions

Several intermediaries offer B2B auction sites (e.g., see **assetnation.com** and **liquidation.com**). Some companies specialize in government auctions, while others focus on surplus stock auctions (e.g., **govliquidation.com**). An intermediary can conduct private auctions either from the intermediary's or the seller's sites. Alternatively, a company can conduct auctions in a public marketplace, using an intermediary (e.g., eBay, which has a special "business exchange" for small companies).

Using an intermediary to conduct auctions has many benefits. The first is that no additional resources (e.g., hardware, bandwidth, engineering resources, or IT personnel) are required. There are no hiring costs for using corporate resources. B2B auction intermediary sites also offer fast time to market as they are capable of running the auction immediately. Without the intermediary, it can take weeks for a company to prepare an auction site in-house. Intermediaries may also be able to provide technical solutions that would be unavailable using in-house IT, such as mobile apps and logistics solution (see **bstock.com**).

Another benefit of using intermediaries relates to payments, which are handled by the intermediary.

For an example of using an intermediary in B2B auction services, see Liquidity Services Inc. (**liquidityservicesinc.com**).

For more about B2B online auctions, see **vasthouse.com/b2b-online-auctions.php** and **essexb2b.com**. For a directory of providers, see **wholesaledir.com/category/Auctions/1**.

Examples of B2B Forward Auctions

The following are examples of B2B auctions:

- Sam's Club (**samsclub.com**) auctions thousands of items (especially electronics) at Sam's Club Auctions (**auctions.samsclub.com**). Featured auctions include the current bid, the number of bids, and the open and close date. They liquidate overstock items, returns, and out-of-style goods.
- Yahoo! conducts both B2C and B2B auctions in Hong Kong, Taiwan, and Japan.

To learn more about B2B auctions, see **vasthouse.com**.

SECTION 4.3 REVIEW QUESTIONS

1. List the benefits of using B2B auctions for selling.
2. List the benefits of using auction intermediaries. What services can they provide?
3. What are the major purposes of forward auctions, and how are they conducted?
4. Comment on the number of bidders and bids using an online auction as compared to using an offline auction.

4.4 ONE-FROM-MANY: E-PROCUREMENT AT BUY-SIDE E-MARKETPLACES

The term *procurement* refers to the purchase of goods and services by organizations. Procurement is usually done by *purchasing agents*, also known as *corporate buyers*.

The buyer's purchasing department sometimes has to enter the order information manually into its own corporate information system. Furthermore, manually searching webstores and e-malls to find and compare suppliers and products can be slow and costly. As a solution, large buyers can open their own marketplaces called **buy-side e-marketplaces** and invite sellers to browse and offer to fulfill demand.

Inefficiencies in Traditional Procurement Management

Procurement management refers to the process of planning, organizing, and coordinating of all the activities pertaining to the purchasing of the goods and services needed by an organization. It involves the B2B purchase and sale of supplies and services, as well as the flow of required information. Approximately 80% of an organization's purchased items, mostly MROs (maintenance, repair, and operations items), constitute 20–25% of the total purchase value. In this case, much of the buyers' time is spent on clerical activities, such as entering data and correcting errors in paperwork (see **grainger.com/content/supplylink-mro-inventory-management**).

The procurement process may be lengthy and complex due to the many activities performed. The following are the major activities that may be included in a single purchase:

- *Search for items* using search engines, catalogs, virtual fairs and showrooms, and sellers' sales presentations.
- *Learn details of items and buying terms* using comparison engines and quality reports, and research industry report and vendors' information.
- *Negotiate or join group purchasing* using software support (if available).
- *Determine when and how much to order each time.* Authorize corporate buyers.
- *Join business-oriented social networks* such as **linkedin.com**.
- *Sign agreements or contracts* using e-contract management (e.g., from Ariba, Inc. **ariba.com**; a SAP company); arrange financing, escrow insurance, etc.
- *Create specific purchasing order(s)* using a computerized system.
- *Arrange packing, shipments, and deliveries* using electronic tracking, RFID, etc.
- *Arrange invoicing, payments, expense management, and purchasing budgetary control* using software packages (e.g., from **ariba.com**).

An example of the traditional procurement process that is often inefficient is shown in Fig. 4.5. For high-value items, purchasing personnel need to spend considerable time and effort on procurement activities. However, the purchasers may not have time to do a quality job since they are busy with the many items of small value such as MROs.

Other inefficiencies, ranging from delays in deliveries to the high cost of rush orders, also may occur in conventional procurement. This situation is called **maverick buying,** which occurs when a buyer makes unplanned purchases of items needed quickly, resulting in buying at non-pre-negotiated, and usually higher, prices.

To correct the situation(s) that may result from traditional procurement, companies must reengineer their procurement systems, implement new purchasing models, and, in particular, introduce e-procurement. Let us elaborate on the generic procurement methods first.

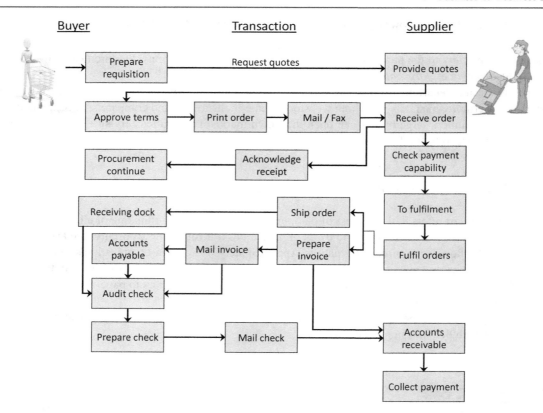

Fig. 4.5 Traditional (manual) procurement process

Procurement Methods

Companies use different methods to procure goods and services depending on factors such as what and where they buy, the quantities needed, and how much money is involved. Each method has its own process benefits and limitations. To minimize the inefficiencies described earlier, companies automate activities in the process. This is the major objective of e-procurement. Examples of companies utilizing efficient methods are Walmart (**walmart.com**), Dell (**dell.com**), and Starbucks (**starbucks.com**) to name a few. The major procurement methods include the following:

- Buy directly from the catalogs of manufacturers, wholesalers, or retailers, and possibly by negotiation (sections "B2B Marketing: Sell-Side E-Marketplaces" and "Selling via E-Auctions").
- Buy at private or public auction sites in which the buying organization is one of many (section "Reverse Auctions at Buy-Side E-Marketplaces (E-Tendering)").
- Conduct bidding in a reverse auction system where suppliers compete against each other. This method is used for high-value items or when large quantities are involved (section "Reverse Auctions at Buy-Side E-Marketplaces (E-Tendering)").
- Buy from the catalog of an intermediary (e-distributor) that aggregates sellers' catalogs (section "Other E-Procurement Methods").
- Buy from the company's own internal buyer catalog. Such catalogs usually include agreed-upon prices of items from many suppliers. This is part of *desktop purchasing*, which allows the users to bypass the procurement department (section "Other E-Procurement Methods").
- Join a group purchasing system that aggregates participants' demands, creating a large volume. Then the group may negotiate prices or initiate a tendering process (section "Other E-Procurement Methods").
- Buy at an exchange or industrial mall (section "B2B Exchanges (E-Marketplaces): Definitions and Concepts").

E-Procurement Concepts

E-procurement (electronic procurement) is the online purchase of supplies, materials, energy, work, and services. It can be done via the Internet or via a private network such as an electronic data exchange (EDI). For the different types of EDI and the trading community, see **edibasics.com/types-of-edi**.

Some activities done by e-procurement include enabling buyers to search for products and suppliers, comparing prices, facilitating reverse auctions for buyers, and automating paperwork and documentation.

Some of these activities are done in private marketplaces, others in public exchanges.

The Goals and Process of E-Procurement

As stated earlier, e-procurement frequently automates activities in the purchasing process from multiple suppliers via the Web for better execution and control.

Improvements to procurement have been attempted for decades, usually by using information technologies. Using e-procurement results in a major improvement. For comprehensive coverage and case studies, see **zdnet.com**.

Essentially, e-procurement automates the process of auctions, contract management, vendor selection, management, etc.

For an overview of e-procurement goals and processes, see **plenitude-solutions.com/index.php?option=com_content &view=article&id=54&Itemid=62**.

Example: Volvo's E-Procurement

Volvo is a premium Swedish car manufacturer (now owned by a Chinese company). The company operates in dozens of countries worldwide. The company has more than 30 purchasing centers on six continents. In the past, this has resulted in inconsistent purchasing practices, lack of collaboration among the centers, and inefficient and inconsistent procurement processes. To overcome the problems, management decided to use a unified e-procurement system. They selected Ariba's Sourcing and Ariba's Contract Management Solutions (Ariba is a B2B SAP company). The system assures standardization of the purchasing processes, sharing of best practices activities, and streamlining of the contracting process and its management. All these systems are digital. The e-procurement resulted in a greater cohesion among the sourcing centers, better use of best practices, and reduced cost of procurement while its effectiveness increases.

Example: Thermo Fisher Scientific E-Procurement

Thermo Fisher Scientific (**thermofisher.com**) is a distributor of materials and equipment for laboratories and scientific needs. In this market, purchasing is not generally a business focus, and it is possible for companies to drastically overpay without controls. Thermo Fisher Scientific attempts to assist laboratories with this issue by providing a suite of e-procurement tools and processes to make the sourcing of materials and equipment hassle-free. See more at **thermofisher.com/us/ en/home/products-and-services/eprocurement.html**.

Types of E-Procurement

Four major methods of e-procurement are available: (1) Buy at buyer's own website, (2) buy at sellers' store, (3) buy at exchanges, and (4) buy at others' e-market sites. Each method includes several activities, as illustrated in Fig. 4.6. Some of these will be described in section "B2B Exchanges (E-Marketplaces): Definitions and Concepts".

The seven main types of e-procurement are as follows: (1) e-sourcing, (2) e-tendering, (3) e-reverse auctioning, (4) e-informing, (5) Web-based ERP (enterprise resource planning), (6) e-market sites, and (7) E-MRO (maintenance, repair, and operating).

The Benefits and Limitations of E-Procurement

E-procurement has the ability of improving supply chain management and providing real-time information on what is going on in the supply chain (known as *visibility* of the supply chain), starting with the customers' needs.

Fig. 4.6 E-procurement
methods

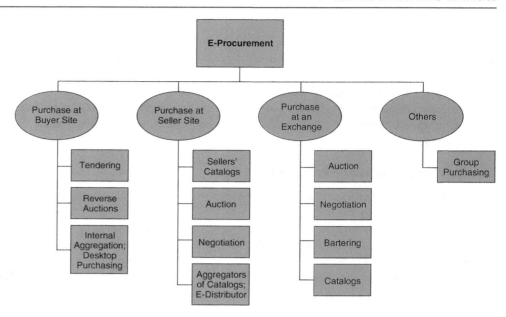

The Benefits of E-Procurement

By automating and streamlining the procurement process, corporate purchasing buyers can focus on more strategic activities that result in:

- Increasing the productivity of purchasing agents, providing them with more non-routine time and reducing job pressures, and possibly reducing purchasing departments' overhead
- Lowering purchase per item prices through activities such as product standardization, reverse auctions, volume discounts, and consolidation of purchases from fewer suppliers
- Improving information flow and its control (e.g., price comparisons)
- Reducing the frequency and cost of maverick buying
- Improving the payment process and sellers' savings due to expedited payment cycle
- Establishing more efficient and collaborative partner relations due to information sharing
- Improving the manufacturing process for the suppliers
- Ensuring on-time delivery and fewer stockouts
- Reducing the skill requirements and training needs of purchasing agents
- Reducing the number of suppliers
- Streamlining and expediting the purchasing process
- Controlling inventories more effectively at the buyers' end
- Streamlining invoice reconciliation and dispute resolution
- Reducing the administrative processing cost per order by as much as 90% by reducing purchasing overheads and intermediary fees
- Finding new suppliers that can provide goods and services faster and/or less expensively (e.g., by going global and use online price comparisons)
- Integrating budgetary controls into the procurement process (e.g., **ariba.com**)
- Minimizing human errors in the buying or shipping processes

For more on the benefits of e-procurement and on implementation issues, see **oxfordcollegeofprocurementandsupply. com/the-benefits-of-e-procurement** and the video titled "eProcurement Case Study: Oldcastle Materials" (3:16 min) at **youtube.com/watch?v=PPVC_CaG1S4**.

The Limitations and Challenges of E-Procurement

Unfortunately, e-procurement practices have some limitations and risks such as:

- The total cost (TCO) may be too high.
- It may be subject to hacker attacks.
- It may be difficult to get suppliers to cooperate electronically.
- The system may be too complex.
- It may be difficult to have internal and external integration (sometimes it involves different standards).
- The technology may change frequently.

For software issues, see **eprocurementsoftware.org**. For an example of how procurement is used in government, see NC E-Procurement (**eprocurement.nc.gov**). Governments frequently use reverse auctions for procurement, which we present next.

Procurement is an extremely important success factor for many companies. Therefore, it is important to learn about the future of e-procurement as well. For ideas about procurement, see Tradeshift (2015). To learn about Shoplet's platform for e-procurement, see Choi (2015) and **shoplet.com/about** or watch the video at youtube.com/watch?v=FyGsDYOqeSg.

SECTION 4.4 REVIEW QUESTIONS

1. Define the procurement process.
2. Describe the inefficiencies of traditional procurement.
3. List the major procurement methods.
4. Define e-procurement and list its goals.
5. List the major e-procurement methods, and list some activities in each.
6. List the major benefits of e-procurement.

4.5   REVERSE AUCTIONS AT BUY -SIDE E-MARKETPLACES (E-TENDERING)

A major method of e-procurement is using reverse auctions. A **reverse auction** is a process in which many sellers (suppliers) compete to fulfill orders requested by one buyer. Recall from our earlier discussion that a *reverse auction* is a tendering system where suppliers are invited to bid on the fulfillment of an order and the lowest bid wins. In B2B usage of a reverse auction, a buyer may open an e-market on its own server (or use an independent auctioneer such as eBay) and invite potential suppliers to bid on the items. This "invitation" to such reverse auctions is a form or document called a **request for quote (RFQ)**. Traditional tendering usually implies one-time sealed bidding, whereas an e-reverse auction opens the process to competing *sequential bidding*. For a comprehensive overview of reverse auctions, see **reverseauctions.com**, **epiqtech.com/reverse_auctions-Overview.htm**, and **reverseauctions.gsa.gov**.

Governments and large corporations frequently mandate reverse auctions, which may provide considerable savings because more suppliers are participating in a more competitive process. The electronic process is faster and administratively much less expensive. It also can benefit suppliers in finding RFQs. Reverse auctions are very important B2B mechanisms in e-procurement.

The Major Benefits of Reverse Auctions

The major benefits of the technology to a buyer are (a) lower cost of items purchased, (b) reduction of administrative costs of procurement, (c) reduction of corruption and bribes, and (d) decrease in time to receive the goods, which may result from the suppliers' ability to produce their products and services faster (see closing case).

Step I   Posting Bid Invitations

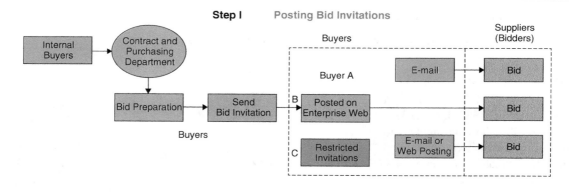

Step II   Evaluation of Bids by Buyer

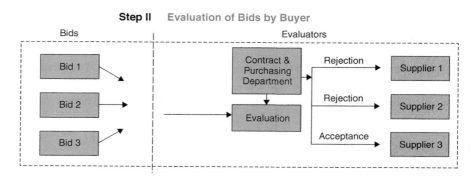

Fig. 4.7 The reverse auction process

For suppliers, as seen in the opening case, savings comes from a reduction in (a) time required to find customers, (b) administrative costs, and (c) time needed by managers to conduct manual bids.

Note that some question the value of reverse auctions (e.g., see Kelman 2015).

Conducting Reverse Auctions

As the number of reverse auction sites increases, suppliers may not be able to monitor all relevant open RFQs manually. This problem has been addressed with the introduction of online directories that list open RFQs. Another way to solve this problem is through the use of monitoring software agents. Software agents also can aid in the bidding process itself. Examples of agents that monitor and support the bidding process are **auctionsniper.com** and **auctionflex.com**.

Alternatively, third-party intermediaries may run the electronic bidding, as they do in forward auctions (e.g., see Opentext Corporation; **opentext.com**). Auction sites such as **ebay.com** and **liquidation.com** also belong to this category. Conducting reverse auctions in B2B can be a fairly complex process. This is why using an intermediary may be beneficial.

The reverse auction process is demonstrated in Fig. 4.7. As shown in the figure, the first step for the would-be buyer is to post bid invitations. When bids arrive, contract and purchasing personnel for the buyer evaluate the bids and decide which one(s) to accept.

CASE 4.1: EC APPLICATION
AMAZON ENTERS THE B2B MARKET

Amazon is well known for its industry-leading innovations in B2C e-commerce. These inventive strategies, along with investments in infrastructure, have allowed the company to be the number one online retailer in the United States. But while these operations have been successful, the company's attempts to work with business customers have been inconsistent.

The Problem

Amazon has historically been the market leader in business-to-consumer sales, but its business-to-business sales have lagged behind. The company hopes to remedy this situation with the expansion of its Amazon Business (**amazon.com/b2b/info/amazon-business**) B2B offering. In the past, the company has relied on its B2C capabilities to cross over into the B2B space. While this was somewhat effective, it did not provide the specific tools to meet the needs of mid- to large-sized businesses. Because of this, the company is only ranked 104 in the B2B top 300 (see **b2becommerceworld.com/b2b-ecommerce/#!/**).

The Solution

Amazon Business is a subset of Amazon.com targeted at business owners of all sizes. The service is meant to provide savings for business clients on commonly purchased items, frequently restocked items, and bulk purchases. Features within the site allow businesses to compare pricing options and offers from different vendors. For larger businesses, the system can be integrated into a variety of back-end purchase and fulfillment systems. This can include multiple accounts with different spending limits and purchase rules, purchasing cards, and detailed workflows with analytics. You can take a video tour of the service at **amazon.com/b2b/info/features**.

This offering from Amazon is meant to compete with other pure B2B office supply and equipment sellers, as well as more commonly known B2B/B2C companies such as Staples (**staples.com**), OfficeMax (**officemax.com**), or Office Depot (**officedeot.com**) (Lunden 2015).

While Amazon has historically been the market leader in business-to-consumer sales, its business-to-business sales have lagged behind. Amazon has high hopes for this new business unit and hopes to add over 100,000 jobs in the next 18 months to support its growth and development. The company is actively developing both processes and systems to support growth and better compete with more established B2B providers (Demery 2017).

The Results

The results of Amazon's experiment in B2B are yet to be seen. This new initiative appears to be a major focus in 2017. Many analysts believe that Amazon will be successful in this endeavor, because of its ability to leverage existing technologies in the B2C space, as well as having deep pockets for both marketing and systems development.

Questions

1. Why would Amazon want to expand into the B2B Market when it has been so successful in B2C e-commerce?
2. What challenges will Amazon face as it enters this new market with existing players?
3. What strengths does the company have from its B2C operations that it may be able to leverage in this new market?

E-Tendering by Governments

Most governments must conduct tendering when they buy or sell goods and services. Doing this manually is slow and expensive. Therefore, many governments are moving to e-reverse auctions for their purchasing.

Group Reverse Auctions

To increase their bargaining power and get price discounts, companies, like individuals, can buy in a group, and the group can use a reverse auction to get an even better deal than a quantity discount.

B2B reverse auctions can be done in a private exchange or at an aggregator's site for a group of buying companies. Such *group reverse auctions* are popular in South Korea and usually involve large conglomerates. For example, the LG Group operates the LG MRO Auction for its member companies, and Samsung Group operates the Samsung iMarketKorea (**imarketkorea.com**), which provides procurement services and MRO goods. Samsung's iMarketKorea's revenue comes primarily from B2B transactions. This practice is popular in the healthcare industry in the United Kingdom, the United States, and other countries where hospitals are banding together to buy their supplies at a quantity-discounted low price.

SECTION 4.5 REVIEW QUESTIONS

1. Describe the manual tendering system and its deficiencies.
2. How do online reverse auctions work?
3. List the benefits of Web-based reverse auctions.
4. Describe group reverse auctions.

4.6   OTHER E-PROCUREMENT METHODS

Other innovative e-procurement methods have been implemented by companies. Some common ones are described in this section.

Desktop Purchasing

Desktop purchasing refers to purchasing by employees without the approval of supervisors and without the involvement of a procurement department. This usually is done by using a *purchasing card (P-card)*. Desktop purchasing reduces the administrative cost and the cycle time involved in purchasing urgently needed or frequently purchased items of small dollar value. This approach is especially effective for MRO purchases.

The desktop purchasing approach can be implemented by collaborating with external private exchanges. For instance, Samsung Electronics of South Korea, a huge global manufacturer, and its subsidiaries have integrated its iMarketKorea (**imarketkorea.com**) exchange with the e-procurement systems of its buying agents. This platform can also be linked easily with *group purchasing*, which is described next.

Group Purchasing

Many companies, especially small ones, are moving to *group purchasing*. With **group purchasing,** orders from several buyers are aggregated so that better prices due to larger quantities purchased can be negotiated. This model is similar to the one we described for B2C. For B2B group purchasing in China, see Young (2015). Two sub-models are in use: internal aggregation and external (third-party) aggregation.

Internal Aggregation of Purchasing Orders

Large companies, such as GE, spend many millions of dollars on MROs every year. These companies aggregate the orders from their subsidiaries and various departments (sometimes there are hundreds of them) for quantity discounts. They can cut administrative costs by 20%.

External Aggregation for Group Purchasing

Many SMEs would like to enjoy quantity discounts but have difficulty finding others to join a group purchasing organization to increase the procurement volume. Finding partners can be accomplished by an external third party such as BuyerZone (**buyerzone.com**), the Healthcare Supply Chain Association (**supplychainassociation.org**), or the United Sourcing Alliance (**usa-llc.com**). The idea is to provide SMEs with better prices, larger selections, and improved services by aggregating demand online and then either negotiating with suppliers or conducting reverse auctions. The external aggregation/group purchasing process is shown in Fig. 4.8.

Several large companies, including large CPA firms and software companies such as EDS Technologies (**edstechnologies.com**) and Ariba, Inc. (**ariba.com**), provide external aggregation services, mainly to their regular customers. Yahoo! also offers such services. A key to the success of these companies is a critical mass of buyers.

Example

The larger the group, the better the deals. Many companies may be too small to gain access to a group purchasing contract or may not gain the leverage they desire. To assist with this issue, many will join purchasing groups like PRIMEAdvantage (**primeadvantage.com**). This group, designed primarily for manufacturers, helps businesses to leverage the larger group to secure volume price discounts.

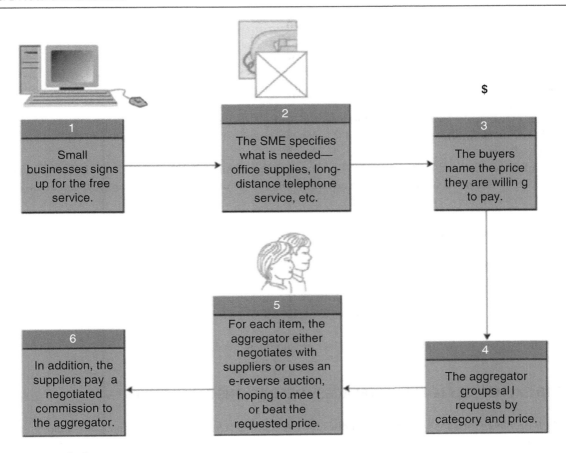

Fig. 4.8 The group purchasing process

Buying from Other Sources

Section "B2B Marketing: Sell-Side E-Marketplaces" described how companies use e-distributors as sales channels. When buying small quantities, purchasers often buy from an e-distributor. Another option for e-procurement is to buy at a B2B exchange using one of several available methods. In all of these options, one may automate some actions in the process, such as the generation of a purchasing order (e.g., see **esker.com** and **ariba.com**).

Acquisition Via Electronic Bartering

Bartering is the exchange of goods or services without the use of money. The basic idea is for a company to exchange its surplus for something that it needs. Companies can advertise their surpluses in classified ads and may find a partner to make an exchange, but in many cases, a company will have little success in finding an exact match on its own. Therefore, companies usually ask an intermediary to help.

A bartering intermediary can use a manual search-and-match approach, or it can create an electronic bartering exchange. With a **bartering exchange,** a company submits its surplus to the exchange and receives points of credit, which the company can then use to buy items that it needs. Popular bartering items are office spaces, idle facilities and labor, products, and even banner ads. For examples of bartering companies, see U-Exchange (**u-exchange.com**), B2B Barter (**b2bbarter.trade**), and Itex (**itex.com**). For a video on how B2B bartering works in the First Canadian Barter Exchange, see the video "How to use barter in your business" at youtube.com/watch?v=z417imNLIho.

Selecting an Appropriate E-Procurement Solution

Having many procurement methods, consultants, and software makes the selection of the right method(s) difficult. Ariba, Inc. (**ariba.com**) provides an innovative score sheet that companies use to evaluate vendors based on the described success factors. The success factors are grouped by cost reduction, increased agility, managing complete commerce, and fulfilling tactical requirements.

When organizations make such decisions, these decisions may be influenced by factors such as: Who is buying? What are you buying? How much information do you need to make the decisions? What is the reputation of the vendor(s)? What testimonials are available?

For more information download the e-book "The State of eProcurement in 2015: 22 World-class Procurement Leaders Rate Today's eProcurement Technology" from **tradeshift.com/confirmation/the-state-of-eprocurement-in-2015**.

SECTION 4.6 REVIEW QUESTIONS

1. Describe a buyer-operated procurement marketplace and list its benefits.
2. Describe the benefits of desktop purchasing.
3. Discuss the relationship of desktop purchasing with group purchasing.
4. Explain the logic of group purchasing and how it is organized.
5. How does B2B bartering work?
6. What are the major considerations for selecting an e-procurement vendor and solution?

4.7   B2B EXCHANGES (E-MARKETPLACES): DEFINITIONS AND CONCEPTS

The term *B2B exchange*, or simply *exchange*, implies the existence of a marketplace with many potential buyers and many potential sellers. In addition to being online trading venues, many exchanges provide support services such as payments and logistics software and consulting services. They also act as industry portals.

Exchanges are known by a variety of names: *e-marketplaces*, *trading exchanges*, *trading communities*, *exchange hubs*, *Internet exchanges*, *Net marketplaces*, and *B2B portals*. We will use the term *exchange* in this book to describe the general many-to-many e-marketplaces, but we will use some of the other terms in more specific contexts (e.g., see **epiqtech.com/others-B2B-Exchanges.htm**).

Despite their variety, all exchanges share one major characteristic: Exchanges are electronic trading community meeting places for many sellers and many buyers and possibly for other business partners, as shown in Fig. 4.9. At the center of every exchange, there is a market maker that operates the exchange and, in some cases, may also own it.

Exchanges can be horizontal, serving many industries (e.g., **ariba.com** or **alibaba.com**), or vertical, serving one or a few connected industries (e.g., see **supplyon.com** for automotive and **oceanconnect.com** for refineries and shipping services). In an exchange, just as in a traditional open-air marketplace, buyers and sellers can interact and negotiate prices, quantities, and other terms.

Global Exchanges

Most large exchanges, such as Alibaba and Amazon Business, operate in many countries. Such activities require special arrangement such as dealing with country regulations, money transfers, language translation, and more.

Functions of and Services Provided by Exchanges

Exchanges have the following four major sets of functions: (1) matching and connecting buyers and sellers, (2) facilitating transactions, (3) developing and maintaining exchange policies and infrastructure, and (4) providing services to buyers and sellers. Details of these functions are provided next.

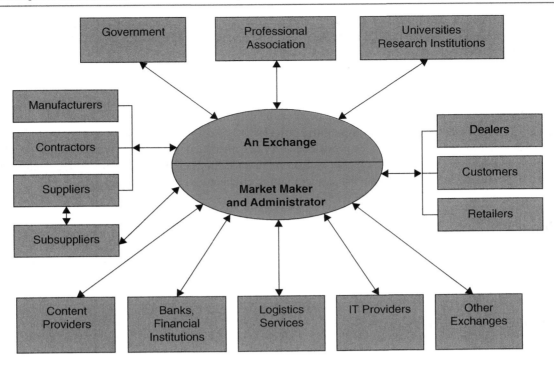

Fig. 4.9 The community of an exchange: flow and access to information

Functions and Services of B2B Exchanges

The following are the major functions of B2B exchanges (compiled from Demery 2015, E-Commerce Wiki 2015 and the authors' experiences):

1. Matching buyers and sellers. The matching of buyers and sellers includes such activities as:

   - Presentation of product offering (e.g., the company's catalogs)
   - Aggregating and posting different products for sale—to meet buyers' need
   - Providing price comparisons
   - Organizing bids (bartering) and (auctions)
   - Providing sellers' profiles and product information
   - Matching suppliers' offerings with buyers' requests
   - Supporting negotiations between buyers and sellers
   - Providing directories of sellers
   - Maintaining security, privacy, and anonymity

2. Facilitating transactions. Facilitating transactions by optimizing the purchasing and sales processes, including the following activities:

   - Allowing for efficient trading between participants
   - Providing for B2B auctions
   - Providing the trading platform with mechanisms such as arranging payment, insurance, order fulfillment, and security
   - Providing escrow services
   - Arranging for group (volume) purchasing and other discounts
   - Defining terms and other transaction values, including negotiation
   - Inputting searchable information, including industry news

- "Grant[ing] exchange access to users and identify[ing] company users eligible to use exchange"
- Collecting transaction fees and providing the necessary software and its integration with buyers and/or sellers systems, including EDI, XML, etc.
- Providing analysis and statistics of products' transactions
- "Registering and qualifying buyers and suppliers"

The types of services provided by an exchange depend on the nature of the exchange. For example, the services provided by a stock exchange are completely different from those provided by a steel or food exchange or by an intellectual property or patent exchange. However, most exchanges provide the services illustrated above. Note that, some B2B exchanges may have individuals as either sellers or buyers, in addition to corporations. An example is **localdirt.com**, an online marketplace that connects thousands of farmers with many buyers, promoting efficient trading of local produce.

Ownership of B2B Exchanges

Exchanges, portals, and directories are usually owned by a third-party operator. Both sellers and buyers prefer such an arrangement. Alternatively, exchanges may be owned by a few very large sellers or buyers. This kind of arrangement is referred to as a *consortium*.

Third-Party Independent Exchanges

Third-party exchanges are electronic intermediaries. The intermediary not only presents catalogs but also tries to *match* buyers and sellers and encourages them to make transactions by providing electronic trading tools and rooms.

Example 1: Intercontinental Exchange Group (ICE)

Intercontinental Exchange (**theice.com**) is an Internet-based global network of B2B exchanges (11 regulated exchanges, 12,000 listed contracts and securities, $9.3 million in daily trade volume (2016 data)) that operates marketplaces that trade commodity contracts and over-the-counter (OTC) energy and commodity features as well as related financial products. While the company's original focus was energy products, recent acquisitions have expanded its activity into "soft" commodities (grains, sugar, cotton, and coffee), foreign exchange, and equity index features. For details, see **intercontinentalexchange.com/about**.

ICE is linked electronically to all its customers (members). Trading is global and is done 24/7. Currently, ICE is organized into three business lines:

- **ICE Markets.** Futures, options, and OTC markets. Energy futures are traded via ICE Futures Europe; soft commodity futures/options are handled by ICE Futures in the United States.
- **ICE Services.** Electronic trade confirmations and education.
- **ICE Data.** Electronic delivery of market data, including real-time trades, historical prices, and daily indices.

ICE offers market participants a range of trading and risk management services globally:

1. Benchmark futures contracts
2. Risk management via a global central counterparty clearinghouse
3. Integrated access to global derivative markets
4. Leading electronic trading platform
5. Transparency and regulation
6. Independence governance

Intercontinental Exchange owns several pioneering exchanges such as ChemConnect.

For a list of exchanges all over the world, see **internetworldstats.com/links2.htm**.

Example 3: Solarexchange.com

SolarExchange.com is a global *solar marketplace* facilitating B2B online *auctions* for solar-related materials and finished goods. This exchange is a global community where suppliers collaborate with buyers from anywhere in the world.

According to the company, their service portfolio "spans the solar supply chain, delivering procurement management, risk management, online auctions, price indexes, human resource sourcing, and a knowledge base serving the solar industry."

The major benefits, according to the company, are:

- Connect with the global solar trading community.
- Reduce costs by automating solar procurement and sale activities.
- React rapidly to changing market conditions for greater competitive advantage.
- Extend your market reach through access to new trading partners and suppliers.
- Accelerate sales cycles and minimize inventory risk.
- Lower operating costs and improve margins.
- Promote your brand to increase awareness and drive commerce activities.
- Source global talent.

(see **solarexchange.com/solarxpages/StaticAboutUs.aspx**).

For how this exchange works and the bidding process, see **solarexchange.com/solarxpages/StaticGetStarted.aspx** and **solarexchange.com/solarxpages/StaticBiddingProcess.aspx**.

Consortium Trading Exchanges (CTE)

A **consortium trading exchange (CTE)** is an exchange formed and operated by a group of major companies in one industry. They can be suppliers, buyers, or both. The major declared goal of CTEs (also called consortia) is to provide services that support trading activities. These services include links to the participants' back-end processing systems as well as collaborative planning and design services. Examples of consortia exchanges are **avendra.com** in the hospitality industry and OceanConnect **oceanconnect.com** in the shipping industry.

Note that some consortia have hundreds of members in the same industry.

Dynamic Pricing in B2B Exchanges

The market makers in both vertical and horizontal exchanges match supply and demand in their exchanges, and this matching determines prices, which are usually *dynamic* and are based on changes in supply and demand. **Dynamic pricing** refers to the rapid movement of prices over time and possibly across customers. Stock exchanges are a prime example of dynamic pricing. Another good example of dynamic pricing occurs in auctions, where prices vary all the time.

The typical process that results in dynamic pricing in most exchanges includes the following steps:

1. A company posts a bid to buy a product or an offer to sell one.
2. An auction (forward or reverse) is activated.
3. Buyers and sellers can see the consecutive bids and offers but usually do not see who is making them. Anonymity often is a key ingredient of dynamic pricing (e.g., in stock markets).
4. Buyers and sellers interact with bids and offers in real time.
5. Sometimes buyers join together to obtain a volume discount price (group purchasing).
6. A deal is struck when there is an exact match between a buyer and a seller on price, volume, delivery date, and other variables, such as location or quality.
7. The deal is finalized, and payment and delivery are arranged.

Advantages, Limitations, and the Revenue Model of Exchanges

Exchanges have several benefits, for buyers and sellers, including making markets more efficient, providing opportunities for sellers and buyers to find new business partners, reducing the administrative costs of ordering MROs, and expediting trading processes. They also facilitate global trade and create communities of informed buyers and sellers.

Table 4.2 Potential gains and risks in B2B exchanges

	For buyers	For sellers
Potential gains	One-stop shopping, huge	New sales channel
	Search and comparison shopping	No physical store is needed
	Volume discounts	Reduced ordering errors
	24/7 ordering from any location	Sell 24/7
	Make one order from several suppliers	Community participation
	Huge, detailed information	Reach new customers spending only little cost
	Access to new suppliers	Promote the business via the exchange
	Status review and easy reordering	An outlet for surplus inventory
	Community participation	Can go global more easily
	Fast delivery	Efficient inventory management
	Less maverick buying	Better partner relationship management
	Better partner relationship management	Loss of direct CRM and PRM
Potential risks	Unknown vendors; may not be reliable	More price wars
	Loss of customer service quality (inability to compare all services)	Competition for value-added services
		Must pay transaction fees; possible loss of customers to competitors

Despite these benefits, beginning in 2000, exchanges started to collapse, and both buyers and sellers realized that they faced the risks of exchange failure or deterioration. The potential benefits and risks of B2B exchanges for buyers and for sellers are summarized in Table 4.2. As the table shows, the benefits outnumber the risks.

Revenue Models

Exchanges, like all organizations, require revenue to survive. Therefore, an exchange's owners, whoever they are, must decide how they will earn revenue. They include transaction fees, membership fees, service fees, advertising fees, and auction fees (paid by the sellers and/or buyers). In addition, for a fee, exchanges offer software, computer services, management consultation, and so forth.

Note: For many new B2B e-marketplaces, see Demery (2015).

SECTION 4.7 REVIEW QUESTIONS

1. Define B2B exchanges and list the various types of exchanges.
2. List the major functions of exchanges and the services they provide.
3. What is dynamic pricing? How does it work?
4. List the potential advantages, gains, limitations, and risks of exchanges to buyers.
5. List the major advantages and limitations to sellers.
6. List the major ownership types in B2B exchanges.
7. Define consortium trading exchanges.

4.8 B2B IN WEB 2.0 AND SOCIAL NETWORKING

Although a large number of companies conduct social networking activities that target individual consumers (B2C), there also is increasing activity in the B2B arena. However, the potential in B2B is large, and new applications are added daily. The opportunities of B2B social networking depends on the companies' goals and the perceived benefits and risks involved (for more information, see **adage.com/article/btob/social-media-increasingly-important-b-b-marketers/291033**).

E-Communities in B2B

B2B applications may involve many participants: buyers and sellers, service providers, industry associations, and others. In such cases, the B2B market maker needs to provide community services, such as chat rooms, bulletin boards, and possibly personalized Web pages.

E-communities connect employees, partners, customers, and any combination of the three. E-communities offer a powerful resource for e-businesses to leverage online discussions and interactions in order to maximize innovation and responsiveness. It is therefore beneficial to study the tools, methods, and best practices of building and managing B2B e-communities. Although the technological support of B2B e-communities is basically the same as for any other online community, the nature of the community itself and the information provided by the community are different. For a list of B2B communities, see DiMauro (2016).

B2B e-communities are mostly communities of transactions, and, as such, members' major interests are trading and business-related information gathering. Many of the communities are associated with vertical exchanges; therefore, their needs may be specific. Communities also support partner-to-partner collaboration and networking. For example, see **partners. salesforce.com** for partnership software. However, it is common to find generic services such as classified ads, job vacancies, announcements, industry news, and so on. For B2B social communities, see Burt (2017). Communities promote collaboration. The newest variation of these communities is the business-oriented or professional social network such as **linkedin.com**.

The Opportunities of Social Commerce in B2B

Companies that use B2B social networking may experience the following advantages:

- Use the network to advertise to large audiences and create brand awareness.
- Discover new business partners and sales prospects.
- Enhance their ability to learn about new technologies, competitors, customers and the business environment.
- Generate sales leads via "contacts," especially on **linkedin.com**, and by tweeting (**twitter.com**) or engaging on **facebook.com** (see Templeman (2015).
- Post questions and facilitate discussions on **linkedin.com** by searching the "Help Center," asking the community a question through the "Help Forum," or by using the posting module on your homepage to ask your network a question. Post questions on the question and answer forums on other social networks.
- Improve participation in industry association activities (including lobbying).
- Create buzz about upcoming product releases.
- Drive traffic to their Facebook page and other social sites and engage visitors there (e.g., provide games, prizes, competitions, etc.). Word of mouth also may increase traffic.
- Create social communities to encourage discussions among business partners (e.g., customers and suppliers) about their products.
- Use social networks, such as **facebook.com** and **linkedin.com** to recruit new talent.

For more opportunities using **linkedin.com**, see Tepper (2015).

More uses of B2B social networking are seen in *enterprise social networks,* which are private social networks within enterprises.

The Use of Web 2.0 Tools in B2B

Many companies are using blogs, microblogs, wikis, RSS feeds, video ads, podcasts, and other tools in B2B EC. For example, Eastern Mountain Sports (**ems.com**) uses blogs (**blog.emsoutdoors.com**), RSS feeds, and wikis to communicate and collaborate with their suppliers and distributors. Thousands of other companies are using (or experimenting with) these tools. For a study on using YouTube for B2B, see **scgpr.com/41-stories/youtube-for-b2b-marketers**; and on using Twitter, see Tepper (2015). For comprehensive coverage, see Zhukova (2017). For case studies, see Ueland (2015).

Example

GoToMeeting (**gotomeeting.com**) provides users with a diverse suite of Web conferencing tools. While the service is targeted at both individuals and businesses, the company has developed a number of features and pricing models to attract business users. The company determined that one factor that may affect adoption is a lack of understanding of the product's abilities and uses. To help address this issue, the company has produced a number of short use cases and highlighted them on the social media image-sharing site Instagram (**Instagram.com**). Pictures highlight not only the product features but ways that clients have leveraged the technology to create benefits that could be emulated by others. (For more information, see **clickz.com/10-b2b-brands-that-are-killing-it-on-social-media/24243/**.)

B2B Games (Gamification)

Virtual games, or **gamification**, refer to virtual games designed to support B2B training and decision-making. Players compete against each other and make market predictions. For details, see Petersen (2015).

Virtual Trade Shows and Trade Fairs

Virtual trade shows and fairs are gaining popularity. They are primarily B2B oriented.

Virtual trade shows are an application of virtual worlds. A **virtual trade show**, also known as a *virtual trade fair*, is the online analogy of a physical trade show. These are temporary or permanent showplaces where exhibitors present their new products to potential customers.

For a large number of screenshots of virtual trade show, conduct a Google search for "Virtual Trade Show."

Example: MarketPlace365

MarketPlace365 (marketplace365.com/Marketing/about.aspx) is a vendor that gives companies tools to build virtual trade shows and attract traffic to the shows. For details, see **marketplace365.com/Marketing/faq.aspx** and **marketplace365.com/Marketing/features.aspx**.

Note: Social media can be used to support exhibits even in physical trade shows. For more on using social media at trade shows, see Carter (2015), and download his free "Social Media Tradeshow Marketing Checklist" at **tradeshowguyblog.com/downloads/Social-Media-Tradeshow-Marketing-Checklist.pdf**.

Social Networking in B2B

Businesses can use B2B social networking to improve knowledge sharing, collaboration, and feedback. Furthermore, social networking sites may also prove beneficial in aiding troubleshooting and problem-solving efforts. Companies (especially small ones) are using social networks and Yahoo! Answers (**answers.yahoo.com**) and specialized groups within LinkedIn, for example, for problem solving. B2B participants need to look into social networking as part of their overall EC strategy; otherwise, they may miss an opportunity to reach the B2B audience and differentiate themselves from the competition.

In 2017, social networking is playing a much more important role in B2B. Both small and large businesses are using social networks quite successfully to find and retain new business. Other applications include:

- Several companies globally use social networks for various networking functions.
- Some businesses have found new customers via social networks.
- Some companies include social networking activity to both acquire and retain customers in the marketing budget.

The main uses of social networks are keeping in contact with business contacts, meeting with special interest groups, learning useful business intelligence, and organizing, managing, and connecting with customer groups.

Social media use among B2B marketers is already very high. However, many do not calculate the return on investment for social media. In 2013, Twitter and LinkedIn were the most used social networks in B2B. By 2016 LinkedIn and Facebook were at the top.

Using Twitter in B2B

Twitter is used extensively in B2C mainly as a communication tool for customer service advertising campaigns, customer engagement platforms, CRM, and market research. Similar uses are evidenced in B2B. The applications include the monitoring of conversations for identifying business opportunities, enabling small businesses to engage with potential customers, making contacts with potential customers, and customers discovering potential suppliers.

Examples of Other Activities of B2B Social Networks

The following are examples of some social networking-oriented B2B activities:

- **Location-based services.** These may provide opportunities for B2B.
- **Corporate profiles on social networks.** LinkedIn and Facebook include substantial information on companies and their individual employees. In fact, employee profiles can be part of a company's brand. For example, as early as 2016, IBM had over 350,000 employees registered on LinkedIn; Microsoft had approximately 200,000 as of late 2016. In addition, some sites feature company profiles, with comments by employees and customers.

Success Stories

It is important to use social tools correctly depending on the business setting. B2C applications may not be effective in a B2B market and may actually be harmful. Ben Green Oktopost details the appropriate networks and approaches for both B2C and B2B applications with a concentration successful B2B examples. Read the guide at **oktopost.com/blog/differences-b2c-and-b2b-social-media-marketing**.

For additional case studies, read True Influence's report titled "Top B2B Social Media Case Studies for 2016" at **trueinfluence.com/blog/b2b-social-media-case-studies-for-2016**.

The Future of B2B Social Networking

Marketing users are developing social media and search tools. Products such as Google's OpenSocial may increase interest in social networking.

Businesses must embrace social networking in order to better understand their customers and business partners.

Convergence of B2B, B2C, and Social Networking

The lines between B2C and B2B e-commerce may not have always been distinct, but the growth of new technologies and social networking continues to blur them. Many experts believe that there will be a convergence between these once semi-distinct business areas in the near future. Many of the technologies and practices that are used in one area are also beneficial to the other two. Leveraging organizational capacities across all different distribution networks and marketing methods will be a defining characteristic of successful businesses. Advances in marketing and social networking have great applicability to B2B models. Better understanding of logistics and ongoing CRM functions can be applied to B2C customers. Synchronizing these demands represents an important internal capacity for companies with multiple market outlets.

In a recent Aberdeen Group report, the authors (Heaney and Ball 2014) contend that understanding of these different systems and the ability to apply those learnings across markets will help define successful companies in the next decade (see Heaney and Ball 2014 and **oracle.com/us/products/applications/aberdeen-b2b-commerce-convergence-2431539.pdf**). For a video explaining how e-commerce systems from IBM can bridge this gap, see youtube.com/watch?v=ojfNgP0eyLc.

CASE 4.2: EC APPLICATION: E-PROCUREMENT IN HEALTHCARE

Procurement management systems can play a vital role in helping many businesses control discretionary spending and overall expenses within the organization. However, many early e-procurement systems lacked the functionality and ease of use necessary to drive adoption and utilization within an organization. Researchers have identified that procurement systems that focus on easy-to-use interfaces and social aspects, similar to B2C e-commerce systems, will have the greatest impact within organizations because of the ease of adoption as well as compliance by employees (Traxpay 2015). The same report outlined the huge potential impact of B2B purchasing and overall procurement management in the US marketplace. It has found:

- 68% of B2B buyers now purchase goods online.
- 18% of B2B buyers spend more than 90% of their budget online (doubling from 9% in 2013).
- 30% of B2B buyers research at least 90% of products online before making a purchase.
- 44% of B2B buyers research company products on a smartphone or tablet.

Others have identified key features and philosophies behind next-generation e-procurement systems and the convergence of B2C models that will be adopted by forward-thinking businesses. This feature set includes social network integration, ease-of-use and configuration, ease of search, automatic replenishment, and robust desktop and mobile clients (Sourcing 2015).

The Problem

This type of spending issues can be particularly important in healthcare organizations, where expenses can be highly variable and organizations may be distributed geographically. An excellent example of this type of dilemma was faced by Avalon Health Care (**avalonhealthcare.com**). This company provides long-term care, skilled nursing rehabilitation, and memory care services in the Western United States. Their greatest issue was managing overall spend within the organization. They identified that over 60% of those expenses were not actively controlled within the system.

The Solution

To help them eliminate this problem, they worked with Coupa Software (**coupa.com**). Coupa is a provider of diverse and integrated spend management systems that rely on a distributed, cloud-based architecture. These systems cover the entirety of spend management, with solutions for the end user all the way to sourcing and analytics for administrators (see solution details at **coupa.com/solutions/business-need** and a video demonstration at youtube.com/watch?v=rbrQNDm9wQY).

The Results

Avalon implemented the Coupa spend management system and has seen significant positive results. The software has been an excellent fit within the company, and its cloud-based deployment has made the process easier. By using a variety of the available tools, including the mobile apps, the company has been able to decrease uncontrolled spending and has much better visibility of spending and the categories in which it fits.
   (see the case study at **coupa.com/pdf/case-study/AvalonHealthCare.pdf**).

Questions

1. Why is spend management a critical factor for companies?
2. How can a procurement systems help address this concern?
3. What issues did Avalon Health Care bring to Coupa Software?
4. What were the solution and results?

SECTION 4.8 REVIEW QUESTIONS

1. List some of the opportunities for corporations to use social networking in B2B EC.
2. What are some of the benefits of social networking for B2B EC?
3. List some Web 2.0 social software for B2B applications.
4. Describe some of the applications of B2B in social networks.
5. Discuss the strategies for B2B social networking.
6. Define e-communities in B2B.
7. Why is convergence between B2B and B2C significant?

4.9   COLLABORATIVE COMMERCE

Collaborative commerce is an e-commerce technology that can be used to improve collaboration within and among organizations, frequently in supply chain relationships.

Essentials of Collaborative Commerce

Collaborative commerce (c-commerce) refers to electronic support for business collaboration. It enables companies to collaboratively plan, design, develop, manage, and research products, services, and innovative business processes, including EC applications. An example would be a manufacturer who is collaborating electronically with an engineering company that designs a product or a part for the manufacturer. C-commerce implies communication, information sharing, and collaborative planning done online by using tools such as groupware, blogs, wikis, and specially designed EC collaboration tools. Sometimes as a digital partnership, c-commerce can drive significant business success. Many collaboration efforts are done along the supply chain where the major benefits are cost reduction, increased revenue, fewer delays, faster movement of goods, fewer rush orders, fewer stockouts, and better inventory management. C-commerce is strongly related to **e-collaboration**, which is collaboration using digital technologies among people for accomplishing a common task.

The Elements and Processes of C-Commerce

The elements of the processes of c-commerce vary according to situations. For example, in many cases, c-commerce involves a manufacturer (or an assembler) who collaborates with its suppliers, designers, and other business partners, as well as with its customers and possibly the government. The major elements of the collaboration process are illustrated in Fig. 4.10. Notice that the collaboration process is based on the analysis of internal and external data that are made visible via a visualization portal. On the lower left side of the figure, we show the cyclical process of c-commerce. The people involved in this cycle use the information in the displays as well as the interactions among the major groups of participants (shown on the right side of the figure). The elements of c-commerce can be arranged in different configurations, one of which is a hub.

Collaboration Hubs

A popular form of c-commerce is the *collaboration hub*, which is often used by the members of a supply chain. A **collaboration hub (c-hub)** is the central point of interaction and of a company's supply chain. A single e-hub can host multiple *collaboration spaces* in which trading partners transact, collaborate, communicate, and share information.

Improving Collaborative Commerce

C-commerce can be divided into two major categories: internal and external. *Internal collaboration* refers to interdepartmental collaboration such as collaboration among organizational employees and collaboration of departments with their mobile employees. It also refers to collaboration among teams and individual employees who are off the premises. *External collaboration* refers to any collaboration between an organization and others in the external environment.

A large number of electronic tools are available to improve collaboration, starting with e-mail and wikis and ending with collaborative spaces and comprehensive tools such as Microsoft SharePoint (**office.microsoft.com/en-us/sharepoint**), Salesforce Chatter (**salesforce.com/ap/chatter/overview**), and Jive Software (**jivesoftware.com**). For example, SAP Inc. provides a social-based layer of software products that optimizes collaboration.

A large number of publications are available on how to improve c-collaboration. For a 2016 list of collaboration software products, see **captera.com**.

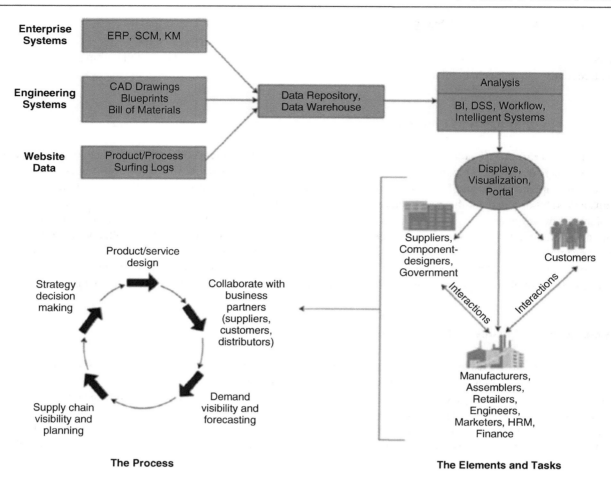

Fig. 4.10 Elements and process of c-commerce systems

Representative Examples of Collaborative Commerce

Leading technology companies such as Dell, Cisco, and HP use collaborative commerce mostly for supply chain improvement such as e-procurement. Other collaboration EC initiatives are used to increase efficiency and effectiveness of operation as can be seen in the following examples.

Vendor-Managed Inventory Systems

Vendor-managed inventory (VMI) refers to a process in which retailers make their suppliers responsible for monitoring the inventory of each item they supply and determining when to order each item and how much to order each time. Then the orders are generated electronically and fulfilled by the vendors. (A third-party logistics provider (3PL) can also be involved in VMI by organizing the shipments as needed.) The retailer provides the supplier with real-time usage (depletion) information (e.g., point-of-sale data), inventory levels, and the threshold below which orders need to be replenished. With this approach, the retailer is no longer involved with inventory management, and the demand forecasting becomes the responsibility of the supplier who can calculate the need for an item before the item is depleted. In addition, instead of sending purchase orders, customers electronically send daily information to the supplier, who generates the replenishment orders for the customer based on this demand information (see **datalliance.com/whatisvmi.html**). Thus, administrative costs are reduced, inventories are kept low, and stockouts become rare. A VMI also can be conducted between a supplier and its sub-suppliers. For more information, see **en.wikipedia.org/wiki/Vendor-managed_inventory**, **vendormanaged-inventory.com**, and JDA Software Group, Inc. (**jda.com**).

Example: VMI and Information Sharing Between a Retailer (Walmart) and a Supplier (P&G)

Walmart provides P&G access to sales information on every item P&G sells to Walmart. The sales information is collected electronically by P&G on a daily basis from every Walmart store. By monitoring the inventory level of its items, P&G knows when the inventories fall below the threshold that triggers an automatic order fulfillment and a shipment. Everything is done electronically. The benefit for P&G is accurate demand information, the benefit for Walmart is adequate inventory, and both enjoy reduced administrative costs (minimum paper orders and manual work). P&G has similar agreements with other major retailers; Walmart has similar agreements with other major suppliers.

Retailer–Supplier Collaboration

In addition to VMI, retailers and the suppliers can collaborate in other areas as illustrated in the following example:

Example: H. Paulin & Co.

H. Paulin & Co. (**hpaulin.com/welcome.html**) is a distributor and manufacturer of fasteners, fluid system products, automotive parts, and screw machine components. Working with their many retailers, it is important to make sure that stock levels are always kept above zero and that reorders come in a timely manner. Being out of stock means that a customer may not be able to complete an important job for lack of a small, relatively inexpensive part. The company uses a supply chain management system from Askuity (**askuity.com**). This system allows them to have accurate real-time information on stock levels, which can also be compared to historical depletion rates. This data allows the retailer and distributor to collaborate on restocking levels and timelines (Fiorletta 2014).

Reducing Transportation and Inventory Costs

Cost reduction in shipping and inventory can be achieved through collaboration. An example is the collaboration between Amazon.com (**amazon.com**) and shippers such as UPS (**ups.com**). Amazon.com delivers millions of items every week from its distribution centers. Rapid delivery is critical, and collaboration with the shippers is essential.

Reduction of Design Cycle Time

The following examples demonstrate cycle time reduction through c-collaboration:

Example 1: Clarion Malaysia

Clarion Malaysia (**clarion.com/my/en/top.html**), a subsidiary of the global car–audio electronics company Clarion Group, manufactures audio electronic systems for cars.

Using computerized technologies provided by IBM, such as computer-aided design (CAD) and product cycle management, the two companies reduced the time to market by about 40% while at the same time improving the design of the products because engineers were able to spend more time creating innovative designs. In addition, closer interaction with Clarion's customers is easier now throughout the design process. Finally, there is also a reduction in tooling preparation time.

Companies such as Commerce Guys (**commerceguys.com**) offer a socially oriented collaboration platform (e.g., see **drupalcommerce.org**).

Elimination of Channel Conflict: Collaboration with Dealers and Retailers

A conflict between manufacturers and their distributors, including retailers and/or dealers, may arise when customers order online directly from the manufacturer. One solution mentioned earlier is to order from the manufacturer and pick up the merchandise from a local retailer or dealer instead. This requires collaboration between the manufacturer and the local vendor. One company that provides the support for such collaborative EC is JG Sullivan Interactive, Inc. (see **jgsullivan.com**). Their product allows manufacturers to sell online with minimal channel conflict. Another example is Cisco Systems (see **cisco.com/c/en/us/solutions/collaboration/index.html**).

Example: Whirlpool Corporation

Whirlpool (**whirlpool.com**) is another company that experienced the problem of channel conflict. Consumers prefer to buy appliances (sometimes customized) online, directly from Whirlpool. Whirlpool's nationwide network of dealers was not happy with the direct ordering. Note that some appliances (e.g., a dishwasher, a washing machine) need to be installed, a job usually organized by the dealers.

JG Sullivan's system for Whirlpool was then used globally. The system was designed to enable direct online ordering and at the same time manage the delivery, installation, warranty, and services by the local dealers. This made customers as well as dealers happy, since marketing and sales expenses decreased significantly. Also, the direct contact with customers allowed Whirlpool to know their customers better.

Social Collaboration

A growing area in c-commerce is **social collaboration**, which refers to the process where people, individually or in groups, interact and share information and knowledge while in social networks, or when pursuing social goals. According to Carr (2015), online collaboration should be social enough to enable employees to be more productive yet not distracted in their work.

A large number of collaborative software is available to support social collaboration (e.g., see **g2crowd.com/categories/team-collaboration**; for more information, see the social collaboration entry in Wikipedia).

Barriers to C-Commerce

Despite the many potential benefits, and with the exception of some very large companies, c-commerce adaptation is moving ahead slowly. Reasons cited in various studies include technical factors involving a lack of internal integration and standards. Other reasons include network security and privacy concerns, and some distrust over who has access to and control of information stored in a partner's database. Internal resistance to information sharing and to new approaches and lack of company skills to conduct c-commerce are also possible factors. Gaining agreement on how to share costs and benefits can also prove problematic.

Finally, global collaboration may be complicated by additional barriers ranging from language and cultural misunderstandings to insufficient budgeting.

Overcoming Barriers to C-Collaboration

Specialized c-commerce software tools may lessen some of the barriers to c-commerce. In addition, as companies learn more about the major benefits of c-commerce—such as smoothing the supply chain, reducing inventories and operating costs, and increasing customer satisfaction—it is expected that more companies will implement c-commerce. New approaches, such as the use of cloud computing and its variants and the use of Web services, could significantly lessen the implementation problem. The use of collaborative Web 2.0 tools based on open source could help as well. Finally, it is essential to have a collaborative culture within and among organizations.

Collaboration Processes and Software

A large number of proprietary methods and supportive communication and collaborative software are available to support c-commerce (Fig. 4.11).

SECTION 4.9 REVIEW QUESTIONS

1. Define c-commerce.
2. List the major types and characteristics of c-commerce.
3. Describe some examples of c-commerce.
4. Describe the elements and processes of c-commerce.
5. List some major barriers to c-commerce. How can a company overcome these limitations?
6. How is C2C practiced in social networking?

MANAGERIAL ISSUES

Some managerial issues related to this chapter are as follows:

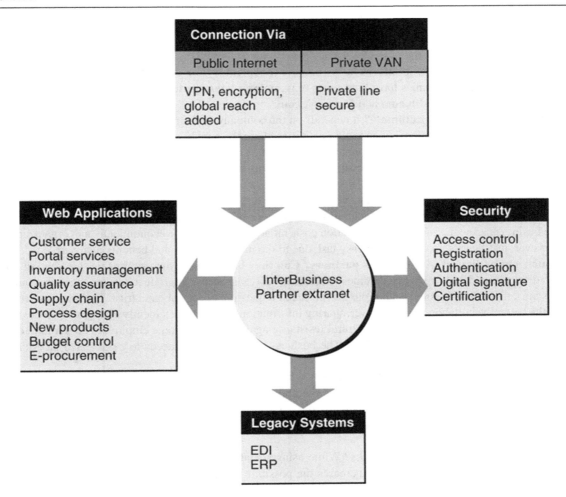

Fig. 4.11 Target's extranet

1. **Which B2B model(s) should we use for e-procurement?** When evaluating the various upstream B2B models, we need to match the suitable e-procurement goals with solution strategies depending upon whether the purchases are direct material or indirect material. Four typical goals that should be distinguished are organizational operational efficiency, minimum price, minimum inventory and stockouts, and low administrative costs. For each of these goals, the appropriate solution and system should be designed accordingly. Managing many small and medium suppliers that do not have sophisticated systems is a challenging goal.

2. **Which B2B model(s) should we use for online B2B sales?** A key issue for B2B sales is how to reconcile with the multiple buyers who adopt different EDI and ERP systems. The Enterprise Application Integration (EAI) solution transforms the internal data of multiple EDI formats used by different buyers. The integration of various types of EDI standards with ERP solutions is another challenge to overcome. In addition to contract management, B2B marketers use auctions, liquidations, and social networks to increase sales.

3. **Which solutions and vendor(s) should we select?** Vendors normally develop and deploy B2B applications, even for large organizations. Two basic approaches to vendor selection exist: (1) Select a primary vendor such as IBM (**ibm. com**), Microsoft (**microsoft.com**), or Oracle (**oracle.com**). This vendor will use its software and procedures and add partners as needed. (2) Use an integrator that will mix and match existing products and vendors to create "the best of breed" for your needs.

4. **What is the organizational impact of B2B?** The B2B system will change the role of the procurement department by redefining the role and procedures of that department. The function of the procurement department may be completely outsourced. A procurement policy portfolio is necessary to balance strategic sourcing items and spot purchasing items and design a supply relationship management system.

5. **What are some ethical issues in B2B?** Because B2B EC requires the sharing of proprietary information, business ethics are necessary. Employees should not be able to access unauthorized areas in the trading system, and the privacy of trading partners should be protected.

6. **Which type of social network should we use—private (proprietary) or public?** There are successes and failures in both types. Some large companies have both types (e.g., **northwesternmutual.com**). In most cases, it is better to use public networks such as **linkedin.com** and **facebook.com**.

7. **Which business processes to automate?** It depends on the company, industry, and value chain. However, as illustrated in this chapter, selling and purchasing and other activities along the supply chains are the prime targets. These include payments (financial supply chains). Also important are logistics, shipments, and inventory management.

8. **How difficult is it to introduce e-collaboration?** Dealing with the technological aspects of e-collaboration may be the easy part. Tackling the behavioral changes needed within an organization and its interactions with the trading partners may be the greater challenge. Change management may be needed for the newly created collaborations, to deal with issues such as the resistance to change. In addition, the responsibilities of the collaborative partners must be articulated with the business partners. Finally, e-collaboration costs money and needs to be economically and organizationally justified; however, justification may not be an easy task due to the intangible risks and benefits involved.

9. **How much can be shared with business partners? Can they be trusted?** Many companies are sharing forecast data and actual sales data. However, when it comes to allowing real-time access to product design, inventory, and interface to ERP systems, there may be some hesitation. It is basically a question of security and trust. The more information that is shared, the better the collaboration. However, sharing information can lead to accidently giving away some trade secrets. In some cases, there is an organizational cultural resistance against sharing (some employees do not like to share information, even within their own organization). The business value of sharing needs to be assessed carefully against its risks.

10. **Who benefits from vendor-managed inventory?** When VMI systems are deployed, both sellers and retailers reap benefits. However, small suppliers may not have the ability to systematically monitor and manage inventory of their business customers. In this case, the large buyer will need to support the inventory management system on behalf of its suppliers. Sensitive issues must be agreed upon when initiating VMI. One such issue is how to deal with item shortages created in the system.

11. **What is our expose using social networks?** While using social networks allows for greater communication between employees and business partners, it also increases the possibility of potential issues due to that increased interaction. Businesses need to consider who and what type of interactions are sanctioned, as well as creating standard operating procedures for collaboration.

SUMMARY

In this chapter, you learned about the following EC issues as they relate to the chapter's learning objectives.

1. **The B2B field.** The B2B field comprises e-commerce activities between businesses. B2B activities account for 85% of all EC. B2B e-commerce can be done by using different models.

2. **The major B2B models.** The B2B field is quite diversified. It can be divided into the following segments: sell-side marketplaces (one seller to many buyers), buy-side marketplaces (one buyer from many sellers), and trading exchanges (many sellers to many buyers). Each segment includes several business models. Intermediaries play an important role in some B2B models.

3. **The characteristics and models of sell-side marketplaces.** Sell-side B2B EC is the online direct sale by one seller (a manufacturer or an intermediary) to many buyers. The major technology used is electronic catalogs, which also allow for efficient customization, configuration, and purchase by customers. In addition, forward auctions are becoming popular, especially for liquidating surplus inventory. Sell-side auctions can be conducted from the seller's own site or from an intermediary's auction site. Sell-side activities can be accompanied by extensive customer service. E-commerce allows customization of products and services in personalized catalogs.

4. **Sell-side intermediaries.** The primary role of intermediaries in B2B is to provide value-added services for manufacturers and business customers. Intermediaries can also support group buyers, conduct auctions, and aggregate catalogs of many sellers.

5. **The characteristics of buy-side marketplaces and e-procurement.** Today, companies are moving to e-procurement to expedite purchasing, save on item and administrative costs, and gain better control over the purchasing process. Major procurement methods are reverse auctions (bidding systems), buying from webstores and catalogs, negotiation, buying from an intermediary that aggregates sellers' catalogs, internal marketplaces and group purchasing, desktop purchasing, buying in exchanges or industrial malls, and e-bartering. E-procurement offers the opportunity to achieve significant cost and time savings.

6. **B2B reverse auctions.** A reverse auction is a tendering system used by buyers to get better prices from suppliers competing to fulfill the buyers' needs. Auctions can be done on a company's website or on a third-party auction site. Reverse auctions can lower buyers' costs dramatically, both in product costs and in the time and cost of the tendering process.

7. **B2B aggregation and group purchasing.** Increasing the bargaining power and efficiency of companies can be done by aggregating either the buyers or the sellers. Aggregating suppliers' catalogs into a buyer's catalog, for example, gives buying companies better control of purchasing costs. In desktop purchasing, employees are empowered to buy up to a certain limit without the need for additional approval. Employees view internal catalogs with pre-agreed-upon prices with the approved suppliers and then buy within their budget. Industrial malls or large distributors specialize in one industry (e.g., computers) or in industrial MROs. They aggregate the catalogs of thousands of suppliers. A purchasing agent can place an order for parts or materials, and shipping is arranged by the supplier or the mall owner. Buyer aggregation through group purchasing is very popular because it enables even SMEs to get better prices on their purchases. In addition to direct purchasing, items can be acquired via bartering.

8. **Exchanges defined and the major types of exchanges.** Exchanges are e-marketplaces that provide a trading platform for conducting business among many buyers, many sellers, and other business partners. Types of public e-marketplaces include B2B third-party trading exchanges and consortium trading exchanges. Exchanges may be vertical (industry oriented) or horizontal.

9. **Third-party exchanges.** Third-party exchanges are owned by an independent company and usually are operated in highly fragmented markets. They are open to anyone and, therefore, are considered public exchanges. They try to maintain neutral relations with both buyers and sellers.

10. **B2B in Web 2.0 and social networks.** Although considerable B2C social are more commonly known, B2B activities are also quite significant. A major success has been seen in the use of blogs and wikis to collaborate with suppliers and customers, as well as the use of business-oriented social networks to communicate between firms. Large companies use social networking to create and foster business relationships. Smaller companies use social networking for soliciting expert opinions. Other companies use it for finding business partners, cultivating business opportunities, recruiting employees, and finding sales leads.

11. **C-commerce.** Collaborative commerce (c-commerce) refers to a planned use of digital technology by business partners. It includes planning, designing, researching, managing, and servicing various partners and tasks, frequently along the supply chain. C-commerce can be conducted between different pairs of business partners or among many partners participating in a collaborative network. Collaboration with Web 2.0 tools and in social networks adds a social dimension that could improve communication, participation, and trust. There are many new tools, some of which are being added to traditional collaboration tools. Better collaboration may improve supply chain operation, knowledge management, and individual and organizational performance.

KEY TERMS

Bartering exchange
Business-to-business e-commerce (B2B EC)
Buy-side e-marketplace
Collaborative commerce (c-commerce)
Collaborative hubs (c-hubs)
Company-centric EC
Consortium trading exchange (CTE)
Desktop purchasing
Direct materials
Dynamic pricing
E-collaboration

E-procurement (electronic procurement)
Exchanges (trading communities or trading exchanges)
Gamification
Group purchasing
Horizontal marketplaces
Indirect materials
Maintenance, repair, and operation (MRO)
Maverick buying
Online intermediary
Procurement management
Public e-marketplaces
Request for quote (RFQ)
Reverse auction
Sell-side e-marketplace
Social collaboration
Vendor-managed inventory
Vertical marketplaces
Virtual trade shows

DISCUSSION QUESTIONS

1. Explain how a catalog-based sell-side e-marketplace works and describe its benefits.
2. Discuss the advantages of selling through online auctions over selling from catalogs. What are the disadvantages?
3. Discuss and compare all of the mechanisms that group purchasing aggregators can use.
4. Should desktop purchasing only be implemented through an internal marketplace?
5. Compare and contrast a privately owned exchange with a private e-marketplace.
6. Compare external and internal aggregation of catalogs.
7. Relate social commerce to B2B group buying.
8. Compare an organizational buyer to an individual consumer.
9. Which emerging technologies will have the largest impacts on B2B EC?
10. It is said that c-commerce signifies a move from a transaction focus to a relationship focus among supply chain members. Discuss.

TOPICS FOR CLASS DISCUSSION AND DEBATES

1. Discuss B2B opportunities in social networking.
2. Discuss the risks in B2B social networking.
3. Discuss how globalization is related to B2B.
4. Relate B2B to the four Ps of marketing (product, pricing, placement, and promotion) and the four Cs (content, connection, communication, and conversion).
5. Discuss potential channel conflicts in B2B.
6. What is the contribution of B2B directories such as Alibaba.com to global trade? What are the potential limitations?
7. Debate: Some say that exchanges must be owned by a third-party intermediary and that consortiums should not be allowed.
8. Discuss why **facebook.com** is not as good as **linkedin.com** in generating sales leads.
9. In class, watch the video "B2B Marketing in a Digital Age" (4:11 min) at youtube.com/watch?v=nSngph5EC6U. Discuss the implications for a progressive marketing manager.
10. Research companies that conduct liquidations. Concentrate on **liquidation.com**, **govliquidation.com**, and **govdeals.com**. Examine the similarities and uniqueness in the services provided. Discuss the value added to the companies that use these services.
11. Who is at greater risk when there is a convergence between B2C and B2B EC? (Hint: see the video at youtube.com/watch?v=krH4SDB1jPQ, and consider the impact of Amazon's entry to B2B markets).

INTERNET EXERCISES

1. **Tripadvisor.com** launched a B2B division in 2010. Find information about the benefits to a company using it and to its business customers.
2. Examine the following sites: **ariba.com**, **ibm.com**, and **ibxplatform.com**. Review their products and services. How do they support mobile marketing and social commerce?
3. Match a B2B business model with the services on each site listed in the previous question.
4. Visit **ebay.com** and identify all of the activities related to its small business auctions. What services are provided by eBay? Then, enter eBay Business & Industrial area at **ebay.com/rpp/business-industrial**. What kind of e-marketplace is this? What are its major capabilities?
5. Enter **ondemandsourcing.com**, and use the free registration to view the product demo. Prepare a list of benefits to small- and medium-sized organizations.
6. Enter **bitpipe.com**, and find recent B2B vendor reports related to e-procurement. Identify topics not covered in this chapter.
7. Visit **cognizant.com**. Examine the major tools they sell for conducting various types of e-procurement. List and analyze each tool.
8. Enter navigatorhms.com/gpo and two other group purchasing sites. Report on B2B group buying activities available at each site.
9. Enter **blog.marketo.com**, and find eight recent successful applications of social B2B. Prepare a list of topics covered at the site. Write a brief summary about the content, including tips and guides, and lessons learned.
10. Enter **smallbusiness.yahoo.com/ecommerce**, and summarize one of the "Success Stories."
11. Enter **eprocurement.nc.gov**. What e-procurement methods does it provide? What are the benefits of each method?
12. Enter **equinix.com**, and identify the B2B services they provide.
13. Enter **collaborativeshift.com** or other c-collaborative sites, and read about recent issues related to e-collaboration. Prepare a report.
14. Enter **opentext.com** or **kintone.cybozu.com/us**. Read the company vision for collaborative commerce, and view the demo. Explain in a report how the company facilitates c-commerce.
15. Enter **lightwellinc.com**, and watch the six-part video series on "B2B and B2C Convergence in Commerce" at youtube.com/playlist?list=PLLL8kmgDjbGlIiQJJoUwQq940iTelZaM_. Identify the areas where they predict B2B and B2B technologies and practices will overlap.

TEAM ASSIGNMENTS AND PROJECTS

1. **Assignment for the Opening Case**
   Read the opening case and answer the following questions:

   (a) What directory services are provided by Alibaba.com?
   (b) Identify the revenue sources of Alibaba.com.
   (c) Find information about the 2014 IPO. Do you think that the company valuation is realistic?
   (d) Enter **slideshare.net/yanhufei/case-study-alibaba-final-v-11**, and review the Alibaba.com case study. Expand on the answers to questions which are designated by your teacher.
   (e) Describe Alibaba's business model.
   (f) Enter **sa.alibaba.com**, and watch the video about supplier assessment at Alibaba.com (3:31 min); summarize its content.
   (g) Watch the video titled "e-Riches 2.0: – The Best Online Marketing Book by Scott Fox" (6:18 min) at **youtube.com/watch?v=6O747UHN9Mw**.

   What did you learn from this video?
2. Each team should explore a different social networking B2B activity and prepare a summary paper for a class presentation. The paper should include the following about the activity or method:

   (a) The mechanisms and technologies used
   (b) The benefits to buyers, suppliers, and others (if applicable)

(c) The limitations to buyers, suppliers, and others (if applicable)

(d) The situations for which each method is recommended

Hint: Look at King (2015) and vendors' products.

3. Each team finds a global B2B intermediary that competes with **alibaba.com** (e.g., **globalsources.com**). Prepare a list of services available to sellers and to buyers from both Alibaba.com and your chosen competitor.

4. Enter **amazon.com/Amazon-Business-Tour/dp/B00WN5U03W**, and view the video tutorial. Also explore the site. Describe the benefits to manufacturers and distributors as well as customers.

5. Enter **ariba.com**, and find out what its software solutions such as Ariba Commerce Cloud can do to facilitate inter-enterprise commerce. Also examine the company's solution for sourcing, procurement, and contract management. Present your findings to the class.

6. Read the article from TradeShift "The Future and Promise of E-Procurement" (2015) available at **spendmatters.com/2015/10/08/the-future-and-promise-of-e-procurement**. Each team analyzes the ideas of several contributors and presents the highlights to the class.

7. Watch the video titled "eProcurement Case Study: HOYER Group" (3:44 min) at **youtube.com/watch?v=BFaJPeDQyIs&noredirect=1**. Answer the following questions:

(a) What problems did the Hoyer Group face?

(b) What were some of the software requirements?

(c) How did they evaluate the software? What criteria did they use?

(d) What have you learned from the video?

8. The class researches Ariba's supplier network and compares it to several similar networks (e.g., to IBM Sterling B2B Collaboration Network). Each team examines one comparison and makes a presentation to the class.

9. View the video "Panel Discussion on Collaborative Commerce (Pt.1) @ Ariba LIVE 2011" (12:36 min) at **youtube.com/watch?v=bucxXpDvWDI**. (Part 2 (11:11 min) at **youtube.com/watch?v=dV_KUJ0eVuE** is optional.) Answer the following questions:

(a) What benefits do the buyers see? Relate these benefits to collaborative commerce.

(b) How is EC used to support c-commerce?

(c) How can buyer/supplier relationships be fostered with c-commerce?

(d) Run a similar panel discussion in class. If possible, ask large buyers to attend and take part.

(e) How is bringing business partners online accomplished?

(f) What role does Ariba play? (Check its website **ariba.com**.)

(g) What have you learned from this video about the benefits of c-commerce and e-commerce?

10. Download and reach the white paper "The Forrester Wave™ B2B Commerce Suites" at **www-cmswire.simplermedia.com/cw-cp-ibm-ogilvy-2015-02.html?utm_source=internal&utm_medium=WIR-150412-WP5&utm_campaign=cw-cp-ibm-ogilvy-2015-02&mkt_tok=3RkMMJWWfF9wsRomrfCcI63Em2iQPJWpsrB0B%2FDC18kX3RUnJbubfkz6htBZF5s8TM3DVlJGXqlI4UEKTLE%3D** . Write a report comparing the different vendor solutions.

11. Watch the video on selecting e-commerce software at **ecommerceandb2b.com/the-basics-and-foundation-of-b2b-e-commerce** . Download the guide at **ecommerceandb2b.com/download/5169**. Write a report on the criteria that can be used to select a B2B software solution.

12. Watch the Frost & Sullivan presentation on "Renault Nissan Alliance CEO Carlos Ghosn Talks About The Future of The Auto Industry" at youtube.com/watch?v=gYg2XNEugJ8. What are the drivers of change in the automotive industry? Which of the these trends relate to e-commerce and to B2B?

CLOSING CASE: MAYBELLINE USES COLLABORATIVE COMMERCE TO MANAGE DISTRIBUTION

Maybelline (**maybelline.com**) is an international producer and distributor of cosmetics. They distribute their products through a wide variety of retail outlets including department stores, drug stores, and specialty retailers.

The Problem

This industry is greatly influenced by the preferences of its customers which can vary quickly over time or drastically by geographic location. These variations can create large problems for both the distributor and the retailer. Retailers who do not track sales of popular items risk being sold out. Additionally, retailers can order additional stock without understanding sales trends and may be stuck with items that are no longer popular. In the same way, distributors need to understand what retailers will plan to order in the future based on the current fashion and also understand those trends enough to direct manufacturing of products to meet those needs. Because of the quick shifts in this segment, it is imperative that both groups have a good understanding of the market forces.

The Solution

To combat these shifting demands, it is critical for the company to have constant awareness of not only sales trends but also stock levels of products and planned manufacturing cycles. To assist in aggregating this information, Maybelline partnered with Market6 (a provider of collaborative commerce solutions **market6.com**) to monitor sales at retailers, to help track both item popularity and demand, and also to help inform production scheduling. This system provides benefits not only to Maybelline but also to retailers as they can better react to customers changing preferences (Fiorletta 2014).

The Results

These variations can create large problems for both the distributor and the retailer. Retailers who do not track sales of popular items risk being so loud. Additionally, retailers to order additional stock without understanding sales trends may be stuck with items that are no longer popular. In the same way, distributors need to understand what retailers will plan to order in the future based on the current fashion and also understand those trends enough to direct manufacturing of products to meet those demands. Because of the quick shifts in this market, it is imperative that both groups have a good understanding of the market forces.

   (**Sources:** Fiorletta (2014) and **supermarketnews.com/kroger/krogers-analytics-arm-acquires-market6** (all accessed January 2017)).

Questions

1. Why is understanding market trends important in this industry?
2. Why is it mutually beneficial for retailers and distributors to work together?
3. Is it important that this system shares real-time data with both parties?
4. How can the system be used to inform product decisions and marketing?

REFERENCES

Burt, T., "B2B marketers look to private social communities to nurture, generate leads" 2017. **fiercecmo.com/special-report/b2b-marketers-look-to-private-social-communities-to-nurture-generate-leads** (accessed January 2017).

Carr, D. F. "How Social Should Social Collaboration Be?" *Forbes Tech*, April 27, 2015. **forbes.com/sites/davidcarr/2015/04/27/how-social-should-social-collaboration-be**. (accessed January 2017).

Carter, T., "14 Tips To Incorporate Social Media Into Event Marketing." March 5, 2015. **marketingland.com/14-tips-incorporate-social-media-event-marketing-118227. (accessed January 2017).**

Clark, D. *Alibaba: The House That Jack Ma Built*, New York, NY: Ecco, 2016.

Chen, L. Y. "Alibaba Beats Estimates as Ma's Push into Rural China Pays Off." *Bloomberg Business*, January 28, 2016. **bloomberg.com/news/articles/2016-01-28/alibaba-sales-beat-estimates-after-making-mobile-rural-inroads** (accessed January 2017).

Choi, J. "The Magic of E-Procurement." Shoplet Blog, February 25, 2015. **blog.shoplet.com/work-better/the-magic-of-e-procurement/** (accessed January 2017).

Demery, P. "A Deep Dive into B2B Web Marketplaces." *Internet Retailer*, May 22, 2015. **internetretailer.com/2015/05/22/deep-dive-b2b-web-marketplaces** (accessed January 2017).

Demery, P., "Amazon's billion-dollar B2B portal is growing rapidly" May 4, 2016a. **b2becommerceworld.com/2016/05/04/amazons-billion-dollar-b2b-portal-growing-rapidly** (accessed January 2017a).

Demery, P., "Amazon Business wants help to get beyond 'Day One'" January 12, 2017. **b2becommerceworld.com/2017/01/12/amazon-business-wants-help-get-beyond-day-one** (accessed January 2017b).

Demery, P., "NeweggBusiness is on a fast-growth track in B2B e-commerce" July 25, 2016. **b2becommerceworld.com/2016/07/25/neweggbusi-ness-growing-fast-b2b-e-commerce** (accessed January 2017).

DiMauro, V. "7 Key Trends in Online B2B Customer Communities." Leader Networks, November 11, 2016. **leadernetworks.com/2016/10/7-key-trends-online-b2b-customer-communities.html** (accessed January 2017).

E-Commerce Wiki. "B2B Exchanges." (Last modified by W. Petersen: October 2, 2015). **en.ecommercewiki.info/fundamentals/market_places/exchanges** (accessed January 2017).

Econsultancy. "B2B Internet Statistics Compendium" January 2017. **econsultancy.com/reports/b2b-internet-statistics-compendium/** (accessed January 2017).

eMarketer. "B2B Ecommerce Market Is Still Maturing" August 8, 2016a. **emarketer.com/Article/B2B-Ecommerce-Market-Still-Maturing/1014311** (accessed January 2017).

eMarketer. "B2B Marketing Trends Roundup." *SilverPop*, February 2016b.

Erisman, P. *Alibaba's World: How a Remarkable Chinese Company is Changing the Face of Global Business.* Shanghai: **Palgrave MacMillan**, 2015.

Fiorletta, A. "Collaboration Becomes Key To Success For Retailers And Suppliers" September 2, 2014. **retailtouchpoints.com/topics/inventory-merchandising-supply-chain/collaboration-becomes-key-to-success-for-retailers-and-suppliers** (accessed January 2017).

Fullerton, L. "Face to face trade shows are increasingly favored by B2B marketers" The Drum, July 18, 2016. **thedrum.com/news/2016/07/18/face-face-trade-shows-are-increasingly-favored-b2b-marketers** (accessed January 2017).

Heaney, B. & Ball, B. "Answering the Call: 5 Best Practice Steps for B2B and B2C Convergence" Aberdeen Group. 2014.

Kelman, S. "A return to normalcy for reverse auctions?" June 10, 2015. **fcw.com/Blogs/Lectern/2015/06/Kelman-reverse-auctions.aspx** (accessed January 2017).

King, K., *The Complete Guide to B2B Marketing: New Tactics, Tools, and Techniques to Compete in the Digital Economy.* Upper Saddle River, New Jersey: 2015.

Lunden, I. (2015). Sources: Amazon plans 'prime for business', folding AmazonSupply into big B2B Play.

Paradis, Z. "The Future of B2B" Sapient, 2016. **sapient.com/content/dam/sapient/sapientnitro/pdfs/insights/TR1_FutureB2B.pdf** (accessed January 2017).

Parekh, S. "Fast is the New Big: B2B E-Commerce Trends for 2016" APTTUS, January 12, 2016. **apttus.com/blog/b2b-ecommerce-trends-2016** (accessed January 2017).

Petersen, R. "33 Inspiring B2B Digital Marketing Case Studies." *Grow*, May 21, 2015. **businessesgrow.com/2015/05/21/b2b-digital-marketing-case-studies** (accessed January 2017).

Pick, T. "20 Brilliant B2B Marketing and Digital Business Stats and Facts." *Meltwater*, August 28, 2015. **meltwater.com/blog** (accessed January 2017).

Sourcing. "B2C cannot replace B2B, but B2B can learn from B2C" August 14, 2015. **sourcinginnovation.com/wordpress/2015/08/14/in-sourc-ing-b2c-cannot-replace-b2b-but-b2b-can-learn-from-b2c/** (accessed January 2017).

Templeman, M. "How Facebook and Twitter fit into B2B Marketing." *Forbes.com*, July 23, 2015. **forbes.com/sites/miketempleman/2015/07/23/how-facebook-and-twitter-fit-into-b2b-marketing/#24a3aedc61dd** (accessed January 2017).

Tradeshift. "The Future and Promise of E-Procurement." Spend Matter, October 8, 2015. **spendmatters.com/2015/10/08/the-future-and-prom-ise-of-e-procurement** (accessed January 2017).

Traxpay. "E-Procurement: The New Focus for B2B Commerce" April 21, 2015. **traxpay.com/2015/04/e-procurement-part-1-the-new-focus-for-b2b-commerce** (accessed January 2017).

Tepper, N. "Nearly All B2B Companies Use Twitter and LinkedIn to Increase Brand Awareness." *Internet Retailer*, August 31, 2015.

Ueland, S. "9 B2B Companies That Excel at Social Media." *PracticalEcommerce*, January 6, 2015.

Wirthwein, C., and J. Bannon. *The People Powered Brand: A Blueprint for B2B Brand and Culture Transformation.* Ithaca, NY: Paramount Market Publishing, Inc., 2014.

Young, D. "Wowo Transforms Through Food Service Buy." *Seeking Alpha*, June 8, 2015.

Zhukova, V. *The Role of Social Media in B2B Communication.* New York, NY: Grin, 2017.

Innovative EC Systems: From E-Government to E-Learning, E-Health, Sharing Economy, and P2P Commerce

5

Contents

Learning Objectives

Upon completion of this chapter, you will be able to:

1. Describe various e-government initiatives.
2. Describe e-government activities and implementation issues including government 2.0 and m-government.
3. Describe e-learning, virtual universities, and e-training.
4. Describe e-books and their readers.
5. Describe e-health.
6. Describe digital disruption.
7. Describe ride sharing and accommodation sharing.
8. Describe P2P models in e-commerce.

OPENING CASE
E-GOVERNMENT IN ESTONIA

Estonia is a small country in Eastern Europe (less than 1.5 million residents). It developed one of the most successful e-government programs.

© Springer International Publishing AG 2018
E. Turban et al., *Electronic Commerce 2018*, Springer Texts in Business and Economics, DOI 10.1007/978-3-319-58715-8_5

The Problem

Estonia was a fairly poor country after it became independent of the Soviet Union. Its information technology was undeveloped despite its proximity to the nordic countries which are technologically advanced. By the end of the 1990s, it became clear that the country must develop the needed information technology, including EC, in order to transform its government services to an e-government.

The Solution

Fortunately, politicians and officials were willing to get involved, providing the necessary efforts and funds. Estonia managed to take the concept of e-society and make it reality.

Being a poor country, Estonia could not afford to simply transfer paper bureaucracy to digital one. So, it was necessary not only to get the financing but also the backing of the entire population. Since the country was in a transitional phase, where new norms were just formed, it was easy to introduce behavioral and other changes.

In addition, Estonia is using flexible strategy. The country monitors global ICT trends and domestic digital society and EC and acts accordingly. Also, they received the cooperation of the private sector, academicians, and any one that has had relevant knowledge, including the politicians and the Prime Minister. Finally, the project was coordinated with the European Union and the OECD in Europe.

Sample Applications (per Kwang 2017a)

- **Electronic ID Card**. Each Estonia citizen carries ID smart card which provides access to over 1000 public services. The chip on the card carries embedded files which, using 2048-bit public key encryption, enable it to be used as definitive proof of ID in an electronic environment. The ID card can be used for numerous purposes—digital signatures, accessing government databases, electronic voting, prepaid transport, and logging into bank accounts.
- **E-Residency.** The country is known as "the country-as-a-service." This service is open to anyone in the world. E-residents can set up a company online within a day, digitally sign documents and contracts, encrypt and transmit documents securely, and administer the company from anywhere in the world. All these services have been available for over a decade. Over 13,000 e-residency cards have been issued by January 2017. This service aims at attracting foreign investors.
- **Digital Signature.** Estonia's digital signature system has paved the way for its numerous e-services, from i-voting systems to electronic tax filing. The system is freely used by businesses as well and has been applied to a variety of Web-based services. More than 242 million digital signatures have been made since its inception in 2000. Electronic signatures have the same legal weight as traditional paper signatures. The nation's electronic ID infrastructure created an effective and universal system for secured identification.
- **X-Road Data Exchange.** The backbone of e-Estonia, X-Road, is the data exchange layer that connects the nation's various services and databases, both in the public and private sector. X-Road enables a range of complex services for citizens. Over 2000 services and 900 organizations make use of X-Road daily in Estonia.
- **i-Voting.** Estonia's Internet voting system allows voters to login using an ID card and cast their ballots from any Internet-connected computer, anywhere in the world.

  In 2005, Estonia became the first country in the world to hold nationwide elections using this method and, in 2007, the first country to use i-voting in parliamentary elections.
- **E-Cabinet.** E-Cabinet is used by the government to streamline the decision-making process, allowing ministers to prepare for cabinet meetings, conduct them, and review minutes, entirely without paper.

  With the e-Cabinet system, the average length of weekly cabinet meetings was cut from 4 to 5 h to just 90 min. The government also eliminated the need to print and deliver thousands of pages of documents each week—a significant reduction in environmental impact and cost.
- **E-School.** E-school is a platform for education stakeholders to collaborate and organize teaching and learning programs and information. Teachers enter grades and attendance information in the system, post homework assignments, and evaluate students' behavior. Over 85% of Estonia's schools e-school, covering 95% of all grade school students.
- **E-Healthcare.** Estonia's nationwide electronic health record system integrates data from different healthcare providers to create a common record for each patient.

Doctors can access a patient's record from a single electronic file, read test results and x-ray scans as soon as they are ready, and prescribe medication to patients electronically. The system also compiles data for national statistics to measure health trends, track epidemics, and ensure that health resources are being spent wisely.

The Results

Here are some concrete examples of the benefits that e-governance brings to Estonia:

- It makes people's lives easier and more convenient—as digital signing and online voting have done.
- It improves the business environment—you can reduce red tape and hassles for company registration and management (as done with easy annual reporting solutions in the electronic business registry).
- It makes government more efficient—from top-level decision-making in the Cabinet (e.g., via the use of e-Cabinet), to everyday frontline services and back offices.
- It makes government more effective, allowing better delivery policy goals—for example, the introduction of real-time database access for police patrols (e-police) leads to cases being quickly solved.
- It enhances transparency of governance and citizen participation—e-Cabinet and e-consultation contribute greatly to hearing people's opinions in national decision-making and for publishing relevant information almost instantly.
- The cumulative time saving in Estonia parliamentary election in 2011, for example, was 11,000 working days.
- Estonians in 116 countries casted votes during the 2015 parliamentary election.

Sources: Compiled from Kwang (2017a) and **estonia.com/estonias-road-e-governance-went-right** (accessed January 2017)

LESSONS LEARNED FROM THE CASE

Even small and not affluent countries are embarking on digitization of their governments. The objective is to improve services, cut costs, and have the citizens involved. Estonia did it successfully (the small size of the country helped, but the collaboration of all and the wide support were critical success factors). The major activities of e-government are the subject of this chapter. We also present the related activities of e-learning and training and e-health. Finally, we present the innovative EC applications delivered by shared economy models as well as the person-to-person EC major activities.

5.1 DIGITAL GOVERNMENT: AN OVERVIEW

Electronic government, also known as *e-government* or *digital government*, is a growing e-commerce application area that encompasses many topics as illustrated in the opening case. It refers to the various levels of government: city, county, and country. The area's major objective is to bring public sector institutions into the digital age. For an overview, see Brown et al. (2014). This section presents the major topic areas.

Definition and Scope

E-government refers to the use of information technology and communication (ITC) in general, and e-commerce in particular, to improve the delivery of government services and activities in the public sector, such as providing citizens with more convenient access to information and services and providing effective delivery of government services to citizens and businesses as well as improving the performance of government employees. It also is an efficient and effective way for governments to interact with citizens, businesses, and other entities and to improve governmental business transactions (such as buying and selling goods and services) and to operate effectively within the governments themselves. E-government includes a large number of activities, as can be seen in the opening case and in **en.wikipedia.org/wiki/E-Government**. For details, see Anderson et al. (2015). For resources, see **w3.org/egov**.

Note that e-government also offers an opportunity to improve the efficiency and effectiveness of the internal operation of a government.

Table 5.1 Representative categories of e-government performance objectives

G2C	G2B
Reduce the time needed to interact with the government	Increase the ability for businesses to find, view, and comment on rules and regulations
Create a friendly single point of access to government services for individuals	Reduce the burden on businesses by enabling online filing of taxes and other documents
Reduce the time spent in finding federal jobs	Reduce the time to fill out export forms and locate related information
Reduce the average time for citizens to find benefits and determine eligibility	Reduce the time for businesses to comply with government regulations
Increase the number of citizens who use the Internet to find information on recreational opportunities	
Meet the high public demand for information	
Improve the value of government services to its citizens	
Expand access to information for people with disabilities	
Make obtaining financial assistance from the government easier, cheaper, quicker, and more comprehensible	
G2G	IEE
Decrease time needed to respond to emergency incidents by government agencies	Increase availability of training programs for government employees
Reduce the time to verify public records	Reduce the average time to process clearance forms
Increase the number of grant programs available for electronic applications	Increase the use of e-travel services within each agency
Increase efficiency of communication between federal, state, local, and tribal governments	Reduce time and overhead costs to purchase goods and services throughout the federal government
Improve collaboration with foreign partners, including governments and institutions	Plan IT investments more effectively
Automate internal processes to reduce costs within the federal government by disseminating the best practices across agencies	Secure better services at a lower cost
	Cut government operating costs

Sources: Based on Egov (2003) and the authors' experiences

E-government includes the following major categories: government-to-citizens (G2C), government-to-business (G2B), government-to-government (G2G), internal efficiency and effectiveness (IEE), and government-to-employees (G2E). The major activities of the first four categories are provided in Table 5.1 (also see Digital Government Strategy 2012). For a description of the range of e-government activities in the United States, see Digital Government Strategy (2012) and **whitehouse.gov/omb/e-gov**. Of special interest is the recent document titled "Digital Government" (**whitehouse.gov/sites/default/files/omb/egov/digital-government/digital-government.htm**). For examples of e-government in Singapore, see **gov.sg**.

Example: The European Commission

The European Commission's Digital Agenda website (**ec.europa.eu/digital-agenda/welcome-digital-agenda**) is an example of a comprehensive e-government system. It is one of the European Union's seven flagships for achieving its 10-year growth strategy. The site is divided into several topics—notably, life and work, public services, ongoing studies, smart cities, and e-health and aging. For details, see **ec.europa.eu/digital-agenda/welcome-digital-agenda**.

The above categories are based on different entities with whom the government is interacting. However, these entities are also interconnected, as shown in the broken lines of Fig. 5.1.

The following is a brief description of the major activities conducted between the government and each major entity.

Government-to-Citizens

The **government-to-citizens (G2C)** category includes all the interactions between a government and its citizens that take place electronically. G2C can involve dozens of different initiatives. The basic idea is to enable citizens to interact electronically with the government from anywhere and at any time. G2C applications enable citizens to ask questions of government agencies and receive answers, pay taxes, receive payments and documents, and schedule services, such as employment interviews and medical appointments. For example, in many US states, residents can renew driver's licenses, pay traffic tickets, and make appointments for vehicle emission inspections and driving tests—all online.

Fig. 5.1 E-government categories of activities

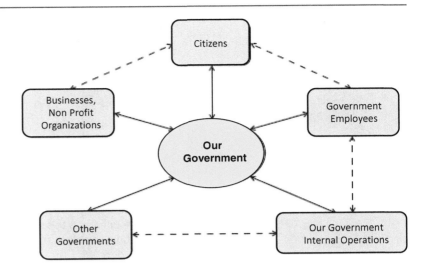

The major features of government websites are information on how to contact the government, public notices to citizens, links to other sites, educational material, publications, statistics, legal notes, and databases. The major areas of such G2C activities are social services, tourism and recreation, public safety, research and education, downloadable forms, discovery of government services, tax filing, information about public policy, and advice about health and safety issues. G2C is now available on mobile/wireless devices in many countries and local governments.

Another area of G2C activity takes place by solving citizens' problems. The government (or a politician) can use CRM-type software to assign inquiries and problem cases to appropriate staff members (as shown on **ict.govt.nz**). Subsequently, workflow CRM software can be used to track the progress of the problems' resolution.

Note that over 20 countries (e.g., China, North Korea, Iran, Syria) block some websites for political, social, or other reasons. For more on G2C, see **usa.gov/Citizen/Topics/All-Topics.shtml**. For an overview of major citizens' groups and the services provided to them by the US Department of Labor, see **dol.gov/_sec/e_government_plan/p41-43_appendixe.htm**.

Two popular examples of G2C are provided next.

Electronic Voting

Voting processes may be subject to errors, manipulation, and fraud. In many countries, there are attempts to "rig" the votes; in others, the losers want a manual recount. Voting may result in major political crises, as has happened in several countries. Problems with the US 2000 and 2004 presidential elections have accelerated the trend toward electronic voting.

The voting process encompasses a broad spectrum of technological and social activities from voter registration and voter authentication to the casting of ballots and subsequent tallying of results. For an example of this process, see Fig. 5.2. Electronic voting automates some or all steps in the process.

Fully electronic voting systems have raised considerable controversy because of a variety of relevant factors, such as the proprietary nature of the software. Typical issues are the difficulties in selling the systems to voters, complex auditing, and the lack of experience in some steps of the process.

Hackable Elections

A debatable issue is the possibility of fraud in electronic voting (Madden 2015). The possibility of fraud is larger if the e-voting machines that do not have paper trails are used. For a discussion, see Gross (2016). Note that it is difficult to hack e-voting systems that are not on the Internet but on government-protected networks. However, some have suggested during the 2016 presidential elections in the United States, that some non-voting systems (e.g., the Democratic National Commission's files) were compromised.

For more information on e-voting, see **en.wikipedia.org/wiki/Electronic_voting** and the Electronic Frontier Foundation (**eff.org**).

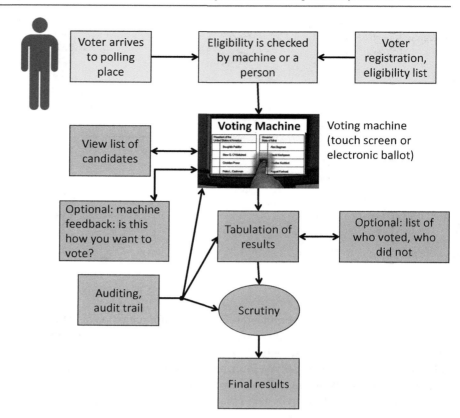

Fig. 5.2 The process of using a voting machine

Electronic Benefits Transfer

One e-government application that is not new is the electronic benefits transfer (EBT). It has been available since the early 1990s and is now in use in many countries. The US government transfers billions of dollars in benefits to many of its citizens on a regular basis. Beginning in 1993, an attempt was made to deliver benefits to recipients' bank accounts. However, more than 20% of payments go to citizens who do not have a bank account. To solve this problem, the government initiated the use of smart cards (see Chap. 12). Lately, some governments provide money transfer to smartphones. Benefit recipients can load the money they receive onto the cards and use the cards at automated teller machines (ATMs), point-of-sale locations, and grocery and other stores, just like other prepaid value cards. The advantage is not only the reduction in processing costs (from about 50¢ per paper check to 2¢ for electronic payment) but also the reduction of fraud. With biometrics (see Chap. 11) coming to smart cards and PCs, officials expect a substantial reduction in fraud. EBT has been implemented in all states since 2004. For more information on EBT in government, see **www.fns.usda.gov/ebt/general-electronic-benefit-transfer-ebt-information**.

In several developing countries (e.g., India, Brazil), governments are using mobile payments to transfer benefits to citizens.

Government-to-Business

Governments seek to automate their interactions with businesses. Although we call this category **government-to-business (G2B)**, the relationship works in two ways: government-to-business and business-to-government. Thus, G2B refers to activities where the government sells products to businesses or provides businesses with services and vice versa. Two key G2B activities are e-procurement and the auctioning of government surpluses. For other US G2B initiatives for businesses and nonprofits, see **usa.gov/Business/Business-Gateway.shtml**.

Government E-Procurement

Governments buy large amounts of MROs (maintenance, repair, and operations; Chap. 4) and other materials directly from suppliers. In many cases, RFQ (or tendering) systems are mandated by law. For years, these RFQs were done manually; the systems are now moving online. These systems utilize reverse (buy-side) auction systems, such as those described in Chap. 4. Governments provide all the support for such tendering systems. For additional information about such reverse auctions, see

GSA Auctions (**gsaauctions.gov/gsaauctions/gsaauctions**). In the United States, for example, the local housing projects of HUD (Housing and Urban Development), which provides housing to low-income residents, are moving to e-procurement.

Example 1: Procurement at GSA

The US General Services Administration (**gsa.gov**) uses technologies such as demand aggregation and reverse auctions to buy items for various units of the federal government (see also **governmentauctions.org** and **liquidation.com**).

Example 2: The US SBA

The Procurement Marketing and Access Network of the Small Business Administration (**sba.gov**) has developed a service called PRO-Net (**pro-net.sba.gov**). It is a searchable database that contracting officers in various US government units can use to find products and services sold by small, disadvantaged businesses or businesses owned by women.

Group Purchasing

Many government agencies also utilize online group purchasing, which was described in Chaps. 3 and 4. A related aspect is *quantity discount*, where suppliers post prices that get lower as quantities of orders increase. A similar method occurs when government buyers initiate group purchasing by posting product requests that other buyers may review and then join the group(s).

Forward and Reverse E-Auctions

Many governments auction equipment surpluses or other goods, ranging from vehicles to foreclosed real estate. These auctions are now moving to the Internet. Governments can auction from a government website, or they can use third-party auction sites such as **ebay.com**, **bid4assets.com**, or **governmentauctions.org**. The US General Services Administration (GSA) in the United States operates a property auction site online (see **gsaauctions.gov**), where real-time auctions for surplus and seized goods are conducted. Some of these auctions are restricted to dealers; others are open to the public (see **governmentauctions.org**). More common is the use of reverse auctions for purchasing goods and services, as described in Chap. 4.

Government-to-Government

The **government-to-government (G2G)** category consists of EC activities between different units of governments, including those within one governmental body. Many of these are aimed at improving the effectiveness and the efficiency of government operations. Here are G2G examples from the United States:

- **Intelink**. Intelink (**intelink.gov**) is an intranet that contains classified information that is shared by the numerous US intelligence agencies. It is a US government computer system that is provided only for authorized US government use.

Government-to-Employees and Internal Efficiency and Effectiveness

Governments are introducing various EC initiatives internally. Two areas are illustrated next.

Government-to-Employees (G2E)

Governments are just as interested, as private sector organizations are, in providing services and information electronically to their employees. **Government-to-employees (G2E)** applications refer to e-commerce activities between the government and its employees. Such activities may be especially useful in enabling efficient e-training of new employees, e-learning for upgrading skills, and communication and collaboration activities. Other typical services are e-payroll, e-human resource management, and e-recruiting.

Internal Efficiency and Effectiveness (IEE)

Governments have to improve the efficiency and effectiveness of their operations in order to stay within their budgets and avoid criticism. Unfortunately, not all governments (or units within governments) are efficient or effective. Automation, including e-commerce, provides an opportunity to significantly improve operations.

The following example illustrates some e-commerce applications for improving IEE.

Example

The US Office of Management and Budget (OMB) (whitehouse.gov/omb) provides a list of activities related to IEE in their FY 2011 "Report to Congress" (see Office of Management and Budget 2012).

This list includes topics such as:

- Federal Cloud Computing Program Management
- Innovative Wireless and Mobile Apps Platform
- FedSpace (a collaborative platform for Federal employees)
- Federal Data Center Consolidation Initiative
- Small Business Dashboard
- IT Dashboard (also available via mobile devices)
- Performance.gov (a website with information about performance improvement activities)

In addition, there are traditional IEE-related initiatives such as e-payroll, e-record management, e-training, integrated acquisition, and e-HRM.

Implementing E-Government

Like most other organizations, government entities want to become digital. Therefore, one can find a large number of EC applications in government organizations. For many practices and examples, see Mei Hua and Rohman (2015), Wohlers and Bernier (2016), and the Government Innovator Network at **innovations.harvard.edu**.

This section examines some of the trends and issues involved in implementing e-government. Note that one of the major implementation inhibitors is the desire of many governments to maintain control over the use and dissemination of data and knowledge.

The Transformation to E-Government

The transformation from traditional delivery of government services to full implementation of e-government may be a lengthy process. For the digitization process, see Corydon et al. (2016).

All major software companies provide tools and solutions for conducting e-government. One example is Cognos (an IBM Company; see **ibm.com/analytics/us/en/technology/cognos-software**). The company also provides free white papers.

E-Government 2.0 and Social Media and Networking

By employing social media tools and new business models and embracing social networks and user participation, government agencies can raise the effectiveness of their online activities to meet users' needs at a reasonable cost. Such initiatives are referred to as **Government 2.0**. For extensive coverage of content and applications of this topic, see Dalton (2016), Imholt (2015), and Grogan (2015). Government agencies around the world are now experimenting with social media tools as well as with their own pages and presence on public social network sites. Governments are using Web 2.0 tools mainly for collaboration, dissemination of information, e-learning, and citizen engagement.

Example

The US Coast Guard uses YouTube, Twitter, and Flickr to disseminate information and discuss their rescue operations. Notable is FEMA's Twitter feed (previously "FEMA in Focus"), a channel that provides dissemination of FEMA-related information (see **twitter.com/fema**). Law enforcement agencies use social media (such as Facebook and Twitter) to hunt for criminals. (For some examples, see **digitaltrends.com/social-media/the-new-inside-source-for-police-forces-social-networks**.) For more on how government agencies are expanding their uses of social media, see **federalnewsradio.**

com/445/3547907/Agencies-open-the-door-to-innovative-uses-of-social-media. For more examples, see Grogan (2015). For case studies in e-government 2.0, see Boughzala et al. (2015). For case studies about how e-government 2.0 is changing citizens' relationships, see Boughzala et al. (2016).

The Potential of E-Government 2.0 (Social Media)

Many governments are embarking on e-government 2.0 initiatives.

For an extensive list of resources on social networks in governments, including reports, applications, and policies, see **adobe.com/solutions/government.html?romoid=DJHAZ**. For extensive coverage of e-government, see **wisegeek.com/what-is-e-government.htm**.

M-Government

Mobile government (m-government) is the implementation of e-government applications using wireless platforms and mobile devices, especially smartphones. It is done mostly in G2C (e.g., see Government of Canada Wireless Portal; **mgov-world.org**). M-government uses wireless Internet infrastructure and devices. It is a value-added service, because it enables governments to reach a larger number of citizens (e.g., via smartphone or Twitter) and it can be more cost-effective than wireline-based EC platforms. It is very useful in disasters (e.g., emergency notifications), is fast (e.g., in conducting surveys and polls), and is convenient for citizens as well. In addition, governments employ large numbers of mobile workers who are supported by wireless devices.

M-government is offered mostly in education, health, financial services, welfare, and environment control. For data regarding the percentage of m-government offered by governments in each category in 2014 and 2016, see **statista.com/statistics/421693/e-government-availability-mobile-serevices**. For innovative mobile applications for citizens, see Kwang (2016a).

Example: Public Buses in Honolulu

An example of a mobile government project is the city government–run bus location system (an app) in Honolulu, Hawaii, called "DaBus" (**honolulu.gov/mobile**). Using your cell phone, you can find the estimated arrival time of any of the buses at more than 4000 bus stops. Buses are equipped with GPS devices that transmit the bus's location in real time. The system then calculates the estimated arrival time for each stop. Similar systems exist in many other places (e.g., in Singapore "IRIS," in the USA "NextBus," and in the United Kingdom "JourneyPlanner" apps).

M-government can help make public information and government services available anytime and anywhere. See **usa.gov/mobileapps.shtml**. A specific example of m-government would be texting a mass alert to the public in the event of a major disaster.

Smart Cities

Smart cities are frequently implemented as e-government projects, and they include digitization of government services, transportation, education, e-health, etc. (see details in Chap. 7). For how this is done in Nigeria, see Akwaja (2017).

The Benefits of M-Government

The major benefits of m-government are:

- More citizens and employees can be reached (anyplace, anytime).
- Cost reduction (e.g., by increasing productivity of employees, reduced budgets).
- Modernizing the operations of the government (e.g., employ mobile devices).
- Employees can bring their own mobile devices to work, saving hardware and software costs.
- Providing quality, flexible services to the public.
- Increasing the reach and speed for public dissemination of information.

In addition, many of the generic benefits of m-commerce (Chap. 6) are valid in m-government too.

Some Implementation Issues

Representative issues of implementing m-government are:

- An expensive infrastructure may be needed to supplement the existing traditional infrastructure. More infrastructures are needed for the wireless systems as well as for the increased volume of information flow (see the closing case in this chapter).
- It may be difficult to maintain security and privacy of information on public mobile networks.
- For many citizens, mobile devices are too small or complex to use.
- In many countries, there is a lack of standards and legislation regarding the use of data delivered wirelessly.

Cutting-Edge Technologies in e-Government

Many city, state and even country governments are implementing or experimenting with cutting-edge technologies, mostly artificial intelligent-related.

Here are few examples:

Artificial Intelligence (AI) Applications

Many believe that AI is the next big thing for governments (e.g., Newcombe 2016). Kwang (2017b) reports about publications of the US Government Office for Science on the future of artificial intelligence (AI) and its impact on society. In general, AI is expected to increase innovation and productivity, enable more efficient use of resources, enable new business models, enable improved health (see section "E-Health"), reduce the burden of search, and improve governmental decision-making. In addition, it will help to make more use of data and make government departments to better understand those people and other departments that they serve. In addition AI will act as a virtual advisor.

Virtual Advisors

Virtual advisors (Chap. 7) are getting smarter and can assist both government employees and citizens in providing information and in decision-making.

Chatbots

These are already used in airports, government offices, public museums, etc. as guides. These are robots equipped with knowledge about the areas they serve. Users can conduct Q&A sessions with them. Spinosa (2016) describes potential applications. Chatbots are parts of the virtual advising.

For an overview, see Haisler (2016).

Virtual Reality and Augmented Reality

Virtual and augmented reality may have huge impact for governments in their contacts with citizens, in increasing productivity, in training provide by governments (see section "E-Learning, E-Training, and E-Books"), and in their research and development activities. For details, see Lohrmann (2016); Thomas (2016) explores the impact on government analytics.

How Chatbots Will Affect Government

According to Haisler (2016), chatbots will have the following effects:

1. Personal chatbots will enable citizens to experience government without visiting physical government facilities (e.g., via Q&A sessions).
2. Enterprise chatbots can help in optimizing customer service provided by government employees.
3. Chatbots will facilitate civic engagements, eliminating the need to go to council meetings, and search lots of information to find answers to questions.
4. Chatbots will facilitate collective intelligence, enabling citizens to interact with data.

For further discussions, see Estopace (2016c).

Other Areas

In section "E-Learning, E-Training, and E-Books", we describe how AI and chatbot facilitate e-learning. Smart computers, such as IBM Watson, can help governments to better anticipate citizens' needs. The Internet of Things (Chap. 7), predictive analytics, and robots can increase the efficiency of the governments.

SECTION 5.1 REVIEW QUESTIONS

1. Define e-government.
2. What are the four major categories of e-government services?
3. Describe G2C.
4. Describe how e-voting works.
5. Describe the two main areas of G2B activities.
6. How does government use EC internally and when dealing with other governments?
7. Describe e-government social networking activities. What are some potential benefits?
8. Describe m-government and its implementation issues.
9. Describe some cutting-edge technologies for e-government.

5.2   E-LEARNING, E-TRAINING, AND E-BOOKS

The topic of e-learning is gaining much attention, especially because even first-rate universities such as MIT, Harvard, and Stanford in the United States and Oxford in the United Kingdom are implementing it. Figure 5.3 shows the forces that are driving the transition from traditional education to online learning. E-learning also is growing as a method for training and knowledge creation in the business world and is becoming a major e-business activity. In this section, we will discuss several topics related to e-learning. For a comprehensive coverage of e-learning in higher education, see Garrison (2016).

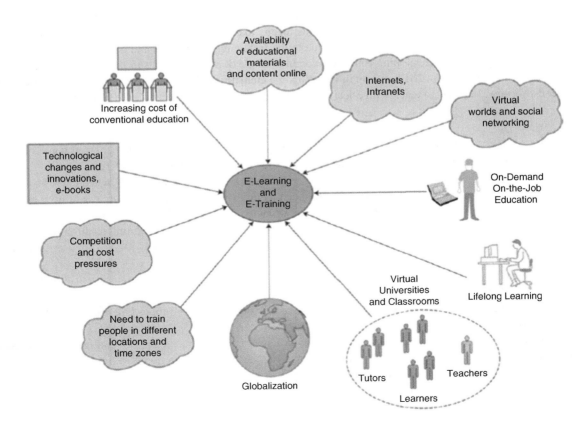

Fig. 5.3 The drivers of e-learning

The Basics of E-Learning: Definitions and Concepts

There are several definitions of e-learning. A working definition of **e-learning** is the use of online delivery of educational materials and methods, using information technologies, for the purposes of learning, teaching, training, or gaining knowledge at any time and at many different locations (see **people.howstuffworks.com/elearning1.htm, en.wikipedia.org/wiki/E-learning,** and **webopedia.com/TERM/E/e_learning.html**).

E-learning is broader than the term *online learning*, which generally refers exclusively to Web-based learning. E-learning includes *m-learning* (or *mobile learning*) that is used when the material is delivered wirelessly to smartphones, tablets, or other mobile devices (description to follow). E-learning is synonymous with *computer-based instruction, computer-based training, online education*, and other terms.

It appears in a variety of electronically supported learning and teaching activities, ranging from virtual classrooms to mobile conferences. E-learning includes a variety of methods of computer-facilitated learning ranging, from self-study with DVDs to online degrees offered by universities. E-learning may also include the use of Web-based teaching materials and hypermedia, multimedia CD-ROMs, learning and teaching portals, discussion boards, collaborative software, e-mail, blogs, wikis, chat rooms, computer-aided assessments, educational animation, simulations, games, learning management software, and more.

An interesting school without classrooms is the Hellerup School in Denmark. Students there "learn by doing" and even determine the best way they can learn. For how the school operates, **see theglobeandmail.com/report-on-business/economy/canada-competes/no-classrooms-and-lots-of-technology-a-danish-schools-approach/article12688441** and Millar (2013). For more on e-learning, see **en.wikipedia.org/wiki/E-learning**. For a community and resources for e-learning professionals, see **elearningguild.com**.

Benefits and Drawbacks of E-Learning

E-learning has many benefits both to the teaching institutions and to the learners. However, it also has several drawbacks, thus making it a controversial topic.

Benefits of E-Learning

In the Internet age, skills and knowledge need to be *continually updated* and refreshed (lifetime learning) to keep up with today's fast-paced business and technological changes. This means that more people need to learn and frequently do so in nontraditional ways. E-learning supports such learning due to the following capabilities and benefits:

E-learning can be very useful in developing countries. For an example of positive results in Jamaica, see Thompson (2014). For the top ten e-learning statistics in 2014 with an infographic, see **elearningindustry.com/top-10-e-learning-statistics-for-2014-you-need-to-know**. For how to teach with e-learning including the design of material, see Clark and Mayer (2016).

- **Education.** Students can learn at home and keep their regular jobs while in school. Busy homemakers can earn degrees.
- **Learning and training time reduction.** E-learning can expedite training time by up to 50%.
- **Cost reduction.** The cost of providing a learning experience can be reduced by 50–70% when classroom lectures are replaced by e-learning sessions. This includes reduced faculty cost, no classrooms, and less or no travel time.
- **Large number and diversity of learners.** E-learning can provide training to a large number of people from diverse cultural backgrounds and educational levels, even though they are at different locations in different time zones. Large companies such as Cisco Systems, Inc. (**cisco.com**), provide online training courses to a large number of employees, customers, and business partners.
- **Innovative teaching.** Ability to provide innovative teaching methods such as special engagements, interaction with experts, interaction with learners in other countries, and so forth.
- **Measurement and assessment of progress.** Ability to assess progress in real time, find areas of difficulties, and design remedial work.
- **Self-paced and motivation learning.** E-learning students usually are self-paced and self-motivated. These characteristics may result in higher content retention (25 to 60% higher than with traditional lecture-based training).
- **Richness and quality.** E-learning enables the use of top instructors as well as employing rich multimedia support. This may make learning more enjoyable. Difficult content can be made interesting and easy to understand. Overall, the quality of learning may increase.

- **Flexibility.** E-learners are able to adjust the time, location, content, and speed of learning according to their own personal schedules.
- **Updated and consistent teaching material.** It is almost impossible to economically update the information in textbooks more frequently than every 2 or 3 years; e-learning can offer real-time access to the most updated knowledge. Delivery of e-learning may be more consistent than that of material presented in traditional classroom learning, because variations among teachers and teaching materials are minimized.
- **Ability to learn from mobile devices.** This helps learning in any place and at any time as well as providing support to learners by teachers and peers.
- **Expert knowledge.** In contrast with the knowledge of a single instructor in the classroom, e-learning may include the knowledge of several experts, each of whom prepares a teaching module in his or her area of expertise.
- **Fear-free environment.** E-learning can facilitate learning for students who may not wish to join a face-to-face group discussion to interact with peers or teachers.

Drawbacks and Challenges of E-Learning

Despite the numerous benefits for both the learners and the teaching organizations, e-learning does have some drawbacks, such as the following:

- **Need for instructor retraining.** Some instructors do not have the knowledge to teach by electronic means and may require training, which costs money.
- **Equipment needs and support services.** Additional funds are needed (by the teaching institute) to purchase e-learning systems that supplement traditional ones. These are needed for e-learning creation, use, and maintenance.
- **Lack of face-to-face interaction and campus lifestyle.** Many feel that the intellectual stimulation that takes place through interaction in a classroom with "live" instructors and peers cannot fully be replicated with e-learning.
- **Assessments and examinations.** In the higher education environment, one criticism is that professors may not be able to adequately assess student work completed through e-learning. There is no way of knowing, for example, who actually completed the assignments or exams. (Nevertheless, the same is true for any homework done outside the classroom.)
- **Creation, maintenance, and updating.** It is not simple to prepare material and design courses online. (For how to do it, see Vai and Sosulski (2015).) Although e-learning materials seem to be easier to update than traditionally published materials, there are practical difficulties (e.g., cost, instructors' time) in keeping e-learning materials current. The content of e-learning material can be difficult to maintain due to the lack of ownership of, and accountability for, website material. The developers of online content might not be those who update it.
- **Need for reliable wireline and wireless communication networks and devices.** Privacy needs to be protected as well as systems need to be secured.
- **Protection of intellectual property.** It is difficult and expensive to control the transmission of copyrighted works downloaded from the e-learning platform.
- **Student retention.** Without some human feedback and intervention, it may be difficult to keep certain students engaged and energetic.

The top constraints for corporate e-learning are (1) too costly to create and maintain, (2) difficulties persuading people to learn in new ways, (3) insufficient technological support, (4) employee hesitation to contribute to social learning, and (5) learners may prefer traditional classroom instruction.

Advanced technologies can reduce some of the above and other drawbacks and constraints. For example, some online software products have features that help stimulate student thinking. Biometric controls can be used to verify the identity of students who are taking examinations from a distance. However, these features add to the costs of e-learning.

For more about the disadvantages of e-learning, see **academia.edu/4052785/Advantages_and_Disadvantages_of_e_Learning**.

Distance Learning and Online Universities

The term **distance learning**, also known as *distance education*, refers to education where the teacher and students are in different locations. In such a case, the student is separated from a classroom by distance and possibly time. Sometimes students meet once or twice at a physical location in order to get to know each other, meet the instructor or coordinator, or take examinations. Distance learning is becoming widely used in universities and learning institutions around the globe. Major universities offer courses and degrees via this mode, which is becoming more recognized and acceptable. For details, see **onlineeducation.net**.

Virtual Universities: Real Degrees

The concept of **virtual universities**, online universities where students take classes from home via the Internet, is expanding rapidly. Hundreds of thousands of students in many countries, from the United Kingdom to Israel to Thailand, are taking online classes. A large number of existing universities, including Stanford University and other top-tier universities, offer online education of some form; for example, MIT offers thousands of their courses online (see courses at **ocw.mit.edu/index.htm**). Millions of independent learners from all over the world (students, professors, self-learners) log on to the MIT OpenCourseWare site each year (see **ocw.mit.edu/about** and **ocw.mit.edu/about/site-statistics**). Some universities, such as the University of Phoenix (**phoenix.edu**), National University (**nu.edu**), and University of Maryland (**umuc.edu**), offer hundreds of courses and dozens of degrees online to students worldwide. The California Virtual Campus (cvc.edu) provides a directory and links to thousands of courses and online degree programs offered by colleges and universities in California (see **cvc.edu/courses**). For information about distance learning resources and online universities, see **distancelearn.about.com**. For a list of the top online MBA programs in the world, see **onlinemba.com/rankings**.

Innovations in E-Learning

There are many innovations in e-learning, one of which is shown in the following example.

Example: E-Learning via Robots

In December 2010, the city of Daegu in South Korea introduced 29 robots into 19 elementary schools. Each robot, about 3.2-feet tall, was designed to teach English to the students. Developed by the Korea Institute of Science and Technology (KIST), the robots roll around on wheels and ask questions in English (see Fig. 5.4). (For details, see **cnet.com/news/korean-schools-welcome-more-robot-teachers**.)

The robots can be moved around the classroom by the instructor (via remote control), which facilitates the interaction of teachers with students. The robots can read books to the students and even "dance" to music. The robots display the face of a "teacher." The tutoring is actually provided by experienced teachers in the Philippines, who are paid much less than Korean teachers. The robots are programed to use the most effective and current teaching methods (e.g., using multimedia games).

Fig. 5.4 EngKey—a robot English teacher (Source: The Korea Advanced Institute of Science and Technology. Used with permission)

Cameras detect the Filipino teachers' facial expressions and instantly reflect them on the robot's avatar face. The students participate more actively, especially the shy ones who are afraid of speaking out loud. The robots are also used in remote rural areas where English teachers are in short supply.

For more examples on educational robotic teachers, see **nytimes.com/2010/07/11/science/11robots.html?pagewanted= all&_r=0**.

Online Corporate Training

With the increased use of smart technologies (Chap. 7) comes the possibility of massive replacement of jobs by machines. Therefore, companies will need to retrain many of their employees (see Gaikwad 2016).

Like educational institutions, a large number of business organizations are using e-learning on a large scale. Many companies, such as Cisco Systems (**cisco.com**), offer online training. A study by the American Society for Training and Development found that nearly one third of corporate training content was delivered electronically.

Corporate training is driven by multiple factors and is often done via intranets and corporate portals. However, the students use the Internet as well. It has several variations, one of which is *on-demand online training*, which is offered by software companies such as Citrix Systems (**citrix.com**). However, in large corporations with multiple sites, and for studies from home, the Internet is used to access the online material. Vendors' success stories of online training and educational materials can be found at **adobe.com/resources/elearning** and at **brightwave.co.uk**. For a comprehensive guide to online training, see Kaattari and Trottier (2013).

Example
Dresser-Rand is a global US corporation that makes compression equipment. It has over 5500 employees in 50 different locations in 26 countries that speak 14 different languages. The company needs to do extensive training due to growth and employee retirement. Previously, the company used over 600 training vendors to conduct training. A major challenge was the update of the teaching material due to technological changes. Using the learning management system (LMS) from Coastal eLearning (**training.dupont.com**, now a part of DuPont Sustainable Solutions), the company deployed a comprehensive online training program via Dresser-Rand University, saving over $1 million per year. To read the case study, see **training.dupont.com/content/pdf/case-studies/dresser-rand-elearning-case-study.pdf**.

Using Computer Games for Training Current and New Employees

There is a trend to use computer simulation games for training.

Example
Marriott International developed a game "My Marriott Hotel," available on Facebook, for help in recruiting and training. The players learn how hotels and their restaurants operate. Initially, Marriott developed a game for the kitchen. The players needed to choose what ingredients to use for different foods (based on price and quality). The players also learned how to select employees from a pool of candidates and make decisions about equipment purchasing. They also learned about food quality.

For a free e-book on how gamification reshapes learning, see **elearningindustry.com/free-ebooks/gamification-reshapes-learning?pushcrew_powered**.

M-Learning

A special category of e-learning is **m-learning**, or mobile learning, which refers to e-learning, or other forms of education using mobile devices. Thus, one can learn at any place where a mobile device works. M-learning deals with communication and teaching in wireless environments. Special attention is given to situations where the instructors and the teaching materials are mobile. This technology enables learners to work and collaborate more easily than in offline situations. An example is Mobile Learn (**waldenu.edu/experience/learning/mobilelearn**), an online learning program offered by Walden University (**waldenu.edu**), an online university that extensively uses m-learning. Some offline universities are using mobile learning as well. One such university is Abilene Christian University (**acu.edu**); faculties are focused on using tablets for learning and teaching (see **legacy.acu.aem.host/technology/mobilelearning/**). For further details including case studies and resources, see **m-learning.org** and **en.wikipedia.org/wiki/M-learning**. See also a slide presentation titled "What is M-Learning" at **slideshare.net/aurionlearning/what-is-mlearning**.

Social Networks and E-Learning

Since its inception, social networking has been interrelated with learning. A new term, **social learning**, also known as *e-learning 2.0*, has been coined to describe the learning, training, and knowledge sharing in social networks and/or facilitated with social software tools. Social environments facilitate high-tech-based training, making it possible for learners to share their experiences with others. Thus, several companies already are using social media for training and development purposes (e.g., see **advancinginsights.com**). Social learning is based on *social learning theory*. For details, see **en.wikipedia.org/wiki/Social_learning_theory**.

Some students use Facebook, LinkedIn, Pinterest, Twitter, and so forth to connect with other pupils. For example, learners can study together, discuss topics, or brainstorm online. Unfortunately, the distractions found on some networks can make it difficult to focus on learning. Some companies use social media to engage employees in group learning via knowledge sharing.

According to News (2016), user-generated content which is a key property of social media is an important trend in corporate e-learning.

Several social networks (or communities) are dedicated to learning and training (e.g., see **elearning.co.uk**). An example of a social network for learning is TestDen or LearnHub (**getlearnhub.com**), which is dedicated to international education. Some scholars believe that the future of e-learning is social learning.

Social networking technology possesses the following capabilities that may facilitate learning:

- *Connect learners in a learning project.* It enables people to connect in real time for discussion, collaboration, and problem solving.
- *Make social part of the company's learning strategy.*
- *Build the know-how of experts.*
- *Enable learners to engage.* Generation X and millennial workers use Web 2.0 tools extensively for interacting among themselves and with others. Organizations can reach out to this group and use social networks for training.
- *Use platforms such as Pinterest to develop creativity in design and to use images to sharpen some learning skills.*
- *Provide relevant content prior to offline meetings for voting or requesting supplements.* This can enrich and facilitate classroom delivery.
- *Link learners to relevant resources and let them rate and share opinions.*
- *Quickly identify the training needs and implementation issues of individuals and groups.*
- *Have learners provide social support to each other.*
- *Improve and expedite learning-related communication (e.g., via Twitter).*

Many universities combine e-learning and social networking; additionally, numerous professors have blogs and wikis for their classes and encourage communication and collaboration via Facebook or other social networks.

Some Recent Technology Support of E-Learning

Several recent technology innovations are used to facilitate learning. Here is an example:

Example

SJI International School (Singapore) is using a social mobile platform to create a collaborative learning environment. The platform allows students and teachers to ask questions, discuss topics, share resources, and work collaboratively on projects. For details and the benefits attained, see Kwang (2016b).

Visual Interactive Simulation

An effective technology for e-training and e-learning is *visual interactive simulation* (VIS), which uses computer graphic displays to present the impact of evaluating alternative solutions to problems. It differs from regular graphics in that the user can manipulate the decision-making process and see the results of the interventions. Some learners respond better to graphic displays, especially when they are interactive. For example, VIS was used to examine the operations of a physician clinic environment within a physician network in an effort to provide high-quality medical care. The simulation system identified the most important input factors that significantly affected performance. These inputs, when properly managed, led to lower costs and a higher level of medical care.

VIS systems provide the following major potential benefits:

- Shorten learning time.
- Aid in teaching how to operate complex equipment.
- Enable self-paced learning, any place, any time.
- Aid in memorization.
- Lower overall training costs.
- Record an individual's learning progress and improve on it.

Visual interactive simulation is closely related to virtual reality (Chap. 2).

Robotics, Chatbots, Telepreser, Robots, and More

Earlier in the chapter, we provided an example of robots which are used as instructors to teach English in Korea. Nowadays, robotics and other artificial intelligence techniques are extensively used to facilitate learning. For an overview, see Anderson (2016).

Using Chatbots

Chatbots are conversational robots (see Chap. 7) that people can communicate with in a natural language. According to Sujatha (2016), chatbots can be used for social interaction to facilitate learning. They are also used in simulation (simulator robots) and as a source of reinforcement.

Recent Technologies

Augmented reality, big data, gamification, personalized e-learning, and other recent technologies are presented by Anderson (2016). Also related is the use of e-learning in e-government (section "Digital Government: An Overview") and smart cities (Chap. 7), for an example, how e-learning is related to smart cities, see Akwaja (2017).

Virtual Assistants

These can be used as advisors to students and teachers. For the use of chatbots for the interface and knowledge base of wisdom, see Chap. 7. Virtual assistants play an increased role in e-learning.

A list of all learning-related chatbots, virtual assistants, conversational agents, and virtual agents, available as of 2016, is provided by **chatbots.org/applications/e-learning**. For a list of vendors and products (including AI based) for small businesses, see Beattie (2016).

E-Learning Management Systems

A **learning management system (LMS)** (also known as a course management system) consists of software applications for managing e-training and e-learning programs including content, scheduling, delivery tips, and so forth. Capterra Inc. Learning Management System Software (**capterra.com/learning-management-system-software**) and similar systems exhibit these capabilities:

- Provide effective student–instructor interactions
- Centralize and automate program administration
- Enable the use of self-service and self-guided e-learning services
- Create and rapidly deliver learning content modules
- Provide a single point of access to all e-learning online materials
- Help manage compliance requirements
- Consolidate training initiatives on a scalable Web-based platform
- Support the portability of systems
- Increase the efficiency and effectiveness of e-learning
- Personalize content and enable knowledge reuse

Many companies (e.g., Saba Software, Inc.; **saba.com/us/apps/learning-work**, SumTotal Systems; **sumtotalsystems. com**) provide methodologies, software, hardware, and consultation about e-learning and its management. For more on LMS, see **en.wikipedia.org/wiki/Learning_management_system** and watch the video titled "What is a Learning Management System?" (2:51 min) at **proprofs.com/c/category/lms**.

Note that it is possible to control what the students are doing when they self-study. For example, according to Streitfeld (2013), teachers can find out when students are skipping pages, not bothering to take notes, or failing to highlight significant passages.

One of the most effective tools for learning management is Blackboard Inc. (**blackboard.com**, now combined with WebCT). A brief description follows.

Example 1: Blackboard

Blackboard Inc. (**blackboard.com**) is the world's largest supplier of course management system software for educational institutions. How do Blackboard products work? A textbook publisher places a book's content, teaching notes, quizzes, and other materials on a Blackboard in a standardized format. Instructors can access modules and transfer them on to their university's Blackboard sites, which can be accessed by their students.

A professor can easily incorporate a book's content into Blackboard's software. As of 2009, Blackboard also delivers corporate and government employee training programs worldwide, which increases productivity and reduces costs. For details, see **blackboard.com** and **en.wikipedia.org/wiki/Blackboard_Inc**.

Example 2: Moodle

An alternative to Blackboard is a mostly free open source system called Moodle (see **moodle.org**).

For an example of how a vendor implemented a new suite of technologically advanced solutions into its cloud-based multichannel LMS, see Lechner (2016).

Electronic Books (E-Books)

An **electronic book (e-book)** is a book in digital format that can be read on a computer screen, on a mobile device, or on a dedicated device known as an *e-reader*. A major event in electronic publishing occurred in 2000, when Stephen King's book *Riding the Bullet* was published exclusively online. For $2.50, readers were able to purchase the e-book on Amazon.com and other e-book providers. Several hundred thousand copies were sold in a few days. However, hackers broke the security protection, copied the book, and distributed free copies of the book online. (See **bookbusinessmag.com/article/ after-riding-bullet-12555/1#**.)

Publishers of e-books have since become more sophisticated, and online publishing has become more secure. Today there are several types of e-books that can be delivered and read in various ways:

- **Via a dedicated reader**. The book must be downloaded to an e-reader such as Amazon's Kindle.
- **Via Web access**. Readers can locate a book on the publisher's website and read it there. The book cannot be downloaded.
- **Via Web download and smartphones**. Readers can download the book to a PC.
- **Via a general-purpose reader**. The book can be downloaded to a mobile device such as an iPad or iPhone.
- **Via a Web server**. The contents of a book are stored on a Web server and downloaded for print-on-demand (which is discussed later in this book).

Most e-books require some type of payment. Readers either pay before they download a book from a website, such as buying a Kindle copy on Amazon.com, or they pay when they order the special CD-ROM edition of a book. Today, Amazon. com offers hundreds of thousands of e-books, e-newspapers (including international ones), and other digital products. All are cheaper than the hard copy version (e.g., new release books may cost $10 or less). There are many free e-books as well (e.g., **free-ebooks.net** and **onlinebooks.library.upenn.edu**).

Devices for Reading E-Books

The major device used to read an e-book is an e-reader. Most e-readers are lightweight (about 10 ounces) and are convenient to carry. The major e-readers and tablets are listed and compared at **the-ebook-reader.com**.

Several other aids are available to help readers who want to read a large amount of material online. For example, Microsoft ClearType (**microsoft.com/en-us/Typography/ClearTypeInfo.aspx**) and CoolType from Adobe (**adobe.com**) can be used to improve screen display, colors, and font sizes. Glowing screens can help you read in the dark (e.g., Kindle Touch and the Kindle Fire have a built-in light).

Combining E-Readers and Tablets

The trend today is to combine e-readers with tablet computers as was initiated with Amazon's Kindle Fire. The 7-inch portable devices allow people to read books, magazines, and documents and listen to audio books. Users can play games, listen to music, watch movies and TV shows, and much more. Kindle has Internet access via Wi-Fi, social network access, and e-mail is available also. Finally, with Amazon's Kindle Owner's Lending Library, Kindle owners who have Amazon Prime can choose from a selection of hundreds of thousands of books to borrow, for free, with no due dates.

Note: Tablet manufacturers also offer a combination of e-readers and tablets. The difference is that e-reader-based products such as Kindle Fire have less computing capabilities, while tablets such as iPad have a less capable e-reader and are more expensive.

Advantages and Limitations of E-Books

For e-books to make an impact, they must offer advantages to both readers and publishers. Otherwise, there would be little incentive to change from traditional books. Indeed, e-book sales are exploding due to the following advantages:

- Ability to store hundreds of books on a small mobile device. (External storage can hold much more.)
- Lower cost to buyers. The simple e-reader model costs less than $75; the tablet based costs less than $200.
- Searchable text—you can show links and connect easily to the Web.
- Instant delivery via downloads from anywhere. The tablet-based models provide you with many of the capabilities of other types of mobile computers.
- Portability—they go where you go.
- Easy integration of content from several sources.
- Durability—they are built stronger than a traditional book (but they can break if you are not careful). In addition, readers tend not to lose them (again, you need to be careful).
- Ability to enlarge the font size for easy reading and to add light if needed.
- Media rich (audio, color, video, etc.).
- Minimal cost for printing out a hard copy.
- Good readability in bright sunlight (ability to read books outdoors).
- Easy updating of content.
- Almost no wear and tear.
- Easy to find out-of-print books.

For additional benefits and advantage of e-books, see **successconsciousness.com/ebooks_benefits.htm**.

The primary advantage that e-books offer publishers is lower production, marketing, and distribution (shipment) costs, which have a significant impact on the price of books (e-textbooks are about 50% cheaper than print versions). Other advantages for publishers are the lower updating and reproduction costs, the ability to reach many readers, and the ease of combining chapters from several books to create customized textbooks, so professors can use materials from different books (usually by the same publisher) in one course.

Finally, the light weight of the tablet can eliminate the back pain that people, especially school children, have from carrying backpacks full of heavy books.

Of course, e-books have some limitations: They require hardware and software that may be too expensive for some readers; some people have difficulty reading large amounts of material on a relatively small computer screen; batteries may run out; and there are multiple, competing software and hardware standards to choose from, confusing the buyers. Several of these obstacles may lessen in time.

A Final Note: Is This the End of Printed Books?

According to Amazon.com, in 2011, the e-book sales on their site considerably exceeded the sales of hardcover and paperback books. (See **nytimes.com/2011/05/20/technology/20amazon.html**.) By 2014, e-book sales surpassed the sales of paper-based books (for all publishers). However, according to Nuwer (2016), e-book sales have plateaued.

Despite the limitations, e-books have become very popular, especially due to sophisticated e-readers. For example, even the Harry Potter books are now available in electronic format, and they are not encrypted, so that readers can move the books between mobile devices and even to a PC. For a comparison between e-books and printed books, see **thrall.org/docs/ebooksandbooks.pdf** and **en.wikipedia.org/wiki/E-book**.

According to Alsever (2017), the $1 billion e-book industry is spawning a whole new ecosystem of businesses that serve the burgeoning world of digital publishing.

The question is: Will most printed books be eliminated? The trend is very clear. Sales of printed books are on the decline, while e-books are up. With Amazon's free loan of Kindle books to their prime members, we expect even more people reading e-books. Are paper books going to disappear? (See discussion by Vaughan-Nichols 2012.) For the advantages of e-books versus traditional books, see **online-bookstores-review.toptenreviews.com/the-advantages-of-ebooks-versus-traditional-books.html**.

SECTION 5.2 REVIEW QUESTIONS

1. Define e-learning and describe its drivers and benefits.
2. List some of the major drawbacks of e-learning and describe how they can be prevented.
3. Describe virtual universities and distance learning.
4. Define e-training and describe how it is done.
5. Describe the connection between e-learning, social networking, and mobile technologies.
6. List some e-learning tools, and describe Blackboard and visual interactive simulation (VIS).
7. How are robots, chatbots, and other artificial intelligence technologies used to facilitate e-learning?
8. Describe e-books.
9. What is an e-reader? What are its major capabilities?
10. List the major advantages and limitations of e-books to their users.

5.3   E-HEALTH

One of the major application areas of e-commerce is e-health.

Definition

The term has many definitions (Wikipedia reports about 51 of them). The *World Health Organization* (WHO) defines e-health as follows: "*E-health* is the transfer of health resources and healthcare by electronic means. It encompasses three main areas:

- The delivery of health information, for health professionals and health consumers, through the Internet and telecommunications
- Using the power of IT and e-commerce to improve public health services (e.g., through the education and training of health workers)
- The use of e-commerce and e-business practices in health systems management

The major concern of WHO (**telehealthcode.eu/glossary-of-terms.html**) is the efficient use of health resources for providing better and safer healthcare worldwide. E-health is an extremely broad field (see **en.wikipedia.org/wiki/Ehealth**). E-health is completely changing healthcare (see Elton and O'Riordan (2016)). For use of artificial intelligence in e-health, see Estopace (2016a). For the use of cloud computing in e-health, see Amazon Web Services Report (2016).

Here we cover only a few representative areas that are directly related to e-commerce.

Electronic Medical Record Systems (EMR)

One of the earliest applications of e-health was the electronic medical record system. The objective was to enable accessibility to patient medical records from any location, even from other cities and countries. With the spread of the Web, this application is growing rapidly. For example, one of the authors of this book can see the results of all his blood tests and certain medical records from any place at anytime, on the Web. Your doctor can pull the medical records whenever she or he needs to see them. One problem is the protection of privacy and assuring the appropriate use of data. In addition, there is an issue of accessibility to the medical records of patients by outsiders, such as researchers.

Doctors' System

Today doctors have immediate access to patient records. They can place orders directly to testing facilities (both internal and external). They can order medications directly from pharmacies, contact specialists, discharge patients in remote locations, and review results of tests from faraway locations. For many additional applications and for comprehensive coverage, see Wachter (2015).

Patient Services

A large number of patient services are available today due to advances in electronic medical record applications. Scheduling appointments from home, reading results of tests from anywhere and anytime are common. Patients enjoy better care due to the availability of Wi-Fi networks (see closing case in this chapter) that enable fast access to information by providers. For use of robots, see Anandan (2015). Patients can find a vast amount of information on hundreds of websites such as WebMD. com. They enjoy the advancements in medicine due to computerized systems. For comprehensive coverage, see Combs et al. (2016). For patient-centric uses of the Internet of Things (IoT) Chap. 7, see Bresnick (2015).

An interesting smartphone application during the 2016 Brazil Olympic was developed by the Brazilian government. It allowed the athletes to record their own health. For details, see Estopace (2016b).

Social Media and Commerce

The healthcare industry was a lagger in adopting social media and social commerce. However, as reported by Lawson (2015) and Mayo Clinic Center for Social Media (2012), this situation is changing. The healthcare participants are becoming actively engaged with one another. Patients report their experiences so others can learn. Doctors have their own professional social networks and other caregivers have similar networks. Medical portals, such as WebMD, disseminate information about many topics, inviting the public to comment. Many healthcare providers have a presence on Facebook, LinkedIn, and other social networks. Large numbers of bloggers provide their opinions on legal, medical, political, financial, and other related topics. One can find a lot of advice on what to eat, how to exercise, and what prescription medicine pills are good for you. Of course, there is extensive advertising all over the social media outlets. For a discussion, see Rogers (2014).

Medical Devices and Patient Surveillance

Large numbers of EC medical devices are used in the health industry. Some of the most well-known ones are robots that help in surgeries and sensors that monitor vital signs of patients and the location of handicapped patients. Considerable use of telecommunication is evidenced in medical facilities (see closing case in this chapter). Known as *telematics*, telemedicine information technologies are used to diagnose and treat diseases from the distance (e.g., in rural areas that have no doctors). A futuristic area is that of the *Internet of Things* (see Chap. 6), where many medical devices and sensors will be combined for new medical treatments. (See **healthitanalytics.com/news**.) A related area is patient monitoring (e.g., see Behr (2016)). For the use of the IoT, see a solution brief at **extremenetworks.com**.

Medical Research

Computer-assisted telecommunication provides access to medical knowledge and help in collaboration among researchers. Such collaboration may expedite new discoveries and save the lives of many patients. For an example of transmission of brain signals, see **enterpriseinnovation.net/article/ntu-develops-smart-chip-wireless-transmissions-brain-signals-1166441949**.

Administrative Purposes

Healthcare providers can save a lot of money by using e-commerce models such as e-procurement, group purchasing of supplies, advertising in social networks, recruitment with the help of LinkedIn and Facebook, and much more. For an example of medical schedules, see Zocdoc.com. Another example is the use of *predictive analysis* to predict which employees might get sick. Healthcare facilities can use B2B to make supply chain-related decision on medical supplies, saving a considerable amount of money (see Insitesoft (2015)).

A final note: A MIT robot helps deliver babies (see O'Brien (2016)).

SECTION 5.3 REVIEW QUESTIONS

1. Define e-health.
2. Describe EMR. Why is it important?
3. Describe social media and commerce in e-health.
4. Describe the major e-health applications in brief.

5.4 DIGITAL DISRUPTION AND SHARING ECONOMY MODELS: RIDE AND ACCOMMODATION SHARING

Digital disruption can take many forms having an impact on industries, companies, business processes, and individual people. In this section, we discuss some of the issues and strategies related to EC disruption and provide several examples, including ride sharing and accommodation sharing. In section "Person-to-Person Electronic Commerce Models", we will present more examples of disruption created by person-to-person EC models.

Digital Disruption: An Introduction

In Chap. 1, we briefly introduced the topic of **digital disruption** of which EC models are a major component. The examples of Amazon.com, Uber, and many other EC companies vividly illustrate how EC companies disrupt whole industries, Expedia and Priceline changed the travel reservation, and E* Trade and TD Ameritrade changed the stock brokerage business. Many more EC companies are doing (or try to do) just that.

Therefore, many businesses are concerned about the new disruptive technologies that threaten their operations, competitive edge, and even survival (e.g., see McCafferty (2016)).

For definition, examples, and discussion, see Poremba (2016). For successful examples, see the slideshow at **itbusinessedge.com/slideshows/9-successful-digital-disruption-examples-02.html**. For a guide to digital disruption, see Bradley and O'Toole (2016).

The disruptive force of e-commerce is discussed by Abcede et al. (2014). The authors describe the top relevant issues and discuss major impacts.

In addition to disrupting whole industries, EC can disrupt certain functions or business processes. For example, EC can change the manner in which customer service is delivered or the manner in which you pay for purchases.

Example: Customer Experience

One area where EC has been a major factor is the customer service experience. Mah et al. (2015) provide a report (as a part of *CMO Innovation Guide*) which shows how EC ("digital") disrupts and innovates the customer's experience (e.g., engagement, analytics, and mobile).

Disruptive technologies may pose a "do-or-die" challenge to many companies. When Starbucks saw decline in sales in 2014, it introduced a disruptive strategy, hoping to increase its sales.

Example: Starbucks Disrupts Its Own Marketing Strategy

Starbucks enabled its customers to make online reservations for lunches and dinners using smartphones. This changed the nature of the company from a coffeehouse to a diversified eatery. For details, see Beuker (2014).

Dealing with Disruptive Forces

Many experts are making suggestions of how to deal with digital disruptions. A comprehensive guide of how to handle such situations is provided by Bradley and O'Toole (2016) of McKinsey & Company (Management Consulting Company). The guide includes advice on how to transform businesses. The authors provide an example of a media company that added online classified ads to its business. In a few years, this addition was generating 80% of their earnings.

For more on how to harness the disruptive forces, see Beard (2016).

Disruptive Companies and Technologies

CNBC provides an annual list of 50 disrupting companies. The 2016 list (CNBC 2016) includes many EC companies (e.g., Uber, Ezetap, Airbnb, DAQRI, Snapchat, Teespring, and Venian). Gartner Inc. also provides an annual list of emerging disruptive technologies. Similar lists are provided by other consultants and technology magazines.

Sharing Economy

In Chap. 1, we introduced the concept of **sharing economy**, which may create some disruptive models and applications (e.g., see Kontzer (2016)). Also known as *collaborative consumption*, and *peer economy*, the concept is actually an umbrella term that covers multiple models, several of which are related directly to e-commerce. A list of sharing economy companies in the areas of food, travel, financial, mobility, travel, logistics, and others is available at **en.wikipedia.org/wiki/Sharing_economy**. In this section, we present two major models: ride sharing and accommodation sharing. In section "Person-to-Person Electronic Commerce Models", we cover the related models of person-to-person (also known as consumer-to-consumer). For a detailed overview, the driving forces, the benefits, and the criticism, see **en.wikipedia.org/wiki/Sharing_economy**.

Ride (Transportation) Sharing

Ride sharing has been around for several decades. People of the same workplaces and students have been using car sharing to save money or to free a family car for other members to use. However, only with the introduction of the smartphones, sharing becomes a mega business. Car sharing basically moved from collaborative commerce ("let's share a car to go to work") to B2C (contact Uber to arrange for a ride). The most impressive case is that of Uber, which despite legal and political obstacles has become a successful multibillion global enterprise. (See the closing case in Chap. 6.)

Example: GM and Lyft

GM provides cars to Lyft drivers (on a rental basis). The project started in Chicago where many potential drivers do not have cars. Called Express Drive, the project is moving to Boston, Washington DC, and Baltimore. Eventually, the cars will become in the future driverless. GM is part owner of Lyft. For details, see Lunden (2016).

In addition to Uber and its competitors, it is interesting to cite some similar ventures.

- Several car manufacturers are joining Uber, Lyft, etc., providing cars (e.g., electric, luxury) for the drivers.
- Ford and MIT University provide electronic cars to students to ride on the campus, on demand. Known as Dynamic Shuttle, the project explores the best way to provide secure and effective transportation to students. For details, see Etherington (2016).
- Explore Bike Share launched a nonprofit program for bike sharing in Memphis, Tenn. in July 2016. The program involved 600 bicycles in 60 stations. For details, see Risher (2016). Bike sharing is available in many cities worldwide.
- ZAPCAB (Chap. 1) pioneered an Uber-like system in Miami, New York, and Vermont. The company encounters several legal and political problems (in addition to disrupting the taxi business).
- In July 2016, Uber joined forces with its major competitor in China (see Young (2016)). Note that this venture has implications for the global competition of ride sharing since both companies compete in other countries.

Note: According to Mack (2017), if we all opt to ride sharing, our city streets would be transformed. But carpool apps could take 10,000 taxis off NY streets, creating unemployment problems.

Accommodation Sharing

With hotel fees mushrooming and shortages prevailing during peak seasons, travelers are seeking innovative reasonable priced accommodations. One solution is *home exchange* (swapping). The idea is simple: I am willing to let someone to stay free in my home while EI am travelling, in exchange of me staying free in that individual's home. There are several variations for how such exchanging is done (e.g., see Lagier (2014)).

Example: Home Exchange Co.

Home exchange is a global company, operating in over 150 countries. The company has (August 2016) 65,000 community members (each pays membership fees). Here is how it works (per **homeexchange.com/en/how-it-works**):

(a) Members list their homes. "Take a few minutes and list your house or your apartment so our Community can see it. Your home is unique. Show it off! Let our Community know what makes your Listing one-of-a-kind!"
(b) A vacation planning member searches for accommodation and exchange information. "It's easy: browse countless Listings for homes and locations you love, and use our simple messaging system to get in touch with those Members. Check our Inquiries sent to you from Members, and when you are ready, simply arrange your Exchange."
(c) An Exchange is finalized if a match is found. "Your Exchange can be anything you want it to be. Plan it on your time, travel where you want, on your schedule. Partner with like-minded Members to get everyone's ideal vacation. Travel your way and live like a local."

Several other companies exist (e.g., HomeLink House Exchange). For a guide, see **nomadicmatt.com/travel-tips/finding-cheap-accommodation**.

Free Home Sharing

If you do not have a home to exchange (e.g., you live with your parents or friends), you may try to find a free accommodation provided by someone who lives where you are going. Not only do you get a free bed, but you also can get local information and possibly make friends. Here are a few companies that can help you: Couchsurfing, Global Freeloaders, and Hospitality Club and Stay4Free (can also help with home swapping). For details and safety advice, see Nomadic Matt Inc. (**nomadicmatt.com**).

SECTION 5.4 REVIEW QUESTIONS

1. List some EC companies that disrupt their industries.
2. Describe ride sharing and its benefits.
3. List some issues in ride sharing.
4. List some variations of ride sharing.
5. How can people exchange accommodations?
6. How does home exchange work?

5.5   PERSON-TO-PERSON ELECTRONIC COMMERCE MODELS

Person-to-person (P2P) e-commerce, which is sometimes called consumer-to-consumer (C2C) EC, refers to electronic transactions conducted between and among individuals. These transactions can also include intermediaries, such as eBay (**ebay.com**), or social network sites or marketplaces, that organize, manage, and facilitate the P2P transactions. P2P activities may include transactions resulting from classified ads, music and file sharing, career and job matching (e.g., at **linkedin.com** and **careerone.com.au**), money lending (e.g., lendingclub.com), and personal matchmaking services (e.g., **match.com**).

P2P EC has given online shopping and trading a new dimension. Although this sort of trading is prevalent in the offline world (newspaper classified ads, garage sales, etc.), it was not expected to succeed online because of problems regarding trust due to the anonymity of the traders, especially those who are in different locations. This problem was solved by using a third-party payment provider (e.g., **paypal.com**) and escrow or insurance services provided by eBay and others. One advantage of P2P EC is that it reduces the administrative and commission costs for both buyers and sellers. It also gives many individuals and small business owners a low-cost way to sell their goods and services by reaching many customers.

Social networks have become a popular place for P2P activities such as selling products and services via classified ads on **craigslist.org** or **facebook.com** and other social networks. People are sharing, bartering or selling music, bartering, selling virtual properties, and providing personal services.

E-Commerce: P2P Applications

Many websites facilitate P2P activities between individuals. We cover several representative applications next.

P2P Auctions

A very successful example of a P2P application is participation in auctions. In dozens of countries, selling and buying on auction sites is growing rapidly. Most auctions are managed by intermediaries (the most well-known intermediary is eBay). Consumers can visit auctions at general sites such as **ebay.com** or **auctionanything.com**, or they can use specialized sites. In addition, many individuals conduct their own auctions with the use of special software. For example, ProcurePort.com (see **procureport.com/reverse-auction-services.html**) provides software to create P2P reverse auction communities online.

Selling and Buying in P2P

In addition to auctions, eBay enables individuals to sell goods to other individuals at fixed prices. Amazon.com and Etsy (Chap. 3) do the same. Hundreds of other sites facilitate P2P trading, including those that use classified ads.

Peer-to-Peer Money Lending

The introduction of online money transfer enables the move of personal loans to the Web in what is called online *person-to-person or peer-to-peer money lending* or, in short, *P2P lending*. This model allows people to lend money and to borrow from each other via the Internet. For how P2P loan works, see **thebalance.com/a-quick-timeline-of-peer-to-peer-landing-985114**. Online File W5.3 provides overview of the logic of peer-to peer money lending.

Examples

Two pioneering examples are Zopa Limited in the United Kingdom (**zopa.com**) and Prosper Marketplace in the United States (prosper.com), which offer P2P online lending (see en.wikipedia.org/wiki/Zopa and **en.wikipedia.org/wiki/Prosper_marketplace**), respectively. Note that, despite the global credit crunch of 2008–2012 and the fact that neither has a government-backed guarantee, both Zopa and Prosper have been enjoying solid growth. For example, as of April 2014, Zopa's 50,000 active members had lent more than £528 million at negotiated rates to UK customers, mainly for car payments, credit card payments, and home improvement financing. The default rate of these P2P lenders is very low (e.g., Zopa's historical bad debt is 0.19% since 2010) since money is lent only to the most credit-worthy borrowers. For Prosper's company overview, see Online File W5.3 and **prosper.com/about**. To learn more about the topic, see an exhaustive review by Cunningham (2015) and Martin and Amy (2016).

Lending Club Is the Largest Commercial Marketplace for P2P Lending

It is registered on the New York stock exchanges, and it also uses institutional investors as sources of funding. Yet, it has several problems that slow the development of the P2P lending business; see Application Case 5.1 for details.

CASE 5.1: EC APPLICATION
THE LENDING CLUB CORP.

The Lending Club Corp. (LC) is the world's largest P2P lending platform. The company claims that $22 billion in loans had been originated through its platform up to January 15, 2017, of which about $2 billion funded in the last quarter of 2016. It was the first P2P lender to register with the SEC. For the history of LC, see Davidson (2013).

The Business Model

According to **lendingclub.com/about-us-action** and **en.wikipedia.org/wiki/lending-club**, Lending Club enables borrowers to create "loan needed" listings on its website by supplying details about themselves and the loans that they would like to obtain. All loans are unsecured personal loans and can be between $1000 and $40,000. On the basis of the borrower's credit score, credit history, desired loan amount requested, and the borrower's debt-to-income ratio, Lending Club determines whether the borrower is *credit worthy* and assigns to its approved loans a credit grade that determines payable interest rate and origination fees. The standard loan period is 3 years.

Investors can browse the "loan listing needed" on Lending Club website and select loans that they want to invest in, based on the information supplied about the borrower, amount of loan, loan grade, and loan purpose. The loans can only be chosen at the interest rates assigned by Lending Club, but investors can decide how much to fund each borrower.

The Revenue Model

Investors make money from interest. Rates vary from 6.03% to 26.06%, depending on the credit grade assigned to the loans. Lending Club makes money by charging the borrowers an origination fee and the investors a service fee. The size of the origination fee depends on the credit grade, and it ranges 1.1–5.0% of the loan amount. The size of the service fee is 1% on all amounts the borrower pays. The company facilitates interest rates that are better for lenders and borrowers than they would receive from (or pay to) most banks.

Note: Because lenders are making personal loans to individuals, their gains are taxable as personal income, instead of investment income (i.e., they pay more tax).

The Secondary Market

The investors have the ability to place the unsecured notes they receive from LC for sale before the notes have reached maturity. This service is offered in a partnership with FOLIOfn Investments which charges a 1% fee on note sales, making Lending Club the first peer-to-peer lending network to offer a secondary market for peer-to-peer loans.

Problems Faced by Lending Club

During its first year, LC grew very fast, added business partners, and involved financial institutions (e.g., hedge funds) in its operation. Then a slew of problems emerged that resulted in the stock price to lose over 80% of its value, its CEO left, and the SEC launched an investigation of the business. The SEC realized that individual lenders have no experience in assessing credit risk nor they have access to information that a bank does. The borrowers and the lenders depend on what they are told by LC. LC itself aims to take no risk, selling the loans to others. In short, the P2P lending business pushes loan volume at the expense of credit equity. Therefore, some argue that LC troubles show why P2P does not work (e.g., see Hutchinson (2016)). For more about LC problems, see Chafkin and Buhayar (2016).

Finally, delinquencies of borrowers climbed in recent years. As a result, LC tightened its credit and increased its fees and interest rates (per Buhayar (2016)).

Conclusion

Despite all the problems, LC is alive and growing. The quality measures resulted in losses in 2016. But its share price is slowly climbing, and financial analysts are willing to wait rather than recommend to sell the shares of LC.

Sources: Compiled from Buhayar (2016), **en.wikipedia.org/wiki/Lending_Club**, Chafkin and Buhayar (2016), and **lendingclub.com**.

Questions

1. It is said that "LC is a kind of eBay for loans." Discuss.
2. Search information about the SEC investigation. Write a report.
3. Find the B2B activities on the site.

4. Compare LC with Funding Circle in the United Kingdom. Write a report. (See Lunden (2017).)

A word of caution about virtual banking, including P2P lending: Before sending money to any company, especially one that promises high interest rates for your deposits, make sure that the service is a legitimate one.

Selling via Classified Ads

Internet-based classified ads have several advantages over newspaper classified ads. They cover a national, rather than a local, audience and can be updated quickly and easily. Most of them are free to sellers and buyers or they charge very little. This greatly increases the supply of goods and services available and the number of potential buyers. One of the most successful sites of C2C classified ads is **craigslist.org** as seen in Chap. 2. Classified ads also include apartments for rent and real estate for sale across the United States (powered by **forrent.com**). **Freeclassifieds.com** allows you to buy or sell anything for free. Many newspapers also offer their classified ads online. In some cases, placing an ad in the classified section of one website automatically directs it into the classified sections of numerous partners (known as cross posting).

Classified ads appear on thousands of websites, including popular social networks such as **facebook.com/ PostFreeAdsToday** and **linkedin.com**.

Personal Services Online

Numerous personal services are available on the Internet (lawyers, handy helpers, tax preparers, investment clubs, dating services). Some are located in the classified ad section, but others are listed on specialized websites (e.g., **hireahelper.com**) and directories. Some are offered free; others charge a fee.

Note: Be very careful before looking for any personal services online. Fraud or crime could be involved (e.g., a lawyer online may not be an expert in the area professed or may not even be a lawyer at all).

Vacation (Short-Term) Rentals

Vacation rentals are short-term rentals offered usually by individuals who own a rental unit or an extra room. The offers can be significantly lower than hotels. Renters can also get a one or two bedroom units, living room, and a kitchen. Vacation rentals are very popular in Hawaii and other vacation areas. E-commerce offers a mechanism that connects sellers and buyers, i.e., people that want to provide accommodations with travelers. In the past, the communication mode was classified newspapers and telephone. EC offers an efficient, fast, and safer mode that supports such transactions. The most well-known name in 2016 is Airbnb (see Application Case 5.2). Other companies are Wimdu, Roomorama, and HomeAway.

CASE 5.2: EC APPLICATION
AIRBNB: AN E-COMMERCE DISRUPTION IN THE HOSPITALITY INDUSTRY

Airbnb is a portal that connects travelers with local hosts that provide lodging. This lodging can include single or shared rooms, suites, or entire apartments/houses. The firm acts as an intermediary and matches travelers with hosts for a fee. Customers enjoy using the service because it is often less expensive than traditional hotels and can provide greater flexibility in the type of lodging being provided. The company was founded in 2008 and has quickly grown to over 190 countries and more than 34,000 cities worldwide (see **nextjuggernaut.com/blog/airbnb-business-model-canvas-how-airbnb-works-revenue-insights**).

Many consider Airbnb's growth to be quite significant, with a revenue growth of 113% between 2014 and 2015 (see **skift.com/2016/05/03/state-of-travel-2016-airbnb-vs-hotel-rivals-in-6-charts**). And while the company is still private, some put its value at up to $30 billion (see **bloomberg.com/news/articles/2016-06-28/airbnb-seeks-new-funding-at-30-billion-valuation**). This growth began in the United States, but international expansion has a dwarf rows domestically (see **growth-hackers.com/growth-studies/airbnb**). Currently only 16% of the company's bookings are in the United States. The fastest-growing host cities for Airbnb are primarily in Asia with other strong growth in Europe (Taylor 2016).

One major question about this growth is if it is dislodging travelers from traditional hotels and if so how much. It is difficult to evaluate all of the potential impacts on hotel occupancy rates and with it the possible impact of Airbnb. While Airbnb rentals are significant, they are small compared to the annual use of hotels in the United States. Many are analyzing this issue and attempting to determine the effect this may have on the lodging industry as a whole (Salvioni 2016).

This growth has not been without challenges. One issue that potential hosts must contend with is the potential for their lodging to be damaged. Because these hosts do not have insurance that is typical of a hotel, these damages may not be covered (see **mashable.com/2015/04/30/house-destroyed-airbnb-renters/#ztIl4rFrFiqm**). To address these concerns, the company is working on systems to better vet potential renters as well as providing some relief to hosts.

Another issue is the legality and regulatory requirements for Airbnb itself. Many localities view Airbnb as they would a traditional hotel or hostel. This may be because the laws currently on the books are not created with this business model in mind. In any case, the company is spending large sums of money and has engaged many employees to work with municipalities to clarify laws and their enforcement as it relates to the company (Taylor 2016).

A major issue for Airbnb and similar companies is taxation. For example, in New York City, there is an accommodation tax of 17%. In 2016, Airbnb agreed to collect money from the renters and pay the fees to the city.

Questions

1. What factors have allowed Airbnb to grow as rapidly as it has?
2. Will Airbnb disrupt the traditional lodging industry?
3. What can renters and hosts do to protect themselves when using Airbnb?
4. Select a city that you would like to travel to. Compare the cost of a traditional hotel (Travelocity.com) to the cost of an Airbnb host (Airbnb.com).

File-Sharing Utilities: Napster and Others

It all started in 1999. By logging onto services such as Napster, people were able to download files that others were willing to share for free. Such *P2P networks* enabled users to search other members' hard drives for a particular file, including data files created by users or copied from elsewhere. Digital music and games were the most popular files accessed. Movies, TV shows, and videos followed shortly thereafter. Napster had over 60 million members in 2002 before it was forced to stop its service due to copyright violations.

The Napster server, and others that followed, functioned as a directory that listed the files being shared by other users. Once logged onto the server, users could search the directory for specific songs and locate the file's owner. They could then directly access the owner's computer and download the songs they had chosen. Napster also included chat rooms to connect its millions of users.

However, a US federal court found Napster to be in violation of copyright laws because it enabled people to obtain music files without paying royalties to the creators of the music. Following this ruling, in March 2002, Napster was forced to shut down and filed for bankruptcy. In 2011, Napster was acquired by Rhapsody (**rhapsody.com**), a subscription-based music downloading site. For a history of Napster, see **theguardian.com/music/2013/feb/24/napster-music-free-file-sharing**. Note: Napster is an independent unit now.

A number of free file-sharing programs still exist. For example, an even purer version of P2P is BitTorrent (**bittorrent. com**), software that makes downloading files fast. To access games over P2P networks, try TrustyFiles (**trustyfiles.com**). Despite the temptation to get "something for nothing," remember that downloading copyrighted materials for free is usually against the law.

P2P Activities in Social Networks and Trading Virtual Properties

P2P activities in social networks include the sharing of photos, videos, music, and other files, trading of virtual properties, and conducting other activities. Trading virtual properties is discussed in Chap. 8.

SECTION 5.5 REVIEW QUESTIONS

1. Define P2P e-commerce.
2. Describe the benefits of P2P e-commerce to all participants.
3. Describe the major e-commerce P2P applications.
4. Describe P2P lending.
5. Describe P2P vacation rentals.

6. Define file sharing.
7. Describe file sharing and the legal issues involved.

MANAGERIAL ISSUES

Some managerial issues related to this chapter are as follows:

1. **How do we design the most cost-efficient government e-procurement system?** Several issues are involved and questions may be raised in planning e-government: How much can the governmental e-procurement system save on procurement costs? How can the system be used for procuring small quantities? How do you deal with bidders from outside your country? How can illegal bribery be prevented? What criteria besides cost need to be considered? How should the online and offline procurement systems be designed? How do you advertise RFQs online? How should the portfolio of auctions and desktop purchasing be constructed? Can the government use commercial B2B sites for procurement? Can businesses use the government procurement system for their own procurement? All these must be considered in an effective design.

2. **How do we design the portfolio of e-learning knowledge sources?** There are many sources of e-learning services. The e-learning management team needs to design the portfolio of the online and offline training applications and the internal and external knowledge sources (paid and nonpaid sources). The internal knowledge management system is an important source of training materials for large corporations, whereas external sources could be more cost-effective for small organizations. Obviously, justification of each item in the portfolio is needed, which is related to vendor selection. For illustrative case studies, see **brightwave.co.uk**.

3. **How do we incorporate social networking-based learning and services in our organization?** With the proliferation of social networking initiatives in the enterprise comes the issue of how to integrate these with the enterprise system, including CRM, KM, training, and other applications and business processes. One issue is how to balance the quality of knowledge with the scope of knowledge in e-learning and training programs.

4. **What will be the impact of the e-book platform?** If the e-book is widely adopted by readers, the distribution channel of online book sales may be disruptive. This new platform may cannibalize the offline book retail business. Additionally, there is the need for the protection of intellectual property of digital contents since it is easy to copy and distribute electronic files (see Online Chap. 12). In general, more e-books will be published and read.

5. **How to recognize a digital disruption?** It depends, but usually a disruption may drive some businesses to lose market share or they end in a bankruptcy. Many times the disruption will be covered by the media and changes in stock prices. Several conferences and management consultants call attention to industry disruptions.

6. **What is the impact of ride sharing?** Ride sharing usually benefits riders by cutting costs. It disrupts the taxi business and may result in political, legal, and social changes.

7. What is the future of P2P commerce? It certainly going to increase in areas such as money lending, marketing of arts and crafts, and delivery of services such as accommodation. It is clearly a disruptor in the hospitality field.

SUMMARY

In this chapter, you learned about the following EC issues as they relate to the chapter's learning objectives:

1. **E-government activities.** Governments, like any other organization, can use EC applications for great savings and increased effectiveness. Notable applications are e-procurement using reverse auctions, e-payments to and from citizens and businesses, auctioning of surplus goods, and electronic travel and expense management systems. Governments also conduct electronic business with other governments. As a result, governments can do a better job with less money.

2. **Implementing e-government to citizens, businesses, and its own operations.** Governments worldwide are providing a variety of services to citizens over the Internet. Such initiatives increase citizen satisfaction and decrease government expenses for providing citizens' service applications, including electronic voting. Governments also are active in electronic trading with businesses. Finally, EC can be conducted within and between governments. E-government's growth can be strengthened by the use of wireless systems in what is described as mobile or m-government. In addition, e-government 2.0 is becoming increasingly popular with tools such as wikis, blogs, social networks, and Twitter.

3. **E-learning and training.** E-learning is the delivery of educational content through electronic media via the Internet and intranets. Degree programs, lifelong learning topics, and corporate training are delivered online by thousands of organizations worldwide. A growing area is distance learning via online university offerings; and virtual universities are becoming quite popular. Some are virtual; others are delivered as a combination of online and offline offerings. Online corporate training is increasing also and is sometimes conducted at formal corporate learning centers. Implementation is done in steps starting with just an online presence and ending with activities on social networks. New e-readers contain easy-to-read text, search capabilities, rich media, as well as other functions. Add to this the low cost of e-books and the capability of storing hundreds of books on a single e-reader, and you can understand the increased popularity of these devices.

4. **E-books and their readers.** There is an increased interest in e-books due to their many benefits (Amazon.com sells more e-books than hardcover ones). There is intense competition among e-reader and tablet manufacturers, and the products' capabilities are increasing while their prices are declining. E-books are used both for pleasure reading and for studying. E-books can be read on several portable devices including tablets.

5. **E-health.** E-commerce, m-commerce, and social commerce applications are increasingly penetrating the healthcare field. Practically, B2B, B2C, c-commerce, and even P2P services are practiced all over the world. The most well-known is the electronic medical record area that helps in rapid care and accessibility in rural areas. Another well-known area is patient care applications ranging from monitoring patients 24/7 to improving medical testing, enabling the use of better medical equipment, and increasing patients' satisfaction and comfort. Patients' education is greatly facilitated by using medical portals. Physicians have rapid access to all data they need and they can transmit orders electronically.

   Social media and networks assist patients and administrators in many ways and foster sharing and collaboration. Other areas that benefit from e-commerce are medical services acquisition, maintenance, and use. Many administrative processes and medical research are supported by EC. However, a major problem in e-health is the protection of patients' medical records and privacy.

6. **Digital disruption and sharing economy.** E-commerce sharing economy models such as ride sharing are a major source of digital disruption, which may impact entire industries, companies, business processes, and/or people. Sharing economy models such as ride sharing and accommodation sharing are becoming popular. There is a variety of other models. The models save money to those who share. Current issues relate to taxation and security.

   P2P activities. P2P consists of individual consumers conducting e-commerce with other individual consumers, mainly in auctions (such as at eBay), classified ads, matching services, and specialty webstores at eBay and Etsy. Also, there are illegal file-sharing activities of music, videos, and games (see Chap. 15).

5.6   KEY TERMS

Digital disruption
Distance learning
E-government
E-health
E-learning
Electronic book (e-book)
Government 2.0
Government-to-business (G2B)
Government-to-citizens (G2C)
Government-to-employees (G2E)
Government-to-government (G2G)
Learning management system (LMS)
Mobile government (m-government)
M-learning
Person-to-person (P2P)
Shared economy
Social learning (e-learning 2.0)
Virtual universities

DISCUSSION QUESTIONS

1. Discuss the advantages and disadvantages of e-government using social networking versus the traditional e-government portal.
2. Discuss the advantages and shortcomings of e-voting.
3. Discuss the advantages and disadvantages of e-books.
4. Discuss the advantages of e-learning in the corporate training environment.
5. Discuss the advantages and disadvantages of ride sharing.
6. Find information about the disruption force of e-commerce.
7. Discuss the critical success factors of Airbnb and similar companies.
8. Discuss why disruption may create do-or-die situation.
9. Summarize the legal problems of Uber and other ride-sharing companies.
10. Some say that B2G is simply B2B. Explain.
11. Compare and contrast B2E with G2E.
12. Which e-government EC activities are intrabusiness activities? Explain why they are categorized as intrabusiness.
13. Identify the benefits of G2C to citizens and to governments.
14. Discuss the improvements in healthcare provided by e-commerce.
15. Discuss the potential impacts of AI on e-government and e-health.

TOPICS FOR CLASS DISCUSSION AND DEBATES

1. Discuss the advantages and disadvantages of e-learning for an undergraduate student and for an MBA student.
2. Discuss the benefits of using e-commerce in the healthcare field. What are the limitations? The disadvantages?
3. One of the major initiatives of many governments (e.g., European Commission) is Smart Cities (see Chap. 6 for the technology). Discuss the content of such initiatives and explain why they are a part of e-government.
4. Uber China and Didi merge their operation in China, but work separately, as competitors in several other countries. Find recent information about the relationship between the two companies.
5. Provide examples of business processes which are disrupted by e-commerce.
6. What industries, companies, and business processes were disrupted by e-commerce?
7. The valuation of Airbnb went from $5B to $30B in a year (July 2015 to Aug. 2016). Is this realistic? Debate.
8. Some consider crowdsourcing and crowdfunding to be examples of sharing economy models; others disagree. Debate.
9. Debate: E-books will replace traditional books.
10. Debate: Analyze the pros and cons of electronic voting.
11. Enter **en.wikipedia.org/wiki/E-Government** and find the "controversies of e-government" section. Discuss the advantages and disadvantages. Write a report.
12. Debate the issue: Is e-learning really working?
13. Discuss the content and benefits of the UN E-Government Development Database (**unpan3.un.org/egovkb**).
14. Debate the issue of electronic vs. manual voting.
15. Debate the value of robo-advisors in e-government and e-health.

INTERNET EXERCISES

1. Enter **e-learningcentre.co.uk**, **elearnmag.acm.org**, and **elearningpost.com**. Identify current discussion issues and find two articles related to the effectiveness of e-training. Write a report. In addition, prepare a list of the resources available on these sites.
2. Enter **adobe.com**, and find the tutorials and tools it offers for e-learning, knowledge management, and online publishing. Prepare and give a presentation on your findings.
3. Enter **blackboard.com** and also view **en.wikipedia.org/wiki/Blackboard_Inc.**. Find the major services provided by the company, including its community system. Write a report.

4. Enter **fcw.com** and read the latest news on e-government. Identify initiatives not covered in this chapter. Then enter **gcn.com**. Finally, enter **egovstrategies.com**. Compare the information presented on the three websites.
5. Enter **lendingclub.com** and find their revenue model.
6. Imagine you are going to New Zealand. Find free accommodation there. Summarize your experience.
7. Investigate **airbnb.com**. Identify factors that give them a competitive advantage.
8. Enter **stay4free.com**. Examine their "true free" and "for free" services.
9. Enter **en.wikipedia.org/wiki/Sharing_economy** and read about the various types of collaborative consumption. In addition, prepare a summary of the driving forces and the benefits.
10. Enter **procurement.org** and **govexec.com**. Identify recent e-government procurement initiatives and summarize their unique aspects.
11. Enter **amazon.com**, **barnesandnoble.com**, and **sony.com**, and find the latest information about their e-readers. Compare their capabilities and write a report. (Consult **the-ebook-reader.com**.)
12. Enter **chegg.com** and similar sites that are learning platforms. Explain what they do.
13. Find two companies that enable C2C (or P2P) e-commerce (such as **egrovesys.com**). Comment on their capabilities.
14. Find successful examples of e-government. Start by posing questions on **quora.com**.
15. Will P2P profoundly transform traditional banking over the next decade? Debate.
16. Debate the pros and cons of ride sharing and its impact on the taxi industry.

TEAM ASSIGNMENTS AND PROJECTS

1. Read the opening case and answer the following questions:

   (a) What drives the e-government in Estonia?
   (b) What were the major critical success factors?
   (c) Given the hacking situation, does the idea of using the Internet for vote in Estonia make sense?
   (d) Enter **e-estonia.com/case_study**, and list all the cases. View the videos of three cases and summarize their contents.

2. Conduct a comparative study on e-government in the following countries:

   (a) Denmark (start with **egov_in_denmark_-_17_0_final.pdf**).
   (b) New Zealand (start with **ict.govt.nz**).
   (c) Singapore (start with **centreforpublicimpact.org/case-study/building-digital-government-singapore**).
       Assign teams to each country. Identify the critical success factors and the special feature of each country. Make a presentation.

3. Create four teams, each representing one of the following: G2C, G2B, G2E, and G2G. Each team will prepare a description of the activities in the assigned area (e.g., G2C) in a small country, such as Holland, Denmark, Finland, or Singapore. A fifth team will deal with the coordination and collaboration of all e-government activities in each of the four countries chosen. Prepare a report.
4. Find newer trends. Explore each of the trends and find examples of how governments deal with these trends. Compare to findings of the UN E-Government Survey of 2016. Prepare a class presentation.
5. Find information about strategies for dealing with disruptions that may endanger your company. Write a summary.
6. Research the relationship between disruption and innovation.
7. Ride sharing disrupts the taxi business. Find information regarding action taken by taxi drivers to deal with the competition.
8. Both Ford and Volvo are working with Uber to offer self-driving cars. Find the status of this and similar projects (e.g., GM and Lyft). Prepare a report. Outline the potential benefits to all participants including renters.
9. Review the list of 50 disruptors provided by CNBC (2016) and identify the EC-related companies (in addition to Uber, Lyft, Pinterest, and Airbnb). Briefly explain why each is an e-commerce company.
10. Research the viability of P2P money lending. Start with the Lending Club Company.

11. View the video "E-Learning Debate 2010 – Highlights" (4:51 min) at **youtube.com/watch?v=Q42f1blFnck**. Debate the pros and cons regarding the value of e-learning.

   (a) List all the pro and con statements from the video.
   (b) For each statement, have two teams (or individuals) explain why each agrees or disagrees with the statement.
   (c) Add several pro and con statements from what you learned in class or discovered on the Web.
   (d) For each added statement, have two teams (or individuals) explain why each agrees or disagrees with the statement.
   (e) Jointly prepare a summary. The use of a wiki is advisable.

12. Have each team represent one of the following sites: **netlibrary.net** and **ebooks.com**. Each team will examine the technology, legal issues, prices, and business alliances associated with its site. Each team will then prepare a report answering the question, "Will e-books succeed?" (Read Nuwer (2016).)

CLOSING CASE: HENRY FORD HEALTH SYSTEM PROVIDES SUPERIOR PATIENT EXPERIENCE USING IT AND E-COMMERCE

Henry Ford Health System (HFHS) is a comprehensive health system that provides care to 2.2 million patients annually in Metro Detroit and several other cities. The HFHS complex includes 5 medical centers and 24,000 employees.

The Challenges

The system's mission is to support the communication and collaboration of the mobile employees, patients, insurers, physicians, visitors, and vendors and to assure the operation of the many mobile biomedical devices. HFHS needed a massive electronic network. Furthermore, it was necessary to support the patient data flow, some of which is in real time (data accessibility at point of care). All this required continued availability with protection of privacy and security. The challenges include the support of a multitude of mobile devices that patients and visitors bring with them. In addition, the mobile and biomedical devices are from many manufacturers and are used for many applications (e.g., x-ray carts, IV pumps, mobile ultrasound, EKG machines, etc.). Parts of the medical facilities are within 6-foot concrete walls, which made radio-frequency (RF) penetration difficult. The hospital needed a wall-to-wall coverage by wireless connection that would work without interferences and enable a large volume of wireless traffic.

The Solution

HFHS decided to install an advanced Wi-Fi system. This required experimentation with different software and hardware and with the locations and numbers of Wi-Fi access points.

   The resultant solution enabled the integration of over 3500 biomedical devices into the Wi-Fi network. This required collaboration with those that are purchasing the devices. To support the wireless, it was necessary to bring access point antennas in over 90 elevators and many stairway corridors (a multiple year project). The solution also included penetration of information flow in lead walls and through 6-foot concrete shelters. In addition, the solution enabled connecting with the many brands of mobile devices belonging to patients and visitors. The system covers over 60 sites of HFHS in many locations. Overall, more than 7 million square feet of facilities are covered. In 2016, there were over 3200 access points and 1200 security sensors. In addition to the Wi-Fi, the HFHS is using several e-commerce information systems such as Philips' CareSage predictive analytics and 3M 360 Encompass system.

The Results

The success of Wi-Fi was featured in a best practice article in the "Association for the Advancement of Medical Instrumentation." Patient satisfaction has increased drastically and so has the productivity and quality of the hospital's employees and the physicians. The networks also enable members of the community to access the educational material disseminated by the hospital. The Wi-Fi enables the biomedical devices to operate smoothly, to enable safe access to all needed information, and to facilitate communication, collaboration, and teamwork. All these were done while meeting all compliance requirements.

   Sources: Based on Extreme Networks (2016) and Philips Media (2016)

Questions

1. Why was Wi-Fi the only reasonable solution?
2. Why was this project so complex?
3. What are the major benefits? To whom?

REFERENCES

Abcede, A., A. Lewis, and M. V. Haar. "Cover Story: Brick, Click, Boom." *CSP Daily News*, May 2014. **cspdailynews.com/print/csp-magazine/article/cover-story-brick-click-boom** (accessed January 2017).

Akwaja, C. "How Nigeria's 4G LTE will Accelerate e-Commerce, Smart City Development." *Leadership*, January 1, 2017. **leadership.ng/business/565722/how-nigerias-4g-lte-will-accelerate-e-commerce-smart-city-development** (accessed January 2017).

Alsever, J. "The Kindle Effect." *Fortune*, January 1, 2017.

Amazon Web Services Report. "How the Cloud Helps Healthcare Focus on What Matters." *Enterprise Innovation*, August 16, 2016.

Anandan, T. M. "Robots and Healthcare Saving Lives Together." *Robotics Online*, November 23, 2015.

Anderson, D., et al. *E-Government Strategy, ICT and Innovation for Citizen Engagement (SpringersBriefs in Electrical and Computer Engineering)* [Kindle Edition]. New York: Springer, 2015.

Anderson, K. "Augmented Reality, Big Data and other E-learning Trends for 2016." *Techco*, May 31, 2016.

Beard, R. "How to Harness Disruptive Forces for Disrupting Innovation" *Business2Community.com*, July 22, 2016.

Beattie, A. "E-Learning Makes Sense for Time-Poor Small Business Owners." *The Huffington Post Australia*, September 28, 2016.

Behr, A. "MocaCare's Latest Health Monitor Tracks Heart Health Metrics." *eWeek*, February 8, 2016.

Beuker, I. "How Starbucks Disrupts Its Own Marketing Strategy?" *Math Men Magazine*, December 19, 2014.

Boughzala, I., et al. *Case Studies in e-Government 2.0: Changing Citizen Relationships.* 2nd ed. New York: Springer, 2016.

Boughzala, I., et al. *Case Studies in e-Government 2.0: Changing Citizen Relationships.* [Kindle Edition]. New York: Springer, 2015.

Bradley, C. and C. O'Toole. "An Incumbent's Guide to Digital Disruption." *McKinsey Quarterly*, May 2016.

Bresnick, J. "4 Patient-Centric Uses for the Healthcare Internet of Things." *Health IT Analytics*, December 29, 2015.

Brown, A., J. Fishenden, and M. Thompson. *Digitizing Government: Understanding and Implementing New Digital Business Models (Business in the Digital Economy)*. New York: Palgrave Macmillan, 2014.

Buhayar, N. "Lending Club Raises Rates, Tightens Credit as Delinquencies Climb." *Bloomberg.com,* October 14, 2016.

CNBC. "Meet the 2016 CNBC Disruptor 50 Companies." *CNBC*, June 7, 2016. **cnbc.com/2016/06/07/2016-cnbcs-disruptor-50.html** (accessed January 2017).

Chafkin, M. and N. Buhayar. "How Lending Club's Biggest Fanboy Uncovered Shady Loans." *Bloomberg Business Week*, August 17, 2016.

Clark, R. C., and R. E. Mayer. *e-Learning and the Science of Instruction*, 4th ed. San Francisco: Pfeiffer/Wiley & Sons, 2016.

Combs, C.D., J. A. Sokolowski, and C. M. Banks. *The Digital Patient: Advancing Healthcare, Research, and Education.* (Wiley Series in Modelling and Simulation) Hoboken, NJ: Wiley, 2016.

Corydon, B., V. Ganesan, and M. Lundqvist. "Transforming Government through Digitization." *McKinsey&Company*, November 2016.

Cunningham, S. "What is Peer to Peer Lending?" *Lending Memo*, March 20, 2015. **lendingmemo.com/what-is-peer-to-peer-lending** (accessed January 2017).

Dalton, K. "3Ways to Make Social Media in Government a Team Effort." *Government Social Media*, October 16, 2016.

Davidson, A. *A Beginner's Guide to Lending Club: An Investment Guide to Peer-to-Peer Lending* [Kindle Edition]. Seattle, WA: Amazon Digital Services, 2013.

Digital Government Strategy. "Building a 21st Century Platform to Better Serve the American People." A Whitehouse Report, 2012. **whitehouse.gov/sites/default/files/omb/egov/digital-government/digital-government.html** (accessed January 2017).

Egov. "E-Government Strategy: Implementing the President's Management Agenda for E-Government." April 2003. **sites.nationalacademies.org/cs/groups/pgasite/documents/webpage/pga_055959.pdf** (accessed January 2017).

Elton, J., and A. O'Riordan. *Healthcare Disrupted: Next Generation Business Models and Strategies.* Hoboken, NJ: Wiley, 2016.

Estopace, E. "AI Personal Health Assistant Now on Global Messaging Services." *Enterprise Innovation*, February 16, 2016a. **enterpriseinnovation.net/article/ai-personal-health-assistant-now-global-messaging-services-902506163** (accessed January 2017).

Estopace, E. "Brazil launches App for Olympic Athletes, Visitors to Report Health Conditions." *Enterprise Innovation*, July 15, 2016b.

Estopace, E. "Singapore to Use 'Chatbots' for Next-Gen Digital Government Services." *Enterprise Innovation*, July 13, 2016c.

Etherington, D. "Ford and MIT project Provides On-Demand Electric Shuttles for Students." *Techcrunch*, July 27, 2016. **techcrunch.com/2016/07/27/ford-and-mit-project-provides-on-demand-electric-shuttles-for-students** (accessed January 2017).

Extreme Networks. "Case Study: Henry Ford Health System." *Extreme Networks Inc.*, 2016. **learn.extremenetworks.com/rs/extreme/images/Henry-Ford-CS.pdf** (February 2017).

Gaikwad, S. "Big Boost to Skilling India." *The Pioneer*, December 28, 2016.

Garrison, R. *E-Learning in the 21st Century: A Community of Inquiry Framework for Research and Practice.* 3rd ed., London, UK: Routhledge Pub., 2016.

Grogan, B. J. *33 Social Media Tips, Tricks & Shortcuts: Helping Digital Marketers in Government and Business Succeed.* Colorado Spring, CO: Van Sant Publishing LLC, 2015.

Gross, G. "A Hackable Election? 5 Things to Know About E-Voting." *IDG News Service*, July 22, 2016.

Haisler, D. "The Chatbots Are Coming: How Facebook's New Bots Will Impact Public Sector?" *Govtech.com*, April 13, 2016.

Hutchinson, M. "Lending Club Troubles Show Why P2P Doesn't Work." *Wall Street Daily*, May 17, 2016.

Imholt, S. J. *User Guide to Government 2.0*. San Antonio, Texas: Top Wing Books, 2015.

Insitesoft. "Medical and Healthcare Suppliers Have Big Growth Potential with eCommerce Websites." *Insitesoft*, October 20, 2015.

Kaattari, J., and V. Trottier. *Guide to Effective Technologies for Online Learning* [Kindle Edition]. Ontario, Canada, Community Literacy of Ontario, 2012 (revised and updated October 2013).

Kontzer, T. "The Sharing Economy Helps Firms Make or Save Money" *Baseline*, June 2, 2016.

Kwang, T. W. "6 Innovative Mobile Apps for Citizens." *eGov Innovation*, August 2, 2016a.

Kwang, T. W. "A Look into Estonia's Digital Society." *eGov Innovation*, January 10, 2017a.

Kwang, T. W. "Social Mobile Platform Transforms Learning at SJI International School." *Enterprise Innovation*, August 8, 2016b.

Kwang, T.W. "UK Government on the Future of Artificial Intelligence." *Enterprise Innovation*, January 3, 2017b.

Lagier, S. "You Take My House, I'll Take Yours." *The Wall Street Journal*, March 31, 2014.

Lawson, G. W. *Healthcare Social Media: Transformation 3.0*. Seattle, WA: CreateSpace Inc., 2015.

Lechner, I. "Bringing Virtual Reality and Telepresence Robotic to E-Learning." *PSFK*, August 29, 2016. **psfk.com/2016/08/bringing-virtual-reality-and-telepresence-robotics-to-e-learning.html** (accessed January 2017).

Lohrmann, D. "3D Government: How Will Augmented Reality (AR) Disrupt the Future of Technology?" *Govtech.com*, June 12, 2016.

Lunden, I. "Lyft and GM Partner on Express Drive, a Rental Service That Paves the Way for Autonomous Cars." *Techcrunch*, March 14, 2016.

Lunden, I. "P2P Lending Site Funding Circle Raises Another $100M Led by Accel." *Techcrunch.com*, January 11, 2017.

Mack, E. "How Carpool Apps Could Take 10,000 Taxis off NY Streets." *CNET News*, January 2, 2017. **cnet.com/news/uber-lyft-carpool-apps-take-10000-taxis-new-york-mit** (accessed January 2017).

Madden, R. *Voting Fraud* [Kindle Edition]. New York: Guardian Press, 2015.

Mah, et al. "Redefining Business in a Disruptive World." *Questex Media Group*, 2015.

Martin and Amy. "Peer-to-Peer Lending." *MoneySavingExpert.com*, July 11, 2016.

Mayo Clinic Center for Social Media. *Bringing the Social Media Revolution to Health Care*. Scottsdale, AZ: Mayo Foundation, 2012.

McCafferty, D. "Disruptive Tech Poses a Do-or-Die Challenge." *Baseline*, July 19, 2016.

Mei Hua, S. R. and I. K. Rohman. "Challenges in E-Government Implementation." *The Jakarta Post*, July 27, 2015.

Millar, E. "No Classrooms and Lots of Technology: A Danish School's Approach." June 20, 2013. **theglobeandmail.com/report-on-business/economy/canada-competes/no-classrooms-and-lots-of-technology-a-danish-schools-approach/article12688441** (accessed January 2017).

Newcombe, T. "Artificial Intelligence: the Next Big Thing in Government." *Tech Talk*, October 2016.

News. "User-Generated Content to be a Key Trend in Corporate E-Learning." *Training Journal*, Aril 5, 2016. **trainingjournal.com/articles/news/user-generated-content-be-key-trend-corporate-e-learning** (accessed February 2017).

Nuwer, R. "If the Word Becomes a Thing of the Past, It May Affect How We Think." *BBC.com*, January 25, 2016. **bbc.com/future/story/20160124-are-paper-books-really-disappearing** (accessed January 2017).

O'Brien, A. "MIT Robot Helps Deliver Babies." *Money.cnn.com*, July 11, 2016. **money.cnn.com/2016/07/11/technology/mit-robot-labor/index.html?iid=ob_article-footer** (accessed January 2017).

Office of Management and Budget. "FY 2011 Report to Congress on the Implementation of the E-Government Act of 2002." March 7, 2012. **whitehouse.gov/sites/default/files/omb/assets/egov_docs/fy11__e-gov_act_report.pdf** (accessed January 2017).

Philips Media. "Henry Ford Health System Is Eighth U.S. Health System in Six Months' Time to Adopt Philips' Predictive Analytics Solution as Health Systems Seek to Identify At-Risk Elderly Patients at Home." February 9, 2016. **philips.com/a-w/about/news/archive/standard/news/press/2016/20160209-Henry-Ford-Health-System-is-eighth-US-health-system-in-six-months-time-to-adopt-Philips-predictive-analytics-solution.html** (accessed February 2017).

Poremba, S.M. "The Digital Disruption Revolution." *ITBusinessEdge*, August 29, 2016.

Risher, W., "Bike-Sharing Demos Set in Memphis This Week." *The Commercial Appeal*, July 25, 2016. **commercialappeal.com/business/tourism/Bike-sharing-demos-set-in-Memphis-this-week-388148622.html** (accessed January 2017).

Rogers, B. "Transforming Healthcare Using an E-Commerce Model." *Forbes*, August 28, 2014.

Salvioni, D. M. (2016). Hotel Chains and the Sharing Economy in Global Tourism. Symphonya, (1).

Spinosa, B. "Is There a Chatbot in Your Agency's Future?" *GCN*, June 30, 2016. **gcn.com/articles/2016/06/30/chatbots-customer-service.aspx** (accessed January 2017).

Streitfeld, D. "Teacher Knows if You've Done the E-Reading." April 8, 2013. **nytimes.com/2013/04/09/technology/coursesmart-e-textbooks-track-students-progress-for-teachers.html?pagewanted=all&_r=0** (accessed January 2017).

Sujatha, B. "Using Chatbots in E-Learning- Why & How." *Commlan India*, December 8, 2016.

Taylor, H. "How Airbnb Is Growing a Far-Flung Global Empire." CNBC, June 8, 2016. **cnbc.com/2016/06/01/how-airbnb-is-growing-a-far-flung-global-empire.html** (accessed February 2017).

Thomas, M. "When Virtual and Augmented Reality Meet Government Analytics." *GCN*, September 23, 2016. **gcn.com/articles/2016/09/23/virtual-augmented-reality.aspx** (accessed January 2017).

Thompson, K., "Managers of E-Learning Project Tout Positive Results." February 13, 2014. **jamaicaobserver.com/news/Managers-of-e-learning-project-tout-positive-results_16006381** (accessed January 2017).

Vai, M. and K. Sosulski. *Essentials of Online Course Design: A Standards-Based Guide (Essentials Online Learning)*. 2nd ed. London, UK: Routhledge, 2015.

Vaughan-Nichols, S. J. "Good-Bye Books, Hello E-Books." December 27, 2012. **zdnet.com/good-bye-books-hello-e-books-7000009208** (accessed January 2017).

Wachter, R. *The Digital Doctor: Hope, Hype, and Harm at the Dawn of Medicine's Computer Age*. New York: Mc Graw-Hill, 2015.

Wohlers, T. E. and L. L. Bernier. *Setting Sail into the Age of Digital Local Government: Trends and Best Practices (Public Administration and Information Technology)*. New York: Springer, 2016.

Young, D. "Didi-Uber China Marriage to Shake Up Global Alliances." *Seeking Alpha*, August 7, 2016. **seekingalpha.com/article/3997034-didi-uber-china-marriage-shake-global-alliances** (accessed January 2017).

Mobile Commerce and the Internet of Things

6

Contents

Learning Objectives

Upon completion of this chapter, you will be able to:

1. Discuss the value-added attributes, benefits, and fundamental drivers of m-commerce.
2. Describe the mobile computing infrastructure that supports m-commerce (devices, software, and services).
3. Discuss m-commerce applications in banking and financial services.
4. Describe enterprise mobility applications.
5. Describe consumer and personal applications of m-commerce, including entertainment.
6. Explain what location-based commerce is.
7. Define and describe ubiquitous computing and sensory networks.
8. Describe wearables, Google Glass, smartwatches, and fitness trackers.
9. Describe the major implementation issues from security and privacy to barriers of m-commerce.

© Springer International Publishing AG 2018
E. Turban et al., *Electronic Commerce 2018*, Springer Texts in Business and Economics, DOI 10.1007/978-3-319-58715-8_6

OPENING CASE
HERTZ GOES MOBILE ALL THE WAY

The Problem

The car rental industry is very competitive, and Hertz Corporation (**hertz.com**), the world's largest car rental company, competes against hundreds of companies in approximately 10,000 locations in 150 countries. The strong competition negatively impacted profits. For Hertz Global Holdings, Inc.'s business profile and statistics, see **hoovers.com/company-information/cs/company-profile.hertz_global_holdings_inc.a13218fdab48db66.html**. Hertz needs to constantly maintain a mobile presence. Customers can easily connect with the company through its mobile site. The Hertz mobile app is available for iPhone, iPad, Android, and Windows phone.

The Solution

Hertz pioneered several mobile commerce applications to increase its competitiveness. Mobile commerce is now embedded in the company's national wireless network. This information is needed to reserve a car, confirm or change reservations, and other customer-related services (e.g., review rental history, direct credit mileage to the proper loyalty program, etc.).

Here are some of Hertz's mobile services:

- **Easy and quick rentals.** Reservations can be made by phone, e-mail, and on the website (via smartphone, tablet, or desktop). Confirmations are e-mailed (or texted) within seconds of making the reservation. Upon arrival in a city, the renter receives a text message pinpointing the car's location in Hertz's parking area. In many rental locations, the cars are equipped with an RFID system. In such a case, the renter sweeps the Hertz key fob/card over the RFID reader to unlock the doors. Alternatively, in some locations, Hertz's curbside attendant confirms the reservation on a handheld device and transmits the arrival information wirelessly to the rental booth. This in return reveals the location of the car. All the renter needs to do is go to the slot where the car is parked and drive away. For interesting new features, see Elliott (2013).
- **Instant returns (eReturn).** There is no longer any need to wait in line in Hertz's office to return the car. An attendant with a handheld device connected to the wireless system enters the return time, and the system calculates the cost of the rental and prints a receipt. The checkout time takes about a minute, right in the parking lot.
- **NeverLost® GPS navigation system.** Many Hertz cars are equipped with the Hertz NeverLost® GPS system (**neverlost.com**) that includes a display screen and voice prompts (e.g., when to make a turn). A map (either Google Maps or MapQuest) shows the routes and business information (e.g., public and consumer services, such as the location of the nearest hospitals, gas stations, and eateries displayed). Hertz also offers the MyExplore™ NeverLost® Mobile Companion app (see **www.neverlost.com/Products/ProductDetail?ProductName=hertzneverlostcompanion**). This app allows you to plan your trip on your smartphone and use the app to navigate over 40 cities such as Washington, DC, and New York. Some of the app's features include augmented reality (turn your camera phone into a live map); social media integration (share your experiences on social networks such as Facebook and Twitter); and weather information (get live weather information and 5-day forecasts).

Hertz also installed inward-facing video cameras in an attempt to upgrade its NeverLost® service.

For more functionalities, see **finance.yahoo.com/news/navigation-solutions-hertz-neverlost-r-221503204.html**.

Additional customer services. In addition to the location guide, the NeverLost® system provides driving directions, emergency telephone numbers, city maps, shopping guides, customer reviews of hotels, restaurants, and other consumer services. This content also is available to Hertz's club members at home, where they can print the information or load it into their mobile devices. For more on customer service at Hertz, see Gingiss (2015).

- **Car locations.** Hertz is experimenting with a GPS-based tracking system, which enables the company to find the location of a rental car at any given time. Furthermore, the system may be able to report in real time the *speed at which the* car is being driven. Although the company promises to keep the collected information secure, many view it as an *invasion of privacy*. However, some renters may feel safer knowing that they are being tracked at all times. Note: Currently (Marsh et al. 2016), Hertz is using the system only to track stolen cars and to find out when cars are returned.
- **Hertz On Demand.** According to their website, Hertz On Demand, available 24/7, offers self-service access to a rental vehicle for a short period of time (by the hour or a day), competing with car-sharing company Zipcar Inc. (**zipcar.com**). The Hertz 24/7 mobile app is available for download at **hertz.com/rentacar/productservice/index.**

jsp?targetPage=hertzmobilesite.jsp and can be used to find car rental locations. This application is available on PCs and mobile devices at the same site. The application includes ride sharing (e.g., rate comparisons of public transportation versus car rental).

- **Wi-Fi connection.** Free high-speed Internet access is available in Hertz's offices in all major Hertz locations in the United States, Canada, and some other countries.
- **PlatePass for toll payments.** Using this device, drivers can pay tolls for participating roads. Depending on the region, rented cars are equipped with a wireless transponder (an electric tag). If there is no such equipment on the car, the toll road will read automatically the auto plate number to bill the driver later. A daily service fee of $4.25 is paid to Hertz plus the fees for the toll road. For details, visit **platepass.com**.
- **Hertz mobile apps.** With the Hertz apps, which are available for iPhone, iPad, Windows, and Android, you can make reservations, search for store locations, enjoy special offers, and much more. See the Hertz mobile page at **hertz.com/rentacar/productservice/index.jsp?targetPage=hertzmobilesite.jsp**. For mobile apps, see *PR Newswire* (2014).
- **Social media.** Hertz is active in social network applications.

For details on the above, see Barris (2014).

The Results

Despite the economic problems of 2008–2014, Hertz has retained the number one position in the car rental industry. Its earnings, which declined in 2008 and 2009, rebounded between 2010 and 2014. Hertz did better than most of its competitors. Its stock market share price, which bottomed out in 2009, more than tripled in 2010 and continued to climb from 2011 to 2014. The company is expanding its operations and maintaining an excellent reputation among customers, due in part to its mobile applications.

Sources: Based on Barris (2014), Gingiss (2015), and **hertz.com** (accessed January 2017).

LESSONS LEARNED FROM THE CASE

The Hertz case illustrates several mobile applications in the transportation industry that can help improve both customer service and the company's operations. The applications are run on mobile devices and supported by a wireless network. (Both topics are discussed in section "The Enabling Infrastructure: Components and Services of Mobile Computing".) The mobile technology is based on a set of unique attributes (section "Mobile Commerce: Concepts, Landscape, Attributes, Drivers, Applications, and Benefits") that enable the use of many applications (sections "Mobile Banking and Financial Applications," "Mobile Enterprise Solutions: From Supporting the Workforce to Improving Internal Operations," "Mobile Entertainment, Gaming, Consumer Services, and Mobile Marketing," "Location-Based Commerce," "Ubiquitous (Pervasive) Computing," "Wearable Computing and Smart Gadgets: Watches, Fitness Trackers, and Smart Glasses," and "Implementation Issues in Mobile Commerce: From Security and Privacy to Barriers to M-Commerce").

The Hertz case is only one example of the impact of growing mobile and wireless technologies on business and electronic commerce (EC). In this chapter, we explore a number of these emerging mobile and wireless technologies as well as their potential applications in the commercial and societal arenas. The chapter also deals with the mobile enterprise, location-based services, and ubiquitous computing, which are emerging EC technologies.

6.1 MOBILE COMMERCE: CONCEPTS, LANDSCAPE, ATTRIBUTES, DRIVERS, APPLICATIONS, AND BENEFITS

As described in Chap. 1, businesses are becoming digital. In addition, many enterprises are going multi-locationally and globally, and the need for mobile communication is increasing rapidly (see the closing case in Chap. 7). According to GSMA (2016), the mobile industry is already a major contributor to the global economy. More than 75% of the world's population already own mobile phones, most of which are smartphones. Obviously, all the above are drivers of mobile commerce.

For definitions, topics, key issues, and so forth, see **mobileinfo.com/mcommerce/index.htm**.

Mobile commerce has its own framework, attributes, landscape, concepts, and terminology. These provide many benefits. For an overview, watch the 2:45 min video titled "What is M-Commerce?" at **youtube.com/watch?v=QtpTTpgpELg**.

One of the clearest trends in computing and e-commerce is that mobile computing is increasing exponentially. Each year, Gartner, Inc. compiles an annual list of the top ten strategic technology trends that have the potential to offer numerous benefits to individuals, businesses, and IT organizations during the following 3 years. Mobile computing topics are listed in all the 2010–2017 reports. Mobile commerce accounts now (2017) for about 40% of all EC transactions. Several countries are leapfrogging to mobile economy. One example is China (Ma 2016). In addition, see examples for mobile payments in Chap. 12. For mobile commerce in SMEs, see Diffly (2016).

Basic Concepts, Magnitude, and the Landscape

Mobile commerce (m-commerce), also known as *m-business*, refers to conducting e-commerce by using mobile devices and wireless networks. Activities include B2C, B2B, m-government, CRM and m-learning transactions, as well as the transfer of information and money. Like regular EC applications, m-commerce involves electronic transaction conducted by using mobile devices via the Internet, corporate intranets, private communication lines, or over other wireless networks. For example, paying for an item in a vending machine or paying taxes with an iPhone is considered m-commerce. M-commerce provides an opportunity to deliver new services to existing customers and to attract new customers to EC anytime, anywhere. Initially, the small screen size and slow bandwidth limited the usefulness to consumers. However, this situation is changing rapidly due to the widespread use of smartphones and tablet computers. In addition, now consumers are more accepting of the handheld culture. Furthermore, the adoption of m-commerce is accelerating due to the spread of 4G networks (and soon 5G). Finally, free Wi-Fi Internet access in many locations helps.

Note that m-commerce is quite different from traditional e-commerce and frequently uses specialized business models (see Swilley 2015 and **mobileinfo.com/mcommerce/differences.htm**). Mobile capabilities have resulted in many new applications and a change in the relationship between buyers and sellers (see **ibm.com/software/genservers/commerce/mobile**).

The Magnitude of M-Commerce

According to a 2013 eMarketer study, by 2017, approximately 25% of all online retail transactions in the United States will take place on mobile devices (reported by **mashable.com/2013/04/24/mcommerce-sales-forecast**). A 2014 InMobi report found that 83% of customers plan to conduct mobile commerce in 2014, a 15% increase from the previous year. Here are some more data to consider:

Mobile services contributed 4.2% of the GDP worldwide in 2015, forecasted to contribute close to 5% in 2020. By 2020, there could be close to 5.8 billion smartphones used by almost 90% of all Internet users. For more statistics, see **gsma.com/mobileeconomy/global/2016/**.

For statistics on m-commerce, see **statista.com/topics/1185/mobile-commerce**. For more details, see **gartner.com/newsroom/id/3270418**.

In this chapter, we consider some of the distinguishing attributes and key drivers of m-commerce, some technical issues relevant to m-commerce, and some of the major m-commerce applications. For the relationship, see **mobilepaymentstoday.com/blogs/social-media-becomes-more-of-a-mobile-commerce-tool-worldwide/**.

The Landscape of M-Commerce

The overall landscape of m-commerce is summarized in Fig. 6.1.

Note that, in the figure, the enabling technologies (e.g., devices, networks) are on the left side and the resulting capabilities and attributes are in the middle. These provide the foundation for the applications that are shown on the right side of the figure. In this section, we describe the attributes and provide an overview of the applications. In section "The Enabling Infrastructure: Components and Services of Mobile Computing", we present the essentials of the major technologies.

Mobile and Social: A Powerful EC Combination

M-commerce is a very powerful platform, but it can be even more powerful when combined with social commerce, as we will describe in Chaps. 7 and 8. This combination will shape the future of e-commerce and could be its major facilitator in the future.

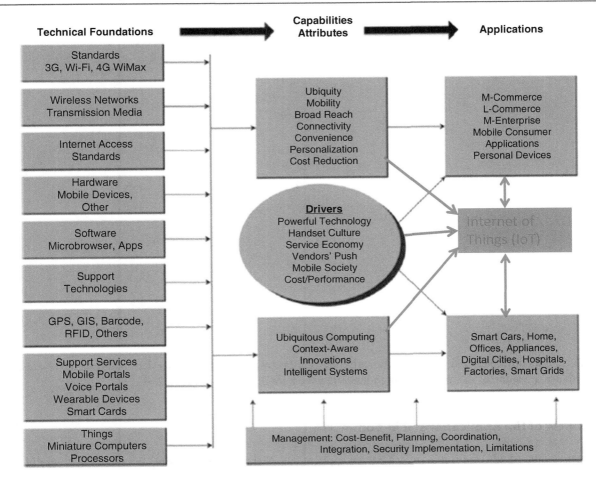

Fig. 6.1 The landscape of mobile computing and m-commerce

The Attributes of M-Commerce

Many of the EC applications described in this book also apply to m-commerce. For example, online shopping, e-travel, e-learning, e-entertainment, and online gaming are all gaining popularity in mobile B2C. Auction sites use m-commerce to send messages to bidders during the auction process; governments encourage m-government (Chap. 5); and wireless collaborative commerce in B2B EC is on the rise. Some key attributes that enable new applications are possible only in the mobile environment. The major attributes include:

- **Ubiquity.** *Ubiquity* means being everywhere, especially at the same time. It is facilitated by wireless computing. Given that Wi-Fi access is available in more and more places, and that about half of all mobile phones are smartphones, we have easier ubiquity.
- **Convenience and capabilities.** Having a mobile device increases the convenience of communication. The functionality and usability of mobile devices are increasing, while their physical size remains small and the cost is affordable. Unlike traditional computers, mobile devices connect to the Internet almost instantly.
- **Interactivity.** Mobile systems allow for fast and easy interactions (e.g., via Twitter, tablets, or smartphones).
- **Personalization.** Mobile devices are personal devices. While several people may share the same PC, a specific mobile device is usually used by one person.
- **Localization.** Knowing where a user is physically located in real time provides an opportunity to offer him or her relevant mobile advertisements, coupons, or other services. Such services are known as location-based m-commerce.

Fig. 6.2 The drivers of m-commerce

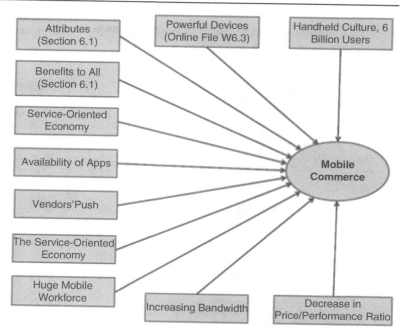

Mobile vendors differentiate themselves from wireline vendors by offering unique services based on the above attributes. These attributes are some of the drivers of m-commerce, which are illustrated in Fig. 6.2.

An Overview of the Applications of M-Commerce

There are many thousands of different m-commerce applications. Many of these are similar to those in a wireline environment, as described in Chaps. 3 and 4. Others are available only for mobile devices.

To simplify our presentation, we divided the applications in this chapter into the following categories, adding consumer applications to the framework:

- Banking and financial services—section "Mobile Banking and Financial Applications"
- Mobile enterprise applications—section "Mobile Enterprise Solutions: From Supporting the Workforce to Improving Internal Operations"
- Consumer services (including shopping and entertainment)—section "Mobile Entertainment, Gaming, Consumer Services, and Mobile Marketing"
- Ubiquitous computing—section "Ubiquitous (Pervasive) Computing"
- Emerging applications: wearables, Google Glass, smart grid, and driverless cars—section "Wearable Computing and Smart Gadgets: Watches, Fitness Trackers, and Smart Glasses"
- Internet of things (IoT) applications are covered in Chap. 7
- Mobile shopping is covered in Chap. 8
- Mobile marketing and advertising are covered in Chap. 10
- Mobile payment is introduced in Chap. 12
- Mobile ride-hailing (Uber, see closing case)

We categorized the *enterprise-related applications* according to the framework used by Motorola Corp. See **motorolasolutions.com/US-EN/enterprise+mobility**. Note: Zebra Tech. acquired Motorola Solutions' Enterprise Business in April 2014.

Fig. 6.3 M-commerce applications and their classifications

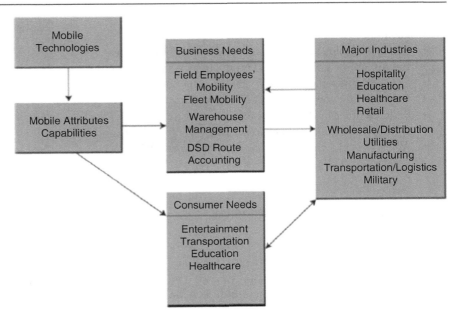

According to this framework, *enterprise applications* are created to meet specific business needs. These needs have some generic aspects as well as industry-specific aspects (see Fig. 6.3). The four needs are:

1. **Field mobility**—the support of the mobile workforce
2. **Fleet mobility**—the support of vehicles in order to minimize downtime and increase effectiveness, efficiency, and utilization
3. **Warehouse management**—the improvement of the operations inside warehouses
4. **Direct store delivery (DSD) route accounting**—the increased usefulness by conducting predelivery activities (e.g., by texting information about a new shipment from the shipper to the receiver)

This chapter discusses the techniques and applications in the m-commerce field from a managerial point of view. A related application, ubiquitous computing, will be discussed in section "Ubiquitous (Pervasive) Computing".

Also of interest is the emerging field of *mobile intelligence* (see Saylor 2012 and Chap. 7).

The Benefits of M-Commerce

M-commerce has many benefits to organizations, individuals, and society. As a result, many believe that the future of EC is mobile applications (watch the 5:06 min video titled "The Future of E-Commerce Is: Mobile Applications" at **youtube.com/watch?v=kYSMP_RH67w**).

Benefits for Organizations

- Increases sales due to ease of ordering by customers from anywhere, anytime
- Allows location-based commerce for more sales and revenue (section "Location-Based Commerce")
- Provides an additional channel for advertising and distribution of coupons (wider reach)
- Increases customers' loyalty
- Improves customer satisfaction through real-time apps
- Increases collaboration, advertisement, customer service, and sales by using IoT (Chap. 7)
- Enables many enterprise applications (section "Mobile Enterprise Solutions: From Supporting the Workforce to Improving Internal Operations")

(continued)

- Facilitates CRM and collaboration
- Reduces employee training time and help desk resources
- Improves time utilization and productivity of mobile employees
- Expedites information flow to and from mobile employees
- Delivers digitized products and services directly to mobile devices
- Reduces order lead-time and fulfillment cycle
- Allows for lower, competitive pricing
- Ability to work at home and have flextime (Barry 2017)

Benefits for Individuals and Customers

- Allows e-commerce from any place, anytime
- Assists in shopping by providing real-time information and other shopping aids
- Helps organization and communication while traveling
- Expedites banking and financial services
- Provides rich media entertainment anytime and anywhere
- Facilitates the finding of new friends and whereabouts of existing ones
- Provides a choice of mobile devices for transactions
- Expedites communication (e.g., locate people, get fast answers to queries, compare prices while in physical stores or via shopping comparison sites/apps)
- Increases affordability over the cost of using desktop computing in some countries
- Allows "smart" applications

Benefits to Society

There are many benefits to society. For example, self-driving cars can reduce accidents; smart cities can benefit the dwellers and visitors. Contributions are in almost any field, from medical care and education to law enforcement. Significant reductions in energy expenses are achieved by using smart grids. Traffic jams can be reduced by using wireless sensors and much more.

There are some limitations to m-commerce, which are discussed in Section 6.9.

Mobile Commerce Trends

According to Moovweb (2016), the following are the major 2016 m-commerce trends:

1. Physical and online worlds will continue to converge.
2. Social commerce will remain hot, but will "buy" buttons deliver?
3. Over 85% of mobile time is spent in apps. However, only 25% sales come from apps.
4. Consumer expectations will drive retailers to focus on mobile services.
5. Loyalty will eclipse convenience in driving mobile payments.
6. IoT is still chasing full potential, but wearables are poised for growth.
7. The growth of mobile will force brands to optimize mobile checkouts.

Note: Figures for 2017 were not available at the time this chapter was written.

SECTION 6.1 REVIEW QUESTIONS

1. Define m-commerce.
2. Briefly describe the five value-added attributes of m-commerce.
3. List and briefly describe eight major drivers of m-commerce (see Fig. 6.2).
4. Describe the framework of m-commerce applications.
5. What are the major categories of m-commerce applications?
6. Describe the landscape of m-commerce.
7. What are the major benefits of m-commerce?
8. Describe the major online enterprise applications.
9. List five major mobility trends

6.2   THE ENABLING INFRASTRUCTURE: COMPONENTS AND SERVICES OF MOBILE COMPUTING

The technology that supports m-commerce is very diversified. Here we concentrate on some major technology items.

Overview of Mobile Computing

In the traditional computing environment, users were confined to desktop computers in fixed locations. A solution to this situation is **wireless mobile computing** (**mobile computing**), where computing is done by using mobile devices at any place connected wirelessly to networks. According to TechTarget Bitpipe, wireless mobile computing, also known as nomadic computing, is the use of portable computing devices (such as tablets and smartphones) in conjunction with mobile communications technologies to enable users' access to the Internet and to data from anywhere with Internet access (see **bitpipe.com/tlist/Wireless-Computing.html**).

For mobile statistics for 2016, see Steinberg (2016).

This section briefly discusses the major technologies and application areas of mobile computing systems. For an extensive list of related terms, see **mobileinfo.com/Glossary/index.htm** and **en.wikipedia.org/wiki/Mobile_computing**. For the introduction and history of mobile computing, see Livingston's presentation at **slideshare.net/davidjlivi/introduction-history-of-mobile-computing**.

Mobile Devices

Mobile devices come in all shapes and sizes—laptops, thin-and-light notebooks, tablet computers, smartphones, ultra-portables, wearables, and ultra-mobile PCs (UMPCs). What distinguishes one type of mobile computer from another are its different capabilities, such as physical dimensions, shape, and the executions of the capabilities. Most of the major computer manufacturers (HP, Apple, Dell, ASUS, Toshiba, Acer, and Lenovo) produce thin laptops and ultraportables.

A few years ago, portable computers, cell phones, and other mobile devices were different from each other and had unique features. Today, all of these devices are converging so that it is sometimes difficult to tell them apart (from a functional perspective).

Mobile devices can be large. Several manufacturers offer special handheld devices, and 23″ laptops or mobile worksta-tions are available (e.g., Dell, HP, and Lenovo). For an example, see Weiss (2015). Tablets are available in a 7″ to 15″ screen. Smartphones also come in a variety of sizes.

Smartphones

A **smartphone** is a mobile phone (such as an iPhone) with Internet access and PC-like functionality.

There is a wide range and variety of smartphone manufacturers. Note that smartphones get "smarter" with time and add features and capabilities. There is also a wide variety of operating systems, including Symbian, Google Apps, Android, Windows Mobile, Apple IOS and OS/X, RIM BlackBerry, and Google's Chrome OS. Like PDAs, smartphones have small screens, keyboards, memory, and storage. Most smartphones have built-in cameras and many are GPS-enabled.

Tablets

A fast-growing category of mobile devices is the *tablet computer*. Tablet computers received a major boost in 2010 with the introduction of the Apple iPad and its competitors, all with a virtual keyboard (but a portable physical keyboard can be attached). Since then, many companies are manufacturing tablets. Notable are Apple, Amazon.com, Samsung, HP, Dell, Microsoft, HTC, and Google. Like laptops, tablets can access the Web via Wi-Fi hotspots. The *iPad* weighs about 1 pound (in between a smartphone and a small laptop). Tablets are replacing PCs and laptops in enterprises and schools. Tablets are also replacing hardcover textbooks in many schools. Tablets can be used as e-readers and can be used to access the Internet. Note that the price of tablets is declining, while their capabilities are increasing. In India, for instance, Aakash students can buy tablets for as little as $35.

Tablets are becoming popular in enterprises as well. For example, Waste Management Inc. (**wm.com**) provides 7″ tablets to their truckers for finding optimal routes. For a comprehensive description, see **informationweek.com/mobile.asp** and **apple.com/ipad**. A major use of a tablet is to facilitate communication and collaboration. However, they are increasingly used in entertainment, learning, and shopping.

Wearable Devices

The smallest mobile devices are wearable. Notable are many devices used in the enterprise (e.g., mounted on the arm, head, or body and carried by employees). Samsung's Galaxy Gear smartwatch, which was released in 2013, is one example. In April 2014, Samsung released its Gear Fit device, a "fitness tracker-smartwatch hybrid" (see **mashable.com/2014/04/08/samsung-gear-fit-review**). Both Fitbit and Apple Watch appeared in 2015. For more about wearable devices, see section "Ubiquitous (Pervasive) Computing".

Radio-Frequency Identification (RFID)

Radio-frequency identification (RFID) enables the transfer of data wirelessly, usually for the purpose of automatically identifying and tracking tags attached to objects. RFID does this by employing radio-frequency electromagnetic fields (see Online Tutorial T2). Most of the enterprise applications relate to logistics and inventory control. For details, see Chap. 13. Also related to EC is the use of RFID to improve security and enable mobile payments (e.g., in paying for toll roads). For images of RFID applications, search Google Images for "RFID applications." For a comprehensive guide to RFID (e.g., white papers, case studies, definition), see the RFID Technology Primer at **impinj.com/guide-to-rfid/what-is-rfid.aspx**. Finally, for 100 uses of RFID, see **rfid.thingmagic.com/rfid-blog/bid/52243/100-Uses-of-RFID**.

Mobile Computing Software and Services

Mobile devices offer some capabilities that desktops do not. These capabilities provide a foundation for new applications.

Mobile Portals and Content Providers

A **mobile portal** is a gateway to the Internet from mobile devices. It combines content from several sources and can be personalized for mobile users. These portals offer services similar to those of desktop portals (see **gartner.com/it-glossary/mobile-portal** and **ehow.com/facts_7631652_definition-mobile-portal.html** for an additional discussion of mobile portals). An example of a pure mobile portal is Zed (**zed.com**; a wholly owned subsidiary of Finnish telecommunication company Sonera) headquartered in Spain. Japan's largest mobile provider, with over 60 million customers, is i-mode from NTT DOCOMO (see **www.nttdocomo.co.jp/english/service/imode** for the capabilities of i-mode).

The services provided by mobile portals are similar to those provided by desktop portals (e.g., news, health, sports, and downloading music). Mobile portals sometimes charge for their services.

Short Message Service

Short message service (SMS) is frequently referred to as *text messaging* or simply *texting*; the technology supports the transmittal of short text messages (up to 140 or 160 characters) between wireless devices. The cost of texting is very low compared to the charge per minute to talk on cell phones. The limited message length makes users use acronyms to convey standard messages. Examples of such acronyms include "how are you" becoming "HOW RU," or "HRU," and "in my opinion" becoming "IMO." Texting is popular worldwide due to the use of smartphones and microblogging (e.g., Twitter).

Multimedia Messaging Services (MMS)

Multimedia messaging service (MMS) is the new type of wireless messaging, delivering rich media content, such as videos, images, and audio to mobile devices. MMS is an extension of SMS (no extra charge with an SMS "bundle"). It allows for longer messages than with SMS.

For the difference between SMS and MMS and their benefits for mobile marketing, see **mogreet.wordpress. com/2012/03/15/understanding-mobile-marketing-what-is-sms-mms-message-marketing**.

The Internet of Things (IoT)

A most discussed topic in EC lately is the IoT. This ecosystem views billions of computing devices connected to the Internet. Most of the connections are wireless. In Chap. 7, we introduce IoT with many of its applications.

Location-Based Services

Retailers who use location-based services use the *global positioning system (GPS)* or other positioning techniques to find a customer's location and then deliver services, such as ads and coupons for products and services, in real time. GPS is also used in emergency services, traffic management, and other applications.

Voice-Support Services

The most natural mode of human communication is voice. Voice recognition and voice synthesizing in m-commerce applications offer advantages such as hands- and eyes-free operation, better operation in dirty or moving environments, faster input (people talk about two and a half times faster than they type), and ease of use for disabled people.

IVR Systems

Voice-support applications, such as **interactive voice response (IVR) systems,** enable users to interact by telephones (of any kind) with a computerized system and to request and receive information. These systems have been around since the 1980s but are now becoming more capable and widespread as artificial intelligence-based voice recognition capabilities continue to improve (see Chap. 7).

Intelligent Personal Assistants and Robo-advisors

As described in Chap. 7, companies use AI to understand spoken natural languages. It is the basis for the development of chatbots and robots (Chap. 7). This application is used for **intelligent personal assistants**, which are offered today by major corporations. Well known are Google Now, Microsoft's Cortana, Apple's Siri, and Amazon's Alexa. Other companies create competing products (e.g., SoundHound). Note that these products are integrated with smartwatches, smart TVs, and cars.

Of special interest is Amazon's Echo, which is a screenless, voice-controlled device that operates with Amazon's Alexa and excels in smart home applications. For details, see Chap. 7, Rubin (2016), Manjoo (2016), and Mayo (2016).

Voice Portals

A **voice portal** is a website with an audio interface that can be accessed through a telephone call. A user requests information by speaking, and the voice portal finds the information on the Web, transforms it into a computer-generated voice reply, and provides the answer by voice. For example, Bing Tell voice assistant (**bing.com/partners/developers# BingSpeechApis**; a Microsoft company) allows callers to request information ranging from weather to current traffic conditions. IVR and voice portals are likely to become important ways of delivering m-commerce services over audio. Popular applications are used for banking, hospitals, airlines, government services, and online entertainment. A similar service, called Siri, is available on iPhones where you can place commands by voice, including sending messages, asking questions, and receiving answers.

Note: Some companies are trying to connect to the Internet by sending signals from high in the sky and even from outer space (e.g., watch the video titled "Beaming the Internet from Outer Space" (1:36 min) at **money.cnn.com/video/ technology/2014/02/26/t-beaming-internet-from-space-outernet-cubesat.cnnmoney**). Also, note that there is an increase in mobile cloud computing (see **prezi.com/dpniferapgzh/examples-of-mobile-cloud-computing**).

Other Mobile Devices

There are other kinds of mobile devices as well. For example, Microsoft offers a tablet with an attachable keyboard, and Dell offers a foldable tablet with a keyboard, combining the capabilities of a laptop and a tablet. A representative list of mobile devices is available at **pcmag.com/article/342695/the-best-mobile-device-management-mdm-software-of-2016**.

Mobile Apps

Mobile Apps and Their Management

According to WhatIs.com, a **mobile app** "is a software application developed specifically for use on small, wireless computing devices, such as smartphones and tablets, rather than desktop or laptop computers. Mobile apps are designed with consideration for the demands and constraints of the devices and also to take advantage of any specialized capabilities they have. A gaming app, for example, might take advantage of the iPhone's accelerometer" (**whatis.techtarget.com/definition/mobile-app**).

Mobile applications are very popular for both consumers and in use inside the enterprise. For example, as of spring 2016, Apple had about 1.2 million approved applications in its App Store.

Mobile apps can run on smartphones and tablets and on other devices such as smartwatches and glasses. Most devices are sold with many preinstalled apps, such as a Web browser. There are probably millions of mobile apps. Many can be downloaded for free, others for a small fee. PC Magazine and CNET provide up-to-date reviews. For a mobile app directory for government agencies categorized by platform and topic, see **usa.gov/mobile-apps**. According to Fox News (2016), the US Federal and Drug Administration launched a mobile app competition for crowdsourcing that will solicit public opinions about drug use.

Because their small size mobile apps are easy to develop and their cost is minimal, many companies provide such apps to their customers. Mobile apps have grown mostly in the areas of social networking, sports, business finance, shopping, health, and enterprise mobility applications.

A vivid example of a mobile app is ride-hailing. Companies such as Uber (see closing case) and Lyft are growing rapidly, disrupting the taxi industry.

Putting It All Together

The previously mentioned software, hardware, and telecommunications are connected by a management system to support wireless electronic trading, as shown in Fig. 6.4. The figure, which is self-explanatory, shows the flow of information from the user (Step 1) to the conclusion of the transaction (Step 9).

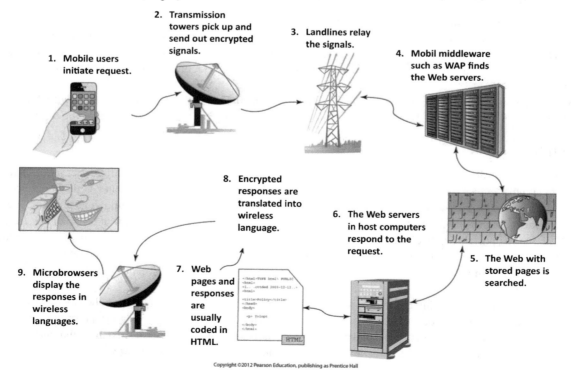

Fig. 6.4 An m-commerce system at work

SECTION 6.2 REVIEW QUESTIONS

1. Briefly describe some of the key differences and similarities among the major mobile devices.
2. Briefly describe the types of messaging services offered for mobile devices.
3. Define mobile portal and voice portal.
4. Distinguish between MMS and SMS.
5. Define IVR.
6. Describe smartphone apps and list their advantages.

6.3   MOBILE BANKING AND FINANCIAL APPLICATIONS

Most mobile financial services are mobile versions of their wireline counterparts. However, they can be used anytime, anywhere. We divided these services into two broad categories: mobile banking and other mobile financial services. Mobile payments are described in Chap. 12. For an overview of mobile financial services, see **ericsson.com/m-commerce/node/11**.

Mobile Banking

Mobile banking (m-banking) describes the conducting of banking activities via a mobile device (mostly via smartphones, tablets, texting, or mobile website). The influx of smartphones and tablets has led to an increased utilization of mobile banking. For details, a conceptual model, and challenges for mobile banking solutions, see Krishnan (2014). A popular service is a mobile deposit of checks. You sign the front and back of the check, snap pictures of both sides, including the endorsement on the back, and submit it.

Throughout the world, more and more banks are offering mobile-based financial and accounting information and transaction capabilities.

Examples
Most banks deploy mobile services through a variety of channels, although the Internet and SMS are the most widely used. A blog written by Brandon McGee (**bmcgee.com**) provides links to a number of banking websites throughout the world that provide comprehensive wireless financial services. The Chase Mobile app and other mobile banking services offered by JPMorgan Chase Bank at **chase.com** enable customers to access their accounts via smartphones and send text messages to request and receive account information.

In February 2014, mBank (**mbank.pl/en**) launched a mobile banking platform in Poland. The app allows access to their banking services, such as checking an account balance or credit card limit (see **telecompaper.com/news/mbank-launches-new-mobile-banking-app-in-Poland**). American First Credit Union offers many mobile services including location-based offers.

Banks and financial services' customers are utilizing their smartphones and cell phones to obtain current financial information and perform real-time transactions. For comprehensive coverage, see Knowledge@Wharton and Ernst & Young (2013).

Mobile Banking Apps

Mobile banking apps are increasingly becoming more important than physical branches. Actually, many banks (e.g., Bank of America) are closing branches. According to Clements (2016), customers are getting more satisfied with mobile apps. This writer also reports that Chase Bank has the best apps. These include fingerprint sign on, mobile check deposits, and the ability to view images of deposited checks.

Example
Citizens Bank lists the following smartphone apps (January 2017):

- Securely check balances quickly and easily with Fast Balance.
- Securely check balances with Fast Balance from the convenience of your Apple Watch, Android Wear, or widget.
- Pay bills and add billers.
- Deposit checks remotely.

- View check images.
- Transfer funds.
- Pay other people with Popmoney personal payment service.
- Review up to 18 months of account history.
- Locate ATMs and branches. Also available on Apple Watch and Android Wear.
- Use Touch ID or a PIN to log in.
- Receive alerts.

For details, see **citizensbank.com/online-and-mobile-banking/ap;ps.aspx**.

Finally, *mobile payments*, including payments withdrawn from bank accounts via mobile devices and depositing checks via smartphone photos, have become very popular (see Chap. 11).

Internet-Only Banks

Internet-only banks are virtual banks that have no physical branches. The more banks closing their physical branches, and the more people using mobile devices, the more people are getting used to transactions online.

Online-only banks' costs are substantially lower than that of conventional banks. Therefore, they can offer more free services, such as free checks or free bill paying. In addition, you do not need to worry about the closing of your branch. Online banks may give users more and/or quicker information, since all the data are digitized. Most Internet banks provide mobile access.

Internet-only banks have some disadvantages. When you need cash, you must go to an ATM, which may cost you money, if it is not maintained by your bank; or, when you cannot get cash from an ATM, you must use your debit card in the supermarket trying to get some extra change. In addition, you will need to mail deposits if you cannot transfer money online, not to mention getting cashier's checks or buying traveler's checks for your trips. Finally, when you have coins, you may need to pay 10% to change them to paper money.

Despite all the negatives, people may like the Internet-only banks.

Selecting a Bank

There are several banks to choose from. Well known are Ally Bank and the Bank of Internet USA. Others are Bank5 Connect, EverBank, Discover Bank, FNBO Direct, and State Farm Bank. To help you select one, you may use Gomez Internet Banker Scorecard. This service uses criteria such as services provided, interest paid to you, charges made, security measures, support provided, and reward programs.

Bank of Internet USA (BOFI)

This bank is one of the oldest Internet-only banks and the first to be listed on a stock exchange (NASDAQ). It is a nationwide bank that received a "Best Banks of 2017" award from **GOBankingRates.com** (GoBankingRate is similar to Gomez Internet Banker Scorecard). Being the oldest FDIC-insured Internet bank in the United States, the bank is the most trusted and is growing rapidly. For more information, see **bankofinternet.com**.

Using Cutting Edge Technologies in Mobile Banking

Since mobile banking requires that all data are digitized, it is easier to implement cutting edge technologies, such as AI and virtual and augmented reality. According to Oxagile (2016), cutting edge technologies will disrupt banking and financial services. Oxagile sees the following areas to be impacted: wealth management, trading, new channels for reaching millennials, and providing immersive experiences through data visualization.

Other Mobile Finance Applications

There are several other mobile finance applications (search Google for "future of mobile finance"). Two applications follow.

Mobile Stock Trading

Several brokerage companies offer extensive mobile services and stock-trading mobile tools. For the best online brokers for stock trading (2017) and the services they offer and their fees, see Yochim (2017).

Real Estate Mobile Applications

The real estate market can be an ideal place for mobile commerce since real estate brokers and buyers and sellers are constantly on the move. Most realtors offer a photo gallery for each property on your desktop or mobile device, but m-commerce can do more than that. Let us look at two examples.

Example: Using Augmented Realty

Using augmented reality (see Chap. 2), some companies in Europe and the United States allow you to point your smartphone at certain buildings in a city (e.g., Paris) and then see the property value superimposed on the image of the particular building. This technology is combined with a GPS to let the system know your location.

HomeScan is an iPhone and McIntosh application developed by California-based **ZipRealty.com** that allows prospective real estate customers to find, see, and download properties in a mobile environment. For more about the HomeScan app, see **ziprealty.com/iphone**. A more generic application is available from HomeSpotter. For an example, watch the 3:21 min video at **youtube.com/watch?v=LgBCkIDQjb0**.

Several other mobile real estate applications, combining Google Maps and Google Earth with mobile applications, are available or are being developed. Note that some people object to other people taking photos of their houses on the basis that it is an invasion of privacy.

Related to real estate, but used elsewhere, is the electronic signature. A leading provider is DocuSign Inc.

SECTION 6.3 REVIEW QUESTIONS

1. Describe some of the services provided by mobile banking.
2. List some of the benefits derived from e-banking.
3. What is Internet-only banking?
4. What is a mobile banking app?
5. Describe mobile applications in real estate.
6. How is virtual reality and virtual augmented reality used in real estate?

6.4   MOBILE ENTERPRISE SOLUTIONS: FROM SUPPORTING THE WORKFORCE TO IMPROVING INTERNAL OPERATIONS

Although B2C m-commerce gets considerable publicity in the media, for most organizations, the greatest benefit from m-commerce is likely to come from applications within the enterprise. These applications mostly support the mobile workforce employees who spend a substantial part of their workday away from the corporate premises.

The majority of enterprise mobile applications are included in **enterprise mobility** or *mobile enterprise*. Enterprise mobility includes the people and technology (e.g., devices and networks) that enable mobile computing applications within the enterprise. Enterprise mobility was one of the top 10 items in Gartner's strategic technology lists since 2013. Mobile enterprise apps are gaining momentum in 2016 (see Weiss 2015). For the top mobility trends for 2016, see Gordon (2015).

Defining Mobile Enterprise (Enterprise Mobility)

Mobile technology is rapidly proliferating in the enterprise. In the previous sections, we introduced several business-oriented examples, in what we survey "mobile enterprise applications" or, in short, "mobile enterprise." This term refers to mobile applications in enterprises (to distinguish from consumer-oriented applications, such as mobile entertainment). Obviously, there are many mobile enterprise applications; examples are illustrated in section "Mobile Commerce: Concepts, Landscape, Attributes, Drivers, Applications, and Benefits", Fig. 6.3.

A Working Definition of Mobile Enterprise

Mobile enterprise refers to mobile applications used by companies to improve the operations of the employees, facilities, and relevant supply chains within the enterprise and with its business partners. The term is also known as *enterprise mobility*.

For a comprehensive description of mobile enterprise, including guidelines for implementation, best practices, and case studies, see Diogenes (2017).

For details, see **searchconsumerization.techtarget.com/definition/Enterprise-mobility**. For a large collection of enterprise mobility and enterprise mobility applications, conduct a Google search. Also, do a Google Images search for "enterprise mobility." For Gartner's analysis (with figures) of enterprise mobility and the impact on IT, see **gartner.com/doc/1985016/enterprise-mobility-impact-it**.

Many companies and experts believe that mobility can transform businesses. For the 2017 trends in enterprise mobility, see Marsh et al. (2016).

The Framework and Content of Mobile Enterprise Applications

There are several proprietary frameworks for classifying mobile applications. For example, AT&T Enterprise Business provides categories such as vertical industry, healthcare, mobility, and mobile productivity. Also well known is Motorola's framework. For development and testing of apps, see Mobile Labs (2016).

Mobile Workers

A **mobile worker** is usually defined as any employee who is away from his or her primary workspace at least 10 h a week (or 25% of the time). According to a new forecast from International Data Corporation (IDC), the US mobile worker population will grow at a steady rate over the next 5 years, increasing from 96.2 million in 2015 to 105.4 million mobile workers in 2020. By the end of the forecast period, IDC expects mobile workers will account for nearly three quarters (72.3%) of the total US workforce. See **businesswire.com/news/home/20150623005073/en/IDC-Forecasts-U.S.-Mobile-Worker-Population-Surpass**.

Examples of mobile workers include members of sales teams, traveling professionals and managers, telecommuters, and repair people or installation employees who work off the company's premises. These individuals need access to the same office and work applications and data as those who work in the office.

Mobile CRM

This is a growing application area. For definitions of CRM and CRM apps, see **ringdna.com/inside-sales-glossary/inside-sales-glossaryinside-sales-glossarywhat-is-mobile-crm** and **bitpipe.com/tlist/mobile-crm.html**. For an overview, benefits, and a case study, see **powershow.com/view/1497bd-M2JiN/Mobile-CRM-a_Case_Study_powerpoint_ppt_presentation**. In addition, see the 2015 slideshow: **slideshare.net/Sage_software_solutions/mobile-crm-ppt-from-sage-software-solutions**. For comprehensive coverage of mobile CRM, including a 2:59 min video, cases, etc., see **salesforce.com/eu/crm/mobile-crm**. For the strategic advantages of mobile CRM, see Maximizer (2015).

Using Messaging in CRM
Thouin (2016) lists the following help scenarios:

1. When someone needs help
2. When someone needs customer service
3. When a shopper needs help
4. When there is an urgency

Other Enterprise Mobile Applications

Hundreds of other mobile applications exist. For examples, see Motorola Solutions Enterprise Mobility (**motorolasolutions.com/US**; now Zebra).

An example of a popular mobile application in the field of medical care is the use of communication devices in clinics, physicians' offices, and hospitals. For an interesting case study on Maryland's Frederick Memorial Hospital and their use of Panasonic laptops, see **business.panasonic.com/industries-healthcarelifesciences-casestudies-frederickmemorial**.

Transportation Management

Another popular mobile application area is that of transportation management (e.g., trucks, forklifts, buses, vans, and so forth). In this area, mobility is used in communication with drivers, use of control systems, surveillance, and dispatching. Examples of these applications can be seen in the Hertz Corp. opening case. Mobile devices are used extensively in airports and by airlines, traffic control systems, public bus systems, and more.

For examples of the importance of enterprise and cars' mobility, see Ford's new division called Smart Mobility. It covers both enterprise and the car's applications (Austin 2016).

Trends for 2015 And Beyond

It is clear that the number of applications and their benefits is increasing. The large global software company Infosys ("Building Tomorrow's Enterprise") provides a paper titled (search **infosys.com/mobility**). The website describes the challenges and opportunities of enterprise mobility and provides a large collection of mobility-related resources (e.g., case studies, white papers).

Enterprise Mobility 2017

For the trends of mobile enterprise in 2016, see Peng (2016). Peng explains that there is focus on knowledge workers by providing them with productivity mobile apps (e.g., Box, Evernote). Another area is *mobile workers,* by providing them with apps such as Invoice2go and PlanGrid, which can increase their productivity. For the near future, Peng sees utilization of all the functionalities of smartphones (e.g., real-time location data to collect real data in the field). For the 2017 trends, see Matteson (2017). For 2018–2023 outlook, see ICON Group (2017). For a pragmatic vision, see Beauduin et al. (2015).

SECTION 6.4 REVIEW QUESTIONS

1. Define mobile enterprise.
2. Describe the content of mobile enterprise applications.
3. Define mobile workers.
4. List the major segments of the mobile workforce.
5. What are some of the common benefits of mobile SFA, FFA, and CRM?

6.5   MOBILE ENTERTAINMENT, GAMING, CONSUMER SERVICES, AND MOBILE MARKETING

Mobile entertainment applications have been around for years, but they have only recently expanded rapidly due to developments in wireless devices and mobile technology. Consumer applications started in the 1990s but really soared after 2000. This section mainly describes mobile entertainment and briefly discusses some other areas of consumer services and mobile shopping.

Overview of Mobile Entertainment

There is some debate about what actually constitutes mobile entertainment and which of its segments is really m-commerce. For example, assume you purchase a song from the Web and download it to your PC and then download it to your MP3 player. Is this a form of mobile entertainment? What if you copy the song to a smartphone rather than to an MP3 player? What if you buy the song and download it directly from the Web to your smartphone? There are many similar "what ifs." A popular definition is **mobile entertainment** refers to entertainment delivered on mobile devices over wireless networks or that interacts with mobile service providers. For an overview of mobile entertainment in 2016, watch the 4:40 min video at **youtube.com/watch?v=9opLALHrFQ8**.

This section discusses some of the major types of mobile entertainment, including mobile music and video, mobile gaming, mobile gambling, and mobility and sports. Mobile entertainment in social networks is covered in Chap. 8.

Mobile Streaming Music and Video Providers

Apple is the clear leader in the digital distribution of music and video. Since 2001, Apple has offered consumers the ability to download songs and videos from the Apple iTunes store. iTunes customers purchase billions of songs annually. Other major Internet music providers are **spotify.com**, **youtube.com**, and **pandora.com**. Note that cell phones today can display analog TV (popular in developing countries). Smartphones can display any programs offered on the Internet. Note that with their Dish Anywhere mobile app, Dish Network works anywhere customers can access the Internet through their smartphone or tablet, and, with their Sling Technology, customers can watch live TV or DVR content on their iPhone, iPad, Android, and Kindle Fire (see **dish.com/technology/dish-anywhere**). Netflix has a free app for its subscribers to watch TV shows and movies streaming from Netflix on their mobile device (e.g., iPhone, iPad, Android). See **get.it/netflix**. TallScreen (formerly imDown) provides a mobile entertainment network that focuses on 1-minute *vertical videos* (categorized by subjects); see details at Perez (2016).

Entertainment in Cars

Entertainment is coming to cars directly from the Internet. For example, in March 2014, Apple announced that it is teaming up with a major carmaker for its *CarPlay* system. The system enables iPhones to plug into cars so drivers can request music with voice commands or with a touch on a vehicle dashboard screen. For details, see Liedtke (2014). JVC ("Experience Apps in a New Mobile Way") allows you to connect an iPod to a JVC receiver and "watch it come alive with your favorite apps." The JVC feature works with compatible car receivers and apps only. For more about JVC and its mobile features for cars, see **www3.jvckenwood.com/english/car/applink**. Future opportunities include car diagnosis, driver health monitoring, usage-based insurance, and even parental alerts. Some car brands already provide communication, telematics, social networking, and mobile commerce.

Mobile Games

A mobile game is a video game played on a mobile device. A wide range of mobile games has been developed for different types of players. The vast majority of players use smartphones and tablets. Many computer games can be played on mobile devices. For example, trading card games like "Magic: The Gathering" are online or plan to be (see **accounts.onlinegaming.wizards.com**). Mobile games can be classified according to:

- **Technology.** Embedded, SMS/MMS, Web browsing, J2ME, BREW, native OS.
- **Number of players.** Solo play or multiplay (from few to many players).
- **Social network-based.** Using smartphones, people can play games available on social networks, such as FarmVille on Facebook.

Several blogs provide information and discussions about the current state of the mobile gaming market, including various game offerings, as well as the technologies and platforms used to develop the games. One of the best is **pocketgamer.biz**. Venture Beat provides mobile game news very frequently; see **venturebeat.com/mobile-games**.

The drivers of the popularity of mobile games are:

- Increasing spread of mobile devices. The more people use smartphones, the more people will play e-games.
- The inclusion of games on social networks and particularly on Facebook.
- The streaming of quality videos is improving. The quantity is also increasing.
- The support for the gamification movement.
- The ability of vendors to generate money from ads attached to games.
- Technological improvements for downloading complex games.
- The availability of free games online.

The potential size and growth of the overall online gaming market are enormous. This explains the large number of companies involved in creating, distributing, and running mobile games.

Hurdles for Growth

Although the market is growing rapidly, game publishers (especially in China and India) are facing some major hurdles. For example, there is a lack of standards, lack of different types of software and hardware, and increasing costs. The newest generation of games requires advanced capabilities available only in higher-end mobile devices and with 3G networks (at a minimum). The ad spending in mobile games has remained low, but it is growing.

To address these hurdles, game publishers are focusing their attention on Apple's iPhone and iPad and on similar popular devices.

A final note: Mobile games can be used for medical research. For example, Chester (2016) reports that data from mobile game players is being used to boost Alzheimer's research.

Mobile Gambling

Unlike some of the other forms of mobile entertainment, the mobile gambling market has a high demand but also some unique hurdles. First, mobile gambling requires two-way financial transactions. Second, online gambling sites face major trust issues. Gamblers and bettors have to believe that the site is trustworthy and fair. Finally, while the legislative and regulatory picture is very restrictive, it is also unclear and keeps changing.

Online gambling is booming despite the fact that it is illegal in almost all US states. In 2013, Delaware and Nevada were the first US states to allow some online gambling, followed by New Jersey (in October 2013, Delaware became the first state to allow a "full suite" of Internet gambling). In February 2014, both Delaware and Nevada signed a deal to allow interstate online gambling. Note that federal law limits online gambling to players while they are physically present within each state. (This can be verified by using geolocation software.) Therefore, if one state allows online gambling, you can play only when you are in that state. As of February 2016, many states legalized gambling or were considering legalizing or expanding online gambling (**washingtonpost.com/blogs/govbeat/wp/2014/02/05/at-least-10-states-expected-to-consider-allowing-online-gambling-this-year**). However, in March of 2014, a bill was introduced in Congress to outlaw any Internet gambling, including in the states where it is already legal (**reviewjournal.com/news/new-bill-would-prohibit-internet-gambling-including-where-already-legal**). As far as we know, the federal government in the United States is still considering the issue (January 2017).

Mobility and Sports

There are many sports mobile applications (e.g., see the closing case about the NFL in Chap. 1).

Here are some representative examples of unique sports mobile applications:

- Nike and Apple introduced an iPod shoe called Nano (a best seller), which can calculate how many calories are burned during workouts. This is done via wireless sensors. In addition to calories burned, users can get information about the distance they run. The data collected by the sensors are transmitted to the runner's iPod and headphones. In addition, the Nike+iPod system delivers music and voice entertainment, including podcasts on different sports topics. For details, see Frakes (2010).
- Personalized live sport events can be viewed on mobile devices. The user can select the event to watch. In the future, systems will be able even to predict users' preferred events during several simultaneous live sports competitions. Streaming live sports to mobile devices is becoming very popular. Unfortunately, there may be a fee to enjoy this.
- ESPN's SportsCenter offers WatchESPN, a system where subscribers can watch ESPN on a desktop or on a mobile device. For details, see **espn.go.com/watchespn/index**.
- Eventbrite **eventbrite.com** is a company that provides several applications for event management online (e.g., creating tickets, promoting events, managing event entry).

Service Industry Consumer Applications

A large number of mobile applications are used in different service industries. Here are two examples:

Healthcare

Mobile devices are everywhere in the field of healthcare, as illustrated next:

- Using a handheld device, a physician can submit a prescription directly to participating pharmacies from her office or patient's bedside. In addition, your physician can order tests, access medical information, scan billable items, and check costs and fees for services.
- Remote devices not only monitor patient vital signs while he/she is at home but also can adjust operating medical equipment. This is done by using sensors.
- To reduce errors, mobile devices can validate the managing, tracking, and verifying of blood collected for transfusions. Promises Treatment Centers (alcohol and drug rehabilitation) uses a free mobile app (iPromises for iPhone; **ipromises.org**) that works as a virtual recovery tool (e.g., list of AA meetings in the United States and Canada, add friends, track progress, etc.). While the iPromises Recovery Companion does not generate revenue for the company, "it is aimed at bolstering Promises' reputation among patients and doctors."

For more applications, see **motorolasolutions.com/US-EN/Business+Solutions/Industry+Solutions/Healthcare** (now Zebra).

Hospitality Management: Hotels, Resorts, and Restaurants

Many applications exist from travel reservations to ensuring safety in hotel rooms. Examples are two-way radio communication, wireless hotspot solutions, food safety checks, parking lot management, asset location and management, guest services, safety and security on the premises, entertainment, inventory management, and much more. For details, see **motorolasolutions.com/en_us/solutions/hospitality.html**.

Example: Leading Hotels

All rooms and public areas are equipped with Wi-Fi. You do not need to stand in line to register. Just go to a room that its number is texted to your smartphone. No keys needed; your smartphone will help you to enter the room. An online guide will tell you about all facilities in the hotels and resorts, as well as information about nearby restaurants and attractions. All are supplemented by maps.

One area in hospitality that benefits from a wireless system is restaurant operations.

Example: Dolphin Fast Food

Dolphin Fast Food Inc. operates 19 Burger King franchises in Minnesota. The company uses a wireless system to streamline operations, control costs, increase staff and customer satisfaction, and comply with regulations. The system includes free Wi-Fi access both in the restaurants and in a corporate management wireless network. The company realized that customers can use their mobile devices while waiting and while dining. Managers use mobile devices to increase effectiveness. The wireless system is also used to improve security on the premises (e.g., video surveillance). The secure Internet access is protected by a VPN, and it can block inappropriate content. The wireless system also operates the payment gateways and the POS terminals. For more recent material, see **dolphinfastfood.com**.

Note: In many full-service restaurants, there are several additional applications such as customers placing orders on handheld devices, where the orders go directly to the kitchen and to the cashiers and mobile devices for advising waiting customers to come in when their tables are ready. A vendor that provides mobile programs for tablets for menus, food ordering, entertainment, and payments is Ziosk.

Tablets and Other Mobile Devices in Restaurants

Several restaurants worldwide are introducing tablets or smartphones as a substitute to paper menus. For example, Au Bon Pain is using iPads in several of their locations. One option is to provide the customers with iPads with a built-in menu. This way they can submit the order directly to the kitchen. Using the tablets, customers can order food by themselves and provide their credit card information. It seems that the use of tablets also facilitates customer relationships since self-ordering expedites the service and reduces errors in ordering.

Fig. 6.5 Genski Sushi's tablet-based system (Photo taken by Deborrah Turban)

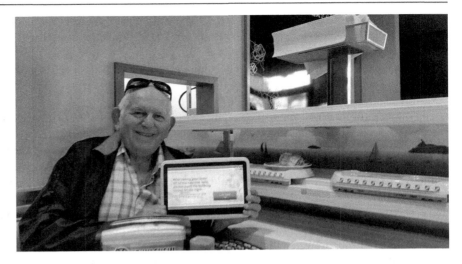

Example: Genki Sushi

This Japan-based company has restaurants in several Asian countries, as well as in California and Hawaii. If you love sushi, you should try Genki Sushi at any of their locations. When you sit at the counter, you are provided with a wireless tablet. Using the tablet, you can find the foods and drinks you would like to order (listed by categories; photos are provided). Once you complete your selection on the tablet, a summary list is returned to you for final approval. Once you approve the list on the tablet, the order is delivered to you on a train-like tray. You pick up the food, push a button to send the tray back to the kitchen, and enjoy the meal (see Fig. 6.5). It is fast, clean, and error-free. Several videos are available at **genkisushiusa.com**. For example, watch the 6:54 min. video titled "Bullet Train Sushi" at **youtube.com/watch?v=PkzBGjjNzPU** or **youtube.com/watch?v=C6ISPgtrqOo**.

Many other mobile apps exist. For example, Taco Bell, Wendy's, Shake Shack, and others let you order from your smartphone, so you can skip the waiting line. You select from the menu, select location and time of arrival, and pay (of course). You get confirmation, go to the restaurant, and get seated immediately. Finally, in some Starbucks, you can order by voice on your smartphone instead of using the store's touchscreen menu.

Note: Such a system may not be available in your town, especially if it is a small one.

Other Industries

Mobile systems and applications can be found in almost all industries. For example, extensive applications can be found in m-government and m-learning (see Chap. 5). The Department of Homeland Security applies many apps and devices, as do the transportation industry and the military. In agriculture, wireless devices can even guide tractors to work at night.

Mobile Marketing: Shopping and Advertising

Mobile marketing refers to all marketing communication activities conducted with wireless devices. Generally speaking, the use of mobile marketing is increasing exponentially. For statistics of the growth, see Strout (2015). For BI mobile marketing statistics, see Sukhraj (2016). This discussion is a preview of the coverage of the topic in Chap. 10.

Mobile Shopping

Online shopping can be easier when done from your smartphone or tablet. For shopping, one needs a mobile shopping platform such as the one provided by ADCentricity Corporation (**omni-channeltechnologies.com**; acquired by Omni-channel Technologies) or by adMobile Corp. (**admobile.com**). Many apps for iPhones facilitate advertising and shopping. For example, you can download the Costco Mobile App for easy coupon redemption (see **costco.com/costco-app.html**). For a list of smartphone applications for businesses, see the iPhone apps. Wishpond Technologies Ltd. (2014) shows how smartphone shoppers use their devices for different shopping-related activities (e.g., checking prices, searching for reviews). Note that about 50% of all customers do mobile research before buying!

A popular app on Facebook is its "stores." There are tens of thousands of stores on Facebook. In 2015, Facebook introduced a shopping section for retail (see **wired.com/2015/10/facebook-testing-shopping-section-app**. For mobile shopping statistics and trends, see Meola (2016).

For examples of mobile advertising and shopping, see CSS Author (2014).

Example: Delta Airlines

Delta offers in-flight Wi-Fi connection on many of its flights (called *Delta Connect*). With Delta Connect, there is free access to many shopping and entertainment sites, including eBay. For a nominal fee, you can purchase a Wi-Fi Mobile Pass and be able to connect to the Internet via your smartphone and send and receive mobile messages, check your e-mail, and browse the Web. For more about Delta Connect and Wi-Fi Mobile Pass, see **delta.com/content/www/en_US/traveling-with-us/onboard-experience/entertainment.html#wifi**. Other airlines offer similar capabilities.

Philippine Airlines provides extensive Wi-Fi services (named iN AiR-mobile services). Users can access the Internet (for a fee). Users can send or receive text messages, make or receive phone calls, send multi-mail messages, and use other mobile services. Users can download the PAL iN AiR Player app for many services. Once you connect to the airplane Wi-Fi hotspot, you can open the app to watch movies, TV shows, etc.

In addition, consumers use mobile devices to locate stores, compare prices, and place orders. For example, Chinese consumers can make purchases from inside WeChat (Millward 2014). China's largest e-tailers, Taobao and Tmall, offered special discounts in 2014, in order to encourage shoppers to buy from their smartphones. Finally, using text messages greatly facilitates recommendations and advice for shoppers, especially in social networks (see Chap. 7). To see how mobile shopping is done, visit Amazon.com, JCPenney, Target, REI, and Crate & Barrel to download their shopping apps.

Example: METRO Group (AG)

METRO Group (AG) is offering an application for high-capacity mobile phones to use in its Future Store in Rheinberg, Germany. According to their site, the Mobile Shopping Assistant (MSA) "is a software package which allows customers to scan items independently, receive current pricing information and a quick overview of the value of their goods." An MSA provides online access to product descriptions and pictures, pricing information, and store maps. It also enables scanning items before they are placed in the cart, calculating the total cost of the items. At checkout, the MSA allows a shopper to "pay in passing" by using the MSA to pass scanned data to a payment terminal. For more about METRO's Future Store Initiative and functionalities of the MSA, see **future-store.org/internet/site/ts_fsi/node/25216/Len/index.html**. METRO has measured the reactions and satisfaction of the Future Store shoppers. The results indicate that customers are more satisfied and visit the store more often than when the store was regular. For the 2016 mobile marketing guide, see **ebooks.localytics.com/2016-app-marketing-guide#new-page**.

Mobile Advertising

Mobile advertising is growing even faster than mobile shopping. This topic is covered in detail in Chap. 10.

SECTION 6.5 REVIEW QUESTIONS

1. Briefly describe the growth patterns of the various segments of mobile entertainment.
2. Discuss the basic components of the mobile music market.
3. What are some of the key barriers to the growth of the mobile games market?
4. Discuss some of the key legal issues impeding the growth of mobile gambling.
5. Describe the use of mobility in sports and in restaurants.
6. Describe some hospitality management mobile applications.
7. Describe mobile shopping and advertising.

6.6   LOCATION-BASED COMMERCE

Location-based commerce (l-commerce), or LBC, refers to the use of location-finding systems such as GPS-enabled devices or similar technologies (e.g., triangulation of radio- or cell-based stations) to find where a customer with a mobile device or an object is located and provide relevant services, such as an advertisement or vehicle route optimization. LBC is also known as LBS (location-based systems). According to TechTarget, LBS is "a software application for a[n] IP-capable mobile device that requires knowledge about where the mobile device is located" (see **searchnetworking.techtarget.com/definition/location-based-service-LBS**). L-commerce involves *context-aware computing technology* (section "Ubiquitous (Pervasive) Computing"). For images, search Google Images for "location-based commerce." L-commerce offers convenient services to consumers such as connections with friends, the ability to receive relevant and timely sales information, safety features (e.g., emergency assistance), and convenience (a user can locate what facility needed is nearby without consulting a directory or a map). Sellers get the opportunity to advertise and provide or meet a customer's needs in real time. In essence, LBC is the delivery of m-commerce transactions to individuals who are in a known specific location, at a specific time. The location-based systems also are referred to location-aware systems. Today (2017), they include mainly smartphones and tablets with location tracking that allows various apps to use the information on the whereabouts of people for social commercial uses.

Basic Concepts in L-Commerce

Location-based m-commerce mainly includes five possible activities, all done in real time:

1. **Location.** Finding where a person (with a smartphone) or another mobile device or a thing (e.g., a truck) is located
2. **Navigation.** Finding and illustrating a route from one location to another (e.g., as is done in Google Maps)
3. **Tracking.** Monitoring the movements and whereabouts of people or objects (e.g., a truck, airplane)
4. **Mapping.** Creating maps of certain geographical locations with superimposed data if needed (e.g., GIS, Google Maps)
5. **Timing.** Determining the arrival or departure time of something at a specific location (e.g., arrival of a bus to a specific bus stop or an airplane to an airport)

For example, WeatherBug (**weather.weatherbug.com**) and Send Word Now (**sendwordnow.com**) have combined some of these five services to ensure the safety of customers, employees, and stores during severe weather and other emergencies.

A recent development of l-commerce is known as **real-time location systems (RTLS)**, which are used to track and identify the location of objects in real time. For an overview, see **searchmobilecomputing.techtarget.com/definition/real-time-location-system-RTLS** and **computerlearningcentre.blogspot.com/2014/04/l-commerce.html**.

L-Commerce Infrastructure

L-commerce is based on an infrastructure. The components depend on the applications. However, the following conditions usually exist:

1. **Location finder (positioning) component.** A GPS (or other device) that finds the location of a person or a thing.
2. **Mobile Positioning Center.** This includes a server that manages the location information received from the location finder.
3. **User.** The user can be a person or thing (e.g., a vehicle).
4. **Mobile devices.** The user needs a mobile device (e.g., a smartphone) that includes a GPS or other feature that locates the location (position) of something or someone.
5. **Mobile communication network.** The network(s) that transfers user requests to the service providers and then transmits the reply to the user.
6. **Service or application providers.** Providers are responsible for servicing a user's request. They may use applications such as GIS.

(continued)

7. **Data or content provider.** Service providers usually need to acquire (e.g., geographic, financial, or other data) in order to provide a reply to requests. Data may include maps, coupons, and GIS information.
8. **Geographical information system (GIS).** This includes maps, location of businesses, and more.
9. **Opt-in application.** In the United States and some other countries, LBS can be used only with people's permission (opt-in). This requires an additional software app.

These components work together as illustrated in Fig. 6.6.
For additional components, see **www.gps.gov/technical/icwg**.
Here is how the LBS works (see Fig. 6.6):

1. The user expresses his or her wish by clicking on a function (e.g., "find me the nearest gas station").
2. The mobile network service finds where the user is located using satellite and GPS.
3. The request is transferred via a wireless network to the application service provider software that activates a search for the needed data.
4. The server goes to a database, to find, for example, the nearest requested business and check if it is open, what it serves, and so forth.
5. Using a GIS, the service delivers the reply to the user, including a map and driving directions if necessary.

A similar system can be used for vehicle or asset location. A GPS is then attached to the object.

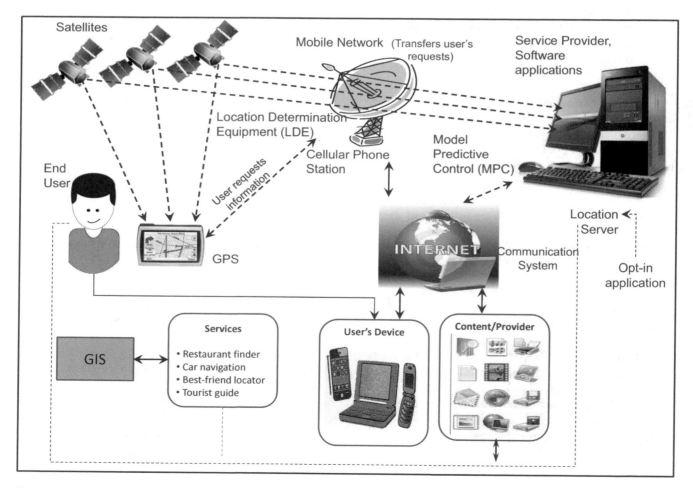

Fig. 6.6 Location-based commerce system

Geolocation

LBS is related to the concept of *geolocation*. **Geolocation** refers to the ability to find the location of a user who is connected to the Web via a mobile device. Geolocation works with all Web browsers.

L-commerce is distinguished from general m-commerce by the *positioning component*, the compulsory opt-in, and the mash-up with GIS or other data sources.

The GPS: Positioning Component

The major device in l-commerce is a global positioning system (GPS). Here is how it works:

According to GPS.gov (2017), "the **Global positioning system (GPS)** is a U.S.-owned utility, satellite-based, that provides users with positioning, navigation, and timing (PNT) services. This system consists of three segments: the *space segment*, the *control segment*, and the *user segment*."

Space Segment
The space segment consists of 24 satellites that transmit signals. The signals designate the satellites' positions at any given time (using an atomic clock). Each satellite orbits the earth once every 12 h at an altitude of 10,900 miles.

Control Segment
The control segment includes a global monitoring system and control station to monitor the satellites.

User Segment
The user's equipment, which is the GPS receiver, receives information from the satellites and calculates the user's position at the given time.

The US government describes these segments as follows:

In recent years, GPS locators have become a part of the consumer electronics market. They are available in many smartphones and today are used widely for business and recreation.

Note: GPS dating applications let you sort through lists of people you may want to date based on their location at any given time (see applications such as Skout (**skout.com**; "the global network for meeting new people")).

Location-Based Data

Location-based services and l-commerce are based on a series of location-based questions or queries.

Using Data Collections
GPS-enabled smartphones and other mobile devices help in collecting large amounts of data, which can be used in decision-making to save millions of dollars.

Locating Customers in Physical Stores

When shoppers equipped with smartphones are in physical stores, it is possible to track their movements in specific stores and malls. The information collected may give retailers ideas about the customers' shopping habits. The companies that collect the information say that it is anonymous. The tracking is done via the smartphone's MAC address (the smartphone's unique identifier code). Any smartphone that is connected to Wi-Fi sends signals with the MAC address, which a store can capture. Smartphone users can opt-out of the use of their MAC address by going to the Smart Store Privacy website at **smartstoreprivacy.org**. For a discussion, see Kerr (2014). For more information on what happens to the information collected on your smartphone and disabling "geotagging" (locating geographical information), see **fouche.net/what-happens-to-the-gps-location-information-collected-on-your-smartphone.html**.

Geographical Information Systems

Some data, information, and processes that are needed to answer location-based queries are usually handled by a *geographical information system (GIS)*. A **geographical information system (GIS)** is a computer-based system whose function is to capture, store, analyze, and display geographically related data. For example, suppose a person is using his or her mobile device to ask an online directory service to provide a list of Italian restaurants that are close by. In order to service this query, the directory service would need access to a GIS containing information about local restaurants by geographical coordinates and type. For more on GIS, see **en.wikipedia.org/wiki/Geographic_information_system, and esri.com/what-is-gis/howgisworks**.

Geographical information systems are frequently combined with GPS, as shown next.

Example: Hailing Taxis from a Smartphone

Hailing taxis from smartphones is spreading slowly around the globe. ZabKab (now "ZabCab") (**zabcab.com**; "connecting taxicabs and passengers") provides an app by which a user with a GPS-enabled smartphone can push a button and GPS technology identifies their location. An icon with a map appears on the mobile devices of participating taxi drivers, letting the driver know the location of the passenger who needs to be picked up. Currently (2017), ZabCab is only available in certain cities in New York, Burlington, Vermont, and South Florida. The HAIL A CAB™ app (**hailacabapp.com**), a product of Yellow Cab, offers the taxi-hailing service in several cities in Texas (Austin, Houston, San Antonio, and Galveston), with more locations forthcoming. The Alibaba Group also offers a cab-hailing app in Beijing (see **online.wsj.com/news/articles/SB10001424052702303287804579442993327079748**.

Note: Taxi company Comfort Transportation, located in Singapore, offers a taxi-booking system in which the booking is done by SMS (see **cdgtaxi.com.sg/commuters_services_booking.mvn**). They also offer taxi-booking apps and online taxi booking. It is not location-based, but it solves the problem of busy telephone lines. Finally, GetTaxi (operating in New York as "Gett"; **gett.com**), available in New York and other major cities worldwide (e.g., Moscow, London, Tel Aviv), offers a free app that allows you to order taxis directly from your smartphone.

Location-Based Services and Applications

A *location-based service (LBS)* is a mobile device-based computerized service, which utilizes information about the geographical position of a user's mobile device (e.g., mobile phone tracking) for delivering a service (e.g., advertisers can target ads to specific location), to the user.

There are a large number of LBS applications. For a list of location-based services (applications), see **geoawesomeness.com/knowledge-base/location-based-services/location-based-services-applications**.

Location-based services can be used in marketing, operations, services, finance, and so forth. LBS technologies determine the location of a person (or an object) and act upon this information. LBS also works in asset tracking (e.g., of parcels at USPS or FedEx) and in vehicle tracking (see the "Tracking" section at **geoawesomeness.com/knowledge-base/location-based-services/location-based-services-applications**). LBS also includes location-based games.

Other examples of location-based services are:

- Recommending public events in a city to tourists and residents
- Asset recovery, for example, finding stolen cars
- Pointing a user to the nearest business (e.g., a gas station) to his (her) location
- Providing detailed navigation from any place to any address (sometimes with voice prompts)
- Locating things (such as trucks) and displaying them on the mobile device map
- Inventory tracking in warehouses
- Delivering alerts, such as notification of a real-time sale in a specific store

RFID technologies wirelessly track objects in warehouses (see Tutorial T2 and Chap. 13).

Four Labs, Inc. and Swarm

A pioneering LBC company is Foursquare. Today it is a local search-and-discovery mobile service app. The app provides personal recommendations. It provides a city guide and is a competitor of Yelp. The original LBC capabilities of Foursquare are available in its subsidiary—Swarm.

Personnel Tracking
Different technologies are used by managers and employees for tracking personnel on the company premises and while they are off premises.

Social Location-Based Marketing

Social location-based marketing occurs when users share their location with vendors in real time (opt-in), usually within social media environments. The vendors then deliver targeted ads, coupons, or rebates to the users. In addition, the vendors may conduct market research about the user's preferences and collect feedback about product quality. For more information, watch the video titled "The Future of M-Commerce - Did You Know?" (4:30 min) at **youtube.com/watch?v=F58q6yUAsHE**.

Location-Based Applications 2016

Toms Guide **tomsguide.com/us/best-location-aware-apps,review-2405.html** provides the following list of the ten best location-based applications (per Corpuz 2016). Most applications are free.

Foursquare and Swarm
Foursquare is the pioneer of check-in location. (It is now two parts.) It helps the discovery of restaurants, events, etc., that are located near a user, in real time (based on users' preferences). In addition, you can meet with your friends when the system lets them know where you are.

GasBuddy
This mobile app helps users track down the cheapest gas stations which are near their present location. Prices are reported by users who receive points for reporting and updating prices. The points make users eligible to participate in regular raffles of prizes.

Waze
Similar to GasBuddy, Waze is based on user reporting. However, the contributions are more organized, so Waze may be considered a social network. In addition, the company is using the concept of *crowdsourcing* (Chap. 9). Waze lets drivers report traffic conditions and incidents, sharing them in real time on dynamically changing maps. Waze also provides optimal routings. The suggestions are based on users' reporting and data collected from other sources (including the cheapest fuel near users' locations). Waze, which is owned by Google, is an intelligent app that can learn users' commuting behaviors and preferred routes. Therefore, the app can make more personal recommendations. You can see which friends are driving to your destination and use Facebook to coordinate all arrival times.

Waze's community is the world's largest traffic and navigation social network. It originated in Israel and now is operational in dozens of countries. Waze works with all mobile devices that have Internet access and GPS support.

In some countries when you get Waze's maps and routing, you see paid advertisers' icons. This is why Google was willing to invest $1.3 billion for the company.

A final note: If you use Waze, you run the risk of being stalked by hackers (see Hill 2016).

Glympse
Glympse is a mobile app that allows you to share your location in real time with others. You can see those people who use Glympse, but who are not on time where they need to be (e.g., to meet you). The app is based on GPS. It can run on any Internet-enabled device. The app is fast and free. Your location is presented on a digital map.

Dark Sky
It is a local weather app that provides an accurate local forecast in real time. The predictions are based on radar mapping. It also can connect users to long-term forecasting (24 h and week ahead). The radar maps are similar to what you see on TV. Of course, the system needs to know your location.

Happn
This app allows you to share location data. This enables people to meet (e.g., for dating a new partner or meeting a potential employer). For example, let us say that you are jogging in the park, when you cross paths with another jogger, who is a Happn user, you can view her (his) profile. Then, you can communicate and possibly set something up.

Trigger

This app can automatically trigger a variety of phone actions based on NFC tags, Wi-Fi network connections, and Bluetooth. Users can set geofences.

Barriers to Location-Based M-Commerce

The following are some factors that are slowing down the widespread use of location-based m-commerce:

- **Lack of GPS in some mobile phones.** Without GPS, it is difficult to use LBS. However, GPS-enabled phones are increasing in availability. In addition, the use of cell phone towers helps.
- **Accuracy of devices.** Some of the location-finding tools are not too accurate. A good, but expensive, GPS provides accuracy of 10 ft. Less accurate locators provide accuracy of about 1500 ft.
- **The cost–benefit justification.** The benefits of location-based services may not justify the cost. For customers, it may be inconvenient to utilize the service. As you may recall from Chap. 1, Starbucks discontinued their LBS.
- **Limited network bandwidth.** Wireless bandwidth is still limited. As bandwidth improves with 4G and 5G, applications will expand, which will increase the use of the technology.
- **Invasion of privacy.** Many people are reluctant to disclose their whereabouts and have their movements tracked (see Chap. 15 for a discussion).

The Viability of LBC

During 2009–2013, the concept of LBC gained momentum due to Foursquare and its competitors. The major problem was lack of profitability. The objective of using LBC for advertising and marketing was not attainable. However, since 2016, there is a revival of the concepts due to advances in mobile apps. Companies such as Waze attract millions of visitors. Will LBC become profitable? We will have to wait for an answer (see Chap. 10 for marketing/advertising applications).

SECTION 6.6 REVIEW QUESTIONS

1. Describe the key elements of the l-commerce infrastructure.
2. What is GPS? How does it work?
3. What are some of the basic questions addressed by location-based services?
4. Define geographical information systems. How do they relate to LBS?
5. List the services enabled by LBS.
6. Describe social location-based marketing.
7. List some applications of LBC.
8. List the major barriers to LBC.

6.7   UBIQUITOUS (PERVASIVE) COMPUTING

Many experts believe that the next major step in the evolution of computing will be *ubiquitous computing (ubicom)*. In a ubiquitous computing environment, almost every object in the system has a processing power (i.e., microprocessor) and a wireless or wireline connection to a network (usually the Internet or intranets). This way, the objects can both communicate and process information. This section provides an overview of ubiquitous computing and briefly examines a number of related applications. (Note: The words *ubiquitous* and *pervasive* mean "existing everywhere.")

Overview of Ubiquitous Computing

Ubiquitous computing is a comprehensive field that includes many topics (e.g., see **en.wikipedia.org/wiki/Ubiquitous_computing**). Here we present only the essentials that are related to EC.

Definitions and Basic Concepts

Ubiquitous computing (ubicom) has computing capabilities embedded into a relevant system, usually not visible, which may be mobile or stationary. It is a form of human–computer interaction. In contrast, mobile computing is usually represented by visible devices (e.g., smartphones) possessed by users. Ubiquitous computing is also called *embedded computing*, *augmented computing*, or *pervasive computing*. The distinction revolves around the notion of mobility. **Pervasive computing** is embedded in the environment but typically is not mobile. In contrast, ubiquitous computing possesses a high degree of mobility. Therefore, for example, most smart appliances in a smart home represent wired, *pervasive computing*, while mobile objects with embedded computing, such as in clothes, cars, and personal communication systems, represent *ubiquitous computing*. In this chapter, however, we treat pervasive and ubiquitous as equivalent terms, and we use them interchangeably.

The Internet of Things (IoT)

Ubiquitous computing is the basis for IoT. When the connections in a network are done via the Internet (e.g., using Cloud computing), the network is referred to as the Internet of things (IoT).

For more on the IoT (e.g., definition, history), see **internetofthingsagenda.techtarget.com/definition/Internet-of-Things-IoT**.

The IoT will include many everyday things, ranging from smart cars to smart homes, clothes, cities, and many others, all being networked.

The IoT applications are related to intelligent systems and are described in Chap. 7.

The field of pervasive computing has been developed rapidly since it provides the theoretical background for the IoT, wearable computing, and sensors. Google, Amazon, Facebook, and Apple are active in this area (see Ungureanu 2016).

Context-Aware Computing

Context-aware computing is a technology that is capable of predicting people's needs and providing fulfillment options (sometimes even before a request by the end user is made). The system is fed with data about the person, such as location and preferences. Regardless of the types of the end user, the system can sense the nature of personalized data needed for different environments. In its 2014 predictions, cited earlier, Gartner, Inc. cited context awareness as one of the top ten futuristic technologies; see **gartner.com/technology/research/top-10-technology-trends**.

In general, the technology is expected to increase productivity and result in many new applications. Carnegie Mellon University is a leader in the research of business applications in this technology.

From Theory to Practice

Here we describe one topic: Smart Grids. In Chap. 7, we describe more applications.

Smart Meters and Grids

An example of a simple application of pervasive computing is the use of smart meters for measuring electricity use. With smart meters, there is no need to go from house to house to read the meters. In addition, electricity consumption can be optimized.

According to the US Department of Energy, a **smart grid** (**smartgrid.gov**) is an electricity network managed by utilizing digital technology. Like the Internet, the smart grid consists of controls, computers, automation, and new technologies and equipment working together, but, in this case, these technologies work with the electrical grid to improve usage by responding to the quickly changing electric demand.

The benefits associated with the smart grid include:

- More efficient transmission of electricity
- Quicker restoration of electricity after power disturbances
- Reduced operations and management costs for utilities and ultimately lower-power costs for consumers
- Reduced peak demand, which will also help lower electric rates
- Increased integration of large-scale renewable energy systems
- Better integration of customer–owner power generation systems, including improved security of renewable energy systems
- Goal of zero carbon emissions

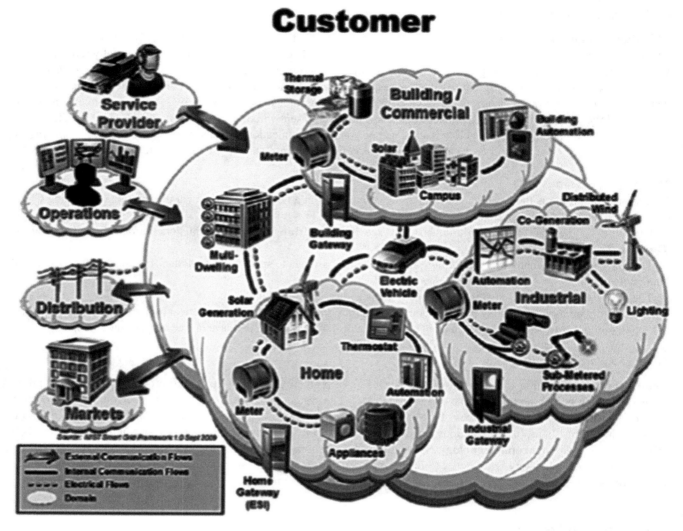

Fig. 6.7 Smart grid environment (Source: National Institute of Standards and Technology, US Department of Commerce, *nist.gov/smartgrid/ upload/FinalSGDoc2010019-corr010411-2.pdf* accessed January 2017)

The US Department of Energy (DOE) Office of Electricity Delivery and Energy Reliability provides substantial information about the smart grid (see **energy.gov/oe/technology-development/smart-grid**). According to the DOE, the smart grid devices have sensors to gather data and two-way digital communication between the device in the field and the utility's network operations center. The essentials of the grid are shown in Fig. 6.7 and in the "Smart Grid Basics" infographic at **edf. org/energy/infographic-smart-grid-basics**.

For more information, see **en.wikipedia.org/wiki/Smart_grid**. Smart grids enable the use of smart homes and appliances. For more, see **edf.org/climate/smart-grid-brings-us-power-21st-century** and **smartgrid.gov**.

Implementation Issues in Ubiquitous Computing

For ubiquitous systems to be widely deployed, it is necessary to overcome many of the technical, ethical, and legal barriers associated with mobile computing (section "Implementation Issues in Mobile Commerce: From Security and Privacy to Barriers to M-Commerce"), as well as a few barriers unique to ubiquitous, invisible computing.

Among the nontechnical issues, the possible loss of individual privacy seems to be at the forefront. There is a concern about "Big Brother" watching. In some cases, privacy groups have expressed a concern that the tags and sensors embedded in items, especially retail items, make it possible to track the owners or buyers of those items. A larger problem is that the information processed by tags, sensors, and other devices may be misused or mishandled.

SECTION 6.7 REVIEW QUESTIONS

1. Define ubiquitous computing.
2. What is the Internet of things (IoT)?
3. Describe the smart grid and the role of sensors there.
4. In what ways can pervasive computing impinge on an individual's right to privacy?

6.8   WEARABLE COMPUTING AND SMART GADGETS: WATCHES, FITNESS TRACKERS, AND SMART GLASSES

In this section, we will briefly describe several emerging topics related to wireless computing.

Wearable Computing Applications and Devices

Wearable computing applications and devices have received a major boost since 2015 due to the expansion of the Internet of things. For a comprehensive slide presentation, see Chamberlin (2014). Wearable computing devices have been used in industry since the mid-1990s. Typical devices were wireless computers tied to people's wrists, digital cameras mounted on the head, mobile devices attached to a belt, and much more. These became popular in the consumer market when Samsung came out with a computer mounted on a watch (smartwatch), and Apple released its Apple Watch in April 2015. Wearable devices are an important part of the annual CES and computer electronics show in Las Vegas. For a list of wearables and other mobile accessories presented in the 2017 CES, see Diaz (2017). Google has released a Nexus-like platform for wearables, called Android Wear.

Wearables are getting popular. For example, medical tracking of patients with chronic diseases is on the increase, and, for $130, you can place a device on your dog's collar to track its movements.

Vijayan (2014) stated, "Wearable computers, like fitness bands, digital glasses, medical devices, and smartphones promise to radically transform the manner in which information is collected, delivered, and used by, and about, people. Many of the emerging technologies promise significant, and potentially revolutionary, user benefits. But as with most Internet-connected devices, the growing proliferation of wearables has spawned both privacy and security concerns." Vijayan presents seven devices and their hidden dangers. These devices are digital glasses (e.g., eyewear like Google Glass), wearable/embedded medical devices, police cameras (wearable "cop cams"), smartwatches, smart clothing, and fitness bands/activity monitors. We describe some later in this section.

Dale (2014) describes a wearable headband that can read the brain's activity. The Canadian company Interaxon developed the device, called Muse (see **interaxon.ca/muse**). In 2014, Amazon opened a special store for wearable devices. For more on wearable technology, see Hunter (2015).

Sensors

Sensors are devices that collect information from the environment. The device can be a camera, a motion detector, a thermometer, or any of other hundreds of devices. Sensors can be a part of the wearables, or they can be stationary. They are an integral part of many mobile devices (e.g., in facial recognition) and the host of IoT applications. We cannot have self-driven cars or smart homes without sensors. For the use of sensors in mobile devices, see **mobiledevicesensors.com/sensor-applications/**. There, you will find categories of devices and their applications. For a handbook of modern sensors, see Fraden (2016). Wireless sensors and their networks are gaining attention and are used extensively in IoT (watch the 13:20 min video at **libelium.com/video-wsn-introduction**. For 50 sensor applications, see **libelium.com/resources/top_50_iot_sensor_applications_ranking**. Many of these relate to wearables.

Enterprise Wearables

Wearables are used extensively in consumer products. However, many companies are using wearables for enterprise applications. There are a large number of wearables, which already have been used for a long time in enterprises. For a report on products, manufacturers case studies and applications, see the 2016 white paper titled: "Enterprise Wearable Technology Case Studies/Tractica." It includes 40 different applications. See **tractica.com/resources/white-papers/enterprise-wearable-technology-case-studies/**.

According to the PWC report (**pwc.com/us/en/advisory/business-digital-technology-trends-wearables.html**), "Wearables hold so much promise because they provide a hands-free way for employees to engage in real-time with context-specific business information, customers, or one another. For example, companies across industries can provide tailored, in-the-moment and job training to workers equipped with smart badges or wearable displays. In industrial settings, goggles, lanyards, or sensor-embedded clothing could help workers who are performing repetitive or dangerous tasks increase productivity and reduce injuries."

Note: Wearable devices are subject to serious privacy and security problems. For a discussion, see Maddox (2015).

State of the Art

Japan is one of the leaders in developing wearable devices. For example, Patrizio (2014) reports the following: "A Japanese university has shown off a tiny personal computer that is worn on the ear and isn't much larger than many Bluetooth headsets, but it can be controlled with the blink of an eye or the click of a tongue."

For the state of the art in 2016, see McDowell (2016). For a slideshow of wearable devices and their applications, see Khillare and Bobade (2015).

Three representative devices, smartwatches, fitness trackers, and smart glasses, are presented next.

Smartwatches

A **smartwatch** is a computerized wristwatch with a functionality that is enhanced beyond timekeeping. Today, smartwatches are wearable computers. Many run mobile apps, using a mobile operating system.

They can function as portable media players; others also feature full smartphone capabilities.

Like other computers, a smartwatch may collect information from internal or external sensors. It may control or retrieve data from other instruments or computers. It may support wireless technologies like Bluetooth, Wi-Fi, GPS, and communication technologies.

For specific features, see the websites of smartwatches' manufacturers, such as Apple, Google, Pebble, Sony, Samsung, and several more. For a 2016 review, see Lamkin (2016a). For an overview, see **en.wikipedia.org/wiki/Smartwatch**. For the capability to shop, see Arthur (2015). A special category of smartwatches is fitness (or activity) trackers. Some watches can be used as medical devices (e.g., Apple's Kardia; see Broussard 2016). Large numbers of companies make smartwatches. Examples are Apple, Google, Samsung, Fossil, Casio, ZTE, and more. Nixon and Qualcomm make sports watches. Smartwatches are combined frequently with fitness and tracker gadgets.

Fitness (Activity) Trackers

An activity tracker is a device or application for monitoring and tracking health and fitness-related metrics such as distance walked or run, calorie consumption, heartbeats and even the quality of sleep. Today, many of these devices are wearable, which may be connected to a computer. For an overview, see **en.wikipedia.org/wiki/Activity_tracker**. For the 2016 major manufacturers (e.g., Fitbit, Jawbone, Misfit, and Garmin), see Stables (2016).

Note that some trackers and regular smartwatches look very fashionable (e.g., Fitbit Blaze). These are becoming more stylish with time. For the best fitness trackers of 2016, see **pcmag.com/article2/0,2817,2404445,00.asp**. For how fitness trackers work, see Nield (2016). Fitness- and health-related gadgets can be on watches, headphones, shoes, and other wearables. For current apps, see Fuller (2017).

Digital (Smart) Glasses

A digital glass is an optical, head-mounted device that looks like regular eyeglasses. It was pioneered by Google (see **en. wikipedia.org/wiki/Google_Glass**). The device displays Internet information and it responds to voice commands. Smart glasses are closely related to virtual reality and augmented reality (see Chap. 2). The most well-known glasses are Google Glass. For the best smart glasses of 2016, see Lamkin (2016b).

In 2012, Google introduced its *Project Glass*, which takes the major functionalities of a smartphone and embeds them into a wearable device that looks like virtual reality glasses. Google Glass has a smartphone-like display, allowing you to take basic smartphone features (messaging, e-mail) and making them hands-free. For more on the features of Google Glass, see **newatlas.com/google-glass-review/30300**. The Google Glass Field Trip app can now be activated by voice commands (**mashable.com/2014/04/29/field-trip-google-glass-update**).

Google Glasses

According to Petroff (2013), Google Glass (and other "smart glasses") may save companies $1 billion a year by 2017 due to an increased productivity of employees, especially those who need to use both hands to perform complex tasks (e.g., by surgeons, technicians). In addition, the devices can be used, for example, by insurance agents to video damaged property while simultaneously checking on the costs of replacements. Several of the benefits of smart glasses are the same as those of other wearable devices.

Other companies in the United States, Japan, and Korea have smart glasses (e.g., Sony). Note that Google Glass is getting more stylish by adopting the look of Ray-Ban and Oakley eyeglasses' top brands.

Some people love smart glasses; others hate them. A 2014 poll, conducted by the research firm Toluna, found that 72% of Americans did not want to wear Google Glass due to privacy and security issues (see **mashable.com/2014/04/07/google-glass-privacy**). Google is trying to counter what they call "the top 10 myths" about Google Glass.

Augmented Reality Glasses

Augmented reality is the basis for several wearables. Two types of glasses are on the market. HoloLens from Microsoft can help you to find your lost items in the house or workplace (e.g., your keys). Using a special camera, the device can make a special map of a room. Machine vision technology can then identify or track objects. For details, see Robertson (2016). Aira is a smart glasses-based service that helps people with visual impairment to navigate in the world. A camera that the blind person wears sends the relevant photos in front of the user to a live agent who can then navigate them. For details, see Bosniak (2017).

SECTION 6.8 REVIEW QUESTIONS

1. Describe wearable computing devices.
2. What are the benefits of wearable devices?
3. Describe sensors.
4. What are smart glasses? Why do some people have issues with them?
5. Describe smartwatches.
6. Define fitness trackers.
7. How can smart glasses help the blind?

6.9   IMPLEMENTATION ISSUES IN MOBILE COMMERCE: FROM SECURITY AND PRIVACY TO BARRIERS TO M-COMMERCE

Several issues need to be considered before applying mobile applications. Here, we discuss only a few of them.

Despite the vast potential benefits for mobile commerce, it is not easy to change the way many companies do business. Several barriers are slowing down the deployment of m-commerce applications. The major barriers to m-commerce are security, performance, availability, cost-benefit, lack of clear strategy, difficulty in integrating with wireline IT, and difficulty in customizing applications. In this section, we examine only some of these barriers, starting with the issue of security. For more on implementation issues, see the three-part video series on mobile commerce. Part 1 is titled "Mobile Commerce: Part 1: Where Are We Now?" (8:03 min), available at **youtube.com/watch?v=aO--a5yhJCg**. Part 2 is titled "Mobile Commerce: Part 2, The Evolution" (8:51 min), available at **youtube.com/watch?v=fBlLxVeCouo**. Part 3 is titled "Mobile Commerce: Part 3, How to Make mCommerce Work" (8:23 min), available at **youtube.com/watch?v=DsDGNLjYPxQ**.

M-Commerce Security and Privacy Issues

In 2004, Cabir became the first known wireless worm that infects mobile phones. It spreads through Bluetooth devices. Since then, attacks on phones, including smartphones, have increased rapidly. For more on the Cabir worm, see **f-secure.com/v-descs/cabir.shtml**.

Most Internet-enabled cell phones in operation today have basic software embedded in the hardware. This makes attackers' programming malware difficult. However, as the capabilities of smartphones and tablets improve, the threat of malware attacks increases. The same applies to mobile apps and IoT applications. The widespread use of smartphones opens up the possibility of viruses coming from Internet downloads. Although m-commerce shares some of the same security issues as general e-commerce (see Chap. 11), there are some differences between the two.

The basic security goals of confidentiality, authentication, authorization, and integrity (Chap. 11) are just as important for m-commerce as they are for e-commerce, but they are more difficult to ensure. Specifically, m-commerce transactions usually pass through several networks, both wireless and wired. An appropriate level of security must be maintained on each network, despite the fact that interoperability among the various networks is difficult.

In general, many of the defense mechanisms used in IT and e-commerce security are also used in m-commerce. However, given the unique nature of mobile security, additional defense methods may be needed. For example, there are many antitheft apps that can help you find your phone and keep your personal data safe from identity theft.

Privacy

Invasion of privacy is one of the major issues related to the use of mobile computing technologies, especially LBS, tracking, RFID, and context-aware applications (see Chap. 15 for a discussion of privacy issues).

Related to this is the issue of combating fraud; see presentation in Chap. 11.

Technological Barriers to M-Commerce

The navigation systems for mobile applications have to be fast in order to enable rapid and easy search and shopping. Similarly, the information content needs to meet the user's needs. Other technical barriers related to mobile computing technology include limited battery life and transmission interference with home appliances. These barriers and others are listed in Table 6.1. Note that, with the passage of time, the technological barriers are decreasing.

Failures in Mobile Computing and M-Commerce

As with many new technologies, there have been many failures of m-commerce initiatives as there are entire m-commerce companies that collapse. It is important to anticipate and plan for possible failures and to learn from those failures.

Table 6.1 Technical limitations of mobile computing

Limitation	Description
Insufficient bandwidth	Sufficient bandwidth is necessary for widespread mobile computing, and it must be inexpensive. It will take a few years until 4G and LTE are the norm in many places. Wi-Fi solves some of the problems for short-range connections
Security standards	Universal standards are still under development. It may take a few more years for sufficient standards to be in place
Power consumption	The longer the life of a battery, the better the devices are (constantly improving)
Transmission interferences	Weather and terrain, including tall buildings, can limit reception. Microwave ovens, cordless phones, and other devices are free but crowded. A range of 2.4 GHz may interfere with Bluetooth and Wi-Fi 802.11b transmissions
GPS accuracy	Tall buildings may limit the use of location-based m-commerce
Potential health hazards	Potential health damages (e.g., cancer) from cellular radio-frequency emission are under investigation. Known health hazards include cell phone addiction, thumb-overuse syndrome, and accidents caused by people using cell phones (e.g., texting) while driving
Human–computer interface	Some people, especially the elderly or those with vision problems, may have difficulty using a small monitor and keypad on cell phones
Complexity	Many add-ons and features may make the device difficult to use

Ethical, Legal, Privacy, and Health Issues in M-Commerce

The increasing use of mobile devices in business and society raises new ethical, legal, and health issues that individuals, organizations, and society will have to resolve.

One workplace issue is the isolation that mobile devices can impose on a workforce. Some workers have had difficulty adjusting to the m-commerce environment since there is less need for face-to-face interactions that some people prefer.

The personal nature of mobile devices also raises ethical and legal issues. Most employees have desktop computers both at home and at work, and they can easily separate business and personal work accordingly. However, it is not so easy to separate work and personal life on a cell phone, unless one carries two phones. The concept of "bring your own device" (BYOD) is spreading rapidly, introducing issues of management, monitoring, and security. For example, if an organization has the right to monitor e-mail communications on its own network, does it also have the right to monitor voice communications on a company-owned or on a BYOD smartphone? For an overview, see Diogenes et al. (2015).

A widely publicized but unproven potential risk is the potential health problems (e.g., cancer) from cellular radio-frequency emissions. Cell phone addiction also is a problem.

Other ethical, legal, and health issues include the ethics of monitoring staff's movements. Finally, there is the issue of privacy infringement and protection while implementing some m-commerce applications. For a comprehensive guide to improving security in a BYOD in the enterprise, see Caspi (2016).

Enterprise Mobility Management

According to TechTarget, *enterprise mobility management* (EMM) is "an all-encompassing approach to securing and enabling business workers' use of smartphones and tablets." It includes data and access security, physical device tracking and configuration, and application management (see **i.zdnet.com/whitepapers/SAP_Enterprise_Mobility_for_Dummies_Guide.pdf**). Since more workers are bringing smartphones and tablets and using them in the enterprise, it is necessary to support these devices. This is where enterprise mobility management enters the picture. With an increasing number of people using mobile devices for many applications, mobility management has become a significant and challenging task.

Mobility management can be divided into the following areas:

- **Mobile device management (MDM).** Some companies allow their IT department to have full control over all mobile devices. Others allow users to maintain their devices mostly on their own (see a discussion on BYOD later in this section). Special software can help companies with their MDM. For the 2017 issues in MDM, see Matteson (2017).
- **Mobile application management (MAM).** Similar to MDM, MAM attempts to control all applications in a company.
- **Mobile information management (MIM).** This is a newer area that deals with cloud computing.

Related to these are two specific areas: Bring your own device ("BYOD") and mobile apps. These are briefly described next.

The BYOD Issue

The proliferation of mobile devices in the enterprise raises the issue of "bring your own device" (BYOD). Many employees like to use their personal devices for work-related activities (e.g., their iPhones for corporate mail, travel reservations, etc.). They bring their devices to their workplace and use those devices to access the company's network. BYOD may save the company money. On the other hand, there are many implementation issues ranging from security to reimbursement policy to technical support.

There are many suggestions regarding the management and control of BYOD. Major consulting companies such as Gartner, Inc. (**gartner.com**) and Forrester Research, Inc. (**forrester.com**) provide free white papers, webinars, and reports on BYOD. For more BYOD for wearables and IoT, see **techproresearch.com/downloads/research-byod-wearables-and-iot**.

Build (or Bring) Your Own App (BYOA)

BYOA is an increasing trend toward the creation of applications by users rather than by software developers. Unfortunately, BYOA creates security challenges. For a practical guide to affordable mobile app development, see Salz and Moranz (2013).

Everything "On-Demand" via Mobile Apps

There are hundreds of thousands of apps to get things on demand. We can get food delivery, make reservations, make payments, and much more. This is becoming a culture. Soon, this phenomenon may make PCs and other devices obsolete. The issue of how to secure and manage these apps, some of which are developed by users, will be even more important in the future.

Other Managerial Issues

Several other issues are related to mobility management. Examples are the issues of ROI measurement, determining the mobility platform, training, budget and cost control, and justification. Other issues are integration, collaboration, and communication. An interesting issue is the increased flow of data traffic and how to handle it (see Knight 2015). For a comprehensive coverage of mobile technology trends for 2017 and some managerial implications, all presented in an infographic, see Gazdecki (2017).

Conclusion

Despite the many obstacles, mobile commerce is growing rapidly, faster than EC in general. Wearables and IoT are growing the fastest.

SECTION 6.9 REVIEW QUESTIONS

1. How is m-commerce security similar to e-commerce security? How is it different?
2. Discuss a few of the technical limitations of m-commerce.
3. Describe the potential impact of mobile devices on organizational, health, and privacy issues.
4. Describe mobility management.
5. Define BYOD and its challenges.
6. Describe mobile apps. Why are they so popular?

MANAGERIAL ISSUES

Some managerial issues related to this chapter are as follows:

1. **What is your m-commerce strategy?** M-commerce is composed of these elements: support for internal business processes; an extension of existing e-business customer services, availability of suppliers, and other business partners; and an extension of Web-based services to smartphone and tablet users. The key to success in the m-commerce world is to define your overall e-commerce and m-commerce business strategy and determine which segments are critical to the strategy and the order in which they need to be addressed and which of the available mobile technologies will support the strategy and the critical segments.
2. **Are there any clear technical winners?** Among mobile devices, the answer is yes. Many like the all-in-one devices, such as smartphones or tablets. There still is a confusing multiplicity of standards, devices, and supporting hardware. The key is to select a suitable platform and infrastructure that can support the existing needs of most users. While m-commerce is becoming very popular in marketing, payments, manufacturing, and services, l-commerce applications are still in their infancy.
3. **How should BYOD be managed?** Device management becomes a complex issue since employees started to bring and use their mobile devices at work. Mobile devices are made by different manufacturers and use different operating systems. Add to this the thousands of apps and you need a good system and policies to manage BYOD. For a comprehensive strategy for managing BYOD, see **cisco.com/c/en/us/solutions/byod-smart-solution/overview.html** and Reisinger (2013).
4. **Which applications should be implemented first?** Although there is little interest associated in various m-commerce applications, especially location-based services, mobile applications must be judged like any other business technology—by ROI, cost-benefit analysis, potential cost reductions, and improved efficiency. Enterprise applications such as supporting the mobile workforce, fleets, and warehouses have resulted in the highest returns. Implementers need to remember that the m-commerce platform is the platform most preferred by younger generations. It is also important to

understand why Japan and Korea have a much higher penetration rate in m-commerce, while other countries with the same level of mobile telecommunication infrastructure do not have a similar level of penetration. Implementation includes the topic of mobile device management (see Oliver 2008).

SUMMARY

In this chapter, you learned about the following EC issues as they relate to the chapter's learning objectives.

1. **What is m-commerce, its value-added attributes, and fundamental drivers?** M-commerce is any e-commerce activity conducted with mobile devices over a wireless telecommunications network. M-commerce complements e-commerce. M-commerce can help a business improve its value proposition to customers by utilizing its unique attributes: ubiquity, convenience, interactivity, personalization, and localization. Currently, m-commerce is driven by the large number of users of mobile devices, a developing "smartphone culture" among youth, demands from service-oriented customers, vendor marketing, declining prices, an increase in size of the mobile workforce, improved ratio of performance to price, and the increasing bandwidth.

2. **What is the mobile computing environment that supports m-commerce?** The mobile computing environment consists of three key elements: mobile devices, wireless networks, and services. Although mobile computing devices vary in size and functionality, they are rapidly moving toward an all-in-one device that is overcoming some of the limitations associated with poor usability, such as small screen size, limited bandwidth, and restricted input capabilities. Even with their limitations, mobile devices offer a series of support services, principally SMS, voice, and location-based services, which differentiate m-commerce from e-commerce.

3. **Financial and banking applications.** Many EC applications in the financial services industries (such as e-banking) can be conducted with wireless devices. Most mobile financial applications are simply wireless versions of their wireline counterparts, and they are conducted via SMS or the mobile Web system. Mobile banking and mobile payments are examples of this activity. More and more, banks throughout the world are enabling their customers to use mobile devices to make payments, view paid checks, compare bank services, transfer funds, and locate branches.

4. **Enterprise mobility applications.** The major application is that of supporting the various types of workforce (e.g., salespeople, repair people, and field force). Other areas are mobile CRM, inventory management, and wireless job dispatch. These applications offer high return on investment, even in the short run. Additional areas are fleet and transportation management and applications in warehouses.

5. **Consumer and personal applications and mobile entertainment.** One of the fastest-growing markets in m-commerce is mobile entertainment. Mobile entertainment encompasses mobile music, games, gambling, adult entertainment, and specialized user-generated content. Among these, mobile music is the largest segment, but mobile video is the fastest growing. Mobile gambling is also growing rapidly despite the legal restrictions by various government bodies. Also growing are mobile sports applications. Service industries using mobile applications include healthcare, hospitality, public safety, crime prevention, and homeland security.

6. **Location-based commerce.** Knowing when people are in real time enables many social interactions. In addition, you can use this information to advertise businesses and products and to induce people to check into certain establishments. This technology can also be used to enhance customer service, to improve driving, to save on gasoline, and to engage people in different tasks.

7. **Ubiquitous computing.** The *Internet of things (IoT)* is upon us, and so are cutting-edge and futuristic systems that involve many embedded and invisible processors. These systems appear in several formats, notably those that are context aware, and they enable intelligent and useful applications. They are interrelated with sensory systems and provide for smart applications such as smart electric grids, smart homes, smart buildings, smart cars, and much more.

8. **Wearable devices: Google Glass, smartwatches, and fitness trackers.** Wearables are getting more important as they relate to the Internet of things and to improved productivity in the enterprise. Wearables improve communication and collaboration. They free people's hands so business processes can be improved. They can be controlled by voice and even by the brain. Many benefits are derived when the wearables are connected to the Internet. Wearable devices that get a lot of publicity are smart glasses. On one hand, these can increase productivity, but, on the other hand, many fear the potential of invasion of privacy. Wearables and other mobile devices are important components in smart cities. Both smartwatches and smart fitness trackers are some of the many mobile consumer-oriented gadgets that are improving every year and increasing our quality of life.

9. **Security and other implementation issues.** Even though the potential benefits of m-commerce applications may be substantial, their implementation faces a number of challenges, including technical interruptions and gaps in network coverage, performance problems created by slow mobile networks and applications, managing and securing mobile devices, and managing mobile network bandwidth. The mobile computing environment offers special challenges for security, including the need to secure transmission over the open air and through multiple connecting networks. The biggest technological challenges relate to the usability and technological changes of mobile devices. Finally, privacy concerns, such as legal, ethical, and health issues, that can arise from the use of m-commerce, especially in the workplace, need to be considered.

KEY TERMS

Context-aware computing
Enterprise mobility
Geographical information system (GIS)
Geolocation
Global positioning system (GPS)
Intelligent personal assistants
Interactive voice response (IVR) system
Location-based commerce (l-commerce; LBS)
Mobile app
Mobile banking (m-banking)
Mobile commerce (m-commerce; m-business)
Mobile enterprises
Mobile entertainment
Mobile portal
Mobile worker
Multimedia messaging service (MMS)
Pervasive computing
Radio-frequency identification (RFID)
Real-time location system
Short message service (SMS)
Smartphone
Smart grid
Smartwatch
Ubiquitous computing (ubicom)
Voice portal
Wireless mobile computing (mobile computing)

DISCUSSION QUESTIONS

1. Discuss how m-commerce can expand the reach of EC.
2. Which of the m-commerce limitations listed in this chapter do you think will have the biggest near-term negative impact on the growth of m-commence? Which ones will be minimized within 5 years? Which ones will not?
3. Discuss the value of Internet-only banks. Check the mobile services of BOFI and compare them to that of the Bank of America.
4. Discuss the factors that are critical to the overall growth of mobile banking.
5. Why are many of the more popular mobile gambling sites located in small island countries?
6. Discuss the need to manage BYOD and BYOA.
7. Discuss the advantages of m-commerce over wired EC.

TOPICS FOR CLASS DISCUSSION AND DEBATES

1. Discuss the potential benefits and drawbacks of conducting m-commerce on social networks.
2. Discuss the strategic advantage of m-commerce.
3. Google acquired AdMob (**google.com/ads/admob**) partly to compete with Apple's iAd. Discuss the strategic implications of AdMob versus iAd.
4. Debate the issue of tracking the whereabouts of employees. Related to this is the privacy issue of tracking people and cars. Discuss the pros and cons.
5. Debate the issue of a company's right to check all employee's e-mails and voice communications, done on either their own or the company's devices during work hours.
6. Examine the use of mobile devices in restaurants and debate the possibility of the elimination of paper menus.
7. Search the issue of m-commerce usability. Start with **baymard.com/mcommerce-usability**.
8. Research the evolvement of Google Glass. Write a report. Start with the evolution of Google Glass at **redmondpie.com/the-evolution-of-google-glass-in-two-years-since-its-inception-image**. What will be the benefits of the device to users? (See **golocalworcester.com/business/smart-benefits-vision-coverage-for-google-glass-is-clear**.) Compare to competitors' products.
9. Discuss the role of augmented reality in mobility and its relationship to smart glasses.
10. Find information about Cisco's "BYOD smart solution." Examine the benefits and discuss the possibility of using this solution in medium or small companies. (See **cisco.com/web/solutions/trends/byod_smart_solution/index.html**.)
11. Discuss the value of Waze. What are its limitations?
12. In-store mobile tracking of shoppers in brick-and-mortar retailers is increasing. Examine the benefits and the necessary protection of the customers (e.g., choice to opt-out). Under what circumstances would you allow customer tracking?
13. Join the discussion at **iotcommunity.com**. Write a report.
14. Is Uber's business part of the sharing economy or just B2C matching? Debate.

INTERNET EXERCISES

1. Research the status of 4G and 5G. You can find information by conducting a Google search and by going to Verizon Wireless (see **verizonwireless.com/wcms/consumer/4g-lte.html**). Also read **pcmag.com/article/345387/what-is-5g?ipmat=345235&lpmtype=3**. Prepare a report on the status of 4G and 5G based on your findings.
2. You have been asked to assemble a directory of Wi-Fi hotspots in your local area. There are a number of sites such as **hotspot-locations.com** that offer search capabilities for finding hotspots in a specific area. Make a list of locations that offer this feature.
3. Juniper Research has created a variety of white papers dealing with different segments of the mobile entertainment market (e.g., mobile games). Go to Juniper Research (**juniperresearch.com**) and download a white paper regarding one of these market segments. Use the white paper as a guide to write a summary of the market segment you selected—the size of the market, the major vendors, the factors encouraging and impeding its growth, and the future of the market segment.
4. Enter **meetup.com** and review their mobile apps. Write a summary.
5. Find information about Google Maps for mobile devices. In addition, review the capabilities of Google SMS and other related Google applications. Write a report on your findings.
6. Enter **mobile.fandango.com** and find the services they offer to mobile customers. Write a report.
7. Enter **waze.com** and other sources about Waze. Identify all the features of a social network. What is shared there?
8. Enter Facebook and find all their features that facilitate mobile shopping. In addition, see **shopify.com/facebook**. Write a report.
9. Enter meetup.com and find their mobile apps. Write a summary.

TEAM ASSIGNMENTS AND PROJECTS

1. Assignment for the Opening Case

   Read the opening case and answer the following questions:

(a) Do you really need the NeverLost GPS (fee of $13.99/day) when you can get almost the same information with a smartphone like the iPhone (or iPad) and a portable GPS? Why or why not? For example, compare the information sheet provided by Hertz on Hawaii on their website to one that you can get on a smartphone from TripAdvisor.
(b) Which one of Hertz's mobile applications can be considered a mobile enterprise and which one can be considered mobile customer service?
(c) Identify finance- and marketing-oriented applications in this case.
(d) What are the benefits of offering mobile apps to Hertz?
(e) As a customer, how do you feel about Hertz knowing where you are at all times?
(f) Enter neverlost.com and identify recent services. View their Companion app. Write a report.
(g) Find information about the NeverLost Companion app. What are its benefits?

2. Each team should examine a major vendor of enterprise-oriented mobile devices (Nokia, Kyocera, Motorola; a Google company, BlackBerry, etc.). Each team will research the capabilities of the devices offered by each company and then present the findings to the class. The objective of the presentation is to convince the rest of the class to buy that company's products.
3. Each team should explore the commercial applications of m-commerce in one of the following areas: financial services (including banking), stocks, insurance, marketing and advertising, travel and transportation, human resources management, public services, restaurants, and healthcare. Each team will present a report to the class based on their findings.
4. Indiana University, with eight campuses, has over 110,000 students and over 18,000 employees, including faculty and support staff. The information systems include the use of many BYOD mobile devices. Enter **citrix.com/products/enterprise-mobility.html** and read the story about Indiana University. Watch the 2:28 min video titled "Indiana University Customer Story" and conduct an additional search regarding how the university controls mobile device security. Write a report. (Start with the university's IT services at **uits.iu.edu/page/bcnh**.)
5. Watch the video titled "Technology Advances Fuelling M-Commerce Today" (7:43 min) at **youtube.com/watch?v=398EztRwPiY** and answer the following questions:

(a) What EC services are provided by m-commerce?
(b) Discuss the role of m-commerce in retailing.
(c) Discuss the lack of m-commerce strategy vs. its wide acceptance.
(d) Why is m-commerce such a fragmented market?
(e) Why do retailers spend much of their IT budget on m-commerce?
(f) Discuss the impact of m-commerce on competition among retailers.
(g) What are the difficulties in managing mobile technology?
(h) What are the advantages of mobile payments?
(i) Research the major methods and vendors of m-payments.

CLOSING CASE: CAN UBER CONTINUE TO GROW IN AN EVOLVING MARKET?

Uber, then called UberCab, began in 2009 in San Francisco, California. The company boasted the ability to hail a cab using a smartphone application. This initial idea has grown worldwide to 81 countries, with a combination of smart technologies and a large decentralized base of independent drivers (**uber.com/our-story**). The company relies on drivers to be available to transport customers on their own schedules. A suite of technology solutions, focused around a smartphone application, allows customers to match themselves with the driver nearest to them. The company's offering has grown and now includes several different classes of cars and even self-driving cars in limited markets (see **nextjuggernaut.com/blog/how-uber-**

works-business-model-revenue-uber-insights). All of this success has spread talks of an IPO in 2017. The company's current valuation is $68 billion (Vellanki 2016). Uber is now a global company operating in hundreds of cities.

Uber is considered a major disruptor (Chap. 5), but can the company be expected to grow in the future or at least grow at the current rate? While Uber has seen many successes in the past, there are several hurdles visible in its future. These challenges may affect the company's ability to remain competitive and profitable in the years ahead. Leaders at Uber will need to face issues with the company's overall business model, growing regulatory burdens, and competition from similar providers.

Business Model

One issue that Uber has always faced is the fundamental soundness of its business model. While the company is growing quickly, so are its losses (Solomon 2016). Company leaders see these losses as a prelude to future growth and a sign that the company is aggressively expanding and maintaining its market dominance. Others are concerned that these losses may never cross over into profits, as the company is faced with competition and legal issues. While an exact description of the businesses profit and loss is not completely available since the company is private. However, leaked information has allowed analysts to make some estimates. It is estimated that the company lost $570 million in Q1 2016 and $750 million in Q2 2016 (Vellanki 2016 and Kolodny 2016).

Part of the business model is collaboration with auto manufacturers and with Hertz and Enterprise Rent-A-Car (for short-term car rental programs). The company also collaborates with Sears.

Regulation

In addition to financial issues, the company faces a wide variety of regulatory challenges. The first set of challenges strike directly at the company's business model and the ability to use independent drivers. A number of legal issues around this model have sprung up. The first issue is that Uber is acting as a taxi service, but is not paying the appropriate licensing fees for that service. Cities argue that Uber must pay the same licensing fees as taxis and that, by not, they are defrauding the city of revenue and competing unfairly (Posen 2015). Plaintiffs in another case contend that Uber's drivers are not truly independent but are acting as employees. In this role, employees would be eligible for benefits as well as overtime, which Uber does not provide (Ross 2015). The final issue is in direct relation to Uber's new driverless car service. In California, the state has held that driverless cars are illegal, and Uber has recently canceled its pilot project in San Francisco, largely due to this complaint (see **nytimes.com/2016/12/21/technology/san-francisco-california-uber-driverless-car-.html**).

Competition

As Uber has continued to grow, others have noticed their success, and that success has brought about competition that did not initially exist. This competition can take the form of a direct competitor, such as Lyft, or changes in the business models from existing companies like Yellow Cab. Lyft has a business model that is very similar to Uber, using independent drivers and a smartphone app to connect them (**lyft.com**). Lyft has a smaller domestic footprint but sees its potential in international markets where firm business boundary is not yet established (see **cnbc.com/2017/01/13/lyft-to-go-global-take-on-uber-outside-the-us.html**). Companies with a history in the taxi business, such as Yellow Cab, are changing their business models to meet some of the same demands of Uber's customers. This includes smartphone applications and lower prices in some markets (see **theverge. com/2016/9/26/13035642/nyc-taxi-cab-android-touchscreen-tablet-verifone**).

Future Plans

Uber started to test driverless cars (Griffith 2016). They already encounter difficulties in testing as discussed earlier. Self-driving car may kill jobs (McFarland 2016). Therefore, there could be political oppositions.

Note: Walton's history has been one of fast growth and many successes. The changes in competitive landscape and lingering issues about the business may cause concern for its future.

Sources: Compiled from Griffith (2016), Kolodny (2016), Posen (2015), Ross (2015), McFarland (2016), and **uber.com** (accessed February 2017)

Questions

1. What is the reason for Uber's rapid growth in both users and revenue?
2. Why is Uber valued at $68 billion, at the time that it is not profitable?
3. Should Uber drivers be treated as employees or independent contractors?
4. Should cities and states be allowed to charge Uber license fees like taxi companies?
5. What can Uber do to remain competitive against companies like Lyft?
6. Are self-driving cars the future of Uber's success? Why or why not?
7. Comment on Uber's partnership with car manufacturers and car rental companies.

REFERENCES

Arthur, R. "Are We Really Going to Shop from the Apple Watch? What Retail Apps Are Trying to Achieve." *Forbes.com*, May 7, 2015.

Austin, L. "Ford Motor Co. (NSYE: F) Energetically Grow and Invest in Emerging Mobility Services-VeriFone Systems (NSYE:PAY)." *Senecaglobe* (News Item) March 12, 2016.

Barris, M. "Hertz App Blends Travel Planner, GPS to Enhance Rental Experience." *Mobile Marketer*, August 13, 2014.

Barry, E. "Say Goodbye to 9–5 and the Commute, More and More Jobs Are Becoming 'Flexible'." *CNBC.com*, January 7, 2017.

Beauduin, A., et al. *The Mobile Enterprise: A Pragmatic Vision*. [Kindle Edition]. Seattle, WA: Amazon Digital Services, 2015.

Bosniak, D. "Aira is a Smart Glasses-Based Service for Blind People." *Androidheadlines.com*, January 4, 2017. **androidheadlines.com/2017/01/aira-smart-glasses-based-service-blind-people.html**. (accessed February 2017).

Broussard, M. "AliveCor Announces Apple Watch 'Kardia Band' for Medical Grade EKG Analysis." March 16, 2016. **macrumors.com/2016/03/16/alivecor-apple-watch-kardia-band** (accessed February 2017).

Caspi, G. "How to Improve Security in a BYOD Enterprise Environment." *Betanews*, February 22, 2016. **betanews.com/2016/02/22/security-mobile-byod-enterprise** (accessed February 2017).

Chamberlin, B. "Wearable Computing: A 2014 Horizon Watching trend Summary Report." *IBM Expert Network*, April 7, 2014. **slideshare.net/HorizonWatching/s11-wearable-computing-2014-horizon-watching-trend-summary-report-01apr2014** (accessed February 2017).

Chester, T. "This Mobile Game Is Using Data from Players to Boost Alzheimer's Research." *Mashable*, May 4, 2016.

Clements, N. "The Best Mobile Banking Apps of 2016." *Forbes.com*, December 17, 2016.

Corpuz, J. "10 Best Location Aware Apps." *Tom's Guide*, August 26, 2016.

CSS Author. "10 of the Great Examples of Mobile Friendly Ecommerce Sites." December 22, 2014 (Last Updated August 3, 2016). **cssauthor.com/great-examples-mobile-friendly-ecommerce-sites** (accessed February 2017).

Dale, B. "This Wearable Device Reads Your Brain Waves. Is There a Market for It?" *Forbes*, February 10, 2014. **fortune.com/2014/02/10/this-wearable-device-reads-your-brain-waves-is-there-a-market-for-it/?** (accessed February 2017).

Diaz, J. "CES 2017 Wrap Up: January 4th." *Androidheadlines.com*, January 4, 2017. **androidheadlines.com/2017/01/ces-2017-wrap-january-4th.html**. (accessed February 2017).

Diffly, A. "Wrapping it Up: 2016 E-Commerce Challenges & Trends." *SMB Retail*, December 2016. **smbretail.com/wrapping-it-up-2016-e-commerce-challenges-trends** (accessed February 2017).

Diogenes, Y., et al. *Enterprise Mobility with App Management, Office 365, and Threat Mitigation: Beyond BYOD*. Seattle, WA: Microsoft Press, 2017.

Elliott, C. "What Will Your Next Rental Car Know about You? Everything." August 14, 2013. **elliott.org/blog/what-will-your-next-rental-car-know-about-you-everything** (accessed February 2017).

FoxNews.com. "FDA Launches Mobile App Competition to Aid Opioid Abuse Epidemic." *FoxNews.com*, September 21, 2016.

Fraden, J. *Handbook of Modern Sensors: Physics, Designs and Applications*. 5th ed. New York, NY: Springer, 2016.

Frakes, D. "iPod Nano (Sixth Generation, Late 2010)." *Macworld*, September 7, 2010. **macworld.com/article/1153921/6G_iPod_nano.html** (accessed February 2017).

Fuller, D. "Sensoria and VIVOBAREFOOT Bring IoT Down to Foot Level." *Androidheadlines.com*, January 4, 2017.

Gazdecki, A. "9 Mobile Technology Trends For 2017 (Infographic)." *BiznessApps.com*, January 2017.

Gingiss, D. "Focus on Customer Service: Hertz [PODCAST]." *Social Media Today*, October 21, 2015.

Gordon, J. "Top 3 Mobility Trends for 2016." *Enterprise Mobility*, December 7, 2015. **enterprisemobile.com/top-3-mobility-trends-for-2016** (accessed February 2017).

GPS.gov. "The Global Positioning System." (Last modified February 2017.) **gps.gov** (accessed February 2017).

Griffith, E. "Who Will Build the Next Great Car Company?" *Fortune.com*, June 23, 2016. **fortune.com/self-driving-cars-silicon-valley-detroit**. (accessed February 2017).

GSMA. "The Mobile Economy 2016." Special Report. **gsmamobileeconomy.com/2016/global** (accessed February 2017).

Hill, K. "If You Use Waze, Hackers Can Stalk You." *Fusion.net*. April 26, 2016. **fusion.net/story/293157/waze-hack**. (accessed February 2017).

Hunter, E. *Wearable Technology: Discover 20 Trends and Interactive Mobile Sensor Devices to Include Medical, Wearable, and Children's Devices (Wearable Camera, Electronic…Trackers, Fashion of the Future)*. Louisville, KY: CreateSpace Independent Publisher, 2015.

ICON Group. *The 2018–2023 World Outlook for Enterprise Mobility Management*. San Diego, CA: ICON Group International, 2017.

Kerr, J. C. "Stores Can See Where You Go by Tracking Your Phone." *AP News*, February 19, 2014. **bigstory.ap.org/article/stores-can-track-where-you-go-using-your-phone** (accessed February 2017).

Khillare, G. B., and S. A. Bobade. "Wearable Computing Devices and Its Application." *Slideshare*, 2015. **slideshare.net/gautamkhillare90/wearable-computing-devices-its-appllcation** (accessed February 2017).

Knight, K. "Mobile Roundup: Mobile Data to Skyrocket." *BizReport*, March 20, 2015.

Knowledge@Wharton and Ernst & Young. *Mobile Banking: Financial Services Meet the Electronic Wallet* [Kindle edition with Audio/Video]. Philadelphia, PA: Knowledge@Wharton, 2013.

Kolodny, L. "Uber Losses Expected to Hit $3 Billion in 2016 Despite Revenue Growth." *TechCrunch*, Dec 21, 2016. **techcrunch.com/2016/12/21/uber-losses-expected-to-hit-3-billion-in-2016-despite-revenue-growth** (accessed February 2017).

Krishnan, S. *The Power of Mobile Banking: How to Profit from the Revolution in Retail Financial Services.* Hoboken, NJ: Wiley, 2014.

Lamkin, P. "Best Smartwatch 2016: Apple, Pebble, Samsung, Sony, Tag and More." *Wareable.com*, March 21, 2016a. **wareable.com/smart-watches/the-best-smartwatches-in-the-world.** (accessed February 2017).

Lamkin, P. "The Best Smartglasses 2016: Sony, Vuzix and More." *Wareable.com*, March 21, 2016b. **www.wareable.com/headgear/the-best-smartglasses-google-glass-and-the-rest.** (accessed February 2017).

Liedtke, M. "Apple Hopes CarPlay Will Drive Further Success." *Irish Examiner*, March 5, 2014. **irishexaminer.com/ireland/apple-hopes-car-play-will-drive-further-success-260832.html** (accessed February 2017).

Ma, W. *China's Mobile Economy: Opportunities in the Largest and Fastest Information Consumption Boom.* Hoboken, NJ: Wiley, 2016.

Maddox, T. "The Dark Side of Wearables: How They're Secretly Jeopardizing Your Security and Privacy." *Tech Republic*, October 7, 2015.

Manjoo, F. "The Echo from Amazon Brims with Groundbreaking Promise." *The New York Times*, March 9, 2016.

Marsh, C., J. McKee, R. Castanon-Martinez, M. Incera, and C. Lehmann. "2017 Trends in Enterprise Mobility." *451 Research*, December 12, 2016. **451research.com/report-long?icid=4101** (accessed February 2017).

Matteson, S. "Mobility in 2017: More Location-Based Apps and IoT Advancements." *Tech Republic*, January 18, 2017.

Maximizer. "5 Strategic Advantages to Using a Mobile Customer Relationship Management Software." *Maximizer.com*, June 24, 2015.

Mayo, B. "Amazon Releases New 'Amazon Tap' and 'Echo Dot': More Competition for Apple's Siri Voice Assistant." *9to5Mac*, March 3, 2016.

McDowell, M. "CES 2016: The Best of Wearable Technology." *WWD*, January 11, 2016.

McFarland, "Is Uber's push for self-driving cars a job killer? *Money.cnn.com*, August 19, 2016. money.cnn.com/2016/08/19/technology/uber-self-driving-cars-jobs/ (accessed March 2017)

Meola, A. "The Rise of M-Commerce: Mobile Shopping Stats & Trends." *Business Insider*, December 21, 2016.

Millward, S. "Starting Today, Chinese Consumers Will Be Able to Buy Almost Anything Inside WeChat." *TechAsia.com*, March 4, 2014.

Mobile Labs. *Enterprise Mobile App Development & Testing: Challenges to Watch Out for In 2017,* [Kindle Edition]. Seattle, WA: Amazon Digital Services, 2016.

Moovweb. "7 Mobile Commerce Trends for 2016." January 4, 2016. **moovweb.com/blog/mobile-commerce-trends-2016** (accessed February 2017).

Nield, D. "How It Works: We Explain How Your Fitness Tracker Measures Daily Steps." *Wareable.com*, December 26, 2016.

Oliver, M. *Mobile Device Management for Dummies (An e-Book).* New York: Wiley & Sons, 2008. (Available in .pdf format at **content.energy-central.com/reference/whitepapers/103292/Mobile-Device-Management-for-Dummies** (accessed February 2017).

Oxagile. "Virtual and Augmented Reality to Disrupt Banking and Finance." *Oxagile.com*, August 16, 2016. **oxagile.com/company/blog/virtual-augmented-reality-disrupt-banking-finance** (accessed February 2017).

Patrizio, A. "Japan Produces Its Own Wearable PC." March 5, 2014. **itworld.com/mobile-wireless/408274/japan-produces-its-own-wearable-pc** (accessed February 2017).

Peng, V. "Mobile Enterprise in 2016 -- The Next Wave of Mobile-First." *The StartUp*, January 22, 2016. **medium.com/swlh/mobile-enterprise-in-2016-the-next-wave-of-mobile-first-540d23f14b95#.rtfidlmpo** (accessed February 2017).

Perez, S. "imDown's Mobile Entertainment Network Focuses on One-Minute Vertical Videos." *TechCrunch*, March 3, 2016.

Petroff, A. "Google Glass May Save Firms $1 Billion." *CNN Tech*, November 11, 2013. **money.cnn.com/2013/11/11/technology/google-glass-report/index.html?iid=s_mpm** (accessed February 2017).

Posen, H. A. (2015). "Ridesharing in the Sharing Economy: Should Regulators Impose Über Regulations on Uber?" Iowa Law Review, 101(1), 405–433.

PR Newswire. "Hertz Debuts A Redesigned and Improved Mobile App." January 21, 2014. **ir.hertz.com/2014-01-21-Hertz-Debuts-A-Rede-signed-And-Improved-Mobile-App** (accessed February 2017).

Reisinger, D. "BYOD: A Cost-Saving Must-Have for Your Enterprise." February 11, 2013. **cioinsight.com/it-strategy/tech-trends/slideshows/byod-a-cost-saving-must-have-for-your-enterprise-02** (accessed February 2017).

Robertson, A. "Microsoft HoloLens Could Help You Find Your Keys, and Also Stalk Your Every More." *TheVerge.com*, December 30, 2016.

Ross, H. (2015). "Ridesharing's House of Cards: O'Connor v. Uber Technologies, Inc. and the Viability of Uber's Labor Model in Washington." Washington Law Review, 90(3), 1431–1469.

Rubin, B. F. "Echo Effect: How Amazon's Alexa Will Give Voice to More Devices." *CNET.com*, March 11, 2016. **cnet.com/aa/news/echo-effect-how-amazons-alexa-will-give-voice-to-more-devices.** (accessed February 2017).

Salz, P. A., and J. Moranz. *The Everything Guide to Mobile Apps: A Practical Guide to Affordable Mobile App Development for Your Business.* Avon, MA: Adams Media, 2013.

Saylor, M. *The Mobile Wave: How Mobile Intelligence Will Change Everything,* New York: (Da Capo Press, a Member of the Perseus Books Group)/Vanguard Press Edition, 2012.

Solomon, B. "Leaked: Uber's Financials Show Huge Growth, Even Bigger Losses." *Forbes*, January 12, 2016. **forbes.com/sites/briansolomon/2016/01/12/leaked-ubers-financials-show-huge-growth-even-bigger-losses/#50200fbf5c99** (accessed February 2017).

Stables, J. "Best Fitness Trackers 2016: Jawbone, Misfit, Fitbit, Garmin and More." *Wareable.com*, March 7, 2016.

Steinberg S. "Twenty Surprising Mobile Stats for 2016: The Smartphone Takeover" *Mobile Business Insights*, June 29, 2016.

Strout, A. "13 Mobile Marketing Stats You Need To Know." *Marketing Land*, June 8, 2015.

Sukhraj, R. "31 Mobile Marketing Statistics to Help You Plan for 2017." *Impact*, October 30, 2016. **impactbnd.com/blog/mobile-marketing-statistics-for-2016** (accessed February 2017).

Swilley, E. *Mobile Commerce: How It Contrasts, Challenges, and Enhances Electronic Commerce.* New York: Business Expert Press, 2015.

Thouin, B. "4 Ways to Use Messaging to Enhance the Customer Experience." *Social Media Today*, March 6, 2016.

Ungureanu, H. "Apple's $200 Million Turi Acquisition to Challenge Google, Amazon and Facebook in Pervasive Computing." *Tech Times,* August 6, 2016.

Vellanki, M. "Here's What A 2017 Uber IPO Could Look Like." *Mahesh VC.* November 14, 2016. **mahesh-vc.com/blog/heres-what-a-2017-uber-ipo-could-look-like** (accessed February 2017).

Vijayan, J. "7 Hidden Dangers of Wearable Computers." *Computerworld*, February 25, 2014. **computerworld.com/article/2474554/emerging-technology/141686-7-hidden-dangers-of-wearable-computers.html** (accessed February 2017).

Weiss, T.R. "Janam's New Mobile Handheld Business Computer Handles RFID UHF Tags." *eWeek*, July 7, 2015.

Wishpond Technologies Ltd. "New Trends of Mobile Users and Their Shopping Behaviour." A White paper, 2014. **corp. wishpond.com/mobile-marketing-resources/new-trends-of-mobile-users-and-their-shopping-behaviour** (accessed February 2017).

Yochim, D. "Best Online Broker for Stock Trading 2017." *Nerdwallet*, January 6, 2017. **nerdwallet.com/blog/investing/best-online-brokers-for-stock-trading** (accessed February 2017).

Contents

Learning Objectives

1. Understand the reasons for intelligent e-commerce systems
2. Become familiar with the essentials of artificial intelligence
3. Cite the major AI applications in e-commerce
4. Understand knowledge systems and their management
5. Understand intelligent computerized personal assistants and their availability
6. Gain knowledge about IoT
7. Describe self-driving cars, smart homes and appliances, and smart cities

OPENING CASE
INRIX SOLVES TRANSPORTATION PROBLEMS

The Problem

The traffic congestion problem is on the rise in many large metropolitan areas. Drivers may spend hours on the roads each day. Air pollution is increasing and more accidents are occurring.

© Springer International Publishing AG 2018

E. Turban et al., *Electronic Commerce 2018*, Springer Texts in Business and Economics, DOI 10.1007/978-3-319-58715-8_7

The Solution

INRIX (**inrix.com**) enables drivers to get real-time traffic information. Drivers can download INRIX-XD Traffic App for iOS and Android. This information is generated by *predictive analysis* of massive data obtained from consumers and the environment (e.g., road construction, accidents). Information sources include:

- Real-time traffic flow and accident information collected in real time by driver services (e.g., helicopters, drones)
- Flow of traffic statuses collected by participating delivery companies and by over 100 million anonymous volunteer drivers that have GPS-enabled smartphones, all reporting in real time
- Public reports about road conditions, current weather, and forecasts
- Traffic congestion reports (e.g., due to road maintenance)

INRIX processes the collected information with proprietary analytical tools and formulas. The processed information is used to generate traffic predictions. For example, it creates a picture of anticipated traffic flows and delays for the next 15–20 min, the next few hours, and the next few days, for many locations. These predictions enable drivers to plan their optimal routes. As of 2016, INRIX offers global coverage in 41 countries and in many major cities, and the company analyzes traffic information from over 100 sources. This service is combined with digital maps. In Seattle, for example, traffic information is disseminated via smartphones and color codes on billboards along the freeways. Smartphones also display estimated times for the roads to be either clear or become jammed. By 2016, the company covered about 5,000,000 miles of highways worldwide, delivering upon request the best recommended routes to use, all in real time.

The INRIX system provides information (or recommendations) for decisions such as:

- Optional routes for delivery vehicles and other travelers
- The best time to go to work or to other places
- How to reroute a trip to avoid encountering a traffic jam that just occurred
- Fees to be paid on highways, which are based on traffic conditions and time of the day

The technologies used to collect data are:

- Closed-circuit TV cameras and radar monitoring traffic conditions
- Public safety reports and traffic information
- Information about freeway access and departure flows
- Toll collection queues
- Magnetic sensing detectors embedded under the road surface (expensive)
- 276 million vehicles, smartphones, and other data collection devices collect data for INRIX

Several of the sources of information are connected to the company via the *Internet of things* (section "The Internet of Things (IoT) and E-Commerce"). According to their website, INRIX has partnered with Clear Channel Radio to broadcast real-time traffic data directly to vehicles via in-car or portable navigation systems, broadcast media, and wireless and Internet-based services. Clear Channel's Total Traffic Network is available in more than 125 metropolitan areas in 4 countries (**inrix. com/why-inrix/customers-partners**).

The Results

In addition to use by individual drivers, the information is used by companies and city planners for planning purposes. In addition, less traffic congestion has been recorded in participating cities, which results in less pollution and road accidents, and in increased productivity of happier employees, who spend less time commuting.

The INRIX Traffic App (available for download at **inrix.com/mobile-apps**) is suitable for all smartphones, and it supports ten languages, including English, French, Spanish, and Hungarian. For the INRIX traffic free features, see **inrixtraffic.com/features**. For interesting case studies, see **inrix.com/global-resources/case-studies**.

Sources: Based on **inrix.com**, Gitlin (2016), **inrix.com/mobile-apps**, and **inrix.com/why-inrix/customers-partners** (all accessed December 2016).

LESSONS LEARNED FROM THE CASE

The INRIX case illustrates to us how the collection and analysis of a very large amount of information (*big data*) can improve cars' mobility in large cities. Specifically, by collecting information from drivers and other sources, instead of collecting it from just expensive sensors, the company was able to optimize mobility. Furthermore, the company is using applications of the *Internet of things* (IoT) to connect vehicles and devices with its computing system. This application is one of the building blocks of *smart cities*. Analysis is done by using powerful algorithms, some of which are applications of artificial intelligence (AI).

7.1 INTRODUCTION TO INTELLIGENT E-COMMERCE

We would all like to see e-commerce simpler, easier to use, intuitive, and less threatening. In addition, indeed, efforts have been made over time to simplify and automate many tasks of e-commerce. Just think of the day that your refrigerator will be able to measure and evaluate its contents and place orders for goods that need replenishment. Such a day is not too far in the future and the task will be supported by the IoT. This is an example of what we call "smart" or "intelligent" e-commerce—the subject of this chapter.

CIO Insight projected that by 2035, intelligent computer technologies will have $5–$8.3 trillion in economic value (**cio-insight.com/print/ot-strategy/tech-trends/slideshow/ten-technologies-that-will-disrupt-business-07**). Among the technologies listed as intelligent ones are the Internet of things, advanced robotics, and self-driven vehicles. All are described in this chapter. Gartner, a leading technology consultant, lists the following in their 2016 Hype Cycle for Emerging Technologies: expert advisors, natural language questions and answering, commercial drones, smart workspaces, IoT platforms, smart data discovery, context brokering, general-purpose machine intelligence, and personal analytics. All these are described or cited in this chapter (see Greengard 2016a, b).

An Overview of Intelligent E-Commerce

There is an increasing trend to make e-commerce "smarter" (as seen in Chap. 2). For example, Web 3.0 supposes to enable systems to exhibit more intelligence. Several applications are already based on *artificial intelligence (AI)*. This means that we can see more automation in various e-commerce activities. For example, the area of machine translation of languages is already helping people buy online products that are advertised in languages they do not speak. Similarly, machine translation can help people that know only their own language to converse, in real time, with people speaking other languages.

Other smart or intelligent applications include those that can help with machines answering customers' questions asked in natural languages. Another area is that of *knowledge-based systems* (also known as *expert systems*). These systems can provide advice, assist people to make decisions, and even make decisions on their own. For example, such systems can approve or reject buyers' requests to purchase online (if they are not preapproved or do not have a line of credit). Other examples include the automatic generating of online purchasing orders and arranging fulfillment of orders placed online. Both Google and Facebook are experimenting with projects that attempt to teach machines how to learn (*machine learning*) and make decisions. Other companies are doing the same (e.g., Toyota; see Markoff 2015). For more smart applications in the enterprise, see Dodge (2016).

Smart EC systems are also important for *innovation*, and they are related to the areas of analytics and big data processing. One of the most advanced projects in this area is IBM's Watson Analytics (e.g., see Taft 2014, Niccolai 2015, and section "Intelligent Personal Assistants and Robot Advisers").

Smart EC can be recognized by its smart applications. The major applications are supported by foundations; smart technology is mostly related to artificial intelligence. Both the foundations and the applications are illustrated in Fig. 7.1.

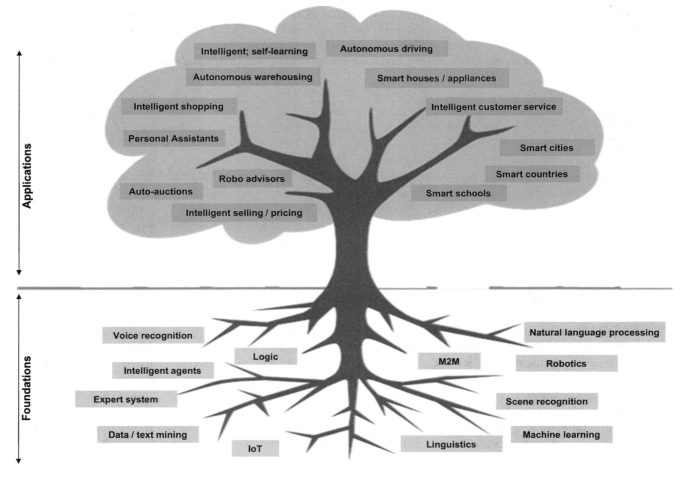

Fig. 7.1 The functionalities and applications of artificial intelligence

In January 2016, Mark Zuckerberg, the CEO of Facebook, announced that his goal in 2016 is to build an AI-based assistant to help with his personal and business activities and decisions. Zuckerberg is teaching a machine to understand his voice and follow his basic commands as well as to recognize faces of his friends and business partners (see Bell 2016 and Ulanoff 2016).

Example: Pitney Bowes Is Getting Smarter with AI

Pitney Bowes Inc. is a US-based global e-commerce solution provider in areas such as shipping products, location intelligence, customer engagement, and customer information management. The company powers billions of physical and digital transactions annually, across the connected and borderless world of commerce.

Today, shipping prices are calculated automatically based on the dimensions, weight, and packaging of each product. The fees' calculations create data that are fed into algorithms. The more data that are collected, the more accurate are the calculations. The company estimates a 25% improvement in an accuracy yield from their algorithms. This gives the company an accurate base for pricing, better customer satisfaction, and improved competitive advantage.

The above example shows an application of artificial intelligence (AI), which is the major driving force in intelligent e-commerce systems. And indeed, AI adoption is on the rise (Khani 2016).

SECTION 7.1 REVIEW QUESTIONS

1. Why do we need intelligent EC?
2. List some of technologies that provide intelligence to EC.
3. List some benefits of smart EC.

7.2   THE ESSENTIALS OF ARTIFICIAL INTELLIGENCE

The major building technology in intelligent e-commerce is artificial intelligence (AI). For an overview, see Russell (2015).

Artificial Intelligence (AI): Definitions and Characteristics

Artificial intelligence (AI) has several definitions; however, many experts agree that AI is concerned with two basic ideas: (1) the study of human thought processes (to understand what intelligence is) and (2) the representation and duplication of those thought processes in machines (e.g., computers, robots).

One well-publicized definition of AI is "behavior by a machine that, if performed by a human being, would be called intelligent."

A well-known application of artificial intelligence is the chess program hosted at a supercomputer. (Deep Blue was developed by a research team at IBM.) The system beat the famous world champion, Grand Master Garry Kasparov.

The Capabilities of Intelligence

To understand what artificial intelligence is, it is useful to examine those abilities that are considered signs of intelligence:

- Learning or understanding from experience
- Making sense out of ambiguous, incomplete, or even contradictory messages and information
- Responding quickly and successfully to a new situation (i.e., the most correct responses)
- Understanding and inferring in a rational way, solving problems, and directing conduct effectively
- Applying knowledge to manipulate the environment and situations
- Recognizing and judging the relative importance of different elements in a situation

Artificial intelligence attempts to provide these capabilities, but in general, it still does not match human intelligence.

How Intelligent Is AI?

AI machines demonstrated superiority over human in playing games such as chess (beating the world champion), Jeopardy (beating the best players), and Go (a complex Chinese game), whose top players were beaten by a computer. A well-known program is Google's DeepMind (see Hughes 2016). Despite these remarkable demonstrations (that cost extremely large amounts of money), many AI applications are still showing significantly less intelligence than humans. To define what we consider intelligent machines, let us look at the Turing test.

Turing Test
Alan Turing designed an interesting test to determine whether a computer exhibits intelligent behavior; the test is called the **Turing test**. According to this test, a computer can be considered smart only when a human interviewer posing the same questions to both an unseen human being and an unseen computer (see Fig. 7.2) cannot determine which is which.

The Content of the AI Field

The AI field is very broad since we can find AI technologies and applications in hundreds of disciplines ranging from medicine to sports. Here we present only some major AI derivatives, which are used in e-commerce.

Intelligent Agents

An **intelligent agent (IA)** is an autonomous, relatively small, computer program that observes and acts upon a changing environment and directs its activities toward achieving specific goals, related to the above changes, by running specific tasks, autonomously. Intelligent agents may have the ability to learn by using and expanding the knowledge embedded in them. Intelligent agents are powerful tools for overcoming the most critical burden of the Internet— *information overload*—and making e-commerce a more viable organizational tool. Interest in using intelligent agents for e-commerce started in the

Fig. 7.2 A pictorial representation of the Turing test

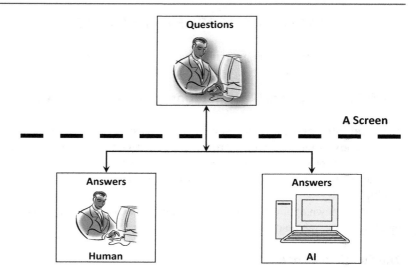

academic world soon after the birth of EC, in the mid-1990s. However, it is only since 2014, when the capabilities of IA increased remarkably, that we started to see many applications, which will be presented in section "Recent AI Applications in E-Commerce".

Initially, intelligent agents were used mainly to support routine activities such as searching for products, getting recommendations, determining products' pricing, planning marketing, conducting negotiations, improving computer security, managing auctions, facilitating payments, and improving inventory management. However, these applications were very simple, using a lower level of intelligence. Their major benefit was increasing speed, reducing cost, reducing errors, and improving customer service. Today's applications, as we will see throughout this chapter, are more sophisticated.

For more on EC/IA, see **ai.ijs.si/sandi/docs/ECIAgents.pdf**.

Example: Virus Detection Program

A simple example of an intelligent software agent is a virus detection program. It resides in your computer, scans all incoming data, and removes found viruses automatically while learning new virus types and detection methods.

Intelligent agents are also applied in personal digital assistants, e-mail servers, news filtering and distribution, appointment handling, and automated information gathering.

Machine Learning

AI systems do not have the same learning capabilities that humans have; rather, they have simplistic (but improving) learning capabilities (modeled after human learning methods) called **machine learning**. The machine learning scientists try to teach computers to identify patterns and make connections by showing it a large volume of examples and related data. Machine learning allows computer systems to monitor and sense their environmental activities and adjust their behavior to match changes in the environment. Technically speaking, machine learning is a scientific discipline that is concerned with the design and development of algorithms that allow computers to learn, based on data coming from sensors, databases, or other sources.

Machine learning algorithms are used today by many companies. Well-known examples are product recommendation services. For an executive guide to machine learning, see Pyle and San Jose (2015).

According to Taylor (2016), the "increased computing power, coupled with other improvements including better algorithms and deep neural networks for image processing and ultra-fast in-memory databases like SAP HANA are the reason why Machine Learning is one of the hottest areas of development in enterprise software today." Machine learning applications also expand due to availability of big data sources, especially those provided by the Internet of things (section "The Internet of Things (IoT) and E-Commerce").

Robotics Systems

Sensory systems, such as scene recognition systems, and signal-processing systems, when combined with AI, define a broad category of complex systems generally called *robots*. There are several definitions of robots and they are changing over time. A classical definition is that a **robot** is an electromechanical device that can be programmed to perform manual and/or mental tasks.

The Robotics Institute of America formally defines a *robot* as "a programmable multifunctional manipulator designed to move materials, parts, tools, or specialized devices through variable programmed motions for the performance of a variety of tasks." This definition ignores the many mental tasks done by today's robots.

An "intelligent" robot or a *bot* has some kind of sensory apparatus, such as a camera, that collects information about the robot's surroundings and its operations. The collected data are interpreted by the "brain" of the robot, allowing it to respond to the changes in the environment.

Robots can be fully autonomous, programmed to do tasks completely on their own, or they can be remotely controlled by a human. Some robots resemble humans and are known as *androids*. Most industrial robots are not. The autonomous robots are equipped with an AI intelligent agent. The more advanced smart robots are not only autonomous, but they can learn from their environment, building on their capabilities. Robots today can learn complex tasks by watching what humans do. This leads to better human–robot collaboration. The Interactive Group at MIT experiments with this capability, aiming to teach robots to make complex decisions. For details, see Shah (2016). For an overview of the robots revolution, see Waxer (2016).

Robots are used extensively in EC warehouses (e.g., tens of thousands are used by Amazon.com; see Chap. 13). They also are used in make-to-order manufacturing (Chap. 13) and lately in self-driven machines and in drones. A new generation of robots is designed to work as advisors as described in section "Intelligent Personal Assistants and Robot Advisers." Notably, they are planned for use in areas such as investments, travel, medicine, and academic advising. They can serve as recipients and be used as teachers and trainers.

Robots can help in online shopping by collecting shopping information (search) and conduct price and capability comparisons. These are known as **shopbots** (e.g., see **igi-global.com/dictionary/shopbot/26826**). Robots can carry goods in open-air markets. Walmart is experimenting now with robotic shopping carts (Knight 2016). For a video (4:41 min.), see **businessinsider.com/personal-robots-for-shopping-and-e-commerce-2016-9?IR=T**.

A special category of robots is the *chatbot*, which are described later in this section. Intelligent personal advisors, including *robo advisors* for investments, are described in section "Intelligent Personal Assistants and Robot Advisers".

Robots are Taking Our Jobs

There are major concerns about robots taking not only industrial jobs but also many white-collar jobs. Oxford University in the United Kingdom looked at 700 jobs and ranked them from 0 (no risk of automation) to 1 (very high risk of automation). Rickard-Straus provided the list of the top 100 most-at-risk jobs (all above .95) and the least-at-risk 100 jobs (with .02 or less). The top 10 "safe" and 10 at risk are listed in Table 7.1.

Table 7.1 Top ten Safe and at-risk occupations

Probability	Title
	Low-risk jobs
0.0036	First-line supervisor of fire fighting and prevention workers
0.0036	Oral and maxillofacial surgeons
0.0035	Healthcare social workers
0.0035	Orthotists and prosthetists
0.0033	Audiologists
0.0031	Mental health and substance abuse social workers
0.0030	Emergency management directors
0.0030	First-line supervisors of mechanics, installers, and repairers
0.0028	Recreational therapists
	High-risk jobs
0.99	Telemarketers
0.99	Title examiners, abstractors, and searchers
0.99	Sewers, hand
0.99	Mathematical technicians
0.99	Insurance underwriters
0.99	Watch repairer
099	Cargo and freight agents
0.99	Tax preparers
0.99	Photographic process workers and processing machine operators
0.99	New account clerks

Based on Rickard-Straus (2014)

Chui et al. (2016) provide an analysis on where machines could replace humans—and where they cannot (yet). The major reason for the concern is that many jobs are in danger; the advantages of robots are growing rapidly—together with their capabilities, and the large number of occupations with high level of risk. (See discussion by Reich 2015.)

Natural Language Processing

Natural language processing (NLP) technology gives computer users the ability to communicate with a computer in their native language. This technology allows for a conversational type of interface, in contrast to using a programming language that consists of computer jargon, syntax, and commands. It includes two subfields:

- *Natural language understanding* that investigates methods of enabling computers to comprehend instructions or queries provided in ordinary English or other languages
- *Natural language generation* that strives to have computers produce ordinary spoken language so that people can understand the computers more easily

NLP is related to voice-generated data, as well as text and other data.

Speech (Voice) Understanding

A **speech (voice) understanding** is the recognition and understanding of spoken languages by a computer. Applications of this technology have become more and more popular. For instance, many companies have adopted this technology in their call centers. For an interesting application, see **cs.cmu.edu/~./listen**.

Related to NLP is machine translation of languages, which is done both of written text (e.g., Web content) and of voice conversation (e.g., by Skype).

Language Translation

Machine translation uses computer programs to translate words and sentences from one language to another. For example, you can use Babel Fish translation, available at **babelfish.com**, to try more than 25 different combinations of language translation. Similarly, you can also use Google's free Translate to translate dozens of different languages (**translate.google.com**). Finally, users can post their status in Facebook in any language. Then translation can be made (per Keating 2016).

Another AI technology related to NLP and robots is *chatbots*.

Chatbots

Short for *chat robot*, a **chatbot** is a computerized service that enables conversations between human and computers, usually over the Internet. The conversations are frequently done by short questions and answers. More intelligent chatbots are equipped with natural language processors, so the computer can *understand unstructured* dialog. Some companies experiment with learning chatbots, which gain more knowledge with experience. The ability of the computer to converse with a human is provided by a knowledge system (usually rule-based; see section "Knowledge (Expert) Systems"). The computer side can look like a person or an avatar. The service is also available at messaging services such as Facebook's Messenger and on Twitter.

Chatbots in E-Commerce

The most common use of chatbots (bots in short) in EC is in customer service. For example, Taco Bell is experimenting with a food ordering chatbot on Slack (a messaging service). Schlicht (2016) provides a beginner's guide to chatbots. He presents the following hypothetical example about today's shopping at Nordstrom (a department store) vs. the use of chatbots.

Example: Nordstrom Uses Chatbots

"If you wanted to buy shoes from Nordstrom online, you would go to their website, look around until you find the shoes you wanted, and then you would purchase them. If Nordstrom makes a bot, which I am sure they will, you would simply be able to message Nordstrom on Facebook. It would ask you what you are looking for and you would simply tell it.

Instead of browsing a website, you will have a conversation with the Nordstrom bot, mirroring the type of experience you would get when you go into the retail store."

A 5-min Facebook video is available at **cnbc.com/2016/04/13/why-facebook-is-going-all-in-on-chatbots.html**. It shows a Q&A. A session with David Marcus on why Facebook is going all in for chatbots.

O'Brien (2016b) provides a discussion of what chatbots can do for e-commerce. This presentation includes Amazon's Alexa, which is presented in section "Intelligent Personal Assistants and Robot Advisers". Mah (2016) discusses the increasing role of chatbots in marketing.

Chatbots are also used in advertising and marketing. Quoc (2016) provides 11 examples of conversational bots in 2016. These include Allo from Google, Slack, Operator Amazon's Echo, Snapchat Discover, Apple TV and Siri Magic, Telegram, Kik, and WeChat. WeChat provides a popular Chinese bot that enables you to:

- Hail a taxi
- Order food delivery
- Buy movie tickets
- Customize and order a pair of Nikes
- Send an order to the nearest Starbucks
- Track your daily fitness progress
- Shop Burberry's latest collection
- Book doctor's appointments
- Pay your water bill
- Host a business conference call
- And much more

For a list of bots, see **botlist.co/bots**

Example 1: LinkedIn
LinkedIn is introducing chatbots, which will conduct tasks such as comparing the calendars of people participating in meetings, and suggesting times and meeting places. For details, see CBS News (2016).

Example 2: Mastercard
Mastercard is launching two AI-backed massaging platforms: Mastercard bot for banks and Mastercard bot for merchants.

Knowledge Systems

These systems, which are presented in section "Knowledge (Expert) Systems", are computer programs that store knowledge, which the applications use to generate expert advice and/or solve problems. It also helps people verify communications and can make certain types of routine decisions.

SECTION 7.2 REVIEW QUESTIONS

1. Define artificial intelligence.
2. List some capabilities of AI.
3. What is the Turing test?
4. Define intelligent agents and list some of their capabilities.
5. Prepare a list of applications of intelligent agents (IA) in EC.
6. What is machine learning? How can it be used in EC?
7. Define robotics and explain its importance for EC.
8. Describe robotic systems.
9. What is natural language processing (NLP)? What are its two major formats?
10. Describe machine translation of languages. Why is it important in EC?
11. Describe chatbots and list some of their applications in EC.
12. What are knowledge systems?

7.3 RECENT AI APPLICATIONS IN E-COMMERCE

Since 2014, we have witnessed increasing numbers of AI applications in various EC activities. This increase is due to several reasons such as technological innovations, the widespread use of smartphones, the increased competition between retailers and e-tailers, and several success stories that show that AI-supported EC can provide strategic advantages. In this section, we provide several illustrative examples, after a general discussion about the potential benefits of AI in EC.

The AI Contribution to E-Commerce

As described earlier, AI enhanced EC since its inception. However, it is only now that we see a wave of powerful applications. Here is what the major technology companies do with AI:

- **Apple.** According to Fingas (2016), AI and augmented reality are core technologies in Apple's future. Apple is continuously improving Siri (its personal assistant robot; see section "The Internet of Things (IoT) and E-Commerce"). Apple has several other AI initiatives, including making the iPhone "smarter" (see Statt 2016).
- **Google.** Google is involved in several AI initiatives. One major effort is *Google Brain*, a secretive project that includes *machine learning*. We already mentioned the company's DeepMind in section "Introduction to Intelligent E-Commerce". Google believes that AI will be able to solve the world's biggest problems. O'Brien (2016a), a scientist at Google Brain, stresses that it "will take some smart humans to get it there."
- **Facebook.** Facebook's CEO is a great believer in AI. He is developing a personal assistant robot for his own use (section "The Internet of Things (IoT) and E-Commerce"). Facebook is working on several other projects related to advertising and customer service. Facebook says that its new AI can understand text with near-human accuracy.
- **IBM.** IBM pioneered the concept of *smart commerce* in 2013/2014 (e.g., see Taft 2014). At that time, they concentrated on big data and analytics. A major part was the use of *data mining technologies* (an AI product) for discovering hidden correlations. This enables a better *predictive analysis*, which is used in EC strategy and decision-making. Deep Blue was the powerful computer that defeated the world's chess champion in the 1990s. IBM is also known for its Watson, the supercomputer that won the Jeopardy game, and for its contribution to medical research. Watson is also used to psychoanalyze people from their tweets to help marketers.
- **Amazon.com.** This company pioneered the use of AI in the 1990s. The most well known are their book recommendation engines. Today, the company is experimenting or using AI in many activities of its e-tailing. Well known is the use of smart robots in the warehouse. The company is also using predictive analysis and machine learning to assess demand for its products. AI is also used for inventory management.

Many other companies are installing, or at least experimenting with, AI applications related to EC. For example, ViSenze of Singapore is a start-up that brings the benefits of AI to e-commerce users (mostly in Asia; see Russel 2016). In summary, it looks like AI is changing the "face" of e-commerce (e.g., Choudhury 2016).

Tverdohleb (2016) describes how AI is helping the world of e-commerce using a special platform called Deep Agent. AI is especially appealing to Internet start-ups and those interested in "deep learning." Several illustrative examples are presented next.

AI in E-Commerce: Some Illustrative Examples

Here are examples of recent applications:

Marketing and Advertising

AI is being used in many marketing and advertising online tasks such as:

- Predictive analytics and AI are used to customize and automate e-mail marketing campaigns (Insightly Blog 2015).
- ClickZ Intelligence (2013) lists the following areas: new customer experience, new product launching, programmatic advertising, content creation, and designing websites.

- Rossi (2016) describes three ways AI helps customers: improve search, help buyers to understand their preferences, and serve as a personal assistant to shoppers.
- Blog (2016) provides a list of 13 companies that use AI in marketing, advertising, and sales.
- 15 examples of AI in marketing are provided by Davis (2016), starting with product recommendation.
- Salesforce's AI Einstein Service facilitates sales transactions (see Womack 2016).
- Kohl (2016) describes the use of AI to boost customer engagement. This is especially important, since shopping is evolving to transactions, which will take place without human interaction (e.g., see IoT and section "Selective Demonstrations of IoT in Action").
- IBM's Watson is learning about people from their tweets. This will help companies predict consumer behavior, deciding what to offer and when (see details by Russell 2014).
- In general, AI is believed to have a big role in retailing's future (Arthur 2016).
- Chatbots are used extensively in marketing (Mah 2016).
- For using AI in e-auctions, watch the video at **youtube.com/watch?v=O65XJd7j2BE**.
- For a comprehensive discussion, see Sutton (2016).

Customer Service and Advice

Related to marketing is customer service. Chatbots (section "The Essentials of Artificial Intelligence") are used extensively to answer customers' questions (Friedman 2016).

Example: Chatbots Advising in Healthcare

As will be seen in section "Intelligent Personal Assistants and Robot Advisers", chatbots are used as the user–computer interface in personal assistants. One company that promotes chatbots in healthcare is Baidu of China. Baidu's *Melody* is an intelligent chatbot that can help patients to determine whether or not they should go to see a doctor. The dialog is currently text-based and the mode is questions and answers. The system is integrated with Baidu's *Doctor*, which lets patients ask doctors questions, make appointments, and search for health- and medical-related information. Melody gains her wisdom by pulling data from digitized material, including research papers and online forums. For details, see Larson (2016).

- Google's computers are using chatbots for its Google Cloud Platform to answer a customer's queries. This improves the efficiency of IBM's data centers (see Clark 2016b for details).
- Using AI (machine learning) and cloud computing enables smarter CRM, as demonstrated by Salesforce's Einstein (see Nicolaus 2016).

AI in B2B

AI applications in B2B are mostly in e-procurement (Clinton 2016), supply chain management (Chandra and Darbhe 2016), and Smart Robotics (see McMahon, undated).

Other Applications

Many other applications emerge:

- Applications in social networks (Smith 2014).
- Applications in travel (e.g., trip planning, Brady 2016). Examine **utip.com** and **eurovacations.com**).
- Robot advisers (see section "Intelligent Personal Assistants and Robot Advisers").
- AI in e-learning is in its initial development. For the future of AI in e-learning, see Smith (2016). However, some wonder if the industry is ready for this (e.g., see Taylor 2016).

Conclusion

There is increasing evidence that AI is transforming many businesses (see Pickup 2016 on how this is done). A major area in this transformation will be automation of many EC tasks and the replacement of humans with AI (is it a good or a bad thing?). See River Logic (2016).

SECTION 7.3 REVIEW QUESTIONS

1. What are the reasons for using AI in EC?
2. What are the major technology companies doing in this area?
3. How can AI assist in marketing?
4. How can AI assist in advertising?
5. What contributions can AI provide to customer service and CRM?
6. How can AI facilitate B2B?

7.4   KNOWLEDGE (EXPERT) SYSTEMS

A major derivative of AI is the knowledge system. Such a system has several e-commerce related applications. The major trust of such a system is the creation and use of knowledge.

The terms *knowledge systems and management* are frequently mentioned in discussions about smart EC. Why is this? To answer this question, you first need to understand what knowledge management is.

An Overview of Knowledge Management

Knowledge is one of the most important assets in any organization, and thus it is important to capture, store, secure, and reuse (share) it, and these are the major purposes of knowledge management. Thus, **knowledge management (KM)** refers to the process of capturing or creating knowledge, storing and protecting it, updating it constantly, disseminating it, and using it whenever necessary (see **en.wikipedia.org/wiki/Knowledge_management** and Milton and Lambe 2016).

Knowledge in organizations is collected from both external and internal sources. It can also be created by AI systems. It is then examined, interpreted, refined, and stored in what is called an *organizational knowledge base*, the repository for the enterprise's knowledge, or it can immediately be used in different applications. A major purpose of an organizational knowledge base is to allow for *knowledge sharing*.

Knowledge Management Types and Activities

Organizational knowledge is embedded in the following key resources: (1) human capital, which includes employee knowledge, competencies, intelligence, and creativity; (2) organizational capital, which includes stored organizational experiences (e.g., best practices, patents, manuals, teaching materials); (3) knowledge generated by AI systems; (4) customer and partner knowledge, which includes the experience of working with customers and business partners.

This organizational knowledge must be managed properly and leveraged through sharing and dissemination. This is the major purpose of KM, which has the following major tasks:

- **Create knowledge.** Knowledge is created as people gain more experience (e.g., trial and error) and education. Sometimes, external knowledge is brought in (e.g., provided by vendors and consultants).
- **Capture knowledge.** Existing knowledge must be identified and assembled. Remember that a considerable amount of knowledge is not documented, and it just dwells in people's memory.
- **Refine knowledge.** New knowledge must be placed in context so that it is actionable. This is why human insights (tacit qualities) must be captured along with explicit facts.
- **Store knowledge.** Useful knowledge must be stored into an easily retrievable format in a secured knowledge repository.
- **Update knowledge.** The knowledge must be kept current. It must be reviewed to verify that it is relevant and accurate; if not, it must be updated.
- **Disseminate knowledge.** Knowledge must be made available in a useful format to anyone in the organization who needs it and who is authorized to access it.

Fig. 7.3 Knowledge management cycle

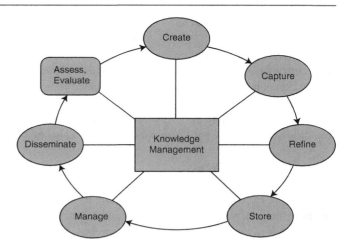

These tasks can be viewed as a cyclical process, as shown in Fig. 7.3. The objective of e-commerce is to automate KM activities as well as help in using the stored knowledge.

For a comprehensive list of KM activities and tools, see **en.wikipedia.org/wiki/Knowledge_management** and **kmworld.com**.

Knowledge Sharing

Knowledge is of limited value if not updated and shared. The ability to share and then distribute knowledge decreases its cost per user and increases its effectiveness. Shared knowledge can also decrease risk and uncertainty and facilitate problem solving. Knowledge is a major component in intelligent EC applications. An example of a knowledge-sharing system at Infosys Technologies is provided in Morin (2014).

How Is Knowledge Management Related to E-Commerce?

Organizations need knowledge, which is provided by KM, in order to better perform their tasks.

In the past, KM and EC initiatives were dealt with independently; however, now they are used together for mutual benefits.

Examples
According to Britt (2013), "E-commerce retailers are using knowledge management solutions to pull together purchasing orders, inventory, sales, and other transaction information, as well as to improve customer feedback and to enhance the overall e-commerce experience." Britt provides the following examples:

- Dog Is Good Inc. (a merchant of "canine-themed apparel") is using KM to help in the integration of EC subsystems (ordering, inventory, order fulfillment, accounting, and EC stores) using the offerings from NetSuite.
- Ideeli, Inc., an online daily flash retailer, uses KM analytics (ForeSee's Satisfaction Analytics) to learn about customer experiences from collected feedback.
- Ideeli, Inc. also uses KM analytics (ForeSee's mobile analytics solution) to identify the needs of frequent visitors (by segments on mobile devices). As a result, the company modified its e-commerce strategies.
- Retina-X Studios provides tracking and monitoring of activities on mobile phones, computing devices, etc. The KM system is used to improve the handling of EC chargebacks due to cancellation. The company turned to Avangate's e-commerce solution that cut costs and improved customer service.

For more on KM-enabling technologies and how they can be applied to business unit initiatives, see **kmworld.com** and **knowledgestorm.com**.

KM and Social Networks

A major venue of knowledge creation is in online communities, including social networks. This is done by *crowdsourcing* and customer and employee discussions and feedbacks. This area has several variations. One variety is limited within a single company. Knowledge can also be created by *user-generated content* (see Chap. 8) and in the "answer" function of some social networks.

Web 2.0 applications help aggregate corporate knowledge, facilitate communication and collaboration, and simplify the building of repositories of best practices, as demonstrated by the following example.

Example: IBM Jam Events

Since 2001, IBM has been using communities for online brainstorming sessions, idea generation, and problem solving. These sessions are called "Jam Events." According to their Web page, "IBM's Jams and other Web 2.0 collaborative mediums are opening up tremendous possibilities for collaborative innovation…" (**collaborationjam.com**). Each Jam has a different topic. For example, a large IBM online brainstorming session held, called the *Innovation Jam*, brought a community of over 150,000 employees from 104 countries and 67 companies to launch new IBM businesses (see **collaborationjam.com**).

Virtual meetings where IBM employees can participate in Innovation Jam launches were conducted in Second Life (SL). IBM's former CEO even created an avatar to represent himself. Besides business, recent topics that have been explored by IBM Jams include social issues. See **collaborationjam.com/IBMJam**. Other topics that have been explored are new technologies for water filtration, 3-D Internet, and branchless banking. For the history of IBM Jams, see **collaborationjam.com/IBMJam**.

Knowledge management is a major activity needed to create expert systems.

Expert Systems

An **expert system**, also referred to as **knowledge-based system**, is a computer system that uses knowledge to solve problems that require expertise and provide advice to nonexperts, usually in specific domains. Thus, it emulates the decision-making of human experts. It is considered a derivative of artificial intelligence. Knowledge required for this capability is stored in a *knowledge base* and organized there such that it can be disseminated to nonexpert users upon request. Expert systems (ES) are used extensively in many AI applications in EC (e.g., in product recommenders and in advisory systems).

The Major Components of an Expert System

The major components are illustrated in Fig. 7.4. They include:

- *Users*—who need the expertise
- *Human experts*—who provide the specific knowledge to the system

Fig. 7.4 The components and processes of expert systems

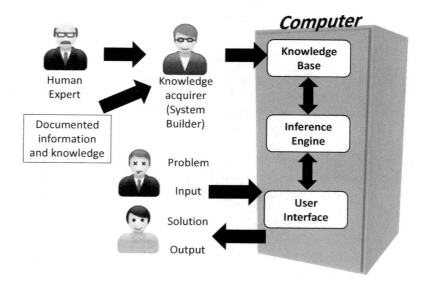

- *System builders*—who acquire the knowledge from expert(s) and documented sources
- *Knowledge base*—the repository where the acquired knowledge is organized, frequently as if then rules and stored
- *Inference engine*—the program that matches the users' requests with computerized answers (that are derived from the rules)
- *User interface*—the interface that enables the user–machine communication. Users can select from several input–output communication modes (written, voice, images)
- *Explanation mechanism*—provides the logic of the system output

For details, see **en.wikibooks.org/wiki/Expert_Systems/Components_of_Expert_Systems**.

The Process and Capabilities of Expert Systems

Knowledge of specific domain, or expertise, resides with human experts and/or in documented sources. This knowledge is collected by a knowledge acquirer, who uses it to program the system (or she/he asks a system builder to do it).

The knowledge is stored in a knowledge base where it is organized. This knowledge can be in the "cloud," namely, it can be shared by many users. When a user interacts with the system, a dialog between the user and the inference engine takes place. The inference engine then selects the appropriate knowledge (e.g., rules) and, at the end of a Q&A dialog, provides a solution or advice. Some systems have an explanation mechanism that shows the reasoning process (e.g., all the rules used).

- Analyzing symptoms
- Identifying problems
- Interpreting user input
- Driving solutions and advices
- Instructing and assisting humans in decision-making
- Displaying and demonstrating processes
- Predicting results
- Justifying conclusions, providing explanations

Expert systems have the following major capabilities:

For details, see Beard (2014) and **en.wikipedia.org/wiki/Expert_system**.

These capabilities enable many applications. However, remember, the quality of the output is highly dependent on the quality of the knowledge and the input of the symptoms provided by the user.

Knowledge-Based System

Expert systems are often used synonymously with the *knowledge-based system*. However, some distinguish between the two. According to **en.wikipedia.org/wiki/knowledge-based_systems**, "Expert system refers to the type of task the system is trying to solve, to replace or aid a human expert in a complete task. Knowledge-based system refers to the architecture of the system, that it represents knowledge explicitly rather than as procedural code. While the earliest knowledge-based system were almost all expert systems, the same tools and architectures can and have since been used for a whole host of other types of systems. That is, virtually all expert systems are knowledge-based systems, but many knowledge-based systems are not expert systems."

There are a large number of applications of knowledge-based and expert systems. For example, the chatbots described earlier usually use expert systems to generate their output. Similarly, the virtual personal assistants described in section "The Internet of Things (IoT) and E-Commerce" are equipped with knowledge-based systems and so is the Allstate case (see Case 7.1). In summary, expert systems and knowledge-based systems provide a quick, consistent, and inexpensive expertise to nonexperts as well as enable sharing knowledge in a fast and economic way.

CASE 7.1
EC APPLICATION
ALLSTATE IS USING KNOWLEDGE SYSTEMS

Allstate Corp. is using a virtual assistant to help call center employees. Allstate insurance business has been growing rapidly, supplemented by *Allstate Business Insurance* that targets small businesses with less than 50 employees.

The Problem

Allstate agents tried to develop expertise in the many types of small businesses they encounter. The agents tried to be qualified as trusted advisors, that is, to make themselves experts in the different industries and be more "customer centric rather than product centric." The agents needed help to get up to speed in the new role. With 10,000 exclusive agents and 2000 independent ones, this was not a simple task. To deal with the many calls received from customers, the agents needed time to research the answers to questions customers ask, and if they did not know the answers, call the Allstate call center for advice. The result was that customers and the agents wasted time. Instead of dealing only with difficult issues, the agents called the center even for small issues; thus, the center was bogged down by training the agents all the time.

The Solution

The company decided to construct a knowledge-based system that would be able to provide quick answers to the agents, even during the time they are working with customer clients. Allstate acquired such a system from an AI vendor, called Earley Information Science. The system acts as an intelligent virtual assistant that helps to make information accessible and usable. To build the system, the vendor collected information from the call center employees and from the sales and marketing team agents. This helps the AI vendor identify large amounts of "common scenarios" (such as providing proof of insurance for contractors). For each scenario, the AI vendor then developed step-by-step instructions. The total knowledge then was packaged in a knowledge system for the agents to use when needed.

The Results

The knowledge system, known as the *Allstate Business Insurance Expert (ABIe)*, a Web-based, real-time system, is available as to all the company's agents. When logged in, the agents see an avatar with which they can communicate. According to PRWeb, "ABIe has become the primary communications channel for Allstate to engage with its agents and ensures they always have the most accurate and up-to-date information available. As a result, the company has been able to dramatically reduce its call center call volume while improving the efficiency and performance of its agents." The impact on the growth of commercial policy sales and on the operational efficiency of the business since the arrival of ABIe has been significant. In addition, the agents are becoming self-sufficient in knowledge and building skills and are more productive. The system was recognized by KMWorld as a "leader in knowledge management."

    Source: Based on McCooey (2016) and **prweb.com/printer/13154986.htm**

Questions for the Case

1. Explain why this is an intelligent advisory system.
2. How is the knowledge based used?
3. How is time saved by the sales agents?
4. How is time saved by the call center employees?
5. Read the "Allstate case study summary" at **earley.com/knowledge/case-studies/allstate's-intelligent-agent-reduces-call-center-traffic-and-provides-help** and analyze the impact on Allstate.

In section "Intelligent Personal Assistants and Robot Advisers", we will introduce the intelligent personal assistants who use expert systems to generate intelligent answers to queries.

SECTION 7.4 REVIEW QUESTIONS

1. Define knowledge management (KM).
2. Describe the major activities of KM and its cyclical process.
3. Describe the relationships between KM, EC, and social networks.
4. Define expert systems.
5. List and briefly describe the major components of expert systems.
6. Describe the process of operating an expert system.
7. List the major capabilities of expert systems.
8. Distinguish between expert systems and a knowledge-based system.

7.5 INTELLIGENT PERSONAL ASSISTANTS AND ROBOT ADVISERS

In the previous sections, we introduced you to chatbots, machines with which you can conduct limited conversations and which are used mostly for providing information or conducting a simple Q&A dialog with users. Chatbots and similar machines have been improved over time. For example, several hospitals employ robot receptionists to direct patients to their place of treatment. Zora Robotics created a robot named Nao to act as a chatting companion for the sick elderly, offering it as a form of therapy for those suffering from dementia.

The coming generations of the above-cited machines are much more intelligent. Their knowledge bases are more capable and frequently maintained centrally, in the "cloud," which makes it more economical for a large amount of users. Users can get even complex assistance and advice from them. These assistants are known as **intelligent personal assistants** which help people to improve their work or their lifestyle. In this section, we will provide you with some interesting applications. The first set of applications involves virtual personal assistants, notably Amazon's Alexa and Apple's Siri. The second set is about personal robots, who act mostly as advisers on specific topics (e.g., investments).

Amazon's Alexa

Of the several virtual personal assistants, the one considered the best (in 2016) is Alexa. Alexa was developed to compete with Apple's Siri, and it turned to be a superior product. (See Fig. 7.5.)

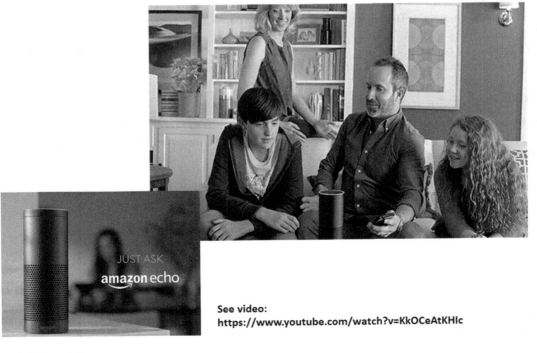

See video:
https://www.youtube.com/watch?v=KkOCeAtKHlc

Fig. 7.5 Amazon's Echo and Alexa

Amazon Alexa is a cloud-based intelligent personal voice assistant product that can do many things such as:

- Answer questions in several domains
- Control your smartphone operations by voice commands
- Provide real-time weather and traffic updates
- Control smart home (Section 7.6) appliances and devices using itself as a home automation hub
- Make to-do lists
- Arrange music Playbox
- Set your alarms
- Play audio books for you
- Control home automation devices
- Analyze shopping lists

To see how Alexa works, watch the 3:55 min video: **youtube.com/watch?v=KkOCeAtKHIc**.

Alexa Skills

In addition to the standard (native) capabilities listed above, people can use Alexa apps (referred to as skills) to download customized capabilities to Alexa (via your smartphone). *Skills* are intended to teach Alexa something new.

Examples of Skills Apps

- Call an Uber for you and let you know the cost.
- Order a pizza (e.g., from Domino).
- Provide financial advice from Capital One.
- Start your Hyundai Genesis car from your house (Korosec 2016).

These skills are provided by third-party vendors; they require invocation commands to activate.

For example, you need to tell Alexa: "Alexa, call Uber to pick me up at my office at 4:30 pm." For more on Amazon's Alexa, see Crist (2016); for its benefits, see Reisinger (2016).

Alexa is equipped with NLP (section "Recent AI Applications in E-Commerce") user interface, so all you need to activate it is to provide a voice command. This is done by combining the Alexa software with an intelligent speaker called Echo.

Voice Interface and Speakers in Alexa

Amazon has a family of three types of speakers for Alexa: Echo, Dot, and Tag. Alexa can also be accessed by Fire TV line and by some non-Amazon devices. For the relationship of Alexa and Echo, see Gikas (2016).

Amazon Echo

Amazon Echo is a hands-free intelligent wireless speaker that is controlled by voice. It is the hardware part of Alexa, so the two operate hand in hand. Echo is always on, always listening. When Echo hears your questions, commands, or requests, it will send the audio up to the "cloud." From there, Amazon's servers will match a respond to the questions, delivering it to Alexa to tell it to you.

Amazon Echo Dot

Amazon Echo Dot is the "little brother" of Echo. It offers full Alexa functionality, but it only has one very small speaker inside. It can be linked to any existing speaker systems to provide an Echo-like experience.

Amazon Echo Tap

Amazon Echo Tap is another "little brother" of Echo that can be used on the go. It is completely wireless and portable, and it is charged via a charging dock.

Both Dot and Tap are less expensive than Echo, but offer less functionalities and quality. However, if you already have good home speakers, you can use Dot.

For a discussion about the three speakers, see Trusted Reviews at **trustedreviews.com/news/amazon-echo-vs-amazon-dot-vs-amazon-tap-difference**.

Apple's Siri

Siri (short for Speech Interpretation and Recognition Interface) is an intelligent virtual personal assistant and knowledge navigator. It is a part of Apple's several operating systems. According to **en.wikipedia.org/wiki/Siri**, Siri can "answer questions, make recommendations and perform action by delegating requests to a set of *Web services*. The software, both in its original version and as an iOS feature, adapts to the user's individual language usage and individual searches (preferences) with continuing use, and returns results that are individualized."

Siri can be integrated into Apple's *Siri Remote*. Using CarPlay, Siri is available in some car models, where it can be controlled by iPhones (5 and higher).

Viv

In 2016 Dag Kittlaus, the creator of Siri, introduced its Viv, "an intelligent Interface for everything." Viv is expected to be the next generation of intelligent virtual interactions (see Matney 2016 for details). In contrast with Siri, the Viv as a platform is open to all developers (third-party ecosystem products). Viv is now a Samsung Company. Samsung plans to launch its own personal assistant with the Galaxy S8.

Other Personal Assistants

Several other companies have virtual personal assistants. For example, Google Home (see Kelly 2016) and Microsoft Cortana are well known. In September 2016, Microsoft combined Cortana and Bing (see Hachman 2016).

Facebook and Its CEO

Mark Zuckerberg, Facebook's CEO, is busy perfecting its own virtual assistant. For details see Ulamoff (2016). Initially, the personal assistant will help Mark to run his home (e.g., follow commands related to music and home appliances operations) and do his work.

IBM Watson

Probably the smartest virtual personal assistant is IBM Watson. It costs billions of dollars. However, its services can be purchased by organizations, paying back some of the expense. The machine can understand and speak eight different languages. It can read close to a billion (1000 million) pages each second. It can learn, understand, reason, and interact. It is built with 50 different AI technologies ranging from NLP to machine vision. It contains a powerful analytical capability. Watson can be accessed via the Web—it is a "cloud" utility. IBM works with several hundred developers in 36 countries to create the necessary knowledge bases for more and more applications. Here are some examples:

- Macy's developed a service to help customers navigate its stores while they shop. Using location-based software, the app knows where you are in the store. Customers can ask questions regarding products and services in the stores. Then, they get a customized response from "Macy's On Call."
- Watson can help physicians to make quicker diagnosis and suggest the best treatment using Medical Advisor. It can analyze images faster and look for things that physicians may miss. Watson already is used extensively in India, where there is a large shortage of doctors.
- Deep Thunder provides accurate weather-forecasting service.
- Hilton Hotels is using Watson-based "Connie robot" in the front desks of their hotels. The service is improving and in experiments did a superb job.
- Clark (2016a) reports that one billion people will use Watson by 2018. This is due in part because IBM Watson is coming to the iPhone (DeNisco 2016).

For more, see Noyes (2016).

Alfie: Sears Voice-Controlled Shopping Assistant

Alfie is a Kenmore-branded device similar to Alexa, but less capable and much cheaper. According to Kenmore **kenmore. com/products/Kenmore-alfie-voice-controlled-intelligent-shopper**, all you need to do is to connect to your Wi-Fi, and you will be able to:

- "**Personal Shopping**: Get what you want, product reviews you require, prices you approve and delivery to your liking.
- **Groceries**: Shop item by item, schedule reorders, or build a shopping list. Perishable grocery delivery available in selected areas.
- **Perfect gifts**: Describe the recipient and Alfie does the shopping for you, saving time.
- **Gets Smarter**: Alfie learns your needs and preferences the more you use it.
- **Human Touch**: Alfie is backed by real human intelligence, not just computer processing. Avoid virtual assistant frustrations. Alfie works hard to offer great solutions. Response time can vary depending on the request.
- **Kenmore Alfie App**: Available for free download on App Store and Google Play Store.
- **Use Alfie anywhere in your home**: Alfie uses your home Wi-Fi network and can be placed anywhere with its convenient rechargeable battery with built in magnetic base."

Find out more at **alfietech.com**. This site includes helpful manuals, instruction videos, FAQs, and troubleshooting and guides.

Personal Robots

Built on the capabilities of chatbots and personal assistants, we see *personal robots* coming to the world. Some of these robots can also do physical tasks. For example, while chatbots are used to provide information as receptionists and in airports as guides, personal robots can improve the service. For example, see Application Case 7.2.

APPLICATION CASE 7.2
EC APPLICATION
AUTONOMOUS' PERSONAL ROBOT

You do not need to be jealous of Mark Zuckerberg, the CEO of Facebook, for having his own personal assistant. You can buy one if you can afford to pay $1499. The expense can be considered as a business expense for tax purposes, if you use your robot to help you at work. Looking at its capabilities, the personal assistant can be of considerable help.

The Personal Robot of Autonomous

It is called a **personal robots**, this assistant (**autonomous.ai/personal-robot**) is designed to live with its owner/s. The personal robot, according to the vendor, is able to:

- Recognize your face.
- Know your mood.
- Understand what you say.
- Know what you really mean.
- Learn and get smarter every day.
- Manage the smart/connected home and its appliances (described in section "Selective Demonstrations of IoT in Action").
- Keep your home secure and save on energy.
- Buy your dinner and automatically track your calorie intake.
- Call you a cab.
- Help with your shopping.

A significantly less expensive solution is to buy Amazon's Alexa, which provides you with many of the above capabilities.

Questions for the Case

1. Why do people need a personal robot?
2. Compare Autonomous' personal robot with Amazon's Alexa/Echo.
3. Both Autonomous' robot and Alexa can help with online shopping. Find out how they do it.

Robo Advisors

The personal assistants described earlier can provide you with information and rudimentary advice. However, now there are robots that can provide you with much more complex advice in specific domains.

Example: Robo Financial Advisors

According to A.T. Kearney's survey (Reported by Regan 2015), **robo advisors** are defined as online providers that offer automated, low-cost, *investment advisory* services through mobile platforms. The robo advisors machine uses algorithms that allocate, deploy, rebalance, and trade investments. Once you enroll for the robo service, you enter your investment objectives and references using advanced AI algorithms. Then, the robo will offer *alternative personalized* investment options for you to choose from (this is different from investing in a mutual funds or ETFs that are not personalized). Conducting a dialog with the robot, the machine will refine your investment portfolio. This is all done digitally without you having to talk to a live person.

You may wonder how good the advice is. The answer is that it will depend on the knowledge base of the robot, on the type of investment, on the interference engine of the machine, etc. However, you need to remember that the robots are not biased and they are consistent. They may prove to be even better than humans at one of the most important aspects in investment advising: know how to legally minimize the related tax. This implies that institutional-grade tax-loss harvesting is now within the reach of all investors.

It is known that the vast majority of buy and sell decision of stocks, trading in the major exchanges, for financial institutions, are made by computers. However, computers can manage individual people's accounts, as well.

For the best robo advisors, see Bundrick (2015) and O'Shea (2016). For more, see **investorjunkie.com/35919/robo-advisors**. For a comprehensive coverage of robo advisors in finance and investment, including the major companies in the advisory industry, see McClellan (2016).

An emerging commercial robo advisor was developed at Cornell University under the name Gsphere.

Regan (2015) reports that the robo advisors business could reach $2 billion a year by 2020.

In addition to investment advisors, there are several other types of robo advisors, ranging from travel to medicine to legal.

A closing note: While current robo advisors are impersonal, future robots will have a personality. Nadine is an experimental social robot that is being developed in Singapore, and it has personality (see **upi.com/Science_News/2015/30/ New-social-robot-Nadine-has-a-personality**.

SECTION 7.5 REVIEW QUESTIONS

1. Describe an intelligent virtual personal assistant.
2. Describe the capabilities of Amazon Alexa.
3. Relate Amazon's Alexa to Echo.
4. Describe Echo Dot and Tap.
5. Describe Apple's Siri.
6. Define personal robots.
7. Explain how robo advisors for investment work.
8. Describe IBM Watson.

7.6 THE INTERNET OF THINGS AND E-COMMERCE

The topic of the Internet of things (IoT) has been receiving significant attention since 2014. While its applications are still emerging, it has a tremendous potential for creating value and innovations in many fields, including e-commerce (e.g., see Manyika et al. 2015). In this section, we present the essentials of IoT. Some evolving applications that are related to e-commerce are described in section "Selective Demonstrations of IoT in Action". For the impact of IoT on e-commerce, see Constantinou and Sellebraten (2015) and Mehra (2015). For existing applications, see Karwatka (2015).

The Essentials of IoT

The **Internet of things (IoT)** is an evolving term with several definitions. In general, the IoT refers to a situation where many objects (people, animals, items) with embedded microprocessors are connected mostly wirelessly to the Internet. That is, it uses *ubiquitous computing*. Analysts predict that by the year 2020, there will be more than 50 billion devices connected to the Internet, creating the backbone of the IoT. The challenges and opportunities of this disruptive technology are discussed in an interview with Peter Utzschneider, the vice president of product management for Java at Oracle (see Kvita 2014). In addition, you can join the conversations at **iotcommunity.net**. For an overview, see Nagpure (2016). For Intel's vision for fully connected world, see Murray (2016).

Embedding computers and other devices into items everywhere and connecting all devices to the Internet permits extensive communication and collaboration between users and items (e.g., see Zuora 2015). This kind of interaction opens the door to many applications. For business applications of the Internet of things, see Jamthe (2016). In addition, check the "Internet of Things Consortium" (**iofthings.org**) and their annual conferences. For an infographic and a guide, see **intel.com/content/www/us/internet-of-things/infographics/guide-to-iot.html**. An interesting example is provided in the closing case of this chapter.

Definitions and Characteristics

There are many definitions of IoT. Wikipedia provides this definition: "*The Internet of Things* (IoT) is the network of physical objects-devices, vehicles, buildings, and other items embedded with electronics, software, sensors, and network connectivity--that enables these objects to collect and exchange data. The Internet of things allows objects to be sensed and controlled remotely across existing network infrastructure, creating opportunities for more direct integration of the physical world into computer-based systems, and resulting in improved efficiency, accuracy, and economic benefit; when IoT is augmented with sensors and actuators, the technology becomes an instance of the more general class of cyber-physical systems, which also encompasses technologies such as smart grids, smart homes, intelligent transportation, and smart cities. Each thing is uniquely identifiable through its embedded computing system but is able to interoperate within the existing Internet infrastructure."

According to Miller (2015), these are the major characteristics of the Internet: IoT is a connected ecosystem in which:

- Large numbers of objects (things) can be connected.
- Each thing has a unique definition (IP address).
- Ability to receive, send, and store data, automatically.
- Delivered mostly over the wireless Internet.
- Built upon machine to machine (M2M) communication.

The Structure of IoT Applications

Things in IoT refers to a variety of objects and devices ranging from cars and home appliances to medical devices, computers, fitness tracers, hardware, software, data, sensors, and much more. Connecting "things" and allowing them to communicate is a necessary capability of an IoT application; but for more sophisticated applications, we need additional components: a control system and a business model. The IoT enables the "things" to sense or be sensed wirelessly across the network (see the closing case). A non-Internet example will be a temperature control system in a room. Another non-Internet example is a traffic light at intersections of roads where cameras photograph the number of cars coming from each direction and a control system adjusts the time for changing the lights according to programmed rules. Later on, we will introduce some Internet-based applications.

The Major Benefits of IoT

The major objective of IoT systems is to improve productivity, quality, speed, and the quality of life.

According to Basu and Didyala (2014) and Miller (2015), the major benefits of IoT are:

- Creates new revenue stream.
- Optimizes asset utilization.
- Improves sustainability.
- Improves workers' productivity.
- The Internet of things is changing and improving everything (McCafferty 2015).
- Systems will anticipate our needs.
- People will make smarter decisions/purchases.
- Greater accuracy.
- Identifies problems quickly (even before they occur).
- Reduces cost by automating processes.
- Instant information availability.
- Quick and inexpensive tracking.
- Expedites problem resolution and recovery.
- Supports facility integration.

The Drivers of IoT

The following are the major drivers of IoT:

- 50 to75 billion "things" may be connected (by 2020–2025).
- Connected autonomous "things"/systems (e.g., cars) are all over the IoT.
- Broadband Internet is more widely available and increasing with time.
- Cost of connecting devices is decreasing.
- More devices are created (via innovation) and they are interconnected (e.g., see Fenwick 2016).
- More sensors are built into devices.
- Smartphones' penetration is skyrocketing.
- Wearable devices are all over.
- Speed of moving data is increasing, to 60HTz.
- Protocols are developing for IoT (e.g., WiGig).
- Customer expectations are on the rise.

How the IoT Works

The following is a comprehensive process for IoT. In many cases, IoT follows only portions of this process.

The process is explained in Fig. 7.6. The Internet ecosystem (top of the figure) includes a large number of things. Sensors and other devices collect information from the ecosystem. This information can be displayed, stored, and/or processed (including data mining). This analysis converts the information into knowledge and/or intelligence. Machine learning may help in turning the knowledge into decision support (made by people and/or machines), which is evidenced by some actions.

The generated decisions can help in creating innovative applications, new business models, and improvements in business processes. These result in "actions," which may impact the original scenario other things.

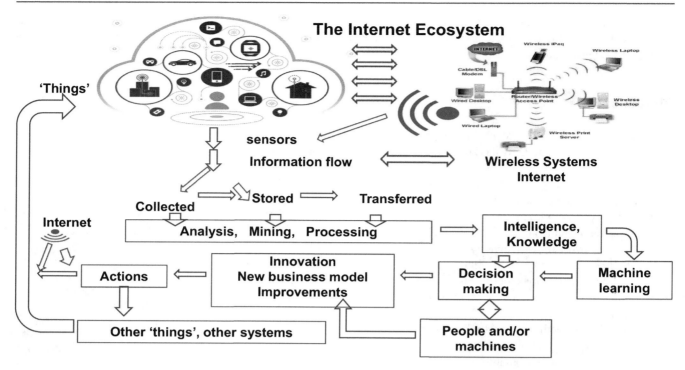

Fig. 7.6 How the IoT works

Fig. 7.7 Google's self-driving car

Note that most of the existing applications are in the upper part of the figure, which is called "sensor-to-insight," meaning opt to the creation of, knowledge, or to the delivery of new information. However, now, the focus is moving to the entire cycle, i.e., *sensor-to-action* (see Ricktun 2016).

The IoT may generate huge amount of data (big data) that needs to be analyzed by various business intelligence methods, including *deep analytics*.

Some Issues in Implementing the IoT

The following are several important issues:

- **Security**. Given that the Internet is not well secured, applying IoT requires special security measures. Perkins (2016) summarizes the situation as follow: "IoT creates a pervasive digital presence connecting organizations and society as a whole. New actors include data scientists; external integrators; and exposed endpoints. Security decision-makers must embrace fundamental principles of risk and resilience to drive change." For details see **gartner.com/analyst/25748**.

- **Connecting the silos of data**. There are millions of silos of data on the Internet, and many of them need to be interconnected. This issue is known as the need for a "fabric" and the need for connectivity. This can be a complex issue for applications that involve many different silos belonging to different organizations. For a discussion and some solutions, see Lucero (2015) and **machineshop.io/blog/the-fabric-of-the-internet-of-things**.
- **Preparing existing IT architectures and operating models for IoT can be a complex issue in many organizations.** For a complete analysis and guide, see Deichmann, et al. (2015).

SECTION 7.6 REVIEW QUESTIONS

1. Define the Internet of things.
2. Describe its major components.
3. List the major drivers of the IoT.
4. Explain how the IoT works using Fig. 7.6.
5. Describe the major issues in implementing the IoT.

7.7   SELECTIVE DEMONSTRATIONS OF IOT IN ACTION

We start with a well-known example. Your refrigerator can sense the quantity of food and texts you when inventory is low (sensor-to-insight). One day the fridge will be able to place an order for items that need replenishment, pay for them, and arrange delivery (sensor-to-action).

A Sampler of Existing Applications

The following examples are IoT applications related to e-commerce, based on Koufopoulos (2015):

- **Hilton Hotel.** Guests can check in directly to their rooms with their smartphones (no check-in lobby is needed; no keys are needed). Other hotel chains follow suit.
- **Ford.** Users can connect to apps by voice. Coming up: autopay for gas and preorder from Ford's cars at Starbucks.
- **Tesla.** Tesla's software autonomously schedules a valet to pick up a car and drives it to Tesla's facility when a need for repair or service arises.
- **Johnnie Walker.** The whiskey company connected 100,000 whiskey bottles to the Internet for Brazil's Father's Day. Using smart labeling, buyers can create a personalized video. Fathers can share the videos on social networks. Fathers get promotions to buy the whiskey if they like it.
- **Apple.** Enables users of iPhone, Apple Watch, and HomeKit with Apple Pay to streamline shopping.
- **Starbucks Clover Net in the Cloud.** This system connects coffee brewers to customers' preferences. The system also monitors employee's performance, improves recipes, tracks consumption patterns, and more.

A large number of consumer applications of the IoT are reported by Jamthe (2016) and Miller (2015). Here is another example:

Nest: A Google Company

A leading manufacturer of IoT applications is Google's Nest. The company is a producer of programmable self-learning, sensor-driven, Wi-Fi-enabled products. In spring 2016, the company had three products:

- **The learning thermostat.** The device learns what temperature and humidity level people like and controls the air conditioner/heater accordingly. The company claims it has an average savings of 13% of energy, which is good enough to pay for the device in 2 years; see **nest.com/thermostat/meet-nest-thermostat/?alt=3**.
- **Smoke detector and alarm.** This device tests itself automatically and lasts for about a decade. It is controlled from a smartphone. For details, see **nest.com/smoke-co-alarm/meet-nest-protect**.

- **Nest.com.** It is a webcam-based system that enables you to see from your smartphone or your desktop computer what is going on in your home when you are away. The system turns itself on automatically when nobody is at home. You can monitor your pets, babies, etc. There is a recorder that allows you to go back in time. For details, see **nest.com/camera/ meet-nest-cam**. For how Nest can use your phone to find out when you have left your house, see Kastrenakes (2016).

For more on Nest, see **en.wikipedia.org/wiki/Nest_Labs**.

Many companies are experimenting with IoT products for retailing (B2C); for B2B operations; for transportation, logistics, and factory warehousing; and more. For details, see Miller (2015) and Jamthe (2016).

Note: For many case studies and examples of the IoT, see **ptc.com/internet-of-things/customer-success**, **divante.co/ blog/internet-e-commerce**, Greengard (2016b), and Kuntz and Becker (2015).

Of all the consumer-related products, three are well known: smart homes and appliances, smart cars, and smart cities.

Smart Homes and Appliances

In a **smart home**, the appliances such as computers, refrigerators, washers, dryers, lights, air conditioners, heaters, televisions, and security systems are interconnected and can be controlled remotely by smartphones via the Internet. For an overview, see **smarthomeenergy.co.uk/what-smart-home** and Miller (2015).

In the United States, thousands of homes are already connected to such systems and other countries are following. Currently, smart home systems support a number of different tasks:

- **Lighting.** Users can manage their home lighting from wherever they are.
- **Energy management.** Home heating and cooling systems can be controlled via remote to adjust the thermostat in the house (e.g., Nest **nest.com/works-with-nest**).
- **Water control.** WaterCop (**watercop.com**) is a system that reduces water damage by monitoring leaking water via a sensor, which sends a signal to the valve, causing the valve to close.
- **Home entertainment.** Audio and video equipment can be programmed to respond to a remote control device. For instance, a Wi-Fi-based remote control for a stereo system located in the family room can command the system to play on speakers installed anywhere else in the house. Home automation performs for the user all from one remote and all from one button.
- **Home security and safety.** Home security and safety systems can be programmed to alert you to a security-related event on your property. Home security can also be supported by cameras, so you can remotely view your property in real time. Sensors can be used at home to detect intruders, keep an eye on working appliances, and much more.

Example: iHealthHome

Security measures are common in assisted living facilities in senior communities and for seniors who live independently. For example, the iHealthHome Touchscreen system collects data and communicates with the company's software. According to their website, it is a comprehensive monitoring and communication system for professional caregivers and independent living communities. Family caregivers and physicians are given remote access to the patient's health data. Using this technology, the iHealthHome program reminds seniors of their daily appointments, makes the Internet useful, keeps their mind occupied, and much more. iHealthHome also reminds seniors to take their medicine, monitor their blood pressure, and stay in touch with their caregiver.

More on Smart Appliances

According to **smartgrid.gov**, a smart appliance is "an appliance that includes the intelligence and communications to be automatic or remote-controlled based on user preferences or external signals, from a utility or third-party energy service provider. A *smart appliance* may utilize a *Home Area Network* to communicate with other devices in the customer's premise, or other channels to communicate with utility systems."

McGrath (2016) provides an overview of smart appliances that includes all coming appliances from Haier (a large China-based manufacturer). The company wants everything in a house to communicate, even across other device makers. Examples are smart refrigerators, air conditioners, and washers. The company offers a control board for all appliances, regardless of the manufacturers. Apple is working on a single control for all smart appliances in a home (Heater 2016).

New Home Appliances in CES 2016

The following new smart appliances were exhibited in the CES show in Las Vegas in January 2016 (per Morris 2016).

- **Samsung smart fridge.** Cameras check content, and sensors check temperature and humidity.
- **Gourmet Robotic Cooker.** It does work for you.
- **10-in-1 device for your kitchen.** Stirring food: stir-fry, scrambled eggs, etc. Also choose ten cooking style: baking, sauce making, etc.
- **LG HOM-BOT Turbo+.** It lets you specify an area in your home that needs special attention. A camera lets you monitor your home remotely while you are away (one similar to Google's Nest).
- **Haier R2D2 refrigerator.** According to Morris (2016), "Is this the most practical refrigerator at CES? Of course not, but it's certainly the one with the most entertainment value. It's a very authentic replica of Star Wars' most famous droid, with authentic light and sound effect. It'll hold a six-pack of your beverage of choice and will bring the drinks to you (with a top speed of 0.62 miles per hour). It also has a built-in projector, allowing you to watch films as you enjoy your drink."
- **Whirlpool's smart top load washer.** A fully automated machine with smart controls. It also saves energy and even encourages philanthropy by sending a small amount of money to "Habitat for Humanity," each time you load your washer. The company also offers a smart dryer.
- **LG LDT8786ST dishwasher.** The machine's camera's sensors keep track of what has already been cleaned in order to save water. In addition, it gives you flexibility in operations.

Cericola (2016) noticed the following smart home trends for 2016 at the CES conference:

- Using the TV as a smart hub for the home appliances is coming from Samsung.
- Dolby Atmos products include speakers, receivers, and other entertainment items.
- DIY home smart security cameras (e.g., it makes sure it is not just the cat before alerting the police).
- Water controls for faucets, sprinklers, and flood detectors. In addition, a robot, which will teach you how to save water indoors (**hydro.fr/en**).

For details and references, see Cericola (2016).

For more about home automation, see **smarthome.com/sh-learning-center-what-can-i-control.html**. To see the various apps used for home control, see **smarthome.com/android_apps.html**.

Smart Cities

The idea of smart cities took off around 2007 when IBM launched their Smart Planet project and Cisco began its Smart Cities and Communities program. The idea is that, in **smart cities**, digital technologies (mostly mobile-based) facilitate better public services for citizens, better utilization of resources, and less negative environmental impact. For resources, see **ec. europa.eu/digital-agenda/en/about-smart-cities**. Townsend (2013) provides a broad historical look and coverage of the technologies. In an overview of his book, he provides the following examples: "In Zaragoza, Spain, a 'citizen card' can get you on the free city-wide Wi-Fi network, unlock a bike share, check a book out of the library, and pay for your bus ride home. In New York, a guerrilla group of citizen-scientists installed sensors in local sewers to alert you when storm water runoff overwhelms the system, dumping waste into local waterways." According to Editors (2015), smart cities will use 1.6 billion connected things in 2016. For more on smart cities, see Schwartz (2015) and Hean (2015). In addition, watch the video "Cisco Bets Big on 'Smart Cities'" at **money.cnn.com/video/technology/2016/03/21/cisco-ceo-smart-cities.cnnmoney**. Finally, in a smart city, you can find smart campuses, as in Singapore (see Kwang 2016 and Lacy 2016).

In many countries, governments and others (e.g., Google) are developing smart city applications. For example, India is planning to develop 100 smart cities (see **enterpriseinnovation.net/article/india-eyes-development-100-smart-cities-1301232910**).

Related to smart cities are smart factories (Libelium 2015). In addition, in smart cities, one will be able to find connected and self-driven cars (see Hamblen 2016 and our next section).

Smart Cars (Self-Driven)

Smart cars, also known as **driverless cars**, robot-driven cars, self-driving cars, and autonomous cars, are already on the roads in several places. The concept was initiated by Google (named Google Chauffeur), and it is becoming a reality, with several states in the United States getting ready to allow them on the road. These cars are electric, and they can create a revolution by their ability to reduce emissions, accidents, and traffic jams (e.g., see Neckermann 2015 and Tokuaka 2016). Greenough (2015) estimated ten million such cars to be on the road in the United States by 2020. Thus far, these cars are being tested in several cities worldwide.

The cars have sensor systems that may prevent collisions, and the cars can be completely autonomous. (Today, they still include a human safety driver.) Among the many implementation issues are legal issues, cost, privacy invasion, safety, and more.

Despite these issues, several car manufacturers are ready to sell such cars soon (e.g., BMW, Mercedes, Ford, GM, Tesla, and—of course—Google). For more information, see Bridges (2015).

In addition to passenger cars, we see new developments related to other vehicles. For example, self-driving buses are new in Finland. Here are some more:

- Uber and other ride-sharing companies plan for self-driving cars (Mitchell and Lien 2016).
- Mail is delivered to the home **uspsoig.gov/blog/no-driver-needed**.
- Driverless buses are being tested in Finland. Watch **money.cnn.com/video/technology/2016/08/18/self-driving-buses-hit-the-road-in-helsinki.cnnmoney** by self-driving buses (McFarland 2016).
- Self-driving taxis operate in Singapore (Watts 2016).

Note: Driverless cars are closer to getting the US green light (Levin (2016)).

SECTION 7.7 REVIEW QUESTIONS

1. Provide a list of five new IoT applications with a brief description.
2. Describe the IoT for home security and appliances.
3. List all home appliances in a smart home.
4. How can one control all smart appliances?
5. Describe smart cities.
6. What are self-driving cars? How are they related to the IoT?

MANAGERIAL ISSUES

1. **How can one justify the investment in AI systems?** Like the justification of any investment, one should assess the costs and benefits (Chap. 14). The problem is that some of the benefits are intangible and some of the future benefits and costs are unclear. Some companies venture as leaders in innovations; others are followers. Look at the competition. Remember that AI projects may be expensive.
2. **Chatbots are all over. Should we follow?** The concept is appealing. The cost may be reasonable, but the accuracy of the answers you get from a machine clearly depends on the investment you will make in the machine's knowledge and its training. Chatbots can save a lot of money and make customers happy. However, they can frustrate customers with "stupid" conversations.
3. **Our employees contribute their wisdom to the company's knowledge base. Should we give them extra compensation?** It depends on the labor contract and on the nature and size of the contribution. If the contribution to AI projects is not related to the regular work of the employees, management should consider special rewards.
4. **Robots and other AI innovations will result in some people losing their jobs in our business. What to do?** This is a major problem that will intensify in the future. Most companies are installing robots where the benefits are large, and they try to reassign the affected employees. Robots will cause people to lose their jobs, like other automations did.
5. **Our company considers the introduction of robo assistant. How to approach the issue?** Robo assistants (or advisors) are used by companies for various purposes. Most frequent uses are internal advisors to employees (such as in the Allstate case), as assistants to customers (such as used by airlines), and as assistant to decision-makers, such as the use of *robo*

advisors in investments or in approving small loans in banks. Depending on the nature of the application, you need to select a vendor and a product (consult an introduction to IT book on how to do it). Finally, you need to conduct a cost–benefit analysis (see Chap. 14).

6. **Internet of things' applications have lots of promises and potential benefits. Is it for us?** The IoT has many potential advantages, but it is in its early stages of life. As shown in the closing case, large companies can reap considerable benefits. While small applications for a home and appliances are feasible now, large-scale implementation in organizations may involve several problems, such as security, system integration, financial justification, and selection of implementing vendor. It is advisable to seek the advice of an IT management company (such as Gartner) as well as consult a major technology vendor (such as Cisco).

SUMMARY

In this chapter, you learned about the following EC issues as they relate to the chapter's learning objectives.

1. **The reasons for intelligent EC systems.** The major reasons are to make EC easier to use, more capable (enable new applications), more intuitive, and less threatening. Intelligent EC systems can work automatically and autonomously, saving time and money, and perform consistent work. They can also work in rural and remote areas where human expertise is rare or not available. Intelligence can be observed in all EC activities, from buying to customer service. Intelligent virtual systems can also act as assistance to humans.

2. **The essentials of AI.** AI systems are computer systems that exhibit low level (but increasing) intelligence. This enables more automation of EC activities, such as machine translation of languages (e.g., for global trading). Intelligent EC systems can facilitate training and decision-making. AI has several definitions and derivatives and its importance is growing rapidly. Many companies and governments recognize the importance of AI. For example, the US government postulated that AI will be a "critical driver of the U.S. economy" (Gaudin 2016). The major derivatives of AI are intelligent agents, machine learning, robotics systems, natural languages processing and recognition, and knowledge systems.

3. **The major AI applications.** These include robotics and chatbots, intelligent personal assistants, machine translation of languages, expert systems of different variety, advisory systems, and automatic ordering systems. AI is also a critical element in driverless cars.

4. **4. Knowledge systems and management.** Knowledge management creates, captures, stores, processes, refines, protects, and disseminates knowledge. The major objective is to preserve knowledge and enable its sharing by many. Knowledge is stored in knowledge bases in organizations. Knowledge is also a major component of expert systems. Such systems act as an advisory to nonexperts by providing them with answers to inquiries, directing them to what to do, and helping them to solve problems. By matching the stored knowledge with symptoms and other input data provided by the nonexperts, the systems' inference engines generate the advice. Some systems can provide explanations of how the advice was generated. Expert systems are very good with tasks that use low level logic (e.g., match items, do simple computations).

5. **Intelligent personal assistants.** A relatively new application of knowledge systems is the intelligent personal assistant. Major examples of such assistants are Amazon Alexa, Apple's Siri, and Google Home. The knowledge is centrally maintained (in the "cloud") and usually disseminated via a Q&A dialog (user with machine). The assistants can be personalized to their owner's traits. Special breeds of assistance are the personal advisors, such as robo advisors, that provide advice to investors.

6. **The essentials of the Internet of things (IoT).** The IoT refers to an ecosystem in which a large number of objects (like people, sensors, and computers) are interconnected via the Internet (usually wirelessly). By the year 2020, there could be as many as 50 billion connected objects. A system of such connected things can be used for many purposes (e.g., see the CNH closing case). The use of the IoT can provide for improved or new EC applications.

7. **Self-driving cars, smart homes and appliances, and smart cities.** These are some of the major applications of consumer-related IoT. Self-driven cars may reduce accidents, pollution, and traffic jams. Such driverless autos can reduce transportation costs as well. While self-driving cars are not fully implemented yet (we may see them in 2017–2018), smart homes and appliances are all over the place. For a small investment, you can use several applications in your home, ranging from home security to controlling your appliances. The concept of smart cities is taking off globally with projects in Singapore, India, Germany, and the United States. Their objective is to provide a better life to the residents of the cities. Major areas are transportation, healthcare, education, and government services.

KEY TERMS

Amazon Alexa
Amazon Echo
Artificial intelligence (AI)
Chatbot
Driverless cars
Expert systems (knowledge-based systems)
Intelligent agents
Internet of things (IoT)
Knowledge management (KM)
Machine learning
Natural language processing (NLP)
Personal robot (also personal assistant, virtual personal assistant)
Robo advisors
Robot
Shopbot
Siri
Smart cities
Smart homes
Speech (voice) understanding
Turing test

DISCUSSION QUESTIONS

1. Relate the concepts of knowledge sharing to knowledge management and to expert systems.
2. Discuss the flow of expertise and knowledge from the "cloud" (via the Internet) to expert systems' users. What are the benefits of such a flow?
3. Find recent information about the progress of India's 100 smart cities. Write a summary.
4. Why is the IoT considered a disruptive technology?
5. Watch the video "What Is a Smart City?" at **youtube.com/watch?v=Br5aJa6MkBc** (3:28 min), and discuss the issues of smart cities.
6. IBM Watson is related to *cognitive computing*. Explain the relationship.
7. Find information on the competition between Google's DeepMind and the World Go Champion. Summarize the reasons for the advantage for the winner of the competition.
8. Find the status of legalizing driverless cars in your country.

TOPICS FOR CLASS DISCUSSION AND DEBATE

1. Many are concerned with the rapid expansions of robots and the jobs they eliminate. Others claim that in the end, more new jobs will be created than eliminated. Given the rapid globally spread of robots, the threat seems logical. See Table 7.1, Rickard-Strauss (2014), and Egan (2015). Debate the issue.
2. It is said that virtual assistants are not as capable (yet) as Ironman's Jarvis, or as HAL 9000. However, their intended functions are largely the same. Discuss.
3. Is replacing humans with AI a good or bad thing? Debate the issue. Start by reading River Logic (2016).
4. According to the June 23, 2016, article "Self-Driving Cars May One Day Face Decision of Whom to Save, Kill" at **abcnews.go.com/Technology/driving-cars-day-face-decision-save-kill/story?id=40072003**, read the article and discuss its assertions.

5. Watch the 16-min video regarding applying AI to auctions ("Applying Artificial Intelligence to Auctions: Colin Rowat at TEDxUniversityofBirmingham" **youtube.com/watch?v=O65XJd7j2BE**). Answer the following questions:

  (a) What are the major advantages of such systems?
  (b) What are the major obstacles and limitations?
  (c) For what types of auctions would you recommend AI systems? Why?
  (d) Comment on possible applications not cited in the video.

6. It is said that the IoT will enable new customer service and B2B interactions. Explain how.
7. Discuss the relationship between knowledge systems and social networking.
8. The IoT has a growing impact on business and e-commerce. Find evidence. Also read Jamthe (2016).
9. Are consumers, automakers, insurers, and politicians really ready for self-driving cars? Discuss and debate.
10. Discuss how IBM Watson will reach 1 billion people by 2018 and what the implications are. Do some research, write a report.

INTERNET EXERCISES

1. Read **saleforce.com/products/Einstein/overview**, a story about *Salesforce Einstein*. Then enter **salesforce.com** and find more information about the service. Prepare a list of all the tasks that "Einstein" supports. Why use it?
2. Enter **purveya.com** and examine the features of their technology. Relate the features to specific benefits for organizations.
3. Enter **theinternetofthings.eu** and find information about the *IoT Council*. Write a summary.
4. Enter **kmworld.com** and find recent information on knowledge management and expert systems which is related to e-commerce. Write a report.
5. Enter **gravityinvestments.com/digital-advice-platform-demo**. Would you invest in this project? Research and write a report.
6. Enter **ptc.com/internet-of-things/customer-success** and select three cases. Write a summary of each.
7. Enter **nuance.com** and find information about Dragon Medical Advice. Describe the benefits. Find other applications by the company. Write a report.
8. Enter **shopadvisor.com/1/platform** and review the platform 3 components. Examine their capabilities and compare them to other shopping advisors.

TEAM ASSIGNMENTS AND PROJECTS

Questions for the Opening Case

1. Read the opening case and research related material, and answer the following questions:

  (a) Explain why traffic may be down while congestion is up (see the case of London at **inrix.com**).
  (b) How does this case relate to m-commerce?
  (c) Identify the intelligent elements in this system.
  (d) Explore the revenue model of the system.
  (e) Enter the press releases from the recent 4 months at **index.com/global-resources/press-releases** and identify developments related to smart commerce. Write a report.
  (f) According to Gitlin (2016), INRIX's new mobile traffic app is a threat to Waze. (Waze is introduced in Chap. 6.) Explain why.

2. Sales intelligence systems are getting very popular both for online and offline sales. Have teams research the major software vendors and then make a comparison as a class project. Suggested vendors are Salesforce, LinkedIn, Sales Navigator, Nimble, InsideView for Sales, DiscoverOrg, RainKing, ZoomInfo, and Salestools.10 (you can find more). Read Dunhill (2016).
3. A major concern of the IoT is its security and privacy protection. The team or teams are assigned to investigate this topic. Begin by reading Schuman (2016), and prepare a presentation that will concentrate on the threats to IoT (under various scenarios; e.g., in the house, in the enterprise, for a country). Then, examine the existing and proposed defense mechanisms. Finally, discuss the organizational issues related to implementation.
4. Find information about Nest's thermostats and then explain how Amazon's Alexa can control this product.

5. Examine **autonomous.ai/personal-robot**. Compare its capabilities to that of Amazon's Alexa, Google Home, and Apple's Siri. There are significant differences in the product costs. Prepare an analysis that will justify (or not justify) the difference in costs.

6. Join the "smart e-commerce" group and blog on LinkedIn (**linkedin.com/company/smart-e-commerce**). Describe the major current topics discussed there. Find similar groups that are interested in smart commerce. Write a report.

7. Several vendors offer trip advising. Well-known ones are Utrip in Europe and TripAdvisor in the United States. Check several of these as to the quality of the advice provided by machines.

8. Find the status of *smart cities* as it is related to Cisco. Write a report.

9. Read the Fintech Editors (2016) article about Mastercard bots and search for more information. Write a report.

CLOSING CASE: CNH INDUSTRIAL USES THE INTERNET OF THINGS TO EXCEL

CNH Industrial N.V. (CNH) is a Netherlands-based global manufacturer of vehicles for the agriculture, construction, and commercial vehicle markets. The company produces and services more than 300 types of vehicles and operates in 190 countries (it employs over 65,000 people). The company's business is continuously growing while operating in a very competitive environment.

The Problem

To manage and coordinate such a complex business from its corporate office in London, the company needed a superb communication system as well as an effective customer service network. For example, parts availability is critical. Customer's equipment does not work until a broken part is replaced. Competitive pressures are very strong, especially in the agriculture sector where weather conditions, seasonal, and harvesting pressure may complicate operations. Monitoring and controlling of equipment are important competitive factors. Ideally, predicting equipment failures is very desirable. Rapid connectivity with the customers and the equipment they purchase from CNH is essential, as well as efficient data monitoring and data collection.

The Solution

Using PTC Transformational, as a vendor, the company implemented an IoT system together with internal structural transformation, in order to solve its problems and reshape its connected industrial vehicles. The initial implementation was in the agricultural sector. The details of the implementation are provided by PTC, Inc. (2015). The highlights are summarized next.

- The IoT connects all vehicles, in hundreds of locations worldwide (those that are equipped with the connectivity to the system), to CNH's command and control center. This connection enables monitoring performance.
- The IoT monitors the products' condition and operation, as well as the surrounding environments, through sensors, and to collect external data.
- The IoT enables customization of products' performance at customers' sites.
- The IoT provides the data necessary for optimizing equipment's operation.
- Using the IoT to analyze the behaviors of the people that drive CNH's produced trucks and recommend changes that can improve the efficiency of the vehicles.
- Predicts the range of the fuel supply in the vehicles.
- Alerts owners to the needs of preventive maintenance and orders the necessary parts for such services (e.g., by monitoring usage and/or predicting failures). This enables proactive maintenance practice.
- Finds when trucks are overloaded, violating the warranty contracts.
- Provides fast diagnosis of products' failures.
- Enables trucks' deliveries on schedule by connecting the trucks to planners and delivery sources and destinations.
- Helps farmers to optimally plan the entire farming cycle, from preparing the soil to harvesting.
- Analyzes collected data as compared to standards.
- All this is done mostly wirelessly.

The Results

According to Marcus (2015), CNH halved the downtime of the participating equipment at customer sites by using the IoT. It also helps farmers monitor their fields and equipment to improve efficiency. The company is now helping customers by showing examples to less effective users of superb operating practices. Parts of incoming orders can be fulfilled very quickly. In addition, product development benefits from the analysis of collected data.

Sources: Compiled from PTC, Inc. (2015), Marcus (2015), and **cnhindustrial.com/en-us/pages/homepage.aspx**

Questions for the Case

1. Why is the IoT the only viable solution to CNH's problems?
2. List and discuss the major benefits of the IoT in this case.
3. How can product development benefit from the collected data about usage?
4. It is said that the IoT enables telematics and connected vehicles. Explain.
5. Why is the IoT considered the "core of the future business strategy?"
6. It is said that the IoT will enable new services for CNH (e.g., for customers and for B2B partners).
7. View Fig. 7.5 (the process of IoT) and relate it to the usage of IoT at CNH.

REFERENCES

Arthur, R. "Future of Retail: Artificial Intelligence and Virtual Reality have Big Roles to Play." *Forbes*, June 15, 2016.
Basu, A and P. Didyala. "The Internet of a Billion Things." *The Economy Times*, August 31, 2014.
Beard, M. *Expert Systems: An Introduction* [Kindle Edition]. Seattle, WA: Matthew Beard, 2014.
Bell, K. "Facebook Says Its New AI Can Understand Text with 'Near-Human Accuracy'." *Mashable*, June 1, 2016. **mashable.com/2016/06/01/facebook-deeptext-ai** (accessed December 2016).
Blog. "All in Ads: 13 High-Momentum Companies Using Machine Learning in Marketing, Ads, and Sales." *CB Insights.com*, May 31, 2016.
Brady, P. "This New App Uses Artificial Intelligence to Plan Your Trip." *Traveler*, May 12, 2016.
Bridges, R. *Driverless Car Revolution: Buy Mobility, Not Metal*. [Kindle edition] Seattle, WA: Amazon Digital Service, 2015.
Britt, P. "E-Commerce Buys into KM." October 2013. **kmworld.com/Articles/Editorial/Features/E-commerce-buys-into-KM-92023.aspx** (accessed December 2016).
Bundrick, H. M. "10 Best Robo Advisors Ranked: Find the Best Automated Online Investing Services." *The Street*, August 14, 2015.
CBS News. "LinkedIn Adding New Training Features, News Feeds and "Bots"." *CBS News*, September 22, 2016. **cbsnews.com/news/linkedin-adding-new-training-features-news-feeds-and-bots** (accessed December 2016).
Cericola, R. "Top 5 Smart Home Trends for 2016." *Electronic House*, January 16, 2016. **electronichouse.com/smart-home/top-5-smart-home-trends-for-2016** (accessed December 2016).
Chandra, M., and A. Darbhe. "Artificial Intelligence: The Next Big Thing in Supply Chain Management." *The Financial Express*, July 26, 2016.
Choudhury, V. "How Artificial Intelligence is Changing the Face of Ecommerce Industry." *I am Wire*, September 26, 2016.
Chui, M., J. Manyika, and M. Miremadi. "Where Machines Could Replace Humans- and Where They Can't (Yet)." *McKinsey & Company*, July 2016. **mckinsey.com/business-functions/digital-mckinsey/our-insights/where-machines-could-replace-humans-and-where-they-cant-yet** (accessed December 2016).
Clark, D. "IBM: A Billion People to Use Watson by 2018." *The Wall Street Journal*, October 26, 2016a.
Clark, J. "New Google AI Brings Automation to Customer Service." *Bloomberg News*, July 20, 2016b.
ClickZ Intelligence. "Seven Ways Artificial Intelligence Can Be Used for Marketing." *ClickZ*, May 31, 2013. **clickz.com/seven-ways-artificial-intelligence-can-be-used-for-marketing/96572** (accessed December 2016).
Clinton, N. "Artificial Intelligence Can Help Procurement Solve Some of the Big Challenges." *Spend Matters UK*, April 28, 2016. **spendmatters.com/uk/artificial-intelligence-help-businesses-save-thousands** (accessed December 2016).
Constantinou, A. and M. Sellebraten. "The Internet of Things is About to Reshape E-Commerce." *Vision Mobile*, December 9, 2015. **visionmobile.com/blog/2015/the-internet-of-things-is-about-to-reshape-e-commerce** (accessed December 2016).
Crist, R. "Amazon Alexa: Device Compatibility, How-Tos and Much More." *CNET.com*, April 8, 2016. **cnet.com/how-to/amazon-alexa-device-compatibility-how-tos-and-much-more.** (accessed December 2016).
Davis, B. "15 Examples of Artificial Intelligence in Marketing." *Econsultancy*, April 19, 2016. **econsultancy.com/blog/67745-15-examples-of-artificial-intelligence-in-marketing** (accessed December 2016).
Deichmann, J., M. Roggendorf, and D. Wee. "Preparing IT Systems and Organizations for the Internet of Things." *McKinsey & Company*, December 2015.
DeNisco, A. "IBM Watson Is Coming to the iPhone, and That's Big News for Business Users." *Tech Republic*, October 25, 2016.
Dodge, J. "Artificial Intelligence in the Enterprise: It's On." *Computer World*, February 10, 2016.
Dunhill, A. "The Secret to Finding New Leads with Sales Intelligence Software." *LinkedIn.com*, February 1, 2016. **linkedin.com/pulse/secret-finding-new-leads-sales-intelligence-software-adam-dunhill.** (accessed December 2016).

Editors. "Smart Cities Will Use 1.6B Connected Things in 2016." *Enterprise Innovation*, December 21, 2015.

Egan, M. "Robots Threaten These 8 Jobs." *CNNMoney News*, New York, May 13, 2015.

Fenwick, N. "IoT Devices Are Exploding on the Market." *Information Management*, January 19, 2016.

Fingas, R. "Tim Cook Says AI & Augmented Reality are Core Technologies in Apple's Future." *Apple Insider*, August 14, 2016.

Fintech Editors. "Mastercard to Launch AI-Backed Messaging Platforms for Merchants and Banks." *Fintech Innovation Editors*, November 2, 2016.

Friedman, L. "Chatbots and Millennials: How Smart Brands Should be Using Artificial Intelligence." *Forbes*, June 22, 2016.

Gaudin, S. "White House: A.I. Will Be Critical Driver of U.S. Economy." *Computerworld*, October 12, 2016.

Gikas, M. "What the Amazon Echo and Alexa Do Best." *Consumer Reports*, July 29, 2016. **consumerreports.org/wireless-speakers/what-amazon-echo-and-alexa-do-best** (accessed December 2016).

Gitlin, J. M. "Watch Out, Waze: INRIX's New Traffic App Is Coming for You." *Ars Technica*, March 30, 2016. **arstechnica.com/cars/2016/watch-out-waze-inrixs-new-traffic-app-is-coming-for-you/** (accessed December 2016).

Greengard, S. "Delving into Gartner's 2016 Hype Cycle." *Baseline*, September 7, 2016a.

Greengard, S. "How AI Will Impact the Global Economy." *CIO Insight*, October 7, 2016b.

Greenough, J. "10 Million Self-Driving Cars Will Be on the Road by 2020." *Business Insider*, July 29, 2015.

Hachman, M. "Microsoft combines Cortana and Bing with Microsoft Research to Accelerate New Features." *PC World*, September 29, 2016.

Hamblen, M. "Innovators Can Air Quality Sensors on Bicycles, While Wireless Connections Help Pave the Way for Driverless Cars." *Computer World*, February 22, 2016.

Hean, C.K. "How We Design and Build a Smart City and Nation." *TEDxSingapore*, December 17, 2015. **youtube.com/watch?v=m45SshJqOP4** (accessed December 2016).

Heater, B. "Apple works to fit the smart home under a single roof." *Techcrunch.com*, September 13, 2016. **techcrunch.com/2016/09/13/apple-home/.** (accessed December 2016).

Hughes, T. "Google DeepMind's Program Beat Human at Go." *USA Today*, January 27, 2016.

Insightly Blog. "Using Artificial Intelligence and Predictive Analytics to Customize and Automate Email Marketing Campaigns." *Insightly*, December 30, 2015.

Jamthe, S. *IoT Disruptions 2020: Getting to the Connected World of 2020 with Deep Learning IoT*. Seattle, WA: Create Space Independent Publishing Platform, 2016.

Karwatka, T. "Internet of Things and E-Commerce." *Divante*, May 25, 2015. **divante.co/blog/internet-e-commerce** (accessed December 2016).

Kastrenakes, J. "Nest Can Now Use Your Phone to Tell When You've Left the House." *The Verge*, March 10, 2016. **theverge.com/2016/3/10/11188888/nest-now-uses-location-for-home-away-states-launches-family-accounts** (accessed December 2016).

Keating, L. "Facebook Users can Now Post a Status in any Language: Here's How the Translation Tool Works." *Tech Times*, July 1, 2016.

Kelly, H. "Battle of the smart speakers: Google Home vs. Amazon Echo." *CNN Tech*, May 20, 2016. **money.cnn.com/2016/05/20/technology/google-home-amazon-echo/index.html?iid=EL** (accessed December 2016).

Khani, T. "AI Sees Increased Adoption by E-Commerce Companies." *The Times of India*, July 20, 2016.

Knight, W. "Walmart's Robotic Shopping Carts Are the Latest Sign that Automation Is Eating Commerce." *Technology Review*, June 15, 2016.

Kohl, R. "2 Ways Artificial Intelligence is Changing Customers Engagement." *The Future Customer Engagement and Commerce*. February 18, 2016. **the-future-of-commerce.com/2016/02/18/commerce-artificial-intelligence** (accessed December 2016).

Korosec, K. "Start Your Car from Inside Your Home Using Amazon's Alexa." *Fortune.com*, August 18, 2016.

Kuntz, C. and R. Becker. "Monetizing the Internet of Things: Creating a Connected Customer Experience." *Zuora Inc.*, 2015. **slideshare.net/Zuora/monetizing-the-internet-of-things-creating-a-connected-customer-experience** (accessed December 2016).

Kvita, C. "Navigate the Internet of Things." January/February 2014. **oracle.com/technetwork/issue-archive/2014/14-jan/o14interview-utzschneider-2074127.html** (accessed December 2016).

Kwang, T.W. "Singapore Polytechnic to Transform into a Smart Campus." *Enterprise Innovation*, January 25, 2016.

Lacey, K. "Higher Ed Prepares for the Internet of Things." *University Business*, July 27, 2016. **universitybusiness.com/article/higher-prepares-internet-things** (accessed December 2016).

Larson, S. "Baidu is Bringing AI Chatbots to Healthcare." *CNN Tech*, October 11, 2016. **money.cnn.com/2016/10/11/technology/baidu-doctor-ai-melody** (accessed December 2016).

Levin, A. "Watch Out, Motorists: Driverless Cars Closer to U.S. Green Light." *Bloomberg News*, March 11, 2016.

Libelium. "Smart Factory: Reducing Maintenance Costs and Ensuring Quality in the Manufacturing Process." *Libelium World*, March 2, 2015.

Lucero, S. "The Internet of Everything Needs a "Fabric."" *HIS Market*, May 13, 2015. **technology.ihs.com/531114/the-internet-of-everything-needs-a-fabric** (accessed December 2016).

Mah, P. "The State of Chatbots in Marketing." *Enterprise Innovation*, November 4, 2016.

Manyika, J., M. Chui, P. Bisson, J. Woetzel, R. Dobbs, J. Bughin, and D. Aharon. "Unlocking the Potential of the Internet of Things." *Insights & Publications*, June 2015.

Marcus, J. "CNH Industrial Halves Product Downtime with IoT." *Product Lifecycle Report*, May 6, 2015.

Markoff, J. "Toyota Planning an Artificial Intelligence Research Center in California." *The New York Times*, November 6, 2015. **gilesmorgan.wordpress.com/2015/11/06/toyota-planning-an-artificial-intelligence-research-center-in-california-by-john-markoff** (accessed December 2016).

Matney, L. "Siri-Creator Shows Off First Public Demo of Viv, 'The Intelligent Interface for Everything'." *Tech Crunch*, May 9, 2016. **techcrunch.com/2016/05/09/siri-creator-shows-off-first-public-demo-of-viv-the-intelligent-interface-for-everything** (accessed December 2016).

McCafferty, D. "How the Internet of Things is Changing Everything." *Baseline*, June 6, 2015.

McClellan. "What the Evolving Robo Advisory Industry Offers." *AAII Journal*, October 2016.

McCooey, E. "Expert System Eases Crunch at Allstate Call Center." *Baseline*, July 22, 2016. **baselinemag.com/crm/expert-system-eases-crunch-at-allstate-call-center.html** (accessed December 2016).

McFarland, M. "Switzerland Enlists Robots to Help Deliver Mail." *CNN Tech*, August 24, 2016. **money.cnn.com/2016/08/24/technology/Switzerland-swiss-post-ground-robot/index.html** (accessed December 2016).

McGrath, J. "Haier Wants You to Live Smaller and Smarter with Its New Appliances." *Digital Trends*, January 5, 2016. **digitaltrends.com/home/haier-shows-off-u-smart-appliances-at-ces-2016** (accessed December 2016).

McMahon, J. "Smart Robotics Meet E-Commerce." *World Trade 100*, undated.

Mehra, G. "Internet of Things Helping Ecommerce." *Practical Ecommerce*, October 8, 2015.

Miller, M. *The Internet of Things: How Smart TVs, Smart Cars, Smart Homes, and Smart Cities are Changing the World*. 1ˢᵗ edition, Indianapolis: Que Publishing, 2015.

Milton, N. and P. Lambe. *The Knowledge Manager's Handbook: A Step-by-Step Guide to Embedding Effective Knowledge Management in your Organization*. London, UK: Kogan Page, 2016.

Mitchell, R. and T. Lien. "Uber Is About to Start Giving Rides in Self-Driving Cars." *LA Times*, August 18, 2016.

Morin, J. *Infosys 94 Success Secrets – 94 Most Asked Questions On Infosys – What You Need To Know* [Kindle Edition]. Queensland, Australia: Emereo Publishing, 2014.

Morris, C. "Ordinary Home Appliances are About to Get Really Sexy." *Fortune.com*, January 6, 2016. **fortune.com/2016/01/06/home-appliances-ces-2016**. (accessed December 2016).

Murray, M. "Intel Lays Out Its Vision for a Fully Connected World." *PC Magazine*, August 16, 2016.

Nagpure, A. *IoT Enabled: Internet of Things Enabled, This Book Is Must If You Want to Make Career in IoT*. [Kindle Edition] Seattle, WA: Amazon Digital Services, 2016.

Neckermann, L. *The Mobility Revolution: Zero Emissions, Zero Accidents, Zero Ownership*. San Francisco, CA: Matador Publishing, 2015.

Niccolai, J. "IBM Watson Will Know What You Did Last Summer." *PC World*, September 23, 2015.

Nicolaus, M. "Welcome Salesforce Einstein: AI for the World's Smartest CRM." *Salesforce.com*, September 19, 2016. **salesforce.com/uk/blog/2016/09/welcome-salesforce-einstein-ai-for-the-worlds-smartest-crm.html**. (accessed December 2016).

Noyes, K. "Watson's the Name, Data's the Game." *PC World*, October 7, 2016.

O'Brien, A. "AI Can Solve World's Biggest Problems'- Google Brain Engineer." *Google Brain Engineer*. February 22, 2016a.

O'Brien, M. "What Can Chatbots Do for Ecommerce?" *ClickZ.com*, April 11, 2016b.

O'Shea, A. "Best Robo-Advisors: 2016 Top Picks." *NerdWallet*, March 14, 2016. **nerdwallet.com/blog/investing/best-robo-advisors/** (accessed December 2016).

Perkins, E. "Securing the Internet of Things." *Gartner Inc.* Report #G00300281, May 12, 2016.

Pickup, O. "How Artificial Intelligence will Transform your Business." *The Telegraph*, July 2, 2016.

PTC, Inc. "Internal Transformation for IoT Business Model Reshapes Connected Industrial Vehicles" *PTC Transformational Case Study*, November 12, 2015.

Pyle, D. and C. San Jose. "An Executive's Guide to Machine Learning." *McKinsey & Company*, June 2015.

Quoc, M. "The State of Bots: 11 Examples of Conversational Commerce." *Venture Beat*, June 16, 2016. **venturebeat.com/2016/06/16/the-state-of-bots-11-examples-of-conversational-commerce-in-2016** (accessed December 2016).

Regan, M.P. "Robo Advisers to Run $2 Trillion by 2020 if this Model is Right." *Bloomberg Business*, June 18, 2015.

Reich, R. "What Happens When Robots Replace All of Our Jobs?" *The Christian Science Monitor*, March 16, 2015.

Reisinger, D. "10 Reasons to Buy the Amazon Echo Virtual Personal Assistant." A Slide Show. *eWeek*, February 9, 2016.

Rickard-Straus, R. "Will You Be Replaced By a Robot? We Reveal the 100 Occupations Judged Most and Least at Risk OF Automation." *This is Money*, May 31, 2014. **thisismoney.co.uk/money/news/article-2642880/Table-700-jobs-reveals-professions-likely-replaced-robots.html** (accessed December 2016).

Ricktun, P. "Internet-of-Things Becomes Internet-of-Everything." *Information Management*, February 5, 2016.

River Logic. "Replacing Humans with Artificial Intelligence: It's a Good Thing." *River Logic*, February 22, 2016. **riverlogic.com/blog/replacing-humans-with-artificial-intelligence-its-a-good-thing** (accessed December 2016).

Rossi, B. "3 Ways Artificial Intelligence is Transforming E-Commerce." *Information Age*, July 18, 2016.

Russell, K. "IBM is Using Watson to Psychoanalyze People from their Tweets." *Business Insider*, February 4, 2014.

Russell, S. *Artificial Intelligence: A Modern Approach*. New York, NY: Pearson, 2015.

Schlicht, M. "The Complete Beginner's Guide to Chatbots." *Chatbots Magazine*, April 20, 2016. **chatbotsmagazine.com/the-complete-beginner's-guide-to-chatbots-8280b7b906ca#.I32ok23cf** (accessed December 2016).

Schuman, E. "Let's Get Serious About IoT Security." *Computerworld*, October 11, 2016.

Schwartz, S.I. *Street Smart: The Rise of Cities and the Fall of Cars* [Kindle Edition]. New York, NY: Public Affairs, 2015.

Shah, J. "Robots Are Learning Complex Tasks Just By Watching Humans Do Them." *Harvard Business Review*, June 21, 2016.

Smith, C. "Artificial Intelligence Is the Next Frontier for Social Networks." *Business Insider*, April 4, 2014.

Smith, S. "The Future of Artificial Intelligence in eLearning Systems." *Elearning Industry*, April 23, 2016. **elearningindustry.com/future-artificial-intelligence-in-elearning-systems** (accessed December 2016).

Statt, N. "Apple Is Trying to Turn the iPhone into a DSLR Using Artificial Intelligence." *Circuit Breaker*, September 8, 2016. **theverge.com/2016/9/8/12839838/apple-iphone-7-plus-ai-machine-bokeh-photography** (accessed December 2016).

Sutton, J. "Demystifying the Role of Artificial Intelligence in Marketing and Advertising." *eMarketer*, April 22, 2016.

Taft, D.K. "IBM Showcases Experience One at Smarter Commerce Global Summit." *eWeek*, May 14, 2014.

Taylor, C. "Artificial Intelligence: Is the E-learning Industry Ready?" *HT2Labs*, February 2, 2016. **ht2labs.com/blog/artificial-intelligence-is-the-elearning-industry-ready** (accessed December 2016).

Tokuoka *Emerging Technologies: Autonomous Cars*. Raleigh, NC: Lulu.com, 2016.

Townsend, A. M. *Smart Cities: Big Data, Civic, Hackers and the Quest for a New Utopia*. New York: W. W. Norton & Company, 2013.

Tverdohleb, V. "Artificial Intelligence Helps the World of E-Commerce." *Parent Herald*, February 2, 2016.

Ulanoff, L. "Mark Zuckerberg's AI Is Already Making Him Toast." *Mashable*, July 22, 2016.

Watts, J. M. "World's First Self-Driving Taxis Hit the Road in Singapore." *The Wall Street Journal*, August 25, 2016. **wsj.com/articles/worlds-first-self-driving-taxis-hit-the-road-in-singapore-1472102747** (accessed December 2016).

Waxer, C. "Get Ready for the BOT Revolution." *Computer World*, October 17, 2016.

Womack, B. "Salesforce Unveils Artificial Intelligence 'Einstein' Service." *Bloomberg News*, September 18, 2016. **bloomberg.com/news/articles/2016-09-18/salesforce-unveils-artificial-intelligence-einstein-service** (accessed December 2016).

Zuora. "Mapping the Connected World- Forrester Report." *Zuora*, (2015, updated) **info.zuora.com/IoT-analyst-report-mapping-the-connected-world-ty.html?aliId=17642926/** (accessed December 2016).

Social Commerce: Foundations, Social Marketing, and Advertising

8

Contents

Learning Objectives

Upon completion of this chapter, you will be able to:

1. Define social commerce and describe its roots and evolution.
2. Describe the scope, drivers, and content of the social commerce field.
3. Summarize the benefits and limitations of social commerce.
4. Describe the major models of social shopping.
5. Explain how advertising and promotions are conducted in social networking environments.
6. Describe how social networking can facilitate customer service, customer support, and CRM.

OPENING CASE
SOCIAL MEDIA WANTS YOUR MARKETING DOLLARS

A common concern for social networks is the lack of a coherent or well-defined business model. Many social networks struggled to create or implement a business model during their infancy and growth stages (Facebook.com), while others are still in the process (Twitter.com). Until any business is able to clearly articulate its revenue model, as well as prove that that revenue model works, its future viability is unknown. One well-known social network that had this issue in its early history is Facebook. Facebook has had a very complex growth and development over the last 10 years (see an infographic at **ignite-visibility.com/history-of-facebook-infographic** or **en.wikipedia.org/wiki/History_of_Facebook**).

© Springer International Publishing AG 2018

E. Turban et al., *Electronic Commerce 2018*, Springer Texts in Business and Economics, DOI 10.1007/978-3-319-58715-8_8

The Problem

Facebook now has developed viable revenue streams, many based around marketing, advertising, and sponsorship. Other revenue streams include online games and services (see the infographic at **business-management-degree.net/facebook**). These activities have been very successful, and Facebook recently reported earnings growth of over 52% on the year (King 2016).

The growth of social media has provided a viable secondary option for businesses wishing to advertise to potential customers. In the past, much of this online advertising was focused around search engine advertising techniques, specifically search engine marketing (SEM). The undisputed leader in this area is Google. The company earned over $75 billion in revenue in 2015, with most of that coming search revenues (Rosenberg 2016). The company is strongly committed to this business model and continues to innovate with its AdWords product across all platforms, including mobile devices.

This competition between the titans of social media and search has had mixed results for advertisers. While additional competition has allowed businesses to target potential customers in different ways, understanding which platform to use, or how much of each platform to use, has become a difficult question for many (Sullivan 2015). Each business has attempted to define its place in the market, but these definitions do not always hold. Google maintains its lead in search, but the two companies are now focusing on the ability to display targeted ads to users based on their preferences. Neither has established supremacy in this area, and the definitions of success seem to be changing (see **wordstream.com/facebook-vs-google**).

The Solution

Business owners and marketing managers must now determine where their marketing dollars should be spent, based on where they can most efficiently be used. A huge advantage that today's marketer has over advertisers of the past is the mountain of metrics and data available from both providers. Today, businesses are able to examine the profitability and effectiveness of campaigns using any search provider or social network (Hague 2016). These metrics can show marketers which products, targeting plans, and search terms have the greatest impact for the money spent. Impact can be measured in traffic or sales.

The Results

Using this available data, companies are able to identify an optimal marketing mix and can balance their media spend between many different providers such as Google and Facebook. While this is all possible, it may not be as easy as it sounds. Many businesses use specialized software products to manage this data (see **hubspot.com**) or outsource their operations to marketing companies who are better able to do these analyses and balance their marketing mix (see **distilled.net**).

To learn more about advertising with Facebook, see **blog.hootsuite.com/how-to-advertise-on-facebook** and **youtu.be/XYY6zn3c8Xk**. To learn more about advertising with Google, see **fitsmallbusiness.com/advertise-on-google** and **youtu.be/_KEzjdWATYQ**.

LESSONS LEARNED FROM THE CASE

In this case we see that social networks are challenging other providers in the quest for businesses marketing dollars. By defining a revenue model based around marketing, social media sites have been able to monetize their activities and ensure that they will be solvent in the future. Businesses today are given more choices, but these choices lead to greater complexity when decisions about marketing budgets are evaluated. Tools and solutions that exist help make these decisions, but the decisions may not be simple.

8.1 SOCIAL COMMERCE: DEFINITIONS AND EVOLUTION

Social commerce (SC), also known as *social business*, refers to e-commerce transactions delivered via social media.

Definitions

As it is a new field that involves several academic and professional disciplines, there is no agreed-upon definition or description of the content and boundaries of the social commerce field. Regardless of its definition, the field is growing rapidly both in the United States and elsewhere. For statics and trends for 2017 and beyond, see Smith (2016). For the impact of the technology, see DeLuca (2015). The magnitude of the field can be seen in Quirk (2016).

For additional discussion, see **bazaarvoice.com/research-and-insight/social-commerce-statistics** and **yotpo.com/blog/the-4-most-powerful-social-commerce-trends**.

The Evolution of Social Commerce

Social commerce emerged from the integration of several fields, which are shown in Fig. 8.1. For example, Marsden and Chaney (2012) show how social media contributes to sales, making it a social commerce application.

A major origin of social commerce (SC) was the development of Web 2.0 technologies, as previously mentioned. With these came commercial applications, which included activities in social networks and the use of social software such as blogs and wikis. A major driver of SC is the globalization of business. This prompted the need for collaboration of employees, partners, and customers, sometimes worldwide. Web 2.0 applications created an efficient and effective platforms for such collaboration. Web 2.0 is a major contributor to social media, which is the major driver of social commerce. For details, see Turban et al. (2016).

The development and rapid growth of mobile computing and smartphones have also facilitated social commerce. Mobile commerce is the basis for SC models such as location-based applications, social networks, and consumer/company networking.

A major emphasis of SC is its marketing orientation. Traditional marketing activities were applied to Internet marketing in the mid-1990s, when companies began building websites and using e-mail to advertise their products for sale offline. As the Web developed, marketers applied the Internet to facilitate e-commerce *transactions*. Until that point, marketers

Fig. 8.1 The major roots of social commerce

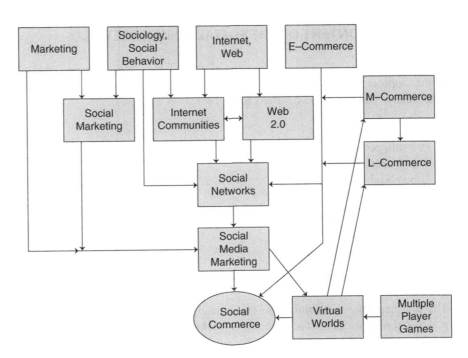

Table 8.1   The major differences between e-commerce and social commerce

Property	E-commerce	Social commerce
Major objective	Transactions	Social interactions
Major activity	Publishing	Engagement
Content	Company generated	User generated
Problem solving	Company experts, consultants	Crowdsourcing
Collaboration	Traditional, unified communications	Web 2.0 tools
Product information	Product descriptions on websites	Peer product reviews
Marketplaces	E-tailers (e.g., Amazon.com) and direct from manufacturers' stores (Dell)	Social networks (f-commerce), collaborative markets
Targeting	Mass marketing, segmentation	Behavioral targeting, microsegmentation
CRM	Seller/manufacturer support	Social support by peers and by vendors and employees
Online marketing strategy	Website selling	Multichannel, direct at social network sites
Integration	System integration	Mashups and system integration
Data management	Reports and analytics	Analytics

controlled brand messages and continued their advertising and other communication monologues to customers and potential buyers (prospects). With the emergence of social media, marketing communication changed to a dialog with Internet users, and many marketing strategies evolved or completely transformed to support social commerce.

For comprehensive coverage of social media marketing, see Williams (2016) and Van Looy (2016). For a complete guide to social commerce (free), see **pixlee.com/download/the-complete-guide-to-social-commerce**. The major differences between social commerce and e-commerce are illustrated in Table 8.1.

For a chronicle presentation and an infographic of historical milestones in the development of social commerce, see **socialtimes.com/social-commerce-infographic-2_b84120**.

SECTION 8.1 REVIEW QUESTIONS

1. Define social commerce and list its major characteristics.
2. Trace the evolution of social commerce.
3. Describe the major differences between e-commerce and social commerce.

8.2   THE CONTENT OF THE SOCIAL COMMERCE FIELD

The content of the SC field is very diversified. For example, Johnson (2015) focuses on the landscape from a company-centric approach, detailing the five main players of social commerce (Twitter, Pinterest, Facebook, Instagram, and YouTube). Alternately, viewing the ecosystem from a function standpoint, Hossain (2016) describes the progressive development of species of the field:

- Peer-to-peer sales
- Social network-driven sales
- Group buying
- Peer recommendations
- User-curated shopping
- Participatory commerce

The Landscape and Major Components of the Field

The landscape of social commerce is multidisciplinary (Turban et al. 2016). Most of the activities center around e-marketing conducted with social media, particularly marketing communication, techniques of advertising, sales promotions, and public relations, usually expressed as *social media marketing* activities. However, several other areas are emerging in the field,

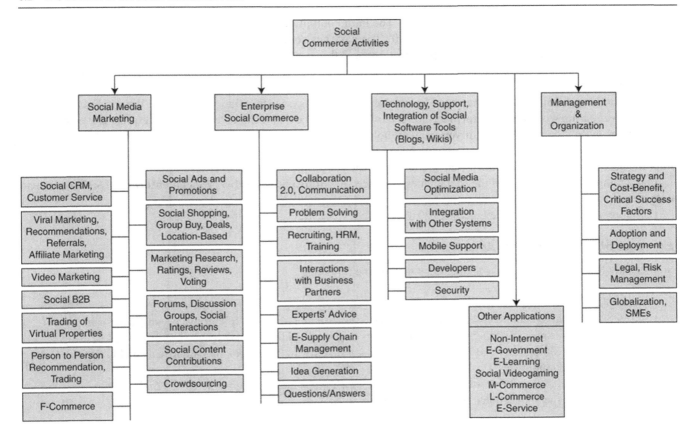

Fig. 8.2 The major dimensions of social commerce

especially activities within organizations that are referred to as *social enterprise or Enterprise 2.0*. Liang and Turban (2011–2012) illustrate the social commerce landscape in Fig. 8.2 and an infographic describe only some of the areas here. Discussions of the other activities of the figure are provided throughout the book.

For a detailed discussion, see Marsden's slide presentation "Social Commerce Opportunities for Brands" at **digitalinnovationtoday.com/new-presentation-social-commerce-opportunities-for-brands**. For statistics about social commerce and its use, see "Social Commerce Statistics" at **bazaarvoice.com/research-and-insight/social-commerce-statistics**. For a specialized textbook, see Turban et al. (2016). The two major elements in social commerce, social media marketing and Enterprise 2.0, are described next.

Social Media Marketing

Social media marketing (SMM) is the application of marketing communication and other marketing tools using social media. Social media marketing facilitates social commerce, builds brands, repairs brand reputation damage in social media, and fosters long-term customer relationships, among other things. For a free toolkit, see **act-on.com/resources/social-media-marketing-toolkit**.

For the industries that benefit most from social media, see Carranza (2015). For predictions of 50 experts on the development of social media and social media marketing for 2016, see Gil (2015). For an infographic, see Wood (2014).

Enterprise 2.0

The second major type of social commerce is *Enterprise 2.0*, also known as *social media-based enterprise*, which is used by an increasing number of companies to conduct several social media and social commerce activities inside the enterprises (e.g., idea generation, problem solving, joint design, and recruiting).

There are several definitions of **Enterprise 2.0**. The initial definition connected the term to Web 2.0 and to collaboration. A refined definition is "What is Enterprise 2.0? The easy answer is that Enterprise 2.0 is bringing Web 2.0 into the office, but that is not entirely accurate. In part, Enterprise 2.0 is a push toward integrating the social and collaborative tools of Web 2.0 into the office environment, but Enterprise 2.0 also represents a fundamental change in how businesses operate" Nation (2016).

Note: For more definitions and concepts of Enterprise 2.0 technology, see the slide presentation "What is Enterprise 2.0?" at **slideshare.net/norwiz/what-is-enterprise-20**. The following are the major characteristics of Enterprise 2.0: ease of information flow, agility, flexibility, user-driven content, bottom-up communication, global teams, fuzzy boundaries, transparency, folksonomies (rather than taxonomies), open standards, and on-demand (rather than scheduled) activities. Also important are flat organizations (rather than hierarchical) and short time-to-market cycles.

For a comprehensive article on the social enterprise, see **worldlibrary.org/Articles/Social enterprise?&Words=social enterprise.**

For more on Enterprise 2.0, see Forrester (2016).

Examples of Social Enterprise Applications

Some examples of social enterprise applications include the following:

- Dell, Sony, IBM, and many other companies solicit ideas from large groups of employees, customers, and business partners on how to improve their business operations (e.g., Dell's IdeaStorm site).
- More than 50% of medium and large corporations use LinkedIn and Facebook to announce available positions and to find potential employees.
- Best Buy provided state-of-the-art customer service via a Twitter-based system where thousands of employees used to answer customers' questions, sometimes within minutes.

The Future

While social commerce today can be described based on the component parts of social media marketing and Enterprise 2.0, the future is less clear. Social media and its attached commerce activities are evolving rapidly and have the ability to expand, diversify, or redefine the field. By evaluating current trends in the market, it is possible to see that other areas may also become a part of social commerce through the convergence of other related technologies. Some of these technologies are software-based and can include artificial intelligence and virtual reality; other technologies are hardware-based and may focus around logistics (such as drone-based same-day delivery) and advanced mobile devices (Smith 2016).

SECTION 8.2 REVIEW QUESTIONS

1. Describe the major components of social commerce.
2. What is social media marketing?
3. Describe Enterprise 2.0.

8.3   THE BENEFITS AND LIMITATIONS OF SOCIAL COMMERCE

According to many practitioners and researchers, social commerce is making significant impacts on organizations and industries. A major impact has been seen in the fashion industry.

Several surveys (e.g., SUMO 2016, get a copy of the report at **info.sumoheavy.com/2016**) have confirmed that social commerce results in significant monetary and strategic benefits to businesses. The report found that:

- 72% use social media on a daily basis.
- 47% use it multiple times per day.
- Only 11% say they don't use it at all.

- 42% are influenced by what they see on Facebook.
- 56% are influenced by posts from family members' and friends' about a brand and its product.
- 62% have shared information about products and offers on social media.
- 83% would share information about a product on Facebook if they loved their purchase.

SC benefits fall, in general, into three categories: benefits to customers, benefits to retailers, and benefits to other types of enterprises. Some are described in the following section.

Benefits to Customers

The success of social commerce depends on its benefits to customers. The major benefits appear in the following list:

- It is easy to get recommendations from friends and other customers (e.g., via Twitter, in social network discussion groups, and on product review sites).
- Recommendations result in more confidence and trust helping customers decide about purchasing products and services.
- Added convenience in online shopping.
- Customers are exposed to special deals (e.g., via Groupon) for large savings.
- Purchases are better matched with specific needs, wants, tastes, and wishes of customers; this increases satisfaction and reduces product choice decision time.
- It is easy for customers to use the SC technology.
- Social commerce fits the mobile device lifestyle well.
- Authentic interactions with vendors
- Increased trust in vendors is developed (via closer relationships).
- Social commerce allows customers to help other customers (social support).
- Customers can get better customer service from vendors.
- Customers can meet new friends (e.g., for travel) and socialize online.
- Customers can get rich social context and relevancy during their purchase decisions.
- Customers can connect with individuals and businesses who otherwise are inaccessible to them.
- (See **businessnewsdaily.com/8430-social-commerce-trends.html** and **academia.edu/1364232/The_benefits_of_social_commerce_for_suppliers_and_customers**.)

Benefits to Retailers

Retailers are major benefactors of social commerce. For example, about 50% of businesses globally find new customers via social networks. In addition, about 30% of companies invest in social networking in order to acquire and retain customers.

Retailers may benefit from social commerce in the following ways:

- Consumers can provide feedback on market communication strategy and on product (service) design.
- Improved customer loyalty.
- Vendors get free word-of-mouth marketing.
- Increased website traffic which increases revenue and sales.
- Better search engine rankings.
- Increased sales as collaborative filtering and other social influence methods are used.
- Better data and metrics on customer preferences.
- (See **blog.pixlee.com/5-business-benefits-of-social-commerce** and **trendwatching.com/trends/TWINSUMER.htm**.)

For more on benefits to retailers, see the video titled "Social Media a Powerful Tool for Online Retailers" (4:08 min) at **youtube.com/watch?v=1ByDmQICXs4**.

Example

GoPro Inc., producer of rugged adventure cameras, uses social media intensively to help reach its target audience of young, active users. The company uses a combination of social media networks and focuses on sites that allow customers to share their pictures and video (like Instagram and YouTube). The company credits its social media marketing as a big factor in its early adoption by customers and revenue growth (even though that growth began to stall in 2016). The company believes that continuing to use social media to target its customer base will help it roll out new products in 2017 (Oaks 2016). For more see **youtu.be/oCUjAmW5yCA** and **gorilla360.com.au/blog/gopro-user-generated-content-marketing**.

Benefits to Other Types of Enterprises

In addition to increased sales and revenue, enterprises can benefit from social commerce in several ways:

- Conduct faster and less costly recruitment with a larger reach to large number of candidates.
- Reduce costs via innovative methods such as using the collective intelligence of employees and business partners.
- Foster better external relationships, for example, with partners and channel distribution members.
- Increase collaboration and improve communication within the enterprise and with business partners (e.g., by using blogs, microblogs, and wikis).
- Foster better internal relationships (e.g., by increasing employee productivity and satisfaction).
- Provide free advice to small enterprises by other enterprises and experts (e.g., via LinkedIn groups).
- Understand that it is usually not expensive to install and operate SC systems.
- Locate experts quickly, both internally and externally, whenever needed (e.g., see **guru.com**).
- Conduct market research quickly and inexpensively and get feedback from customers, employees, and business partners.
- Better understand customer needs.
- Increase market share and margins.
- Build brands through conversations and social media promotions.
- Microsegment for reaching very small markets with brand offerings at a low cost.
- Manage company and brand reputations online.
- Build brand communities for positive word of mouth online.
- Enhance customer service and support.
- Generate more authentic customer feedback.
- Increase traffic and sales at the company website and at physical retailers.
- Facilitate market research by monitoring conversations online.
- Increase company and brand rankings on search engine results pages.

The potential benefits in the previous list may increase productivity and value and could provide a *strategic advantage*, and they encourage companies to at least experiment with social commerce.

The Social Business: An IBM Approach

The previously noted benefits to enterprises make it desirable for enterprises to transform to what IBM calls a *social business*. A **social business** is "a business that embraces networks of people to create business value." Many consider this term equivalent to social commerce and use the two interchangeably. However, IBM is more concerned with the structure and operations of enterprises.

IBM strategically integrates social media into various business processes (e.g., procurement) and is developing an organizational culture to support the integration process for delivering rapid and impressive outcomes. For details see **ibm.com/social-business/us/en** and the slideshow at **slideshare.net/AndersQuitzauIbm/social-business-innovation-in-ibm-cbs-2016**.

IBM takes social media seriously and developed a system for their Watson supercomputer to analyze social media content. The company describes the innovation as "IBM Watson Analytics for Social Media guides you through the traffic of social networks and automatically creates data visualizations for exceptionally insightful discoveries, all on the cloud. Identify a topic and quickly get relevant content that shows you interesting relationships and patterns. You can easily take the pulse of your audience, gain greater visibility into a topic or market and compare results with other data sources for new insights derived from different views of information." This application was first used internally and is now available for other businesses to leverage. For details see **ibm.com/us-en/marketplace/social-media-data-analysis**.

New or Improved Business Models

Social commerce provides innovative e-commerce business models. Some are new, while others are improvements of regular EC models (e.g., group buying). A large number of SC models are in the area of social shopping as described in section "Social Shopping: Concepts, Benefits, and Models". Several other new models are in the area of enterprise commerce. Here are some brief examples:

- Shopping business models include widgets on social media sites to "buy now."
- Marketing and shopping systems tied to the location of a mobile device (l-commerce).
- Online software agents that put buyers and sellers together, such as when TripAdvisor refers users to online travel sites to purchase hotel rooms.
- Content sponsorship—selling advertising on a site that supports content development (YouTube).
- Crowdsourcing models that allow companies to design their products or logos by involving their customers.
- Sales promotions conducted in social networks that drive traffic to the company's site, such as contests, discounts, and downloading free music and software.
- Recruiting in social networks, as exemplified by LinkedIn.
- Collaboration models that are facilitated by blogs, wikis, and crowdsourcing.

Many start-ups have invented these and other business models. For example, Webkinz (**webkinz.com**) created a huge business around virtual pet world for kids. IZEA Inc. (**izea.com**), a pioneer of social sponsorship, created a marketplace for connecting advertisers with social media creators of content (e.g., bloggers). Kate Spade, a New York fashion designer, created shoppable videos in the #missadventures series (**youtube.com/user/katespadenewyork**).

For the opportunities for business created by social commerce, see Drell (2014). For new models in the fashion industry, see Hope (2016) and **businessfashion.com**.

Concerns and Limitations of Conducting Social Commerce

Although social commerce presents many opportunities for organizations, its implementation may involve some potential risks and possibly complex issues such as integration of new and existing information systems. Representative risk factors are difficulties in justification of SC initiatives to upper management, security and privacy issues, possibilities of fraud, legal concerns, quality of UGC, and time wasting by employees during work hours. Companies also risk loss of control over their brand images and reputations in social media conversations and product review sites, which can affect product sales (Pownall 2015). The major barriers to adoption of Enterprise 2.0 are resistance to change, difficulty in measuring ROI, and difficulties of integration with existing IT systems and security.

SECTION 8.3 REVIEW QUESTIONS

1. List the major benefits to customers.
2. List the major benefits to retailers.
3. List the major benefits to other companies than retailers.

4. Describe new or improved social commerce business models.
5. Describe some concerns and limitations of social commerce.
6. How does IBM support better understanding of social media metrics?

8.4   SOCIAL SHOPPING: CONCEPTS, BENEFITS, AND MODELS

Involvement in shopping is a natural area for social networks. Although shopping in social networks is only beginning to grow, it has enormous potential. Leading the movement of social shopping are Facebook and Google (Knight 2016). In this section, we cover the essentials of social shopping.

Definitions and Drivers of Social Shopping

Shopping is, by nature, a social activity. **Social shopping** (also known as *sales 2.0*) is online shopping with social media tools and platforms including five social networks. It is about sharing shopping experiences with friends. Social shopping blends e-commerce and social media. Thus, social commerce takes the key features of social media (e.g., discussion groups, blogs, recommendations, reviews, etc.) and uses them before, during, and after shopping.

   An overview of social shopping is provided by Turban et al. (2016).

The Drivers of Social Commerce

The following are the major drivers of social shopping:

- A large number of people visiting social networks attract advertisers.
- The increasing number of recommendations/suggestions made by friends and the ease and speed of accessing them.
- The need to compete (e.g., by differentiation) and to satisfy the social customer.
- The emergence of social customers with knowledge and competence in using the Internet (e.g., in finding reviews and comparing prices).
- The need to collaborate with business partners.
- The huge discounts provided by some of the new business models (e.g., flash sales).
- The socially oriented shopping models (e.g., group buying).
- The ease of shopping while you are inside some social networks (e.g., from Facebook's "Buy" button).
- The ease of communicating with friends in real time using Twitter and smartphones.

   For more on social shopping, see Bradburn (2016) and **webtrends.about.com/od/web20/a/social-shopping.htm**.

Concepts and Content of Social Shopping

Social shopping is done in social networks (e.g., Polyvore, Wanelo), in vendors' socially oriented stores, in stores of special intermediaries (such as Groupon.com), and on social networks. The buyers are *social customers* that trust and/or enjoy social shopping. As will be seen later in this section, there is a wide range of social shopping models that utilize many of the Web 2.0 tools as well as social communities. The nature of shopping is changing, especially for brand name clothes and related items. For example, popular brands are sold by e-tailers such as Gap (**gap.com**), Shopbop (**shopbop.com**), and InStyle (**instyle.com**). In addition, fashion communities such as Stylehive (**stylehive.com**) and Polyvore (**polyvore.com**) help promote the season's latest fashion collections. Social shoppers are logging on to sites like Net-a-Porter (**net-a-porter.com**) to buy designer clothes online. They can also log on to sites such as ThisNext (**thisnext.com**), create profiles, and blog about their favorite brands. For practical issues of social commerce, see **digitalintelligencetoday.com/social-shopping-101-a-practitioners-prime** and **sage.ie/business-advice/growing-and-running/small-business-guide-to-social-media**.

   There are two basic practices for deployment of social shopping:

1. Add social software, apps, and features (e.g., polling) to existing e-commerce sites.
2. Add e-commerce functionalities (e.g., e-catalogs, payment gateways, and shopping carts) to social media and network sites, where many vendors offer their stores.

Why Shoppers Go Social

Many shoppers like to hear from others prior to purchasing. Therefore, they ask for recommendations from friends or use the concept of communal shopping.

Communal shopping (also known as *collaborative shopping*) is a method of shopping where shoppers enlist friends and other people they trust to advise them on what products to shop for. This results in more confidence in decisions made to buy or not to buy (a phenomenon known as the "bandwagon effect"). For examples, watch the video "New Frontiers in the Communal Shopping Experience" (2:58 min) at **bloomberg.com/video/eden-s-communal-shopping-experience-Exvm-RAIhTE2AZapKKd5aVA.html**.

The Roles in Social Commerce

The following roles people play in social media and e-commerce:

- **Connectors.** These are the people with contacts that introduce people to each other. Connectors try to influence people to buy. Consultants and connected people play this role.
- **Salespeople.** Like their offline counterparts, salespeople's major effort is to influence shoppers to buy. They are well connected so they can impress buyers.
- **Seekers.** These consumers seek advice and information about shopping and services from experts, friends, and mavens.
- **Mavens.** Mavens are recognized but are unofficial experts in certain domains that can provide positive or negative recommendations to advice seekers.
- **Self-sufficients.** These people work on their own and do not like to be influenced.
- **Unclassifieds.** Most people do not belong to any one of the above categories.

The major influencers are friends, other consumers, salespeople, connectors, and mavens (experts).

Benefits of Social Shopping

Many of the benefits of social commerce (section "The Benefits and Limitations of Social Commerce") apply to social shopping. Additional benefits are:

- You can socialize while shopping.
- You can quickly get honest feedback.
- You can discover products/services you never knew existed (e.g., see **thisnext.com**).
- You can interact with vendor (brand) representatives easily and quickly (e.g., feature available at the blog on **stylehive.com**).
- Your confidence and trust in online shopping may increase due to engagement and interactions with friends.
- You can get super deals via group buying, daily specials, and more. Join Groupon just to see the super daily deals.
- You can exchange shopping tips with your friends, fans, and others. Thus, you can learn from experiences of others.
- You can build and share wish lists.
- You can shop together with people like you.

For more benefits, including for sellers, see Turban et al. (2016) and **digitalintelligencetoday.com/social-shopping-101-a-practitioners-prime**.

Note that social shopping sites may generate additional revenue from advertising, commissions on actual sales, sharing customer information with retailers, and affiliate marketing.

The use of social media marketing is justified financially in many cases. For a free e-book of examples, see Petersen (2014) and **stuartjdavidson.com/how-to-win-in-social-media**.

Note: Both Pinterest and Twitter are providing activities with some or all of these models directly and indirectly. For Twitter, see **business.twitter.com/twitter-101**.

What Elements to Expect in a Social Shopping Site

Depending on the social shopping model, on the products offered and related information, and on the supporting information systems, one may find a diversity of elements in a site. The following are the major elements that help shoppers in making purchasing decisions:

- **Visual sharing.** Photos, videos, and other images enable shoppers to visually share their product experiences.
- **Online discussions.** Ratings, reviews, interactions, recommendations, blogging, and comments facilitate discussions regarding features and benefits of products.
- **Journals of products and their use.** These demonstrate how to use products via videos, blogs, and step-by-step instructions.
- **Guides.** Guides are created by users who can be experienced consumers, experts, or employees. The guides are supported by case studies, testimonials, and videos.

Traditional E-Commerce Sites with Social Media Additions

In addition to pure social shopping sites, there are many traditional e-commerce sites that add social media tools (e.g., see Helmrich 2017). A prominent example is Amazon.com, which adds recommendations, reviews, ratings, and more.

Example: The Cheetos Museum Engages Customers' Imaginations

Cheetos are a unique American snack food made from puffed corn coated with artificial cheese flavor. They are very common in the United States and well known by most customers. As Americans grow more conscious of their diets, the consumption of snack foods has the possibility of decreasing. To keep their product in customers' minds, Cheetos interacts regularly through social media with its customer group, reinforcing the snack food's positive and fun image.

Cheetos has found that the most successful social media campaigns are the ones that directly elicit participation from its users. The most recent example is the Cheetos Museum (**cheetosmuseum.com**). The Cheetos Museum seeks to find uniquely shaped Cheetos snacks that bear resemblances to animals, objects, and famous persons. The museum allows customers to upload images using their web browsers or mobile devices with pictures of their misshapen snack food and a description of what it supposedly looks like. To help encourage customers to participate, Cheetos offers a cash prize for the best submission and also allows voting across all submissions to help select the winner (Gioglio 2016).

This type of brand promotion through social media leverages an immersive experience and is common in other brands with successful social media campaigns. Many of these campaigns also include curated museums (Monllos 2016). Not only does this campaign engage customers but also allows the company to better understand their preferences as well as their patterns of consumption. Because of the submissions, voting, and prizes, a company is able to extend the length of the campaign and thus maintain awareness with users for a longer period of time.

For more see **twitter.com/ChesterCheetah/status/755895976359931904**.

The Major Types and Models of Social Shopping

A large number of social shopping models and strategies have appeared in recent years, many created by start-ups such as Groupon.com. Some are extensions of EC generic models; others are unique to social shopping. These models can be stand alone, combined, or used within social networks. We have grouped them into the following categories:

- Group buying
- Deal purchases (flash sales), such as daily special offers
- Shopping together in real time
- Communities and clubs

- Marketplaces
- Innovative models
- Shopping for virtual products and services
- Location-based shopping (presented in section "Social Advertising: From Viral Advertising to Microblogging and Other Promotions")
- Shopping presentation sites (e.g., on YouTube) and gaming sites
- Peer-to-peer models (e.g., money lending)
- Private online clubs
- B2B shopping

For these, there are several shopping aids which we describe after we elaborate on some of these categories.

Group Buying

The group buying B2C model was unpopular and seldom used in many countries, including the United States. However, in other countries (e.g., China), group buying has had good success. The problem with this model was the difficulty in organizing the groups, even with an intermediary. Furthermore, even if a group was organized, the negotiations about discounts could have been difficult, unless a very large volume was negotiated. In order to rally shoppers, group-shopping sites like LivingSocial and BuyWithMe offer major discounts or special deals during a short time frame. These start-up companies act as intermediaries to negotiate the deals with vendors. Group buying is closely associated with daily deals (flash sales). The social commerce approach revived the not so successful original e-commerce model and frequently is combined with flash sales.

Note: The model is not so popular today (2016) in the United States but is very popular in China.

Group Buying in China

Group buying is very popular in China ("tuangou" in Chinese). In the first half of 2015, about 1000 companies were active all over China with an estimated 180 million shoppers who purchased more than $12 billion in goods and services (Yoo 2015). Almost 1 in 5 people used group buying in June, 2015 alone. For example, Lashou.com (**lashou.com**) operates in more than 100 cities. Major companies there are Nuomi and Meituan. Meituan has more than 50% of China's group buying market share in terms of gross merchandise volume and currently has a $7 billion valuation and recently raised over $3.3bn to grow its offering (Clover 2016).

The Process

For several years, Chinese buyers were organizing groups to buy a product (e.g., a car). Then, the group leader bargained with potential sellers. Sometimes the leader brought the entire buying group to a face-to-face collective negotiation (e.g., see a video [1:59 min] "Group Shopping Tuangou" at **vimeo.com/8619105**).

All major Chinese Internet companies have launched, or plan to launch, group buying and flash deals. These includes **ir. baidu.com**, **sina.com**, **tencent.com**, and **alibaba.com**. For details, watch the video titled "Group Buying in China" (2:10 min) at **cnn.com/video/data/2.0/video/business/2011/01/26/yoon.china.coupon.gen.cnn.html** or read **eggplantdigital.cn/china-buying-trends-2016-this-article-could-change-your-entire-business-model-for-2016**.

Deal Purchases (Flash Sales)

Short period deals are practiced offline usually to attract people who are already in a store, or vendors advertise a sale for a day, or for several days (in a newspaper, radio, and TV), or for "doorbuster" sales between certain hours on a certain day. There are several variations of this model when done online, and it is frequently offered together with other models.

A common strategy of flash sale sites is to focus on an industry. For example, **gilt.com** focuses on designer apparel, jewelry, bags, and upscale home furnishings.

Woot.com (an Amazon.com company) offers community information related to its deals. For example, there is a "discussion about today's deal," a Woot blog, top past deals, deal news, and what percentage of community members bought which product and what quantities of the products. Testimonials by members are also available. Woot is known as a favorite place for gadget geeks. Thus, Woot is not only a brand but also a culture. Other interesting flash sale companies are Jetsetter (a TripAdvisor company) and Rue La La. Flash sales may offer discounts up to 80%.

Shopping Together Online in Real Time

Shoppers on social networks can invite their friends to shop online at the same time, while in different locations. Using Facebook e-mail (or other networks) or Twitter, they interact to discuss shopping-related subjects and provide opinions.

Shopping Together Sites

Dozens of sites facilitate shopping together models. For example, Select2gether allows you to join a conversation in a chat room; create a wish list; shop online in real time with your friends; find inspirations, ideas, and advice; start a live showroom with your friends; and get access to the latest fashion-related products in which the site specializes. For details and explanations, see **select2gether.com/about/help**.

Co-Shopping

Co-shopping is an IBM software tool that enables two online shoppers to browse a store, view products, and chat together, all in real time. It also enables employees in customer care centers to conduct live interactions with customers.

Online Social Shopping Communities

According to **socialecart.com/category/stories**, "*shopping communities* bring like-minded people together to discuss, share, and shop. The community platforms and forums connect people with each other, with businesses and with other communities." To date, fashion communities are the most popular (e.g., Polyvore, Stylefeeder, and ShopStyle). However, other shopping communities are organized around food, pets, toys, and so forth. For example, Listia (**listia.com**) is an online community for buying and selling used or new items, along with fashion, in online auctions using virtual currency. DJdoodleVILLE (**djdoodleville.com**) is an online shopping community specializing in arts and crafts.

For a summary about social shopping communities, see **digitalinnovationtoday.com/speed-summary-ijec-social-commerce-special-edition-social-shopping-communities**.

Examples of Shopping Communities

There are many sites that can be classified as pure shopping communities. A prime example is **polyvore.com**, which is presented in Case 8.1.

CASE 8.1: EC APPLICATION
POLYVORE A TRENDSETTER IN SOCIAL SHOPPING

According to its website, Polyvore **polyvore.com** is a community site for online fashion and style where users are empowered to discover and develop their style and possibly set fashion trends. Users do this by creating "sets" which are shared across the Web. The company collaborates with prominent brands such as Calvin Klein (**calvinklein.com**), Lancome (**lancome-usa.com**), and Coach (**coach.com**) and retailers such as Net-a-Porter, to drive product engagement; the user-generated fashion products on its site are then judged by community members and by celebrities such as Selena Gomez and Katy Perry. Today, the company is also using mobile technologies. For example, it has a new app for that will automatically suggest and mix selected fashions (see **venturebeat.com/2015/04/07/polyvores-new-mobile-app-chooses-outfits-for-you**). Note: Some celebrities, such as Blake Lively, post their own products for sale on the site.

The story of the now-profitable Polyvore is described in detail by Silverbean (2014) as well as by Volusion (2015; an infographic at **volusion.com/ecommerce-blog/articles/success-tips-polyvore-infographic**). Users create "sets," of their wardrobe designs, using a special editor provided free on the site. These "sets" can then be posted and shared on Polyvore's site, Facebook, and Twitter. Merchants (e.g., designers) can use the site for free by (a) creating a profile, (b) uploading existing products, and (c) creating sets.

Once merchants create a profile and upload products, Polyvore encourages the merchants to engage with other community members by reviewing and evaluating the sets. Polyvore believes that the merchants' activity will be reciprocated. To facilitate actual shopping, the sets link to the creators' sites.

Polyvore can be viewed as a crowdsourcing fashion operation that reflects the creativity and opinion of many; thus, it can be viewed as expressing current fashion trends (they now do the same with interior design). In 2015 Remix created an app to help those who want to browse or buy, and not to create outfits (see Perez 2015).

According to TrueShip (2016), Polyvore has over 20 million users importing 2.2 million items to the site each month, creating about 2.5 million fashion sets per month, and viewing sets 1 billion times a month. Users spend hours browsing, following favorite taste streams, asking questions, and sharing ideas. Polyvore is considered by many to be the best place to discover or evaluate fashion trends, which are facilitated by contests managed by the company. Polyvore was acquired by Yahoo in 2015.

Polyvore can be used together with Pinterest to increase traffic to the site.

Sources: Based on Porcellana (2016) Perez (2015), Silverbean (2014), **polyvore.com/cgi/about**, and **crunchbase.com/organization/polyvore** (all accessed January 2017).

Questions

1. How can one use the Polyvore Editor to create designs (see the short video (2:02 min) by Polyvore titled "How to Create a Set in the Polyvore Editor" at **vimeo.com/7800846**).
2. The company added supermodel Tyra Banks as an investor in 2013. Comment on the logic of such an addition.
3. Comment on the logic of creating Remix.
4. Read Porcellana (2016) and explain what and how people create at Polyvore. Also identify the critical success factors of this site.
5. Explain the statement made by Polyvore's vice president of product management: "Our mission is to democratize fashion."
6. Identify all the features of a shopping community in this case.

Private Online Shopping Clubs

One Kings Lane (**onekingslane.com**) is an upscale private shopping club that focuses on unique home furnishing and home decor items. The club offers discounts to members, although the exact amounts are not published. Many of the items available are limited runs, and not available at other merchants. The company believes that its members enjoy the ability to shop a variety of unique and tasteful items with limited availability. The store has recently opened a members-only showroom in New York City.

Examples of Private Clubs

Some private (or "members only") clubs are Beyond the Rack (**beyondtherack.com**; in the United States and Canada posts flash deals), Gilt Groupe (**gilt.com**), Rue La La (**ruelala.com**), men's fashions at JackThreads (**jackthreads.com**), Ideeli (**ideeli.com**), and BestSecret (**bestsecret.com**). Note that, to minimize conflict with department stores, luxury brands now offer select items at Internet prices in stores such as Target Inc. (**target.com**).

Other Innovative Models

There are hundreds of start-ups in social commerce. Here are some representative examples:

- **Wanelo.** This popular social shopping marketplace (especially with young shoppers) combines bookmarking and product sharing. Members can follow others to find trendy shopping. Wanelo (**wanelo.com**) is an online community-based e-commerce site that brings together products from a vast array of stores into one pinboard-style platform. It also has an app on iTunes and Google Play as well as a Facebook fan page. For more information about Wanelo, see **crunchbase.com/organization/wanelo**.
- **Virtual gifts.** There is a rapidly increasing market on social networks for virtual gifts. Facebook sells virtual gifts in its marketplace.
- **Getting help from friends.** To get help from friends, you may go to sites such as **shopshocially.com**. You can post a question, share a purchase, and much more.
- **Shopping without leaving Facebook.** There are several ways to use Facebook fan pages for shopping, so fans do not have to leave Facebook. Payment is one implementation issue and security is another (see **facebook.com/auctionitems**).

- **Social auctions.** Facebook now has a store app for eBay sellers, called Auction Items (previously "eBay items"), where members can send private invitations to their friends to invite them to their store. The Auction Items app is available in several languages. For more details see **facebook.com/AuctionItems**. Facebook also offers an app for Etsy stores.
- **Crowdsourcing shopping advice.** You can get advice from many people (the crowd), as is done by Cloud Shopper. Cloud Shopper allows users to organize the advice given by their friends. Users select products and start a conversation on Facebook about their items of interest. The company also provides price comparisons and price alerts about the selected items; see **cloudshopper.com** for details.
- **Helping sellers and bloggers sell products.** Etsy is a socially oriented marketplace which helps bloggers and sellers (mostly artists) monetize their businesses by making it easy for them to sell products directly to consumer.
- **Event shopping.** There are many sites that will help you shop for a special event (e.g., a wedding) with the assistance of your friends. Many variations of this model exist.
- **Get involved.** Social site Tumblr has recently integrated social donations/shopping into the platform to support user-defined worthy causes. Users can share links from a select partner sites (currently Artsy, Etsy, Kickstarter, and Do Something) and action buttons appear in the top right corner of the posts for people to "buy," "browse," "pledge," or "do something."

Social Shopping Aids: From Recommendations to Reviews, Ratings, and Marketplaces

In addition to the typical e-commerce shopping aids such as comparison engines and recommendations a la Amazon.com style, there are special aids for social commerce.

Recommendations in Social Commerce

Online customers use shopping aids (e.g., price comparison sites like **nextag.com**), looking at product review sites such as **epinions.com**, and researching other sources. Examining and participating in social networking forums is another way to compare prices and read product and service reviews. A variety of SC models and tools is available for this purpose. We present two major categories here.

Ratings and Reviews

Ratings and reviews by friends, even by people that you do not know (e.g., experts or independent third-party evaluators), are usually available for social shoppers. In addition, any user has the opportunity to contribute reviews and participate in relevant discussions. Some tools for conducting rating and reviews can be found at **bazaarvoice.com/solutions/conversations**. Examples are:

- **Customer ratings and reviews.** Customer ratings are popular. They can be found on vendors' product (or service) sites, such as Buzzillions, or on independent review sites (e.g., TripAdvisor), and/or in customer news feeds (e.g., Amazon.com, Epinions). Customer ratings can be summarized by votes or polls.
- **Customer testimonials.** Customer experiences are typically published on vendors' sites and third-party sites such as **tripadvisor.com**. Many sites encourage discussion (e.g., **bazaarvoice.com/solutions/conversations**).
- **Expert ratings and reviews.** Ratings or reviews can also be generated by domain experts and appear in different online publications.
- **Sponsored reviews.** These are written by paid bloggers or domain experts. Advertisers and bloggers find each other by searching through websites such as **sponsoredreviews.com**, which connects bloggers with marketers and advertisers.
- **Conversational marketing.** People communicate via e-mail, blog, live chat, discussion groups, and tweets. Monitoring conversations may yield rich data for market research and customer service (e.g., as practiced by Dell; see their social media command center).
- **Video product review.** Reviews can be generated by using videos. YouTube offers reviews that are uploaded, viewed, commented on, and shared.
- **Bloggers reviews.** This is a questionable method since some bloggers are paid and may use a biased approach. However, many bloggers have the reputation to be unbiased.

Example

Maui Jim (**mauijim.com**) is a designer of high-quality polarized sunglasses. The company is using Bazaarvoice Ratings & Reviews to enable customers to rate the company's sunglasses and accessories.

The company is relying on word-of-mouth marketing to advertise its products and help shoppers. Customers are invited to share their opinions on the style, fit, and quality of specific sunglass models. The invitations appear when customers are conducting a search. Maui Jim sends customers an e-mail asking them to review products and the company has reviews on its pages in selected social network sites.

Social Recommendations and Referrals

Recommendation engines allow shoppers to receive advice from other shoppers and to give advice to others.

Social shopping may combine recommendations in a social network platform with actual sales. Social recommendations and referrals are closely related to ratings and reviews and are sometimes integrated with them.

Example

Amazon (**amazon.com**) is a huge global retailer specializing in B2C sales. One huge advantage that Amazon has over other e-tailers is its large customer base. Amazon is able to leverage that customer base to provide additional product information to potential buyers during the purchase decision-making process. In addition to providing product descriptions, pictures, videos, user rankings, and user reviews, Amazon has also enabled a system that allows potential buyers to ask past buyers questions about a product. For example, if a potential buyer is interested in purchasing a new rug, they may ask previous buyers how well the rug has resisted wear or if the color in the picture is an accurate representation of the actual rug's color. Potential purchasers are able to ask these questions to past buyers anonymously, and past buyers are able to reply if they choose to. Additionally, these answered questions are stored for reference for future customers (see Steiner 2014 and **amazon.com/gp/forum/content/db-guidelines.html**).

It makes sense to combine recommendations with marketing communications and shopping. Sites in this category allow shoppers to receive and provide advice to specific friends, in contrast with traditional online product reviews that include advice provided by unknown shoppers. Furthermore, these sites sell ad space and provide coupons, and some offer automatic cash-back rewards for shopping with local merchants.

Sometimes, social recommendations are embedded in social shopping portals that offer shopping tools as well as bundling recommendations with ratings and reviews.

Common recommendation methods are:

- **Social bookmarking.** Recommended products, services, etc. are bookmarked so members of social networks can easily find them.
- **Personal social recommendations.** These are based on finding people with similar profiles. By using these customers' actual purchases, conclusions can be reached about general and targeted recommendations (e.g., see Apple's Near Me [**getnearme.com**]; applications that are popular based on a user's current location), Amazon Recommendations, and Snoox (**snoox.com**; "your friends' recommendations on everything").
- **Referral programs.** Affiliate programs (e.g., Amazon Associates [**affiliate-program.amazon.com**] and Apple's iTunes Affiliate Program [**apple.com/itunes/affiliates**]) pay people for referring new customers. For more about referral programs, see **slideshare.net/getAmbassador/building-an-effective-referral-program**.
- **Matching algorithms.** Consulting companies and vendors (e.g., Netflix) provide recommendations based on similarity algorithms.

Illustrative Examples of Recommendation Sites

A typical example is provided next.

Buzzillions

Buzzillions (**buzzillions.com**) is a user-generated product review site. It gets reviews from its parent company, PowerReviews (acquired by Bazaarvoice), which provides customer review software to e-commerce sites. It also incorporates product reviews from companies that use other third-party providers or have an in-house review system. The site provides several useful tools for tagging and researching the reviews. It also provides ranking. By 2016 it had over 17 million product reviews.

Buzzillions' business model is based on selling traffic, or product leads, from Buzzillions right back to the merchant network that uses PowerReviews. In other words, Buzzillions' readers read reviews imported from many other sites, and they can then click on products of interest, giving them the opportunity to read more about these products and possibly purchase them at the seller's site.

The company is unique because:

1. The rankings are based on feedback from customers. The company provides the tools to narrow down the search, but the consumers have to read the reviews to see if the product is right for them.
2. Positive or negative, all reviews are encouraged on Buzzillions. Unless a review is profane or violates the company's terms, it will be shown on the site.
3. Buzzillions does not sell products, although the company has retail partners listed on the site for direct contact by consumers.

Concerns about Social Reviews and Recommendations

Some people raise the issue of how accurate the reported reviews and recommendations are. Fake reviews and claims are suspected to be 30–40% of the total reviews in some sites. For example, see the "allegations against business owners" at **en.wikipedia.org/wiki/Yelp**. There is also a concern about businesses paying money to review sites to manipulate the reviews. Another concern is that in cases of small number of reviewers a bias (positive or negative) may be shown.

Concerns about fake reviews are growing as the use of social recommendations becomes more and more important in the customer decision-making process (see **bbb.org/hawaii/news-events/news-releases/2016/11/increase-in-fake-retail-apps-as-the-holidays-approach**). Unscrupulous sellers have found that the use of fake reviews can significantly increase the purchase of their products, even if the product attributes are not described correctly. This is a large concern for both merchants and customers. From the merchant's perspective, fake reviews can influence purchases away from better or more appropriate products, and this can result in returns and dissatisfaction with the retailer themselves. From a customer perspective, fake reviews can drive people to make incorrect decisions about products that may not have all of the functionality or may not have the value-for-money that they were expecting. Tutorials have sprung up to help users understand when the review they are reading maybe fake (**howtogeek.com/282802/how-to-spot-fake-reviews-on-amazon-yelp-and-other-sites**). Amazon, one of the largest users of customer reviews, is cracking down on the practice. Amazon has begun to sue sellers who have posted or purchased fake reviews to be posted on their site (**techcrunch.com/2016/10/27/amazon-sues-more-sellers-for-buying-fake-reviews**). The company hopes that these actions will put the dishonest on notice and decrease the frequency of fake reviews.

For a discussion, see Barnett (2015), or for an infographic, see **vendasta.com/blog/50-stats-you-need-to-know-about-online-reviews**.

Other Shopping Aids and Services

In addition to recommendations and marketplaces, there are several sites that provide social shopping aids, as illustrated in the following examples.

Yelp: The Shoppers' Best Helper

Yelp (**yelp.com**) is company that operates a local guide for helping people find in a specific city services ranging from mechanics to restaurants based on reviews and recommendations of users. In this way, it connects people with great local businesses. Community members, known as "Yelpers," write reviews of the businesses and then rate them. Yelpers also find events and special offers and can "talk" with each other (e.g., see **yelp.com/talk**).

The site is also a place for businesses to advertise their products and services (paying fees to Yelp for posting a "Yelp Deal"). Yelp is also accessible via mobile devices. The site offers several social networking features such as discussion forums, photo posting, and creation of groups and have followers. Yelp has a company blog (**officialblog.yelp.com**), along with a community blog for Elite Yelpers worldwide (**communityblog.yelp.com**). Yelpers who frequently become actively involved and engage on the site can apply to become an "Elite Squad" member (see **yelp.com/elite**).

How Yelp Works

Users look for a business in a specific location. Yelp's search engine finds available businesses and presents them with ratings and reviews as well as with accessibility and directions.

Yelp connects with Google Maps to show the business location and further aids in discovering related businesses.

Adding social features to user reviews creates a reputation system, whereby site visitors can see the good and the bad. For the topic of reputation management, see **seofriendly.com/tag/reputation-management**. For more on Yelp's operation, see the video "Yelp Explained" at **youtu.be/RPRDZgYSZ_c**. For further information, see **yelp.com/faq** and **en.wikipedia.org/wiki/Yelp**.

Note that some shopping aids can be used for both online and offline shopping. One such aid is the touchscreen PC available at kiosks in physical stores, (e.g., Kohl's) where you can examine catalogs and place your order to be shipped to your home, while you are in the store.

Collaborative Product Reviews

Sites such as ProductWiki (**productwiki.com**) are structured like a wiki; thus, every user can contribute to the site. The goal is to create a comprehensive resource collection. The companies believe that a need exists for unbiased, accurate, and community-based resources for product information. These sites use *collaborative reviews*, a collection of pros and cons about a product submitted by and voted on by the consumers. The result is a comprehensive review that takes the opinions of many people into account and highlights the most important aspects of a product. A collaborative review is made up of two things—short statements and votes. Community members submit and vote on specific statements that are separated by pros and cons, making it easy to see what is good and bad about each product. For further information on collaborative reviews, see **productwiki.com/home/article/collaborative-reviews.html**.

Dealing with Complaints

As seen earlier, customers have learned how to use social media to air their complaints. For a UK survey that shows that customers are more likely to complain via social media, see **xlgroup.com/press/new-survey-finds-customers-increasingly-likely-to-use-social-media-to-complain**. See also **gocompare.com/covered/2016/05/how-to-complain-on-social-media-and-get-what-you-want/**.

Social Marketplaces and Direct Sales

The term **social marketplace** refers to a marketplace that uses social media tools and platforms and acts as an online intermediary between buyers and sellers. Ideally, a social marketplace should enable the marketing of members' own creations as Polyvore does.

Some examples of social marketplaces include:

- **Craigslist.** Craigslist (**craigslist.org**) can be considered a social network marketplace in that it provides online classified ads and discussion areas and supports social activities (meetings, dating, events).
- **Backpage.** Backpage (**backpage.com**) is similar to Craigslist and provides classified ads for local communities.
- **Fotolia.** Fotolia (**fotolia.com**) is a social marketplace for royalty-free photos, images, and video clips. In 2014, there were more than 31 million images available on the site. It serves a community of artists, designers, and other creative people who express themselves through images, forums, and blogs. Buyers can legally buy images (pay only one time for each or periodically) and then use these images and photos as they wish (e.g., resell them, modify them, etc.). For details see **us.fotolia.com/info/AboutUs**.
- **Flipsy.** Anyone can use Flipsy (**flipsy.com**) to list, buy, and sell books, music, movies, and games. It was created to fill the need for a free and trustworthy media marketplace. Flipsy does not charge commissions in order to increase the trading volume. Payment processing for items purchased is handled by a third party, such as PayPal.
- **ShopSocially.** ShopSocially (**shopsocially.com**) is a consumer-to-consumer marketing communication and experience-sharing platform for shopping. This platform also enables shoppers to recommend products to their friends. ShopSocially combines the concepts of online shopping and social networks, creating a new business model of online social shopping. Users can solicit shopping information from friends via Facebook, Twitter, and e-mail. A combination of shopping questions, their answers, and purchases shared by friends creates a powerful experience and shopping knowledge base. For details and benefits to retailers, see **shopsocially.com**.

Direct Sales from within Social Networks

There is an increased volume of direct sales, mostly on Facebook. Here is an example:

Example: How Musicians Sell Online via Social Networks like Spotify

Spotify is becoming a very prominent new music-based social network. Launched in 2008, the service currently has over 70 million users. It offers a wide variety of music from different artists signed under different music labels. The system allows users to share songs and artists they enjoy through other social networks like Facebook and Twitter. Because of the social interaction that it facilitates, Spotify can be considered its own social network with a user group that is very interested in music (see **businessonmarketst.com/blog/spotify-the-social-network**).

Artists are able to distribute their music on Spotify, either through their labels or through self-distribution. In this way, Spotify offers options to new and lesser-known artists that may not have been available to be heard through traditional radio or CD distribution channels. Many artists gained their initial notoriety through Spotify. Unfortunately, the economics of licensing music through Spotify, or other similar channels, is not lucrative for the artist. Many will need to use other means to generate significant income from their work, such as album sales and concerts. (See **digitalmusicnews.com/2016/06/03/artist-sales-equal-spotify-salary**.)

Example: How buy Button Work

Following Facebook, other social networks and retailers introduced "buy buttons." Examples are Twitter, Pinterest, Instagram (Kuchler 2015), Google, and many more. These buttons help to convert social views into purchases by presenting buying options in locations that are convent and relevant to users' interests.

Socially Oriented Person-to-Person (P2P) Selling, Buying, Renting, or Bartering

When individuals trade online, they may do so with some social elements. For example, some consider **craigslist.org** to be a socially oriented virtual community and so is **altimetergroup.com**. Here are some more examples:

P2P Sharing (Also Known as *Collaborative Consumption*)

SnapGoods facilitates P2P sharing. Some other sites, like SwapBabyGoods.com (**swapbabygoods.com**), Swapmamas (**swapmamas.com**), and Neighborhood Fruit (**neighborhoodfruit.com**; helps people share fruit that are growing in their yards or find fruit trees on public lands), have a niche market. The sharing and renting trend is booming, especially during the economic recession; and there is a "green" aspect as well—saving on the use of resources. There is also the social aspect of sharing, allowing people to make meaningful connections with others (see Hickman 2015 for details).

Several variations exist. Some people share cars for a price (ride sharing, e.g., Uber and Lyft), and others invite travelers to stay free in their homes or exchange homes (e.g., **couchsurfing.com**) for a short periods and much more.

Shopping for Virtual Goods in a Virtual Economy

An increasing number of shoppers purchase all kinds of virtual products and services online. **Virtual goods** are computer images of real or imaginary goods. These include, but are not limited to, properties and merchandise on Second Life (such as virtual mobile phones to equip your avatar) and a large number of items sold in multiplayer games in on social networks (e.g., FarmVille on Facebook).

The Virtual Economy

A **virtual economy** is an emerging economy existing in several virtual worlds, where people exchange virtual goods frequently related to an Internet game or to a virtual business. People go there primarily for entertainment. However, some people trade their virtual goods or properties. A virtual property can be any resource that is controlled by virtual objects, avatars, or user accounts. For the characteristics of these properties, see **en.wikipedia.org/wiki/Virtual_economy**.

Why People buy Virtual Goods

There are several reasons why people buy virtual goods. For example, many people in China buy virtual properties because they cannot afford to buy properties in the real world. According to Savitz (2011) and further detailed by Hamari (2015), there are four major reasons for such purchases made in any country:

1. **Generating special experiences.**
2. **Generating emotions.**
3. **Small purchases make people happier.**
4. **Virtual goods are low cost and low hassle.**

Real-Time Online Shopping

In real-time online shopping, shoppers can log onto a site and then either connect with Facebook or with another social network instantly from a smartphone or computer or invite their friends and family via Twitter or e-mail. Friends shop online together *at the same time*, exchanging ideas and comparing experiences.

Some real-time shopping platforms are Facebook's social graph-based shopping platforms. Another player in this area is BevyUP (see **bevyup.com/resources** and **samesurf.com/about.html**). These empower multiple users to share their experiences in real time.

Note: Facebook is considering building a shopping mall to compete with Amazon.com. Facebook will add a strong social flavor to the mall (see King 2015).

Social Shopping in the Near Future

Imagine this scenario: A retailer will ask you to log in with Facebook on your mobile device as soon as you step into a physical store. Many of Facebook's partners have custom Facebook applications (Partner Apps) that users can download through their app stores, including Blackberry and Windows Phone (see **facebook.com/Mobile**).

In this way users can receive *customized recommendations* on their mobile phones. You can expect that your friends who have been in that store will indicate electronically which clothes may be the best fit for you (e.g., using "likes") and then walk in and find what to buy. Privacy is a concern to many but less important to "millennials" who frequently share their experiences with others. In addition, sometimes people do not need to reveal their full identity on an in-store screen. See a related video titled "The Future of Shopping" (48 s) at **youtube.com/watch?v=R_TAP0OY1Bk**.

For example, when you walk into a dressing room in a department store, the mirror reflects your image, but you also see the images of apparel items (you like and certain) celebrities wear, all on an interactive display. A webcam also projects an image of a consumer wearing the item on a website, for everyone to see. This creates an interaction between the consumers inside the store and their social network (friends) outside the store. The technology behind this system uses RFID (radio-frequency identification) and has already been tried by the Prada store in New York City for showing customers which shoes and purses would go with the clothes they are trying on in the dressing room. You can watch a video titled "Future Store (Smart Dressing Room)" (2:53 min) of how a "smart" dressing room works at **youtube.com/watch?v=0VII-xdg5Ak&feature=related**. Note that due to privacy concerns, Prada (and others) discontinued their RFID experiments.

SECTION 8.4 REVIEW QUESTIONS

1. Define social shopping and describe its drivers.
2. List the major benefits of social shopping.
3. List the major models of social shopping. Briefly describe their functionalities.
4. Describe ratings, reviews, and recommendations.
5. Define group buying.
6. Define social communities and social clubs as they relate to marketing. How do they work?
7. Define social marketplaces. What is going on there?
8. Describe the major shopping aids.
9. Describe shopping for virtual goods.
10. Describe social shopping in the near future.

8.5   SOCIAL ADVERTISING: FROM VIRAL ADVERTISING TO MICROBLOGGING AND OTHER PROMOTIONS

The major current revenue source for many social commerce companies is advertising. The reason is that seeing the large number of members and visitors in the social networks, and the amount of time they spend there, has given advertisers the motivation and justification to pay a great deal for placing ads and running promotions in those networks. Like other SC activities, advertising is done both in public, as well as in private company-owned social networks.

Many advertisers are placing ads on Facebook, YouTube, LinkedIn, Instagram, Pinterest, or Twitter. Although social media campaigns may have a small impact on actual online retail sales, they may have huge benefits with regard to increasing *brand awareness*. Millions of companies have pages and a presence on all major social networks. The value of social media marketing is significant. Hootsuite details a number of social media advertising statistics at **blog.hootsuite.com/social-media-advertising-stats**; they include:

- Social media advertising budgets have doubled worldwide over the past 2 years—going from US $16 billion in 2014 to $31 billion in 2016.
- Social media spending in the United States alone is expected to increase to $17.34 billion in 2019.
- Social media ad spending is likely to exceed $35 billion in 2017, representing 16% of all digital ad spending globally.

Social ads and Social Apps

Most ads in social commerce are branded content paid for by advertisers. These come in two major categories: *social ads* and *social apps*.

1. **Social ads.** These display ads and banners are placed in social games and discussion boards in social networks.
2. **Social apps.** These applications support social interactions and user contributions. These are more complex to implement than social ads.

Facebook features hundreds of thousands of third-party software applications on its site. One popular application area is travel. For example, one specific application is "Where I've Been," which includes a map of places where users have visited or hope to visit. You can plan trips, organize group travel, and find and rate paid or free accommodations (e.g., at Couchswap). This information can be sold to travel-oriented vendors, who in turn advertise their products to Facebook members. Of special interest is TripAdvisor's "Cities I've Visited" with its interactive map. Research has shown that social media users are greatly influenced by the travel recommendations and experiences of others (see **independenttraveler.com/travel-tips/travelers-ed/social-media-the-ultimate-travel-guidebook**).

Viral (Word-of-Mouth) Marketing and Social Networking

Viral marketing refers to electronic word-of-mouth (WOM) method by which people tell others (frequently their friends) about a product they like or dislike. Viral marketing and advertising has several variations and it plays a major role in e-commerce and social commerce. For more, see Logan (2014), **learningmarketing.net**, and Turban et al. (2016).

Young adults are especially good at viral marketing. If members like a certain product or service, word-of-mouth advertising will spread rapidly sometimes to millions of people at a minimal cost to companies' advertisers. For example, when YouTube first started up, the site conducted almost no traditional advertising in its first few months, but millions joined because of WOM. For the "power of WOM," see **bazaarvoice.com/research-and-insight/social-commerce-statistics** and see HigherVisibility (2015) for examples of recent successful campaigns and Smith (2015) and Griffith (2014) for examples using Instagram to acquire customers.

Viral Blogging

Many retailers are capitalizing on WOM marketing by using bloggers. See some examples at **viralbloggingsystem.com**. When viral marketing is done by bloggers, it is referred to as **viral blogging**. Viral blogging can be very effective with the use of tools such as Twitter (e.g., do a Google search for "Dell Uses Twitter to Drive Sales").

Note that paid bloggers may be biased in favor of those that hire them. This could be a concern for the blogs' readers.

Other Viral Marketing Methods

Viral marketing is done in most social networks through internal e-mail, text messages, and forwarding of videos, stories, and special offers. In addition, there are other innovative ways to go viral.

Using YouTube and Other Social Presentation Sites for Advertising

Using videos for advertising is becoming a major successful strategy. Sellers introduce new products or try to improve a brand image by attaching video clips to their product pages on social networks or their corporate portal.

Viral Videos

A **viral video** is any video that is forwarded rapidly from one person to others, sometimes with a recommendation to watch it. Social networks are an ideal place to disseminate such videos, which became popular due to Internet sharing (mostly through video sharing websites, e-mail, texting, blogs, etc.). This method is inexpensive.

   Here we briefly describe how viral videos work with social commerce. Social media can be most powerful when a video goes viral, because it is an attention grabber (e.g., funny). People forward videos or their URLs to their friends and acquaintances, and as a result, many watch a video that may contain an ad or show a brand logo. Certain videos can receive several million hits in less than a week. Big brands do not always dominate here. For example, some of the most well-known viral videos of 2016 were those produced by HBO, Visa, and the Democratic National Committee (DNC), and others were created by start-up companies or individuals.

Why It Works

Interesting videos seen on YouTube are usually shared through Facebook, Twitter, or e-mail. These posts are in turn shared through the same channels from the recipients.

   Interesting examples are available at **blog.socialmaximizer.com/youtube-business-use-cases**.

Using Twitter as an Advertising and Marketing Tool

Twitter and some other microblogging sites have added social networking capabilities to their sites such as creating profiles and lists of fans and friends. Sellers can reach out to these friends to create strong WOM.

   Twitter is becoming a little more of a business. The company launched its first ad product—"promoted tweets"—in 2010 and netted $45 million in ad dollars. That was due in part because brands like Virgin America, Coke, Ford, and Verizon were willing to experiment with the idea. Twitter earned about $2.2 billion in 2015, up from $1.4 billion in 2014. In 2016, Twitter's revenues began to falter, and there were decreases in the value of its stock (see **recode.net/2016/4/26/11586438/ twitter-earnings-q1-added-new-users**).

   Companies can tweet about their business and product offerings, including promotions. This way, they can attract Twitter followers to visit their stores. Twitter may help disseminate ads resulting in increased sales. Twitter's software suites help merchants reach their Twitter followers by posting "tweets" when the merchants add new products or create promotions. For successful examples, do Google searches for "twitter simply speakers" and "twitter SBL publishing." Twitter is already the world's second-largest social networking platform (about 317 million registered users in September 2016) (see reports at **mediabistro.com**). This may help the microblogging site compete with Facebook in attracting advertisers.

   Finally, here are some more ways one can do business or advertise on Twitter. These are:

- **Recruiting and finding jobs.** These can be facilitated by direct contacts or contacts via an intermediary.
- **Brand display.** A company's blog, display ads, and marketing communications can be displayed on Twitter. Bloggers can display their capabilities.
- **Market research.** By listening to tweets, companies can learn what customers and competitors say. Also, companies can actively participate in discussions.
- **Delivering offers.** Companies can offer promotions, coupons, and discounts to those that opt-in. For example, American Express synchronized their customers' accounts with the customers' Twitter account to provide discounts from participating merchants.
- **Collaboration.** Twitter provides for efficient collaboration within and between organizations.
- **Customer service.** As will be described in section "Social Advertising: From Viral Advertising to Microblogging and Other Promotions", Twitter can facilitate CRM and customer service.
- **Using professionals to enhance company presence on Twitter.** Twitter is used by many professionals, some of who are social commerce influencers. Companies can interact with these professionals and with active bloggers.
- **Cost-effectiveness.** Interacting with customers and business partners using Twitter is very cost-effective. An example is American Apparel, which is using Twitter to solicit and discuss ideas for ads.

Twitter gained significant notoriety during the 2016 US presidential elections. Most political candidates, parties, and special interest groups used the platform extensively to talk to voters and to each other. Twitter's platform allows for the direct communication between candidates and voters, leaving out media sources that often distribute this information. The platform also allowed individuals to reply back to the candidates and the message that they had posted. The social aspects of the system allowed like-minded individuals to communicate with each other, but some argued that this resulted in "echo chambers" of people only agreeing with themselves. The effects of Twitter in the 2016 election will certainly be studied and debated in the future, possibly on Twitter (Kapko 2016).

A major success factor is the mobility of Twitter. Most people tweet from mobile devices. As a matter of fact, the majority of its advertising revenue comes from mobile ads. For more information on how to advertise on Twitter, see this comprehensive guide **blog.kissmetrics.com/twitter-marketing-guide**.

Using Facebook for Advertising

With a huge number of users and even more traffic, Facebook is a likely location for social media advertising. There are many ways to use Facebook to advertise a company's product or service, and the method used is often based on the goals of the company.

Banners and Other ads

One direct way to use Facebook is by the use of banner and other types of display ads. These ads can be targeted to users based on search results as well as personal preferences and interests. These ads can then be used to drive traffic to a business in main page or microsite.

Facebook Offers

This feature allows companies to post coupons on their Facebook page. Fans as well as other users can "claim" the offers (click on "get offer") that come as a mobile newsfeed. Any offer that is claimed is e-mailed to the person who claimed it for printing or sharing with friends. Offers can be daily deals and other promotions.

Community Presence

Another option that can be used by itself or combined with other advertising methods is simply maintaining a space and activity within the community. Facebook page allows for users to find out more information about products, services, and current events. This may be more appropriate than an external Web page, or used in conjunction with it, since users are already within the social network.

Using LinkedIn

With its large professional audience, LinkedIn is another possibility for business marketing. Unlike many other social networks, LinkedIn is focused on a professional audience, and so the types of products and services that may be effective in this venue would be limited to items that would be purchased by individuals related to or supporting their profession, or businesses themselves. LinkedIn offers several different ways for companies to advertise. Firms can create a page within LinkedIn that describe and market their firm. Companies can purchase display ads that take users to their external website or internal LinkedIn page. A new option allows companies to sponsor activities within LinkedIn to build brand awareness and goodwill with other users.

Other Innovative Ways to Advertise in Social Media

A major objective of social advertising is to increase traffic to the digital and or physical sites. There are many innovative ways to do this. 3dCart (**3dcart.com**) lists the following: Advertise your Facebook store on your company's Facebook page, place a "like" button linked to a customer story to your product page, and use social e-mail marketing on Facebook; advertise your store using customer stories through Twitter; advertise in videos on YouTube; and use mobile apps; social bookmarking will improve communications from your product page.

- Use a Facebook page for your company, and add a Facebook store. Customers will become "fans" of your business to check on updates and meet others with similar interests.
- Tweet about the business, any promotions/new products.
- Blog to your customers to keep them updated about new products.
- Integrate videos (e.g., YouTube) on your website.
- Add social bookmarking to your product's page for easy return.
- Embrace mobile apps.
- Add a Facebook "Like" button with its sponsored story to your product (e.g., Gatorade brand scored 1.2 million conversations in 6 months using their "Mission Control" campaign).

For details on each of the above and more, see **blog.3dcart.com/7-social-commerce-tools-to-increase-traffic** and Sukhraj (2016) and download the e-book "Social Commerce: Monetizing Social Media" at **digitalintelligencetoday.com/ downloads/White_Paper_Social_Commerce_EN.pdf**.

For how ZIPCAR is using social campaigns on Facebook to drive traffic to their website, see Belosic (2015).

The Changing Rules of Branding

Many aspects of product branding have changed with the advent of social networks. New rules apply, and they require authentic engagement with customers (see **allbusiness.com/transparency-changed-rules-branding-23303-1.html**).

Using Blogs

Blogs are Web 2.0 tools known as being an effective means of market communication, information dissemination, recommendations, and discussions about products (including upcoming ones). For example, merchants can post ideas about new products to start a discussion and collect opinions. Blogs can be added to a company's Facebook page (or pages of other social networks) as well as to the company's in-house webstore. In addition, companies can place click-on banners on bloggers' pages.

Using Coupons

Coupons can be distributed in several ways in social commerce. One method is to distribute coupons by deploying LBS. Once a vendor knows your location and how to e-mail or text you, targeted coupons can be sent to you. Another way is to offer coupons on a company's Facebook Offers page. This is done via *Facebook Offers*. Coupons are used by Groupon.

Using Snapchat

This social network is emerging as a serous venture for advertising and sales. For an overview, see Quensenberry (2016).

Mobile Advertising

Mobile advertising is a rapidly developing area. It refers to advertisements on smartphones and other mobile devices. The competition for mobile ad revenue is intensifying, especially with the increased use of smartphones. Advertisers are starting to attach ads to video clips. Finally, advertisers use microblogging, especially Twitter, to reach large audiences.

SECTION 8.5 REVIEW QUESTIONS

1. Describe advertising in social commerce.
2. Define social ads and social apps.
3. Define viral marketing.
4. Describe viral blogging.
5. Define geolocation and geosocial networks.
6. How does location-based advertising work?
7. List some concerns of LBS advertising.
8. Describe viral videos.
9. How is Twitter used for advertising?
10. Describe mobile advertising.

8.6   SOCIAL CUSTOMER SERVICE AND CRM

The customer service landscape is undergoing significant transformation. The change is reflected both in the way that customers interact with organizations and the manner in which the company's employees interact with customers. For an overview see Goldenberg (2015).

These changes resulted from the introduction of social media, and at first, one may think that not much of a connection exists between customer service and social commerce. However, the opposite is true. Managing customer relationships is a major business challenge related to social business implementation.

How Does Social Networking Empower Customers?

It is said that one angry tweet can torpedo a brand, but one sweet tweet can correct a problem. Many customers have ended a relationship with vendors due to perceived poor customer service. Let's examine how Facebook helped change a policy for one company.

Example: Using Customers and Social Media to Design a New Flavor of Mountain Dew

It is possible for social media to empower customers in many ways. Some customers may use social media to help solve problems and overcome customer service issues. Others may use social media to recommend products and services to friends and others on their social network. Still others may engage with companies to help design and perfect products that are targeted toward them. An interesting example of this is the PepsiCo beverage company and their work with Mountain Dew.

Mountain Dew has a loyal following of users, and PepsiCo has recently begun creating flavor derivatives of the original citrus Mountain Dew formula. Some of these derivatives have been successful and others have been shunned by the market.

To increase the odds of their next flavor that would be appreciated by fans, the company extended a request to customers through social media to determine what their preferences in beverage flavors were. By evaluating this customer feedback, the company was able to determine which flavor profiles might be most readily accepted and embraced by customers. This resulted in the new Mountain Dew "Voltage" flavor. This experiment was a success, and the new flavor derivative was more widely accepted then other initial efforts (see **visioncritical.com/power-of-customer**).

Social CRM

Customer relationship management (CRM) is a customer service approach that focuses on building long-term and sustainable customer relationships that adds value for both the customers and the merchants. When delivered online, it is referred to as e-CRM. A major area of e-CRM is social CRM.

Definition

Social customer relationship management (SCRM) (also known as **CRM 2.0**) is CRM supported by social media (e.g., Web 2.0 tools, social network sites), which is designed to engage the customer in conversations, sharing, and other interactions in order to provide benefits to all participants and increase trust. SCRM is based on social media, in support of companies' stated goals and objectives of optimizing the customer's experience, and building trust and loyalty. Success requires considering people, business processes, and technology associated with the interactions between customers and enterprises. Like CRM, a major goal of SCRM is building trust and brand loyalty.

Unlike traditional CRM systems that rely on independent collection and communication systems, SCRM system can be integrated into social platforms to gather customer issues and to provide solutions. Conversocial reports that 71% of users will turn to social media to for service, and SCRM systems meet the customer in the environment they are comfortable in (see **conversocial.com/social-crm**).

SCRM is an extension of CRM, not a replacement. It adds two dimensions: social media and people. It is designed to engage customers in conversations using social media tools. An important goal of SCRM is to add benefits to the sellers (e.g., increased trust, loyalty, and sales from their customers) and to the customers (e.g., better and quicker service, and more engagement). SCRM is the segment of business strategy that addresses the issue of how companies adapt to the *social customers* and their expectations regarding the treatment by the companies with which they interact. For a detailed presentation of social CRM, download the free e-book by Fagan (2014). For coverage of social CRM, see Goldenberg (2015) and **salesforce.com/eu/crm/ social-crm**.

The Components of Social CRM

The major elements and characteristics of SCRM are shown in Fig. 8.3. As the figure illustrates, these characteristics are the foundations of a social customer who is driven by social networking. The social customer's needs are different from those of the customer who does not use social media. Social customers, for example, want to communicate with vendors by using the Internet and specifically want to engage with them from with the social platforms they use frequently. The social environment is also a major element of social CRM, since it is the source of interactions with the social customer.

How to Serve the Social Customers

Empowered customers are referred to as **social customers**. These are customers who usually are members in social networks, do social shopping, and understand their shopper's rights and how to use them to their advantage. Social customers select the mode of interaction with companies. These customers are influenced by friends, mavens, and family. Merchants must understand how social customers differ from conventional customers and provide them with socially based customer service (see Goldenberg 2015 for details).

Methods and Guidelines for Social Customer Service

How does a company serve the social media customer?

Companies are looking for an answer to this question not only because they are afraid of the negative comments posted by social network members but also because they see an opportunity to involve customers in providing feedback and ideas on how to improve customer service and operations. Furthermore, companies can solicit feedback from customers to improve customer loyalty and make their own customer service people more satisfied at work. For more on how this is done, see Fagan (2014). Procedures, guidelines, and software are available for social CRM (e.g., see Goldenberg 2015).

Fig. 8.3 The elements of social CRM

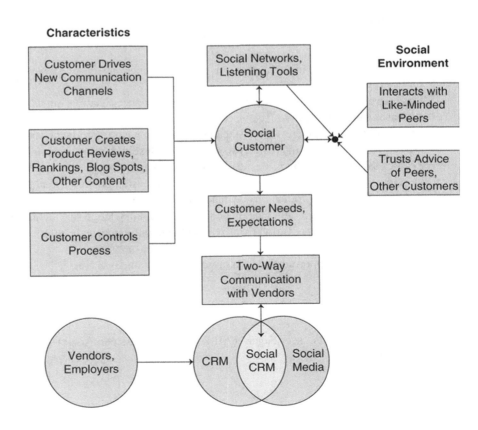

Social Listening

Companies can actively respond to direct customer inquiries as they are sent in. Another option is to monitor posts in social media and flag negative experiences to be addressed whether the customer complains or not. This process is referred to as "social listening" by many practitioners (Davey 2015). Social listening involves scouring social media for all posts concerning a business product or brand. This is similar to "clipping service" that would have been used in the past with print journalism. These mentions can be quickly identified and then responded to appropriately. Many companies who engage in social listening believe that they are able to:

1. Proactively diffuse situations that could have a negative impact on the brand.
2. Create positive buzz when they solve a problem without being asked.

Effective social listening is often achieved through the use of social media management software products.
For additional details see **sproutsocial.com/insights/social-listening** and **blog.hootsuite.com/social-listening-business**.

The Benefits of Social CRM

Social customers place new demands on organizations. However, social media tools meet these demands nicely, usually at a low cost. Social media provides for engagement and collaboration that eventually results in a competitive advantage to the organization if implemented properly (see Turban et al. 2016).

Social CRM offers the following potential benefits to customers ("c") and enterprise ("e"):

(Note: Several of these are illustrated in Case 8.2 (iRobot, presented later in this chapter). These benefits to iRobot are marked with an [I].)

- Drives quick resolution of customers' problems (c)
- Provides for effective and efficient business–customer collaboration (c), (e)
- Improves the reputation of companies (e), (I)
- Provides better understanding of customer needs and wants (e)
- Provides focused, intuitive, and easy-to-use CRM applications (e)
- Provides better marketing, better targeting, and improved products/services due to customers' creation of content and WOM (e)
- Provides customer input for market research at a quicker rate and at a low cost for improving products and customer service (e)
- Provides customers with more information about products/services quickly (c), (I)
- Increases trust and loyalty (e)
- Provides a more complete view of the customer than what traditional CRM can provide (e)
- Decreases overall customer care costs (e.g., through self-helping communities) (e)
- Enables salespeople to find sales leads quickly and easily (e)
- Develops new revenue opportunities and turns new customers into repeat customers (c)
- Increases CRM staff productivity by teaching them to use analytics and collaboration 2.0 techniques (e)
- Improves employee performance by benefiting from knowledge sharing gained in social networks (e)
- Improves customer satisfaction by providing them with opportunities for engagement using social media platforms (c), (I)
- Converts leads to opportunities with more effective campaigns (e)

For additional benefits, see Fagan (2014) and **business.com/social-media-marketing/leveraging-the-power-and-benefits-of-social-crm**.

CASE 8.2: EC APPLICATION
IROBOT USES SOCIAL MEDIA FOR MULTICHANNEL CRM

iRobot (**irobot.com**), which was founded in 1990 by three roboticists at MIT with the vision of making practical robots a reality, designs and builds some of the world's most important nonmilitary robots. According to their website, in 2015, iRobot generated $617 million in revenue and is forecasting 2016 revenue of $650–$655 million. iRobot makes robots for the government, defense and security, military and civil defense forces worldwide, commercial applications, industry, and home use. The public is mostly familiar with the Roomba vacuuming robot. Due to the technical nature of its products, the company's customers may require specialized support and service. On their customer care website, the company provides self-diagnosis, support videos, live chat, product FAQs (go to "customer help" and type in a problem and receive automatic answers), and more (e.g., see **homesupport.irobot.com/app/answers/list/session/L3RpbWUvMTQwMDQzNjk4NS9za WQvODJsX1ZBVWw%3D**). However, there are home market customers who may need more technical assistance since many are new at using robots. The company's objective is to expand the sale of home market products. Therefore, they must provide extensive assistance to inexperienced customers. The company supports a community and provides discussion boards, community search capability, and live chat.

Social CRM: Serve the Customers While Learning from Them

iRobot utilizes a CRM system with the help of Oracle RightNow Inc. (see Oracle Service Cloud at **oracle.com/us/products/applications/rightnow/overview/index.html**). The system enables customers to contact iRobot's service group via several different communication channels, including e-mail, live chat, social networks, and Web self-service. This way, iRobot can respond to any online customer communication in a timely manner, regardless of the channel used. All this needs to be done at a low cost; therefore, it is necessary to automate the services.

Specific Social Media CRM Activities

iRobot customers can post service and support requests or complaints on **homesupport.irobot.com** or they can contact the help desk. Customers can also communicate with each other. The company monitors these messages and tries to provide immediate responses. iRobot tries to find the identity of the customers that have problems by monitoring relevant conversations in the various social channels (e.g., in forums on social networks). Once identified, iRobot communicates with the customers privately to resolve the issues.

The social media-oriented activities are integrated with documents and videos in a knowledge base managed by RightNow. The company uses RightNow's monitoring tools to identify the customers who post the comments. Some customers may provide their real names. Anonymous customers are encouraged to contact iRobot directly. For how the company listens to social media, see **informationweek.com/software/social/roomba-robots-listen-to-social-media/d/d-id/1100404**. For a podcast, see **moneybasicsradio.com/2013/04/irobot-social-media**.

Responding to issues quickly is important because, as discussed earlier, customers can attract a considerable amount of attention using YouTube or Twitter (the company runs promotions, such as giveaways and games on Twitter) to publicize their complaints. In addition to problem resolution, the company gets valuable feedback from the customers so it can improve its products and services.

General Social Media Activities

An interesting facet of using social media to serve customers is that customers must be talking about the product and be active in social media networks in order for this to occur. In order to drive the conversation and encourage activities surrounding their product on social media, iRobot encourages customers to discuss their products in these channels.

For example, the company also uses social media to engage customers. In early 2017, the company encouraged users to follow #HappyBirthdayRoomba on Twitter for a chance to win prizes. Other examples include encouraging users to post pictures and stories about their Roombas and their strange interactions with cats, dogs, and Christmas trees (see **medium.com/@invoker/social-media-lessons-from-a-robotic-vacuum-2941a65b5cff#.cckabj4yx**).

These social activities serve as positive marketing items by educating non-customers about the benefits of the product. But they also ensure that customers are actively engaged in the discussion of their product and feel like the ownership of the product itself make them part of a community. This community can then be serviced through SCRM.

iRobot has a presence on Facebook, Twitter, Pinterest, YouTube, and Tumblr. The company uses these sites to disseminate information and collect customer feedback and complaints.

Sources: Based on HigherVisibility (2015) and **irobot.com/About-irobot.aspx** (accessed January 2017).

Questions

1. What is meant by the term *multichannel service support*? What is the benefit of multichanneling?
2. What are the activities related to social media at iRobot? What are their benefits?
3. Describe how the company listens to their customers' complaints, and how they resolve the problems.

The Evolution of Social CRM

Now that you have a basic understanding of CRM, e-CRM, and SCRM, we can look at the evolution of SCRM as well as some differences between SCRM and e-CRM. SCRM can be viewed as an extension of e-CRM. Most e-CRM software companies, such as Salesforce Inc. (**salesforce.com**), offer social media features in their products. However, there are some significant differences between e-CRM and SCRM. These differences can be seen at **slideshare.net/ JatinKalra/e-crm-112520123741** and Turban et al. (2016). Social CRM today is delivered in many cases by mobile devices (see Goldenberg 2015) and can be implemented by small businesses (Jamieson 2014).

Multidimensional Presentation SCRM

Ken Tucker (2013) outlines the difference between CRM and SCRM (referred to as CRM 1.0 and CRM 2.0) along the following dimensions: landscape, customer touch points, and business processing modeling, technology, and organizational mindset. The differences between CRM 1.0 and CRM 2.0 are illustrated in Figs. 8.4 and 8.5.

Example: Get Satisfaction for CRM

Get Satisfaction (**getsatisfaction.com/corp/about**) is a platform where customers can interact with one another and voice their opinions and complaints. Using a forum, they can quickly get resolutions to their problems. Each community is organized around four topics:

1. **Ask a question**. Customers can answer one another's questions.
2. **Share an idea**. Aggregated feedback is provided from customers (by topic, product, and vendor).
3. **Report a problem**. Search to see if anyone posted a similar problem. Post yours.
4. **Give praise**. Customers can praise a product or vendor.

Get Satisfaction provides information on the customers' conversations to interested vendors at no charge.
For an example of a Get Satisfaction Support Community, see **getsatisfaction.com/safarichallenge**.

Conclusions

Implementing social CRM requires empowering the employees, which means that a new set of employee skills may be needed. For a long time, marketers have said that everything starts with the needs of consumers. With social CRM and all the social media product discussions, marketers must now learn how to incorporate this philosophy in their strategies. These implementations also require purpose-built software tools to function well. These tools are available from traditional CRM vendors (Salesforce) as well as social media management software firms (Sprout Social).

Examples of Implementation of Social Customer Service and CRM

There are several models and methods for implementing social customer service. First let us look at what Safeway is doing in this area.

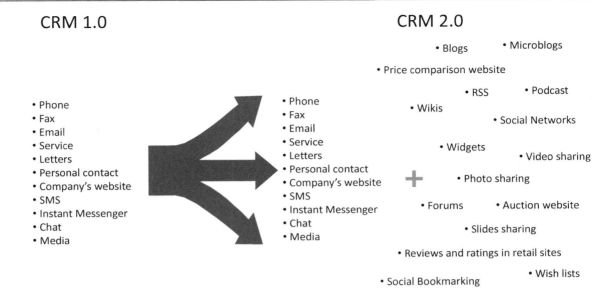

CRM 1.0

- Phone
- Fax
- Email
- Service
- Letters
- Personal contact
- Company's website
- SMS
- Instant Messenger
- Chat
- Media

CRM 2.0

- Phone
- Fax
- Email
- Service
- Letters
- Personal contact
- Company's website
- SMS
- Instant Messenger
- Chat
- Media

+

- Blogs
- Microblogs
- Price comparison website
- RSS
- Podcast
- Wikis
- Social Networks
- Widgets
- Video sharing
- Photo sharing
- Forums
- Auction website
- Slides sharing
- Reviews and ratings in retail sites
- Social Bookmarking
- Wish lists

- Single view of the customer based on the interactions history, customer profile data residing in the company's base and data integration with internal systems
- Company owns the data but it is limited to previous interactions

- Single view of the customer is far more complex to achieve. Besides internal information, the company must rely on external information such as customer profiles in social networks and his behavior when participating in a community.
- Customer and other web 2.0 sites own part of the precious data

Source: Courtesy of F. Cipriani, "Social CRM: Concept, Benefits, and Approach to Adopt," November 2008. **<URL>slideshare.net/fhcipriani/social-crm-presentation-761225</URL>** (accessed January 2012). Used with permission.

Fig. 8.4 Touch points in CRM versus SCRM (Source: Courtesy of F. Cipriani, "Social CRM: Concept, Benefits, and Approach to Adopt," November 2008. **slideshare.net/fhcipriani/social-crm-presentation-761225** (accessed January 2017). Used with permission)

Fig. 8.5 The business model and process of Groupon

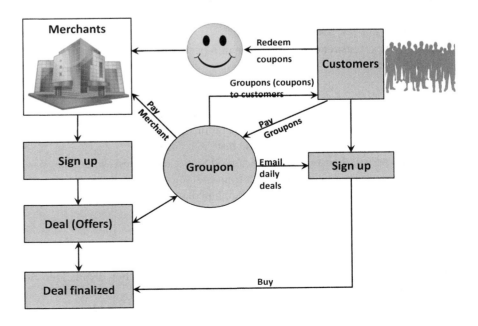

Example 1: How Safeway Provides Social Customer Service

Safeway, a large grocery chain, has a virtual customer club. Members can get in-store discounts as well as e-mails with coupons and a description of what is on sale. An online newsletter with health news and recipes, shopping tips, etc. is also available to members. To extend this service, Safeway invites their customers to become Safeway Fans on Facebook and follow the company on Twitter. This allows customers/members to know about exclusive promotions. Also, members can connect and share information with other Safeway shoppers.

In their "Just for U" program, shoppers can get digital coupons and personalized deals when they click on a certain coupon, say for milk; then, when they buy milk, they get a 10–20% discount. There is no need to clip coupons anymore. For more information, see **safeway.com/ShopStores/Justforu-FAQ.page**.

Additionally, customers can visit the company's blog, *Today at Safeway!*, where the company's team members post items from floral, bakery, and other departments throughout the store. Safeway's experts also publish information about nutrition, environmental sustainability, and more. Members of the virtual customer club can comment on the blog and are asked to post original content only.

Example 2: REI Adventure

This fast-growing adventure travel company has a trip planning division that sells outdoor clothing and gear. For customers who want to travel to a specific destination with others who share similar interests, REI Adventure puts together groups of people and fully plans the group trip. The planning documents are prepared manually and shipped to the customers. A fully computerized solution is initiated around Salesforce Sales Cloud. The system has two parts: One for employees and another one for customers. This is basically a social CRM system on both parts. It permits customization of trips to individuals in the groups. The system has a friendly interface, and all documents are sent quickly online. Overall, the system makes customers very satisfied, the employees can serve more customers, and the customers can communicate with each other as they discover their adventure destinations. For details see Brown (2016).

Example 3: How Best Buy Uses Twitter to Provide Real-Time Customer Service

Best Buy is a large appliance retailer. The company uses their Twitter account @twelpforce to interact with customers.

Best Buy empowered its technical support service (called Geek Squad) and other corporate employees (total 4000 participants). There, any employee who finds a relevant tweeted question can answer the customer. The answers are visible on the website, allowing other employees to add information.

For additional examples, see **thesocialcustomer.com/sites/thesocialcustomer.com/files/TheSocialContract.pdf**.

Social Networking Helps Customer Service in Small Companies

Most of the examples provided so far have dealt with large companies. What about the small ones? Obviously, there are some applications the SMEs cannot afford. But many other applications can be deployed.

Example

Teusner Wines (**teusner.com.au**) is a small 3-person boutique winery in Australia. Using Twitter, the company's one-person marketing department:

- Initiates online conversations about wine with influential people in the wine industry
- Sends tweets to people he finds talking online (e.g., in communities) about Teusner Wines, praising them for trying the wine
- Starts to build trust with customers via online conversations
- Invites people to tour the winery and taste the wines
- Advises potential customers in the United States and Canada where they can buy the Australian wine
- Monitors real-time online feedback from customers
- Encourages customer-to-customer social media conversations
- Posts customer reviews using Twitter
- Shares all information with Twitter followers
- Use Instagram to show photos and get "likes"

All this is done in a tiny company at virtually no cost. For details, see **dottedlinecollaborations.com/social-media/case-study-using-twitter-attract-new-customers**.

For large companies, it is necessary to integrate marketing, customer services, and social networks.

Reputation Management System

Not all postings in social networks are positive. The problem is what companies do when they see negative comments. Historically, companies may have tried to hide or downplay negative news or bad customer reviews. The nature of social media however is open, honest engagement. Because of the nature of social networks and the Internet, in general, it is very difficult or impossible to hide negative feedback. Companies cannot block people from posting negative comments on social platforms, including Facebook pages. If a company blocks such postings, it eliminates the potential positive comments from its fans, losing the positive WOM and customer feedback. If companies delete posts, the poster and others may retaliate.

This results in the need to change the paradigm in responding to customer complaints in the social space. Many suggest that instead of seeing negative feedback as something to hide, that companies should use it as an opportunity to demonstrate that they listen to the customer and can make the issue right. Some have referred to this as reputation management, and others refer to it as "proactive damage control" (Bloomberg 2015). Reputation systems should:

- Allow for quick identification and response to issues.
- Build trust in the sellers.
- Promote quality of the products and services.
- Sustain loyalty.

These systems can be implemented using the social platforms themselves or using systems that aid businesses in managing their social media interactions (like hootesuite.com). The ability to monitor is critical to being able to address issues quickly. Regardless of the methods used, there are best practices in the creation of social media reputation management systems as described by York (2016) with **sproutsocial.com**:

1. Know what you're monitoring.
2. Connect your social media accounts to a platform.
3. Focus your efforts on engagement.
4. Encourage more social reviews.
5. Scale reputation management to track ROI.

Many acknowledge that support systems make these practices more attainable, regardless of the size of the business that engages in them.

For additional coverage, see **reputationinstitute.com**, Christman (2014), and York (2016).

SECTION 8.6 REVIEW QUESTIONS

1. Define the social customer and describe their characteristics.
2. Why and how are customers empowered by social networks?
3. Define social CRM.
4. What are the needs of social customers?
5. List 5–8 benefits of social CRM.
6. How does social CRM differ from traditional CRM?
7. Describe a reputation management system.

MANAGERIAL ISSUES

Some managerial issues related to this chapter are as follows.

1. **How will social commerce influence businesses?** The impacts of social marketing can change the manner in which many shoppers make purchasing decisions. Social commerce will change both B2B and B2C by increasing interactions, engagement, and collaboration. The impact will change business processes, the manner in which companies treat customers and employees, and may even restructure some organizations. A strong impact will be felt in advertising, viral marketing, collaboration, and brand recognition. The impact will also be strong on delivering customer service, conducting market research, and organizing collaboration. For more information see Jamieson (2014).

2. **Do companies need to sponsor a social network?** Although sponsoring a social network might sound like a good idea, it may not be simple to execute. Community members need services, which cost money to provide. The most difficult task is to find an existing community that matches your business. In many cases, the cost of a social network may be justified by its contribution to advertising. However, social network service providers need to create various revenue models to maintain sustainable services. Creating revenue is the most challenging issue to social network service providers.

3. **Which social networks should we be a part of?** There are many social media networks that businesses could have a presence on. The decision could be based on the size of the network, the specific purpose of the network (like photo sharing), and the amount of employee time available to manage company interactions.

4. **Is it wise for a small business to be on Facebook?** The answer depends on the business and on what you are trying to achieve. It could be helpful for those that need to constantly reach customers and/or suppliers. Facebook, at present, may not be very helpful for direct sales. However, just having a presence costs little and therefore should be considered. A major issue for SMBs is the loose security in social networks. See **entrepreneur.com/article/239539** for comprehensive coverage of this topic.

5. **How to deal with false reviews and fake followers?** Unfortunately, there are many fake followers. Some are paid by companies to boost their image; others are paid by competitors. It is possible to use software to detect some fake accounts. These fictitious data can mislead companies when deciding, for example, where to advertise.

6. **Should we embark on selling via social networking?** For most cases the answer would be yes. Just view it as an additional channel to increase sales. Which model to use will depend on the product, the competition, and the potential risks. For justification see cases by Petersen (2014).

7. **Should we engage in social media reputation management?** New tools will allow businesses react to customer issues posted in social networks and businesses can pro-actively respond to issues as they arise. There are definite benefits, but software systems, significant employee time, and corporate policies would be required.

SUMMARY

In this chapter, you learned about the following EC issues as they related to the chapter's learning objectives.

1. **Social commerce definition and evolution.** Social commerce (SC) refers to conducting EC in the social media environment. It can be viewed as a subset of EC where activities are done in social networks and by using social media tools. It operates at the intersection of social media, EC, e-marketing, and supporting theories from several disciplines including social psychology, marketing, sociology, and information technology.

2. **The scope, content, and drivers of social commerce.** Social commerce is a comprehensive field comprised mostly of social media marketing (advertising, market research, and customer service) and social enterprise (problem solving, recruiting, and collaboration). It also includes social entertainment, social games, and crowdsourcing. Social commerce is driven by the existence of giant social networks, Web 2.0 tools, and the emergence of social customers.

3. **Benefits and limitations of social commerce.** A large number of benefits are available for customers, retailers, and other businesses. Customers can get better prices, improve customer service, and also receive social support (e.g., product recommendations) from friends. They can find new friends as well and establish new contacts. Retailers can reach more customers, get quick feedback, improve relationships with customers, go global, and use free word-of-mouth marketing communication. There are also benefits to businesses. Businesses can conduct fast and inexpensive market research, recruit employees from all over the globe, innovate, collaborate, and locate experts when needed.

4. **Describe social shopping.** Social shopping refers to online shopping that is supported by social media and involves friends and online social media communities. The major drivers are the large number of people who are engaged in social networking, reliance on friends' recommendations, and the potential of receiving large discounts for the buyers, the increase of sales volume for the sellers, the socially oriented shopping models, and the rise of the social customer.

5. **How advertisements and promotions are conducted in social networking.** The major driver of SC is the money spent by advertisers who see a huge potential market. Advertising can be done in many ways. Using word of mouth is almost free for companies, but it can be dangerous (e.g., negative comments). The use of banner ads and other paid advertisement and social search models generate billions for social networks (mostly to Google and Facebook). Large numbers of advertising apps exist. Also, bloggers can provide positive (but sometimes negative) comments. Many companies have developed special campaigns that engage community members in advertising-related activities (play games, vote, generate ideas, etc.). In addition, advertising on Facebook, LinkedIn, Pinterest, Instagram, Twitter, and YouTube is becoming popular.

6. **Conducting social customer service and CRM.** When the CRM platform involves social media (e.g., Web 2.0 tools and social network sites), CRM is referred to as social CRM (SCRM). SCRM provides many benefits for customers, vendors, and public institutions that include an improved relationship between the empowered customers and the vendors and service providers as well as providing better service to customers. The evolution to SCRM can be described along the following five dimensions: the landscape (e.g., structure and focus), the touch points (e.g., the use of social media tools), business processes (e.g., how to listen to customers), the technology (e.g., socially oriented tools), and the organizational mindset (e.g., patterns of interactions). This evolution is driven by the explosive use of social network sites, the rise of the social customer, and the importance buyers place on social recommendations. Customers are empowered by social networks so they can get attention quickly for problem resolution. Customers can make suggestions for improvements and vote on them. Businesses can engage in social networks to maintain their brand reputations and can also use social listening to proactively address negative items.

KEY TERMS

Communal shopping (collaborative shopping)
Customer relationship management (CRM)
Enterprise 2.0
Social business
Social commerce (SC)
Social customer
Social customer relationship management (SCRM; CRM 2.0)
Social marketplace
Social media marketing (SMM)
Social shopping (sales 2.0)
Viral blogging
Viral marketing
Viral video
Virtual economy
Virtual goods

DISCUSSION QUESTIONS

1. Compare social computing to traditional computing.
2. Discuss the social element in social media.
3. Discuss the contribution of social commerce to e-commerce.
4. Compare Polyvore to Pinterest.
5. Discuss the reasons why people buy virtual goods.
6. Discuss how traditional online vendors can add social networking capabilities to their sites.
7. Under what circumstances would you trust an expert's recommendation rather than a friend's?
8. How can marketers use social networks for viral marketing?
9. What are the major differences between social media marketing and search engine marketing?
10. Why are advertisers so interested in social networks?
11. Discuss the issue of possible fraud in P2P transactions.
12. Discuss the shortcomings of user-generated reviews and recommendations.

TOPICS FOR CLASS DISCUSSION AND DEBATES

1. Debate the privacy dangers to social shoppers.
2. Debate: "Is the social media influence on purchasing overrated?" Start by reading the article titled "Digital Shopping Behavior Report: Is Social Media Overrated?" (Hong 2014) at **linkdex.com/en-us/inked/digital-shopping-behavior-report-is-social-media-overrated/**.

3. Debate: One day all e-commerce will be social.
4. Daily deals are being offered today by many offline and online retailers and other organizations (e.g., newspapers). Only on the Internet are these offers common. Is there a need for intermediaries? Debate.
5. Discuss how trust is affected in social shopping. (Skim **pdfs.semanticscholar.org/674e/4c8b395c35be6bca11a5b909dc 25f602d4ed.pdf**).
6. Why do you think that Wanelo is popular?
7. Examine Facebook Offers. What is the potential of the viral service? What is the advantage of mobile newsfeeds? Explain the competition with LivingSocial.

INTERNET EXERCISES

1. Enter **smartmobs.com**. Go to the blogroll. Find three blogs related to social commerce, and summarize their major features.
2. Enter **thisnext.com**. What are the features of the site? What do you like? Dislike?
3. Enter **salesforce.com** and identify all SCRM activities supported by the company, especially those related to their Chatter product. View the slide show at **slideshare.net/Salesforce/salesforce-customer-servicebest-practices-25640141**. Write a report.
4. Enter **salesforce.com/dreamforce/DF14**. Find topics that deal with SCRM. Write a summary.
5. Enter **bazaarvoice.com**. Summarize its major services. Examine SocialConnect.
6. Enter **hootsuite.com**. Summarize its major services.
7. Enter **hubspot.com**. Summarize its major services.
8. Enter **thisnext.com**. What are the features of the site? What do you like? Dislike? Why?
9. Enter **tkg.com/social-media-marketing**. Prepare a list of information you can get there about social shopping.
10. Enter **https://hootsuite.com/pages/social-media-marketing-certification** and gather information about the Hootsuite Social Marketing Certification. What are its major benefits?
11. Enter **powerreviews.com**. Compare their activities to those of similar sites.
12. Enter **deal-of-the-day-review.toptenreviews.com**, and summarize the lesson learned.
13. Enter **socialshoppingnetwork.org**. Find material related to this chapter. Write a report.
14. Enter **socialmediaexaminer.com/smmworld/**. Find out about the conference. Discuss the key features and a session you are most interested in.

TEAM ASSIGNMENTS AND PROJECTS

1. Assignment for the Opening
2. Case

   (a) Why is it important for a social media company to have a revenue model?
   (b) What is Facebook's revenue model?
   (c) Select another social network and identify its business model.
   (d) How can Facebook compete with Google for business marketing expenditures?
   (e) How can a business determine where to spend their marketing money efficiently?

3. Facebook is increasingly offering marketing tools (e.g., Open Graph, Social Plugins). Identify all the tools offered. Each group concentrates on the business implications in one of the following areas: advertising and search engine optimization (SEO), shopping, market research, customer service, CRM, and others. Make a class presentation.
4. Each group adopts one or two of the following companies that actively advertise and engage on Facebook and Twitter: Coca-Cola, Starbucks, Ford, Pepsi, Levi's, Disney, Victoria's Secret, iTunes, Toyota, Sony, or P&G. Find and summarize what advertising methods they use and how they do their campaigns.
5. The class will investigate group buying in China and India. What is the prospect for group buying in Asia? (Start with Yoo's article "Almost 1 in 5 People In China Group-Bought In June 2015, And It's Rising" at **technode.com/2015/07/30/ chinas-group-buying-market-turnover-reaches-77b-rmb/**. Also check Meituan in China.
6. The class reads Gil (2015) and divides the 50 predictions among groups. Research progress and submit reports.

7. Download "The Retailer's Guide to Social Commerce Channels" from **cpcstrategy.com/blog/social-commerce-guide-small-2** and outline the steps a small business would take to select which socials channels it should utilize to attach customers.
8. Watch the video "Enterprise 2.0 and Social Business" (2:37 min) with Andrew McAfee at **youtu.be/XeIQRBmSgqk**. Summarize the key aspects of Enterprise 2.0. This video was created in 2012, have the principles of Enterprise 2.0 held up over time?

CLOSING CASE: HOW SONY USES SOCIAL MEDIA FOR IMPROVING CRM

Sony, the giant consumer electronics producer, has been struggling during the last few years.
Now, by using social media, improvement is in being realized.

The Problem

Sony Corporation (**sony.com**) faces fierce competition from Samsung (**samsung.com/us**), Sharp Electronics (**sharpusa.com**), LG Electronics (**lg.com/us**), and other large, global companies. This competition has intensified during the economic slowdown in recent years. As a result, total revenues for Sony have declined every year from 2008 to 2012. The company suffered heavy losses in 2009 and 2012, causing its share price to drop from \$35/share in 2010 and 2011 to \$9.57 in late 2012. In 2013, the stock rose mostly due to the recovery in Tokyo's stock exchange. Consumer electronic products are fairly mature, so the differences in quality and prices are not substantial. Therefore, the competitors in the field are promoting their customer service as a strategic differentiator. Sony is trying to do this with the help of their social media communities and initiatives.

The Solution

Sony Corporation embarked on social CRM as a vehicle for improving customer service. According to Jack (2013), Sony combined a customer support and direct marketing program, mostly using social channels. The various initiatives are managed by Sony's Customer Experience Management Team. The team organized *Sony's Community Site* (**community.sony. com**), which is a central hub for customer information and support. It includes *idea boards*, *discussion groups*, *blogs*, *Twitter feeds*, and other content-generating channels. The site is used also for marketing campaigns.

The following are representative activities, many of which are done at Sony Europe:

- Active social communities; some are for specific products; others are general for the entire Sony brand. The company's staff members and consumers are involved in these communities. Members of these communities are helping each other and providing feedback. Customer service employees are "listening" to the feedback and using the information to improve service.
- YouTube videos provide training for customers on the use of Sony's products.
- Using Lithium Social Web software (a SAP company), relevant sites are monitored for reviews and comments (positive and negative). This allows Sony to improve operations, resolve problems, and capitalize on opportunities.
- There is a special "Customer Relations" tab located on Sony's Community Site, the company's central social network, for easy communication.
- The company created a "Facebook Support Community" within their Facebook page (**facebook.com/sony**), Twitter "Sony Support USA" (**twitter.com/sonysupportusa**), Tumblr Support (**sony.tumblr.com**), and a YouTube Sony Support Channel "Sony Listens" (**youtube.com/user/SonyListens**).
- In the communities, the company's staff demonstrates how problems are resolved quickly and efficiently. For example, there is an "Experts" tab for "How To" videos and technical support. See **community.sony.com/t5/Meet-Our-Experts/ bg-p/experts**.
- Sony is using all its social media channels, including LinkedIn, to proactively engage users and provide customer service in a timely fashion (see Sony 2016).
- Sony Electronic integrates Pinterest (**pinterest.com/sonyprousa**) to send information about its products to community members (see details at Eckerle 2013 and **ohsopinteresting.com/lessons-from-sony-on-pinterest**).

Sony monitors social media conversations and conducts sentiment analysis (Brand24 2015) to improve customer service and product improvement and design. Note that Sony is using social media campaigns for customer engagement. For an overview of how Sony is using social networks, see Moth (2013). Finally, software from Reevoo.com helps Sony to automatically translate reviews from one language to another.

The Results

Significant results realized in 2014/2015 after the deployment of most SC initiatives. However, some improvements have materialized in 2013. For example, according to Jack (2013), the improved communication resulted in a 22% increase in "clicks" (over 100% in some cases). Other results are:

- Customer trust in Sony increased.
- Page views, conversation rates, and engagement activities (e.g., posting) increased by 100% (Jack 2013).
- Follower growth increased 200% with a charitable Pinterest board (Eckerle 2013).
- Customer service was combined with marketing promotions, which resulted in new sources of revenue for Sony.
- In March 2014, PlayStation had about 2.5 million followers on Twitter and 35 million fans on Facebook. For a case study about PlayStation and social media, see Brand24 (2015).

Sony's share price recovered in 2015 and 2016.

Sources: Based on Taylor (2013), Eckerle (2013), Reevoo (2014), Brand24 (2015), and Sony (2016).

Questions

1. What social media tools and platforms does Sony use?
2. How does each tool facilitate customer service?
3. What are the major benefits of social CRM to Sony?
4. Relate Sony's use of Pinterest to social CRM. (Start by entering **community.sony.com**.)
5. Find CRM-related activities. Summarize.
6. Go to Sony's community and ask a question. Get results. Summarize four experiences.

REFERENCES

Bradburn, L. "How Social Media Changed The Way We Shop" Online Ventures Group, November 4, 2016. **onlineventuresgroup.co.uk/how-social-media-changed-the-way-we-shop/b50440** (accessed January 2017).

Barnett, S. "Let's Kill Fake Reviews: How to Make Feedback Fair." *Social Media Today*, June 15, 2015.

Belosic, J. "How the World's Largest Car-Sharing Company Uses Social Campaigns to Drive Traffic to their Website." *Social Media Today*, June 16, 2015.

Bloomberg, J. "Reputation Management With Digital And Social Media." *Forbes*, January 29, 2015. **forbes.com/sites/jasonbloomberg/2015/01/29/reputation-management-with-digital-and-social-media/** (accessed January 2017).

Brand24. "What You Can Learn from Sony PlayStation Social Media Monitoring." *Blog.brand24.net*, February 11, 2015. **blog.brand24.net/what-you-can-learn-from-sony-playstation-social-media-monitoring** (accessed January 2017).

Brown, A. "A Company That Plans Adventure Trips Turns to a Cloud-Based CRM System to Eliminate Paper, Improve Customer Satisfaction, Save Money and Increase Business." *Baseline Magazine*, February 24, 2014.

Carranza A. "7 Industries That Benefit Most from Social Media." *Social Media Today*, June 16, 2015.

Christman, C. "Reputation Management through Social Media and Online Reviews." March 3, 2014. **smallbusiness.yahoo.com/advisor/reputation-management-social-media-online-reviews-212958979.html** (accessed January 2017).

Clover, C. "Chinese Online Group Meituan Dianping Raises $3.3BN." *Financial Times*, January 19, 2016. **ft.com/content/f6714d4c-be9e-11e5-846f-79b0e3d20eaf** (accessed January 2017).

Davey, N. "Being smart about social: How to build a social listening strategy." MyCustomer, June 25, 2015. **mycustomer.com/experience/voice-of-the-customer/being-smart-about-social-how-to-build-a-social-listening-strategy** (accessed January 2017).

DeLuca, L. "The Social Effect of Commerce." U.S. Chamber of Commerce Foundation, September 4, 2015. **uschamberfoundation.org/blog/post/social-effect-commerce/43693** (accessed January 2017).

Drell, L. "17 Business Models Shaking Up the Marketplace." *Mashable*, June 16, 2014. **linkdex.com/en-us/inked/digital-shopping-behavior-report-is-social-media-overrated** (accessed January 2017).

Eckerle, C. "Social Email Integration: Sony Electronics Nets 3,000 Clickthroughs from Email to "Pin" on Pinterest." Case Study. April 23, 2013. **marketingsherpa.com/article/case-study/sony-nets-3000-clickthroughs-pinterest** (accessed January 2017).

Fagan, L. "Free Ebook: How Social CRM Connects You to Customers." April 3, 2014. **blogs.salesforce.com/company/2014/04/free-ebook-socialcrm.html** (accessed January 2017).

Forrester. "Digital Experience Technology and Delivery Priorities," May, 2016. **acquia.com/resources/collateral/forrester-report-digital-experience-technology-and-delivery-priorities-may-2016** (accessed January 2017).

Gil, C. "Social Media Marketing: 50+ Predictions for 2016." *Social Media Today*, December 31, 2015.

Gioglio, J. "Why Cheetos Is Crowdsourcing Its Latest Campaign." Convince & Convert, August 31, 2016. **convinceandconvert.com/social-media-case-studies/cheetos-crowdsourcing-campaign** (accessed January 2017).

Goldenberg, B. *The Definitive Guide to Social CRM: Maximizing Customer Relationships with Social Media to Gain Market Insights, Customers, and Profits*. London, UK: Pearson FT Press, 2015.

Griffith, E. "How One Founder Used Instagram Likes to Earn $500K in New Business." *Fortune.com*, February 14, 2014. **tech.fortune.cnn.com/2014/02/14/lovematically-instagram** (accessed January 2017).

Hague, A. "Google Ads vs. Facebook Ads: Picking the Perfect Marketing Platform." Omni Digital Marketing, January 31, 2016. **omnidigitalmarketing.co.uk/google-ads-vs-facebook-ads-picking-the-perfect-marketing-platform** (accessed January 2017).

Hamari, J. "Why Do People Buy Virtual Goods? Attitude Toward Virtual Good Purchases Versus Game Enjoyment." *International Journal of Information Management*, June 2015. **sciencedirect.com/science/article/pii/S0268401215000080** (accessed January 2017).

Helmrich, B. "Social Media for Business: A Marketer's Guide." Business News Daily, January 23, 2017. **businessnewsdaily.com/7832-social-media-for-business.html** (accessed January 2017).

Hickman, M. "An App That Promotes Neighborly Bonding Through the Borrowing of Stuff." *Mother Nature Network*, January 6, 2015. **mnn.com/your-home/at-home/blogs/an-app-that-promotes-neighborly-bonding-through-the-borrowing-of-stuff** (accessed January 2017).

HigherVisibility. "Here are Some of the Best Viral Campaigns of 2015." *Small Business Trends*, December 9, 2015. **smallbiztrends.com/2015/12/best-viral-campaigns-2015.html** (accessed January 2017).

Hong, P. "Digital Shopping Behavior Report: Is Social Media Overrated?" Linkdex, October 7, 2014. **linkdex.com/en-us/inked/digital-shopping-behavior-report-is-social-media-overrated/** (accessed January 2017).

Hope, K. "How Social Media Is Transforming the Fashion Industry." *BBC News*, February 5, 2016. **bbc.com/news/business-35483480** (accessed January 2017).

Hossain, M. "The Evolution of Social Commerce: Types, Trends and Future." Iammoulude, October 14, 2016. **iammoulude.wordpress.com/2016/10/14/the-evolution-of-social-commerce-types-trends-and-future** (accessed January 2017).

Jack, D. "2013 Forrester Groundswell Entry- Sony Electronics: Support Channels Show Dramatic Improvements in Consumer Engagement and Help Boost Sales." *Lithium Technologies*, August 27, 2013 (ed. September 3, 2013). **lithosphere.lithium.com/t5/lithium-s-view-blog/2013-Forrester-Groundswell-Entry-Sony-Electronics-Support/ba-p/100214** (accessed January 2017).

Jamieson, C. M. *The Small Business Guide to Social CRM*. Birmingham, UK: Packt Publishing, 2014.

Johnson, L. "What Marketers Need to Know About 5 New Types of Social Commerce." *AdWeek*, June 25, 2015. **adweek.com/digital/what-marketers-need-know-about-5-new-types-social-commerce-165552** (accessed January 2017).

Kapko, M. "Twitter's Impact on 2016 Presidential Election Is Unmistakable." *CIO*, November 3, 2016. **cio.com/article/3137513/social-networking/twitters-impact-on-2016-presidential-election-is-unmistakable.html** (accessed January 2017).

King, H. "Facebook Is Making More Money Off You Than Ever Before." CNN Tech, January 27, 2016. **money.cnn.com/2016/01/27/technology/facebook-earnings** (accessed January 2017).

King, H. "Facebook Is Taking on Amazon with Shopping Pages." July 16, 2015. **money.cnn.com/2015/07/16/technology-buy/index.html?iid=hp-stack-dom** (accessed January 2017).

Knight, K. "Social Roundup: Facebook, Google Leading the Way." *BizReport*, January 27, 2016.

Kuchler, H. "Pinterest and Instagram Launch 'Buy Buttons'." *Financial Times*, June 2, 2015.

Liang, T.P., and E. Turban. "Introduction to the Special Issue: Social Commerce: A Research Framework for Social Commerce." *International Journal of Electronic Commerce*, Winter 2011–2012.

Logan, N. *Go Viral!: The Most Effective Viral Marketing strategies to Launch Your Online Business* [Kindle Edition]. Seattle, WA: Amazon Digital Services, Inc., 2014.

Marsden, P., and P. Chaney. *The Social Commerce Handbook: 20 Secrets for Turning Social Media Into Social Sales*. New York: McGraw-Hill, 2012.

Moth, D. "How Sony Uses Facebook, Twitter, Pinterest and Google+." *Econsultancy*, May 29, 2013.

Monllos, K. "Why Brands Are Building Their Own 'Museums' Where Immersion Is the Price of Entry." *AdWeek*, August 7, 2016. **adweek.com/brand-marketing/why-brands-are-building-their-own-museums-where-immersion-price-entry-172822/** (accessed January 2017).

Nation, D. "What is Enterprise 2.0?" *Lifewire*, February 19, 2016. **lifewire.com/what-is-enterprise-2-0-3486260** (accessed January 2017).

Oaks, J. "GoPro and 3 Other Brands that Understand Importance of Social Media Integration" *Social Media Today*, January 13, 2016. **socialmediatoday.com/social-networks/gopro-and-3-other-brands-understand-importance-social-media-integration** (accessed January 2017).

Perez, S. "Polyvore Launches Remix, A New App for Style Advice and Shopping." *TechCrunch*, April 7, 2015.

Petersen, R. "166 Case Studies Prove Social Media ROI (Free eBook)." *BarnRaisers*, April 27, 2014. **barnraisersllc.com/2014/04/166-case-studiess-prove-social-media-roi** (accessed January 2017).

Porcellana, S. "Social Commerce is Still Growing: Facebook, Pinterest and Polyvore Case Study." SEM Rush, June 27, 2016. **semrush.com/blog/social-commerce-is-still-growing-facebook-pinterest-and-polyvore-case-study** (accessed January 2017).

Pownall, C. *Managing Online Reputation: How to Protect Your Company on Social Media*, New York: Palgrave Macmillan, 2015.

Quensenberry, K. "Snapchat has Grown Up: What You Need to Know as a Marketer." *Social Media Today*, March 07, 2016.

Quirk, D. "The Evolving Social E-Commerce Landscape." Centric Digital, November 17, 2016. **centricdigital.com/blog/digital-trends/the-evolving-social-e-commerce-landscape/** (accessed January 2017).

Reevoo. "New Automated Translation Tool Brings Immediate International Social Commerce Benefits to Sony." 2014. **reevoo.com/pages/press_sony_international_reviews** (accessed January 2017).

Rosenberg, E. "The Business of Google (GOOG)." *Investopedia*, August 5, 2016. **investopedia.com/articles/investing/020515/business-google.asp** (accessed January 2017).

Savitz, E. "Four Reasons Why Virtual Goods Make Us Happy." *CIO Network*, October 25, 2011. **forbes.com/sites/ciocentral/2011/10/25/four-reasons-why-virtual-goods-make-us-happy** (accessed January 2017).

Silverbean. "The Power of Polyvore: Social Commerce Case Study." April 14, 2014. **silverbean.com/blog/power-polyvore-social-commerce-case-study** (accessed January 2017).

Smith, B. "How to Use Instagram for Business [Infographic]." *Social Media Today*, January 6, 2015. **socialmediatoday.com/content/how-use-instagram-business** (accessed January 2017).

Smith, K. "E-Commerce Trends: 7 Predictions on What to Expect in 2017." Brandwatch, December 7, 2016. **brandwatch.com/blog/ecommerce-trends-2017** (accessed January 2017).

Sony. "Company News." *Social Media*, Periodical, March 2016. **sony.com/en_us/SCA/company-news/social-media.html** (accessed January 2017).

Steiner, I. "Amazon Launches New Twist on Product Reviews." *Ecommerce Bytes*, April 15, 2014. **ecommercebytes.com/cab/abn/y14/m04/i15/s03** (accessed January 2017).

Sukhraj, R. "25 Social Media Campaign Ideas from Big Brands You Want to Be." *Impact Brand & Design*, September 9, 2016. **impactbnd.com/blog/25-social-media-campaign-ideas** (accessed January 2017).

Sullivan, L. "Google Dominates Search, Struggles in Display Targeting Against Facebook." *Search Marketing Daily*, October 21, 2015. **mediapost.com/publications/article/260871/google-dominates-search-struggles-in-display-targ.html** (accessed January 2017).

SUMO. "2016 Social Commerce Survey" 2016. **info.sumoheavy.com/2016/** (accessed January 2017).

Taylor, J. "Social CRM Case Study: Sony Europe Creates a Community of Super Fans." *OurSocialTimes*, May 14, 2013.

TrueShip. "Polyvore Statistics Illustrate Rise of Social Giant." TrueShip, January 12, 2016. **trueship.com/blog/2016/01/12/polyvore-statistics-illustrate-rise-of-new-social-giant/#.VuzHselrI2w** (accessed January 2017).

Tucker, K. "Social Customer Relationship Management (sCRM)." July 2013. **slideshare.net/KenTucker/s-crm-presentation** (accessed January 2017).

Turban, E., et al. *Social Commerce*. New York: Springer, 2016.

Van Looy, A. *Social Media Management: Technologies and Strategies for Creating Business Value*. New York: Springer, 2016.

Williams, B. *Social Media: Master and Dominate Social Media Marketing Using Facebook, Instagram, Twitter, YouTube, LinkedIn, Snap Chat, Pinterest, Google+, Vine, and Much more!* Seattle, WA: Amazon Digital Services, Inc., 2016.

Wood, T. "The Marketers Guide to the Social Media Galaxy [Infographic]." January 2, 2014. **business2community.com/infographics/marketers-guide-social-media-galaxy-infographic-0729381** (accessed January 2017).

Yoo, E. "Almost 1 in 5 People in China Group-Bought in June 2015, and It's Rising." TechNode, July 30, 2015. **technode.com/2015/07/30/chinas-group-buying-market-turnover-reaches-77b-rmb** (accessed January 2017).

York, A. "The 5-Step Social Media & Online Reputation Management Plan." Sprout Social, November 9, 2016. **sproutsocial.com/insights/social-media-reputation-management** (accessed January 2017).

Social Enterprise and Other Social Commerce Topics

Contents

Learning Objectives

Upon completion of this chapter, you will be able to:

1. Understand the concept of the social enterprise and its variants.
2. Describe business-oriented public social networks, their characteristics, and benefits.
3. Describe the major social commerce activities that can be conducted within and by enterprises and the characteristics of such private social networks.
4. Review the social commerce activities and their relationship with e-entertainment and gaming.
5. Describe social gaming and gamification.
6. Define crowdsourcing and describe its use in social commerce.
7. Describe social collaboration and its benefits.
8. Comment of the future of social commerce.

© Springer International Publishing AG 2018
E. Turban et al., *Electronic Commerce 2018*, Springer Texts in Business and Economics, DOI 10.1007/978-3-319-58715-8_9

OPENING CASE
MAXIMIZING THE IMPACT OF SOCIAL MEDIA WITH A MINIMUM
OF EFFORT IN MORTGAGE LENDING

The use of social media has the ability to transform a business and allow it to tap into customers in ways never thought of before. Using public social networks, employees have the ability to communicate in a direct and authentic manner with both customers and potential customers. These efforts can be seen as marketing or customer relationship management, but in either case they break down the walls traditionally in place between a company and the people it serves.

The Problem

Unfortunately, using social media is also fraught with potential disadvantages, for both the company that implements it and the employee that is utilizing it. These concerns are detailed by Accenture in their 2015 e-book *A Comprehensive Approach to Managing Social Media Risk and Compliance*. Principal among the concerns are the potential downfalls employees attempting to manage very diverse and potentially busy social media streams (Accenture 2015). This is even more of a concern when the employees are not digital natives, but are beginning to use social media networks later in life (Zur & Zur 2016).

These issues are compounded with the diversity of social media networks. Many companies strive to be active on multiple networks in order to cast a wide net to engage with customers. While this plan sounds good in concept, in execution it increases the workflow for employees and makes it more likely that social media errors or gaffs may occur. While it is possible to be efficient in social media use (see the free e-book from Leaning 2015 "How to Monitor Social Media in Only 10 Minutes a Day"), these practices are not always practical if social media is a primary method of customer interaction.

The Mortgage Industry

The desire to connect more authentically with customers and potential customers can be felt within the mortgage loan industry. Over the past several years, there have been many upheavals in the industry related to changes in government regulation as well as internal processes. To remain competitive, many large firms have identified the need to form stronger bonds with customers, and they view social media as an ideal outlet to achieve this goal (Hearsay Social 2016).

RPM Mortgage (**rpm-mtg.com**) is an independently owned and operated residential mortgage lender located in Alamo, California. RPM seeks to provide knowledge and resources to its customers in every transaction and identified social networks as a way to help achieve this goal. RPM faces similar hurdles in the use of social media as other mortgage lenders in the United States.

The Solution

Hearsay Social (**hearsaysystems.com**) is a San Francisco-based technology start-up company that provides social media management systems designed to help streamline social interactions with customers. The company's Predictive Omnichannel Suite (**hearsaysystems.com/product/**) allows the integration of multiple social networks and streams of information. Additionally, the solution uses predictive technology to allow financial service professionals to better deliver content and messages to customers at the time when they are most needed and appropriate. These features are particularly important due to the changes in the overall mortgage market. According to Clara Shih, the CEO and Founder of Hearsay Social, "Digital-native millennials are at the age where they're purchasing their first homes, representing a huge opportunity that's at stake for loan officers who aren't on social media, aren't appearing in search engine results, and aren't accessible via email or text" (Shih 2016).

The Results

RPM Mortgage was able to adopt the Hearsay Social platform, and the system has allowed them to automate and control their significantly enhanced social media profile. The system has allowed them to connect more consistently with customers at appropriate times to build stronger relationships. The company firmly believes that these efforts have helped to not only grow their existing business but to forge bonds that will catalyze further transactions when they are needed. For more on how Hearsay Social's system works with RPM Mortgage, see their case study and the video at **hearsaysystems.com/2016/03/digital-technology-transformation-and-adoption-at-rpm-mortgage**.

Sources: Accenture (2015), Zur & Zur (2016), Shih (2016) and **hearsaysystems.com**.

LESSONS LEARNED FROM THE CASE

Engaging in social media activities can help transform a business and allow them to better connect with customers. This transformation is not always simple and may require the use of supplemental systems that allow for better control of social media activities and timing. The financial services industry in the United States use social media as an important tool to connect with their customer base, and specialized software systems to allow them to do this more efficiently and effectively.

9.1 SOCIAL BUSINESS AND SOCIAL ENTERPRISE

A major forthcoming trend in social commerce is its move to the enterprise level. This trend is related to the concept of social business. Let us define both terms.

Definitions: Social Business and Social Enterprise

The social enterprise concept has several names, definitions and explanations. The concept is sometimes confused with the related concept of social business. Generally, one can distinguish between the two concepts that often are used interchangeably. Let us explain.

Social Business

A **social business** is a name for a commercial for-profit or nonprofit organization that is designed to achieve some social goal(s), such as improving human well-being, rather than just make a profit. Social Firms UK (**socialfirmsuk.co.uk**) provides several other definitions (of what they call *social enterprise*). They cite the following UK government definition: "A social enterprise is a business with primarily social objectives whose surpluses are reinvested for that purpose in the business or in the community, rather than being driven by the need to deliver profit to shareholders and owners" (see details at **socialfirmsuk.co.uk/faq/faq-what-social-enterprise-and-what-types-are-there**).

In the United States, social businesses are designated as "B Corps." According to **bcorporation.net**, B Corps are "for-profit companies certified by the nonprofit B Lab to meet rigorous standards of social and environmental performance, accountability, and transparency." There is a growing community of more than 1,600 Certified B Corps across 42 countries in 120 industries working to "redefine success in business" (watch the explanation video at **bcorporation.net/what-are-b-corps**).

About.com distinguishes between two types of social business: one type that describes companies that "aspire to social purposes more than to profit-making" and a second type that describes companies that "use social media to advance their business objectives." (See **webtrends.about.com/od/web20/a/social-media.htm**.)

The above second type is the basis for the *social enterprise*. In summary, we view a *social business* as one that is built mainly around social objective(s), while a *social enterprise* uses social networking to facilitate its commercial objectives.

A major organization dedicated to social business (referring to itself as "social enterprise") is the *Social Enterprise Alliance* (see **se-alliance.org/what-is-social-enterprise**).

Social Employees

The successful social business needs to empower their employees (e.g., using IBM Connections). For how it is done in IBM, AT&T, and other large corporations, see Nolinske (2016).

The Social Enterprise (Enterprise 2.0)

Social enterprise refers to the use of social media tools and platforms and conducting social networking activities in organizations as its major objectives (World Library 2015).

The concept of the social enterprise has become a buzzword in recent years. For an example, see **innov8social.com/2011/05/5-buzzwords-to-know-in-sustainable**. Social enterprise applications are growing rapidly. They appear under different names, mostly as social enterprises and Enterprise 2.0. Enterprise applications are conducted inside enterprises, on companies' private social networks or portals. They also are conducted on public social networks, both pure business-oriented (e.g., LinkedIn), and other networks, mostly Facebook and Twitter. Major applications are recruitment, collaboration, and problem-solving. Enterprise social capabilities facilitate a new type of collaboration, encourage business upgrades, and enable more vendor and customer applications.

Many workers use social media for business purposes at daily. Corporations are rushing to get involved in several innovative ways, as will be described later in this chapter.

For additional definitions, characteristics, and discussion on social enterprise, see **centreforso-cialenterprise.com/what.html**. For a comprehensive description, see Ridley-Duff and Bull (2015).

More Complex Definitions

In addition to the above definitions, there are some definitions that are more complex, as illustrated next.

The Social Business Forum's Definition

The Social Business Forum defines *social business* as "an organization that has put in place the strategies, technologies and processes to systematically engage all the individuals of its ecosystem (employees, customers, partners, suppliers) to maximize the co-created value" (**2012.social-businessforum.com/what-is-social-business**). The Forum also discusses the implications of this definition and its relevance, across and outside organizations. Note that an efficient creation of value using technology is emphasized.

Six interesting videos are recommended for a better understanding of the concept:

1. "What is Web/Enterprise 2.0" with Andrew McAfee (3:29 minutes) at **youtu.be/6xKSJfQh89k**
2. "Social PHD Sandy Carter: How Do You Become a Social Business?"(1:05 minutes) at **youtube.com/watch?v=OZy0dNQbotg**
3. "How Do You Become a Social Business?" (3:27 minutes) at **youtube.com/watch?v=3Hov0l7SvAo**
4. "How to create a successful social enterprise" with Marquis Cabrera at TEDxTeachersCollege (10:33 minutes), at (**youtu.be/M3fl1R2lZFk**)
5. "Social Business at IBM" – An Interview with Luis Suarez, Social Computing Evangelist (8:50 minutes), at (**youtube.com/watch?v=enudW2gHek0&feature=related**)
6. "Enterprise 2.0: The Pros and Cons of Social Media" with Mohammed Alnaqaa (59:40 minutes), at (**youtu.be/RvJ7oxTQaGc**)

Notice that our definition of social enterprise is based on the use of social media tools and platforms. A related topic is *business networks*.

Business Networks

Business networks are a core component in the social enterprise. A *business network* refers to a group of people with a professional business relationship; for example, the relationships between sellers and buyers, buyers and suppliers, and professionals and their colleagues. In this chapter, we use the term *buyers* to refer to agents buying something for a business (e.g., a purchasing agent). Such a network of people can form **business social networks**, which are business-oriented networks that are built on social relationships and can exist offline or online. For example, public places, such as airports or golf courses, provide opportunities to make new face-to-face business contacts if an individual has good social skills. Similarly, the Internet is proving to be a good place to network and connect. In this book, we address online networks. The most well-known network is LinkedIn (**linkedin.com**). For a discussion about business social networks, see Krans (2015) and a list of business social networks at **lifewire.com/business-social-networks-3486557**.

Types of Business Social Networks

There are three major types of business social networks:

(a) *Public networks*, such as LinkedIn, which are owned and operated by independent companies and are open to anyone for business networking. The networks connect, for example, sellers and buyers or employers and potential employees.
(b) *Enterprise private networks*, which operate inside companies. These usually restrict membership to employees and sometimes to business partners. An example is USAA that has an internal social network for employees who can ask for help from their peers.
(c) *Company-owned and company-hosted networks* that are controlled by a company but open to the public, usually for brand-related networking (e.g., Starbucks, Dell Computer).

The Benefits and Limitations of Enterprise Social Networking

Social networking appeals to business users for many reasons. For example, networking makes it easy to find people and discover information about companies, understands the relationships and communication patterns that make a company tick, and creates a common culture across large organizations.

- Improve collaboration inside the enterprise and with business partners
- Facilitate knowledge capture and distribution (increase access to specialized knowledge)
- Build better customer, vendor, and employee relationships
- Facilitate recruiting and employee retention activities
- Increase business and marketing opportunities (e.g., meet new potential business partners and/or customers)
- Reduce operation, communication, and travel costs
- Increase sales and revenue (e.g., more sales leads)
- Improve customer satisfaction
- Reduce marketing and advertising costs
- Reduce other operational costs
- Improve employee and organizational performance
- Foster internal and external relationships
- Collect feedback from employees
- Build an effective workforce
- Improve decision-making capabilities including forecasting
- Find experts and advice (internally and externally)
- Improve customer service and CRM
- Accelerate innovation and competitive advantage

The major reasons an organization becomes a social enterprise are the abilities to:
For details of these and other benefits, see Krans (2015) and section "Business-Oriented Public Social Networking".
Enterprises that use social media extensively can reap the benefits found in the previous list and be transformed into social businesses. For details, see **ibm.com/social-business/us/en**. For how to select the best organizational model for a social business, see Terpening (2015).

Obstacles and Limitations

Some limitations, such as security of information and information pollution, slow down the growth of social enterprising. In their e-book *A Comprehensive Approach to Managing Social Media Risk and Compliance*, Accenture (2015) details nine major concerns as social business is implemented in an organization:

1. Improper or under-performing software platform
2. Exposure of organizational weaknesses
3. Data misuse

4. Intellectual property loss
5. Financial loss
6. Privacy violations
7. Brand damage
8. Noncompliance

All of these issues can be overcome, but must be considered as social media is incorporated into a business and social enterprise applications are deployed.

For more details, see **slideshare.net/norwiz/what-is-enterprise-20**.

How Web 2.0 Tools Are Used by Enterprises

Web 2.0 tools are used in different ways by various corporations. Typical uses are increasing speed of access to knowledge, reducing communication costs, increasing speed of access to internal exports, decreasing travel costs, increasing employee satisfaction, reducing operational costs, reducing time to market for products/services, and increasing the number of successful innovations for new products or services.

Some of the uses outside the enterprises include recruitment, advice in problem-solving, joint design, collaboration on supply chain issues, and marketing communication. For a comprehensive slide presentation on Enterprise 2.0, see **slideshare.net/norwiz/what-is-enterprise-20**. For an e-book, see World Library (2015).

Implementing a firm foundation for the successful use of social media within a business can be problematic. It is very important for businesses to understand all of the potential issues, as well as the necessary steps to the completion of this type of project. Consulting for this type of implementation has become big business, with several firms providing services to businesses that want to jump into the social networking fray. Services can be provided by traditional business consultants, as well as software and service providers.

Accenture

Accenture (**accenture.com**), a traditional business consulting firm, offers a wide variety of services for companies that are interested in integrating social media interaction with their current business operations and customer relationship management activities. While being mindful of the risks, they focus on a three-step process to effectively implementing social media and social media risk management. These areas are:

- **Governance.** Ensuring that structures are in place that allow for defined protocols related to social media use, as well as systems to audit that use and respond two crises.
- **Processes.** Adjusting and developing corporate standards that can be used for social media interactions and risk management evaluation.
- **Systems.** Managing technology and data to mitigate risk in social media as well as optimizing the efficiency of employees.

Salesforce

Salesforce (**salesforce.com**), a leader in corporate CRM systems, has also developed a framework for companies that wish to implement social media strategies within their existing business structures. Being a software company, Salesforce focuses more on the implementation of these systems and the methods by which they can be optimized to allow the most positive and influential contact with customers and potential customers. When designing and implementation, the company recommends that businesses complete the following four steps first:

- Define the vision of the social media efforts
- Set clear goals for the use of social media that are attainable
- Define the purpose and types of activities that will be undertaken
- Establish a social task force to guide the implementation and evaluation

After these initial steps are completed, Salesforce follows an implementation plan that is meant to use their proprietary systems to help expand the customer relationship, facilitate greater collaboration, build deeper relationships, and allow for information gathering through both private and public networks.

For more information on both approaches, download the implementation guides for each provider. Accenture's *A Comprehensive Approach to Managing Social Media Risk and Compliance* (2015) is available at **accenture.com/ t20150523T022413__w__/us-en/_acnmedia/Accenture/Conversion-Assets/DotCom/Documents/Global/PDF/ Dualpub_1/accenture-comprehensive-approach-managing-social-media-risk-compliance.pdf**, while Salesforce's (2014) *The Little Blue Book of Social Transformation Salesforce* is available at **secure2.sfdcstatic.com/assets/pdf/misc/ Salesforce_ebook.pdf**.

SECTION 9.1 REVIEW QUESTIONS

1. Define social business and relate it to the social enterprise.
2. How does IBM define social business?
3. What is a business network?
4. List five reasons why organizations want to become social enterprises.
5. Why are there various approaches to implementing social media systems in businesses?

9.2   BUSINESS-ORIENTED PUBLIC SOCIAL NETWORKING

Social networking activities are conducted in both public and/or private social networking sites. For example, LinkedIn is a business-oriented public network, whereas Facebook is primarily a public social network used for socially oriented activities. Facebook, however, allows its members to conduct business-oriented activities. "My Starbucks Idea" (**mystarbucksidea. force.com**) is an example of a company-hosted social network that is open to the public. In this section, we will concentrate on public social networks.

The following are some examples of business-oriented public social networks.

- **Google+.** Google+ ("one Google account for everything"), which began operating in 2011, designated itself as a business-oriented social network. In its fourth year of operation, it has over 1.1 million users. For an overview, see **socialmediatoday.com/content/google-overview-breaking-through-misconceptions**.
- **LinkedIn.** Referred to as the premier business-oriented network, LinkedIn (**linkedin.com**) is known as the most popular network for business, as illustrated in the closing case of this chapter. For an overview, see **lifewire.com/ what-is-linkedin-3486382**. Also see the infographic at **blog.hoot-suite.com/social-network-for-work**.

LinkedIn shows content and provides customer service in a multitude of languages, including English, Spanish, French, and Tagalog, among others, with a plan for considering other languages in the future.

Several other networks similar to LinkedIn are Wealink (**wealink.com**) in China, Rediff (**rediff.com**) in India, International High Potential Network (iHipo) (**ihipo.com**) in Sweden, and Moikrug (My Circle) (**moikrug.ru**) in Russia.

There are many public business-oriented networks that focus on specific industries or types of professional specialties; one example is the Network of Entrepreneurial Women (**networkwomen.org**).

Example: Could Facebook Be a Business Network Too?

Facebook has been primarily designed to be a personal social network, allowing friends and acquaintances to share information and news. This is different than a purely business Network such as LinkedIn that is designed around professional networking with profile presentations very similar to a resume. But many use Facebook for business tasks (Turner 2016). Some use Facebook for professional networking while others may use it to search for jobs. The reason for this crossover is the critical mass of users on Facebook and individuals' decreasing sensitivity to mixing work and personal lives (especially among millennials). With these activities in mind, some have wondered if Facebook truly can be used as a business network.

While the number of users and specific features related to job search certainly indicate that it could be, other factors are weight against it (Vahl 2015). The design of the system is not meant to showcase professional skills in the same way that other networks such as LinkedIn are. Additionally, some users are concerned about the bleed-over between personal activities and professional activities. Privacy also plays into this concern as well. Supporting more business network features would be possible for Facebook, but does not appear to be the current strategic direction the company is moving in. That being said, only time will tell if Facebook chooses to expand into this complementary yet contradictory direction.

Entrepreneur Networks

Some business-oriented public networks concentrate on entrepreneurial activities. A few examples are listed next. Gottlieb (2015) lists 42 social networks for entrepreneurs. Here are some more in detail:

- **Startup Nation (startupnation.com).** Participants in this community of start-up owners and experts are helping people start and operate new businesses. Sharing knowledge and ideas is the main objective.
- **Entrepreneur Connect (econnect.entrepreneur.com).** From the company that produces Entrepreneur Magazine, this social network was created specifically for entrepreneurs and small business owners and allows them to leverage relationships with service providers, suppliers, advisers, and colleagues.
- **Biznik (biznik.com).** Biznik is a community of entrepreneurs and small business owners dedicated to helping each other by sharing ideas and knowledge. Their motto is "collaboration beats the competition" (see **biznik.com/articles/collaboration-beats-the-competition**). According to **biznik.com**, their policy is that members must use their real names on the site and Biznik supplements its interactions with face-to-face meetings.
- **EFactor (efactor.com).** The world's largest network of entrepreneurs (over 1 million members in 222 countries across 240 industries) provides members with people, tools, marketing, and expertise to succeed and make real, trustworthy, and lasting connections (2011 data). Members connect with like-minded people and with investors.
- **Inspiration Station (inspiration.entre-preneur.com).** Inspiration Station is one of the best portals for small businesses and start-ups. It not only has a lot of useful information for business owners, it has a great community for you to take advantage of, and to connect with fellow business owners from around the globe.

For how social entrepreneurship works, see Martin et al. (2015) and the video "What is a social entrepreneur?" at **youtu.be/bWAxdYN0dlc**.

SECTION 9.2 REVIEW QUESTIONS

1. Distinguish between private and public business-oriented networks.
2. List and briefly describe public business-oriented networks.
3. Define entrepreneur networks and list two examples.
4. Why do some many business social networks exist?

9.3   ENTERPRISE SOCIAL NETWORKS

An increasing number of companies have created their own in-house, enterprise social networks. Some of these networks can be private, developed for use only by their employees, former employees, and business partners. Others are open to the public, although these are mostly used by their customers. Many networks are now utilizing a hybrid format, with much of the system only available in-house, but with some customer service functions available publicly. Additionally, many of these systems connect to other social media networks such as LinkedIn and Facebook to increase their functionality and audience. Private networks are considered to be secured ("behind the firewall") and are often referred to as *corporate social networks*. Such networks come in several formats, depending on their purpose, the industry, the country, and so forth. For the evolution of the networked enterprise, see Bughin (2015) and Krans (2015).

Taxonomy of Social Enterprise Applications

The following terms are frequently used in enterprise networking. Most will be discussed in this chapter.

1. **Networking and community building.** Conducting networking and community building involving employees, executives, business partners, and customers.
2. **Crowdsourcing.** Gathering ideas, insights, and feedback from crowds (e.g., employees, customers, and business partners; see section "Business-Oriented Public Social Networking"). Salesforce Success Community (**success.salesforce.com**) and My Starbucks Idea (**mystarbucksidea.force.com**) are examples.
3. **Social collaboration.** Collaborative work and problem-solving using wikis, blogs, instant messaging, voice and video chat, collaborative office documents, and other special purpose Web-based collaboration platforms such as Laboranova (**laboranova.com**) and WebEx (**webex.com**).
4. **Social publishing.** This is the creation of user-generated content in the enterprise, which is accessible to all (e.g., **slideshare.net** and **youtube.com**).
5. **Social views and feedback.** Getting feedback and opinions from the enterprise's internal and external communities on specific issues.

Characteristics of Enterprise Social Networks

Enterprise social networks, like any social network, enable employees to create profiles and interact with one another. By encouraging interactions among members, a company can foster collaboration and teamwork and increase employee satisfaction. For more benefits, see **zdnet.com/blog/hinchcliffe** and the SocialCast video "Why Companies Need Enterprise Social Networking" at **youtu.be/xxHJLXXAask**.

For additional information, see the *International Journal of Social and Humanistic Computing* **inderscience.com/jhome.php?jcode=ijshc**. For additional tips and sources, see **socialcast.com**.

An Example of a Private Enterprise Network

Many corporations maintain private enterprise social networks. Examples include Starbucks' hosted enterprise network and Sony's and iRobot's hosted enterprise social networks. Many other companies also have enterprise networks of all kinds. Here is an example of another private network:

Example: IBM'S Business and Professional Community

The Greater IBM Connection (**ibm.com/ibm/greateribm**) is an internal social networking site that gives IBM employees and former IBMers a rich connection to the people with whom they work, on both a personal and a professional level. The network helps employees make new connections, track current friends and coworkers, and renew contacts with people they have worked with in the past, including retirees. When employees join the network, they get a profile page. They can use the status message field and the free-form "MyIBM" section on their profile page to let other people at IBM know where they are, what they are doing, and even what they are thinking. By 2017, about 500,000 IBMers were connected to one another using IBM Connections platform.

Employees can also use the network to post photos, create lists, and organize events. If users are hosting an event, they can create an event page on the network and invite people to attend. The page can also be a place to spread the buzz about the event and get people talking about it through the comments feature.

In addition to the social goal, the network team created the site to help IBM employees meet the challenge of building professional relationships that are vital to working in large, distributed enterprises. The network can help IBM employees discover people with common interests or the right skills for a project. Learning more about someone—personally and professionally—facilitates making contacts and might entice people to learn about the ongoing projects and activities of other people. This network can also provide valuable insights for managers evaluating employees for promotion.

The IBM network is related to IBM's social business Innovation Projects, cited later in this chapter. It is also related to *IBM's Connections*, the company's social software platform.

Note: Gartner Inc. named IBM a leader for social software in 2015.

How Enterprise Social Networking Helps Employees and Organizations

Enterprise social networking can help employees in one or more of the following ways:

1. **Quick access to knowledge, knowhow, and "know-who."** As people list their skills, expertise, and experience, enterprise social networks can help simplify the job of locating people with specified knowledge and skills.
2. **Expansion of social connections and broadening of affiliations.** Enterprise social networks help managers and professionals to know people better by interacting with them in online communities and by keeping up with their personal information. Such interaction and information about others can decrease the social distance in a company.
3. **Self-branding.** People can become creative in building their profiles the way they want to be known. It helps them promote their personal brand within the corporation.
4. **Referrals, testimonials, and benchmarking.** Enterprise social networks can help employees prepare and display referrals and testimonials about their work and also benchmark them with their colleagues.

Benefits to Organizations

The benefits to organizations, as well as to employees, were presented in section "Social Business and Social Enterprise". In addition, the benefits to employees can develop into benefits to organizations in the long run. For additional insights, see Alex Hannant's TEDx presentation "Why social enterprise is a good idea, and how we can get more of it" at **youtu.be/Kx9tizvS8NY**.

Support Services for Enterprise Social Networks

Businesses can use a variety of services and vendors to support their social networking. Three examples are as follows.

Example 1: Tibbr

Tibbr (**tibco.com**) is an enterprise social collaboration platform that creates a joint workspace that enables discussion, task management, content, and personal contacts. The suite of tools are designed to help individuals within an organization communicate easily and openly with each other and also reach out to the company's customers and business partners. The platform accomplishes this by a combination of Web- and mobile-based applications. The system also allows for a number of integrations with other social tools such as Facebook, Twitter, LinkedIn, WebEx, Google Drive, Skype, and SharePoint. In 2017, Tipper had over 6 million users in 100 countries worldwide active on the platform. For more information, visit **tibco.com/products/tibbr** or watch the video at **vimeo.com/video/80391600**.

Example 2: Socialtext

Socialtext (**socialtext.com**) is a vendor of enterprise social software, providing an integrated suite of Web-based applications including social media tools and platforms. The company also provides Web security services. Businesses can benefit by keeping employees connected to the enterprise strategy and operations. For details, see **socialtext.com/about**.

Example 3: Yammer—A Collaboration Platform

Yammer, Inc. (**yammer.com**), is a Microsoft company. According to its website, Yammer is a private social network that helps employees collaborate across departments, locations, and business apps in over 500,000 companies (in 2016). Yammer brings together people for conversations, content, and business data in a single location. With Yammer, you can easily stay connected to coworkers and information, collaborate with team members, and make an impact at work. It is used for communication and collaboration within organizations or between organizational members and predesignated groups.

Key Features

Yammer's social networks allow users to (compiled from **about.yammer.com**):

- **Converse using enterprise microblogging.** Start a conversation, read posts, and actively collaborate with coworkers in real time using microblogging.
- **Create profiles.** Report your expertise, work experience, and contact information. You can upload photos, images, and documents. This will help you share information with others and become easier to find.
- **Manage groups.** Create new groups or join private or public groups and then discuss issues or collaborate with the group members. (Discover and join groups, invite team members to join, and start collaborating.)
- **Conduct secure and private messaging.** Create a private dialog with one or multiple coworkers, similar to what you can do on Facebook. Secure the messages with Yammer's security features.
- **Create external networks.** Create external networks for working with business partners.
- **Create a company directory.** Create a directory of all employees.
- **Archive knowledge.** Archive all online conversations to be fully searchable.
- **Use administrative tools.** Keep the Yammer network running smoothly with a suite of features built to increase managerial control.
- **Employ tagging.** Tag the content and message in the company's network to make content easy to search for and to organize.
- **Integrate applications.** Install third-party applications into Yammer to increase the functionality of the company's network.
- **Deploy mobile capabilities.** Connect to the company's network from anywhere, at any time. Download free iPhone, Blackberry, Android, and Windows Mobile applications.

You can view a short video on how to use Yammer at youtu.be/Fz5yi4Cyj5o. Note that in 2017 Microsoft is planning to change Yammer and roll its functionality into its Office360 product. For details see Buckley (2015).

How Companies Interface with Social Networking

Enterprises can interface with public and/or private social networks in several ways. The major interfaces, which are shown in Fig. 9.1, are described next.

Fig. 9.1 The major interfaces with social networking

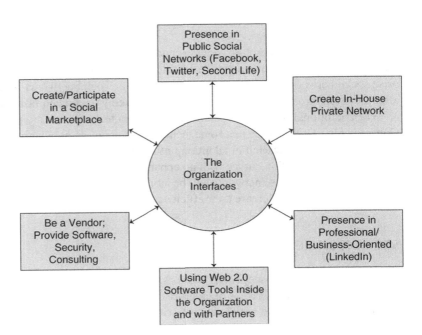

- Use existing public social networks, such as Facebook and LinkedIn, to create pages and microcommunities, advertise products or services, and post requests for advice, job openings, and so forth.
- Create an in-house private social network and then use it for communication and collaboration among employees and retirees or with outsiders (e.g., customers, suppliers, designers). Employees can create virtual rooms in their company's social networks where they can deploy applications to share information or to collaborate.
- Conduct business activities in a business-oriented or professional social network (e.g., LinkedIn or Sermo).
- Create services for social networks, such as software development, security, consulting services, and more (e.g., Oracle, IBM, Microsoft).
- Use Web 2.0 software tools, mostly blogs, wikis, workspaces, microblogging (Twitter), VOIP communication, and team rooms, and create innovative applications for both internal and external users.
- Create and/or participate in a social marketplace (such as Fotolia; **us.fotolia.com**; now an Adobe company).

Integration with Other Tools

Many systems are now highly dependent on integration with other social networks to provide a portion of their functionality. The determination of how much integration is needed is a function of both the capabilities of the enterprise social network software itself, and management decisions about how private or public the network itself should be.

Many networks allow integration to a large number of social media systems, and these systems are used to help grow the audience that is available to corporate users. In some cases these integrations are customer-facing and meant to facilitate customer interaction and support. Examples of these types of integrations would be with Facebook, Instagram, and Twitter. Other integrations are meant to augment the feature set of the enterprise social network itself. In many cases these integrations are used to add functionality to the system it would not otherwise exist or that would not be as ubiquitous. Examples include using WebEx for voice and video chat and using Google Drive for document storage and sharing.

Patterns and Speed of Adoption

The growth of enterprise social networks has slowed since their initial introduction, but much of this is due to saturation within businesses. In many cases the question is not if social enterprise networks being used but how are they being used and to what extent. Bughin (2015) from McKinsey & Company noted at as early as 2008 two thirds of companies they tracked used some sort of this technology but that diffusion within the company was very low with only 20% of employees actively using the system. This observation is confirmed by Li (2015), who notes that networks need to have critical mass to achieve acceptance in organizations.

Overtime, this diffusion has grown as additional features, and integrations have been added into the system, especially those that allow for communication to outside networks such as Facebook and LinkedIn. Evaluation further shows that enterprise social networks did act as a "copycat" to public social networks by adopting many of their features and technologies after they were proven in the public space and us taking on a much faster adoption curve.

When additional options of specific social media technologies are taken into consideration as seen in the McKinsey & Company report, we can see that some technologies are more popular in the corporate space than others. For example, video sharing had a very quick initial adoption until it plateaued. By contrast both blogs and integration to other social networks have had steady adoption curves with no apparent plateau.

Future growth of these networks will be largely dependent not on corporate acceptance but on tools and features that businesses can leverage to increase their efficiency and provide enhanced customer service.

SECTION 9.3 REVIEW QUESTIONS

1. Define enterprise (private) social networks.
2. List the major characteristics of enterprise social networks.
3. Describe the enterprise social network within IBM.

4. List the benefits to organizations.
5. Describe Yammer and identify its connections with social networks.
6. List the different ways that companies interface with social networking.
7. What tools and features drive usage of enterprise social networks?
8. Why would enterprise social networks integrate with public social networks?

9.4   SOCIAL NETWORK-BASED JOB MARKETS

A major enterprise area of activity in social networks, private and public, relates to job seeking and recruitment.

Social Recruiting

Finding qualified employees in certain fields may be a difficult task. To accomplish this task, companies pay considerable fees to executive recruiters or third-party online companies.

If job seekers are online and active in their search and in posting their résumés, there is a good chance that they will be discovered by recruiters. In addition, many so-called passive job seekers are employed and are not actively looking for a new job. Therefore, it is important that both active and passive job seekers maintain a *profile* online that present them in a positive light, especially on LinkedIn and Facebook.

Both recruiters and job seekers are moving to a new recruiting platform—the online social networks—mostly LinkedIn, Facebook, and Twitter (e.g., using TwitJobSearch; **twitjobsearch.com**), a job search engine that allows employers to post job ads on Twitter). Enterprise recruiters are scanning online social networks, blogs, and other sources to identify and find information about potential employees. This transition is especially important as the methods for recruitment change. Today, studies estimate that as many as 85% of all positions are filled through networking instead of more traditional processes (see **linkedin.com/pulse/new-survey-reveals-85-all-jobs-filled-via-networking-lou-adler**). In this environment, it is critical for both recruiters and applicants to be active in the ecosystem (social networks) where decisions are being made.

Clearly, the electronic job market has benefits, but it can also create high turnover costs for employers by facilitating employees' movements to look for better jobs. This is compounded by millennials proclivity to change jobs more frequently than prior generations. In addition, finding candidates online is more complicated than most people think, mostly due to the large number of résumés available in social media sites. To facilitate recruitment, top recruiters are using electronic aids, like interviewing candidates by video from remote locations. Recruiters use social media tools and multiple social networking sites to find candidates faster. Some recruiters send Facebook "friend" invitations to candidates whom they have interviewed. However, this can be a controversial practice due to ethical implications. Recruiters are also using social networks and other online tools to vet potential hires.

Facebook has many features that help people find jobs (see **jobcast.net** for jobseekers and employers to connect; Social Jobs Partnership (**facebook.com/socialjobs**), a collaboration between Facebook and the US Department of Labor).

LinkedIn provides a similar service. LinkedIn's search engine can help employers quickly find an appropriate candidate. For finding employees (jobs) in other countries, one can use LinkedIn or Xing (**xing.com**). An interesting global recruiting community is EURES (**ec.europa.eu/eures**), which specializes in online recruiting in Europe. LinkedIn has also recently launched a mobile app aimed at first-time job seekers in colleges and universities.

Lately, there has been an increased use of mobile recruiting tools in general and Twitter and LinkedIn in particular, as aids for people who are searching for jobs. The following are possible activities:

- Search for posted positions
- Follow job search experts
- Follow and read about people in your field
- Engage, communicate with people, and ask for help
- Evaluate hiring companies through their social media accounts
- Connect with people at your target companies to evaluate the company or ask for referrals

For a slideshow showing how using social media can help you land a new job, see **money.usnews.com/money/careers/slideshows/10-ways-social-media-can-help-you-land-a-job**. For details on which networks to use, see **thebalance.com/best-social-media-sites-for-job-searching-2062617**.

Recruiting and Job Searching Using Social Networks

Most public social networks, especially those that are business-oriented, facilitate recruiting and job finding. For example, recruiting is a major activity at LinkedIn and was the driver for the site's development (see closing case to this chapter). To be competitive, companies must also look at the global market for talents. Luckily, they can use global social networking sites to find them. Large companies are using their in-house social networks to find in-house talents for vacant positions. Furthermore, some claim that social media significantly changed the hiring process (e.g., see Huff 2014). For how to use social media to impress recruiters, see Thomas (2016).

According to a Jobvite survey on social recruiting **jobvite.com/wp-content/uploads/2016/09/RecruiterNation2016. pdf**, 95% of companies use, or plan to use, social media to recruit and hire new employees, with 87% of recruiters find LinkedIn most effective when vetting candidates during the hiring process. Recruiters also use Facebook (43%), Twitter (22%), Blogs (11%), YouTube (6%), and Snapchat (3%). Conversely, 67% of job seekers use Facebook in their job search. Additionally, 45% of recruiters have mobile career sites. See **jobvite.com/wp-content/uploads/2016/09/ RecruiterNation2016.pdf**.

As described earlier, LinkedIn, Facebook, Google+, and Craigslist provide job listings, in competition with nonsocial networks online recruiters such as Monster. Several other social networks offer job listings as well.

Note that, while over 90% of recruiters use social networks while seeking and researching qualified candidates, nearly 69% have rejected candidates due to the content posted on their social networking sites. It is important for jobs seekers to keep their social media personal information secure (or as private as possible). Another issue for employed candidates is that many times employers have discovered through social networks that their employees are looking for a job elsewhere. For recruiting via gamification, see Zielinski (2015). For a current guide to job searching with social media, see Deligiannis (2017).

Note to job seekers: It is important you write your Internet profile in a correct way. For suggestions how to do it and what not to do, see Bernstein (2015).

Virtual Job Fairs and Recruiting Events

Virtual job fairs are other new strategies for quickly finding qualified candidates at a reduced cost. These are done using special vendor sites (e.g., **on24.com**, **expos2.com**, and **brazencareerist.com**) or employers' websites.

The following are few examples:

- IBM needed qualified employees for leadership positions in Africa. To quickly attract qualified employees, it used ON24 to conduct a job fair. For the complete story, see **on24.com/case-studies/ibm-job-fair**.
- P&G of Western Europe conducts annual virtual recruiting conferences using INXPO platform. The event is successful and it is used as a model for other European companies. For a complete description, see **inxpo.com/assets/pdfs/CS_P&G. pdf**.
- The state of Michigan periodically conducts virtual career fairs where job seekers and recruiters meet online. The latest one was held in November 2015. For details, see **michiganvirtualcareerfair.com**.

Training Employees

Several companies use enterprise social networking, for training purposes. Black & Decker is using user-generated videos posted on YouTube to help users of its products. These videos help reduce training time.

Social Network Privacy and Job Search

While social media is seen as a boon too many job seekers, others worry about their privacy as they use systems that may have been designed for friendly interaction in a business environment. Many Facebook users have found that potential employers not only check references but also check Facebook accounts to better understand the temperament and history of an applicant (see **huffingtonpost.com/2013/06/28/facebook-posts-employers_n_3517130.html**). Other users are simply concerned that their personal details be visible two recruiters, whether it is part of the selection process or not.

Many employment consultants recommend that job applicants evaluate their public social media presence and determine if anything available could cast them in a bad light during interviews or job selection. If that is the case, they recommend scrubbing or disabling social media content and features that could give this impression (Walker 2015). Others simply recommend that users accept the fact that nothing online can be truly private and that they should always be thinking of their reputation when they post to any publicly available network (Davidson 2014).

For more information on how social media could hurt your job search, see **forbes.com/sites/jacquelynsmith/2013/04/16/ how-social-media-can-help-or-hurt-your-job-search/#3b272a5b24fd**, and for information on how to protect your Facebook account, see **breakingnews.ie/discover/5-easy-ways-to-make-your-facebook-account-more-private-634953.htm**l.

REVIEW QUESTIONS FOR SECTION 9.4

1. List the benefits of social networking to job seekers.
2. List the benefits to corporate recruiters.
3. What special services are provided by social networks such as LinkedIn?
4. Describe virtual job fairs.
5. Why would applicants be concerned about their privacy when engaging in online job seeking?

9.5 SOCIAL ENTERTAINMENT

The rich media capabilities of Web 2.0 technologies, the ability to engage millions of people who congregate in social networks and who are interested in online entertainment, the availability of innovative social media tools, and the creative and collaborative nature of Web 2.0 all facilitate social entertainment (e.g., *Carpool Karaoke with Adele* was YouTube's most watched video in 2016). Web 2.0 tools also are aiding in the proliferation of on-demand entertainment. The most well-known entertainment application is streaming music (e.g., iTunes; **apple.com/itunes**). Also popular are Spotify, Pandora, and Google's All Access (**play.google.com/about/music**) and Amazon's Prime Music (**www.amazon.com/PrimeMusic**). The trend today is to stream music on-demand usually for free or with a monthly/annual subscription, which gives listeners the ability to enjoy whatever they want, whenever they want. Jurgensen (2014) provides a comprehensive coverage of digital music today and tomorrow, including information about providers and about. Finally, Facebook and Twitter entered this area. This section describes some of the entertainment-centered social networks, as well as other issues related to entertainment in social commerce.

Entertainment and Social Networks

A large number of social networks are fully or partially dedicated to entertainment. Well-known examples in 2016 are Vimeo, Netflix, Vudo, and Amazon Prime Video. The following are representative examples of the use of Web 2.0 applications for entertainment.

Mixi

In Japan, Mixi, Inc. (**mixi.com**) is a highly visited social networking service even though users must be invited to join. Mixi's goal is to allow users to build friendships with other users who share common interests. The site has about 27 million members and over 1 million small communities of friends and interests. Mixi is going global, while Facebook is overtaking it in Japan.

Last.fm

Last.fm (**last.fm**) is not just an Internet radio station. It is considered an online music catalog with free music streaming, videos, lyrics, etc. It also recommends music to its listeners. Musical profiles are constructed when users listen to a personal music collection with a Last.fm plug-in or when they listen to the Last.fm Internet radio service. As of 2017, regular membership is free; premium membership is $3 per month. The site, which operates in 12 major languages (as of 2017), won the Digital Music Award for Best Music Community Site in 2006.

Pandora

Similar to Last.fm, Pandora (**pandora.com**) is a site for music lovers. It mostly acts as a personal radio. The site is based on user-centered music recommendations. Pandora can create a personalized "radio station" based on a user's search for a particular artist, song, or genre.

Amazon's Prime Music

This service allows users to stream a wide catalog of music to a variety of devices that are connected to the Internet. These can include Wi-Fi-enabled MP3 players, smartphones, tablets, and Amazon's own ecosystem. Prime Music is configured in two tiers of service. Customers who have an Amazon Prime account can access a large array of free music that they are able to stream. Customers who want an expanded catalog can choose to pay a monthly or annual fee for access to this expanded music listing. This includes a significant increase in the number of available songs, including many that are not available on other streaming services (see **amazon.com/PrimeMusic**).

Web Series and Streaming Movies

Web series are similar to episodic series on TV (e.g., soap operas). The number of Web series is increasing, and some are already available on DVD. Examples include *Stranger Things*, *House of Cards*, and *Mozart in the Park*. For more about Web series and other examples, see **webserieschannel.com/web-series-101** and **geekwire.com/2016/amazon-netflix-challenge-major-tv-networks-in-spending-on-original-shows-study-says**.

Hulu

Hulu (**hulu.com**) offers advertisement-supported streaming on-demand videos of TV shows and movies from NBC, Fox, Disney (including ABC programs), and other networks and studios. While Amazon and Netflix are the largest streaming providers   (**geekwire.com/2016/study-amazon-video-now-third-largest-streaming-service-behind-netflix-youtube**), Hulu has a unique niche in offering current broadcast content. Due to copyright laws, Hulu offers videos only to users in the United States and a few other countries. Hulu provides video in Flash Video format. In addition, Hulu offers some TV shows and movies in high definition in a manner similar to Google Sites, Fox Interactive Media, and Yahoo! Sites. Users can manually share videos they like on their Facebook pages by using the "Facebook" button. It is not necessary to connect their Hulu and Facebook accounts to do this. Hulu is one of the most popular Internet video sites (see **screencrush.com/nielsen-streaming-data-hulu-netflix**). Hulu offers some of its services free, supported by advertising. It also offers Hulu Plus, which includes premium shows and the ability to watch on more devices for a monthly fee of $7.99. This service, however, also features limited advertising. Like other streaming services, Hulu is also beginning to create original content (see **comingsoon.net/tv/features/695179-the-10-best-hulu-original-series**). For more about their offerings and difference between Hulu and Hulu Plus, click on the "frequently asked questions" tab at **hulu.com/plus**.

Advertising and subscriptions are the primary social commerce business models for most streaming entertainment sites.

Funny-or-Die and Cracked.com

According to their website, Funny or Die (**funnyordie.com**) is a comedy video website created by actor and comedian Will Ferrell, among others. Unlike other viral video sites, members of Funny or Die are encouraged to vote on videos that they view. If they think the video is funny, viewers cast a vote for "Funny." The video then gets a score of the total percentage of people who voted the video "Funny." If the video receives an 80% or greater "Funny" rating after 100,000 views, it gets an "Immortal" ranking. If the video receives a 20% or less "Funny" rating after 1,000 views, it "dies" and is relegated to the Crypt section of the site.

Cracked.com, another humor website (which includes videos), also uses crowdsourcing to solicit material from the Internet crowd.

Multimedia Presentation and Sharing Sites

Multimedia sharing can be done in several ways, and its purpose is entertainment, advertising, training, and socialization. The following are some representative types of sharing and companies in each area:

- **Photography and art sharing.** Flickr, Instagram, Picasa, SmugMug, Photobucket, Imgur
- **Video sharing.** YouTube, Vimeo, Metacafe, Openfilm, Japan's Niconico (**nicovideo.jp**; now available in English as well)
- **Livecasting.** Twitch.tv, Livestream, Skype, Ustream, Facebook
- **Mobile social networks:** Path, Liveme, Vine
- **Music and audio sharing.** ccMixter, FreeSound, Last.fm, MySpace, Reverb-Nation, The Hype Machine (**hypem. com/popular**)
- **Presentation sharing.** SlideSnack, SlideShare, authorSTREAM, SlideBoom
- **Virtual worlds.** Second Life, The Sims, Activeworlds, IMVU
- **Game sharing.** Miniclip, Kongregate, Techcult, GameTap

Note that many of these have some features of social networks; therefore, they may be referred to as such. In addition, most of these generate revenue from advertising and/or subscriptions, including from mobile devices. For more, see Accenture Consulting at **accenture.com/us-en/industry/media-entertainment/Pages/media-entertainment-index.aspx**.

SECTION 9.5 REVIEW QUESTIONS

1. Relate social networks to streaming music.
2. Describe the ways you can watch videos on the Web (streaming videos on-demand).
3. Describe some of the multimedia presentation sites.

9.6   SOCIAL GAMES AND GAMIFICATION

A **social game** is a video multiplayer game played on the Internet, mostly in social networks or in virtual worlds. Gamers can play against computers or against each other. Many social games are "massively" multiplayer online games (known as MMOG or MMO), which are capable of supporting hundreds to many thousands of players simultaneously. MMOG players can compete, collaborate, or just interact with other players around the globe. Many game consoles, including the PSP, PlayStation, Xbox, Nintendo, and Wii, can be played on the Internet. Additionally, mobile devices and smartphones based on such operating systems as Android, iOS, and Windows Mobile are seeing an increase in the number of MMO available games. Social games are very popular.

Games on Social Networks

A **social network game** is a video game that is played in social networks and usually involves multiplayers. Social (network) games may have little or nothing to do with how *social* the games are played. However, some games have social elements such as educating the public, gift-giving, and helping other or sharing playing strategies.

For a game to be more social, it should facilitate and encourage engagement and communication about the environment outside the game, run on or integrated with a social network, and use that network to enhance game play between players.

Example: Popular Games on Facebook

Players can choose from several thousands of games on Facebook. Some games are played by 50–150 million people each. The most popular games each attract tens of millions of players. Facebook's list of popular games for October 2016 includes Candy Crush Saga (most popular in 2016), Clash of Clans, Candy Crush Soda Saga, Farm Heroes Saga, 8 Ball Pool, and Criminal case. (See **statista.com/statistics/267003/most-popular-social-games-on-facebook-based-on-daily-active-users**.)

Representative major Facebook developers for games are King, Zynga, Social Point, and Pretty Simple. Note that there is a trend to play more casino-type games. To enhance the game experience, some platforms utilize the players' social graphs. To learn more about social games, go to **museumstuff.com/learn/topics/Social_network_game**.

The Business Aspects of Social Games

To understand the variety of games and their properties and commercial possibilities, we suggest you watch the video "Social Media Games: Worldwide Gamification Is the New Paradigm for Life and Business" at **youtube.com/watch?v=xCWsgBHY_VU**. The video presents opportunities for advertising, marketing, and training, among others. Also, visit the site of Zynga (**zynga.com**), a major vendor in the field.

For the relationship between YouTube and gamers, see Hutchinson (2015).

CASE 9.1: EC APPLICATION
POKÉMON GO

Pokémon GO (**pokemongo.com**) is a mobile game that is designed around physical locations and actions that users must take to play the game. Pokémon is a popular franchise of "pocket monsters" that can be collected and used to interact with other players through battles. The original game and subsequent television show are popular in the 1990s but maintain their cachet today.

The game is a mobile app that is available for both Apple's iOS and Android. It is free to play but also includes in-game purchases. The game uses the GPS system in the phone and augmented reality to allow you to find and capture Pokémon characters. Capturing characters requires physical actions that can include both walking and running after the characters. Pokémon can be found and a wide variety of physical locations and the search for these characters can lead users to a variety of odd places. Users enjoy the game because it's tie in with the classic series, as well as the augmented reality of using the mobile device (Lee 2016). Detail guides on how to be successful in the game are also available (see **primagames.com/games/pokemon-go/coverage/pokemon-go-guide-and-tips-legendary-pokemon-gym-combat-strategies**).

Augmented reality is an important component of the game, as it displays the fictional character in a real location using the camera on a mobile device as well as the games software. This gives the impression that its character may be in front of you through augmented reality, when it is not actually there. Pokémon GO is the first large-scale implementation of augmented reality that has become very successful in the United States (see Anderton 2016 and the infographic at **forbes.com/sites/kevinanderton/2016/11/14/augmented-reality-the-future-and-pokemon-go-infographic/#53a8a5344e66**).

The game is not without its detractors and disadvantages. Individuals playing the game may become caught up in the augmented reality and hurt themselves as they move about the physical world. Individuals may also venture into areas that they do not belong such as private property while playing the game. There have been many reports of gamers being hurt or even killed playing the game (Bowerman 2016).

The business aspects of the game are also very interesting; in the period during its initial launch the game enjoyed a very steep adoption curve as a significant number of users began using the game during a very short period of time. During this initial high adoption phase, the game was able to generate a huge amount of in-game purchases. At the height of its popularity, the game had an estimated 7.5 million downloads and an average daily revenue of $1.6 million. From this revenue, some estimated that the value of the game was over $3.65 billion (Kelly 2016). Unfortunately, this level of use, spending, and valuation has not kept pace, as the number of users of the game has dropped precipitously since its initial launch.

During the height of its popularity, many businesses looked for ways to capitalize on the phenomenon, including potential joint ventures with the company in order to place Pokémon characters at their business locations to generate foot traffic.

Pokémon GO has had a very interesting run of popularity and is an excellent example of both augmented reality technologies and social gaming and social commerce.

Sources: Lee (2016), Anderton (2016) and Kelly (2016).

Questions

1. Why were users so infatuated with Pokémon GO?
2. How is this game an example of augmented reality?
3. How is this game an example of social commerce?
4. Why do you think the game did not retain its initial popularity?

Educational Social Games

Games can also be educational as the following examples show. Environmental apps for adults and kids (e.g., for tablets) can be found at **ecogamer.org/environmental-games**.

Example 1: Pollution Reduction Game
The Philippine-made Facebook game called Alter Space aims to educate the people on how to reduce pollution. Specifically, it educates the players about the concepts of carbon footprints and cleaner energy and how people can help achieve a cleaner world (inactive now).

Example 2: Economic and Finance Game—Empire Avenue
Empire Avenue (**empireavenue.com**) is a social media stock market simulation game where individuals and businesses buy and sell virtual shares from each other. The shares can be of individuals, companies, etc. The share price is based on the shares' trading activity coupled with the players' influence on the major social networks. The trading is done with reward points called *Eaves* and *Vees*. In the game, there are financial data and decision-making capabilities about dividends, number of shares outstanding, and share prices, to name just a few. Empire has many variables within the game. The reward points can also be used as virtual currency to play the Social Market game. Players can interact via popular social networks (e.g., Facebook, Twitter, and Instagram) across the Web. The more social the player is, the more virtual currency the player will earn, and the bigger the player's Empire will become. Several major brands are already using this site (e.g., Toyota, AT&T, Audi, and Ford). For details, see Empire Avenue at **businessesgrow.com/2014/01/08/how-empire-avenue-crushed-my-soul**.

Gamers Helped Scientists

For decades, scientists were unable to unfold the chemical chain of an enzyme of an AIDS-like virus. However, researchers at the University of Washington turned Foldit, a "fun for purpose" program created by the university, which transfers scientific problems into competitive computer games.

The gamers were divided into groups and were challenged to compete by using their problem-solving skills to build 3D models of a protein that scientists had been unable to find for years. The players solved the chemical chain problem accurately in just 3 weeks. (See **balita.com/online-gamers-crack-aids-enzyme-puzzle**.) For more about Foldit ("Solve Puzzles for Science"), see **fold.it/portal**.

Gamification

Some social games are designed so that players will connect with vendors or brands in the game environments. This is only one aspect of **gamification**, which refers to the introduction of gaming into social networking. Gamification can also be viewed as the introduction of social networking activities into online games. Our interest is in those applications that are related to social commerce and e-commerce. For more definitions and limitations, see the Gamification Wiki (**gamification. org**) and Harrison (2014).

Social activities are not new to online gaming. For example, players collectively agree to the rules of the games. Also, gamers need trust between the players. What is new here is the integration of traditional multiplayer games and social networking. Given that so many people play online games, it is not surprising that vendors are encouraging players (e.g., via rewards) to engage in desired behavior (e.g., problem-solving or collaboration). Vendors also use games as advertising platforms. For a gamification framework, see Chou (2015) and his TED talk (**youtu.be/v5Qjuegtiyc**).

According to Findlay (2016) and Florentine (2014), companies can use gamification to create winning social customer experiences such as increasing loyalty, building trust, accelerating innovation, providing brand engagement, and increasing relevant knowledge. For how to use gamification to engage employees, see White (2016).

For commercial possibilities and strategies of social games and gamification, see Burke (2014).

For additional information, you can download the e-book titled *The Essential Social Playbook: 8 Steps to Turn Social into Sales* at **powerreviews.com/assets/new/ebooks/powerreviewsessential social playbook.pdf** and also consider attending Yu-kai Chou's free 21-day gamification course at **join.yukaichou.com/21-day-gamification-course**.

SECTION 9.6 REVIEW QUESTIONS

1. Describe online games.
2. Describe games in social networks.
3. Discuss the business aspects of social games.
4. What is gamification? Relate it to social commerce.

9.7   CROWDSOURCING AND CROWDFUNDING

Both crowdfunding and crowdsourcing draw on the idea of the "wisdom of crowds" that a large group may be able to find solutions to a problem that individuals are not able to determine. One major applications of crowdsourcing is the facilitation of problem-solving.

Crowdsourcing as a Distributed Problem-Solving Enabler

Crowdsourcing actually describes a set of tools, concepts, and methodologies that deal with the process of outsourcing work, including problem-solving and idea generation to a *community* of potential solvers known as the "crowd."

More than just brainstorming or ideation, crowdsourcing uses proven techniques to focus on the crowd's innovation, creativity, and problem-solving capacity on topics of vital interest to the host organization. An overview of crowdsourcing is provided in Jeff Howe's video titled "Crowdsourcing" (3:20 minutes) at **youtube.com/watch?v=F0-UtNg3ots** and **crowdsourcing.org** and in Zoref (2015). Also watch the video "Crowdsourcing As a Model for Problem Solving" (6.1 minutes) at **youtube.com/watch?v=hLGhKyiJ8Xo**.

Crowdsourcing Models

Howe (2008) has classified applications of crowdsourcing into functional models, and these distinctions are still being utilized (Reffell 2016). The following four categories described are:

1. **Collective intelligence (or wisdom).** Here, people are solving problems and providing new insights and ideas leading to product, process, or service innovations.
2. **Crowd creation.** Here, people are creating various types of content and sharing it with others (paid or for free). The content may be used for problem-solving, advertising, or knowledge accumulation. This can be done by splitting large tasks into small segments (e.g., contributing content to create the Wikipedia).
3. **Crowd voting.** Here, people are giving their opinions and ratings on ideas, products, or services, as well as evaluating and filtering information presented to them. An example would be voting on American Idol.
4. **Crowd support and funding.** Here, people are contributing and supporting endeavors for social causes, which might include volunteering their effort and time, offering donations, and microfinancing.

Chaordix Inc. (**chaordix.com**) classifies crowdsourcing into the following three models:

1. **Secretive.** Individuals submit ideas, and the winner is selected by the company. Ideas are not visible to all participants.
2. **Collaborative.** Individuals submit ideas, the crowd evaluates the ideas, and the crowd picks the winners. Ideas are visible to all participants.
3. **Panel selects.** Individuals submit ideas, the crowd evolves ideas, a panel selects finalists, and the crowd votes for the winner.

A *crowdsortium* is a community of industry practitioners whose mission is to advance the crowdsourcing industry through best practices and education (see **crowdsortium.org**).

These theories have been tested and can be applied into real-world business models. In his book *The Business Idea Factory: A World-Class System for Creating Successful Business Ideas*, Sedniev (2016) details systems and processes that can be used to generate business and social ideas that can be successful. The author argues that by using the wisdom of crowds in research supported methodologies, that effective models can be identified.

Crowdsourcing also has the potential to be a problem-solving mechanism for governments and nonprofit use via community participation. Urban and transit planning are prime areas for crowdsourcing. One project used crowdsourcing to encourage public participation in the planning process for the Salt Lake City transit system. Another notable application of crowdsourcing to government problem-solving is the Peer to Patent Community Patent Review project for the US Patent and Trademark Office (see **peertopatent.org**). For more details and examples of crowdsourcing in the public sector, see Brabham (2015), and in law in Finland see the video at **youtu.be/wIHMmhngrq4**.

Progressive companies and organizations now recognize the value of tapping into the wisdom of the crowd to capture the best answers and the most innovative ideas.

Crowdsourcing can be used for many purposes. For an overview, see Zoref (2015).

The Process of Crowdsourcing

The process of crowdsourcing differs from application to application depending on the models of the specific problem to be solved and the method used. However, the following steps exist in most enterprise applications, even though the details of the execution differ. The major steps are based on the generic process are:

1. Identify the task (problem) you want to investigate or accomplish.
2. Select the target crowd.
3. Broadcast the task to the crowd (frequently to an unidentified crowd in an open call, as Starbucks and Dell do).
4. Engage the crowd in accomplishing the task (e.g., idea generation).
5. Collect the user-generated content. (This may include a submission of solutions, voting, new ideas, etc.)
6. Evaluate the quality of submitted material—by the management that initiated the request, by experts, or by the crowd.
7. Accept or reject a solution.
8. Compensate the crowd.

For a more detail, see Cancialosi (2015) and the video "Crowdsourcing intelligence: - the right crowd, the right process" at **youtu.be/KcbTDhhceaU**.

Successfully Deployed Crowdsourcing Systems: Some Representative Examples

The following are some representative examples of implemented crowdsourcing systems.

- **Dell's IdeaStorm (ideastorm.com)** enables customers to vote on Dell's product features they prefer, including new ones. Dell is using a technically oriented crowd, such as the Linux (**linux.org**) community. The crowd submits ideas and sometimes members of the community vote on them.
- **Procter & Gamble's** researchers post their problems at **innocentive.com**, and at **ninesigma.com**, offering cash rewards to problem solvers. P&G uses other crowdsourcing service providers such as **yourencore.com**.
- **Amazon Mechanical Turk (mturk.com)** is a marketplace for distributing large-scale work that requires human intelligence. It is limited to large tasks that can be divided (known as HITs—human intelligence tasks) and is posted by companies that need assistance. Then, Amazon arranges workers (the "Mechanical Turk Workers"), each of whom is allocated a small subtask and is paid when the work is completed. For details see **mturk.com**.
- **Facebook (facebook.com)** used crowdsourcing to translate its site into more than 65 different languages. The completion of the English to French translated by over 4,000 volunteers only took 1 day; however, Facebook had to hire a team of professional translators to oversee the whole crowdsourcing process to ensure that the resulting translations were accurate.

- **McDonald's Burger Builder (mcdonalds.com)**, a well-known US fast food chain, created a system that allowed customers to customize hamburgers and toppings. Customers were then able to vote on their favorite combinations. The winning burgers were released in select locations, along with details about their creators.
- **Frito-Lay (fritolay.com)** used crowdsourcing for designing a successful annual Super Bowl advertising campaign.
- **Wikipedia (wikipedia.org)** is considered by many to be the "granddaddy" of crowdsourcing and is certainly the world's largest crowdsourcing project.

CASE 9.2: EC APPLICATION
KICKSTARTER

Kickstarter (**kickstarter.com**) is a popular crowdfunding site that allows individuals to market their ideas for products and then have those products funded by potential or future buyers. The premise behind Kickstarter is that individual creativity will generate new and unique ideas and that funding by the community will allow those ideas to come to fruition. Kickstarter is different than other crowdfunding sites, such as GoFundMe, in that they do not allow fundraising for charity.

Users who are interested in creating a Kickstarter can register a project on the website and provide as much detail as they would like. Users then indicate the amount of support that would be needed to fund the idea and an indication of what potential reward from that funding is available. For example, Kickstarter is often used to develop new products, and individuals who fund at a certain level are generally promised one of those products after it goes into production (Kickstarter, n.d.).

Kickstarter's Revenue model is straightforward in that they take 5% of all fees collected by creators. Additionally, if fees are paid by credit card, the credit card processing company will take an additional 3–5%. But if an inventor does not reach the required funding level, then no fees are charged.

Kickstarter has been very popular since its inception and has helped to create a number of very innovative and interesting products.

1. Vue Smart glasses (smart glasses)
2. Kingdom Death: Monster 1.5 (a board game)
3. Fidget Cube (a toy)

For more, see a listing of completed products at **digitaltrends.com/cool-tech/best-kickstarters-2016**.

Unfortunately, the history of the site has not always been positive. There have been several Kickstarter projects that were never fully developed and really end product released to funders. This is always a disappointment to backers, and in some cases users felt that the creators had scammed them, meaning that they had never intended to actually develop a product. For examples, see **digitaltrends.com/cool-tech/biggest-kickstarter-and-indiegogo-scams**. In order to avoid this type of issue, Kickstarter has become more explicit on the types of projects that it will accept and the lack of guarantees that the company provides to backers. Backers are also more familiar with the possibility of scams or failed projects due to the recent press (Nanalyze 2016).

For videos on how to use Kickstarter, see **youtu.be/MXKEccRiMeQ** and **youtu.be/tpy3pWye5Rg**

Sources: Nanalyze (2016) and **kickstarter.com**.

Questions

1. How can an inventor list of project on Kickstarter?
2. What is Kickstarter's business model?
3. How can backers avoid scams on Kickstarter?
4. Find a product on Kickstarter and discuss why it appeals to you.

Tools for Crowdsourcing

To launch crowdsourcing initiatives, businesses and developers can make use of crowdsourcing tools and platforms, such as NineSigma, InnoCentive, YourEncore, yet2, UserVoice, Get Satisfaction, and IdeaScale.

Example: Crowdsourcing Software Development with Topcoder

Topcoder (**www.topcoder**) is a company that engages a community of over 1 million design and technology experts to help businesses complete their software development projects faster, with better quality and more innovation. Businesses interested in working with Topcoder submit ideas and goals to the network. A coach from the system curates those ideas and then generates challenges for the Topcoder network. Typically projects are broken down into many small components to make both understanding and idea generation easier. These challenges are then released to Topcoder's network. Developers who are interested in participating in the challenge examine the specifications and submit ideas for the most efficient and innovative methods to solve the problems. The coach and sponsor business then select the best ideas. Solutions for all components are aggregated and developed. The Topcoder system uses both crowdsourcing and gamification in its challenges. For more information, see the explanation video at **youtu.be/Qc_PcN6ECjg** or whitepapers at **topcoder.com/research/**.

Crowdfunding and Kickstarter

Raising funds from the crowd for different purposes is gaining popularity with several start-ups operating in this area. A notable company is Kickstarter. For how they help small businesses, see the video at **youtube.com/watch?v=xudOhEYIwyU**.

Examples of Crowdfunding

An increased number of start-ups are using crowdfunding to raise funds for their businesses. Here are four examples:

- Filmmaker Zach Braff used Kickstarter to raise money for his film (watch the video "Zach Braff Uses Kickstarter to Get Money for Next Film" (0:51 minutes) at **youtube.com/watch?v=CIyJtcxjWhw**).
- Zach Danger Brown collected over $52,000 on Kickstarter in July 2014 for his "potato salad" idea. For details, see Root (2014) and a video about how the collection went global at **abcnews.go.com/GMA/video/zach-danger-browns-potato-salad-kickstarter-global-24464503**.
- The digital music phenomenon, Kawehi, is raising money via Kickstarter to promote her music projects in Hawaii. For details, see Russo (2014).
- Next Thing Co. raised $700,000 from 15,000 people, using Kickstarter in May 2015. The company boasted to produce $9 computer. For details see della Cava (2015).

For eight successful Kickstarter campaigns, see Serino (2015). For a crowdfunding strategy guide, see Stegmaier (2015). For tools for crowdfunding, see Roth (2016).

Example: Innovation Excellence—A Marketplace for Crowdsourcing

According to its website, Innovation Excellence (**innovationexcellence.com**) is a multinational social marketplace with about 1,000,000 registered experts in more than 170 countries. As a problem-solving individual or research organization, one can create a profile, make professional contacts, and connect with colleagues (for a fee), peers, and friends. If you are a problem solver and only want to solve problems on Innovation Excellence, you choose what information you want to disclose and decide who can see it. In Innovation Excellence, users can share activities with their contacts on other social networks. You can develop your own networks or join one of the many networks that already exist on Innovation Excellence. Users can meet with people who share their interests and follow their friends' activities. After seeing what their friends are working on, people can decide to either compete or collaborate with their friends on problem-solving.

For more information, download the State of Crowdsourcing in 2016 report from **innovationexcellence.com/blog/2016/10/17/the-state-of-crowdsourcing-in-2016**.

SECTION 9.7 REVIEW QUESTIONS

1. Define crowdsourcing.
2. List the seven crowdsourcing models.
3. List the major steps of the crowdsourcing process.
4. What are the capabilities of Kickstarter and Innovation Excellence?

9.8 SOCIAL COLLABORATION (COLLABORATION 2.0)

One of the major applications of Web 2.0 and social media in the enterprise is in the area of collaboration. Some even equate Web 2.0 with enterprise collaboration. Social collaboration is used for many purposes, an important one being product design.

Essentials of Social Collaboration

Collaboration in business can be defined as *people working with other people toward a common outcome or goal*. For many images of social collaboration, search Google for "images of social collaboration."

Social collaboration refers to people's collaboration within and between communities enabled by social media tools and platforms. The processes help people interact and share information to achieve a common goal. It is also known as *Collaboration 2.0*. Collaboration 2.0 is recognized as a major element in social business that can provide considerable benefits. For implementation of social collaboration, see Dalbec (2016). For a comprehensive report including benefits and lessons learned, see Avanade (2013).

Social Collaboration (Collaboration 2.0)

Collaboration drives business value up by enabling people to work together more efficiently. Wikis and other social software tools can be used effectively by all types and sizes of enterprises for a wide range of tasks and activities. Collaboration helps with solving business problems and uncovering new opportunities, especially with the help of social media tools (see details at Morgan 2014). Collaboration in social networking is done both internally, among employees from different units working in virtual teams, and externally, when working with suppliers, customers, and other business partners. In fact, surveys have shown that employees desire this type of interaction and that social networks that do not focus on social functions or achieve critical masses of engaged users do not thrive (Li 2015). For example, collaboration occurs in forums and other types of groups and by using wikis and blogs. For the benefits of social collaboration, see Buckley (2015). For the use of Collaboration 2.0 in the enterprise, see Turban et al. (2016), and for guidelines for enabling collaboration, see Bratteteig (2016).

Social collaboration has several dimensions as illustrated in Fig. 9.2.

Some believe that in the future, people will use mostly Web 2.0 tools, rather than e-mail, for collaboration. For a discussion, see **thefutureorganization.com** and "Will Generation Z be the death of email?" at **4thoffice.com/blog/?p=142**.

A large number of Web 2.0 tools are used to support social collaboration. The support is given to idea sharing, communication, working together on the same documents, and more. The Web 2.0 tools range from wikis to virtual worlds. For the success story of Walgreens, see **rightpoint.com/case-studies/Walgreens**. Barr (2017) describes the uses of webinars within enterprise social networks for internal collaboration in his video presentation at **highq.com/resources/webinars/four-use-cases-collaboration-software-corporates-webinar**.

The development of tools, philosophies, and procedures of social media support for collaboration allows employees and managers to engage much more fully in the collaboration process. Furthermore, social collaboration has improved the organizational culture.

Social collaboration is supported mainly by:

- Wikis, blogs, and microblogging (e.g., Twitter)
- Collaborative communities (forums and discussion groups)
- Early vintage Web 2.0 technologies
- Crowdsourcing
- Integrations with public networks (e.g., LinkedIn)
- Other tools (e.g., Yammer)

Fig. 9.2 The various dimensions of social collaboration

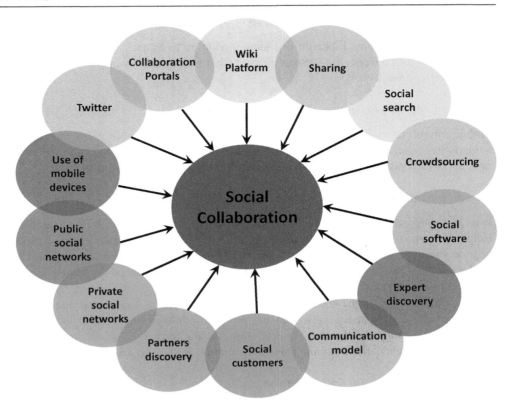

Most collaboration software vendors are adding Web 2.0 tools to their collaboration suites (e.g., Binfire, Podio Unily, etc.).

Using Blogs and Wikis Inside the Enterprise

Blogs and wikis are used within enterprises. The use of these tools is expanding rapidly. Companies use blogs and wikis for the following activities:

- Project collaboration and communication
- Process and procedure documentation
- Knowledge sharing and knowledge management
- FAQs
- E-learning and e-training
- Forums for new ideas
- Corporate-specific dynamic glossary and terminology
- Collaboration with customers

As you can see, most of the activities in the previous list relate to collaboration. For additional information, see **zdnet.com/blog/hinchcliffe** (several blogs).

Using Twitter to Support Collaboration

Twitter already is used extensively in the enterprise to support collaboration. Twitter is used extensively for interaction with customers and prospects as well as for conducting market research.

Using LinkedIn to Support Collaboration

Due to its wide audience, LinkedIn is a natural addition to business collaboration plans. Many professionals are already members, and the networks tools makes it easy to find colleagues within the system. LinkedIn is often integrated into private collaboration networks.

The Role of Mobile Commerce in Social Collaboration

Mobile commerce is growing very rapidly. Most enterprise social applications can be done on wireless devices. This is particularly true for communication and collaboration. For a list of popular collaboration mobile apps, see **pastemagazine.com/articles/2016/03/stay-in-the-know-with-these-10-collaboration-apps.html**.

Questions and Answers in Social Networks

In a Q&A "answer" function individuals and companies can post questions. For example, in LinkedIn community, go to the Help Forum and use the posting module on your home page to ask your network a question, and the community usually will provide you with answers. You can also ask a question on the "share box" on the home page. Many other professional networks and their internal groups provide advice and supporting material for helping in decision-making. These services can be either paid or for free. For example, according to the medical social network, "Sermo" (**sermo.com**; "Social Media Meets Healthcare"), a large online community exclusive to physicians, has an app that allows physicians to author and discuss urgent and interesting patient cases from any Web- or mobile-enabled device, and based on market tests, be almost assured feedback from multiple colleagues. Typical questions and responses include requested/suggested diagnoses and treatments with the best insights often resulting from collaboration among the doctors. (see sermo.com/news/press-releases/54).

Suites of Tools for Social Collaboration

Several companies offer suites of social collaboration tools, either as stand-alone products or as added tools in existing collaboration suites.

Example 1: IBM Connections

IBM Connections provides tools such as forums, wikis, and blogs and new capabilities like advanced social analytics, which enable users to expand their network of connections and engagement. For details, see press release "IBM Launches New Software and Social Business Consulting Services" at **ibm.com/press/us/en/pressrelease/32949.wss**.

You can download many free white papers at the IBM Jam Events page (**collaborationjam.com**). IBM has about 20,000 internal blogs (used by over 100,000 people), over 70,000 members are in SocialBlue (an internal clone of Facebook), 350,000 members are on LinkedIn (January 2016), and over 500,000 are participants in crowdsourcing. Today these numbers are probably larger. IBM also provides the tools needed to support innovation.

Example 2: Cisco WebEx Meeting Center (Formerly Cisco Quad)

Cisco WebEx, according to Cisco's website, is an enterprise collaboration platform, which is designed for today's workforce. It is characterized by social, mobile, visual, and virtual features. WebEx connects people to the information and expertise they need, when they need it. Knowledge and ideas are easily shared across the enterprise, and teams collaborate across geographical and organizational boundaries. For details, see **webex.com/products/enterprise_meeting.html**.

WebEx Meetings is a universal app available for all major smartphones and tablets. For other WebEx social features, see **webex.com/products/web-conferencing/mobile.html**.

Example 3: Smartsheet to Mange Projects

Smartsheet (**Smartsheet.com**) is a web-based tool that allows teams to plan and manage projects collaboratively. The system allows teams to set up Gantt charts and other project management templates to better understand the process flow and schedules needed to complete company initiatives. Because the system is Web-based, teams can collaborate on the creation of these documents, as well as seeing updates when they are made. The system additionally allows resources, people, or systems to be assigned to projects. Team members can set permissions on files so some users may add and edit content, while others may only view content. The system was designed to be as easy to use as a spreadsheet, and in 2014, the application won "Best Business App of 2014" by Evernote's Platform Awards. For more information see the how to videos at **smartsheet.com/videos/how-to-use-smartsheet**.

For a list of vendors, the tools they use, the type of collaboration/communication supported and the benefits of social collaboration, see Buckley (2015) and **capterra.com/collaboration-software**.

The Future of Social Commerce

In determining justification and strategy of social commerce, we need to look into the future. Many researchers and consultants are speculating on the future (e.g., **slideshare.net/YairCarmel1/e-commerce-trendsesenglish?related=3**). The predictions are diverse, ranging from "SC will dominate EC" to "it is a buzz word and will disappear soon." See Gebauer (2015) for 132 case studies, both successes and failures. Given the popularity of Facebook, Twitter, Pinterest, YouTube, social games, social shopping, and social advertising, it is difficult to side with the pessimistic predictions. In fact it appears that the growth of social commerce is inextricably linked to these networks. Social commerce provides the business case to justify many of these services (see the infographic by Forte 2016). It looks as if mobile social commerce will be a major area of EC growth. Also, several of the social shopping and social collaboration models could be very successful. In the enterprise area, there is a trend to have a "social as a service" rather than as an application approach (due to the influence of cloud computing).

The future of social commerce depends largely on social media trends. Social commerce is anchored to these trends and technologies and should continue to grow as they do (Walker 2016). For some 2017 trends, see Rohampton (2017) and Holmes (2017).

Conclusion: IBM's Watson and Social Commerce

There are many opinions on what the future of SC will be. Instead of presenting them, we decided to end this chapter by looking at IBM's Watson supercomputer. In February 2011, IBM's Watson won a *Jeopardy* 8-day tournament against two world champions. This was a great achievement for what IBM calls Social Business and Smart Computing. Aided by intelligent systems such as IBM's Pure Systems, Watson will be able to do much more. According to **research.ibm.com/smarterplanet/us/en/ibm**, Watson may assist people in the following social commerce-related tasks:

- **Personal investment advisor.** There is no need to conduct research any longer. All you have to do is to state your investment goals and Watson will make recommendations after checking all the needed input data. Given what goals you have, Watson can figure out what you need, recommending what stocks to buy or sell. Upon your approval, Watson can complete the deal for you.
- **Language translator.** In EC we sometimes need language translation for introducing websites to people who understand other languages, in order to exploit global opportunities. We need it also for translating a natural human language to a language that a computer can understand. Today's automatic machine translation is not optimal, but it is improving. Computer systems, such as IBM's Watson, have powerful natural language processors that are getting even better with time and thus provide better machine translation.
- **Customer service.** Providing technical support is critical for success. Watson's intelligence will enable automatic guides for people who need help, taking them through all the necessary steps. The service will be consistent, top quality, and available in real time.
- **Q&A service.** Watson will provide the best answers to any business, medical, legal, or personal question you have. It can answer any question and subsequent sub-questions.
- **Matchmaking.** Watson can match sellers and buyers, products and markets, job seekers and job offers, partners to bartering, P2P lending participants, or any other match you can think of. For example, Watson will be able to find you a partner who will fit your stated goals. IBM's Watson is related to IBM's Smarter plant activities (see ibm.com/smarterplanet/us/en/).

SECTION 9.8 REVIEW QUESTIONS

1. Define social collaboration.
2. List and describe the major benefits of social collaboration briefly.
3. List social collaboration tools.
4. What are the major points related to the future of social commerce?

MANAGERIAL ISSUES

Some managerial issues related to this chapter are as follows:

1. **What are some of the ethical issues that may be involved in deploying social commerce?** Using social commerce can lead to several ethical issues such as privacy and accountability. In addition, mistakes can cause harm to users as well as to the company. Another important ethical issue is human judgment, which is frequently a key factor in social commerce. Human judgment may be subjective or corrupt, and therefore, it may lead to unethical consequences. Companies should provide an ethical code for system builders and users. There are ethical issues related to the implementation of idea generation and other problem-solving-related considerations. One issue to consider is whether an organization should employ productivity-saving devices that are not ethical. Another ethical issue is the use of knowledge extracted from people in crowdsourcing. A further related issue is whether a company should compensate an employee when others use knowledge that he or she contributed. This issue is related to the motivation issue. It also is related to privacy. Should people be informed as to who contributed certain knowledge?

2. **How should we deal with social commerce risks?** There are several possible risks in implementing social commerce, depending on the applications. For example, to protect the security of the SC open source system, you need to consult your internal security experts, and you may need some outside legal advice. There is also the risk of information pollution and biased or falsified user-generated content. You may also need to use a consultant for large projects to examine and evaluate the associated risks. Weighing the benefits of social media against security and other potential risks is a major strategy issue.

3. **Can we recruit using social media?** Many businesses can use social media as a method to recruit and seek referrals for open positions. This requires adjustments in the HR function as well as clear policies for current employees.

4. **Should we move to be a social business?** It depends on the estimated costs and benefits. Also, it is possible to introduce some, but not all, features of social enterprise. For example, using crowdsourcing can be very beneficial. Social collaboration may be cost-effective as well.

5. **What about a private, in-house social network?** Such a venture may bring many benefits, and it can be combined with internal activities of crowdsourcing, as well as with social collaboration with business partners. Most successful in-house networks are used for idea generation, internal collaboration, recruitment, and public relations.

6. **Shall we try gamification?** In most cases it is wise to wait and see the results of other companies. The deployment requires skilled employees. In certain applications the reward can be large. But in most cases we are not sure at this time. As one says: "Try it, you make like it."

7. **Can we use crowdsourcing?** Business may look at the possibility of using crowdsourcing as the concepts begin to mature. Tools can be used to generate or validate ideas, while support companies like Topcoder can assist in application development.

SUMMARY

In this chapter, you learned about the following EC issues as they relate to the chapter's learning objectives:

1. **The social enterprise.** Conducting social networking activities in the enterprise can result in substantial benefits. Two types of business social networks exist, public and private. The private network is company owned; it may have restricted access, or it may be open to the public. The public network (e.g., LinkedIn) is used mainly for recruiting, connections, collaboration, and marketing communication. The private, in-house social enterprise uses Collaboration 2.0, social CRM, social marketing media, and more. You can even "spy" on your competitors (see **entre-preneur.com/article/229350**). All this translates to improved relationships with employees, customers, and business partners. Significant cost reduction, productivity increase, and competitive advantage can be achieved as well.

2. **Business-oriented public social networks.** Following the successful examples of LinkedIn and Xing, many public business-oriented networks were created. Applications vary from recruiting to market research and advertising. One major activity in public networks is external collaboration. Several entrepreneurship networks also exist.

3. **Social networking to find a job.** Networking is still the predominate method of finding a position. Social media can make this processes easier by placing recruiters and applicants together. Both groups use these technologies extensively.

4. **Major enterprise social commerce activities.** Currently, collaboration and communication, as well as community building, are the major activities. In addition, problem-solving via idea generation and finding expertise are becoming more

and more important. Related to this is knowledge creation and management. Companies recruit, train, and conduct other HRM activities in enterprise networks. Several companies also use the enterprise social network for interactions with customers, suppliers, and other business partners.

5. **Social commerce, entertainment, and gaming.** Rich media, user-created content, and groups and subgroups with common interests have opened many possibilities for a second generation of online entertainment. Add to this the wireless revolution and the increased capabilities in mobile devices to support Web 2.0 tools and social networking activities, and you will discover a new and exciting world of online entertainment ranging from music and videos to comedy.

6. **Social gaming and gamification.** Many Internet-based games include some social activities. Players collectively agree to the rules and act as community members. Companies such as King and Zynga create the games which are played on Facebook and other social networks. This is one aspect of gamification. Another aspect is the introduction of social media into games.

7. **Crowdsourcing and social networking.** Crowdsourcing in the enterprise is used mostly for idea generation, voting, and problem identification. Content creation and updating projects, such as volunteers translating the Facebook website to French and German, falls into this category. Crowdfunding is an application for raising funds only from a large number of people. The concept is maturing, but users are wary of scams.

8. **Social collaboration.** Many see social collaboration (Collaboration 2.0) as the major activity that social media supports. Activities supported range from joint design to problem-solving.

9. **The future of social commerce.** The general consensus is social commerce will grow rapidly; but some disagree. Most agree that social networking will continue to expand through both market acceptance and new technologies and that social commerce will be tied to this grow as the business model that supports them.

KEY TERMS

Business social networks
Gamification
Social business
Social collaboration (Collaboration 2.0)
Social enterprise
Social game
Social network game

DISCUSSION QUESTIONS

1. How do public business-oriented networks and private enterprise social networks differ?
2. Discuss the role of crowdsourcing in idea generation and in other enterprise activities.
3. Corporate social networking: booster or time waster? What are the pitfalls of enterprise social networking? Discuss.
4. How can crowdsourcing reduce risks to inventors? To merchants?
5. What are some of the risks companies may face if they decide to use public social networks?
6. Review the features of Socialtext (**socialtext.com**). Discuss how you would make use of this platform in a small enterprise in retail, manufacturing, or financial services.
7. Discuss how social collaboration can support commercial activities.
8. Why are social games so popular?
9. How can gamification be used in business?
10. Compare and contrast social collaboration and crowdsourcing.
11. What will derive social commerce growth in the future?

TOPICS FOR CLASS DISCUSSION AND DEBATES

1. Debate: Should a crowd have professional knowledge of the task it has been given or not?
2. Some claim that using social collaboration may be slow and ineffective. Others disagree. Debate the issue.
3. Idea generation by the employees or customers using crowdsourcing is becoming popular. However, some say it is only an electronic suggestion box. Others disagree. Discuss.

4. Enter **quara.com** and ask for the benefits and limitations of social enterprises. Write a report.
5. Debate: Should companies build in-house social networks for external activities (e.g., marketing, CRM) or use existing public social networks?
6. Examine the Candy Crush Saga game. Why the game is so popular? Are there any social elements there?
7. Why does one need a special entrepreneur network? What features make it effective?
8. What are some of the risks companies may face if they decide to use public social networks?
9. Review the features of Socialtext (**socialtext.com**). Discuss how you would make use of this platform in a small enterprise in (a) retail, (b) manufacturing, and (c) financial services.
10. Would you use **monster.com**, **linkedin.com**, or **facebook.com** for recruiting top managers, or would you rather use a traditional agency? Why?
11. Crowdfunding is becoming very popular. Find recent information about its success. What are some of the implementation challenges?

INTERNET EXERCISES

1. Enter **xing.com** and **linkedin.com** and compare their functionalities (capabilities). Also, enter **youtube.com/watch?v=pBAghmYMG0M** and view the video "Ryze Business Networking Tutorial" (7:20 minutes). Compare Ryze's capabilities with those of LinkedIn.com. Write a report.
2. Enter **pandora.com**. Find out how you can create and share music with friends.
3. Check several crowdfunding sites such as Kickstarter and Indiegogo and compare their processes. Find information about crowdfunding in China. Can it be a $50 billion by 2025? Write a report.
4. Post a question on **quara.com** about the future of social commerce. Summarize the answers and comment.
5. Enter **innocentive.com**. Describe how this site works. List their major products and services. Identify benefits and challenges.
6. Enter **hulu.com/plus**. Why is it an online entertainment service? What are the benefits to viewers? Compare this site to **hbogo.com**.
7. Enter **gaiaonline.com** and find all socially oriented activities. Write a report.
8. Enter the **yammer.com** and find information related to enterprise applications of social commerce technologies. Write a report.
9. Enter **brazencareerist.com/company** check the services Brazen provides. Compare services to the virtual event hosted at **expos2.com**.
10. Compare what **jobserve.com** and **aspireme-diagroup.net** offer regarding solutions for recruitment. Differentiate services to employees from services to employers. Write a report.
11. Identify a difficult business problem. Post the problem on **linkedin.com** and **answers.com**. Summarize the results or offers you received to solve the problem.
12. Enter **huddle.com** and take the interactive demo (registration required). Also, view the video on the main page. Write a report on social collaboration activities.
13. Enter **kickstarter.com** and examine the available products. Select one that you feel will be produced and another that will not be. Defend your reasoning.
14. Enter **topcoder.com** and examine how a coding challenge is offered. Find an example of a successful collaboration. Write a report.

TEAM ASSIGNMENTS AND PROJECTS

1. Assignment for the Opening Case
   Read the opening case and answer the following questions:

   (a) How can social media allow companies to better connect with customers?
   (b) Why can the use of social media be problematic for a company? For an employee?
   (c) Why would a company want to forge a stronger bond with customers?
   (d) How does the Hearsay Social platform work?
   (e) View the video case study at **hearsaysystems.com/2016/03/digital-technology-transformation-and-adoption-at-rpm-mortgage**. What part of the system was most beneficial for RPM Mortgage?

2. The crowdsourcing model works with designers, like this: (1) A company outlines an area for which they need a design. (2) The company turns the design outline into a competition (e.g., among experts, among amateurs, or between amateur and professional designers). (3) A winner is selected by management, consultants, or by the crowd. This is done at little cost.

   (a) If this model becomes widespread, how will it affect the design industry?
   (b) What is the purpose of the competition?
   (c) Some believe that amateurs can do the best job. Others disagree. Find information and discuss.
   (d) Compare this situation to the Polyvore model. Discuss.

3. Some consider gamification to be a major social commerce technology of the future. Enter **badgeville.com/wiki/ External_Resources.** Find additional resources. Write a report on the existing and potential applications of gamification in e-commerce and social commerce.
4. All students register as members at LinkedIn.

   (a) Each team member joins two LinkedIn groups and observes their activities.
   (b) All join the EC group: (group-digest@LinkedIn.com). Follow some of the discussions there. Have a joint class presentation on the value of groups at LinkedIn.

5. Check the competition in the area of streaming music services (e.g., check Spotify, Amazon, Apple, Google, etc.). Write a report.
6. Yammer, Huddle, Chatter, and Jive Software are cloud-based social networking services. They are considered very useful, replacing traditional enterprise tools. Investigate the issue and write a report.
7. Enter **hearsaysystem.com** and examine their product offerings. Compare the different features in different vertical markets. Write a report.

CLOSING CASE: LINKEDIN—THE PREMIER PUBLIC BUSINESS-ORIENTED SOCIAL NETWORK

Let us look at LinkedIn (**linkedin.com**), the world's largest professional network. LinkedIn is a global business-oriented social networking site (has offered in 23 languages), used mainly for professional networking. By January 2016, it had about 414 million registered users spanning 200 countries and territories. By the end of 2016 there were 2.2 million different groups, each with a special interest. LinkedIn can be used to find jobs, people, potential clients, service providers, subject experts, and other business opportunities. The company became profitable in 2010 with revenue approaching $3 billion in 2016. The company filed for an initial public offering in January 2011, and its stock is one of the best performing on the stock market. A major objective of LinkedIn is to allow registered users to maintain a list of professional contacts (see **en.wikipedia.org/wiki/LinkedIn**), i.e., people with whom they have a relationship. The people in each person's network are called *connections*. Users can invite anyone, whether he or she is a LinkedIn user or not, to become a connection. When people join LinkedIn, they create a profile that summarizes their professional accomplishments. This profile makes it easier to be found by recruiters, former colleagues, and others. Members can also meet new people and find opportunities for collaboration and marketing. For 2016 statistics about LinkedIn, see **expandedramblings.com/index.php/ by-the-numbers-a-few-important-linkedin-stats**.

LinkedIn is based on the concept of "degrees of connections." A *contact network* consists of a user's direct connections (called first-degree connections), people connected to their first-degree connections (called second-degree connections), and people connected to the second-degree connections (called third-degree connections). Degree "icons" appear next to a contact's name. The contact network makes it possible for a professional to gain an introduction, through a mutual, trusted contact, to someone he or she wishes to know. LinkedIn's administrators themselves are also members and have hundreds of connections each (see Elad 2016 and **linkedin.com**).

The "gated-access approach," where contact with any professional requires either a preexisting relationship or the intervention of a mutual contact, is intended to build trust among the site's users.

The searchable LinkedIn groups feature allows users to establish new business relationships by joining alumni, industry, professional, or other relevant groups.

LinkedIn is especially useful in helping job seekers and employers find one another. According to Ahmad (2014), 94% of all US recruiters use LinkedIn to examine potential candidates. Job seekers can list their résumés, search for open positions, check companies' profiles, and even review the profiles of the hiring managers. Applicants can also discover connections with existing contacts (people) who can introduce them to a specific hiring manager. They can even see who has viewed their profiles. For details see **linkedin.com/company/linkedin/careers** and **linkedin.com/directory/job.** For a LinkedIn guide for job searchers, see Boone (2015).

Companies can use the site to post available jobs and find and recruit employees, especially those who may not actively be searching for a new position.

Smart Ways to Use LinkedIn

LinkedIn is known mostly as a platform for recruitment, job searches, and making connections. However, there are many opportunities in the network for marketing, advertising, sales, and more (e.g., see Cole 2015). Members can ask others to write recommendations (endorsements) for them. For a list of opportunities, see **linkedintelligence.com/ smart-ways-to-use-linkedin**.

In lieu of LinkedIn Answers that was discontinued in 2013, a new service is available, per **help.linkedin.com/app/ answers/detail/a_id/35227**.

In 2011, LinkedIn launched LinkedIn "Ads." Ads, which is their version of Google's AdWords, is a self-service, text-based advertising product that allows advertisers to reach a targeted professional audience of their choosing (see their FAQ's at **help.linkedin.com/app/answers/detail/a_id/1015**). For a comparison between Ads and AdWords, see **shoutex.com/ linkedin-directads-vs-google-adwords-2**.

According to Ahmad (2014), LinkedIn has three times higher "visitor-to-lead" conversion rate than Facebook and Twitter.

As of 2014, LinkedIn can provide job matching to positions available, by using a computer algorithm that determines potential employee's fitness to potential jobs.

LinkedIn can also be used for several marketing strategies such as creating special groups to promote interest in events, purchasing paid media space, and seeing what your competitors are doing (e.g., **linkedin.com/about-us**). Note that about 75% of LinkedIn members are located outside the United States. For example, many users are in Brazil, India, the United Kingdom, and France. Over 1.5 million teachers are on LinkedIn and use the site for educational purposes.

As previously mentioned, LinkedIn is a public company. It was an instant success, as the share price almost tripled the first day of trading. In contrast, shares of Monster, a major online recruiting company, plunged more than 60% during 2011, mainly due to investors' fear that LinkedIn would take business away from Monster.

LinkedIn constantly adds capabilities to its site. For example, in 2014, the company launched features that help increase local relevance.

Mobile Applications

A mobile version of LinkedIn, launched in February 2008, offers access to most features in the site by using mobile devices. The mobile service is supported in many languages, including Chinese, English, French, German, Japanese, and Spanish (for mobile devices and supported languages, see **help.linkedin.com/app/answers/detail/a_id/999**).

The Future of LinkedIn

LinkedIn continues its aggressive growth in both number of users and features offered. In late 2016, LinkedIn was acquired by Microsoft Corporation. The two companies feel that they will be able to leverage their combined user bases as well as product functionality to continue to grow business social networking for the enterprise (see **wsj.com/articles/ microsoft-closes-acquisition-of-linkedin-1481215151**).

LinkedIn is also continuing to expand its recruiting activities, with a dramatic expansion into the higher education market. In 2016, the company launched a new initiative to bring college students into the network with the promise of special tools to allow them to apply for positions and be noticed by recruiters (see **university.linkedin.com**).

Some Resources for LinkedIn

The following are some useful resources on LinkedIn: **blog.linkedin.com**, **mylinkedinpow-erforum.com**, and **linkedin. com/search**.

For LinkedIn success stories, see Elad (2016) and **cbsnews.com/news/linkedin-5-job-search-success-stories**

Sources: Based upon Elad (2016), Ahmad (2014), Bernstein (2015), **en.wikipedia.org/wiki/LinkedIn**, and **press.linkedin.com/about-linkedin** (both accessed March 2016).

Questions

1. Enter **linkedin.com** and explore the site. Why do you think the site is so successful?
2. What features are related to recruiting and job search?
3. Conduct an investigation to find the company's revenue sources. Prepare a list.
4. Several companies have attempted to clone LinkedIn with little success. Why do you think LinkedIn is dominating?
5. Join the group called "eMarketing Association Network" on LinkedIn (free; it is a private group so you must request to join), and observe their group's activities regarding social media and commerce for 1 week. Write a report.
6. Research the issue of falsified profiles on LinkedIn.

REFERENCES

Accenture. *A Comprehensive Approach to Managing Social Media Risk and Compliance.* Accenture, 2015. **accenture.com/t20150523T022413__w__/us-en/_acnmedia/Accenture/Conversion-Assets/DotCom/Documents/Global/PDF/Dualpub_1/accenture-comprehensive-approach-managing-social-media-risk-compliance.pdf** (accessed January 2017).

Anderton, K. "Augmented Reality, the Future, and Pokemon Go." *Forbes*, November 14, 2016. **forbes.com/sites/kevinanderton/2016/11/14/augmented-reality-the-future-and-pokemon-go-infographic/#53a8a5344e66** (accessed January 2017).

Ahmad, I. "How to Boost LinkedIn Engagement [Infographic]."*Social Media Today*, January 3, 2014.

Avanade. "Achieving Social Collaboration Success." A white paper from Accenture and Microsoft, 2013. **avanade.com/~/media/documents/enterprise-social-collaboration-pov.pdf** (accessed January 2017).

Barr, S. "The Four Core Use Cases of Collaboration Software for Corporates." HighQ, 2017. **highq.com/resources/webinars/four-use-cases-collaboration-software-corporates-webinar** (accessed January 2017).

Bernstein, B. *How to Write a KILLER LinkedIn Profile... and 18 Mistakes to Avoid.* Madison, WI: The Essay Expert, 2015.

Boone, R.S. *LinkedIn: Guide To Making Your LinkedIn Profile Awesome: 25 Powerful Hacks for Your LinkedIn Profile to Attract Recruiters and Employers (Career Search... Profile, LinkedIn Makeover, Career Search).* Kindle edition. Seattle, WA: Amazon Digital Services, 2015.

Bowerman, M. "Man Killed While Playing 'Pokemon Go' at San Francisco Park." *USA Today*, August 8, 2016. **usatoday.com/story/news/nation-now/2016/08/08/man-killed-playing-pokemon-san-francisco-aquatic-park/88384200** (accessed January 2017).

Brabham, D. *Crowdsourcing in the Public Sector.* Kindle Edition. Seattle, WA: Amazon Digital Services, 2015.

Bratteteig, T. *Disentangling Participation: Power and Decision-making in Participatory Design.* New York: Springer, 2016.

Buckley, C. "Understanding the Business Benefits of Social Collaboration." *Beezy, Business Culture*, September 2015.

Bughin, J. "Taking the Measure of the Networked Enterprise." *McKinsey Quarterly*, October 2015. **mckinsey.com/business-functions/digital-mckinsey/our-insights/taking-the-measure-of-the-networked-enterprise** (accessed January 2017).

Burke, B. *Gamify: How Gamification Motivates People to Do Extraordinary Things.* New York: Bibliomotion, 2014.

Cancialosi, C. "Crowdsourcing: Your Key To A More Effective, Engaged Organization?" *Forbes*, August 31, 2015. **forbes.com/sites/chriscancialosi/2015/08/03/crowdsourcing-your-key-to-a-more-effective-engaged-organization/#3f59f167193e** (accessed January 2017).

Chou, Y. *Actionable Gamification: Beyond Points, Badges, and Leaderboards*, Kindle Edition. Seattle, WA: Octalysis Media, 2015.

Cole, D. *Go From Zero to Hero on LinkedIn: Jump Start Your Prospecting Success in as Little as 7 Days.* Kindle Edition. Seattle, WA: Amazon Digital Services, 2015.

della Cava, M. "$9 Computer Killing it on Kickstarter." *USA Today*, May 11, 2015.

Dalbec, B. "The Benefits of Internal Social Media? Engaged Employees" APCO, January, 25, 2016. **apcoworldwide.com/blog/detail/apcoforum/2016/01/25/the-benefits-of-internal-social-media-engaged-employees** (accessed January 2017).

Davidson, J. "The 7 Social Media Mistakes Most Likely to Cost You a Job." *Time*, October 16, 2014. **time.com/money/3510967/jobvite-social-media-profiles-job-applicants** (accessed January 2017).

Deligiannis, N. "How to Use Social Media to Enhance Your Job Serach in 2017." Hays Recruiting, January 25, 2017. **social.hays.com/2017/01/25/how-to-use-social-media-to-enhance-your-2017-job-search** (accessed January 2017).

Elad, J. *LinkedIn for Dummies.* Hoboken, NJ: Wiley & Sons, 2016.

Findlay, J. "How Gamification Enhances the Customer Experience." CMS Wire, September 30, 2016. **cmswire.com/customer-experience/how-gamification-enhances-the-customer-experience/** (accessed January 2017).

Florentine, S. "How Gamification Makes Customer Services Fun." *Computer World*, March 3, 2014.

Forte, D. "The Evolution and Future of Social Commerce." Multichannel Merchant, September 20, 2016. **multichannelmerchant.com/infographics/evolution-future-social-commerce-20092016** (accessed January 2017).

Gebauer, S. "132 Social Media Case Studies—Successes and Failures." *The Social MS*, April 2015. **blog.thesocialms.com/132-social-media-case-studies-successes-and-failures** (accessed January 2017).

Gottlieb, M. "42 Leading Social Networking Sites for Business Professionals and Entrepreneurs You May Not Know." *LinkedIn Pulse*, April 25, 2015.

Harrison, L. *Gamification for Business.* New York, NY: Motivational Press, 2014.

Hearsay Social. "Hearsay Social Empowers Mortgage Lenders and Loan Officers to Maximize Referrals and Compliantly Engage Clients Across Digital Channels." Hearsay Systems, April 4, 2016. **hearsaysystems.com/hs-press/hearsay-social-empowers-mortgage-lenders-and-loan-officers-to-maximize-referrals-and-compliantly-engage-clients-across-digital-channels** (accessed January 2017).

Holmes, R. "Top 5 Social Media Trends for Businesses in 2017." Hootsuite. January 3, 2017. **blog.hootsuite.com/social-media-trends-2017** (accessed January 2017).

Howe, J. *Crowdsourcing: Why the Power of the Crowd Is Driving the Future of Business.* New York: Crown Business, 2008.

Huff, T. "How Social Media Changed the Hiring Process." August 10, 2014. **socialmediatoday.com/content/how-social-media-changed-hiring-process** (accessed January 2017).

Hutchinson, A. "Why YouTube is Seeking to Win over Gamers with YouTube Gaming." *Social Media Today*, June 16, 2015.

Jurgensen, J. "An Ode to Joyful Streaming." *The Wall Street Journal*, January 4–5, 2014.

Kelly, H. "Pokemon Go breaks Apple download records." CNN Tech, July 22, 2016. **money.cnn.com/2016/07/22/technology/pokemon-go-apple-download-records/?iid=EL** (accessed January 2017).

Kickstarter. "Kickstarter Basics." Undated. **kickstarter.com/help/faq/kickstarter+basics** (accessed January 2017).

Krans, J. "The Intelligent Networked Enterprise: New Paradigm for the Digital Age." Ascent, July 15, 2015. **ascent.atos.net/intelligent-networked-enterprise-new-paradigm-digital-age** (accessed January 2017).

Leaning, B. "How to Monitor Social Media in Only 10 Minutes a Day." Hubspot, January 8, 2015. **blog.hubspot.com/marketing/monitor-social-media-effectively#sm.001ai11nzh0xf7611rs1x190h6plu** (accessed January 2017).

Lee, S. "What Is Pokémon Go and Why Is Everyone Talking About It?" Lifehacker, July 11, 2016. **lifehacker.com/what-is-pokemon-go-and-why-is-everyone-talking-about-it-1783420761** (accessed January 2017).

Li, C. "Why No One Uses the Corporate Social Network." *Harvard Business Review*, April 25, 2015. **hbr.org/2015/04/why-no-one-uses-the-corporate-social-network.** (accessed January 2017).

Martin, R. L. et al. *Getting Beyond Better: How Social Entrepreneurship Works.* Boston: Harvard Business Review, 2015.

Morgan, J. *The Future of Work: Attract New Talent, Build Better Leaders, and Create a Competitive Organization.* New York: McGraw-Hill, 2014.

Nanalyze. "How Easy Is It to Run Scams on Kickstarter?" Nanalyze, June 9, 2016. **nanalyze.com/2016/06/kickstarter-scams** (accessed January 2017).

Nolinske, T. "Social Networks Benefit Employees and Customers." National Business Research Institute, 2016. **nbrii.com/employee-survey-white-papers/social-networks-benefit-employees-and-customers** (accessed January 2017).

Reffell, C. "Diverse Crowdfunding Models Across Sectors Highlighted at CSW Europe 2016." CrowdsourcingWeek.org, December 7, 2016. **crowdsourcingweek.com/blog/crowdfunding-models-energy-sustainability-innovation.** (accessed March 2017).

Ridley-Duff, R. and M. Bull. *Understanding Social Enterprise: Theory and Practice,* 2nd edition. Thousand Oaks, CA: Sage Publications, 2015.

Rohampton, J. "5 Social Media Trends That Will Dominate 2017." *Forbes*, January 3, 2017. **forbes.com/sites/jimmyrohampton/2017/01/03/5-social-media-trends-that-will-dominate-2017** (accessed January 2017).

Root, A. "Potato Salad Tops $50k in Pledges." July 8, 2014. **crowdsourcing.org/editorial/potato-salad-tops-50k-in-pledges/32674** (accessed January 2017).

Roth, J. *Crowdfunding: How to Raise Money for your Startup and Other Projects! (Crowdfunding, Funding, Raise, Business, Money, Startup, Guide, Capital).* Publisher: John Roth, 2016.

Russo, J. "Talking Story with Kawehi on Her Upcoming Hawaii Tour." July 1, 2014. **mauitime.com/2014/07/01/talking-story-with-kawehi-on-her-upcoming-hawaii-tour** (accessed January 2017).

Salesforce. *The Little Blue Book of Social Transformation* Salesforce, 2014. **salesforce.com/form/conf/social-enterprise-bluebook.jsp** (accessed January 2017).

Serino, L. "8 Kickstarter Campaigns that Nailed It (and How You Can, Too)." *ECommercefuel*, May 29, 2015. **ecommercefuel.com/kickstarter-campaign-tips** (accessed January 2017).

Sedniev, A. *The Business Idea Factory: A World-Class System for Creating Successful Business Ideas.* Kindle edition. Seattle, WA: Amazon Digital Services, 2016.

Shih, C. "Empowering Mortgage Lenders and Loan Officers to Thrive in the Digital Era." Hearsay Systems, April 4, 2016. **hearsaysystems.com/2016/04/empowering-mortgage-lenders-and-loan-officers-to-thrive-in-the-digital-era** (accessed January 2017).

Stegmaier, J. *A Crowdfunder's Strategy Guide: Build a Better Business by Building Community.* Oakland, CA: Berrett-Koehler Pub., 2015.

Terpening, E. "How to Choose the Best Organizational Model for Social Business." *Altimeter Group*, September 2015.

Thomas, S. "2016 Best Career Apps and Websites to Land Your Dream Job." *Huffington Post*, February 3, 2016. **huffingtonpost.com/sherri-thomas/2016-best-career-apps-and_b_9125474.html** (accessed January 2017).

Turban, E. et al. *Social Commerce.* New York: Springer 2016.

Turner, A. "20 Social Networking Sites for Business Professionals." SitePoint, July 27, 2016. **sitepoint.com/social-networking-sites-for-business** (accessed January 2017).

Vahl, A. "How to Network with Facebook Groups." *Social Media Examiner*, January 19, 2015. **socialmediaexaminer.com/network-with-facebook-groups** (accessed January 2017).

Walker, R. "Protecting Privacy in a Job Search." New York Times, January 24, 2015. **nytimes.com/2015/01/25/business/protecting-privacy-in-job-search.html?_r=0** (accessed January 2017).

Walker, T. "The Future of Advertising Is Native Social Commerce." Hubspot, February 25, 2016. **blog.hubspot.com/marketing/future-of-advertising-native-social-commerce#sm.001ai11nzh0xf7611rs1x190h6plu** (accessed January 2017).

White, S. "How to Use Gamification to Improve Employee Engagement." *CIO.com*, November 23, 2016. **cio.com/article/3143955/gamification/how-to-use-gamification-to-improve-employee-engagement.html.** (accessed January 2017).

World Library. *Social Enterprise Handbook.* (e-book), World Public Library, 2015. **worldlibrary.org/articles/Social_enterprise** (accessed January 2017).

Zielinski, D. "The Gamification of Recruitment" SHRM, November 1, 2015. **shrm.org/hr-today/news/hr-magazine/pages/1115-gamification-recruitment.aspx** (accessed January 2017).

Zoref, L. *Mindsharing: The Art of Crowdsourcing Everything.* New York, NY: Portfolio, 2015.

Zur, O. & Zur, A. (2016): "On Digital Immigrants and Digital Natives: How the Digital Divide Affects Families, Educational Institutions, and the Workplace." Zur Institute – Online. 2016. **zurinstitute.com/digital_divide.html** (accessed January 2017).

Part IV

EC Support Services

Marketing and Advertising in E-Commerce

Contents

Learning Objectives

Upon completion of this chapter, you will be able to:

1. Describe factors that influence online consumer behavior.
2. Explain how consumer behavior can be analyzed for creating personalized services.
3. Understand consumer market research in e-commerce.
4. Describe the objectives and characteristics of Web advertising.
5. Describe the major advertising methods used on the Web.
6. Learn mobile marketing concepts and techniques.
7. Describe various online advertising strategies and types of promotions.
8. Understand some implementation issues.

OPENING CASE
IKEA USES MOBILE AND AUGMENTED REALITY

IKEA (ikea.com) is a global leader in retail furniture sales. It is a Swedish multinational company that designs and sells a wide variety of ready-to-assemble furniture and is the world's largest furniture retailer. IKEA sells furniture through a series of 392 stores in 48 countries as well as online using Web-based and mobile catalogs.

The Problem

Because of the personal nature of furniture and how it fits into an individual's home or apartment, a key issue is ensuring that whatever is purchased will fit in both size and style. This is difficult because the product is never in the home environment until after purchase (Teixeira and Gupta 2015). This creates the possibility of regret for purchases which can spawn decreased brand satisfaction or costly reverse logistics (returns). Customers at the store must picture the furniture in their home, and customers in their home must picture the furniture available on the website at that location. This creates distinct disadvantages for sales of furniture, creates cognitive dissonance before and after the sale, and lengthens the overall sales cycle. If customers were confident in how furniture would look in their home, it would make the selection process easier and quicker.

The Solution

IKEA recognized that its customers, typically in younger demographics, were quickly adopting mobile technologies and were very comfortable with the use of mobile apps. Additionally, the company had studied the possible uses of augmented reality. The company decided that a mobile-based augmented reality application would be a viable solution to the concern about how furniture fit and feel in a customer's home (Allen 2016).

The company launched its augmented reality app for both Apple's iOS and Android in 2013 and have been making significant updates to it through 2016 (see **ikea.com/ms/en_CA/customer-service/about-shopping/free-ikea-apps/index.html**). The app allows customers to take pictures of their surroundings and then select from a wide array of IKEA furniture and place it within those surroundings. This idea calls back to early IKEA catalogs that encouraged customers to cut out pictures of furniture and hold them up in their home environment to see how things would look. Customers are able to select different patterns and adjust the size and perspective of furniture pieces. See a video of how the app works at **youtu.be/xC6t2eEPkPc**.

The Results

The app was very well-received by customers. Due to its popularity, IKEA has continued to add additional furniture items (over 200 in 2017) for customers to virtually evaluate. As of early 2017, the app had been downloaded more than 200,000 times across both platforms. The company credits the use of augmented reality for increases in overall sales, as well as decreases in the amount of time sales are being considered (Carpenter 2016). The company plans to continue to update the application to keep it current with its existing catalog of furniture items.

LESSONS LEARNED FROM THE CASE

Some items are difficult to sell online, but by using technology we can make this process easier for customers. The adoption of mobile devices and their ability to use augmented reality systems presents unique opportunities to some retailers, including those that sell home furnishings. IKEA was able to leverage an augmented reality application to boost sales, increase customer confidence, and decrease post-sale regrets.

10.1   ONLINE CONSUMER BEHAVIOR

Companies are operating in an increasingly competitive environment. Therefore, sellers try to understand customers' needs and influence them to buy their products and services. Customer acquisition and retention are key success factors, both offline and online. This is particularly important for online businesses, as most interactions with their customers are online. For a summary of factors affecting consumer behavior, see **iresearchservices.com/5-common-factors-influencing-consumer-behavior/**.

A Model of Online Consumer Behavior

For decades, market researchers have tried to understand consumer shopping behavior and develop various models to summarize their findings. A consumer behavior model is designed to help vendors understand how a consumer makes a purchasing decision. Through understanding the decision process, a business may be better able to influence the buyer's decision through improved product design or advertising.

Consumers can be divided into two groups: individual consumers and organizational buyers including governments, private corporations, resellers, and nonprofit organizations. These two types of buyers tend to have different purchasing behaviors and usually are analyzed differently. In this chapter, we focus on individual buyers. An individual consumer behavior model often includes *influential internal and external factors* that affect the buyer's *decision process* and the process for making a purchasing decision. Figure 10.1 shows a consumer behavior model, and this video (**youtu.be/dcV9y_LLdR8**) explains the process.

- **Influential factors.** Factors influencing purchasing decisions fall into five major dimensions. They are *consumer factors, environmental factors, merchant and intermediary factors, product/service factors* (which include market stimuli), and *EC selling systems*. The first three dimensions are not controllable by the sellers, while the last two are mostly controlled by the sellers. The dimensions are shown in Fig. 10.1. The influential factors affect the buyers' decision process.
- **The attitude–behavior decision process.** The second part in a consumer behavior model is the decision-making process, which usually starts with awareness of the situation and a positive attitude and ends with the buyer's decision to purchase and/or repurchase (see the oval part in Fig. 10.1). A *favorable attitude* would lead to a stronger *buying intention*, which in turn would result in the *actual buying behavior*. Previous research has shown that the links between attitude, purchase intention, and actual purchase behavior are quite strong. Marketers are working to control as much of this process as possible, and one way is to try to move as much of the experience online as possible. These tactics also involve converging the online and physical environments to establish an ideal marketing playing field (van Bommel et al. 2014).

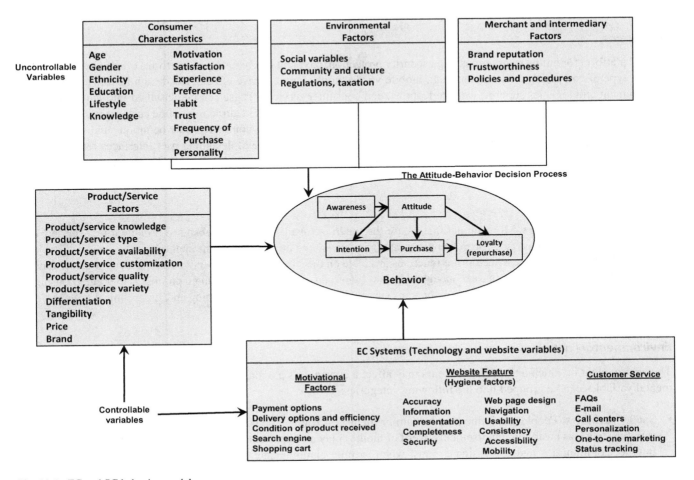

Fig. 10.1 EC and SC behavior model

The Major Influential Factors

Major influential factors of consumer purchasing behavior fall into the following categories:

Consumer Characteristics

Consumer (personal) characteristics, which are shown in the top-left portion of Fig. 10.1, refer to demographic factors, individual preferences, and behavioral characteristics of the consumer. Several websites provide information on customer buying habits online (e.g., **emarketer.com**, **clickz.com**, and **comscore.com**). The major demographics that such sites track are gender, age, marital status, education level, ethnicity, occupation, and household income, which can be correlated with Internet usage and EC data. Both men and women have been found to perceive information differently depending on their levels of purchase confidence and internal knowledge. Marketers also study the psychological variables such as personality and lifestyle characteristics. Several studies show that shopping experience has a significant effect on consumer attitude and intention to purchase and repurchase online (e.g., Chiu et al. 2014).

Merchant and Intermediary-Related Factors

Online transactions may also be affected by the merchant that provides the product/service. This group of factors includes merchant reputation, size of the transaction, trust in the merchant, and so on. For example, a customer may feel more secure when making a purchase from Amazon.com (due to its reputation) than from an unknown seller. Other factors such as marketing strategy and advertising can also play a major role.

Product/Service Factors

The second group of factors is related to the product/service itself. The consumer's decision to make a purchase is affected by the nature of the product/service in the transaction. These may include the price, quality, design, brand, and other related attributes of the product.

EC Systems

The EC platform for online transactions (e.g., security protection, payment mechanism, and so forth) offered by the merchant and the type of computing environment (e.g., mobile vs. desktop) may also have effects. EC design factors can be divided into payment and logistics support, website features, and consumer services. These can be classified into *motivational* and *hygiene* factors with motivational factors being important than hygiene factors in attracting online customers. Another factor that we include here is the type of EC. For example, consumer behavior in m-commerce may be unique and so is behavior during social shopping. Understanding these factors highlights the importance of designing user interfaces that are reactive to the device being used, with a focus on ensuring mobile availability as detailed in a study by Pantano and Priporas at **sciencedirect.com/science/article/pii/S0747563216302448**.

- **Motivational factors.** Motivational factors are the functions available on the website to provide direct support in the purchasing process (e.g., search engines, shopping carts, and multiple payment methods).
- **Hygiene factors.** Hygiene factors are functions available on the website whose objective is to make the website functional and serviceable (e.g., ease of navigation, show items added to the cart); their main purpose is to protect consumers from risks or unexpected events in the transaction process (e.g., security breaching and site technical failure).

Environmental Factors

The environment in which a transaction occurs may affect a consumer's purchase decision. As shown in Fig. 10.1, environmental variables can be grouped into the following categories:

- **Social variables.** People are influenced by family members, friends, coworkers, and current styles. Therefore, social variables (such as customer endorsements, word of mouth) play an important role in EC. Of special importance in EC are Internet communities and discussion groups, where people communicate via chat rooms, electronic bulletin boards, tweeting, and newsgroups.

- **Cultural/community variables.** The influence of culture on buying behavior varies from country to country. It makes a big difference in what people buy if a consumer lives near Silicon Valley in California or in the mountains in Nepal. Chinese shoppers may differ from French shoppers, and rural shoppers may differ from urban ones.
- **Other environmental variables.** These include aspects such as available public information, government regulations, legal constraints, and situational factors. For example, tax rates may affect online shopping (see Einav et al. 2014).

Lately, attention has been given to customers' behavior in the mobile environment. For more information, see **mobile-marketer.com**.

Enhancing Customer Loyalty

One factor that has a significant impact on consumer behavior, both online and offline, is loyalty. Customers who have had positive past experiences with a brand or retailer will show that brand or retailer preferential treatment during the buying process. This is because the customer shortcuts some of the evaluation process steps because they have trust based on previous outcomes. A report by Bain & Company (available for download **bain.com/Images/Value_online_customer_loyalty_you_capture.pdf**) shows the importance of loyalty in the e-commerce environment. The report shows several key factors in customer loyalty:

- Loyalty is needed for repeat buyers, and repeat buyers drive firm profitability.
- Repeat purchasers spend more and have larger transactions.
- Repeat customers generate referrals and drive more business.
- Loyal customers will buy additional products, even if they are dissimilar from the original product.

With these facts in mind, it becomes apparent that maintaining or growing customer loyalty is an important part of any e-commerce business. While many experts suggest methods to increase customer loyalty (see Kissmetrics 2016; Charlton 2015; Thompson, 2015), many agree that the most important factors are:

- Recognition of customer importance
- Honest engagement and customer service
- Convenience in using e-commerce systems
- Economic factors such as discounts or access to special promotions

By building customer loyalty, businesses are able to leverage our understanding of consumer behavior models, explicitly specifically decision and purchase models. Jackie Huba presents some interesting points on online customer loyalty in this video **youtu.be/UMWw6V_ZtvI**.

SECTION 10.1 REVIEW QUESTIONS

1. Describe the major components of the model of online consumer behavior.
2. List some major personal characteristics that influence consumer behavior.
3. List the major environmental variables of the purchasing environment.
4. List and describe five major merchant-related variables.
5. Describe the relationships among attitude, intention, and actual behavior in the behavior process model.
6. Why is loyalty an important part of the purchase decision model?

10.2 PERSONALIZATION AND BEHAVIORAL MARKETING

As the Internet provides a huge amount of data for customer profiling, one-to-one marketing becomes effective. There are three generic strategies for one-to-one marketing: *personalization*, *behavioral targeting*, and *collaborative filtering*.

Personalization in E-Commerce

Personalization refers to the matching of advertising content and vendors' services with customers based on their preferences and individual needs. Personalized content on a website has been found to increase conversion rates (see **searchenginewatch.com/article/2334157/How-Personalizing-Websites-With-Dynamic-Content-Increases-Engagement**). The matching process is based on the *user profile*. The **user profile** describes customer preferences, behaviors, and demographics. It can be generated by getting information directly from the users; for example, observing what people are doing online through the use of tools such as a **cookie**—a data file that, frequently, without the knowledge of users, is placed on their computers' hard drives. Alternatively, profiles can be built from previous purchase patterns. Profiles can be structured from market research or by making inferences from information known about similar consumers.

One-to-one matching can be done by methods such as *collaborative filtering* (discussed later in this section). Many vendors provide personalization tools that help with customer acquisition and retention. An example of these vendors is Magnify360 (**magnify360.com**).

Web Cookies for Data Collection

Cookies are small files sent from a website and stored in a designated area in your computer. They allow companies to save certain information for future use. The use of cookies is a popular method that allows computers to look smarter and simplifies Internet access. According to Webopedia, "the main purpose of cookies is to identify users and possibly prepare customized Web pages for them" (per **webopedia.com/TERM/C/cookie.html**).

Are cookies bad or good? The answer is "both." When users revisit Amazon.com or other sites, they are greeted by their first name. Amazon.com knows the users' identity by using cookies. Vendors can provide consumers with considerable personalized information if they use cookies that signal a consumer's return to a site. Cookies can provide marketers with a wealth of information, which then can be used to target specific ads to them. Thus, marketers get higher rates of "click-throughs," and customers can view information that is relevant to them. Cookies can also prevent repetitive ads because vendors can arrange for a consumer not to see the same ad twice. Finally, advanced data mining companies (e.g., provided by SPSS and Sift), can analyze information in cookie files so companies can better meet their customers' needs.

However, some people object to cookies because they do not like the idea that "someone" is watching their activity on the Internet. Users who do not like cookies can disable them. On the other hand, some consumers may want to keep the "friendly" cookies. For example, many sites recognize a person as a subscriber by accessing their cookies so that they do not need to reregister every time they visit the site.

Cookies can be removed if the user does not like them. For instructions on deleting cookie files from your Internet browser (e.g., Internet Explorer, Google Chrome, Firefox), see **whitecanyon.com/delete-cookie**.

Example: Using Cookies at DotMailer

DotMailer (**dotmailer.com**) is a marketing automation platform that focuses on e-mail campaigns. Like most other companies, DotMailer tracks cookies on their website. The policy states that:

> Cookies are small text files which a website may put on your computer or mobile device when you first visit a site or page. The cookie will help the website, or another website, to recognize your device the next time you visit. Web beacons or other similar files can also do the same thing. We use the term "cookies" in this policy to refer to all files that collect information in this way.

The company further categorizes the cookies it uses into three groups:

1. Essential cookies—so subscribers can access content
2. Performance cookies—to evaluate website use and performance
3. Functionality cookies—to remember user preferences

So are these cookies harmful? Like their uses on so many other sites, the jury is still out. In many cases the uses of cookies are benign and are only meant to help a website run more effectively and give the business a basic understanding of its users.

Individuals that are concerned about their online privacy can always block the use of cookies (see this site for details **allaboutcookies.org/manage-cookies**). If you are interested in more information about how cookies work, visit **allaboutcookies.org**.

Other Methods for Data Collection

While cookies been the primary method for tracking user activity online historically, there are new technologies that offer other ways to track users. These new technologies are being used as customers begin to restrict the use of cookies in their browsers and as the available technologies allow greater specificity and understanding of user behavior using these new software ideas. In an article in Kompyte, Sergio Ramirez (2015) details the following five methods that can, that are, or that could be used to track users:

1. Using the user's IP address as a unique identifier
2. Using LocalStorage, a new feature in HTML5
3. Using canvas fingerprinting, a method to embed material in Web pages that changes as the user advances
4. User behavior, identifying the user paste on a profile of their type of behavior online
5. Using ETAG, matching past user behavior on server logs with active user behavior

For additional research in this area, see **consumer.ftc.gov/articles/0042-online-tracking**

Using Personalized Techniques to Increase Sales

It has become a common practice for vendors to provide personalized services to customers in order to increase customer satisfaction and loyalty. A prime example is Amazon.com, which provides many personalized services where the most common activity is product recommendations. Amazon.com automatically generates such recommendations based on the buyers' purchasing and browsing histories, and upon the purchasing history of other customers with similar purchasing histories.

Personalized services can be facilitated when the companies know more about their customers. TowerData (**towerdata.com**) offers a service that helps businesses learn more about their customers, so they can personalize content (go to **intelligence.towerdata.com**). For a free e-book about the 40 best ways to personalize website, see **qubitproducts.com/content/40-best-ways-to-personalize**.

CASE 10.1: EC APPLICATION
USING AI AT THE NORTH FACE

The Problem

Online retailing is a crowded and competitive space. Businesses must work diligently to provide shopping experiences for customers that will meet their needs and keep them coming back. One issue that many retailers struggle with is personalization of the shopping experience based on customer needs. These systems are especially limited within the mobile environment. Retailers that are truly able to customize interactions with customers and recommendations of products have the opportunity to prosper.

The North Face (**thenorthface.com**) is an outdoor clothing and equipment company that offers a wide variety of products for both the professional and casual user. The company identified a deficiency in the personalization of its e-commerce experience and decided to do something about it.

The Solution

To solve this issue, The North Face partnered with IBM's Watson supercomputer and Fluid's Expert Personal Shopper (XPS) software to create an artificial intelligence recommendation system. The system relies on Fluid's cognitive computing platform that allows for rapid, complex personalization based on user requests and interactions. Visitors to The North Face site can provide basic information about their needs in a jacket (see **thenorthface.com/xps**), and products would then be recommended or even potentially customized to meet those needs (Marshall 2016). This system allows the company to better understand customer needs and behaviors. This data can then be used in the initial interaction with the customer and potentially future interactions as well (Greengard 2016).

The initial product launch was in late December 2015, and during that time over 55,000 customizations were performed with a session time of approximately 2 minutes. Because of the interactivity, there was a 60% click-through rate, and 75% of users enjoyed the system and said they would use it again (see **fluid.com/portfolio/the-north-face-xps**)

Questions

1. Why is personalization important for retailers and shoppers?
2. How is The North Face using artificial intelligence?
3. Why would this system generate repeat purchases?

Behavioral Marketing and Collaborative Filtering

A major goal of marketing is to enhance customer value through delivering the right product or service to the customer. One of the most popular ways of matching ads with customers is *behavioral marketing*, which is identifying customer behavior on the Web and designing a marketing plan accordingly.

Behavioral Targeting

Behavioral targeting uses consumer browsing behavior information, and other information about consumers, to design personalized ads that may influence consumers better than mass advertising does. It also assumes that users with similar profiles and past shopping behavior may have similar product preferences. Google tests its "interest-based advertising" to make ads more relevant and useful. Representative vendors of behavioral targeting tools are **predictad.com**, **criteo.com**, and **conversantmedia.com**. A major method of behavioral targeting is *collaborative filtering*.

Collaborative Filtering

When new customers come to a business, it would be useful if a company could predict what products or services are of interest to them without asking or viewing their previous records. A method that attempts to do just that is **collaborative filtering**. Using proprietary formulas, collaborative filtering automatically connects the preferences and activities of many customers that have similar characteristics to predict preferences of new customers and recommend products to them. For a free tutorial of 119 slides about collaborative filtering from Carnegie Mellon University, see Cohen (Undated). Many commercial systems are based on collaborative filtering.

Amazon's "Customers who bought this item also bought…" is a typical statement generated by collaborative filtering, which intends to persuade a consumer to purchase the recommended items by pointing to preferences of similar consumers.

Trouvus Inc., a provider of collaborative filtering software, describes how their product works in this short video **youtu.be/u_V9o2HDCTE**.

Other Methods

In addition to collaborative filtering, a few other methods for identifying users' profiles are described below:

Rule-Based Filtering

A company queries consumers about their preferences via multiple choice questions and uses the collected information to build patterns for predicting customers' needs. From this information, the collaborative filtering system derives behavioral and demographic rules such as, "If the customer's age is greater than 35, and the customer's income is above $100,000, show the Jeep Cherokee ad; otherwise, show the Mazda Protégé ad."

Content-Based Filtering

This technique allows vendors to identify customer preferences by the attributes of the product(s) they buy or intend to buy. Knowing the customers' preferences, the vendor will recommend products with similar attributes to the user. For instance, the system may recommend a text-mining book to customers who have shown interest in data mining or recommend more action movies after a consumer has rented one in this category.

Activity-Based Filtering

Filtering rules can also be built by logging the user's activities on the Web. For example, a vendor may want to find potential customers who visit bookstores more than three times a month. This can be done by analyzing the website's visiting level and activities. For a comprehensive discussion and more information about data collection, targeted advertising, and 104 companies that catch data, and so forth (including an infographic), see Weise (2016).

Legal and Ethical Issues in Collaborative Filtering

A major issue in using collaborative filtering for personalization is the collection of information from users without their consent or knowledge. Such a practice is illegal in many countries (e.g., the United States) because of the violation of privacy laws. Permission-based practices solve this problem. In fact, empirical research indicates that permission-based practices are able to generate better positive attitude in mobile advertising (Lin et al. 2015).

Social Psychology and Morphing in Behavioral Marketing

Cognitive styles that define how people process information has become a subject of research in Internet marketing and advertising. The underlying rationale is that people with different cognitive styles have different preferences in website design and marketing messages. Specifically, an attempt is made to connect the Web with users in their preferred cognitive style. This can make one-to-one advertising messages more effective. MIT designed an empathetic Web that is utilized to figure out how a user processes information and then responds to each visitor's cognitive style.

CASE 10.2: EC APPLICATION
NETFLIX USES TECHNICAL AND SOCIAL SYSTEMS SO YOU CAN FIND SOMETHING TO WATCH

A key benefit of streaming TV companies is the variety of their catalog of movies and shows and an individual's ability to view those on demand. Unfortunately, this is also a disadvantage; with so many options, how can an enjoyable selection be found? There are several ways to address this problem, and industry leader Netflix (**netflix.com**) has applied several of them. Two ways that may be used are software-based systems that recommend movies and shows based on an individual's past preferences, and the other option is social: allowing users to make recommendations to others.

The Technical Approach

There are another number of challenges to a technical approach of recommending content to individual users. These challenges are detailed by Raimond and Basilico (2016) and include:

- Challenge 1: Uneven video availability
- Challenge 2: Cultural awareness
- Challenge 3: Language
- Challenge 4: Tracking quality

But another significant issue is the wide variability in the amount of content available based on different regions. Because of different contract stipulations with content providers, some content is available in some countries, but not others. For example, a BBC show may be available in the United States but not in England. This means that recommendation software must segment users by geographic location as well.

The system uses a very detailed algorithm that looks at both content descriptors as well as preferences in peer groups. Different pieces of content are grouped based on their type, genre, age, rating, cast, and so on. These data points can be used to make a recommendation if an individual has expressed a preference for one of these categories. For example, if a user likes the movie *Predator* with Arnold Schwarzenegger, the system may recommend other movies starring Schwarzenegger. The system also looks at peer groups. Based on an individual's past preferences, they can be filtered into similar groups of users. Then other movies that were like by this peer group, but not watched yet by the individual user, can be recommended. These systems interact with each other and also are tied to viewing regions (Popper 2016).

The Social Approach

In 2014 Netflix launched social recommendations that allowed users to share their feelings about different content available within the Netflix platform. The idea was that when searching for a movie to watch, users would trust reviews by both known and unknown individuals. The rollout initially focused on an integration with Facebook and allowed people to publicize their like or dislike for content they had recently seen (Page 2014). Functionality was later added to the Android app that also made it easy to place these recommendations.

In addition to efforts from Netflix itself, a number of third-party websites and apps have taken up the challenge of helping users find something good to watch. Examples include **agoodmovietowatch.com**, **whatisonnetflix.com**, and **netflixroulette.net**.

Understanding what users want is a very complicated matter. Making recommendations is an important part of customer satisfaction when a large amount of choice exists or the product offerings are complex. Netflix follows both a technical and social approach to attempt to keep users satisfied with their viewing options.

Questions

1. Why does making choices get harder when you have more options?
2. Why does Netflix use both a technical and a social approach two recommendations?
3. How do the technical recommendations work?
4. Why is it important for Netflix to be able to make appropriate recommendations for their users?

SECTION 10.2 REVIEW QUESTIONS

1. Define and describe the benefits and costs of personalization.
2. Describe how websites can track users and the benefits to companies of this tracking.
3. Define behavioral targeting and find a sample application on the Internet.
4. Define collaborative filtering and find a sample application on the Internet.
5. Explain how one-to-one advertising is done using cookies and behavioral targeting.

10.3   MARKET RESEARCH FOR E-COMMERCE

In order to sell more effectively, it is important to conduct proper market research to find information and knowledge about consumers and products. The market researcher's goal is to identify marketing opportunities and problems, to provide input for marketing planning, to find out how to influence the purchasing process, and to evaluate the success of promotions and advertisements. Market research aims to investigate the behavior of customers on the Web (see Strauss and Frost 2014). Market researchers gather information about competition, regulations, pricing, strategies, and consumer behavior.

Objectives and Concepts of Online Market Research

Investigation of EC markets can be conducted through conventional methods (e.g., in-person surveys; focus groups), or it can be done by using the Internet. Internet-based market research is frequently faster, allowing researchers to reach remote or diverse audiences. In addition, market researchers can conduct very large studies on the Web at a much lower price than using offline methods. Telephone surveys can cost as much as $50 per interview, and their quality may be poor. Such cost can accumulate to thousands of dollars when several hundred respondents are needed. An online survey will cost a fraction of a similarly sized telephone survey and can expedite research considerably. On the other hand, the increased sample size in online surveys can increase the accuracy of the results. McDaniel and Gates (2014) provide a comprehensive review of online market research technologies, methods, tools, issues, and ethical considerations.

What are Marketers Looking for in EC Market Research?

By looking at a customer's personal profile that includes observed behaviors on the Web, it is possible for marketers to predict online buying behavior. For example, companies want to know why some customers are online shoppers and why others are not. Major factors that are used for predicting customer online purchasing behavior are (in descending order of importance) product information requested, number of related e-mails, number of orders made, products/services ordered, and gender.

Typical questions that online market research attempts to answer are: What are the purchase patterns for typical individuals, and what are the patterns for specific groups? How can we identify those who are real buyers from those who are just browsing? What is the optimal Web page design? Knowing the answers to these questions can help a vendor advertise properly, price items, design a website, and provide appropriate customer service. Online marketing research can provide data to help answer these questions. More information about market research on the Web can be found in the tutorials at **webmonkey.com** and **inc.com/guides/biz_online/online-market-research.html**.

Representative Market Research Approaches

To conduct online marketing, it is necessary to know what the customer wants or needs. Such information can be collected by:

- Soliciting information from customers online (e.g., via interviews, questionnaires, use of focus groups, or blogging)
- Observing what customers are doing on the Web by using transaction logs and cookies
- Using data, text, and Web mining or collaborative filtering techniques to analyze the available data

Data Collection and Analysis

Specific methods for collecting online data include e-mail communication with individual customers, questionnaires placed on websites, monitoring conversations in social networks, and tracking customers' movements on the Web.

Online Surveys

An online survey is a major method for collecting EC data, and it is considered the most cost-effective mode of survey research. It has several other advantages, including lower overall preparation and administration costs, better control of the process of filling out the questionnaire (which may lead to fewer response errors, and easier follow-up), and more flexibility in the questionnaire design. In addition, the cycle time can be much shorter. However, online surveys also have some limitations, including the lack of anonymity, data errors due to nonresponses, reporting biases, and poor data privacy.

Web-Based Surveys

A special type of online survey is done by placing questions on selected websites and inviting potential consumers to reply. For example, General Mills used a Web-based survey to help understand how consumers use Chex cereal. Web surveys may be passive (a fill-in questionnaire) or interactive (respondents download the questionnaires, add comments, ask questions, and discuss issues). The surveys may include both approaches.

Online Focus Groups

Several research firms create panels of qualified Web visitors to participate in online focus groups. For example, see NPD Group, Inc. (go to **npd.com/wps/portal/npd/us/about-npd/consumer-panel**). This panel consists of 2 million consumers recruited online and verified by telephone to provide information for NPD's consumer tracking services. The use of preselected focus group participants helps to overcome some of the research limitations (e.g., small sample size and partial responses) that sometimes limit the effectiveness of Web-based surveys.

Hearing Directly from Customers

Instead of using focus groups, a company may ask customers directly what they think about a product or service. Companies can use chat rooms, social network discussion groups, blogs, wikis, podcasts, and electronic consumer forums to interact with consumers. For example, toymaker LEGO used a market research company to establish a direct survey on an electronic bulletin board where millions of visitors read each other's comments and share opinions about LEGO toys. The researchers analyzed the responses daily and submitted the information to LEGO. Netflix is using this approach extensively by encouraging customers to report their likes and dislikes. Software tools can facilitate obtaining input directly from customers. For examples, see **millwardbrowndigital.com**, a leading provider of media analytics and marketing solutions.

Data Collection in Social Networks and Other Web 2.0 Environments

Collecting data in social networks and Web 2.0 environments provides new and exciting opportunities. Here are some methods:

- **Polling.** People like to vote (e.g., the US television show *American Idol*), expressing their opinions on certain issues. People provide opinions on products, services, performances of artists and politicians, and so forth. Voting is popular in social networks.
- **Blogging.** Bloggers can raise issues or motivate others to express opinions in blogs.
- **Chatting.** Community members love to chat in public chat rooms. By following the chats, you can collect current data.
- **Tweeting.** Following what travels on Twitter can be enlightening.
- **Live chat.** Here, you can collect interactive data from customers in real time.
- **Chatterbots.** These can be partially interactive. You can analyze logs of communications. Sometimes people are more honest when they chat with an avatar.
- **Collective wisdom (intelligence).** This is a type of community brainstorming. It is used in crowdsourcing where communication is encouraged.
- **Find expertise.** Expertise is frequently found in the Web 2.0 environment; many times it is provided for free (e.g., Yahoo! Answers).
- **Folksonomy.** This social tagging makes data easier to find and access.
- **Data in videos, photos, and other rich media.** Places where these media are shared contribute to valuable data collection.
- **Discussion forums.** Subgroups in social networks use a discussion format where members exchange opinions on many topics.

Example: Xiaomi's Data Collection from Social Media in China

Xiaomi, Inc. (**mi.com/en**) is a Chinese company that designs and sells smartphones and consumer electronics. The company has grown unprecedentedly to become one of the top five smartphone brands in China in three years. It sold 18.7 million smartphones in 2013, only three years after its launch. A key to its success story is the effective use of social media as a marketing research tool. Xiaomi engages fans on social media sites. For example, the company organized a flash sale in 2014, using social media to notify their fans about their upcoming sale. According to the company's global director of marketing, social media is very important to Xiaomi, as it is the most direct and effective way to interact with its fans. Within a year, the market research website had enrolled over 6 million registered users (called Mi Fen). The company analyzed user contributions on the Xiaomi website to design a user interface called MIUI. Xiaomi's first smartphone model was released in August 2011, which received more than 300,000 preorders. Two years later, its sales reached $5 billion in 2013 and started entering the market of other electronic products. Xiaomi's success story shows the importance of market research on social media. By November 2014, the Millet Forum (**bbs.xiaomi.cn**) had more than 221 million posts from its 30 million members. For more information about Xiaomi and its social media engagement, see **thenextweb.com/asia/2014/04/09/xiaomis-social-media-strategy-drives-fan-loyalty-books-it-242m-in-sales-in-12-hours**.

Observing Customers' Movements Online

To avoid some of the problems of online surveys, especially the reporting bias that occurs when people give false or biased information, some marketers choose to learn about customers by observing their behavior rather than by asking them questions. Keeping track of consumer's online behavior can be done by using transaction logs (log files) or cookie files. This allows activity-based filtering to be done.

Transaction Logs

A **transaction log** (for Web applications) is a user file that records the user's activities on a company's website from the computer log. A transaction log can be further analyzed with log file analysis tools (e.g., from Oracle) to get a good idea about online visitors' activities, such as how often they visit the site.

Note that, as customers move from site to site, they establish their **clickstream behavior**, a pattern of their movements on the Internet, which can be seen in their transaction logs (see upcoming discussion of clickstream analysis).

Cookies and Web Bugs

Cookies and Web bugs can be used to supplement transaction log methods. Cookies allow a website to store data on the user's personal device. When the customer returns to a site visited previously, the website can find what the customer did in the past from the cookie. The customer can be greeted by their name, or a targeted ad can be sent to them. For a comprehensive description of cookies, including examples and privacy concerns, see the Indiana University Knowledge Base (**kb. iu.edu/d/agwm**). Cookies are frequently combined with **Web bugs** that are tiny (usually invisible) objects concealed in a Web page or in e-mail messages. Web bugs transmit information about the user and his or her movements to a monitoring site (e.g., to find out if the user has viewed certain content on the Web page). Many believe that cookies and Web bugs are an invasion of a user's privacy.

Spyware

Spyware is software that enters your computer like a virus does, without your knowledge. It then enables an outsider to gather information about your browsing habits. Originally designed to allow freeware authors to make money on their products, spyware applications are typically bundled together with freeware that is downloaded onto users' computers. Many users do not realize that they are downloading spyware with the freeware. The best defense against spyware is to install anti-virus software, which should detect and remove any viruses or other harmful intrusions.

Web Analytics and Mining

Web analytics deal with the monitoring, collecting, measuring and evaluating, and reporting tasks related to Internet data and activities (e.g., see Kahn 2015 and Batrinca and Treleaven 2014). Web analytics help us understand and optimize Web usage. Such analysis is done, for example, by retailers for market research. For example, see IBM Coremetrics (**ibm.com/software/ marketing-solutions/coremetrics**; now part of IBM Customer Experience Analytics). A company can also use Web analytics software to improve its website's look and operation. Web analytics can provide quick feedback from customers to help marketers decide which products to promote. For tutorials on data, text, and Web mining, see **mydatamine.com**, **tutorialspoint.com/data_mining/index.htm**, and the video series "Introduction to Data Mining" that begins at **youtube.com/watch?v=EtFQv_B7YA8**.

For details and methods used, see Alhlou et al. (2016). A special type of Web analytics is *clickstream analysis*, or just *click analysis*.

Clickstream Analysis

Clickstream data are data that describe which websites users visit, in what order, and the time spent on each. This is done by tracking the succession of "clicks" each visitor makes. Clickstream analysis is a widely used component of overall website and e-commerce system analysis. It provides a detailed set of information about user activities online, specifically how they respond to a website or e-commerce store. By evaluating this data, site owners can get a better picture of their users' aggregate interest and activity patterns. These patterns can help influence a variety of areas including website design, e-commerce system design, and product/recommended product placement. These systems generate a huge amount of data, and this type of analysis is usually associated with big data analytics and tools such as Hadoop that allow for the evaluation and understanding of what has been recorded.

Several companies offer tools that enable such an analysis. For example, Analytics 10 from Webtrends, Inc. (**analytics. webtrends.com**) features several advanced tools for analyzing clickstream data (**webtrends.com/solutions/digital-measurement/streams**). Finally, **clickstreamr.com** configures Google Analytics standards and can be used for such analysis.

Web Mining

Web mining refers to the use of data mining techniques for both Web content and usage in Web documents in order to discover patterns and hidden relationships. Web mining has the potential to change the way we access and use the information available on the Web. For mining the social web, see Khan (2015).

The growth of more advanced Web-based systems and social media has enabled the generation of significant amounts of customer data concerning online activities, patterns, and behavior. As the amount available information grows, so does the ability to analyze that information and the potential business uses that this information can be used for. For an infographic that details the type of information that Google collects and how it may be used, see **welivesecurity.com/wp-content/media_files/Google-Privacy-Infographic-780p.jpg**.

Limitations of Online Market Research and How to Overcome Them

Online market research has technical and behavioral limitations. One technical problem with online market research is that there may be an abundance of data. To use data properly, one needs to organize, edit, condense, and summarize them. However, such a task may be expensive and time-consuming. One solution to this problem is to automate the process by using data warehousing and data mining.

Behavioral limitations of online research methods are responding biases, sample representatives that are hard to control, and the ethics and legality of Web tracking. As Web-based surveys often use an "open call" to recruit respondents, the response rate is hard to know, and the respondent control is limited. Anonymity in Web-based surveys may encourage people to be more honest in their replies. However, anonymity may result in the loss of valuable information about the demographics, preferences, and behaviors of the respondents. To overcome some of the above limitations, online market research methods need to be designed carefully and rigorously. Small companies without proper expertise may outsource their market research to large and experienced companies that have specialized market research departments and expertise.

Privacy Issues in Market Research

Collecting data from customers, sometimes without their knowledge, may constitute an invasion of privacy. For an overview, guidelines, and standards, see **esomar.org/knowledge-and-standards/codes-and-guidelines.php** and **marketingresearch. org/issues-policies/mra-code-marketing-research-standards**.

Biometric and Smartphone Marketing Helps Market Research

Many households have several users; thus, the data collected may not represent any one person's preferences (unless, of course, we are sure that there is one user per device, as in the case of smartphones). Potential solutions are using biometric marketing or smartphones to access individuals.

A **biometric** is one of an individual's unique physical or behavioral traits that can be used to authenticate an individual. By applying the technology to computer users, we can improve security and learn about the user's profile. The question is how to do it. Indeed, there are programs by which users identify themselves to the computer by biometrics, and these are spreading rapidly. Note that utilizing the technology for market research involves social and legal acceptability.

Mobile market research is a method of collecting data though mobile devices including mobile phones, smartphones, and tablets. Typical methods for collecting information are through apps, short message systems (SMS), WAP, mobile Web, and location-based services. A major advantage of mobile market research is that it can be conducted virtually anywhere at any time. However, it does suffer from the limitation that it is hard to define the sampling frame and cannot access the sample without the users' mobile devices. Privacy protection is another key concern for conducting mobile market research. Hence, an organization called ESOMAR has released guidelines for conducting mobile market research (**esomar.org**).

As mobile adoption continues to grow, so does the field of mobile research. While some of these tools are based on the mobile device itself, others are simply conversions of Web-based tools that can be used in the mobile environment (as responsive websites or apps). In the mobile environment, several of these tools may in fact have greater efficiency. Mobile users can take surveys in physical locations or can react to surveys or requests for information based on their location data. For more information about how mobile marketing can be conducted, see **mmra-global.org**.

SECTION 10.3 REVIEW QUESTIONS

1. Describe the objectives of market research.
2. Describe the role of transaction logs and clickstream analysis.
3. Define cookies, Web bugs, and spyware, and describe how they can be used in online market research.
4. Describe how the issue of privacy relates to online market research.
5. Describe the limitations of online market research.
6. Describe how biometrics and smartphones can improve market research.

10.4   WHY WEB ADVERTISING

Advertising on the Web plays an extremely important role in e-commerce. Internet advertising is growing very rapidly, especially in B2C, and companies are changing their advertising strategies to gain a competitive edge. Since the Internet provides interactivity, online ads are also useful for brand building directly through response ads. Based on a 2016 IAB Internet Advertising Report conducted by the professional service network PricewaterhouseCoopers (**pwc.com**), online ad revenue reached a record high of $17.6 billion in Q3 of 2016 in the United States alone, which is a 20% increase from the previous year (see **iab.com/news/q3-2016-internet-ad-revenues-hit-17-6-billion-climbing-20-year-year-according-iab**). In the full year of 2015, mobile advertising jumped 66% from the previous year and overall advertising grew 20.4% for a total of $59.6 billion (see **iab.com/wp-content/uploads/2016/04/IAB_Internet_Advertising_Revenue_Report_FY_2015-final.pdf**).

Search, display/banner ads, and mobile ads are the three most popular types of Internet ads. Social media advertising is another fast-growing area. Statistical trends and predictions reported by **Statistica.com** in late 2016 indicate that in social media advertising:

- Revenue in 2016 will be $14.8 billion.
- A 32.2% increase over 2015.
- There is a predicted a 20% increase in 2017.
- The revenue from each mobile user will grow from $55.95 in 2016 to $65.91 in 2017 (a 17.8% increase).

When individual social media networks are examined, we find (LePage 2016a):

- By the third quarter of 2016, Facebook brought in $6.8 billion in advertising revenue, up from $4.3 billion the year before.
- Twitter advertising revenue totaled $545 million in Q3 of 2016, an increase of 60% year-over-year.
- LinkedIn Marketing Solutions revenue increased 26% year-over-year to $175 million in Q3 of 2016.
- Instagram has over 500 million active monthly users.
- By the third quarter of 2016, Facebook brought in $6.8 billion in advertising revenue, up from $4.3 billion the year before.
- 150 million people use Pinterest every month.
- The number of YouTube channels earning 6 figures per year is up 50% year-over-year.

All these numbers indicate the fast-growing trend in online and mobile advertising. In this section, we concentrate on generic Web advertising.

Overview of Web Advertising

Advertising is the delivery of ads to Internet users in order to influence people to buy a product or a service. Traditional advertising (also known as marketing communication) is an impersonal, one-way mass communication. Telemarketing and direct mail ads attempted to overcome the deficiencies of mass advertising, but they are expensive and their response rate was not too high. For example, a direct mail campaign costs about $1 per person and has a response rate of only 1% to 3%. This makes the cost per responding person in the range of $20 (for a 5% response) to $100 for 1% response. Such an expense can be justified only for high-ticket items (e.g., cars). For a video on how to calculate the cost of responses, see **youtu.be/AcPbfP7Cxg0**.

One of the problems with direct mail advertising was that the advertisers knew very little about the recipients. Market segmentation by various characteristics (e.g., age, income, gender) helped a bit but did not solve the problem. The concept of **interactive marketing** enables marketers and advertisers to interact directly with customers.

On the Internet, a consumer can click an ad to obtain more information or send an e-mail to ask a question. The customer can chat live with the merchant (person or avatar) or with peers in a social network chat room. The Internet enables truly one-to-one advertising.

The Advertising Cycle

Many companies are treating advertising as a cyclical process, as shown in Fig. 10.2. The cyclical process requires a plan to determine the target audience of a campaign and how to reach that audience. Analyzing a campaign after its completion assists a company in understanding the campaign's success or failure. This knowledge is then used for planning future campaigns.

Before we describe the steps in the cycle as it is implemented in Web advertising, let us learn some basic Internet advertising terminology.

Fig. 10.2 The advertising cycle

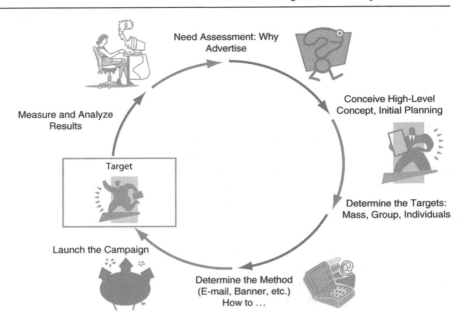

Basic Internet Advertising Terminology

The following terms and their definitions will be of use as you read about Web advertising.

- **Ad views**: The number of times users call up a page that has a banner on it during a specific period; known as *impressions* or *page views.*
- **Click (ad click)**: A count made each time a visitor clicks on an advertising banner to access the advertiser's website.
- **CPM (cost per mille, i.e., thousand impressions)**: The fee an advertiser pays for each 1,000 times a page with a banner ad is shown.
- **Conversion rate**: The percentage of clickers who actually make a purchase.
- **Click-through rate/ratio (CTR)**: The percentage of visitors who are exposed to a banner ad and click on it.
- **Hit**: A request for data from a Web page or file.
- **Landing page**: The page a viewer is directed to after having clicked on a link. In online marketing, this page is used to convert the person from a viewer to a buyer.

Why Internet Advertising?

The major traditional advertising media are television, newspapers, magazines, and radio. However, the market is changing, as many consumers are spending more time on the Internet (about a 32% annual growth) and using mobile devices. For children, the time spent online has overtaken the time spent watching television (Coughlan 2017). Internet advertising is getting more attention. The advertising revenue of Internet advertising exceeded that of broadcast TV, cable TV, and newspapers in 2013, and we can foresee this trend continuing. Hence, online advertising is a clear choice for the future.

Advertising Online and Its Advantages

The major advantages of Internet ads over traditional media advertising are the ability to interact one-to-one with customers and the ability to use rich media (e.g., videos) to grab attention. In addition, ads can be changed easily, and campaigns are usually less costly. In comparison with traditional media, the Internet is the fastest-growing communication medium by far. Worldwide, as of April 2016, the number of Internet users was getting close to 3.6 billion (see **internetlivestats.com/internet-users/**). Of course, advertisers are interested in such a fast-growing community.

Other reasons why Web advertising is growing rapidly include:

- **Cost.** Online ads usually are cheaper than ads in traditional media.
- **Media richness.** Web ads can include rich and diversified media (e.g., videos, animation). In addition, ads can be combined with games and entertainment.
- **Easy updating.** Updating can be done quickly and inexpensively.
- **Personalization.** Web ads can be either one-to-one or addressed to population segments.
- **Location-based.** Using wireless technology and GPS, Web advertising can be location based.
- **Linking to shopping.** It is easy to link from an online ad to a vendor's webstore. Usually, it can be done in one click.

Traditional Versus Online Advertising

Each advertising medium, including the Internet, has its advantages and limitations. Bilos et al. in 2014 compares traditional advertising against Internet advertising (including social networks). They concluded that not only is Internet advertising more cost efficient but also the business impact of Internet ads is larger than traditional ads.

The synergy between TV and online advertising can help attract more attention than either medium on its own. It has been found that a TV campaign increases brand awareness by 27%, whereas a combined TV and online campaign increases it by 45%. A TV campaign increases intent to purchase by 2%, whereas a combined TV and online campaign increases it by 12%.

The impact of Internet ads on newspaper viability is devastating. Many newspapers are disappearing, merging, or losing money. One solution is to increase their digital ads, as the *New York Times* is doing. For more details, see **absolutemg. com/2014/12/23/traditional-media-balancing-effect**.

Internet ads are subject to limitations such as screen size, space, and policies.

SECTION 10.4 REVIEW QUESTIONS

1. Define Web advertising and the major terms associated with it.
2. Describe the reasons for the growth in Web advertising.
3. Describe emerging Internet advertising approaches.
4. List the major benefits of Web advertising.
5. Draw and explain the advertising cycle.
6. What is the impact of online advertising on the viability of newspapers and TV?

10.5 ONLINE ADVERTISING METHODS

A large number of online advertising methods exist. For a list and description, please see **en.wikipedia.org/wiki/Online_ advertising**. Next, we discuss the three major categories of ads.

Major Categories of Ads

Ads can be classified into three major categories: *classified*, *display,* and *interactive*.

Classified Ads

These ads usually use text, but lately may include photos. The ads are grouped according to classification (e.g., cars, rentals). They are the least expensive.

Classified ads can be found on special sites (e.g., see classified ads at **craigslist.org** and **backpage.com**), as well as on online newspapers, e-markets, and portals. In many cases, posting regular-size classified ads is free, but placing them in a larger size, in color, or with some other noticeable features is done for a fee. For examples, see **traderonline.com** and **advertising.microsoft.com.**

Display Ads

These are illustrated advertisements that use graphics, logos, colors, or special designs. These ads are usually not classified, but they can be combined. Display ads are popular offline in billboards, yellow pages, and movies. They are becoming very popular on the Internet as well. All major search-based advertising companies (e.g., Google, Yahoo!, Microsoft) are leveraging their online positions in search advertising into the display ad business.

Interactive Ads

These ads use online or offline interactive media to interact with consumers and to promote products, brands, and services. This is most commonly performed through the Internet, often using video as a delivery medium.

There are several variations in each of these categories. The major methods are presented next.

Banners

A **banner** is a display that is used for advertising on a Web page (words, logos, etc. embedded in the page). A banner ad is frequently linked to an advertiser's Web page. When users "click" on the banner, they are transferred to the advertiser's site. A banner must be designed to catch a consumer's attention. Banners often include images and sometimes video clips and sound. Banner advertising, including pop-up banners, is a popular advertising method on the Web.

There are several sizes and types of banners. The sizes, which are standardized by the Interactive Advertising Bureau (IAB) (**iab.com**), are measured in pixels. **Random banners** appear randomly, not as a result of some action by the user. Companies that want to introduce their new products (e.g., a new movie or CD) or promote their brand use random banners. **Static banners** stay on a Web page regularly. Finally, **pop-up banners** appear in a separate window when its affiliated Web page is activated.

If an advertiser knows something about a visitor, such as his/her user profile, or area of interest, the advertiser will try to match a specific banner with that visitor. Obviously, this kind of targeted, personalized banner is usually most effective. Such **personalized banners** that are tailored to meet the need of target customers are being developed, for example, by Conversant (**conversantmedia.com**).

Live banners are ads where the content can be created or modified at the time the ads pop up instead of being preprogrammed like banner ads. They usually are rich media. For details and examples, see **en.wikipedia.org/wiki/Live_banner**.

Benefits and Limitations of Banner Ads

The major benefit of banner ads is that, by clicking on a banner, users are transferred to an advertiser's site, frequently directly to the shopping page of that site. Another advantage of using banners is the ability to customize them for individual surfers or a market segment of surfers. In many cases, customers are forced to see banner ads while waiting for a page to load, or before they can get the page they requested (a strategy called *forced advertising*). Finally, banners may include attention-grabbing rich multimedia.

The major disadvantage of banners is their cost. If a company demands a successful marketing campaign, it will need to pay high fees for placing banners on websites with high traffic.

However, it seems that viewers have become somewhat immune to banners and simply ignore them. The click-through rate has been declining over time. Because of these drawbacks, it is important to decide where on the screen to place banners (e.g., right side is better than left side, top is better than bottom). Companies such as QQ.com and Taobao.com in China have built behavior labs to track eye movements of consumers to understand how screen location and Web page design may affect viewer attention. Ad blocking tools are also available to install on a browser to remove all banner ads when a Web page is accessed. This also reduces the number of click-throughs.

Pop-Up and Similar-Type Ads

One of the most annoying phenomena in Web surfing is the increased use of pop-ups and similar ads. A **pop-up ad**, also known as *ad spawning*, appears due to the automatic launching of a new browser window when a visitor accesses or leaves a website, when a delay occurs. Pop-ups cover the user's current screen and may be difficult to close. They may include images, audio, or video. They can gain a user's immediate attention, but their use is controversial. Many users strongly object to this advertising method, which they consider to be intrusive. Most browsers provide some options that allow the viewer to block pop-up windows. Some users resort to using specialized applications to block pop-ups and other ads (see **adblockplus.org**). Legal attempts have also been made to control pop-ups because they are basically a form of spam.

Several other tactics, some of them very aggressive, are being used by advertisers, and their use is increasing. These tactics may be accompanied by music, voice, and other rich multimedia.

Pop-Up Videos

Along with the increase in popularity of free viral videos (e.g., on YouTube) comes the pop-up commercial before them. Some can be skipped; others cannot. These commercials usually last for 10 to 20 seconds. These pop-ups may or may not be related to the content of the video you want to watch. Sometimes, video ads come with an incentive, called *incentivized video ads*, which will be described later. In place of standardized videos, some sites, like Hulu, are allowing users to select the video ad that is most interesting to them.

E-Mail Advertising

E-mail marketing refers to the use of e-mails for sending commercial messages to users. E-mail marketing may occur in different formats and for different purposes. Typical e-mail marketing formats are:

1. Using **e-mail advertising** means that ads are attached to e-mails
2. Sending e-mail messages for facilitating vendor-customer relationships (CRM types)
3. Sending e-mail messages for attempting to acquire new customers
4. Sending messages via microblogs or other social media platforms

E-mail messages may be combined with brief audio or video clips to promote a product; some messages provide links that users can click on to make a purchase. Sending coupons and special offers is done by all major retailers, including department stores and supermarkets. Airlines, banks, educational institutions, and anyone else who can get your e-mail will send you e-mail ads.

Major Advantages and Limitations of E-Mail Advertising

The major advantages of e-mail advertising are:

- Low cost
- Target fans of your brand
- Market segmentation
- Calls to action
- Easy to create
- Easy to track
- Easy to share
- Immediacy
- Return on investment

For more details, see **pure360.com/10-benefits-of-email-marketing**, or download a report on e-mail marketing maturity at **pure360.com/maturity-benchmarking-report-2015**.

Using an infographic, Hanford (2016) explains the benefits of e-mail marketing for customer acquisition and retention, increased sales, and CRM.

Limitations

A major limitation of e-mail ads is that these messages are often treated as spam and are blocked by the user's spam control software. In general, using e-mail to send ads (sometimes floods of ads) without the receivers' permission is considered *spamming*.

As the volume of e-mail increases, consumers' tendency to screen and block messages is on the rise as well. Today, most e-mail services permit users to block messages from specific sources or automatically filter certain ads as junk mail.

Implementing E-Mail Advertising

A segmented list of e-mail addresses can be a very powerful tool for a company, helping it to target a group of people that share common characteristics. In many cases, the mailing list is based on membership and loyalty programs, such as an airline's frequent flyer program. For information on how to create a mailing list, consult **topica.com**.

E-mail can also be sent to mobile devices. Mobile phones, in particular, offer advertisers a real chance to advertise interactively and on a one-to-one basis with consumers—anytime, anyplace. Now e-mail ads are targeted to individuals based not only on their user profiles but also on their physical location at any point in time.

A wide variety of software systems exist to help businesses manage e-mail marketing campaigns. These systems allow users to create and send messages, track responses, build customer data, and maintain regulatory compliance. Some leaders in the field are **constantcontact.com**, **mailchimp.com**, and **infusionsoft.com**.

E-Mail Hoaxes

E-mail hoaxes are very popular; some of them have been going on for years (e.g., Neiman Marcus's cookie recipe, the Nigerian Letters, the Homeland Security cashier check hoax). Some of these are scams. For details, see US Federal Trade Commission (**ftc.gov**).

Fraud

Fraud may happen in e-mail ads. For example, a person may receive an e-mail stating that his or her credit card number is invalid or that his or her MSN service will be terminated unless another credit card number is provided by the recipient of the mail. For protection against such fraudulent practices, see **scambusters.org**.

Regulatory Compliance

In the United States, marketers are also required to maintain compliance with the CAN-SPAM act that also users to remove themselves from mailing lists; see **ftc.gov/tips-advice/business-center/guidance/can-spam-act-compliance-guide-business**.

Search Engine Advertisement and Optimization

Search engines are a good mechanism for most people to find information and, therefore, a good platform for online advertising. Placing online ads on Web pages that show results from querying a search engine is known as **search advertising**. If the search result includes your company and product, it is a free advertisement for you. The problem is that the results of a search may include thousands of items, and your product may be not on the first or second page of the results. Note that search advertising includes mobile search and social network search (see **pipl.com**).

Keyword advertising links the appearance of ads with keywords specified by the advertiser. It includes "pay per click." Businesses select the keywords to which they want their advertisements to be searched and matched. Advertisements appear on the screen along with the search results when the chosen keywords are searched. This can substantially increase the likelihood that the advertisement will be viewed and possibly acted on because of its high relevance to user interests. For an example of how this works, see **google.com/adwords/how-it-works/ads-on-google.html**. Google is using two major methods (to be described later) to implement its advertisement strategy. In fact, more than 92% of Google's revenue is in Q3 of 2016 and was generated from advertising.

Other search engines also focus on this type of advertising. The second largest US search engine is Bing (a Microsoft product). In mid-2016, Bing held 21% of the search engine market. For an example of keyword advertising works with Bing, see **advertise.bingads.microsoft.com/en-us/solutions/tools/keyword-planner**.

Search Engine Optimization (SEO)

Search engine optimization (SEO) is a process that improves the visibility of a company or brands on the results page displayed by a search engine. Ideally, the results should be in the top 5 to 10 on the first page. Companies hire search optimizers or try to optimize by themselves. SEO can increase the number of visitors to a website, and therefore companies are willing to pay for this service. For how to do this, see Duermyer (2016). SEO is performed in all types of online searches, including video search, social network search, and image search. According to Google AdWords, "to get your ads to appear when people search for your product or service, the keywords you choose need to match the words or phrases that people use, or should be related to the content of the websites your customers visit." Figure 10.3 shows the general process of SEO. For further details, see Amerland (2015) and **blog.kissmetrics.com/minimalist-seo**. For a free e-book on SEO, visit **offers.hubspot.com/learning-seo-from-the-experts**.

Fig. 10.3 The process of
search engine optimization

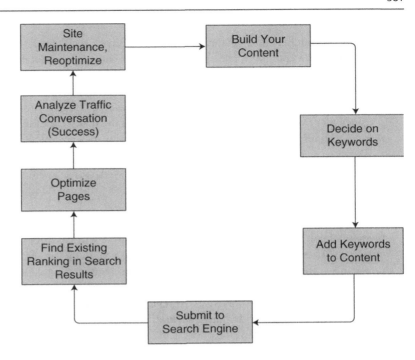

Sponsored Ads (Paid Inclusion)

In addition to optimizing your Web pages so that they will appear on the first page of the search results, you can buy keyword ads to appear on the first page of the results. This is referred to as *paid inclusion* or *sponsored ads*. Your ads will show up on the first page of the results, at the top of the page, or on the right side based on the amount you decide to spend. Google uses auctions (first page bids) to sell the best locations to advertisers. For how keywords work in Google, see **support.google. com/adwords/answer/1704371?hl=en**; for Bing, see **secure.azure.bingads.microsoft.com**.

Google: The Online Advertising King

Google provides several methods of search engine advertising to their clients, generating most of its billions of dollars in revenue and profits from them. Google uses a behavioral marketing algorithm to determine users' interests while they search for information and then targets (matches) advertisements to them. Google is continuously improving its matching algorithms (see Williams 2016).

Google's major advertising platform is composed of two programs: Google's AdWords and AdSense, and it can be supported by Google Analytics.

Google's Major Advertising Methods: AdWords and AdSense

The mechanisms of how AdWords and AdSense work are described below:

Google AdWords

AdWords is an advertising program for sponsored ads. Whenever you use Google to search for something, you will notice URLs with colored backgrounds, titled "sponsored links" on the right hand side or on the top of the page. These include Google AdWords participants. According to Google.com, these URLs are created by advertisers who select a few key terms related to their brands. They also choose how much they want to spend to "buy" these key terms (up to a daily dollar limit). Google uses ranking algorithms to match the advertisers' selected key terms with the searchers' search activities. Typically, if a searcher types in a selected keyword, a banner ad will appear in the sponsored links column.

Then, if the searcher clicks on the ad (to go to the advertiser's page), the sponsor vendor is billed according to the agreed upon rate (payments are made from the prepaid budget). For details and success stories, see **adwords.google.com**. Google AdWords is a "pay-per-click" type of advertising. You pay only if people click on your ads. How it works: You create your ads and choose your keywords (you can also target your ads); when someone searches on Google using your keyword, your ad may appear next to the search results; you gain more customers.

Since all advertisers like their ads to appear on the first page of the search results, Google devised a bidding system that determines which ads are shown where and how fees are calculated.

Despite its success, AdWords by itself does not provide the best one-to-one targeting. Better results may be achieved in many cases through a complementary program—AdSense (both are offered on mobile devices).

Google AdSense

Google's AdSense is an *affiliate program*. In other words, website publishers can earn money by displaying targeted Google ads on their website. In collaboration with Google, participating website owners (publishers) can add search engines to their own sites. Then, when someone is searching for a term related to the content of the affiliated websites, they can see the Google ad and, if interested, will be directed to the advertisers' text, video, or image ads, which are crafted by Google.

The matching of the displayed ad to content of the affiliates is based on Google's proprietary algorithm. This matching algorithm is known to be fairly accurate. The key for success is the quality and appearance of both the affiliate's pages and the ads, as well as the popularity of the affiliate's sites. Hundreds of thousands of companies and individuals participate in the affiliate program. Google provides the affiliates with analytic tools and procedures that help convert visitors to customers (see the information at **google.com/adsense**). Google's affiliates earn money when visitors click on the ads. The advertisers pay Google. Google shares the revenue generated from advertisers with the affiliates. For a tutorial video on using AdSense, visit **youtu.be/TmFB_kz8fyc**.

AdSense has become a popular method of advertising on websites because the advertisements are less intrusive than in other programs, and the content is often better targeted. For an example of a site using AdSense, see **rtcmagazine.com**.

Google's success is attributed to the accuracy of the matches, the large number of advertisers in its network, the ability to use ads in many languages, and the clarity of the ads. Google offers several types of AdSense programs. See details at **webopedia.com/TERM/A/adsense.html**. Competing programs are offered by eBay and Yahoo! (see eBay Partner Network at **partnernetwork.ebay.com**). For an overview on how AdSense works, see **google.com/adsense/start/how-it-works.html**.

Example: Using Cookies at DotMailer

Google the AdWords platform is meant to help businesses advertise their websites and products by purchasing keywords within the Google search engine. Many times these activities help drive traffic to a website and offer a good return on investment (ROI) for the owner. In some cases, however, the return is much more than expected.

In 2016, Charismatico Dancewear, Dresses, and Costumes (**charismatico-dancewear.com**) engaged the help of an AdWords consulting firm to try to drive traffic to their website. As a part of the consultative process, it was determined that this company filled a unique niche in the market with its showgirl dresses. Based on this knowledge of the company, it was possible to identify seldom-used keywords at low values that could be used to support the company's unique selling proposition.

Over the course of one year, following this strategy the company was able to leverage its AdWords usage and earned over $345,000 from just over $22,000 in marketing spend. For more information, see **aliraza.co/google-adwords-case-study**

Viral Marketing

Viral marketing (viral advertising) refers to electronic *word-of-mouth* (WOM) marketing—the spreading of a word, story, or some media. It is a marketing strategy where a company encourages the spreading of information and opinions from person to person about a product or service. This can be done by e-mails, text messaging, in chat rooms, via instant messaging, by posting messages on social network walls (e.g., Facebook), and in discussion groups or by microblogging (e.g., using Twitter). It is especially popular in social networks. Having people forward messages to friends, telling them about a good product is an example of viral marketing. Viral marketing has been used offline for generations, but now, being online, its speed and reach are multiplied and is done at minimal cost to vendors, because the people who transmit the messages are usually paid nothing. The process is analogous to the spread of computer (or regular) viruses using a self-replication process. Viral messages may take the form of text messages, video clips, or interactive games.

An ad agency supplies Internet users with something of value for free, which encourages them to share with others, so as many people as possible can see the message. For example, advertisers might distribute a small e-game or a video embedded within a sponsor's e-mail sent to thousands of people hoping that they will forward it to tens of thousands of people. Viral marketing also was used at the pioneering of Hotmail (now closed), a free e-mail service that grew from zero to 12 million subscribers in its initial 18 months, and to more than 50 million subscribers in about four years. Each e-mail sent via Hotmail carried an embedded advertisement to the recipient to sign up for a free Hotmail account. Facebook's initial reputation was achieved in a similar way, but much faster. Viral marketing can be effective, efficient, and relatively inexpensive when used properly. eWOM can also influence consumer judgment about products. For further details, see **learnmarketing.net**. For six steps to an effective viral marketing strategy, see Burton (2016). For a strategy, see Wright (2014).

eWOM constitutes a multitude of activities, which can be divided into specific categories (see Weisfeld-Spolter et al. 2014). One category is a "higher degree" of e-word of mouth (e.g., viral marketing, e-referral marketing), and the other is "lower degree" marketing (e.g., social networks, brand communities).

One of the downsides of eWOM marketing is that many customers complain about receiving unsolicited e-mails, comparing them to telemarketing calls. Consumers may use spam blockers to filter out unsolicited e-mails, which may appear to be spam.

The messages circulated in viral marketing may be in different formats and serve different purposes. A typical one is a text message about a product or service sent for persuading consumers.

Example: Netflix Socks

Netflix is a streaming video service with fans who are sometimes concerned with "first-world problems" such as falling asleep while watching television. In collaboration with MakeIt, the company created a DIY set of socks with accelerometers that could determine if the user had fallen asleep, allowing the show they were watching to be paused. Netflix shared all these details with users and even included patterns for knitting. This low-cost, low-effort activity quickly went viral. To see the video: **youtube.com/watch?v=PMtqy8edUq8**. Viral campaigns are so important that they even receive industry awards.

For details, see **webbyawards.com/winners/2016/advertising-media/individual/viral-marketing/**.

Video Advertising

Video advertising refers to the insertion of video ads into advertisements or regular online contents. The Internet Advertising Bureau (IAB) believes in the importance of video ads and created a guide to the topic; see **slideshare.net/hardnoyz/iab-guide-to-video-advertising-online** and the accompanying document transcript. Video ads are common in Internet TV programs.

Video ads are growing rapidly, mainly due to the popularity of YouTube and similar sites. Online video is growing nearly 42% annually, while TV viewing continues to fall. For statistics, see **marketingcharts.com**.

Video ads appear all over the Web both as unsolicited pop-ups and when you give permission to see a demo or information about a product. Video ads have become very popular in the Web 2.0 environment and in social networking. An April 2016 IAB report shows a growth of digital video ads revenue of 85% from 2014 in the United States (download a copy at **iab.com/wp-content/uploads/2016/04/2016-IAB-Video-Ad-Spend-Study.pdf**).

The major reason for the popularity of videos is that almost everyone who uses the Internet now watches online videos. Videos are also viewed on all mobile devices (e.g., smartphones, tablets), and they can be posted on Twitter. Social media and the accessibility to increased broadband mobile access are also reasons for the growth of online video usage. Watching videos on mobile devices has become very popular on airplanes and other public transportation.

There are primarily two approaches to incorporating videos in Web advertising: (1) per-product videos that are embedded in regular product pages, adding product details, and (2) editorial-style videos that allow consumers to discover such products. Many retailers are adding product-specific videos to their e-commerce sites. For a complete overview of video marketing and advertising, see **webvideomarketing.org/video-advertising** and Le Vu (2016).

According to a Cisco survey, most large online retailers are using videos to help sell products. Forrester Research found that most major retailers are making product videos central to their marketing strategies. According to a statistical digest (per Insivia 2017):

- By 2017, online video will account for 74% of all online traffic.
- 55% of people watch videos online every day.
- Using the word "video" in an e-mail subject line boosts the open rates by 19%.
- Including video in a landing page can increase conversion by 80%.
- Almost 50% of Internet users look for videos related to a product or service before visiting a store.

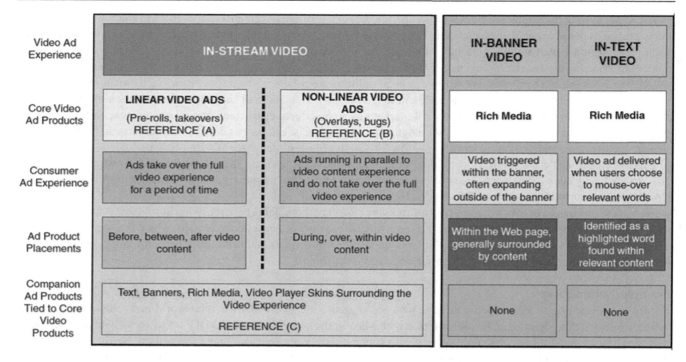

Fig. 10.4 IAB model of video advertising (Source: Interactive Advertising Bureau. "A Digital Video Advertising Overview." January 2008. iab.net/media/file/dv-report-v3.pdf (accessed April 2016). Used with permission)

Some of the leading companies in this area are YouTube, Vimeo, Dailymotion, and Veoh. Figure 10.4 illustrates the IAB Model of video advertising. For information on Google's video advertising platform, see **google.com/ads/video**.

Almost any video that you click on is preceded by a 10 to 30 second commercial that can be skipped only some of the time. This kind of "forced view" commercial has been found to be effective because people are used to seeing commercials when watching TV programs. More TV shows are coming to the Internet, frequently with video ads.

Viral Videos

A **viral video** is a video that is spread rapidly through the process of online information sharing. These videos become popular when they are circulated via e-mail, SMSs, blogs, discussion forums, and so forth. This way, people share videos that receive more attention, sometimes drawing millions of viewers in a short time. Popular sites that are used for sharing viral videos include YouTube (**youtube.com**) and Vimeo (**vimeo.com**). For the top viral video ad campaigns, see **www.visible-measures.com/insights/charts/adage**.

Viral videos are liked (or disliked) so much that viewers send them to others, spreading the word about them quickly across the Internet. Marketers are using viral videos by inserting ads in videos or by using ads as pop-ups prior to the start of presentations; see **adage.com/section/the-viral-video-chart/674**. Note that if the reactions to a video are positive, the buzz can be useful, but negative reactions can hurt the brand. *Baseline* magazine (**baselinemag.com**) periodically provides a list of the 10 best viral marketing videos. For viral video marketing case studies (the best virals of 2016), see **time.com/4602738/best-viral-videos-2016/**.

Consumer-Generated Videos

Many companies are utilizing user-generated videos for their online ads and even for their TV commercials.

YouTube is the largest advertising platform for video ads. It has billions of videos and is growing rapidly. YouTube permits selected marketers to upload videos with ads to the site. Google's AdSense ad distribution network also offers ad-supported video clips. Another way for advertisers to use viral video is by creating contests (see **onlinevideocontests.com**).

Example: QuickBooks' Small Business Big Game Competition

Beginning in 2016, QuickBooks, a provider of small and medium-sized business accounting software, offered its users the chance to win a TV spot during the Super Bowl. The company narrowed down the applicants and then allowed the public to vote on their favorite ad. In 2016, Death Wish Coffee Company won with their depiction of Vikings and coffee. See the video at **deathwishcoffee.com/blogs/news/54920833-thank-you-for-voting-we-won**.

Interactive Videos

The term **interactive video** refers to a technique that is used to mix user interaction with videos. The interaction is controlled by a computer for entertainment, advertisement, or educational activities. Interactive videos are popular because:

- Increased bandwidth enables rapid downloading of videos.
- Good search engines find videos that have been developed.
- Both the media and advertisers have increased the use of videos.
- Incentives such as contests and gifts are offered for the use of interactive videos.

The following are representative types of interactive videos:

Video Click-Throughs
VideoClix.tv and Clickthrough.com have developed tools that allow people who watch videos to click on any person, place, banner ad, and so forth in the video.

Live Interactive Videos
In live interactive videos, you can see certain events in real time and sometimes interact with those in the video. For example, GE presented the company's annual report in a banner ad during a live Webcast of its annual meeting. Viewers were able to interact with the presenters, asking questions or making comments.

Example: Interactive Dressing Room
Metail.com created an interactive online video dressing room. It includes a wide variety of women's fashions and styles. The animated models appear with your selected brands, and you can control their movements (e.g., turn them around). For details, see **metail.com**.

Augmented Reality in Advertising

Augmented reality (AR) can be utilized by advertisers and marketers, especially in the fashion industry.

Examples of AR Applications
In the opening case, IKEA used an augmented reality application to help customers visualize how furniture would look in their homes. Several examples of interactive applications are provided at **en.wikipedia.org/wiki/Augmented_reality**. These include real estate and architecture, product and industries design, tourism, and more. Companies such as Nissan, Best Buy, Walt Disney, and Burger King have experimented with using AR in advertising. For more examples, see Schrack (2016).

Retailers in the clothing, fashion, and jewelry industries are using this technology, because in their industries, visualization is critical. For example, ClothiaCorp combines AR with real-time merchandise recommendations. It allows shoppers to "try on" clothing and share the "how they look" with family and friends, in real time.

Advertising in Chat Rooms and Forums

Chat rooms can be used for advertising. For example, Mattel Corp. sells about one-third of its Barbie dolls to collectors. These collectors use chat rooms to make comments or ask questions that are subsequently answered by Mattel's staff. The Xiaomi case in this chapter runs a smartphone forum for its product design and advertising.

Advertisers sometimes use online fantasy sports (e.g., available at Yahoo!, ESPN, and more) to send ads to specific sports fans (e.g., fans of the National Football League or Major League Baseball). Online fantasy sports attract millions of visitors every month.

CASE 10.3: EC APPLICATION
SUPPORTING MARKETING CAMPAIGNS WITH SOFTWARE SYSTEMS

The Problem

As the options and opportunities for online advertising grow, so does the complexity. Businesses have the ability to market online in a vast number of ways. This can include everything from search engine marketing, e-mail marketing, to social media marketing. Keeping track of all of these activities may be difficult, especially for small businesses. Managing data, calculating efficiency, placing orders, and generating reports on results can be a heavy burden.

The Solution

To help resolve these issues, there are many software applications and services that are available to help businesses manage this workload. Many of these applications are specific to the type of marketing being undertaken.

- **Search engine marketing example: Kenshoo (kenshoo.com)**
  Kenshoo allows you to manage, automate, and optimize multiple search engine marketing campaigns. The system provides a suite of tools that allow you to plan, execute, and evaluate keyword purchases across a number of search engines including Google Bing Yahoo and AOL. The system has advanced workflows that allow for the automation of this process with intelligent agents that suggest the most beneficial mix of keywords and search engine providers.
- **Social media example: Hootsuite (hootsuite.com)**
  HootSuite is an integrated package that allows you to manage all of your social media marketing activities from one central location. The system allows you to have oversight of all current running campaigns, the ability to schedule campaigns, interact with customers, and collaborate with your team. The system helps you manage any amounts being spent and allows you to collect and analyze data on your social media endeavors.
- **E-mail marketing example: MailChimp (metail.com)**
  MailChimp is a comprehensive e-mail marketing system that allows users to create marketing e-mails using well-designed templates and special interactive features, send those messages to defined user groups, and track the results of those messages. Campaigns of multiple messages can be created, and different rules can be set for users based on their levels of interaction. The system also allows you to generate detail reports on the results of your campaigns.

Questions

1. Why would businesses want to use supportive software systems for their online marketing activities?
2. For each of the selected systems, what is the main advantage?
3. For each of the name systems, go online and find an alternative.

SECTION 10.5 REVIEW QUESTIONS

1. Define banner ads and describe their benefits and limitations.
2. Describe the issues surrounding pop-ups and similar ads.
3. Explain how e-mail is used for advertising.
4. Describe the search engine optimization technique and what it is designed for.
5. Describe Google's AdWords and AdSense.
6. Describe video ads and their growing popularity.
7. Describe augmented reality advertising.

10.6   MOBILE MARKETING AND ADVERTISING

As the adoption of mobile devices grows, so does the growth of mobile commerce and the associated advertising. Mobile devices both in the United States and internationally are becoming more and more ubiquitous.

In 2016, it was estimated that there were more than 2.6 billion smartphone users worldwide, and 37% of all website visits came from mobile devices (see **deviceatlas.com/blog/16-mobile-market-statistics-you-should-know-2016**). In fact, the number of mobile users exceeded the number of desktop Internet users for the first time (see **smartinsights.com/mobile-marketing/mobile-marketing-analytics/mobile-marketing-statistics**). Other important developments include:

- 77% of Americans own a smartphone.
- 1 out of 10 US users only uses a smartphone for Internet access.
- Younger Americans are more likely to have smartphones and use them more frequently.

(from pewinternet.org/fact-sheet/mobile)

This is a major shift in end user behavior and expectations for e-commerce. These changes demand a response from businesses that market to individuals and employ e-commerce systems. Because of the volume of traffic and users in this mobile market, businesses must address this market if they wish to maintain their existing market share.

The rapid growth of mobile devices provides another arena for EC marketing and advertising. For example, the ratio of mobile handsets, including smartphones, to desktop and laptop computers is approximately 2 to 1 and growing. A 2016 estimation by eMarketer indicates that the global annual mobile ad spending has an increase of 38%, reaching $43.6 billion in 2016, and is predicted to reach $67 billion in 2017, a 54% growth. This represents a great opportunity for online mobile marketing and advertising. (See **emarketer.com/Article/Digital-Ad-Spending-Surpass-TV-Next-Year/1013671** and **emarketer.com/Article/Three-Agencies-Release-Estimates-2017-Ad-Spending/1014804**.)

Mobile Marketing and Mobile Commerce

Mobile marketing and advertising are generally considered a subset of both mobile commerce and mobile marketing. Mobile marketing takes several forms, such as using SMS (e.g., Twitter), as well as games and videos. Their major elements are described next.

Defining Mobile Marketing

Mobile marketing is frequently defined as the use of mobile devices and wireless infrastructure as a means of marketing and advertising. The marketer intends to access potential customers through wireless information channels. The Mobile Marketing Association (**mmaglobal.com**) provides definitions of advertising, apps, messaging, m-commerce, and CRM on all mobile devices, including smartphones and tablets.

Mobile marketing includes sales, market research, customer service, and advertising, all supported by mobile computing. Companies can devise contests where customers describe the quality of a new product, and the sellers can post coupons and promotions. You can make ads interactive since mobile computing provides a direct link between vendors and consumers.

Mobile Advertising

Mobile advertising (m-advertising) is defined by the IAB (2016) as "Advertising tailored to and delivered through wireless mobile devices such as smartphones (e.g. Blackberry, iPhone, Android, etc.), feature phones (e.g. lower-end mobile phones capable of accessing mobile content), and media tablets (e.g. iPad, Samsung Galaxy Tablet, etc.)." Mobile advertising ranges from simple text messaging to intelligent interactive messaging on mobile devices. It involves several key players, such as the advertisers, mobile ad networks, mobile apps, and mobile devices.

Figure 10.5 shows how mobile ads work. A company hires a mobile advertiser to create a mobile ad and specifies the promotional criteria. The mobile ad is then sent to a mobile advertising network. The original network forwards these ads to multiple mobile networks and keeps track of the distribution and responses to these ads. The ad will reach the mobile user through proper mobile devices and apps. The user's response is then transmitted to the advertiser and the company through mobile networks.

Fig. 10.5 The process of
mobile advertising

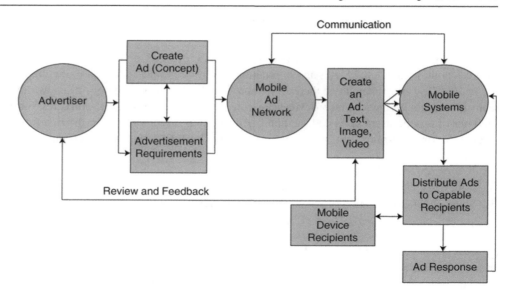

Interactive Mobile Advertising

Interactive mobile advertising refers to the delivery of interactive marketing contents via mobile devices, mostly tablets and smartphones. The inclusion of the word "interactive" points to the fact that this is a two-way communication that may include a customer response (e.g., placing an order or asking a question). For a comprehensive guideline, see the IAB Mobile Web Advertising Measurement Guidelines at **iab.com/guidelines/iab-measurement-guidelines**.

Types of Mobile Ads

Mobile ads may appear in different forms. The most popular one is short text messages. Other forms include rich media advertising, advergaming, and ads appearing during TV shows and movies on mobile devices.

Short Message Ads

SMS ads are commercial messages sent in the form of short text messages. They are quite popular and SMS mobile banner ads are growing rapidly due to the increased popularity of smartphones and 4G networks. Several major advertising portals have been launched by both private mobile advertisers and portals (e.g., D2 in Japan). This type of ad is best for existing customers that have opted into the system because they see particular value in the products or services being offered.

One advantage of SMS is that users can send them quickly and privately from any place and almost any time. A major drawback, however, is that short messages may interrupt and annoy the recipients.

Location-Based Ads

Location-sensitive businesses can take advantage of this feature to deliver location-based ads. Location-based mobile ads have the potential to change many existing advertising paradigms by using the GPS system available in phones. Marketers may be able to determine the location of consumers and based on that location target advertisements to them.

This adds another layer to the ability to target an individual consumer. Not only can marketers understand an individual's preferences, but they can now isolate that consumer at a particular place and time.

For example, if a fast food restaurant knows a customer's preferences for food items, they can now note when that user is close to the restaurant and then target advertisements and potentially coupons to the user based on this confluence of preferences and location.

Location-based ads are also potentially beneficial for brick-and-mortar locations. By knowing when an individual is in a store, it is possible to converge the physical experience and the virtual experience using a mobile app or other location-based tools.

For example, a-mobile app may be able to remember personal information like clothing sizes, and this information can be integrated into the selection process at a store.

There are several mobile location-based advertising techniques that are available, and the most often cited are:

- Hyper-contextual targeting—using location targeted ads to provide additional experiences
- Geo-aware targeting—using real-time location information to target specific advertisements
- Place-based targeting—using locations and a specific time frame to provide access to features
- Geo-fencing—targeting users with in particular geographic boundaries
- Geo-conquesting—targeting users when they are close to a location and convincing them to move to a different location

Each of these strategies has unique properties that could be implemented depending on the specific marketing and advertising goals of a business. While some of these techniques are very specialized, others could be used by a wide variety of retailers or other businesses (Mobile Ads 2016).

Mobile Marketing and Advertising Campaigns

There are basically four classes of online campaigns: information, entertainment, raffles, and coupons. These classes focus on one or more of the following six objectives:

1. **Building brand awareness.** Increase customers' ability to recognize and recall a brand.
2. **Changing brand image.** Change the customers' perception of the brand.
3. **Promoting sales.** Stimulate quicker or greater purchase of products or services.
4. **Enhancing brand loyalty.** Increase consumers' commitment to repurchase the brand.
5. **Building customer databases.** Collect data about the mobile device, data network, or profiles of customers.
6. **Stimulating mobile word of mouth.** Encourage customers to share ads with other customers via their mobile devices.

Obviously, these are the same types of campaigns and objectives underlying traditional marketing approaches. Currently, SMS and e-mails are the principal technologies used to deliver advertisements to mobile devices. However, richer content and advertising is expanding with improved bandwidth.

Recent mobile marketing campaigns conducted by retailers have been very successful. For example, the "Singles Day" (November 11, 2016) sales resulted in over $17.8 billion, with 84% generating from mobile devices. (See **https://techcrunch.com/2016/11/11/alibaba-singles-day-2016**.)

Mobile Marketing Implementation Guidelines

Although organizations such as the Direct Marketing Association have established codes of practice for Internet marketing, including the use of mobile media, most industry pundits agree that the codes are not well suited for the dynamic nature of mobile commerce. Therefore, the mobile media industry has established a set of guidelines and "best practices" for mobile advertising. The Global Code of Conduct from the Mobile Marketing Association (MMA; **mmaglobal.com**) is indicative of the types of practices promoted by the industry. The basic principles of the code include four sections: Notice, choice and consent, customization and constraints, and enforcement and accountability. For practical tactics by large advertising companies, see Eslinger (2014). See also Rowles (2017).

Tools to Support Mobile Advertisement

A large number of applications, tools, and methods are available to support advertising in m-commerce. There are millions of applications (apps) that have been developed for iPhone and Android-based mobile devices that can be downloaded from App Stores (e.g., Google Play and Apple store). Applications include features such as: finding products, places, or events. For details and a marketing glossary, see **where2getit.com**.

Mobile Ad Trends

Several positive predictions have been made about the future of mobile ads. According to **entrepreneur.com/slide-show/254425** and Van Camp (2016), the following are the important trends that advertisers need to watch:

1. Content marketing will improve the mobile marketing experience.
2. Instead of Big Data, it's about accurate data on mobile—and this data will be coveted.
3. Video on mobile is growing, and targeting by location is key.
4. Higher-resolution video will be supported and available.
5. Virtual reality will create new ad formats.
6. Mobile accessories/wearables will increase functionality and marketing opportunities.
7. Beyond cross-screen, mobile marketers will align unified screens with in-store touch points.

Example: Innovative Sticker Advertising

In addition to these five trends, we also see the increasing importance of mobile social media, such as **whatsapp.com**, **wechat.com**, and **line.me/en**. Creative advertising methods such as stickers offer new ways of advertising. A sticker is a small image (like an "emoticon") that can be used to show certain emotions such as love, hate, and so forth. It is very popular for Line users. Line allows a business to develop a set of eight sponsored fun stickers (with company logo or advertising messages) at a fixed cost. Line users can download free chat stickers from Google Play and iTunes.

Note: For a comprehensive collection of articles about mobile advertising, see **mashable.com/category/mobile-advertising** and Mobile Commerce Daily (**mobilecommercedaily.com**).

Marketing Through Apps

Traditional e-commerce activities could be expected to take place within a website, but mobile commerce may be different. While websites can be designed to be responsive to both desktop and mobile devices, some cases may demand a mobile app instead of a traditional website. Advantages of apps over responsive websites (from VentureBeat 2016) include:

- Apps have the benefit of being resident on a user's smartphone, and they can be designed to work perfectly within that operating system environment.
- Users may also be more comfortable using an app on a smartphone for security reasons.
- Interface design for an app may be more intuitive.
- Apps are generally the best choice when there is a mobile commerce transaction that will take place often or when the transaction has detailed steps or configurations that are needed.
- Faster response times are possible with an app.
- Apps are always available on a smartphone reminding the customer of the business.

Some companies may choose to have both a responsive website and an app, giving the customer the choice of which method they want to use. Many experts believe that because of its inherent flexibility and ability to be customized, the app has the upper hand versus the website. Apps are generally more time-consuming and expensive for businesses to create, but many feel that these costs are outweighed by the benefits that have been presented.

There are many examples of innovative mobile applications with ties to mobile Commerce. These applications can serve as customized catalogs, auction clients, product configuration systems, menus and food ordering lists, augmented reality systems, or gamified commerce (see **practicalecommerce.com/articles/78916-13-Innovative-Mobile-Commerce-Apps**).

SECTION 10.6 REVIEW QUESTIONS

1. Why is it important for businesses to respond to the growth of mobile devices?
2. Define mobile marketing (provide at least three definitions). Why are there several definitions?
3. What drives mobile advertising?
4. What is the role of SMS in mobile ads?
5. Define interactive mobile advertising.

6. Describe the process of mobile advertising.
7. What are the benefits of location-based ads?
8. What are the similarities and differences between traditional media and mobile marketing/ad campaigns?
9. What are the trends in mobile advertising in the near future?
10. When are mobile apps superior to responsive websites?

10.7 ADVERTISING STRATEGIES AND PROMOTIONS

Several advertising strategies can be used on the Internet. In this section, we present some major strategies and implementation concerns.

Permission Advertising

One solution to the flood of ads that people receive via e-mail that is used by advertisers is **permission advertising** or *permission marketing* (or the *opt-in approach*), in which users register with vendors and agree to accept advertisements (see **returnpath.com**). For example, one of the authors of this book agreed to receive a number of e-commerce newsletters via e-mail, knowing that some would include ads. This way, the authors of this book, for example, can keep abreast of what is happening in the field. The authors also agreed to accept e-mails from certain research companies, newspapers, travel agencies, and more. These include ads. The vendors publish and send valuable (and usually free) information to us. Note that some vendors ask permission from consumers to send them other users' recommendations, but they do not ask whether they can use historical purchasing data to create the recommendations.

For extensive information from Seth Godin, see **sethgodin.com/permission/thanks.asp**, or for a short video that summarizes the concepts, see the video at **youtu.be/V8xw9J0EbhA**.

Other Advertising Strategies

Many advertising strategies exist both for wired and wireless advertisement systems. For examples, see **www.opentracker.net/article/online-advertising-strategies** and **ultracart.com/resources/articles/ecommerce-advertising**.

Affiliate Marketing and Advertising

Affiliate marketing is a type of "performance-based-marketing" used mainly as a revenue source for the referring organization and as a marketing tool for the sellers. Earlier in this chapter, we introduced Google's AdSense. This is an example of *affiliate marketing*. However, the fact that the vendor's logo is placed on many other websites is free advertising as well. Consider Amazon.com, whose logo can be seen on more than 1 million affiliate sites! Moreover, CDNow (a subsidiary of Amazon.com) and Amazon.com both are pioneers in the "get paid to view" or "listen to" commercials also used in affiliate marketing.

Affiliate Networks

A key to successful affiliate advertising is to have a good affiliate partner network. An **affiliate network** is a network created as a marketplace where publishers (affiliates) and merchants (affiliate programs) can collaborate. Examples of affiliate networks are: Rakuten LinkShare (**linkshare.com**) and CJ Affiliate by Conversant (**cj.com**). For the Top Affiliate Marketing Networks of 2016, see **mthink.com/top-20-affiliate-networks-2016**.

Ads as a Commodity: Paying People to Watch Ads

In some cases, people are paid by advertisers (money or discounts) to view ads (also called "*ads as a commodity*"). This approach is used, for example, at Bing Rewards (get rewards for watching videos, playing games) at CreationsRewards searching the Web with Bing, and others. The HitBliss app pays you to watch commercials (but you must pay attention!). Consumers usually need to show some personal interest in the material viewed and then they receive targeted ads based on their personal interests. Each banner is labeled with the amount to be paid if the consumer reads the ad. If interested, the consumer clicks the banner to read it, and after he or she passes some tests to assure they read the content, the customer is paid for the effort. Readers can sort and choose what they read, and the advertisers can vary the payments to reflect the frequency and enthusiasm of the readers. Payments may be cash, credit, or product discounts. This method is used with smartphones, too.

Personalized Ads

Since the Internet contains too many irrelevant ads, customized ads can help. The heart of e-marketing is a customer database, which includes registration data and information gleaned from site visits. Companies use the one-to-one approach to send customized ads to consumers. Using this feature, a marketing manager can customize display ads based on user profiles.

Advertising as a Revenue Model

Many of the dot-com failures from 2000 to 2002 were caused by a revenue model that contained advertising income as the only or the major revenue source. Many small portals failed, but several large ones are dominating the field: Google, Facebook, AOL, and Yahoo!. However, even these heavy-traffic sites only started to show a significant profit after 2004. Too many websites are competing with limited advertising money. Thus, almost all portals are adding other sources of revenue.

However, if careful, a small site can survive by concentrating on a niche area. For example, NFL Rush (**nflrush.com**) is doing it well. It generates millions of dollars in advertising and sponsorship fees by concentrating on NFL fans, mostly kids 6 to 13 years old. The site attracts millions of visitors by providing comprehensive and interactive content and a chance to win prizes. It directs you to the NFL Shop for each team where sponsors such as Visa and U.S. Bank pay for the free games and the prize.

An important component in a revenue model is the *pay-per-click (PPC)* formula.

Pay per click (PPC) is a popular Internet advertising payment formula where advertisers pay sites only when someone clicks on their ad. Payments are made to search engines and other sites (e.g., affiliates). For tips on how to economize the cost of using PPC, see **advertise.com/ad-solutions/contextual/overview**.

Choose-Your-Own-Ad Format

AdSelector is a format created in 2010, which lets viewers choose their own ads. The AdSelector allows consumers to select what ads they like to view within the video clips (they are presented with two or three options). This model has been in use mostly for online videos with Hulu leadership. Users like this option and, according to research, are twice as likely to click on an ad. Recently the video content streaming service Hulu.com began using a similar system that allows viewers to select the commercial they would like to watch before beginning a program (Hulu, LLC 2015).

Live Web Events for Advertising

Live Web events (concerts, shows, interviews, debates, webcasts, videos), if done properly, can generate tremendous public excitement and drive massive traffic to a website. Some of the best practices for successful live Web events are:

- Carefully planning content, audiences, interactivity levels, and schedules
- Including as much rich media as possible
- Conducting appropriate promotions via e-mails, social media sites, and streaming media, as well as conducting proper offline and online advertisements
- Preparing for quality delivery
- Analyzing audience feedback so that improvements can be made

A global event can allow a product to debut in different locations. Facebook is experimenting with real-time ads in live videos (see **digiday.com/platforms/facebook-live-real-time-ads**).

Note: Web-based seminars, often called *webinars*, are becoming more popular to promote more knowledge-intensive products (see **gotomeeting.com**).

Localization in Advertising

The reach of Internet marketing is quite broad. An ad may be viewed around the world. This is an advantage but could also be a drawback because culture differences may cause different interpretations of the same message in different communities. Hence, localization of ad messages is an important consideration for advertisers.

Localization in EC refers to the transformation and adaptation of Web content media products and advertising materials to fit the Web environment of a certain region or country. It is usually done following a set of international guidelines. An important aspect is that of language localization. Web page translation (see **lionbridge.com**) is just one aspect of localization. However, several other aspects, such as culture, are also important. For example, a US jewelry manufacturer that displayed its products on a white background was astonished to find that this display might not appeal to customers in some countries where a blue background is preferred.

If a company aims at the global market where there are millions of potential customers, it must make an effort to localize its Web pages. This may not be a simple task because of the following factors:

- Many countries do business in English, but the English used may differ in terminology, spelling, and culture (e.g., United States versus United Kingdom versus Australia).
- Without a proper translation program, accented characters cannot be converted to English and other languages. Thus, the translation may be inaccurate. If text includes an accented character, the accent will disappear when converted into English, which may result in an incorrect translation.
- Hard-coded text and fonts cannot be changed, so they will stay in their original format in the translated material.
- Graphics and icons look different to viewers in different countries. For example, a US mailbox resembles a European trash can.
- When translating into Asian languages, and so forth, significant cultural issues must be addressed, for example, how to address older adults in a culturally correct manner.
- Date formats that are written as mm/dd/yy (e.g., June 8, 2016) in the United States are written as dd/mm/yy (e.g., 8 June 2016) in many other countries. Therefore, "6/8" would have two meanings (June 8 or August 6), depending on the location of the writer.
- Consistency in document translation in several different documents can be very difficult to achieve.

For more details on localization, download the 2016 State of E-Commerce Localization Report at **translatemedia.com/ us/blog-usa/state-ecommerce-localisation-2016-report/** or watch an interesting video on "How to Conduct Successful Cross-border E-commerce in China" at **youtu.be/L7ZwMwHfqzI**.

Developing an Online Advertising Plan

Advertising online is a competitive necessity for most businesses these days. With so many different media and advertising methods available, a challenge is to develop an effective advertising plan within budget constraints. A life cycle process composed of six steps to build and maintain an advertising plan is illustrated in Fig. 10.6.

1. **Determine the goal of the advertising project:** The goal needs to be specific—is it for gaining brand awareness, traffic to the website, or higher revenue?
2. **Identify the target customers:** A group of target customers must be determined for the advertising plan. As we have discussed in this chapter, customer segmentation is useful for reducing costs and increasing effectiveness. Depending on the nature of the campaign, segmentation may be based on demographics or other criteria.

Fig. 10.6 Life cycle of advertising plans

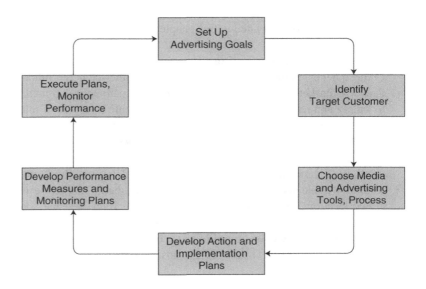

3. **Choose media and advertising tools:** Once the target customer is chosen, the advertising plan should select proper media and tools that can access the target customers. For instance, many firms use mobile social media to enhance their brand awareness in the younger generation in Taiwan.
4. **Develop action and implementation plans:** After choosing media and tools, a number of implementation issues must be planned, such as budget, time frame for advertising, advertising designs (e.g., video), and so on.
5. **Develop performance measurement and monitoring plans:** In order to ensure that the money spent on advertising is not wasted, performance measurement and monitoring plans must be developed before the plan is put into action. The performance measurement must be clearly defined and objectively measurable.
6. **Execute plans and evaluate performance:** After the advertising plan is approved, attention must be given to its execution, and finally, its performance must be evaluated to see whether the originally planned goals are achieved. For preparing a promotion plan, see The Balance (2016); for mobile marketing, see Wong (2016); and for a social media marketing plan, see LePage (2016b).

Many publications and vendors generate planning templates and e-books on creating one marketing plans. Some of these resources are listed below:

- The Essential Guide to Internet Marketing (**offers.hubspot.com/essential-guide-internet-marketing**)
- The Beginner's Guide to Online Marketing (**wrike.com/blog/beginners-guide-to-online-marketing-free-ebook**)
- Online marketing strategy toolkit (**smartinsights.com/solution/online-marketing-strategy**)
- Online Advertising Plan Template (**demandmetric.com/content/online-advertising-plan-template**)
- 25 Actionable Social Media Strategies You Can Implement Today (**blog.bufferapp.com/social-media-strategies-ebook**)

SECTION 10.7 REVIEW QUESTIONS

1. Describe permission advertising.
2. Describe video ads and their sudden increase in appearance.
3. Discuss the process and value of affiliate marketing.
4. How does the "ads as a commodity" strategy work?
5. Describe other kinds of online advertising methods.
6. What is localization? What are the major issues in localizing Web pages?
7. Describe choose-your-own-ad format.
8. Describe the six-step process life cycle for an advertising plan.

MANAGERIAL ISSUES

Some managerial issues related to this chapter are as follows:

1. **Do we focus on value-creating customers?** Understanding customers, specifically what they need and how to respond to those needs, is the most critical part of consumer-centered marketing. This was not possible before the solutions for database marketing, one-to-one marketing, and customer relationship marketing became available. What tools do we use to satisfy and retain customers and monitor the entire process of marketing, sales, maintenance, and follow-up services? Do we focus resources effectively on VIP customers (e.g., giving them high priority)?
2. **Which Internet marketing/advertising channel(s) do we use?** An increasing number of online methods are available from which advertisers can choose. These include banners, search engines, video ads, blogging, social networks, and more. Businesses must be able to quantitatively determine the results of a channel to determine its comparative ROI.
3. **Should we use social media channels?** Social media marketing is growing quickly. Firms need to determine if these networks allow access to markets more efficiently than other methods. They must also determine if they are able to manage any additional required management efforts associated with social media.
4. **What metrics do we use to guide advertisers?** A large amount of information has been developed to guide advertisers as to where to advertise, how to design ads, and so on. Specific metrics such as CPM (cost per million impressions), click-

through rate, stickiness, and actual purchase rate may be used to assess the effectiveness of advertising and calculate the return on investment from an organization's online advertising campaign. The metrics can be monitored by third-party monitoring companies. For example, the Mobile Marketing Association and IAB developed the industry standards for measuring mobile ad delivery.

5. **What is our commitment to Web advertising?** Once a company has committed to advertising on the Web, it must remember that a successful program requires the collaboration of the marketing, legal, and IT departments. In addition, coordination with non-Web advertising as well as support from top management is needed.

6. **Should we integrate our Internet and non-Internet marketing campaigns?** Many companies are integrating their TV and Internet marketing campaigns. For example, a company's TV or newspaper ads direct the viewers/readers to their website, where short videos and sound ads, known as *rich media*, are used. With click-through ratios of banner ads down to less than 0.5% at many sites, innovations such as the integration of offline and online marketing are needed to increase click-through rates/ratios.

7. **Who will conduct the market research?** B2C requires extensive market research that may be costly and difficult to conduct. Thus, it may be necessary to outsource some or all of the marketing research activities. If a company owns a large-scale customer database, the research on the internal database itself can be an important market research activity, and data mining techniques may be helpful.

8. **Should we use mobile coupons?** Consumers and advertisers are curious about mobile coupons, but current usage is still low. Advertisers do not yet feel pressured to launch a nationwide coupon effort, but they should start to plan for it. Forrester Research Corp. claims that Instagram is the king of social engagement. Mobile coupons are gaining more popularity. The advantage of mobile coupons is that you can see them when you need them. Showing the coupon to a vendor may be sufficient to get the discount (there is no need to print the coupons). In general, the benefits of mobile coupons are larger than their limitations.

   Many large retailers (e.g., Walmart) offer coupons on their websites. Smaller companies may use intermediaries that have coupons of many companies in their database.

9. **What ethical issues should we consider in online marketing?** Several ethical issues relate to online advertising. One issue that receives a great deal of attention is spam. Another issue is the selling of mailing lists and customer information. Some people believe that not only does a company need the consent of customers before selling a list, but that the company should also share the profits derived from the sale of such lists with the customers. Using cookies without an individual's consent is considered by many to be unethical. The negative impacts of advertising need to be considered.

SUMMARY

In this chapter, you learned about the following EC issues as they relate to the chapter's learning objectives.

1. **Factors influencing online consumer behavior.** Consumer behavior in EC is similar to that of any consumer behavior, but it has some unique features. It is described in a stimuli-based decision model that is influenced by factors that include the consumer's personal characteristics, environmental characteristics, product/service features, merchants and intermediaries, and the EC systems (logistics, technology, and customer service). All of these characteristics and systems interact to influence the decision-making process and produce an eventual buyer decision.

2. **Online personalization.** Using personalized Web pages, customers can interact with a company, learn about its products or services in real time, or receive customized products or services. Companies can allow customers to self-configure the products or services they want. Customization also can be done by matching products with customer profiles. Personalization includes the recommendation of products (services) and delivering content that customers want.

3. **EC consumer market research.** Several fast and economical methods of online market research are available. The two major approaches to data collection are (1) soliciting voluntary information from customers and (2) using cookies, transaction logs, or clickstream data to track customer movements on the Internet and discover their interests. Understanding market segmentation by grouping consumers into categories is also an effective EC market research method. However, online market research has several limitations, including data accuracy and representation of the statistical population generated by using an incorrect sample.

4. **Objectives and characteristics of Web advertising.** Web advertising attempts to attract surfers to an advertiser's site. Once at the advertiser's site, consumers can receive information, interact with the seller (e.g., chat with an online representative), and in many cases, are given a chance to easily place an order. With Web advertising, ads can be customized

to fit groups of people with similar interests (segmentation) or even individuals (one-to-one). In addition, Web advertising can be interactive, is easily updated, can reach millions at a reasonable cost, and offers dynamic presentation and rich multimedia.

5. **Major online advertising methods.** Banners are the most popular online advertising method. Other frequently used methods are pop-ups and similar ads, e-mail (including e-mail sent to mobile devices), classified ads, registration of URLs with search engines, and advertising in chat rooms. Some of these are related to search results obtained through search engines, such as keyword advertising (especially on Google). Social network communities provide new opportunities for marketing by enabling segmentation, viral marketing, user-generated ads, and more. Advertising in videos is gaining popularity as well.

6. **Mobile marketing.** With the increased use of mobile devices comes the opportunity to reach individuals wherever they are at any time. Despite the small screen size, advertisers use clever designs to show not only banners but video ads as well. Mobile ads are designed for the young generation, and some of these are interactive. The younger generation is especially active in viral advertising. Next technologies also allow for the creation of specific mobile apps that may provide benefits for customers. Location-based systems may allow better targeting.

7. **Various advertising strategies and types of promotions.** The major advertising strategies are ads associated with search results (text links), affiliate marketing, monetary or other types of incentives for customers to view ads, viral marketing, ads customized on a one-to-one basis, and online events and promotions. Web promotions are similar to offline promotions. They include giveaways, contests, quizzes, entertainment, coupons, and so on. Customization and interactivity distinguish Internet promotions from conventional ones. It is also important that marketing projects are localized to meet the unique needs of different cultures.

8. **Implementation topics.** In permission marketing, customers are willing to accept ads in exchange for special (personalized) information or monetary incentives. Ad management deals with planning, organizing, and controlling ad campaigns and ad use. Ads can be localized to culture, country, and so forth. Market research can be facilitated by feedback from bloggers, chats in social networks, recommendations of friends, reading members' opinions, and so forth. Advertising is enhanced by user-generated ad content, viral marketing, and better segmentation.

KEY TERMS

Ad views
Affiliate marketing
Affiliate network
Banner
Behavioral targeting
Biometrics
Click (ad click)
Clickstream behavior
Clickstream data
Click-through rate/ratio (CTR)
Collaborative filtering
Conversion rate
Cookie
CPM (cost per mille, i.e., thousand impressions)
E-mail advertising
E-mail marketing
Hit
Interactive marketing
Interactive video
Landing page
Live banner
Localization
Mobile advertising (m-advertising)
Mobile marketing

Mobile market research
Pay per click (PPC)
Permission advertising
Personalization
Personalized banner
Pop-up ad
Pop-up banner
Random banners
Search advertising
Search engine optimization (SEO)
Spyware
Static banner
Transaction log
User profile
Viral marketing (viral advertising)
Viral video
Web bugs
Web mining

DISCUSSION QUESTIONS

1. How can you describe the buying decision process when the customer is online and looking for an iPhone? What can a webstore do to attract this customer to purchase from their store?
2. Discuss the advantages and limitations of three methods of data collection about individual online consumer behavior.
3. Why is personalization becoming an important element in EC? What techniques can be used to learn about consumer behavior? How can personalization be used to facilitate customer service? Give an example.
4. Watch the videos "Wherever You Want to Go" (from BMW; **youtube.com/playlist?list=PL53450A123A3ADCE2**) and Burger King's "Sign and Race" (**youtube.com/watch?v=qab5PH43sok**), and also find articles about them. Write a report on what made these videos so successful.
5. Discuss why banners are popular in Internet advertising. What kinds of products may or may not be suitable for banners?
6. Discuss the advantages and limitations of using keyword advertising with a search engine.
7. Explain why online ad management is critical. What are the major concerns for a company managing its own online ad program?
8. Discuss the evolving landscape of mobile advertising. Select a topic and explain its importance.
9. Discuss the potential ethical implications of location-based advertising.
10. Discuss the benefits of video ads in the social networking environment.

TOPICS FOR CLASS DISCUSSION AND DEBATES

1. Discuss the similarities and differences between data mining, text mining, and Web mining for online market research.
2. Some say that people come to social networks to socialize, and they will disregard, disable, or not accept ads. Others say that people do not mind the ads, but they ignore them. Discuss.
3. What strategic implications do you see for companies that use videos, mobile devices, and social networks as platforms for advertising? Discuss.
4. Debate: Will traditional advertising (TV, newspapers, billboards) disappear in the future?
5. Debate: Netflix.com, Amazon.com, and others view historical purchases as input in their recommendation systems. Some believe that this is an invasion of privacy.
6. Some people claim that they trust traditional media advertising (e.g., newspaper) over online ads (e.g., Richter 2014). Others disagree. Debate the issue.
7. Will advertising be more effective as an app or a website in a mobile environment?

INTERNET EXERCISES

1. Examine a market research website (e.g., **nielsen.com**). Discuss what might motivate a consumer to provide feedback to market research questions used by this company.
2. Enter **marketingterms.com** and conduct a search by keywords and by category. Look at their marketing glossary. Check the definitions of any 10 key terms in this chapter.
3. Enter **2020research.com**, **infosurv.com**, and **marketingsherpa.com** and identify areas about market research on consumer behavior. Write a summary of your findings.
4. Enter **yume.com** and find their video ad activities and reports. Write a summary.
5. Enter **selfpromotion.com** and **nielsen-online.com**. What Internet traffic management, Web results, and auditing services are provided? What are the benefits of each service? Compare the services provided and their costs.
6. Enter **adweek.com**, **wdfm.com**, **ad-tech.com**, **adage.com**, and other online advertising websites to find new developments in Internet advertising. Write a report based on your findings.
7. Enter **clickz.com** and find its market research topics. Summarize your findings.
8. Enter **adobe.com/marketing-cloud.html**. How does this product help with site optimization? What other services does it provide?
9. What resources do you find to be most useful at **targetmarketingmag.com**, **clickz.com**, **admedia.org**, **marketresearch.com**, and **wdfm.com**? Describe useful information for online marketing that you have found from these websites.
10. Enter **zoomerang.com** and learn how it facilitates online surveys. Examine the various products, including those that supplement the surveys. Write a report.
11. Enter **pewinternet.org** and **pewresearch.org**. What research do they conduct that is relevant to B2C? To B2B? Write a report.
12. Enter **hootsuite.com** and sign up for a free trial of the system. Write a report.
13. Enter **mailchimp.com** and sign up for a free trial of the system. Write a report.

TEAM ASSIGNMENTS AND PROJECTS

1. **Assignment for the Opening Case**

   Read the opening case and answer the following questions:

   (a) Why are some items difficult to sell online?
   (b) What is augmented reality?
   (c) Why is augmented reality a good fit for online furniture sales?
   (d) How could IKEA enhance their augmented reality app to make it more convenient for customers?

2. Apple is encroaching onto Google's turf by buying Quattro Wireless, a mobile advertising company, and by initiating the iAd mobile device platform. Research the reason for Apple's venture into the field and the Apple vs. Google battle. Give a presentation to the class.
3. The field of video ads is growing rapidly, with many companies introducing innovative models and services (e.g., see **yume.com**). The class examines the major models and services available, including mobile ads and video clips on Twitter. Write a report.
4. Each team will choose one advertising method and conduct an in-depth investigation of the major players in that part of the ad industry. For example, direct e-mail is relatively inexpensive. Visit **thedma.org** to learn about direct mail. Also visit **ezinedirector.com** and similar sites. Each team will prepare and present an argument as to why its method is superior.
5. In this exercise, each team member will enter **pogo.com** and a similar site to play games and win prizes. Relate the games to advertising and marketing. Write a report.
6. Enter **autonlab.org** and download tools for conducting data mining analysis (these downloads are free). Write a report about the capabilities of the tools.

7. Watch the video "Beginning Analytics: Interpreting and Acting on Your Data" at **youtube.com/watch?v=Hdsb_uH2yPU** and answer the following questions:

   (a) To what metrics does the video refer?
   (b) How can Google Analytics be used?
   (c) What can analytics contribute to competitive intelligence?
   (d) Why is the average time spent on a site so important?
   (e) What decisions can be supported by analytics?
   (f) What have you learned from this video?
   (g) Compare Bing's Content Ads with Google's AdSense. Give a presentation.

8. Watch the video "Complete Google AdWords Tutorial 2016" at **youtu.be/zhSnj3jR_6c** and answer the following questions:

   (a) What is required to setup an AdWords account?
   (b) How is AdWords integrated with your website?
   (c) How do you bid on keywords?
   (d) How can you control costs?
   (e) How can you evaluate your results?

CLOSING CASE: ROLEX USES NEW MEDIA MARKETING

Rolex (**rolex.com**) is a purveyor of luxury watches founded in 1905. Historically, the company's business strategy has always been to produce an exceptionally high-quality product and market that product to a high-end clientele. *Forbes* ranked Rolex 64th in its list of the world's most powerful brands in 2016 (Forbes 2016). Rolex does not concentrate on volume of sales, but instead concentrates on being able to maintain a high margin on each individual sale. Prices for new Rolex watches can range significantly in retail stores but are generally available between 3000 and $12,000.

The Problem

Because of its notoriety and high-end segmented brand strategy, Rolex did not need to use Web-based marketing or social media to grow sales or interest in the brand. While the company dabbled in Internet advertising beginning in 2006, they did not focus on the Web as a marketing channel until 2012 (Bhasin 2016). The company recognized that in order to maintain its brand identity with younger demographics, it would need to be active in the types of media that those individuals were consuming. Specifically, the company did not want to become the "old man's watch" (see NewsCred 2014 and Paton 2014).

Even with this goal in mind, the company's marketing department wanted to ensure that Rolex launch online and, especially in social media, was very deliberate. One of the company's marketing axioms is that no advertising should be haphazard, but instead all uses of the brand image should be deliberate and curated. To this end, the brand's activities both online and in social media have been reserved. The brand works through planned, distinct marketing campaigns that are used to highlight the history, quality, and luxury of Rolex. (See **mashable.com/2014/04/17/rolex-marketing-strategy/#4YfvzomoFPqD** for both historical and new media examples.)

The Solution

Rolex began its foray into social media with a deliberate launch of a YouTube channel in 2012. The channel included well-produced videos that focused on the unique characteristics of Rolex watches, as well as their premier status through the use of celebrity referrals. After seeing success with YouTube, the company branched out into Facebook in 2013. Using this social media network, the company continued a minimalist approach focusing on brand quality and testimonials. Additionally, the company used the Facebook platform to gather data on brand mentions to help determine the interest and preferences of potential customers.

In 2014 and 2015 the brand added custom Pinterest and Instagram pages that display select product images as well as allowing shared photos from customers. While the company has adopted a number of social media systems, the company has shunned Twitter. This is consistent with Rolex his brand strategy that embraces focused, limited marketing efforts (Soliday 2016).

Results

Quantifying the benefits of Web-based marketing and social media attention is a challenge with a product that has such a small number of sales like Rolex. It is difficult for the company to directly attribute these marketing efforts to individual sales. However, the company feels that its overall advertising efforts are more importantly focused on building and maintaining the Rolex brand. Marketing managers feel that the company's activities online and in social media have been consistent with their historical approach to brand building but have extended that philosophy into a new medium. The company plans to continue their work online and evaluate their use of different social media outlets as they evolve.

Questions

1. Why is Rolex not interested in a mass-market advertising strategy?
2. Why does Rolex limit its marketing activities online?
3. How does the company maintain its brand image online?
4. What steps could the company take to improve its image using social networks?

REFERENCES

Allen, R. "7 Examples of Effective Mobile Marketing Campaigns." Smart Insights, April 29, 2016. **smartinsights.com/mobile-marketing/mobile-advertising/7-effective-mobile-marketing-campaigns** (accessed January 2017).

Alhlou, F., E. Fettman, and S. Asif. *Google Analytics Breakthrough: From Zero to Business Impact*, Hoboken, NJ: Wiley, 2016.

Amerland, D. *Google Semantic Search: Search Engine Optimization (SEO) Techniques That Get Your Company More Traffic, Increase Brand Impact, and Amplify Your Online Presence (Que Biz-Tech Series)*. Hoboken, NJ: Que Publishing, 2015.

Batrinca, B. and P. Treleaven. (2014). Social Media Analytics: A Survey of Techniques, Tools and Platforms. *AI & Society*, July 26, 2014.

Bhasin, H. "Marketing Mix of Rolex." Marketing91, November 30, 2016. **marketing91.com/marketing-mix-of-rolex** (accessed January 2017).

Bilos, A., I. Ruzic, I. Kelic. "An Enterprise Odyssey." *International Conference Proceedings: 1195-1207*. Zagreb: University of Zagreb, Faculty of Economics and Business. (2014)

Burton, R. "Six Steps for Creating a Viral Marketing Campaign." SEO Site Checkup, March 24, 2016. **seositecheckup.com/articles/six-steps-for-creating-a-viral-marketing-campaign** (accessed January 2017).

Carpenter, J. "Could Ikea Furniture Assembly Be a Tipping Point for Augmented Reality?" *Forbes*, June 10, 2016. **forbes.com/sites/johncarpenter1/2016/06/10/could-ikea-furniture-assembly-be-a-tipping-point-for-augmented-reality/** (accessed January 2017).

Charlton, G. "21 Ways Online Retailers Can Improve Customer Retention Rates." Econsultancy, July 3, 2015. **econsultancy.com/blog/11051-21-ways-online-retailers-can-improve-customer-retention-rates** (accessed January 2017).

Chiu, C.-M., E. T. C. Wang, Y. H. Fang, and Y. H. Huang. "Understanding Customers' Repeat Purchase Intentions in B2C E-Commerce: The Roles of Utilitarian Value, Hedonic Value and Perceived Risk." DOI: 10.1111/j.1365-2575.2012.00407.x *Information Systems Journal*, Volume 24, Issue 1, (2014).

Cohen, W. W. "Collaborative Filtering: A Tutorial." *Carnegie Mellon University* (Undated). Available for download at **google.com/url?sa=t&rct=j&q=&esrc=s&source=web&cd=1&ved=0ahUKEwiBhduAgZLMAhWMHD4KHRSMBlkQFggdMAA&url=https%3A%2F%2Fwww.cs.cmu.edu%2F~wcohen%2Fcollab-filtering-tutorial.ppt&usg=AFQjCNGxEZhzDumFZBRKESQ2gpqB9kAPBw&cad=rja** (accessed January 2017).

Coughlan, S. "Time Spent Online 'Overtakes TV' Among Youngsters." BBC News, January 26, 2017. **bbc.com/news/education-35399658** (accessed January 2017).

Duermyer, R. "Search Engine Optimization Tutorial." The Balance, July 4, 2016. **thebalance.com/search-engine-optimization-tutorial-1794804** (accessed January 2017).

Einav, L., D. Knoepfle, J. Levin, and N. Sundaresan. "Consumer Behavior in Online Shopping Is Affected by Sales Tax." *London School of Economics and Political Science*, January 14, 2014. **blogs.lse.ac.uk/usappblog/2014/01/14/sales-tax-internet** (accessed January 2017).

Eslinger, T. *Mobile Magic: The Saatchi and Saatchi Guide to Mobile Marketing and Design.* Hoboken, NJ: Wiley, 2014.

Forbes. "The World's Most Valuable Brands." Forbes, 2016. **forbes.com/companies/rolex** (accessed January 2017).

Hanford, J." Why Email Marketing Is Essential for Business [Infographic]." Business 2 Community, March 7, 2016. **business2community.com/infographics/email-marketing-essential-business-infographic-01473089#Z9Ywc1bSJgBDxMME.97** (accessed January 2017).

Greengard, S. "AI Helps North Face Get Personal With Customers." *Baseline*, February 2, 2016. **baselinemag.com/crm/ai-helps-north-face-get-personal-with-customers.html** (accessed January 2017).

Hulu, LLC. "Patent Issued for Video Ad Swapping in a Video Streaming System." (2015). *Marketing Weekly News,* 485.

IAB. *IAB Internet Advertising Revenue Report: 2016 Q3 Results.* December 2016.

Insivia. "27 Video Stats for 2017." January 27, 2017. **insivia.com/27-video-stats-2017/** (accessed January 2017).

Khan, G. *Seven Layers of Social Media Analytics: Mining Business Insights from Social Media Text, Actions, Networks, Hyperlinks, Apps, Search Engine, and Location Data.* New York: CreateSpace Independent Publishing Platform. 2015.

Kissmetrics. "10 Tactics for Increasing Your Customer Lifetime Value and Loyalty." Kissmetrics, 2016. **blog.kissmetrics.com/increasing-customer-ltv-and-loyalty** (accessed January 2017).

Le Vu, M. *The Video Marketers Cookbook: Video Marketing Explained: 4 Ingredients that Turn Views into Brand Awareness, Leads and Sales,* Seattle, WA: Amazon Digital Services, 2016.

LePage, E. "All the Social Media Advertising Stats You Need to Know." Hootesuite, November 29, 2016a. **blog.hootsuite.com/social-media-advertising-stats/** (accessed January 2017).

LePage, E. "How To Create a Social Media Marketing Plan In 6 Steps." Hootsuite, August 4, 2016b. **blog.hootsuite.com/how-to-create-a-social-media-marketing-plan** (accessed January 2017).

Lin, H., H. Li, and Y. Wang. (2015). "Permission-Based E-Mail Marketing Websites Success: An Integrated Perspective." *Journal of Global Information Management (JGIM),* 23(2), 1-23.

NewsCred. "Time for Social: 5 Lessons Luxury Brands Can Learn From Rolex." NewsCred Insights, July 5, 2014. **insights.newscred.com/lessons-luxury-brands-learn-from-rolex/** (accessed January 2017).

Marshall, M. "The North Face to Launch Insanely Smart Watson-Powered Mobile Shopping App Next Month." *VentureBeat,* March 4, 2016. **venturebeat.com/2016/03/04/the-north-face-to-launch-insanely-smart-watson-powered-shopping-app-next-month** (accessed January 2017).

McDaniel, C. Jr., and R. Gates. *Marketing Research,* 10th ed. Hoboken, NJ: Wiley, 2014.

Mobile Ads. "Location-Based Mobile Advertising: A Step-by-Step Guide for Small Businesses." Mobile Ads Blog, December 22, 2016. **mobileads.com/blog/location-based-mobile-advertising-small-business** (accessed January 2017).

Page, C. "Netflix Launches Social Recommendations for Sharing Guilty Pleasures with Friends." *The Inquirer,* September 2, 2014. **theinquirer.net/inquirer/news/2363001/netflix-launches-social-recommendations-for-sharing-guilty-pleasures-with-friends** (accessed January 2017).

Paton, E. "Rolex Races to Reclaim Market Share." *Financial Times,* June 5, 2014. **ft.com/content/01eb4294-cae1-11e3-9c6a-00144feabdc0** (accessed January 2017).

Popper, B. "How Netflix Completely Revamped Recommendations for Its New Global Audience." *The Verge,* February 17, 2016. **theverge.com/2016/2/17/11030200/netflix-new-recommendation-system-global-regional** (accessed January 2017).

Raimond, Y. and J. Basilico. "Recommending for the World." Netflix Tech Blog, February 17, 2016. **techblog.netflix.com/2016/02/recommending-for-world.html** (accessed January 2017).

Ramírez, S. "5 Ways To Identify Your Users Without Using Cookies." Kompyte, October 27, 2015. **kompyte.com/5-ways-to-identify-your-users-without-using-cookies/** (accessed January 2017).

Richter, F. "Consumers Still Trust Traditional Media Advertising Over Online Ads." January 8, 2014. **statista.com/chart/1473/consumer-trust-in-advertising** (accessed January 2017).

Rowles, D. *Mobile Marketing: How Mobile Technology is Revolutionizing Marketing, Communications and Advertising.* London, UK: Kogan Press, 2017.

Schrack, M. "Augmented Reality: The Best Examples and Activations." Sanborn Agency, October 27, 2016. **sanbornagency.com/best-augmented-reality-examples** (accessed January 2017).

Soliday, C. "Rolex Doesn't Care About Twitter." *Huffington Post,* April 11, 2016. **huffingtonpost.com/courtney-m-soliday/rolex-fashions-anti-socia_b_9666784.html** (accessed January 2017).

Strauss, J., and R. Frost. *E-Marketing,* 7th ed. Upper Saddle River, NJ: Pearson Education, 2014.

Statistica. "Social Media Advertising." 2016. **statista.com/outlook/220/109/social-media-advertising/united-states** (accessed January 2017).

The Balance. "7 Steps to Planning a Successful Promotional Campaign." *The Balance,* August 30, 2016. **thebalance.com/steps-successful-promotion-campaign-2295836** (accessed January 2017).

Teixeira, T. and S. Gupta. "Case Study: Can Retailers Win Back Shoppers Who Browse then Buy Online?" *Harvard Business Review,* September 2015. **hbr.org/2015/06/case-study-can-retailers-win-back-shoppers-who-browse-then-buy-online** (accessed January 2017).

Thompson, D. "3 Ways to Increase Customer Loyalty." *Entrepreneur,* March 30, 2015. **entrepreneur.com/article/244138** (accessed January 2017).

Van Bommel, E., Edelman, D., and Ungerman, K. "Digitizing the consumer decision journey." *McKinsey & Company* June 2014. **mckinsey.com/business-functions/marketing-and-sales/our-insights/digitizing-the-consumer-decision-journey** (accessed January 2017).

Van Camp, J. "16 Trends from Mobile World Congress That Will Reshape the Year Ahead." *Digital Trends,* February 27, 2016. **digitaltrends.com/mobile/16-crazy-mobile-trends-for-2016** (accessed January 2017).

VentureBeat. " Mobile Commerce Wars: Apps Versus Mobile Web." *VentureBeat,* September 6, 2016. **venturebeat.com/2016/09/06/mobile-commerce-wars-apps-versus-mobile-web** (accessed January 2017)

Weise, E. "They Really Are Watching You: Web Tracking Surges with Online Ads." USA Today, August 16, 2016. **usatoday.com/story/tech/news/2016/08/16/web-trackers-cookies-third-party-doubleclick-google-university-of-washington/88864172** (accessed January 2017).

Weisfeld-Spolter, S., F. Sussan, and S. Gould. "An Integrative Approach to eWOM and Marketing Communications." *Corporate Communications an International Journal,* July 2014.

Williams, A. *SEO 2017 & Beyond: A Complete SEO Strategy - Dominate the Search Engines!* Seattle, WA: CreateSpace Independent Publishing Platform, 2016.

Wong, J. "A Step-By-Step Guide to Setting Up a Mobile Marketing Campaign." Convince & Convert, 2016. **convinceandconvert.com/mobile/a-step-by-step-guide-to-setting-up-a-mobile-marketing-campaign** (accessed January 2017).

Wright, T. *Fizz: Harness the Power of Word of Mouth Marketing to Drive Brand Growth.* New York: McGraw-Hill, 2014.

E-Commerce Security and Fraud Issues and Protections

11

Contents

Learning Objectives

Upon completion of this chapter, you will be able to:

1. Understand the importance and scope of security of information systems for EC.
2. Describe the major concepts and terminology of EC security.
3. Understand about the major EC security threats, vulnerabilities, and technical attacks.
4. Understand Internet fraud, phishing, and spam.
5. Describe the information assurance security principles.
6. Describe the major technologies for protection of EC networks, including access control.
7. Describe various types of controls and special defense mechanisms.
8. Describe consumer and seller protection from fraud.
9. Discuss enterprisewide implementation issues for EC security.
10. Understand why it is so difficult to stop computer crimes.
11. Discuss the future of EC.

© Springer International Publishing AG 2018

E. Turban et al., *Electronic Commerce 2018*, Springer Texts in Business and Economics, DOI 10.1007/978-3-319-58715-8_11

OPENING CASE
KANSAS HEART HOSPITAL BECOMES A VICTIM TO RANSOM

Kansas Heart Hospital of Wichita, Kansas, provides specialized comprehensive cardiovascular care to Kansas residents at its hospital and clinical services. The hospital is known for its quality surgical services, and it is well respected, except by ransom attackers.

The Incident

In May 2016, the hospital became a victim of ransomware attacks. Hackers demanded a ransom payment in order to release data which the hackers were able to lock up after they infiltrated the hospital computers (probably from outside the United States). In section "Nontechnical Methods: From Phishing to Spam and Fraud", we will present this topic, explaining the process.

In short, the hackers locked up the data files, refusing to give back access unless the hospital paid a ransom in Bitcoins (Chap. 12), to avoid tracking.

Hospitals are common targets of attacks since they have sensitive patient data. If the hackers succeed, the hospital usually pays the ransom.

(In 2016, Hollywood Presbyterian Medical Center in Los Angeles, California, paid $17,000 after a long negotiation. During the negotiation, nearly 1000 patients had to be sent to nearby hospitals.)

The attack in Kansas occurred at 9:00 pm and within minutes, hospital employees lost access to the files. Within a short time, the problem was felt throughout the hospital.

The hospital negotiated the ransom and paid the money. The hackers provided access to some, but not all, of the files, demanding more money.

Repeated attacks on hospitals are common. However, usually a second attack will be made by different hackers. This time, the same hackers had the nerve to hold some of the files. However, the hospital refused to pay.

The Solution

The hospital immediately activated a preplanned defense system.

The hackers encrypted the data in the file; the plan was ready for this, and the defense system was able to minimize the damage the encrypted malware agent was able to do.

The Results

According to the hospital, no patient information was jeopardized. The incident helped the hospital improve its defense security system.

Sources: Compiled from Newman (2016) and Sun (2016).

LESSONS LEARNED FROM THE CASE

Hackers' attacks are getting to be more innovative and sophisticated. Recently, demand for ransoms mushroomed. Hospitals are major targets for hacking. However, hospital administrators are aware of this risk and have found ways to try to protect patient information. Ransomware is only one attack method of information systems. Several other major methods are used. It is an endless war between the attackers and the defenders. A growing area closely related to e-commerce is *fraud*, which is committed by sellers, buyers, and intermediaries. This chapter provides an overview of information systems security with special attention to topics related to e-commerce.

11.1 THE INFORMATION SECURITY PROBLEM

Information security, or information systems security, refers to a variety of activities and methods that protect information systems, data, and procedures from any action designed to destroy, modify, or degrade the systems and their operations (see Kim and Solomon 2016). In this chapter, we provide an overview of some generic information security problems and solutions as they relate to EC and IT. In this section, we look at the nature of the security problems and the magnitude of the problems and introduce some essential terminology of information security. For an overview, see John (2016) and Smith (2015).

What Is EC Security?

Computer security in general refers to the risks and protection of data, networks, computer programs, computer power, and other elements of computerized information systems. It is a very broad field due to the many methods of attack as well as the many modes of defense. The attacks on and defenses for computers can affect individuals, organizations, countries, or the entire Web. Computer security aims to prevent, repair, or at least minimize the attacks.

Information security has been ranked consistently as one of the top management concerns in the United States and many other countries. Fig. 11.1 illustrates the major topics cited in various studies as being the most important in information security.

The Status of Computer Security in the United States

Several private and government organizations try to assess the status of computer security in the United States annually. Notable is the annual CSI report, which is described next.

Comprehensive annual security surveys are published periodically by IBM, Symantec, and other organizations.

In addition to organizational security issues, there is also the issue of personal security.

Fig. 11.1 Major EC security management concerns

Personal Security

Fraud on the Web is aimed mostly at individuals. In addition, loose security may mean danger to personal safety due to sex offenders who find their victims on the Internet.

National Security

Protection of US computer networks is handled by the Department of Homeland Security (DHS). It includes the following programs:

- **Cyber Security Preparedness and the National Cyber Alert System.** Computer users can stay up-to-date on cyber threats through this program.
- **United States Computer Emergency Readiness Team (US-CERT Operations).** Provides information about vulnerabilities and threats, proactively manages cyber risks to the nation, and operates a database to provide technical descriptions of vulnerabilities.
- **National Cyber Response Coordination Group (NCRCG).** Comprised of representatives from 13 federal agencies, it reviews threat assessments and recommends actions to incidents, including allocation of federal resources.
- **CyberCop Portal.** A portal designed for law enforcement and government officials to use the Internet to collaborate and share sensitive information with one another in a secure environment.

Hackers are increasingly attacking the most critical infrastructures of the United States (e.g., power, nuclear, and water facilities). They even tried to influence the US presidential elections.

On February 17, 2013, President Obama issued an executive order for combating cyberwars. This order gave federal agencies greater authority to share "cyber threat" information with the public sector.

Security Risks for 2017 and 2018

The major security risks for the near future are:

- Cyberespionage and cyberwars, including terrorist attacks, are growing threats (see Laudicina 2016 and Armerding 2016).
- Attacks are now also occurring against mobile assets, including smartphones, tablets, and other mobile devices. Enterprise mobile devices are particular targets.
- Ransomware is growing very rapidly.
- Attacks on social networks and social software tools are growing. User-generated content is a major source of malware.
- Attacks on BYOD ("bring your own device") and DOYA ("develop your own applications") are increasing.
- Identity theft is exploding, increasing the criminal use of the stolen identities.
- Profit motive—as long as cybercriminals can make money, security threats and phishing attacks will continue to grow.
- Social engineering tools such as phishing via texting, e-mail, and web content are growing rapidly.
- Cybergang consolidation—underground groups are multiplying and getting bigger, especially in Internet fraud and cyberwars.
- Business-oriented spam (including image-based spam) is increasing.
- Attackers are using more sophisticated spyware tools.
- Attacks on new technologies such as cloud computing, IoT, and virtualization are growing.
- Attacks on mobile apps are rapidly growing.
- Fake news products and services are mushrooming.
- More analytics invite more attacks.

For more, see Olavsrud (2016).

We cover all the major topics on the above list in the rest of this chapter. The major attacks on corporations are on customers or employees' personal data, companies' strategies and plans, and on executives (plans and strategy) and sales. While most of the attacks are against large enterprises, hackers attack medium and small companies as well. Additionally, 93% of companies affected are in the healthcare, high technology, retail, banking, or IT industries. For more information, see SlideShare by Singh (2016), **sans.org**, **baselinemag.com/security**, **enisa.europa.eu/topics/threat-risk-management/risk-management**, and the Information Systems Security Certification Consortium (**isc2.org**).

Security Risks in Mobile Devices

The major security concerns of mobile devices are loss of devices that include sensitive information, data leaks, mobile devices infected by malware, theft of data from the device, users downloading malicious apps, identity theft, and other user personal loss. For more security risks for mobile commerce, see **usa.kaspersky.com/internet-security-center/threats/mobile-device-security-threats#.WKsaeG_yvIU**. This security company points to the unsecured nature of Wi-Fi, network, spoofing, phishing attacks, spyware, and broken encryption.

According to Kang (2017), the old smartphone used by President Trump for tweeting could be an opening to security threats.

Cyberwars and Cyberespionage Across Borders

Using computers as a tool to attack information systems and computers is growing rapidly and becoming more and more dangerous.

Cyberwarfare

According to the UN Crime and Justice Research Institute (UNICRI), *cyberwarfare* or *cyberwar* refers to any action by a nation, state, or international organization to penetrate another nation's computer networks for the purpose of causing damage or disruption. However, broader definitions claim that cyberwarfare also includes acts of "cyberhooliganism," cybervandalism, or cyberterrorism. The attack usually is done through viruses, DoS, or botnets. According to Laudicina (2016), 2017 will be the year of cyberwarfare.

- Cyberwarfare, which is an illegal activity in most countries, includes the following major threats: online acts of espionage and security breaches—which are done to obtain national material and information of a sensitive or classified nature through the exploitation of the Internet (e.g., exploitation of network flaws through malicious software).
- Sabotage—the use of the Internet to disrupt online communications with the intent to cause damage.
- Attacks on SCADA (supervisory control and data acquisition) network and NCIs (National Computational Infrastructure). For example, in 2015, hackers attacked the German Parliament's computer network (Troinovski 2015).

According to Khanal (2016), the United States and Russia are on the brink of an open cyberwar.

Cyberespionage

Cyberespionage refers to unauthorized spying using a computer system. Espionage involves obtaining secrets without the permission of the holder of the information (individual, group, or organization). Cyberespionage is an illegal activity in most countries. For cyberspying on US firms by the Chinese, see Yan (2016).

Attacking Information Systems

The GhostNet attack was not an isolated case of cross-border cyberattacks. The US Congress is working on legislation to protect the country from what some call the "Cyber Pearl Harbor" attack or a digital 9/11. In May 2014, the US government named five Chinese military hackers who were responsible for stealing data and spying on several thousand companies in the United States, stealing trade secrets (Kravets 2014).

Types of Cyberwar Attacks

Cyberattacks can be classified into two major interrelated categories:

1. **Corporate espionage.** Many attacks target energy-related companies because their inside information is valuable. Almost half of all power plants and other infrastructures surveyed have been infiltrated by "sophisticated adversaries," with extortion being a common motive. Foreign hackers targeted a water plant control system in Illinois, causing the pump to fail. The attackers also gained unauthorized access to the system database. The attackers' Internet address used was tracked back to Russia. There were suspected cyberattacks against Iranian oil production and refineries. Cyberattackers hacked into 30,000 of Saudi Aramco's computers in 2012, and crippled the national oil company's networks, but failed to disrupt gas or oil output.

   In 2011, cyber thieves (known as the "Rove group") based in Eastern Europe hijacked at least four million computers in more than 100 countries before they were caught. The attackers used malware and rerouted Internet traffic illegally. The cyber thieves stole $14 million before they were captured. The hackers also attacked US government agencies and large corporations.

   In 2013, Chinese hackers allegedly attacked the *New York Times*' computers to intimidate the American news media into not reporting on China's negative image and the journalists' sources of this information.

2. **Political espionage and warfare.** Political espionage and cyberwars are increasing in magnitude. Sometimes, these are related to corporate espionage. In 2014, US hackers in Illinois used DDoS malware to attack the official website of the Crimean referendum. A few days later, major Russian government Web resources and state media websites were also attacked by DDoS malware.

Example 1

According to US Intelligence Reports, the Russians were actively involved in hacking the US Democratic Party e-mails (e.g., the DNC e-mails) during the 2016 presidential election. There was a clear attempt to influence the results of the election (see Khanal 2016).

Example 2

A suspected cyberespionage network, known as GhostNet, compromised computer systems in 103 countries, including computer systems belonging to the Dalai Lama's exile network, embassies, and foreign ministries. The attacks allegedly came from China. For more on GhostNet, see Chalakkal (2016).

Example 3

One of the most complex cyberespionage incidents that has ever occurred is the suspected Russian spyware Turla, which was used to attack hundreds of government computers in the United States and Western Europe.

   The above incidents illustrate the ineffectiveness of some information security systems. For an overview of how cyberwarfare works, see **forbes.com/sites/quora/2013/07/18/how-does-cyber-warfare-work**.

The Drivers of EC Security Problems

There are many drivers (and inhibitors) that can cause security problems to EC. Here, we describe several major ones: the *Internet's vulnerable design*, the *shift to profit-induced crimes*, the *wireless revolution*, the *underground Internet economy*, the *dynamic nature of EC systems, and the role of insiders* and the *sophistication of the attacks*.

The Internet's Vulnerable Design

The Internet and its network protocols were never intended to protect against cybercriminals. They were designed to accommodate computer-based communications in a *trusted community*. However, the Internet is now a global place for communication, search, and trading. Furthermore, the Internet was designed for maximum efficiency without regard for security. Despite improvements, the Internet is still fundamentally insecure.

The Spread of Computerized Medical Data

With the requirements to computerize medical and healthcare data came the danger of breaches; see Greengard (2016a).

The Shift to Profit-Induced Crimes

There is a clear shift in the nature of the operation of computer criminals. In the early days of e-commerce, many hackers simply wanted to gain fame or notoriety by defacing websites. There are many more criminals today, and they are profit-oriented and sophisticated. Most popular is the theft of personal information such as credit card numbers, bank accounts, Internet IDs, and passwords. According to the Privacy Rights Clearinghouse (**privacyrights.org**), millions of records containing personal information are breached every year. In 2016, Yahoo! admitted that hackers stole data associated with 1 billion of its user accounts. The data that were stolen were to be sold to criminals.

Ransomware

Criminals today are even holding data for ransom and trying to extort payments from their victims. An illustrative CNN video (2:30 min) titled "Hackers Are Holding Data for Ransom" is available at **money.cnn.com/video/technology/2012/10/08/t-ransomware-hackers.cnnmoney**. In 2016, a hospital was forced to pay a ransom (with Bitcoins) to get back its data, which were not backed up (see Winton 2016). CryptoLocker is a new ransomware virus (Trojan type) used for such crimes (see **usatoday.com/story/news/nation/2014/05/14/ransom-ware-computer-dark-web-criminal/8843633**). For more on ransomware, see section "Nontechnical Methods: From Phishing to Spam and Fraud".

Thefts of Devices

Lemos (2016) provides a slideshow that illustrates the 2016 top secret trends that include ransomware and cyberspying.

Note that laptop computers, tablets, and smartphones are stolen for two reasons: selling them (e.g., to pawnshops and on eBay) and trying to find the owners' personal information (e.g., social security number, driver's license details, and so forth). In January 2014, a former Coca-Cola employee stole laptops containing information on 74,000 individuals belonging to current and past employees of the company. The company did not have a data loss prevention program in place nor were the laptops encrypted.

Computers Everywhere

As described in Chap. 7, computers are everywhere, from your home to your work, study place, entertainment area, etc. Even your car can be hacked (see Pagliery 2014b).

The Increased Volume of Wireless Activities and the Number of Mobile Devices

Wireless networks are more difficult to protect than wireline. For example, many smartphones are equipped with near-field communication (NFC) chips, which are necessary for mobile payments. Additionally, BYOD (Chap. 6) may create security problems. In addition, hackers can exploit the features of smartphones and related devices (e.g., Bluetooth) with relative ease.

The Globalization of the Attackers

Many countries have cyberattackers (e.g., China, Russia, Nigeria, Iran, and India). For an example of Iranian attacks on US banks, see Nakashima and Zapotosky (2016).

The Explosion of Social Networking

The huge growth of social networking and the proliferation of platforms and tools make it difficult to protect against hackers. Social networks are easy targets for phishing and other social engineering attacks.

The Dynamic Nature of EC Systems and the Acts of Insiders

EC systems are changing all the time due to a stream of innovations. Security problems often accompany change. In recent years, we have experienced many security problems in the new areas of social networks, mobile commerce, and wireless systems (some will be explored later in this book). Note that insiders (people who work for the attacked organizations) are responsible for almost half of the security problems. New employees are being added frequently to organizations, and they may bring security threats with them.

The Sophistication of the Attacks

Cybercriminals are sharpening their weapons continuously, using technological innovations. In addition, criminals are getting organized in very powerful groups, such as LulzSec and Anonymous. Cybercriminals change their tactics because of improved security (i.e., they are adapting quickly to a changing environment).

The Darknet and the Underground Economy

The **darknet** can be viewed as a separate Internet that can be accessed via the regular Internet and a connection to the TOR network (TOR is a network of VPNs that allows privacy and security on the Internet). The darknet has restricted access to trusted people ("friends") by using nonstandard protocols (IP addresses that are not listed). Darknet allows anonymous surfing. The darknet's contents are not accessible through Google or other search engines. The TOR technology is used in file sharing (e.g., in the well-known Pirate Bay case). The darknet is often used for political dissent and conducting illegal transactions, such as selling drugs and pirating intellectual property via file sharing. The latter activity is known as the *underground Internet economy*. In November 2014, law enforcement authorities in Europe and the United States shut down many of TOR websites. However, it seems they have not cracked TOR encryptions yet. In 2015, the US government shut down a market for stolen personal data called Darkode. See Victor (2015).

The Underground Internet Economy

The **underground Internet economy** refers to the e-markets for stolen information. These markets includes thousands of websites that sell credit card numbers, social security numbers, e-mail addresses, bank account numbers, social network IDs, passwords, and much more. Stolen data are sold to spammers or to criminals, from less than a dollar a piece to several hundred dollars each. The purchasers use them to send spam or conduct illegal financial transactions such as transferring other people's money into their own accounts or paying the spammers' credit card bills. It is estimated that about 30% of all the transactions in the underground market are made with stolen credit cards. Symantec estimates the potential worth of just the credit cards and banking information for sale is about a billion annually. Forty-one percent of the underground economy is in the United States, while 13% is in Romania. For a discussion of the digital underground, see Goodman (2016).

The Internet Silk Road

This was one of the underground sites where hundreds of drug dealers and other "black market" merchants conduct their business. In October 2013, law enforcement authorities in the United States shut down the site and arrested its founder, who was sentenced to more than 20 years in jail. However, shortly thereafter, Silk Road was "resurrected" as Silk Road 2.0.

Transactions on Silk Road are paid only by *Bitcoins* (Chap. 12). In February 2014, hackers stole over 4400 Bitcoins that were held in escrow (between buyers and sellers); over $2.7 million value of Bitcoins are gone forever (see Pagliery 2014a). The owner of the Silk Road site declared bankruptcy. However, by May 2014, the site was back in business as Silk Road 2.0 and back online in May 2016 as Silk Road 3.0.

The Cost of Cybercrime

It is not clear how much cybercrime costs. Many companies do not disclose their losses. However, HP Enterprise Security's "2013 Cost of Cyber Crime Study: Global Report" found that the average annualized cost of cybercrime per company surveyed was $7.2 million per year, which is an increase of 30% from the previous year's global cyber cost study. Data breaches can be very costly to organizations. For an infographic regarding the cost of cyberattacks, see Alto (2016).

SECTION 10.1 REVIEW QUESTIONS

1. Define computer security.
2. List the major current security risks.
3. Describe the vulnerable design of the Internet.
4. Describe some profit-induced computer crimes.
5. Describe the dynamic nature of EC systems.
6. Describe the underground Internet economy and the darknet.

11.2 BASIC E-COMMERCE SECURITY ISSUES AND LANDSCAPE

In order to understand security problems better, we need to understand some commonly used concepts in EC and IT security. We begin with basic terminology.

Basic Security Terminology

In section "The Information Security Problem", we introduced some key concepts and security terms. We begin this section by introducing alphabetically the major terms needed to understand EC security issues:

Business continuity plan: A plan that keeps the business running after a disaster occurs. Each function in the business should have a valid recovery capability plan.

Cybercrime: Intentional crimes carried out on by using the Internet.

Cybercriminal: A person who intentionally carries out crimes over the Internet.

Exposure: An instance of being exposed to losses from an attack that exploits vulnerability (including estimate of damages).

Fraud: Any business activity that uses deceitful practices or devices to deprive another of property or other rights.

Conclusion

Cybercrime is a diversified phenomenon with many methods and potential damages. It keeps changing since criminals are getting more innovative and sophisticated. For the state of cybercrime in 2016, see the White Paper by RSA (2016).

Malware (malicious software): A generic term for malicious software.

Phishing: A fraudulent process of attempting to acquire sensitive information by masquerading as a trustworthy entity.

Ransomware: A method of attack where the attacker encrypts files so the victim cannot open them unless they pay a ransom.

Risk: The probability that a vulnerability will be known and exploited.

Social engineering: A type of nontechnical attack that uses some ruse to trick users into revealing information or performing an action that compromises a computer or network.

Spam: The electronic equivalent of junk mail.

Vulnerability: Weakness in software or other mechanisms that threatens the confidentiality, integrity, or availability of an asset. It can be used directly by a hacker to gain access to a system or network.

Zombie: Computers infected with malware that are under the control of a spammer, hacker, or other criminal.

Detailed definitions of these terms are provided at **webopedia.com/TERM**.

The EC Security Battleground

The essence of EC security can be viewed as a battleground between attackers and defenders of the EC and IT systems. This battleground includes the following components, as shown in Fig. 11.2:

- The attacks, the attackers, and their strategies
- The assets that are being attacked (the targets) in vulnerable areas
- The security defense, the defenders, and their methods and strategies

The Threats, Attacks, and Attackers

Information systems, including EC, are vulnerable to both unintentional and intentional threats.

Unintentional Threats

Unintentional threats fall into three major categories: human error, environmental hazards, and malfunctions in the computer system.

HUMAN ERROR

Human errors can occur in the design of the hardware, software, or information systems. It can also occur in programming (e.g., forgetting to factor in leap year), testing, data collection, data entry, authorization, system operation, and instructions. Errors can occur because of negligence, outdated security procedures, or inadequate employee training or because passwords are not changed or are shared with others.

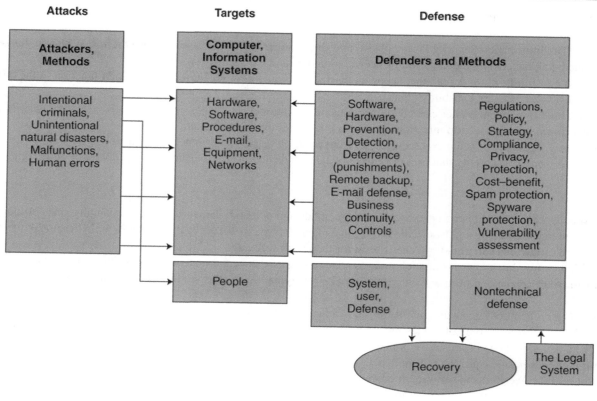

Fig. 11.2 The EC security battleground

ENVIRONMENTAL HAZARDS

These include natural disasters and other environmental conditions outside of human control (e.g., acts of God, large-scale acts of nature, and accidents such as earthquakes, severe storms, hurricanes, blizzards, or sandstorms), floods, power failures or strong fluctuations, fires (the most common hazard), explosions, radioactive fallout, and water-cooling system failures. Computer resources also can be damaged by side effects such as smoke and water.

MALFUNCTIONS IN THE COMPUTER SYSTEM

Defects can be the result of poor manufacturing, defective materials, memory leaks, and outdated or poorly maintained networks. Unintentional malfunctions can also happen for other causes, ranging from lack of user experience to inadequate testing.

In January 29, 2017, a computer outage grounded Delta Airline flights in the United States. One hundred and fifty flights were canceled (CNN News, January 29, 2017).

Another example is Amazon's Cloud (EC2), which hosts many major websites (e.g., Reddit, Airbnb, Foursquare). In the past, the cloud hosting service crashed due to problems with the company's data centers. The crash took down Netflix, Foursquare, Dropbox, Instagram, and Pinterest due to severe weather hitting the North Virginia data center. These problems were fixed after few hours.

Intentional Attacks and Crimes

Intentional attacks are committed by cybercriminals. Types of intentional attacks include theft of data, inappropriate use of data (e.g., changing it or presenting it for fraudulent purposes), theft of laptops and other devices and equipment, and/or inserting computer programs to steal data, vandalism or sabotage directed toward the computer or its information system, damaging computer resources, losses from malware attacks, creating and distributing viruses, and causing monetary losses due to Internet fraud. Most of these are described in Sects. "Technical Malware Attack Methods: From Viruses to Denial of Service" and "Nontechnical Methods: From Phishing to Spam and Fraud". The opening and closing cases of this chapter provide examples of intentional attacks.

The Criminals and Their Methods

Intentional crimes carried out using computers and the Internet are called *cybercrimes*, which are done by *cybercriminals* (*criminals* for short) that include *hackers and crackers*. A **hacker** describes someone who gains unauthorized access to a computer system. A **cracker** (also known as a *black hat hacker*) is a *malicious hacker* with extensive computer experience who may be more damaging. Some hacker groups (such as the international group Anonymous) are considered unstoppable in penetrating organizations of all kinds (many US government agencies, including the US Army and the Department of Energy). The danger is that some companies may not take even minimal precautions to protect their customer information placing the blame for the attacks on the cybercriminals.

Criminals use a variety of methods for the attacks. Some use computers as a weapon; some attack computing assets depending on the targets. For a short history of hacking (with an infographic), see **i-programmer.info/news/149-security/3972-a-short-history-of-hacking.html**.

Money Mules

Hackers and crackers may recruit unsuspecting people, including company insiders, to assist in their crimes. For example, according to Malwarebytes, a "*money mule*" is a person who is local to the compromised account, who can receive money transfers with a lesser chance of alerting the banking authorities.

These money mules retrieve the funds and then transfer them to the cybercriminal. Since the mules are used to transfer stolen money, they can face criminal charges and become victims of identity theft.

Example: The Bangladesh Bank

Some hackers installed malware in the Bangladesh Central Bank computer systems that enabled them to watch, for weeks, how funds were being withdrawn from the bank's US account. The hackers then attempted to steal about $1 billion but were stopped after stealing $80 million from the reserves of Bangladesh at the Federal Reserve Bank of New York. For details, see Reuters (2016).

The Targets of the Attacks in Vulnerable Areas

As seen in Fig. 11.2, the targets can be people, computers, or information systems. Fraud usually aims to steal money or other assets such as real estate. Computers are also used to harass people (e.g., cyberbullying), damage their reputation, violate their privacy, and so forth.

Vulnerable Areas Are Being Attacked

Any part of an information system can be attacked. PCs, tablets, or smartphones can easily be stolen or attacked by viruses and/or malware. Users can become victims of a variety of fraudulent actions. Databases can be attacked by unauthorized intruders, and data are very vulnerable in many places in a computerized system. For example, data can be copied, altered, or stolen. Networks can be attacked, and information flow can be stopped or altered. Computer terminals, printers, and any other pieces of equipment can be damaged in different ways. Software programs can be manipulated. Procedures and policies may be altered and much more. *Vulnerable* areas are frequently attacked.

Vulnerability Information

A *vulnerability* is where an attacker finds a weakness in the system and then exploits that weakness. Vulnerability creates opportunities for attackers to damage information systems. MITRE Corporation publishes a dictionary of publicly known security vulnerabilities called *common vulnerabilities and exposures (CVE)* (**cve.mitre.org**). *Exposure* can result when a cybercriminal exploits a vulnerability. See Microsoft's guide to threats and vulnerabilities at **technet.microsoft.com/en-us/library/dd159785.aspx**.

Attacking E-Mail

One of the easiest places to attack is a user's e-mail, since it travels via the unsecured Internet.

Attacking Smartphones and Wireless Systems

Since mobile devices are more vulnerable than wired systems, attacking smartphones and tablets is becoming popular due to the explosive growth of mobile computing. According to Fink (2014), hackers can even steal your phone password wearing digital glasses.

The Vulnerability of RFID Chips

These chips are embedded everywhere, including in credit cards and US passports. Cards are designed to be read from some distance (contactless), which also creates a vulnerability. When you carry a credit card in your wallet or pocket, anyone with a RFID reader that gets close enough to you may be able to read the RFID information on your card. For a presentation, watch the video "How to Hack RFID-Enabled Credit Cards for $8 (BBtv)" at **youtube.com/watch?v=vmajlKJlT3U**.

The Vulnerabilities in Business IT and EC Systems

Vulnerabilities can be of *technical nature* (e.g., unencrypted communications, insufficient use of security programs and firewalls), or they can possess *organizational weaknesses* (e.g., lack of user training and security awareness and an insider who steals data and engages in inappropriate use of business computers).

Pirated Videos, Music, and Other Copyrighted Material

It is relatively easy to illegally download, copy, or distribute music, videos, books, software, and other intellectual property when it is on the Web. For example, online piracy occurs when illegal software is downloaded illegally from a peer-to-peer network. An example is the pirating of live sports events. At stake are millions of dollars in lost revenue to sports leagues and media companies. These institutions are joining forces in lobbying for stronger copyright legislation and by filing lawsuits against violators. For facts and statistics about online piracy around the globe, see Ernesto (2016).For additional coverage, see Chap. 15.

EC Security Requirements

Good security is a key success factor in EC.

The following set of security requirements is used to assure success and to minimize EC transaction risks:

- **Authentication. Authentication** is a process used to verify (assure) the real identity of an EC entity, which could be an individual, software agent, computer program, or EC website. For electronic messages, authentication verifies that the sender/receiver of the message is who the person or organization claims to be (the ability to detect the identity of a person/entity with whom you are doing business).
- **Authorization. Authorization** is the provision of permission to an authenticated person to access systems and perform certain operations in those specific systems.
- **Auditing.** When a person or program accesses a website or queries a database, various pieces of information are recorded or logged into a file. The process of maintaining or revisiting the sequence of events during the transaction, when and by whom, is known as *auditing*.
- **Availability.** Assuring that systems and information are available to the user when needed and that the site continues to function. Appropriate hardware, software, and procedures ensure availability.
- **Nonrepudiation.** Closely associated with authentication is **nonrepudiation**, which is the assurance that online customers or trading partners will not be able to falsely deny (repudiate) their purchase, transaction, sale, or other obligation. Nonrepudiation involves several assurances, including providing proof of delivery from the sender and proof of sender and recipient identities and the identity of the delivery company.

Authentication and nonrepudiation are potential defenses against phishing and identity theft. To protect and ensure trust in EC transactions, *digital signatures*, or *digital certificates*, are often added to validate the senders and the times of the transactions so buyers are not able to deny that they authorized a transaction or that it never occurred.

The Defense: Defenders, Strategy, and Methods

Everybody should be concerned about security. However, in a company, the information systems department and security vendors provide the technical side, while management provides the administrative aspects. Such activities are done via security and strategy procedures that users need to follow.

EC Defense Programs and Strategy

An **EC security strategy** consists of multiple layers of defense that includes several methods. This defense aims to deter, prevent, and detect unauthorized entry into an organization's computer and information systems. **Deterrent methods** are countermeasures that make criminals abandon their idea of attacking a specific system (e.g., a possible deterrent is a realistic expectation of being caught and punished). **Prevention measures** help stop unauthorized people from accessing the EC system (e.g., by using authentication devices and firewalls or by using *intrusion prevention* which is, according to TechTarget, "a preemptive approach to network security used to identify potential threats and respond to them swiftly"). **Detection measures** help find security breaches in computer systems. Usually this means to find out whether intruders are attempting (or have attempted) to break into the EC system, whether they were successful, whether they are still damaging the system, and what damage they may have done.

Information Assurance

Making sure that a customer is safe and secure while shopping online is a crucial part of improving the online buyer's experience. **Information assurance (IA)** is measures taken to protect information systems and their processes against all risks.

Possible Punishment

A part of the defense is to deter criminals by punishing them heavily if they are caught. Judges now are giving more and harsher punishments than a decade ago. For example, in March 2010, a federal judge sentenced 28-year-old TJX hacker Albert Gonzalez to 20 years in prison for his role in stealing millions of credit and debit card numbers and selling them. Such severe sentences send a powerful message to hackers and help the defense. Unfortunately, in many cases the punishment is too light to deter the cybercriminals.

Defense Methods and Technologies

There are hundreds of security defense methods, technologies, and vendors, and these can be classified in different ways so their analyses and selection may be difficult. We introduce only some of them later in this chapter.

Recovery

In security battles, there are winners and losers in each security episode, but it is difficult to win the security war. There are many reasons for this. On the other hand, organizations and individuals usually recover after a security breach. Recovery is especially critical in cases of a disaster or a major attack, and it must be speedy. Organizations need to continue their business until the information systems are fully restored, and they need to restore them fast. This is accomplished by activating *business continuity and disaster recovery plans.*

Because of the complexity of EC and network security, comprehensive coverage requires an entire book or even several books. Here, we cover only selected topics. Those readers interested in a more comprehensive discussion should check **issa. org/** and search Google.

SECTION 11.2 REVIEW QUESTIONS

1. List five major EC security terms.
2. Describe the major unintentional security hazards.
3. List five examples of intentional EC security crimes.
4. Describe the security battleground, who participates, and how. What are the possible results?
5. Define hacker and cracker.
6. List all security requirements and define authentication and authorization requirements.
7. What is nonrepudiation?
8. Describe vulnerability and provide some examples of potential attacks.
9. Describe deterring, preventing, and detecting in EC security systems.
10. What is a security strategy, and why is it needed?

11.3   TECHNICAL MALWARE ATTACK METHODS: FROM VIRUSES TO DENIAL OF SERVICE

There are many ways criminals attack information EC systems and users. Here, we cover only major representative methods. For an example from India (32 slides), see Singh (2016).

It is helpful to distinguish between two common types of attacks—*technical* (which we discuss in this section) and *nontechnical* ones, which we discuss in section "Nontechnical Methods: From Phishing to Spam and Fraud".

Technical and Nontechnical Attacks: An Overview

Software and systems knowledge are used to perpetrate *technical attacks*. Insufficient use of antivirus and personal firewalls and unencrypted communication are the major reasons for technical vulnerabilities.

Nontechnical organizational attacks are those where the security of a network or the computer is compromised (e.g., lack of proper security awareness training). We consider *financial fraud*, *spam*, *social engineering*, that includes *phishing*, *ransomware*, and other fraud methods, as *nontechnical*. Many nontechnical methods also use some malware in their attacks. The goals of social engineering are to gain unauthorized access to systems or information by persuading unsuspected people to disclose personal information that is used by criminals to commit fraud and other crimes. The major nontechnical methods are described in section "Nontechnical Methods: From Phishing to Spam and Fraud". For lists of top 10 attacks by category, see **www.secpoint.com**. Then, search for virus, spyware, etc.

The Major Technical Attack Methods

Hackers often use several software tools (which unfortunately are readily and freely available over the Internet together with tutorials on how to use them) in order to learn about vulnerabilities as well as attack procedures. The major technical attack methods are illustrated in Fig. 11.3 and are briefly described next. Note that there are many other methods such as "mass SQL injection" attacks that can be very damaging.

Malware (Malicious Software): Viruses, Worms, and Trojan Horses

Malware is a software program that, when spread, is designed to infect, alter, damage, delete, or replace data or an information system without the owner's knowledge or consent. Malware is a comprehensive term that describes any malicious program or software (e.g., a virus is a "subset" of malware). Malware attacks are the most frequent security breaches. Computer systems infected by malware take orders from the criminals and do things such as send spam or steal the user's stored passwords.

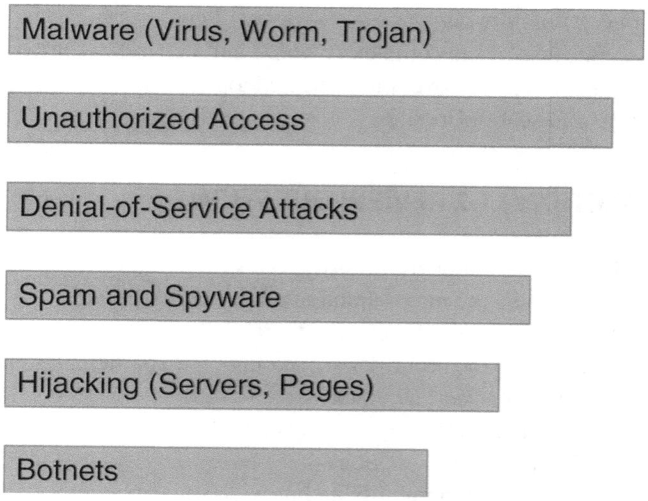

Fig. 11.3 The major technical security attack methods (in descending order of importance)

Malware (Virus, Worm, Trojan)

Unauthorized Access

Denial-of-Service Attacks

Spam and Spyware

Hijacking (Servers, Pages)

Botnets

Malware includes computer viruses, worms, botnets, Trojan horses, phishing tools, spyware tools, and other malicious and unwanted software. According to Harrison and Pagliery (2015), nearly one million new malware threats are released worldwide every day.

According to Adhikari (2016), an Android malware called Gooligan breached more than one million Google accounts. The malware affected devices running Androids 4 and 5.

Viruses

A **virus** is programmed software inserted by criminals into a computer to damage the system; running the infected host program activates the virus. A virus has two basic capabilities. First, it has a mechanism by which it spreads. Second, it can carry out damaging activities once it is activated. Sometimes a particular event triggers the virus's execution. The problem is that existing virus protection systems may not work against new viruses, and unfortunately, new viruses are created all the time. For instance, Michelangelo's birth date triggered the infamous Michelangelo virus. On April 1, 2009, the entire world was waiting for a virus named Conficker. In 2014, a virus by the name of "Pony" infected hundreds of thousands of computers to steal Bitcoins and other virtual currencies (see Finkle 2014). Finally, Finkle reports that a virus named Agent BTZ attacked over 400,000 computers in Russia, the United States, and Europe. This big attack was not successful, but viruses continue to spread all the time. For how computer viruses work, see **computer.howstuffworks.com/virus.htm**.

Web-based malware is very common today. Virus attacks are the most frequent computer attacks. The process of a virus attack is illustrated in Fig. 11.4.

Viruses are dangerous, especially for small companies. In 2013, the CryptoLocker virus was used to blackmail companies after seizing their computer files and threatening to erase their content.

For tutorials on, and information about, viruses, see Scott (2014) and Dawn Ontario (undated). For the scariest viruses of 2001–2015, see Van Allen (2016). Note that in Microsoft tutorials, you will learn how to identify a computer virus, how to know if you are infected, and how to protect yourself against viruses (see the Microsoft Safety and Security Center at **microsoft.com/security/default.aspx**).

The ILOVEYOU Virus

The ILOVEYOU virus was one of the most damaging viruses in history. It was sent via an e-mail note with "I LOVE YOU" in the subject line, and it contained an attachment that, when opened, resulted in the message being resent to everyone in the recipient's Microsoft Outlook address book and, perhaps more seriously, led to the loss of every JPEG, MP3, and certain

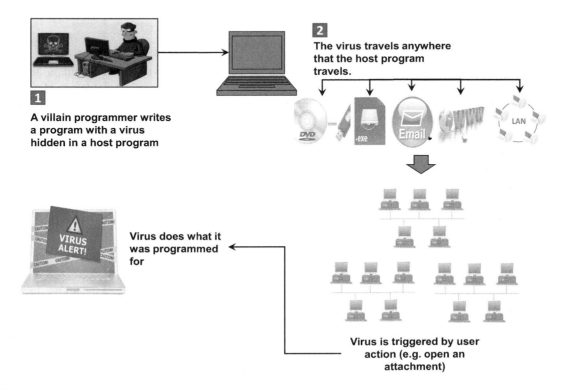

1 A villain programmer writes a program with a virus hidden in a host program

2 The virus travels anywhere that the host program travels.

Virus does what it was programmed for

Virus is triggered by user action (e.g. open an attachment)

Fig. 11.4 How a computer virus can spread

other files on the recipient's hard drive. Therefore, it was able to spread rapidly from user to user within a corporation. On May 4, 2000, when the virus first showed up, it spread so quickly that e-mail had to be shut down in a number of major enterprises. The virus reached an estimated 45 million users in a single day.

One of the first steps companies used to ward off the ILOVEYOU virus was to screen out notes with ILOVEYOU in the subject line. However, the hackers quickly introduced copycat variations. The total damage was estimated at $10 billion. Other damaging viruses/worms were Code Red, Melissa, and Sasser.

Worms

Unlike a virus, a **worm** can replicate itself automatically (as a "stand-alone"—without any host or human activation). Worms use networks to propagate and infect a computer or handheld device and can even spread via instant messages or e-mail. In addition, unlike viruses that generally are confined within a target computer, a worm can infect many devices in a network as well as degrade the network's performance. According to Cisco, "worms either exploit a vulnerability on the target system or use some kind of social engineering to trick users into executing them." Because worms spread much more rapidly than viruses, they may be more dangerous.

Macro Viruses and Micro Worms

A **macro virus (macro worm)** is a malware code that is attached to a data file rather than to an executable program (e.g., a Word file). According to Microsoft, macro viruses can attack Word files as well as any other application that uses a programming language. When the document is opened or closed, the virus can spread to other documents on the computer's system. For information about Word macro viruses, see Microsoft Support at **support.microsoft.com/kb/187243/en**. Computer programs that are very similar to viruses are worms and Trojan horses.

Trojan Horse

A **Trojan horse** is a program that seems to be harmless or even looks useful but actually contains a hidden malicious code. Users are tricked into executing an infected file, where it attacks the host, anywhere from inserting pop-up windows to damaging the host by deleting files, spreading malware, and so forth. The name is derived from the Trojan horse in Greek mythology. Legend has it that during the Trojan War, the city of Troy was presented with a large wooden horse as a gift to the goddess Athena. The Trojans hauled the horse inside the city gates. During the night, Greek soldiers who were hiding in the hollow horse opened the gates of Troy and let in the Greek army. The army was able to take the city and win the war.

Trojans are spread only by user interaction (e.g., such as operating under the guise of an e-mail allegedly sent by Verizon), and there are many variants of Trojans (e.g., Zeus, W32).

Example 1: Trojan-Phisher-Rebery

In 2006, a variant of a Trojan horse program named *Trojan-Phisher-Rebery* was used to steal tens of thousands of identities from people in 125 different countries. The Rebery malicious software is an example of a **banking Trojan**, which is programmed to create damage when users visit certain online banking or e-commerce sites. For an infographic describing the state of financial Trojans, see Wueest (2013).

Example 2: The DDOS Attacks on WordPress Corporation

In March 2014, hackers used a botnet to attack more than 162,000 WordPress sites. Given that WordPress powers about 17% of the world's blogging websites, any attack can be devastating.

Some Security Bugs: Heartbleed and CryptoLocker

Two dangerous computer bugs were discovered in 2013 and 2014.

Heartbleed

According to Russell (2014), "Heartbleed is a flaw in OpenSSL, the open-source encryption standard used by the majority of websites that need to transmit the data that users want to keep secure. It basically gives you a secure line when you're sending an e-mail or chatting on IM."

The potential damage may be large. In theory, any data kept in the active memory can be pulled out by the bug. Hackers can even steal encryption keys that enable them to read encrypted messages. About 650 million websites may be affected. The only advice provided by experts is to change the online passwords.

CryptoLocker

Discovered in September 2013, CryptoLocker is a ransomware Trojan bug. This malware can come from many sources including e-mail attachments and can encrypt files on your computer, so that you cannot read these files. The malware owner then offers to decrypt the data in exchange for a Bitcoin or similar untraceable payment system.

For information on what to do if you are being blackmailed and how to protect yourself, see Cannell (2013).

Mirai (Malware)

According to Wikipedia, "**Mirai** (Japanese for "the future") is malware that turns computer systems running Linux into remotely controlled "bots" that can be used as part of a botnet in large-scale network attacks. It primarily targets online consumer devices such as remote cameras and home routers…The Mirai botnet has been used in some of the largest and most disruptive distributed denial of service (DDoS) attacks, including an attack on 20 September 2016 on computer security journalist Brian Krebs's web site,… and the October 2016 Dyn cyberattack…." (see closing case).

Denial of Service (DoS and DDoS)

According to Incapsula, Inc., a **denial-of-service (DoS) attack** is "a malicious attempt to make a server or network resource unavailable to users, usually by temporarily interrupting or suspending the services of a host connected to the Internet." This causes the system to crash or become unable to respond in time, so the site becomes unavailable. One of the most popular types of DoS attacks occurs when a hacker "floods" the system by overloading the system with "useless traffic" so a user is prevented from accessing their e-mail, websites, etc.

Note: A DoS attack is a malicious attack caused by one computer and one Internet connection as opposed to a distributed denial-of-service (DDoS) attack, which involves many devices and multiple Internet connections. For example, the attack on the Dyn (closing case) was done by thousands of computers taken hostage by the hackers. Hackers also use the IoT (Chap. 7) to capture computers and to bombard the victims; see Mello Jr. (2016). An attacker can also use spam e-mail messages to launch a similar attack on your e-mail account. A common method of launching DoS attacks is by using *zombie (hijacked) computers*, which enable the hijacked computer to be controlled remotely by a hacker without the knowledge of the computer's owner. The zombie computer (also known as a "botnet") launches an overwhelming number of requests toward an attacked website, creating the DoS. For example, DoS attackers target social networks, especially Facebook and Twitter.

Example

On Oct 22, 2016, during the attack on Dyn (see closing case), several social networks were off for over an hour. These included Twitter, Spotify, and Reddit; see Lake (2016).

DoS attacks can be difficult to stop. Fortunately, the security community has developed tools for combating them. For comprehensive coverage, see **us-cert.gov/ncas/tips/ST04-015**.

Note: In 2014, a hacking group called Lizard Stresser offered to take down any website by employing DoS, for a fee of $3 (see Goldman 2014a).

Web Server and Web Page Hijacking

Page hijacking *or pagejacking* is illegally copying website content so that a user can be misdirected to a different website. Social media accounts are sometimes hijacked for the purpose of stealing the accountholder's personal information. For example, Justin Bieber's 50 million followers fell victim to this method when Bieber's Twitter account was hijacked in March 2014. The account was embedded with a malicious link to an application that was used to hijack accounts retweeted to more friends.

Botnets

According to the Microsoft Safety and Security Center, a **botnet** (also known as "zombie army") is a malicious software that criminals distribute to infect a large number of hijacked Internet-connected computers controlled by hackers. These infected computers then form a "botnet," causing the personal computer to "perform unauthorized attacks over the Internet" without the user's knowledge. Unauthorized tasks include sending spam and e-mail messages, attacking computers and servers, and committing other kinds of fraud, causing the user's computer to slow down (**microsoft.com/security/resources/botnet-whatis.aspx**).

Each attacking computer is considered *computer robot*. A botnet made up of 75,000 systems infected, in 2010, with Zeus Trojan contaminated computers. Botnets are used in scams, spams, and frauds or just to damage systems. Botnets appear in different forms and can include worms or viruses. Famous botnets include Zeus, Srizbi, Pushdo/Cutwail, Torpig, and Conficker.

Example

Rustock was a botnet made up of about one million hijacked PCs, which evaded discovery for years. The botnet, which sent out up to 30 billion spam messages per day, placed "booby-trapped" advertisements and links on websites visited by the victims. The spammers camouflaged the updates to PCs to look like comments in discussion boards, which made them hard to find by security software. Microsoft was one of the companies that helped shut down Rustock. In 2013, Microsoft and the FBI "disrupted" over 1000 botnets used to steal banking information and identities. Both Microsoft and the FBI had been trying to take down the malware "Citadel," which affected millions of people located in more than 90 countries. For an analysis of malicious botnet attacks, see Katz (2014).

Home Appliance "Botnet"

The Internet of things (IoT) can also be hacked. Since participating smart home appliances (Chap. 7) have a connection to the Internet, they can become computers that can be hacked and controlled. The first home attack, which involved television sets and at least one refrigerator, occurred between December 2013 and January 2014 and was referred to as "the first home appliance 'botnet' and the first cyberattack from the Internet of Things." Hackers broke into more than 100,000 connected home appliances and used them to send over 750,000 malicious e-mails to enterprises and individuals worldwide (see Bort 2014).

For criminal attacks using botnets, see Mello, Jr. (2016).

Malvertising

According to Techopedia, *malvertising* is "a malicious form of Internet advertising used to spread malware." Malvertising is accomplished by hiding malicious code within relatively safe online advertisements (see **techopedia.com/definition/4016/malvertising**).

Note that hackers are targeting ads to hide malware at accelerating rates. For example, in 2013, Google disabled ads from over 400,000 sites that were hiding malware (see Yadron 2014). A final word: If you get an e-mail that congratulates you on winning a large amount of money and asks you to "Please view the attachment," don't!

Keystroke Logging in the Underground Economy

Keystroke logging (keylogging) is the process of using a device or software program that tracks and records the activity of a user in real time (without the user's knowledge or consent) by the keyboard keys they press. Since personal information such as passwords and user names are entered on a keyboard, the keylogger can use the keystrokes to obtain them.

SECTION 11.3 REVIEW QUESTIONS

1. Describe the difference between a nontechnical and a technical cyberattack.
2. What are the major forms of malicious code?
3. What factors account for the increase in malicious code?
4. Define a virus and explain how it works.
5. Define worm and Trojan horse.
6. Define DoS. How are DoS attacks perpetrated?
7. Define malvertising.
8. Describe botnet attacks.

11.4 NONTECHNICAL METHODS: FROM PHISHING TO SPAM AND FRAUD

As discussed in section "The Information Security Problem", there has been a shift to profit-related Internet crimes. These crimes are conducted with the help of both technical tools, such as malicious code, that can access confidential information that may be used to steal money from your online bank account, and nontechnical methods, such as social engineering.

Note: Most of the nontechnical methods listed here use some technical malware (e.g., virus). Then, the criminals employ some nontechnical approach (e.g., psychological pressure).

Fraud can take many forms. The major ones are covered in this chapter. Some methods are a combination of technical and nontechnical (e.g., ransomware). For the global EC fraud trends, see Altshull (2017). For methods, business impacts, and solutions, see Perret (2016).

Social Engineering and Fraud

Social engineering refers to a collection of methods where criminals use human psychology to persuade or manipulate people into revealing their confidential information, or their employment information, so they can collect information for illegal activities. The hacker may also attempt to get access to the user's computer in order to install malicious software that will give hackers control over the person's computer. The major social engineering attacks are *phishing* (several submethods; typically, a phisher sends an e-mail that appears to come from a legitimate source), *pretexting* (e.g., an e-mail allegedly sent from a friend asking for money), and *diversion theft* (when a social engineer convinces a courier company that he is the real recipient of the package but it should be "rerouted" to another address, whereupon the social engineer accepts the package). Once information is obtained from a victim (e.g., via phishing), it is used for committing crimes, mostly for financial gain, as shown in Fig. 11.5. The growth rate of unpatched vulnerabilities and the volume of e-mail, text, or Web scam/phishing activities are increasing rapidly (for predictions, see Damri 2016).

As you can see in the figure, phishers obtain confidential information by using methods ranging from social engineering to physical theft. The stolen information (e.g., credit card numbers, users' identity) is used by the thieves to commit fraud for financial gain, or it is sold in the underground Internet marketplace to another set of criminals, who then use the information to conduct financial crimes themselves. For details, see Wallen (2016). In this section, we will describe how phishing, which is a subset of social engineering, is used.

Notorious hacker Kevin Mitnick, who served jail time for hacking, used social engineering as his primary method to gain access to computer systems.

Social Phishing

In the field of computer security, *phishing* is a fraudulent process of acquiring confidential information, such as credit card or banking details, from unsuspecting computer users. A phisher sends an e-mail, IM, comment, or text message that appears to come from a legitimate, well-known, popular company, bank, school, or public institution. The user is instructed to enter a corrupted website, where he or she may be tricked into submitting confidential information (e.g., being asked to "update" information). Sometimes phishers install malware to facilitate the extraction of information. For an interesting novel that "cries out an alarm about cyber security," read "*Marlins Cry A Phishing Story*" by Swann (2012). The process of Web-based phishing is illustrated in Fig. 11.6. For a quarterly report, see APWG (2016).

Fig. 11.5 Social engineering: from phishing to financial fraud and crime

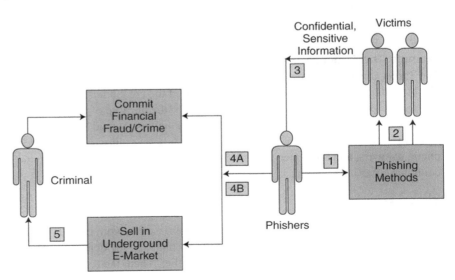

Fig. 11.6 How phishing is
accomplished

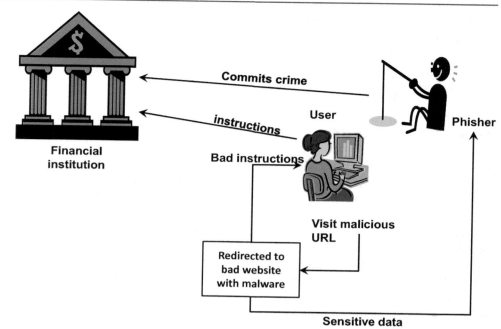

Example: The Amazon 2016 Phishing Scam

According to Jones (2016b), "Just in time for the holiday shopping season, a massive email phishing scam is making the rounds. You really need to watch out for this fake Amazon email.

What's happening is people are getting emails claiming to be from Amazon, but they are actually from scammers. The email warns the recipient that there is a problem processing an order that they placed and that it will not be shipped.

It goes on to say you won't be able to access your account or place orders with Amazon until your information is confirmed. Inside the email is a malicious link that takes you to a fake Amazon page where you need to confirm your information. It asks for your name, address and all of your credit card information." Jones suggested sending the suspicious e-mail to stop-spoofing@amazon.com.

According to Shepard (2017), Amazon scams are on the rise.

For a discussion of what phishing is and how to recognize it, see **ehow.com/how_2003277_yahoo-messenger-scam. html**. See also **www.phishing.org/phishing-techniques** for how phishing works. Anti-phishing companies provide educational reports (see APWG 2016). The quarterly reports include comprehensive coverage of phishing with statistics and forecasts. Casti (2014) describes a phishing scam on Netflix where users were tricked into contacting phony customer service representatives and handing over personal account data. Scammers have now targeted many other companies, such as AT&T and Comcast, by drawing users to fake websites via phony sponsored ads. For 2015 phishing attacks, see Lemos (2016). See also Forrest (2016) for why phishing is getting more dangerous.

Selling stolen information, like selling any stolen goods, can be profitable and unstoppable.

Example: The Target Security Breach

The Target Corp. 2013 security breach, where millions of customers had their debit and credit card data stolen, started as a phishing attack (see Schwartz 2014). Hackers used the credentials of an employee of one of Target's vendors to gain access to Target's security system and install malware for the purpose of accessing the data of every card used. A Target employee would swipe the customer's card and the installed malware would "capture the shopper's credit card number. Once the hackers gained access to the data, they were able to steal 40 million credit and debit card numbers—and 70 million addresses, phone numbers, and other pieces of personal information. To see an infographic of how the hackers broke in and how Target could have prevented the hack, see Smith (2014).

Spear Phishing

Spear phishing is a variant of phishing that targets victims with e-mails purporting to be from colleagues, or family members, or friends. For example, a well-known spear phishing incident is one that you get from a friend that tells you that she is in another country and she was robbed of her wallet. Then, the request for money for a ticket comes so that she can return home and return the money to you. According to Perret (2016), there is a significant increase in such attacks, especially on businesses. Another example is that you can get an e-mail, allegedly from your boss, who is traveling, to transfer money to a "client" in Korea or to e-mail the "boss" the list of customers with their e-mails. Perret (2016) presents possible solutions for both phishing and spear phishing. For the top 10 phishing scams, see **secpoint.com/top-10-spam-attacks.html**. Jones (2016c) reports that Russia's Fancy Bear, which targeted the Democratic National Commission, launched a spear phishing attack and exploited vulnerabilities in Adobe Flash and Microsoft Windows.

Other Phishing Methods

Bisson (2016) lists the following additional methods: deceptive phishing, CEO fraud, Dropbox phishing, Google Docs phishing, and pharming. Bisson also provides protection measures.

Pharming

Similar to phishing, **pharming** is a scam where malicious code installed on a computer is used to redirect victims to bogus websites without the victims' knowledge or consent. Pharming can be more dangerous than phishing since users have no idea that they have been redirected to a fake website. Pharming is directed toward large groups of people at one time via *domain spoofing*. Pharming can be used for identity theft scams (discussed later in this section). For details, see **en.wikipedia.org/wiki/Pharming**.

Fraud and Scams on the Internet

Potential e-commerce customers list "the potential risk of fraud" and "the mistrust of online merchants that you do not know" as their primary reasons for not shopping online.

Phishing can lead to many fraud schemes. The EC environment, where buyers and sellers cannot see each other, facilitates fraud. There are many types of fraud on the Internet (see **fbi.gov/scams-and-safety/common-fraud-schemes/internet-fraud**). Fraud is a problem for online retailers and customers alike. Fortunately, even though actual losses per incident increase, there are fewer incidents, and thus the total monetary damage may be declining. Visit **dmoz.org/Society/Issues/Fraud/Internet** for a comprehensive collection of fraud resources. Mobile fraud attacks are growing rapidly; see Damri (2016). For a discussion, see section "Consumer and Seller Protection from Online Fraud".

Examples of Typical Online Fraud Attacks

The following are some characteristic fraud attacks perpetrated on the Internet.

- When one of the authors of this book advertised online that he had a house to rent, several "doctors" and "nurses" pretending to be from the United Kingdom and South America applied. They agreed to pay a premium price for a short-term lease and said they would pay with a cashier's check. They asked if the author would accept a check from $6000 to $10,000 and send them back the balance of $4000 to $8000. When advised that this would be fine, but that the difference would be returned only after their check had cleared, none of the would-be renters followed up.
- Extortion rings in the United Kingdom and Russia have extorted hundreds of thousands of dollars from online sports betting websites. Any site refusing to pay "protection fees" has been threatened with DoS attacks.

For a video titled "How Hackers Can Invade Your Home" (2:26 min), see **money.cnn.com/video/technology/2013/08/14/t-hack-my-baby-monitor-and-house.cnnmoney**. For a comprehensive discussion of fraud, see CyberSource (2016).

For a discussion on social engineering, phishing, and other methods of fraudulently obtaining confidential information online, see Pontrioli (2013).

Types of Scams

The following are some representative types of scams (per Spamlaws, see **spamlaws.com/scams.html**): literary scams, jury duty scams, banking scams, e-mail scams, lottery scams, Nigerian scams (or "419" fraud), credit cards scams (several types), work at/from home scams, IRS e-mail scams, and free vacation scams. Many more can be found at **fbi.gov/scams-safety/fraud/internet_fraud**.

E-Mail Scams

E-mail scams are the most popular type of scam since they are so easy to commit. Dog Breed Info Center posts common examples at (**dogbreedinfo.com/internetfraud/scamemailexamples.htm**). The examples are both educational and entertaining. The most dangerous are e-mails scams that look like they come from well-known organizations (banks, telecommunication companies) that tell you that you must provide information in order to keep your account active. An example of an e-mail purportedly sent by Yahoo! is provided below.

YAHOO ACCOUNT

Verification Alert!!! (KMM69467VL55834KM)

Dear Valued Member,

Due to the congestion in all Yahoo Accounts, Yahoo would be shutting down all unused Accounts. You will have to confirm your E-mail by filling out your Login Information below after clicking the reply button, or your account will be suspended within 24 h for security reasons.

Yahoo! ID Card

Name:...

Yahoo! ID:...............................

Yahoo! Mail Address:................

Password:..................................

Member Information

Gender:.....................................

Birth Date:...............................

Occupation:...............................

Country:....................................

If you are a Yahoo! Account Premium subscriber, we will refund the unused portion of your Premium subscription. The refund will appear as a credit via the billing method we have on file for you. So please make sure that your billing information is correct and up-to-date. For more information, please visit **payments.mail.yahoo.com**.
    After following the instruction on this sheet your account will not be interrupted and will continue as normal.
    We appreciate your being a Yahoo! Account user.

Sincerely,

Yahoo! Customer Support

Any e-mail you receive asking for personal details is most likely a scam or phishing attempt since a legitimate organization will already have all your personal information. For tips from Yahoo! on how to protect yourself online, see Yahoo! Safety (**safety.yahoo.com**).

Top 10 Attacks and Remedies

IT security site SecPoint.com provides a list of the top 10 security-related attacks on the following topics: top viruses, spyware, spam, worms, phishing, hacker attacks, and hackers and social engineering tactics. In addition, the site provides related pages on IT security resources such as the top ten hackers; top ten security tips and tools; pages relating to anti-phishing, anti-DoS, antispam, and more. For SecPoint IT resources for top ten spam attacks, see **secpoint.com/Top-10-Spam-Attacks.html**.

Identity Theft and Identify Fraud

Identity theft, according to the US Department of Justice website, is a crime. It refers to wrongfully obtaining and using the identity of another person in some way to commit crimes that involve fraud or deception (e.g., for economic gain). Victims can suffer serious damages. In many countries, it is a crime to assume another person's identity. According to the US Federal Trade Commission (**ftc.gov**), identity theft is one of the major concerns of EC shoppers. According to Safe Smart Living statistics, identity theft affects over 12 million Americans each year, (2015) for a loss of over $55 billion, and is growing about 20% annually. According to Alt (2016), over 1 billion leaked records affected 500,000 victims in June 2014. Identity thieves collect $5.8 billion each year. In addition, 19 people become victims of identity theft every minute. Finally, children are easy prey. For an entertaining comedy movie, see the 2013's "Identity Thief."

Example
According to Constantin (2016a), in January 2016, identity thieves stole 100,000 social security numbers and other personal data from the US IRS files.

Identity Fraud

Identity fraud refers to assuming the identity of another person or creating a fictitious person and then unlawfully using that identity to commit a crime. Typical activities include:

- Opening a credit card account in the victim's name
- Making a purchase using a false identity (e.g., using another's identity to buy goods)
- Business identity theft is using another's business name to obtain credit or to get into a partnership
- Posing as another to commit a crime
- Conducting money laundering (e.g., organized crime) using a fake identity

For information and protection, see **idtheftcenter.org** and **fdic.gov/consumers/assistance/protection/IdTheft.html** and Velasco (2016).

Cyber Bank Robberies

Cyberattacks can happen to individuals and organizations, including banks.

Example
Secureworks.com uncovered the following check fraud operations: Russian cybercriminals used "money mules" (people who thought they were signing up for a legitimate job), 2000 computers, and sophisticated hacking methods to steal archived check images from five companies and wire the collected money overseas.

Next, the scammers printed counterfeit checks, which the money mules deposited in their own accounts. Then, the mules were ordered to wire (transfer) the money to a bank in Russia. The "mules," as usual, were innocent people who were hired and paid to do the transfer. Some of the mules became suspicious and reported the scam to the authorities.

Ransomware

File-encrypting ransomware programs become one of the biggest threats to organizations' networks. Unfortunately, ransomware programs are constantly evolving and get more sophisticated. Some believe that ransomware is becoming an epidemic (Greengard 2016b). The opening case is one example of an attack. According to Fitzpatrick and Griffin (2016), the FBI received 2453 complaints in 2015, where the victims paid $24 million in ransom. In 2016/2017, the magnitude of the problem is much larger. For example, security firm Malwarebytes checked over 50,000 incidents and found that Las Vegas is the most attacked region in the USA (per capita).

What Is Ransomware?

In a nutshell, criminals encrypt and lock digital files by using malware and demand a ransom before the system is unlocked. The process of ransomware is illustrated in Fig. 11.7.

Fig. 11.7 The process of ransomware

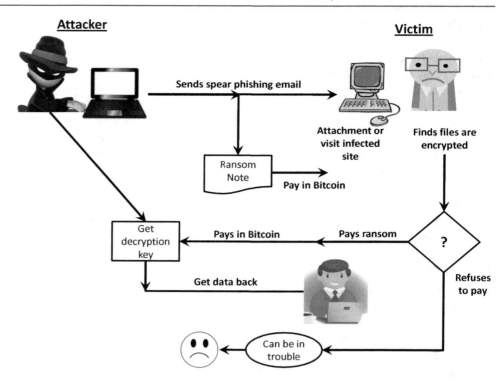

The hackers can use an e-mail with an attachment sent to the victim. Using spear phishing or other social engineering trick, they persuade the unsuspecting employee to open the attachment, which has a virus. A few hours later, all the loosely protected files get encrypted. The data in the files are then taken hostage and a ransom demand is made.

The decryption price asked by ransomware author(s) is calculated per system locked. Payments are usually made in Bitcoins (Chap. 12). The victims need to get decryption keys for the affected systems. Otherwise, the malware may spread even further. Therefore, it is necessary to detect the malware as soon as possible before it spreads inside a network, affecting more systems.

Possible Solutions

The most obvious solutions are having a good antivirus package, good backup of the data, and well-trained users. These solutions are good, but they may not stop all hackers. Most security vendors provide additional solutions and security tips. For example, Tripwire provides 22 ransomware prevention tips at **tripwire.com/state-of-security/security-data-protection/cyber-security/22-ransomware-prevention-tips**.

Mello Jr. (2017) provides an overview of the problem and discusses solutions. For a free 2016 e-book, see Staff (2016b).

Hassell (2016) also suggests some methods to fight ransomware. The future is looking brighter. The security industry is finding new ways to block ransomware. For example, according to Constantin (2016b), machine learning (Chap. 7) could help companies react faster to ransomware. This AI method can significantly improve ransomware detection and reaction time, enabling to stop the fast spread of malware in organizations.

A special (2016) comprehensive e-book is available for free from Symantec. You can get it at **symantec.com/content/en/us/enterprise/media/security_response/whitepapers/ISTR2016_Ransomware_and_Businesses.pdf**.

Example 1

Even the President of the United States can be affected by ransomware. According to Constantin (2017), "around 70 percent of the cameras hooked up to the police's closed-circuit TC (CCTV) system in Washington D.C. were reportedly unable to record footage for several days before President Donald Trump's inauguration due to a ransomware attack.

The attack affected 123 of the 187 network video recorders that form the city's CCTV system. Each of these devices is used to store video footage captured by up to four cameras installed in public spaces.

The incident occurred on January 12, 2017, eight days before the inauguration of President Trump, and it took three days to restore the system. The city refused to pay the ransom and sent teams at each site to take the affected devices offline, replace their software and restart them." If the criminal would have been clever enough and started the incident 1 day before the inauguration, the city would have had little choice but to pay the ransom or put the President at a security risk.

Example 2

Even a small company can be attacked. Bolton (2016) provides an example of a small taxi firm with 12 networked PCs in East London (UK). Malware penetrated the system via an e-mail attachment. An attempt to remove the culprit by Spy Hunter failed. A ransom of 1.2 Bitcoins was demanded. Luckily, the company was in the process of replacing the old PCs, so they did this and did not pay the ransom. Bolton's suggestions for SMEs are to (1) have an e-mail scanner and (2) back up your data frequently.

Spam Attacks

E-mail spam, also known as *junk e-mail* or just *spam*, occurs when almost identical messages are e-mailed to many recipients in bulk (sometimes millions of unsolicited e-mails). According to Symantec, most of messages on corporate networks are e-mail spam. Nearly 58% of spam came from botnets; the worst botnet was called *Dotnet*. The situation is better today (2017) due to improved filtering of junk mail. Spammers can purchase millions of e-mail addresses and then format the addresses, cut and paste the messages, and press "send." Mass e-mail software that generates, sends, and automates spam e-mail sending is called *Ratware*. The messages can be advertisements (to buy a product), fraud-based, or just annoying viruses. For current statistics on spam, see **securelist.com/statistics**. Securelist is a comprehensive site that also provides descriptions of spam and viruses, a glossary, and information on threats. More than 130 billion spam e-mails are sent each day as of 2013, but this growth rate has stabilized. Note that approximately 80% of all spam is sent by fewer than 200 spammers. These spammers are using spyware and other tools mostly for sending unsolicited advertising. The spammers are getting more clever and more sophisticated (e.g., see Ban 2015 for an analysis of cases). Clever spam techniques require advanced antispam technologies (Ban 2015).

Typical Examples of Spamming

Each month, Symantec provides a report titled "The State of Spam: A Monthly Report." The report provides examples of current popular scams, categories of spam, originating countries, volume, and much more.

Spyware

Spyware is a tracking software that is installed by criminals, without the user's consent, in order to gather information about the user and direct it to advertisers or other third parties. Once installed the spyware program tracks and records the user's movements on the Internet. Spyware may contain malicious code redirecting Web browser activity. Spyware can also slow surfing speeds and damage a program's functionality. Spyware usually is installed when you download freeware or shareware. For news and a video titled "Ethiopian Government Spying on U.S.-Based Journalists" (2:23 min) of how some regimes use spyware against journalists, see Timberg (2014).

Social Networking Makes Social Engineering Easy

Social networking sites are vulnerable and fertile areas for hackers and con artists to gain a user's trust, according to a study by Danish-owned IT security company CSIS.

How Hackers Are Attacking Social Networks

Hackers are exploiting the trusted environment of social networks that contain personal information (especially Facebook) to launch different social engineering attacks. Unfortunately, many social networking sites have poor track records for security controls. There is a growing trend to use social networking sites as platforms for stealing users' personal data.

Examples

Here are some examples of security problems in social networking:

- Users may unknowingly insert malicious code into their profile page or even their list of friends.
- Most antispam solutions cannot differentiate between real and criminal requests to connect to a network. This enables criminals to obtain personal information about the members in a network.
- Facebook and other popular social networking sites offer free, useful, attractive applications. These applications may have been built by developers who used weak security.
- Scammers may create a fake profile and use it in a phishing scam.

Spam in Social Networks and in the Web 2.0 Environment

Social networks attract spammers due to the large number of potential recipients and the less secure Internet and social networking platforms. Spammers like to attack Facebook in particular. Another problem area is blog spam.

Automated Blog Spam

Bloggers are spammed by automatically generated commercials (some real and some fake) for items ranging from herbal Viagra to gambling vendors. Blog writers can use tools to ensure that a human, and not an automated system, posts comments on their blogs.

Search Engine Spam and Splogs

Search engine spam is a technology that enables the creation of pages called **spam sites** that trick search engines into offering biased search results so that the ranking of certain pages is inflated. A similar tactic involves the use of **splogs** (short for *spam blog sites*), which are blogs created by spammers solely for advertising. The spammer creates many splogs and links them to the sites of those that pay him (her) to increase certain page ranking. As you may recall from Chap. 10, companies are looking for search engine optimization (SEO), which is conducted unethically by the above techniques.

Examples

Some examples of spam attacks in social networks (social spam) are:

- Instant messaging in social networks is frequently vulnerable to spam attacks.
- King (2016) describes phishing attacks on the major social networks (Facebook, Twitter, LinkedIn). These attacks have increased 150% in 1 year.

King listed the following five examples:

1. Fake customer service accounts on Twitter
2. Fake comments on popular posts
3. Fake livestream videos
4. Fake online discounts
5. Fake online surveys and contests

Data Breach (Leak)

A **data breach** (also known as *data leak* or *data loss*) is a security incident in which data are obtained illegally and then published or processed. There are many purposes for data breaches. For instance, one person in the US military used a USB to download classified information and then posted the stolen information on the Internet. For drivers of data breaches and how to protect yourself, see Goldman (2014b). For the most frightening data breaches, see TechRepublic Staff (2015).

The discussion so far has concentrated on attacks. Defense mechanisms, including those related to spam and other cybercrimes, are provided in section "Defending Information Systems and E-Commerce Including Mobile Systems". First, let us examine what is involved in assuring information security.

SECTION 11.4 REVIEW QUESTIONS

1. Define phishing.
2. Describe the relationship of phishing to financial fraud.
3. Briefly describe some phishing tactics.
4. Define pharming.
5. Describe spam and its methods.
6. Define splogs and explain how sploggers make money.
7. Why and how are social networks being attacked?
8. Describe data breaches (data leaks).
9. Describe the process of ransomware.

11.5   THE INFORMATION ASSURANCE MODEL AND DEFENSE STRATEGY

The *information assurance (IA) model*, known as the **CIA security triad**, is a point of reference used to identify problem areas and evaluate the information security of an organization. The use of the model includes three necessary attributes: *confidentiality*, *integrity*, and *availability*. This model is described next. (For a discussion, see **whatis.techtarget.com/definition/Confidentiality-integrity-and-availability-CIA**.)

Note: The assurance model can be adapted to several EC activities. For example, securing the EC supply chain is critical.

Confidentiality, Integrity, and Availability

The success and security of EC can be measured by these attributes:

1. **Confidentiality** is the assurance of data secrecy and privacy. Namely, the data is disclosed only to authorized people. Confidentiality is achieved by using several methods, such as encryption and passwords.
2. **Integrity** is the assurance that data are accurate and that they cannot be altered. The integrity attribute needs to be able to detect and prevent the unauthorized creation, modification, or deletion of data or messages in transit.
3. **Availability** is the assurance that access to any relevant data, information websites, or other EC services and their use is available in real time, whenever and wherever needed. The information must be reliable.

Authentication, Authorization, and Nonrepudiation

Three concepts are related to the IA model: *authentication, authorization*, and *nonrepudiation*. These important concepts are:

- *Authentication* is a security measure making sure that data information, ECD participants and transactions, and all other EC-related objects are valid. *Authentication* requires verification. For example, a person can be authenticated by something he knows (e.g., a password), something he possesses (e.g., an entry token), or something unique to that person (e.g., a fingerprint).
- *Authorization* requires comparing information provided by a person or a program during a login with stored information associated with the access requested.
- *Nonrepudiation* is the concept of ensuring that a party in an EC transaction cannot repudiate (or refute) the validity of an EC contract and that she or he will fulfill their obligation in the transactions. According to the National Information Systems Security (INFOSEC)'s glossary, nonrepudiation is the "[a]ssurance the sender of data is provided with proof of delivery and the recipient is provided with proof of the sender's identity, so that neither can later deny having processed the data."

Note: See the list of key terms in section "Basic E-Commerce Security Issues and Landscape". Some sources list more concepts (e.g., Techopedia).

To assure these attributes, e-commerce applies technologies such as encryption, digital signature, and certification. For example, the use of a *digital signature* makes it difficult for people to deny their involvement in an EC transaction.

In e-commerce, new or improved methods to ensure the confidentiality of credit card numbers, the integrity of transaction-related messages, the authentication of buyers and sellers, and nonrepudiation of transactions need to be constantly updated as older methods become obsolete.

E-Commerce Security Strategy

EC security needs to address the IA model and its components. In Fig. 11.7, an EC security framework that defines the high-level categories of assurance and their controls is presented. The major categories are regulatory, financial, and marketing operations. Only the key areas are listed in the figure.

The Defense Side EC Systems

We organize the defense into eight categories:

1. **Defending access to computing systems, data flow, and EC transactions.** This includes three topics: Access control (including biometrics), encryption of contents, and public key infrastructure (PKI).

   This line of defense provides comprehensive protection when applied together. Intruders that circumvent the access control will face encrypted material even if they pass a firewall.
2. **Defending EC networks.** This includes mainly protection by firewalls. The firewall isolates the corporate network and computing devices from the Internet that are poorly secured. To make the Internet more secure, we can use virtual private networks. In addition to these measures, it is wise to use intrusion detection systems. A protected network means securing the incoming e-mail, which is usually unencrypted. It is also necessary to protect against viruses and other malware that are transmitted via the networks.
3. **General, administrative, and application controls.** These are a variety of safeguards that are intended to protect computing assets by establishing guidelines, checking procedures, and so forth.
4. **Protection against social engineering and fraud.** Several defense methods are used against spam, phishing, and spyware.
5. **Disaster preparation, business continuity, and risk management.** These topics are managerial issues that are supported by software.
6. **Implementing enterprisewide security programs.** To deploy the abovementioned defense methods, one needs to use appropriate implementation strategy.
7. **Conduct a vulnerability assessment and a penetration test.** (See the following text.)
8. **Back up the data.**

For a comprehensive coverage of all aspects of information protection, see Harwood (2015).

To implement the above defense, first conduct some assessment and then plan and execute. Two possible activities are *vulnerability assessments* and *penetration tests*.

Assessing Vulnerabilities and Security Needs

A key task in security strategy is to find the weaknesses and strengths of the existing security strategies and solutions. This is part of a risk assessment and can be accomplished in different ways. Here are two representative suggestions:

1. Conduct a vulnerability assessment of your EC systems. A **vulnerability assessment** is a process of identifying and evaluating problem areas that are vulnerable to attack on a computerized system. The EC system includes online ordering, communication networks, payment gates, product database, fraud protection, and so forth. The most critical vulnerabili-

ties are those that can interrupt or shut down the business. For example, a DoS can prevent order taking; a virus attack can prevent communication. The assessment will determine the need for, and priority of, the defense mechanisms. For an overview of vulnerability assessment including the process, see searchmidmarketsecurity.techtarget.com/definition/vulnerability-analysis.

2. Conduct *penetration (pen) tests* (possibly implemented by hiring ex-hackers) to find the vulnerabilities and security weaknesses of a system. These tests are designed to simulate outside (external) attacks. This is also called "black-box" testing. In contrast, software development companies conduct intensive "white-hat" testing, which involves a careful inspection of the system—both hardware and software. Other types of pen testing include targeted texting, blind testing, and double-blind testing.

For more information, see **searchsoftwarequality.techtarget.com/definition/penetration-testing**.

Penetration Test

A **penetration test (pen test)** is a method of assessing the vulnerability of a computer system. It can be done manually, by allowing experts to act as hackers to simulate malicious attacks. The process checks the weak (vulnerable) points that an attacker may find and exploit. Any weakness that is discovered is presented to management, together with the potential impact and a proposed solution. A pen test can be one step in a comprehensive security audit.

Several methods can be used to execute pen tests (e.g., automated process). In addition, many software tools are available for this purpose. For a review and a tutorial, see **pen-tests.com** and **coresecurity.com/penetration-testing-overview**. For more on penetration tests, see Maxwell (2016).

SECTION 11.5 REVIEW QUESTIONS

1. What is information assurance? List its major components.
2. Define confidentiality, integrity, and availability.
3. Define authentication, authorization, and nonrepudiation.
4. List the objectives of EC strategy.
5. List the eight categories of defense in EC systems.
6. Describe vulnerability assessment.
7. What is a penetration test?

11.6   DEFENDING INFORMATION SYSTEMS AND E-COMMERCE

Defending information systems regardless of their nature is similar and is described in generic IT books (e.g., by Kim and Solomon 2016).

We provide only highlights of this security, dividing it into three categories: (1) access control, encryption, and PKI; (2) security e-commerce networks; and (3) general controls, spam, pop-ups, and social engineering. In section "Consumer and Seller Protection from Online Fraud", we describe fraud protection.

Comprehensive coverage of cybersecurity threats and defense is provided by Scott in several volumes titled *Cybersecurity 101*. Volume 1 (Scott 2016a) covers mostly nontechnical areas, while Volume 2 (Scott 2016b) covers mostly technical areas. A comprehensive book regarding defense against attacks on the Web is provided by Harwood (2015).

The Defense I: Access Control, Encryption, and PKI

In this section, we describe the following topics: access control methods, biometric systems, encryption, and PKI encryption. For an overview of this area of defense, see Cloud (2015).

Access Control

Access control determines who (person, program, or machine) can legitimately use the organization's computing resources (which resources, when, and how).

Authorization and Authentication

Access control involves *authorization* (having the right to access) and *authentication*, which is also called *user identification* (user ID), i.e., proving that the user is who he or she claims to be. Each user has a distinctive identification that differentiates it from other users. Typically, user identification is used together with a password.

Authentication

After a user has been *identified*, the user must be *authenticated*. *Authentication* is the process of verifying the user's identity and access rights. Verification of the user's identity usually is based on one or more characteristics that distinguish one individual from another.

Antivirus Protection

A large number of companies provide basic to super protection. Some are free. Representative names are McAfee, Norton, and Kaspersky (from Symantec), Webroot, and Bitdefender, and PC Magazine and other technical publications review different products. For the best of 2017, see Rubenking (2017).

Biometric Systems

A **biometric authentication** is a technology that measures and analyzes the identity of people based on measurable biological or behavioral characteristics or physiological signals.

Biometric systems can *identify* a previously registered person by searching through a database for a possible *match* based on the person's observed physical, biological, or behavioral traits, or the system can *verify* a person's identity by matching an individual's measured biometric traits against a previously stored version.

Examples of biometric features include fingerprints, facial recognition, DNA, palm print, hand geometry, iris recognition, and even odor/scent. Behavioral traits include voice ID, typing rhythm (keystroke dynamics), and signature verification. A brief description of some of these follows:

- **Thumbprint or fingerprint.** A thumb- or fingerprint (finger scan) of users requesting access is matched against a template containing the fingerprints of authorized people (e.g., used by Apple Pay).
- **Retinal scan.** A match is sought between the patterns of the blood vessels in the retina of the access seekers against the retinal images of authorized people stored in a source database.
- **Voice ID (voice authentication).** A match is sought between the voice pattern of the access seekers and the stored voice patterns of the authorized people.
- **Facial recognition.** Computer software that views an image or video of a person and compares it to an image stored in a database (used by Amazon.com and Alibaba).
- **Signature recognition.** Signatures of access seekers are matched against stored authentic signatures.

In 2017, Apple was exploring two-step touch ID and facial recognition for iPhones; see Hardwick (2017).

Note that Alibaba is using facial recognition for online payments. You scan your face in front of the camera on your smartphone (see Kan 2015 for details). Amazon is using a similar system (Hinckley 2016).

Other biometric types are thermal infrared face recognition, hand geometry, and hand veins. For details, comparisons with regard to human characteristics, and cost–benefit analyses, see **findbiometrics.com/solutions.** For more on biometrics, see **biometricsociety.org**.

Encryption and the One-Key (Symmetric) System

Encryption is the process of encoding data into a form (called a *ciphertext*) that will be difficult, expensive, or time-consuming for an unauthorized person to understand. All encryption methods have five basic components: *plaintext, ciphertext*, an *encryption algorithm*, the *key*, and *key space*. **Plaintext** is a human-readable text or message. **Ciphertext** is an encrypted plaintext. The **encryption algorithm** is the set of procedures or mathematical algorithms used to encrypt or decrypt a message. Typically, the algorithm is not the secret piece of the encryption process. The **key (key value)** is the secret piece used with the algorithm to encrypt (or decrypt) the message. For how encryption works, see **computer.howstuffworks.com/encryption.htm**.

The major benefits of encryption are:

- Allows users to carry data on their laptops, mobile devices, and storage devices (e.g., USB flash drives)
- Protects backup media while people and data are offsite
- Allows for highly secure virtual private networks (VPNs; see section "Advertising Strategies and Promotions")
- Enforces policies regarding who is authorized to handle specific corporate data
- Ensures compliance with privacy laws and government regulations and reduces the risk of lawsuits
- Protects the organization's reputation and secrets

Encryption has two basic options: the *symmetric system*, with one secret key, and the *asymmetric system*, with two keys.

Symmetric (Private) Key Encryption

In a **symmetric (private) key encryption**, the same key is used to encrypt and decrypt the plaintext (see Fig. 11.8). The sender and receiver of the text must share the same key without revealing it to anyone else—making it a so-called *private* system.

A strong key is only one requirement. Transferring the key between individuals and organizations may make it insecure. Therefore, in EC, a PKI system is used.

Public Key Infrastructure

A **public key infrastructure (PKI)** is a comprehensive framework for securing data flow and information exchange that overcomes some of the shortcomings of the one-key system. For example, the symmetric one-key encryption requires the writer of a message to reveal the key to the message's recipient. A person that is sending a message (e.g., vendor) may need to distribute the key to thousands of recipients (e.g., buyers), and then the key probably would not remain secret. The PKI solution is using two keys, public and private, as well as additional features that create a highly secured system. In addition to the keys, PKI includes digital signatures, hash digests (function), and digital certificates.

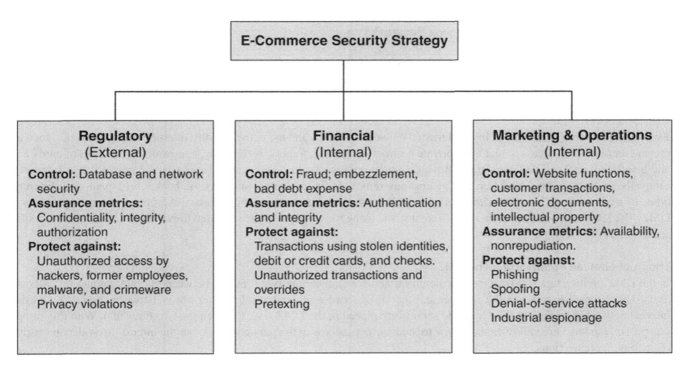

Fig. 11.8 E-commerce security strategy framework

Public (Asymmetric) Key Encryption

Public (asymmetric) key encryption uses two keys—a **public key** that is known to all and a **private key** that only its owner knows. The two keys must be used together. If a message is encrypted with a public key, then only the associated private key can decrypt the message (and vice versa). If, for example, a person wants to send a purchase order to a vendor and have the contents remain private, the sender encrypts the message with the buyer's public key. When the vendor, who is the *only one able* to read the purchase order, receives the order, the vendor decrypts it with the associated private key.

The PKI Process: Digital Signatures and Certificate Authorities

Digital signatures are the electronic equivalent of personal signatures on paper. They are difficult to forge since they authenticate the identity of the sender that uses the public key. Digital signatures are legally treated as signatures on paper. To see how a digital signature works, go to **searchsecurity.techtarget.com/definition/digital-signature**.

Certificate Authority

Independent agencies called **certificate authorities (CAs)** issue digital certificates or SSL certificates, which are electronic files that uniquely identify individuals and websites and enable encrypted communication. The certificate contains personal information and other information related to the public key and the encryption method, as well as a signed hash of the certificate data.

Secure Sockets Layer (SSL)

PKI systems are further secured with SSL—a protocol for e-commerce. The PKI with SSL makes e-commerce very secure but cumbersome for users. One of the major protocols in use today is Secure Sockets Layer (SSL). SSL has been succeeded by Transport Layer Security (TLS), which is based on SSL. For further details, see **searchsecurity.techtarget.com/definition/Transport-Layer-Security-TLS**.

Other Controls

Several other methods are used for access control. For example, Shipley (2017) provides a list of the best DDos services of 2017 (e.g., f5, Arbor Network, Akamai, and Incapsula). Some are free.

In the next section, the focus is on the company's digital perimeters—the networks.

The Defense II: Securing E-Commerce Networks

Several technologies exist that ensure that an organization's network boundaries are secure from cyberattack or intrusion and that if the organization's boundaries are compromised the intrusion is detected quickly and combated.

Firewalls

Firewalls are barriers between an internal trusted network (or a PC) and the untrustworthy Internet. A firewall is designed to prevent unauthorized access to and from private networks, such as intranets. Technically, a firewall is composed of hardware and a software package that separates a private computer network (e.g., your LAN) from a public network (the Internet). Firewalls are designed mainly to protect against any remote login, access by intruders via backdoors, spam, and different types of malware (e.g., viruses or macros). Firewalls come in several shapes and formats. A popular defense system is a DMZ. The DMZ can be designed in two different ways, using a single firewall or with dual firewalls. For intelligent firewalls, see Teo (2016).

The Dual-Firewall Architecture: The DMZ

In the DMZ architecture (DMZ stands for demilitarized zone), there are two firewalls between the Internet and the internal users. One firewall is between the Internet and the DMZ (border firewall), and another one is between the DMZ and the internal network (see Fig. 11.9). All public servers are placed in the DMZ (i.e., between the two firewalls). With this setup, it is possible to have firewall rules that allow trusted partners access to the public servers, but the interior firewall can restrict all incoming connections.

For more on DMZ and its benefits, see Mitchell (2016).

Fig. 11.9 Symmetric (private) key encryption

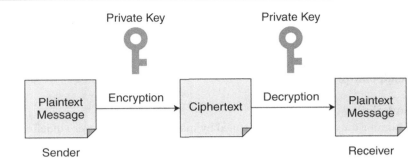

Virtual Private Networks (VPNs)

Suppose a company wants to establish a B2B application, providing suppliers, partners, and others access not only to data residing on its internal website but also to data contained in other files (e.g., Word documents) or in legacy systems (e.g., large relational databases). Traditionally, communications with the company would have taken place over a secure but expensive *value-added private leased line* or through a dial-up line connected to modems or a remote access server (RAS). Unfortunately, using the Internet instead, which is free, may not be secure. A more secure use of the Internet is provided by using a VPN.

A **virtual private network (VPN)** refers to the use of the Internet to transfer information but in a more secure manner. A VPN behaves like a private network by using encryption and other security features to keep the information secure. For example, a VPN verifies the identity of anyone using the network.

For details on VPNs, see **searchenterprisewan.techtarget.com/definition/virtual-private-network**. For the best VPN services, see **pcmag.com/article2/0,2817,2403388,00.asp**.

Intrusion Detection Systems (IDS)

No matter how protected an organization is, it still can be a target for attempted security attacks. For example, most organizations have antivirus software, yet they are subjected to virus attacks by new viruses. This is why an organization must continually monitor for attempted, as well as actual, security breaches. The monitoring can be done by using intrusion detectors.

An **intrusion detection system (IDS)** is a device composed of software and/or hardware designed to monitor the activities of computer networks and computer systems in order to detect and define unauthorized and malicious attempts to access, manipulate, and/or disable these networks and systems. For details, the technology, benefits, and limitations, see Parker II (2016) and **searchsecurity.techtarget.com/guides/Introduction-to-IDS-IPS-Network-intrusion-detection-system-basics**. For the future of IDS, see Guri (2016). For defeating DDos attacks, see Cisco (2014).

Dealing with DoS Attacks

DoS attacks, as described earlier, are designed to bombard websites with all types of useless information, which clogs the sites. The faster a DoS attack is discovered, the easier is the defense. DoS attacks grow rapidly. Therefore, detecting an intrusion early can help. Since there are several types of DoS attacks (e.g., DDoS), there are several defense methods. For examples, see **learn-networking.com/network-security/how-to-prevent-denial-of-service-attacks**. Intrusion detecting software also identifies the DoS type, which makes the defense easier and faster.

The Defense III: General Controls, Spam, Pop-Ups, and Social Engineering Controls

The objective of IT security management practices is to defend information systems. A defense strategy requires several *controls*.

The major types of controls are (1) **general controls**, which are designed to protect all system applications, and (2) **application controls** which guard applications. In this and the following sections, we discuss representative types of these two groups of information system controls. Later in the section, we cover spam and fraud mitigation.

General, Administrative, and Other Controls

The major categories of general controls are physical controls, administrative controls, and other controls. A brief description of general controls is provided next.

Physical Controls

Physical controls protect computer facilities and resources, including the physical area where computing facilities are located. The controls provide protection against natural hazards, criminal attacks, and some human error.

Network access control software is offered by all major security vendors (e.g., see **symantec.com/campaigns/ endpoint-protection**).

Administrative Controls

Administrative controls are defined by management and cover guidelines and compliance issuing and monitoring.

Protecting Against Spam

Sending spam that includes a sales pitch and looks like personal, legitimate e-mail and may bypass filters is a violation of the US Controlling the Assault of Non-Solicited Pornography and Marketing (CAN-SPAM) Act of 2003. However, many spammers hide their identity by using hijacked PCs or spam zombies to avoid detection and identification.

Protecting Your Computer from Pop-Up Ads

The use of pop-ups and similar advertising methods is growing rapidly. Sometimes it is even difficult to close these ads when they appear on the screen. Some of these ads may be part of a consumer's permitted marketing agreement, but most are unsolicited. What can a user do about unsolicited pop-up ads? Here are some resources:

Panicware, Inc.'s Pop-Up Stopper Free Edition (**pop-up-stopper-free-edition.software.informer.com**), Softonic's Pop up Blocker (**pop-up-blocker.en.softonic.com/download**), and AdFender (**adfender.com**); others are available for a fee. For a list, see **snapfiles.com**, and for a list of blocker software for Windows, see **download.cnet.com/windows/popup-blocker-software**. Many ISPs and major browser makers (e.g., Google, Microsoft, Yahoo!, Mozilla) offer tools to stop pop-ups.

Protecting Against Other Social Engineering Attacks

With the increasing number of social engineering attacks via websites and in social networks comes the need for better protection. The open source environment and the interactive nature of the technology also create risks. Thus, EC security becomes a necessity for any successful social networking initiative.

Mangis (2016) provides an interesting example of an attempt to extort money by using social engineering and locking up an individual's PC. It was a clever scam, but it failed.

Social networking spans many different applications and services. Therefore, many methods and tools are available to defend such systems. Many of the solutions are technical in nature and are outside the scope of this book.

Protecting Against Phishing

Because there are many phishing methods, there are many defense methods as well. Illustrative examples are provided by Symantec (2009) and the FTC Consumer Information at **consumer.ftc.gov/articles/0003-phishing**. For risk and fraud insights, see **sas.com/en_us/insights/risk-fraud.html**.

Protecting Against Malvertising

According to TechTarget, *malvertising (malicious advertising)* "is an advertisement on the Internet that is capable of infecting the viewer's computer with malware." Microsoft combats malvertising by taking legal action against malvertisers.

Bisson (2016) classifies phishing into six categories and suggests a solution for each category.

Protecting Against Spyware

In response to the emergence of spyware, a large variety of antispyware software exists. Antispyware laws, available in many jurisdictions, usually target any malicious software that is installed without the knowledge of users. The US Federal Trade Commission advises consumers about spyware infections. For details and resources, see **ftc.gov/news-events/media-resources/identity-theft-and-data-security/spyware-and-malware**.

Protecting Against Cyberwars

This is a difficult task since these attacks usually come from foreign countries. The US government is developing tools that will mine social media sites to predict cyberattacks. The tools will monitor all Facebook, Twitter, and other social networks sites to interpret content. The idea is to automate the process.

Protecting Users of Social Media

As indicated earlier, there is an increased threat to users of social media and members of social networks. It can be difficult to defend, particularly against social media impersonators who try to commit fraud. Velasco (2016) suggests the following:

- "Make use of any security settings offered by social media platforms. Examples of these include privacy settings, captcha puzzles and warning pages informing you that you are being redirected offsite.
- Do not share login info, not even with people you trust. Close friends and family might still accidentally make you vulnerable if they are using your account.
- Be wary of what information you share. Keep your personal info under lock and key, and never give out highly sensitive information like your social number or driver's license number.
- Do not reuse passwords. Have a unique password for every account you hold.
- Consider changing inessential info. You don't have to put your real birthday on Facebook.
- Only accept friend requests from people seem familiar."

Business Continuity and Disaster Recovery

Disasters may occur without warning. A prudent defense is to have a *business continuity plan*, mainly consisting of a *disaster recovery plan*. Such a plan describes the details of the recovery process from major disasters such as loss of all (or most) of the computing facilities or data.

Example: Hospital Paid Ransom After Malware Attack Because They Had No Disaster Recovery Plan

Hollywood Presbyterian Medical Center paid a ransom of $17,000 in Bitcoins (so the blackmailer/hacker could not be identified; see Chap. 12 for Bitcoins). The hacker encrypted the data that were not backed up. The hospital failed with its disaster recovery plan, so there was no choice (per the hospital management) but to pay the ransom. For details, see Jennings (2016). This case is similar to the opening case.

SANS's CIS Critical Security Controls

SANS Institute is a company that specializes in information security. The company is well known for its training, education, and certification programs. One of the company's most known projects is the "Monitoring and Measuring the CIS Critical Security." These 20 controls are the core of the recommended security configuration of computer network infrastructure. They are recommended for effective cyber defense. SANS provides a free poster that includes the highlights of the controls; see **sans.org/media/critical-security-controls/SANS_CSC_Poster.pdf**. The 20 items are the considered first priority items. The poster includes the major vendors and their products, along with a matrix that shows the degree to which the products can satisfy each of the 20 items. A description of the 20 items is available on the poster as well as at **sans.org/critical-security-controls**. Greene (2015) provides additional discussion. SANS provided case studies, Internet monitoring systems staffed by global experts, research documents, and news. A notable development is *NetWars*, a suite of interactive learning tools for simulating scenarios such as cyberattacks. NetWars is used by the US Air Force and the US Army.

Several of the critical controls (e.g., access controls, data protection, data recovery, firewalls, and penetrating tests) are discussed in this chapter.

SECTION 11.6 REVIEW QUESTIONS

1. Define access control.
2. What are the basic elements of an authentication system?
3. Define biometric systems and list five of their methods.
4. Define a symmetric (one-key) encryption.
5. List some of the disadvantages of the symmetric system.
6. What are the key components of PKI?
7. Describe the PKI process.
8. How does a digital signature work?
9. Describe digital certification.
10. List the basic types of firewalls and briefly describe each.
11. How does a VPN work and how does it benefit users?

12. Briefly describe the major types of IDSs.
13. What are general controls? List the various types.
14. How does one protect against spam?
15. How does one protect against pop-ups?
16. How does one protect against phishing, spyware, and malvertising?
17. How does one protect against ransomware?

11.7 CONSUMER AND SELLER PROTECTION FROM ONLINE FRAUD

Internet fraud is a major problem in e-commerce and it is growing rapidly. The fraud is mostly against consumers, but there is some against sellers and merchants. Governments are especially eager to educate the public about the many types of fraud, which target senior citizen in particular. General information on what are common frauds are provided by agencies such as the FBI (see **fbi.gov/scams-and-safety/common-fraud-schemes/internet-fraud**). FBI also operates the Internet Crime Complaint Center, IC3 at **ic3.gov**. Internet fraud is a growing problem (about 25% of all consumers are victims). The problem is growing due to the blending of social commerce and e-commerce and the increase use of m-commerce (see Frenkel 2016). For an overview, see **paypal.com/us/webapps/mpp/paypal-safety-and-security**. Online fraud attacks are growing at an alarming rate in the United States, according to Meola (2016). Fraud activities exist in many formats, as discussed in section "Nontechnical Methods: From Phishing to Spam and Fraud". See also Lonergan (2016). For trends in global e-commerce fraud, see Khaitan (2016).

For 20 tips for keeping your EC website protected against hacking and fraud, see Karol (2017).

It is necessary to protect EC consumers, which the IC3 attempts to do, by informing the public about Internet scams and by publishing public service announcements.

Consumer (Buyer) Protection

Consumer protection is critical to the success of any commerce, especially electronic ones, where transactions between buyers and sellers are not face-to-face. The Federal Trade Commission (FTC) enforces consumer protection laws in the United States. The FTC provides a list of common online scams (see **onguardonline.gov/articles/0002-common-online-scams**). In addition, the European Union and the United States are attempting to develop joint consumer protection policies. For details, see the Transatlantic Consumer Dialogue website at **tacd.org**.

In 2016, the FTC released the OECD's recommendations on consumer protection in e-commerce. The recommendations aim to increase payment protection, reduce privacy and security risks, expand product safety, and encourage the use of plain language in advertising. For details, see Law Blog (2016) and **oecd.org/sti/consumer/ECommerce-Recommendation-2016.pdf**.

Representative Tips and Sources for Your Protection

A representative list follows:

- Users should make sure that they enter the real website of well-known companies, such as Walmart, Disney, and Amazon.com, by going directly to the site rather than through a link.
- Check any unfamiliar site for an address and telephone and fax numbers. Call and quiz a salesperson about the company and the products.
- Investigate sellers with the local chamber of commerce, Better Business Bureau (**bbb.org**), or TRUSTe (**truste.com**).
- Investigate how secure the seller's site is and how well it is organized.
- Examine the money-back guarantees, warranties, and service agreements before making a purchase.
- Compare prices online with those in regular stores—prices that are too low may be too good to be true.
- Ask friends what they know about the websites. Find testimonials and endorsements (be careful, some may be biased).
- Find out what remedy is available in case of a dispute.
- Consult the National Consumers League Fraud Center (**fraud.org**).
- Check the resources available at **consumerworld.org**.
- Amazon.com provides comprehensive protection. See **pay.amazon.com/us/merchant**.

In addition to these tips, consumers and shoppers also have rights on the Internet, as described in the following list of sources:

- The Federal Trade Commission (**ftc.gov**): Protecting America's Consumers. Abusive e-mail should be forwarded to spam@uce.go. For tips and advice see **ftc.gov/tips-advice**.
- The Federal Government Safety Online (**usa.gov/online-safety**)
- National Consumers League Fraud Center (**fraud.org**).
- Federal Citizen Information Center at (**gsa.gov/portal/**).
- US Department of Justice (**justice.gov**).
  - Internet Crime Complaint Center (**ic3.gov**).
- The American Bar Association provides online shopping tips at **americanbar.org/groups/business_law/migrated/safeshopping.html**.
- The Better Business Bureau (**bbb.org**).
- The US Food and Drug Administration provides information on buying medicine and medical products online (**www.fda.gov/forconsumers/protectyourself/default.htm**).
- The Direct Marketing Association (**thedma.org**).

For specific tips on how to spot fake sites and products, see Horowitz and Horowitz (2015).For fighting fake news that may include fraud, see LaCapria (2017).

Disclaimer: This is general information on consumer rights. It is not legal advice on how any particular individual should proceed. If you require specific legal advice, consult an attorney.

Third-Party Assurance Services

Several public organizations and private companies also attempt to protect consumers. The following are just a few examples.

Protection by a Third-Party Intermediary

Intermediaries who manage electronic markets try to protect buyers and sellers. A good example is eBay, which provides an extensive protection program (see eBay Money Back Guarantee (**pages.ebay.com/ebay-money-back-guarantee/**) and Dispute Resolution Center).

TRUSTe's "Trustmark"

TRUSTe (**truste.com**) is a for-profit company whose mission is to ensure that "businesses adhere to best practices regarding the collection and use of personal information on their website" (see **truste.com/about-TRUSTe/**).

The TRUSTe program is voluntary. The licensing fee for use of the Trustmark is paid by sellers, depending on the size of the online business.

Better Business Bureau

The Better Business Bureau (BBB; **bbb.org**), a nonprofit organization supported largely by membership, collects and provides reports on businesses that consumers can review before making a purchase. The BBB responds to millions of inquiries each year. The BBB also handles customer disputes against businesses.

WebTrust Seal

The WebTrust seal program is similar to TRUSTe. The American Institute of Certified Public Accountants (**aicpa.org**) sponsors it (see **webtrust.org/item64428.aspx**).

Evaluation by Consumers

A large number of sites include product and vendor evaluations offered by consumers. For example, on Yelp!, community members rate and comment on businesses.

The Computer Fraud and Abuse Act (CFAA)

The **Computer Fraud and Abuse Act (CFAA)**, passed in 1984 and amended several times, is an important milestone in EC legislation. Initially, the scope and intent of CFAA was to protect government computers and financial industry computers from criminal theft by outsiders. In 1986, the CFAA was amended to include stiffer penalties for violations, but it still only protected computers used by the federal government or financial institutions. As the Internet expanded in scope, so did the CFAA.

Seller (Merchant) Protection

The Internet also makes it easy for buyers engaging in EC to commit fraud against merchants.

For an example of how buyers attempt to trick money or goods out of sellers, see Shrubb (2015). Mellor (2016) discusses the issue and makes some suggestions for making use of available data by researching customers' profiles and behavior.

- Customers who deny that they placed an order
- Customers who download copyrighted software and sell it to others
- Customers who give fraudulent payment information (fake credit card or a bad check) for products and services that they buy
- Customers with a false identity
- Imposters—sellers using the name of another seller (see the CyberSource Annual Reports)
- Other sellers using the original seller's names, trademarks, and other unique features and even their Web addresses (or similar to it)

Sellers must be protected against:

Payment fraud by consumers and by criminals (e.g., use of invalid credit cards).

Sellers also can be attacked illegally or unethically by competitors. Merchants also are subject to piracy. This issue is described in Chap. 15.

Example

A class action lawsuit was filed against McAfee in the US District Court for the Northern District of California (Case No. 10-1455-HRL) alleging that after the plaintiffs purchased McAfee software from McAfee's website, a deceptive pop-up ad (from one of McAfee's partners) that looks like a McAfee page appeared and thanked the plaintiffs for their software purchase. The pop-up ad asked them to click on a "Try it Now" button, which they assumed would download the software they had just purchased, but unbeknownst to them, they received a 30-day trial subscription to Arpu, Inc. (a non-McAfee product). They found out later that McAfee transmits customer credit/debit card and billing information to Arpu (customers are charged $4.95 per month after the trial period) and collects an undisclosed fee for each customer who "tries" Arpu via the McAfee website.

What Can Sellers Do?

Companies like Chargeback Stopper (**chargebackstopper.com**) and Chargeback Protection (**chargebackprotection.org**) provide merchants with a database of credit card numbers that have had "chargeback orders" recorded against them. Sellers who have access to the database can use this information to decide whether to proceed with a sale. In the future, the credit card industry is planning to use biometrics to manage electronic shoplifting. In addition, sellers can use PKI and digital certificates, especially the SET protocol, to help prevent fraud.

Other possible solutions include the following:

- Use intelligent software to identify questionable customers (or in small companies, do this identification manually). One technique, for example, involves comparing credit card billing and requested shipping addresses.
- Identify warning signals—i.e., red flags—for possible fraudulent transactions.
- Ask customers whose billing address is different from the shipping address to call their bank and have the alternate address added to their bank account. Retailers will agree to ship the goods to the alternate address only if this is done.
- Ask the customer to disclose the credit card verification code.
- Delay shipment until money is received.

For security merchant terminals and EC systems, see the Report by the Retail Cyber Intelligence Sharing Center (R-CISC); see details at ISAC (2016).

For a further discussion of what merchants can do to protect themselves from fraud, see CyberSource (e.g., **www.cyber-source.com/products/fraud_management**). For ten measures to reduce credit card fraud for Internet Merchants (a FraudLabs.com White Paper), see **fraudlabs.com/docs/fraudlabs_white_paper.pdf**.

Grant (2016) provides a list of the following scams against business: (1) the old switcheroo, (2) fake returns, (3) phony audit, (4) the altered, and (5) the international overpayment. Grant (2016) also suggests how to avoid these frauds and scams.

Protecting Marketplaces and Social Networking Services

Marketplaces such as eBay, Yahoo!, Amazon.com, and Alibaba face a problem of sellers who try to sell counterfeit products online. The problem is especially acute for Alibaba and eBay, whose business model is to connect sellers and buyers, in contrast with Amazon.com and other e-tailers that mostly buy products and retail them to consumers. Marketplaces try to crack down on the counterfeiter, but it is not an easy job.

Facebook and other social networks that have moved to commercialization are facing the problem of fake accounts. For the problem and solutions, see Jones (2016a).

Fraud Detection Software

A large number of software products are available to detect fraud by consumers, other businesses, compliance losses, etc. For an evaluation of the major software products, see **capterra.com/financial-fraud-detection-software**.

Protecting Both Buyers and Sellers: Using Electronic Signatures and Other Security Features

There are several methods that protect EC transactions and both the customers and sellers. For details, see Hyatt (2016).

One method to help distinguish between legitimate and fraudulent transactions is electronic signatures.

An **electronic signature** is "the electronic equivalent of a handwritten signature" (per **pcmag.com/encyclopedia/term/42500/electronic-signature**). Electronic signatures provide high level of security and are recognized by most legal entities as being equivalent to handwritten signatures. All electronic signatures are represented digitally. Signed electronic documents and contracts are as legally binding as paper-based documents and contracts.

Authentication

In the online environment where consumers and merchants do not have physical contact with one another, proving the authenticity of each person is necessary since buyers and sellers do not see each other. However, if one can be sure of the identity of the person on the other end of the line, there could be more e-commerce applications. For example, students would be able to take exams online from anywhere without the need for proctors. Fraud among recipients of government payments would be minimized. Buyers would be assured who the sellers are, and sellers would know, with a very high degree of confidence, who the buyers really are. Online job interviews would be accurate because it would be almost impossible for an applicant to impersonate another person. Overall, trust in online transactions and in EC in general would increase significantly. Authentication can be achieved in several ways, including the use of biometrics.

Fraud Detecting Systems

There are a large number of fraud detection systems such as the use of data mining for credit card fraud. CyberSource also has developed several tools for detecting fraud. For details, see CyberSource periodic reports and **authorize.net/resources/files/fdswhitepaper.pdf**.

SECTION 11.7 REVIEW QUESTIONS

1. Describe consumer protection measures.
2. Describe assurance services.
3. What must a seller do to protect itself against fraud? How?
4. Describe types of electronic signatures. Who is protected? Why?
5. Describe authentication.

11.8   IMPLEMENTING ENTERPRISEWIDE E-COMMERCE SECURITY

Güldenast (2016) recommends following these four steps: (1) define clear requirements, (2) set your standards, (3) search for flows, and (4) conduct continuous monitoring.

Now that you have learned about both the threats and the defenses, we can discuss some implementation issues starting with the reasons why it is difficult, or even impossible, to stop computer crimes and the malfunction of information systems. For security management in general, see Sennewald and Baillie (2015).

The Drivers of EC Security Management

The explosive growth of EC and SC, together with an increase in the ever-changing strategies of cybercriminals, combined with regulatory requirements and demands by insurance companies, drives the need for comprehensive EC security management. Additional drivers are:

- The laws and regulations with which organizations must comply.
- The conduct of global EC. More protection is needed when doing business with a foreign country.
- Information assets have become critical to the operation of many businesses.
- New and faster information technologies are shared throughout organizations. Organizational collaboration is needed.
- The complexity of both the attacks and the defense require an organization-wide collaboration approach.

How Serious Is Cybersecurity?

According to Editors (2016), $1 trillion will be spent globally on cybersecurity (the defense side alone) from 2017 to 2021. Cybercrime predicted in 2016 report that cybercrimes will cost the world $6 trillion. Obviously, senior management must be involved. For comprehensive coverage of management of information security, see Whitman and Matford (2016).

Senior Management Commitment and Support

The success of an EC security strategy and program depends on the commitment and involvement of senior management. Many forms of security are unpopular because they are inconvenient, restrictive, time-consuming, and expensive. Security practices may not be a top organizational priority unless they are mandated.

Therefore, an EC security and privacy model for effective enterprisewide security should begin with senior management's commitment and support, as shown in Fig. 10.10. The model views EC security (as well as the broader IT security) as a combination of commitment and support, policies and training, procedures and enforcement, and tools, all executed as a continuous process (Figs. 11.10 and 11.11).

According to the *Delta Risk* White Paper (see Staff 2016a), the Board of Directors' involvement in cybersecurity should follow the following four key areas:

- "Ensuring that board members themselves receive cybersecurity training that is appropriate for their level and role.
- Incorporating cybersecurity protection into the organization's Statement of Risk Appetite.
- Driving the implementation of a cyber risk management program that is integrated with the institution's broader enterprise management of all risks, such as financial risk (e.g., market, liquidity, credit), compliance risk and other operational risks (e.g., fraud, litigation, reporting, safety, physical security).
- Fostering a cybersecurity throughout the institution."

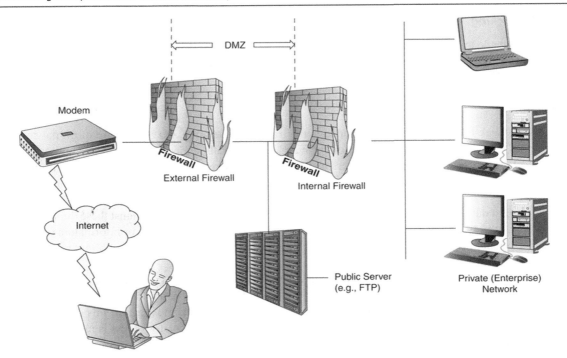

Fig. 11.10   The two firewalls: DMZ architecture

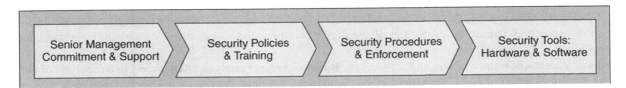

Fig. 11.11   Enterprisewide EC security and privacy process

EC Security Policies and Training

An important security task is developing an organizational EC security policy, as well as procedures for specific security and EC activities such as access control and protecting customer data. Customers should:

- Know that data is being collected and when this is done
- Give their permission for the data to be collected
- Have knowledge and some control over how the data is controlled and used
- Be informed that the information collected is not to be shared with other organizations

To protect against criminal use of social media, you can:

- Develop policies and procedures to exploit opportunities but provide customer protection
- Educate employees and others about what is acceptable and what is not acceptable

Training to Do Hacking

While some train people to hack in order to make money, others believe that if you learn how to hack, you will be better in defending your system. For a video that shows how to hack Facebook using phishing, see the 10-min video at **youtube.com/watch?v=Z2z9zncsYW8**.

Cyber Intelligence

According to WiseGeek (2017), "Cyber intelligence is the tracking, analyzing and countering of digital security threats. This type of intelligence is a blend of physical espionage and defense with modern information technology. Various cyber intelligence efforts help to combat viruses, hackers and terrorists that exist on the Internet with the aim to steal sensitive information. Protecting parties, like a government, from these threats is a major part of this field, but so is aggressively fighting these threats."

"One of the biggest duties of the cyber intelligence community is providing security against these digital threats. An intelligence professional will likely have a dual background in espionage and Internet security or information technology. Setting up firewalls, virus scanning programs, and routinely checking for breaches in security are important roles that keep a computer system secure from outside forces."

"Analyzing terror threats is another important aspect of cyber intelligence. This aspect of the field is most like traditional intelligence and espionage tactics of information gathering. Using third party sources, either informants or one of the many independent companies that help identify cyber threats, professionals must gather this data and determine how it threatens what is being protected. Often, creating reports and recommendations for others is more common in this area than electronic work."

According to **sans.org**, cyber intelligence is an important defense tool.

EC Risk Analysis and Ethical Issues

EC security procedures require an evaluation of the digital and financial assets at risk—including cost and operational considerations.

A related assessment is the *business impact analysis.* **Business impact analysis (BIA)** refers to an analysis of the impact of losing the functionality of an EC activity (e.g., e-procurement, e-ordering) to an organization. Once such risks are computed, the organization should focus its defense strategy on the largest risks.

Ethical Issues

Implementing security programs raises several ethical issues. First, some people are against the monitoring of any individual's activities. Imposing certain controls is seen by some as a violation of freedom of speech or other civil rights. A survey by the Gartner Group found that even after the terrorist attacks of September 11, 2001, only 26% of Americans approved a national ID database. Many even consider using biometrics to be a violation of privacy.

Note: In 2015, the US Congress pressured President Obama to institute national biometric IDs for all Americans (Newman 2015). This suggestion is still being discussed.

Handling the privacy versus security dilemma is difficult. There are other ethical and legal obligations that may require companies to "invade the privacy" of employees and monitor their actions. In particular, IT security measures are needed to protect against loss, liability, and litigation.

Why Is It Difficult to Stop Internet Crime?

The following are the major reasons Internet crime is so difficult to stop.

Making Shopping Inconvenient

Strong EC security may make online shopping inconvenient and may slow shopping time as well. Therefore, shoppers may not like some security measures.

Lack of Cooperation by Business Partners

There is a potential lack of cooperation from credit card issuers, suppliers, local and especially foreign ISPs, and other business partners. If the source ISP would cooperate and suspend the hacker's access, it would be very difficult for hackers to gain access to the systems.

Shoppers' Negligence

Many online shoppers are not taking the necessary (but inconvenient) precautions to avoid becoming victims of identity theft or fraud (e.g., changing passwords).

Ignoring EC Security Best Practices

Many companies do not have prudent IT security management or employee security awareness. Many widespread threats in the United States stem from the lack of user awareness of malware and hacking attacks. In addition, many businesses do not meet security compliance standards (see Blog 2016).

Design and Architecture Issues

It is well known that preventing vulnerability during the EC design and pre-implementation stage is far less expensive than mitigating problems later; unfortunately, such prevention is not always made. Even minor design errors can increase hacking.

Lack of Due Care in Business Practices

Another reason for the difficulty is the lack of due care in conducting many business processes (e.g., in crowdsourcing). The **standard of due care** is the minimum and customary practice that a company is reasonably expected to take to protect the company and its resources from possible risks. For a major survey, see PwC (2013).

Protecting Mobile Devices and Mobile Apps

With the explosive growth of mobility and m-commerce comes the task of protecting these systems from the security problems described earlier in this chapter and from some new ones. For an overview, see Faulkner (2016). For a prediction made by Gartner Consulting, see Krishnan (2016).

Mobile Security Issues

Typical security issues range from wireless transmissions not being encrypted to lack of firewalls or passwords on mobile devices or connecting to an unsecured Wi-Fi network.

Reisinger (2014) lists additional security issues such as data theft and unlocked jailbreaking devices. The proliferation of BYOD also brings threats to the enterprise (see Faulkner 2016) and Security News (2016).

The Defense of Mobile Systems

To defend mobile systems, it is necessary to implement tools and procedures such as those described in section "Defending Information Systems and E-Commerce Including Mobile Systems" and modify them for the mobile environment. A practical checklist for reducing security risks is offered by Lenovo (2013). Finally, a major problem is the theft of mobile devices. Two solutions are at work: first, automatic security that enables only the owners to use their devices and, second, make a kill switch a mandatory feature in all smartphones. In 2016, this feature was still only available in California.

The Internet of Things Security

The IoT is very vulnerable to cybercrime. In the IoT, one can find a large number of devices from different manufacturers and vintages connected to one system. If the connection is via the Internet, the situation can be even worse. According to DeNisco (2017), there are a lot of security risks in the IoT. The author based his conclusion on Gartner's report. The report estimates that more than 8.4 billion devices are already connected to the Internet. Most users are individual consumers (5.2 billion devices) and enterprises 3.1 billion (devices). Cars and trucks are getting connected to the Internet as well. Gartner also predicts that by 2018, there will be 1 billion cross industry devices. All of these contribute to security risks.

McLellan (2017) provides a very comprehensive, 47-page, free report on how to harness the IoT in the enterprise (you need to register, but pay no fees, to get the report).

SECTION 11.8 REVIEW QUESTIONS

1. If senior management is not committed to EC security, how might that impact the e-business?
2. What is a benefit of using the risk exposure method for EC security planning?
3. Why should every company implement an acceptable use policy?
4. Why is training required?
5. List the major reasons why it is difficult to stop computer crimes.

MANAGERIAL ISSUES

Some managerial issues related to this chapter are as follows.

1. **What steps should businesses follow in establishing a security plan?** Security management is an ongoing process involving three phases: asset identification, risk assessment, and implementation. By actively monitoring existing security policies and procedures, companies can determine which of them are successful or unsuccessful and, in turn, which should be modified or eliminated. However, it also is important to monitor changes in business processes and business environments and adjust the plans accordingly. In this way, an organization can keep its security policies and measures up-to-date.

2. **Should organizations be concerned with internal security threats?** Except for malware, breaches committed by insiders may be much more frequent than those done by outsiders. This is true for both B2C and B2B sites. Security policies and measures for EC sites need to address the insider threats. In addition, insiders can be victims of security crimes. Therefore, companies should educate employees, especially new hires, about such threats.

3. **What is the key to establishing strong e-commerce security?** Most discussions about security focus on technology, with statements like, "all messages should be encrypted." Although technologies are important, no security solution is useful unless it is adopted by the employees. Determining business requirements is the first step in creating a security solution. Business requirements, in turn, determine information requirements.

4. **What should we do in case we are victims of ransomware?** It is not good for you if you do not have a backup system. However, you may have to pay to get your data back. If a ransom is requested to avoid a DoS, quickly try to set up protection to avoid the problem spreading. In either case, report the incident to the police.

SUMMARY

In this chapter, you learned about the following EC issues as they relate to the chapter's learning objectives.

1. **The importance and scope of EC information security.** For EC to succeed, it must be secure. Unfortunately, this is not an easy task due to many unintentional and intentional hazards. Security incidents and breaches interrupt EC transactions and increase the cost of doing business online. Internet design is vulnerable, and the temptation to commit computer crime is increasing with the increased applications and volume of EC. Criminals are expanding operations, creating an underground economy of valuable information that was stolen. A strategy is needed to handle the costly defense technology and operation, which includes training, education, project management, and the ability to enforce security policy. EC security will remain an evolving discipline because threats are changing continuously. Therefore, e-business needs to adapt. An EC security strategy is needed to optimize EC security programs for efficiency and effectiveness.

2. **Basic EC security issues.** The security issue can be viewed as a battleground between attackers and attacks and defenders and defense. There are many variations on both sides and many possible collision scenarios. Owners of EC sites need to be concerned with multiple security issues: authentication, verifying the identity of the participants in a transaction; authorization, ensuring that a person or process has access rights to particular systems or data; and auditing, being able to determine whether particular actions have been taken and by whom.

3. **Threats, vulnerabilities, and technical attacks.** EC sites are exposed to a wide range of attacks. Attacks may be non-technical (social engineering), in which a criminal lures people into revealing sensitive personal information. Alternatively,

attacks may be technical, whereby software and systems expertise are used to attack networks, databases, or programs. DoS attacks bring operations to a halt by sending a flood of data to target specific computers and websites. Malicious code attacks include viruses, worms, Trojan horses, or some combination of these. Over the past few years, new malware trends have emerged, such as Blackhole and ZeroAccess (see Wang 2013). The new trends include an increase in the speed and volume of new attack methods and the shorter time between the discovery of a vulnerability and the release of an attack (to exploit the vulnerability). Finally, the new trends include the growing use of bots to launch attacks; an increase in attacks on mobile systems, social networks, and Web applications; and a shift to profit-motivated attacks.

4. **Internet fraud, phishing, and spam.** A large variety of Internet crimes exist. Notable are identify theft and misuse, stock market frauds, get-rich-quick scams, and phishing. Phishing attempts to obtain valuable information from people by masquerading as a trustworthy entity. Personal information is extracted from people (or stolen) and sold to criminals, who use it to commit financial crimes such as transferring money to their own accounts. A related area is the use of unsolicited advertising or sales via spam.

5. **Security measures slow our EC transactions.** E-commerce can be greatly affected by delays and interruption of service known as *friction*. According to Mello, Jr. (2017), both ransomware and DDoS, or other security attacks, can damage EC. "Consumers do not respond well to any delays doing what they want to do online. That's why so many shopping carts are abandoned before shoppers pull the trigger on a purchase. More than two out of three carts (68.81 percent) are deserted by shoppers, according to the Baymard Institute. Friction creates a ticklish problem for security teams, because protecting merchants and consumers from fraud can create friction. Ideally, the best security scheme is one that gives consumers their cake and lets them eat it, too, one that offers maximum protection but is invisible to shoppers."

6. **Information assurance.** The information assurance model represents a process for managing the protection of data and computer systems by ensuring their confidentiality, integrity, and availability. Confidentiality is the assurance of data privacy. Integrity is the assurance that data is accurate or that a message has not been altered. Availability is the assurance that access to data, the website, or EC systems and applications is available, reliable, and restricted to authorized users whenever they need it.

7. **Securing EC access control and communications.** In EC, issues of communication among trading partners are paramount. In many cases, EC partners do not know their counterparts, so they need secured communication and trust building. Trust starts with the authentication of the parties involved in a transaction, that is, identifying the parties in a transaction along with the actions they are authorized to perform. Authentication can be established with something one knows (e.g., a password), something one has (e.g., an entry card), or some physical characteristic (e.g., a fingerprint). Biometric systems can confirm a person's identity. Fingerprint scanners, iris scanners, facial recognition, and voice recognition are examples of biometric systems.

8. **The different controls and special defense mechanisms.** The major controls are general (including physical, access controls, biometrics, administrative controls, application controls, and internal controls for security and compliance). Each type has several variations.

9. **Fraud on the Internet and how to protect consumers and sellers against it.** Protection is needed because there is no face-to-face contact between buyers and sellers; there is a great possibility of fraud; there are insufficient legal constraints; and new issues and scams appear constantly. Several organizations, private and public, attempt to provide the protection needed to build the trust that is essential for the success of widespread EC. Of note are electronic contracts (including digital signatures), the control of gambling, and what taxes should be paid to whom on interstate, intrastate, and international transactions. The practice of no sales tax on the Internet is changing. States are starting to collect sales tax on Internet transactions.

Many procedures are used to protect consumers. In addition to legislation, the FTC tries to educate consumers so they know the major scams. The use of seals on sites (such as TRUSTe) can help, as well as tips and measures taken by vendors. Sellers can be cheated by buyers, by other sellers, or by criminals. Protective measures include using contacts and encryption (PKI) keeping databases of past criminals, sharing information with other sellers, educating employees, and using artificial intelligence software.

Given the large number of ways to commit Internet fraud, it is difficult to protect against all of them. Fraud protection is done by companies, security vendors, government regulations, and, perhaps most important, consumer education. Knowing the most common methods used by criminals is the first step of defense. Remember, most criminals are very experienced. They are able to invest in new and clever attack methods.

9. **Enterprisewide EC security.** EC security procedures are inconvenient, expensive, tedious, and never ending. Implementing a defensive in-depth model that views EC security as a combination of commitment, people, processes, and technology is essential. An effective program starts with senior management's commitment and budgeting support.

This sets the tone that EC security is important to the organization. Other components are security policies and training. Security procedures must be clearly defined. Positive incentives for compliance can help, and negative consequences need to be enforced for violations. The last stage is the deployment of hardware and software tools based on the policies and procedures defined by the management team.

10. **Why is it so difficult to stop computer crimes?** Responsibility or blame for cybercrimes can be placed on criminals, victimized people, and organizations. Online shoppers fail to take necessary precautions to avoid becoming victims. Security system designs and architectures are still incredibly vulnerable. Organizations may fail to exercise due care in business or hiring and practices, opening the doors to security attacks. Every EC business knows that there are threats of stolen credit cards, data breaches, phishing, malware, and viruses that never end and that these threats must be addressed comprehensively and strategically.

11. **The future of EC.** EC is growing steadily and rapidly, expanding to include new products, services, business models, and countries. The most notable areas of growth are the integration of online and offline commerce, mobile commerce (mostly due to smartphone apps), video-based marketing, and social media and networks. Several emerging technologies, ranging from intelligent applications to wearable devices, are facilitating the growth of EC. On the other hand, several factors are slowing down the spread of EC such as security and privacy concerns, limited bandwidth, and lack of standards in some areas of EC.

KEY TERMS

Access control
Application controls
Authentication
Authorization
Availability
Banking Trojan
Biometric authentication
Biometric systems
Botnet
Business continuity plan
Business impact analysis (BIA)
Certificate authorities (CAs)
CIA security triad (CIA triad)
Ciphertext
Computer Fraud and Abuse Act (CFAA)
Confidentiality
Cracker
Cybercrime
Cybercriminal
Darknet
Data breach
Denial-of-service (DoS) attack
Detection measures
Deterrent methods
Digital signature
EC security strategy
Electronic signature
E-mail spam
Encryption
Encryption algorithm
Exposure
Firewall
Fraud

General controls
Hacker
Identity theft
Information assurance (IA)
Information security
Integrity
Intrusion detection system (IDS)
Key (key value)
Keystroke logging (keylogging)
Macro virus (macro worm)
Malware (malicious software)
Nonrepudiation
Page hijacking
Penetration test (pen test)
Pharming
Phishing
Plaintext
Prevention measures
Private key
Public key
Public (asymmetric) key encryption
Public key infrastructure (PKI)
Ransomware
Risk
Search engine spam
Social engineering
Spam
Spam site
Spear phishing
Splog
Spyware
Standard of due care
Symmetric (private) key encryption
Trojan horse
Underground Internet economy
Virtual private network (VPN)
Virus
Vulnerability
Vulnerability assessment
Worm
Zombies

DISCUSSION QUESTIONS

1. Consider how a hacker might trick people into divulging their user IDs and passwords to their Amazon.com accounts. What are some of the specific ways that a hacker might accomplish this? What crimes can be performed with such information?
2. B2C EC sites and social networks continue to experience DoS and DDoS attacks. How are these attacks executed? Why is it so difficult to safeguard against them? What are some of the things a site can do to mitigate such attacks?
3. How are botnets, identity theft, DoS attacks, and website hijackings perpetrated? Why are they so dangerous to e-commerce?
4. Discuss some of the difficulties of eliminating online financial fraud.

5. Enter **zvetcobiometrics.com**. Discuss the benefits of these products over other biometrics.
6. Find information about the Zeus Trojan virus. Discuss why it is so effective at stealing financial data. Why is it so difficult to protect against this Trojan?
7. Visit the National Vulnerability Database (**nvd.nist.gov**) and review five recent CVE vulnerabilities. For each vulnerability, list its published date, CVSS severity, impact type, and the operating system or software with the vulnerability.
8. Report on the status of using biometrics in mobile commerce. (Start with **nxt-id.com**.)
9. Find several definitions of "information warfare" and discuss the major attributes of the definitions.
10. What contribution does TRUSTe make to e-commerce?
11. Describe the issue of ransomware.

TOPICS FOR CLASS DISCUSSION AND DEBATES

1. A business wants to share its customer data with a trading partner and provide its business customers with access to marketing data. What types of security components (e.g., firewalls, VPNs, etc.) could be used to ensure that the partners and customers have access to the account information while those who are unauthorized do not? What types of network administrative procedures will provide the appropriate security?
2. Why is it so difficult to fight computer criminals? What strategies can be implemented by financial institutions, airlines, and other heavy users of EC?
3. All EC sites share common security threats and vulnerabilities. Do you think that B2C websites face different threats and vulnerabilities than do B2B sites? Explain.
4. Why is phishing so difficult to control? What can be done? Discuss.
5. Debate this statement: "The best strategy is to invest very little and only in proven technologies such as encryption and firewalls."
6. Debate: Can the underground Internet marketplace be controlled? Why or why not?
7. Debate: Is taking your fingerprints or other biometrics to assure EC security a violation of your privacy?
8. Watch the video "How to hack Facebook with phishing" (10 min, 2016). Also, learn how to protect your Facebook account.
9. Discuss the issue of providing credit card details on Facebook. Would you do it?
10. Discuss the recent security trends pointed out by Lemos (2016).
11. Examine the identity theft and identity crime topics from the FBI site **fbi.gov/about-us/investigate/cyber/identity-theft**. Report the highlights.
12. Research the state of the art of fake posting and fake comments about popular posts. Review the defense measures. Write a summary report.
13. Under what circumstances should a company pay a ransom? Debate the issue.

INTERNET EXERCISES

1. Your B2C site has been hacked with a new, innovative method. List two organizations where you would report this incident so that they can alert other sites. How do you do this and what type of information do you have to provide?
2. Determine the IP address of your computer by visiting at least two websites that provide that feature. You can use a search engine to locate websites or visit **ip-adress.com** or **whatismyipaddress.com**. What other information does the search reveal about your connections? Based on this finding, how could a hacker use that information?
3. Conduct a Google search for "Institutional Identity Theft." Compare institutional identity theft with personal identity theft. How can a company protect itself against identity theft? Write a report.
4. The Symantec Annual Internet Security Threat Report provides details about the trends in attacks and vulnerabilities in Internet security. Obtain a copy of the latest report and summarize the major findings of the report for both attacks and vulnerabilities.
5. Conduct a Google search for examples of underground Internet activities in five different countries. Prepare a summary.
6. Enter **verisign.com** (a Symantec company) and find information about PKI and encryption. Write a report.
7. Enter **hijackthis.com**. What is offered on the site? Write a report.

8. Enter **blackhat.com**. Find out what the site is about. Describe some of the site's activities.
9. Enter **ftc.gov** and identify some of the typical types of fraud and scams on the Internet. List ten of them.
10. Enter **scambusters.org** and identify and list its antifraud and anti-scam activities.

TEAM ASSIGNMENTS AND PROJECTS

1. **Assignment for the opening case**

   Read the opening case and answer the following questions:

   (a) Why did the hackers attack this hospital?
   (b) Research the case to find out why the hospital paid a small ransom to begin with.
   (c) Why it is difficult, sometimes impossible, to find the hackers that receive a ransom?
   (d) Read section "Nontechnical Methods: From Phishing to Spam and Fraud" about ransomware and the tactics hacker use.

2. Assign teams to report on the latest major spam and scam threats. Look at examples provided by **ftc.gov**, the latest Symantec report on the State of Spam, and white papers from IBM, VeriSign, McAfee, and other security firms.
3. Watch the video "Cyberattacks and Extortion" (13:55 min) at **searchsecurity.techtarget.com/video/Cyberattacks-and-extortion**. Answer the following questions:

   (a) Why are there more extortions online today? How are they accomplished?
   (b) What is involved in targeted e-mail attacks?
   (c) What is an SQL injection attack?

4. Data leaks can be a major problem. Find some major defense methods. Check some major security vendors (e.g., Symantec). Find white papers and Webinars on the subject. Write a report.
5. Each team is assigned one method of fighting against online fraud. Each method should involve a different type of fraud (e.g., in banking). Identify suspicious e-mails, dealing with cookies in Web browsers, credit card protection, securing wireless networks, installing anti-phishing protection for your browser with a phishing filter, and so forth.
6. Armies of botnets were used in the 2016 US presidential elections to boost candidate popularity. Is this the end of democracy? Discuss.
7. In class, watch the video how to protect yourself from fraud at **youtube.com/watch?v=gsSQqSSHrAI**. Summarize the lessons learned.

CLOSING CASE: HOW DYN WAS ATTACKED BY DDOS?

Dyn is a cloud-based Internet performance management (IPM) company that provides visibility and control into cloud and public Internet resources (an Oracle company). The company controls and optimizes infrastructure to be faster, safer, and provides more reliable service. Dyn offers domain name system (DNS) services, essentially acting as an address book for the Internet. The company serves networks with many thousands of customers each. For more on the IPM industry and Dyn, see **dyn.com/blog/what-is-internet-performance-management-industry-tech-talk-with-dyn-executive**.

The Incident

If you were on a Dyn-served network and tried to surf the Internet for buying from Amazon.com, reading news, reading some tweets, using Reddit, or trying to connect to Netflix or Spotify, you were unable to do so during most of the day on October 21, 2016, if the site was served by Dyn. Dyn's attacker, which used DDoS, targeted Dyn's headquarters in New Hampshire.

The first attack was launched at 7 am and was resolved by Dyn in about 2 h. A second attack began around noon and a third one around 4 pm. The attackers bombarded Dyn with a flood of malicious requests, sent from tens of millions of IP addresses. The result was that Dyn's Internet directory service was stopped, primarily on the East Coast of the United States and later in other parts of the country. The attack was complex and sophisticated.

The Results

According to Newman (2016), "Dyn offers Domain Name System (DNS) services, essentially acting as an address book for the Internet. DNS is a system that resolves the web addresses we see every day, like wired.com, into IP addresses needed to find and connect with the right servers so browsers can deliver requested content, (like news, finding products and prices or conducting a search). A DDoS attack overwhelms a DNS server with lookup requests, rendering it incapable of completing any. That's what makes attacking DNS so effective; rather than targeting individual sites, an attacker can take out the entire Internet for any end user whose DNS requests route through a given server."

In addition, "DDoS is a particularly effective type of attack on DNS services because in addition to overwhelming servers with malicious traffic, those same servers also have to deal with automatic re-requests, and even just well-meaning users hitting refresh over and over to summon up an uncooperative page."

Dyn experienced DDoS attacks before and successfully fought them, but they were on a much smaller scale. The scale and sophistication of this attack were too much for Dyn to defend, so access to hundreds of sites and services has been disrupted by the attack. This attack highlights how critical DNS is to maintaining stable and secure Internet service.

Using Botnet

The attacker hijacked thousands of Internet-connected computing devices and appliances (e.g., DVRs, routers, home appliances) which are not so secured and infected them with malware. The infected devices became part of a botnet (section "Technical Malware Attack Methods: From Viruses to Denial of Service") that drove malicious traffic to Dyn. The major malware was Mirai (see section "Technical Malware Attack Methods: From Viruses to Denial of Service"). Note that the attackers hijacked devices that were connected to the Internet of things. The botnet addition is the "distributed" part of DDoS, and the attack was the largest of its kind in history.

The Motive

The question is why the attackers attacked Dyn. In many DDoS and DoS attacks, a ransom is requested. Not this time. Maybe the attackers wanted to punish Dyn because the attackers failed previously in small-scale attacks. Other DDoS attacks were done to "show off," were used for protesting against companies, and were used in cyberwars and for intimidation and extortion. The motive in the case of Dyn is not really known. Some speculate that the perpetrators were most likely mad at Dyn for helping Brian Krebs be identified, and the FBI arrested two Israeli hackers who were running a DDoS-for-hire ring.

Sources: Compiled from Newman (2016), Blaine (2016), Gallagher (2016), and Krebs (2016).

Questions

1. Why did the hackers recruit innocent computers and create a botnet?
2. Explain why Dyn was unable to counter the attack.
3. Explain the role of DSN in the IPM process.
4. Relate the case to conducting business on the Internet.
5. Relate the case to IoT.

REFERENCES

Adhikari, R. "Gooligan Ransacks More than 1M Android Accounts." *TechNewsWorld*, December 2, 2016.
Alt, K. "7Alarming Identity Theft Statistics." *Safesmartliving.com*, June 15, 2016.
Alto, P. "Infographic: The Real Cost of Cyberattacks." *Enterprise Innovation*, March 21, 2016.

Altshull, Y. "Global eCommerce & Fraud Trends for 2017." *Riskified.com*, January 12, 2017.

APWG. "Phishing Activity Trends Report." *APWG.org/Reports*, (July-Sept., 2016), December 20, 2016. **docs.apwg.org/reports/apwg_trends_report_q2_2016.pdf** (accessed March 2017).

Armerding, T. "Top 15 Security Predictions for 2016." *CSO News*, April 15, 2016.

Ban, E. "Spammers Getting More Clever-An Analysis of Recent Spam Attacks." *OEM Hub*, June 25, 2015. **oem.hub.bitdefender.com/spammers-getting-more-clever-analysis-spam-attacks** (accessed February 2017).

Bisson, D. "6 Common Phishing Attacks and How to Protect Against Them." *Tripwire*, June 5, 2016.

Blaine, G. "DDoS Attack on Dyn Reveals New Threat Actor Strategies." *AIO Networks, Inc.*, October 21, 2016.

Blog. "Does Your Business Meet IT Security Compliance Standards?" *Guardian Data Destruction*, March 13, 2016.

Bolton, D. "A Case Study in Dealing with Ransomware." *Dice.com*, June 7, 2016. **insights.dice.com/2016/06/07/a-case-study-in-dealing-with-ransomware** (accessed February 2017).

Bort, J. "For the First Time, Hackers Have Used a Refrigerator to Attack Businesses." *Business Insider*, January 16, 2014.

Cannell, J. "Cryptolocker Ransomware: What You Need to Know." *Malwarebytes Labs*, October 8, 2013. **blog.malwarebytes.org/intelligence/2013/10/cryptolocker-ransom** (accessed February 2017).

Casti, T. "Phishing Scam Targeting Netflix May Trick You with Phony Customer Service Reps." *The Huffington Post Tech*, March 3, 2014. **huffingtonpost.com/2014/03/03/netflix-phishing-scam-customer-support_n_4892048.html** (accessed February 2017).

Chalakkal, S. "Study of Ghostnet." *University of Berlin*, April 2016. **priyachalakkal.files.wordpress/2016/06/ghostnet_sreepriyachalakkal.pdf** (accessed February 2017).

Cisco. "Defeating DDOS Attacks." *White Paper*, January 23, 2014.

Cloud, J. *Internet Security: Online Protection from Computer Hacking*. North Charleston, USA: CreateSpace Publishing Platform, 2015.

Constantin, L. "Identity Thieves Obtain 100,000 Electronic Filing PINs from IRS System." *IDG News Service*, February 10, 2016a.

Constantin, L. "Machine Learning could Help Companies React Faster to Ransomware." *IDG News Service*, June 13, 2016b.

Constantin, L. "Ransomware disrupts Washington DC's CCTV system." *IDG News Service*, January 30, 2017.

CyberSource. "Annual Fraud Benchmark Report: A Balancing Act." 2016. **NA_2016_Fraud_Benchmark_Report.pdf** (accessed March 2017).

Damri, L. "E-Commerce Fraud Predictions for 2017." *Internet Retailer*, October 20, 2016.

Dawn Ontario. "Virus Information: Guide to Computer Viruses." Undated.

DeNisco, A. "There Will Soon Be More IoT Devices in the World than People, Security Risks Abound." *TechRepublic.com*, February 7, 2017.

Editors. "Cybersecurity Market Report." *CyberSecurity Ventures*, Q4 2016.

Ernesto. "Europe Has The Highest Online Piracy Rates, By Far." *Torrentfreak*, August 1, 2016.

Faulkner, A. "Protecting Against the Top Mobile Security Threats in 2016." *RCA Conference Paper*, February 10, 2016. **rsaconference.com/blogs/protecting-against-the-top-mobile-security-threats-in-2016** (accessed February 2017).

Fink, E. "Google Glass Wearers Can Steal Your Password." *CNN News*, July 7, 2014. **money.cnn.com/2014/07/07/technology/security/google-glass-password-hack** (accessed February 2017).

Finkle, J. "'Pony' Botnet Steals Bitcoins, Digital Currencies: Trustwave." *Reuters.com US Edition*, February 24, 2014. **reuters.com/article/2014/02/24/us-bitcoin-security-idUSBREA1N1JO20140224** (accessed February 2017).

Fitzpatrick, D. and D. Griffin. "'Ransomware' crime wave growing." *CNNTech*, April 4, 2016.

Forrest, C. "Phishing Gets More Dangerous: New Report Analyzes the Weapons of Choice." *TechRepublic*, January 27, 2016.

Frenkel, K. A. "2016 Has the Markings of a Perfect Storm for Fraud." *CIO Insight*, January 28, 2016.

Gallagher, S. "DoS Attack on Major DNS Provider Brings Internet to Morning Crawl [updated]." *ARS Technica*, October 21, 2016.

Goldman, D. "Take Down Any Website for $3." *CNN Tech*, December 31, 2014a. **money.cnn.com/2014/12/31/technology/lizard-squad-attack** (accessed April 2016).

Goldman, J. "Data Breach Roundup: January 2014." *eSecurity Planet*, February 14, 2014b. **esecurityplanet.com/network-security/data-breach-roundup-january-2014.html** (accessed February 2017).

Goodman, M. *Future Crimes: Inside the Digital Underground and the Battle for our Connected World*. New York, NY: Anchor Reprint, 2016.

Grant, E. "How to Avoid Frauds & Scams Targeting Ecommerce Businesses." *Ecommerce Platforms*, June 20, 2016.

Greene, T. "SANS: 20 Critical Security Controls You Need to Add: A List of the Controls You Need Plus How to Implement Them." *NetworkWorld*, October 13, 2015. **networkworld.com/article/2992503/security/sans-20-critical-security-controls-you-need-to-add.html** (accessed February 2017).

Greengard, S. "Breaches of Health Care Data: A Growing Epidemic." *Baseline*, February 12, 2016a.

Greengard, S. "Is Ransomware Becoming an Epidemic?" *Baseline*, August 8, 2016b.

Güldenast, G. "Four Steps to a Secure E-Commerce Solution." *Service Plan*, October 12, 2016.

Guri, M. "The Future of Intrusion Detection." *Help Net Security*, June 16, 2016.

Hardwick, T. "Apple Exploring Two-Step Touch ID and Facial Recognition System for iPhone 8." *MacRumors.com*, January 21, 2017.

Harrison, V., and J. Pagliery. "Nearly 1 Million New Malware Threats Released Everyday." *CNN Tech*, April 14, 2015. **money.cnn.com/2015/04/14/technology/security/cyber-attack-hacks-security** (accessed February 2017).

Harwood, M. *Internet Security: How to Defend Against Attackers on the Web (Jones & Bartlett Learning Information Systems Security & Assurance)*. 2nd ed. Burlington, MA: John Bartlett Learning, 2015.

Hassell, J. "Fighting Ransomware: A fresh look at Windows Server approaches." *Computer World*, December 8, 2016.

Hinckley, S. "Pay by Selfie? Amazon Says Your Portrait Can Protect Online Purchases." *Christian Science Monitor*, March 15, 2016.

Horowitz, D., and A. Horowitz. "Online Merchandise Scams Target Students." *The Costco Connection*, December 2015.

Hyatt, P. "How to protect your company and customers in e-commerce transactions." *TradeReady.com*, July 29, 2016.

ISAC. "Securing Merchant Terminals and Ecommerce Systems." *R-CISC, TLP White Alert*, December 2016.

Jennings, R. "This Hollywood Hospital Didn't Backup Its Data? 'Ransomware' Payday for Evil Hackers." *Computerworld*, February 18, 2016.

John, A. *Internet Security*. Publisher: Self-Publishing, 2016.

Jones, M. "Facebook Tests Tool that Identifies Fake Accounts." *Value Walk*, March 24, 2016a.

Jones, M. "New Amazon Phishing Scam Spreading Like Wildfire!" *Komando.com*, November 18, 2016b.

Jones, D. "Russia's Fancy Bear Attacks Microsoft, Adobe as Election Nears." *Tech News World*, November 4, 2016c. **technewsworld.com/ story/84059.html** (accessed February 2017).

Kan, M. "Alibaba Uses Facial Recognition Tech for Online Payments." *Computerworld*, March 16, 2015.

Kang, C. "That Old Phone Trump Uses for Twitter Could Be an Opening to Security Threats." *The New York Times*, January 25, 2017.

Karol, K. "20 Simple Tricks to Secure Your WordPress Website in 2017." *Codeinwp*, January 7, 2017.

Katz, O. "Analyzing a Malicious Botnet Attack Campaign through the Security Big Data Prism." January 6, 2014. **blogs.akamai.com/2014/01/ analyzing-a-malicious-botnet-attack-campaign-through-the-security-big-data-prism.html** (accessed February 2017).

Khaitan, S. "2016 Trends in Global E-Commerce Fraud." *Rippleshot*, July 21, 2016.

Khanal, S. "U.S. & Russia on the Brink of an Open Cyber War: What to Expect?" *Inquisitr*, December 17, 2016. **inquisitr.com/3804493/cyber- war-us-russia-obama-putin-hacking** (accessed February 2017).

Kim, D. and M. G. Solomon. *Fundamentals of Information Systems Security*. 3rd edition. Burlington, MA: Jones & Barlett Learning, 2016.

King, H. "Top 5 social media scams to avoid." *CNN News*, April 22, 2016. **money.cnn.com/2016/04/22/technology/facebook-twitter-phishing- scams** (accessed February 2017).

Kravets, D. "How China's Army Hacked America." *ARS Technica*, May 19, 2014. **arstechnica.com/tech-policy/2014/05/how-chinas-army- hacked-american-companies** (accessed February 2017).

Krebs, B. "Hacked Cameras, DVRs Powered Today's Massive Internet Outage." *KrebsonSecurity.com*, October 21, 2016.

Krishnan, S. "It Starts Now: 2017 Mobile Security Predictions from Gartner." *Lookoutblog.com*, December 1, 2016. **blog.lookout.com/ blog/2016/12/01/gartner-mobile-security-predictions** (accessed February 2017).

LaCapria, K. "Snopes' Field Guide to Fake News Sites and Hoax Purveyors." *Snopes.com*, January 25, 2017.

Lake, E. "Anti-Social Twitter, Spotify and Reddit among Social Media Sites Taken Offline After Major Cyber Attack." *The SUN*, October 21, 2016.

Laudicina, P. "2017 Will Be the Year of Cyber Warfare." *Forbes.com*, December 16, 2016.

Law Blog. "FTC Releases OECS's Recommendation on Consumer Protection in E-Commerce." *Hunton Privacy Blog*, April 7, 2016.

Lemos, R. "Phishing Attacks Continue to Sneak Past Defenses." *eWeek*, February 11, 2016.

Lenovo. "Lenovo Recommends 15 Steps to Reducing Security Risks in Enterprise Mobility." White Paper, August 2013. Available for download in pdf format at **techrepublic.com/resource-library/whitepapers/Lenovo-recommend-15-steps-to-reducing-security-risks-in-enterprise- mobility/post** (accessed March 2017).

Lonergan, K. "The Seven Types of E-Commerce Fraud Explained." *Information Age*, April 15, 2016.

Mangis, C. "How My Neighbor Beat a Social-Engineering Scam." *PCMagazine.com*, June 21, 2016.

Maxwell, D. *Hacking: Bootcamp--How to Hack Computers, Basic Security and Penetration Testing (Hacking The Common Core)*. [Kindle Edition] Seattle, WA: Amazon Digital Services, 2016.

McLellan, C. "Harnessing IoT in the Enterprise." *ZdNet Special Feature*, February 1, 2017. **zdnet.com/topic/harnessing-iot-in-the-enterprise** (accessed March 2017).

Mello, Jr. P. "Cyber Grinches Could Disrupt Holidays' Biggest Shopping Weekend." *TechNewsWorld*, November 23, 2016. **ecommercetimes. com/story/84109.html** (accessed February 2017).

Mello, Jr. P. "Las Vegas Capture Ransomware Crown." *TechNewsWorld*, January 7, 2017. **ecommercetimes.com/story/84211.html** (accessed February 2017).

Mellor, R. "Managing Fraud in E-Commerce: Is your Online Business Bulletproof?" *Security*, July 12, 2016.

Meola, A. "Online Fraud Attacks in the U.S. Are Growing at an Alarming Rate." *Business Insider*, April 20, 2016.

Mitchell, B. "DMZ-De-Militarized Zone (Computer Networking)" *Lifewire*, April 30, 2016.

Nakashima, E., and M. Zapotosky. "U.S. Charges Iran-Linked Hackers with Targeting Banks, N.Y. Dam." *The Washington Post*, March 24, 2016.

Newman, A. "Congress Pushes Obama-Backed National Biometric ID for Americans." *News American*, March 28, 2015.

Newman, L.H. "What We Know About Friday's Massive East Coast Internet Outage." *Wired*, October 21, 2016.

Olavsrud, T. "9 Biggest Information Security Threats through 2018." *CIO*, March 22, 2016.

Pagliery, J. "Drug Site Silk Road Wiped Out by Bitcoin Glitch." *CNN Tech*, February 14, 2014a. **money.cnn.com/2014/02/technology/secu- rity/silk-road-bitcoin** (accessed April 2016).

Pagliery, J. "Your Car Is a Giant Computer- and It Can Be Hacked." *CNN Money*, June 2, 2014b. **money.cnn.com/2014/06/01/technology/secu- rity/car-hack** (accessed February 2017).

Parker II, C. "Intrusion Detection Systems (IDS): Finally for the Vehicles: *National Cybersecurity Institute*, August 19, 2016.

Perret, D. "E-commerce Security Issues: Phishing and Spear Phishing." *Vade Secure*, March 17, 2016.

Pontrioli, S. "Social Engineering, Hacking the Human OS." *Kaspersky Lab Daily*, December 20, 2013. **blog.kaspersky.com/social-engineering- hacking-the-human-os** (accessed February 2017).

PWC. "Key Findings from the 2013 U.S. State of Cybercrime Survey." June 2013. **pwc.com/en_US/us/increasing-it-effectiveness/publications/ assets/us-state-of-cybercrime.pdf** (accessed February 2017).

RSA. "2016: Current State of Cybercrime- RSA." **rsa.com/content/dam/rsa/PDF/2016/05/2016-current-state-of-cybercrime.pdf** (accessed February 2017).

Reisinger, D. "10 Mobile Security Issues that Should Worry You." *eWeek*, February 11, 2014.

Reuters. "Malware Suspected in Bangladesh Bank Heist." *Fortune.com*, March 12, 2016. **fortune.com/2016/03/12/malware-bangladesh-bank- heist** (accessed February 2017).

Rubenking, N. J. "The Best Antivirus Protection of 2017." *PCMag.com*, January 13, 2017.

Russell, K. "Here's How to Protect Yourself from the Massive Security Flaw That's Taken over the Internet." *Business Insider*, April 8, 2014.

Schwartz, M. J. "Target Breach: Phishing Attack Implicated." *Information Week Dark Reading*, February 13, 2014. **darkreading.com/attacks- and-breaches/target-breach-phishing-attack-implicated/d/d-id/1113829** (accessed February 2017).

Scott, J. *Cybersecurity 101: What You Absolutely Must Know! - Volume 1: Learn How Not to be Pawned, Thwart Spear Phishing and Zero Day Exploits, Cloud Security Basics and Much More.* [Kindle Edition] Seattle, WA: Amazon Digital Services, 2016a.

Scott, J. *Cybersecurity 101: What You Absolutely Must Know! - Volume 2: Learn JavaScript Threat Basics, USB Attacks, Easy Steps to Strong Cybersecurity, Defense Against Cookie Vulnerabilities, and Much More!* [Kindle Edition] Seattle, WA: Amazon Digital Services, 2016b.

Scott, W. *Information Security 249 Success Secrets - 249 Most Asked Questions on Information Security - What You Need to Know.* Brisbane, Queensland, Australia: Emereo Publishing, 2014.

Security News. "Security 101: Protecting your BYOD Environment." *VIPRE News*, November 5, 2016. **blog.vipreantivirus.com/viper-for-business/security-101-protecting-byod-environment** (accessed February 2017).

Sennewald, C. and C. Baillie. *Effective Security Management*, 6th edition. Oxford, UK: Butterworth-Heinemann, 2015.

Shepard, W. "Amazon Scams on the Rise in 2017 as Fraudulent Sellers Run Amok and Profit Big." *Forbes.com*, January 2, 2017.

Shipley, R. "The Best DDoS Protection Services of 2017." *Top10reviews.com*, January 24, 2017.

Shrubb, R. "How Do You Beat Bad Buyers on Amazon and eBay." *WebRetailer*, December 7, 2015.

Singh, I. "E Commerce-Security Threats and Challenges." *SlideShare* (32 slides), February 15, 2016. **slideshare.net/InderBarara1/ecommerce-security-threats-and-challenges-58271913/** (accessed February 2017).

Smith, C. "It Turns Out Target Could Have Easily Prevented Its Massive Security Breach." *BGR Media*, March 13, 2014. **bgr.com/2014/03/13/target-data-hack-how-it-happened** .(accessed February 2017).

Smith, R. *Elementary Information Security*. 2nd Edition, Burlington, MA: Jones Bartlett, 2015.

Staff. "Cybersecurity and the Board of Directors." A White Paper, *Delta Risk*, April 2016a.

Staff. "eBook: Defending Against Crypto Ransomware." *Help Net Security*, August 16, 2016b. **helpnetsecurity.com/2016/08/16/ebook-defending-crypto-ransomware** (accessed March 2017).

Sun, D. "Hackers Demand Ransom Payment from Kansas Heart Hospital for Files." *News KWCH12*, May 20, 2016.

Swann, C. T. *Marlins Cry a Phishing Story*. Spokane, WA: Cutting Edge Communications, Inc., 2012.

Symantec. "Web Based Attacks." White paper, #20016955, February 2009. **symantec.com/content/en/us/enterprise/media/security_response/whitepapers/web_based_attacks_02-2009.pdf** (accessed February 2017).

TechRepublic Staff. "The 15 Most Frightening Data Breaches." *TechRepublic*, October 29, 2015.

Teo, F. "Monitoring Your Internal Network with Intelligent Firewalls." *Enterprise Innovation*, January 19, 2016.

Timberg, C. "Foreign Regimes Use Spyware against Journalists, Even in U.S." *Washington Post*, February 12, 2014. **washingtonpost.com/business/technology/foreign-regimes-use-spyware-against-journalists-even-in-us/2014/02/12/9501a20e-9043-11e3-84e1-27626c5ef5fb_story.html** (accessed February 2017).

Troinovski, A. "German Parliament Struggles to Purge Hackers from Computer Network." *The Wall Street Journal*, June 12, 2015.

Van Allen, F. "The 18 Scariest Computer Viruses of All Time." *TechRepublic*, January 22, 2016.

Velasco, J. "4 Case Studies in Fraud: Social Media and Identity Theft." *Socialnomics*, January 13, 2016.

Victor, D. "Authorities Shutdown Darkode, a Marketplace for Stolen Personal Data." *New York Times*, July 15, 2015.

Wallen, J. "10 Social Engineering Exploits Your Users Should Be Aware Of." *TechRepublic*, January 27, 2016. **techrepublic.com/blog/10-things/10-social-engineering-ploys-your-users-should-be-aware-of** (accessed February 2017).

Wang, R. "Malware B-Z: Inside the Threat from Blackhole to ZeroAccess." A Sophos White Paper, Sophos Ltd., January 2013. **sophos.com/en-us/medialibrary/Gated%20Assets/white%20papers/sophos_from_blackhole_to_zeroaccess_wpna.pdf** (accessed February 2017).

Whitman, M.E. and H. Mattord. *Management of Information Security*, 5th edition. Boston: MA: Cengage Learning, 2016.

Winton, R. "Hollywood Hospital Pays $17,000 in Bitcoin to Hackers: FBI Investigating." *Los Angeles Times*, February 18, 2016.

WiseGeek. "What is Cyber Intelligence? (with pictures)." *WiseGeek.com*, January 29, 2017. **wisegeek.com/what-is-cyber-intelligence.htm** (accessed March 2017).

Wueest, C. "The State of Financial Trojans 2013." *Symantec Official Blog*, December 17, 2013. **symantec.com/connect/blogs/state-financial-trojans-2013** (accessed February 2017).

Yadron, D. "Newest Hacker Target: Ads." *The Wall Street Journal Tech*, January 31, 2014. **online.wsj.com/news/articles/SB10001424052702303743604579350654103483462** (accessed February 2017).

Yan, S. "Chinese Man Admits to Cyber Spying on Boeing and Other U.S. Firms." *Money CNN News*, March 24, 2016.

Electronic Commerce Payment Systems

12

Contents

Learning Objectives

Upon completion of this chapter, you will be able to:

1. Describe cross-border EC and the issues that arise in EC payments.
2. Describe the major changes in retail and their impacts on EC payments.
3. Discuss the different payment cards used online and processing methods.
4. Discuss the different categories and potential uses of smart cards.
5. Describe the issues with and solutions to online micropayments.
6. Understand PayPal and third-party payment gateways.
7. Understand the major types and methods of mobile payments.
8. Describe the differences and key characteristics of digital and virtual currencies.

OPENING CASE
CROSS-BORDER EC—COSTCO PARTNERS WITH CHINA'S TMALL

The Problem

In EC, "the world is your oyster." It can transcend borders, opening product lines and services to a growing international market. The problem is that like the original line from Shakespeare's "The Merry Wives of Windsor," it may take a substantial sword to open it.

© Springer International Publishing AG 2018
E. Turban et al., *Electronic Commerce 2018*, Springer Texts in Business and Economics, DOI 10.1007/978-3-319-58715-8_12

When a buyer makes an online purchase from a merchant or seller in another country, it's called international e-commerce or **cross-border e-commerce**; the two concepts are synonymous. Sometimes, researchers and practitioners refine the definition to exclude EC trade between countries that share a common language, border, and currencies (Goodale 2014). For example, trade between the United States and Canada is treated as international because their currencies and financial regulations differ and the free-flow of goods is restricted by law, while trade between many of the neighbors in the European Union is considered domestic because they share a common currency (the Euro), common payment resolution (SEPA—see section "Smart Cards"), and open borders. Because of the polyglot nature of many of these countries, they often share one or more languages in common. When countries share common geography, language, payment systems, and currencies, a number of the key barriers to cross-border commerce are eliminated.

According to a recent report (Alizilia.com 2015) by Accenture and AliResearch (the research arm of the Chinese Alibaba Group), in 2015 there were approximately 300 billion global cross-border B2C transactions which represented around 16% of all B2C transactions. These transactions were the combined result of the purchases of 360 million B2C shoppers worldwide which was only 25% of all online buyers that year. So, only one out of every seven transactions was cross-border and only one out of every four buyers made cross-border purchases.

Based on additional figures from survey of 24,000 adult consumers in 29 countries across the globe (PayPal 2015), in virtually every region of the world, the United States and China are by far the most popular online cross-border purchase destinations. The only exception is in Western Europe where cross-border purchases tend to be made within the region. From the buyer's standpoint, the countries with the strong proclivities for cross-border purchasing (i.e., those with more than 70% of their online purchases being cross-border) are scattered across the globe and include Canada, Ireland, Austria, Israel, Nigeria, Singapore, and Australia. Those with the weakest proclivities include the United States, the United Kingdom, Germany, the Netherlands, Poland, Turkey, Japan, South Korea, and China.

By 2020 (Alizilia.com 2015), the outlook for cross-border transactions is predicted to change substantially. The volume of cross-border transactions is projected to have a compound growth rate of close to 30% between now and then, so that cross-border transactions will reach around one trillion. This will represent about 30% of the estimated total for that year. At that time, close to one out of every two of the estimated two billion shoppers will make cross-border purchases. For merchants and sellers, these estimates paint a picture of massive opportunity—the "oyster." It also represents a substantial opportunity for banks and payment service providers, So, where's the "sword?" What's needed to take advantage of the opportunity? For the inefficiencies of cross-border payments, see Park (2015).

The Solution

Suppose a merchant wants to expand his or her online B2C specialty clothing and apparel business to handle overseas buyers. Point of fact, there are more cross-border purchases for clothing and apparel than any other product category by a wide margin. Given this fact, how hard could it be to sell clothing on the international market? With English and credit cards being de facto standards on the Internet, it seems like most merchants could engage in cross-border EC by simply adding support for international credit cards and delivery. While this might work for a handful of transactions in some parts of the world, experience tells us it would not work for even the average number of sales transactions handled by most EC retailers.

A recent study of a sample of 180 online B2C merchants in ten countries by Pymnts.com (2015) assessed the characteristics of those already successfully engaged in international B2C, as well as the readiness of the sample to participate in cross-border transactions. Based on their analysis of 60 features, the number one key finding was that the top ten merchants "think local." They treat international customers as if they were domestic. They offer multiple languages, multiple currencies, and multiple payment systems. They customize pages to the customer's country (e.g., simple things like address and phone fields). They support access through a variety of devices, especially mobile. They simplify the checkout process, eliminating the need for extensive user profiles. They also offer free shipping and rewards to encourage repeat business.

The second key finding of the study (Pymnts.com 2015) was that the vast majority of businesses in the sample were far from ready to engage in cross-border transactions. It's understandable given that there are currently 195 countries in the world with a combined total of 6500 spoken languages and 180 currencies, not to mention differing customs procedures, logistics, physical infrastructures, and other regulatory and legal systems.

Treating potential cross-border customers as if they were all "local" is almost an impossible task. Because the barriers and issues that need to be addressed in cross-border sales are so intertwined, it is hard to do it in a phased approach or piecemeal fashion. This is why most businesses start by offering a small segment of their product or service listings to a handful of countries. Also, instead of setting up local legal entities within the countries of interest or creating on their own with fully localized features for each of the countries to be served, many companies start by working with a partner who is conversant in the world of cross-border commerce and who has a site or portal that is already serving a broad spectrum of cross-border consumers.

The Costco Solution

This was the approached used by Costco when they decided to offer some of their products to the burgeoning B2C market in China.

Costco's 2015 annual report provides an overview of the company and the general strategy and operating principles (Costco.com 2015). Costco Wholesale Corporation began operations in 1983 in Seattle, Washington. From the beginning they have focused on operating membership warehouses in the United States and Canada, as well as a handful of foreign countries including the United Kingdom, Mexico, Japan, Australia, Spain, Taiwan, and Korea. Worldwide there are 686 warehouses, the bulk (569) of which are located in the United States and Canada. These warehouses, which average about 144,000 sq. ft., run by 200,000 employees and service 81 million cardholders. Cardholders pay annual fees that vary by country, although they are around $55 in the United States.

Their basic strategy is to offer lower-priced, high-quality, nationally branded, and Costco private-label (Kirkland Signature) products across a range of categories including food, sundries, hardlines, softlines, fresh foods, and ancillary products (e.g., gas stations and pharmacy). Given the low-price strategy, the profits come from selling focused inventory (3700 SKUs) with high sales volumes and rapid turnover coupled with "operating efficiencies achieved by volume purchasing, efficient distribution and reduced handling of merchandise in no-frills, self-service warehouse facilities." They also come from membership fees.

In 2015, Costco's sales totaled $114B with an annual growth rate of 20% annually. The overwhelming majority (97%) of these sales were in store. Costco was late getting to EC, and, as a consequence, they lag behind their competitors. Their anemic EC sales are also a consequence of their expressed strategy. EC sales don't generate memberships, nor do they encourage much foot traffic along with in-store impulse buying.

While Costco's international presence is limited, it was hard for Costco to ignore China's astounding retail growth, especially from online sales. In order to test the retail market in China, Costco decided in 2014 to enter the market by setting up shop on Alibaba's Tmall Global site without capital investments in Chinese real estate.

The Alibaba Group and Their Tmall and Alipay

In recent years the Alibaba Group has made a concerted effort to encourage cross-border online B2C imports. Toward this end, in 2014 they launched a new cross-border EC website called Tmall Global. It's a platform that enables foreign companies to sell to Chinese consumers without having a physical presence in China. This was particularly attractive to Costco because they were wary of following the same path of the big box stores.

Tmall has a number of key features supporting cross-border EC, but two of the more important are Alipay and Tmall's bonded warehouses and logistics partner network (Tran 2015). Alipay is Alibaba's payment platform (sort of like PayPal). It is the largest payment system in China, used much more than credit or debit cards which Tmall also supports. The platform automatically handles currency conversion so that Chinese buyers pay in Yuan and retailers are paid in their home currency (once a buyer has received their goods). Basically, once a merchant is hooked up to Alipay, it provides entrée to China's 300 M online buyers. The other key feature revolves around a set of bonded warehouses located in five major cities (Shanghai, Guangzhou, Hangzhou, Zhengzhou, and Ningo) where merchants can pre-ship products in large quantities. The warehouses are in duty-free zones dedicated to handling imports and delivery for international merchandise purchased online. They not only enable faster shipping times to customers but also lower fees on customs and duties. Technically, the warehouses are operated by customs, but in reality the actual goods are the responsibility of Alibaba's logistics subsidiary, Cainiao, who uses a network of third-party logistics providers (3PLs) to perform the necessary warehouse activities including the sorting, picking, delivery, and custom clearance.

Criteria for Collaboration

In exchange for these types of key services, which aren't free, retailers must meet certain criteria. Among other things they have to (Tran 2015):

- Have a retail or trading license.
- Prove they own the brands or have rights to distribute them.
- Provide their Tmall site in Chinese.
- Have products manufactured outside inspected and approved by Tmall.
- Provide customer service including Chinese language service support.
- Support customer returns and provide a return location in China.
- Provide shipping direct to the consumer in China.

Many of the required services can be and are often outsourced to third-party providers, who are preapproved and endorsed by Tmall Global.

The Results

Today, Costco's Tmall Global site sells around 200 items from its food, healthcare, and private-label Kirkland Signature product offerings. They also used their base in Taiwan to help support operations and rely on Tmall's inventory storage and 20-day delivery to limit operating expenses.

Unlike some of the other 5400 Tmall Global customers, Costco has enjoyed a modicum of success. While there are no official annual statistics provided by Costco or Tmall, Tmall did report that Costco sold over $6.4 million in the first month of operation and that during the 2014 Singles' Day Sale Costco sold $3.5 million in merchandise.

Because of Costco's razor thin margins, whatever revenues are made have to be weighed against the benefits and costs of operating accrued from the site and partnership. On the benefit side, the operation (Mahajan 2015):

- Enables them to test the market without having to invest in real estate; this was the mistake that many big box retailers (e.g., Home Depot and Best Buy) made when they entered the Chinese market.
- Allows them to experiment with the market to determine those products that will sell, the features that are important to Chinese customers, the prices they can charge, and the general spending patterns of Chinese consumers with respect to their offerings.
- Alleviates the need for a local business license to establish an online store. This can be a complex, lengthy, and costly endeavor.
- Eliminates many of the typical interchange costs associated with card-based payment systems and reduces overall logistical costs by speeding transit time.

In terms of limitations, the operation:

- Restricts them from advertising on Tmall Mainland and Taobao which accounts for 80% for China's online sales. They have to rely on company name and brand recognition to drive business.
- Charges merchants a deposit fee ($25,000), an annual fee (somewhere between $5000 and $10,000), a sales commission fee of 2–5% of the product price and logistics fees, and an Alipay fee of 1% of the product price and logistics fees.
- Eliminates a key element of their business strategy—membership fees.

There's no assurance that Costco will succeed in the Chinese online B2C market. There is tremendous competitive pressure coming from leading Chinese retailers and from other cross-border retailers and manufacturers. If they are successful, eventually they will probably have to go the local route and establish an independent online presence in China in order to reduce their overall costs.

Sources: Alizila.com (2015), Costco.com (2015), Goodale (2014), Mahajan (2015), PayPal (2015), Pymnts.com (2015), and Tran (2015) (all accessed December 2016).

LESSONS LEARNED FROM THE CASE

From the consumer's point of view, the world of online retail is pretty simple—select, pay, confirm, and wait for delivery. From the merchant's point of view, online life is anything but simple. Regardless of whether a merchant is running a domestic or international operation, there are a large number of complex issues that need to be addressed in making a business successful. A major difference between the two types of operations is that when a merchant tries to expand her or his online business by going international, the problems are exacerbated—almost like running separate, local businesses in the different countries.reference list.

As the opening case highlighted, among the litany of issues that have to be addressed by merchants, some of the key issues revolve around (1) handling electronic currencies and payments, (2) managing and fulfilling orders once payment has been made, and (3) ensuring that the linkage between the financial side and the logistical side appears seamless to customers. This chapter focuses on these issues.

Almost since the inception of e-commerce, the world of e-payments has been dominated by credit cards, debit cards, and third-party surrogates like PayPal tied directly to cards or bank accounts. Today, this world is in flux. While the traditional e-payment methods still dominate worldwide, this is changing rapidly. The changes are being driven by the rise of omni-channel retail, the expanding use of mobile devices, innovations in the world of digital or virtual currencies, as well as the changing demographics of B2C consumers.

This chapter deals with this changing payment world. First, it examines the underlying shifts driving the changes. Next, it looks at the major forms of payment worldwide, including cards, third-party systems, mobile payments, and virtual currencies. The chapter also explores the players and processes associated with the various payment alternatives along with the underlying reasons why some have been widely adopted while others have not.

A subsequent chapter (Chap. 13) presents the second part of the story—order fulfillment and logistics.

12.1 CHANGING RETAIL LANDSCAPE

"Retail stores will completely die." "Cash is King no more." "The PC is dead." It's easy to find any number of pundits proclaiming the imminent demise of some historical pillar of offline or online retail. However, as the writer Mark Twain was once quoted as saying "…the report of my death has been grossly exaggerated." Clearly, online shopping, digital payments, and mobile devices are all growing at substantial rates relative to their historical counterparts, but as Bill Gates has said "we always overestimate the change that will occur in the next 2 years and underestimate the change that will occur in the next ten." None of these are in immediate danger of passing, especially when they are viewed from a global perspective.

Omni-Channel Retail

Overall, worldwide retail sales are growing, but EC retail sales are growing faster (eMarketer 2015). In 2015, global retail sales were close to $24 trillion. By 2019, they will be around $29 trillion, a growth rate of 6% annually. In contrast, EC retail sales were estimated at $1.7 trillion in 2015 which was 7% of the total figure. This online segment of sales is projected to grow at over 8% annually for the next few years and will reach $3.6 trillion in 2019. By that time, they will be 12% of the total. Loosely translated, this means that for every $1 of EC sales, there are $9 sold elsewhere (primarily in stores).

In today's world of omni-channel retail, it's misleading to look at in-store versus online as a zero sum game. Online and offline activities are intertwined. If I spend time on my smartphone checking on the prices, reviews, and availability of some product, I may then decide to go to the store and buy it. The store will get the credit, but the sale was really the result of my "webrooming" activities.

While these and other combinations aren't possible with every product and every retailer, they are rapidly becoming so for leading retailers. A few years ago, retailers' store systems and online systems—both front office and back—were completely separate. This made it difficult to offer and service customers with all these possible combinations. However, today many of the world's leading retailers are transitioning systems so they can provide their customers an array of browsing, buying, and delivery choices.

There is no doubt that the number of retail stores and retail square footage are on the decline. So is the foot traffic within most stores. A lot of this decline is a function of online shopping, but this doesn't mean that stores are completely dying. It does mean that the shopping experiences we know today are morphing into something different, so that strictly keeping score of in-store versus online dollars may be moot. This is why, for example, Forrester Research (reported by O'Grady 2016) has been stating the relative position of online, Web-influenced, and non-Web-influenced offline sales. When these distinctions are made, they estimate that the $3.6 trillion in global retail sales for 2016 sales will be divided among the three categories: online = 8%, Web-influenced = 44%, and non-Web-influenced = 48%.

Cash Versus Non-cash Transactions

Both offline and online non-cash payments are on the rise. In absolute terms this doesn't mean that cash payments are declining and ultimately dying. In fact they are actually increasing but at a slower rate than non-cash payments.

Unlike non-cash payments, it is very difficult to track and accurately measure the total use of cash in a country. Governments try to track how much cash is in circulation, but most governments have no way of accurately knowing who's using how much cash to buy what. In fact, this is one of the reasons that some people like cash, as well as the digital counterparts like bitcoins.

One thing we can measure is ATM activity. The ATM business is booming (Gordon 2015). In 2014, the installed base of ATMs worldwide was three million and is expected to be at four million by 2020. Indeed, China with the fast-growing economy had 600,000 ATMs that year, an increase of 500% from the year before. In 2014, there were over 90 billion cash withdrawals worth around $14 trillion. That was an increase of over 4%. Of course, in the future we'll be able to load our electronic wallets from ATMs, so we'll have to make a distinction between cash versus electronic withdrawals.

From a cash standpoint, another thing we can estimate is the relative number of consumer transactions that are cash versus non-cash. A widely cited report from MasterCard (2015) noted that cash accounts for 85% of global consumer transactions, although this percentage varies widely by country. Actually, in the vast majority of countries, the percent exceeds 85%. Included in this majority are China, Spain, Brazil, Japan, India, and Russia. This is followed by a group of countries like the United States, Australia, Germany, and South Korea where the percent of consumer cash transactions falls between 55 and 70%. Finally, there is a very small handful of countries where the percent is between 40 and 50%. These are the closest thing we get to a cashless society and include Singapore, the Netherlands, France, Sweden, Canada, and Belgium.

There is a substantial push by a number of governments to eliminate cash transactions as much as possible. However, because of its ubiquitous role in small-value transactions and among lower-income populations who have few financial alternatives, it's close to impossible for a government to eliminate cash even in a country that is economically advanced.

This pattern between cash and non-cash consumer transactions mirrors the pattern between offline and online retail sales. More specifically, like in-store retail cash is king and increasing. However, non-cash transactions are increasing more rapidly and gaining market share. These gains are being driven by EC sales transactions. While cash can be used for EC purchases (e.g., cash on delivery or transfers from cash accounts), the vast majority of these sales involve non-cash payments of various sorts.

Like cash in the broader world, cards—credit and debit—have been the king of global non-cash payments since the early 2000s. Looking at figures from a Capgemini Financial Services Analysis (2016), overall non-cash payments fall into one of four groups—cards, direct debit, credit transfers, and checks. Except for Europe where cards represent about 45% of all non-cash payments, in every other region of the world the share of card transactions ranges from a low of 50% in Latin America to a high of over 80% in emerging Asia.

Usage of EC Payment Methods

Data from worldwide survey of 13,000 consumers in 26 countries conducted by Nielsen (2016) provides a closer look at how non-cash transactions are used globally in the online world. Respondents were asked to indicate what methods they used to make B2C online purchases in the last 3 months. Payments were divided into five categories—credit card, debit cards (third party), digital payment systems (e.g., PayPal), direct debit, and cash on delivery (COD). The top three payment methods for a number of key geographical areas are shown in Table 12.1.

Globally, cards (credit and debit) are the most frequently used, followed by digital payment systems. However, it's obvious that the relative importance of a particular method varies from one region to another. Clearly, China is an anomaly because neither credit cards nor debit cards are in its top three. In China digital payments are used most frequently by a wide margin. In China the popularity of digital payments results from the fact that Alibaba is by far the largest EC site in the

Table 12.1 Percent of respondents using EC payment method in the last 3 months

Country	Credit	Debit	Digital	Direct debit	COD
Global	53	49	43	–	–
China	–	–	86	53	49
India	–	71	–	61	83
SE Asia	57	–	37	35	–
Western Europe	44	56	56	–	–
Eastern Europe	46	–	–	55	57
North America	74	–	38	–	–
Africa	–	52	–	42	54
Latin America	65	31	46	–	–
Middle East	46	11	–	–	64

Source: Based on data from Nielsen (2016)

county and Alibaba relies on its own proprietary payment system called Alipay. Again, it is also important to point out that COD is the leading payment method in four out of the nine areas which all happened to be developing economies where there is a large portion of "unbanked."

Amazon's GO is Changing Retail

In early 2017 Amazon.com is changing the brick-and-mortar retailing by introducing stores that let customers bypass the manual checkout. Using several AI technologies, machine learning, sensors, computer vision, and deep learning (see Chap. 7), a smart store is keeping track of what shoppers place in their shopping carts. When shoppers leave the physical store, they do not stay in line to pay. There are no cashiers, no credit card to swipe, and no wait in line. Amazon simply charges customer's accounts and send them e-receipt. Shoppers use Amazon's special app, this is all. Initially, an experimental store is opened only for Amazon's employees in Seattle. However, Amazon plans to open such 2000 stores.

- How will it catch thieves?
- How will it spot fast shoppers?
- What if you consume items in store and put the package back on the shelf?
- How the system handles returns?
- What if you put an item in someone else's cart by mistake?

Brandon (2016) raised the following five questions regarding the viability of such stores:

For all grocery shopping methods including self-checkout and self-scanning, see Rossman et al. (2016). This case is an example of the use of smartphones in shopping.

Move to Mobile

It should be no surprise that the world is rapidly adopting smartphones. According to Ericson (Lunden 2015), in 2015 there were just under two million smartphone users globally, around 25% of the world population. By 2016, they expect the number to rise to over six million users or 70% of the world population. Much of this astounding growth is being fueled by developing economies and by the "digital natives" between the ages of 18 and 24.

Not surprisingly, the rapid adoption of smartphones is also highlighted by the number of global shipments of new smartphones versus the combined shipments of other computer-based devices including tablets, 2-in-1 hybrid tablets, portable PCs, and desktop PCs (Lunden 2015). At the end of 2011, new shipments of smartphones exceeded the shipments of PCs of all sorts for the first time. Today, smartphones account for 70% of all new shipments. By 2019 the percent may be close to 80%.

Clearly, the PC is on its last breath, but not so fast. First, ignoring the fact that Apple still refuses to provide touch screens on the MacBooks, most PCs are morphing into tablet devices which have mobile capabilities. Second, many smartphone users still have PCs that they use on a daily basis. Finally, when you look at the EC world, it's clear that PCs still rule the roost in terms of online purchases.

With respect to this latter claim, consider the data in Fig. 12.1. This figure shows the percent of online purchases made with tablets, smartphones, and PCs. With the exception of two countries—Japan and South Korea where cell phone and smartphone usage is historically very high—PCs account for at least 70% of the purchases. Even in Japan and South Korea, the numbers are around 50%.

Why is the percent of online purchases with PCs still higher than it is for smartphones? There are a number of reasons. One reason is that sizeable percentage of smartphone users are still hesitant to put personal and credit information on their phones, fearing it might be stolen and hacked. This is the same sort of fear that slowed the use of credit cards for online purchases when EC was first getting started. Obviously, consumers got over it and they will get over it again with mobile devices. A second reason is found in the demographics of the buyers. Adoption of mobile devices is strongest among younger cohorts. Yet, the purchasing power of older cohorts is much larger than it is for younger cohorts. Globally, the median net worth of those over 65 is close to 50 times larger than those under 35! Older consumers still use PCs. What this is likely to mean in the longer run is that the percent of purchases by smartphones will begin to climb rapidly. However, the dollar value purchased with PCs will be larger than it is for smartphones for the foreseeable future.

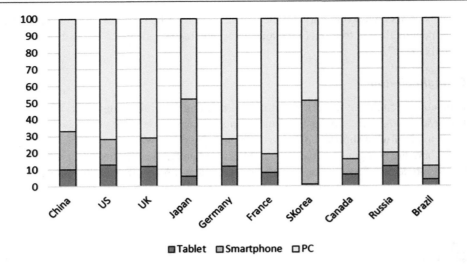

Fig. 12.1 Percent of Total Country Online EC Spend by Device (Source: Based on Keith, M. Global eCommerce Sales, Trends and Statistics 2015. September 2, 2015. remarkety.com/global-ecommerce-sales-trends-and-statistics-2015)

The Cashless Society

Despite all its obstacles, the move is toward cashless society (see Desjardins 2016). According to Beilfuss (2016), the shift to cashless payment is set to spur trillions of dollars in consumer spending (estimated an additional ten trillion dollars over a decade). The major driver for such cashless society is the fact that over 3.2 billion people have Internet access (2016 data). By 2020 there will be over 4.4 billion. In addition, the smartphones are spreading even in developing countries, enabling money transfers (see the closing case). As a matter of fact, India is already on the path toward a cashless society (see Sharma 2016). Note that over 50% of all dollar payments in the United States and Canada are already cashless. In Western Europe, Australia, and Southeast Asia, it is over 35%. In other countries it is around 10%.

Implications for EC Payments

Since its inception in 1995, B2C EC has been dominated by a relatively simple set of business models, transactions, and payment types. Crudely put, at the beginning of the twenty-first century, it was enough for the average merchant to offer a catalog of products and prices via a browser, to enable payment by cards (credit and debit) or some third-party payment processor (e.g., PayPal), to provide systems for shipping the product and handling returns, and to provide customer support. Those merchants with both a physical and digital presence tended to run their online business as a simple, albeit separate, extension of their offline world. Basically, it was as if a catalog business had gone digital. Like most catalog businesses, the primary focus has been on nonperishable products (not on customers) and on domestic markets, not on international buyers. Even today a large portion of EC sites still operate this way with a number of bells and whistles thrown in.

   For the last 10 years, the underlying tenets and practices of this model have been under assault by the operational, technical, and demographic changes briefly described in this section. In the last 4–5 years, these changes have picked up a full head of steam. Nowhere is this more apparent than in the area of payments, both from the buyers' and sellers' sides. The size of the assault in this area has been described as a tsunami. Literally, innovations aimed at supplementing, modifying, or replacing some aspect of electronic payments number in the thousands. Many of these are coming from new players and start-ups in the financial technology (fintech) industry.

   While there are no industry standard categories for classifying these efforts and, thus, no official data for estimating associated volume and value, Capgemini Financial Services Analysis (2016) has attempted to address these deficiencies. They coined the term "hidden digital payments" to describe this overall collection of activities and divided the payments into four main types including:

- *Closed-loop cards and mobile apps*, enabling online and offline payments and aimed at promoting loyalty
- *Digital wallets* (nonbanks), supporting a variety of EC transactions
- *Mobile money*, enabling mobile financial transactions for the "unbanked" and "underbanked"
- *Virtual currencies*, supporting the instantaneous transfer of "value" without the aid of traditional financial institutions

For 2015, they estimated the total volume of hidden payments between 25 and 40 billion, a small percent of all non-cash transactions (between 6% and 10%).

Critical Mass

Before credit cards became the standard in EC, many companies tried to introduce nontraditional payment systems. With the exception of PayPal, they all died an early death. Today, the number of new systems far exceeds the number from those early years. A handful will probably gain widespread acceptance, another handful will gain regional acceptance, and the overwhelming majority of these will suffer the same fate as their predecessors. Even notoriety and a faithful group of followers is any guarantee of success.

A case in point is the well-publicized virtual currency Bitcoin (**bitcoin.org**). Bitcoin is a peer-to-peer, encrypted digital currency powered by open source software (discussed in detail in section "Digital and Virtual Currencies"). It has a sizeable number of users and supporters. It has a rocky history. At this point in time, some pundits are forecasting its demise as a currency. However, they are also forecasting that there's a good chance that its underlying technical foundation may be repurposed for other financial applications.

As Evans and Schmalensee (2005) pointed out back in 2005, it takes years for any payment system to gain widespread acceptance. For example, credit cards were introduced in the 1950s but did not reach widespread use until the 1980s. A crucial element in the success of any e-payment method is the "chicken-and-egg" problem: How do you get sellers to adopt a payment method when there are few buyers using it? Further, how do you get buyers to adopt a method when there are few sellers using it? In physics terms, how do the payment systems reach critical mass?

Factors for Critical Mass

Critical mass depends on a number of key factors such as those listed below:

- **Independence.** Most forms of e-payment require the buyer to adopt some new technology in order to initiate a payment and the merchant to install specialized software and hardware to accept, authorize, and process a payment. If the new system can piggyback on existing technologies and practices, it has an easier road to success.
- **Interoperability and portability.** An e-payment method must be integrated with existing information systems before it can be adopted.
- **Security.** How safe is the payment transaction? What if the transfer is compromised? Only safe systems will succeed.
- **Anonymity.** Some buyers want their identities and purchase records to be anonymous. This can be done only when cash is used. To succeed, special payment methods, such as virtual currencies, have to maintain anonymity.
- **Divisibility.** It is difficult for most payment systems to efficiently scale across a range of purchase prices. For example, on one end try using a credit card to buy a candy bar. On the other, try using a credit card to purchase a plane. Any method that can service one or the other of the extremes or can cover a wide range in the middle has a chance of succeeding.
- **Ease of use.** Credit cards are used for B2C and B2B e-payments because of their ease of use. E-payments must complement the trading methods.
- **Transaction fees.** Outside of cash, virtually any payment system costs one or more service fees. When a credit card is used, the merchant pays processing fees. When a card is used to withdraw money, the cardholder usually pays. If the aggregate fees prove too costly for one of the parties, the system is likely to fail.
- **International support.** EC is a worldwide phenomenon. An e-payment method must be easily adapted to fit buying needs and local legal requirements before it can be widely adopted. The major exceptions are systems that are mandated by law.
- **Regulations.** A number of international, federal, and state regulations govern all payment methods. Any changes or new methods need approval of the regulators. PayPal, for instance, faced several lawsuits brought against them by several US states for alleged violations of banking regulations.

SECTION 12.1 REVIEW QUESTIONS

1. What is omni-channel retail? "Webrooming?"
2. Why is it difficult to track the global use of cash?
3. What are the different types of non-cash EC payment used in different regions of the world?
4. Describe the relative use of smartphones, tablets, and PC for EC purchases?
5. What are the main types of "hidden payments?"
6. What is the "chicken-egg" problem in EC payment adoption?
7. What factors are key to the successful adoption of an EC payment method?

12.2 USING PAYMENT CARDS ONLINE

Payment cards are electronic cards that contain payment-related data. They come in three forms:

1. **Credit cards.** A credit card enables its holder to charge items (and pay later) or obtain cash up to the cardholder's authorized limit. With each purchase, the credit card holder receives a loan from the credit card issuers. Most credit cards do not have an annual fee. However, holders are charged interest if the balance is not paid in full by the due date. Visa and MasterCard are the leading cards.
2. **Charge cards.** These are special credit cards where the balance must be paid in full by the due date and usually have annual fees. Examples of issuers are American Express and Diner's Club (they both offer regular credit cards as well).
3. **Debit cards.** Payments made with a debit card are withdrawn from the holder's checking or savings account. The actual transfer of funds usually takes place in real time from the holder's account (if an ATM card is used). However, a settlement to a merchant's checking account may take place within one to 2 days. Again, MasterCard and Visa are examples of debit card issuers. For a discussion of some best practices for debit card usage, see **usatoday.com/story/tech/columnist/komando/2014/04/11/4-places-you-should-not-swipe-your-debit-card/7436229** .

Credit Card Reading

When paying with a credit card, it is necessary for merchants to read the content of the card and then transfer the content for approval and processing. This must be done in almost real time.

Several methods are available.

- **Stationary card readers.** The most common readers available are physical POS in stores. They are wirelined to the authorization and processing system.
- **Portable card readers.** These are used in places where wirelines do not exist (e.g., on airplanes). They may be connected wirelessly to the processing system or may be stand-alone systems (sellers then take risks, usually for small payments).
- **Mobile readers.** These systems enable payments from mobile devices. They include credit card readers, which are plugged into the smartphones. The Square Reader (**squareup.com**), which has a "swiper" that plugs into the smartphone's headphone jack and reads the information from the magnetic strip of the customer's card, is such a device (see section "PayPal and Other Third-Party Payment Gateways").

Processing Cards Online

The processing of credit card payments has two major phases: *authorization* and *settlement*. **Authorization** determines whether a buyer's card is valid (e.g., not expired) and whether the customer has sufficient credit or funds in his or her account. **Settlement** involves the transfer of money from the buyer's account to the merchant's. There are a number of parties involved in both processes including:

- **Customer.** The individual possessing the card.
- **Merchant.** The vendor that sells goods or services.
- **Issuing bank.** The issuer (usually a bank) of the credit (debit) card to customer (or businesses). Services customer accounts including billing and collecting month payments.
- **Merchant acquiring bank.** Enrolls merchants into a program that accept a specific card brand (e.g., Visa) and, on the merchant's behalf, processes debit or credit card payments made using that particular card brand.
- **Credit card (association) network.** Credit card networks determine where credit cards can be used and facilitate the payment process between credit card users, merchants, and credit card issuers.
- **Payment service provider.** The company that provides electronic connections and transaction services among all the parties involved in electronic payments (including authorizations). A payment service provider is also called a *payment gateway provider.*

Authorization and Settlement

The roles that the participants play, the linkages among them, and the general flow of the authorization and settlement processes are depicted in Fig. 12.2. For any given card and merchant, there can be variations in the exact players and in the details of the process. However, regardless of whether the payment is being made offline or online, they usually include:

- **Authorization cycle**—The customer initiates a payment transaction (fills out Web page, swipes a card, etc.). The merchant receives the transaction information. This information is passed to its PSP where it is routed to the merchant's acquiring bank (processor). The acquiring bank passes the information to the issuing bank through the credit card network. If the issuing bank approves the transaction, an authorization code is sent back to the merchant via the same linkages. The issuing bank also holds an authorization associated with that merchant and consumer for the approved amount. Finally, the merchant notifies the customer and fulfills the order.
- **Settlement**—At the end of the day, the merchant submits in *batch* all the approved authorizations they have received to the acquiring bank via its PSP. Again, the acquiring bank makes the batch settlement request to the issuing bank via the card network. The credit card issuer makes a settlement payment to the acquiring bank via the card network (the next day).

Fig. 12.2 Credit card payment procedure (Drawn by D. King)

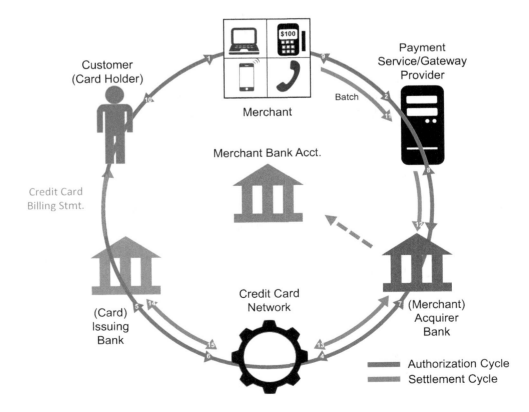

The acquiring bank subsequently deposits approved funds into the merchant's *nominated* account. This could be an account with the acquiring bank if the merchant does their banking with the same bank or an account with another bank. The entire process from authorization to settlement to funding typically takes 3 days.

Although the entire authorization process involves a number of parties, it usually takes a few seconds. Some of that time involves various security measures—encrypting the information is transmitted and checking for fraudulent transactions along the way. In contrast the settlement process usually takes a few days. The settlement process can be slowed if the transaction depends on the customer actually receiving the order.

While cards are obviously convenient for both the consumer and the merchant, they cost the merchant money. This is one of the reasons smaller businesses are hesitant to support a laundry list of card brands and types because of the size and complexity of the charges that come with this support. The main fee that a merchant pays for offering credit card payments is called **discount rate**. It might be something like 2%, 3%, or more of the transaction value. There are a number of factors that impact the rate like the size of the transaction, the type of transaction (e.g., card present or not), the particular brand of card, etc. A major portion of the discount rate (e.g., 85%) goes to the issuing bank—these are the fees charged by the issuing bank for handling authorization and settlement requests. This segment of the fees are called the **interchange rate**. The remaining amount is split between the credit card association (around one third) and the acquiring bank (around two thirds).

One way to eliminate or reduce some of the complexities and costs associated with card payments is by eliminating or consolidating some of the steps in the process—especially the processing options that link the merchant to the issuing bank. The following are the major processing options. The EC merchant may:

1. **Own the payment software.** A merchant can purchase a payment processing module and integrate it with its other EC software. This module communicates with a payment gateway run by an acquiring bank or another third party.
2. **Use a point-of-sale (POS) system operated by a card acquirer.** Merchants can redirect cardholders to a POS system run by an acquirer. The POS handles the complete payment process and directs the cardholder back to the merchant's site once payment is complete. In this case, the merchant's system deals only with order information. In this configuration, it is important to find an acquirer that handles multiple cards and payment instruments. If not, the merchant will need to connect with a multitude of acquirers.
3. **Use a POS system operated by a payment service provider.** Merchants can rely on **payment service providers (PSPs)**, which are third-party companies that provide services to merchants so they can accept all kinds of electronic payments. The PSPs connect all participants in the electronic transactions. See an example at **usa.visa.com/content/dam/VCOM/download/merchants/bulletin-mobile-best-practices.pdf**

Option number 1 is simply the base method that is shown in Fig. 12.2. With option 2 the merchant steps to the side and lets the acquirer deal with the customer's payment. In option 3, the merchant simply deals with a third-party processor that handles not only card payments but other types of payments as well. These third-party companies can also alleviate the need for merchants to establish relations with acquiring banks.

Fraudulent Card Transactions

Although the processes used for authorizing and settling card payments offline and online are very similar, there is one substantial difference between the two. In e-commerce, the merchants usually are liable for fraudulent transactions. In addition to the cost of lost merchandise and shipping charges, merchants who accept fraudulent or unauthorized cards for payments may have to pay penalties to the credit card companies. However, these are not the only costs.

There also are the costs associated with combating fraudulent transactions. These include the costs of tools and systems to review orders, the costs of manually reviewing orders, and the revenue that is lost from erroneously rejecting valid orders. According to CyberSource's 16th annual survey (CyberSource.com 2016) of online fraud management, fraudulent online card transactions still result in substantial losses although the rate of e-commerce revenue loss has remained steady (at.9%) for the past 5 years. The stability is a function of the measures that merchants have adopted to manage fraud. Over the years, the CyberSource surveys (CyberSource is a subsidiary of Visa) also have monitored the steps taken by merchants to combat fraud. Today, virtually every merchant has instituted automated processes backed by manual review to detect fraudulent transactions. The exact automated procedures vary from one merchant to the next. However, there are some tools that are used by a majority.

Methods for Combating Fraud

The key tools used in combating fraud are:

- **Card verification number (CVN).** More than 86% of all merchants use the **card verification number (CVN)** method, which detects fraud by matching the three-digit verification number printed on the signature strip on the back of the credit card (or the four-digit number on the front of the card, such as American Express cards) to the number stored by the cardholder's issuing bank. However, if a fraudster possesses a stolen card, the number is in plain view and verification becomes difficult. Attempts are made to check the habits of the card user (e.g., to check unusually large purchases or purchases made overseas). In such cases, a cardholder may get a telephone call from the card issuer or the credit card company, asking for verification of identity. In such a case, the verification may be done by intelligent software agents automatically.
- **Address verification.** A vast majority of merchants (better than 86%) use the **Address Verification System (AVS)**, which detects fraud by comparing the address provided by the buyer at checkout with the card address on file. Unfortunately, this method may result in a number of false positives, meaning that the merchant may reject a valid order. Cardholders may have a new address or simply make mistakes in inputting numeric street addresses or zip codes. AVS is available only in the United States and Canada.
- **Customer order history.** The purchases made with a particular card (and cardholder) tend to follow regular patterns with respect to place, amounts, types, and frequency. Order data from the card's used can be mathematically and statistically mined to discern these patterns. Current card purchases can be matched against these patterns to detect anomalies in real time in order to flag them as potential fraud. Close to 78% of merchants employ this process.
- **Negative lists.** Close to 70% of the merchants use *negative lists*. A negative list is a database of card numbers that could potentially be used by fraudsters. It is also a database of card numbers used to avoid further fraud from repeat offenders. The merchants can match each customer's card against this database to find customers and cards with known problems.
- **Postal address validation service.** Checks to see if the shipping address received with an order is a valid postal address. Just under 70% use this technique.

While automated procedures are key to fraud detection, the CyberSource survey indicated that close to one out of every four card transactions is flagged as potentially fraudulent, requiring manual review. The average length of a manual review is about 5 min. This adds up to a lot of time and labor expense. In fact half of the money spent combating card transaction fraud goes to these costs. The future key to reducing these costs is clearly better automated procedures.

SECTION 12.2 REVIEW QUESTIONS

1. Describe the three types of payment cards.
2. Describe credit card readers.
3. List the major participants in processing cards online.
4. Describe the key processes in card settlement and authorization.
5. What options does a merchant have in setting up an e-payment system?
6. What costs does an online merchant incur if it accepts a fraudulent card transaction?
7. What steps are often taken by online merchants to combat fraudulent orders?

12.3 SMART CARDS

A **smart card** is a plastic payment card that contains data in an embedded microchip. The embedded chip can be a microprocessor combined with a memory chip or just a memory chip with nonprogrammable logic. Information on a microprocessor card can be added, deleted, or otherwise manipulated; a memory-chip card is usually a "read-only" card, similar to a magnetic stripe card. The card's programs and data must be downloaded from, and activated by, some other device (such as an ATM). Smart cards are used for a wide variety of purposes including:

- Telecom—SIM cards
- Financial—cards issued by banks, retailers, and service providers for payment services (debit, credit, prepaid), loyalty, and social cards with payment apps
- Government and healthcare—cards issued by governments for citizen identification and online services and cards issued by private health insurance companies
- Device manufactures—mobile phones, tablets, navigation devices, and other connected devices including secure element without SIM application
- Others—cards issued by operators for transport, tolls, car park service, pay TV, and physical and logical access to cards

A little over 9.2 billion smart cards were shipped in 2015, a 12% increase over the previous year. In 2016, the number is expected to only grow about 6% to 9.8 billion units. The majority of smart cards are currently found in telephones (5.4 billion out of the 9.2 billion), followed by the number of cards used for payments (which is 2.6 billion). The growth that has been experienced is being driven primarily by the migration of payment cards from swipe to (EMV) chips, the rise in mobile devices (excluding SIM cards), and increasing e-government services.

Types of Smart Cards: Contact and Contactless

There are two distinct types of smart cards. The first type is a **contact card**, which is activated when it is inserted into a smart card reader. The second type of card is a **contactless (proximity) card**, meaning that the card only has to be within a certain proximity of a smart card reader to process a transaction. On the front or back of the contact smart cards, there is a small gold (or silver) plate about one half inch in diameter that contains a chip. When the card is inserted into the card reader, the plate makes electronic contact and data are transferred to and from the chip. A contactless card has an embedded antenna that facilitates data transfer to another antenna (e.g., attached to another device). Contactless cards are especially useful where data must be processed (e.g., paying toll road fees, bus or train fares) or when contact may be difficult. Most proximity cards work at short range (just a few inches). For some applications, such as payments at highway tollbooths, longer range proximity cards are available.

In 2015, over 50% of the smart cards shipped to the United States and Europe were contactless. For Asia Pacific, the figure was close to 75%.

Smart Card Readers

Hybrid cards and *combi cards* combine the properties of contact and proximity cards into one card. A hybrid smart card has two separate chips embedded in a card: contact and contactless. In contrast, a combi card (dual-interface) smart card has a single chip that supports both types of interfaces. The benefit of either card is that it eliminates the need of carrying both contact and contactless cards to use with different applications. In addition, you need only one card reader.

With both types of cards, *smart card readers* are crucial to the operation of the system. Technically speaking, a smart card reader is actually a read/write device. The primary purpose of the **smart card reader** is to act as a mediator between the card and the host system that stores application data and processes transactions. Just as there are two basic types of cards, there are two types of smart card readers—*contact* and *proximity*—that match the particular type of card. Smart card readers can be transparent, requiring a host device to operate, or stand alone, functioning independently. Smart card readers are a key element in determining the overall cost of a smart card application. Although the cost of a single reader is usually low, the cost can be quite high when they are used with a large population of users (e.g., passengers traveling on a metropolitan mass transit system).

Stored-Value Cards

The **stored-value card** is a card where a monetary value is prepaid and can be loaded on the card once or several times. From a physical and technical standpoint, a stored-value card is indistinguishable from a regular credit or debit card. In the past, the money value was stored on the magnetic strip, but recently, most stored-value cards use the technology of smart cards. With stored-value cards, the chip stores the prepaid value. Consumers can use stored-value cards to make purchases, offline or online, in the same way that they use credit and debit cards—relying on the same networks, encrypted communications, and electronic banking protocols. What is different about a stored-value card is there is no need for authorization, but there is a limit set by how much money is stored on the card. The most popular applications of stored-value cards are the transportation cards that are very popular in the large cities in Asia. It is a necessity for the citizens in Seoul, Hong Kong, and Singapore to hold smart cards that pay for subways, buses, taxis, and other applications. The transportation cards do not require any fees, but the bank that initiates prepaid cards may require fixed monthly fees or a registration fee. Stored-value cards are also popular to pay for telephone calls and texting.

Stored-value cards come in two varieties: *closed-loop* (single purpose) and *open-loop* (multiple purposes). Closed-loop cards are issued by a specific merchant or merchant group (e.g., a shopping mall) and can be used to make purchases only from the card issuer. Mall cards, refund cards, some toll-pay cards, prepaid telephone cards, and Internet use cards are all examples of closed-loop cards.

Among closed-loop cards, gift cards have traditionally represented a strong growth area, especially in the United States (CardCash 2015). Over 90% of US consumers purchase or receive a gift card annually. In the United States, over $100 billion is spent annually on gift cards. The figure has been averaging about a 6% annual increase over the last 5 years.

An open-loop card is a multipurpose card that can be used for transactions at several retailers or service providers. Open-loop cards also can be used for other purposes, such as a prepaid debit card or for withdrawing cash from an ATM. Financial institutions with card-association branding, such as Visa or MasterCard®, issue some open-loop cards. They can be used anywhere that the branded cards are accepted. *Full open-loop cards* (e.g., the MasterCard Mondex® card) allow the transfer of money between cards without the bank's intervention.

Stored-value cards may be acquired in a variety of ways. Employers or government agencies may issue them as payroll cards or benefit cards in lieu of checks or direct deposits. Merchants or merchant groups sell and load gift cards. Various financial institutions and nonfinancial outlets sell prepaid cards by telephone, online, or in person. Cash, bank wire transfers, money orders, cashier's checks, other credit cards, or direct payroll or government deposits fund prepaid cards.

Applications of Smart Cards

In many parts of the world, smart cards with magnetic stripes are used as credit cards for retail purchases and paying for transportation. They also are used to support nonretail and nonfinancial applications. A general discussion of all types of smart card applications can be found at **globalplatform.org** .

Retail Purchases

Credit card companies and financial institutions are transitioning their traditional credit and debit cards to multi-application smart cards. In many parts of the world, smart cards have reached mass-market adoption rates. This is especially true in Europe, where the goal was to have all bank cards be smart cards with strong authentication and digital signature capabilities as of 2010.

In 2000, the European Commission established an initiative known as the Single Euro Payments Area (SEPA), encompassing 33 European countries. To bring this initiative to fruition, all the EU banks agreed to use the same basic bank card standard, enabling the use of credit and debit cards throughout the EU. The standard (EMV) is named after the three major card associations that developed its initial specifications (Europay, MasterCard, and Visa). It is based on smart cards with a microprocessor chip. The chip is capable of storing not only financial information, but other applications as well, such as strong authentication and digital signatures. The history of SEPA along with its key principles is detailed in Wikipedia (**en.wikipedia.org/wiki/Single_Euro_Payments_Area**).

Originally, the 33 countries agreed to convert all their magnetic strip cards to EMV smart cards by December 2010. None did. Today, European adoption varies by region. In Western Europe 97% of all card transactions are EMV. For Eastern Europe it's around 65%. Outside of Europe, there have also been high rates of adoption in the Middle East, Africa, Canada, and Latin and South America. In these areas, it's 85% or higher. In Asia Pacific reception has been modest with around 35% of the card transactions involving EMV. Likewise in the United States, adoption has been very slow.

In the United States, the major card associations had self-imposed October 1, 2015, as the date for mandatory adoption of EMV cards. As of that date, those merchants who had not adopted the format would be held liable for any losses they incurred from credit card fraud. The date came and went. By the end of 2015, the estimate was that less than 40% of the merchants had EMV terminals and around 40% of cardholders have cards with EMV chips. While the United States has been slow to move, the rate of adoption has picked up substantially during 2016. The exception is gas stations, which are not expected to accept EMV cards until 2017.

Cards Security

The impetus for smart cards versus standard usage is that they are more secure. Because they are often used to store more valuable or sensitive information (e.g., cash or medical records), smart cards often are secured against theft, fraud, or misuse. In contrast, if someone steals a regular payment card, he (she) can see the card's number, the owner's signature, and the security code. In many cases only the card number and the security code are required to make a purchase. However, criminals can use the cards up to the authorized value, which is a loss to the bank and Visa or MasterCard.

On the other hand, if someone steals a smart card, the thief is usually out of luck (with the major exception of contactless, or "wave and go," cards used for retail purchases). Before the smart card can be used, the holder may be required to enter a PIN. The other benefit of smart cards versus standard payment cards is that they can be widened to include other payment services. In the retail arena, many of these services are aimed at those establishments where payments are usually made in cash, and speed and convenience are important. These include convenience stores, gas stations, fast food or quick-service restaurants, and cinemas. Contactless payments exemplify this sort of value-added service.

Contactless in Retailing

A few years ago, card companies began piloting contactless payment systems in retail operations where speed and convenience are crucial. All these systems utilize the existing POS and magnetic strip payment infrastructure used with traditional credit and debit cards. The only difference is that a special contactless smart card reader is required. To make a purchase, a cardholder simply waves his or her card near the terminal, and the terminal reads the financial information on the card. Despite their convenience and speed, the overall uptake of contactless payment cards in retail stores has been relatively slow until recently. For example, according to data from the Smart Payment Association (2016), 40% of the 1.5 billion smart payment cards shipped in 2014 were contactless. That's a 35% increase from the year before.

Transit Fares

In the United States, several European countries, and large Japanese cities, commuters need to drive to a parking lot near a train station, board a train, and then change to one or more subways or buses to arrive at work. The entire trip may require several payments. Many major transit operators in the United States and Asia have introduced smart card fare-ticketing systems to help these commuters. The transit systems in Washington, D.C., Seoul, Hong Kong, San Francisco Bay area, Singapore, and most other major cities all use smart card payment systems. In addition to handling transit fares, the public transport smart cards and other e-payment systems (e.g., smartphones) are being used for paying parking fees and even for purchasing certain goods. For an example, see the Philadelphia Parking Authority (**philapark.org**). Similarly, many of the major toll roads in the United States and elsewhere accept electronic payments rendered by devices called *transponders* that operate much like contactless smart cards but from a much larger distance. Singapore's ERP (electronic road pricing) system, shown in Fig. 12.3, monitors the roads in downtown Singapore to control traffic, especially during rush hour, by using remote transponders in the car.

Fig. 12.3 Singapore electronic road pricing system (Source: Photo taken by J. K. Lee, March 2013)

Note: Despite their popularity, smart card use will decline in the future, replaced by payments from smartphones. One area where it is already happening is EC micropayments.

SECTION 12.3 REVIEW QUESTIONS

1. What is a smart card? Contact card? Contactless card?
2. Describe some of the general where smart cards are used?
3. What is a stored-value card? Closed-loop card? Open-loop card?
4. What is the EMV standard?
5. Why is a smart card more secure than a regular credit card?
6. Describe the use of smart cards in metropolitan transportation systems.

12.4   EC MICROPAYMENTS

Micropayments or **e-micropayments** are small payments made online, usually under $10. From the viewpoint of many vendors, credit cards are too expensive for processing small payments. The same is true for debit cards, where the fixed transaction fees are greater, even though there are no percentage charges. These fees are relatively small (in percentage) only for card purchases over $10. Regardless of the vendor's point of view, there is substantial evidence, at least in the offline world, that consumers are willing to use their credit or debit cards for small-value purchases. In the online world, the evidence suggests that consumers are interested in making small-value purchases, but not with credit or debit card payments. A good example is Apple's iTunes music store and their App Store. There have been more than 35 billion songs downloaded from iTunes (Lee 2014) and over 100 billion apps downloaded from their App Store (Statista-1 2015). A substantial percentage of the songs that were downloaded cost $1.29 a piece, while many of the apps cost somewhere between $.99 and $5. Although most of Apple's customers paid for these downloads with a credit or debit card, the payments were not on a per-transaction basis. Instead, their customers created accounts with Apple, and Apple then aggregated multiple purchases before charging a user's credit or debit card.

Other areas where consumers have shown a willingness to purchase items under $5 using a credit card are cell phone ringtones, ringback tones, and online games. The annual market for ringtones and ringback tones is in the billions of dollars. The download of both types of tones is charged to the consumer's cell phone bill. Similarly, the annual market for online games is in the billions of dollars. Like songs and tones, downloading a game is usually charged to the consumer's account, which is paid by a credit or debit card. Consumers also pay parking fees, fees for renting carts in airports, and fees for other services.

Micropayment Models

Currently, there are five basic micropayment models that do not depend solely or directly on credit or debit cards and that have enjoyed some amount of success. Some of these are better suited for offline payments than online payments, although there is nothing that precludes the application of any of the models to the online world. The models include:

- **Aggregation.** Payments from a single consumer are accumulated and processed periodically (e.g., once a month), or as a certain level is reached (e.g., $100). This model fits vendors with a high volume of repeat business. Both Apple's iTunes and App Store use this model. The transportation card used in Seoul, Korea, and many other places is of this nature.
- **Direct payment.** In this case, an aggregation is used, but the micropayments are processed with an existing monthly bill (e.g., a mobile phone bill).
- **Stored-value.** Funds are loaded into a debit account from which the money value of purchases is deducted when purchases are made. Offline vendors (e.g., Starbucks) use this model, and music download services use variants of this model. This system is being used by several online gaming companies and social media sites.
- **Subscriptions.** A single payment (e.g., monthly) provides access to content. Online gaming companies and a number of online newspapers and journals have used this model.
- **À la carte.** Payments are made for transactions as they occur; volume discounts may be negotiated. This model is used in stock trading, such as at E-Trade.

Micropayment Options and Costs

The world of micropayments has been billed as $13 billion opportunity being driven by the rapid growth in digital content (news, music, videos, etc.), mobile apps, and the social network and online gaming communities (LPT Team 2014). In spite of this opportunity, the micropayment arena continues to be a graveyard filled with the remains of companies who expired in their infancy. Some companies and payment options that support micropayments and seem to have some staying power are Amazon Payments, PayPal Micropayments, and the mobile payment companies Boku (**boku.com**) and Fortumo (**fortumo.com**). Prior to their acquisition by PayPal, Zong was a relatively successful mobile payment company that specialized in micropayments for online gaming and social networking.

   Except for a handful of situations, all of these options still cost the merchants and consumers money depending on nature of the purchases and on how the customer backs the payment (by credit cards, bank accounts, mobile accounts, etc.). So, the long-term answer to the issues with micropayments may ultimately rest with the credit card associations. In some cases, the solution might be for the card associations to adjust their fees, which Visa and MasterCard have done for some vendors with high transaction volumes. In other cases it may require changes in the way that the cards are traditionally processed by the vendors. A good example of this is found in Case 12.1 which discusses the use of credit cards for real-time payment of transit fares in South Korea.

CASE 12.1
EC APPLICATION
INNOVATIVE CREDIT CARD MICROPAYMENTS FOR THE KOREAN METROPOLITAN UNIFIED FARE SYSTEM

In many Asian countries, daily commuters often use a combination of public trains and buses to travel to and from work, necessitating the use of a combination of stored-value or regular credit cards for each mode. This was the situation facing commuters in Seoul, Korea, a few years ago. As the details of this case explain, the eventual solution was the creation of a *unified transportation smart card*.

The Problem

Boram, a banker in Seoul, Korea, commutes by MRT and public buses. She uses a credit card that allows her to pay for both MRT and buses, not only in Seoul but also in other major Korean cities without having to recharge the card. The accumulated monthly charges are automatically paid by her bank. Boram recalls the days when she had to carry two different transportation cards in addition to credit cards.

   In the past, Boram used to pay for the subway by using a Seoul MRT Card, which is a stored-value card. The card is issued by the city-owned Seoul MRT Corporation and could be recharged only at MRT stations. To ride a bus, she had to use a Seoul Bus Card that is another stored-value card issued by the private Seoul Bus Transport Association (SBTA). The Seoul Bus Card was introduced in 1996 as the first RF-type bus card in the world. Thus, she had to recharge both cards individually because they could not be used interchangeably. Other cities have similar governance structures. Therefore, to take the subway in another city, Boram had to buy one-time subway tickets at the subway station.

   Credit cards, as described in this chapter, are not cost-effective enough to be used for the micropayment of transportation because the card company could not justify its service fee. Therefore, as described earlier, Boram needed to carry at least one credit card and two transportation cards in her wallet.

   Large cities in Asia such as Seoul, Hong Kong, and Singapore have adopted similar types of stored-value transportation cards. As such, credit cards and stored-value cards coexist as two major card services. The two types of card issuers compete to expand their application territory. The transportation card company wants to extend the card's application so users can pay for parking fees, for various toll fees, and at restaurants and stores. However, the users have to load the cards for prepayment.

   At the same time, for credit card issuers to expand their application to include payments for transportation, they need to simplify the authorization process and reduce the service fee for the participating transporters. The question is: which business model will eventually win? In Seoul, it is the credit card issuer that includes payments for transportation.

The Solution

In order to pay transportation fares quickly, credit card payments for subways and buses must be processed without the full authorization procedure. This risk is tolerable because the frequency and amount of micropayment abuse is low in Korea. Therefore, the transportation ticket gate merely automatically checks whether the card is valid and not on a "blacklist." The gate displays not only the fare but also the charges incurred during the current month as shown in Fig. 12.4. The first credit-based MRT card was adopted by Kookmin Bank in 1998. Today, several issuers support this type of card.

The credit-based transportation card has revolutionized the recharge service process. In the early stage, both MRT cards and bus cards had to be recharged at manned booths. To reduce the expense of the recharge service, unmanned booths were installed at MRT stations. However, with the credit card, recharge booths can be eliminated altogether, and users do not have to spend time recharging their cards. Therefore, both the users and the city transportation authority benefit.

Another benefit of the smart transportation card is that it can restructure the city's transportation system by aligning and coordinating the routes of subways and buses. In the past, bus routes were designed in consideration of the departure and destination points of citizens' trips. This approach intended to make it convenient for citizens to take only one bus to reach their destination. However, too many buses created bottlenecks in busy streets, causing traffic jams. To avoid such congestion, the MRT and main bus companies planned to design the transportation system so that bus branch routes are connected to the subway and to the main bus routes. However, if citizens are required to pay an additional fee for branch routes, they may resist the new structure. Therefore, the transportation fare card should be interconnected.

To solve this problem, the transportation card, credit or stored-value, is designed to memorize the departure time from the MRT station so that the connecting buses do not charge passengers again if the elapsed time is less than 30 min. Taking a branch bus is regarded as a transfer for single trip. This means that the owners of transport systems need to agree on about how to allocate the collected fees. Therefore, the city of Seoul adopted the Metropolitan Unified Fare System in 2009.

The Results

Due to the national standardization and integration effort, nationwide transportation cards are now unified using smart cards. Credit card companies do not really make enough money through transportation payment services, but this service is essential for them to gain new customers and retain the existing ones.

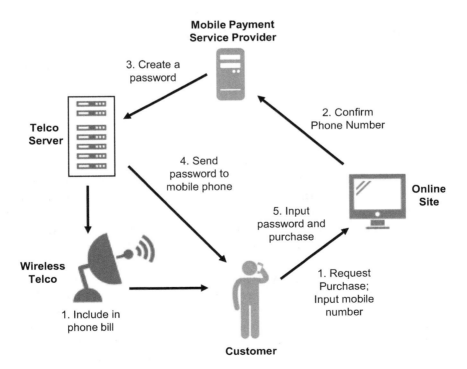

Fig. 12.4 Process of mobile payment service (Drawn by D. King and J. K. Lee)

The city also can collect data about commuters so that additional buses can be dispatched depending upon the passenger load by route and time. Note that, at midnight, regular bus services stop. For midnight bus service, the control center analyzes the frequency of mobile phone usage in certain areas to estimate the number of potential commuters and dynamically determine the routes of midnight buses.

Another lesson that can be learned from Korea's experience is the C2C payment system use of credit cards. In C2C auction markets, escrow services that are based on credit cards allow individual buyers to pay eBay Korea directly. The sellers can receive payment through eBay Korea if delivery is confirmed by the buyer. Therefore, there is no need for an e-mail payment system such as PayPal that charges high service fees. The function of a debit card, combined with a credit card, has also virtually replaced the function of electronic checks, so e-checks are no longer needed. In this manner, payments by credit cards in Korea are electronically integrated for e-commerce, physical stores, and micropayments for transportation.

Sources: Case written by Jae K. Lee, Seoul, Korea.

Questions for the Case

1. How can credit cards be processed as quickly as stored-value cards at the ticket gate?
2. What is the major benefit of owning a credit-based transportation card for commuters?
3. What is the major benefit of credit-based transportation cards to the city government?
4. How can the Metropolitan Unified Fare System enable the restructuring of public transportation infrastructure?

Note: Value cards may eventually be obsolete due to the increased smartphone apps that allow micropayments. For example, iPhone supports trains' payments in Japan (see McCormick 2016). Also, payments for taxis from smartphones are in operation in several cities worldwide.

SECTION 12.4 REVIEW QUESTIONS

1. What is a micropayment?
2. List some of the circumstances where micropayments can be used.
3. Besides credit or debit cards, what are some alternate ways that an online merchant can process micropayments?

12.5 PAYPAL AND OTHER THIRD-PARTY PAYMENT GATEWAYS

An alternative to credit cards is third-party payment gateways. Some are very popular in person-to-person payments such as on eBay and Craigslist. The pioneer and most well-known gateway is PayPal.

PayPal

While credit and debit cards dominate e-commerce payments, one alternative that has succeeded is PayPal (and its clones). PayPal was formed in the late 1990s from the merger of two small start-up companies, Confinity and **X.com**. Their initial success came from providing a payment system that was used for eBay transactions (PayPal is now an eBay company). How did the system work? Essentially, eBay sellers and buyers opened up PayPal accounts that were secured by a bank or credit card account. At the completion of an auction, the payment transactions were conducted via the seller's and buyer's PayPal accounts. In this way, the bank or credit card accounts remained confidential. It is important to remember that in those days, buyers were often wary of revealing their credit card numbers online. For the seller, it also eliminated the transaction fees charged by the credit card companies, although PayPal eventually began charging similar, though somewhat lower, transaction fees.

Even though eBay had a payment system called Billpoint, PayPal became so successful that eBay eventually decided to close Billpoint and acquired PayPal in October 2002. Why did eBay select PayPal over Billpoint? This is a tough question that has generated a multitude of answers. PayPal had a better user interface, better marketing, a better mix of services, and is user-friendly for both buyers and sellers. Regardless, neither Billpoint nor PayPal had to find the market of potential buyers and sellers; eBay had already done this. What Billpoint and PayPal had to do was convince eBay consumers and merchants to use their systems. PayPal was simply more successful at it than Billpoint.

Because of their ongoing success and the percentage of their non-eBay business, PayPal was spun off from eBay in July 2015. According to their 2015 annual report, PayPal operates in 203 global markets and has 184 million active user accounts. PayPal supports payments in 26 currencies. As a stand-alone company, their 2015 revenue was about $9.2 billion up 15% from the prior year. Part of this growth comes from the acquisition of a number of key payment companies focused on the future of digital payments including:

- Braintree—payment gateway with key customers in sharing economy space (e.g., Airbnb and Uber)
- Venmo—mobile P2P company that was part of Braintree (see section "Mobile Payments" for details of mobile P2P)
- Xoom—international remittance (the closing case in this chapter discusses and illustrates new approaches to digital remittance)
- Paydiant—technology for creating branded (private-label) mobile e-wallets for retail chains

While PayPal provides a number of services, at their core they are a full-service third-party payment gateway. Basically, they eliminate the need for a merchant to deal with the intricacies and complexities of authorization and settlement in online payment. They also eliminate the need for merchants to handle card information and for customers to provide their financial information with every transaction. The way it works is that in a given purchase transaction, the customer is presented with a payment Web page containing PayPal as an option. If the customer selects this option, they are directed to a Web page on PayPal's site. If the customer has a PayPal account, they simply confirm the purchase and payment instrument (e.g., card). If not, they provide information about their card, and PayPal takes it from there. In both cases, the customer is returned to the merchant site along with approval of the payment. At this point, PayPal transfers the settlement payment to the merchant's bank.

Other Third-Party Gateways

Several US and global competitors entered the market, competing both with smart cards and PayPal.

Apple Pay and Google's Android Pay

Two new and growing e-wallets are Apple Pay and Google's Android.

Apple Pay (apple.Com/pay)

This is a mobile payment and digital wallet service that enables users of Apple's iPhone 6 and later models, and other Apple products, to make payments with their devices. It can store your credit and debit cards which are charged when you make payments. You also can get points in your loyalty account (e.g., when you buy an airline ticket). Apple Pay can work with contactless terminals. For how this is done, see Wikipedia and Leary (2016). The card offers secure shopping.

Android Pay (Android.Com/pay)

What Apple Pay is doing for Apple device users is what Google's Android Pay is doing for Android system users. The app can easily be downloaded from Google devices, where it is preloaded (e.g., *Google Play*). For a comprehensive coverage, see Betters (2016). The card offers secure shopping.

Note: According to Wang (2016), Alipay is taking on Apple Pay and PayPal on their home turf.

Amazon Payments

Domestically, PayPal is the leading third-party payment gateway. In recent years, Amazon, the leading online retailer, has started to make forays into this third-party payment arena with their Amazon Payments system (**payments.amazon.com**). It is a comprehensive set of online payment tools and APIs that enable businesses and developers to offer Amazon's payment capabilities as an alternative to paying with credit or debit cards or PayPal. Like PayPal this alternative is surfaced by incorporating a "Pay with Amazon" button on the merchant's checkout Web page or mobile app. If a customer clicks the button, they are taken to Amazon's familiar "Login and Pay" screen. If he or she already has an account with Amazon, then the customer will be asked to confirm or select from the cards and shipping addresses that are associated with the account. If he or she doesn't have an account, they will be guided through the enrollment process. While Amazon is not an immediate threat to PayPal, they may be in the future. It is estimated there are over 50 million US Amazon Prime members, which represents close to 50% of US households. Amazon already has their payment information on hand, and these customers are all familiar with the simplicity of their patented "By now with 1-Click" button.

Global Gateways

Globally, PayPal is also the market-leading gateway. PayPal is used extensively throughout the world. In a number of countries, PayPal is one of the preferred payment methods behind cards, often handling between 10% and 15% of all payments (Adyen.com 2015). This is the case, for example, in France, Germany, the United Kingdom, and Australia. However, in select countries there are other gateways that are used more often. Included in this group are:

- Sofort (**sofort.com**) in Germany. Gateway that relies on direct bank transfers rather than cards.
- Wirecard AG (**wirecard.com**) in Germany. Offers cashless payment and other services on a one-stop basis as well as offers a vast range of e-commerce industries worldwide.
- Yandex.Money (**wirecard.com**) in Russia. Partnership between Sberbank and the search company Yandex. Handles cash, bank cards and e-money.
- Qiwi (**qiwi.com**) in Russia. Payment service that is publicly traded on NASDAQ and headquartered in Cyprus. It also operates in Kazakhstan, Moldova, Belarus, Romania, the United States, and the United Arab Emirates.
- Alipay (**global.alipay.com**) in China. Part of the Alibaba Group discussed in the opening case of this chapter. Like PayPal, it is a full-service payment gateway servicing domestic and cross-border transactions in China.
- Tenpay (**global.tenpay.com**) in China. Second largest payment service. It's owned by Tencent who also owns China's largest social network Weibo.
- iDEAL (**ideal.nl**) in the Netherlands. A payment service in the Netherlands that uses direct bank transfers.

With the exception of China, in each of these countries, PayPal is still used.

SECTION 12.5 QUESTIONS

1. What is PayPal?
2. Why was PayPal more successful than its competitors?
3. What is a third-party payment gateway? Describe how one works.
4. What is Amazon Payments? What competitive threat does it pose for PayPal?
5. What are some of the key gateways used in other regions of the world?
6. Describe Apple Pay and Google Android Pay.

12.6   MOBILE PAYMENTS

Because of the strong growth in mobile usage worldwide (see section "Changing Retail Landscape"), there continues to be a strong belief that mobile payments (made by using mobile devices) will emerge as a primary way to pay, potentially eliminating dependence on cash, cards, and other modes of EC payment. While mobile payments are growing rapidly, they will not supplant cash, cards, or even other forms of EC payments anytime soon. According to eMarketer (2016), mobile payments reached $450 billion in 2015 and will grow to $1 trillion by 2019. To put this in context, in 2015 mobile payments accounted for 24% of all EC retail sales and 1% of total retail sales. By 2019, they will account for 30% and 4%, respectively. In November 2016, mobile shopping accounted for 33% of Thanksgiving and Black Friday sales (Perez 2016). These shifts reflect a substantial amount of growth in mobile payments that sellers cannot ignore, and it is important to remember that in relative terms usage is still low when compared to all other forms of payment. However, this situation may change soon.

Another sign of increased of mobile payments is the fact that Bank of America reduced the number of branches from close to 6000 in 2011 to less than 4800 in 2016. At the same time, the number of customers that adopted mobile banking in the bank increased by 30%.

Types of Mobile Payments

The term **mobile payment** refers to payment transactions initiated or confirmed using a person's mobile device, usually a smartphone although payments can be made with other mobile devices such as tablets and wearables. The term actually covers a number of different types of solutions, as well as different combinations of hardware and software technologists.

Fig. 12.5 The credit-based transportation card displays the fare and accumulated charges for the current month at the ticket gate (Photos by J. K. Lee)

Mobile payments are a popular method for government's payments to people, especially in developing countries, such as India and Brazil, where more people have smartphones than bank accounts.

Just like online payments, there are many parties involved in any mobile payment system (see Fig. 12.5). From the standpoint of the various parties, any successful mobile system needs to overcome the following sorts of issues:

For buyer: Security (fraud protection), privacy, ease of use, and choice of mobile device.
For seller: Security (getting paid on time), low cost of operations, adoption by sufficient number of users, and improved speed of transactions.
For network operator: Availability of open standards, cost of operation, interoperability, and flexibility and roaming.
For financial institutions: Fraud protection and reduction, security (authentication, integrity, nonrepudiation; see Chap. 11), and reputation.

Most of today's mobile payment solutions are designed to replace existing payment methods including non-digital (cash or credit) digital (PC-based). As such, they tend to fall into one of four payment types (distinguished by "who pays whom") including (Allum 2014):

- **Consumer.** Buyer pays a merchant for goods and services. This is the purview of most digital wallets (e.g., Apple Pay).
- **Merchant.** Receiving money from a customer in exchange for goods and services. Often enabled by mobile POS (e.g., Square).
- **Person-to-person (P2P).** Money exchange between two or more people, as a gift or payback (e.g., PayPal's Venmo).
- **Institutional.** Managing and paying bills from an institution (like a utility company) for services rendered (e.g., Finovera or Mint).

The fact that these payment types are all designed to supplant or cannibalize existing nonmobile payment systems may be one of the reasons for their slower than expected uptake. To many potential users, mobile payment applications are simply "credit card surrogates: they're a veneer over what already exists." So, why change especially since they are all underpinned by substantial technological ecosystems?

We won't discuss institutional payments in this chapter, but we will describe the other three types of mobile payments in this section along with their underlying technologies.

Mobile Consumer Payments: Wallets, Clouds, and Loops

As a recent Accenture (2015) survey of 4000 respondents in North America shows, the average consumer's exposure to mobile payments is through his or her mobile digital wallet. Among the more popular wallets are PayPal, Apple Pay, and the recently morphed Google Wallet (in that order).

The term **mobile digital wallet** refers to the combination of an electronic account along with a smartphone and mobile app designed to make purchases digitally and to redeem rewards from loyalty programs and targeted digital promotions. There are two main types of wallets—device-based and cloud-based.

Device-Based Digital Wallets

These are proximity payment systems enabled by near-field communication (NFC) technology. On the consumer side, the system requires that the mobile device being used is equipped with NFC antenna and an integrated chip or a smart card inside the phone that holds payment card information (credit or debit). On the merchant's side, it requires a specialized NFC reader used to recognize the chip when the chip comes within a short distance of the reader and a network for handling the payment. Essentially, a buyer first enters his or her credit card information into the wallet app on the phone prior to shopping. At the time of the purchase, the buyer then "waves" the specially equipped mobile phone near a reader to initiate a payment. The reader collects the info and passes to the payment network. The card is charged and the purchase is complete. These proximity payments are also called *contactless payments* where the phone plays the surrogate roll of a contactless card with a chip (see section "Smart Cards").

In the past there were few wallets on the market. Today, while there a large number of device-based wallets (last count over 1000), the most popular are PayPal wallet (**paypal.com**), Apple Pay (**apple.com/apple-pay**), and Android Pay (**android.com/pay**).

Over the years, a number of protocols and technologies have been proposed to support proximity payments (e.g., from mobile devices). NFC has won out. It is now used for a wide variety of purchases including those in-store, from vending machines, and from transit ticket dispensers or fare collection. As of 2015 (Statista-2 2016), around 13% of smartphone users in the United States were active users of these sorts of proximity payments. In that same year, the total value of these transactions was about $27 billion. By 2019 this figure is projected to (magically) climb to $210 billion.

It will require extraordinary growth (a sevenfold increase in a 4-year period) in the number of installed NFC readers for these estimates to pan out. Thus far, many merchants have been hesitant to install the readers. Part of this hesitancy is due to the fact that while NFC is a standard, there is still disagreement about the specific handsets, chips, readers, and networks to be used. A case in point is the Google Wallet. Originally, Google Wallet had a fixed set of operational partners (Sprint, Citibank, MasterCard, and First Data) and was available only on the Sprint Nexus S 4G handset, supporting two credit cards (Citibank MasterCard PayPass terminals and Google Prepaid cards). Then they shifted to MasterCard and MasterCard PayPass terminals. Just recently, they turned Google Wallet solely into a P2P application and shifted general purchasing to a newer wallet called Android Pay, which operates on both Android and Apple smartphones. This is simply another example of the "chicken-egg" problem (section "Changing Retail Landscape").

It is also an example of another reason why there is hesitancy to adopt a particular NFC configuration because the mobile payment field is changing so fast that there is no assurance that the current form of NFC proximity payments won't be supplanted by some other technologies. A good case in point is the diminishing role of the integrated (payment) chips inside smartphones. These chips were used to bolster security. However, they only worked with specific readers. Today, wallets like Apple Pay and Android Pay store card and other information on the phone, not in a chip. During a purchase, card information is not transmitted to the reader; instead, a secure numerical token (one-time payment number and dynamic security code) is generated and transmitted. They open up the number of types of readers that the mobile wallet can work with.

Example: Wearable Wallets from MasterCard and Coin (onlycoin.Com)

In October of 2015, MasterCard (2015) announced a new program—*Commerce for Every Device*—aimed at bringing mobile payment capabilities to a range of consumer products across the automotive, fashion, technology, and wearable worlds. The goal is to provide consumers with the ability to shop and pay with the device or thing that is most convenient and secure. The announcement named a number of partners like Bulgari, GM, the Parsons School of Design, and Ringly (jewelry) along with a number of "wearables" companies including Nymi, Atlas Wearables, Moov, and Omate. The program is an extension of the MasterCard Digital Enablement Service and the Digital Enablement Express programs and support their vision to enable virtually every device for commerce.

From a technology standpoint, a key partner is Coin. Currently, the primary product that Coin provides is a combined EMV and NFC compliant smart card called the Coin. The smart card holds information of all the credit and debit cards that the card owner wants to use for purchases. A companion smartphone app is used for initial setup and for adding and changing cards. Given its combined EMV and NFC capabilities, purchases can be made with the Coin card by swiping, tapping, or waving like other EMV or NFC smart cards. The advantage is that the Coin eliminates the need to carry multiple cards or even a smartphone. The Coin card provides the means to switch from one card to the next depending on the owners' preferences at the time of purchase.

Initially, Coin was solely focused on using the technology for their own card. With the MasterCard partnership, they have expanded their horizons and plan to provide other companies with their *Payment of Things* hardware and software platform (Cipriani 2016). This will enable these companies to embed Coin's smart card payment capabilities into these devices. The fact that the partnership is nonexclusive means that Coin's platform will eventually be available to companies affiliated with the other card associations.

Cloud-Based Digital Wallets

An alternative to device-based mobile wallets is cloud-based mobile wallets. The infrastructure for these wallets is not as onerous as a system based on NFC. Basically, a customer enrolls his or her card with a secure Web service. Requests for payments are made to the service and charged to enrolled card(s). In this way no card information is transmitted during a purchase. Instead, transactions are initiated by scanning a barcode or Quick Response (QR) code created specifically for the customer and stored and displayed on the smartphone by wallet app. A QR code is a 2D barcode consisting of a collection of black square dots placed on a square grid with a white background. What is required on the merchant's end is a barcode or QR code image reader that is networked into the service via the Web. The whole system operates much like the way PayPal operates without using a Web page with a PayPal button to start the process. Instead, it's started when the code is scanned. As a point of fact, PayPal employs a cloud-based mobile wallet instead of device-based.

This architecture is also being used to create Walmart Pay (**walmart.com/cp/walmart-pay/5998388**) and Chase Pay (**chase.com/digital/digital-payments/chase-pay**). Actually, both Walmart and Chase are using a cloud-based mobile platform called *CurrentC* being created by the Merchant Customer Exchange (MCX) consortium (**mcx.com**) which is being funded by over 30 retailers who are its members. Not only will the platform support initiating a purchase by scanning a QR code on the customer's screen, but it will also support initiating a purchase by having the customer use his or her phone to scan a QR code on the merchant's screen.

Compared to device-based wallets, it's much simpler to create and develop a cloud-based wallet. Because these systems are basically hardware agnostic, the main barriers revolve around PCI security compliance, customer authentication, and integration with a settlement system. Of course, building it is one thing, having merchants adopt it is another. While these systems require a barcode and QR code reader hooked to the backend Web service (not too onerous), these transactions are "card not present." CNP transactions have higher authorization and settlement fees. Additionally, since a cloud-based wallet relies on the Web, a merchant will need uninterrupted and reliable Internet service with consistent speed throughout business hours—not a sure bet.

Closed-Loop Systems

Closely tied to the cloud-based wallets are the closed-loop payment applications. These systems are much like the closed-loop, stored-value, or prepaid (gift) cards offered by a single retailer. The main difference is that the value is stored in an application on your phone and redeemed with your phone by again having an application barcode or QR code scanned by the merchant. In essence it is a cloud-based digital wallet that can only be used with a single retailer (although this isn't a hard and fast rule). One advantage of the phone is that you can reload the application at virtually anytime rather than having the retailer do it in the store.

Example: Starbucks Closed-Loop Wallet (starbucks.Com)

One of the better known and most widely used closed-loop mobile payment system is the Starbucks mobile wallet app that works on Apple and Android smartphones. Because it is closed-loop, the app can only be used to do business with Starbucks. The card enables Starbucks customers to use their smartphones to locate stores, by gift cards online, to place and order for pickup at a designated local Starbucks and most importantly to use their smartphones to pay for in-store purchases using an electronic version of the loyalty reward cards which are basically prepaid stored-value cards. The electronic version displays a QR code on the smartphone screen which is scanned by an image reader connected to a POS. Each time a purchase is made with the app, the stored value of the card is debited and associated Starbucks rewards are increased. The app is also used to automatically reload the card when the value falls below a customer specified minimum.

Automatic reload obviously encourages regular consumption, and it's working (Taylor 2015). Starbucks has 10.4 million loyalty card members. A third of all purchases are made with these cards. On initial rollout the mobile version was accounting for over 20% of all transactions. Given the demographic of their customers, this will only increase.

Mobile Point of Sale

Up to this point the discussion has all been about supporting mobile purchases from the customer's point of view. Mobile payment apps are also used to meet the needs of the merchant during the purchase process. One key area where mobile payment applications are being employed by merchants is at the point of sale (POS). Instead of taking payments at a traditional

POS register or computer that is stationary, mobile POS (mPOS) devices are used in their place. Initially, mPOS systems were designed to run on specialized hardware and networks, just like their tethered counterparts. Today, they run on tablets and smartphones and are cloud-based. The cost of these cloud-based mPOS is substantially less. Not only is the hardware less expensive but so are the network costs.

Because of their lower costs, mPOS were originally targeted at small businesses and independent operators such doctors, dentists, delivery companies, taxis, and retail kiosks. More recently, these devices are being used in-store by retailers of all sizes. They are also being integrated with mobile *clienteling* applications designed to help sales staff with in-store, personalized customer support and service. A major mPO vendor is Square, Inc. (see Case 12.2).

CASE 12.2
EC APPLICATION
USING THE SQUARE MAGSTRIPE READER

One of the leading vendors of mPOS hardware and software is Square, Inc. (**squareup.com**).

They are a "financial services, merchant services, and mobile payment company" that was started in 2008 by Jack Dorsey (also the CEO and founder of Twitter). Square is probably best known for their Square *magstripe reader*, a small square dongle device that plugs into the headset jack of an iPhone, iPad, or Android and enables a merchant to accept payments made with credit cards. There are actually two parts of the reader. There's the card swipe device, and there's the Square Wallet application. The way it works for a merchant is the following:

1. Download the Square app from the Apple App Store or Google's Android Market.
2. Register with Square, providing US-based bank account, US mailing address, and Social Security number and the business employer ID (if there is one). Once the registration is accepted, Square will send the free card reader.
3. With the bank registration information, Square will next run a test to ensure that your bank account will accept deposits from the Square app. After that, funds from card transactions will be directly deposited to the account within 24 h of the transaction.
4. Start using the reader and application. For each transaction, the amount and description of the product or service is input, then the card is swiped. The app transmits the information to Square's proprietary card service (via the Internet) for approval. Once approved, the customer signs with their finger. The receipt is then delivered by text message or e-mail to the customer. If the reader happens to fail, the information can be put into the application manually.

Square has a simple pricing policy. The reader is free and so is setup. There is a 2.75% fee "per swipe for Visa, MasterCard, Discover, and American Express."

The Square magstripe reader is used by major vendors such as AT&T, Walgreens, FedEx Office, Walmart, Starbucks, and Whole Foods. For example, Starbucks uses the Square mobile POS in-store as well as allows customers to pay with Square Wallet. Likewise, Whole Foods has Square checkout stands at the food venues (e.g., sandwich counters, juice and coffee bars, and beer and wine bars); see **media.wholefoodsmarket.com/news/square-and-whole-foods-market-partner-to-create-faster-easier-payment-and-c**.

More recently, Square has added additional input devices including a combined contactless NFC and EMV chip card reader and an iPad POS stand with a card reader (called Square Stand).

Square's success has generated a raft of competitors including various offerings from the major POS players like Oracle Micros and NCR. PayPal has essentially cloned Square's hardware and application with a service called PayPal Here. Just like Square, they provide a dongle and EMV chip card reader along with a mobile wallet app. They also have the same fee structure. For details, see **paypal.com/webapps/mpp/credit-card-reader**.

QUESTIONS FOR THE CASE

1. What is mPOS?
2. What is a magstripe reader? What are its benefits?
3. How Square works?
4. Find information about Square's success against its competitors.

Person-to-Person (P2P) Payments

Financial transactions among individuals—friends, colleagues, family members, and the like—occur all the time. We lend money to a friend, we pay somebody back for lunch, we send or receive money from home, or we send money as a birthday present. Most of the time, these transactions involve cash or check.

Increasingly, these person-to-person (P2P) transactions are being handled by online payment systems using either a computer, tablet, smartphone, or even prepaid cards. Many of the more popular P2P systems are actually provided by the major payment gateways (like PayPal) either as a component of the larger payment system or as a separate application. These online P2P systems transcend distance and time, eliminate the need carry cash and checks for smaller transactions of this sort, and in some cases offer the "unbanked" and "underbanked" an entry into the larger financial. They enable us not only to pay friends but also merchants for lower-priced products and services. The closing case at the end of this chapter discusses in detail Kenya's M-Pesa system, which is an exceptional success story of how a mobile P2P system provides benefits of these sorts and much more (see the Closing Case to this chapter). For more on P2P money lending, see Chap. 5.

SECTION 12.6 REVIEW QUESTIONS

1. What are the four types of mobile payment?
2. Who are the key players in a mobile payment system?
3. What is mobile wallet? Devised-based wallet? Cloud-based wallet? Wearable wallet?
4. Describe closed-loop payment systems. What is a good example of this type of system?
5. What is a mobile POS? Who is the leading provider of these systems?
6. What is a person-to-person payment?

12.7 DIGITAL AND VIRTUAL CURRENCIES

In some discussions the terms *digital currency*, *virtual currency*, and *e-money* are often used interchangeably. In other discussions, they are recognized as being different, although there seems to be little consistency about which is which. In this discussion, the definitions that are used come from the Financial Action Task Force (FATF 2014). This is an inter-government body with 35 member countries (including all the major players in EC) charged with examining and addressing anti-money laundering and countering the financing of terrorism (AML/CFT) worldwide. They are one of the few official bodies that has a critical stake in defining the differences among the concepts so they can craft language to be used by legal and regulatory bodies.

Types of Currencies: Physical and Digital

To understand the differences among these three concepts, let us start at the other end of the currency spectrum—*fiat currency*. **Fiat currency** (aka real currency, real money, or national currency) is the "coin and paper money of a country that is designated as legal tender, circulates, and is customarily used and accepted as the medium of exchange in the issuing country and other countries." **Electronic money** (abbreviated e-money) is a digital representation of fiat currency used for purposes of electronic transfer (e.g., the digital representation funds used to settle a merchant account after an EC purchase is made). In contract **virtual currency** is the "digital representation of value that can be digitally traded and functions as (1) a medium of exchange; and/or (2) a unit of account; and/or (3) a store of value, but does not have legal status in any jurisdiction." Basically, it only functions as a currency because there is a community of users willing to treat it as such. Finally, **digital currency** is a generic term that refers to the digital representation (0 s and 1 s) of either e-money (fiat) or virtual currency (non-fiat). So, e-money and virtual currency are types of digital currency but not vice versa.

Virtual Currency

Virtual currency covers two sub-types: *nonconvertible* (closed) and *convertible* (open). According to the US Treasury's Financial Crimes Enforcement Network (**fincen.gov**, **convertible virtual currency** is a virtual currency that has "an equivalent value in real currency, or acts as a substitute for real currency." Some examples include the cryptocurrencies like Bitcoin and most retail e-coupons. In contrast, a **nonconvertible virtual currency** is a virtual currency used in a specific virtual world or domain that cannot (theoretically) be exchanged for fiat currency. Many of the better known examples come from online games. Some examples of this would include World of Warcraft Gold, Farm(ville) Cash, and Q Coin from Tencent QQ. In these games, success is based on obtaining virtual money, which is earned by completing various tasks or purchased using real money (which is often the primary source of income for the game company). Technically, these currencies cannot be used or exchanged in the outside world. However, in many cases secondary markets (black or not) have arisen that are willing to exchange the nonconvertible currency into a fiat currency or some other virtual currencies.

A key feature of nonconvertible, virtualized currencies is that they are *centralized*. This means that there is a single administrative authority in charge of regulating the currency—issuing the currency, establishing rules of use and exchange rates, tracking payments, and controlling the amount in circulation. In contrast convertible virtual currencies can be either centralized or decentralized. A *decentralized* virtual currency is distributed, open-sourced, and peer-to-peer. There is no single administrate authority who oversees and monitors the currency. This is the nature of many of the *cryptocurrencies* like Bitcoin which we'll discuss momentarily.

Size of the Virtual Currency Market

A couple of years back, the Yankee Group (McKee 2013) accessed the size of the virtual currency market. Their analysis included both the mature virtual currencies like loyalty points, credit card points, air miles, and physical coupons and the up-and-coming (digital) virtual currencies including app-based coins and tokens, personal information and time (exchanged) for apps and tokens, and Bitcoins. At that time (2012), the total value of all the virtual currency markets was close to $48 billion with the mature currencies making up close to 97% of the total. They estimated that by 2017, the mature markets would grow steadily, while the up-and-comers would experience rapid growth (in the 130% to 200% range). Yet, the mature markets would still garner the lion's share.

However, the problem with the estimates is that, then and now, it is very difficult to assess the exact values associated with the game-based and Bitcoin currencies, although for different reasons. For game-based you not only have to calculate an exchange rate, but many of the game companies don't provide the necessary data to do a reasonable assessment. For Bitcoin the number of coins in circulation is known; however, their exact value is dependent on exchange rates that can fluctuate substantially at any given time. At the moment, the Bitcoin value can change on any given day. The value is subjective and based on market volatility and the going rates paid by the Bitcoin exchanges. For example, in the spring of 2016, the total number of Bitcoins in circulation was around 15.5 billion and the price was fluctuating between $400 and $450. That's a difference of around $6.2 billion, to $6.7 billion which is fairly substantial.

Digital Currency Exchanges

Digital currency exchanges are services that allow customers to trade digital currencies for conventional fiat money (e.g., US dollars) or for different digital currencies. They operate similar to stock exchanges. They take bids and ask to determine the transactions which they execute. You can buy bitcoins and other digital currencies there. These exchanges can be of the brick-and-mortar type, or most frequently they are online. Most of them operate outside of Western countries to avoid regulatory issues. For an overview and list of exchanges, see Wikipedia. For a list of exchanges for bitcoins, see **toptenreviews. com/money/investing/best-bitcoin-exchanges** . For how they operate, see **coinpursuit.com/articles/how-to-do-digital-currency-exchanges-work.138** . Well-known exchanges are CoinPursuit, Bitstamp, BTC Market, itBit, and Coinbase.

Note: in 2016 a federal judge authorized a summons requiring Coinbase, America's largest Bitcoin exchange, to provide the IRS with records of millions of customers who traded on the site during 2014 and 2015. The objective is to try to identify those tax evaders who use virtual currency to cover certain transactions.

Bitcoin and Other Cryptocurrencies

Among the (digital) virtual currencies, the one that has garnered the most attention is Bitcoin. From previous discussion, it was stated that Bitcoin is an encrypted, decentralized (peer-to-peer), convertible, virtual currency. Taken together it sounds complex, and it is. That is why we will simply touch the surface of how it works along with its advantages and disadvantages. For those who are interested, there are several books (e.g., Antonopoulos 2015) and some YouTube videos devoted to various aspects of its history, underlying mathematics, structure, operation, and uses. Instead, in this discussion we will hit the highlights of these elements.

Bitcoin Background

The origin of Bitcoin comes from a specification and proof of concept developed in 2009 by Satoshi Nakamoto and published in a paper entitled "Bitcoin: A Peer-to-Peer Electronic Cash System." That is not his real name, it's a pen name. The real identity of the inventor is still unknown. After the initial development, Satoshi left the project in the hands of a community of open source developers (see **bitcoin.org**), meaning that the development and maintenance of the underlying code is being done by a community in much same ways as projects like Linux and Apache.

Bitcoin was not the first system to propose a decentralized virtual currency. However, it was the first to come up with a decentralized system that offered a usable solution to what is known as the *double-spend problem*. As the concept implies, in a virtual currency double-spending refers to the result of spending the same money more than once. For instance, if money is held in a digital file, what prevents a clever user from simply duplicating the file and using it again for a purchase or investment? In most systems, this is handled by having a central (automated) authority review transactions before they are committed. In Bitcoin, there is no central authority, but it relies on an innovative *proof-of-work* scheme that uses consensus among peer-to-peer nodes to verify transactions and to protect against assaults like double-spending.

When we talk about the Bitcoin ecosystem, the term is capitalized. When we speak about the unit of currency in this system, it is designated in small letters ("bitcoin") which in abbreviated form is designated as BTC (similar to USD). There is an upper limit on the number of bitcoins that can be produced (21 million BTC), a governor on the number of bitcoins that are produced on the average every 10 min (i.e., 1 block), and an end date for their production (2040).

Bitcoin Characteristics

Like the dollar or any other currency, a bitcoin is a *unit of account* that possesses a number of the key characteristics (Tomaino 2015):

- *Durable*—This means that it retains its shape, form, and substance over an extended period of time, so that in the future it will still work as a medium of exchange. While bitcoins have only been around for 7 years, they are widely accepted at merchants, traded on currency exchanges, recognized (or tolerated) by many countries, and owned by sizeable numbers of individuals. There's no assurance about its future, but it has lasted longer than virtually all of its digital predecessors.

- *Divisible*—This characteristic means that a currency can be divided into smaller increments so that the sum of the increments equals the original value. In this way bitcoins can be used to purchase products and services of varying values. The smallest unit of the a bitcoin is .00000001BTC (that's 1 hundred millionth). This unit is called a Satoshi. It serves the same role as $.01 or a penny in USD.
- *Countable*—This implies that the units are subject to the rules of mathematics so they can be added, subtracted, multiplied, and divided. In accounting terms it means we can employ these operations to measure profit, loss, income, expenses, debt, and wealth and determine the net worth of an entity possessing units.
- *Transportable*—Currency is needed to easily support transactions and exchanges across the world. Because bitcoins run on the Internet is a decentralized fashion, they are more transportable than most fiat currencies.
- *Fungible*—This means that one unit of a currency is interchangeable with all others regardless of when or where it was obtained. For example, in the corn commodities market, all No. 2 corn has the same value regardless of where it was grown. Similarly, one bit coin is the same as any other bitcoin regardless of how it was produced or who holds it.
- *Verifiable* (non-counterfeitable)—This means that it is not easily counterfeited, and if it is, it's easily detected. This is one of the key characteristics and strengths of a cryptocurrency like bitcoins. Before any bitcoins are accepted for payment, there is a strong vetting process to ensure its authenticity.

For comprehensive tutorial, see Kleinman (2016). For more on Bitcoin's background, see Geissinger (2016).

How Does Bitcoin Work?

At its foundation, the Bitcoin currency is nothing more than a *public ledger*. Essentially, it is a digital file tracking every Bitcoin transaction—time, date, participants, amount, and transfer of ownership of bitcoins—that has ever occurred since the first bitcoin was issued. It's much like a company's general ledger that provides a complete record of all the transactions that have occurred over the life of the company except in this case the company consists of everyone worldwide who has ever owned some fraction of a bitcoin. At the present time, the ledger file is about 20GB.

The Bitcoin ledger is called the **blockchain**. As the name suggests, it is a collection of blocks each containing a grouping of bitcoin transactions that occurred around the same time, much like a single page in a ledger. These blocks are linked or chained together in the order in which they occurred.

Unlike a company ledger, the Bitcoin blockchain is *public*, as opposed to private or secret. This means that anyone can view it. In fact there are websites (e.g., **blockchain.info**) where you can watch the transactions in action. Also, unlike a company ledger, there is no central body (like the finance department) or trusted third party that is in charge of the ledger or central place where the official copy is held. Instead there is one digital file that is fully distributed across Bitcoins decentralized peer-to-peer network. Each node or computer on the network has a full copy of the file. Using complex mathematical computations, the transactions are verified by *bitcoin miners* (computers and computer programs) that maintain the ledger. The computations also ensure that there is agreement among all the nodes on the network about the current state of the blockchain and every transaction in it. If an attempt is made to corrupt a transaction within a block, then the nodes will fail to reach consensus and the transaction and the associated block verified.

With the right equipment and software, anyone can run a node on the network and can be bitcoin miner. The incentive for doing so is that miners can earn bitcoins for their "verification" efforts. Crudely put, verification is a bit like a "hackathon" or coding contest. There are very specific mathematical criteria and hurdles that are required to combine transactions into a block. The miner who does it first while adhering to criteria receives 25 new bitcoins. It doesn't sound like much, but remember there are a lot of transactions in a day (ergo a number of blocks created), and each bitcoin is currently worth around $450 which is over $11,000. Also, if you are thinking about joining the ranks of the miners, these days it takes a lot of computing power to handle the computations. As a consequence, groups of miners have formed *Bitcoin mining pools* that share computing resources and split the bitcoin payoff.

There are easier ways to obtain bitcoins besides mining for them. Someone who has their own bitcoins could give some of them to you. You can buy them from any one of the commercial bitcoin exchanges (e.g., **coinbase.com** or **cex.io**) using another currency (e.g., USD). Also, you could sell someone goods or services in exchange for bitcoins. Regardless of the method, how do they "give" them to you, and where do they go after you get them? After all, bitcoins aren't physical, they are digital, and there is no bank where you can deposit them.

While Bitcoin is a payment system for exchanging value, at its technical base, it is a messaging system built on its peer-to-peer (Internet) network. The messages that are sent are the transactions. These messages are sent and received in much the same way that encrypted messages are sent and received over the Internet using asymmetrical public and private keys (similar to those described in section "Mobile Marketing and Advertising"). However, in this instance the type of encryption that is used is called Elliptical Curve Digital Signature Algorithm (ECDSA).

In order to send or receive a message over the Bitcoin network, a user needs a private key and a Bitcoin address. A **Bitcoin private key** is a randomly generated number between 1 and 2^{256} (i.e., 2 raised to the 256th power) that is used by the owner to initiate and digitally sign transactions and used by the network to verify those. You can think of it like a password or PIN that is used to gain access to funds in a bank account, although in this case the funds are not stored in an account but are recorded in a ledger. Just like any password, this private key can be used by anyone who has it to gain access to the protected bitcoins whether they are the rightful owner or not. So it pays to keep it secret. Also, like any other password, if the owner loses or forgets it, then the funds it protects can no longer be accessed. In this case, however, they are lost for eternity because there is no way for anyone to reset it.

A **Bitcoin address** is an alphanumeric string that identifies the recipient of a Bitcoin transaction. You can think of the Bitcoin address like the bank account number that is password protected by the private key. Bitcoin addresses are generated in a two-step process. First, elliptical curve mathematics is a paired *public key* from the private key. Second, a special mathematical function called a "hash function" is used to generate a Bitcoin address from the public key. A Bitcoin address starts with either a 1 or a 3 and has between 27 and 34 alphanumeric characters (except for 0 or O and 1 or l because these pairs are easily mistaken for one another). The identifier can also be represented as a QR code which is easily displayed on a mobile device so the address can be scanned instead of typing the character representation.

When someone wants to execute a transaction, he or she uses his or her private key to digitally sign a message that includes:

- Input—the funds to be transferred or more specifically the source transactions that assigned ownership to the bitcoins being sent
- Amount—the amount of bitcoins being sent
- Output—the Bitcoin address of the recipient

The message is broadcast to the nodes on the Bitcoin network at which point the verification process begins. Sometime later if it is verified by one or more machines, it will be posted. Typically, this process takes about 10 min.

In reality, if a user had to remember and handle all of the details of a transaction, the Bitcoin ecosystem would have never gained much traction. Fortunately, most of these details are hidden by the Bitcoin wallets which are client software that are used to create the keys and addresses and to send and receive bitcoins. Electronic Bitcoin wallets come in three versions: desktop, mobile (apps), and Web. Figure 12.6 displays the Web wallet for a dummy account. The first panel of this figure shows the initial screen which displays the Bitcoin address and its associated QR code and shows pertinent transaction data including the balance for this user and menu selections for sending and receiving bitcoins. The second panel shows the entries required to send bitcoins. In this case you only need to enter an address and an amount. The address can either be the alphanumeric string or the scanned image of the associated QR code.

There are a lot of details about how the Bitcoin ecosystem operates. This discussion has only touched on a few. For those who are interested, refer to Antonopoulos (2015), the diagram at **bitcoin.stackexchange.com/questions/4838/what-does-a-bitcoin-transaction-consist-of**, and **en.wikipedia.org/wiki/Bitcoin_network**.

Fig. 12.6 Bitcoin Web Wallet (Drawn by D. King)

Advantages of Bitcoin

The adherents and supporters of Bitcoin, of which there many, point to number of advantages of Bitcoin over fiat currencies and other virtual currencies. Most of these revolve around it's decentralized structure. Some of the more frequently cited advantages include (Hochstein 2016):

- *Anonymity.* Even though transactions are public, there is nothing to tie a user's name to the particular encrypted address or signatures unless the user wants to make the connection public. It's also the case that users can have multiple addresses, even a new one for every transaction. This increases the anonymity. However, the shear fact that transactions and addresses are public leaves open the possibility of tying transactions to real-life identity. For this reason Bitcoin is often referred to as *pseudo-anonymous.*
- *Simplifying financial transactions.* There are no pre-requisites and no minimum levels required to participate. Transactions between parties can transpire without the assistance of any bank or financial institution. Because transactions are basically frictionless, fees are held to a minimum.
- *Merchant friendly.* For merchants, it's easy to set up a payment system without relying on third-party gateways or intermediaries. The setup costs are minimal and there are none of the chargebacks associated with cards.
- *Supporting cross-border commerce.* Architecturally, Bitcoin can easily support cross-border transactions simply because it utilizes the Internet. Also, it's an open system that allows anyone to join regardless of their location. In most countries they can operate pretty much with impunity largely because of the regulatory confusion over virtual currencies. However, it is the case that Bitcoin is outlawed in a handful of countries (e.g., Russia) and is increasingly subject to the regulations governing banks and institutions in a number of countries, especially those dealing with money laundering and financing terrorism.
- *Free from government manipulation.* In many developing countries and a number of developed countries, the currencies have been subject to governmental fraud and illegal manipulation. On an individual level, accounts have been frozen or expropriated by national governments. On a national level, governments have illegally manipulated the circulation of currency, defaulted on debts, etc., all of which impact currency valuations. In Bitcoin no one, governments or otherwise, directs control of accounts, the bitcoins in circulation, nor their valuation.

Disadvantages of Bitcoin

On the other side of the coin, Bitcoin has equally vociferous detractors and opponents. The list of disadvantages they cite includes (CoinReport 2014):

- *Not yet widely accepted.* Even though there has been substantial growth in the number of merchants accepting Bitcoins, the number of transactions, and the valuations of the currency, it has yet to reach the "critical minimum." The pace may get increasingly slower as governments move to place regulatory controls on aspects like the anonymity of accounts which provides cover for money laundering and the finance of terrorism.
- *Fluctuating valuation.* While all currencies have swings in valuation, the value of a bitcoin has had a history of volatile swings. This means there is substantial risk for owners, much like the risk associated with stock investments. For example, the value went from $120 in October 2013 to $600 in January 2014 to $225 in July 2015, to $408 in November 2015, to $367 in January 2016, to $462 in April 2016. While it's been on the rise lately, there's no assurance that it will continue this way in the future. Besides the risk, this also makes it hard for merchants to know how many bitcoins to charge and how to handle returns. For merchants it is more like dealing with the exchange rates for a foreign currency rather than the domestic currency.
- *Transactions are irreversible.* This is both good and bad. It's bad in the sense that if a buyer makes a purchase and the merchant fails to deliver the goods, there is no recourse because the transactions will already be committed. A variety of external controls have been suggested, but many of them are an anathema to the underlying tenets on which the system operates.
- *Private keys can be lost.* As noted earlier, if a user loses his or her encryption private key(s), they are simply out of luck. Keys can be lost in a variety of inadvertent ways (e.g., disk crashes, file corruption, stolen hardware, and the like). Even though the transactions and public account numbers are visible, there is no way to sign a message to execute a transaction, and there is no central authority or administrator who can issue a new key. It's not like losing a password. This is why users are encouraged to back up their private keys to paper or some other medium.
- *Problems with everyday use.* Traditional currencies and cards are easier to use both offline and online and are accepted virtually everywhere. Virtually every online retailer who accepts bitcoins sets their prices in a conventional currencies and determines the bitcoin cost based on exchange rates against those same currencies. So, from the perspective of everyday use, bitcoins offer little advantage.

- *Network latency and issues of scalability.* While the system is designed to verify transactions on average every 10 min, sometimes it can take hours. It is hard to image how this could support the transaction volume of even a reasonable sized retailer or replace a system like Visa that handles thousands of transactions per second.
- Despite these disadvantages, Bitcoin is becoming more popular. There is even a Visa bitcoin card, and its value in dollars is increasing.

Bitcoin Competitors and the Future of Math-Based Currencies

There are over 700 cryptocurrencies being traded in online markets. Only ten of them have market caps above $10 million, and only three have market caps above $100 million (recall that Bitcoin's was about $7 billion). The three include (**coinmarketcap.com**):

- *Ethereum* (**ethereum.org**). Valued at close to $750 million, Ethereum was crowdfunded in 2014 and developed by the Ethereum Foundation, a Swiss nonprofit foundation. While Ethereum is a decentralized blockchain technology that is traded as a virtual currency, it is actually a development platform with its own language that can be used to create other distributed applications like smart contracts that can be run "without any downtime, fraud, or third-party control." In contrast to Bitcoins, it confirms blocks in seconds, not minutes. Recently, Ethereum has partnered with Microsoft to offer Ethereum Blockchain as a service on Microsoft's Azure cloud.
- *Ripple* (**ripple.com**). Ripple has 35 billion shares versus Bitcoin's max of 21.5 million. Each share is valued at $.007 per share for a market cap close to $230 million. Ripple was originally targeted as a distributed, open source, consensus ledger with its own currency XRP (ripples). More recently, the system has been repurposed for banks and payment networks as a real-time cross-currency settlement system that can support applications like international money transfer.
- *Litecoin* (**litecoin.com**). Valued at $170 million, this distributed, peer-to-peer cryptocurrency is almost a clone of Bitcoin. Where it differs is it's speed (about 4× faster), its proof-of-work algorithm (called "scrypt" vs. "SHA-256"), and the maximum units of currency (84 million vs. 21.5 million).

While individual cryptocurrencies (including Bitcoin) may fade away, the underlying platforms and algorithms will likely morph to other uses similar to the types of shifts that have occurred with Ethereum and ripple. For other potential uses in banks, see Roberts (2016).

SECTION 12.7 REVIEW QUESTIONS

1. Distinguish electronic money, virtual currency, and digital currency.
2. What is the difference between convertible and nonconvertible virtual currency?
3. What are the major product categories in the virtual currency market?
4. What characteristics does Bitcoin possess that make it a currency?
5. What is a blockchain?
6. What is a bitcoin miner?
7. How are a Bitcoin private key, public key, and address interrelated?
8. What are the key advantages of Bitcoin? Key disadvantages?
9. Who are some of the main competitors of Bitcoin?

MANAGERIAL ISSUES

Some managerial issues related to this chapter are as follows:

1. **How will you address the omni-channel imperative?** Today, most "brick-and-mortar" retailers have multiple sales channels—stores and branches, catalogs, call centers, kiosks, vending machines, websites, and mobile apps. Historically, these channels have been managed as silos with separate personnel, practices, and information systems (both front office and back) with the lead channel getting preferential treatment. In the past this was sufficient because the customers were less demanding. This has changed. Customers expect a seamless experience across all these channels. They want to buy what they want and where they want, receive it when and where they want, and return it where they want. To meet these

expectations, retailers will have to accept orders and payments from any channel, as well as fulfill orders from anywhere (e.g., distribution centers, stores and branches, manufacturers (drop-ships), 3PLs, and vending machines). For most retailers, this will obviously require substantial redesign of their payment and order fulfillment systems, as well as the redesign of a number of processes and systems along their supply chains.

2. **What payment methods should you support?** Many EC merchants in the United States who are focused primarily on domestic sales can get by supporting only payments made by card or PayPal. It's the same way for many merchants in other parts of the world, although the alternative to cards is likely to be some other digital payment systems besides PayPal. However, there are a number of exceptions like China where cards are rarely used and other countries where cash payments (COD or direct withdrawals) are widely used. The implication is that if you plan to expand your EC business by encouraging cross-border purchases, then at a minimum you will need to accept a variety of payment methods. The studies also point out that successful sites support multiple languages, currencies, and access devices along with pages customized for particular countries, simplified checkout processes, and free shipping to name a few.

3. **What micropayment strategy should your e-marketplace support?** If your EC site sells items priced less than $10, credit cards are not a viable solution. Many digital content products cost less than $1. For small-value products, micropayments should be supported. Fees may be taken from a prepaid account that is connected to the buyer's bank account or credit card, or the fee may be charged to the buyer's cell phone bill. The use of stored-value smart cards on the Internet has emerged but has not widely penetrated the market because buyers need to install the card reader/writer. Companies should support multiple options so that customers can choose their preferred payment method.

4. **Which mobile systems could influence your business?** Over the next few years, the market for smartphones will continue to grow and may eventually become the primary way that people pay for digital and physical goods, both online and off. Mobile payments have the potential to replace the direct use of credit and debit cards, as well as cash. At the present time, mobile payment technologies and protocols are in a state of flux, making it difficult to decide which systems to adopt. The key is to determine which forms of mobile payment are required for a particular business—remote or proximate—and, in the short term, rely on those vendors and organizations that already have a strong presence in the online world (for instance, PayPal or the protocols and systems supported by major credit card vendors).

5. **Should we outsource our payment gateway service?** It takes time, skill, money, software, and hardware to build and maintain a comprehensive self-payment system. For this reason, even a large online business usually outsources its e-payment service. Many third-party vendors provide comprehensive payment gateways. Furthermore, if a website is hosted by a third party (e.g., Yahoo! Stores), an e-payment service will already be provided by the host.

6. **Should we accept virtual currencies as a form of payment?** Even though there are a variety of virtual currencies, this question really translates into "should we accept Bitcoin?" A number of merchants have answered in the affirmative because the transaction fees are minimal and there are no charge backs. Yet, the lower cost does not eliminate the facts that bitcoins are not backed by any government agency, that there are potential issues with determining the taxes assessed to bitcoin payments, and that the exchange rates can fluctuate substantially and depend on the usage and country of payment. Bottom line, if you plan to accept bitcoins, then you need to carefully determine the associated risks.

7. **How secure are e-payments?** Security and fraud continue to be major concerns in different online e-payments. This is true with regard to the use of credit cards for online purchases, especially for cross-border purchases. B2C merchants are employing a wide variety of tools (e.g., address verification and other authentication services) to combat fraudulent orders. These cannot be used in isolation but need to be an integral part of a business security program (Chap. 10). For more on payment security, see European Banking Authority (2014).

SUMMARY

In this chapter, you learned about the following EC issues as they relate to the chapter's learning objectives:

1. **Cross-border EC.** Many B2C companies are looking to grow their businesses by increasing sales to international customers. These sales are part of what is called cross-border EC. The problem is that most B2C companies are ill-prepared to engage in cross-border commerce. As demonstrated by B2C companies that already have strong international sales, those companies that want to successfully engage in cross-border EC will have to "think local," meaning that they need to treat international customers as if they were domestic. More specifically, their online sites will need to (1) provide support for multiple languages, currencies, payment systems, and input devices (especially mobile), (2) customize Web pages based on country (e.g., handle international addresses and phone numbers), (3) simplify checkouts by eliminating the need for detailed user profiles, and (4) offer free shipping and rewards to encourage repeat traffic. Because this is such a

daunting task for most companies, they usually rely on third-party partners who have successfully done this to assist with the transition. For example, this was what Costco did a couple of years back when they decided to start selling online to Chinese consumers. Instead of establishing their own in-country operation, they partnered with Alibaba's Tmall Global EC marketplace which provided access to a substantial percentage China's online consumers, immensely simplified the handling of payments from these consumers, and eliminated many of the logistical issues that confront businesses trying to deliver orders originating from outside the country to Chinese consumers. Besides removing many of the barriers to cross-border EC, working with a partner enables a business to more easily test an international market and experiment with its product offerings without having to make very large upfront investments and incurring substantial card usage fees and logistical costs.

2. **Changing retail landscape.** In the rapidly changing retail landscape, retailers are faced with a series of conundrums. First, while EC retail sales are growing much faster than in-store sales, the overwhelming majority of sales are not online. This means that those retailers who support multiple sales channels will have to determine how to best combine the channels so that customers are provided with a seamless omni-channel experience. Second, cards continue to be the payment method used in most EC transactions. Yet, cash is still used in the vast majority of retail sales, and in some regions of the world, other forms of EC payment predominate. The implication is EC retailers who sell worldwide will have to support alternative methods of payment including cash on delivery and cash transfers. Finally, although payment by smartphones is growing substantially faster than payments by other devices, overall purchases made by PCs swamp the number of purchases made by smartphones. This suggests that for the near term, most EC retailers will have to provide interfaces that support different devices including smartphones, tablets, and PCs.

   The various dilemmas facing e-tailers indicate that the models on which EC was originally built are undergoing rapid transformation. This has given rise to a literally hundreds of new payment initiatives, especially in the areas of closed-loop cards and mobile payments, digital wallets, mobile money of all sorts, and virtual currencies. Unfortunately, the vast majority will suffer the same fate as most of the predecessors—death from failure to reach a critical mass of buyers and sellers who are willing to adopt the new schemes and technologies.

3. **Using payment cards online.** The processing of online card payments is essentially the same as it is for brick-and-mortar stores and involves essentially the same players and the same systems—banks, card associations, payment processing services, and the like. This is one of the reasons why payment cards are predominant in the online world. Even so, this doesn't mean that EC card payments don't present challenges to online merchants who accept them. First, the discount rate and interchange fees charged with each card transaction are substantial. This is one of the reasons merchants are always looking for ways to reduce these fees (like using third-party digital gateways such as PayPal). Second, online merchants experience more card fraud than offline merchants. Surveys, such as those conducted annually by CyberSource, indicate that over the past few years, merchants have adopted a wide variety of methods including card verification services, address verification, customer order history, negative lists, and postal address verifications.

4. **Smart cards.** A smart card is a plastic payment card that contains data in an embedded microchip. Some cards have memory chips for read/write data. Smart cards can be rechargeable. Applications include telecom SIM cards, contactless financial payments and services, paying for mass transit, identifying cardholders for government services, and verifying eligibility for healthcare. There are two types of smart cards—contact and contactless. With both types smart card readers are critical and a key element in determining the cost of a smart card application.

   Stored-value cards are a particular type of smart card where a monetary value is prepaid and can be loaded on the card once or several times. They can be used like a credit or debit card to make purchases online or off. They come in two forms—closed-loop and open-loop. Closed-loop stored-value cards are issued for a single purpose by a specific merchant (e.g., a Starbucks gift card). In contrast, open-loop stored-value cards are more like standard credit or debit cards and can be used for multiple purposes (e.g., a payroll card).

5. **EC micropayments.** In the online world, most purchases are made with credit and debit cards. When the value of a purchase is under $10, it is called a micropayment. The problem is that the fees associated with card purchases make these low-value transactions cost prohibitive. As an alternative, most merchants rely on one of five methods such as aggregation, direct payment, stored-value card, subscription, and à la carte to avoid the individual transaction costs. Aggregation adds the value of a number of purchases before submitting the transaction to the card companies; direct payments aggregate payments by adding them to an existing bill (e.g., mobile phone bill); a stored-value card enables up-front payments to a debit account from which purchases are deducted as they are made; a subscription is a single payment that covers access to content for a defined period of time; and with à la carte payments are made as they occur with reduced fees based on pre-negotiated volume discounts. Companies like Amazon and PayPal support micropayments, and, while their fees are lower, they're still costly. More recently, Visa and MasterCard have started lowering their fees on low-cost transactions primarily for those merchants with high volumes of card sales.

6. **PayPal and third-party payment gateways.** A third-party gateway is a company that provides electronic connections and transaction services among all the parties involved in electronic payments. Essentially, they eliminate the need for a merchant to deal with the intricacies and complexities of authorization and settlement in online payment. Among these gateways, PayPal is oldest and most successful worldwide. Recently, other gateways have started gaining market share in specific regions of the world, for example, Alipay in China, Sofort in Germany, Yandex.Money in Russia, and iDEAL in the Netherlands. In the United States, Amazon has recently entered the gateway market with their Amazon Payments which is modeled after their extremely successful "one click" payment system used by Amazon customers.

7. **Mobile payments.** The term refers to payment transactions initiated or confirmed using a person's mobile device, usually a smartphone although payments can be made with other mobile devices such as tablets and wearables. They generally fall into one of four payment types (distinguished by "who pays whom") including (1) consumer where a buyer pays a merchant for goods and services, often using either a device-based digital wallet like Apple Pay or a cloud-based wallet like Walmart Pay that is built on the cloud-based mobile platform called *CurrentC*; (2) merchant mobile POS, such as Square's *magstripe reader*, that is used by merchants to take customer card payments instead of relying on stationary POS; and (3) person-to-person (P2P) systems, like Kenya's M-Pesa (see closing case), used for exchanging money between people both within and across country boundaries.

8. **Digital and virtual currencies.** Digital currency refers to the digital representation of money or currency. Electronic money is the digital representation of a national (fiat) currency. Virtual currency functions as a digital medium of exchange but has no legal status as a fiat currency. Virtual currencies are either convertible or nonconvertible, meaning either it can be converted thru exchange into a fiat currency (like Bitcoin) or it cannot be converted and only has value in a particular virtual world (like World of Warcraft Gold). Among the multitude of virtual convertible currencies, Bitcoin has garnered the most attention for a couple of reasons. First, it was the first decentralized virtual currency which means there is no central authority that issues or administers the currency, and as a consequence there are only very minimal fees even for international transactions. Instead, it is administered by a distributed peer-to-peer network of computers (called bitcoin miners). Second, the currency is pseudo-anonymous. This means that while all Bitcoin transactions are displayed in a public digital ledger called the blockchain, the recipients of any exchange are denoted by their encrypted public keys generated from their private keys, and the senders are designated by encrypted digital signatures again generated by their private keys. There is virtually no way to decipher these keys. Finally, through the combination of the distributed network along with the public (private) key cryptography, Bitcoin has addressed the "double-spend problem" which prevents any participant from digitally copying their coins and spending them twice. Because of its success, Bitcoin has spawned a number of competitive currencies. None of these have attracted the same volume of investment. As a consequence, these groups have started ignoring the currency side and started promoting the use of these distributed, decentralized architectures for other types of transactions (e.g., legal contracts or international remittances).

KEY TERMS

Address Verification System (AVS)
Authorization
Bitcoin address
Bitcoin private key
Blockchain
Card verification number (CVN)
Contact card
Contactless (proximity) card
Convertible virtual currency
Cross-border e-commerce
Digital currency
Digital currency exchanges
Discount rate
Electronic money
Fiat currency
Interchange rate
Micropayments (e-micropayments)

Mobile payment
Mobile (digital) wallet
Nonconvertible virtual currency
Payment cards
Payment service providers (PSPs)
Settlement
Smart card
Smart card reader
Stored-value card
Virtual currency

DISCUSSION QUESTIONS

1. Five years from now, do you think credit and debit cards will still be the primary payment method for online purchases? What about cash for offline purchases? In both instances explain why or why not.
2. What type of payment service does Boku (**boku.com**) provide? How does it work? What are some of the countries where it works? Who are some of the companies that utilize the service? What is their chance of success? What factors do you think will pay a role in its success or failure? Start by reading the press release at **boku.com/#merchants** and **boku. com/#carriers** .
3. In B2C EC criminals may use fake or stolen credit cards to pay merchants. What steps should the merchants take to combat the fraud?
4. A metropolitan area wants to provide users of its public transportation system with the ability to pay transit fares and make retail purchases, using a single contactless smart card. What sorts of problems can it encounter in setting up the system, and what types of problems could the riders encounter by using the cards?
5. Discuss the differences between Litecoin and Bitcoin? How likely is it that Litecoin will become a widely used global virtual currency? What will be the key reasons for its success or failure?
6. Bitcoin has often been criticized because of its potential support for money laundering activities. What is "money laundering?" What are the features of Bitcoin that support and hinder these activities? Based on what has happened in recent court cases involving money laundering and virtual currencies, is the criticism justified or overblown?
7. Will Amazon Go replace jobs? Can this loss be stopped? How?

TOPICS FOR CLASS DISCUSSION AND DEBATES

1. Debate: Why was PayPal able to succeed where other e-payment alternatives were not? Does the company present a threat to the banking industry?
2. Several years ago Facebook declared that all Facebook applications, including games, would have to use Facebook Credits as their currency. A short time later they rescinded this policy. Why would Facebook issue such a policy? Why did they rescind it? Do you agree with their actions?
3. Besides music and apps, what are some of the other places where EC micropayments could be used?
4. Which would you prefer, paying for goods and services with a physical debit or credit card or paying with your smartphone? What are some of the benefits and limitations of each?
5. What is MasterPass™ and how does it work? Some question the longer-term viability of MasterPass™. Find pro and con information and debate the issue.
6. Discuss the differences between convertible and nonconvertible virtual currencies. What are some examples of each? Contrary to the strict definition, are there some instances where the nonconvertible virtual currencies have actually been used as a medium exchange in the "real" world?
7. Digital currencies are used extensively by criminals and tax evaders. But, they also are used extensively by honest customers due to their convenience and anonymity. Should they be outlawed if governments cannot control them? Debate.
8. According to Wang (2016), Alipay is challenging Apple Pay and PayPal on their home turf. Research what is going on. Write a report.

INTERNET EXERCISES

1. Select a major retail B2C merchant in the United States and one outside of North America. Detail the similarities and differences in the e-payment systems they offer. What other payment systems could the sites offer? Write a short report.
2. Go to **worldpay.com/sites/default/files/WPUK-Omni-channel-payments-store-of-the-future.pdf** . Based on the implications of this short report, in what ways do current payment systems impede the growth of omni-channel retail? What sorts of changes in payment systems can be made to bolster in-store retail in the future?
3. Who is Authorize.Net? What sorts of services do they provide and how do they work? Who are their major competitors and what accounts for their success against them?
4. A number of companies are providing digital (mobile) wallet systems. What is a digital wallet? Make a list of these companies and their products. Compare their various capabilities. Do you think any of these products will be popular in the near future? Why or why not?
5. Go to **smartcardalliance.org/smart-cards-applications-transit-open-payments-resources** . The site lists a number of existing transit systems that are using contactless smart cards effectively. Select two of the systems and compare and contrast them.
6. Read about Starbucks gift cards and stored-value mobile app. In recent years, these have been victimized by cybercriminals. What types of cybercrimes have been committed, what has been the impact, and how have the problems been addressed?
7. Download the latest version of the CyberSource Fraud Benchmark Report at **cybersource.com** . In the report, is mobile commerce more or less susceptible to fraud than nonmobile EC, which mobile operating systems are most susceptible to fraud, and what techniques are most often used to combat it?
8. Bitcoin exchange Bitfinex was hacked in 2016. Compare it to Mt. Gox hack in 2014. Why these hacks continue? What is the impact on Bitcoin?

TEAM ASSIGNMENTS AND PROJECTS

Assignment for the Opening Case

1. Read the opening case and answer the following questions:

   (a) What is cross-border research, and under this definition, is trade between two member countries of the European Union cross-border or not? Explain.
   (b) Describe the current and estimated size of the cross-border market.
   (c) What are the key elements of success for an EC company wanting to expand into global markets?
   (d) What is the basic approach that Costco used in entering the Chinese EC market?
   (e) Would the approach used by Costco work for a company like Walmart? Explain.

2. The competition within the mobile payment reader industry is very intense. Each team selects a company in this field (e.g., Square, PayPal, Groupon) and presents the company's capabilities and weaknesses.
3. Have each member of a (4+ member) team keep a 2-week diary tracking their online and offline purchases—noting time, seller, products or services purchased, type of payment method used, the POS device, and the total amount (only noting less than or more than $10US)? Compare and contrast the team's overall results with the payment and payment system patterns discussed throughout the chapter.
4. Write a report comparing smart card applications in two or more European and/or Asian countries. In the report, discuss whether those applications would succeed in North America.
5. Have one team represent MasterCard® *PayPass*™ (**mastercard.us/paypass.html**) and another represent Visa payWave (**usa.visa.com/personal/security/card-technology/visa-paywave.jsp**)? The task of each team is to convince a company that its product is superior to the other.
6. Research and write a report on the differences among the cloud-based and device-based digital wallets, giving examples of each and noting the pros and cons of each approach.
7. Research the issue of B2B EC payments. Begin with a guide at **ecommerceguide.com/guides/b2b-ecommerce-payment-systems**, and read **ecommerceandb2b.com/b2b-e-commerce-payments** . Write a report and make a class presentation.

8. View the case study about payment marketplace Goat Rodeo (8:43 min) at **youtube.com/watch?v=AdqyiwLmx7k** .

Answer the following questions:

(a) What is the role of the marketplace?
(b) What is the significance of the Goat Rodeo?
(c) Relate it to Amazon.com, Apple, Google, and Facebook.
(d) What lessons have you learned from the video?

CLOSING CASE

Send Money Home: M-PESA and the Kenya Experience

The slang term *unbanked* refers to people who do not use banks or other financial institutions. Instead of using checks and cards, they conduct most of their financial transactions in cash. While there are many reasons for people to be unbanked, most of them are poor and either lack the credit standing to have a bank account or they are located in poorer regions where there are no banking services. In many countries around the world, moving from the ranks of the unbanked is almost a necessary step for getting out of poverty.

From 2011 to 2014, the number of "unbanked" adults declined an astounding 20% to 2 billion (World Bank 2015). The drop was not the result of declines in the number of unbanked living in the more advanced or growing economies. Instead it was almost solely attributable to shifts in the number of unbanked residing in sub-Saharan Africa and more specifically in Kenya. It was due to a program called M-Pesa originally intended to provide person-to-person international remittances conducted via cell phones. This closing case describes in detail the M-Pesa program including the problems it was designed to address, the structure and operation of the program, and its long-term results on the unbanked poor in Kenya and other parts of the world.

The Problem

In developing countries, immigration is "a way of life." When done voluntarily, people often migrate for the express purpose of finding work or taking advantage of opportunities outside of the countries or areas where they live. Worldwide, this migration results in a massive transfer of money from workers to their families and friends back home. These transfers are known as remittances. While any single remittance is usually small, the aggregate amounts are substantial. For example, according to figures from the World Bank (2016), "official" global remittances involving foreign workers from developing countries totaled over $430 billion in 2015. To put this in perspective, for many developing countries, the yearly total is often more than the development assistance they receive from all sources and larger the monies from direct foreign investments.

These sums not only represent big money from the developing countries' perspective; they also represent big money for the money transfer operators like Western Union who handle these transfers. The MTOs charge fees for their services and are making money from currency conversion. While most of these operators follow strict guidelines and rules, even small charges can have a major impact on the amounts received by the individual families.

In addition to these global remittances, developing countries also have sizeable "internal" remittances generated by workers who have moved from the rural parts of the country to take jobs in the cities. Because the workers and their families are unbanked, most of these remittances take place the old fashion way. Either the workers take the cash home themselves or they have someone do it for them. While this certainly avoids the fees charged by the MTOs, it is still a costly and dangerous undertaking—it takes time to transport the money (usually by bus) and places both the person and the money at risk given the high rates of robbery in many of these countries. Also, because the transfers occur outside any formal financial system, there is no way to measure the numbers of people, cash, and transactions involved.

In the past a number of countries have sought to address either directly or indirectly the issues and inefficiencies in global and domestic remittances. Many of these programs revolved around the idea of somehow turning the "unbanked" into the "banked." Theoretically, if both the sender and the receiver had bank accounts, this could certainly simplify the domestic transfers of funds and would open other possibilities for international transfers. It might also address the larger issues of poverty, thus alleviating the need for family members to separate in the first place. Ignoring the fact that it costs money to have a bank account and the fact that banking systems in many developing countries are suspect, this approach is a massive, costly, and long-term undertaking. As the last few years have demonstrated, the real answer might be in mobile money and the "un-banking" of the banking system. At least, that is what the experience in Kenya over the last few years have shown.

The Solution

The history of the M-Pesa is well documented in *Money, Real Quick* by Omwansa and Sullivan (2012) and touched on more recently by Runde (2016). The discussion that follows briefly covers some of the key events that these discussions highlight.

Kenya is an East African country of approximately 40 million people with high unemployment and poverty. Approximately 10 years ago, an in-depth survey of the Kenyan financial sector found, much to the surprise of the Central Bank of Kenya, that only 20% of the adults in the country were "banked." Basically, the bank was servicing urban elites and slowly dying in the process. The same could be said for the government-owned telecom system which historically had provided landlines in urban areas. As a result, only 2% of the population had phone service. In contrast, Kenya's mobile operators, of which Safaricom Network Company was by far the largest, had managed in a relatively short period of time to get ten million mobile phones in the hands of the Kenyans (for a 35% penetration rate). So, instead of thinking about how to spread a dying landline business or branch banking business to the rural populace or for that matter to the slums of the cities, maybe it would be easier to figure out how to use mobile phones to help bring financial services to the poor.

The original pilot for Kenya's mobile money system was run under the auspices of Britain's governmental development agency (DFID) and focused on reducing the costs of microfinance loan repayments and lowering the associated interest rates. After the initial foray, control of the program was shifted to Safaricom, and the focus morphed away from loan repayments toward person-to-person money transfer. The new system was called M-PESA—the "M" stands for mobile and "PESA" is the Swahili word for money. The marketing slogan for the new system was simply "Send money home," although the system had broader financial capabilities.

The task of sending money was relatively straightforward. First, the sender and the receiver had to have mobile phones that supported texting, which virtually every mobile phone has regardless of the underlying technology. Next, they had to get Safaricom SIM cards. Once they had the SIM cards, they had to register with an M-PESA agent. All that was required to register was an identity card, something that every Kenyan had. Once registered, the network sends an updated menu to the registered customer's mobile phone. At this point, the system is ready to go. To actually send money, a registered customer first deposits cash to his or her account. This is done by giving cash to an M-PESA agent who immediately credits it to the customer's account. The network sends a text message to verify the deposit. Once it's in the customer's account, he or she can send money at any time by selecting "Send money" from the M-PESA menu and then entering the recipient's phone number. At this point, the sender is prompted for his or her M-PESA PIN and then selects "Ok." At this point, the system sends a message to the sender confirming the transfer and the recipient's name. In turn the recipient receives a message with the sender's name and the amount transferred to his or her account.

On the other end, a recipient can now go to a local M-PESA agent to pick up the money. Actually, the recipient is basically making a cash withdrawal from his or her account. It's done by showing the agent his or her identity card, choosing "Withdraw" cash from menu, entering the agent's ID number, and then entering his or her M-PESA PIN. Once the transaction is confirmed, the agent distributes the cash.

Obviously, a major key to the success of the system is the M-PESA agent network (Stahl 2015). It has been described as a network of "human ATMs." An agent might be a local grocer, or gas station owner, or a post person, etc. They were recruited through a thorough selection and vetting process. Many of them were also selling mobile airtime for Safaricom. They receive regular training and are frequently monitored. They are also restricted from doing business with other mobile operators. Outside of the due diligence process, the major hurdle for an agent is monetary. Agents have to pre-purchase mobile money so they can sell it to customers for cash. Likewise, they have to sell cash for mobile money so customers can withdraw funds. Both the cash and the mobile money they manage are theirs, not M-PESA's. Some agents do well, but for the majority, it is a part-time job.

Less obvious is the fact that M-PESA is modeled after a "prepaid" mobile phone system where consumers pay upfront for minutes rather than relying on credit and paying for minutes after they are used. In M-PESA you don't need credit approval upfront to open and use the system. Essentially, you open an account and then deposit money. There are no fees for making deposits nor are there fees for adding airtime to a phone. There are fees for transferring and withdrawing funds. They pale in comparison to fees charged by the MTOs and by ATMs. There are also restrictions on the maximum amount of money you can store in your account and the amount of money you can transfer at any given time. There are a variety of reasons for these restrictions. First, a majority of customers are poor so the system is focused on their needs. Second, they don't want the system to be used for illegal purposes (e.g., money laundering). Third, and most importantly, M-PESA is not a bank. Monies are held in a trust owned by Vodafone (the major shareholder) and deposited in commercial banks.

The Results

By virtually every measure, M-PESA has been a major success (Vodafone 2016). The program started in Kenya but now operates in 11 countries. In 2014/2015 it had 23.4 million customers and 240 thousand agents and handled 3.4 billion transactions. In Kenya there are over 20 million subscribers (which is about 50% of the entire population and 90% of the adults). There are also over 80,000 M-PESA agents. The value of transactions flowing through the system in Kenya is around 2 trillion Kenyan Shillings (which converts to about 20 billion US dollars).

The capabilities of the system have also expanded and now include sending money to another M-PESA customer, paying bills (e.g., utilities), buying goods from merchants, withdrawing money from ATMs, receiving money from abroad, and receiving or paying salaries. Essentially, M-PESA has become a mobile e-wallet.

Additional systems have also been integrated to M-PESA to provide other financial services. For instance, the M-SHWARI system and a new entry (KCB M-PESA) offer M-PESA customers savings and loan capabilities. By early 2015, M-SHWARI had about ten million customers.

As noted above, M-PESA now operates in ten other countries besides Kenya. This includes places inside of Africa (e.g., Tanzania), as well as outside of Africa like Afghanistan, India, South Africa, and Romania. In virtually all of these other countries, the Kenyan success has not been replicated, although the jury is still out in some of these (e.g., India). A number of critics have suggested that the success M-PESA of Kenya rests on a series of circumstances that are hard to replicate in other countries, including (*Economist* 2013):

1. The financial sector basically had a hands-off policy that eliminated a number of regulatory hurdles encountered in countries.
2. Safaricom was close to a mobile monopoly in Kenya. In the other countries the competition is much greater which makes it harder, for example, to control things like the SIM cards used in phones or the mobile airtime.
3. Unlike a number of similar projects, Safaricom recognized that the biggest hurdles were people related not technological in nature. This was the reason for the original marketing theme, the simplified phone capabilities, and the establishment of network of agents located close to the potential customer base.
4. Finally, in the beginning the percent of the "unbanked" population was close to 90% at the beginning of the project. In most of the other countries where M-PESA is present, the percent is much higher (e.g., 30–50%).

Sources: *Economist* (2013), Omwansa and Sullivan (2012), Runde (2016), Vodafone (2016), and World Bank (2016).

Questions

1. What are remittances and why are they important in developing countries?
2. What is an MTO? What role have they historically played in remittances?
3. What is M-Pesa? Briefly describe how M-Pesa works.
4. What evidence is there that M-Pesa was successful?
5. What is the major benefit of owning a credit-based transportation card for commuters? What role did the M-Pesa agent network play in this success?
6. What has M-Pesa been successful in Kenya but not in other countries?

REFERENCES

Accenture. "2015 North America Consumer Digital Payments Survey." October 21, 2015. **accenture.com/t20151021T165757__w__/us-en/_ acnmedia/Accenture/next-gen/na-payment-survey/pdfs/Accenture-Digital-Payments-Survey-North-America-Accenture-Executive-Summary.pdf** (accessed December 2016).

Adyen.com. "Cross-Border Payments Opportunities and Best Practices for Going Global." 2015. **adyen.com/blog/report-cross-border-payments-will-drive-your-growth** (accessed December 2016).

Alizilia.com. "Cross-Border E-Commerce to Reach $1 Trillion in 2020." June 11, 2015. **alizila.com/cross-border-e-commerce-to-reach-1-trillion-in-2020** (accessed December 2016).

Allum, S. Designing Mobile Payment Experiences. *O'Reilly Media* (2014).

Antonopoulos, A. *Mastering Bitcoin*. O'Reilly Media, 2015. **alizila.com/cross-border-e-commerce-to-reach-1-trillion-in-2020** (accessed December 2016).

Beilfuss, L. "Move to Cashless Payments Set to Spur Trillions in Consumer Spending, Report Says." *Dow Jones*, August 2, 2016.

Betters, E. "Android Pay Explained: How It Works and Where It's Supported." *Pocket-lint*, September 13, 2016.

Brandon, J. "5 Big Questions I Have about Amazon Go's Cashier-Less Grocery Store." *Computerworld*, December 5, 2016.

Capgemini Financial Services Analysis. "Top Ten Trends in Payments 2016." 2016. **capgemini.com/resource-file-access/resource/pdf/payments_trends_2016.pdf** (accessed December 2016).

CardCash. "Gift Card Statistics." 2015. **cardcash.com/gift-card-statistics** (accessed December 2016).

Cipriani, J. "Coin Looks Beyond Smart Cards by Teaming With MasterCard." *Fortune*, January 6, 2016. **fortune.com/2016/01/06/coin-mastercard-mobile-payments** (accessed December 2016).

CoinReport. "What Are the Advantages and Disadvantages of Bitcoin?" 2014. **coinreport.net/coin-101/advantages-and-disadvantages-of-bitcoin** (accessed December 2016).

Costco.com. "CostCo Annual Report 2015." October 2015. **phx.corporate-ir.net/External.File?item=UGFyZW50SUQ9NjA1NzM5fENoaWWx kSUQ9MzE3NzEwfFR5cGU9MQ==&t=1** (accessed December 2016).

CyberSource.com. "Annual Fraud Benchmark Report: A Balancing Act." 2016. **www.cybersource.com/learn/fraud_management** (accessed November 2016).

Desjardins, J. "The Shift to a Cashless Society is Snowballing." *Visual Capitalist*, May 17, 2016.

Economist. "Why Does Kenya Lead the World in Mobile Money." May 27, 2013. **economist.com/blogs/economist-explains/2013/05/economist-explains-18** (accessed December 2016).

eMarketer. "Mobile Payments Will Triple in the US in 2015." October 26, 2016. **emarketer.com/Article/Mobile-PaymentsWill-Triple-US-2016/1013147#sthash.dj6IbXrS.dpuf** (accessed December 2016).

eMarketer. "Worldwide Retail Ecommerce Sales: eMarketer's Updated Estimates and Forecast Through 2019." December 23, 2015. **www.emarketer.com/Report/Worldwide-Retail-Ecommerce-Sales-eMarketers-Updated-Estimates-Forecast-Through-2019/2001716** (accessed December 2016).

European Banking Authority. "Guidelines on the Security of Internet Payments." December 19, 2014. **eba.europa.eu/regulation-and-policy/consumer-protection-and-financial-innovation/guidelines-on-the-security-of-internet-payments** (accessed December 2016).

Evans, D. S., and R Schmalensee. Paying with Plastic: The Digital Revolution in Buying and Borrowing, 2nd ed., Cambridge, MA: *MIT Press*, 2005.

FATF. "Virtual Currencies Key Definitions and Potential AML/CFT Risks." *FATF Report* 2014. **fatf-gafi.org/media/fatf/documents/reports/Virtual-currency-key-definitions-and-potential-aml-cft-risks.pdf** (accessed December 2016).

Geissinger, E. *Virtual Billions: The Genius, the Drug Lord, and the Ivy League Twins behind the Rise of Bitcoin*. Amherst, NY: Prometheus Book, 2016.

Goodale, D. "Everything You Need to Know about Cross-Border Fees." October 12, 2014. **foxycart.com/blog/everything-you-need-to-know-about-cross-border-fees#.Vylu2PkrKuU** (accessed December 2016).

Gordon, C. "Cash Use and the ATM – Going from Strength to Strength." November 26, 2015. **ncr.com/company/blogs/financial/76286** (accessed December 2016).

Hochstein, M. "Why Bitcoin Matters to Banks." *American Banker*. May 11, 2016. **americanbanker.com/magazine/124_02/why-bitcoin-matters-for-bankers-1065590-1.html** (accessed December 2016).

Kleinman, B. *The Bitcoin Tutorial: Develop an Intuitive Understanding of the Currency and Blockchain Technology*. Seattle, WA: Amazon Digital Services, 2016.

Leary, K. "How to Use Apple Pay to Buy Things in Stores and Online." *Digital Trend*, December 11, 2016.

Lee, C. "iTunes Surpasses 35 Billion Songs Sold, itunes Radio Hits 40 Million Listeners." May 29, 2014. **idownloadblog.com/2014/05/29/itunes-35-itunes-radio-40** (accessed December 2016).

LPT Team. "Payment Entrepreneurs Go after MicroPayments Segment, $13 B+ Opportunity Globally." January 31, 2014. **letstalkpayments.com/payment-entrepreneurs-go-micropayments-segment-13-b-opportunity-globally** (accessed December 2016).

Lunden, I. "Basic Fixed Phone Subscriptions." June 2, 2015. **techcrunch.com/2015/06/02/6-1b-smartphone-users-globally-by-2020-overtaking-basic-fixed-phone-subscriptions** (accessed December 2016).

Mahajan, N. "Why Costco's Online-First Approach in China Is a Smart Strategy." May 4, 2015. **foundingfuel.com/column/dispatches-from-china/why-costcos-onlinefirst-approach-in-china-is-a-smart-strategy** (accessed December 2016).

MasterCard. "MasterCard Launches New Program That Can Turn Any Consumer Gadget, Accessory or Wearable into a Payment Device." October 26, 2015. **newsroom.mastercard.com/press-releases/mastercard-launches-new-program-that-can-turn-any-consumer-gadget-accessory-or-wearable-into-a-payment-device** (accessed December 2016).

McCormick, R. "Apple's Next iPhones Could Support Tap-To-Pay for Japan's Trains." *The Verge*, August 25, 2016. **theverge.com/2016/8/25/12653774/apple-iphone-felica-tap-to-pay-subway-japan** (accessed December 2016).

McKee, J. "Redefining Virtual Currency." Yankee Group. May 2013. **home.tapjoy.com/info/wp-content/uploads/sites/4/2013/05/RedefiningVirtualCurrency_WhitePaper-1MAY2013-v1.pdf** (accessed December 2016).

Nielsen. "Global Connected Commerce: is e-Tail Therapy the New Retail Therapy." January 28, 2016. **studylib.net/doc/8306358/nielsen-global-connected-commerce** (accessed December 2016).

O'Grady, M. "Forrester Data Web-Influenced Retail Sales Forecast, 2016 To 2021." *Forrester Research* 2016. **forrester.com/report/Forrester+Data+WebInfluenced+Retail+Sales+Forecast+2016+To+2021+EU7/-/E-RES133600** (accessed December 2016).

Omwansa, T. and Sullivan, N. Money, Real Quick: The M-Pesa Story. *Guardian Books* (2012).

Park, Y.S, "The Inefficiencies of Cross-Border Payment: How Current Forces are Shaping the Future." *Visa Commercial*, 2015.

PayPal. "PayPal Cross-Border Consumer Research 2015." 2015. **paypalobjects.com/digitalassets/c/website/marketing/global/pages/jobs/pay-pal-insights-2015-global-report-appendix-added.pdf** (accessed December 2016).

Perez, S. "PayPal Says Mobile Shopping Accounted for a Third of Thanksgiving & Black Friday Sales." *TechCrunch*, November 28, 2016.

Pymnts.com. "X-Border Payments Optimization Index." 2015. **pymnts.com/x-border-payments-optimization** (accessed December 2016).

Roberts, D. "How Big Banks Are Paying Lip Service to the Blockchain." Yahoo! Finance February 17, 2016. **finance.yahoo.com/news/big-banks-interest-in-blockchain-r3-052723646.html?soc_src=mediacontentstory&soc_trk=tw** (accessed December 2016).

Rossman, S., E. Weise, and E. Baig. "Can Amazon Fix the Grocery Game?" *USA Today*, December 6, 2016.

Runde, D. "M-Pesa and The Rise of the Global Mobile Money Market." *Forbes*, August 12, 2016. **forbes.com/sites/danielrunde/2015/08/12/m-pesa-and-the-rise-of-the-global-mobile-money-market/#1831c30923f5** (accessed December 2016).

Sharma, A. "India Along the Path Towards a Cashless Society." *Fintech Innovation*, November 30, 2016.

Smart Payment Association. "More Than Half of Payment Cards Shipped in 2015 Were Contactless." April 27, 2016. **nfcworld.com/2016/04/27/344298/half-payment-cards-shipped-2015-contactless** (accessed December 2016).

Stahl, L. "The Future of Money." November 22, 2015. **cbsnews.com/news/future-of-money-kenya-m-pesa-60-minutes** (accessed December 2016).

Statista-1. "Cumulative Number of Apps Downloaded from the Apple App Store from July 2008 to June 2015 (in billions)." 2015. **statista.com/statistics/263794/number-of-downloads-from-the-apple-app-store** (accessed December 2016).

Statista-2. "Proximity Mobile Payment Transaction Value in the United States from 2014 to 2019 (in Billion U.S. Dollars)." 2016. **statista.com/statistics/244475/proximity-mobile-payment-transaction-value-in-the-united-states** (accessed December 2016).

Taylor, K. "Starbucks Is Conquering a Huge Challenge in Retail — and Even Apple and Chipotle Should Be Jealous." November 20, 2015. **businessinsider.com/starbucks-mobile-payment-numbers-2015-11** (accessed December 2016).

Tomaino, N. "Bitcoin is Good Money." February 10, 2015. **businessoffashion.com/articles/opinion/good-money** (accessed December 2016).

Tran, M. "Tmall and Tmall Global: The 'Fast Track into China' for U.S. Retailers." 2015. **cpcstrategy.com/blog/2015/05/tmall-tmall-global-fast-track-china-u-s-retailer**s (accessed December 2016).

Vodafone. "M-Pesa FAQs." 2016. **vodafone.com/content/index/what/m-pesa/m-pesa-faqs.html#** (accessed December 2016).

Wang, H. "AliPay Takes on Apple Pay and PayPal on Their Home Turf." *Seeking Alpha*, November 6, 2016.

World Bank. "Remittances to Developing Countries Edge Up Slightly in 2015." April 13, 2016. **worldbank.org/en/news/press-release/2016/04/13/remittances-to-developing-countries-edge-up-slightly-in-2015** (accessed December 2016).

World Bank. "Massive Drop in Number of Unbanked, says New Report." April 15, 2015. **www.worldbank.org/en/news/press-release/2015/04/15/massive-drop-in-number-of-unbanked-says-new-report** (accessed December 2016).

Order Fulfillment Along the Supply Chain in e-Commerce

13

Learning Objectives

Upon completion of this chapter, you will be able to:

1. Define EC order fulfillment and describe the EC order fulfillment process.
2. Describe the make-to-order approach and 3D printing.
3. Describe the role of warehousing in order fulfillment and the use of robots there.
4. Describe EC delivery methods including futuristic ones.
5. Describe the major problems of EC order fulfillment along the supply chains.
6. Describe various solutions to EC order fulfillment problems.
7. Describe RFID supply chain applications.
8. Describe B2B order fulfillment.
9. Describe other supply chain topics.

© Springer International Publishing AG 2018

E. Turban et al., *Electronic Commerce 2018*, Springer Texts in Business and Economics, DOI 10.1007/978-3-319-58715-8_13

OPENING CASE
HOW AMAZON.COM FULFILLS ORDERS

The Problem

With traditional retailing, customers go to a physical store and purchase items that they like and then take them home. Large quantities are delivered to each store or supermarket; there are not too many delivery destinations. With e-tailing, customers want the goods quickly and have them shipped to their homes. Deliveries of small quantities need to go to a large number of destinations. In addition, items must be available for immediate delivery. Therefore, maintaining an inventory of items becomes critical. Maintaining inventory and shipping products costs money and takes time, which may negate some of the advantages of e-tailing. Let us see how Amazon.com, the "king" of e-tailing, handles the situation.

In 1994, Amazon started with "virtual retailing" as a business model—no warehouses, no inventory, and no shipments (also called *dropshipping*). The idea was to take orders and receive payments electronically and then let others fill the orders. It soon became clear that this model, although appropriate for a small company, would not work for the world's largest e-tailer.

The Solution

In 1997, Amazon.com decided to change its business model and handle its own inventory and logistics. Furthermore, for a fee, the company provides logistics services to any seller—even its competitors. The company spent billions of dollars to construct their own distribution network around the United States and the world and in the process became a world-class leader in warehouse management, warehouse automation (including robots), packaging, and inventory management.

Amazon began by opening their own fulfillment centers (warehouses) in Seattle and Delaware, both occupying many thousand square feet. This rapidly expanded to eight more in 1999, including three centers in Europe. Because of economic issues, they slowed their growth until 2005, when they began a period of incredible facility expansion.

The expansion started with a series of larger distribution centers that were located in states with favorable tax breaks and incentives, especially states where they did not have to pay sales tax because technically they were not a retail store. This provided them with a substantial economic advantage over the "brick-and-mortar" retailers until the states started reinterpreting their laws and treated Amazon like any other retailer. In 2013, Amazon shifted their supply chain strategy to optimize their delivery speed, so they could support new programs aimed at one-day delivery and same-day delivery of food and other items.

Picking and Packing

How is Amazon.com able to efficiently fulfill many millions of orders every month? Part of the answer lies in the way they operate their centers. For the larger facilities, fulfillment of an order goes sort of like this:

- **Step 1.** When you place an order at Amazon.com and designate a delivery destination, the computer program knows from where the order is going to be shipped. It is usually shipped from an Amazon's fulfillment center or from the sellers' locations. Sellers have an option to ship their merchandise to Amazon.com for storage and processing. Amazon lists the products in its online catalog and may advertise the product(s). When an order arrives, a computer program will route the order to where it will be fulfilled. Amazon.com has dozens of distribution centers. In general, a typical Amazon.com distribution center operates in the following way.
- **Step 2.** All orders received are routed electronically by the dispatcher to specific parts pickers for fulfillment.
- **Step 3.** The items (such as books, games, and CDs) are stocked in bins in the warehouses. Each bin is equipped with a red light. When an item in the bin needs to be picked up, the red light turns on. Pickers then pick up the items from the bins with red lights and then turn off the lights.
- **Step 4.** Each picked item is placed in a basket with a barcode designating the order number. The baskets are placed on a 10-mile-long winding conveyor belt in the warehouse. Each basket is directed automatically to a specific destination point guided by barcode readers.
- **Step 5.** Each full basket is checked to assure that the barcodes are matched with a specific order. Then the items are moved to appropriate chutes, where they slide into delivery boxes. The system arranges for multiple items to reach this same box if there are several items in one order.

- **Step 6.** The boxes are then sealed for delivery. If gift wrapping was selected, this is done by hand.
- **Step 7.** The full boxes are then taped, weighed, labeled, and routed to one of the truck bays in the warehouse for shipment; some are owned by UPS, the US Postal Service (USPS), and other shippers.

Del Rey (2013) provides a photo slideshow of the operation of one of Amazon.com's largest centers located in Phoenix, AZ.

- *Fulfillment Centers* differentiated by the size of the products being packaged.
- *Replenishment Centers* for receiving incoming goods from vendors.
- *Customer Return Centers* obviously dedicated to returns.
- *Sortation Centers* receiving pallets of packages from Fulfillment Centers, the aggregating and sorting of the pallets by zip code so they can be distributed to the USPS facility handling the associated zip codes. The USPS is one of the vendors that deliver the packages the "last mile."
- *Delivery Stations*, which are midsized centers, networked together with smaller *Amazon Fresh & Pantry* sites to handle same-day home delivery in urban areas of groceries and general merchandise.
- *Specialty Sites* are for dealing with smaller packages of textbooks, clothing, jewelry, and shoes.
- *Prime Now* and *Flex Hubs* are smaller facilities for handling a limited number of high-demand items (especially for *Prime* customers) to be delivered in 1–2 h in urban areas.

Specialization of Distribution Centers

Yet, that is only part of the story. The real optimization comes from the division of labor and specialization of the various centers, especially their new "sortation" centers. For a detailed discussion of the changes, see Wulfraat (2014, 2016).
Today, the facilities include:

The Army of Robots

To expedite fulfillments, Amazon is using tens of thousands of robots in its fulfillment centers. For a description, see section "Warehousing, Robots, and Warehouse Management Systems".

Delivery by Drones

The fastest possible way to deliver items to individual customers is by using drones. This method will be used when several legal and other obstacles are overcome. See the description in section "Delivery to Customers: From Robots to Drones".

The Results

Table 13.1 provides some sense of the distribution of the centers across the various types, as well as the size of the various facilities. Overall, there are around 290 facilities occupying over 110 million square feet. The majority of these (160) are *Fulfillment Centers* taking up the majority of the square footage (over 100 million).

Table 13.1 Amazon distribution center network

	Type	#Centers	SqFt(M)	F# Centers	FSqFt(M)
United States	Fulfillment	76	59.9	17	12.7
	Sortation	26	7.1	3	0.8
	Prime Now	43	0.7	0	0
	Delivery/sort	16	1.3	0	0
	Subtotal	161	69.0	20	13.5
Rest of the world	Fulfillment	83	41.4	6	5
	Prime Now	23	0.1	1	0.1
	Delivery/sort	24	1.6	0	0
	Subtotal	131	43.1	7	5.1
Global	Total	292	112.1	27	18.6

Source: Based on data from Wulfraat (2016)
M million, *F* future

While all of these serve as key roles, the ones with probably the greatest impact have been the 26 *Sortation Centers*. These have not only helped Amazon to accomplish their goal of same-day delivery, but, more importantly, they have also enabled Amazon to substantially reduce their reliance on UPS and FedEx transportation and have enabled Amazon to gain control over their shipping and delivery. Unlike offline retailers who have their own carriers and fleets, Amazon has had to utilize UPS, FedEx, and other third-party carriers due to the large volume and the number of destinations. During peak selling seasons (e.g., the winter holidays), Amazon has to vie with other retailers for UPS and FedEx services. The *Sortation Centers* have cut much of that reliance by shifting to USPS delivery. The cost reductions have been massive and there is no competition with other retailers. There is little doubt that they are laying the groundwork for their own fleet—not only on the ground but also in the air.

The success of Amazon's supply chain has been amazing. They have been a first mover on a number of supply chain fronts, especially in the EC world, and continue to do so. During 2015, not only did they become the fastest company to reach $100 billion in annual sales, but also they were recognized (by their peers) as #1 on the Gartner (2015) rankings of the top 25 supply chain companies. The company is attributing this success to a program called *Fulfillment by Amazon*. In their words:

You sell it, we ship it. Amazon has created one of the most advanced fulfillment networks in the world, and your business can benefit from our expertise. With Fulfillment by Amazon (FBA), you store your products in Amazon's fulfillment centers, and we pick, pack, ship, and provide customer service for these products. Best of all, FBA can help you scale your business and reach more customers.

Toward this end, they have recently taken a large minority stake in Atlas Air that has the largest fleet of 747 freighter aircraft.

Sources: Based on Del Rey (2013), Wulfraat (2014, 2016), and Amazon *Annual Report* 2015 available at **services.amazon.com/fulfillment-by-amazon/how-it-works.htm** (accessed January 2017).

LESSONS LEARNED FROM THE CASE

The opening case illustrates to us how the world's largest e-tailer fulfills the many millions of orders arriving every week. The major activities are acquisition, storage, picking up, packaging, and delivery of physical items worldwide. The success of Amazon is based on their control of the supply chain, automating their warehouses (e.g., using many robots) and controlling their supply chains. Finally, Amazon strives to deliver very quickly. Several of these topics are described in this chapter.

13.1   ORDER FULFILLMENT AND LOGISTICS: AN OVERVIEW

Comparatively speaking, taking orders and payments over the Internet may be the easy part of B2C. Fulfilling orders and delivering the ordered items to the customers' doors can be the tricky part. For example, consider Amazon.com that initially started out as a totally virtual company accepting orders and payments but relying on third parties to fulfill and deliver the orders. Eventually, they came to realize that they needed physical warehouses with thousands of employees and robots in order to expedite deliveries and substantially reduce order fulfillment costs. In order to understand the importance of order fulfillment and delivery in EC, as well as the complexities and problems associated with each, you first have to have a general understanding of the following concepts.

Basic Concepts of Order Fulfillment and Logistics

Regardless of the type of product and the type of commerce involved—online or off—**order fulfillment** refers to all the operations a company undertakes from the time it receives an order to the time the items are delivered to the customers, including all related customer service. For example, a customer must receive assembly and operation instructions with a new appliance. This can be done by including a paper document with the product or by providing the instructions on the Web. In addition, if the customer is dissatisfied with a product, an exchange or return must be arranged.

Order fulfillment encompasses a number of *back-office operations*, which are the activities that support the fulfillment of orders, such as packing, delivery, accounting, inventory management, and shipping. It also is strongly related to the *front-office operations*, or *customer-facing activities*, such as advertising and order taking, that are visible to customers.

Obviously, the overall objective of order fulfillment is to deliver the right product, to the right customer in a timely, cost-effective, and profitable manner. The way these objectives are achieved varies between e-tailing and offline retailing because e-tailers are focused on delivering smaller numbers of items directly to the individual consumer, while many retailers are focused on delivering volumes of products to stores' shelves. Of course, these days' e-tailing and conventional retailing are intertwined because most retailers have multiple sales and service channels—the Web, mobile, in store, call center, etc. This requires them to integrate the various channels, enabling customers to order from anywhere and pick up or receive from anywhere.

For a comprehensive guide, see **shopify.com/blog/14069585-the-beginners-guide-to-ecommerce-shipping-and-fulfillment**.

The EC Order Fulfillment Process and Elements

In order to understand why there are problems in order fulfillment, it is beneficial to look at a typical EC fulfillment process and elements, as shown in Fig. 13.1. The process starts on the left, when an order is received, and after verification that it is a real order, several activities take place, some of which can be done simultaneously; others must be done in sequence. These activities include the following steps:

1. Customer places an order and pays for it
2. Payment verification by the seller if needed
3. Check for in-stock availability. Notify buyer if and when available

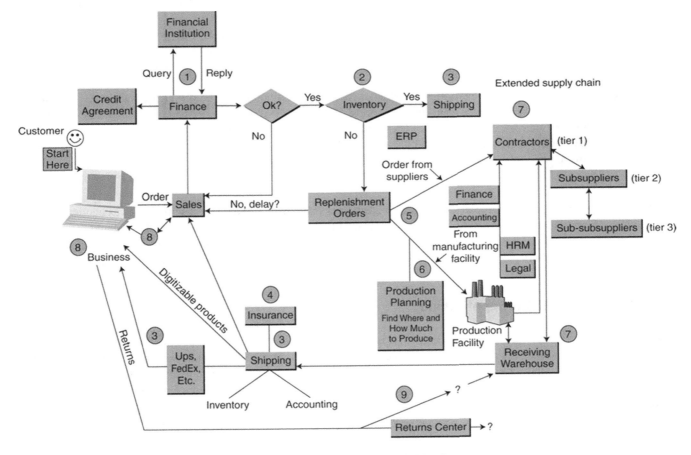

Note: Demand forecasts and accounting are conducted at various points throughout the process.

Fig. 13.1 Order fulfillment activities

4. Determine whether inventory should be replenished (and whether additional production is required)
5. Locate the warehouse where each order can be handled. Transmit the order to a warehouse (or fulfillment center)
6. Pick and pack order for shipment
7. Dispatch fulfilled orders to customer
8. Customer receives the goods
9. Sellers manage returns if needed

Operation Models

Order fulfillment processes may vary, depending on the types of products (e.g., by size, perishability, etc.), whether third parties are involved in warehousing and shipping and whether the business is primarily B2C or B2B, and on the company's strategies and operation models. Often, retailers and the manufacturing partners are differentiated by these strategies and models. The basic operation models, which predate EC by 20 years, are well known to supply chain experts and practitioners, and they include:

- **Engineer-to-order (ETO).** Here, the product is designed and built to customer specifications; this approach is the most common in customized products (e.g., jewelry).
- **Make-to-order (MTO).** Aka *build-to-order* (BTO) is used with low-demand products that are manufactured to customer specifications (custom made). They are only built after the order is actually in hand. Most typical in e-commerce.
- **Assemble-to-order (ATO).** Aka *assemble-to-request*, these are products built to customer specifications from a stock of existing components. This requires a modular product architecture for the finished products. The best known example of this approach is the way in which Dell manufactures their computers. Very typical in e-commerce.
- **Make-to-stock (MTS).** For standardized products that sell in high volumes. The product is built against a sales forecast and sold to the customer from finished goods. This means that demand can be quickly met. For example, many of the consumer packaged goods (CPG) in grocery stores are of this sort.
- **Digital copy (DC).** Where products are digital assets and inventory is created from a digital master. Copies are created on demand and downloaded to a customer's storage device.

Because clothing and apparel, (packaged) food, and electronics equipment are the largest selling B2C categories, the most frequently used models are MTS and ATO. While managing and fulfilling orders for these types of products would seem straightforward, they can suffer from the characteristics of the generic supply chain because of spikes in demand (e.g., Black Friday), or disruptions caused by a shortage of source component parts or materials, or the sudden comings and goings of popular styles.

Order Fulfillment and the Supply Chain

The nine-activity order fulfillment process (Fig. 13.1) is an integral part of the *supply chain*. The flows of orders, payments, information, materials, and parts need to be coordinated among all the company's relevant departments' participants, as well as with and among all relevant external partners. The procedures of supply chain management (SCM) must be considered when planning and managing the order fulfillment process, which, due to its complexity, may have problems. Many of these factors are covered in the opening case, which describes how Amazon.com fulfills its orders. It also provides a brief look at Amazon's underlying strategies, the processes involved, and some of the issues that are encountered.

In this chapter, we cover only the major activities in the process, which are illustrated in Fig. 13.1. These major activities are summarized in Fig. 13.2 together with the section number in this chapter where they are discussed.

The major problems along the supply chain are discussed in detail in section "Problems in Order Fulfillment Along the Supply Chain", and the solutions to several of these problems are found in section "Solutions for Order Fulfillment Problems Along the Supply Chain".

Fig. 13.2 Highlights of EC
order fulfillment

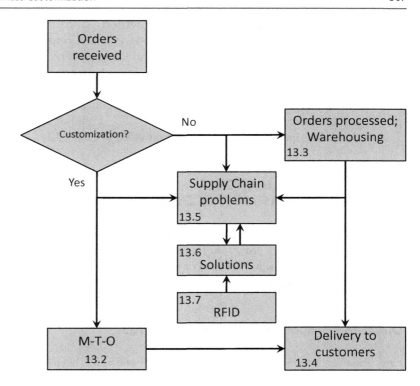

SECTION 13.1 REVIEW QUESTIONS

1. Define order fulfillment.
2. Compare traditional logistics with e-logistics.
3. List the nine activities of the order fulfillment process.
4. Describe the major operation models.
5. Relate order fulfillment to supply chains.

13.2   ORDER FULFILLMENT IN MAKE-TO-ORDER (MTO) AND MASS CUSTOMIZATION

As you may recall from Chap. 1, one of the advantages of EC is the ability to easily customize products and personalize services. Although taking customized orders is done online, the fulfillment of such orders may not be simple when physical items are involved. Mass production enabled companies to reduce the price per unit. Customization is usually more expensive, since each item must be handled separately. Customization also requires time, especially for large products like cars. However, consumers usually want customized products to be delivered in a timely fashion at prices that are not much higher than those of similar standard products that are mass-produced. Therefore, the question is how do suppliers, manufacturers, or retailers do this at a reasonable cost to themselves and in a reasonable time for their customers?

Mass Customization, Make-to-Order, and Assemble-to-Order

Companies like to sell large quantities of similar products, which are customized. It is similar to ordering a hamburger from Burger King or McDonald's, which is done the way you like it. To do so, companies use a **mass customization** approach.

Example: Dell Computer Assemble-to-Order Method

Dell was a pioneer in providing customized products to end consumers in a timely and cost-effective fashion using mass customization approach. They were able to do this using mass-produced components that were assembled to meet the customized orders of their customers. This approach has been adopted by many other manufacturers. Most customized are computers, cars, shoes, toys, textbooks, and wedding rings. Of course, when you talk about millions of computers at Dell, the supply chain, the logistics, and the delivery of components are critical to its success and survival. Dell is a classic example of assemble-to-order.

A detailed description of Dell's system is provided in Case 13.1.

CASE 13.1: EC APPLICATION
DELL'S WORLD-CLASS SUPPLY CHAIN AND ORDER FULFILLMENT SYSTEM

Dell Computer is a pioneer of self-configuration PCs from standard components. To deal with the huge number of orders, the company needed a superb order fulfillment system. Furthermore, frequently it was necessary to ship parts (e.g., monitors and towers) from different locations so the customers would get a complete system at the same time. Dell was so successful that it was ranked for years at the top of US supply chain companies.

Direct-to-Consumer and Configure-to-Order

One of the key reasons for Dell's continued high ranking has been the quality of their logistics and order fulfillment systems. Dell was a pioneer in the direct-to-order consumer business model, as well as the *configure-to-order* method of manufacturing which is used today by most computer manufacturers. For much of the time period between 2004 and present day, this business model and manufacturing method served Dell well. Dell was able to automate both the order-taking and fulfillment processes, enabling the company to coordinate with their suppliers to produce the specific components and finished products required to fill the various customer orders at various locations.

This system enabled Dell to handle the overwhelming majority of their online purchase orders through an Internet portal. The portal was used by suppliers to view the requirements of various orders and to work with Dell on forecasted requirements and delivery dates. In this way, only those components required to fulfill current orders were shipped to Dell's factories. The result was a substantial reduction in the flow of parts, the warehouse space required to manage the parts, and idle inventory. Compared to other competitors, Dell had less than 4 days of inventory at any given time, while their competitors had more than 30 days of inventory on hand.

In both computer electronics, components and models have a short life span. Today's computer models are rapidly becoming obsolete. Dell's automated system has enabled the company to deal with the short life problem, as well as helping their suppliers respond rapidly to changing demand. For details, see Dudovskiy (2015).

Assemble-to-Order

A large portion of Dell's business is B2B. Organizations purchase hundreds or thousands of PCs, tablets, printers, etc. As indicated earlier, Dell is minimizing its in-house inventory of components. The fulfillment process is shown in Fig. 13.3 and it is self-explanatory.

Segmented Supply Chain

In 2008, things began to change for Dell. Dell found that their online configure-to-order system was too inflexible and resulted in configurations that were too expensive as compared with other, faster-growing business segments—their retail stores, enterprise customers, and high-volume consumer products. In each case, fewer, cheaper configurations were required. Because of the mismatch between their supply chain model and the expectations of their newer customers in newer channels, Dell's competitors were able to capture a significant market share. In response, Dell decided to transform its supply chain into a segmented model, with different procedures for different types of customers. The result was four supply chain segments, each focusing on a different type of customer. The four segments are displayed in Table 13.2 along with their distinguishing characteristics.

Fig. 13.3 Changes in the
supply chain (linear vs. hub)

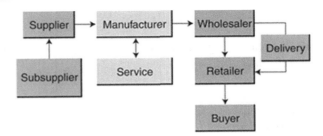

Traditional Linear Supply Chain

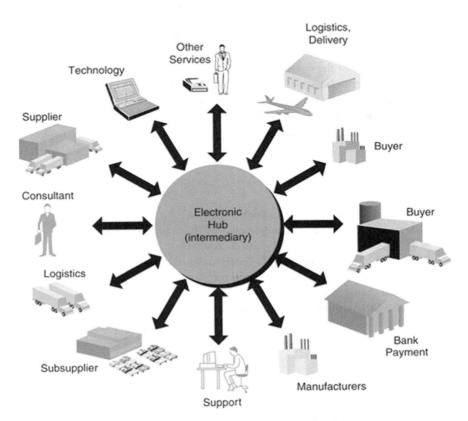

Hub-Based Structure of the Supply Chain

Copyright ©2012 Pearson Education, publishing as Prentice Hall

Table 13.2 Dell's segmented supply chain

SC production policy	*Build-to-order:* built when configured order received	*Build-to-plan:* built in anticipation of forecasted demand	*Build-to-stock:* built and stocked in anticipation of demand	*Build-to-spec:* built in short time period according to corporate specs with no inventory stocks
SC segment	Online	Retail	Online	Corporate
Volume	Low	High	High	Med-high
Product batch size	One	Large	Large	Med-large
Finished goods inventory	No	Yes, at retailer	Yes, at Dell	No
Lead time	Short	Long	Long	Long

Source: Based on Simchi-Levi et al. (2012) and Thomas (2016)

Dell is using this and other innovations to reach emerging markets (Blanchard 2012). Dell supply chain's complexity can be seen in a Google search for images of "Dell computer supply chain." See also Fig. 2 in Dubovsky (2015).

Results

Dell's shift to a segmented supply chain substantially impacted the efficiencies and effectiveness of their supply chain. Some of the major benefits included:

- Improved product availability
- Reduced order-to-delivery times
- Fewer configurations required to meet customer demand
- Improved forecast accuracy
- Reduced transportation and manufacturing costs

Up until 2011, these improvements served Dell's bottom line well. In 2011, they were ranked number 2 on the supply chain list of the top 25; in 2012, they were number 4, and in 2013, they were number 11. The shift in rankings in 2013 was primarily a result of the declining revenues in their PC business and had little to do with the performance of their supply chain. Dell's overall business model was built on providing PC systems for businesses and consumers. This business has been severely impacted by the rapid increase in smartphones and tablets, which has eroded the demand for PCs. It will take more than improvements in the supply chain to address the declining demand.

Sources: Based on Hofman et al. (2013), Simchi-Levi et al. (2012), Dubovsky (2015), and Thomas (2016).

Questions

1. Describe the process of self-configuration.
2. How does Dell manage its component flow from its suppliers?
3. Why is Dell's business model mass customization?
4. What type of supply chain did Dell originally have? What were its benefits?
5. Why did Dell encounter supply chain problems around 2008?
6. What is a segmented supply chain?
7. Describe Dell's segmented supply chain.
8. View the slide show at **slideshare.net/thushan89/supply-chain-in-dell** and find material relevant to this case. Write a summary.

Make-to-Order and Assemble-to-Order

In MTO and ATO, you also need to closely collaborate with your suppliers. In addition, you need to have flexible production lines where changes are made quickly and inexpensively (e.g., painting cars at Toyota), and you need tools that enable quick and not-so-expensive production changes (usually driven by computerized systems). The technology of 3D printing is often used for these purposes. This is usually a part of an *intelligent factory* or production line, like those of Siemens AG, IBM, and General Electric. It is also like the distributed mass customization approach used at Etsy (**etsy.com**). Etsy is an online market for goods that are custom made by small producers and sold online in one electronic marketplace. For sources on intelligent factories and mass customization, see the *International Journal of Mass Customization*, for *Smart Factory*, and (**belden.com/blog/industrialethernet/The-Smart-Factory-of-the-Future-Part-1.cfm**).

Using 3D Printing for Mass Customization

Of the several technologies that can be used to support customization in e-commerce, probably the most promising one is 3D printing.

3D printing, also known as *additive manufacturing*, is a manufacturing process that uses a computer-aided design (CAD) to create a *digital model* which is sliced into very thin cross sections, called layers. The 3D layers are placed one over the other to create three-dimensional physical objects. In reality, the process is not as simple as it sounds. According to Stratasys, a large 3D vendor:

The vendor of 3D printing is at times a tangled web of technologies, materials, and new processes and capabilities and that can make navigating the 3D ecosystem difficult. 3D printing doesn't refer to one kind of manufacturing or technological process and therefore a well-rounded understanding requires an in-depth look into all available 3D printing systems.

To help you with understanding 3D, the company provides you with a free tutorial: **stratasys.com/resources/what-is-3d-printing**. The tutorial includes a 3:33 min video.

The technology is significant because it offers a process that lets you go from design (CAD) directly to physical product via a computer and a printer (of the layers). This process enables the creation of products of almost any shape and forms plastic and other materials, fairly inexpensively, since you do not need to build a prototype of the objects. Furthermore, this technology enables buyers to get instant, custom-generated quotations for their desired objects.

Some believe that 3D printing will change the world (e.g., Homic 2015). Many call it a manufacturing revolution (e.g., Wallach-Kloski and Kloski 2016, and Turney 2016).

3D and e-Commerce

3D is one of the best technologies for supporting EC mass customization due to its relatively low cost and the speed with which items can be produced (see Fabian 2015). Some believe that the future of e-commerce will depend on 3D. Industries such as fashion, jewelry, and toys can greatly be impacted by 3D. For example, Koslow (2015) describes the fashion industry, e-commerce, and 3D printing connection. For a case study about jewelry 3D support, see **3dsystems.com/learning-center/case-studies/3d–printing-helps-jewelry-start-ride-mass-customization-wave**.

An interesting example of make-to-order shoes is presented in Case 13.2.

CASE 13.2: EC APPLICATION
FEETZ INC. IS USING 3D FOR MASS CUSTOMIZATION IN E-COMMERCE

Finding the proper shoes may be difficult. It is not only the size, it is also the material used, the color, the style, and the look and feel. You can go to a make-to-order physical store. There, they will measure your feet. There, however, you will have only limited options for styles and colors. In addition, when you order your shoes, you usually will pay a lot, and you are limited by store location and the available options.

How about self-configuration online; you will have over seven million possible combinations of materials, styles, sizes, and colors to choose from. It sure is better than finding shoes in a brick-and-mortar store, and you get what you really want and you may even pay less. All you have to do is to go to **feetz.com**.

How Does Feetz Work?

1. Download an app to your mobile device.
2. Follow the instructions for creating a 3D digital model of your feet.
3. Feetz will use a 3D printer to customize your shoes. The shoes will be delivered to your home in less than 2 weeks.

Furthermore, should your shoes wear out, ship them back and Feetz will recycle them and deliver a new pair to you (for a small fee).

The company did considerable trials to assure the look and quality of their shoes. They are using the Airwolf 3D printer for this purpose.

Sources: Condensed from **airwolf3d.com/2016/06/29/mass-customization-3d-printers-feetz** and from **feetz.com/story.php**.

Questions

1. Enter the above-cited Airwolf website and view the 4:43 min video. Answer the following questions:
   (a) How was the idea for the business started?
   (b) List some of the technical challenges encountered by Lucy Beard.
   (c) What is the future vision for 3D manufactured shoes?

2. What is the contribution of the 3D printing?
3. View buying shoes online without customization (e.g., at Zappos.com or Kickz.com). Write a comparison between buying from Feetz.

Using Robots with Make-to-Order Fulfillment

Robots have long been involved in manufacturing, especially in the auto industry. Most of the older versions deployed in auto factories were large, cumbersome, and dedicated to a single task like welding or painting. More recently, smaller bots are being produced that are "smarter, more mobile, more collaborative, and more adaptable" (Hagerty 2015). Some of these have been designed to handle the tricky job of assembling consumer electronic items from standard parts, which is still mostly done by hand in many places. Robots are also designed to assist humans rather than replacing them. A case in point is a bot product from the partnership of ABB Ltd. and Rethink Robotics, Inc. They are designed to handle small parts and to sense when parts are being assembled incorrectly. They are also more programmable so they can adapt very quickly to new requirements and uses. To see the bot in action, go to **rethinkrobotics.com**. For using robots in mass customization, watch the video at **youtube.com/watch?v = HJzzPXeDdX8**.

Robots are also used in warehousing as illustrated in section "Warehousing, Robots, and Warehouse Management SystemsS54S54". Some even see robots as major player in the future of e-commerce.

SECTION 13.2 REVIEW QUESTIONS

1. Define customization.
2. Define mass customization.
3. Describe mass customization.
4. What is make-to-order? What is assemble-to-order?
5. Explain the use of 3D printing to facilitate MTO.
6. Explain the use of robots in MTO production.
7. Relate this section to mass customization.

13.3 WAREHOUSING, ROBOTS, AND WAREHOUSE MANAGEMENT SYSTEMS

Warehousing plays a major role in EC fulfillment of standard (not make-to-order) objects. Most EC businesses are fulfilled from make-to-stock standard items. Alternatively, as described earlier, EC vendors can take orders and let someone else fulfill them (dropshipping), or they can stock the items in their own warehouses to enable fast fulfillment. The warehousing activities include:

- Receiving merchandise
- Storing merchandise
- Picking up items when orders are received
- Packing up the items (e.g., see Mohan 2014)
- Arranging delivery (Williams 2016)

These activities can be done in *distribution centers*, as was described in Amazon's opening case. For detail on warehousing and the related inventory management system, see **dlca.logcluster.org/display/LOG/Warehousing+and+Inventory+Management**.

In EC, there is a need to automate as much as possible due to the large number of orders and shipments. This is done by robots and warehouse management systems.

Example of a distribution center is provided by the Newegg example.

Example: Newegg's Distribution Center

Newegg is a very large EC electronic e-tailer in the United States. The company has several distribution centers in the United States and Canada. One of their newest centers is a 400,000 square foot large in Indianapolis, IN. The system includes, according to Bastian Solution (2016), the following key technologies:

- Hybrid of OPEX Perfect Pick (solutions/technology/goods-to-person/perfect-pick) and operator pick modules.
- High-velocity picking are using pick to light (solutions/technology/supply-chain-software/picking-technology/pick-to-light) devices.

- Pick to voice (solutions/technology/supply-chain-software/picking-tecnology/voice-picking) used in remaining pick areas.
- Automated print and apply systems for order induction and shipping.
- Determine machine size for unique order case sizes.
- 3000 feet each of zip line (**bastiansolutions.com/shop/conveyor/zipline-conveyor**) and Hytrol conveyor (**bastiansolutions.com/shop/conveyor/hytrol-conveyors-and-parts**).
- Human Machine Interface (**bastiansolutions.com/solutions/service/industrial-controls/human-machine-interface**) for system visibility and monitoring.
- Exacta Warehouse Control System (WCS) (**bastiansolutions.com/solutions/technology/supply-chain-software/warehouse-control-system**).

The major results are:

- **High system throughput**—up to 18,000 orders per day during peak season, 6–8000 per day on average.
- **Reduced order cycle time** to 20 min.
- **High system accuracy**—picking allows for scanning of each item.
- **Low shipping cost**—pack size machine produces 200 different shipping containers for best cube.
- **Security**—high-end items safely in OPEX Perfect Pick.
- **Scalability**—easily expand Perfect Pick aisles to accommodate growth.

You can watch the system in a video (5.36 min) at **bastiansolutions.com/case-studies/e-commerce/newegg**. (Click on the OPEX picture.)

Using Robots (Bots) in Warehouses

In 2012, Amazon bought a robot company called Kiva Systems for $775 million. By 2016, more than 30,000 Kiva robots have been deployed to about 15 of Amazon's larger fulfillment centers. The robots are used to assist workers with picking and packing activities. There are several videos on the Web that illustrate how they go about their work (e.g., **vimeo.com/113374910**).

Robots operate a bit differently than one might think (Valerio 2015). The items to be picked and packed reside in bins on moveable pallets called pods. A single pod can hold hundreds of items. Fully loaded, the pods can weigh up to 3000 lbs. At first blush, the logical thing to do would be to use the *man-to-goods* method. In other words, if you need an item, simply send a bot to retrieve it. In reality, Kiva works the other way around—the *goods-to-man* method.

There are two types of bots, both of which look sort of like big Roombas, the robot vacuum cleaners from iRobot company, except they are square, not round. One type, the S model, is 2 × 2.5 × 1 foot and can lift close to 1000 lbs. The other type, a G model, is a bigger version and can lift up to 3000 lbs. Both of them can fit under the bottom section of the pods. When an item order is received, it is entered into a database of the computer that controls the robots. Software on the same computer searches for the bot that is closest to the pod and directs the bot via Wi-Fi to retrieve the pod holding the item. At this point, the bot follows a series of QR code reflectors placed on the floor (like lane markers on a road) to find the correct pod, and the bot slides under the pod, lifts it, and carries it back to a specified human operator. The operator picks out the correct item and puts it in a shipment package, hence, the moniker *goods-to-man*. At this point, the bot is ready to go again. Bots travel about 1.3 m a second and require recharging about every hour for 5 min.

Kiva's approach to automated handling systems for e-fulfillment also works well with in-store restocking, part distribution, and medical device distribution operations. Thus far, the system has proven to be more accurate and efficient than humans.

At the time Kiva was originally purchased, it was also being used by other retailers like Walgreens, Staples, Crate & Barrel, and the Gap. Almost immediately, Amazon ended Kiva support for these outside companies. In the interim, a series of new robot competitors moved to fill the void. Some examples are Swisslog's CarryPick (**swisslog.com/carrypick**), GrayOrange's Butler (**greyorange.com/products/butler**), and Grenzeback's Carry AGV (**grenzebach.com**). While there are some differences in terms of speed, strength, and delivery targets (e.g., conveyors), almost all operate on the same goods-to-man principle. See Tobe (2015) for details about these and other systems.

Robotic automation is believed to play a major role in EC warehouses (see Bhaiya 2016, Technology Story 2016, and Martin 2015).

There is a strong belief among the proponents of these sorts of robotic applications that enable small companies to better compete against larger companies and for companies in higher-wage countries to better compete against the likes of China and other lower-wage countries.

Warehouse Management System (WMS)

Although it seems like a misnomer, one way to manage inventory is with a **warehouse management system (WMS)**. On the surface, WMS refers to a software system that helps managing warehouses, which it does. However, any market-leading WMS also provides:

- **Inbound functions** such as yard management, appointment scheduling, multi-method receiving, cross docking, put-to-store, quality assurance, staging, and put-away
- **Inventory functions** such as inventory visibility, lot-serial control, multilevel holds, counts, replenishments, value-added services (VAS) processing, work order processing, internationalization, and slotting
- **Resource management** such as dynamic pick location assignment, equipment utilization, facility utilization, task management, automation interfaces, and workforce management
- **Outbound functions** such as shipment order management, multi-method order picking, retail in-store and dark-store picking and processing of e-commerce orders, cartonization, shipping and parcel manifesting, sequenced staging and loading, and compliance of shipping documents
- **3PL/divisional support** such as multiclient architecture, client billing, client-based process modeling, cross client optimization, client visibility, and reporting

See **jda.com** for a description of the detailed capabilities of a WMS.

A WMS is useful in reducing inventories and decreasing the number of out-of-stock incidents. Such systems also are useful in maintaining an inventory of repair items so repairs can be expedited, picking items out of storage bins in the warehouse, receiving items at the receiving docks, and automating the warehouse operations. For example, introducing a make-to-order production process and providing timely and accurate demand information to suppliers can minimize inventories and out-of-stock incidents. In some instances, the ultimate inventory improvement is to have no inventory at all; for products that can be digitized (e.g., software), order fulfillment can be instantaneous and can eliminate the need for inventory.

SECTION 13.3 REVIEW QUESTIONS

1. List the activities done in warehousing.
2. How are robots used in warehousing?
3. Describe the "goods-to-man" concept.
4. Describe the functions of WMS.
5. What are the benefits of WMS?

13.4 DELIVERY TO CUSTOMERS: FROM ROBOTS TO DRONES

An integral part of EC order fulfillment is the delivery of physical objects to customers. The difficulty here is the large number of deliveries to the large number of customers. Most EC vendors outsource the delivery to companies such as UPS, USPS, FedEx, and HDL. The major issue here is *speed*. Customers want the items they buy as quickly as possible. In addition, perishable items need to be delivered quickly. And indeed, delivery time in certain cities has already been reduced to hours. The future trend here is to automate delivery by using drones and robots.

Speeding Up Deliveries: From Same Day to a Few Hours

As discussed earlier, a major success factor in EC is the speed within which shoppers receive their orders. And indeed, the competition for fast delivery is intensifying.

Same- Day Delivery

We covered this topic in Chap. 3 as it related to groceries. Also cited there is the increased competition. In addition to Amazon Fresh, many other companies are active in the market. Notable are Instacart, Postmates, and Google Express (see.

Alfs and Harper 2016). However, same-day delivery does not only apply to groceries. Amazon is starting same-day delivery of everything in several large cities. Google Shopping Express is active too and so are eBay, Uber Rush, and others (Bowman 2014). For 1-h delivery, see Halkias (2015).

FedEx initiated the concept of "next-day" delivery in. It was a revolution in door-to-door logistics. A few years later, FedEx introduced its "next-morning delivery" service. In the digital age, however, even the next morning may not be fast enough. Today, we talk about same-day delivery and even delivery within an hour. Deliveries of urgent materials to and from hospitals, shipping auto parts to car service shops, and delivering medicine to patients are additional examples of such a service. The opening case describes the restructuring of Amazon.com's distribution centers for the express purpose of achieving same-day and even hourly delivery service for most US households. Two other newcomers to this area are eFulfillment Service (**efulfillmentservice.com**) and One World Direct (**owd.com**). These companies have created networks for the rapid distribution of products, mostly EC-related ones. They offer national distribution systems across the United States in collaboration with shipping companies, such as FedEx and UPS.

Delivering groceries is another area where speed is important, as discussed in Chap. 3. Quick pizza deliveries have been available for a long time (e.g., Domino's Pizza). Today, many pizza orders can be placed online. Also, many restaurants deliver food to customers who order online. Examples of this service can be found at **gourmetdinnerservice.com.au** and **grubhub.com** companies. Some companies even offer aggregating supply services, processing orders from several restaurants and then making deliveries (e.g., **foodpanda.hk/?ref=dialadinner** in Hong Kong).

Supermarket deliveries are often done same day. Arranging and coordinating such deliveries may be difficult, especially when fresh or perishable food is to be transported. Buyers may need to be home at certain times to accept the deliveries.

Delivery by Drones

Ideally, e-tailers want to deliver faster than you can get products by going to a store and buying there. The futuristic solution is delivery of packages by drones in minutes. **Drones** are self-flying vehicles, which, similarly to self-driving cars, are remotely controlled. A dream? Amazon originally touted that it would come true soon. Obviously, this is going to take longer because of legal, technological (sensors' capabilities), and other constraints; see Black (2014) and watch the video.

Example: Drones Deliver Pizzas

Drones are used extensively by the military and for taking photos from the sky. They are also used for transporting commercial goods in several places. For example, Domino's delivers pizzas in Auckland, New Zealand, where the traffic is often very congested. According to McFarland (2016a), customers that are willing to pay extra for fast delivery receive a notification when the drones are approaching. All the customers have to do is hit a button on their smartphone. Then, the drone will lower the pizza via a tether. The pizza is released and the tether is pulled back to the drone. While there is an extra charge for the service today, in the long term, there will be no extra charge especially when several customers will be served in one drone trip.

Obstacles to Drone Delivery

The major obstacles to drone delivery are the safety and traffic regulations and the rules imposed by the US Federal Aviation Administration in the United States and by similar agencies in other countries. Also, certain situations, cities, or countries may impose additional traffic regulations. In addition, Mehra (2015) sees the following obstacles:

1. *Launching pads* need to be designed and employees need to be trained.
2. *Drones are constrained* by weight limits. It may be necessary to split heavy orders, which adds costs.
3. *Many retailers use dropship vendors*. These vendors will need to invest in drones. Who is going to pay for this?
4. *Distance limits*. Shipping to remote locations may require retailers to transport the drones closer to the customers. This adds to the costs.
5. *Required investment*. It may be a big strain on smaller retailers. Amazon will be happy to pick and deliver to all, but they sure will charge for the service.
6. *Shipping big-ticket items*. Since drones fly only a few hundred feet from the ground, they could be an easy prey for thieves, especially if they know that expensive goods are transported. Insurance costs will go up for sure.
7. *Weather restrictions*. Severe weather can be an obstacle to the drones. Delays are possible.
8. *Uninterrupted service*. Drones are flying machines. They can fall due to accidents, weather conditions, mechanical problems, etc. Therefore, insurance and costs will go up, for sure.

So, what will be the future for drone's delivery? Google is already testing them, see Marsh (2016). Many believe it will be very successful. For example, the US Postal Service is getting ready to use drones (Wing 2016), and Amazon.com already named the service to be *Prime Air*.

However, some are skeptical. For example, Kahn (2016) believes that robots, not drones, are the future of e-commerce deliveries.

Example: Amazon Prime air

One day, we may see a fleet of Prime Air vehicles in the sky, delivering packages to customers' doors. For how the delivery is envisioned, see the video and read the text at **amazon.com/b?node=8037720011**. With Amazon Prime Air, drone delivery is currently being designed and tested for commercial outdoor use under an exemption from FAA regulations. Amazon's current models are designed to deliver packages under 5 lbs. within a 15–20 mile radius. The weight limit covers about 85% of the products they deliver, and the 20 miles covers about 50–65% of the retailer's core "same-day addressable market" (French 2015a).

At the present time, commercial use is banned under FAA regulations unless they give a company an exception. A few years back, Congress asked the FAA to come up with a new set of rules for commercial use. They are expected to issue the rules in 2016 or 2017.

Additional Examples

Amazon is not alone in their quest. Other companies are working on their own tests for small parcel delivery. Some of the more notable efforts include:

- Matternet (**mttr.net**). Working with groups like UNICEF and Doctors Without Borders, a Bay area start-up called Matternet has been using drones to deliver medical supplies and specimens in Switzerland, Haiti, and the Dominican Republic since 2011. Drones provide autonomous transportation. They do not need drivers, are not impeded by traffic congestion, and are low cost and efficient. Currently, their drones can handle loads up to 2 lbs. and can transport items about 10 miles at 40 mph so that the journey takes just under 20 min. Matternet thinks that the medical uses may sway regulators to approve the technology for commercial uses. For a step-by-step description of how the Matternet drones are used, see French (2015b).
- Walmart (**walmart.com**) has some of the same interests in drones as Amazon. They have already tested their use inside their warehouses, and now they have applied for a permit to test them for outdoor package delivery. Initial tests will be focused on deliveries from their retail distribution centers to their own store parking lots within the same locale. From there, the tests will grow to include delivery in small residential neighborhoods. These latter deliveries are of interest because there is a Walmart within 5 miles of 70% of the US population. Walmart is using Chinese-made DJI (**dji.com**) drones in their tests.
- Flirtey (**flirtey.com**). An Australian start-up recently conducted the first FAA-approved drone delivery in the United States. Using GPS guidance, the drone delivered bottled water, emergency food supplies, and a first aid kit to an unoccupied house in Hawthorne, NV. The delivery tested the drone's ability to navigate around buildings, power lines, and streetlights to make the drop in a populated area. Flirtey drones have previously been used to deliver textbooks in Australia and auto parts in New Zealand (Boyle 2016).
- **Google X Project Wing.** Google X has been working on drone delivery since 2014 under the umbrella of a project called Project Wing (Grothaus 2016). Recently, they were awarded a patent for a "mobile receptacle on wheels." The basic idea is to have the drones deliver packages to the receptacles, which will in turn deliver them to the recipient.

Delivery of Medical Supplies

Medical supplies need to be transported quickly. In rural areas and developing countries, such delivery can take hours. The developing country of Rwanda is using drones to deliver medical supplies to hospitals. For details, see McFarland (2016b).

Note: Alibaba and JD.com, Inc., in China deliver healthcare supplies to customers within 3 h! (See Carsten 2015.)

Delivery by Robots

With self-driving cars coming to our roads comes the idea of using a smaller version for EC package deliveries.

Grocery Delivery in Washington DC by Robots

As of fall 2016, rolling *robots* (some call them rolling drones) deliver groceries to homes. The robots use sidewalks. The company, Starship Technologies, already uses the robots in several European countries. According to Etherington (2016):

Starship's decidedly earthbound robots are very reminiscent of wheeled coolers (and they actually can keep things cool, too - useful for grocery delivery), with six wheels and a large antenna for receiving orders from central dispatch. They're pokey when compared to vehicles, with a max speed of 10 mph, but about as fast as a lot of joggers. They can carry around 40 pounds within their gently domed interior, which makes for a decent haul of groceries (especially for single-or double-occupant households).

(This service was in testing during fall 2016.) Robots already deliver mail in Switzerland. For more on robot delivering packages, see Said (2016). For more on drone and robot delivery, see **apparatus.io/Delivery-Robots-The-Future-of-Ecommerce**.

A final note: in China, online deliveries are done using electric bikes. For challenges, see Buckley (2016).

SECTION 13.4 REVIEW QUESTIONS

1. Describe same-day delivery and its importance.
2. Why use drones for deliveries?
3. List the major obstacles for using drones for EC delivery.
4. Provide some examples of drone deliveries.
5. Describe delivery by robots.

13.5   PROBLEMS IN ORDER FULFILLMENT ALONG SUPPLY CHAINS

Order fulfillment is considered a critical success factor for e-commerce. A relatively recent study of close to 600 top supply chain executives conducted by Peerless Research Group (2013) revealed that order fulfillment was very intricate and that management and delivery performance is slipping. As a consequence, customer satisfaction has suffered. The main challenges that these executives and their companies are facing are the following (VanLandingham 2014):

- **Order expectations**. EC orders require higher levels of service and attention. The required delivery times are much shorter, and the order changes and cancelations are frequently done at the last minute.
- **Order accuracy**. If the deliveries to a store are off by a couple of units either way, it is no big deal. If the same thing happens to an EC customer, a merchant might lose the customer's business.
- **Multichannel order management**. Because most companies have separate systems for the various channels, it is very difficult to present one view of the company to consumers. (See the closing case.)
- **Complex distribution**. In contrast to offline orders and deliveries, each EC order is usually small with a few units, and there are many more of them. Packing and shipping is harder. Because consumers cannot "touch, see, and feel" the products before they buy, there are numerous returns.

As a consequence, additional surveys (e.g., Kinnison 2015) frequently show that customer satisfaction suffers because of the fulfillment process. Dissatisfaction is usually the result of (1) inaccurate orders, (2) the lengthy time of the order process, (3) missed delivery schedules, and (4) the lack of visibility as the order moves across the fulfillment process.

These issues and problems are typical of the types of challenges that continue to confront both offline and online businesses. The problems are exacerbated in EC, especially in omni-channel EC, because of the mismatch between standard supply chain structures and processes and the special nature and requirements of EC. For example, most manufacturers' and distributors' warehouses are designed to ship large quantities to a set number of stores; they are not designed to optimally pack and ship small orders to a large number of customers' doors. Improper inventory levels are typical in EC, as are poor delivery scheduling and mixed-up shipments.

At the root of many of the problems and challenges are deficient planning and execution practices. Some of the key causes are:

- **Uncertainties in demand.** Many problems along the EC supply chain stem from demand uncertainties and the difficulties that ensue across the supply chain in trying to meet this uncertain demand. This is where *demand forecasting* comes into play. Here, the major goal is to forecast at a very detailed level in the number of products (at the SKU level) of a certain type that will be needed to meet the demand at specific locations at particular points or time intervals in the future. These forecasts rest on statistical (time series) and business analytic estimates from historical patterns, trends in sales or order data, and causal factors like the weather or promotions. These factors can all change quickly, which is why demand forecasting is as much an art as it is a science. The basic issue is that if the demand plan is wrong, it will ripple across the chain, impacting that planned needs for inventory, raw materials, works in progress, factory capacity, etc. Companies try to address these problems by making adjustments to the forecasts and by sharing the forecasts with the major players in the chain.

- **Lack of information sharing.** In today's world, the flow of information across the supply chain is almost as critical as the flow of goods and services. Information systems support this flow, enabling communication and coordination of the various players and systems in the chain. A good example of the types of issues that arise with poor information flow is the *bullwhip effect*, which is a mismatch between the actual demand for goods and the inventory supplied upstream in the supply chain to meet the assumed demand. The mismatch results in excess inventory and safety stock that is used as a buffer against underestimated demand. In practice, the mismatch grows as you move up the chain from the retailer to the distributor to the supplier to the manufacturer so that variability in inventory and safety stock increases along the way. One way to reduce the mismatch is to ensure that information, and thus visibility, about demand, flows to all the parties involved in real time, so that there is only "one version of the truth."

- **Inadequate logistical infrastructure.** Pure play EC companies are likely to have more problems because they do not have a logistical infrastructure already in place and are forced to use external logistics services rather than in-house departments for these functions—much like Amazon has done with UPS and FedEx. These external logistics services are often called **third-party logistics suppliers (3PL)** or *logistics service providers*. Outsourcing logistics services can be expensive, and it requires more coordination and dependence on outsiders who may not be reliable. For this reason, large online retailers usually have their own physical warehouses, shipping, and distribution systems.

- **Inefficient financial flows.** Note that supply chain problems and improvements refer not only to the flow of goods but also to the flow of information and money. Money flow includes invoicing, payment, collection, and so forth. In spite of the availability of computer-based systems, many suppliers, manufacturers, distributors, and retailers rely on manual and paper-based systems to conduct financial transactions. These inefficient financial processes not only slow the flow of cash across the supply chain but also halt the flow of goods and services and put the various partners at a competitive disadvantage.

SECTION 13.5 REVIEW QUESTIONS

1. What are some of the challenges facing order fulfillment?
2. What are the results of these challenges?
3. What are the four root causes of poor order fulfillment?
4. Describe the bullwhip effect and lack of information sharing.
5. Describe the role of 3PLs.

13.6   SOLUTIONS FOR ORDER FULFILLMENT PROBLEMS ALONG THE SUPPLY CHAIN

Many EC logistics problems are generic; they can be found in the non-Internet world as well. Therefore, many of the solutions that have been developed for these problems in brick-and-mortar companies also work for e-tailers. IT and EC technologies facilitate most of these solutions. They also provide for automation of various processes along the supply chain that usually improve their operations. In this section, we will discuss some of the specific solutions to EC order fulfillment problems along the supply chain.

Improvements in the Order-Taking Activity

One way to excel in order fulfillment is to improve the order-taking activity and its links to fulfillment and logistics. Order taking can be done via e-mail or on a webstore and it may be automated. For example, in B2B, orders can be generated and transmitted automatically to suppliers when inventory levels fall below a certain threshold. It is a part of the *vendor-managed inventory* (VMI) strategy cited in Chap. 4 (for B2B). The result is a fast, inexpensive, and more accurate (no need to rekey data) order-taking process. In B2C, Web-based ordering using electronic forms expedites the process, making it more accurate (e.g., automated processes can check the input data and provide instant feedback), and reduces processing costs for sellers. When EC order taking can interface or integrate with a company's back-office system, it shortens cycle times and eliminates errors.

Order-taking improvements also can take place within an organization, for example, when a manufacturer orders parts from its own warehouse. When delivery of such parts runs smoothly, it minimizes disruptions to the manufacturing process, reducing losses from downtime.

Changing the Structure and Process of the Supply Chain

An efficient solution to many supply chain problems is to change the supply chain structure from a linear to a hub structure as illustrated in Fig. 13.4. Notice that in a hub structure, connection between supply chain partners and elements is much shorter. Also, coordination and control is done at the center of the hub, making the management more efficient, and the structure increases visibility. Long supply chains are usually more susceptible to problems. Also, the hub structure management is usually fully digital, making order fulfillment faster, less expensive, and less problematic. One area of improvement

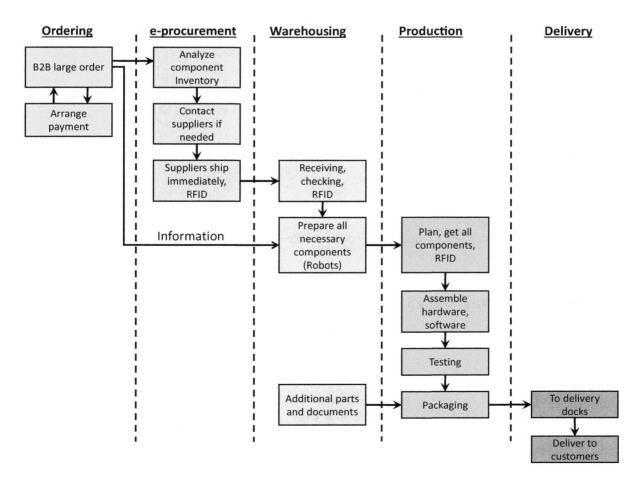

Fig. 13.4 Dell's B2B order fulfillment

is the *visibility* of the inventory, which can be helped by radio frequency identification (RFID) (section "RFID as a Key Enabler in Supply Chain Management"). For the importance of such visibility, see **blog.dydacomp.com/accurate-inventory-visibility-is-key-to-ecommerce-success**.

Integrated Global Logistics Program

An increase in global trading created a need for an effective global logistics system. Order fulfillment problems tend to be even larger in longer supply chains than cross-country borders. The number of partners in such situations is usually larger than in domestic logistics (e.g., customs brokers, global carriers) and so is the need for coordination, communication, and collaboration. Furthermore, such systems require a high level of security, especially when the Internet is the centric technology platform. Integrating separate segments of the supply chain can be very beneficial for minimizing problems in long global chains.

Partnering Efforts and Outsourcing Logistics

An effective way to solve order fulfillment problems is for an organization to partner with other companies. For example, several EC companies have partnered with UPS or FedEx. Similarly, companies outsource Fulfillment by Amazon and Alibaba's Tmall (as discussed in the opening case of this chapter).

Logistics-related partnerships can take many forms. For example, marketplaces may be managed by one of many freight forwarders such as A & A Contract Customs Brokers, a company that helps other companies find "forwarders." Forwarders help prepare goods for shipping and work with carriers to determine the optimal way to ship. Forwarders can also find the least expensive prices on air carriers, and the carriers bid to fill the space with forwarders' goods that need to be shipped.

Supply Chain Segmentation

In Case 13.1(Dell), we introduced the **supply chain segmentation**. Segmentation refers to the creation of several supply chains, each of which fits different types of customers. For how this is done, see Thomas (2016).

SECTION 13.6 REVIEW QUESTIONS

1. How can one improve order taking?
2. Explain the use of a centralized hub in a supply chain.
3. How can one integrate a global supply chain?
4. How can partnering and outsourcing reduce supply chain problems?
5. Describe segmentation and its benefits.

13.7   RFID AS A KEY ENABLER IN SUPPLY CHAIN MANAGEMENT

An effective technology for improving and reducing problems along the end-to-end supply chain is RFID.

The Essentials of RFID

Radio frequency identification (RFID) is a tag technology where RFID tags are attached to or embedded in objects. The tags employ wireless radio wave technology to communicate with the RFID readers, so that the tagged objects can be identified, located, and transmit their data to the readers. Tags are similar to barcodes, but they contain much more information. In addition, they can be read wirelessly from a longer distance (up to 50 feet).

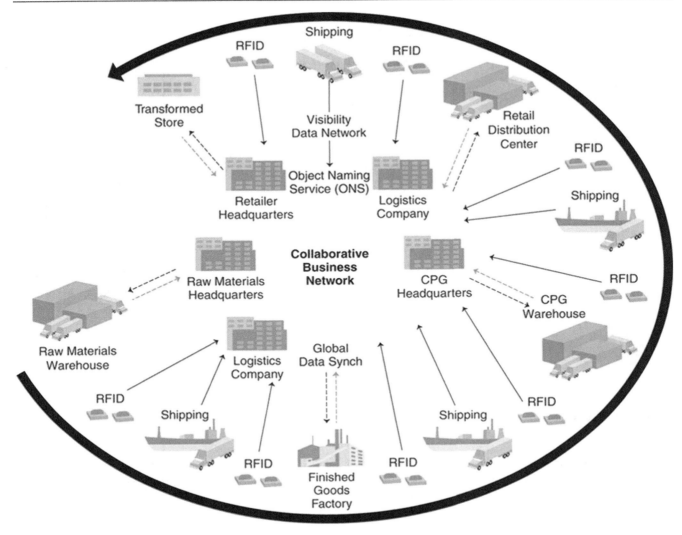

Fig. 13.5 Digital supply chains (Source: Intel, "Building the Digital Supply Chain: An Intel Perspective." Intel Solutions White Pater, January 2005, Figure 5, p. 9.)

Theoretically, RFID can be utilized and read in many places along the supply chain, as illustrated in Fig. 13.5. Over the long run, RFID tags will be attached to most individual items flowing through the supply chain and tracked and monitored at most of the places depicted in Fig. 13.5. To date, cost and privacy issues (e.g., when people carry tagged products, the people can be tracked) have been major inhibitors to the uptake of RFID technology. However, costs are coming down to the point where companies are willing to invest in RFID because they can be more certain of achieving an ROI on their RFID investments. Even when costs are at a reasonable level, organizations still need to learn how to effectively use RFID technologies with their back-office systems. Also, companies need to redesign and retool their business processes so they can accrue solid business benefits from these technologies. RFID technology is used mainly in B2B supply chains. For example, HotSpot, a B2B EC company, increased revenue 50% by using RFID (see **hotspot.com/customers/atlas-rfid**).

Given these developments, what effect will RFID have on supply chains? Such effect is illustrated in Fig. 13.6, which shows the relationship between a retailer (Walmart), a manufacturer (such as P&G), and P&G's suppliers. Note that the tags are read as merchandise travels from the supplier to the retailer (steps 1 and 2). The RFID transmits real-time information on the location of the merchandise. Steps 3 through 6 show the use of the RFID at the retailer, mainly to confirm arrivals (step 3) and to locate merchandise inside the company, control inventory, prevent theft, and expedite processing of relevant information (steps 4 through 6). It is no longer necessary to count inventories, and all business partners are able to view inventory information in real time. This transparency can go several tiers down the supply chain. Additional applications, such as rapid checkout, which eliminates the need to scan each item, will be provided by RFID in the future.

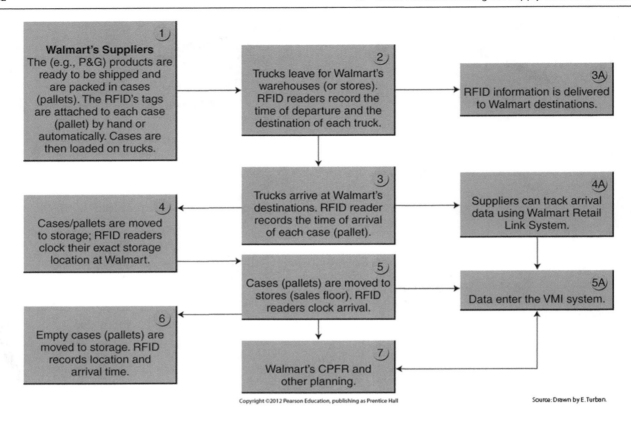

Fig. 13.6 RFID at Walmart

RFID can help improve *supply chain visibility*; see Macy's application Case 13.3, asset visibility and capital goods tracking, returnable asset tracking, work-in-process tracking, as well as managing internal supply chains. For more on RFID, see **rfid.org**. Examples of several applications are presented next.

CASE 13.3: EC APPLICATION
RFID SUPPORTS MACY'S MULTICHANNEL STRATEGY

One innovation in EC is store-based fulfillment for online and mobile orders. In other words, you order online and pick up at the physical store. You can do this at Walmart, Macy's, and many other stores. The strategy is to peg a specific store that is closed to the customers. The problem is that merchants may be reluctant to use RFID (due to privacy concerns) if an item with an RFID tag is carried by people (i.e., if customers carry items with a RFID tag).

A major potential use is when the perpetual inventory in a store is low. The reason is that the perpetual inventory in stores is frequently inaccurate. This may lead to an inability to fulfill orders, resulting in unhappy customers. To solve the problem, Macy's, which adopted the strategy of "order online, pick up in stores" (known as P2LU), decided to use item-level RFID to address the problem. The company hoped that RFID implementation would be a huge sales driver for e-commerce. Macy's roles the program first in a department by department and only in several stores.

According to SCD Staff (2016), RFID allowed, for example, to increase show display compliance from 65–70% to 100%. It also resulted in confidence in-store inventories' level accuracy. Macy's now can accept orders if there is only one item inventory in a specific store. The company is able now to fulfill accurately, even online, fashion order from the last units for sale. In addition, low inventory items are more likely to be sold at or near full price. This saves considerable money, since 15–20% of inventory of last unit is placed on sale without the RFID system.

According to SCD Staff (2016), the system informs the store's associates where the item is located, based on the last RFID cycle count taken, and allows them to find if it has moved since then by using handheld RFID readers, both of which reduce associate search time. Finally, once the online customer picks up the goods, he/she can return it immediately. Also, these customers may purchase additional items in the physical store.

In 2015, Macy's was the superstar award winner by the Retail TouchPoints Organization, for Macy's RFID project. For a complete case study, see **tycoretailsolutions.com/Pages/ArticleDetail.aspx?ItemId=697**.

Sources: Based on SCD Staff (2016).

Questions

1. Why do companies use multichannel marketing?
2. Why does Macy's provide an option for picking up online orders at their stores?
3. The strategy adopted by Macy's with an RFID tag attached to each unit is called "pick to the last unit." Explain how the system works.
4. Find current information about the success of the program.
5. Summarize the benefits to Macy's.

RFID Applications in the Supply Chain Around the Globe

Many potential and actual applications exist in enterprises using RFID (e.g., see *RFID Journal*). The following are representative examples of how RFID is used in the supply chain. For comprehensive coverage, see the *RFID Journal* (**rfi-djournal.com/case-studies**).

RFID at Starbucks

As Starbucks expands its range of fresh foods (such as salads, sandwiches, and the like) available at its stores, the complexity and demands of managing this supply chain increase. Keeping the food fresh depends on keeping it at a steady, cold temperature and ensuring timely delivery. Starbucks is requiring its distributors to employ RFID tags to measure the temperature in the delivery trucks. These tags are programmed to record the temperature inside the truck every few minutes, and on return to the depot, this temperature data can be downloaded and analyzed. If there are unacceptable readings (e.g., the temperature is deemed to have risen too high), efforts are made to determine the cause and remedy of the problem. This can then cause a redesign of critical business processes with regard to the transportation and handling of food. In the future, the tags themselves will be able to detect variations in temperature and send a signal, via IoT, to a thermostat to activate refrigeration fans within the truck.

RFID at Deutsche Post (Germany)

Deutsche Post owns over six million shipping containers that it uses to hold and transport over 70 million letters and other items that pass through its distribution centers daily. In order to process these containers, Deutsche Post was printing in excess of 500 million thick paper labels a month, all of which were thrown away after a single use. It was environmental concerns, rather than purely economic ones, that drove Deutsche Post's RFID initiative.

Deutsche Post uses passive RFID tags with a bistable display, meaning that the text displayed remains on-screen after the power is removed and does not change until the power is restored and an RFID interrogator rewrites the text. Tags on the containers must be readable from all angles and in all types of weather, requiring a robust tag. Furthermore, the tags need to last about 5 years in order for the application to be financially viable.

Deutsche Post developed a custom tag and RFID reader and uses specialized software in this innovative application. Several other post offices around the world use RFID systems (e.g., Canada).

RFID at Atlantic Beef Products (Ontario, Canada)

Cows' ears are tagged with RFID tags. After cows are slaughtered, their ear tags are scanned for food traceability. The carcass goes onto two leg hooks, each equipped with an RFID chip. They are synced to each animal's database record. The RFIDs replace barcodes, which could get contaminated with *E. coli* on the slaughterhouse floor. The RFID tags help tracking the movement of each cow and its meat produced at any time. The system won a gold medal from the Canadian IT organization. For details, see Makepolo (2014).

SECTION 13.7 REVIEW QUESTIONS

1. What is RFID technology?
2. Relate RFID to supply chain visibility.
3. Discuss attaching RFID tags to individual objects.
4. Describe how Macy's is using RFID.

13.8   OTHER ORDER FULFILLMENT TOPICS

Several other topics relate to order fulfillment depending on the objects fulfilled and the location to where shipments are made.

Here we present some typical topics.

Handling Returns (Reverse Logistics)

Allowing for the return of defective or unsatisfactory merchandise and providing for product exchanges or refunds are necessary for maintaining customers' trust and loyalty. Some time ago, it was found that the absence of a good return mechanism was the number two reason for shopper reluctance to buy online. A good return policy is a must in EC.

Dealing with returns is a major logistics problem for EC merchants. Several options for handling returns are:

- **Return the item to the place of purchase.** This is easy to do with a purchase from a brick-and-mortar store, but not a virtual one. To return a product to a virtual store, a customer needs to get authorization, pack everything up, pay to ship it back (if not paid by the retailer), insure it, and wait up to two billing cycles for a credit to show up on his or her credit card statement. The buyer is not happy and neither is the seller, who must unpack, check the paperwork, and resell the item, usually at a loss. This solution is workable only if the number of returns is small or the merchandise is expensive (e.g., diamonds). Some vendors (e.g., Amazon.com) enable customers to print prepaid UPS or USPS shipping labels that make returns easier for the customers.
- **Separate the logistics of returns from the logistics of delivery.** With this option, returns are shipped to an independent return unit and are handled separately. This solution may be more efficient from the seller's point of view, but it does not ease the return process for the buyer.
- **Completely outsource returns.** Several outsourcers, including UPS and FedEx, provide logistics services for returns. The services deal not only with delivery and returns but also with the entire logistics process. FedEx, for example, offers several options for returning goods.
- **Allow the customer to physically drop the returned item at a collection station or at a physical store of the same vendor.** Offer customers locations (such as a convenience store or The UPS Store) where they can drop off returns. In Asia and Australia, returns are accepted in convenience stores and at gas stations. For example, BP Australia Ltd. (gasoline service stations) teamed up with **wishlist.com.au** (now closed), and Caltex Australia is accepting returns at the convenience stores connected to its gasoline stations. The accepting stores may offer in-store computers for ordering and may also offer payment options, as at Japanese 7-Elevens (**7dream.com**). In Taiwan and some other countries, you can order merchandise (e.g., books), pay, pick up the item ordered, and return unwanted items, at a 7-Eleven store. Click-and-mortar stores usually allow customers to return merchandise that was ordered online to their physical stores (e.g., **walmart.com** and **eddiebauer.com**).
- **Auction the returned items.** This option can go hand in hand with any of the previous solutions.

For strategy, guidelines, and other information on returns, see the Reverse Logistics Executive Council publications. Also see **reverselogisticstrends.com**.

Order Fulfillment in B2B

According to recent forecasts by Forrester Research (reported by Demery 2015), online revenues for B2B EC in 2015 were substantially higher than online revenues for B2C EC. The figures in the United States were close to $780 billion for B2B and $304 billion for B2C. The estimate is that B2B will climb to $1.1 trillion in 2020, while B2C will move to $500 billion. In spite of the sizeable difference, B2B EC is far less developed than B2C EC. The differences are found not only in the front-end experience but also in the back-office functionality, including information management, Web content management, and order management.

Some of the major differences in order management capabilities were pinpointed in an earlier survey sponsored by Honeywell and conducted by Peerless Research Group (2013) for *Logistics Management* and *Supply Chain Management Review*. Based on responses from 469 supply chain managers, most of whom were responsible for either B2B or a combination of B2B and B2C EC systems across a range of industries, the survey revealed that:

- The most important missions for their systems were increasing the volume and speed of fulfillment while reducing costs per order, increasing profitability, and improving customer service.
- Many of the inefficiencies and increased costs in order fulfillment were due to increased transportation, packaging, and material costs.
- The keys to addressing the inefficiencies and costs rest with improved supply chain software applications, reengineered (fulfillment) operations, and adoption of supply chain analytics.

B2B fulfillment tends to be more inefficient than in B2C because it is usually more complex. Typically, the shipments are larger, there are multiple distribution channels, the shipment frequency is more varied, the breadth of the carrier services is more uneven, there are fewer EC carrier offerings, and the EC transaction paths are much more complicated. The types of improvements in applications and reengineering of processes needed to resolve these sorts of complications revolve around the automation of physical systems, as well as the use of business process management (BPM) software to automate processes.

For the importance of fulfillment in B2B due to its impact on customers, and for suggestions for improvements, see Insitesoft (2016).

Using e-Marketplaces and Exchanges to Ease Order Fulfillment Problems in B2B

In Chap. 4, we introduced a variety of e-marketplaces and exchanges. One of the major objectives of these entities is to improve the operation of the B2B supply chain. Let us see how this works with different business models.

- A company-centric marketplace can solve several supply chain problems. For example, CSX Technology developed an extranet-based EC system for tracking cross-country train shipments as part of its supply chain initiative and was able to effectively identify bottlenecks and provide more accurately forecast demand.
- Using an extranet, Toshiba America provides an ordering system for its dealers to buy replacement parts for Toshiba's products. The system smooths the supply chain and delivers better customer service.
- HighJump Software suggested taking into account a number of key elements for optimal order fulfillment including the automation of picking, packing, and shipping, the transformation of paper-based processes, and the inclusion of sales and marketing input into various supply chain processes.

For additional discussion on how fulfillment is done in B2B, see **fedex.com/us/supply-chain/services/fulfillment-services** and Demery (2012).

Order Fulfillment in Services

Thus far, we have concentrated on order fulfillment with physical products. Fulfilling service orders (e.g., buy or sell stocks, buy airline tickets, process insurance claims) may involve additional information processing, which requires more sophisticated EC systems.

Innovative e-Fulfillment Strategies

Several innovative e-fulfillment strategies exist. For example, supply chain partners can transmit information flows and hold off shipping physical goods until a point in time when they can make more direct shipments. An example of logistics postponement is merge-in-transit.

Merge-in-transit is a model in which components for a product need to arrive from two or more physical locations. For example, in shipping a desktop PC, the monitor may come from the East Coast of the United States and the CPU from the West Coast. Instead of shipping the components to a central location and then shipping both together to the customer, the components are shipped directly to the customer and merged into one shipment by the local deliverer (so the customer gets all the parts in one delivery), reducing unnecessary transportation.

SECTION 13.8 REVIEW QUESTIONS

1. What are some of the options for handling returns?
2. How does B2B order fulfillment differ from B2C order fulfillment?
3. Give an example of how e-marketplaces are used to alleviate problems with B2B order fulfillment.
4. Describe merge-in-transit.

MANAGERIAL ISSUES

Some managerial issues related to this chapter are as follows:

1. **How will you address the omni-channel imperative?** Today, most "brick-and-mortar" retailers have multiple sales channels—stores and branches, catalogs, call centers, kiosks, vending machines, websites, and mobile apps. Historically, these channels have been managed as silos with separate personnel, practices, and information systems (both front office and back) with the lead channel getting preferential treatment. In the past, this was sufficient because the customers were less demanding. This has changed. Customers expect a seamless experience across all these channels. They want to buy what they want and where they want, receive it when and where they want, and return it where they want. To meet these expectations, retailers will have to accept orders and payments from any channel, as well as fulfill orders from anywhere (e.g., distribution centers, stores and branches, manufacturers (dropships), 3PLs, and vending machines). For most retailers, this will obviously require substantial redesign of their payment and order fulfillment systems, as well as the redesign of a number of processes and systems along their supply chains.
2. **If you are an EC vendor, what are the bottlenecks in your order fulfillment process?** Order fulfillment is an important task, especially for e-tailers. Issues arise with order fulfillment along the entire supply chain, not just with the physical shipment of the order. To enhance the order fulfillment process, vendors need to identify the specific bottlenecks impeding various steps in their process. Potential issues are delayed delivery date, high return rate, high inventory cost, high shipping cost, and poor integration along the supply and demand chains.
3. **How should we manage returns?** Dealing with returns is important for CRM, yet may not be simple. Reverse logistics is very costly, and most companies will fail if the return rate is too high. Use the CRM system to identify the items with higher return rates and resolve the reason or stop the online sales of these items. A company should estimate its percentage of returns and plan a process for receiving and handling them. The logistics of returns may be executed through an external logistics service provider.
4. **For which items should we keep our own inventory?** As Amazon.com has experienced, online vendors try to avoid keeping inventory because it is expensive. However, we should not neglect the fact that retailing with appropriate inventory is a source of extra profit as well. In addition, for certain items, it is not possible to assure on-time delivery without having controllable inventory; the no-inventory policy is not always the best policy. A company has to design the portfolio plan of inventory and distribution centers for the items that have a positive effect of having inventory.
5. **What is the alliance strategy in order fulfillment?** Partnerships and alliances can improve collaboration and increase the efficiency of the supply chain. We need to decide in which part of order fulfillment we should count on partners. The typical activities that may be outsourced are shipping, warehousing, inventory holding, return management, and so on. Decide on the appropriate third-party logistics supplier that can provide reliable service for these activities. For certain

items that you cannot supply well, a partner may take care of the entire merchandising as well as order fulfillment, especially if you have leverage on the online brand image. An example is Newegg, which was described earlier, which provides software for Amazon.com's Fulfillment by Amazon (FBA) sellers.

6. **What logistics information should we provide to customers?** Customers, particularly business customers, want to know the availability of inventory and delivery date at the time of order. To meet these needs, the EC system should be integrated with the back-end information system. Customers may also want to trace the status of order processing, which should be managed by more than one company along the order fulfillment process. To provide seamless information beyond the boundary of the vendor, the partners should collaborate while developing their information systems.

7. **Should we use RFID for the order fulfillment?** If your buyer requires you to use RFID tags, there is no choice but to follow the request; however, RFID equipment and expertise are not always available within the supplier company. Some third-party logistics service providers support the tagging service. One question is who pays for the cost and who gets the benefit? So far, big buyers such as Walmart and the Department of Defense get the benefit, while the suppliers pay the cost. In the long run, suppliers may be able to share the benefit in inventory management. However, it will take time until the penetration becomes pervasive enough to maximize the benefit of RFID technology.

SUMMARY

In this chapter, you learned about the following EC issues as they relate to the chapter's learning objectives.

1. **Order fulfillment process.** Once an item has been ordered and purchased online, the next major phase of the process is order fulfillment. Order fulfillment encompasses all the activities a company undertakes from the time it receives an order to the time the items in the order are delivered to the customer. These can include checking inventory for availability, determining the completeness and accuracy of an order, locating a warehouse with the inventory, picking the items at the warehouse, arranging for shipment, loading and transporting items ordered, and receiving acknowledgment of receipt, as well as handling returns (reverse logistics). These activities are part of a larger supply chain that also deals with demand planning, procurement, manufacturing, and replenishment, to name a few of the other major activities. Ensuring that order fulfillment is well executed so that the right products are delivered to the right person and place in a timely and profitable manner is a complex task, whose difficulty varies by the types of product, whether third parties are involved, and on the company's strategies and operation models (i.e., whether the company primarily engineers-to-order, makes-to-order, assembles-to-order, or makes-to-stock).

2. **Make-to-order and 3D printing.** In EC, MTO refers to customized orders where fulfillment is done after orders are in. Usually, this involves self-customization. Orders are fulfilled using two methods. One method involves assembling products from standard components, as done by Dell and other computer manufacturers. The second method is to manufacture the specialized product. If a large number of similar products are made, one can use 3D printing, such as in the case of making customized shoes by Feetz Corporation. This is an example of mass customization, meaning a large number of similar items, each of which is made to order.

3. **Warehouses and robots in order fulfillment.** Order fulfillment in B2C may involve millions of items a week, to accomplish it. Amazon has hundreds of fulfillment centers (opening case). Other companies own distribution centers or pay Amazon or other companies to fulfill their orders (e.g., Target). Activities in warehousing include receiving and storage and managing inventories, picking items for orders, packaging them, and arranging deliveries. To handle the large volume, companies use robots. For example, Amazon is using over 30,000 of them (2016). The processes are controlled by different software, such as warehouse management systems and order management.

4. **Delivery to customers.** The delivery of EC physical goods is usually outsourced to companies such as UPS, USPS, FedEx, and DHL. The objective here is to deliver as fast as possible. Today, deliveries are done the same day, sometimes within hours. There is strong competition where nontraditional companies such as Google Express and Uber participate. The most discussed futuristic systems are drones and robotics (including self-driving cars). Delivery across national borders can be complex.

5. **Problems with order fulfillment.** Survey results indicate customer satisfaction has declined as a direct result of problematic order fulfillment. It is a challenge to companies because customers expect very short delivery times, as well as very accurate orders. They also want a seamless experience across all of a company's sales channels both online and offline. In B2C retail, most of these problems arise because of uncertainties in demand, lack of information sharing across all the participating companies' supply chains, inadequate logistical infrastructure, and inefficient financial flows (invoicing, payment, collection, etc.).

6. **Solutions to order fulfillment problems.** There are a large number of solutions that are aimed at addressing the problems in order fulfillment. These involve major changes to the order-taking process, improvements to the warehousing and inventory systems, as well as major changes to the structure and process of the broader supply chain. It also involves solutions targeted to specific problems. A case in point is the changes designed to enable much faster fulfillment, including novel approaches like Amazon Prime Air, which envisions small package delivery by drones; faster warehouse picking, packing, and delivery by using robots to assist in the process or using mass customization in make-to-order fulfillment; or even faster and more efficient handling of EC returns (e.g., return to store or special collection stations).

7. **The major objective of RFID** is to provide visibility of items and inventories along the supply chain. RFID readers can read tags, wirelessly from tens of yards away. Thus, it is easy to know when deliveries arrive or depart from each point in the supply chain. Also, using RFID readers, it is easy to find items in warehouses.

8. **Other supply chain topics.** While some of these solutions apply equally well to B2B EC, B2B tends to be more inefficient because it is more complex—larger shipments, multiple distribution channels, varied shipment frequency, and more complicated transaction paths, to name a few. Often solutions to these complexities require major changes to business processes, as well as the incorporation of software systems that can automate the processes.

Regardless of the type of EC or source of the problems, many companies rely on supply chain planning and execution software systems to help address the problems—both structure and processes. Included among the key systems are supply chain planning system of record (SCP SOR), warehouse management (WMS), and transportation management (TMS). Given the complexity of most supply chain problems (order fulfillment included), it can be a multiyear undertaking even with the aid of these systems.

KEY TERMS

3D printing
  Drones
  Mass customization
  Merge-in-transit
  Order fulfillment
  Radio frequency identification (RFID)
  Supply chain segmentation
  Third-party logistics suppliers (3PL)
  Warehouse management system (WMS)

DISCUSSION QUESTIONS

1. Discuss the problem of reverse logistics in EC. What types of companies may suffer the most from this problem?
2. Differentiate order fulfillment in B2C from that of B2B.
3. Watch **youtube.com/watch?v=OTnSXMhqQ-g** to gain a better understanding of the *bullwhip* effect and potential factors that cause it. Based on your understanding, what sorts of factors should demand forecasting incorporate to mitigate these factors?
4. Describe the importance of providing a single demand forecast for improving control along the entire supply chain.
5. Investigate and discuss how artificial intelligence can be used to manage warehouse operations. Begin with **yahoo.com/tech/meet-the-new-boss-the-worlds-first-128660465704.html**.
6. Discuss the benefits of 3D printing to mass customization.

TOPICS FOR CLASS DISCUSSION AND DEBATES

1. Chart the supply chain portion of returns to a virtual store. Check with an e-tailer to see how it handles returns. Prepare a report based on your findings.
2. Some say outsourcing B2B services may hurt the competitive edge. Others disagree. Debate.
3. Which activities are most critical in order fulfillment of B2C? Which are for B2B? Discuss the differences.

4. Write a report about the status of Amazon.com's same-day delivery projects.
5. Debate the futuristic value of drone vs. robot deliveries.
6. Research Microsoft's BizTalk RFID implementation. For order fulfillment, start with **msdn.microsoft.com/en-us/library/dd335979.aspx**.

INTERNET EXERCISES

1. The US Postal Service (USPS) has working relations and special programs with Amazon, UPS, FedEx, and most recently with the Chinese firm Alibaba. What is the nature of these relationships, how do they differ, and are they successful?
2. Visit **freightquote.com** and the sites of two other online freight companies. Compare the features offered by these companies for online delivery.
3. Enter **efulfillmentservice.com**. Review the products you find there. Watch the video about their operation. How does the company organize the network? How is it related to companies such as FedEx? How does this company make money?
4. Enter **kewill.com**. Find the innovations offered there that facilitate order fulfillment. Compare it with a competitor. Write a report.
5. Visit **b2btoday.com**, **socialmediatoday.com**, and other sources. Identify the major B2B logistic vendors. Then select three vendors and examine the services they provide to the B2B community.
6. Go to **ariba.com**. What is SAP Ariba and what supply chain solutions does it provide? Prepare a report describing the solutions they offer in the procurement arena.
7. Enter **reverselogistics.com** and summarize the differences between reverse and forward logistics. "The food industry has been the slowest major consumer sector to expand into e-commerce." First, read **foodlogistics.com/article/12021908/food-and-beverages-push-into-e-commerce-raising-questions-for-the-supply-chain**. Based on the article, what are some of the major issues that the food industry faces with EC? What are some of the solutions that have tried to address these issues?
8. Enter **dlca.logcluster.org/display/LOG/Warehousing+and+Inventory+Management** and identify all the major topics that are related to warehousing and inventory management.

TEAM PROJECTS

1. Assignments Related to the Opening Case
   (a) What were the drivers of the centralized warehousing?
   (b) Amazon.com is using third-party companies for delivery. Can you guess why?
   (c) Can Amazon.com use RFID in its warehouses? If yes, where and when? If no, why not?
   (d) Find out how Amazon.com handles returned merchandise.
   (e) Draw Amazon.com's supply chain for books.
   (f) Where do you think there are intelligent (software) agents in Amazon.com's order fulfillment/logistics?

2. Each team should investigate the order fulfillment process offered at an e-tailer's site, such as **gap.com**, **staples.com**, or **walmart.com**. Contact the company, if necessary, and examine any related business partnerships. Based on the content of this chapter, prepare a report with suggestions for how the company can improve its order fulfillment process. Each group's findings will be discussed in class. Based on the class's findings, draw some conclusions about how companies can improve order fulfillment.
3. FedEx, UPS, the US Postal Service, DHL, and others are competing in the EC logistic market. Each team should examine one company. Contact the company, if necessary, and aggregate the team's findings into a report that will convince classmates or readers that the company is the best. (What are its best features? What are its weaknesses?)
4. The competition for "same-day delivery" is intensifying with more and more competitors entering the race. Investigate the status of the competition including delivery by drones (e.g., FAA's approval). Start with Bowman (2014). Write a report.
5. Read about the warehouse management systems provided by JDA and Manhattan Associates (including some of their warehouse case studies) and answer the following:
   (a) What supply chain processes are supported by both systems?
   (b) What are the major benefits of each system?
   (c) What are the major differences in the capabilities provided?

6. Research the progress regarding the obstacles of drone deliveries. Enter Auburn University RFID Lab and summarize the experiences of two companies they worked with. In addition, comment on the importance of RFID for the omni-channel shopping experience.
7. Conduct research on the progress of the use of 3D printing in e-commerce (start with feetz.com).
8. Debate the advantages and disadvantages of using RFID in the B2C supply chain.

CLOSING CASE: CROSS-BORDER EC (PARTNERING WITH TMALL GLOBAL)

The Problem

In EC, "the world is your oyster." It can transcend borders, opening product lines and services to a growing international market. The problem is that like the original line from Shakespeare's "The Merry Wives of Windsor," it may take a substantial sword to open it.

When a buyer makes an online purchase from a merchant or seller in another country, it's called international e-commerce or **cross-border e-commerce**, and the two concepts are synonymous. Sometimes, researchers and practitioners refine the definition to exclude EC trade between countries that share a common language, border, and currencies (Goodale 2014). For example, trade between the United States and Canada is treated as international because their currencies and financial regulations differ and the free-flow of goods is restricted by law, while trade between many of the neighbors in the European Union is considered domestic because they share a common currency (the Euro), common payment resolution (SEPA—see section "Technical Malware Attack Methods: From Viruses to Denial of Service"), and open borders. Because of the polyglot nature of many of these countries, they often share one or more languages in common. When countries share common geography, language, payment systems, and currencies, a number of the key barriers to cross-border commerce are eliminated.

According to a recent report (Erickson and Najberg 2015) by Accenture and AliResearch (the research arm of the Chinese Alibaba Group), in 2015 there were approximately 300 billion global cross-border B2C transactions which represented around 16% of all B2C transactions. These transactions were the combined result of the purchases of 360 million B2C shoppers worldwide which was only 25% of all online buyers that year. So, only one out of every seven transactions was cross-border, and only one out of every four buyers made cross-border purchases.

Based on additional figures from survey of 24,000 adult consumers in 29 countries across the globe (PayPal 2015), in virtually every region of the world, the United States and China are by far the most popular online cross-border purchase destinations. The only exception is in Western Europe where cross-border purchases tend to be made within the region. From the buyer's standpoint, the countries with the strong proclivities for cross-border purchasing (i.e., those with more than 70% of their online purchases being cross-border) are scattered across the globe and include Canada, Ireland, Austria, Israel, Nigeria, Singapore, and Australia. Those with the weakest proclivities include the United States, the United Kingdom, Germany, the Netherlands, Poland, Turkey, Japan, South Korea, and China.

By 2020 (Erickson and Najberg 2015), the outlook for cross-border transactions is predicted to change substantially. The volume of cross-border transactions is projected to have a compound growth rate of close to 30% between now and then, so that cross-border transactions will reach around 1 trillion. This will represent about 30% of the estimated total for that year. At that time, close to 1 out of every 2 of the estimated 2 billion shoppers will make cross-border purchases. For merchants and sellers, these estimates paint a picture of massive opportunity—the "oyster." It also represents a substantial opportunity for banks and payment service providers. So, where's the "sword"? What's needed to take advantage of the opportunity?

The Solution

Suppose a merchant wants to expand his or her online B2C specialty clothing and apparel business to handle overseas buyers. Point of fact, there are more cross-border purchases for clothing and apparel than any other product category by a wide margin. Given this fact, how hard could it be to sell clothing on the international market? With English and credit cards being de facto standards on the Internet, it seems like most merchants could engage in cross-border EC by simply adding support for international credit cards and delivery. While this might work for a handful of transactions in some parts of the world, experience tells us it would not work for even the average number of sales transactions handled by most EC retailers.

A recent study of a sample of 180 online B2C merchants in 10 countries by Pymnts.com (2015) assessed the characteristics of those already successfully engaged in international B2C, as well as the readiness of the sample to participate in cross-border transactions. Based on their analysis of 60 features, the number one key finding was that the top 10 merchants "think local." They treat international customers as if they were domestic. They offer multiple languages, multiple currencies, and multiple payment systems. They customize pages to the customer's country (e.g., simple things like address and phone fields). They support access through a variety of devices, especially mobile. They simplify the checkout process, eliminating the need for extensive user profiles. They also offer free shipping and rewards to encourage repeat business.

The second key finding of the study (Pymnts.com 2015) was that the vast majority of businesses in the sample were far from ready to engage in cross-border transactions. It's understandable given that there are currently 195 countries in the world with a combined total of 6500 spoken languages and 180 currencies, not to mention differing customs procedures, logistics, physical infrastructures, and other regulatory and legal systems.

Treating potential cross-border customers as if they were all "local" is almost an impossible task. Because the barriers and issues that need to be addressed in cross-border sales are so intertwined, it is hard to do it in a phased approach or piecemeal fashion. This is why most businesses start by offering a small segment of their product or service listings to a handful of countries. Also, instead of setting up local legal entities within the countries of interest or creating on their own with fully localized features for each of the countries to be served, many companies start by working with a partner who is conversant in the world of cross-border commerce and who has a site or portal that is already serving a broad spectrum of cross-border consumers.

This was the approached used by Costco when they decided to offer some of their products to the burgeoning B2C market in China.

Costco's 2015 annual report provides an overview of the company and the general strategy and operating principles (Costco 2015). Costco Wholesale Corporation began operations in 1983 in Seattle, Washington. From the beginning they have focused on operating membership warehouses in the United States and Canada, as well as a handful of foreign countries including the United Kingdom, Mexico, Japan, Australia, Spain, Taiwan, and Korea. Worldwide, there are 686 warehouses, the bulk (569) of which are located in the United States and Canada. These warehouses, which average about 14,400 sq. ft., are run by 200,000 employees and service 81 million cardholders. Cardholders pay annual fees that vary by country, although they are around $55 in the United States.

Their basic strategy is to offer lower-priced, high-quality, nationally branded, and Costco private-label (Kirkland Signature) products across a range of categories including food, sundries, hardlines, softlines, fresh foods, and ancillary products (e.g., gas stations and pharmacy). Given the low price strategy, the profits come from selling focused inventory (3700 SKUs) with high sales volumes and rapid turnover coupled with "operating efficiencies achieved by volume purchasing, efficient distribution, and reduced handling of merchandise in no-frills, self-service warehouse facilities." They also come from membership fees.

In 2015, Costco had total sales of $114B with an annual growth rate of 20% annual. The overwhelming majority (97%) of these sales were in store. Costco was late getting to EC and, as a consequence, they lag behind their competitors. Their anemic EC sales are also a consequence of their expressed strategy. EC sales don't generate memberships, nor do they encourage much foot traffic along with in-store impulse buying.

While Costco's international presence is limited, it was hard for Costco to ignore China's astounding retail growth, especially from online sales. In order to test the retail market in China, Costco decided in 2014 to enter the market by setting up a shop on Alibaba's Tmall Global site without capital investments in Chinese real estate.

In recent years, the Alibaba Group has made a concerted effort to encourage cross-border online B2C imports. Toward this end, in 2014 they launched a new cross-border EC website called Tmall Global. It's a platform that enables foreign companies to sell to Chinese consumers without having a physical presence in China. This was particularly attractive to Costco because they were wary of following the same path of the big box stores.

Tmall has a number of key features supporting cross-border EC, but two of the more important are Alipay and Tmall's bonded warehouses and logistics partner network (Tran 2015). Alipay is Alibaba's payment platform (sort of like PayPal). It is the largest payment system in China, used much more than credit or debit cards which Tmall also supports. The platform automatically handles currency conversion so that Chinese buyers pay in Yuan and retailers are paid in their home currency (once a buyer has received their goods). Basically, once a merchant is hooked up to Alipay, it provides entrée to China's 300 M online buyers. The other key feature revolves around a set of bonded warehouses located in five major cities (Shanghai, Guangzhou, Hangzhou, Zhengzhou, and Ningbo) where merchants can pre-ship products in large quantities. The warehouses are in duty-free zones dedicated to handling imports and delivery for international merchandise purchased online. They not only enable faster shipping times to customers but also lower fees on customs and duties. Technically, the warehouses are operated by customs, but in reality the actual goods are the responsibility of Alibaba's logistics subsidiary, Cainiao, who uses a network of third-party logistics providers (3PLs) to perform the necessary warehouse activities including the sorting, picking, delivery, and customs clearance.

In exchange for these types of key services, which aren't free, retailers must meet certain criteria. Among other things, they have to (Tran 2015):

- Have a retail or trading license.
- Prove they own the brands or have rights to distribute them.
- Provide their Tmall site in Chinese.
- Have products manufactured outside inspected and approved by Tmall.
- Provide customer service including Chinese language service support.
- Support customer returns and provide a return location in China.
- Provide shipping direct to the consumer in China.

Many of the required services can be and are often outsourced to third-party providers, who are preapproved and endorsed by Tmall Global.

The Results

Today, Costco's Tmall Global site sells around 200 items from its food, healthcare, and private-label Kirkland Signature product offerings. They also used their base in Taiwan to help support operations and rely on Tmall's inventory storage and 20-day delivery to limit operating expenses.

Unlike some of the other 5400 Tmall Global customers, Costco has enjoyed a modicum of success. While there are no official annual statistics provided by Costco or Tmall, Tmall did report that Costco sold over $6.4 million in the first month of operation and that during the 2014 Singles' Day Sale, Costco sold $3.5 million in merchandise.

Because of Costco's razor thin margins, whatever revenues are made have to be weighed against the benefits and costs of operating accrued from the site and partnership. On the benefit side, the operation (Mahajan 2015):

- Enables them to test the market without having to invest in real estate; this was the mistake that many big box retailers (e.g., Home Depot and Best Buy) made when they entered the Chinese market.
- Allows them to experiment with the market to determine those products that will sell, the features that are important to Chinese customers, the prices they can charge, and the general spending patterns of Chinese consumers with respect to their offerings.
- Alleviates the need for a local business license to establish an online store. This can be a complex, lengthy, and costly endeavor.
- Eliminates many of the typical interchange costs associated with card-based payment systems and reduces overall logistical costs by speeding transit time.

In terms of limitations, the operation:

- Restricts them from advertising on Tmall Mainland and Taobao which accounts for 80% for China's online sales. They have to rely on company name and brand recognition to drive business.
- Charges merchants a deposit fee ($25,000), an annual fee (somewhere between $5000 and $10,000), a sales commission fee of 2 to 5% of the product price and logistics fees, and an Alipay fee of 1% of the product price and logistics fees.
- Eliminates a key element of their business strategy—membership fees.

There's no assurance that Costco will succeed in the Chinese online B2C market. There is tremendous competitive pressure coming from leading Chinese retailers and from other cross-border retailers and manufacturers. If they are successful, eventually they will probably have to go the local route and establish an independent online presence in China in order to reduce their overall costs.

Sources: Costco (2015), Erickson and Najberg (2015), Goodale (2014), Mahajan (2015), PayPal (2015), Pymnts.com (2015), and Tran (2015) (all accessed February 2017).

Questions

1. What is cross-border research and under this definition is trade between two member countries of the European Union cross-border or not? Explain.
2. Describe the current and estimated size of the cross-border market.
3. What are the key elements of success for an EC company wanting to expand into global markets?
4. What is the basic approach that Costco used in entering the Chinese EC market?
5. Would the approach used by Costco work for a company like Walmart? Explain.

REFERENCES

Alfs, L. and B. Harper. "Google Express Adds Delivery Service in 13 More States." *USA Today*, Oct.26, 2016.

Bastian Solution. "Newegg Opens New Facility to Service Midwest Customers." *Bastian Solutions*, Case Study, 2016. **bastiansolutions.com/case-studies/e-commerce/newegg** (accessed December 2016).

Bhaiya, A. "Is Robotic Automation the Future of Ecommerce Warehouses?" *The Washington Post*, November 2016.

Black, T. "Amazon Drones Set Off Air Delivery Race." June 9, 2014. **stuff.co.nz/technology/gadgets/60094928/amazon-drones-set-off-air-delivery-race** (accessed December 2016).

Blanchard, D. "Supply Chain and Logistics: Dell Taps into Innovation to Reach Emerging Markets." *Industry Week*, November 14, 2012.

Bowman, R. "Will Google Shopping Express Help Retailers Fend Off Challenge from Amazon?" *Forbes*, June 7, 2014.

Boyle, A. "Flirtey Makes First Urban Drone Delivery in FAA Test, Beating Amazon to the Punch." *GeekWire*, March 25, 2016. **geekwire.com/2016/flirtey-makes-an-urban-drone-delivery-in-faa-test-beating-amazon-to-the-punch** (accessed December 2016).

Buckley, C. "Beijing's Electric Bikes, the Wheels of E-Commerce, Face Traffic Backlash." *The New York Times*, May 30, 2016.

Carsten, P. "Alibaba Rolls Out Three-Hour Delivery Service for Healthcare Goods." *Reuters*, May 12, 2015.

Costco. "CostCo Annual Report 2015." October 2015. **phx.corporate-ir.net/External.File?item=UGFyZW50SUQ9NjA1NzM5fENoaWxkSU Q9MzE3NzEwfFR5cGU9MQ==&t=1** (accessed February 2017).

Del Rey, J. "This Is What It Looks Like Inside an Amazon Warehouse (Photos)." *AllThingsD*, December 23, 2013. **allthingsd.com/20131223/this-is-what-it-looks-like-inside-an-amazon-warehouse-slideshow/#slideshow-1-3** (accessed December 2016).

Demery, P. "B2B E-Commerce Sales Will Top $1.13 Trillion by 2020." *Internet Retailer*, April 2, 2015. **internetretailer.com/2015/04/02/new-report-predicts-1-trillion-market-us-b2b-e-commerce** (accessed December 2016).

Demery, P. "UPS Ties Technology to Bridgeline Digital's E-Commerce Software." *Internet Retailer*, June 12, 2012. **internetretailer.com/2012/06/12/ups-ties-technology-bridgeline-digitals-e-commerce-software** (accessed December 2016).

Dudovskiy, J. "Dell Value Chain Analysis." *Research Methodology*, September 3, 2015. **research-methodology.net/dell-value-chain-analysis** (accessed December 2016).

Erickson, J., and A. Najberg. "Cross-Border E-Commerce to Reach $1 Trillion in 2020." June 11, 2015. **alizila.com/cross-border-e-commerce-to-reach-1-trillion-in-2020** (accessed February 2017).

Etherington, D. "Grocery Deliveries via Rolling Drone Will Kick Off in Washington D.C. this Fall." *TechCrunch*, September 22, 2016. **techcrunch.com/2016/09/22/grocery-deliveries-via-rolling-drone-will-kick-off-in-washington-d-c-this-fall** (accessed December 2016).

Fabian. "Empowering Mass Customization: How 'Digital Forming' Is Creating Unique Products with 3D Printing." *I.Materialise*, October 27, 2015. **i.materialise.com/blog/3d-printing-mass-customization/** (accessed December 2016).

French, S. "6 Myths about Amazon Prime Air and Drone Delivery, Debunked." *MarketWatch*, December 2, 2015a. **marketwatch.com/story/6-myths-about-amazon-prime-air-and-drone-delivery-debunked-2015-12-02** (accessed December 2016).

French, S. "Drone Delivery Is Already Here — And It Works." *MarketWatch*, December 15, 2015b. **marketwatch.com/story/drone-delivery-is-already-here-and-it-works-2015-11-30** (accessed December 2016).

Gartner. "Gartner Announces Rankings of Its 2015 Supply Chain Top 25." May 14, 2015. **gartner.com/newsroom/id/3053118** (accessed December 2016).

Goodale, D. "Everything You Need to Know about Cross-Border Fees." October 12, 2014. **foxycart.com/blog/everything-you-need-to-know-about-cross-border-fees#.Vylu2PkrKuU** (accessed February 2017).

Grothaus, M. "This is How Google's Project Wing Drone Delivery Service Could Work." *Fast Company* (2016). **fastcompany.com/3055961/fast-feed/this-is-how-googles-project-wing-drone-delivery-could-work** (accessed December 2016).

Hagerty, J. R. "Meet the New Generation of Robots for Manufacturing." *Wall Street Journal*, June 2, 2015. **wsj.com/articles/meet-the-new-generation-of-robots-for-manufacturing-1433300884** (accessed December 2016).

Halkias, M. "Amazon's One-Hour Delivery Now Available in Dallas; Find Your ZIP Code." *The Dallas Morning News*, March 26, 2015. **biz-beatblog.dallasnews.com/2015/03/amazon-coms-one-hour-deliver-now-available-in-dallas-find-you-zip-code.html** (accessed December 2016).

Hofman, D., S. Aronow, and K. Nilles. "The Gartner Supply Chain Top 25 of 2013." May 2013. **gartner.com/imagesrv/summits/docs/na/supply-chain/Gartner-2013-SupplyChain-Top25.pdf** (accessed December 2016).

Homic, J. *3D Printing will Rock the World.* North Charleston, SC: CreateSpace Independent Publishing Platform, 2015.

Insitesoft. "Order Fulfillment: Important Part of Customer Experience on B2B eCommerce Sites." *Insitesoft*, January 5, 2016. **insitesoft.com/blog/order-fulfillment-important-part-of-customer-experience-on-b2b-e-commerce-sites** (accessed December 2016).

Kahn, J. "Droids Not Drones Are the Future of E-Commerce Deliveries." *Bloomberg Technology*, April 18, 2016.

Koslow, T. "Iconery: Where Fashion, E-Commerce, & 3D Printing Intersect." *3D Printing Industry*, October 2, 2015. **3dprintingindustry.com/news/iconery-where-fashion-e-commerce-3d-printing-intersect-58883** (accessed December 2016).

Kinnison, A. "How Order Management Systems Help Streamline Ecommerce." *Volusion*, June 9, 2015. **volusion.com/ecommerce-blog/articles/how-order-management-systems-help-streamline-ecommerce** (accessed December 2016).

Mahajan, N. "Why Costco's Online-First Approach in China is a Smart Strategy." *Founding Fuel*, May 4, 2015. **foundingfuel.com/column/dispatches-from-china/why-costcos-onlinefirst-approach-in-china-is-a-smart-strategy** (accessed February 2017).

Makepolo. "Canadian Beef Processor Touts RFID Computer Hardware & Software." January 11, 2014. **madeinchinasuppliers.com/canadian-beef-processor-touts-rfid-computer-hardware-software.html** (accessed December 2016).

Marsh, R. "White House: Google Will Start Testing Delivery Drones in the U.S." *News*, August 2, 2016. **money.cnn.com/2016/08/02/technology/drones-white-house-google/index.html?iid=hp-stack-dom** (accessed December 2016).

Martin, G. "New Goods-to-Robot Systems Take E-Fulfillment to the Next Level." *Bastian Solution*, February 23, 2015. **bastiansolution.com/blog/index.php/2015/02/23/goods-to-robot-picking-for-efulfillment/#WBA8ui0rI2w** (accessed December 2016).

McFarland, M. "Domino's Delivers Pizza by Drone in New Zealand." *Money.cnn.com*, August 26, 2016a. **money.cnn.com/2016/08/26/technology/dominos-drone-new-zealand/?iid=EL.** (accessed December 2016).

McFarland, M. "Rwanda's Hospitals Will Use Drones to Deliver Medical Supplies." *Money.cnn.com*, October 13, 2016b. **money.cnn.com/2016/10/13/technology/Rwanda-drone-hospital/index.html?iid=hp-stack-dom.** (accessed December 2016).

Mehra, G. "8 Obstacles to Drone Delivery, for Ecommerce." *Practical Ecommerce*, September 4, 2015.

Mohan, A. M. "E-commerce packaging pitfalls & opportunities." *Packaging World*, December 4, 2014.

Pymnts.com. "X-Border Payments Optimization Index." 2015. **pymnts.com/x-border-payments-optimization** (accessed February 2017).

PayPal. "PayPal Cross-Border Consumer Research 2015." 2015. **paypalobjects.com/digitalassets/c/website/marketing/global/pages/jobs/paypal-insights-2015-global-report-appendix-added.pdf** (accessed February 2017).

Peerless Research Group. "Aligning Order and Fulfillment Channels." June 2013. **country.honeywellaidc.com/CatalogDocuments/honeywell-multichannel-fulfillment-white-paper.pdf** (accessed December 2016).

Said, C. "Robots May Beat Drones in Race to Deliver Packages." *SFGate*, April 6, 2016.

SCD Staff. "Macy's Says RFID Accuracy Enables New Inventory Strategy." *SC Digest, News*, February 17, 2016.

Simchi-Levi, D., A. Clayton, and B. Raven. "When One Size Does Not Fit All." (December 2012). *Operations Management and Research.*, December 2010.

Technology Story. "Are Robots About to Take Over E-Commerce Warehouses?" *IT News Today*, November 7, 2016.

Thomas, K. "Supply Chain Segmentation: 10 Steps to Greater Profits." *Supply Chain Quarterly*, Quarter 1, 2016. **supplychainquarterly.com/topics/Strategy/201201segmentation** (accessed December 2016).

Tobe, F. "Competing Robotic Warehouse Systems." *Robot Report*, April 30, 2015. **therobotreport.com/news/goods-to-man-robotic-systems** (accessed February 2017).

Tran, M. P. "Tmall and Tmall Global: The 'Fast Track into China' for U.S. Retailers." *CPC Strategy Blog*, May 27, 2015. **cpcstrategy.com/blog/2015/05/tmall-tmall-global-fast-track-china-u-s-retailers** (accessed December 2016).

Turney, D. "How 3D Printing to Order Is Changing Manufacturing." *Tech Radar Pro*, April 18, 2016.

Valerio, P. "Amazon Robotics: IoT in the Warehouse." *InformationWeek*, September 28, 2015. **informationweek.com/strategic-cio/amazon-robotics-iot-in-the-warehouse/d/d-id/1322366** (accessed December 2016).

VanLandingham, G. "What's Challenging about E-Commerce Fulfillment? Everything." *SupplyChainDharma.com*, October 10, 2014. **supplychaindharma.com/e-commerce-fulfillment** (accessed December 2016).

Wallach-Kloski, L. and N. Kloski, *Getting Started with 3D Printing: A Hands-on Guide to the Hardware, Software, and Services Behind the New Manufacturing Revolution.* San Francisco, CA: Maker Media Inc., 2016.

Williams, M. *Dropshipping: The Ultimate Dropshipping Blueprint Made Simple (Dropshipping for Beginners, Dropshipping with Amazon, Dropshipping Suppliers)."* [Kindle Edition], Seattle, WA: Amazon Digital Services, 2016.

Wing , T. "From E-Commerce to Drones, USPS Looks for Competitive Edge." *Federal News Radio*, July 15, 2016.

Wulfraat, M. "Amazon Global Fulfillment Center Network." *MWPVL*, 2016. **mwpvl.com/html/amazon_com.html** (accessed December 2016).

Wulfraat, M. "Logistics Comment: Amazon is Building a New Distribution Network - Quickly and Quietly!" *Supply Chain Digest*, July 23, 2014. **scdigest.com/EXPERTS/WULFRAAT_14-07-23.PHP?cid=8309&ctype=content** (accessed December 2016).

Part V

E-Commerce Strategy and Implementation

EC Strategy, Globalization, SMEs, and Implementation

14

Contents

Learning Objectives

Upon completion of this chapter, you will be able to:

1. Describe the EC strategy phases.
2. Describe the need for justifying EC investments.
3. Evaluate the issues involved in global EC.
4. Describe the reasons for success and failure of EC.
5. Describe how small- and medium-sized businesses can use EC.
6. Describe the major components of EC implementation.
7. Discuss the steps in developing an EC system.
8. Describe the major EC development strategies.

OPENING CASE
TELSTRA CORPORATION HELPS ITS CORPORATE CUSTOMERS JUSTIFY EC INITIATIVES

Telstra Corp. is Australia's major telecommunication and information services company, which provides fixed line and mobile communications as well as digital TV and Internet access services. The company operates in a competitive market (e.g., against Vodafone and Optus Corp.). Telstra has expanded its services to several countries in Asia and Europe.

© Springer International Publishing AG 2018
E. Turban et al., *Electronic Commerce 2018*, Springer Texts in Business and Economics, DOI 10.1007/978-3-319-58715-8_14

The Problem

The company is very active in the e-commerce and social media markets, mainly through Telstra Digital and its wireless units. For example, it provided its corporate customers with Facebook apps so they can manage their Telstra accounts. The company also maintains channels at Twitter, Instagram, LinkedIn, Vine, Tumblr, and Google + (see **exchange.telstra.com. au**). One area where the company saw an opportunity but had some marketing difficulties was m-commerce. In particular, the company offered its corporate customers applications that had many intangible benefits. The customers had difficulty getting approval from their own top management for paying for Telstra's services without detailed *justification*.

Telstra was interested in promoting the following four lines of applications:

1. **Fleet and field service management.** This topic involves enterprise mobility applications.
2. **Video conferencing.** This application uses video conferencing in order to save on travel expenses to meeting places and helps expedite decision making. Both fixed line and mobile services can support this initiative.
3. **Web contact centers.** This application is designed to improve CRM.
4. **Teleworking.** Allows employees to work off-site. *Teleworking* (also known as telecommuting) requires sophisticated technology to enable effective communication, collaboration, and collaborative commerce activities.

Both the infrastructure and the software for the above applications are expensive. Many Telstra customers were interested in learning about how to *justify* the investment, but they did not know how to go about it.

The Solution

Telstra developed a white paper to illustrate the use of ROI calculators in each of the above four lines of applications. The unique property of the calculators is that they compute benefits to the users' organizations, to the employees, and to the society. Telstra is known for its concerns for SMEs. In 2015 it took a majority ownership in Neto, an EC platform provider for SMEs (Murtagh 2015). Here, we provide some of the highlights.

Justifying Video Conferencing

Benefits include reduction in travel expenses, work time lost by employees, and so forth. This calculator uses the net present value (NPV) approach.

The cost–benefit analysis calculates the savings to a company (seven variables), some of which are intangible (such as faster decision making). The benefits are compared with both the fixed and variable costs. The benefits to employees are measured by five variables, some of which are intangible (e.g., better job satisfaction). Finally, benefits to society include variables such as reduced car emissions and traffic congestion.

Justifying Teleworking

The benefits to the companies range from reduced office footprints to higher employee retention. Again, some benefits are intangible. The costs are detailed (e.g., cost of equipment). Employees save travel time when they work at home, but they need to pay for the energy used at home. Society enjoys reduced vehicle emissions when people telecommute.

Justifying Web Contact Centers

The above approach is used here, too: The calculator includes savings, benefits, and costs to the company, employees, and society. Both tangible and intangible variables are considered in the calculations.

Justifying Fleet and Field Force Management

The structure of this calculator is similar to those above: savings, benefits, and costs to the company, employees, and society.

The white paper provides comprehensive calculations with sample data for a hypothetical company.

Telstra offers other calculators including one for data usage for mobile devices.

Justifying Green Efficiency

The company has also used similar approaches to these calculators in examining the use of green technologies specifically solar power. These approaches are used to justify the use of solar and other green projects throughout the organization.

The Results

Telstra believes that Australian companies have an opportunity to develop a sustainability strategy using the above technologies that need to be justified. Telstra provides proof of substantial cost–benefits. While the savings to companies are substantial in many cases, the benefits to employees and society should not be ignored.

As far as Telstra itself, the introduction of the calculators helped the company increase its market share and profitability. Also the market value of Telstra stock doubled from 2010 to 2015.

Note: Telstra is known for its EC and IT innovations. For how it is outpacing the United States in IoT adoption, see Barbaschow (2016).

Sources: Based on Telstra (2016), Murtagh (2015), and Barbaschow (2016).

LESSONS LEARNED FROM THE CASE

The Telstra case demonstrates the need for organizations to justify EC-related projects and the fact that this may not be easy to do. Telstra provided calculators to their clients to help them with the justification of IT and EC investments. The case points to intangible benefits, which are difficult to measure and quantify. It also raises the issue of sharing costs among several projects and the need to consider the benefits to employees and to society. These are only some of the topics presented in this chapter. Other topics deal with the use of EC metrics. This chapter also provides a discussion of successes and failures in e-commerce. Other implementation issues covered are the implementation of EC by SMEs and the strategy of going global online. Finally, privacy, ethical issues, and intellectual property are covered. The chapter ends with an assessment of the future of e-commerce.

14.1 ORGANIZATIONAL STRATEGY: CONCEPTS AND OVERVIEW

An organizational **strategy** is a comprehensive framework for expressing the manner in which a business plans to achieve its mission, what goals are needed to support it, and what plans and policies will be needed to accomplish these goals. Strategy also is about making decisions on what activities not to pursue and trade-offs between strategic alternatives. An organization's strategy (including EC and IT strategies) starts with understanding where the company is today with respect to its goals and where it wants to be in the future.

Example: Facebook

Facebook (**facebook.com**) is the leading social media network in the United States. It competes with other social media networks such as YouTube (owned by Google), Twitter, Reddit, Pinterest, Instagram, Tumblr, LinkedIn, and Google + (see **statista.com/statistics/265773/market-share-of-the-most-popular-social-media-websites-in-the-us**). To maintain this superiority, Facebook is continually adding additional features to its product offering. These features come in the form of both innovations and acquisitions. Examples of recent innovations include Facebook Messenger (**messengerplatform.fb.com**) and Facebook Marketplace (**facebook.com/fbmarketplace**). Facebook maintains a listing and description of innovations at **fbinnovation.com**.

Most of Facebook's Innovations are based around acquisitions of complementary technology companies. Notable acquisitions in the last 3 years include:

- **WhatsApp** (mobile instant messaging)—2014
- **Wit.ai** (speech recognition)—2015
- **TheFind** (e-commerce)—2015
- **InfiniLED** (Oculus VR—virtual reality)—2016
- **FacioMetrics** (machine learning)—2016

For a complete listing of Facebook acquisitions, see **crunchbase.com/organization/facebook/acquisitions**.

By continually adding to its platform, Facebook is able to provide new and interesting features that benefit its users. By consistently providing the most feature-rich platform, Facebook ensures that it will continue to maintain its population of users and potentially grow them. For more on Facebooks strategies, see Hoefflinger (2017) and Solon (2016).

Strategy and Performance Cycle

The major objective of a strategy is to improve organizational performance. Therefore, strategy development and performance are interrelated and described here as a five-phase cyclical process.

A strategy is important, but the *process* of developing a strategy can be even more important. No matter how large or how small the organization, the strategic planning process leads managers to assess the current performance of the firm, then determine where the performance should be, and plan how to get from where a company is to where it wants to be.

Any strategic planning process has five major phases, *initiation, formulation, implementation, assessment*, and *performance improvement*, as shown in Fig. 14.1. The major phases of the strategic planning process, and some identifiable activities and outcomes associated with each phase, are discussed briefly in the following text.

Example: Organizational Evaluation Tools
Organizations can use a wide variety of tools and processes to evaluate their current state in the marketplace as well as determining what their future strategy should be. All these tools are often specific to individual companies and industries; there are some that are commonly used in all disciplines.

- **SWOT analysis.** The SWOT analysis looks at an organization's strengths, weaknesses, opportunities, and threats. This is an internal analysis and is meant to focus on the organization's current standing within its existing marketing positioning. When a SWOT analysis is conducted, it is typically presented in a template like the one seen at **strategyexpert.com/downloads/20091026_2**. For more information on SWOT analysis, see an explanation at **mindtools.com/pages/article/newTMC_05.htm**, or watch the video at **youtu.be/GNXYI10Po6A**.
- **Porter model.** The Porter model is a second evaluation system that aims to evaluate a firm's current standing in the marketplace but also evaluate the market itself. The Porter model breaks this evaluation into five forces: supplier power, buyer power, competitive rivalry, threat of substitution, and threat of new entry. The Porter model is typically presented in a graphic much like the one seen at **strategyexpert.com/downloads/20091026**. For more information on the Porter model, see an explanation at **mindtools.com/pages/article/newTMC_08.htm**, or watch the video at **hbr.org/video/3590615226001/the-explainer-porters-five-forces**.

Fig. 14.1 The strategy-performance cycle

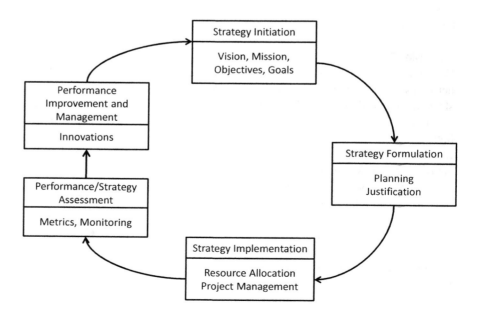

Strategy Initiation

In the **strategy initiation** phase, an organization is setting its vision, goals, and objectives. Looking at its environment, strategy initiation includes an assessment of a company's strengths and weaknesses and examines the external factors that may affect the business. Additionally, a company may undertake a competitive and competitor analysis to determine its strategy. All these activities need to be related to the e-commerce and social networks.

Specific outcomes from this phase include a *company analysis.* One key outcome from this analysis should be a clear statement of the company's *value proposition.* For a description, see Kim (2015) and Hitt and Ireland (2017); and for examples, see Laja (2017).

Example: Amazon.com

While Amazon (**amazon.com**) was originally founded with the value proposition of selling books, the company has greatly expanded into other areas since that time. Today Amazon competes in a number of markets and is the largest Internet-based retailer in the world (Zaczkiewicz 2016). The company sells a wide variety of products including books, music, personal electronics, apparel, toys, jewelry, food, streaming video and audio, and software services (and more). The breadth of its product and service offerings is immense and represents a significant expansion in the company's original value proposition. Amazon has been able to successfully leverage its initial success in books and that underlying technology/competency, to become a multichannel, multi-product, multi-industry competitor.

For more on Amazon's history and competitive strategy, see Rossman (2016) and Saleem (2017).

Core Competencies

A *core competency* refers to the unique capabilities of companies, which are difficult to imitate. For example, Google's core competency is its expertise in information search technology, and eBay's core competency is in conducting online auctions. Facebook's expertise is in creating social communities, and Zillow concentrates on real estate.

- **Forecasts.** *Forecasting* means predicting future behavior and trends of factors that may impact the business.
- **Market research: competitor and industry analyses.** *Competitor analysis* involves scanning the business environment to assess the strategy, strengths, and weakness of all types of competitors. Several methodologies are available to conduct such an analysis, including strengths, weaknesses, opportunities, and threats (SWOT) analysis and competitor analysis (see "competitor analysis" at **tutor2u.net/business/strategy/competitor_analysis.htm**).

First-Mover Advantage

The business, IT, and e-commerce worlds all have examples of companies that have succeeded with first-mover advantage. However, some companies have failed, despite their first-mover advantage. Generally, the advantages of being first include an opportunity to make a first and lasting impression on customers, to establish strong brand recognition, to lock in strategic partners, and to increase switching costs for customers.

Example: Books

Amazon (**amazon.com**) operated the first major online bookstore and laid the groundwork for brick-and-mortar bookstores such as Barnes & Noble to follow suit. Amazon used this first-mover advantage to cement itself as the default provider of books online in the minds of customers. While Barnes & Noble had the advantage of a considerable physical presence, customers did not think of them as online provider. They were never able to significantly overcome Amazon's first-mover advantage, and Amazon is still the leader in online book sales.

In some cases, being the first mover can have some disadvantages. The risks of being a first mover include the high cost of pioneering EC initiatives, making mistakes, the chance that a second wave of competitors will eliminate a first mover's lead through lower cost and innovation, and the risk that the move will be too early. Although the advantage of a speedy market entry cannot be ignored, followers (late movers or second movers, see **insight.kellogg.northwestern.edu/article/the_second_mover_advantage**) can be more profitable than first movers can in the long run.

Example: Jewelry

Blue Nile (**bluenile.com**) was a leader in online jewelry sales, offering a wide variety of jewelry items, including wedding rings, and unique features on its website. While Blue Nile had the first-mover advantage in online jewelry sales, they were quickly eclipsed by other sites such as Amazon that were able to leverage their existing user base and positive public perception. Blue Nile still exists, but they were not able to leverage their first-mover advantage into being a market leader.

Strategy Formulation

Once the goals and objectives are known and prioritized, a company can start to formulate its strategy. **Strategy formulation** refers to the development of specific strategies and tactics to exploit opportunities and manage threats in the business environment in light of corporate strengths and weaknesses. In an EC strategy, the result is likely to be a list of EC applications or projects to be implemented (e.g., online storefront, e-procurement, and social media).

Selecting E-Commerce Opportunities

There are many potential ways to get involved in EC (e.g., see Flierl 2015).

Selecting an appropriate EC project(s) involves a justification, ranking, and cost–benefit analysis. Best results can be achieved with input solicited from both internal and external participants. One approach is to use a strategy driven by existing factors. For example, a problem-driven strategy may help a company if its EC strategy can solve an existing, difficult problem (e.g., using forward e-auctions via e-auctioneers such as **Liquidation.com** to dispose of excess equipment). As noted earlier, a late-mover strategy can be effective if the company can use its brand, technology, superior customer service, or innovative products and strategies to overcome any potential deficiencies resulting from not being the first mover. Examples are Google's emergence as the leading search engine (they were the 11th) and Facebook becoming the top social network.

However, most times it is best to use a systematic methodology that determines which initiatives to pursue. For more on second-mover advantages, see **mfishbein.com/4-second-mover-advantages-why-competitive-markets-can**.

Risk Analysis in Strategy Formulation

While EC, social media, and mobile markets enable new business opportunities, it also may create substantial risks because of the open computing and interactive nature of the technology. **E-commerce risk** is the likelihood that a negative outcome will occur in the course of developing and operating a new e-commerce initiative. Risk in EC, social, and mobile environments is different from those faced by offline companies. For example, an EC financial services company (like **creditkarma. com**) may face unique Internet security threats and vulnerabilities. As a result, a robust online security strategy is essential for fraud protection.

The most dangerous risk to a company engaged in e-commerce is business risk—the possibility that developing and operating a new e-commerce business could negatively impact the well-being of the organization itself.

Collaborative Efforts in Strategy Formulation

Strategy formulation is considered a highly secretive process, which is done by a small team that only seldom involves outsiders (e.g., a consultant). However, this situation is changing, mostly due to the trend of companies transforming into social businesses. The basic idea is to open the planning process to be more participatory. According to Gast and Zanini (2012) and Nketia (2016), companies that are experimenting with this approach see two major benefits. One benefit is "improving the quality of strategy by pulling in diverse and detailed frontline perspectives that are typically overlooked but can make the resulting plans more insightful and actionable." The second benefit involves "building enthusiasm and alignment behind a company's strategic direction—a critical component of long-term organizational health, effective execution, and strong financial performance." Such participation usually helps in strategy implementation.

Software systems such as Cascade (**executestrategy.net**) and OnStrategy (**onstrategyhq.com**) have been developed to help facilitate this type of interactive approach.

Pricing Strategy

Traditional methods for determining price are the *cost-plus* and *competition-based models*. **Cost-plus** means determining the expenses associated with producing a product (production cost) by adding up all the costs involved—materials, labor, rent, overhead, and so forth—and adding an additional amount to generate a profit margin (a percentage markup). The *competition-based model* determines price based on what competitors are charging for similar products in the marketplace. For a comprehensive presentation, see **netmba.com/marketing/pricing**.

Pricing products and services for online sales changes these pricing strategies in the following ways:

- **Price comparison is easier.** In traditional markets, either the buyer or more often the seller has more information than the other party does, and the seller uses this information to determine a product's price. Price comparisons help create the "perfect market"—one in which both the buyer and the seller have ubiquitous and equal access to all relevant information, frequently in the buyer's favor.

- **Buyers sometimes set the price.** Name-your-own-price models, such as Priceline.com and auction sites, provide buyers with the option to set their own prices.
- **Online and offline goods are priced differently.** Pricing strategy may be especially difficult for a click-and-mortar company. Setting online prices lower than those offered by the offline side of the same business may lead to internal conflict, whereas setting prices at the same level might hurt the competitive advantage of the online business.
- **Differentiated pricing can be a pricing strategy.** For decades, airline companies have maximized revenues with *yield management* models—charging different customers different prices for the same product or service. In the B2C EC marketplace, one-on-one marketing can provide price differentiation to a segment of customers (e.g., those buying an airline seat early).

The consumer's buying power is increasing due to Internet technologies and social media that provide easy access to pricing information. Sellers need to implement smarter pricing strategies in order to be profitable and competitive, particularly using the Internet to optimize prices. This can be done by setting prices more competitively, adapting to changing prices, and segmenting customers for differentiated pricing.

For more on cost-plus pricing, see **accountingtools.com/cost-plus-pricing** or the video at **study.com/academy/lesson/cost-plus-pricing-definition-method-formula-examples.html**. For more on competition-based pricing, see **priceintelligently.com/blog/bid/161610/Competitor-Based-Pricing-101-The-Necessities-and-Your-Pricing-Strategy** or the video at **youtu.be/TNP60zjIKZ0**.

Acquisitions, Partnerships, Joint Venture, and Multi-EC Model Strategy

In contrast with early EC companies, which were focused on one product or website, many EC companies today have multiple areas of market focus. Furthermore, many collaborate with other companies in joint ventures or other kinds of partnership. For example, Macy's (**macys.com**) a leading US fashion retailer has begun to sell online in China through a joint venture with Alibaba's Tmall (**tmall.com**) (see **businesswire.com/news/home/20150812005604/en/Macy's-Forms-Joint-Venture-Fung-Retailing-Test**), and Amazon.com is in the business of software services (SaaS—see **aws.amazon.com/marketplace/saas**) in addition to e-tailing. Facebook, Google, Apple, and Amazon are aggressively seeking access to a broad range of online services. Google is even investing in robotics, and Facebook purchased the virtual reality company Oculus VR in 2014 and additional technologies in 2016.

Strategy Implementation

In this phase, the emphasis is on "How do we do it?" The **strategy implementation** phase includes tactics, plans, schedules, deployment strategies, resource allocation, and project management.

E-Commerce and Social Media Strategy Implementation Process

Typically, the first step in e-strategy implementation is to find a **project champion** (the person who ensures that the team is ready to move forward and understands its responsibilities) within the organization and establish an EC team, which then initiates and manages the execution of the plan. As EC implementation continues, the team is likely to introduce changes in the organization. Thus, during the implementation phase, it also becomes necessary to develop an effective system to change business processes to accommodate the EC strategy. For a comprehensive case study on how Cadbury implemented social media, see Link Humans (2016).

Start with a Pilot Project
A clever way to implement EC is to begin with one or a small number of EC pilot projects. Problems can be determined during the pilot stage, allowing plans to be modified before it is too late.

Allocate Resources
The resources required for EC projects depend on the information requirements, the capabilities of the performers, and the requirements of each project. Some resources—software, computers, warehouse capacity, and staff—could be new and unique to the EC project. A project's success depends upon an effective allocation and utilization of shared resources to the project such as human resources, marketing budget, and IT systems.

Manage the Project

Project management tools assist in determining specific project tasks, milestones, and resource requirements. Examples of these tools include Microsoft Project (**products.office.com/en-us/project/project-and-portfolio-management-software**), Basecamp (**launchpad.37signals.com/basecamp**), and Smartsheet (**smartsheet.com**).

E-Commerce Strategy Implementation Issues

There are several e-strategy implementation issues, depending on the circumstances. Here we describe some representative ones.

Build, Buy, or Rent EC Elements

Implementation of an EC or social media solution requires access to the construction of the company's website and integration of the site with the existing corporate information systems (e.g., front end for order taking, back end for order fulfillment). At this point, a number of decisions of whether to build, buy, or outsource various components or an entire project need to be made. Some of the more specific decisions include the development of websites and EC systems, marketing management, IT Resources, and logistics.

Calculating a "buy or build" decision is based on an organization's core abilities and the costs required to perform each function well. For more details on calculating "buy or build," see Doig (2015).

Outsource: What? When? To Whom?

Outsourcing can deliver strategic advantages for firms in that it provides access to highly skilled or low-cost labor and provides potential market opportunities. **Outsourcing** is the process of contracting the company's products, services, or work to another organization that is willing and able to do the job. Alternatively, the company's own employees could carry out these projects in-house. In the context of EC, outsourcing means the use of external vendors to acquire EC applications.

Example: Gartner's Magic Quadrant

An interesting tool to help the "go or no go" outsourcing decisions is Gartner's Magic Quadrant. It analyzes companies (providers) along two scales: the ability to execute and the completeness of vision. Vendors are then placed in one of four resulting quadrants (e.g., high ability to execute and full vision make leaders, while low ability to execute and high vision make visionaries). Companies can use the quadrant to find the right outsourcers. For details, see (**gartner.com/technology/research/methodologies/magicQuadrants.jsp#m**).

Successful implementation of EC projects often requires careful consideration of outsourcing strategies, which involves:

- Evaluating when outsourcing should take place
- Deciding which part(s) of the EC projects to outsource and which to keep in-house
- Choosing an appropriate vendor(s)

Strategy Assessment

Strategy assessment refers to the continuous performance monitoring, the comparison of actual to desired performance, and the evaluation of the progress toward the organization's goals, resulting in corrective action and, if necessary, in strategy reformulation. In strategy assessment, EC metrics are used as a standard against which the performance level of the strategy is compared using analytics.

In this stage, companies will use pre-existing metrics to evaluate their overall success. Metrics are defined measures of success that can be easily quantified and are universally agreed upon. Examples of metrics used in EC projects include revenue, sales, ROI, customer counts, and expenses. The chosen metrics must be monitored on an ongoing basis to evaluate the project. Without these measures in place, it will be difficult or impossible to determine if the project was successful and if it should be continued, expanded, or canceled.

For examples and more on EC metrics, see Teneva (2016) and the infographic at **website-designs.com/online-marketing/conversion-rate-optimization/essential-ecommerce-metrics-infographics**).

Performance Improvement and Innovations

If the analysis shows a negative result, it is necessary to take some corrective action. A key activity here is to improve the performance. However, even if the results are good, the organization may take actions that range from providing bonuses for the best performers identified in the analysis to raising the desired levels of performance in the future. A key activity here is being innovative, because even good performance can be improved by innovation. In addition, techniques such as competitive analysis can be useful.

The Objectives of Assessment

Strategic assessment has several objectives. The most important ones are:

- Measure the extent to which the EC strategy and projects are delivering what they are supposed to deliver.
- Determine if the EC strategy and projects are still viable in the current changing business environment.
- Reassess the initial strategy in order to learn from mistakes and improve future planning.
- Identify failing or lagging projects as soon as possible, and determine why they failed or lagged to avoid the same problems in the future.

The Performance Assessment Process

The performance assessment is a process that is based on the stated strategy, tactics, and implementation plans. The process involves the following steps:

1. Set up performance metrics.
2. Monitor the performance of the business.
3. Compare the actual performance to the metrics.
4. Conduct an analysis using analytics, including Web analytics.
5. Combine the analysis with the methodology of the *balanced scorecard*.
6. Present the results to management in the form of reports, tables, and graphics.

The process is illustrated in Fig. 14.2.

This process is part of the larger cyclical process that starts with strategy initiation and formulation and ends with taking corrective action. The major steps of the process are described in the remainder of this section.

Fig. 14.2 The performance assessment process

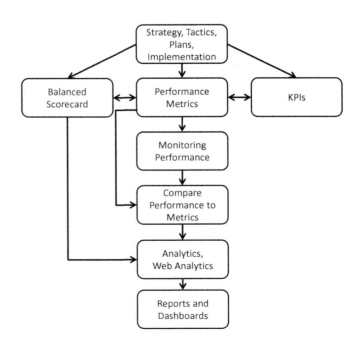

SECTION 14.1 REVIEW QUESTIONS

1. What is strategy?
2. Describe the strategy-performance cycle.
3. Describe the strategy initiation phase.
4. Describe the strategy formulation phase.
5. What is involved in strategy implementation?
6. What is strategy assessment?
7. Describe the phase of performance improvement.

14.2   WHY JUSTIFY E-COMMERCE AND SOCIAL MEDIA INVESTMENTS? HOW CAN THEY BE JUSTIFIED?

Companies need to justify their EC investments for a number of different reasons.

Increased Pressure for Financial Justification

Today, companies are careful with EC expenses and budgets. Managers feel the pressure for financial justification and planning from top executives. However, there is still a long way to go as demonstrated by the following data:

- Most companies lack the knowledge or tools to do ROI calculations for EC or social media projects.
- The vast majority of companies have no formal processes or metrics in place for measuring ROI for EC or social media projects.
- Many companies do not measure how completed EC or social media projects compare with their promised benefits.

At the same time, the demand for expanding or initiating e-business and social media projects is high. Therefore, it is recommended to calculate the projected value of proposed EC or social media projects in order to gain approval for them. For further discussion, see Del Real (2017) and Garver (2014).

Note that in some cases, following the competitors is a major reason to embark on these projects. In such cases, you still need to do a formal justification, but it may be more of a qualitative in nature.

Other Reasons Why EC and Social Media Justification is Needed

The following are some additional reasons for conducting justification:

- Companies now realize that EC and/or social media is not necessarily the solution to all problems. Therefore, these projects must compete with other internal and external projects for funding and resources. The answer usually is provided by ROI.
- Some large companies and many public organizations mandate a formal evaluation of requests for funding.
- There are many levels of social media strategy (scale of interaction and number of networks), and there may be varying returns.
- Companies are required to assess the success of EC and social media projects after their completion.
- The pressure by top management for better alignment of EC and social media strategy with the business strategy.
- The success of EC or social media projects may be assessed in order to pay bonuses to those involved with the projects.

EC Investment Categories and Benefits

Before we look at how to justify EC and social investments, let us examine the nature of such investments. One basic way to categorize different investments is to distinguish between investments in infrastructure, investments in specific EC or social media applications, and staffing.

IT infrastructure provides the foundation for EC or social media projects or applications in the enterprise. IT infrastructure includes servers, intranets, extranets, data centers, data warehouses, knowledge bases, and so forth. In addition, it is necessary to integrate the EC applications with other applications throughout the enterprise that share the infrastructure. Infrastructure investments are made for the long term.

EC applications are specific projects and programs for achieving certain objectives. The number of EC applications can be large. They may be in one functional department, or several departments may share them, which makes the assessment of their costs and benefits more complex.

Social media applications are software and service suites meant to help streamline the process of managing content and interactions in these networks (see Hootsuite and SproutSocial).

Staffing refers to the number of personnel or percentage equivalents that will be needed to set up and operate a project.

Note: Cloud computing may provide a low-cost IT infrastructure and EC applications and must be considered.

The major reasons that companies invest in these projects are to improve business processes, lower costs, increase productivity, increase customer satisfaction and retention, increase revenue and market share, reduce time-to-market, and gain a competitive advantage.

How Is an EC or Social Media Investment Justified?

Justifying an EC or social media investment means comparing the costs of each project against its benefits in what is known as a **cost–benefit analysis**.

A number of different methods are available to measure the *business value* of the project's investments. Traditional methods that support such analyses are *net present value (NPV)* and ROI (see **nucleusresearch.com/research**).

Cost–Benefit Analysis and the Business Case

The cost–benefit analysis and the business value are part of a *business case*. The business case's cost–benefit includes three major components: *benefits* (e.g., revenue increase, cost reduction, customer satisfaction), *costs* (investment and operating costs), and *risks* (e.g., obsolescence, employee resistance). Several vendors provide templates, tools, guidelines, and other aids for preparing the business case in specific areas. For example, you can download a template for an EC business case at **www.ctg.albany.edu/publications/reports/social_media/social_media.pdf** or see **selfstartr.com/ecommerce-business-plan** for a similar social media resource. For a detailed analysis, download the Forrester report "Amplify Your Social Media Business Case Beyond Marketing" (Liousas 2016) from **hootsuite.com/resources/white-paper/forrester-amplify-your-social-media-business-case-beyond-marketing-ty**.

What Needs to Be Justified? When Should Justification Take Place?

Not all investments need to be justified formally. In some cases, a simple one-page qualitative justification is sufficient. The following are cases where formal evaluation may not be needed:

- When the value of the investment is relatively small for the organization.
- When the relevant data are not available, are inaccurate, or are too volatile.

When the EC or social media project is mandated—*it must* be done regardless of the costs involved (e.g., when mandated by the government or when it is necessary to match the competition).

However, even when formal analysis is not required, an organization should conduct at least some qualitative analysis to explain the logic of investing in the project.

Using Metrics in EC and Social Media Justification

Metrics can be used to designate the ratio between costs and benefits or the total costs or do comparisons. They are used not only for justification but also for other economic activities (e.g., to compare employee performance in order to reward those who do the best job). Metrics can produce very positive results in organizations by driving behavior in a number of ways. Metrics can:

- Be the basis for setting up specific goals and plans.
- Describe and measure the value proposition of business models.
- Align the goals of individuals, teams, departments, and other organizational units with the enterprise's objectives.
- Track the characteristics and/or performance of EC or social media systems, including usage, types of visitors, page visits, conversion rate, likes/followers, and so forth.

Metrics, Measurements, and Key Performance Indicators

Metrics need to be defined properly with a clear way to measure them. Figure 14.3 shows the process of using metrics. The cyclical process begins with setting up goals and objectives for organizational and EC performance, which is then expressed by a set of metrics. The metrics are expressed by a set of **key performance indicators (KPIs)**, which are the quantitative expressions of critically important metrics. Often one metric has several KPIs.

The KPIs are continuously monitored by the organization (e.g., via Web analytics, financial reports, marketing data, and so forth). As shown in Fig. 14.3, the KPIs that reflect actual performance are compared to the desired KPIs and planned metrics. If a gap exists, corrective actions take place, and then goals, objectives, and metrics are adjusted if necessary. For a comprehensive coverage, see Turban et al. (2016).

Another example of metrics is shown in the *balanced scorecard method*. This method uses four types of metrics: *customer*, *financial*, *internal business processes*, and *learning growth*. See Fig. 14.4 for an example of the balanced scorecard.

One of the most useful tools for EC management is Web analytics. Web analytics are closely related to metrics.

Fig. 14.3 How metrics are used in performance management

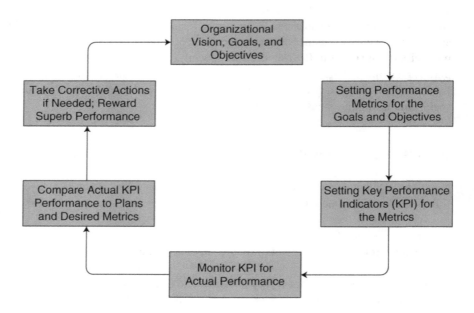

Fig. 14.4 The balanced scorecard approach

CASE 14.1: EC APPLICATION
ALDI SUPERMARKET TRYING E-COMMERCE IN THE UNITED KINGDOM

The Problem

Aldi supermarket is a large Germany-based supermarket chain which is also active in the United Kingdom and Ireland. The grocer is known to be active, with over 10,000 stores in 18 countries and over 500 of those stores in the United Kingdom. The company is a discounter, so profitability is difficult to achieve. The profit margin is very low. The competition is very strong, especially against well-known brands in the United Kingdom (e.g., Primark).

The Solution

Aldi's major competitors do not offer online services. Aldi decided to go online since the company sells many nonperishable goods such as wines and nonfoods. By going online, the company hopes to reach more customers and have its brand be more familiar. The first product went online in early 2016 (it was wine). Clothing home items and electrical products went online in late 2016. Additionally the company has begun using social media to connect with customers and promote products. The results of these efforts have been mixed (see **dailymail.co.uk/news/article-3422192/Internet-users-respond-hilariously-retail-giant-ALDI-s-ill-advised-social-media-campaign-Twitter.html** and **aldi.co.uk/social-media**).

The Results

Given that the EC experiment started in late 2015 and it is the first of its kind in the United Kingdom, the results are not known. Researchers associate the company's online activities with company sales records in 2016, although profits dipped as well (McClean 2016). According to Hobbs (2015), the move is both a risk and an opportunity. The company may increase its cost and turn to EC to be profitable only in several years.

Sources: Based on Hobbs (2015), Baldwin (2015), Chapman (2016), McClean (2016), and **aldi.co.uk**

Questions

1. Read information about the case and identify all the risks and opportunities.
2. The company decided against EC in 2014 but changed its mind a year later. Find the reasons why.
3. Why has the company's social media efforts been both positive and negative? Could Aldi improve in the future?
4. What factors can determine the success and what factors can determine the failure in this venture.

Note: You need to read the sources to answer the questions.

Web Analytics

Web analytics refers to tools and methods that are used to measure, analyze, and optimize Web usage and other Internet activities. A common usage of Web analytics is to evaluate website traffic, but it can also be used as a tool for EC and social media market research. The outcomes of advertising campaigns can also be assessed with Web analytics. For additional information, see Emergent Digital (2017), Khan (2015), and the webinar at **youtu.be/qgyUXQueDSk.**

Now that we understand the need for conducting EC justification and the use of metrics, let us see why EC and social media justification is difficult to accomplish.

The Process of Justifying EC and IT Projects

The major steps of this process are:

1. Establish an appropriate basis for analysis with your vendor, and then conduct your ROI.
2. Investigate what metrics to use (including internal and external metrics), and be sure about their accuracy.
3. Justify the cost–benefit under appropriate assumptions.
4. Verify all data used in the calculation.
5. Include strategic benefits, including long-term ones. Find contributions to competitive advantage. Make sure not to underestimate costs and overestimate benefits (a tendency of many managers).
6. Make data as realistic as possible, and include cost avoidance and risk analysis.
7. Commit all business partners, as well as suppliers and major customers, to your plans.

Quantitative or Qualitative Metrics?

A consistent problem in analyzing the effectiveness of EC or social media projects is the lack of quantitative metrics. While quantitative metrics for both types of projects are readily available in the form of page views, likes, follows, and Web traffic, these may not accurately represent the success of the project based on the specific goals that were laid out. In some cases goals that relate to "popularity" or "effectiveness" may be difficult to weigh. Many times, and especially with social media projects, the value of the investment must be weighed using qualitative metrics as opposed to quantitative metrics. Qualitative metrics are subjective by nature and therefore more difficult to use. It is often quite helpful to identify ahead of time how qualitative metrics will be used and who will determine what those metrics are. Because they are subjective, they may be influenced by individuals who are concerned about the project's overall level of success. For more discussion on this topic, see Levine (2015) or the post at **blog.kissmetrics.com/qualitative-quantitative-analytics**.

SECTION 14.2 REVIEW QUESTIONS

1. List some of the reasons for justifying an EC or social media investment.
2. Describe how an EC or social media investment is justified.
3. List the major investment categories.

4. What are metrics? What benefits do they offer?
5. Describe KPI.
6. Describe the cyclical use of metrics as it relates to organizational performance.
7. What is Web analytics, and what role does it play in the justification of EC or social media projects?
8. Describe the difficulty of using qualitative metrics, especially with social media projects.

14.3   A STRATEGY FOR GLOBAL E-COMMERCE AND SOCIAL MEDIA

Deciding whether to "go global" is a strategic issue. The statistics regarding Internet and smartphone usage worldwide illustrate the enormous potential that exists for companies to expand their market share globally using EC and social media.

The decision to go global is made for many reasons, both reactive and proactive. Reactive reasons include factors such as competitors that are already selling or marketing internationally. Proactive reasons include sellers that are seeking economies of scale; looking for new international markets; gaining access to sufficient or new resources, cost savings, and local government incentives; evaluating products online; and looking to connect with brands. Regardless of the reasons, expanding globally to realize a company's strategic objectives requires extensive planning and responding quickly to opportunities.

A global electronic marketplace can be an attractive opportunity in an EC and social media strategy. Going global means access to new and possibly larger markets, opportunity to minimize taxes, and flexibility to employ a less expensive workforce anywhere. However, going global is a complex and strategic decision process for several reasons. Geographic distance is an obviously important issue in conducting business globally; however, frequently, it is not the most important issue. Cultural differences and political, legal, administrative, and economic issues must be considered. This section briefly examines representative opportunities, problems, and solutions for companies that are going global with EC and social media.

Benefits and Extent of Global Operations

A major advantage of EC is the ability to conduct business at any time, from anywhere, and at a reasonable cost. A major advantage of social media is the ability to interact directly with customers in a format and network in which they are comfortable. Both of these are also the drivers behind global strategies, and there have been some incredible success stories in this area. For example:

- eBay conducts auctions in hundreds of countries worldwide.
- Alibaba.com provides B2C and B2B trading services to millions of companies worldwide.
- Amazon.com sells books and millions of other items to individuals and separate retail websites for 19 countries, including the United States, China, Canada, Japan, the United Kingdom, France, Germany, and Brazil.
- Cisco has expanded its international sales channels to increase sales in Central and South America.
- Major corporations, such as GE and Boeing, have reported an increasing number of international vendors participating in their electronic RFQs. These electronic bids have resulted in a 10–15% cost reduction and more than 50% reduction in cycle time.
- Facebook is working diligently to provide their social network to users in China (see Issac 2016).
- LinkedIn continues to grow its users in India, where it has over 35 million users, 10% of its total user base (see Forbes 2016).

Barriers to Global E-Commerce

Despite the benefits and opportunities offered by globalization, there are several barriers to global EC and social media. Some of these barriers face any venture but become more difficult when international impacts are considered. These barriers include authentication of buyers and sellers, generating and retaining trust, order fulfillment and delivery, security, cultural norms, feature sets, and language. Others are unique to global EC or social media. In this chapter, we will discuss only some of these barriers.

iGlobal Stores (**iglobalstores.com**) and Alibaba.com offer suggestions on what to offer international customers: country-specific checkout experience, up-to-the-minute currency conversion and foreign settlement, global fraud and risk and its protection, calculation of duty and tax, and integration with existing information systems. When social media is considered, Onwuanibe (2015) and the Englishtown case presented by Ross (2014) provide details on different considerations that should be evaluated depending on the product and location being considered.

Cultural Differences

The Internet is a multifaceted marketplace made up of cross-cultural users. The multicultural nature of global EC and social media is important because cultural attributes (such as social norms, local habits, and spoken languages) determine how people interact with companies, agencies, and with each other. Cultural and related differences include spelling differences (e.g., American versus British spelling), information formatting (e.g., dates can be mm/dd/yy or dd/mm/yy), graphics and icons (e.g., mailbox shapes differ from country to country), measurement standards (e.g., metric versus imperial system), and so forth. Additionally, norms may relate to the type of information being shared or who is sharing it. For example, information that is deemed negative to the government in China is banned, and women in some Islamic countries are not encouraged to interact online. Many companies are globalizing their websites by creating different sites for different countries, taking into account site design elements, pricing and payment infrastructures, currency conversion, customer support, and language translation. See the article at **bowerwebsolutions.com/5-social-media-pitfalls-you-must-avoid** for some examples.

Mini Case: Dangdang Inc.

Sometimes companies may view global expansion and e-commerce as an option to drive growth and revenue. Other times, global expansion is necessary purely to keep pace with one's competitors. Chinese e-commerce company Dangdang Inc. (**dangdang.com**) was an early mover in Chinese e-commerce and was once heralded as the "Amazon.com of China." Overtime, Dangdang has continued to be active and profitable in the Chinese market, but it is becoming overshadowed internationally by Alibaba Group (**alibaba.com**) and Jingdong Technology Group Corporation (**jd.com**). These competitors have been able to leverage their success in China into success internationally through expansion and joint ventures. This international success has helped to drive both companies in the Chinese market as well, both through positive perception and additional revenue flows. Dangdang now faces an uphill battle to continue its competitiveness in its home market. For additional details, see Sands (2014) and China Scoop (2016).

Language Translation

Although the world population is over 7.5 billion (2017), only about 1 billion people speak English as their native or second language. In contrast, more than 1.5 billion people speak Chinese. In a study of 3000 shoppers, CSA Research (2014) found that 60% of shoppers in non-English speaking countries would purchase (or only purchase rarely) from websites that were just in English and that 75% would prefer a site in their native tongue. Similarly the research highlighted in GaggleAMP's e-book on "Social Media Globetrotting" indicates that social media efforts that are not in the customer's native language are likely to be ignored, even if English is a common second language in a country (GaggleAMP 2016).

The number one global website in 2017 is Facebook. Other large global sites are Alibaba and Google. Facebook's representative innovations include multilingual plug-ins, an improved global gateway, and multilingual user profiles. The primary problems with language translation are speed and cost. It may take a human translator a week to translate a medium-sized website into another language. For large sites, the cost can be more than $100,000, depending on the complexity of the site and the number of languages for translation, and can be a lengthy process.

Machine Translation

Some companies address the cost and time problems by translating their Web pages into different languages through what is called *machine translations* such as Google Translate. A list of free translation programs can be found at **toptenreviews.com/business/software/best-translation-software/** and **websites.translations.com**. For examples on how Lionbridge Technologies, Inc. uses machine translation to help their clients, see **lionbridge.com/clients**. For example, in 2016, Lionbridge has continued to support Nikon, which is now in 39 locales and 31 languages. Lionbridge provides a team of translators with a detailed knowledge of photography. Product-related content originates from Nikon headquarters in Japan and is then adapted to local markets before being sent to Lionbridge. For more details, see **lionbridge.com/case-study-nikon**.

Example: Stepes for Social Media Translation

Translating content for EC and social media can be quite a challenge, especially for small- and medium-sized businesses. Luckily, there are several vendors that provide this type of service. An excellent example is Stepes (**stepes.com**). Stepes provides a range of services to help businesses translate their social media pages and content into over 100 of target languages. The company provides services to translate both business-generated content and selected user content, like product reviews. Additionally, they provide a machine transcription tool that allows for automatic computer-aided translation of content, as well as a chat-based translation app. For more details, see **stepes.com/social-media** and **gabornemet.com/single-post/2016/1/12/Stepes-world's-first-chatbased-translation-app-now-available-on-iTunes-and-Google-Play**.

Legal Issues

One of the most contentious areas of global EC is the resolution of international legal issues. An ambitious effort to reduce differences in international law governing EC is the United Nations Commission on International Trade Law (UNCITRAL) Model Law on Electronic Commerce. Its purpose is to provide national legislators with a set of guidelines that are internationally acceptable, which specify how to overcome some of the legal constraints in the development of e-commerce. It also provides for a safer legal platform to be constructed through the design of fair, current, and consistent guidelines in e-commerce transactions (see **uncitral.org**). The Model Law has been adopted in some form or another in many countries and legal jurisdictions, including Singapore, Australia, Canada, Haiti, and the United States.

Geographic Issues and Localization

Barriers posed by geography differ based on the transportation and communication infrastructures between and within countries and the type of product or service being delivered. For example, geographic distance is almost irrelevant with online software sales.

Example: Legal Issues and Twitter

Twitter was used significantly as a communication tool in the run-up before and during the 2016 presidential election in the United States. During this time, users on both sides of most issues battled with each other over ideology. Some of these tweets became fairly nasty and personal. In the United States, the vast majority of speech is protected by the First Amendment to the Constitution. In these cases, the largest consequence that users were concerned with was being banned from Twitter's platform. In other countries, this is not the case. Both political and personal speech may have more constraints and possible legal consequences. For example in England, speech that is considered "hate speech" is illegal and can carry possible fines and even jail time (Gale 2016). These variations in laws raise the question about the social media platforms' involvement or responsibility in identifying or enforcing infractions to these laws and speech codes. For a detailed analysis, see **nap.edu/read/15853/chapter/6**.

Web Localization

Many companies use different names, colors, sizes, and packaging for their overseas products and services. This practice is referred to as *localization*. In order to maximize the benefits of global e-commerce, the localization approach also should be used in the design and operation of the supporting information systems. For example, many websites offer different language or currency options, as well as special content. Europcar (**europcar.com**), for example, has a global presence in over 150 countries, each with an option for 1 of 10 languages. The company has a free iPhone and Android app, which is available in eight languages.

Example: Social Media Localization

Localizing social media can be even more difficult than localizing a standard EC page. This is because of the wide variety of social norms and social media practices throughout the world. It is very important for a company to have a comprehensive understanding of these norms and activities before using social media in a particular country, and this is where the localization of the social media efforts becomes very important. For example, Twitter is not as popular in Germany because of the 140 character limit that it is based on. This is because the German language and vocabulary does not generally support such a small space when conveying complex ideas. For more examples, see **welocalize.com/social-media-tips-localization-top-apps**.

Economic and Financial Issues

Economic and financial issues encompassing global efforts include government tariffs, customs, and taxation. In areas subject to government regulation, tax and regulatory agencies have attempted to apply the rules used in traditional commerce to e-commerce, with considerable success. Exceptions include areas such as international tariff duties and taxation. Software shipped in a box would be taxed for duties and tariffs upon arrival. However, software downloaded online may rely on self-reporting and voluntary payment of tax by the purchaser, something that does not happen very often. Social media is greatly affected by these issues as well, as many networks look to embedded commerce and advertising as a sustainable business model.

A major financial barrier to global EC is electronic payment systems. To effectively sell online, EC firms must have flexible payment methods that match the ways people in different countries pay for their online purchases. Although credit cards are used widely in the United States, many European and Asian customers prefer to complete online transactions with offline payments. Even within the category of offline payments, companies must offer different options depending on the country.

Pricing is another economic issue. A vendor may want to price the same product at different prices in different countries based upon local prices and competition. However, if a company has one website, differential pricing will be difficult or impossible. Similarly, what currency will be used for pricing? What currency will be used for payment?

Breaking Down the Barriers to Global E-Commerce

A number of international organizations and experts have offered suggestions on how to break down the barriers to global EC. Some of these suggestions are:

- **Be strategic.** Follow the entire strategy life cycle. A company must consider what countries to target and which languages and how the users in the target countries will react. These considerations need to be included in the strategy.
- **Know your audience.** Consider cultural issues (both in general and online) and legal constraints, which vary around the world.
- **Localize.** Websites need to be localized. In most countries, local languages are essential; translation and machine translation services can help with this. Products are priced in local currencies; and local terms, conditions, and business practices are based on local laws and cultural practices.
- **Think globally, act consistently.** An international company with country-specific websites should be managed locally and must make sure that areas such as brand management, pricing, ad design, and content creation and control are consistent with the company's strategy.
- **Clarify, document, explain.** Pricing, privacy policies, shipping restrictions, contact information, and business practices should be well documented, located on the website, and visible to the customer.
- **Offer services that reduce trade barriers.** It is not feasible to offer prices and payments in all currencies, so provide a link to a currency exchange service (e.g., **xe.com**) or to a currency conversion calculator. In B2B e-commerce, integrate EC transactions with the accounting/finance information system of the major buyers.

SECTION 14.3 REVIEW QUESTIONS

1. Describe globalization in EC and social media and the advantages it presents.
2. Describe the major barriers to global EC and social media expansion.
3. What can companies do to overcome the barriers to global EC and social media use?
4. Discuss the pros and cons of a company offering its website in more than one language.
5. Discuss the legal concerns a company should have using social media in different countries.

14.4 STRATEGY FOR SMALL- AND MEDIUM-SIZED ENTERPRISES

The combination of e-commerce and social media can be one of the most effective business strategies for small- and medium-sized enterprises (SMEs). The potential for SMEs to expand their markets and compete with larger firms through EC and social media is enormous. Some of the first companies to take advantage of Web-based e-commerce and social media were small- and medium-sized enterprises (SMEs). While larger, established, tradition-bound companies hesitated, some forward-thinking SMEs initiated online presence and opened webstores because they realized there were opportunities in marketing, business expansion, cost cutting, procurement, and a wider selection of partner alliances. An example of an active SME that is using social media to expand its EC efforts is Beardbrand (**beardbrand.com**), an e-tailer specializing in products for beards. They use social media and humor to help set themselves apart from other offerings and generate buzz from current and potential customers.

Many SMEs today are adopting social media and EC strategies, either as a means to remain competitive or as the sole business case for their firms. SMEs can join marketplaces such as Alibaba, Amazon.com, and eBay to sell their products there, or they can create their own websites and EC systems using any of the many available website and EC builder applications (see cases in this chapter). According to TrueShip (2016), consumers like to buy in marketplaces with the variety of products they can find there.

Choosing an EC and social media approach is a strategic decision that must be made in the context of the company's overall business strategy. On the positive side, the nature of EC and social media lowers the barriers to entry, and it is a relatively inexpensive way of reaching a larger number of buyers and sellers who can more easily search for, compare prices, and negotiate a purchase. However, there are also some inherent risks associated with the use of EC and social media in SMEs. Table 14.1 provides a list of major advantages and disadvantages of EC for SMEs, while Table 14.2 provides a list of major advantages and disadvantages of EC for SMEs.

Table 14.1 Advantages and disadvantages of EC for small- and medium-sized businesses

Advantages/benefits	Disadvantages/risks
Inexpensive sources of information. A Scandinavian study found that over 90% of SMEs use the Internet for information search (OECD 2001)	Lack of funds to fully exploit the potential of EC
Inexpensive ways of advertising and conducting market research. Banner exchanges, newsletters, chat rooms, and so on are frequently cost-free ways to reach customers	Lack of technical staff or insufficient expertise in legal issues, advertising, etc. These human resources may be unavailable or prohibitively expensive to an SME
Competitor analysis is easier. A Finnish study found that Finnish firms rated competitor analysis third in their use of the Internet, after information search and marketing	Less risk tolerance than a large company. If initial sales are low or the unexpected happens, the typical SME does not have a large reserve of resources to fall back on
Inexpensive ways to build (or rent) a webstore. Creating and maintaining a website are relatively easy and cheap	When the product is not suitable or is difficult for online sales
SMEs are less locked into legacy information technologies and existing relationships with traditional retail channels	Reduced personal contact with customers
Image and public recognition can be generated quickly. A Web presence makes it easier for a small business to compete against larger firms	There is an inability to afford entry or purchase enough volume, to take advantage of digital exchanges
An opportunity to reach worldwide customers. Global marketing, sales, and customer support online can be very efficient	

Table 14.2 Advantages and disadvantages of social media for small- and medium-sized businesses

Advantages/benefits	Disadvantages/risks
Reinforces brand to existing customers, validates their purchase	Human error engaging with the public
Improves search results and provides other avenues for customers to find the business	Legal issues related to privacy, data, and security
Possibly reduces costs for marketing and is easier to target advertising efforts	Costs related to systems and staff time
Easy way to distribute content and FAQs to customers	Reputation loss if issues are not dealt with quickly and correctly

Sources: Adapted from Sitkins (2016) and Belbey (2015)

CASE 14.2: EC APPLICATION WEBSITE BUILDERS

The Problem

In the early days of the Web, building a website was a very technical process. Businesses needed someone who was comfortable with HTML code, or they needed to work with an outside design firm. The development process could take months, and prices for simple websites are easily arranged into thousands or tens of thousands of dollars. Today building a website is much easier, but having a website is more important. A website today is critical for the vast majority of businesses, and that site must have all of the appropriate information about the business which must be kept constantly up to date.

The Solution

For small businesses, this can be a daunting challenge. But luckily there are many products today that are targeted at small businesses with staff that has limited or no experience designing a website. These solutions often come in the form of a website builder application or service. These services are typically Web-based and allow users to quickly develop websites using a series of predesigned templates. While all of the potential product offerings have a variety of features, most focus on the ability to quickly and visually develop Web pages using a WYSIWYG (What You See Is What You Get) editor built into the browser. Services generally include hosting and domain names. Pricing is typically a function of the services used and can be paid by the month (many are less than $10 per month).

Popular options include:

- **Sitebuilder.com**. This solution allows you to quickly create a webpage online as well as securing a domain name and e-mail. There are over 1000 templates to choose from, in a variety of styles and industries. Websites are created with a WYSIWYG editor and allow the user to customize templates. E-commerce options are also available.
- **Wix.com**. This company also allows for the creation of simple websites in a Web-based editor. The templates are smaller in number at 200 but maybe easier to use for a nontechnical employee.
- **Weebly.com**. This service includes how Web-based editor creates and may work better for larger or multipage sites. It includes a number of options for e-commerce and e-mail marketing.

For more examples and reviews, see Muchmore (2017) or **reviews.com/website-builder**.

Questions

1. Why would a small business want to use a website builder application?
2. What would be the benefits and risks of using this type of application?
3. Compare two website builder applications. Which do you prefer and why?

Globalization and SMEs

In addition to increasing their domestic market, EC and social media open up a vast global marketplace for SMEs, but only a small percentage of them conduct a significant part of their business globally. However, a growing number are beginning to use EC and social media to tap into the global marketplace in some way, but even then, SMEs are more likely to purchase globally than to sell globally. This situation is changing thanks to Alibaba.com and similar online directories that help small companies sell globally. For details, see Polk (2015). Very important is the advice provided by Alibaba Group (see Fan 2015).

For resources for SMEs going global, see **sbecouncil.org/resources/going-global**.

Resources to Support SME Activities in EC and Social Media

SME owners often lack strategic management skills and consequently are not always aware of changes in their business environment with respect to emerging technologies. Fortunately, SMEs have a variety of private and public support options (e.g., **sba.gov**, **score.org**, **business.gov.au**).

Today, SMEs have many resources available to support their creation of websites, EC storefronts, mobile apps, and social media campaigns. While some systems were originally developed for large companies [e.g., IBM's small and medium business solutions (**ibm.com/midmarket/us/en**)], many have now been repurposed for this market. Additionally, many services today are focused on serving the needs of this market exclusively and provide products specifically tailored to small businesses. For more details on these services, see the cases in this chapter.

Resources to assist SMEs in going global are also emerging as helpful tools for SMEs that want to expand their horizons. For example, the Global Small Business Blog (GSBB) (**globalsmallbusinessblog.com**) was created in 2004 by Laurel Delaney to help entrepreneurs and small business owners expand their businesses internationally. Another example is the Small Business and Entrepreneurship Council (SBE Council)'s global resources at **sbecouncil.org/resources/going-global**. A good source regarding SMEs' use of e-markets to conduct international business is **emarketservices.com/start/Case-studies-and-reports/index.html**. Also see Goldberg (2016).

SMEs and Social Networks

Social commerce is one of the fastest growing EC technologies that is being adopted by SMEs.

Small businesses can utilize social network sites to market to potential customers, support existing customers, and interact with peer groups outside their immediate geographical area to exchange ideas. Social media efforts can be conducted using many of the same networks and tools used in the United States but may require localization as discussed above. Additionally, SMEs can find websites that are dedicated to small businesses and provide opportunities to make contacts, get start-up information, and receive advice on e-strategies. Not only can sites such as LinkedIn be used to garner advice and make contacts, they can be used in B2B to develop networks that can connect SMEs with other small businesses or foster relationships with partners.

Table 14.3 lists ten steps to success when using social media in SMEs. For tips on how to use YouTube to promote the online content of SMEs, see **masternewmedia.org/online_marketing/youtube-promote-content-viral-marketing/youtube-video-marketing-10-ways-20070503.htm** and **forbes.com/sites/ajagrawal/2016/09/16/5-ways-to-use-video-marketing-for-small-business-growth/#2886e91233f8**.

SMEs are following the growing popularity of social networking sites and using social media to build connected networks, enhance customer relationships, and gather feedback about their services and products.

For implementation issues of social commerce, see Didner (2014) and Wells (2015).

SECTION 14.4 REVIEW QUESTIONS

1. What are the advantages or benefits of EC and social media for small businesses?
2. What are the disadvantages or risks of EC and social media for small businesses?
3. Why are there software solutions tailored to SMEs?
4. How can social networks help SMEs become more competitive?

Table 14.3 Ten steps to a successful social media strategy

Step	Description
1	Understand what social media is and what the benefits of using it are
2	Identify the audience you want to reach and where to find it
3	Identify the resources you currently have available for use for social networking and social networks
4	Identify the most appropriate technologies to use
5	Start a blog and create a social culture in your business
6	Build social media profiles for your business on Facebook, LinkedIn, Twitter, YouTube, Instagram, Pinterest, etc.
7	Make your blog social media friendly
8	Build relationships with your target market
9	Turn friends and followers into customers
10	Decide how you will monitor and measure the performance of your social media initiatives

14.5   THE IMPLEMENTATION LANDSCAPE

Now that you know about EC and social media benefits and applications, you may wonder what to do next. First you need to ask questions such as: "Do I need EC and social media?" and then "How am I going to do it?" The answers to these two and other questions can be very complex since they depend on many factors that we will discuss in this chapter. We refer to these factors as *implementation factors*.

The Major Implementation Factors

Many factors can determine the need and success of EC and social media projects. We organize them in the following categories.

Justification/Economics

The first issue is to find out if you need to get involved in an EC or social media project(s). This issue can be very complex for large-scale projects. We call this EC and social media project justification.

Acquire or Self-Develop Your E-Commerce or Social Media Management System

This issue is not simple either, especially when medium- and large-scale projects are involved. In the case of social media, a system for managing campaigns may not be needed but could be helpful depending on the volume of interaction and the available staff time.

Organizational Readiness and Impacts of E-Commerce

How to organize your EC and social media projects within the organization and how to deal with changing business processes and other changes brought by EC and social media are all part of the implementation considerations. In addition, potential impacts on marketing, manufacturing, and people need to be addressed. Finally, technical issues such as connecting to other information systems need to be considered.

How to Succeed

The last part of this chapter addresses some of the critical success factors of implementing EC projects.

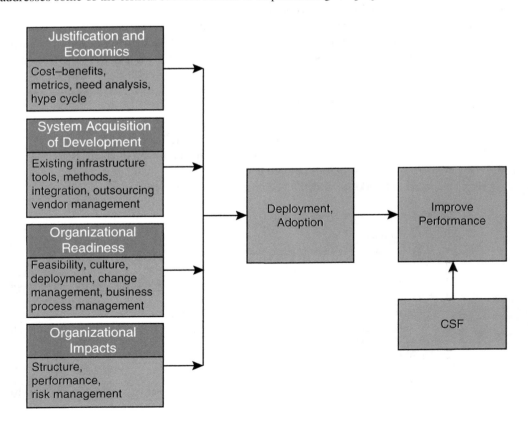

Fig. 14.5 The elements in EC and social media implementation

We have organized the above factors into a framework, which is shown in Fig. 14.5.

On the left side of the figure, we placed the major factors that impact implementation. They all may affect the adoption and deployment of the EC and social media projects. A successful deployment and adoption will lead to improved performance.

CASE 14.3: EC APPLICATION
E-COMMERCE BUILDERS

The Problem

When e-commerce sites begin to be more common in the mid-to-late 1990s, developing, hosting, and maintaining these services were a detailed and expensive process. Many of the initial e-commerce sites were developed in-house from scratch. These systems had the advantage of being exactly what the business wanted but the distinct disadvantage of being very expensive. Other options included the use of software systems that could be customized by the developer or by integrators. These were still expensive but less so than pure insourcing. All of these systems required dedicated hosting with a large upfront cost and/or significant monthly fees.

The Solution

Today, e-commerce systems are much less complex, and many options exist for small businesses that do not require the large upfront expenses, significant ongoing expenses, and technical expertise of previous systems. Much like the Web-based website design tools available, there are also many Web-based e-commerce tools available for businesses. These solutions all focus on ease of setup, ease of use, and integration into existing business processes. These systems use the same WYSIWYG architecture as the website builder applications but add e-commerce capabilities. These packages typically include secure hosting as well as integrated payment solutions.

Popular options include:

- **Shopify.com**. This is the most commonly used service and includes many templates that can be used to set up an online store. It includes built-in payment systems as well as mobile compatibility. Unique to this store is the ability to use the system as a point-of-sale (POS) application as well.
- **Jimbo.com**. This service also includes templates to develop an online storefront with secure payment options by default. This system is unique with its global emphasis, easily allowing localization of different sites as well as localization of the developer interface.
- **Squarespace.com**. This service provides a wide variety of templates to ensure that the e-commerce portions of the site can match an existing website (or it is also possible to develop the website itself inside Squarespace). This service has a number of additional add-ons and services that can be selected to customize a solution.

For more examples and reviews, see Angeles (2016b) or **websitebuilderexpert.com/e-commerce-online-store-builders-comparison-chart**.

Sources: Angeles (2016b).

Questions

1. Why would a small business want to use an e-commerce builder application?
2. What would be the benefits and risks of using this type of application?
3. Compare two e-commerce builder applications. Which do you prefer and why?

Using Vendors and Materials

Many vendors exist with the primary aim of helping small- and medium-sized businesses as they implement EC and social media campaigns. Many of these systems are designed specifically to meet the needs of this market and have feature sets that will be useful for this type of organization. Businesses evaluating the use of vendor products must ensure that the product is a good fit for their organization. This means that the product has all of the required features, has the appropriate level of complexity, and is within the allocated budget. For an EC example, see **nonlinearcreations.com/Digital/how-we-think/ articles/2013/10/7-things-to-consider-before-choosing-an-ecommerce-platform.aspx**.

Many vendors today provide significant documentation of how to use their products, as well as guides on best practices in implementing these types of projects. Using vendor guides, especially when it is the vendor that an organization has selected, can be a useful shortcut in an organization's planning and implementation of a particular product. For an example of an EC guide, see Shopify (**shopify.com/guides**), and for an example of a social media management guide, see Hootsuite (**hootsuite.com/resources/guide/scaling-social-media-a-guide-to-implementing-a-social-center-of-excellence**).

SECTION 14.5 REVIEW QUESTIONS

1. Why is the implementation of EC and social media so complex?
2. What are the major elements of EC and social media implementation (see Fig. 14.5)?
3. What factors determine deployment and adoption (see Fig. 14.5)?
4. Why should businesses be careful in selecting software vendors and using their guides?

14.6   DEVELOPMENT STRATEGIES FOR E-COMMERCE AND SOCIAL MEDIA PROJECTS

When companies are deciding how to implement their EC and social media projects, they have several choices on how to develop and launch those systems. Many of these choices focus around how much work will be done internally within the organization and how much will be outsourced to a software or consulting firm. As a general rule, keeping these activities within the company may be faster or cheaper but may create issues with existing workload and talent. Generally, outsourcing these activities costs more but can result in a higher-quality project. The general approaches that companies can pursue include:

- **Complete insourcing.** Use existing staff to create and manage the project.
- **Insourcing with new hires.** Keep the project internal but bring on staff to help with the workload and specific project talent requirements.
- **Insourcing with applications or tools.** Purchase or rent tools or applications that allow existing staff to complete the project.
- **Insourcing and new hires with applications or tools.** Purchase or rent tools or applications that allow existing staff and new hires to complete the project.
- **Outsource.** All or a portion of the project to a software company or consulting firm.
- **Use a consulting firm.** To help educate and implement using existing staff.

In-House Development: Insourcing

The first generation of EC development and social media campaigns was accomplished largely through proprietary programming, in-house development, and staff trial and error that is widely referred to as **insourcing**.

Although insourcing can be time-consuming and costly, it may lead to implementations that best fit an organization's strategy and needs and differentiate the company from its competition. These in-house developments, however, can be lengthy and expensive. Furthermore, the maintenance and updating may require considerable resources in the future.

Insourcing may be the appropriate option, but additional staff members may be needed. Many companies identify the need for greater expertise in implementing these types of projects and hire staff with that experience in order to meet this talent requirement. Additionally, companies may identify the need for additional personnel to operate the project and higher around that need as well.

Insourcing with Applications or Tools

With a large number of software applications available, it may be easy for businesses to select a tool, suite of tools, or set of services that meet their exact needs. These options have the distinct advantage of being easier to implement and use while generally carrying a lower price tag and then a custom solution. Many of these tools are designed to be used by existing personnel within a company. While there are many possible benefits, there are drawbacks as well.

Advantages and Limitations of Software Solutions

The following are the major advantages of purchasing ready-made EC systems:

- A large variety of off-the-shelf software packages is available.
- It saves time and money (compared to in-house development).
- It may allow existing staff to operate the system.
- The company does not need to hire programmers.
- The company knows the system's capabilities before it invests in it.
- The company is neither the first nor the only user of the package.
- Updating is done by the vendor with little or no cost to the users.

This option also has some major disadvantages:

- Software and services may not exactly meet the company's needs.
- Options may be expensive.
- Options for specific industries or vertical markets may not be available.
- Software may be difficult or impossible to modify, or it may be necessary to modify the company's business processes.
- The using company has little control over software improvements and new versions.
- Applications can be difficult to integrate with existing software systems.
- Vendors may discontinue a product or go out of business (risk factor).

Outsourcing Development and Implementation

Some businesses may opt to outsource the development and implementation of some of these projects. As a general rule, outsourced projects can have very high level of quality and fast turnaround times. Conversely, outsourced projects are typically more expensive and run the risk of not integrating well with a business's existing processes and corporate culture.

Project Outsourcing Options

Typical outsource solutions today include:

- **Building and implementing EC solutions**, including populating the catalog/database as well as integrating required third-party systems. This type of outsourcing is typically performed by a software company or integrator.
- **Launching and maintaining social media campaigns**, including specific advertising campaigns as well as daily interactions. This type of outsourcing is typically performed by a marketing or advertising agency.
- **Development of websites**, including the integration of EC or social media aspects. This type of outsourcing is typically performed by a website or media firm or could also be performed by an integrator or marketing agency.
- **Development of mobile applications**, including the integration of these applications with EC or social media functions. This type of outsourcing is typically performed by a software development company or marketing firm.

CASE 14.4: EC APPLICATION
WOULD YOU BUILD AN APP ONLINE?

The Problem

Many businesses see the benefit of developing mobile applications that integrate with existing e-commerce or social media efforts. Other businesses view apps as a way to attract new potential customers. Start-up businesses may view apps as a primary revenue model. The development of mobile apps is typically viewed as a task left to programmers, working with specific software tools designed for the iOS or Android operating systems. While apps may be available to many businesses or individuals willing to go this route, they are not available to those unwilling or unable to learn the technical proficiencies needed (or to pay for them).

The Solution

Recently several companies have launched that offer solutions that can develop custom applications for individuals and businesses but without using specific software development tools (and the underline technical proficiencies). These companies allow for the development of apps using a Web-based interface, with a wide variety of pre-built features. Most allow for the development across multiple operating systems, generally both iOS and Android.

Example: Appypie.com

Appypie (**appypie.com**) offers the ability to create a wide variety of apps using its Web-based development platform. Apps can be developed from both of functional and design perspective. Additionally, many pre-built app templates are available for different uses and vertical markets. The system allows you to customize most functionality within the app, as well as creating an interface suitable to that functionality. In addition to apps, mobile games may also be developed. Apps can be developed for the iOS, Android, Blackberry, Windows Phone, and FireOS platforms.

There are several different pricing models, each based on a monthly, yearly, or lifetime fee. These fees are a function of the services that are provided by Appypie. A free option exists that is ad-based. Other options exist with no ads, white labeling, and additional marketing services. Free applications that are not upgraded to a paid plan will be deleted after 1 year.

Similar services are provided by **buildfire.com**, **ibuildapp.com**, and **theappbuilder.com**.

For more examples and reviews, see Angeles (2016a) or **websitetooltester.com/en/blog/app-makers**.

Sources: Angeles (2016a).

Questions

1. What benefits can a business obtain through the use of a mobile app?
2. Why has the use of mobile apps been constrained for small businesses?
3. Examine the features of this service and discuss your findings. Would you build an app online?

Selecting a Development Option

Before choosing an appropriate development option, you need to consider the following factors (given here as questions):

- **Customers.** Who are the target customers? What are their needs? What kind of marketing tactics should a business use to promote the webstore and attract traffic? How can a business enhance customer loyalty? How can a business engage the customers and make them happy so they will return? What social media networks do they frequent?
- **Merchandising.** What kinds of products or services will the business sell online? Are soft (digitized) goods or hard goods sold? Are soft goods downloadable?
- **Sales service.** Can customers order online? How? Can they pay online? Can they check the status of their order(s) online? How are customer inquiries handled? Are warranties, service agreements, and guarantees available for the different products? What are the refund procedures? Do customers want to communicate by e-mail, text, or social media?

- **Promotion.** How are the products and services promoted? How will the traffic to special events be organized? Are coupons, manufacturer's rebates, or quantity discounts offered? Is cross selling possible? Will viral marketing be used? What type of media is required?
- **Transaction processing.** Is transaction processing done in real time? How are taxes, shipping and handling fees, and payments processed? What kinds of shipping methods will the site offer? What kind of payment method(s) will the site accept? How will the site conduct order fulfillment?
- **Marketing data and analysis.** What information, such as sales, customer data, and advertising trends, will the site collect? How will the site use such information for future marketing? How is the information secured? How will social media campaigns be assessed? How will customer interaction be assessed?
- **Branding.** What image should the webstore reinforce? How is the company's webstore different from the competition webstore?

The initial list of requirements should be as comprehensive as possible. It is preferable to validate the identified requirements through focus group discussions or surveys with potential customers. The business can then prioritize the requirements based on customer preferences.

For more detail on insourcing versus outsourcing for EC systems, see **practicalecommerce.com/articles/3705-Outsourcing-v-Hiring-In-house-Pros-and-Cons**; for social media decisions, see **smartinsights.com/managing-digital-marketing/resourcing-digital-marketing/insourcing-outsourcing-digital-marketing**.

SECTION 14.6 REVIEW QUESTIONS

1. List the major EC and social media development options.
2. Define insourcing.
3. List some of the pros and cons of using software solutions.
4. List some of the pros and cons of outsourcing.
5. What are the advantages of building with templates or builder applications? What are the disadvantages?
6. What are some of the selection criteria for an EC or social media project?

14.7 OPPORTUNITIES FOR SUCCESS IN E-COMMERCE AND SOCIAL MEDIA AND AVOIDING FAILURE

Now that EC has been around for over 20 years and social media for more than 10 years, it is possible to observe certain patterns that contribute to the success or failure of EC and social media projects. By examining these patterns, one can find indications of the opportunities that lie ahead and avoiding pitfalls along the way. It is not easy to assure success in e-commerce was shown in the case of Aldi supermarket (Case 14.1).

Factors that Determine E-Commerce and Social Media Success

The economic capabilities of EC and social media described earlier influence some industries more than others do. The success factors depend on the industry, the sellers and buyers, and the products sold. Furthermore, the ability of sellers to create economic and personal value for consumers will also determine success. When deciding to sell online or market using social media, looking at the major factors that determine the impact of these types of projects can assist in evaluating the chances for success.

Four categories of e-market success factors exist: *product*, *industry*, *seller*, and *consumer* characteristics.

E-Commerce and Social Media Failures

By examining the economic history of previous innovations, the failure of EC and social media initiatives should come as no surprise. Three economic phenomena suggest why this is the case.

Some of the specific reasons for failure in B2C EC are lack of profitability, excessive risk exposure, the high cost of customer acquisition, poor performance, and poor website design. Two additional financial reasons are lack of funding and incorrect revenue models. For the use of social media, specific reasons for failure are high cost-to-benefit ratios, poorly planned campaigns that hurt company prestige, improper interactions that decrease customer loyalty, and gross errors that become viral.

E-Commerce and Social Marketing Effectiveness

One consistent issue that all businesses need to watch is the effectiveness of their marketing campaigns, to make sure that they are getting value for the money that they spend. Businesses need to determine the rate of return that they can receive on any advertising to ensure that it is the best use of their available money and that it is producing positive revenue for them. This is particularly important in EC, because of the huge amount of competition and also due to possible marketing fraud online. In addition to watching overall effectiveness, businesses need to be on the lookout for fraudulent competitors that can potentially rob them of business. This will also show up in the form of decreased conversions in advertisements and page views.

Example: Factors Effecting Profitability: Fraudulent ads

Fraudulent and misleading ads are a significant issue online. In 2016 Google removed over 1.7 billion fraudulent advertisements from its platform (Jones 2017). Fraudulent ads are designed to mislead customers concerning the features of a product or are meant to be outright scams, pushing customers to purchase nonexistent products or services. Google works hard to ensure that this type of ad does not exist on its platform. For legitimate businesses, fraudulent advertisements create more competition for users' attention and create noise in the market space that can potentially decrease customer confidence. Both of these can negatively affect the amount of attention and sales that a legitimate business is able to garner.

Example: Factors Effecting Profitability: Fake Reviews

Just like fraudulent ads, fake reviews can also be a large issue online. Fake reviews can hurt a business in two different ways. First, the fake review may be about the business's legitimate product, but the review can be negative and that can hurt the products' perception. Second, a fake review may be very positive about a competitor's product, reducing the sales of the legitimate product (Lanford 2017). Fake reviews prey on customers' inherent trust of feedback from other users. Just like with fake ads, different platforms work diligently to ensure that fake reviews are identified and removed as quickly as possible. There are several excellent examples of Amazon identifying and removing fraudulent reviews (Faulkner 2016) and methods a consumer can use to protect themselves (see **laptops.reviewed.com/news/heres-what-you-need-to-know-about-fake-amazon-reviews**).

E-Commerce and Social Media Successes

Despite the failure of hundreds of start-ups and thousands of EC projects, EC is alive and well and continues to grow rapidly. Social media has overcome its awkward and unappreciated beginning to become a mainstay of corporate advertising.

EC success stories abound, primarily in the specialty and niche markets. One example is Puritan's Pride Inc. (**puritan. com**), a successful vitamin and natural healthcare product store. Another is GrubHub, Inc. (**grubhub.com**), which allows people to order food online for either pickup or delivery (previously CampusFood.com). Also doing very well are travel sites, such as Expedia, TripAdvisor, and Priceline.

Social media success stories are also prevalent, in both small businesses and major brands. An example of a small company using social media effectively is the Dollar Shave Club's #RaozorBurn campaign on Twitter. A larger company using social media well is auditing firm PricewaterhouseCoopers using Snapchat to track Oscar balloting in 2016. For details on both, see **cio.com/article/3062615/social-networking/10-top-social-media-marketing-success-stories.html**.

For a comparison of how these and other thriving online businesses have translated critical success factors (CSFs) from the old economy into EC success, see Table 14.4. EC successful companies such as Priceline, Netflix, Amazon.com, Facebook, and Google are becoming major players in their industries, making their shareholders very rich.

Following are some of the reasons for EC and social media success and suggestions from EC experts and consultants on how to succeed in EC.

Table 14.4 Critical success factors: old economy and EC

Old economy CSFs	EC CSFs
Vertically integrate or do it yourself	Create new partnerships and alliances; stay with core competency
Deliver high-value products	Deliver high-value service offerings that encompass products
Build market share to establish economies of scale	Optimize natural scale and scope of business; look at mass customization
Analyze carefully to avoid missteps	Approach with urgency to avoid being left out; use proactive strategies
Leverage physical assets	Leverage intangible assets, capabilities, and relationships – unleash dormant assets
Compete to sell product	Compete to control access to markets, and build relationships with customers; compete with other websites

Strategies for EC and Social Media Success

- Thousands of brick-and-mortar companies are adding online marketing and/or procurement channels with great success.
- For an EC exchange to be successful, it has to create value for *all* participants. A vivid example is Alibaba.com.
- Pricing in EC has continued to be a challenge for sellers because of shipping and handling costs. Often, the seller and market maker will see the potential for profits and ignore the fact that the buyers will subscribe to EC only if they see a benefit in price or product variety. For example, free shipping is available at Dell, Newegg, and many other e-tailers.
- New technologies can boost the success of EC. For example, RFID has great potential for improving the supply chain; however, it will take a large investment in EC infrastructure and applications to realize its full potential.
- Digital partnerships can drive business success (McCafferty 2016).
- Social media engagement must be authentic.
- Campaigns must be memorable and funny to gain traction or go viral (Jackson 2015).

Additional Guidelines for EC and Social Media Success

A number of experts and consultants have proposed many more keys to success. Several studies identified success factors such as:

- Effective marketing and advertising
- User-friendly website
- Good relationships between customers and merchants
- Open, clear communication with customers
- Interacting with customers in the platform they prefer
- Proper supply chain management and order fulfillment
- Integration with internal and external information systems
- The use of appropriate business models (including revenue models)
- Effective and efficient infrastructure
- Organization culture regarding becoming an e-business and social business
- Clear goals and guidelines for social media use
- Effective leadership of the digital business team (Raskino and Waller 2016)

As with any EC or social media business, success cannot be guaranteed, and failure rates remain high. However, if companies learn from the mistakes of others and follow the guidelines offered by experts and researchers, their chances for success are greatly enhanced.

Cultural Differences in EC and Social Media Successes and Failures

Here, we add the issue of *cultural differences* so that appropriate strategies can be developed when doing business globally.

One of the strengths of EC and social media is the ease with which sellers and buyers can reach and communicate with a global population of consumers or suppliers. However, they must recognize existing cultural differences and act upon them. Even the content of online ads can mean different things in different cultures. Due to these differences, the transaction costs, including coordination costs, may vary among the consumer base.

SECTION 14.7 REVIEW QUESTIONS

1. What are the characteristics of EC that are different than traditional commerce?
2. What are the characteristics of social media that are different than traditional advertising?
3. List three reasons why EC and social media failure should not come as a surprise.
4. What are some reasons for EC and social media success?
5. Relate EC and social media to cultural differences.

MANAGERIAL ISSUES

Some managerial issues related to this chapter are as follows:

1. **What is the strategic value of EC and social media to the organization?** It is important for management to understand how EC or social media can improve marketing and promotions, customer service and sales, and the supply chain and procurement processes. More significantly, the greatest potential of these projects is realized when management views these projects from a strategic perspective, not merely as a technological advancement. Management should determine the primary goals of EC and social media projects, such as new market creation, cost avoidance and reduction, and customer service enhancement.
2. **Why do we need an EC and social media planning process?** A strategic plan is both a document and a process. Former US President Dwight D. Eisenhower once said, "Plans are nothing, planning is everything." A planning process that includes management, employees, business partners, and other stakeholders not only produces a planning document that will guide a business into the future but also describes to the participants about where the company is going and how it intends to get there. The same can be said for e-business planning—the process is as important as the plan itself.
3. **How do you relate the EC or social media activities to business objectives and metrics?** Companies first must choose objectives and design-appropriate metrics to measure the goals and actual achievement. The companies need to exercise with caution, because the metrics may accidentally lead employees to behave in the opposite direction of the intended objectives. Organizations must be careful if qualitative metrics are used to ensure their validity. The balanced scorecard is a popular framework adopted to define objectives, establish performance metrics, and then map them. EC and social media planning needs to identify what the role of the project is in achieving the goals in BSC metrics.
4. **How can EC and social media go global?** Going global with EC or social media is a very appealing proposition for companies of all sizes, but it may be difficult to do, especially on a large scale or for SMEs that lack the necessary resources. Companies need to identify, understand, and address the barriers to globalization such as culture, language, and law, as well as customers and suppliers. An e-business needs to decide on a localization strategy.
5. **What can small businesses do to remain competitive?** Both EC and social media provide several opportunities that can allow small businesses to remain competitive against larger firms. Both of these technologies can be said to level the playing field. Small businesses need to examine EC and social media to determine how or if they are to be used to remain competitive both globally and locally.
6. **How can we plan for successful implementation?** Implementing EC and social media projects can be a complicated task. Detailed planning may be necessary in order to assure that defined goals are met within the allocated time and budget. Many different strategies exist including insourcing, outsourcing, and the use of software tools and services.

SUMMARY

In this chapter, you learned about the following EC issues as they relate to the chapter's learning objectives:

1. **Strategy concepts and competitiveness.** Implementing EC and social media projects requires a strategy. The five major phases of developing a business strategy are initiation, formulation, implementation, assessment, and performance improvements. The major generic tools for strategic management are the strategy map, SWOT analysis, competitor analysis, scenario planning, and business plan.
2. **The need for EC and social media justification.** Like any other investment, EC and social media investment (unless it is small) needs to be justified. Many start-up companies have crashed because of incorrect or no justification. In its simplest form, justification looks at revenue minus all relevant costs. Analysis is done by defining performance and comparing actual performance to the desired metrics and KPI related to organizational goals.
3. **Issues in global EC and social media.** Going global with EC or social media can be done quickly and with a relatively small investment. However, businesses must deal with a number of different issues in the cultural, administrative, geographic, legal, and economic dimensions of global trading.
4. **Reasons for EC and social media success and failure.** Products, industries, sellers, and consumer characteristics require different metrics. With the growing worldwide connectivity to the Internet, EC and social media economics will play a major role in supporting buyers and sellers. Some EC failures are the result of problematic website design, lack of sustained funding, and weak revenue models. Some social media failures have come from high cost to benefit ratios, poorly planned campaigns that hurt company prestige, improper interactions that decrease customer loyalty, and gross errors that become viral. Success in EC has come through automating and enhancing familiar strategies, such as branding, morphing, building

trust, and creating value for all trading partners by enriching the human experience with integrated and timely information. Success in social media has come through careful planning, detailed procedures, and solid research on customer needs.

5. **Small- and medium-sized businesses and EC and social media.** Depending on the circumstances, innovative small companies have a tremendous opportunity to adopt EC or social media at little cost and expand rapidly. Being in a niche market provides the best chance for small business to succeed. A variety of Web-based resources are available for small- and medium-sized business owners to get help to ensure success.

6. **The major components of EC and social media implementation.** Four major categories exist for implementation: justification and economics (cost–benefit); acquiring and/or developing systems; assurance of organizational readiness and performance of necessary restructuring, training, and so forth; and cultivating the necessary success factors while avoiding mistakes.

7. **The major EC and social media development strategies, along with their advantages and disadvantages.** EC applications and social media systems are rarely built from scratch. Instead, they can purchase software systems or services and customize them to suit their needs (if possible), or they outsource the development to a vendor. A new generation of Web tools including social software enables more "do it yourself" activities.

KEY TERMS

Cost–benefit analysis
Cost-plus
E-Commerce risk
Insourcing
Key performance indicators (KPIs)
Outsourcing
Project champion
Strategy
Strategy assessment
Strategy formulation
Strategy implementation
Strategy initiation
Web analytics

DISCUSSION QUESTIONS

1. How would you identify competitors of your small business who want to launch an EC or social media project?
2. Find some SME EC success stories and identify the common elements in them.
3. Why must e-businesses consider strategic planning to be a cyclical process?
4. Your state government is considering an online vehicle registration system. Develop a set of EC metrics and discuss how these metrics differ from that of the existing manual system.
5. Your state government is considering a social media campaign to decrease illegal drug use. Develop a set of social media metrics, and why you are using quantitative metrics, qualitative metrics, or both.
6. Enter **businesscase.com** and find material on ROI analysis. Discuss how ROI is related to a business case.
7. A craftsperson operates a small business making wooden musical instruments in a small US town. The business owner is considering using social media to increase the business's market recognition to the nation and the world. How can the business owner use social media to make the products more attractive to consumers?
8. Discuss the pros and cons of going global online to sell a physical product.
9. Discuss the pros and cons of using social media globally.
10. Find some SME EC or social media success stories, and identify the common elements in them.
11. Submit three questions regarding EC or social media strategy for small businesses to **linkedin.com** and **answers.yahoo. com**. Get some answers and summarize your experience.
12. After viewing the video "The Biggest Challenges for International Marketers" (4:00 min) at **youtu.be/6alaVZB_Rk8**, discuss how social media could be used to address these issues.
13. Discuss how a company embarking on global e-commerce would approach each challenge such as payments or logistics, without the assistance of a company like Borderfree.

TOPICS FOR CLASS DISCUSSION AND DEBATES

1. Debate: An airline offers extensive travel services online including hotels, car rentals, vacations, and so forth all over the globe. Its online business should be autonomous.
2. The stock market success of e-commerce and social commerce companies varies greatly from very successful (e.g., Google, LinkedIn) to poor (Groupon, Zynga). Examine the IPOs of 2015 through 2017 and try to explain the CSF. Write a report.
3. As the principal in a small business that already has an effective Web presence, you are considering taking your company global. Discuss the main issues that you will have to consider in making this strategic decision.
4. Has the availability of EC and social media affected the way we assess industry attractiveness? Develop new criteria for assessing the attractiveness of pure online industries.
5. Consider the challenges of a brick-and-mortar company manager who wants to create an integrated (online/offline) business. Discuss the challenges that he or she will face.
6. Examine the seven strategies of Facebook and Twitter at **socialmediatoday.com/christinegallagher/165536/top-7-facebook-and-twitter-strategies,** and comment on them.
7. Is Amazon.com eBay's biggest competitor? What about Walmart.com? What about Alibaba Group?
8. Have technologies needed by small businesses for e-commerce or social media marketing lagged behind those of larger businesses? Why or why not?

INTERNET EXERCISES

1. Survey several online travel agencies (e.g., **travelocity.com, orbitz.com, cheaptickets.com, priceline.com, expedia.com, hotwire.com**), and compare the business strategies of three of them. How do they compete against brick-and-mortar travel agencies?
2. Enter **digitalenterprise.org/metrics/metrics.html**. Read the material on Web analytics, and prepare a report on the use of Web analytics for measuring advertising success.
3. Enter **salesforce.com/form/roi**. Register and download the free ROI kit. Summarize one case study. View two demos. Write a report.
4. One of the most global companies is Amazon.com. Find stories about its global strategies and activities (try **forbes.com**), and conduct a Google search. What are the most important lessons you learned?
5. Visit **business.com/starting-a-business/tech-toolkit-for-startups** and find some of the EC opportunities available to small businesses. Also visit the website of the Small Business Administration (SBA) office in your area. Summarize recent EC-related topics for SMEs.
6. Visit **https://hootsuite.com/resources/toolkit/social-media-planning-toolkit-2016** and download the planning documents. What difficulties would a small business face creating a social media strategy?
7. Conduct research on small businesses and their use of the Internet for EC and social media marketing. Visit sites such as **marketingprofs.com** and **uschamber.com**. Also enter **google.com** or **bing.com**, and type "small businesses + electronic commerce + social media." Use your findings to write a report on current small business EC and social media issues.
8. Enter **baselinemag.com** and find free ROI analysis tools. Download a tool of your choice and identify its major components. Write a report.
9. Read the articles at **socialmediaexaminer.com/10-metrics-to-track-for-social-media-success** and **cio.com/article/2901047/social-media/12-standout-social-media-success-stories.html**. Identify and write a report on the factors in social media campaigns that may be a success.

TEAM ASSIGNMENTS AND PROJECTS

1. **Assignment for the opening case**

   (a) Read the opening case and answer the following questions:
   (b) What motivated Telstra to prepare the calculators?
   (c) Why do the calculators include benefits to employees and to the community?
   (d) The use of NPV is discussed. Explain how it works in this case (hint: **investopedia.com/terms/n/npv.asp**).
   (e) How is the company using social media to engage customers? Does this make it more competitive?

2. Explore the business value of EC. Each member enters a different site (e.g., Nicholas G. Carr (**nicholascarr.com**), Baseline (**baselinemag.com**), Strassmann, Inc. (**strassmann.com**)). Prepare a presentation on issues, value, and directions.

3. Have three teams represent the following units of one click-and-mortar company: (1) an offline division, (2) an online division, and (3) top management. Each team member represents a different functional area within the division. The teams will develop an EC strategy in a specific industry (a group of three teams will represent a company in one industry). Teams will present their strategies to the class.

4. The class will set up a webstore on Facebook. You can use the application from **ecwid.com** or from **bigcommerce.com**. Have several members place products there while others shop. Write a report on your experience.

5. Set up a free website using a website builder app. Write a report discussing your site and website builder you used.

6. Each team needs to find the latest information on one global EC or social media issue (e.g., cultural, administrative, geographic, economic). In addition, check how leading retailers, such as Levi's, serve different content to local audiences, both on their websites and on their Facebook pages. Each team prepares a report based on their findings.

7. Compare the services provided by Yahoo!, Microsoft, and Web.com to SMEs in the e-commerce area. Each team should take one company and give a presentation.

8. Research the topic of going global in the social world. Identify the issues and the practices. Write a report.

9. Enter **youtube.com/watch?v=qh1drAg1jdg** and watch the video titled "Gartner Hype Cycle." Write a summary of the major points. Do the assignment provided there.

CLOSING CASE: BATTLE OF THE B2C TITANS

Amazon.com has been crowned the "King of Online Retailing" in the United States and has enjoyed that title for several years. While many believed that Amazon's constant innovations would ensure that it would retain this title into the foreseeable future, there are new developments from some competitors that may put this at risk.

The Leader: Amazon

Amazon enjoys a first-mover advantage in the online retailing space due to its early entry online selling books. The company rapidly expanded beyond this market to include a wide variety of retail, electronic, media, and grocery items (Saleem 2017). The company is also beginning to focus on B2B items as well (Zaczkiewicz 2016). The company has a culture of innovation, where new products, services, and processes are continually rolled out to benefit the customer. The primary strategic advantages enjoyed by the company include its well-designed user interface, its wide variety of products, and its efficient logistics system.

A Competitor: Walmart

While Amazon may be the king of online retailing, in the United States, Walmart is the king of retail. Walmart is a ubiquitous brand and retail outlet across the country. Walmart is a discount retail store founded in the United States but active internationally. In 2016 it was the world's largest company based on revenue and was also the world's largest private employer. In 2015 it was the most profitable retailer in the United States. It has over 11,000 stores in 28 countries.

Despite this huge infrastructure, Walmart's growth into online has been less than executives had hoped for. The company initially fought with channel issues because of concerns of competition between the online venture and physical locations. The company also identified logistics issues that they report to be mostly corrected in 2016. The company's e-commerce growth has now been reignited with online sales growing 11.8% at the end of the third quarter in 2016 (Wahba 2016).

The company hopes to become significantly more competitive online and specifically with Amazon, using its brand recognition, logistics systems (specifically as developed for Site2Store transactions), and purchasing abilities. The company intends to continue to evaluate the features desired by consumers and to integrate them into its offering. Mobile applications are a specific goal (Francisco 2017). The company hopes to continue to take market share from Amazon as well as from other retailers in 2017.

A Competitor: Alibaba

The Alibaba Group is a Chinese e-commerce company that focuses on both B2C and B2B e-commerce. The company has been very successful in China and has begun its expansion worldwide. Its initial primary strategy was to connect Chinese manufacturers with global buyers (Wells 2016). From this beginning, the company has expanded into B2C activities in China and is planning on similar activities globally. The company completed an IPO in the United States in 2014, raising $25 billion, the largest IPO in history.

Alibaba hopes to leverage its scale and product selection to begin to compete with other retailers worldwide. This is a deviation from its existing business strategy of acting as a product and retailer matchmaker (see **advisoryhq.com/articles/alibaba-vs-amazon**). Competing directly with a company like Amazon would be a challenge due to this major shift in business models. The company hopes that it will be able to leverage its large product catalog as well as its experience in China to this new market.

The State of the Market

Competition in the US B2C retailing is becoming more heated. New entrants and reinvigorated competitors are beginning to eye Amazon's title as the leader of US-based e-tailing. Companies looking to compete with Amazon must focus on their core abilities and how they could be leveraged to create competitive advantages. The needed abilities in this market include customer-facing interfaces and applications, product variety, and logistics efficiency (Petro 2016). While neither Walmart nor Alibaba can compete in all three of these areas today, they each have the possibility to leverage at least one from their current operations to gain a stronger foothold in the US market (Petro 2016). Only time will tell how this battle of the titans will turn out, but in the end, it will drive better pricing and services for US customers.

Questions

1. Why is Amazon the leader in US B2C retail?
2. What core competency can Walmart leverage to compete with Amazon?
3. What core competency can Alibaba leverage to compete with Amazon?
4. What actions should Amazon take to ensure they remain competitive against Walmart and Alibaba?
5. Why is the change in business model so significant in Alibaba's plans to compete with Amazon?
6. Why does Walmart have the logistical infrastructure to compete with Amazon?
7. Why will the competition between these three titans benefit US customers?

REFERENCES

Angeles, S. "Best App Makers of 2017." *Business News Daily*, December 8, 2016a. **businessnewsdaily.com/4901-best-app-makers-creators.html** (accessed January 2017).

Angeles, S. "Best e-Commerce Software 2017." *Business News Daily*, August 24, 2016b. **businessnewsdaily.com/7707-best-ecommerce-software.html** (accessed January 2017).

Baldwin, C. "Will Aldi Justify Its Move into E-Commerce?" *Essential Retail*, September 28, 2015.

Barbaschow, A. "Australia is Outpacing the US in IoT Adoption: Telstra CTO." *ZDNet.com*, April 7, 2016. **zdnet.com/article/Australia-is-outpacing-the-US-in-iot-adoption-telstra-cto** .(accessed January 2017).

Belbey, J. "Protect Your Firm From the 12 Risks of Social Media." *Forbes*, May 21, 2015. **forbes.com/sites/joannabelbey/2015/05/21/protect-your-firm-from-the-13-risks-of-social-media/#57d70c354397** (accessed January 2017).

Chapman, M. "Aldi Puts £35 m Into Ecommerce as It Begins Selling Wine Online." *Marketing Magazine*, January 21, 2016. **campaignlive.co.uk/article/aldi-puts-35m-ecommerce-begins-selling-wine-online/1380384?src_site=marketingmagazine** (accessed March 2017).

China Scoop. "How Dangdang Inc Lost Out in China's E-Commerce Race." China Scoop, June 22, 2016. **chinascoop.net/how-dangdang-inc-lost-out-in-chinas-e-commerce-race** (accessed January 2017).

CSA Research. "Survey of 3,000 Online Shoppers Across 10 Countries Finds that 60% Rarely or Never Buy from English-Only Websites." Common Sense Advisory, April 1, 2014. **commonsenseadvisory.com/default.aspx?Contenttype=ArticleDet&tabID=64&moduleId=392&Aid=21500&PR=PR** (accessed January 2017).

Del Real, M. G. "How To Calculate Your Return on Investment (ROI)." MGR Consulting Group, February 1, 2017. **mgrconsultinggroup.com/ how-to-calculate-your-return-on-investment-roi** (accessed February 2017).

Didner, P. *Global Content Marketing: How to Create Great Content, Reach More Customers, and Build a Worldwide Marketing Strategy.* Columbus, OH: McGraw-Hill Education, 2014.

Doig, C. "How to Determine When to Build or Buy Enterprise Software." *CIO*, November 5, 2015. **cio.com/article/3001357/software/how-to- determine-when-to-build-or-buy-enterprise-software.html** (accessed January 2017).

Emergent Digital. "The Beginner's Guide to Web Analytics." 2017. **emergentdigital.com/web-analytics** (accessed January 2017).

Fan, W. "Alibaba Has Big Plans for Small U.S. Businesses." *Ecns.cn.news*, June 11, 2015. **ecns.cn/business/2015/06-11/168916.shtml** (accessed January 2017).

Faulkner, T. "Fake Amazon Reviews: Amazon Continues To Crack Down On Fakes." Inquisitr, April 26, 2016. **inquisitr.com/3034054/fake- amazon-reviews-amazon-continues-to-crack-down-on-fraudulent-reviews/** (accessed January 2017).

Flierl, T. "7 Questions to Guide Your E-Commerce Initiative." HD Insights, October 22, 2015. **hansondodge.com/blog/2015/october/7-ques- tions-to-guide-your-e-commerce-initiative** (accessed January 2017).

Forbes. "How LinkedIn Is Establishing Itself in India." *Forbes.com*, November 22, 2016. **forbes.com/sites/greatspeculations/2016/06/03/how- linkedin-is-establishing-itself-in-india** (accessed January 2017).

Francisco, M. "Walmart App Lets Buyers Scan Items While Shopping and Skip Checkout Lane." *Tech Times*, January 11, 2017. **techtimes.com/ articles/192184/20170111/walmart-app-walmart-app-scan-and-go-skip-checkout-lane-amazon.htm** (accessed January 2017).

GaggleAMP. *Social Media Globetrotting*. Medford, MA: GaggleAMP 2016. **blog.gaggleamp.com/blog/blog/use-the-native-language-for- your-foreign-social-media-strategy** (accessed January 2017).

Gale, S. L. "Arrests for Offensive Facebook and Twitter Posts Soar in London." *Independent*, June 4, 2016. **independent.co.uk/news/uk/arrests- for-offensive-facebook-and-twitter-posts-soar-in-london-a7064246.html** (accessed January 2017).

Garver, A. "E-Commerce Valuation: Offering Guidance for Buyers and Sellers." Seeking Alpha, March 13, 2014. **seekingalpha.com/ article/2085293-e-commerce-valuation-offering-guidance-for-buyers-and-sellers** (accessed January 2017).

Gast, A. and M. Zanini. "The Social Side of Strategy." *McKinsey Quarterly Insights & Publications*, May 2012. **mckinsey.com/business-func- tions/strategy-and-corporate-finance/our-insights/the-social-side-of-strategy** (accessed January 2017).

Goldberg, J. *Internet Marketing 101: Online Marketing for Small Business*, [Kindle Edition]. Seattle, WA: Simultaneous Device Usage, 2016.

Hitt, M. and Ireland, D. *Strategic Management: Concepts and Cases: Competitiveness and Globalization*. New York: Cengage Learning, 2017.

Hobbs, T. "How Aldi's Move Into Ecommerce Shows It Is Becoming a More 'Conventional' Grocer." *Marketing Week*, September 28, 2015.

Hoefflinger, M. *Becoming Facebook: The 10 Challenges That Defined the Company That's Disrupting the World*. New York: AMACOM, 2017.

Issac, M. "Facebook Said to Create Censorship Tool to Get Back into China." *The New York Times*, November 22, 2016. **nytimes.com/2016/11/22/ technology/facebook-censorship-tool-china.html** (accessed January 2017).

Jackson, D. "How to Go Viral: 8 Things You Need to Know." Sprout Social, September 10, 2015. **sproutsocial.com/insights/how-to-go-viral** (accessed January 2017).

Jones, D. "Google Gets Rid of 1.7 Billion Bad Ads." *E-Commerce Times*, January 25, 2017. **ecommercetimes.com/story/84258.html** (accessed January 2017).

Khan, G. *Seven Layers of Social Media Analytics: Mining Business Insights from Social Media Text, Actions, Networks, Hyperlinks, Apps, Search Engine, and Location Data*. Seattle, WA: CreateSpace Independent Publishing Platform, 2015.

Kim, W. C. *Blue Ocean Strategy, Expanded Edition: How to Create Uncontested Market Space and Make the Competition Irrelevant*. Boston, MA: Harvard Business Review Press, 2015.

Lanford, D. "Fake Reviews Hurt Your Business." BBEX, January, 23, 2017. **bbexmarketing.com/blog/2017/01/fake-reviews-hurt-your-busi- ness** (accessed January 2017).

Laja, P. "Useful Value Proposition Examples (and How to Create a Good One)." CXL, 2017. **conversionxl.com/value-proposition-examples- how-to-create** (accessed January 2017).

Levine, S. "Qualitative Vs. Quantitative Social Media Reporting." Sysomos, July, 28, 2015. **blog.sysomos.com/2015/07/28/qualitative-vs-quan- titative-social-media-reporting** (accessed January 2017).

Link Humans. "How Cadbury Uses Social Media." 2016. **linkhumans.com/case-study/cadbury** (accessed January 2017).

Liousas, E. A. "Amplify Your Social Media Business Case Beyond Marketing." Forrester, February 22, 2016. **hootsuite.com/resources/white- paper/forrester-amplify-your-social-media-business-case-beyond-marketing-ty** (accessed January 2017).

McCafferty, D. "How Digital Partnerships Drive Business Success." *Baseline*, January 15, 2016. **baselinemag.com/intelligence/slideshows/how- digital-partnerships-drive-business-success.html** (accessed January 2017).

McClean, P. "Aldi UK sales hit record but profits dip." *Financial Times*, September 26, 2016. **ft.com/content/98174a58-83dd-11e6-8897- 2359a58ac7a5** (accessed January 2017).

Muchmore, M. "The Best Website Builders of 2017." *PC Magazine*, January 31, 2017. **pcmag.com/article2/0,2817,2484510,00.asp** (accessed January 2017).

Murtagh, R. "The Case for E-Commerce." *Telstra Exchange*, July 21, 2015. **exchange.telstra.com.au/2015/07/21/case-e-commerce** (accessed January 2017).

Nketia, B. A. "The Influence of Open Strategizing on Organizational Members' Commitment to Strategy." 12th International Strategic Management Conference, Antalya, Turkey, October 30, 2016. **sciencedirect.com/science/article/pii/S1877042816315920** (accessed January 2017).

OECD (Organization for Economic Cooperation and Development). Enhancing SME Competitiveness: The OECD Bologna Ministerial Conference, Bologna, 14–15, June 2000. (2001). **oecd.org/cfe/smes/enhancingsmecompetitivenesstheoecdbolognaministerialconference- bologna14-15june2000.htm** (accessed March 2017).

Onwuanibe, U. "The Global Impact of Social Media." Market Mogul, September 7, 2015. **themarketmogul.com/global-impact-social-media** (accessed January 2017).

Petro, G. "Amazon Vs. Walmart: Clash of the Titans." *Forbes*, August 25, 2016. **forbes.com/sites/gregpetro/2016/08/25/amazon-vs-walmart- clash-of-the-titans/#3e94178018d9** (accessed January 2017).

Polk, N. "Jack Ma Calls on Small US Businesses to Join Alibaba." *China Business Review*, June 12, 2015. **chinabusinessreview.com/jack-ma-calls-on-small-us-businesses-to-join-alibaba** (accessed January 2017).

Raskino, M. and G. P. Waller. "Learn How to Lead Your Digital Business Team." *A Gartner Webinar*, March 8, 2016.

Ross, A. "Overcoming Cultural Barriers on Social Media." Adobe Blog, July 30, 2014. **blogs.adobe.com/digitalmarketing/social-media/overcoming-cultural-barriers-social-media/** (accessed January 2017).

Rossman, J. *The Amazon Way: 14 Leadership Principles Behind the World's Most Disruptive Company*. Seattle, WA: Clyde Hill Publishing, 2016.

Saleem, F. "How Amazon.com, Inc.'s (NASDAQ:AMZN) Innovative Strategy is Beating Alphabet Inc. (NASDAQ:GOOGL) and Apple Inc. (NASDAQ:AAPL)." Library of Smart Investors, January 2, 2017. **libraryforsmartinvestors.com/2017/01/amazon-com-inc-nasdaqamzns-innovative-strategy-beating-alphabet-inc-nasdaqgoogl-apple-inc-nasdaqaapl/41369946.htm** .(accessed January 2017).

Sands, J. "E-Commerce China Dangdang Faces an Uphill Climb in China's Highly Competitive E-Commerce Market." Seeking Alpha, April 1, 2014. **seekingalpha.com/research/916375-james-sands/2800443-e-commerce-china-dangdang-faces-an-uphill-climb-in-chinas-highly-competitive-e-commerce-market** (accessed January 2017).

Sitkins, P. "Benefits of Social Media for Small Businesses." *B2C*, January 24, 2016. **business2community.com/small-business/benefits-social-media-small-businesses-01431621#8dX4HrVqbK3BMk7W.99** (accessed January 2017).

Solon, O. "How Facebook Plans to Take Over the World." *The Guardian*, April 23, 2016. **theguardian.com/technology/2016/apr/23/facebook-global-takeover-f8-conference-messenger-chatbots** (accessed January 2017).

Telstra. "Telstra Exchange." 2016. **exchange.telstra.com.au** (accessed January 2017).

Teneva, D. "11 Ecommerce Metrics That Really Show Your Business Performance." Metrilo Blog, May 3, 2016. **metrilo.com/blog/important-ecommerce-metrics** (accessed January 2017).

TrueShip. "The Future of Ecommerce: 10 Predictions for 2016." January 5, 2016. **trueship.com/blog/2016/01/05/the-future-of-ecommerce-10-predictions-for-2016/#VwLle_krI2w** (accessed January 2017).

Turban, et al. *Social Commerce*, New York: Springer, 2016.

Wahba, P. "Here's How Walmart Is Reigniting Its E-Commerce Growth." *Fortune*, August 18, 2016. **fortune.com/2016/08/18/walmart-ecommerce-2** (accessed January 2017).

Wells, N. "A Tale of Two Companies: Matching up Alibaba vs. Amazon." CNBC, May 5, 2016. **cnbc.com/2016/05/05/a-tale-of-two-companies-matching-up-alibaba-vs-amazon.html** (accessed January 2017).

Wells, P. *Building A Global Business With Social Media*, Seattle, WA: CreateSpace Independent Publishing Platform, 2015.

Zaczkiewicz, A. "Amazon, Wal-Mart Lead Top 25 E-Commerce Retail List." WWD, March 7, 2016. **wwd.com/business-news/financial/amazon-walmart-top-ecommerce-retailers-10383750** (accessed January 2017).

E-Commerce: Regulatory, Ethical, and Social Environments

15

Contents

Learning Objectives

Upon completion of this chapter, you will be able to:

1. Understand the foundations of legal and ethical issues in EC.
2. Describe intellectual property law and understand its adjudication.
3. Explain privacy and free speech issues and their challenges.
4. Describe types of fake content on the Web and what can be done about it.
5. Describe EC-related societal issues and loss of jobs in particular.
6. Describe Green EC and IT.
7. Describe the future of e-commerce.

© Springer International Publishing AG 2018

E. Turban et al., *Electronic Commerce 2018*, Springer Texts in Business and Economics, DOI 10.1007/978-3-319-58715-8_15

OPENING CASE
FAKE NEWS: THE AUSTIN, TEXAS, FIASCO

For a period of 3 days, November 9–11, 2016, fake news created unintentionally went viral exponentially on the Web.

The Initial Step

On November 9, a Mr. Tucker of Austin, Texas, posted a tweet about "paid protesters bused to demonstrations against President-elect Trump." Mr. Tucker read about the anti-Trump demonstration in his own city. When he saw an unusually large group of buses in downtown Austin earlier that day, he thought it was related to the demonstrations. Therefore, he took photos of the buses, and when he came home, he tweeted the pictures with his interpretation of what he saw. The truth was that there were no buses packed with paid protestors. The unusual numbers of buses were those hired by Tableau Software to bring participants to their company's conference.

The Story Goes Viral

The fake news went viral very quickly. Mr. Tucker had 40 followers on Twitter. However, within hours, the post was shared over 16,000 times on Twitter and 350,000 times on Facebook. Clearly, speed took over the truth.

Within a few hours, the tweet was also posted to the main "Reddit Community for Mr. Trump." Members went to check and found that the buses were parked just blocks away from the Austin protestors. Therefore, the members spread the fake news even further. Some even implied that George Soros, the liberal billionaire, paid for the busing and the participation. Within 15 h, the story was all over the Internet. Within a few hours after that, the bus company denied the story. However, by that time, the news spread like wildfire. In addition, Mr. Tucker admitted that he just *assumed* that the buses brought demonstrators, but he actually had not seen any. This admission also came too late.

However, Mr. Tucker repeated that the buses were near the demonstrators.

Within 24 h, a conservative blog posted the story, with the Soros money story added on. The entire conservative blogosphere continue to spread the story. The story now was inflated as "a story from an eyewitness."

Further Events

Within 24 h, President-elect Trump tweeted that it is unfair that "professional protestors that were incited by the media are protesting against the election results." This tweet angered Mr. Tucker, who decided not to delete his tweet.

The next morning, more denials from Tableau Software and others came, including the local TV stations. However, the tweet continued to generate many thousands of retweets and comments.

False Rumors Spread Much Faster Than True Ones

Within a few hours after the last denial, Mr. Tucker decided to delete his message. He posted the original message with the word "false" stamped on it. Unfortunately, after a week, that message had only 29 retweets and 27 likes. In section "Fake Content on the Web," we will discuss this phenomenon.

Source: Condensed from Maheshwari (2016), Roberts (2017a, b), and Stetler (2016).

LESSON LEARNED FROM THE CASE

Fake news is one aspect of the fake content phenomenon. We learned from this case that fake news also can be generated unintentionally and can spread very rapidly through several channels on the Web. Fake content and products constitute a major problem on the Web. In this concluding chapter, we also describe other issues that relate to the e-commerce business. They include ethics, privacy, intellectual property and piracy, legal issues, public policy regarding the Web, and social impacts. The chapter concludes with a presentation about the future of e-commerce.

15.1 ETHICAL CHALLENGES AND GUIDELINES

Ethics is a set of moral principles or rules of how people are expected to conduct themselves. It specifies what is considered by society to be right or wrong.

Issues of privacy, ownership, control, and security must be confronted in implementing and understanding the ethical challenges of EC.

Ethical Principles and Guidelines

Public law embodies ethical principles, but the two are not the same. Acts that generally are considered unethical may not be illegal. Lying to someone may be unethical, but it is not illegal. Conversely, the law is not a collection of ethical norms, and not all ethical codes are incorporated into public law.

One example of an ethical issue is the Facebook class action lawsuit of 2009, described next.

Example: Who Owns User-Generated Content?

In August 2009, five Facebook users filed a class action lawsuit against Facebook, claiming that Facebook violated privacy laws by gathering online users' activity and providing their personal information to third parties without the users' permission. They also alleged that Facebook engages in data mining, without informing the users.

The objective of the data collection was to enable Facebook to sell their users' data to advertisers because Facebook needed more revenue sources. The Electronic Privacy Information Center filed a complaint with the FCC, alleging that Facebook's changes in privacy settings made users' information publicly available without giving the users the option to opt out. Facebook was found to be liable for violating the privacy of their users and amended their rules. Facebook has continuously been modifying and changing its privacy settings, letting its users decide how much they want to share with the public.

Business Ethics

Business ethics (also known as *corporate* or *enterprise ethics*) is a code of values, behaviors, and rules, written or unwritten, for how people should behave in the business world. These ethics dictate the operations of organizations. For implementation considerations, see Business for Social Responsibility (**bsr.org**).

The Issues of Internet Abuse in the Workplace

The actual time wasted and productivity losses due to employees spending time on the Web during working hours are very high. In general, employees spent more than 1 h per week during working hours on social media alone, followed by online games and e-mails. Many companies have banned access to social networks such as Facebook, Twitter, and LinkedIn. In 2013, *SFGate* (per Gouveia 2013) conducted a survey in which they found that 69% of the employees were wasting time for 30 min to several hours per day. The top four employee "time wasters" were: checking news (37%), social networking (14%), online shopping (12%), and online entertainment (11%). For more information, see **salary.com/2014-wasting-time-at-work**.

Managing Internet Abuse

Instead of banning the use of social networks in the workplace, some employers are following less draconian measures by setting the following policies in place: employees are encouraged to check their social networks only once or twice a day, consolidate their social networking streams, develop a clear social networking policy, and utilize technology made for consolidation. A social networking policy should communicate clear guidelines from employers to employees. For example, employees should not spend more than 20 min per day of company time browsing social networks.

Monitoring Employees: Is It Ethical?

Google and several other software application providers have incorporated new spyware on company smartphones given to employees, which enables employers to monitor the whereabouts of their employees using the smartphones' built-in GPS tracking systems. Google's Latitude enables companies to know their employees' location at all times. The ethical question is, whether this new power will be used by governments to invade the privacy of an individual's real-time whereabouts. In other words, rules and procedures for ethical behavior are needed for businesspeople practicing EC. Two major risks are criminal charges and civil suits. Table 15.1 lists examples of safeguards to minimize exposure to those risks.

Table 15.1 Typical safeguards to minimize exposure to risks of criminal or civil charges

1. Does the website clearly post shipping policies and guarantees? Can the selling company fulfill its policies and guarantees? Does it comply with Federal Trade Commission (FTC) rules?
2. Does the website clearly articulate procedures for customers to follow when returning a shipment or when seeking a refund for products or services not received or received in bad or damaged condition?
3. Has the company checked partners' backgrounds before entering into agreements with third-party vendors and supply chain partners? Do those agreements include protection of the company against all possible risks?
4 Is there sufficient customer support staff, and are they knowledgeable and adequately trained to process customers' inquiries?

EC Ethical and Legal Issues

There are many EC- and Internet-related ethical issues that are related to legal issues (see Lewis 2014). These issues are often categorized into intellectual property rights, privacy, free speech versus censorship, and fraud protection methods.

- **Intellectual property rights.** Ownership and value of information and intellectual property. Intellectual property is difficult to protect on the Web. Owners are losing a substantial amount of money due to piracy (section "Intellectual Property Law and Copyright Infringement").
- **Privacy.** Because it is so difficult to protect the privacy of individuals on the Web, there are some countries that do not regulate privacy issues while others have strict anti-invasion rules (section "Privacy Rights, Protection, and Free Speech").
- **Free speech versus censorship.** Free speech on the Web may result in offensive and harmful attacks on individuals and organizations. Therefore, some countries have decided to censor material on the Internet.
- **Consumer and merchant protection against fraud.** For e-commerce to succeed, it is necessary to protect all transactions and participants against fraud (see Chap. 1).

Examples of ethical issues discussed elsewhere in this book are channel conflict (Chap. 3), pricing conflict (Chap. 3), disintermediation (Chaps. 3 and 4), and trust (Chap. 9). Two additional EC-related ethical issues are Internet use that is not work related and code of ethics. See also **investopedia.com/terms/c/code-of-ethics.asp**.

Other Issues

Lunka (2015) lists the following ethical issues in EC, asking: Are you violating any of them? The issues are selling counterfeit products (section "Fake Content on the Web"), Web accessibility (section "Public Policy, Taxation, and Political Environments"), accurate product listing (section "Fake Content on the Web"), and the use of EC best practices. Lunka (2015) provides some guidelines on the ethical behavior of the above.

Internet Use That Is Not Work Related

As described earlier, a majority of employees use e-mail and surf the Web for purposes not related to work. The use of company property (i.e., computers, tablets, networks) for e-mail and Internet use may create risk and waste time. The degree of risk depends on the extent to which the company has implemented policies and procedures to prevent and detect illegal uses. For example, companies may be held liable for their employees' use of e-mail to harass other employees, participate in illegal gambling, or distribute child pornography.

According to McCafferty (2016b), Internet distractions are the top productivity killers.

SECTION 15.1 REVIEW QUESTIONS

1. List seven ethical issues related to EC.
2. List the major principles of ethics.
3. Define business ethics.

4. Give an example of an EC activity that is unethical but not illegal.
5. How can employees abuse the Internet? How do small companies handle this?
6. Describe the issues of monitoring employees.

15.2   INTELLECTUAL PROPERTY LAW AND COPYRIGHT INFRINGEMENT

The legal system is faced with the task of maintaining a delicate balance between preserving social order and protecting individual rights. In this section, we explain some types of intellectual property laws and the issues arising from EC.

Intellectual Property in E-Commerce

Intellectual property (IP) refers to property that derives from the creative work of an individual, such as literary or artistic work. Intellectual property can be viewed as the ownership of intangible assets, such as inventions, ideas, and creative work. It is a legal concept protected by patents, copyrights, trademarks, and trade secret law (known as **Intellectual property law**).

There are various intellectual property law specialties, as shown in Table 15.2. Those specialty laws are interrelated and may even overlap.

Recording Movies, Shows, and Other Events

A common method of infringement is to bring video cameras and video-capable cell phones to movie theaters, stadiums, etc. and record the performances. PirateEye (pirateeye.com) is one of the companies that manufactures devices that discover and identify the presence of any digital recording device, monitor remotely in real time, and much more.

A common problem is the illegal copying of e-books, which, according to Scott (2016), is damaging not only to authors and publishers but also to our culture. This situation requires international collaboration.

For intellectual property in social media, see Kankanala (2015).

Copyright Infringement and Protection

Numerous high-profile lawsuits already have been filed regarding online copyright infringement related to EC and the Web. A **copyright** is an exclusive legal right of an author or creator of intellectual property to publish, sell, license, distribute, or use such work in any desired way. In the United States, content is automatically protected by federal copyright laws as soon as a work is produced in a tangible shape or form. A copyright does not last forever; it is good for a set number of years after the death of the author or creator (e.g., 50 years in the United Kingdom). After the copyright expires, the work reverts to the public domain (or becomes publicly available). See **fairuse.stanford.edu/overview/public-domain** and **thepublicdomain. org**. In many cases, corporations own copyrights. In such a case, the copyrights will last up to 120 years, or even longer. The legal term for the use of a work without permission or contracting for payment of a royalty is **copyright infringement**.

Example

One artist made $90,000 by selling someone's Instagram photos without permission. See details at Instagram (2015).

Table 15.2 Intellectual property laws and the protections of intellectual property

Laws	Protection provided by the law
Intellectual property law	Protects the creative work of people
Patent law	Protects inventions and discoveries
Copyright law	Protects original works of authorship, such as music and literary works, artistic design, and writing computer codes
Trademark law	Protects trademarks, logos, etc.
Trade secret law	Protects proprietary business information
Law of licensing	Enables owners of intellectual property to share it via licensing
Law of unfair competition relating to counterfeiting and piracy	Protects against those who use illegal or unfair methods or methods not available to others. Also protects against those pirating intellectual property

File Sharing

One of the major methods of violating copyrights is *file sharing*. File sharing became popular in the late 1990s through facilitating companies such as Napster. One of the players in this area is The Pirate Bay (see this chapter's closing case). The loss to copyright holders is estimated to be several billion dollars annually. The Recording Industry Association of America (RIAA) is fighting back.

Examples

The file sharing business is a major target of the RIAA, which shut down popular sites LimeWire LLC and Kazaa. Additionally, another popular file sharing site, Megaupload.com, was shut down in January 2012. However, the site was relaunched in January 2013 under the domain name **mega.co.nz**.

Illegal Visits to Torrent, Streaming, and Download Sites (i.e., Piracy)

There are billions of visits to websites that provide free videos, music, books, and other media to people that do not pay for the legal versions. Known as piracy, this phenomenon is performed worldwide. In some countries (e.g., Latvia), almost half of the population visit pirate sites (see this chapter's closing case and **torrentfreak.com**; news site).

Legal Aspects of Infringement

In November 2010, the US Senate Judiciary Committee approved the controversial Combating Online Infringement and Counterfeits Act (COICA) that provides the Attorney General with the power to shut down websites without a trial or court order if copyright infringement is considered to be the "central activity of the site." The problem is that, under this bill, most business websites are considered publishers (e.g., even when publishing an online sales brochure) and may be subject to disruptive investigations.

The RIAA Industry Versus the Violators

To protect its interests, the RIAA uses selective lawsuits to stamp out rampant music piracy on the Internet. However, the RIAA spent more than $58 million in pursuit of targeted infringers between 2006 and 2008, yet collected less than $1.4 million (less than about 2%) from judgments. Given that there are thousands of pirate sites, to fight them is not a simple task.

Sometimes legal actions against the owners of pirate websites can be successful. However, while the actions about the Pirate Bay illegal site (closing case) ended with imprisoning the owner, the site is still alive. According to Mello, Jr. (2016b), the owner of Kickass Torrents (KAT), another popular piracy site, was arrested and is facing 20 plus years in jail. However, the site opened again in late 2016.

Note, since 2009, the number of lawsuits has been declining for several reasons. Viacom sued YouTube (Google) for $1 billion for copyright violations. In 2013, Viacom lost its case against YouTube (the appellate court ruled in favor of Google). Finally, pending copyright infringement lawsuits are not favored because they are lengthy and very costly. As an alternative to direct lawsuits, the entertainment industry has begun developing digital rights management (DRM) policies to be enforced through the court system as well as through federal legislation.

Globalization

Much of the media piracy occurs in other countries (e.g., Russia, China, and Sweden, and many developing countries). Therefore, it is difficult to combat piracy, as per the closing case of Pirate Bay.

Digital Rights Management (DRM)

Digital rights management (DRM) describes a system of protecting the copyrights of data circulated over the Internet or digital media. These arrangements are technology-based protection measures (via encryption or using watermarks). Typically, sellers own the rights to their digital content. For details, see **eff.org/issues/drm**. However, DRM systems may restrict the *fair use* of material by individuals. In law, **fair use** refers to the limited use of copyrighted material, without paying a fee or royalty, for certain purposes (e.g., reviews, commentaries, teaching).

Patents

According to **wipo.org**, a **patent** is "an exclusive right to a particular invention, which is a product or a process that provides, in general, a new way of doing something, or offers a new technical solution to a problem." Patents are granted by states or governments to the creator of an invention or to someone who has been designated by them to accept the rights over the invention. The holder of the patent has sole rights over the invention for a specified period of time (e.g., 20 years for applications filed on or after June 8, 1995, in the United States and 20 years in the United Kingdom). Patents serve to protect the idea or design of the invention, rather than any tangible form of the invention.

There is some discrepancy between the United States and Europe over the way certain patents are granted. For example, in 1999, Amazon.com successfully obtained a US patent for its "1-Click" ordering and payment procedure. Using this patent, Amazon.com sued Barnes & Noble in 1999, alleging that its rival had copied its patented technology. Barnes & Noble was enjoined by the courts from using their "Express Lane" payment procedure. However, on May 12, 2006, the USPTO ordered a reexamination of the "1-Click" patent. In March 2010, the Amazon patent was rewritten in the United States to include only a shopping cart and was approved as such. Nevertheless, Expedia and many other e-tailers use similar "checkout" systems today. See **en.wikipedia.org/wiki/1-Click**.

Another example of a legal case involving patents is when Canadian firm i4i Corporation sued Microsoft for patent infringement, alleging that Microsoft had infringed i4i's patent relating to text manipulation software. Microsoft wanted the standard changed by which patents would be deemed invalid. Microsoft took the case all the way to the US Supreme Court and lost.

Oracle Versus Google

In following its legal right of enforcement, Oracle has been mining its newly acquired patent portfolio and actively seeking and suing infringers. In 2012, Oracle sued Google over its Android product for using Oracle's Java technology (copying Java code) without a license. While the trial court ruled that APIs are not subject to copyright, the appeals court disagreed, holding that Java's API packages were copyrightable, although it sent back the case to the trial court to determine whether or not Google's copying was a violation of the Fair Use Doctrine. In 2014, Oracle won the case (see McLaughlin 2014).

Trademarks

According to the USPTO, a *trademark* is "a word, phrase, symbol, and/or design that identifies and distinguishes the source of the goods of one party from those of others." A trademark is used by individuals, business organizations, or other legal entities to notify consumers of a unique source and to tell the difference between a company's products or services and those of others. Although federal registration is not necessary, there are several advantages, such as informing the public that the trademark belongs to the registrants and giving them exclusive right of use (see **uspto.gov/trademarks-getting-started/ trademark-basics/trademark-patent-or-copyright**).

In 2008, eBay won a landmark trademark case against Tiffany, a leading jewelry retailer, who had sued eBay, alleging that many of the items being advertised on eBay as Tiffany merchandise were actually fakes. The US court ruled in 2008 that eBay cannot be held liable for trademark infringements "based solely on their generalized knowledge that trademark infringement might be occurring on their websites."

Protecting Intellectual Property on Websites

According to Verbauwhede (2015), "[a] company's website can be a great tool for promoting business online and generating sales. However, as Web commerce increases, so does the risk that others may copy the look and feel of your website, some of its features or the content on your website. The risk also increases that you may be accused of unauthorized use of other people's intellectual assets."

Verbauwhede (2015) lists the following elements that need to be protected: EC systems, search engines, software, website design, creative content, databases, trademark-protected items, graphic-related items, and confidential information.

(a) Verbauwhede (2015) also suggests the following protecting measures:
   • Register your trademarks.
   • Register a domain name that is user-friendly and reflects your trademark, business name, or character of your business.
   • Think about patenting online business methods, in countries where such protection is available.
   • Register your website and copyright material in countries which provide this option at the national copyright office.
   • Take precautions about disclosure of your trade secrets. Make sure that all who might get to know about your confidential business information (such as employees, maintenance contractors, website hosts, Internet providers) are bound by a confidentiality or nondisclosure agreement.
   • Consider to take an IP insurance policy that would cover your legal costs should you need to take enforcement action against infringers.

(b) Letting people know that the content is protected. Many people assume that material on websites can be used freely. Remind viewers of your IP rights.

- It is a good idea to mark your trademark with the trademark symbol ®, TM, SM, or equivalent symbols. Equally, you can use a copyright notice (the symbol © or the word "Copyright" or abbreviation "Copr."
- Another option is to use watermarks that embed copyright information into the digital content itself.
- Provide access control and encryption (Chap. 11).

More suggestions can be found in the article.

SECTION 15.2 REVIEW QUESTIONS

1. What is intellectual property law? How is it helpful to creators and inventors?
2. Define DRM. Describe one potential impact on privacy and one drawback.
3. What is meant by "fair use"? How does the "jailbreaking" of iPhones fall under "fair use"?
4. Define trademark infringement and discuss why trademarks need to be protected from dilution.

15.3   PRIVACY RIGHTS, PROTECTION, AND FREE SPEECH

Privacy has several meanings and definitions. In general, privacy is the state of not being disturbed by others, being free from others' attention, and having the right to be left alone and not to be intruded upon. (For other definitions of privacy, see the Privacy Rights Clearinghouse at **privacyrights.org**.) Privacy has long been a legal, ethical, and social issue in most countries. Digital privacy is a world of complex paradoxes (see the infographic by EMC 2014).

One issue is the increasing use of online surveillance and knowing who is watching whom (see Angwin 2015).

Privacy in E-Commerce

The reason for privacy concerns stems from the fact that in using the Internet, users are asked to provide some personal data in exchange for access to information (such as getting coupons, allowing downloads, etc.). Data and Web mining companies receive and gather the collected data. As a result, users' privacy may be violated (see the slide presentation titled "Your Data, Yourself" by Justyne Cerulli at **prezi.com/fgxmaftxrxke/your-data-yourself**). Privacy concerns limit EC according to Adhikari (2016a, b).

Privacy rights protection is one of the most debated and frequently emotional issues in EC and social commerce. According to Leggatt (2012), in a survey conducted by TRUSTe, 90% of Internet users "were found to worry about their online privacy." Many EC activities involve privacy issues ranging from collection of information by Facebook to the use of RFID. Here we only explore the major aspects of the privacy problem in EC. For many issues of EC privacy, see Kenyon (2016) and Gupta and Dubey (2016).

Example: Google Glass

In May 2013, eight US lawmakers, concerned about Google Glass (and other smart glasses), wrote a letter to Google asking what the company planned to do to protect people's privacy. See Guynn (2013) for a description. A similar example is that stores can see where you go while you are in the store or at the shopping mall.

Here we explore the major aspects of the problem as it relates to social networking.

Social Networks Changing the Landscape of Privacy and Their Protection

Today's youth seem to be less concerned about privacy than young people were in the past. The younger generations are more interested in blogs, photos, social networking, and texting. Attitudes about what constitutes private information are changing. As a result, there are new opportunities for marketers and marketing communication, mainly in offering experiences that are better personalized, which do not violate Internet user privacy.

This problem has been articulated by Andrews (2012), who studied privacy protection in social networks and concluded that very little privacy protection exists (e.g., college applicants are being rejected because of what they posted on the social networks; criminals read posts about vacations to know when to break into an empty house).

However, in May 2014, Facebook announced the addition of the "Anonymous Login" feature and changes in login procedures, which allow users to try apps without sharing personal information from Facebook. For more about Facebook and users' privacy, see Fox-Brewster (2016).

Information Pollution and Privacy

Information pollution, the adding of irrelevant, fake, or unsolicited information, may raise privacy issues such as the spreading of misinformation about individuals. In addition, polluted information used by decision-makers or by UGC may cause an invasion of privacy.

Global View

Note that the issue of privacy on the Internet is treated differently in different countries. For example, in November 2009, Google was sued in Switzerland over privacy concerns regarding its Street View application. In 2012, Switzerland's highest court ruled that Google may document residential street fronts with its Street View technology (now Google Maps), but imposed some limitations on the kinds of images the company can take (e.g., lowering the height of its Street View cameras so they would not peer over garden walls and hedges). For more about the court's decision and the reaction of the parties, see O'Brien and Streitfeld (2012). In June 2013, the European Union's highest court determined that government agencies cannot force Google to remove links to personal material. However, in May 2014, Europe's highest court ruled that people should have the right to say what information is available when someone Googles them. The ruling applies to 28 nations and all search engines (Google, Bing) in Europe. The decision does not apply to the United States or any other country outside Europe (see Sterling 2014).

Privacy Rights and Protection

Today, virtually all US states and the federal government (and many other countries) recognize the right to privacy, but few government agencies actually follow all the statutes (e.g., citing reasons of national security). One reason is that the definition of privacy can be interpreted quite broadly. However, the following two rules have been followed closely in past US court decisions: (1) The right to privacy is not absolute. Privacy must be balanced against the needs of society; (2) the public's "right to know" is superior to the individual's right to privacy. The vagueness of the two rules shows why it is sometimes difficult to determine and enforce privacy regulations.

Section 5 of the Federal Trade Commission Act protects privacy. For an explanation of the FTC Act, see **ftc.gov/news-events/media-resources/protecting-consumer-privacy**. Those practices extend to protecting consumer privacy, including the "do not track" option, protecting consumers' financial privacy, and the Children's Online Privacy Protection Act (COPPA).

In 2016, the federal government sued Apple in order to force the company to allow the government to open the secured iPhone of an alleged terrorist. Apple refused to cooperate. The government dropped the suit after it was successful in breaking into the phone. In a similar case Amazon claimed that Alexa's speech is protected by the First Amendment, refusing to allow the government to open the files related to a murder case.

Amazon agreed to give the data only after the murder's suspect gave a permission to do so.

Opt-In and Opt-Out

Privacy concerns have been overshadowed by post-9/11 counterterrorism activities, but consumers still want their data protected. One way to manage this issue is the *opt-in* and *opt-out* system, generally used by direct marketing companies. **Opt-out** is a method that gives consumers the choice to refuse to share information about themselves or to avoid receiving unsolicited information. Offering the choice to opt-out is good customer practice, but it is difficult to opt out in some industries, because either consumer demand for opting out is low or the value for the customer information is high.

In contrast, **opt-in** is based on the principle that consumers must approve in advance what information they receive from a company or allow a company to share their information with third parties. That is, information sharing should not occur unless customers affirmatively allow or request it.

See also the Direct Marketing Association (**thedma.org**) for information and resources on consumers' ad choices, opt-in and opt-out, privacy, identity theft, and more.

According to IBM, the following six practices for implementing a successful privacy project are:

1. **Get organized.** This can be done by creating a cross-functional privacy team for guidance.
2. **Define the privacy protection needs.** Decide what needs to be protected.
3. **Conduct inventory of data.** List and analyze all data that need protection.
4. **Select solution(s).** Choose and implement a solution that protects privacy.
5. **Test a prototype system.** Create a prototype of the system and test it under different conditions.
6. **Expand the project scope.** Expand the project to encompass other applications.

For further information on privacy protection, see IBM and the International Association of Privacy Professionals (**iapp.org**).

Some Measures of Privacy Protection

Several government agencies, communities, and security companies specialize in privacy protection. Representative examples in the United States include the Privacy Protection (**privacyprotect.org/about-privacyprotection**), Privacy Choice (**avg.com**), and Home PC Firewall Guide (**firewallguide.com/privacy.htm**). Finally, Cagaoan et al. (2014) describe the issue of privacy awareness in e-commerce. For a complete guide to Internet privacy, anonymity, and security, see Bailey (2015).

Free Speech Online Versus Privacy Protection

Although the First Amendment of the US Constitution grants the right to free speech, as with many rights, the right to free speech is not unlimited. The First Amendment does not give citizens the right to say absolutely anything to anyone. Defamation laws (including privacy violations), child pornography, fighting words, and terrorist threats are some of the traditional restrictions on what may be said freely. For example, it is illegal to scream "fire" in a crowded theater or make bomb threats in an airport, but there is no law against taking pictures in public places. Free speech often conflicts with privacy, protection of children, indecency, and so forth. For a discussion of the First Amendment and the ten rights it does not grant, see **people.howstuffworks.com/10-rights-first-amendment-does-not-grant.htm#page=1**.

For comprehensive coverage of the legal aspects of privacy vs. defamation, see Kenyon (2016). As demonstrated in a study by Gupta and Dubey (2016), privacy is related to security and trust.

Example

Anthony Graber, a motorcyclist in Maryland, was stopped by a plainclothes state police officer driving an unmarked car. He filmed his own traffic stop by using a camera attached to his motorcycle helmet. He posted his video on YouTube in March 2010 and, as a result, was charged with violating state wiretap laws for audio recording the officer and posting the video on the Internet without police consent. Graber was arrested and faced up to 16 years in prison for this undisclosed recording. He pled guilty to speeding but fought the charge of illegal monitoring, citing freedom of speech as a defense. The court ruled that the state trooper had "no legal expectation of privacy," and that videotaping is protected under the First Amendment. The court dismissed all of Graber's charges, except for the traffic violations. See **youtube.com/watch?v=QNcDGqzAB30&feature=related**.

Free Speech Online Versus Child Protection Debate

The debate over free speech versus child protection began in December 2000, after the *Children's Internet Protection Act (CIPA)*, which mandated the use of filtering techniques in libraries and schools that receive federal funding, was signed into law. In June 2003, the Supreme Court handed down a ruling that the CIPA was constitutional, allowing Congress to require some kinds of blocking, but the filters must not block too much material. Their review represented the third time justices had heard arguments pitting free speech against attempts to protect children from offensive online content. See the FCC Children's Internet Protection Act at **fcc.gov/guides/childrens-internet-protection-act**.

The Price of Protecting an Individual's Privacy

In the past, gathering information about individuals that was residing in government agencies' databases was difficult and expensive to do, which helped protect privacy. The Internet, in combination with powerful computers, and targeting algorithms with access to large-scale databases have in all practical terms eliminated the barriers of protecting citizens' privacy.

In the UK in 2010, Heathrow airport security officials were caught circulating printouts of a Hollywood star's full naked body scans downloaded from the full-body security scanners. However, authorities feel that the scanning process is necessary for airport security. Today's technology even enables monitoring people's activities from a distance, which may be considered a violation of their privacy, as shown in Case 15.1.

CASE 15.1: EC APPLICATION
SCHOOL ADMINISTRATORS USED WEBCAMS TO SPY ON STUDENTS AT HOME

Unbeknownst to the students in a Pennsylvania high school, administrators were caught spying on the activities of the underage students. The administrators did this by remotely activating webcams built into each laptop that was issued to the students by the Lower Merion School District, without the permission or knowledge of the students or their parents.

The continued surveillance of the students, even while they were at home, by school officials at Harriton High School revealed that one student was conducting what the school defined as "improper behavior." Based on the video taken at his home, the student was confronted at the school by the assistant principal and shown "photographic evidence." The school told the parents that they can do such monitoring. As a result, one student filed a class action lawsuit representing all the students who received laptops, for invasion of privacy and illegal interception of private information. The case was settled in October 2010 and the school district paid $610,000. In 2011, the same school district was sued by a former student over the secret monitoring of laptops in 2009.

Sources: Based on **courthousenews.com/judge-tells-school-to-stop-spying** (accessed February 2017).

Questions

1. What legitimate excuse could be made to justify this behavior? Why should the school's actions be stopped?
2. What federal laws were broken? What rights in the US Constitution were violated?
3. What precedent did this decision set? Can you see a way that schools will be allowed to continue this behavior for a narrowly construed purpose?
4. Find other similar cases.

The Future of ePrivacy

With advances in technology come more concerns regarding privacy protection. For example, Valerio (2016) suggests that there will be many changes in data privacy issues in 2016 (and probably in 2017). These changes relate to technological developments and the way people interact with technology. Brown (2016) lists the following areas for privacy in 2016: Data localization laws, IoT and ubiquitous computing, more FCC regulations, government surveillance and investigation, cybersecurity standards, big data, trans-Atlantic data transfer framework, more class action suits, and more regulations in Europe regarding data protection.

How Information About Individuals Is Collected and Used Online

An individual's private data can be gathered in a number of ways over the Internet. Comprehensive coverage of how data are collected, the users involved, and the individual rights are provided by Schneier (2016). Representative examples of the ways that the Internet can be used to find information about an individual are provided next; the first three are the most common ways of gathering information on the Internet.

- By a user completing a registration form including personal data
- By tracking users' movement on the Web (e.g., by using cookies)
- By using spyware, keystroke logging, and similar methods
- By website registration
- By finding out where you are by knowing the location
- By reducing your phone and e-mail texts
- By reading an individual's blog(s) or social network postings
- By looking up an individual's name and identity in an Internet directory or social network profile
- By reading an individual's e-mail, IM, or text messages (hacking)
- By monitoring employees in real time
- By wiretapping conversations over communication lines
- By using wearables such as smart glasses (Chap. 6), including invisible ones
- By using a smart TV that records an individual's behavior

For the hidden battles to collect your data and control your world, see Schneier (2016).

Cookies

A popular way for a website to gather information about an individual is by using cookies. *Cookies* enable websites to keep track of users' online movements without asking the users for permission.

Originally, cookies were designed to help with personalization and market research; however, cookies can also be used to disseminate unsolicited commercial information. Cookies allows vendors to collect detailed information about a user's online behavior. The personal data collected by cookies often are more accurate than information provided by users, because users have a tendency to falsify information while filling out registration forms. Although the ethical use of cookies is still being debated, concerns about cookies reached a peak in 1997 at the United States. FTC hearings on online privacy. Cookies can be successfully deleted by informed users with programs such as Cookie Monster and CCleaner; to delete and manage flash cookies, see **flashcookiecleaner.com**. By setting the privacy levels on Web browsers very high, cookies from all websites are blocked, and existing cookies cannot be read.

Spyware as a Threat to Privacy and Intellectual Property

In Chap. 11, we described **spyware** as a tool that some merchants use to gather information about users without their knowledge. Spyware infections are a major threat to privacy and intellectual property.

Spyware may enter the user's computer as a virus or as a result of the user clicking some innocent looking, but harmful, links. Spyware is effective in illegally tracking users' Internet surfing habits. Using spyware clearly is an invasion of the computer user's privacy and may be illegal. It can also slow down computer performance. While specific spyware can harvest data, it can also be used to take pictures from an unsuspecting user's Webcam and e-mail or post the photos all over the Internet.

Unfortunately, antivirus software and Internet firewalls cannot always detect all spyware; therefore, extra protection is needed. Many free and low-cost antispyware software packages are available. Representative free antispyware programs are Microsoft security essentials (**support.microsoft.com/en-us/help/14210/security-essentials-download**), and AVG (**avg. com**). Programs that charge a fee include Trend Micro (**trendmicro.com**) and Kaspersky Lab (**usa.kaspersky.com**). Upgraded versions of free programs are also available for a fee. Symantec and other companies that provide Internet security services also provide anti-spyware software.

RFID's Threat to Privacy

Although several states have mandated or are considering legislation to protect customers from loss of privacy due to RFID tags, as mentioned in Chap. 13 and Online Tutorial T2, privacy advocates fear that the information stored on RFID tags or collected with them may violate an individual's privacy.

Monitoring Employees

There are several issues concerning Internet use at work and employee privacy. In addition to wasting time online, employees may disclose trade secrets and possibly make employers liable for defamation based on their actions on the corporate website. In response to these concerns, many companies monitor their employees' e-mail and Web surfing activities, including postings on social network walls. One tool that enables companies to monitor their employees is Google Location, which works in combination with a compatible device (e.g., Android, iOS).

For workplace privacy and employee monitoring, see PRC (2014).

The issue of monitoring employees is complex and debatable because of the possibility of invasion of privacy. For comprehensive coverage, see PRC (2014). For more about employers and Internet usage monitoring, see **wisegeek.org/how-do-employers-monitor-internet-usage-at-work.htm**.

Other Methods

Other methods of collecting data about people are:

- **Site transaction logs.** These logs show what users are doing on the Internet.
- **EC ordering systems and shopping carts.** These features permit sellers to know buyers' ordering history.
- **Search engines.** Search engines can be used to collect information about users' areas of interest.
- **Web 2.0 tools**. Blogs, discussion groups, chatting, social networks, etc. contain a wealth of information about users' activities and personalities.
- **Behavioral targeting.** Using tools to learn people's preferences (Chap. 10).
- **Polling and surveys.** People's demographics, thoughts, and opinions are collected in surveys.
- **Payment information and e-wallets.** These may include sensitive information about shoppers.

Privacy Protection by Information Technologies

Dozens of software programs and IT policies and procedures are available to protect your privacy. Some were defined in Chap. 11. Representative examples are:

- **Platform for Privacy Preferences Project (P3P)**. Software that communicates privacy policies (described later in this chapter). This will be discussed later.
- **Encryption.** Software programs such as PKI for encrypting e-mail, payment transactions, and other documents.
- **Spam blocking.** Built into browsers and e-mail; blocks pop-ups and unwanted mail.
- **Spyware blocking.** Detects and removes spyware and adware; built into some browsers.
- **Cookie managers.** Prevents the computer from accepting cookies; identifies and blocks specific types of cookies.
- **Anonymous e-mail and surfing.** Allows you to send e-mail and surf without leaving a history.

Privacy Policies and Regulations

A useful practice for companies is to disclose their privacy policies to their customers. For an example, see **arvest.com/pdfs/about/privacy-and-security/privacy-policy-and-notice.pdf**.

E-privacy is especially an important topic in Europe. For regulations and their impact on e-commerce, see Press (2017).

Privacy Issues in Web 2.0 Tools and Social Networks

The rise in social network use raises some special issues of privacy and free speech. Here are a few examples.

Presence, Location-Based Systems, and Privacy

Establishing real-time connections in the social networking world is an important activity. For example, Facebook offers Wave (formerly Nearby Friends), an app that enables users to know where their friends are.

IBM has presence capabilities in its Lotus Software Connections (now called IBM Connections; **ibm.com/software/products/en/conn**), while Microsoft offers similar capabilities with SharePoint (**office.microsoft.com/en-us/sharepoint**). Apple, Google, and other companies offer similar features. Several social networks enable people to share their location with others. What are the privacy implications of such capabilities if used by businesses to locate customers and goods? Who will be held responsible or legally liable for unforeseen harm resulting from so much awareness and connectivity?

Obviously, clear policies are needed to govern what social networks can do with all the data they collect about people.

Privacy Protection by Ethical Principles

Some ethical principles that exist for the collection and use of personal information also apply to information collected in e-commerce. Examples are: proper notification about the possible use of personal data, option of opting-in and/or opting-out, accessibility to stored data, keeping consumers' data secured, and the ability to enforce related policies.

The broadest law in scope is the Communications Privacy and Consumer Empowerment Act (1997), which requires, among other things, that the FTC enforces online privacy rights in EC, including the collection and use of personal data. For the status of pending legislation in the United States, see **govtrack.us/congress/bills/subjects/right_of_privacy/5910**.

Government Spying on Its Citizens

At issue here is the proper balance between personal privacy and national security, whereby innovation and commerce is not stifled. The claim is that social networking sites have technology that has outpaced government law enforcement capabilities. The laws on the books do not cover new communication methods (i.e., texting and social networking). Opponents see this as nothing more than unbridled government eavesdropping. During 2013 and 2014, it was found that the US government did spy on its citizens. In 2014 and 2015, efforts were taken to minimize such government surveillance.

P3P Privacy Platform

The **Platform for Privacy Preferences Project (P3P)** is a protocol for privacy protection on the Web developed by the (W3C). According to W3C, an international standards organization for the Web, the "Platform for Privacy Preferences Project (P3P) enables websites to express their privacy practices in a standard format that can be retrieved automatically and interpreted easily by user agents" (per **w3.org/P3P**). The W3C also explains that P3P is useful because "P3P uses machine readable descriptions to describe the collection and use of data. Sites implementing such policies make their practices explicit and thus open them to public scrutiny." This exposure can increase users' trust and confidence in e-commerce sites and vendors. Figure 15.1 shows the process of P3P.

Privacy Protection in Countries Other Than the United States

In 1998, the European Union passed a privacy directive (EU Data Protection Directive) reaffirming the principles of personal data protection in the Internet age. This directive protects privacy more than US protection laws do.

In many countries, the debate about the rights of the individual versus the rights of society continues. In some countries, like China, there is little protection of an individual's Internet privacy.

Note: According to Ranger (2016), the battle over privacy technologies could define the future of the Web.

Fig. 15.1 How P3P works

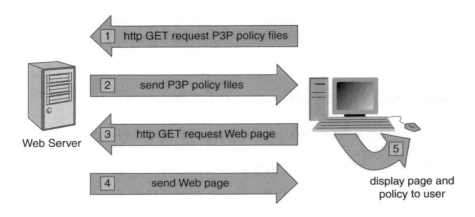

A Simple http Transaction with P3P Added   Source: U.S. Department of Commerce (2009).

SECTION 15.3 REVIEW QUESTIONS

1. Define privacy and free speech. Do your definitions depend on technology?
2. List some of the ways that the Internet can collect information about individuals.
3. What are cookies and spyware, and what do they have to do with online privacy?
4. Describe information pollution and privacy.
5. List four common ethical principles related to the gathering of personal information.
6. Describe privacy issues in social networks. What are the dangers?
7. Define P3P and describe its objectives and procedures.

15.4 OTHER EC LEGAL ISSUES

In addition to the EC law related to privacy, piracy, patents, and other topics discussed in sections "Ethical Challenges and Guidelines," "Intellectual Property Law and Copyright Infringement," and "Privacy Rights, Protection, and Free Speech," there are many other laws related to EC. In this section we will list a sample of them and discuss two in detail.

Note that legal issues are country- or even state-dependent. For comprehensive coverage of these, see Todd and Craig (2017) and Howell (2015). You can find a comprehensive e-commerce law blog at **ecommercelaw.typepad.com**.

Selected Legal and Regulatory Environment: E-Discovery and Cyberbullying

The legal and regulatory environment related to EC is very broad (e.g., Todd and Craig 2017).

Here, we briefly describe two issues: *e-discovery* and *cyberbullying*.

E-Discovery

Electronic discovery (e-discovery) refers to the process of finding any type of electronic data (e.g., text, images, videos) by using computerized systems (see Phillips, et al. 2016). A major application of e-discovery is its use of finding evidence in legal cases. For details, see **en.wikipedia.org/wiki/Electronic_discovery**. For a primer on litigations, see Bennion (2016).

E-discovery frequently deals with e-mail archives. E-mail is the prime target of e-discovery requests. E-discovery must have features such as a full-content index, keyword search, and metadata index. For e-discovery tools for healthcare issues aiding compliance and saving money, see Johnson (2016).

Note: Johnson has several other books for other industries.

E-Discovery and Social Networks

Speaking of discovery, should families of the recently deceased get access to their loved one's social network(s) after they die? How do you manage privacy in the afterlife?

Several social networks have developed policies for such cases. For example, Facebook has developed several policies for the accounts of its users who have passed away. A useful tool is Secret Valet (**secretvalet.com**), an automated system that sends the subscriber's personal information to another person, at a specific time, such as upon the subscriber's death. See also the password manager, PasswordBox. For more, see Ciobanu (undated). For types of e-discovery collections, see Burney (2016).

EDRM

According to Duke Law School, EDRM is a community of e-discovery and legal professionals who create practical resources to improve e-discovery and information governance. The technology is expected to radically transform litigation and the legal profession. EDRM members collaboratively develop vital frameworks, standards, educational tools, and other resources to guide the adoption and use of e-discovery technologies (see **edrm.net/about-us**).

This model illustrates the process of e-discovery; see Fig. 15.2.

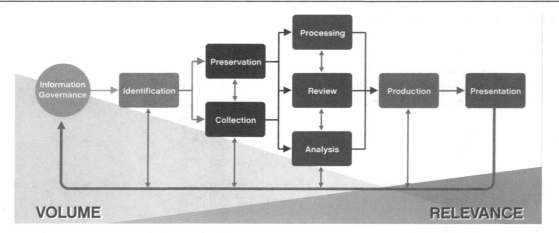

Fig. 15.2 The process of e-discovery

Cyberbullying

According to **stopybullying.gov**, **cyberbullying** is "bullying that takes place using electronic technology. Electronic technology includes devices and equipment such as cell phones, computers and tablets as well as communication tools including social media sites, text messages, chat, and websites." Examples of cyberbullying include mean text messages or e-mails, rumors sent by e-mail or posted on social networking sites, and embarrassing pictures, videos, websites, or fake profiles (per **stopbullying.gov/cyberbullying/what-is-it/index.html**). Bullying means "unwanted, aggressive behavior among school aged children that involves a real or perceived power imbalance." Examples of bullying are "actions such as making threats, spreading rumors, attacking someone physically or verbally, and excluding someone from a group on purpose" (per **stopbullying.gov/what-is-bullying/definition/index.html**). Unfortunately, adults can also be victims of bullying (see **bullyingstatistics.org/content/adult-bullying.html**). For comprehensive coverage, see Harris (2016).

The National Science Foundation (**nsf.gov**) published a series titled "Bullying in the Age of Social Media," which describes how cyberbullying is done, its possible damage to people (some commit suicide), and how to manage it. For legislation and awareness campaigns, see **cyberbullying.org** and **stopcyberbullying.org**.

For more about cyberbullying protection and Internet trolls (section "Fake Content on the Web"), see Elicksen (2015).

Note: In 2016, the First Lady Melania Trump promised to focus on combating cyberbullying if her husband won the election.

Top 10 Internet and EC Legal Issues in 2016

According to Broadcast (2016), the following are the top ten legal issues:

1. Internet privacy
2. Data security
3. The Internet of things
4. The move to mobile and BYOD
5. SaaS and cloud computing
6. Bid data
7. Internet defamation
8. The new generic top-level domains
9. Copyright in the Internet age and the DMCA
10. Online contracting and terms of service

According to Morgan (2016), the IoT introduces many legal issues related to privacy, data ownership, security, and protection of intellectual property.

A Sample of Other Issues

Here is a list of other EC legal issues:

- Disputes between companies regarding patents.
- Legalizing Internet gambling.
- Web monopoly by giant companies (e.g., Google, Tencent in China).
- Use of social media sites for prostitution.
- Regulating online P2P money lending.
- Who has the right to sell?
- Online advertising compliance.
- Laws regarding data protection.
- Refunding policy.

Note: There are many other legal cases related to the Internet and EC. For example, Amazon's e-book business was investigated in 2015/2016 by the European Antitrust regulators (Scott 2015).

Protection is needed not only for buying goods but also from buying services. For a comprehensive collection of legal issues to consider before you open a B2C store, see Guide (2016).

Drivers of EC and Internet Laws

The following are the major drivers of EC and Internet laws:

- Cars as computers
- The Internet of things
- Government policies
- Cracking down on offensive content
- Stronger geographic borders on the Internet
- The ad blocker war
- Who is considered an employee online
- The copyright and piracy battles

We add to the issue of fake information and Internet trolls (see section "Fake Content on the Web").

A Final Note

To illustrate the diversity of the legal issues related to the Internet and EC, consider the following incidents:

According to AP News (2016), a Georgia couple (the Maynards) is suing Snapchat and the driver of a car that crashed into their car (Ms. McGee). "The lawsuit says that in September [2015], McGee was driving down a highway south of Atlanta using a Snapchat filter that places the rate at which a vehicle is traveling over an image. It says McGee was trying to reach 100 miles an hour in her car, which struck the Maynards' car, sending it across the left lane and into an embankment." Mr. Maynard suffered brain damage.

According to Smith (2017), a French man sued Uber for $48 million (USD) for allegedly breaking up his marriage. A notification bug in an Uber app allowed his wife to spy on him without his knowledge. The husband used his wife's iPhone to order Uber trips and then signed out. However, a computer bug made the notifications for the husband's account arriving to the wife's iPhone. As a result, the wife figured out that the husband was lying about certain trips. In addition, she saw all of the Uber drivers' information. Therefore, his "working late at the office" excuse was not good anymore when the wife found out what he was doing late in the day. Therefore, the wife divorced the man who blamed Uber.

SECTION 15.4 REVIEW QUESTIONS

1. List some of the issues that EC will face in the coming years that will affect your daily life.
2. Define e-discovery. How is it related to the law? To e-commerce?
3. Define cyberbullying. What damages can it cause?
4. Enter **hg.org/busecommerce.html**. How do they relate to this section?

15.5 FAKE CONTENT ON THE WEB

The opening case illustrated to us how fake content is produced and spread on the Web. The problem received considerable attention in November 2016. Unfortunately, fake news is only one type of fake content. In this section, we will describe some of the other types as well as some possible solutions.

Fake News

A major type of online fake content is fake news. Fake news can be intentionally set or, as shown in the opening case, be unintentional. In addition to one-time fake news, there are fake news sites. Many claim that the Internet is loosening society's grip on the truth (e.g., Manjoo 2016). Tim Cook, of Apple, said that, "fake news is killing people's minds." Fake news can hurt individuals and/or organizations. One problem is that the fake news spreads very fast. In addition, using bots (Chap. 7), it is possible to send, for example, a huge number of tweets and people can post news on multiple social networks, at once. For how this is done in politics (e.g., 2016 election), see Mello, Jr. (2016a). For a comprehensive discussion, see Shane (2017).

Google and Facebook Actions

Tucker's opening case resulted in continued criticism for companies not addressing the fake news problem. Google responded by banning websites that peddle fake news from using its online advertising service. Facebook changed its Facebook Audience Network policy, saying that it will not display ads in sites that show misleading or illegal content. The Facebook Audience Network policy covers all fake news sites.

Facebook has been at the epicenter of the turmoil. Some accused it for trying to influence voters to vote for President Trump. For details, see Wingfield et al. (2016).

Other Fake Content Types and Activities on the Internet

- In Chap. 11, we presented several methods of fraud involving fake content, products, and sites. Fake sites are used extensively to trick people into providing private information (social engineering). Goel (2016) reported that Russian cyber-forgers stole millions of dollars each day with fake sites. They tricked advertisers to pay for video ads on fake sites (the ads were never watched).
- Plummer (2016a) describes the problem of celebrities that are being attacked by Internet trolls.
- Viner (2016) describes a fake news situation that started in a newspaper, but then went viral on the Internet. (This is similar to the opening case, where fake news was spread both online and offline.)
- Fake reviews are a common problem discussed in Chaps. 8 and 14.
- Amazon.com is trying to fight fake reviews by going after both individuals and website operators. Amazon was able to legally shut down such websites. For details, see Editorial Board (2016).

Internet Trolls

According to Moreau (2016), "an **Internet troll** is a member of an online social community who deliberately tries to disrupt, attack, offend, or generally cause trouble within the community by posting certain comments, photos, videos, graphic interchange formats (GIFs) or some other form of online content.

You can find trolls all over the Internet—on message boards, in your YouTube video comments, on Facebook, on dating sites, in blog comment sections and everywhere else that has an open area where people can freely post to express their thoughts and opinions." A common platform for trolling is Twitter. Trolls have been around since 2010. They do appear in a variety of forms.

Note: Trolls in Internet slang refers to Internet trolls (which are people) or sometimes to the content produced by the Internet trolls themselves. For an overview, see **lifewire.com/what-is-internet-trolling-3485891**.

Types of Trolls

Moreau (2016) lists the following types of trolls:

1. The grammar and spell check troll
2. The forever offended troll
3. The show off, know-it-all troll
4. The one word only troll
5. The exaggeration troll
6. The off-topic troll
7. The insult troll
8. The persistent troll

There are many other classifications of trolls.

Controlling Trolls

It is not easy to control trolls. Moreau (2016) observed that "controlling them can be difficult when there a lot of community members, but the most common ways to get rid of them includes either banning/blocking individual user accounts (and sometime IP addresses altogether) or closing off comment sections entirely on a blog post, video page, or topic thread." Roberts (2017a, b), who was attacked by trolls, describes an ongoing project at Google that tries to use an AI-based tool called a Jigsaw to control trolls, even those generated by bot.

Difficulties Controlling Fake Content

It is not easy to control fake content due to variety of shapes it takes and the way that the fake content is structured. Here are some related issues:

- Even the clever students of Stanford University have had trouble judging the credibility of information published online (Donald 2016).
- Lies spread much faster than truths, as shown in a study of viral content (Silverman 2015).
- The plague of fake content is getting worse.

  Despite the difficulties, there are many possible solutions.

Controlling Fake Content

Many experts make suggestions about how to control fake content. Here are some:

- Kiely and Robertson (2016) provide suggestions on how to spot fake content.
- Kercher (2016) provides a list of fake and misleading news sites to watch videos on AI and their potential role in controlling fake news.
- Stelter (2016) provides suggestions on how to protect against fake news.
- Nicholas (2016) provides advice regarding finding out if an EC website is legitimate.

What to Do When There Is Fake Content About Your Company?

Several years ago, employees of Domino's Pizza in Conover, NC, created five fake videos showing unclean food preparation including food contamination practices at the company. The videos featured Domino's employees in the company's uniform and were posted on YouTube. The videos went viral and within 6 h were featured on a consumer advocacy site (**consumerist. com**). The videos were seen by millions of viewers by the time the company found about them. Damage control worked fast; YouTube removed the videos. The employees lost their jobs and faced criminal charges. However, the reputation of Domino's was damaged. In Chap. 10, we described the issue of reputation management in general. A question was raised by Alaimo (2017): "what to do when the fake news [and content] is about your company[?]" Alaimo reports that "in December 2016, a

28-year-old man drove 6 h to a Washington, D.C., pizza parlor and fired a rifle after reading fake news claiming that Hillary Clinton was leading a child sex slavery operation there" (at the Pizza Parlor). Alaimo suggests that companies plan for and address the possibility of fake content against their businesses. Specific suggested actions are:

- Communicate values in advance.
- Use employees as advocates.
- Do not inadvertently fund nonmainstream new sites.
- Write responses in advance (response time must be very fast).
- Choose your battles.
- Consider legal action (like Domino's did).

Tips for Analyzing and Dealing with Various Types of Fake News

Zimdars (2016) provides a huge list of tips and creative comments to handle the situation. Here we provide only some.

- "Avoid websites that end in 'lo' ex: Newslo. These sites take pieces of accurate information and then packaging that information with other false or misleading 'facts' (sometimes for the purposes of satire or comedy).
- Watch out for common news websites that end in 'com.co' as they are often fake versions of real news sources (remember: this is also the domain for Colombia!)
- Watch out if known/reputable news sites are not also reporting on the story. Sometimes lack of coverage is the result of corporate media bias and other factors, but there should typically be more than one source reporting on a topic or event.
- Odd domain names generally equal odd and rarely truthful news.
- Lack of author attribution may, but not always, signify that the news story is suspect and requires verification.
- Some news organizations are also letting bloggers post under the banner of particular news brands; however, many of these posts do not go through the same editing process (ex: BuzzFeed Community Posts, Kinja blogs, *Forbes* blogs).
- Check the 'About Us' tab on websites or look up the website on Snopes or Wikipedia for more information about the source.
- Bad Web design and use of ALL CAPS can also be a sign that the source you're looking at should be verified and/or read in conjunction with other sources.
- If the story makes you REALLY ANGRY it's probably a good idea to keep reading about the topic via other sources to make sure the story you read wasn't purposefully trying to make you angry (with potentially misleading or false information) in order to generate shares and ad revenue. Thanks to ED Brayton for this tip!
- If the website you're reading encourages you to DOX individuals, it's unlikely to be a legitimate source of news.
- It's always best to read multiple sources of information to get a variety of viewpoints and media frames. Sources such as *The Daily Kos*, *The Huffington Post*, and Fox News vacillate between providing important, legitimate, problematic, and/ or hyperbolic news coverage, requiring readers and viewers to verify and contextualize information with other sources."
- For more tips on analyzing the credibility and reliability of sources, please check out School of Library Journal (they also provide an extensive list of media literacy resources) and the Digital Resource Center.

SECTION 15.5 REVIEW QUESTIONS

1. Define fake news and explain the potential damage.
2. What are Google and Facebook doing to combat the problem?
3. List all major types of fake content.
4. Define Internet trolls and list several of their variations.
5. How can one control Internet trolls?
6. Why is it difficult to control fake content on the Web?
7. List some solutions to control fake content.
8. Describe the problem for enterprises and list some solutions.

15.6 PUBLIC POLICY, TAXATION, AND POLITICAL ENVIRONMENTS

Public policy rules and actions made by elected officials and regulators around the world can impact how EC is conducted. Stay informed of the policy issues facing the EC community and the opportunities to engage your government officials. In this chapter, we include four topics of public policy that are closely related to e-commerce.

Net Neutrality

Internet neutrality (also *network neutrality*, *net neutrality*, or *NN*) has been a hotly debated topic that may shape the future of the Internet (see **businessinsider.com/net-neutralityfor-dummies-and-how-it-effects-you-2014-1**). It became a high-profile topic when telecommunications network operators AT&T and Verizon announced that they wanted to charge an extra fee to deliver content on the Internet at a faster rate of speed. Currently, all Internet traffic is being treated equally (or "neutrally") by telecommunication providers. In response, numerous groups have tried to stop the extra fee. The problem here is that 5–10% of all Internet users occupy 80–90% of the available bandwidth, partially because of the heavy peer-to-peer (P2P) traffic.

On December 21, 2010, the Federal Communications Commission (FCC) approved net neutrality. **Net neutrality** is a network design principle stating that basic protocols of the Internet should enable users to utilize the Web without being discriminated against by Internet service providers. In other words, there should be net equality. Net providers cannot dictate the types of content you see; they must treat all Internet traffic sources equally, and consumers can access anything they want at no extra charge (see **businessinsider.com/net-neutralityfor-dummies-and-how-it-effects-you-2014-1**). Net neutrality puts in place three high-level rules for service providers. For more on net neutrality and its impact, see Gross (2014) and Sommer (2014). Note that implementation of net neutrality is not simple; it involves Web companies, lawmakers and government agencies, fiber-optic owners, content providers, mobile carriers, and consumers. Opponents are fighting the authority of the FCC to enforce net neutrality by circulating and signing petitions, protesting, and so forth. For how net neutrality, or lack thereof, can affect a business, see **entrepreneur.com/article/233991**. For a discussion on the net neutrality debate and an infographic, see **wired.com/2014/06/net_neutrality_missing**.

In April 2014, the FCC announced new rules that might have abolished net neutrality (see Mayton 2014). However, in May 2014, the FCC generated a new *proposal* that is intended to uphold net neutrality. The FCC's proposal includes keeping the Internet open and holding Internet providers to higher levels of transparency. Also in question is how the FCC plans to regulate ISPs. The FCC plans on adopting a new set of rules by the end of 2014 (see Anthony 2014). Well, it sure keeps changing!

Since 2014, there has been an ongoing battle and pressures on the FCC by those who are for and against changes in the net neutrality regulation concept. The Trump administration may reverse the situation. See Reilly (2017) and Breland (2017) for details.

The international implementation of EC taxation is very complicated due to each country's regulations. The trend is to move to destination-based taxes. For details, see Schwanke (2016).

Taxation of EC Transactions in the United States

Several types of taxes are related to e-commerce. The most debatable one is the Internet sales tax, which is imposed by individual states on products sold in their jurisdictions. See **en.wikipedia.org/wiki/Internet_taxes**. When Internet commerce started in the mid-1990s, it was declared free of taxation in the United States at the federal, state, county, and city levels in order to encourage e-commerce. However, not imposing taxes on the Internet was seen as discriminatory against mail-order businesses and traditional retailers who must collect taxes. Over the years, there were several court challenges and modifications. You can read about the history at **libertytax.com/online/taxbrain/**. One development was the 1998 Internet Tax Freedom Act that placed a moratorium on special taxation on the Internet for 1 year. This meant that Internet access could not be taxed by state and local governments. The Act has been renewed by Congress periodically, with a few changes (see **money.howstuffworks.com/personal-finance/personal-income-taxes/internet-tax-freedom-act1.htm**). A bill to permanently extend the Internet Tax Freedom Act was introduced in 2013 and was passed by the House Committee on the Judiciary in June 2014. To read about the bill and track its progress, see **govtrack.us/congress/bills/113/hr3086#overview**.

Therefore, the states' budget and taxing authorities have placed the issue of collecting Internet taxes high on their agendas as a potential means of generating state revenues. Some states are suing online vendors for not collecting sales taxes. It appears that there is a consensus forming among state lawmakers that Internet taxes are inevitable. Obviously, there is consumer resistance.

A major player in the conflict between consumers that are used to not paying taxes and states that need money is Amazon. com. In 2011, California passed a tax collection bill for the Internet and started to pressure Amazon into collecting the sales tax. In 2012, Amazon agreed to collect sales tax from its buyers in California as well as in some other states.

In 2013, the US Senate passed the Marketplace Fairness Act (**marketplacefairness.org**), a law that will require all online and catalog sellers in the United States to collect sales tax at the time of an online transaction. However, states must simplify their sales tax laws. The bill was sent to the House Subcommittee and, as of June 2014, is still being reviewed.

By 2017, Amazon.com agreed to collect tax in some states (e.g., California) but not in others (e.g., Hawaii).

According to Lowry and Lunder (2016), "in certain instances, the taxes are not included in the online prices due to constitutional limitations on the states' authority to require that out-of-state sellers collect them.

Two public policy issues are typically raised concerning the effects of current law.

First, differential tax treatment of similar items creates an economic distortion that affects producer and consumer decisions. Remote sellers may locate operations based on potential sales and use tax consequences, not traditional market factors. Additionally, consumers may choose out-of-state vendors to evade taxes.

Second, current law limits the ability for state and local government to require the collection and use of taxes on goods and services that would otherwise be subject to such collection if sold by a local vendor. This is particularly a significant issue for states that rely relatively more on general sales tax as part of their overall revenue mix."

In addition to sales tax, there are several other taxes related to e-commerce.

For example, in July 2010, in a move to legalize Internet gambling, the US House Committee on Financial Services approved a bill that lays the groundwork for a multibillion-dollar online gambling tax.

Internet Censorship by Countries

Internet censorship refers to restrictions on what can be seen, published, or accessed on the Internet. Internet restrictions can be imposed domestically (e.g., big businesses and corporations restricting employee Internet access) and in foreign countries. Censorship is done using different methods, ranging from blocking access to certain websites to the creation of a whole alternative Internet, as was done in Iran. A popular method of censorship is content filtering. Filtering can be based on a blacklist of offensive website content providers or by other methods. When blacklisted, a website will have all or part of its content censored by a government agency that sees the website's content as offensive to citizens or to the government. For comprehensive information on the different types of Internet censorship in the United States and other countries, see **computer.howstuffworks.com/internet-censorship.htm**. In 2010, Google decided not to do business in China because the Chinese government had asked Google to block certain websites and information in Google searches. Google refused and withdrew from China.

In early 2009, President Obama appointed Cass Sunstein as the White House's "Regulatory Czar." Sunstein is an advocate for Internet censorship, having written several white papers promoting the idea. For examples and infographics of censorship in countries around the world, see **en.wikipedia.org/wiki/Internet_censorship_by_country**.

SECTION 15.6 REVIEW QUESTIONS

1. What is net neutrality and how will it affect the Internet?
2. Why is net neutrality such a hotly debated issue? Find the legal status of this issue.
3. Describe how taxes relate to e-commerce.
4. What is Internet censorship?

15.7 SOCIETAL ISSUES AND GREEN EC

At this point in the chapter, our attention turns to several societal issues of EC. The first societal topic is one that concerns many—the *digital divide*.

The Digital Divide

Despite the factors and trends that contribute to future EC growth, since the inception of the Internet, and e-commerce in particular, a gap has emerged between those who have and those who do not have the ability to engage in e-commerce. This gap is referred to in its generic format as the **digital divide**. According to Internet World Stats, the digital divide "is a social issue referring to the differing amount of information between those who have access to the Internet (especially broadband access) and those who do not have access" (see **internetworldstats.com/links10.htm**). The gap exists both *within* and *between* countries. The US federal and state governments are attempting to close this gap within the United States by encouraging training and supporting education and infrastructure. The gap between countries, however, may be widening rather than narrowing. For an overview and statistics, see **en.wikipedia.org/wiki/Digital_divide**. Many government and international organizations, including the United Nations and Citizens Online, are exploring this issue.

Overcoming the Digital Divide

Governments, companies, and nonprofit organizations are trying to reduce the digital divide. One example is the "One Laptop per Child" project (**one.laptop.org**), a nonprofit organization whose mission is to provide children in low-income communities and developing nations with low-cost "XO" brand laptops.

For a short video, see **laptop.org/en/video/brand/index.html**. The current cost of each laptop (2014) is around $35. For more information about the program and the capabilities of the laptops, see **one.laptop.org/about/faq**. In 2017, Amazon. com offered its cheapest Fire tablet for $39.00.

Telecommuting

One activity of e-commerce is **telecommuting**, which is working at home using a PC, tablet, smartphone, and the Internet. Telecommuting is on the rise in the United States and in several developing countries. For a list of potential benefits, see Table 15.3. For example, one benefit of working from home is that people who live in the suburbs can save one to 2 h of time per day by not having to commute to work (Enviro Boys 2010).

Table 15.3 Potential benefits of telecommuting or virtual work

Individuals	Organizational	Community and Society
Reduces or eliminates travel-related time and expenses	Reduces office space needed	Conserves energy and lessens dependence on foreign oil
Improves health by reducing stress related to compromises made between family and work	Increases labor pool and competitive advantage in recruitment	Preserves the environment by reducing traffic-related pollution and congestion
Allows closer proximity to and involvement with family	Provides compliance with the Americans with Disabilities Act	Reduces traffic accidents and resulting injuries or deaths
Allows closer bonds with the family and the community	Decreases employee turnover, absenteeism, and use of sick leave	Reduces the incidence of disrupted families; telecommuters may be able to keep their job and work from home if a family member needs to relocate for business reasons
Decreases involvement in office politics	Improves job satisfaction and productivity	Increases employment opportunities for the homebound
Increases productivity despite distractions		Allows the transfer of jobs to areas of high unemployment

Example: Ascend One Corporation

Ascend One Corporation, a consumer debt management business, decided to change their networking strategies in order to expand. Ascend One's success was substantially burdened by having to provide its call center agents with daily cumbersome support and application updates on their desktop computers. The company increased productivity and satisfaction of customer care employees by combining telecommuting with virtualization technology. The company stored and managed applications on virtual desktops instead of on remote computers. Call center agent productivity increased by 10%. By allowing telecommuting, there was an increase in employee productivity and a reduction in attrition rates. The technology also allowed the company to maintain high levels of communication with mobile employees. Training programs are accessible 24 h per day to remote workers (see Park 2009 for details).

Note: Some companies do not like their employees to work from home. In 2013, Yahoo's CEO banned the work-from-home policy. For a debate on this policy, see Bercovici (2013) and Ascharya (2013). Although the ban on telecommuting is still enforced, the CEO extended Yahoo's parental leave policy.

Does EC Increase Unemployment?

In January 2017, Amazon.com opened its first physical store (Amazon Go) without cashiers (see Chap. 7). The question is: "Will Amazon Go replace jobs?" While the specific issue is still debatable, the more general question is "will robots take our jobs?" or in general: Where and when can machines replace humans?

Automation and Job Losses

The arguments that automation takes jobs started with the *Industrial Revolution*. What is really happening is difficult to assess. While certain jobs disappear, others are created. Therefore, proponents of automation believe that there is actually total job increase. Opponents say the opposite. The problem is that today the pace of automation is much faster than in the past and the magnitude is much broad. Let us see the implication in EC-related fields, especially robotics.

The Current Automation Impact

If all merchants will replace their checkout employees with robots, there will be millions of additional unemployed people in the world. Foxcom, an iPhone manufacturer in Taiwan, plans to replace almost all of their employees with robots (Statt 2016). The company itself produces 10,000 robots each year for this purpose. A study done in the United Kingdom (cited in Chap. 7) predicts that robots will take 50% of all jobs in about 10 years. Egan (2015) reports that robots already threaten the following jobs: marketers, toll booth operators and cashiers, customer service, financial brokers, journalists, lawyers, and phone workers. Note that automation may affect portions of almost all jobs to a greater or lesser degree. According to Hiner (2016), about 80% of IT jobs will be eliminated by software (i.e., software agents in AI).

According to Manyika et al. (2017), automation is spreading because "robots and computers can only perform a range of routine physical work activities better and more cheaply than humans, but they are also increasingly capable of accomplishing activities that include cognitive capabilities once considered too difficult to automate successfully, such as making tacit judgments, sensing emotion, or even driving. Automation will change the daily work activities of everyone, from miners and landscapers to commercial bankers, fashion designers, welders, and CEOs." When all of this is going to happen will depend on many factors, primarily on human-computer interaction and collaboration.

Amazon.com and other e-tailers are trying to automate operations to stay competitive. Inventions in the IoT, for example, will result in automatic ordering. The more inventions are made, the more competitive advantage of EC against traditional retailers.

So What Can Be Done?

Given that EC is unstoppable, replacement of humans by machines will accelerate. The solutions depend on organizational, political, social, economic, training ability, and other factors. This issue is outside the boundaries of this book.

Note: In February 2017, Bill Gates suggested that industrial robots should be taxed like workers. The tax should be imposed both on manufacturers of robots and on users of the robots. The collected money will be used for retraining displaced employees (see details in Morris 2017).

Green EC and IT

There are many opportunities to make EC green, and here we present some representative ones.

Operating Greener Businesses, Eco-friendly Data Centers, and Cloud Computing

The growing power consumption of computing technology and high energy costs are having a direct negative impact on business profitability. Enterprises are trying to reduce energy costs and increase the use of recyclable materials. **Green computing** refers to the eco-friendly use of computing resources (e.g., see **searchdatacenter.techtarget.com/definition/green-computing**). In this section, we focus on how EC is *going green* by adopting environmentally friendly practices.

Table 15.4 Turning IT green: guidelines for energy-efficient computer use

Use the computer's power management options, such as setting all computers to hibernate and using the standby option
Instruct all personnel to turn off computer monitors when not in use
Shut down all computers automatically after hours or when not in use
Encourage telecommuting whenever possible
Follow the manufacturers' recommendations on all energy-related equipment
Embrace cloud computing. Replace existing servers with virtualization, as money permits
Increase cooling efficiency. For practices, see "Cooling Data Center Costs" in *Baseline*, August 13, 2010 (available online at **baselinemag.com/infrastructure/Cooling-Data-Center-Costs** accessed February 2017)

For example, energy use in data centers is a major concern to corporations. Green EC/IT is a growing movement (see Nelson 2008) that also includes data centers. According to Gartner Inc., Green IT initiatives are expanding to many other areas (see **enterpriseinnovation.net/article/gartner-green-data-center-means-more-energy-efficiency**). For guidelines on how to go green, see Table 15.4.

For practices, see "Cooling Data Center Costs" in *Baseline*, August 13, 2010 (available online at **baselinemag.com/c/a/IT-Management/Cooling-Data-Center-Costs-368334** (accessed February 2017).

The efforts to improve the use of EC (and IT) by minimizing damage to the environment, and at the same time saving money, are major objectives of **Green IT**. Company data center servers are also known to be both power hungry and heat generating. PC monitors consume about 80 to 100 billion kilowatt hours of electricity every year in the United States. Both Intel and AMD are producing new chips aimed at reducing this amount of energy usage. Turning off PCs when they are not in use can save a company money and add to good corporate social health by reducing the damage caused by excess carbon dioxide release. Finally, discarded PCs and other computer equipment can cause serious waste disposal problems. An important issue is how to recycle old computing equipment and whose responsibility it is to take care of the problem (the manufacturers? the users? the government?). *Green software* assists companies save energy and/or comply with EPA requirements.

Comprehensive coverage of Green IT is provided by Murugesan and Gangadharan (2012), who distinguish between making EC (and IT) greener and using IT and EC as an enabling tool to improve environmental sustainability (i.e., make it greener). They also cover implementation and strategy issues. For a guide to Green IT strategy, see IBM (2008).

How to Operate Greener Businesses, Data Centers, and Supply Chains

Chief information officers (CIOs) who are looking to operate greener businesses, data centers, and supply chains should focus on: (1) virtualization, (2) software management, and (3) harnessing the "cloud." *Virtualization* provides energy saving solutions, resulting in both energy and monetary savings. Companies seeking advice, tools, and processes can turn to software management outsourcing to help them achieve their software needs and licensing management needs. Finally, cloud computing is predicted to be included in 45% of all IT applications by 2017.

Gaining energy efficiency in business requires managing these issues: the computers, computing power of the data center, data center power/cooling, and data center storage. Many organizations are turning to server virtualization, such as cloud computing, to cut their energy costs.

Example 1: Wells Fargo

Wells Fargo (**wellsfargo.com**) is a large financial institution that offers a wide range of banking services online. The company is data-dependent and known for its eco-friendliness. The company decided to "go green" in its two data centers. Data centers must ensure security and availability of their services, and when they are planned from scratch, they can be energy efficient with low power consumption. The two new facilities had more than 8000 servers. After major virtualization efforts, the data centers were using significantly less power compared to the previous year.

Wells Fargo introduced several energy saving devices (see Clancy 2010). It constantly expands and renovates its data centers, yet shows high consideration to the environment. Wells Fargo is also eco-friendly in other ways. (For more about "green banking" at Wells Fargo, see **bankrate.com/financing/banking/green-banking-at-wells-fargo**.)

Example 2: Google

Google aimed to reduce the power consumption of its data centers by 30%. This was done by reducing overhead costs: improving the cooling system, lighting, and the power infrastructure. Google closely followed the strategies and recommendations of the company's "Green Energy Czar." Google, whenever possible, embraces free cooling—such as cooling towers and use of fresh air. Google also purchases clean energy from several sources. For details, see Samson (2010).

Global Green Regulations

Global regulations also are influencing green business practices. Sustainability regulations such as the Restriction of Hazardous Substances Directive (RoHS) in the European Union (EU) will increasingly impact how supply chains function regardless of location (see **ec.europa.eu/environment/waste/rohs_eee** and **www.gov.uk/government/organisations/ national-measurement-and-regulation-office**).

Eco-friendly practices reduce costs and improve public relations in the long run. Not surprisingly, demand for green computing is on the rise. A tool to help companies find greener computers and other electronics is the Electronic Product Environmental Assessment Tool (EPEAT).

The Electronic Product Environmental Assessment Tool

Maintained by the Green Electronics Council (GEC), the **Electronic Product Environmental Assessment Tool (EPEAT)**, according to their website, rates electronic products against a range of environmental performance criteria. They are a comprehensive global rating system for greener electronics. For more on e-commerce for a better environment, see **rainforesta- gencies.com.au/egreen.html**.

Telecommuting, which was discussed earlier, also offers several green benefits, including reducing rush-hour traffic, improving air quality, improving highway safety, and even improving healthcare by reducing pollution.

Other Societal Issues

Many other societal issues can be related to EC. Three in which EC has had a generally positive impact are mentioned here: education, public safety, and health.

Education

E-commerce has had a major impact on education and learning. Virtual universities are helping to reduce the digital divide. Companies can use the Internet to help retrain employees, enabling them to defer retirement.

Public Safety, Surveillance, and Homeland Security

With increased concerns about public safety after September 11, 2001, many organizations and individuals have started to look at technologies that will help deter, prevent, or detect criminal activities of various types. Various e-commerce tools can help increase safety both at home and in public places. These include e-911 systems; global collaborative commerce technologies (for collaboration among national and international law enforcement units); e-procurement (of unique equipment to fight crime); e-government efforts at coordinating, information sharing, and expediting legal work and cases; intelligent homes, offices, and public buildings; and e-training of law enforcement officers.

An issue to consider is whether the financial, functional, and social impact of surveillance systems is worth the public's perceived intrusion of privacy. The fact remains that most cities that use the surveillance cameras do so more for the retrieval of images rather than for active monitoring. Thus, as a crime deterrent, these cameras make little financial sense since only one person can effectively monitor ten cameras at one time. The City of Chicago, for example, has installed more than 10,000 cameras. For real-time monitoring, the city would need to hire an additional 1000 city employees, which is impossible with budget shortages and lower tax revenues (per Gallio 2010). Machine interpretation of videos, which is getting more and more accurate, will make surveillance a more cost-effective tool in the future. However, Chicago is adding more surveillance cameras. As of 2014, Chicago has 24,000 cameras, which is raising privacy concerns with citizens and the ACLU (see **foxnews. com/politics/2014/05/12/security-camera-surge-in-chicago-sparks-concerns-massive-surveillance-system**).

Health Aspects

Is EC a health risk? Generally speaking, it is probably safer and healthier to shop from home than in a physical store. However, some believe that exposure to cellular mobile communication radiation may cause health problems. It may take years before the truth of this claim is known. Even if communication radiation may cause health problems, the damage would probably be insignificant due to the small amount of time most people spend on wireless shopping and other m-commerce activities. However, given the concern of some about this issue, protective devices are now available that would minimize this problem (e.g., see **safecell.net**).

Another health-related issue is the addiction to online games, social networks, and EC/Internet-related applications. Several countries (including the United States) have begun prevention and reeducation programs, and some have opened inpatient treatment and recovery centers (e.g., see Geranios 2009 and **netaddiction.com**).

EC technologies such as collaborative commerce can help improve healthcare. For example, using Web technologies during the review process and the approval process of new drugs has been shortened, saving lives and reducing suffering. Wireless computing helps in the delivery of healthcare (see Chap. 6). Intelligent systems facilitate medical diagnoses. Healthcare advice can be provided from a distance. Finally, intelligent hospitals, doctors, and other healthcare facilities use EC tools. In 2009, the major social networks and Twitter were tracking the outbreak of the swine flu pandemic, advising people where not to travel and how to protect themselves. Finally, in Israel and Europe, an ongoing major multinational, collaborative research project called "MobiGuide" combines monitoring patients from a distance and generating medical decisions according to the data collected.

SECTION 15.7 REVIEW QUESTIONS

1. Define the digital divide.
2. Describe the One Laptop per Child project.
3. Describe how EC can improve safety and security.
4. Describe the impact of EC on health services.
5. What is green computing?
6. List three examples in which green computing can help protect the environment or conserve resources.
7. What is a green supply chain? Give one example.
8. How do the new data centers help us to go green?
9. How does telecommuting or virtual work conserve the environment?

15.8 THE FUTURE OF E-COMMERCE

Generally speaking, the consensus is that the future of EC is positive. EC will become an increasingly important method of trading, reaching customers, providing services, and improving organizations' operations. In addition, EC facilitates collaboration, innovation, and people-to-people interactions. Analysts differ in their predictions for the anticipated growth rate of EC and the length of time it will become a substantial portion of the economy. There is also disagreement about the identification of industry segments that will grow the fastest. However, there also is a consensus about the overall direction of the field: full speed ahead! Companies such as Amazon.com, eBay, Alibaba Group, Priceline, and Newegg.com are growing rapidly.

EC will grow all over the globe.

Some Key Factors for the Future of E-Commerce

The future of EC depends on how many factors will have impacts in the future. TrueShip (2016) made the following ten predictions:

1. Amazon will become bigger than Walmart.
2. EC will be 10% of all retail.
3. Facebook will overtake YouTube for branding.
4. Emotionally driven shopping will become a standard.
5. In-store pickup will save the large retail chains (as in the case of Target).
6. Competitors will create Amazon Prime-like shopping portals.
7. Drones will start to deliver.
8. Marketplaces for selling goods will become very popular.
9. Mobile shopping will overtake desktop shopping. It may be required for survival.
10. Hassle-free returns will be mainstreams in EC.

Other factors cited are:

- The shape of net neutrality.
- The extent of developing easy-to-shop and smart applications (e.g., Google's DeepMind).
- The competition between EC giants (e.g., Amazon, Alibaba) and large retailers that are going "brick-and-click" (e.g., Walmart) is intensifying.
- Multichannel shopping is increasing.
- Beacon technology integrates online and offline systems.
- Huge images and videos deliver stunning homepages.
- Real-time analytics become the norm.

For comprehensive reports, see Knight (2016), McCafferty (2016a), and Zorzini (2015).

New Trends That Are Shaping the Future of B2C

According to Smeaton (2016), the following are the six trends that are shaping the future of B2C e-commerce:

1. New EC product categories will take over computer and consumer electronics.
2. Developing countries will become the largest EC markets (mostly Asia Pacific, China, Indonesia, and India).
3. Will Amazon and Alibaba keep up against new EC trends? Yes, but niche players will play a leading role in certain market sectors.
4. Marketplaces vs. direct websites: which business model is the future of EC?
5. Is the future of EC mobile? Yes, but slowly, new technologies make it easier to shop online.
6. Product visualization will become a crucial EC trend, especially for more complicated products.

The B2C Road to 2016

Ovum (2016) outlined the road of B2C EC for the year 2016. In their free e-book, the company talks about the following seven major categories:

1. Consumers of the future.
2. Online retailing is growing more than three times faster than regular retailing.
3. The blurring boundaries of retail and e-tail.
4. Mobile-centric retail experience.
5. Context is King.
6. Key technologies that will shape retail.
7. How to prepare for the future (a guide).

The Future of B2B

B2B is much larger than B2C, but the ratio is getting smaller. From a 6:1 ratio in the 1990s, the ratio will be only 2:1 in a few years. Columbus (2016) provides the following predictions:

- B2B EC will top $1.1 billion, accounting for over 12% of all B2B commerce. (B2C is under 8% of all B2C.)
- New cloud-based platforms are increasing, selling speed, scale, and simplicity.
- There is a conversion of B2B and B2C.

Zorzini's List of Trends for 2016 and Beyond

Zorzini (2015) made the following predictions:

1. Multichannel shopping may make or break your business (namely, you better have one).
2. Connecting with customers through social media is not enough.
3. An integration of online and offline will be done with beacon technology.

4. The pop-up may make an effective comeback (or may not).
5. Huge images and videos deliver stunning homepages.
6. The virtual salesforce becomes highly implemented.
7. Mobile is required for survival.
8. Real-time analytics become the norm.

Other Predictions

Other predictions for 2017 and beyond are:

1. E-commerce competition will increase.
2. President Trump could be good for e-tailers.
3. M-commerce will outperform desktop commerce.
4. EC delivery will get better and faster (Chap. 13).
5. The payment landscape will evolve (Chap. 11).
6. For more predictions, see DeMarco (2016).

Integrating the Marketplace with the Marketspace

Throughout this book, we have commented on the relationship between the physical marketplace and the online marketspace. We have pointed out conflicts in certain areas, as well as successful applications. The fact is that, from the point of view of the consumer, as well as of most of the merchants and suppliers, these two entities exist, and will continue to exist, together.

Probably the most noticeable integration of the two concepts is in the click-and-mortar organization. In the near future, the click-and-mortar organization will be the most prevalent model (e.g., see Sears.com, Target.com, Costco.com, and Walmart.com), although the model may take different forms. Some organizations will use EC as just another sales channel, as most large retailers, airlines, and banks are doing today. Others will use EC only for some products and services and sell other products and services the conventional way (e.g., LEGO Group).

The consumers prefer to have the choice where to shop. As of 2015, consumers love the combination of ordering online and picking up the merchandise in the physical store. Some believe that such a combination saves retailers from extinction (e.g., see Chap. 13 and Douglas 2014).

M-Commerce

There is almost a consensus that the role of m-commerce in e-commerce will increase significantly. There already are millions of innovative mobile apps, and their numbers are growing rapidly. The area where we will see the fastest growth in EC is the proliferation of apps. Many m-commerce start-ups are entering the field. For details, see Chap. 6 and Kemp (2016).

With the advances of the IoT, we see many increasing applications (e.g., see the closing case in Chap. 7).

Social Commerce

Recently, the use of mobile social networks has been accelerating. The increasing number of new wireless Web 2.0 services has assisted many social networks to go wireless, enabling more interactions between people. Nielsen's September 2012 release of its *Social Media Report* indicated that four out of five active Internet users visit social networks and blogs. The report also shows that nearly 82% of social media users access these websites using their mobile phones (Nielsen 2012). These numbers continue to grow with time.

Social commerce is growing rapidly on Facebook, Twitter, Google, Instagram, and many other companies. Mobile advertising and promotions are major areas of growth. For details, see Turban et al. (2016) and Kemp (2016).

Future Technological Trends that May Accelerate the Speed of E-Commerce

The following are a few examples that will facilitate the use of e-commerce (based on Scollay (2015) and McCafferty (2016a)):

- Much wider broadband of technologies and faster networks.
- More powerful search engines (intelligent agent-based).
- Better batteries for mobile devices.
- Development in quantum computing and the semantic Web.
- The arrival of flexible computer screens.
- Better cloud applications.
- Wide use of smartphones and tablets.
- Increased use of wearable devices (will become a platform to m-commerce)
- Possibility of free Internet access 3D printing will grow (Chap. 13).
- Wide applications of AI technologies.
- Using augmented reality (e.g., in order fulfillment; see DHL 2015).
- Going further into the IoT.
- Next generation data centers.
- The proliferation of AI applications (also see Adhikari 2016a, b).

Future Trends That Are Limiting the Spread of EC

The following trends may slow down the growth of EC and Web 2.0 and may even cripple the Internet:

- **Security concerns.** Both shoppers and users of e-banking and other services worry about online security. The Web needs to be made safer; see Constantin (2017).
- **Lack of agreement on net neutrality.** If the big telecom companies are allowed to charge more for faster access, small companies that cannot pay extra may be at a disadvantage. The issue is still in limbo.
- **Copyright violations.** The legal problems of YouTube, Wikipedia, and others may result in a loss of vital outlets of public opinion and creativity.
- **Lack of standards.** There is still a lack of standards for EC, especially for global trade.

Consumer Behavior

The future of B2C EC depends on consumer behavior. The young people that are more computer-oriented will buy more online, especially if they can save time and money. The consumers will interact with AI apps and probably love them. For more on the consumer of the future, see Ovum (2016).

Conclusion

In conclusion, many people believe that the impact of EC on our lives will be as much as, and possibly more profound than, that of the Industrial Revolution. No other phenomenon since the Industrial Revolution has been classified in this category. It is our hope that this book will help you move successfully into this exciting and challenging area of the digital revolution.

For a 537 slideshow, see "Digital in 2016" at **slideshare.net/wearesocialsg/digital-in-2016** by Kemp (2016).

Enjoy Some Interesting Videos About the Future of E-Commerce

The following are some suggested videos about e-commerce:

1. "E-Commerce's Future Ain't What It Used to Be; It's Even Better" (7:48 min) at **youtube.com/watch?v=mJtw1027FYs**
2. "Future of E-Commerce: Trends, Challenges, and Opportunities for Telecom and the Mobile Industry" (7:41 min) at **youtube.com/watch?v=wCZXif3MUEw**

Here are two coming applications of EC. They were taken from 10eCommerce (2017), **10ecommercetrends.com** (accessed February 2017).

L'Oréal of Paris

"L'Oréal Paris has designed five diagnostic tools: skincare, cosmetics (face and eyes), haircare, and hair color. These beauty diagnostics, typically operated on a mobile device, allow consumers to 'try on' different shades of make-up, 'scan' their hair color, etc. Not only can consumers use these tools to play with different looks in real time, but the data collected during each session allows for an unprecedented level of personalization of communications and interactions, not to mention ultra-customized discount coupons, which can have a major influence on purchasing decision."

Chatbots

According to L'Oréal business trends: "In 2017, many consumers will have their first interaction with a chatbot, a fully automated chat agent that will answer their questions and act as the first point of contact with the brand. A chatbot increases the number of platforms on which a brand can transact by offering guided, interactive browsing at all times.

Chatbots will soon become as commonplace as automated phone systems, only much more interactive and interesting. At the same time, store sales staff will become more important than ever, as they'll be increasingly involved in the online experience.

What are the potential impacts of a chatbot on e-commerce?

Live chat users spend an average of 5%–30% more.

The buyer conversion rate is 5 to 10 times higher following a chat session."

SECTION 15.8 REVIEW QUESTIONS

1. How is EC related to traditional commerce?
2. Describe the role of mobility in the future of EC.
3. How will social networks facilitate EC?
4. Which future trends will help EC?
5. Which trends slow down the growth of EC?

MANAGERIAL ISSUES

Some managerial issues related to this chapter are as follows:

1. **What legal and ethical issues are of concern in an EC initiative?** Key issues to consider include the following: (1) What type of proprietary information should we allow and disallow on our site? (2) Who will have access to information that visitors post on our site? (3) Do the content and activities on our site comply with laws in other countries? (4) What disclaimers do we need to post on our website? (5) Are we using trademarked or copyrighted materials without permission? Regardless of the specific issues, an attorney should periodically review the website content, and someone should be responsible for monitoring legal and liability issues. In addition, companies need a privacy policy.
2. **What are the most critical ethical issues?** Negative or defamatory articles published online about people, companies, or products on websites or blogs can lead to charges of libel—and libel can stretch across countries. Issues of privacy, ethics, and legal exposure may seem tangential to running a business, but ignoring them puts the company at risk of fines, customer dissatisfaction, and disruption of an organization's operations. Privacy protection is a necessary investment.

3. **How can intellectual property rights be protected when it comes to digital content?** To protect intellectual property rights such as video, music, and books online, we need to monitor what copyrights, trademarks, and patents are infringed upon over the Internet. Portal sites that allow pirated video and music files should be monitored. This monitoring may require a vast amount of work, so software agents should be employed to continually inspect any pirated material. The risk to the business that can be caused by the infringement and the possibility of legal protection as well as technical protection by current regulation and potential new common law should be analyzed. Consider settling any suit for damages by negotiation.

4. **How can a patent in EC be purchased?** Some people claim that patents should not be awarded to businesses or computer processes related to EC (as is the case in some European countries). Therefore, investing large amounts of money in developing or buying EC patents may be financially unwise in cases where patents may not be granted or protected properly. Some companies that own many business model patents have been unable to create business value out of these patents. Companies like IBM have patents for sale.

5. **How can you handle fake news and information about the company and its products and services?** Large companies need a reputation management strategy. Soon AI programs will be able to monitor all the material about your company. Watch for a possibility of unhappy employees that may generate fake content about the company in all types of media including videos and tweeting.

6. **What is the ethical principle of protecting the privacy of customers?** To provide personalized services, companies need to collect and manage customers' profile data. In practice, the company has to decide whether to use spyware to collect data. Collecting data may make customers unhappy (as in the cases of Google Street View or Facebook privacy settings). The company needs well-established principles of protecting customer privacy: Notify customers before collecting their personal information, inform and get consent on the type and extent of disclosures, allow customers to access their personal data and make sure the data are accurate and securely managed, and apply some method of enforcement and remedy to deter privacy breaches. In this manner, the company can avoid litigation and gain the long-term trust of customers.

7. **How can a company create opportunities in the global trend toward Green EC?** Reducing carbon emissions and saving energy are global issues. (1) EC can save carbon emissions by reducing the need for transportation. This is a generic contribution of EC. (2) EC can provide an electronic exchange platform for trading CO_2 emission rights. This is a new business opportunity. (3) The IT hardware manufacturers may try to earn the Energy Star Excellence Award from the Environmental Protection Agency to prove that their products are contributing to the protection of the environment.

SUMMARY

In this chapter, you learned about the following EC issues as they relate to the chapter's learning objectives:

1. **Understanding legal and ethical challenges and how to contain them.** The global scope and universal accessibility of the Internet create serious questions as to which ethical rules and laws apply. Ignoring laws exposes companies to lawsuits or criminal charges that are disruptive, expensive, and damaging to customer relations. The best strategy is to avoid behaviors that would expose the company to these types of risks. Important safeguards are a corporate code of ethics stating the rules and expected behaviors and actions and an Internet acceptable use policy.

2. **Intellectual property law.** EC operations are subject to various types of intellectual property (IP) laws, some of which judges have created in landmark court cases. IP law provides companies with methods of compensation for damages or misuse of their property rights. IP laws passed by Congress are being amended to better protect EC. These protections are needed because the theft or replication of intellectual works on the Internet is both simple and inexpensive. These actions violate or infringe upon copyrights, trademarks, and patents. Although the legal aspects seem clear, monitoring and catching violators remain difficult.

3. **Privacy, free speech, defamation, and their challenges.** B2C companies use CRM and depend on customer information to improve products and services. Registration and cookies are two ways to collect this information. The key privacy issues are who controls personal information and how private it should remain. Strict privacy laws have been passed recently that carry harsh penalties for any negligence that exposes personal or confidential data. There is ongoing debate about censorship on the Internet. The proponents of censorship feel that it is up to the government and various ISPs and websites to control inappropriate or offensive content. Others oppose any form of censorship; they believe that control is up to the individual. In the United States, most legal attempts to censor content on the Internet have been found unconstitutional. The debate is not likely to be resolved any time soon.

4. **Fake content and possible solutions.** Highlighted by fake news during the 2016 presidential election, the topic of fake content took a central stage in comments, opinions, and debate in late 2016 and 2017. While the problem is not new, fake content was considered a second priority issue until November 2016. In addition to fake websites and so forth, suggestions of how to deal with the problem depend on the types of fake content. Educating the public is important, but taking legal action against violators can be effective.

5. **Societal impacts of EC.** EC brings many societal benefits, ranging from improved security, transportation, and education to better healthcare delivery and international collaboration. Although the digital divide still exists between developed and developing countries, the advent of mobile computing, especially through smartphones, is beginning to close the gap.

6. **Green EC.** EC requires large data centers, but these data centers waste energy and create pollution. Users of large data centers (e.g., Google) are using innovative methods to improve the situation. Other environmental concerns are also caused by the use of EC. There are several ways to make EC greener, including working from home (telecommuting).

7. **The future of EC.** EC is growing steadily and rapidly, expanding to include new products, services, business models, and countries. The most notable areas of growth are the integration of online and offline commerce, mobile commerce (mostly due to smartphone apps), video-based marketing, and social media and networks. Several emerging technologies, ranging from intelligent applications to wearable devices, are facilitating the growth of EC. On the other hand, several factors are slowing down the spread of EC such as security and privacy concerns, limited bandwidth, and lack of standards in some areas of EC.

KEY TERMS

Business ethics
Copyright
Copyright infringement
Cyberbullying
Digital divide
Digital rights management (DRM)
Electronic discovery (e-discovery)
Electronic Product Environmental Assessment Tool (EPEAT)
Ethics
Fair use
Green computing
Green IT
Intellectual property (IP)
Intellectual property law
Internet censorship
Internet troll
Net neutrality
Opt-in
Opt-out
Patent
Platform for Privacy Preferences Project (P3P)
Spyware
Telecommuting

DISCUSSION QUESTIONS

1. What can EC websites and social networks do to control fake content?
2. Privacy is the right to be left alone and free of unreasonable personal intrusions. What are some intrusions that you consider "unreasonable" in e-commerce?
3. Who should control minors' access to "offensive" material on the Internet—parents, the government, or ISPs? Why?
4. Discuss the conflict between freedom of speech and the control of offensive websites.
5. Discuss the possible insufficient protection of opt-in and opt-out options. What measures would satisfy you?

6. Clerks at some convenience stores enter their customers' data (gender, approximate age, etc.) into the computer. These data are then processed for improved decision-making. Customers are not informed about this, nor are they being asked for permission. (Names are not keyed in.) Are the clerks' actions ethical? Compare this with the use of cookies.

7. Why do many companies and professional organizations develop their own codes of ethics? After all, ethics are generic and "one size may fit all."

8. Cyber Promotions, Inc., attempted to use the First Amendment in defense of its flooding AOL subscribers with junk e-mail, which AOL tried to block. A federal judge agreed with AOL that unsolicited e-mail is annoying, a waste of Internet time, and often inappropriate and, therefore, should not be sent. Discuss some of the issues involved, such as freedom of speech, how to distinguish between junk and non-junk e-mail, and the similarity to regular mail. Cyber Promotions is no longer in business.

9. Discuss the different types of fake content on the Web.

TOPICS FOR CLASS DISCUSSION AND DEBATES

1. Discuss what the RIAA hopes to achieve by using lawsuits against college students for copyright infringement. Research the issue of how will the proposed Copyright Enforcement Bill, if enacted, support further RIAA lawsuits? Find the status of the bill. Write a report.

2. The proposed Copyright Enforcement Bill defines everyone that creates a website as a publisher and is liable under the Act. Enforcement under this proposed bill for unintentional use or distribution of copyrighted content on business websites could result in the confiscation of a company's domain name or server, which in turn could potentially disable the company's e-mail capability—substantially killing commerce. What steps should a business take to minimize the risk? Discuss.

3. The IRS buys demographic market research data from private companies. These data contain income statistics that could be compared with tax returns. Many US citizens feel that their rights within the realm of the Electronic Communications Privacy Act (ECPA) are being violated; others say that this is unethical behavior on the part of the government. Discuss.

4. Many hospitals, health maintenance organizations, and federal agencies have converted already or are converting, or plan to convert, all patient medical records from paper to electronic storage (using imaging technology) in compliance with the Patient Protection and Affordable Care Act (PPAC), also known as "Obamacare." The PPAC mandates that all medical records shall be freely disseminated to insurance companies, the US government, and government-approved third-party vendors. Once completed, electronic storage will enable expeditious access to most records anytime and from anywhere. However, the availability of these records in a database or on networks or smart cards may allow people, some of whom are unauthorized, to view another person's private medical data. To protect privacy fully may cost too much money or may considerably slow down the speed of access to the records. What policies could healthcare administrators use to prevent unauthorized access? Discuss.

5. In 2017, Bill Gates suggested that taxes should be put on robots and the collected money used for retraining people displaced by robots. Many disagree. Debate the issue.

6. Facebook and other Web networks should fact-check the content published by others on their websites. Debate the issue.

7. Debate the pros and cons of net neutrality.

8. Research the potential impact of online gambling on physical casinos.

9. Erotic services advertising on Craigslist amounted to a significant portion of the total revenue before being taken down following national publicity over the robbery and murder of a Boston massage therapist, who had advertised on Craigslist. Craigslist denied responsibility, citing the 1996 Federal Telecommunications Act, since Craigslist does not create the content published on its website. Later, Craigslist voluntarily removed the erotic services from its regular pages. Address the following topics in a class discussion:

   (a) Craigslist may have chosen to voluntarily remove its erotic-related advertising for political reasons, even though no laws were being broken. Discuss free speech versus public safety. Take an issue and support the pros and cons of Craigslist's action.

   (b) Do you agree that self-governing Web content is the most effective means of providing public safety or should the federal government step in to enact tougher laws?

   (c) Take the position of an erotic dancer. Determine an argument in favor of reversing Craigslist's decision to remove "erotic services" advertisements. (Use free speech and right to earn money through employment.)

10. Many sports-related leagues, including the NFL and UK Football Association, restrict the players' use of social networks. The NFL prohibits any use of social networks 90 min before and 90 min after games. Debate the issue.
11. Debate Yahoo's "no work from home" policy. Start by reading Ascharya (2013).
12. Have two groups debate the issue of ownership of user-generated content (the Facebook example). One group should be for and one against.
13. Debate: Are privacy standards strict enough to protect electronic health records?
14. Debate: Should the exchange of songs between individuals, without paying royalties, be allowed over the Internet?
15. Debate: Is the Patriot Act too loose or too tight?
16. Debate: It may be too expensive for some companies to "go green." If they "go green," they may not be able to compete against companies in countries that do not practice Green EC. Should the government subsidize Green EC?
17. Debate: Who should own content created by employees during their regular work hours?
18. It was suggested to tax robots if they take American jobs. Debate the issue.

INTERNET EXERCISES

1. You want to set up an ethical blog. Using sites such as CyberJournalist.net: A Bloggers' Code of Ethics at **cyberjournalist.net/news/000215.php**, review the suggested guide to publishing a blog. Make a list of the top 10 ethical issues for blogging.
2. You want to set up a business-oriented website. Prepare a report summarizing the types of materials you can and cannot use (e.g., logos, graphics, etc.) without breaking copyright laws. (Consult some free legal websites.)
3. Conduct a Google search for industry and trade organizations involved in various computer privacy initiatives. One of these groups is the World Wide Web Consortium (W3C). Describe its Platform for Privacy Preferences Project (P3P) (**w3.org/P3P**). Prepare a table with ten initiatives and describe each briefly.
4. Enter **defamationremovalattorneysblog.com/category/other-internet-law-issues** and find five recent posts dealing with fake content. Summarize them. What lessons did you learn?
5. Enter **calastrology.com**. What kind of community is this? Check the revenue model. Then enter **astrocenter.com**. What kind of site is this? Compare and comment on the two sites.
6. Enter **nolo.com**. Find information about various EC legal issues. Find information about international EC issues. Then go to **legalcompliance.org** or **cybertriallawyer.com**. Find information about international legal aspects of EC. Conduct a Google search for additional information on EC legal issues. Prepare a report on the international legal aspects of EC.
7. Find the status of the latest copyright legislation. Try **fairuse.stanford.edu** and **wipo.int/copyright/en**. Is there anything new regarding the international aspects of copyright legislation? Write a report.
8. Enter **econsultancy.com** and find five posts related to the topics of this chapter. Summarize.
9. Enter **wispa.org** and similar organizations that represent the ISP industry. Identify the various initiatives they have undertaken regarding topics discussed in this chapter. Write a report.

TEAM ASSIGNMENTS AND PROJECTS

1. Assignment for the Opening Case
   Read the opening case and answer the following questions:

   (a) What made the initial tweet go viral so quickly?
   (b) Why does fake news sometimes spread faster than true stories?
   (c) How does fake news relate to doing business on the Internet?
   (d) What should Mr. Tucker have done after he saw the buses that could have prevented this incident?

2. The number of lawsuits in the United States and elsewhere involving EC has increased. Have each team prepare a list of five recent EC legal cases on each topic in this chapter (e.g., privacy, digital property, defamation, patents). Prepare a summary of the issues of each case, the parties, the courts, and dates. What were the outcomes of these cases? What was (or might be) the impact of each decision?
3. Form three teams. Have two teams debate free speech versus protection of children. The third team acts as judges. One team is for complete freedom of speech on the Internet; the other team advocates protection of children by censoring offensive and pornographic material. After the debate, have the judges decide which team provided the most compelling legal arguments.

4. Is it legal to monitor employees' Internet activity, e-mail, and instant messages? Note that it is legal to open letters addressed to individuals sent to the company's address. Why is the monitoring necessary? To what extent is it ethical? Are employees' rights being violated? Have two teams debate these issues.

5. Amazon.com is disputing several states that are trying to force the company to collect state taxes ("Amazon laws"). Amazon canceled its affiliate program in certain states (e.g., Colorado, Minnesota) when the sales tax for online retailing was imposed (however, they reinstated their program in California). Check the status of this law (requiring Amazon to collect taxes) and its relationship to Federal law. Start at **illinoisjltp.com/timelytech/ongoing-taxation-disputes-between-amazon-and-state-governments**.

6. Smart computer programs enable employers to monitor their employees' movements online. The objective is to minimize wasting time and computing resources and reduce theft by employees. These actions may invade privacy and reduce confidence and loyalty. Find the various methods used to monitor employees (list their approaches) and list all possible negative aspects. Find case studies about the benefits (including increasing productivity) and the limitations and dangers. Relate monitoring to telecommuting and debate the issue.

7. The new technologies will displace many employees. Research the issue and write a report.

CLOSING CASE: THE PIRATE BAY AND THE FUTURE OF FILE SHARING

What had been considered a landmark 2009 copyright law case involving the Motion Picture Association of America (MPAA) against illegal file sharing in Sweden appears not to have significantly deterred online file sharing. In fact, just the opposite may have occurred.

An Overview

The Pirate Bay (TPB) site was launched in 2003 by hackers and computer activists as a BitTorrent tracker, which made it possible to get free access to most media content (including copyrighted material) using BitTorrent peer-to-peer (P2P) file sharing protocol services (see **en.wikipedia.org/wiki/BitTorrent**). The Pirate Bay site includes links to websites where you can download movies, TV shows, music, e-books, live sport games, software, and more. TPB has been ranked as one of the most popular websites in the world. The site generates revenue by advertisements, donations, and sales of merchandise. The site is probably the most well known among dozens of other sites that provide free access to copyrighted content.

The Legal Situation

The Pirate Bay has been involved in a number of lawsuits, both as a defendant and as a plaintiff. For an overview, see **torrentfreak.com/the-pirate-bay-turns-10-years-old-the-history-130810**. Here are some examples. In Sweden, The Pirate Bay company was raided by the Swedish police in 2006. The site was shut down but reappeared a few days later with servers hosted in different countries. In 2008, the Swedish government began a criminal investigation against the founders of TPB for copyright theft. Three founders and a financier were charged with promoting copyright infringement by facilitating other people's breach of copyright law by using TPB BitTorrent technology. For 34 cases of copyright infringement, the damage claims could have exceeded US $12 million. The trial started on February 16, 2009, and ended on March 3, 2009, with a guilty verdict that carried a 1-year prison sentence and a fine of US $3.5 million. The four founders lost on appeal in 2010 but succeeded in getting reduced prison time; however, the copyright infringement fine was increased. The site is now blocked by several countries. The US government considers TPB (together with the Chinese sites Baidu and Taobao Marketplace) a top market for pirated and counterfeit goods.

Current Operation

As of June 2014, TPB continues to offer torrent files and magnet links to facilitate file sharing for those using the BitTorrent system. The site also offers downloading, watching videos, and searching for all types of media. In fact, much public support for TPB was noted. In 2003, Piratbyrån ("The Pirate Bureau"), a Swedish organization, was established to support the free sharing of information (however, they disbanded in 2010). Political parties in many European countries have adopted the label "The Pirate Party," after a party in Sweden, which was formed in 2006. Other countries followed suit, creating their own

Pirate Parties. The party supports the reform of copyright and patent laws, government transparency, and net neutrality. In 2006, the International Pirate Party Movement was formed as an umbrella organization. In 2009, the Swedish Pirate Party won a seat in the European Parliament, and in 2013, Iceland gained three similar seats. The Pirate Bay advocates copyright and patent law reform and a reduction in government surveillance. In the meantime, in Sweden, TPB's founders have worked on several other decentralized peer-to-peer file sharing websites, which have flourished in filling the enormous global demand for P2P file sharing. TPB has plenty of defenders. In 2014, the supporters of TPB's jailed founder planned an online campaign to bring more attention to his situation.

All along, file sharing technology has been one step ahead of enforcement. Since some countries block access to TPB, there are several proxy URLs now that provide indirect access to TPB's website.

Despite losing its November 2010 appeal, TPB has kept growing. In 2011, TPB's founders launched a new website, called IPredator, offering IP address anonymity to registered users by tunneling traffic into a secure server, which reassigns fake IP addresses to registered users so that they may access TPB or other BitTorrent tracking sites on the Web for file sharing without revealing their true IP addresses. Although TPB continues to thrive today as one of the most popular websites on the Internet, many countries are enacting new stricter copyright protection laws aimed directly at stopping this illegal activity. Note that Facebook blocks all shared links to TPB in both public and private messages (however, TPB does have a Facebook page). In 2012, a UK court ordered a blockade on TPB in the UK because of its violation of copyright law. Some countries are allowing access to TPB. For example, in 2014, the Netherlands court ordered the ban on TPB lifted (see **bbc.com/news/technology-25943716**).

In 2012, The Pirate Bay, to protect itself from raids, moved its operation from physical servers to the cloud. Serving its users from several cloud hosting providers makes it impossible to raid because there are no physical locations; the site is more portable and thus makes it more difficult to shut down. Other benefits include reducing downtime, ensuring better uptime, and cutting costs (see Van Der Sar 2012).

According to Plummer (2016b), "Having returned from its latest exile, The Pirate Bay now is using the Torrents Time plugin to deliver an illegal answer to Netflix. With the plugin installed on a Mac or PC, users can click the new 'Stream It!' button to access a wealth of movies an TV shows without paying a cent to the copyright holders.

Once the plugin has found enough peers, it can stream content without having to buffer—and peer acquisition takes just seconds." Finally, it looks as if The Pirate Bay is vying to become the world's largest streaming site.

Note: Whether pirated content is streamed or downloaded, accessing it is illegal in the United States and many other countries.

The Pirate Bay now uses many proxy sites and torrents. It is well and alive (Protalinski 2016).

Note. In February 2017 a court made the Pirate Bay illegal in Sweden, but OK in other countries.

Discussion

The Pirate Bay is one of a multitude of websites specializing in pirated and counterfeit content. The Pirate Bay does not host content, in contrast to sites, which allows people to upload videos, including pirated ones. The Pirate Bay only provides links to possible illegal downloads. This strategy did not help the site much in its legal battles.

The Pirate Bay case is only one part of a much broader issue of protecting intellectual property on the Internet. An interesting related issue is the hosting of content by sites such as YouTube, which is more complicated.

Note that one aspect of this case is that the US government is pushing the Swedish government to take a stronger stand against pirating.

Sources: Based on Stone (2011), Plummer (2016b), Protalinski (2016), and **medlibrary.org** (accessed February 2017).

Questions

1. Compare TPB's legal problems to those of Napster between 2000 and 2005 and to those of Kazaa (file sharing companies).
2. Debate the issue of freedom of speech on the Internet against the need to protect intellectual property.
3. What is The Pirate Bay's business model? What are its revenue sources? (Find more information; start with Wikipedia.)
4. Explore the international legal aspects of this case. Can one country persuade another country to introduce stricter laws?
5. Read the Stone (2011) article and identify all the measures used to battle piracy of live sporting events. Which of these measures can be used in The Pirate Bay case? Which cannot? Why?
6. Find the status of TPB's website.

REFERENCES

10ecommerce. "10 E-Commerce Trends for 2017. (2017) **10ecommercetrends.com** (accessed February 2017).

Adhikari, R. "Facebook Videos Explain AI in a Nutshell." *TechNewsWorld*, December 5, 2016a. **technewsworld.com/story/84135.html** (accessed February 2017).

Adhikari, R. "Privacy Concerns Curb Online Commerce, Communication." *E-Commerce Times*, May 17, 2016b. **ecommercetimes.com/story/83509.html** (accessed February 2017).

Alaimo, K. "When the Fake News Is About Your Company." *Bloomberg View*, February, 10, 2017. **bloomberg.com/view/articles/2017-02-10/when-the-fake-news-is-about-your-company** (accessed February 2017).

Andrews, L. *I Know Who You Are and I Saw What You Did: Social Networks and the Death of Privacy.* Florence, MA: Free Press, 2012.

Angwin, J. *Dragnet Nation: A Quest for Privacy, Security, and Freedom in a World of Relentless Surveillance.* New York: Times Books, 2015.

Anthony, S. "The FCC's Net Neutrality Proposal: What Does It Mean for You, and the Internet?" May 16, 2014. **extremetech.com/computing/182572-the-fccs-net-neutrality-proposal-what-does-it-mean-for-you-and-the-internet** (accessed February 2017).

AP News. "Georgia Couple Sues Snapchat Over Car Crash." *AP.org*, April 28, 2016. **bigstory.ap.org/article/b67303bb20a945aeb203d986c-1d09a3e/georgia-couple-sues-snapchat-over-car-crash** .(accessed February 2017).

Ascharya, K. "Marissa Mayer and the Telecommuting Debate." March 26, 2013. **2machines.com/articles/178412.html** (accessed February 2017).

Bailey, M. *Complete Guide to Internet Privacy, Anonymity & Security.* 2nd ed. Delhi, India: Nerel Online, 2015.

Bennion, J. "E-Discovery: A Primer for Litigators." *Above the Law*, May 31, 2016.

Bercovici, J. "Yahoo Spins No-Work-From-Home Policy as Morale Booster. Seriously." *Forbes*, March 6, 2013.

Breland, A. "Net Neutrality Fix Faces Hard Sell." *The Hill*, February 11, 2017. **thehill.com/policy/technology/319051-net-neutrality-fix-faces-hard-sell** (accessed February 2017).

Broadcast. "Top Ten Internet Legal Issues, Including Social Media and Employee/Employer Issues." Federal Bar Association, September 26, 2016. **federalbarcle.org/product/top-ten-internet-legal-issues-including-social-media-employeeemployer-issues** (accessed February 2017).

Brown, C. "Top 10 Privacy Issues to Watch This Year." *Law360*, January 7, 2016. **law360.com/articles/743826/top-10-privacy-issues-to-watch-this-year** (accessed February 2017).

Burney, B. "Social Media: A Different Type of E-Discovery Collection." *Legal Tech News*, September 6, 2016.

Cagaoan, K.A.A, M. J. A. V. Buenaobra, A. T. M. Martin, and J. C. Paurillo. "Privacy Awareness in E-Commerce." *International Journal of Education and Research*, January 2014. Vol. 2, No. .1, **ijern.com/journal/January-2014/19.pdf** (accessed February 2017).

Clancy, H. "Virtualization Core to Wells Fargo Green IT Initiative." July 6, 2010. **zdnet.com/blog/green/virtualization-core-to-wells-fargo-green-it-initiative/12852** (accessed February 2017).

Columbus, L. "Predicting the Future of B2B E-Commerce." *Forbes.com*, September 12, 2016. **forbes.com/forbes/welcome/?toURL=https://www.forbes.com/sites/louiscolumbus/2016/09/12/predicting-the-future-of-b2b-e-commerce/&refURL=https://www.google.com/&referrer=https://www.google.com** .(accessed February 2017).

Constantin, L. "Hard-to-Detect Fileless Attacks Target Banks, Other Organizations." *PC World*, February 9, 2017. **pcworld.idg.com.au/article/613963/hard-to-detect-fileless-attacks-target-banks-other-organizations** (accessed February 2017).

DeMarco, T. "7 Ecommerce Predictions for 2017." *Veinteractive.com*, December 16, 2016. **veinteractive.com/us/blog/7-ecommerce-predictions-2017** .(accessed February 2017).

DHL. "Vision Picking in the Warehouse-Augmented Reality in Logistics." *SupplyChain247*, January 29, 2015. **supplychain247.com/article/vision_picking_in_the_warehouse_augmented_reality_in_logistics** (accessed February 2017).

Donald, B. "Stanford Researchers Find Students Have Trouble Judging the Credibility of Information Online." Stanford Education, November 22, 2016. **ed.stanford.edu/news/stanford-researchers-find-students-have-trouble-judging-credibility-information-online** (accessed February 2017).

Douglas, M. "New Retail Strategies: It's a Store! It's a Site! It's a Warehouse!" Inbound Logistics, August 2014. **inboundlogistics.com/cms/article/new-retail-strategies-its-a-store-its-a-site-its-a-warehouse** (accessed February 2017).

Editorial Board. "Anonymity Is a Threat to E-Commerce." *Bloomberg View*, October 28, 2016. **bloomberg.com/view/articles/2015-10-26/amazon-s-case-against-fake-reviews-is-strong** (accessed February 2017).

Egan, M. "Robots Threaten These 8 Jobs." CNN News, May 13, 2015. **money.cnn.com/2015/05/13/news/economy/robots-threaten-jobs-unemployment** (accessed February 2017).

Elicksen, D. *Take Back the Internet: Empower Yourself Against Cyberbullies and Internet Trolls*, Kindle edition. Seattle, WA: Amazon Digital Services, 2015.

EMC. "Infographic: Digital Privacy – A World of Complex Paradoxes." *Enterprise Innovation*, July 7 2014. **enterpriseinnovation.net/infographic/infographic-digital-privacy-world-complex-paradoxes** (accessed February 2017).

Enviro Boys. "Is Telecommuting on the Rise?" November 14, 2010. **enviroboys88.blogspot.com/2010/11/telecommuting-on-rise.html** (accessed February 2017).

Fox-Brewster, T. "Facebook Is Playing Games with Your Privacy and There's Nothing You Can Do About It." *Forbes.com*, June 29, 2016. **forbes.com/forbes/welcome/?toURL=https://www.forbes.com/sites/thomasbrewster/2016/06/29/facebook-location-tracking-friend-games/** .(accessed February 2017).

Gallio, L. "Surveillance Camera: Big Brother and Big Sis are Watching!" August 29, 2010. **examiner.com/article/surveillance-cameras-big-brother-and-big-sis-are-watching** (accessed February 2017).

Geranios, N. K. "Internet Addiction Center Opens in U.S." *USA Today* (by Associated Press) September 3, 2009.

Goel, V. "Russian Cyberforgers Steal Millions a Day with Fake Sites." *The New York Times*, December 20, 2016. **nytimes.com/2016/12/20/technology/forgers-use-fake-web-users-to-steal-real-ad-revenue.html** (accessed February 2017).

Gouveia, A. "2013 Wasting Time at Work Survey." July 28, 2013. **sfgate.com/jobs/salary/article/2013-Wasting-Time-at-Work-Survey-4374026.php** (accessed February 2017).

Gross, D. "Pay to Play on the Web? Net Neutrality Explained." January 15, 2014. **cnn.com/2014/01/15/tech/web/net-neutrality-explained** (accessed February 2017).

Gupta, P., and A. Dubey. "E-Commerce – Study of Privacy, Trust, and Security from Consumer's Perspective." *International Journal of Computer Science and Mobile Computing*, Vol. 5, Issue 6, June 6, 2016, 224–.232. **ijcsmc.com/docs/papers/June2016/V5I6201647.pdf** (accessed February 2017).

Guide. "EC Legal Considerations Before You Launch Your Store." *The Legal Side*, 2016. **ecommerceguide.com/guides/ecommerce-legals** (accessed February 2017).

Guynn, J., "Lawmakers ask Google's Larry Page to address Glass privacy issues." *Los Angeles Times*, May 16, 2013.

Harris, B. C. *Cyberbully (Society of Spies)*, Volume 1″ North Charleston, SC: CreateSpace Independent Publishing Platform, 2016.

Hiner, J. "Video: Vinod Khosla Predicts 80% of IT Jobs Will be Eliminated by Software." *TechRepublic.com*, November 10, 2016. **techrepublic. com/article/video-vinod-khosla-predicts-80-of-it-jobs-will-be-eliminated-by-software** .(accessed February 2017).

Howell, R. F. "E-Commerce's Hidden Legal Issues." *The National Law Review*, May 16, 2015.

IBM. "IBM Software: A Green Strategy for Your Entire Organization." A white paper, June 2008. New York: IBM Software Group.

Instagram. "Artist Richard Prince Made $90,000 by Selling Someone's Instagram Photo Without Permission." *First Post*, May 26, 2015.

Johnson, A. *E-Discovery Nuts and Bolts: The Essentials of E-Discovery for Healthcare Professionals*. North Charleston, SC: CreateSpace Independent Publishing Platform, 2016.

Kankanala, K.C. *Social Media and IP: Social Media, Intellectual Property and Business (Intellectual Property Basics for Business Book 4)*. Kindle Edition, Seattle, WA: Amazon Digital Services, 2015.

Kemp, S. "Digital in 2016." *Wearesocial*, January 27, 2016. **wearesocial.com/uk/special-reports/digital-in-2016** (accessed February 2017).

Kenyon, A. T. *Comparative Defamation and Privacy Law (Cambridge Intellectual Property and Information Law)*. New York: NY: Cambridge University Press, 2016.

Kiely, E., and L. Robertson. "How to Spot Fake News." FactCheck.org, November 18, 2016. **factcheck.org/2016/11/how-to-spot-fake-news** .(accessed February 2017).

Kercher, M. M. "An Extremely Helpful List of Fake and Misleading News Sites to Watch Out For." *NewYorkMag.com*, November 15, 2016. **nymag.com/selectall/2016/11/fake-facebook-news-sites-to-avoid.html** .(accessed February 2017).

Knight, K. "Report: Timeliness Key for Ecommerce." *BizReport*, January 28, 2016.

Leggatt, H. "Online Privacy Real Concern for 90% of U.S. Internet Users." *BizReport,* February 14, 2012. **bizreport.com/2012/02/90-percent-of-online-adults-worry-about-their-online-privacy.html** (accessed February 2017).

Lewis, M. "Ethical Issues Relating to E-commerce." *LinkedIn.com*, June 5, 2014. linkedin.com/pulse/20140605220127-310310-ethical-issues-relating-to-e-commerce (accessed August 2017).

Lowry, S., and E. K. Lunder. "Internet Sales and State Taxes: Policy Issues." CRS Insight, December 1, 2016. **fas.org/sgp/crs/misc/IN10418.pdf** (accessed February 2017).

Lunka, R. "Ethical Issues in E-Commerce: Are You Violating Any of Them?" *Nchannel.com*, April 21, 2015. **nchannel.com/blog/ethical-issues-in-ecommerce** .(accessed February 2017).

Maheshwari, S. "How Fake News Goes Viral: A Case Study." *The New York Times*, November 20, 2016. **nytimes.com/2016/11/20/business/media/how-fake-news-spreads.html?_r=0** (accessed February 2017).

Manjoo, F. "How the Internet Is Loosening Our Grip on the Truth." *The New York Times*, November 3, 2016. **nytimes.com/2016/11/03/technology/how-the-internet-is-loosening-our-grip-on-the-truth.html** (accessed February 2017).

Manyika, J., M. Chui, M. Miremadi, J. Bughin, K. George, P. Willmott, and M. Dewhurst "Harnessing Automation for a Future That Works." Report from the McKinsey Global Institute, January 2017. **mckinsey.com/global-themes/digital-disruption/harnessing-automation-for-a-future-that-works** (accessed February 2017).

Mayton, J. "RIP Net Neutrality? FCC Backs New Rules That Permit Pay-Based Internet 'Fast Lane.'" April 26, 2014. **techtimes.com/articles/6062/20140426/rip-net-neutrality-fcc-backs-new-rules-that-permit-pay-based-internet-fast-lane.htm** (accessed February 2017).

McCafferty, D. "9 Significant Technology Predictions for 2016." *Baseline*, February 24, 2016a.

McCafferty, D. "Tech Distractions Are Top Productivity Killer." Baseline, July 11, 2016b. **baselinemag.com/mobility/slideshows/tech-distractions-are-top-productivity-killers.html** (accessed February 2017).

McLaughlin, K. "Oracle Wins Appeal in Google Android Suit, Court Rules It Can Copyright Java APIs." *CRN News*, May 9, 2014. **crn.com/news/applications-os/300072804/oracle-wins-appeal-in-google-android-suit-court-rules-it-can-copyright-java-APIs** (accessed February 2017).

Mello, J. P. Jr "Bot Armies Boost Candidates' Popularity on Twitter." *Technewworld.com*, October 29, 2016a. **technewsworld.com/story/84044.html** .(accessed February 2017).

Mello, J. P. Jr "Kickass Torrents Owner Faces 20-Plus Years in Stir." E-Commerce Times, July 26, 2016b. **ecommercetimes.com/story/83734.html** (accessed February 2017).

Moreau, E. "10 Types of Internet Trolls You'll Meet Online." Lifewire, Updated November 1, 2016. **lifewire.com/types-of-internet-trolls-3485894** (accessed February 2017).

Morgan, L. "IoT Raises New Legal Challenges for Business." Informationweek.com, January 10, 2016. **informationweek.com/iot/iot-raises-new-legal-challenges-for-business/d/d-id/1323926** .(accessed February 2017).

Morris, D. Z. "Bill Gates Says Robots Should Be Taxed Like Workers." *Venturebeat.com*, February 18, 2017. **venturebeat.com/2017/02/18/bill-gates-says-robots-should-be-taxed-like-workers** .(accessed February 2017).

Murugesan, S., and G. R. Gangadharan (Eds.) *Harnessing Green IT: Principles and Practices*. Hoboken, NJ: Wiley, 2012.

Nelson, N. "How to Estimate Energy Efficiency as Part of a Server Upgrade." *eWeek*, April 28, 2008. **eweek.com/it-management/How-to-Estimate-Energy-Efficiency-as-Part-of-a-Server-Upgrade** (accessed February 2017).

Nicholas, M. "Naughty or Nice? Here's How to tell If an E-Commerce Website is Legit." Dashlane.com, December 6, 2016. **blog.dashlane.com/identifying-fake-ecommerce-websites** (accessed February 2017).

Nielsen. "State of the Media: The Social Media Report 2012." 2012. **nielsen.com/us/en/reports/2012/state-of-the-media-the-social-media-report-2012.html** (accessed February 2017).

O'Brien, K.J. and Streitfeld, D. "Swiss Court Orders Modifications to Google Street View." June 8, 2012. **nytimes.com/2012/06/09/technology/09iht-google09.html?_r=0** (accessed February 2017).

Ovum. "The Future of E-Commerce: The Road to 2026." Ovum, 2016. **criteo.com/media/4094/ovum-the-future-of-e-commerce-the-road-to-2026.pdf** (accessed February 2017).

Park, H. S. "Empowering Employees with Technology." *Baseline*, May 27, 2009.

Phillips, A., et al. *E-Discovery: An Introduction to Digital Evidence (with DVD), Loose-Leaf Version*. Clifton Park, NY: Delmar Cengage Learning, 2016.

Plummer, Q. "Traversing the Social Media Minefield." *Technewsworld.com*, December 9, 2016a. **technewsworld.com/story/84155.html** .(accessed February 2017).

Plummer, Q. "The Pirate Bay Is Now Streaming." *E-Commerce Times*, February 10, 2016b. **ecommercetimes.com/story/83094.html** (accessed February 2017).

Press. "New Proposal for a Regulation on ePrivacy: Pros and Cons for E-Commerce." *Ecommerce Europe,* January 11, 2017. **ecommerce-europe. eu/press-item/new-proposal-regulation-eprivacy-pros-cons-e-commerce** (accessed February 2017).

PRC. "Workplace Privacy and Employee Monitoring." (Revised May 2014). **privacyrights.org/workplace-privacy-and-employee-monitoring** (accessed February 2017).

Protalinski, E. "The Pirate Bay Now Uses Torrents Time to Let You Stream All Its Movies and TV Shows." *Venturebeat.com*, February 5, 2016.

Ranger, S. "The Undercover War on Your Internet Secrets: How Online Surveillance Cracked Our Trust in the Web." *Tech Republic*, February 10, 2016.

Reilly, P. "Net Neutrality: A Top Target for Trump's FCC?" *Christian Science Monitor*, January 21, 2017. **csmonitor.com/Technology/2017/0121/ Net-neutrality-A-top-target-for-Trump-s-FCC** (accessed February 2017).

Roberts, J. J. "Can Artificial Intelligence Silence Internet Trolls." *Fortune.com*, February 1, 2017a. **fortune.com/2017/01/23/jigsaw-google-internet-trolls** .(accessed February 2017).

Roberts, P. C. "A Case in the Creation of False News: Delegitimize Trump's Presidency. *GlobalReseach.org*, January 6, 2017b. **globalresearch. ca/a-case-study-in-the-creation-of-false-news/5567103** .(accessed February 2017).

Samson, T. "GreenNet 2010: Google Shares Its Green Data Center Secrets." *InfoWorld*, April 29, 2010.

Scott, G. *Internet Book Piracy: The Fight to Protect Authors, Publishers, and Our Culture*. New York: Allworth Press, 2016.

Schneier, B. Data and Goliath: The Hidden Battles to Collect Your Data and Control Your World. New York: W. W. Norton and Company, 2016.

Schwanke, A. "Taxation on E-Commerce: The International Implementation." *International Tax Review*, March 2016. **internationaltaxreview. com/Article/3533682/Taxation-on-e-commerce-International-implementation.html** (accessed February 2017).

Scollay, R. "Six Business Technology Predictions for 2016." *Enterprise Innovation,* November 10, 2015. **enterpriseinnovation.net/article/six-business-technology-predictions-2016-150408718** (accessed February 2017).

Scott, M. "Amazon's E-Books Business Investigated by European Antitrust Regulators." *The New York Times*, June 12, 2015. **nytimes. com/2015/06/12/business/international/european-union-amazon-ebooks-antitrust-investigation.html** (accessed February 2017).

Shane, S. "From Headline to Photograph, a Fake News Masterpiece." *The New York Times*, January 18, 2017. **nytimes.com/2017/01/18/us/fake-news-hillary-clinton-cameron-harris.html** (accessed February 2017).

Silverman, C. "How Lies Spread Faster Than Truth: A Study of Viral Content." Mediashift.org, February 18, 2015. **mediashift.org/2015/02/how-lies-spread-faster-than-truth-a-study-of-viral-content** .(accessed February 2017).

Smeaton, C. "6 New Ecommerce Trends Shaping the Future of Online Retail." *Demo-Up video conference*, July 5, 2016. **demoup.com/blog/six-new-ecommerce-trends-shaping-the-future-online-retail** (accessed February 2017).

Smith, C. "French Man Wants $48 Million from Uber for Allegedly Breaking Up His Marriage." *BGR.com*, February 12, 2017. **bgr.com/2017/02/12/ uber-iphone-notifications-bug** .(accessed February 2017).

Sommer, J. "Defending the Open Internet." *The New York Times*, May 11, 2014. **nytimes.com/2014/05/11/business/defending-the-open-internet.html** (accessed February 2017).

Statt, N. "iPhone Manufacturer Foxconn Plans to Replace Almost Every Human Worker with Robots." *The Verge*, December 30, 2016. **theverge. com/2016/12/30/14128870/foxconn-robots-automation-apple-iphone-china-manufacturing** (accessed February 2017).

Sterling, T. "European Court: Google Must Yield on Personal Info." May 13, 2014. **bigstory.ap.org/article/european-court-upholds-right-be-forgotten-says-google-must-edit-some-search-results** (accessed February 2017).

Stetler, B. "The Plague of Fake News Is Getting Worse—Here's How to Protect Yourself." *CNN*, November 1, 2016. **money.cnn.com/2016/10/30/ media/facebook-fake-news-plague/index.html** (accessed February 2017).

Stone, B. "Pro Sports versus the Web Pirates." February 24, 2011. **businessweek.com/magazine/content/11_10/b4218066626285.htm** (accessed February 2017).

Todd, P., and W. Craig. *E-Commerce Law*, 2nd ed. New York: Routledge, 2017.

TrueShip. "The Future of Ecommerce: 10 Predictions for 2016." January 5, 2016. **trueship.com/blog/2016/01/05/the-future-of-ecommerce-10-predictions-for-2016/#VwLle_krI2w** (accessed February 2017).

Turban, et al. *Social Commerce*, New York: Springer, 2016.

Valerio, P. "Top Data Privacy Issues to Scare You in 2016." *InformationWeek*, January 6, 2016.

Van Der Sar, E. "Pirate Bay Moves to the Cloud, Becomes Raid-Proof." October 17, 2012. **torrentfreak.com/pirate-bay-moves-to-the-cloud-becomes-raid-proof-121017** (accessed February 2017).

Verbauwhede, L. "Intellectual Property and E-Commerce: How to Take Care of Your Business' Website." WIPO, 2015. **wipo.int/export/sites/ www/sme/en/documents/pdf/business_website.pdf** (accessed February 2017).

Viner, K. "How Technology Disrupted the Truth. *The Guardian*, July 12, 2016. **theguardian.com/media/2016/jul/12/how-technology-dis-rupted-the-truth** (accessed February 2017).

Wingfield, N., M. Isaac, and K. Benner. "Google and Facebook Take Aim at Fake New Sites." *The New York Times*, November 14, 2016. *New York Times.* **nytimes.com/2016/11/15/technology/google-will-ban-websites-that-host-fake-news-from-using-its-ad-service.html** (accessed February 2017).

Zimdars, M. "False, Misleading, Clickbait-y, and Satirical 'News' Sources." Creative Commons, 2016. **d279m997dpfwgl.cloudfront.net/ wp/2016/11/Resource-False-Misleading-Clickbait-y-and-Satirical-%E2%80%9CNews%E2%80%9D-Sources-1.pdf** (accessed February 2017).

Zorzini, C. "10 Interesting E-Commerce Trends for 2016 and Beyond." E-Commerce Platforms, December 7, 2015. **ecommerce-platforms.com/ ecommerce-news/10-interesting-ecommerce-trends-for-2016-and-beyond** (accessed February 2017).

Glossary

3D printing   A manufacturing process that creates products directly from digital models, by placing many layers one over the top of others.

Access control   A defense mechanism that determines who (person, program, or machine) can legitimately use the organization's computing resources (which resources, when, and how).

Ad views   The number of times users call up a page that has a banner on it during a specific period, known as *impressions* or *page views.*

Address Verification System (AVS)   System that detects fraud by comparing the address provided by the buyer at checkout with the address on file.

Affiliated marketing   A type of "performance-based marketing" used mainly as a revenue source for the referring organization and as a marketing tool for the sellers.

Affiliate network   A network created as a marketplace where publishers (affiliates) and merchant affiliate programs can collaborate.

Amazon Alexa   Cloud-based intelligent personal voice assistant product that can answer questions and provide information.

Amazon Echo   Hand-free intelligent wireless speakers that are controlled by voice and works with Alexa.

Application controls   Controls that guard applications.

Artificial intelligence (AI)   A behavior by a machine that, if performed by a human being, would be called intelligent.

Augmented reality   "A live, copy, view of a physical, real-world environment whose elements are *augmented* (or supplemented) by computer-generated sensory input such as sound, video, graphics, or GPS data" (see **en.wikipedia.org/wiki/Augmented_reality**).

Authentication   A process to verify (assure) the real identity of an EC entity, which could be an individual, software agent, computer program, or EC website.

Authorization   The provision of permission to an authenticated person to access systems and perform certain operations in those specific systems or in a specific case the first phase of processing a credit card transaction that determines whether a buyer's card is valid (e.g., not expired) and whether the customer has sufficient credit or funds in his or her account.

Availability   The assurance that access to any relevant data, information websites, or other EC services and their use is available in real time, whenever and wherever needed.

Back end   Where activities that are related to order aggregation and fulfillment, inventory management, purchasing from suppliers, accounting and finance, insurance, payment processing, packaging, and delivery.

Banking Trojan   Malicious software programmed to create damage when users visit certain online banking or e-commerce sites.

Banner   A display that is used for advertising on a Web page (words, logos, etc. embedded in the page).

Bartering   The exchange of goods and services.

Bartering exchange   A marketplace where an intermediary arranges barter transactions.

Behavioral targeting   Targeting that uses consumer browsing behavior information to design personalized ads that may influence consumers better than mass advertising does.

Biometric   One of an individual's unique physical or behavioral trait that can be used to authenticate an individual precisely (e.g., fingerprints).

Biometric authentication   A technology that measures and analyzes the identity of people based on measurable biological or behavioral characteristics or physiological signals.

Biometric systems   A system that can *identify* a previously registered person by searching through a database for a possible *match* based on the person's observed physical, biological, or behavioral traits, or the system can *verify* a person's identity by matching an individual's measured biometric traits against a previously stored version.

© Springer International Publishing AG 2018

E. Turban et al., *Electronic Commerce 2018*, Springer Texts in Business and Economics, DOI 10.1007/978-3-319-58715-8

Bitcoin address An alphanumeric string that identifies the recipient of a Bitcoin transaction.

Bitcoin private key Key that is a randomly generated number between 1 and $2^{\wedge}$ that is used by the key's owner to initiate and digitally sign transactions and used by the network to verify those transactions.

Blockchain The Bitcoin public ledger containing a complete list of all transactions since the first Bitcoin was issued.

Botnet Malicious software that criminals distribute, usually to infect a large number of computers.

Brick-and-mortar (old economy) organizations Purely physical organizations (corporations) doing business offline.

Brick-and-mortar retailer A retailer that conducts business exclusively in the physical world.

Business continuity plan A plan that keeps the business running after a disaster occurs. Each function in the business should have a valid recovery capability plan.

Business ethics (corporate or enterprise ethics) A code of values, behaviors, and rules, written or unwritten, for conducting business. These ethics dictate the operations of organizations.

Business impact analysis (BIA) An analysis of the impact of losing the functionality of an EC activity (e.g., e-procurement, e-ordering) to an organization.

Business model A description of how an organization intends to generate revenue through its business operations.

Business-oriented social network A social network whose primary objective is to facilitate business.

Business social network A network that is built on social relationships and can exist offline or online. Business social networking can take place in traditional corporate physical environments.

Business-to-business (B2B) All transactions take place between and among organizations.

Business-to-business e-commerce (B2B EC) Transactions between businesses conducted electronically over the Internet, extranets, intranets, or private networks.

Business-to-consumer (B2C) Retail transactions of products or services from businesses to individual shoppers.

Business-to-employees (B2E) The delivery of services, information, or products from organizations to their employees.

Buy-side e-marketplace Where a company purchases from many potential suppliers; this type of purchasing is considered to be *many-to-one*, and it is a B2B activity. These marketplaces are often owned by large buyers that invite sellers to browse and offer to fulfill orders.

Card verification number (CVN) Method for detecting fraud by matching the three-digit verification number printed on the signature strip on the back of the credit card (or the four-digit number on the front of the card, such as American Express cards) with the number stored by the cardholder's issuing bank.

Certificate authorities (CAs) Independent agencies that issue digital certificates or SSL certificates, which are electronic files that uniquely identify individuals and websites and enable encrypted communication.

Channel conflict Refers to the case in which online sales damage the well-being of existing channel partner.

Chatbot An intelligent computerized system that enables written on voice chatting in a natural language.

CIA security triad (CIA triad) A point of reference used to identify problem areas and evaluate the information security of an organization that includes *confidentiality*, *integrity*, and *availability*.

Ciphertext An encrypted plaintext.

Click (ad click) A count made each time a visitor clicks on an advertising banner to access the advertiser's website.

Click-and-mortar (click-and-brick) organizations Organizations that conduct some e-commerce activities, usually as an additional marketing channel.

Click-and-mortar retailer A combination of both the traditional retailer and an online store.

Clickstream behavior A pattern of customer movements on the Internet, which can be seen in their transaction logs.

Clickstream data Data that describe which websites users visit, in what order, and the time spent on each. This is done by tracking the succession of "clicks" each visitor makes.

Click-through rate/ratio (CTR) The percentage of visitors who are exposed to a banner ad and click on it.

Collaborative commerce (c-commerce) Electronic support for business collaboration. It enables companies to collaboratively plan, design, develop, manage, and research products, services, and innovative business processes, including EC applications.

Collaborative filtering A method that attempts to predict what products or services are of interest to new customers without asking or viewing their previous records.

Collaboration hub (c-hub) The central point of interaction and of a company's supply chain. A single e-hub can host multiple *collaboration spaces* in which trading partners trade, collaborate, communicate, and share information.

Communal shopping (collaborative shopping) A method of shopping where shoppers enlist friends and other people they trust to advise them on what products to shop for.

Company-centric EC One-to-many and many-to-one markets where one company does either all the selling (*sell-side market*) or all the buying (*buy-side market*).

Computer Fraud and Abuse Act (CFAA)   Act passed in 1984 and amended several times and is an important milestone in EC legislation. Initially, the scope and intent of CFAA was to protect government computers and financial industry computers from criminal theft by outsiders. In 1986, the CFAA was amended to include stiffer penalties for violations, but it still only protected computers used by the federal government or financial institutions.

Confidentiality   The assurance of data secrecy and privacy. Namely, the data are disclosed only to authorized people.

Consortium trading exchange (CTE)   An exchange formed and operated by a group of major companies in one industry. They can be suppliers, buyers, or both.

Consumer-to-business (C2B)   People use the Internet to sell products or services to individuals and organizations. Alternatively, individuals use C2B to bid on products or services.

Consumer-to-consumer (C2C)   E-commerce category in which individual consumers sell to or buy from other consumers.

Consumer-to-consumer (C2C) EC   Electronic transactions completed between and among individuals.

Contact card   A smart card that is activated when it is inserted into a smart card reader.

Contactless (proximity) card   A smart card that only has to be within a certain proximity of a smart card reader to process a transaction.

Convertible virtual currency   A virtual currency that has an equivalent value in real currency or acts as a substitute for real currency.

Context-aware computing   A technology that is capable in predicting people's needs and providing fulfillment options (sometimes even before a request by the end user is made).

Conversion rate   The percentage of clickers who actually make a purchase.

Cookie   A data file that, without the knowledge of users, is placed on their computer hard drives.

Copyright   An exclusive legal right of an author or creator of intellectual property to publish, sell, license, distribute, or use such work in any desired way.

Copyright infringement   The use of a work without permission or contracting for payment of a royalty.

Corporate portal   A gateway for customers, employees, and partners to reach corporate information and to communicate with the company.

Cost–benefit analysis   A comparison of the costs of each project against its benefits.

Cost-plus   A pricing strategy that determines the expenses associated with producing a product (production cost) by adding up all the costs involved—materials, labor, rent, overhead, and so forth—and adding an additional amount to generate a profit margin (a percentage markup).

CPM (cost per mille, i.e., thousand impressions)   The fee an advertiser pays for each 1000 times a page with a banner ad is shown.

Cracker   A malicious hacker who may be more damaging than a hacker.

Cross-border e-commerce   Online purchases involving buyers and merchants or sellers who are in different countries.

Crowdsourcing   Utilizing crowds to collectively execute tasks such as solving problems, innovating, or getting large projects done by dividing the work among many people.

Customer relationship management (CRM)   A customer service approach that focuses on building long-term and sustainable customer relationships that adds value for both the customers and the merchants.

Cyberbullying   "Bullying that takes place using electronic technology. Electronic technology includes devices and equipment such as cell phones, computers and tablets as well as communication tools including social media sites, text messages, chat, and websites." (per **stopybullying.gov**)

Cybercrime   Intentional crimes carried out on the Internet.

Cybercriminal   A person who intentionally carries out crimes over the Internet.

Darknet   A separate Internet that can be accessed via the regular Internet and a connection to the TOR network (TOR is a network of VPNs that allows privacy and security on the Internet). The darknet has restricted access to trusted people ("friends") by using nonstandard protocols (IP addresses are not listed). Darknet allows anonymous surfing.

Data breach   A security incident in which data are obtained illegally and then published or processed.

Denial-of-service (DoS) attack   "A malicious attempt to make a server or network resource unavailable to users, usually by temporarily interrupting or suspending the services of a host connected to the Internet." (Incapsula, Inc.)

Desktop purchasing   Purchasing done by employees without the approval of supervisors and without the involvement of a procurement department.

Desktop search   The search of a user's own computer files. The search is done by looking through all the information that is available on the user's PC.

Detection measures   Methods that help find security breaches in computer systems. Usually, this means to find out whether intruders are attempting (or have attempted) to break into the EC system, whether they were successful, whether they are still damaging the system, and what damage they may have done.

Deterrent methods   Countermeasures that make criminals abandon their idea of attacking a specific system (e.g., a possible deterrent is a realistic expectation of being caught and punished).

Digital currency   A generic term that refers to the digital representation of either e-money or virtual currency.

Digital currency exchanges   Services that allow customers to trade digital currencies for conventional fiat money (e.g., US dollars) or for different digital currencies.

Digital disruption   Electronic technologies including e-commerce may have a disruptive impact on industries, companies, business models, economies, and people. These impacts can be very positive to some and negative to others.

Digital divide   The gap that has emerged between those who have and those who do not have the ability to engage in e-commerce.

Digital economy   An economy that is based on online transactions, mostly e-commerce. Also called the *Internet economy*.

Digital enterprise   A new business model that uses IT to gain competitive advantage by increasing employee productivity, by improving efficiency and effectiveness of business processes, and by better interactivity between vendors and customers.

Digital products   Goods that can be transformed to digital format.

Digital rights management (DRM)   A system of protecting the copyrights of data circulated over the Internet or digital media. These arrangements are technology-based protection measures (via encryption or using watermarks).

Digital signatures   The electronic equivalent of personal signatures on paper. They are difficult to forge since they authenticate the identity of the sender that uses the public key.

Direct marketing   Describes marketing that takes place without physical stores. Selling takes place directly from manufacturer to customer.

Direct materials   Materials used in making products, such as steel in a car or paper in a book.

Discount rate   The main fee that a merchant pays for offering credit card payments.

Disintermediation   Elimination of intermediaries between sellers and buyers because they offer only services that can be fully automated (usually in a supply chain).

Distance learning   Education conducted from home or other places, anytime.

Double auction   An auction in which multiple buyers and their bidding prices are matched with multiple sellers and their asking prices, considering the quantities on both sides.

Driverless cars   Robot-driven cars, self-driving cars, and autonomous cars.

Drones   Unmanned vehicles that can navigate autonomously. They can be remotely controlled.

Dropshipping   An EC model where an e-tailer sells a product and then buys it from a supplier who packs and sends the product to the buyer.

Dynamic pricing   Prices that are not fixed but that are allowed to fluctuate and are determined by supply and demand.

E-bartering (electronic bartering)   Bartering conducted online, usually in a bartering exchange.

E-business   A broader definition of EC, not just the buying and selling of goods and services, but conducting all kinds of business online such as servicing customers, collaborating with business partners, delivering e-learning, and conducting electronic transactions within an organization.

E-collaboration   The use of digital technologies among people for accomplishing a common task.

E-commerce (EC) risk   The likelihood that a negative outcome will occur in the course of developing and operating an e-commerce initiative.

E-distributor   An entity that basically aggregates product information from many manufacturers, sometimes thousands of them, in the e-distributor's catalog.

E-government   The use of information technology in general, and e-commerce in particular, to improve the delivery of government services and activities in the public sector, such as providing citizens and organizations with more convenient access to government information and services and providing effective delivery of public services to engage citizens and businesses partners, as well as improving the performance of government employees. Also when a government agency buys or provides goods, services, or information from or to businesses (G2B) or from or to individual citizens (G2C). Governments can deal also with other governments (G2G).

E-grocer   A grocer that takes orders online and provides deliveries on a daily or other regular schedule or within a very short period of time, sometimes within an hour.

E-health   The transfer of health resources and healthcare by electronic means.

E-learning   The online delivery of educational materials and methods using information technologies, for the purposes of learning, teaching, training, or gaining knowledge at any time and at many different locations.

E-mail marketing   The use of e-mail for sending commercial messages to users.

E-mail advertising   Ads are attached to e-mails.

E-mall (online mall)   An online shopping center where many online stores present their catalogs.

E-marketplace   An electronic space where sellers and buyers meet and conduct different types of transactions.

E-procurement (electronic procurement)   The online purchase of supplies, materials, energy, work, and services. It can be done via the Internet or via a private network such as EDI.

E-tailers   Sellers who conduct retail business online.

E-tailing   Online retailing, usually B2C.

EC security strategy   Multiple layers of defense that include several methods. This defense aims to deter, prevent, and detect unauthorized entry into an organization's computer and information systems.

Electronic auction (e-auction)   An auction conducted online.

Electronic book (e-book)   A book in digital format that can be read on a computer screen, including mobile devices (e.g., a tablet, iPhone) or on a dedicated device known as an *e-reader*.

Electronic catalog (e-catalog)   The presentation of product information in electronic form, the backbone of most e-selling sites.

Electronic commerce (EC)   Using the Internet and intranets to purchase, sell, transport, or trade data, goods, or services.

Electronic discovery (e-discovery)   The process of finding any type of electronic data (e.g., text, images, videos) by using computerized systems.

Electronic market (e-marketplace)   An online location where buyers and sellers conduct commercial transactions such as selling goods, services, or information.

Electronic money   Abbreviated as e-money, it is a digital representation of fiat currency used for purposes of electronic transfer.

Electronic (online) banking or e-banking   Conducting banking activities online.

Electronic Product Environmental Assessment Tool (EPEAT)   A comprehensive global rating system for greener electronics based on a range of environmental performance criteria.

Electronic retailing (e-tailing)   Retailing conducted over the Internet.

Electronic shopping cart   Software that allows customers to accumulate items they wish to buy before they arrange payment and check out.

Electronic signature   "The electronic equivalent of a handwritten signature" (per **pcmag.com/encyclopedia/term/42500/electronic-signature**).

E-mail spam   Occurs when almost identical messages are e-mailed to many recipients (sometimes millions of unsolicited e-mails).

Encryption   The process of encoding data into a form (called a *ciphertext*) that will be difficult, expensive, or time-consuming for an unauthorized person to understand.

Encryption algorithm   The set of procedures or mathematical algorithms used to encrypt or decrypt a message.

Enterprise 2.0   "The use of social software platforms within companies or between companies and their partners or customers."

Enterprise mobility   The people and technology (e.g., devices and networks) that enable mobile computing applications within the enterprise.

Enterprise search   The search for information *within* the files and databases of an organization.

Ethics   A set of moral principles or rules of how people are expected to conduct themselves.

Event shopping   The B2C model in which sales are designed to meet the needs of special events (e.g., a wedding, Black Friday). This model may be combined with group purchasing (to lower the customers' cost).

Exchanges (trading communities or trading exchanges)   Many-to-many e-marketplaces where many buyers and many sellers meet electronically to trade with one another.

Expert systems (knowledge-based systems)   A computer program that uses a stored knowledge to solve problem or provide advice in specified areas.

Exposure   An instance of being exposed to attackers that exploits vulnerability.

Extranet   A network that uses Internet technology to link intranets of several organizations in a secure manner.

Fair use   The limited use of copyrighted material, without paying a fee or royalty, for certain purposes (e.g., reviews, commentaries, teaching).

Fiat currency   The coin and paper money of a country that is designated as legal tender.

Firewalls   Barriers between an internal trusted network (or a PC) and the untrustworthy Internet. Technically, it is composed of hardware and a software package that separates a private computer network (e.g., your LAN) from a public network (the Internet).

Forward auction   An auction where a seller entertains bids from multiple buyers.

Fraud   Any business activity that uses deceitful practices or devices to deprive another of property or other rights.

Front end   The place where customers interact with a marketspace. The major components of the front end can include the seller's portal, electronic catalogs, a shopping cart, a search engine, an auction engine, a payment gateway, and all other activities related to placing orders.

Gamification   The introduction of gaming into social networking or other platforms (like B2B training). Gamification can also be viewed as the introduction of social networking activities into online games.

General controls   Controls designed to protect all system applications.

Geographical information system (GIS)   A computer-based system that captures, stores, analyzes, and displays geographically related data.

Geolocation   The ability of finding the location of a mobile Web-connected user.

Global positioning system (GPS)   A US government satellite-based system that provides users with positioning, navigation, and timing.

Government 2.0   The employment of social media tools, new business models, and embracing social networks and user participation, government agencies can raise the effectiveness of their online activities to meet users' needs at a reasonable cost.

Government-to-business (G2B)   E-government category that works both ways: government-to-business and business-to-government. Thus, G2B refers to activities where the government sells products to businesses or provides businesses with services and vice versa.

Government-to-citizens (G2C)   E-government category that includes all the interactions between a government and its citizens that take place electronically.

Government-to-employees (G2E)   E-government category that includes activities between the government and their employees.

Government-to-government (G2G)   E-government category that includes EC activities between different units of governments, including those within one governmental body. Many of these are aimed at improving the effectiveness and the efficiency of the government operation.

Green computing   The eco-friendly use of computing resources.

Green IT   The efforts to improve the use of EC (and IT) by minimizing damage to the environment and at the same time saving money.

Group purchasing   Orders from several buyers are aggregated so that better prices due to larger quantities purchased can be negotiated.

Hacker   Someone who gains unauthorized access to a computer system.

Hit   A request for data from a Web page or file.

Horizontal marketplaces   Markets in which trading is in a service or a product that is used in many types of industries. Examples are office supplies, PCs, or travel services.

Identity theft   Wrongfully obtaining and using the identity of another person in some way to commit crimes that involve fraud or deception (e.g., for economic gain).

Indirect materials   Items, such as office supplies or light bulbs, which support operation and production.

Information assurance (IA)   The performance of activities (steps) to protect information systems and their processes against all risks. The assurance includes all tools and defense methods.

Information security   Measures taken to protect information systems and their processes against all risks.

Insourcing   In-house development of applications.

Integrity   The assurance that data are accurate and that they cannot be altered.

Intellectual property (IP)   Property that derives from the creative work of an individual, such as literary or artistic work.

Intellectual property law   Area of the law concerned with the regulation of thinking-related products, including creativity, that are protected by patents, copyrights, trademarks, and trade secret law.

Intelligent agents   Autonomous, small computer program that acts upon changing environment as directed by stored knowledge.

Intelligent personal assistants   An application that uses AI to understand spoken natural languages. Users can receive complex assistance and advice from them.

Interactive marketing   A marketing concept that enables marketers and advertisers to interact directly with customers.

Interactive video   A technique used to mix user interaction with videos.

Interactive voice response (IVR)   A voice support application system that enables users to interact by telephone (of any kind) with a computerized system to request and receive information.

Interchange rate   The fees charged by the issuing bank for handling authorization and settlement requests.

Intermediary   A third party that operates between sellers and buyers.

Internet censorship   Restrictions on what can be seen, published, or accessed on the Internet.

Internet of Things   An ecosystem composed of interconnected objects with microprocessors via the Internet.

Internet Radio   Audio content transmitted live via the Internet.

Internet trolls   Community members who publish online offensive, disruptive, or troublemaking content.

Internet TV   The delivery of TV content via the Internet by video streaming technologies.

Intrabusiness EC   E-commerce category that refers to EC transactions among various organizational departments and individuals.

Intranet   An internal corporate or government network that uses Internet tools, such as Web browsers and Internet protocols.

Intrusion detection system (IDS)   A device composed of software and/or hardware designed to monitor the activities of computer networks and computer systems in order to detect and define unauthorized and malicious attempts to access, manipulate, and/or disable these networks and systems.

Key (key value)   The secret piece used with the algorithm to encrypt (or decrypt) the message.

Key performance indicator (KPI)   A quantifiable measurement that is considered a critical success factor of a company, department, or project.

Keystroke logging (keylogging)   The process of using a device or software program that tracks and records the activity of a user in real time (without the user's knowledge or consent) by the keyboard keys they press.

Knowledge management (KM)   The process of capturing or creating knowledge, storing and protecting it, updating it constantly, disseminating it, and using it whenever necessary.

Landing page   The page a viewer is directed to after having clicked on a link. In online marketing, this page is used to convert the person from a viewer to a buyer.

Learning management system (LMS)   Software applications for managing e-training and e-learning programs including content, scheduling, delivery tips, and so forth.

Live banners   Ads where the content can be created or modified at the time the ads pop up instead of being preprogrammed like banner ads.

Localization   The transformation and adaptation of Web content media products and advertising materials to fit the Web environment of a certain region or country.

Location-based commerce (l-commerce, LBS)   A system that can find the location of people (or objects) and provide with relevant services.

M-learning (mobile learning)   Refers to e-learning or other forms of education using mobile devices.

Machine learning   Teaching computers to learn from examples and large amount of data.

Macro virus (macro worm)   A malware code that is attached to a data file rather than to an executable program (e.g., a Word file).

Maintenance, repair, and operation (MRO)   Indirect materials used in activities that support production.

Malware (malicious software)   A generic term for malicious software.

Mass customization   Producing large number of customized products.

Maverick buying   A buying situation that occurs when a buyer makes unplanned purchases of items needed quickly, resulting in buying at non-pre-negotiated, and usually higher, prices.

Merge-in-transit   Logistics model in which components for a product may come from two (or more) different physical locations and are shipped directly to the customer's location.

Micropayments (e-micropayments)   Small online payments, usually under $10.

Mobile advertising (m-advertising)   "Advertising tailored to and delivered through wireless mobile devices such as smartphones (e.g. Blackberry, iPhone, Android, etc.), feature phones (e.g. lower-end mobile phones capable of accessing mobile content), and media tablets (e.g. iPad, Samsung Galaxy Tablet, etc.)" (IAB 2016).

Mobile app   A software application developed specifically for use on small, wireless computing devices, such as smartphones and tablets, rather than desktop or laptop computers.

Mobile banking (m-banking)   A term used to describe the conducting of banking activities via a mobile device (mostly by texting or via mobile website).

Mobile commerce (m-commerce, m-business)   Conducting e-commerce by using mobile devices and wireless networks.

Mobile (digital) wallet   Proximity payments that are debited to a mobile phone account as a monthly fee or to a debit card account. The technology enables payments as well as processing loyalty programs and performing target promotions all in one mobile device.

Mobile enterprise   Mobile applications conducted by enterprises to improve the operations of the employees, facilities, and relevant supply chains, within the enterprise and with its business partners.

Mobile entertainment   Any entertainment delivered on mobile devices over wireless networks or that interacts with mobile service providers.

Mobile government (m-government)   The implementation of e-government applications using wireless platforms.

Mobile marketing   The use of mobile devices and wireless infrastructure as a means of marketing and advertising.

Mobile market research   A method of collecting data though mobile devices including mobile phones, smartphones, and tablets.

Mobile payment   Payment transactions initiated or confirmed using a person's mobile device, usually a smartphone.

Mobile portal   A portal accessible via a mobile device.

Mobile social networking   Social networking where members converse and connect with one another using any mobile device.

Mobile worker   Any employee who is away from his or her primary work space at least 10 h a week (or 25% of the time).

Multichannel business model   The model or strategy of selling both online and offline.

Multimedia messaging service (MMS)   The new type of wireless messaging, delivering rich media content, such as video, images, and audio to mobile devices. MMS is an extension of SMS (no extra charge with an SMS "bundle"). It allows for longer messages than with SMS.

Name-your-own-price model   Auction model in which a would-be buyer specifies the price (and other terms) he or she is willing to pay to any willing and able seller. It is a C2B model that was pioneered by Priceline.com.

Natural language processing   Technology that allowed people to communicate with a computer in their native language.

Net neutrality   A network design principle stating that basic protocols of the Internet should enable users to utilize the Web without being discriminated against by Internet service providers.

Nonconvertible virtual currency   A virtual currency used in a specific virtual world or domain that cannot (theoretically) be exchanged for fiat currency.

Nonrepudiation   The assurance that online customers or trading partners cannot falsely deny (repudiate) their purchase, transaction, sale, or other obligations.

On-demand delivery service   An express delivery option.

Online intermediary   A third-party entity that brokers the transactions between the buyer and seller and can be either a virtual or a click-and-mortar intermediary.

Opt-in   The principle that consumers must approve, in advance, what they are willing to see. That is, information sharing should not occur unless customers affirmatively allow or request it.

Opt-out   A method that gives consumers the choice to refuse to share information about themselves or to avoid receiving unsolicited information.

Order fulfillment   All the operations a company undertakes from the time it receives an order to the time the items are delivered to the customers, including all related customer services.

Outsourcing   The process of contracting (farming out) the company's products, services, or work to another organization that is willing and able to do the job.

Page hijacking   Illegally copying website content so that a user can be misdirected to a different website.

Patent   "An exclusive right to a particular invention. Patents are granted by states or governments to the creator of an invention, or to someone who has been designated by them to accept the rights over the invention. The holder of the patent has sole rights over the invention for a specified period of time" (per Fedcirc.us).

Pay per click (PPC)   A popular Internet advertising payment formula where advertisers pay sites only when someone clicks on their ad.

Payment cards   Electronic cards that contain payment-related data. They include credit cards, charge cards, and debit cards.

Payment service providers (PSPs)   Are third-party companies that provide services to merchants so they can accept all kinds of electronic payments.

Penetration test (pen test)   A method of assessing the vulnerability of a computer system, which is done by allowing experts to act as malicious attackers.

Penny auction   A new type of forward auction in which participants must pay a small nonrefundable fee each time they place a bid (usually in small increments above the previous bid). When time expires, the last participant to have placed a bid wins the item and also pays the final bid price.

Permission advertising Advertising (marketing) strategy in which customers agree to accept advertising and marketing materials (known as *opt-in*).

Person-to-Person (P2P) Sometimes called consumer-to-consumer (C2C) EC, refers to electronic transactions conducted between and among individuals.

Personal robot (also personal assistant, virtual personal assistant) This assistant is designed to live with its owner(s). The personal robot, according to vendors, is able to recognize your face, know your mood, understand what you say, know what you really mean, and much more. It learns and gets smarter everyday.

Personalization The matching of advertising content and vendors' services with customers based on their preferences and individual needs.

Personalized banners Banners that are tailored to meet the need of target customers.

Pervasive computing Computing capabilities that are embedded in the environment but typically are not mobile.

Pharming A scam where malicious code installed on a computer is used to redirect victims to bogus websites without the victims' knowledge or consent.

Phishing A fraudulent process of attempting to acquire sensitive information by masquerading as a trustworthy entity.

Plaintext A human-readable text or message.

Platform for Privacy Preferences Project (P3P) A protocol for privacy protection on the Web developed by the W3 organization (W3C).

Pop-up ad An ad that appears due to the automatic launching of a new browser window when a visitor accesses or leaves a website and when a delay occurs, also known as *ad spawning*.

Pop-up banner Banners that appear in a separate window when its affiliated Web page is activated.

Prevention measures Ways to help stop unauthorized people from accessing the EC system (e.g., by using authentication devices and firewalls or by using *intrusion prevention* which is, according to TechTarget, "a preemptive approach to network security used to identify potential threats and respond to them swiftly").

Private key A key that only its owner knows.

Private shopping club Enables members to shop at discount, frequently for short periods of time (just few days).

Procurement management The process of planning, organizing, and coordinating of all the activities pertaining to the purchasing of the goods and services needed by an organization.

Project champion The person who ensures that the team is ready to move forward and understands its responsibilities. The project champion is responsible for activities such as identifying the project's objectives, prioritizing phases, allocating resources to ensure completion of the project, and so forth.

Public e-marketplaces Third-party exchanges open to all interested parties (sellers and buyers).

Public key A key that is known to all.

Public (asymmetric) key encryption An encryption method that uses two keys: public key and private key.

Public key infrastructure (PKI) A comprehensive framework for securing data flow and information exchange that overcomes some of the shortcomings of the one-key system.

Radio-frequency identification (RFID) A short-range radio-frequency communication technology for wirelessly identifying and tracking tags attached to objects.

Random banners Banner ads that appear randomly, not as a result of some action by the user.

Ransomware A method of attack where the attacker encrypts files so the victim cannot open them unless they pay a ransom.

Real-time location systems Systems that track and identify the location of people or objects in real time.

Reintermediation The new intermediation that provides valuable help services.

Request for quote (RFQ) A form or document used as an "invitation" to take part in a reverse auction.

Reverse auction The auction process in which many sellers (suppliers) compute to fulfill orders requested by one buyer.

Reverse auction (bidding or tendering system) Auction in which the buyer places an item for bid (tender) on a request for quote (RFQ) system; potential suppliers bid on the job, with the price reducing sequentially; and the lowest bid wins, primarily a B2B or G2B mechanism.

RFID Technology Use of radio frequency (RF) to identify tagged objects.

Risk The probability that a vulnerability will be known and exploited.

Robo advisors Virtual personal assistants that contain knowledge so they can advise people in several fields, mostly in finance and investment.

Robot Electromechanical device that is programmed to perform manual and/or mental work done by people.

Search advertising Placing online ads on Web pages that show results from querying a search engine.

Search engine A computer program that can access databases of Internet resources, search for specific information or keywords, and report the results.

Search engine optimization (SEO) A process that improves the position of a company or brands on the result page displayed by a search engine. Ideally, the results should be in the top five on the first page of the results.

Search engine spam The technology that enables the creation of spam sites.

Sell-side e-marketplace A place where a company sells either standard or customized products to individuals (B2C) or to businesses (B2B); this type of selling is considered to be one-to-many.

Semantic Web A group of methods that focuses on machines (in contrast with Web 2.0 that focuses on people), trying to enable machines to understand the semantics (i.e., the meaning) of information using natural language understanding tools.

Settlement Involves the transfer of money from the buyer's account to the merchant's.

Sharing economy An economic system constructed around the concept of sharing goods and services among the participating people.

Shopbot Robots that help in online shopping by collecting shopping information (search) and conducting price and capability comparisons.

Shopping portals Gateways to webstores and e-malls.

Shopping robots (shopping agents or shopbots) Search engines that look for the lowest prices or for other search criteria.

Short message service (SMS) A service that supports the transmittal of short text messages (up to 140–160 characters) between wireless devices.

Siri Virtual intelligent personal assistant. Similar to Alexa.

Smart card A plastic payment card that contains data in an embedded microchip.

Smart card reader A read/write device that acts as a mediator between the card and the host system that stores application data and processes transactions.

Smart cities Cities where digital technologies and EC facilitate public services and transportation and improve people's life.

Smart grid An electricity network managed by utilizing digital technology.

Smart homes Homes where all the appliances, security, entertainment, etc. are interconnected (frequently wireless) and are controlled centrally (e.g., via smartphone's apps).

Smartphone A mobile phone with Internet access and PC-like functionality.

Smartwatch A computerized wrist watch with functionality that is enhanced beyond timekeeping. Today, smartwatches are wearable computers. Many run mobile apps, using a mobile operating system.

Social business "An organization that has put in place the strategies, technologies and processes to systematically engage all the individuals of its ecosystem (employees, customers, partners, suppliers) to maximize the co-created value" (Social Business Forum).

Social collaboration (Collaboration 2.0) People's collaboration within and between communities enabled by social media tools and platforms.

Social commerce (SC) Refers to the process where people, individually or in groups, interact and share information and knowledge while in social networks or when pursuing social goals.

Social computing Computing systems that involve social interactions and behavior.

Social customers Customers who usually are members in social networks, do social shopping, and understand their shopper's rights and how to use them to their advantage.

Social customer relationship management (SCRM, CRM 2.0) The delivery of CRM by using social media tools and platforms.

Social (digital) customers Members of social networks who share opinions about products, services, and vendors, do online social shopping, and understand their rights and how to use the wisdom and power of social communities to their benefit.

Social engineering A type of nontechnical attack that uses some ruse to trick users into revealing information or performing an action that compromises a computer or network.

Social enterprise The use of social media tools and platforms and conducting social networking in organizations, while the major objectives are either commercial or nonprofit activities (e.g., the government).

Social game A video multiplayer game played on the Internet, mostly in social networks or virtual worlds.

Social learning Learning, training, and knowledge sharing in social networks and/or facilitated by social software tools.

Social marketplace A marketplace that uses social media tools and platforms and acts as an online intermediary between buyers and sellers.

Social media   Involves user-generated online text, image, audio, and video content that are delivered via Web 2.0 platforms and tools. The media is used primarily for social interactions and conversations such as to share opinions, experiences, insights, and perceptions and to collaborate, all online.

Social media marketing (SMM)   The application of marketing communication and other marketing tools using social media.

Social network   A social entity composed of nodes (which are generally individuals, groups, or organizations) that are connected by links such as hobbies, friendship, or profession. The structures are often very complex.

Social network game   A video game that is played in social networks and usually involves multiplayers.

Social networking   The execution of any Web 2.0 activity, such as blogging or having a presence in a social network. It also includes all activities conducted in social networks.

Social networking service (SNS)   A service that builds online communities by providing an online space for people to build free homepages and that provides basic communication and support tools for conducting different activities in the social network.

Social shopping (sales 2.0)   Online shopping with social media tools and platforms. It is about sharing shopping experiences with friends. Social shopping is the combination of social media and e-commerce.

Social TV   An emerging social media technology that enables several TV viewers who are in different locations to interactively share experiences such as discussions, reviews, and recommendations while watching the same show simultaneously.

Spam   The electronic equivalent of junk mail.

Spam site   Pages that trick search engines into offering biased search results so that the ranking of certain pages is inflated.

Spear phishing   A variant of phishing that targets victims with e-mails purporting to be from colleagues, or family members, or friends.

Speech (voice) understanding   Computer system that understands natural language spoken by people.

Splog   Blogs created by spammers solely for advertising.

Spyware   Tracking software that is installed by criminals or advertisers, without the user's consent, in order to gather information about the user and direct it to advertisers or other third parties.

Standard of due care   The minimum and customary practice that a company is reasonably expected to take to protect the company and its resources from possible risks.

Static banner   Banners that stay on a Web page regularly.

Stored-value card   A card where a monetary value is prepaid and can be loaded on the card once or several times.

Strategy   A comprehensive framework for expressing the manner in which a business plans to achieve its mission, what goals are needed to support it, and what plans and policies will be needed to accomplish these goals.

Strategy assessment   The continuous performance monitoring, comparison of actual to desired performance, and evaluation of the progress toward the organization's goals, resulting in corrective actions and, if necessary, in strategy reformulation.

Strategy formulation   The development of specific strategies and tactics to exploit opportunities and manage threats in the business environment in light of corporate strengths and weaknesses.

Strategy implementation   The "How do we do it?" phase that includes tactics, plans, schedules, deployment strategies, resource allocation, and project management.

Strategy initiation   The initial phase of strategic planning in which the organization is setting its vision, goals, and objectives. Looking at its environment, strategy initiation includes an assessment of a company's strengths and weaknesses, examining the external factors that may affect the business.

Supply chain segmentation   Alignment of customer demands in different channels with supplies.

Symmetric (private) key encryption   A scheme in which the same key is used to encrypt and decrypt the plaintext.

Telecommuting   Working at home using a PC, tablet, smartphone, and the Internet.

Tendering (bidding) system   System through which large organizational buyers make large-volume or large-value purchases (also known as a *reverse auction*).

Third-party logistics suppliers (3PL)   External, rather than in-house, providers of logistics services.

Trojan horse   A program that seems to be harmless or even looks useful but actually contains a hidden malicious code.

Turing test   A test of a computers's capablity to mimic equivalent human behaviors.

Ubiquitous computing (ubicom)   Computing capabilities embedded into a relevant system, usually not visible, which may be mobile or stationary.

Underground Internet economy   E-markets for stolen information made up of thousands of websites that sell credit card numbers, social security numbers, e-mail addresses, bank account numbers, social network IDs, passwords, and much more.

User profile   Customer preferences, behaviors, and demographics.

Value proposition Refers to the benefits, including the intangible ones that a company hopes to derive from using its business model.

Vendor-managed inventory (VMI) A process in which retailers make their suppliers responsible for monitoring the inventory of each item they supply and determining when to order each item.

Vertical marketplaces Markets for one industry or one industry segment. Examples include marketplaces specializing in electronics, cars, hospital supplies, steel, or chemicals.

Viral blogging Viral marketing done by bloggers.

Viral marketing Word-of-mouth (WOM) method by which people tell others (frequently their friends) about a product they like (or dislike).

Viral video A video that is spread rapidly through the process of online information sharing. This way, people share videos that receive more attention, sometimes drawing millions of viewers in a short time.

Virtual community A community where the interaction takes place over a computer network, mainly the Internet.

Virtual currency The digital representation of value that can be digitally traded and functions as a medium of exchange, a unit of account, and a store of value but does not have legal status in any jurisdiction.

Virtual economy An emerging economy existing in several virtual worlds, where people exchange virtual goods frequently related to an Internet game or to a virtual business.

Virtual goods Computer images of real or imaginary goods.

Virtual private network (VPN) A network that uses the Internet to transfer information in a secure manner.

Virtual (pure-play) e-tailers Companies with direct online sales that do not need physical stores.

Virtual (pure-play) organizations Organizations that conduct their business activities solely online.

Virtual reality A computer-generated simulation of a real-life environment in which users can be immersed.

Virtual trade show Temporary or permanent showplaces where exhibitors present their new products to potential customers.

Virtual university Online universities where students take classes from home via the Internet.

Virus Programmed software inserted by criminals into a computer to damage the system; running the infected host program activates the virus.

Voice portal A portal with audio interfaces that can be accessed by telephone or cell phone.

Vulnerability Weakness in software or other mechanisms that threatens the confidentiality, integrity, or availability of an asset (recall the CIA model). It can be directly used by a hacker to gain access to a system or network.

Vulnerability assessment A process of identifying and evaluating problem areas that are vulnerable to attack on a computerized system.

Warehouse management system (WMS) A software system that helps in managing warehouses.

Web 2.0 The second generation of Internet-based tools and services that enables users to easily generate content, share media, and communicate and collaborate, in innovative ways.

Web 3.0 A term used to describe the future of the World Wide Web. It is projected to deliver a new generation of business applications that will see business and social computing converge.

Web 4.0 The Web generation after Web 3.0. It is still an unknown entity. However, it is envisioned as being based on islands of intelligence and as being ubiquitous.

Web analytics "The measurement, collection, analysis, and reporting of Internet data for the purposes of understanding and optimizing Web usage" (per Web Analytics Association).

Web bugs Tiny (usually invisible) objects concealed in a Web page or in e-mail messages. Web bugs transmit information about the user and his or her movements to a monitoring site (e.g., to find out if the user has viewed certain content on the Web page).

Web (information) portal A single point of access, through a Web browser, to critical business information located inside and outside organizations.

Web mining The use of data mining techniques for both Web content and usage in Web documents in order to discover patterns and hidden relationships.

Webstore (storefront) A single company's (or individual seller's) website where products or services are sold.

Wireless mobile computing (mobile computing) A computing solution where computing is done using mobile devices at any place connected to a wireless network.

Worm A software code that can replicate itself automatically (as a "standalone"—without any human intervention). Worms use networks to propagate and infect a computer or handheld device and can even spread via instant messages.

Zombies Computers infected with malware that are under the control of a spammer, hacker, or other criminals.

Index

A

Access control
  authentication, 414
  authorization, 414
  biometric systems, 432
  definition, 414
  user identification, 432
Address verification system (AVS)
  cardholders, 469
  detects fraud, 469
  false positives, 469
Administrative controls, 435
Alexa skills, 266
Alibaba.com
  Alipay, 125
  buyers, 125
  competition, 126
  database, 125
  My Alibaba, 125
  services, buyers and suppliers, 125
  suppliers, 124
  Taobao, 124
  tools and resources, 125
Alipay, 478
Allstate Business Insurance Expert (ABIe), 264
Amazon Alexa, 266
Amazon.com
  benefits, 504
  1-click, 118
  description, 502
  logistics services, 502
  personalized services, 80
  support services, 96
  virtual retailing, 502
Amazon Echo, 265, 266
Androids, 255
Antivirus tools, 416
Ariba, Inc., 137, 144, 146
Artificial intelligence (AI), 251
  capabilities, 253
  definitions, 253
  field, 253
  machine learning, 254
  virus detection program, 254
Augmented reality (AR)
  definition, 64
  IKEA, 65
  Net-a-Porter, 65
Authentication
  and nonrepudiation, 429–430
  provision of permission, 414
  verification, user's identity and access rights, 432

Authorization
  processing cards online, 466–468
  stored information, 429
  stored-value card, 471
Availability, 411, 414, 429, 431, 447

B

B2B e-marketplaces and services
  one-to-many and many-to-one (private), 128
  supply chain improvers and collaborative commerce, 128
B2B exchanges
  advantages, limitations, and revenue model, 149–150
  dynamic pricing, 149
  functions and services, 147–148
  ownership, 148–149
Back end, 46
Banking Trojan, 418
Banners
  ads, 378
  benefits and limitations, 378
  description, 378
  disadvantage, 378
  live, 378
  personalized, 378
  pop-up, 378
  random, 378
  static, 378
Bartering (e-bartering), 70
Bartering exchange, 58, 70, 145
Behavioral marketing
  collaborative filtering, 369
  customer database, 389
  social psychology and morphing, 369
  targeting, 368
Behavioral targeting
  collaborative filtering, 368
  consumer browsing information, 368
Biometrics, smartphone marketing, 374
Bitcoin
  advantages, 488
  digital currency, 484
  litecoin, 489
  mining, 486
  peer-to-peer and encrypted digital currency, 465
  public and private keys, 486
  valuation, 488
  wallet, 487
Blue Nile Inc.
  discounts, 47
  success factors, 47
Bluetooth, 232, 236, 238

E. Turban et al., *Electronic Commerce 2018*, Springer Texts in Business and Economics, DOI 10.1007/978-3-319-58715-8

9783319587141